LIFE AN

LIFE AND TEACHING OF JESUS

BASED ON THE URANTIA BOOK

Contents

ings that she had been selected to become the earth mother of the bestowal child.

Paper 122

Birth and Infancy of Jesus

122:0.1 (1344.1) IT WILL hardly be possible fully to explain the many reasons which led to the selection of Palestine as the land for Michael's bestowal, and especially as to just why the family of Joseph and Mary should have been chosen as the immediate setting for the appearance of this Son of God on Urantia.

122:0.2 (1344.2) After a study of the special report on the status of segregated worlds prepared by the Melchizedeks, in counsel with Gabriel, Michael finally chose Urantia as the planet whereon to enact his final bestowal. Subsequent to this decision Gabriel made a personal visit to Urantia, and, as a result of his study of human groups and his survey of the spiritual, intellectual, racial, and geographic features of the world and its peoples, he decided that the Hebrews possessed those relative advantages which warranted their selection as the bestowal race. Upon Michael's approval of this decision, Gabriel appointed and dispatched to Urantia the Family Commission of Twelve—selected from among the higher orders of universe personalities—which was intrusted with the task of making an investigation of Jewish family life. When this commission ended its labors, Gabriel was present on Urantia and received the report nominating three prospective unions as being, in the opinion of the commission, equally favorable as bestowal families for Michael's projected incarnation.

122:0.3 (1344.3) From the three couples nominated, Gabriel made the personal choice of Joseph and Mary, subsequently making his personal appearance to Mary, at which time he imparted to her the glad tid-

1 Joseph and Mary

122:1.1 (1344.4) Joseph, the human father of Jesus (Joshua ben Joseph), was a Hebrew of the Hebrews, albeit he carried many non-Jewish racial strains which had been added to his ancestral tree from time to time by the female lines of his progenitors. The ancestry of the father of Jesus went back to the days of Abraham and through this venerable patriarch to the earlier lines of inheritance leading to the Sumerians and Nodites and, through the southern tribes of the ancient blue man, to Andon and Fonta. David and Solomon were not in the direct line of Joseph's ancestry, neither did Joseph's lineage go directly back to Adam. Joseph's immediate ancestors were mechanics—builders, carpenters, masons, and smiths. Joseph himself was a carpenter and later a contractor. His family belonged to a long and illustrious line of the nobility of the common people, accentuated ever and anon by the appearance of unusual individuals who had distinguished themselves in connection with the evolution of religion on Urantia.

122:1.2 (1345.1) Mary, the earth mother of Jesus, was a descendant of a long line of unique ancestors embracing many of the most remarkable women in the racial history of Urantia. Although Mary was an average woman of her day and generation, possessing a fairly normal temperament, she reckoned among her ancestors such well-known women as Annon, Tamar, Ruth, Bathsheba, Ansie, Cloa, Eve, Enta, and Ratta. No Jewish woman of that day had a more illustrious lineage of common progenitors or one extending back to more auspicious beginnings. Mary's ancestry, like Joseph's, was characterized by the predominance of strong but average individuals, relieved now and then by numerous outstanding personalities in the march of civilization and the progressive evolution of religion. Racially considered, it is hardly proper to regard Mary as a Jewess. In culture and belief she was a Jew, but in hereditary endowment she was more a composite of Syrian, Hittite, Phoenician, Greek, and Egyptian stocks, her racial inheritance being more general than that of Joseph.

122:1.3 (1345.2) Of all couples living in Palestine at about the time of Michael's projected bestowal, Joseph and Mary possessed the most ideal combination of widespread racial connections and superior average of personality endowments. It was the plan of Michael to appear on earth as an average man, that the common people might understand him and receive him; wherefore Gabriel selected just such persons as Joseph and Mary to become the bestowal parents.

2   *Gabriel Appears to Elizabeth*

122:2.1 (1345.3) Jesus' lifework on Urantia was really begun by John the Baptist. Zacharias, John's father, belonged to the Jewish priesthood, while his mother, Elizabeth, was a member of the more prosperous branch of the same large family group to which Mary the mother of Jesus also belonged. Zacharias and Elizabeth, though they had been married many years, were childless.

122:2.2 (1345.4) It was late in the month of June, 8 B.C., about three months after the marriage of Joseph and Mary, that Gabriel appeared to Elizabeth at noontide one day, just as he later made his presence known to Mary. Said Gabriel:

122:2.3 (1345.5) "While your husband, Zacharias, stands before the altar in Jerusalem, and while the assembled people pray for the coming of a deliverer, I, Gabriel, have come to announce that you will shortly bear a son who shall be the forerunner of this divine teacher, and you shall call your son John. He will grow up dedicated to the Lord your God, and when he has come to full years, he will

gladden your heart because he will turn many souls to God, and he will also proclaim the coming of the soul-healer of your people and the spirit-liberator of all mankind. Your kinswoman Mary shall be the mother of this child of promise, and I will also appear to her."

122:2.4 (1345.6) This vision greatly frightened Elizabeth. After Gabriel's departure she turned this experience over in her mind, long pondering the sayings of the majestic visitor, but did not speak of the revelation to anyone save her husband until her subsequent visit with Mary in early February of the following year.

122:2.5 (1345.7) For five months, however, Elizabeth withheld her secret even from her husband. Upon her disclosure of the story of Gabriel's visit, Zacharias was very skeptical and for weeks doubted the entire experience, only consenting half-heartedly to believe in Gabriel's visit to his wife when he could no longer question that she was expectant with child. Zacharias was very much perplexed regarding the prospective motherhood of Elizabeth, but he did not doubt the integrity of his wife, notwithstanding his own advanced age. It was not until about six weeks before John's birth that Zacharias, as the result of an impressive dream, became fully convinced that Elizabeth was to become the mother of a son of destiny, one who was to prepare the way for the coming of the Messiah.

122:2.6 (1346.1) Gabriel appeared to Mary about the middle of November, 8 B.C., while she was at work in her Nazareth home. Later on, after Mary knew without doubt that she was to become a mother, she persuaded Joseph to let her journey to the City of Judah, four miles west of Jerusalem, in the hills, to visit Elizabeth. Gabriel had informed each of these mothers-to-be of his appearance to the other. Naturally they were anxious to get together, compare experiences, and talk over the probable futures of their sons. Mary remained with her distant cousin for three weeks. Elizabeth did much to strengthen Mary's faith in the vision of Gabriel, so that she returned home more fully dedicated to the call to mother the child of destiny whom she was so soon to present to the world as a helpless babe, an average and normal infant of the realm.

122:2.7 (1346.2) John was born in the City of Judah, March 25, 7 B.C. Zacharias and Elizabeth rejoiced greatly in the realization that a son had come to them as Gabriel had promised, and when on the eighth day they presented the child for circumcision, they formally christened him John, as they had been directed aforetime. Already had a nephew of Zacharias departed for Nazareth, carrying the message of Elizabeth to Mary proclaiming that a son had been born to her and that his name was to be John.

122:2.8 (1346.3) From his earliest infancy John was judiciously impressed by his parents with the idea that he was to grow up to become a spiritual leader and religious teacher. And the soil of John's heart was ever responsive to the sowing of such suggestive seeds. Even as a child he was found frequently at the temple during the seasons of his father's service, and he was tremendously impressed with the significance of all that he saw.

3 Gabriel's Announcement to Mary

122:3.1 (1346.4) One evening about sundown, before Joseph had returned home, Gabriel appeared to Mary by the side of a low stone table and, after she had recovered her composure, said: "I come at the bidding of one who is my Master and whom you shall love and nurture. To you, Mary, I bring glad tidings when I announce that the conception within you is ordained by heaven, and that in due time you will become the mother of a son; you shall call him Joshua, and he shall inaugurate the kingdom of heaven on earth and among men. Speak not of this matter save to Joseph and to Elizabeth, your kinswoman, to whom I have also appeared, and who shall presently also bear a son, whose name

shall be John, and who will prepare the way for the message of deliverance which your son shall proclaim to men with great power and deep conviction. And doubt not my word, Mary, for this home has been chosen as the mortal habitat of the child of destiny. My benediction rests upon you, the power of the Most Highs will strengthen you, and the Lord of all the earth shall overshadow you."

122:3.2 (1346.5) Mary pondered this visitation secretly in her heart for many weeks until of a certainty she knew she was with child, before she dared to disclose these unusual events to her husband. When Joseph heard all about this, although he had great confidence in Mary, he was much troubled and could not sleep for many nights. At first Joseph had doubts about the Gabriel visitation. Then when he became well-nigh persuaded that Mary had really heard the voice and beheld the form of the divine messenger, he was torn in mind as he pondered how such things could be. How could the offspring of human beings be a child of divine destiny? Never could Joseph reconcile these conflicting ideas until, after several weeks of thought, both he and Mary reached the conclusion that they had been chosen to become the parents of the Messiah, though it had hardly been the Jewish concept that the expected deliverer was to be of divine nature. Upon arriving at this momentous conclusion, Mary hastened to depart for a visit with Elizabeth.

122:3.3 (1347.1) Upon her return, Mary went to visit her parents, Joachim and Hannah. Her two brothers and two sisters, as well as her parents, were always very skeptical about the divine mission of Jesus, though, of course, at this time they knew nothing of the Gabriel visitation. But Mary did confide to her sister Salome that she thought her son was destined to become a great teacher.

122:3.4 (1347.2) Gabriel's announcement to Mary was made the day following the conception of Jesus and was the only event of supernatural occurrence connected with her entire experience of carrying and bearing the child of promise.

4   *Joseph's Dream*

122:4.1 (1347.3) Joseph did not become reconciled to the idea that Mary was to become the mother of an extraordinary child until after he had experienced a very impressive dream. In this dream a brilliant celestial messenger appeared to him and, among other things, said: "Joseph, I appear by command of Him who now reigns on high, and I am directed to instruct you concerning the son whom Mary shall bear, and who shall become a great light in the world. In him will be life, and his life shall become the light of mankind. He shall first come to his own people, but they will hardly receive him; but to as many as shall receive him to them will he reveal that they are the children of God." After this experience Joseph never again wholly doubted Mary's story of Gabriel's visit and of the promise that the unborn child was to become a divine messenger to the world.

122:4.2 (1347.4) In all these visitations nothing was said about the house of David. Nothing was ever intimated about Jesus' becoming a "deliverer of the Jews," not even that he was to be the long-expected Messiah. Jesus was not such a Messiah as the Jews had anticipated, but he was the world's deliverer. His mission was to all races and peoples, not to any one group.

122:4.3 (1347.5) Joseph was not of the line of King David. Mary had more of the Davidic ancestry than Joseph. True, Joseph did go to the City of David, Bethlehem, to be registered for the Roman census, but that was because, six generations previously, Joseph's paternal ancestor of that generation, being an orphan, was adopted by one Zadoc, who was a direct descendant of David; hence was Joseph also accounted as of the "house of David."

122:4.4 (1347.6) Most of the so-called Messianic prophecies of the Old Testament were made to apply to Jesus long after his life had been lived on earth. For centuries the Hebrew prophets had proclaimed the coming of a deliverer, and these promises had been construed by successive generations as referring to a new Jewish ruler who would sit upon the throne of David and, by the reputed miraculous methods of Moses, proceed to establish the Jews in Palestine as a powerful nation, free from all foreign domination. Again, many figurative passages found throughout the Hebrew scriptures were subsequently misapplied to the life mission of Jesus. Many Old Testament sayings were so distorted as to appear to fit some episode of the Master's earth life. Jesus himself onetime publicly denied any connection with the royal house of David. Even the passage, "a maiden shall bear a son," was made to read, "a virgin shall bear a son." This was also true of the many genealogies of both Joseph and Mary which were constructed subsequent to Michael's career on earth.

Many of these lineages contain much of the Master's ancestry, but on the whole they are not genuine and may not be depended upon as factual. The early followers of Jesus all too often succumbed to the temptation to make all the olden prophetic utterances appear to find fulfillment in the life of their Lord and Master.

5   *Jesus' Earth Parents*

122:5.1 (1348.1) Joseph was a mild-mannered man, extremely conscientious, and in every way faithful to the religious conventions and practices of his people. He talked little but thought much. The sorry plight of the Jewish people caused Joseph much sadness. As a youth, among his eight brothers and sisters, he had been more cheerful, but in the earlier years of married life (during Jesus' childhood) he was subject to periods of mild spiritual discouragement. These temperamental manifestations were greatly improved just before his untimely death and after the economic condition of his family had been enhanced by his advancement from the rank of carpenter to the role of a prosperous contractor.

122:5.2 (1348.2) Mary's temperament was quite opposite to that of her husband. She was usually cheerful, was very rarely downcast, and possessed an ever-sunny disposition. Mary indulged in free and frequent expression of her emotional feelings and was never observed to be sorrowful until after the sudden death of Joseph. And she had hardly recovered from this shock when she had thrust upon her the anxieties and questionings aroused by the extraordinary career of her eldest son, which was so rapidly unfolding before her astonished gaze. But throughout all this unusual experience Mary was composed, courageous, and fairly wise in her relationship with her strange and little-understood first-born son and his surviving brothers and sisters.

122:5.3 (1348.3) Jesus derived much of his unusual gentleness and marvelous sympathetic understanding of human nature from his father; he inherited his gift as a great teacher and his tremendous capacity for righteous indignation from his mother. In emotional reactions to his adult-life environment, Jesus was at one time like his father, meditative and worshipful, sometimes characterized by apparent sadness; but more often he drove forward in the manner of his mother's optimistic and determined disposition. All in all, Mary's temperament tended to dominate the career of the divine Son as he grew up and swung into the momentous strides of his adult life. In some particulars Jesus was a blending of his parents' traits; in other respects he exhibited the traits of one in contrast with those of the other.

122:5.4 (1348.4) From Joseph Jesus secured his strict training in the usages of the Jewish ceremonials and his unusual acquaintance with the Hebrew scriptures; from Mary he derived a broader viewpoint of religious life and a more liberal concept of personal spiritual freedom.

122:5.5 (1349.1) The families of both Joseph and Mary were well educated for their time. Joseph and Mary were educated far above the average for their day and station in life. He was a thinker; she was a planner, expert in adaptation and practical in immediate execution. Joseph was a black-eyed brunet; Mary, a brown-eyed well-nigh blond type.

122:5.6 (1349.2) Had Joseph lived, he undoubtedly would have become a firm believer in the divine mission of his eldest son. Mary alternated between believing and doubting, being greatly influenced by the position taken by her other children and by her friends and relatives, but always was she steadied in her final attitude by the memory of Gabriel's appearance to her immediately after the child was conceived.

122:5.7 (1349.3) Mary was an expert weaver and more than averagely skilled in most of the household arts of that day; she was a good housekeeper and a superior homemaker. Both Joseph and Mary were good teachers, and they saw to it that their children were well versed in the learning of that day.

122:5.8 (1349.4) When Joseph was a young man, he was employed by Mary's father in the work of building an addition to his house, and it was when Mary brought Joseph a cup of water, during a noontime meal, that the courtship of the pair who were destined to become the parents of Jesus really began.

122:5.9 (1349.5) Joseph and Mary were married, in accordance with Jewish custom, at Mary's home in the environs of Nazareth when Joseph was twenty-one years old. This marriage concluded a normal courtship of almost two years' duration. Shortly thereafter they moved into their new home in Nazareth, which had been built by Joseph with the assistance of two of his brothers. The house was located near the foot of the near-by elevated land which so charmingly overlooked the surrounding countryside. In this home, especially prepared, these young and expectant parents had thought to welcome the child of promise, little realizing that this momentous event of a universe was to transpire while they would be absent from home in Bethlehem of Judea.

122:5.10 (1349.6) The larger part of Joseph's family became believers in the teachings of Jesus, but very few of Mary's people ever believed in him until after he departed from this world. Joseph leaned more toward the spiritual concept of the expected Messiah, but Mary and her family, especially her father, held to the idea of the Messiah as a temporal deliverer and political ruler. Mary's ancestors had been prominently identified with the Maccabean activities of the then but recent times.

122:5.11 (1349.7) Joseph held vigorously to the Eastern, or Babylonian, views of the Jewish religion; Mary leaned strongly toward the more liberal and broader Western, or Hellenistic, interpretation of the law and the prophets.

6   The Home at Nazareth

122:6.1 (1349.8) The home of Jesus was not far from the high hill in the northerly part of Nazareth, some distance from the village spring, which was in the eastern section of the town. Jesus' family dwelt in the outskirts of the city, and this made it all the easier for him subsequently to enjoy frequent strolls in the country and to make trips up to the top of this near-by highland, the highest of all the hills of southern Galilee save the Mount Tabor range to the east and the hill of Nain, which was about the same height. Their home was located a little to the south and east of the southern promontory of this hill and about midway between the base of this elevation and the road leading out of Nazareth toward Cana.

Aside from climbing the hill, Jesus' favorite stroll was to follow a narrow trail winding about the base of the hill in a northeasterly direction to a point where it joined the road to Sepphoris.

122:6.2 (1350.1) The home of Joseph and Mary was a one-room stone structure with a flat roof and an adjoining building for housing the animals. The furniture consisted of a low stone table, earthenware and stone dishes and pots, a loom, a lampstand, several small stools, and mats for sleeping on the stone floor. In the back yard, near the animal annex, was the shelter which covered the oven and the mill for grinding grain. It required two persons to operate this type of mill, one to grind and another to feed the grain. As a small boy Jesus often fed grain to this mill while his mother turned the grinder.

122:6.3 (1350.2) In later years, as the family grew in size, they would all squat about the enlarged stone table to enjoy their meals, helping themselves from a common dish, or pot, of food. During the winter, at the evening meal the table would be lighted by a small, flat clay lamp, which was filled with olive oil. After the birth of Martha, Joseph built an addition to this house, a large room, which was used as a carpenter shop during the day and as a sleeping room at night.

7   The Trip to Bethlehem

122:7.1 (1350.3) In the month of March, 8 B.C. (the month Joseph and Mary were married), Caesar Augustus decreed that all inhabitants of the Roman Empire should be numbered, that a census should be made which could be used for effecting better taxation. The Jews had always been greatly prejudiced against any attempt to "number the people," and this, in connection with the serious domestic difficulties of Herod, King of Judea, had conspired to cause the postponement of the taking of this census in the Jewish kingdom for one year. Throughout all the Roman Empire this census was registered in the year 8 B.C., except in the Palestinian kingdom of Herod, where it was taken in 7 B.C., one year later.

122:7.2 (1350.4) It was not necessary that Mary should go to Bethlehem for enrollment—Joseph was authorized to register for his family—but Mary, being an adventurous and aggressive person, insisted on accompanying him. She feared being left alone lest the child be born while Joseph was away, and again, Bethlehem being not far from the City of Judah, Mary foresaw a possible pleasurable visit with her kinswoman Elizabeth.

122:7.3 (1350.5) Joseph virtually forbade Mary to accompany him, but it was of no avail; when the food was packed for the trip of three or four days, she prepared double rations and made ready for the journey. But before they actually set forth, Joseph was reconciled to Mary's going along, and they cheerfully departed from Nazareth at the break of day.

122:7.4 (1350.6) Joseph and Mary were poor, and since they had only one beast of burden, Mary, being large with child, rode on the animal with the provisions while Joseph walked, leading the beast. The building and furnishing of a home had been a great drain on Joseph since he had also to contribute to the support of his parents, as his father had been recently disabled. And so this Jewish couple went forth from their humble home early on the morning of August 18, 7 B.C., on their journey to Bethlehem.

122:7.5 (1351.1) Their first day of travel carried them around the foothills of Mount Gilboa, where they camped for the night by the river Jordan and engaged in many speculations as to what sort of a son would be born to them, Joseph adhering to the concept of a spiritual teacher and Mary holding to the idea of a Jewish Messiah, a deliverer of the Hebrew nation.

122:7.6 (1351.2) Bright and early the morning of August 19, Joseph and Mary were again on their way. They partook of their noontide meal at the foot of Mount Sartaba, overlooking the Jordan valley, and journeyed on, making Jericho for the night, where they stopped at an inn on the highway in the outskirts of the city. Following the evening meal and after much discussion concerning the oppressiveness of Roman rule, Herod, the census enrollment, and the comparative influence of Jerusalem and Alexandria as centers of Jewish learning and culture, the Nazareth travelers retired for the night's rest. Early in the morning of August 20 they resumed their journey, reaching Jerusalem before noon, visiting the temple, and going on to their destination, arriving at Bethlehem in midafternoon.

122:7.7 (1351.3) The inn was overcrowded, and Joseph accordingly sought lodgings with distant relatives, but every room in Bethlehem was filled to overflowing. On returning to the courtyard of the inn, he was informed that the caravan stables, hewn out of the side of the rock and situated just below the inn, had been cleared of animals and cleaned up for the reception of lodgers. Leaving the donkey in the courtyard, Joseph shouldered their bags of clothing and provisions and with Mary descended the stone steps to their lodgings below. They found themselves located in what had been a grain storage room to the front of the stalls and mangers. Tent curtains had been hung, and they counted themselves fortunate to have such comfortable quarters.

122:7.8 (1351.4) Joseph had thought to go out at once and enroll, but Mary was weary; she was considerably distressed and besought him to remain by her side, which he did.

8   The Birth of Jesus

122:8.1 (1351.5) All that night Mary was restless so that neither of them slept much. By the break of day the pangs of childbirth were well in evidence, and at noon, August 21, 7 B.C., with the help and kind ministrations of women fellow travelers, Mary was delivered of a male child. Jesus of Nazareth was born into the world, was wrapped in the clothes which Mary had brought along for such a possible contingency, and laid in a near-by manger.

122:8.2 (1351.6) In just the same manner as all babies before that day and since have come into the world, the promised child was born; and on the eighth day, according to the Jewish practice, he was circumcised and formally named Joshua (Jesus).

122:8.3 (1351.7) The next day after the birth of Jesus, Joseph made his enrollment. Meeting a man they had talked with two nights previously at Jericho, Joseph was taken by him to a well-to-do friend who had a room at the inn, and who said he would gladly exchange quarters with the Nazareth couple. That afternoon they moved up to the inn, where they lived for almost three weeks until they found lodgings in the home of a distant relative of Joseph.

122:8.4 (1351.8) The second day after the birth of Jesus, Mary sent word to Elizabeth that her child had come and received word in return inviting Joseph up to Jerusalem to talk over all their affairs with Zacharias. The following week Joseph went to Jerusalem to confer with Zacharias. Both Zacharias and Elizabeth had become possessed with the sincere conviction that Jesus was indeed to become the Jewish deliverer, the Messiah, and that their son John was to be his chief of aides, his right-hand man of destiny. And since Mary held these same ideas, it was not difficult to prevail upon Joseph to remain in Bethlehem, the City of David, so that Jesus might grow up to become the successor of David on the throne of all Israel. Accordingly, they remained in Bethlehem more than a year, Joseph meantime working some at his carpenter's trade.

122:8.5 (1352.1) At the noontide birth of Jesus the seraphim of Urantia, assembled under their directors, did sing anthems of glory over the Bethlehem manger, but these utterances of praise were not heard by human ears. No shepherds nor any other mortal creatures came to pay homage to the babe of Bethlehem until the day of the arrival of certain priests from Ur, who were sent down from Jerusalem by Zacharias.

122:8.6 (1352.2) These priests from Mesopotamia had been told sometime before by a strange religious teacher of their country that he had had a dream in which he was informed that "the light of life" was about to appear on earth as a babe and among the Jews. And thither went these three teachers looking for this "light of life." After many weeks of futile search in Jerusalem, they were about to return to Ur when Zacharias met them and disclosed his belief that Jesus was the object of their quest and sent them on to Bethlehem, where they found the babe and left their gifts with Mary, his earth mother. The babe was almost three weeks old at the time of their visit.

122:8.7 (1352.3) These wise men saw no star to guide them to Bethlehem. The beautiful legend of the star of Bethlehem originated in this way: Jesus was born August 21 at noon, 7 B.C. On May 29, 7 B.C., there occurred an extraordinary conjunction of Jupiter and Saturn in the constellation of Pisces. And it is a remarkable astronomic fact that similar conjunctions occurred on September 29 and December 5 of the same year. Upon the basis of these extraordinary but wholly natural events the well-meaning zealots of the succeeding generation constructed the appealing legend of the star of Bethlehem and the adoring Magi led thereby to the manger, where they beheld and worshiped the newborn babe.

Oriental and near-Oriental minds delight in fairy stories, and they are continually spinning such beautiful myths about the lives of their religious leaders and political heroes. In the absence of printing, when most human knowledge was passed by word of mouth from one generation to another, it was very easy for myths to become traditions and for traditions eventually to become accepted as facts.

9 *The Presentation in the Temple*

122:9.1 (1352.4) Moses had taught the Jews that every first-born son belonged to the Lord, and that, in lieu of his sacrifice as was the custom among the heathen nations, such a son might live provided his parents would redeem him by the payment of five shekels to any authorized priest. There was also a Mosaic ordinance which directed that a mother, after the passing of a certain period of time, should present herself (or have someone make the proper sacrifice for her) at the temple for purification. It was customary to perform both of these ceremonies at the same time. Accordingly, Joseph and Mary went up to the temple at Jerusalem in person to present Jesus to the priests and effect his redemption and also to make the proper sacrifice to insure Mary's ceremonial purification from the alleged uncleanness of childbirth.

122:9.2 (1353.1) There lingered constantly about the courts of the temple two remarkable characters, Simeon a singer and Anna a poetess. Simeon was a Judean, but Anna was a Galilean. This couple were frequently in each other's company, and both were intimates of the priest Zacharias, who had confided the secret of John and Jesus to them. Both Simeon and Anna longed for the coming of the Messiah, and their confidence in Zacharias led them to believe that Jesus was the expected deliverer of the Jewish people.

122:9.3 (1353.2) Zacharias knew the day Joseph and Mary were expected to appear at the temple with Jesus, and he had prearranged with Simeon and Anna to indicate, by the salute of his upraised hand, which one in the procession of first- born children was Jesus.

122:9.4 (1353.3) For this occasion Anna had written a poem which Simeon proceeded to sing, much to the astonishment of Joseph, Mary, and all who were assembled in the temple courts. And this was their hymn of the redemption of the first- born son:

122:9.5 (1353.4) Blessed be the Lord, the God of Israel,
122:9.6 (1353.5) For he has visited us and wrought redemption for his people;
122:9.7 (1353.6) He has raised up a horn of salvation for all of us
122:9.8 (1353.7) In the house of his servant David.
122:9.9 (1353.8) Even as he spoke by the mouth of his holy prophets —
122:9.10 (1353.9) Salvation from our enemies and from the hand of all who hate us; 122:9.11 (1353.10) To show mercy to our fathers, and remember his holy covenant — 122:9.12 (1353.11) The oath which he swore to Abraham our father,
122:9.13 (1353.12) To grant us that we, being delivered out of the hand of our enemies,
122:9.14 (1353.13) Should serve him without fear,
122:9.15 (1353.14) In holiness and righteousness before him all our days.
122:9.16 (1353.15) Yes, and you, child of promise, shall be called the prophet of the Most High; 122:9.17 (1353.16) For you shall go before the face of the Lord to establish his kingdom; 122:9.18 (1353.17) To give knowledge of salvation to his people
122:9.19 (1353.18) In the remission of their sins.
122:9.20 (1353.19) Rejoice in the tender mercy of our God because the dayspring from on high has now visited us

122:9.21 (1353.20) To shine upon those who sit in darkness and the shadow of death;
122:9.22 (1353.21) To guide our feet into ways of peace.
122:9.23 (1353.22) And now let your servant depart in peace, O Lord, according to your word,
122:9.24 (1353.23)
For my eyes have seen your salvation,

122:9.25 (1353.24) Which you have prepared before the face of all peoples;

122:9.26 (1353.25) A light for even the unveiling of the gentiles

122:9.27 (1353.26) And the glory of your people Israel.

122:9.28 (1353.27) On the way back to Bethlehem, Joseph and Mary were silent—confused and overawed. Mary was much disturbed by the farewell salutation of Anna, the aged poetess, and Joseph was not in harmony with this premature effort to make Jesus out to be the expected Messiah of the Jewish people.

10   *Herod Acts*

122:10.1 (1353.28) But the watchers for Herod were not inactive. When they reported to him the visit of the priests of Ur to Bethlehem, Herod summoned these Chaldeans to appear before him. He inquired diligently of these wise men about the new "king of the Jews," but they gave him little satisfaction, explaining that the babe had been born of a woman who had come down to Bethlehem with her husband for the census enrollment. Herod, not being satisfied with this answer, sent them forth with a purse and directed that they should find the child so that he too might come and worship him, since they had declared that his kingdom was to be spiritual, not temporal. But when the wise men did not return, Herod grew suspicious. As he turned these things over in his mind, his informers returned and made full report of the recent occurrences in the temple, bringing him a copy of parts of the Simeon song which had been sung at the redemption ceremonies of Jesus. But they had failed to follow Joseph and Mary, and Herod was very angry with them when they could not tell him whither the pair had taken the babe. He then dispatched searchers to locate Joseph and Mary.

Knowing Herod pursued the Nazareth family, Zacharias and Elizabeth remained away from Bethlehem. The boy baby was secreted with Joseph's relatives.

122:10.2 (1354.1) Joseph was afraid to seek work, and their small savings were rapidly disappearing. Even at the time of the purification ceremonies at the temple, Joseph deemed himself sufficiently poor to warrant his offering for Mary two young pigeons as Moses had directed for the purification of mothers among the poor.

122:10.3 (1354.2) When, after more than a year of searching, Herod's spies had not located Jesus, and because of the suspicion that the babe was still concealed in Bethlehem, he prepared an order directing that a systematic search be made of every house in Bethlehem, and that all boy babies under two years of age should be killed. In this manner Herod hoped to make sure that this child who was to become "king of the Jews" would be destroyed. And thus perished in one day sixteen boy babies in Bethlehem of Judea. But intrigue and murder, even in his own immediate family, were common occurrences at the court of Herod.

122:10.4 (1354.3) The massacre of these infants took place about the middle of October, 6 B.C., when Jesus was a little over one year of age. But there were believers in the coming Messiah even among Herod's court attachés, and one of these, learning of the order to slaughter the Bethlehem boy babies, communicated with Zacharias, who in turn dispatched a messenger to Joseph; and the night before the massacre Joseph and Mary departed from Bethlehem with the babe for Alexandria in Egypt. In order to avoid attracting attention, they journeyed alone to Egypt with Jesus. They went to Alexandria on funds provided by Zacharias, and there Joseph worked at his trade while Mary and Jesus lodged with well-to-do relatives of Joseph's family. They sojourned in Alexandria two full years, not returning to Bethlehem until after the death of Herod.

Paper 123

The Early Childhood of Jesus

123:0.1 (1355.1) OWING to the uncertainties and anxieties of their sojourn in Bethlehem, Mary did not wean the babe until they had arrived safely in Alexandria, where the family was able to settle down to a normal life. They lived with kinsfolk, and Joseph was well able to support his family as he secured work shortly after their arrival. He was employed as a carpenter for several months and then elevated to the position of foreman of a large group of workmen employed on one of the public buildings then in process of construction. This new experience gave him the idea of becoming a contractor and builder after their return to Nazareth.

123:0.2 (1355.2) All through these early years of Jesus' helpless infancy, Mary maintained one long and constant vigil lest anything befall her child which might jeopardize his welfare or in any way interfere with his future mission on earth; no mother was ever more devoted to her child. In the home where Jesus chanced to be there were two other children about his age, and among the near neighbors there were six others whose ages were sufficiently near his own to make them acceptable play-fellows. At first Mary was disposed to keep Jesus close by her side. She feared something might happen to him if he were allowed to play in the garden with the other children, but Joseph, with the assistance of his kinsfolk, was able to convince her that such a course would deprive Jesus of the helpful experience of learning how to adjust himself to children of his own age. And Mary, realizing that such a program of undue sheltering and unusual protection might tend to make him self-conscious and somewhat self-centered, finally gave assent to the plan of permitting the child of promise to grow up just like any other child; and though she was obedient to this decision, she made it her business always to be on watch while the little folks were at play about the house or in the garden. Only an affectionate mother can know the burden that Mary carried in her heart for the safety of her son during these years of his infancy and early childhood.

123:0.3 (1355.3) Throughout the two years of their sojourn at Alexandria, Jesus enjoyed good health and continued to grow normally. Aside from a few friends and relatives no one was told about Jesus' being a "child of promise." One of Joseph's relatives revealed this to a few friends in Memphis, descendants of the distant Ikhnaton, and they, with a small group of Alexandrian believers, assembled at the palatial home of Joseph's relative-benefactor a short time before the return to Palestine to wish the Nazareth family well and to pay their respects to the child. On this occasion the assembled friends presented Jesus with a complete copy of the Greek translation of the Hebrew scriptures. But this copy of the Jewish sacred writings was not placed in Joseph's hands until both he and Mary had finally declined the invitation of their Memphis and Alexandrian friends to remain in Egypt. These believers insisted that the child of destiny would be able to exert a far greater world influence as a resident of Alexandria than of any designated place in Palestine. These persuasions delayed their departure for Palestine for some time after they received the news of Herod's death.

123:0.4 (1356.1) Joseph and Mary finally took leave of Alexandria on a boat belonging to their friend Ezraeon, bound for Joppa, arriving at that port late in August of the year 4 B.C. They went directly to Bethlehem, where they spent the entire month of September in counsel with their friends and relatives concerning whether they should remain there or return to Nazareth.

123:0.5 (1356.2) Mary had never fully given up the idea that Jesus ought to grow up in Bethlehem, the City of David. Joseph did not really believe that their son was to become a kingly deliverer of Israel. Besides, he knew that he himself was not really a descendant of David; that his being reckoned among the offspring of David was due to the adoption of one of his ancestors into the Davidic line of descent. Mary, of course, thought the City of David the most appropriate place in which the new candidate for David's throne could be reared, but Joseph preferred to take chances with Herod Antipas rather than with his brother Archelaus. He entertained great fears for the child's safety in Bethlehem or in any other city in Judea, and surmised that Archelaus would be more likely to pursue the menacing policies of his father, Herod, than would Antipas in Galilee. And besides all these reasons, Joseph was outspoken in his preference for Galilee as a better place in which to rear and educate the child, but it required three weeks to overcome Mary's objections.

123:0.6 (1356.3) By the first of October Joseph had convinced Mary and all their friends that it was best for them to return to Nazareth. Accordingly, early in October, 4 B.C., they departed from Bethlehem for Nazareth, going by way of Lydda and Scythopolis. They started out early one Sunday morning, Mary and the child riding on their newly acquired beast of burden, while Joseph and five accompanying kinsmen proceeded on foot; Joseph's relatives refused to permit them to make the trip to Nazareth alone. They feared to go to Galilee by Jerusalem and the Jordan valley, and the western routes were not altogether safe for two lone travelers with a child of tender years.

1   Back in Nazareth

123:1.1 (1356.4) On the fourth day of the journey the party reached its destination in safety. They arrived unannounced at the Nazareth home, which had been occupied for more than three years by one of Joseph's married brothers, who was indeed surprised to see them; so quietly had they gone about their business that neither the family of Joseph nor that of Mary knew

they had even left Alexandria. The next day Joseph's brother moved his family, and Mary, for the first time since Jesus' birth, settled down with her little family to enjoy life in their own home. In less than a week Joseph secured work as a carpenter, and they were supremely happy.

123:1.2 (1356.5) Jesus was about three years and two months old at the time of their return to Nazareth. He had stood all these travels very well and was in excellent health and full of childish glee and excitement at having premises of his own to run about in and to enjoy. But he greatly missed the association of his Alexandrian playmates.

123:1.3 (1356.6) On the way to Nazareth Joseph had persuaded Mary that it would be unwise to spread the word among their Galilean friends and relatives that Jesus was a child of promise. They agreed to refrain from all mention of these matters to anyone. And they were both very faithful in keeping this promise.

123:1.4 (1357.1) Jesus' entire fourth year was a period of normal physical development and of unusual mental activity. Meantime he had formed a very close attachment for a neighbor boy about his own age named Jacob. Jesus and Jacob were always happy in their play, and they grew up to be great friends and loyal companions.

123:1.5 (1357.2) The next important event in the life of this Nazareth family was the birth of the second child, James, in the early morning hours of April 2, 3 B.C. Jesus was thrilled by the thought of having a baby brother, and he would stand around by the hour just to observe the baby's early activities.

123:1.6 (1357.3) It was midsummer of this same year that Joseph built a small workshop close to the village spring and near the caravan tarrying lot. After this he did very little carpenter work by the day. He had as associates two of his brothers and several other mechanics, whom he sent out to work while he remained at the shop making yokes and plows and doing other woodwork. He also did some work in leather and with rope and canvas. And Jesus, as he grew up, when not at school, spent his time about equally between helping his mother with home duties and watching his father work at the shop, meanwhile listening to the conversation and gossip of the caravan conductors and passengers from the four corners of the earth.

123:1.7 (1357.4) In July of this year, one month before Jesus was four years old, an outbreak of malignant intestinal trouble spread over all Nazareth from contact with the caravan travelers. Mary became so alarmed by the danger of Jesus being exposed to this epidemic of disease that she bundled up both her children and fled to the country home of her brother, several miles south of Nazareth on the Megiddo road near Sarid. They did not return to Nazareth for more than two months; Jesus greatly enjoyed this, his first experience on a farm.

2   The Fifth Year
(2 B.C.)

123:2.1 (1357.5) In something more than a year after the return to Nazareth the boy Jesus arrived at the age of his first personal and wholehearted moral decision; and there came to abide with him a Thought Adjuster, a divine gift of the Paradise Father, which had aforetime served with Machiventa Melchizedek, thus gaining the experience of functioning in connection with the incarnation of a supermortal being living in the likeness of mortal flesh. This event occurred on February 11, 2 B.C. Jesus was no more aware of the coming of the divine Monitor than are the millions upon millions of other children who, before and since that day, have likewise received these Thought Adjusters to indwell their minds and work for the ultimate spiritualization of these minds and the eternal survival of their evolving immortal souls.

123:2.2 (1357.6) On this day in February the direct and personal supervision of the Universe Rulers, as it was related to the integrity of the childlike incarnation of Michael, terminated. From that time on throughout the human unfolding of the incarnation, the guardianship of Jesus was destined to rest in the keeping of this indwelling Adjuster and the associated seraphic guardians, supplemented from time to time by the ministry of midway creatures assigned for the performance of certain definite duties in accordance with the instruction of their planetary superiors.

123:2.3 (1357.7) Jesus was five years old in August of this year, and we will, therefore, refer to this as his fifth (calendar) year of life. In this year, 2 B.C., a little more than one month before his fifth birthday anniversary, Jesus was made very happy by the coming of his sister Miriam, who was born on the night of July 11. During the evening of the following day Jesus had a long talk with his father concerning the manner in which various groups of living things are born into the world as separate individuals. The most valuable part of Jesus' early education was secured from his parents in answer to his thoughtful and searching inquiries. Joseph never failed to do his full duty in taking pains and spending time answering the boy's numerous questions. From the time Jesus was five years old until he was ten, he was one continuous question mark. While Joseph and Mary could not always answer his questions, they never failed fully to discuss his inquiries and in every other possible way to assist him in his efforts to reach a satisfactory solution of the problem which his alert mind had suggested. *

123:2.4 (1358.1) Since returning to Nazareth, theirs had been a busy household, and Joseph had been unusually occupied building his new shop and getting his business started again. So fully was he occupied that he had found no time to build a cradle for James, but this was corrected long before Miriam came, so that she had a very comfortable crib in which to nestle while the family admired her. And the child Jesus heartily entered into all these natural and normal home experiences. He greatly enjoyed his little brother and his baby sister and was of great help to Mary in their care.

123:2.5 (1358.2) There were few homes in the gentile world of those days that could give a child a better intellectual, moral, and religious training than the Jewish homes of Galilee. These Jews had a systematic program for rearing and educating their children. They divided a child's life into seven stages:

123:2.6 (1358.3) 1. The newborn child, the first to the eighth day.

123:2.7 (1358.4) 2. The suckling child.

123:2.8 (1358.5) 3. The weaned child.

123:2.9 (1358.6) 4. The period of dependence on the mother, lasting up to the end of the fifth year.

123:2.10 (1358.7) 5. The beginning independence of the child and, with sons, the father assuming responsibility for their education.

123:2.11 (1358.8) 6. The adolescent youths and maidens.

123:2.12 (1358.9) 7. The young men and the young women.

123:2.13 (1358.10) It was the custom of the Galilean Jews for the mother to bear the responsibility for a child's training until the fifth birthday, and then, if the child were a boy, to hold the father responsible for the lad's education from that time on. This year, therefore, Jesus entered upon the fifth stage of a Galilean Jewish child's career, and accordingly on August 21, 2 B.C., Mary formally turned him over to Joseph for further instruction.

123:2.14 (1358.11) Though Joseph was now assuming the direct responsibility for Jesus' intellectual and religious education, his mother still interested herself in his home training. She taught him to know and care for the vines and flowers growing about the garden walls which completely surrounded the home plot. She also provided on the roof of the house (the summer bedroom) shallow boxes of sand in which Jesus worked out maps and did much of his early practice at writing Aramaic, Greek,

and later on, Hebrew, for in time he learned to read, write, and speak, fluently, all three languages.

123:2.15 (1358.12) Jesus appeared to be a well-nigh perfect child physically and continued to make normal progress mentally and emotionally. He experienced a mild digestive upset, his first minor illness, in the latter part of this, his fifth (calendar) year.

123:2.16 (1359.1) Though Joseph and Mary often talked about the future of their eldest child, had you been there, you would only have observed the growing up of a normal, healthy, carefree, but exceedingly inquisitive child of that time and place.

3   *Events of the Sixth Year (1 B.C.)*

123:3.1 (1359.2) Already, with his mother's help, Jesus had mastered the Galilean dialect of the Aramaic tongue; and now his father began teaching him Greek. Mary spoke little Greek, but Joseph was a fluent speaker of both Aramaic and Greek. The textbook for the study of the Greek language was the copy of the Hebrew scriptures—a complete version of the law and the prophets, including the Psalms—which had been presented to them on leaving Egypt. There were only two complete copies of the Scriptures in Greek in all Nazareth, and the possession of one of them by the carpenter's family made Joseph's home a much-sought place and enabled Jesus, as he grew up, to meet an almost endless procession of earnest students and sincere truth seekers. Before this year ended, Jesus had assumed custody of this priceless manuscript, having been told on his sixth birthday that the sacred book had been presented to him by Alexandrian friends and relatives. And in a very short time he could read it readily.

123:3.2 (1359.3) The first great shock of Jesus' young life occurred when he was not quite six years old. It had seemed to the lad that his father—at least his father and mother together—knew everything. Imagine, therefore, the surprise of this inquiring child, when he asked his father the cause of a mild earthquake which had just occurred, to hear Joseph say, "My son, I really do not know." Thus began that long and disconcerting disillusionment in the course of which Jesus found out that his earthly parents were not all-wise and all-knowing.

123:3.3 (1359.4) Joseph's first thought was to tell Jesus that the earthquake had been caused by God, but a moment's reflection admonished him that such an answer would immediately be provocative of further and still more embarrassing inquiries. Even at an early age it was very difficult to answer Jesus' questions about physical or social phenomena by thoughtlessly telling him that either God or the devil was responsible. In harmony with the prevailing belief of the Jewish people, Jesus was long willing to accept the doctrine of good spirits and evil spirits as the possible explanation of mental and spiritual phenomena, but he very early became doubtful that such unseen influences were responsible for the physical happenings of the natural world.

123:3.4 (1359.5) Before Jesus was six years of age, in the early summer of 1 B.C., Zacharias and Elizabeth and their son John came to visit the Nazareth family. Jesus and John had a happy time during this, their first visit within their memories. Although the visitors could remain only a few days, the parents talked over many things, including the future plans for their sons. While they were thus engaged, the lads played with blocks in the sand on top of the house and in many other ways enjoyed themselves in true boyish fashion.

123:3.5 (1359.6) Having met John, who came from near Jerusalem, Jesus began to evince an unusual interest in the history of Israel and to inquire in great detail as to the meaning of the Sabbath rites, the synagogue sermons, and the recurring feasts of commemoration. His father explained to him the meaning of all these seasons. The first was the mid-winter festive illumination, lasting eight days, starting out with one candle the first night and adding one each successive night; this commemorated the dedication of the temple after the restoration of the Mosaic services by Judas Maccabee. Next came the early springtime celebration of Purim, the feast of Esther and Israel's deliverance through her. Then followed the solemn Passover, which the adults celebrated in Jerusalem whenever possible, while at home the children would remember that no leavened bread was to be eaten for the whole week. Later came the feast of the first-fruits, the harvest ingathering; and last, the most solemn of all, the feast of the new year, the day of atonement. While some of these celebrations and observances were difficult for Jesus' young mind to understand, he pondered them seriously and then entered fully into the joy of the feast of tabernacles, the annual vacation season of the whole Jewish people, the time when they camped out in leafy booths and gave themselves up to mirth and pleasure.

123:3.6 (1360.1) During this year Joseph and Mary had trouble with Jesus about his prayers. He insisted on talking to his heavenly Father much as he would talk to Joseph, his earthly father. This departure from the more solemn and reverent modes of communication with Deity was a bit disconcerting to his parents, especially to his mother, but there was no persuading him to change; he would say his prayers just as he had been taught, after which he insisted on having "just a little talk with my Father in heaven."

123:3.7 (1360.2) In June of this year Joseph turned the shop in Nazareth over to his brothers and formally entered upon his work as a builder. Before the year was over, the family income had more than trebled. Never again, until after Joseph's death, did the Nazareth family feel the pinch of poverty. The family grew larger and larger, and they spent much money on extra education and travel, but always Joseph's increasing income kept pace with the growing expenses.

123:3.8 (1360.3) The next few years Joseph did considerable work at Cana, Bethlehem (of Galilee), Magdala, Nain, Sepphoris, Capernaum, and Endor, as well as much building in and near Nazareth. As James grew up to be old enough to help his mother with the housework and care of the younger children, Jesus made frequent trips away from home with his father to these surrounding towns and villages. Jesus was a keen observer and gained much practical knowledge from these trips away from home; he was assiduously storing up knowledge regarding man and the way he lived on earth.

123:3.9 (1360.4) This year Jesus made great progress in adjusting his strong feelings and vigorous impulses to the demands of family co-operation and home discipline. Mary was a loving mother but a fairly strict disciplinarian. In many ways, however, Joseph exerted the greater control over Jesus as it was his practice to sit down with the boy and fully explain the real and underlying reasons for the necessity of disciplinary curtailment of personal desires in deference to the welfare and tranquillity of the entire family. When the situation had been explained to Jesus, he was always intelligently and willingly co-operative with parental wishes and family regulations.

123:3.10 (1360.5) Much of his spare time—when his mother did not require his help about the house—was spent studying the flowers and plants by day and the stars by night. He evinced a troublesome penchant for lying on his back and gazing wonderingly up into the starry heavens long after his usual bedtime in this well-ordered Nazareth household.

4   The Seventh Year (A.D. 1)

123:4.1 (1361.1) This was, indeed, an eventful year in Jesus' life. Early in January a great snowstorm occurred in Galilee. Snow fell two feet deep, the heaviest snowfall Jesus saw during his lifetime and one of the deepest at Nazareth in a hundred years.

123:4.2 (1361.2) The play life of Jewish children in the times of Jesus was rather circumscribed; all too often the children played at the more serious things they observed their elders doing. They played much at weddings and funerals, ceremonies which they so frequently saw and which were so spectacular. They danced and sang but had few organized games, such as children of later days so much enjoy.

123:4.3 (1361.3) Jesus, in company with a neighbor boy and later his brother James, delighted to play in the far corner of the family carpenter shop, where they had great fun with the shavings and the blocks of wood. It was always difficult for Jesus to comprehend the harm of certain sorts of play which were forbidden on the Sabbath, but he never failed to conform to his parents' wishes. He had a capacity for humor and play which was afforded little opportunity for

expression in the environment of his day and generation, but up to the age of fourteen he was cheerful and lighthearted most of the time.

123:4.4 (1361.4) Mary maintained a dovecote on top of the animal house adjoining the home, and they used the profits from the sale of doves as a special charity fund, which Jesus administered after he deducted the tithe and turned it over to the officer of the synagogue.

123:4.5 (1361.5) The only real accident Jesus had up to this time was a fall down the back-yard stone stairs which led up to the canvas-roofed bedroom. It happened during an unexpected July sandstorm from the east. The hot winds, carrying blasts of fine sand, usually blew during the rainy season, especially in March and April. It was extraordinary to have such a storm in July. When the storm came up, Jesus was on the housetop playing, as was his habit, for during much of the dry season this was his accustomed playroom. He was blinded by the sand when descending the stairs and fell. After this accident Joseph built a balustrade up both sides of the stairway.

123:4.6 (1361.6) There was no way in which this accident could have been prevented. It was not chargeable to neglect by the midway temporal guardians, one primary and one secondary midwayer having been assigned to the watchcare of the lad; neither was it chargeable to the guardian seraphim. It simply could not have been avoided. But this slight accident, occurring while Joseph was absent in Endor, caused such great anxiety to develop in Mary's mind that she unwisely tried to keep Jesus very close to her side for some months.

123:4.7 (1361.7) Material accidents, commonplace occurrences of a physical nature, are not arbitrarily interfered with by celestial personalities. Under ordinary circumstances only midway creatures can intervene in material conditions to safeguard the persons of men and women of destiny, and even in special situations these beings can so act only in obedience to the specific mandates of their superiors.

123:4.8 (1361.8) And this was but one of a number of such minor accidents which subsequently befell this inquisitive and adventurous youth. If you envisage the average childhood and youth of an aggressive boy, you will have a fairly good idea of the youthful career of Jesus, and you will be able to imagine just about how much anxiety he caused his parents, particularly his mother.

123:4.9 (1362.1) The fourth member of the Nazareth family, Joseph, was born Wednesday morning, March 16, A.D. 1.

5   *School Days in Nazareth*

123:5.1 (1362.2) Jesus was now seven years old, the age when Jewish children were supposed to begin their formal education in the synagogue schools. Accordingly, in August of this year he entered upon his eventful school life at Nazareth. Already this lad was a fluent reader, writer, and speaker of two languages, Aramaic and Greek. He was now to acquaint himself with the task of learning to read, write, and speak the Hebrew language. And he was truly eager for the new school life which was ahead of him.

123:5.2 (1362.3) For three years—until he was ten—he attended the elementary school of the Nazareth synagogue. For these three years he studied the rudiments of the Book of the Law as it was recorded in the Hebrew tongue. For the following three years he studied in the advanced school and committed to memory, by the method of repeating aloud, the deeper teachings of the sacred law. He graduated from this school of the synagogue during his thirteenth year and was turned over to his parents by the synagogue rulers as an educated "son of the commandment"—henceforth a responsible citizen of the commonwealth of Israel, all of which entailed his attendance at the Passovers in Jerusalem; accordingly, he attended his first Passover that year in company with his father and mother.

123:5.3 (1362.4) At Nazareth the pupils sat on the floor in a semicircle, while their teacher, the chazan, an officer of the synagogue, sat facing them. Beginning with the Book of Leviticus, they passed on to the study of the other books of the law, followed by the study of the Prophets and the Psalms. The Nazareth synagogue possessed a complete copy of the Scriptures in Hebrew. Nothing but the Scriptures was studied prior to the twelfth year. In the summer months the hours for school were greatly shortened.

123:5.4 (1362.5) Jesus early became a master of Hebrew, and as a young man, when no visitor of prominence happened to be sojourning in Nazareth, he would often be asked to read the Hebrew scriptures to the faithful assembled in the synagogue at the regular Sabbath services.

123:5.5 (1362.6) These synagogue schools, of course, had no textbooks. In teaching, the chazan would utter a statement while the pupils would in unison repeat it after him. When having access to the written books of the law, the student learned his lesson by reading aloud and by constant repetition.

123:5.6 (1362.7) Next, in addition to his more formal schooling, Jesus began to make contact with human nature from the four quarters of the earth as men from many lands passed in and out of his father's repair shop. When he grew older, he mingled freely with the caravans as they tarried near the spring for rest and nourishment. Being a fluent speaker of Greek, he had little trouble in conversing with the majority of the caravan travelers and conductors.

123:5.7 (1362.8) Nazareth was a caravan way station and crossroads of travel and largely gentile in population; at the same time it was widely known as a center of liberal interpretation of Jewish traditional law. In Galilee the Jews mingled more freely with the gentiles than was their practice in Judea. And of all the cities of Galilee, the Jews of Nazareth were most liberal in their interpretation of the social restrictions based on the fears of contamination as a result of contact with the gentiles. And these conditions gave rise to the common saying in Jerusalem, "Can any good thing come out of Nazareth?"

123:5.8 (1363.1) Jesus received his moral training and spiritual culture chiefly in his own home. He secured much of his intellectual and theological education from the chazan. But his real education—that equipment of mind and heart for the actual test of grappling with the difficult problems of life—he obtained by mingling with his fellow men. It was this close association with his fellow men, young and old, Jew and gentile, that afforded him the opportunity to know the human race. Jesus was highly educated in that he thoroughly understood men and devotedly loved them.

123:5.9 (1363.2) Throughout his years at the synagogue he was a brilliant student, possessing a great advantage since he was conversant with three languages. The

Nazareth chazan, on the occasion of Jesus' finishing the course in his school, remarked to Joseph that he feared he "had learned more from Jesus' searching questions" than he had "been able to teach the lad."

123:5.10 (1363.3) Throughout his course of study Jesus learned much and derived great inspiration from the regular Sabbath sermons in the synagogue. It was customary to ask distinguished visitors, stopping over the Sabbath in Nazareth, to address the synagogue. As Jesus grew up, he heard many great thinkers of the entire Jewish world expound their views, and many also who were hardly orthodox Jews since the synagogue of Nazareth was an advanced and liberal center of Hebrew thought and culture.

123:5.11 (1363.4) When entering school at seven years (at this time the Jews had just inaugurated a compulsory education law), it was customary for the pupils to choose their "birthday text," a sort of golden rule to guide them throughout their studies, one upon which they often expatiated at their graduation when thirteen years old. The text which Jesus chose was from the Prophet Isaiah: "The spirit of the Lord God is upon me, for the Lord has anointed me; he has sent me to bring good news to the meek, to bind up the brokenhearted, to proclaim liberty to the captives, and to set the spiritual prisoners free."

123:5.12 (1363.5) Nazareth was one of the twenty-four priest centers of the Hebrew nation. But the Galilean priesthood was more liberal in the interpretation of the traditional laws than were the Judean scribes and rabbis. And at Nazareth they were also more liberal regarding the observance of the Sabbath. It was therefore the custom for Joseph to take Jesus out for walks on Sabbath afternoons, one of their favorite jaunts being to climb the high hill near their home, from which they could obtain a panoramic view of all Galilee. To the northwest, on clear days, they could see the long ridge of Mount Carmel running down to the sea; and many times Jesus heard his father relate the story of Elijah, one of the first of that long line of Hebrew prophets, who reproved Ahab and exposed the priests of Baal. To the north Mount Hermon raised its snowy peak in majestic splendor and monopolized the skyline, almost 3,000 feet of the upper slopes glistening white with perpetual snow. Far to the east they could discern the Jordan valley and, far beyond, the rocky hills of Moab. Also to the south and the east, when the sun shone upon their marble walls, they could see the Greco-Roman cities of the Decapolis, with their amphitheaters and pretentious temples. And when they lingered toward the going down of the sun, to the west they could make out the sailing vessels on the distant Mediterranean. *

123:5.13 (1364.1) From four directions Jesus could observe the caravan trains as they wended their way in and out of Nazareth, and to the south he could overlook the broad and fertile plain country of Esdraelon, stretching off toward Mount Gilboa and Samaria.

123:5.14 (1364.2) When they did not climb the heights to view the distant landscape, they strolled through the countryside and studied nature in her various moods in accordance with the seasons. Jesus' earliest training, aside from that of the home hearth, had to do with a reverent and sympathetic contact with nature.

123:5.15 (1364.3) Before he was eight years of age, he was known to all the mothers and young women of Nazareth, who had met him and talked with him at the spring, which was not far from his home, and which was one of the social centers of contact and gossip for the entire town. This year Jesus learned to milk the family cow and care for the other animals. During this and the following year he also learned to make cheese and to weave. When he was ten years of age, he was an expert loom operator. It was about this time that Jesus and the neighbor boy Jacob became great friends of the potter who worked near the flowing spring; and as they watched Nathan's deft fingers mold the clay on the

potter's wheel, many times both of them determined to be potters when they grew up. Nathan was very fond of the lads and often gave them clay to play with, seeking to stimulate their creative imaginations by suggesting competitive efforts in modeling various objects and animals.

6 His Eighth Year (A.D. 2)

123:6.1 (1364.4) This was an interesting year at school. Although Jesus was not an unusual student, he was a diligent pupil and belonged to the more progressive third of the class, doing his work so well that he was excused from attendance one week out of each month. This week he usually spent either with his fisherman uncle on the shores of the Sea of Galilee near Magdala or on the farm of another uncle (his mother's brother) five miles south of Nazareth.

123:6.2 (1364.5) Although his mother had become unduly anxious about his health and safety, she gradually became reconciled to these trips away from home. Jesus' uncles and aunts were all very fond of him, and there ensued a lively competition among them to secure his company for these monthly visits throughout this and immediately subsequent years. His first week's sojourn on his uncle's farm (since infancy) was in January of this year; the first week's fishing experience on the Sea of Galilee occurred in the month of May.

123:6.3 (1364.6) About this time Jesus met a teacher of mathematics from Damascus, and learning some new techniques of numbers, he spent much time on mathematics for several years. He developed a keen sense of numbers, distances, and proportions.

123:6.4 (1364.7) Jesus began to enjoy his brother James very much and by the end of this year had begun to teach him the alphabet.

123:6.5 (1364.8) This year Jesus made

arrangements to exchange dairy products for lessons on the harp. He had an unusual liking for everything musical. Later on he did much to promote an interest in vocal music among his youthful associates. By the time he was eleven years of age, he was a skillful harpist and greatly enjoyed entertaining both family and friends with his extraordinary interpretations and able improvisations.

123:6.6 (1365.1) While Jesus continued to make enviable progress at school, all did not run smoothly for either parents or teachers. He persisted in asking many embarrassing questions concerning both science and religion, particularly regarding geography and astronomy. He was especially insistent on finding out why there was a dry season and a rainy season in Palestine. Repeatedly he sought the explanation for the great difference between the temperatures of Nazareth and the Jordan valley. He simply never ceased to ask such intelligent but perplexing questions.

123:6.7 (1365.2) His third brother, Simon, was born on Friday evening, April 14, of this year, A.D. 2.

123:6.8 (1365.3) In February, Nahor, one of the teachers in a Jerusalem academy of the rabbis, came to Nazareth to observe Jesus, having been on a similar mission to Zacharias's home near Jerusalem. He came to Nazareth at the instigation of John's father. While at first he was somewhat shocked by Jesus' frankness and unconventional manner of relating himself to things religious, he attributed it to the remoteness of Galilee from the centers of Hebrew learning and culture and advised Joseph and Mary to allow him to take Jesus back with him to Jerusalem, where he could have the advantages of education and training at the center of Jewish culture. Mary was half persuaded to consent; she was convinced her eldest son was to become the Messiah, the Jewish deliverer; Joseph hesitated; he was equally persuaded that Jesus was to grow up to become a man of destiny, but what that destiny would prove to be he was profoundly uncertain. But he never really doubted that his son was to

fulfill some great mission on earth. The more he thought about Nahor's advice, the more he questioned the wisdom of the proposed sojourn in Jerusalem.

123:6.9 (1365.4) Because of this difference of opinion between Joseph and Mary, Nahor requested permission to lay the whole matter before Jesus. Jesus listened attentively, talked with Joseph, Mary, and a neighbor, Jacob the stone mason, whose son was his favorite playmate, and then, two days later, reported that since there was such a difference of opinion among his parents and advisers, and since he did not feel competent to assume the responsibility for such a decision, not feeling strongly one way or the other, in view of the whole situation, he had finally decided to "talk with my Father who is in heaven"; and while he was not perfectly sure about the answer, he rather felt he should remain at home "with my father and mother," adding, "they who love me so much should be able to do more for me and guide me more safely than strangers who can only view my body and observe my mind but can hardly truly know me." They all marveled, and Nahor went his way, back to Jerusalem. And it was many years before the subject of Jesus' going away from home again came up for consideration.

Paper 124

The Later Childhood of Jesus

124:0.1 (1366.1) ALTHOUGH Jesus might have enjoyed a better opportunity for schooling at Alexandria than in Galilee, he could not have had such a splendid environment for working out his own life problems with a minimum of educational guidance, at the same time enjoying the great advantage of constantly contacting with such a large number of all classes of men and women hailing from every part of the civilized world. Had he remained at Alexandria, his education would have been directed by Jews and along exclusively

Jewish lines. At Nazareth he secured an education and received a training which more acceptably prepared him to understand the gentiles, and which gave him a better and more balanced idea of the relative merits of the Eastern, or Babylonian, and the Western, or Hellenic, views of Hebrew theology.

1　Jesus' Ninth Year (A.D. 3)

124:1.1 (1366.2) Though it could hardly be said that Jesus was ever seriously ill, he did have some of the minor ailments of childhood this year, along with his brothers and baby sister.

124:1.2 (1366.3) School went on and he was still a favored pupil, having one week each month at liberty, and he continued to divide his time about equally between trips to neighboring cities with his father, sojourns on his uncle's farm south of Nazareth, and fishing excursions out from Magdala.

124:1.3 (1366.4) The most serious trouble as yet to come up at school occurred in late winter when Jesus dared to challenge the chazan regarding the teaching that all images, pictures, and drawings were idolatrous in nature. Jesus delighted in drawing landscapes as well as in modeling a great variety of objects in potter's clay. Everything of that sort was strictly forbidden by Jewish law, but up to this time he had managed to disarm his parents' objection to such an extent that they had permitted him to continue in these activities.

124:1.4 (1366.5) But trouble was again stirred up at school when one of the more backward pupils discovered Jesus drawing a charcoal picture of the teacher on the floor of the schoolroom. There it was, plain as day, and many of the elders had viewed it before the committee went to call on Joseph to demand that something be done to suppress the lawlessness of his eldest son. And though this was not the first time complaints had come to Joseph

and Mary about the doings of their versatile and aggressive child, this was the most serious of all the accusations which had thus far been lodged against him. Jesus listened to the indictment of his artistic efforts for some time, being seated on a large stone just outside the back door. He resented their blaming his father for his alleged misdeeds; so in he marched, fearlessly confronting his accusers. The elders were thrown into confusion. Some were inclined to view the episode humorously, while one or two seemed to think the boy was sacrilegious if not blasphemous. Joseph was nonplused, Mary indignant, but Jesus insisted on being heard. He had his say, courageously defended his viewpoint, and with consummate self- control announced that he would abide by the decision of his father in this as in all other matters controversial. And the committee of elders departed in silence.

124:1.5 (1367.1) Mary endeavored to influence Joseph to permit Jesus to model in clay at home, provided he promised not to carry on any of these questionable activities at school, but Joseph felt impelled to rule that the rabbinical interpretation of the second commandment should prevail. And so Jesus no more drew or modeled the likeness of anything from that day as long as he lived in his father's house. But he was unconvinced of the wrong of what he had done, and to give up such a favorite pastime constituted one of the great trials of his young life.

124:1.6 (1367.2) In the latter part of June, Jesus, in company with his father, first climbed to the summit of Mount Tabor. It was a clear day and the view was superb. It seemed to this nine-year-old lad that he had really gazed upon the entire world excepting India, Africa, and Rome.

124:1.7 (1367.3) Jesus' second sister, Martha, was born Thursday night, September 13. Three weeks after the coming of Martha, Joseph, who was home for awhile, started the building of an addition to their house, a combined workshop and bedroom. A small workbench was built for

Jesus, and for the first time he possessed tools of his own. At odd times for many years he worked at this bench and became highly expert in the making of yokes.

124:1.8 (1367.4) This winter and the next were the coldest in Nazareth for many decades. Jesus had seen snow on the mountains, and several times it had fallen in Nazareth, remaining on the ground only a short time; but not until this winter had he seen ice. The fact that water could be had as a solid, a liquid, and a vapor—he had long pondered over the escaping steam from the boiling pots—caused the lad to think a great deal about the physical world and its constitution; and yet the personality embodied in this growing youth was all this while the actual creator and organizer of all these things throughout a far-flung universe.

124:1.9 (1367.5) The climate of Nazareth was not severe. January was the coldest month, the temperature averaging around 50° F. During July and August, the hottest months, the temperature would vary from 75° to 90° F. From the mountains to the Jordan and the Dead Sea valley the climate of Palestine ranged from the frigid to the torrid. And so, in a way, the Jews were prepared to live in about any and all of the world's varying climates.

124:1.10 (1367.6) Even during the warmest summer months a cool sea breeze usually blew from the west from 10:00 A.M. until about 10:00 P.M. But every now and then terrific hot winds from the eastern desert would blow across all Palestine. These hot blasts usually came in February and March, near the end of the rainy season. In those days the rain fell in refreshing showers from November to April, but it did not rain steadily. There were only two seasons in Palestine, summer and winter, the dry and rainy seasons. In January the flowers began to bloom, and by the end of April the whole land was one vast flower garden.

124:1.11 (1367.7) In May of this year, on his uncle's farm, Jesus for the first time helped with the harvest of the grain. Before he was thirteen, he had managed to find out something about practically everything that men and women worked at around Nazareth except metal working, and he spent several months in a smith's shop when older, after the death of his father.

124:1.12 (1368.1) When work and caravan travel were slack, Jesus made many trips with his father on pleasure or business to near-by Cana, Endor, and Nain. Even as a lad he frequently visited Sepphoris, only a little over three miles from Nazareth to the northwest, and from 4 B.C. to about A.D. 25 the capital of Galilee and one of the residences of Herod Antipas. *

124:1.13 (1368.2) Jesus continued to grow physically, intellectually, socially, and spiritually. His trips away from home did much to give him a better and more generous understanding of his own family, and by this time even his parents were beginning to learn from him as well as to teach him. Jesus was an original thinker and a skillful teacher, even in his youth. He was in constant collision with the so-called "oral law," but he always sought to adapt himself to the practices of his family. He got along fairly well with the children of his age, but he often grew discouraged with their slow-acting minds. Before he was ten years old, he had become the leader of a group of seven lads who formed themselves into a society for promoting the acquirements of manhood—physical, intellectual, and religious. Among these boys Jesus succeeded in introducing many new games and various improved methods of physical recreation.

2   The Tenth Year (A.D. 4)

124:2.1 (1368.3) It was the fifth of July, the first Sabbath of the month, when Jesus, while strolling through the countryside with his father, first gave expression to feelings and ideas which indicated that he was becoming self-conscious of the unusual nature of his life mission. Joseph listened attentively to the momentous words of his son but made few comments; he volunteered no information. The next day Jesus had a similar but longer talk with his mother. Mary

likewise listened to the pronouncements of the lad, but neither did she volunteer any information. It was almost two years before Jesus again spoke to his parents concerning this increasing revelation within his own consciousness regarding the nature of his personality and the character of his mission on earth.

124:2.2 (1368.4) He entered the advanced school of the synagogue in August. At school he was constantly creating trouble by the questions he persisted in asking. Increasingly he kept all Nazareth in more or less of a hubbub. His parents were loath to forbid his asking these disquieting questions, and his chief teacher was greatly intrigued by the lad's curiosity, insight, and hunger for knowledge.

124:2.3 (1368.5) Jesus' playmates saw nothing supernatural in his conduct; in most ways he was altogether like themselves. His interest in study was somewhat above the average but not wholly unusual. He did ask more questions at school than others in his class.

124:2.4 (1368.6) Perhaps his most unusual and outstanding trait was his unwillingness to fight for his rights. Since he was such a well-developed lad for his age, it seemed strange to his playfellows that he was disinclined to defend himself even from injustice or when subjected to personal abuse. As it happened, he did not suffer much on account of this trait because of the friendship of Jacob, a neighbor boy, who was one year older. He was the son of the stone mason, a business associate of Joseph. Jacob was a great admirer of Jesus and made it his business to see that no one was permitted to impose upon Jesus because of his aversion to physical combat. Several times older and uncouth youths attacked Jesus, relying upon his reputed docility, but they always suffered swift and certain retribution at the hands of his self-appointed champion and ever-ready defender, Jacob the stone mason's son.

124:2.5 (1369.1) Jesus was the generally accepted leader of the Nazareth lads who stood for the higher ideals of their day and generation. He was really loved by his youthful associates, not only because he was fair, but also because he possessed a rare and understanding sympathy that betokened love and bordered on discreet compassion.

124:2.6 (1369.2) This year he began to show a marked preference for the company of older persons. He delighted in talking over things cultural, educational, social, economic, political, and religious with older minds, and his depth of reasoning and keenness of observation so charmed his adult associates that they were always more than willing to visit with him.

Until he became responsible for the support of the home, his parents were constantly seeking to influence him to associate with those of his own age, or more nearly his age, rather than with older and better-informed individuals for whom he evinced such a preference.

124:2.7 (1369.3) Late this year he had a fishing experience of two months with his uncle on the Sea of Galilee, and he was very successful. Before attaining manhood, he had become an expert fisherman.

124:2.8 (1369.4) His physical development continued; he was an advanced and privileged pupil at school; he got along fairly well at home with his younger brothers and sisters, having the advantage of being three and one-half years older than the oldest of the other children. He was well thought of in Nazareth except by the parents of some of the duller children, who often spoke of Jesus as being too pert, as lacking in proper humility and youthful reserve. He manifested a growing tendency to direct the play activities of his youthful associates into more serious and thoughtful channels. He was a born teacher and simply could not refrain from so functioning, even when supposedly engaged in play.

124:2.9 (1369.5) Joseph early began to instruct Jesus in the diverse means of gaining a livelihood, explaining the advantages of agriculture over industry and trade. Galilee was a more beautiful and prosperous district than Judea, and it cost only about one fourth as much to live there as in Jerusalem and Judea. It was a province of agricultural villages and thriving industrial cities, containing more than two hundred towns of over five thousand population and thirty of over fifteen thousand.

124:2.10 (1369.6) When on his first trip with his father to observe the fishing industry on the lake of Galilee, Jesus had just about made up his mind to become a fisherman; but close association with his father's vocation later on influenced him to become a carpenter, while still later a combination of influences led him to the final choice of becoming a religious teacher of a new order.

3   *The Eleventh Year (A.D. 5)*

124:3.1 (1369.7) Throughout this year the lad continued to make trips away from home with his father, but he also frequently visited his uncle's farm and occasionally went over to Magdala to engage in fishing with the uncle who made his headquarters near that city.

124:3.2 (1369.8) Joseph and Mary were often tempted to show some special favoritism for Jesus or otherwise to betray their knowledge that he was a child of promise, a son of destiny. But both of his parents were extraordinarily wise and sagacious in all these matters. The few times they did in any manner exhibit any preference for him, even in the slightest degree, the lad was quick to refuse all such special consideration.

124:3.3 (1370.1) Jesus spent considerable time at the caravan supply shop, and by conversing with the travelers from all parts of the world, he acquired a store of information about international affairs that was amazing, considering his age. This was the last year in which he enjoyed much free play and youthful joyousness. From this time on difficulties and responsibilities rapidly multiplied in the life of this youth.

124:3.4 (1370.2) On Wednesday evening, June 24, A.D. 5, Jude was born. Complications attended the birth of this, the seventh child. Mary was so very ill for several weeks that Joseph remained at home. Jesus was very much occupied with errands for his father and with many duties occasioned by his mother's serious illness. Never again did this youth find it possible to return to the childlike attitude of his earlier years. From the time of his mother's illness—just before he was eleven years old—he was compelled to assume the responsibilities of the first-born son and to do all this one or two full years before these burdens should normally have fallen on his shoulders.

124:3.5 (1370.3) The chazan spent one evening each week with Jesus, helping him to master the Hebrew scriptures. He was greatly interested in the progress of his promising pupil; therefore was he willing to assist him in many ways. This Jewish pedagogue exerted a great influence upon this growing mind, but he was never able to comprehend why Jesus was so indifferent to all his suggestions regarding the prospects of going to Jerusalem to continue his education under the learned rabbis.

124:3.6 (1370.4) About the middle of May the lad accompanied his father on a business trip to Scythopolis, the chief Greek city of the Decapolis, the ancient Hebrew city of Beth-shean. On the way Joseph recounted much of the olden history of King Saul, the Philistines, and the subsequent events of Israel's turbulent history. Jesus was tremendously impressed with the clean appearance and well-ordered arrangement of this so-called heathen city. He marveled at the open-air theater and admired the beautiful marble temple dedicated to the worship of the "heathen" gods. Joseph was much perturbed by the lad's enthusiasm and sought to counteract these favorable impressions by extolling the beauty and grandeur of the Jewish temple at Jerusalem. Jesus had often gazed curiously upon this magnificent Greek city from the hill of Nazareth and had many times inquired about its extensive public works and ornate buildings, but his father had always sought to avoid answering these questions. Now they were face to face with the beauties of this gentile city, and Joseph could not gracefully ignore Jesus' inquiries.

124:3.7 (1370.5) It so happened that just at this time the annual competitive games and public demonstrations of physical prowess between the Greek cities of the Decapolis were in progress at the Scythopolis amphitheater, and Jesus was insistent that his father take him to see the games, and he was so insistent that Joseph hesitated to deny him. The boy was thrilled with the games and entered most heartily into the spirit of the demonstrations of physical development and athletic skill. Joseph was inexpressibly shocked to observe his son's enthusiasm as he beheld these exhibitions of "heathen" vaingloriousness. After the games were finished, Joseph received the surprise of his life when he heard Jesus express his approval of them and suggest that it would be good for the young men of Nazareth if they could be thus benefited by wholesome outdoor physical activities. Joseph talked earnestly and long with Jesus concerning the evil nature of such practices, but he well knew that the lad was unconvinced.

124:3.8 (1371.1) The only time Jesus ever saw his father angry with him was that night in their room at the inn when, in the course of their discussions, the boy so far forgot the trends of Jewish thought as to suggest that they go back home and work for the building of an amphitheater at Nazareth. When Joseph heard his first-born son express such un-Jewish sentiments, he forgot his usual calm demeanor and, seizing Jesus by the shoulder, angrily exclaimed, "My son, never again let me hear you give utterance to such an evil thought as long as you live." Jesus was

startled by his father's display of emotion; he had never before been made to feel the personal sting of his father's indignation and was astonished and shocked beyond expression. He only replied, "Very well, my father, it shall be so." And never again did the boy even in the slightest manner allude to the games and other athletic activities of the Greeks as long as his father lived.

124:3.9 (1371.2) Later on, Jesus saw the Greek amphitheater at Jerusalem and learned how hateful such things were from the Jewish point of view. Nevertheless, throughout his life he endeavored to introduce the idea of wholesome recreation into his personal plans and, as far as Jewish practice would permit, into the later program of regular activities for his twelve apostles.

124:3.10 (1371.3) At the end of this eleventh year Jesus was a vigorous, well-developed, moderately humorous, and fairly lighthearted youth, but from this year on he was more and more given to peculiar seasons of profound meditation and serious contemplation. He was much given to thinking about how he was to carry out his obligations to his family and at the same time be obedient to the call of his mission to the world; already he had conceived that his ministry was not to be limited to the betterment of the Jewish people.

4 The Twelfth Year (A.D. 6)

124:4.1 (1371.4) This was an eventful year in Jesus' life. He continued to make progress at school and was indefatigable in his study of nature, while increasingly he prosecuted his study of the methods whereby men make a living. He began doing regular work in the home carpenter shop and was permitted to manage his own earnings, a very unusual arrangement to obtain in a Jewish family. This year he also learned the wisdom of keeping such matters a secret in the family. He was becoming conscious of the way in which he had caused trouble in the village, and henceforth he became increasingly discreet in concealing everything which might cause him to be regarded as different from his fellows.

124:4.2 (1371.5) Throughout this year he experienced many seasons of uncertainty, if not actual doubt, regarding the nature of his mission. His naturally developing human mind did not yet fully grasp the reality of his dual nature. The fact that he had a single personality rendered it difficult for his consciousness to recognize the double origin of those factors which composed the nature associated with that selfsame personality.

124:4.3 (1371.6) From this time on he became more successful in getting along with his brothers and sisters. He was increasingly tactful, always compassionate and considerate of their welfare and happiness, and enjoyed good relations with them up to the beginning of his public ministry. To be more explicit: He got along with James, Miriam, and the two younger (as yet unborn) children, Amos and Ruth, most excellently. He always got along with Martha fairly well. What trouble he had at home largely arose out of friction with Joseph and Jude, particularly the latter.

124:4.4 (1372.1) It was a trying experience for Joseph and Mary to undertake the rearing of this unprecedented combination of divinity and humanity, and they deserve great credit for so faithfully and successfully discharging their parental responsibilities. Increasingly Jesus' parents realized that there was something superhuman resident within this eldest son, but they never even faintly dreamed that this son of promise was indeed and in truth the actual creator of this local universe of things and beings. Joseph and Mary lived and died without ever learning that their son Jesus really was the Universe Creator incarnate in mortal flesh.

124:4.5 (1372.2) This year Jesus paid more attention than ever to music, and he continued to teach the home school for his brothers and sisters. It was at about this time that the lad became keenly conscious of the difference between the viewpoints of Joseph and Mary regarding the nature of his mission. He pondered much over his parents' differing opinions, often hearing their discussions when they thought he was sound asleep. More and more he inclined to the view of his father, so that his mother was destined to be hurt by the realization that her son was gradually rejecting her guidance in matters having to do with his life career. And, as the years passed, this breach of understanding widened. Less and less did Mary comprehend the significance of Jesus' mission, and increasingly was this good mother hurt by the failure of her favorite son to fulfill her fond expectations.

124:4.6 (1372.3) Joseph entertained a growing belief in the spiritual nature of Jesus' mission. And but for other and more important reasons it does seem unfortunate that he could not have lived to see the fulfillment of his concept of Jesus' bestowal on earth.

124:4.7 (1372.4) During his last year at school, when he was twelve years old, Jesus remonstrated with his father about the Jewish custom of touching the bit of parchment nailed upon the doorpost each time on going into, or coming out of, the house and then kissing the finger that touched the parchment. As a part of this ritual it was customary to say, "The Lord shall preserve our going out and our coming in, from this time forth and even forevermore." Joseph and Mary had repeatedly instructed Jesus as to the reasons for not making images or drawing pictures, explaining that such creations might be used for idolatrous purposes. Though Jesus failed fully to grasp their proscriptions against images and pictures, he possessed a high concept of consistency and therefore pointed out to his father the essentially idolatrous nature of this habitual obeisance to the doorpost parchment. And Joseph removed the parchment after Jesus had thus remonstrated with him.

124:4.8 (1372.5) As time passed, Jesus did much to modify their practice of religious forms, such as the family prayers and other customs. And it was possible to do many such things at Nazareth, for its synagogue was under the influence of a liberal school of rabbis, exemplified by the renowned Nazareth teacher, Jose.

124:4.9 (1372.6) Throughout this and the two following years Jesus suffered great mental distress as the result of his constant effort to adjust his personal views of religious practices and social amenities to the established beliefs of his parents. He was distraught by the conflict between the urge to be loyal to his own convictions and the conscientious admonition of dutiful submission to his parents; his supreme conflict was between two great commands which were uppermost in his youthful mind. The one was: "Be loyal to the dictates of your highest convictions of truth and righteousness." The other was: "Honor your father and mother, for they have given you life and the nurture thereof." However, he never shirked the responsibility of making the necessary daily adjustments between these realms of loyalty to one's personal convictions and duty toward one's family, and he achieved the satisfaction of effecting an increasingly harmonious blending of personal convictions and family obligations into a masterful concept of group solidarity based upon loyalty, fairness, tolerance, and love.

5   His Thirteenth Year (A.D. 7)

124:5.1 (1373.1) In this year the lad of Nazareth passed from boyhood to the beginning of young manhood; his voice began to change, and other features of mind and body gave evidence of the oncoming status of manhood.

124:5.2 (1373.2) On Sunday night, January 9, A.D. 7, his baby brother, Amos, was born. Jude was not yet two years of age, and the baby sister, Ruth, was yet to come; so it may be seen that Jesus had a sizable family of small children left to his watchcare when his father met his accidental

death the following year.

124:5.3 (1373.3) It was about the middle of February that Jesus became humanly assured that he was destined to perform a mission on earth for the enlightenment of man and the revelation of God. Momentous decisions, coupled with far-reaching plans, were formulating in the mind of this youth, who was, to outward appearances, an average Jewish lad of Nazareth. The intelligent life of all Nebadon looked on with fascination and amazement as all this began to unfold in the thinking and acting of the now adolescent carpenter's son.

124:5.4 (1373.4) On the first day of the week, March 20, A.D. 7, Jesus graduated from the course of training in the local school connected with the Nazareth synagogue. This was a great day in the life of any ambitious Jewish family, the day when the first-born son was pronounced a "son of the commandment" and the ransomed first-born of the Lord God of Israel, a "child of the Most High" and servant of the Lord of all the earth.

124:5.5 (1373.5) Friday of the week before, Joseph had come over from Sepphoris, where he was in charge of the work on a new public building, to be present on this glad occasion. Jesus' teacher confidently believed that his alert and diligent pupil was destined to some outstanding career, some distinguished mission. The elders, notwithstanding all their trouble with Jesus' nonconformist tendencies, were very proud of the lad and had already begun laying plans which would enable him to go to Jerusalem to continue his education in the renowned Hebrew academies.

124:5.6 (1373.6) As Jesus heard these plans discussed from time to time, he became increasingly sure that he would never go to Jerusalem to study with the rabbis. But he little dreamed of the tragedy, so soon to occur, which would insure the abandonment of all such plans by causing him to assume the responsibility for the support and direction of a large family, presently to consist of five brothers and three sisters as well as his mother and himself. Jesus had a larger and longer experience rearing this family than was accorded to Joseph, his father; and he did measure up to the standard which he subsequently set for himself: to become a wise, patient, understanding, and effective teacher and eldest brother to this family—his family— so suddenly sorrow-stricken and so unexpectedly bereaved.

6   The Journey to Jerusalem

124:6.1 (1374.1) Jesus, having now reached the threshold of young manhood and having been formally graduated from the synagogue schools, was qualified to proceed to Jerusalem with his parents to participate with them in the celebration of his first Passover. The Passover feast of this year fell on Saturday, April 9, A.D. 7. A considerable company (103) made ready to depart from Nazareth early Monday morning, April 4, for Jerusalem. They journeyed south toward Samaria, but on reaching Jezreel, they turned east, going around Mount Gilboa into the Jordan valley in order to avoid passing through Samaria. Joseph and his family would have enjoyed going down through Samaria by way of Jacob's well and Bethel, but since the Jews disliked to deal with the Samaritans, they decided to go with their neighbors by way of the Jordan valley.

124:6.2 (1374.2) The much-dreaded Archelaus had been deposed, and they had little to fear in taking Jesus to Jerusalem. Twelve years had passed since the first Herod had sought to destroy the babe of Bethlehem, and no one would now think of associating that affair with this obscure lad of Nazareth.

124:6.3 (1374.3) Before reaching the Jezreel junction, and as they journeyed on, very soon, on the left, they passed the ancient village of Shunem, and Jesus heard again about the most beautiful maiden of all Israel who once lived there and also about the wonderful works Elisha performed there. In passing by Jezreel, Jesus' parents recounted the doings of Ahab and Jezebel and the exploits of Jehu. In passing around Mount Gilboa, they talked much about Saul, who took his life on the slopes of this mountain, King David, and the associations of this historic spot.

124:6.4 (1374.4) As they rounded the base of Gilboa, the pilgrims could see the Greek city of Scythopolis on the right. They gazed upon the marble structures from a distance but went not near the gentile city lest they so defile themselves that they could not participate in the forthcoming solemn and sacred ceremonies of the Passover at Jerusalem. Mary could not understand why neither Joseph nor Jesus would speak of Scythopolis. She did not know about their controversy of the previous year as they had never revealed this episode to her.

124:6.5 (1374.5) The road now led immediately down into the tropical Jordan valley, and soon Jesus was to have exposed to his wondering gaze the crooked and ever-winding Jordan with its glistening and rippling waters as it flowed down toward the Dead Sea. They laid aside their outer garments as they journeyed south in this tropical valley, enjoying the luxurious fields of grain and the beautiful oleanders laden with their pink blossoms, while massive snow-capped Mount Hermon stood far to the north, in majesty looking down on the historic valley. A little over three hours' travel from opposite Scythopolis they came upon a bubbling spring, and here they camped for the night, out under the starlit heavens.

124:6.6 (1374.6) On their second day's journey they passed by where the Jabbok, from the east, flows into the Jordan, and looking east up this river valley, they recounted the days of Gideon, when the Midianites poured into this region to overrun the land. Toward the end of the second day's journey they camped near the base of the highest mountain overlooking the Jordan valley, Mount Sartaba, whose summit was occupied by the Alexandrian fortress where Herod had imprisoned one of his wives and buried his two strangled sons.

124:6.7 (1375.1) The third day they passed by two villages which had been recently built by Herod and noted their superior architecture and their beautiful palm gardens. By nightfall they reached Jericho, where they remained until the morrow. That evening Joseph, Mary, and Jesus walked a mile and a half to the site of the ancient Jericho, where Joshua, for whom Jesus was named, had performed his renowned exploits, according to Jewish tradition.

124:6.8 (1375.2) By the fourth and last day's journey the road was a continuous procession of pilgrims. They now began to climb the hills leading up to Jerusalem. As they neared the top, they could look across the Jordan to the mountains beyond and south over the sluggish waters of the Dead Sea. About halfway up to Jerusalem, Jesus gained his first view of the Mount of Olives (the region to be so much a part of his subsequent life), and Joseph pointed out to him that the Holy City lay just beyond this ridge, and the lad's heart beat fast with joyous anticipation of soon beholding the city and house of his heavenly Father.

124:6.9 (1375.3) On the eastern slopes of Olivet they paused for rest in the borders of a little village called Bethany. The hospitable villagers poured forth to minister to the pilgrims, and it happened that Joseph and his family had stopped near the house of one Simon, who had three children about the same age as Jesus—Mary, Martha, and Lazarus. They invited the Nazareth family in for refreshment, and a lifelong friendship sprang up between the two families. Many times afterward, in his eventful life, Jesus stopped in this home.

124:6.10 (1375.4) They pressed on, soon standing on the brink of Olivet, and Jesus saw for the first time (in his memory) the Holy City, the pretentious palaces, and the inspiring temple of his Father. At no time in his life did Jesus ever experience such a purely human thrill as that which at this time so completely enthralled him as he stood there on this April afternoon on the Mount of Olives, drinking in his first view of Jerusalem. And in after years, on this same spot he stood and wept over the city which was about to reject another prophet, the last and the greatest of her heavenly teachers.

124:6.11 (1375.5) But they hurried on to Jerusalem. It was now Thursday afternoon. On reaching the city, they journeyed past the temple, and never had Jesus beheld such throngs of human beings. He meditated deeply on how these Jews had assembled here from the uttermost parts of the known world.

124:6.12 (1375.6) Soon they reached the place prearranged for their accommodation during the Passover week, the large home of a well-to-do relative of Mary's, one who knew something of the early history of both John and Jesus, through Zacharias. The following day, the day of preparation, they made ready for the appropriate celebration of the Passover Sabbath.

124:6.13 (1375.7) While all Jerusalem was astir in preparation for the Passover, Joseph found time to take his son around to visit the academy where it had been arranged for him to resume his education two years later, as soon as he reached the required age of fifteen. Joseph was truly puzzled when he observed how little interest Jesus evinced in all these carefully laid plans.

124:6.14 (1375.8) Jesus was profoundly impressed by the temple and all the associated services and other activities. For the first time since he was four years old, he was too much preoccupied with his own meditations to ask many questions. He did, however, ask his father several embarrassing questions (as he had on previous occasions) as to why the heavenly Father required the slaughter of so many innocent and helpless animals. And his father well knew from the expression on the lad's face that his answers and attempts at explanation were unsatisfactory to his deep-thinking and keen- reasoning son.

124:6.15 (1376.1) On the day before the Passover Sabbath, flood tides of spiritual illumination swept through the mortal mind of Jesus and filled his human heart to overflowing with affectionate pity for the spiritually blind and morally ignorant multitudes assembled for the celebration of the ancient Passover commemoration. This was one of the most extraordinary days that the Son of God spent in the flesh; and during the night, for the first time in his earth career, there appeared to him an assigned messenger from Salvington, commissioned by Immanuel, who said: "The hour has come. It is time that you began to be about your Father's business."

124:6.16 (1376.2) And so, even ere the heavy responsibilities of the Nazareth family descended upon his youthful shoulders, there now arrived the celestial messenger to remind this lad, not quite thirteen years of age, that the hour had come to begin the resumption of the responsibilities of a universe. This was the first act of a long succession of events which finally culminated in the completion of the Son's bestowal on Urantia and the replacing of "the government of a universe on his human-divine shoulders."

124:6.17 (1376.3) As time passed, the mystery of the incarnation became, to all of us, more and more unfathomable. We could hardly comprehend that this lad of Nazareth was the creator of all Nebadon. Neither do we nowadays understand how the spirit of this same Creator Son and the spirit of his Paradise Father are associated with the souls of mankind.

With the passing of time, we could see that his human mind was increasingly discerning that, while he lived his life in the flesh, in spirit on his shoulders rested the responsibility of a universe.

124:6.18 (1376.4) Thus ends the career of the Nazareth lad, and begins the narrative of that adolescent youth—the increasingly self-conscious divine human—who now begins the contemplation of his world career as he strives to integrate his expanding life purpose with the desires of his parents and his obligations to his family and the society of his day and age.

Paper 125

Jesus at Jerusalem

125:0.1 (1377.1) NO INCIDENT in all Jesus' eventful earth career was more engaging, more humanly thrilling, than this, his first remembered visit to Jerusalem. He was especially stimulated by the experience of attending the temple discussions by himself, and it long stood out in his memory as the great event of his later childhood and early youth.

This was his first opportunity to enjoy a few days of independent living, the exhilaration of going and coming without restraint and restrictions. This brief period of undirected living, during the week following the Passover, was the first complete freedom from responsibility he had ever enjoyed. And it was many years subsequent to this before he again had a like period of freedom from all sense of responsibility, even for a short time.

125:0.2 (1377.2) Women seldom went to the Passover feast at Jerusalem; they were not required to be present. Jesus, however, virtually refused to go unless his mother would accompany them. And when his mother decided to go, many other Nazareth women were led to make the journey, so that the Passover company contained the largest number of women, in proportion to men, ever to go up to the Passover from Nazareth. Ever and anon, on the way to Jerusalem, they chanted the one hundred and thirtieth Psalm.

125:0.3 (1377.3) From the time they left Nazareth until they reached the summit of the Mount of Olives, Jesus experienced one long stress of expectant anticipation. All through a joyful childhood he had reverently heard of Jerusalem and its temple; now he was soon to behold them in reality. From the Mount of Olives and from the outside, on closer inspection, the temple had been all and more than Jesus had expected; but when he once entered its sacred portals, the great disillusionment began.

125:0.4 (1377.4) In company with his parents Jesus passed through the temple precincts on his way to join that group of new sons of the law who were about to be consecrated as citizens of Israel. He was a little disappointed by the general demeanor of the temple throngs, but the first great shock of the day came when his mother took leave of them on her way to the women's gallery. It had never occurred to Jesus that his mother was not to accompany him to the consecration ceremonies, and he was thoroughly indignant that she was made to suffer from such unjust discrimination. While he strongly resented this, aside from a few remarks of protest to his father, he said nothing. But he thought, and thought deeply, as his questions to the scribes and teachers a week later disclosed.

125:0.5 (1377.5) He passed through the consecration rituals but was disappointed by their perfunctory and routine natures. He missed that personal interest which characterized the ceremonies of the synagogue at Nazareth. He then returned to greet his mother and prepared to accompany his father on his first trip about the temple and its various courts, galleries, and corridors. The temple precincts could accommodate over two hundred thousand worshipers at one time, and while the vastness of these buildings—in comparison with any he had ever seen—greatly impressed his mind, he was more intrigued by the contemplation of the spiritual significance of the temple ceremonies and their associated worship.

125:0.6 (1378.1) Though many of the temple rituals very touchingly impressed his sense of the beautiful and the symbolic, he was always disappointed by the explanation of the real meanings of these ceremonies which his parents would offer in answer to his many searching inquiries. Jesus simply would not accept explanations of worship and religious devotion which involved belief in the wrath of God or the anger of the Almighty. In further discussion of these questions, after the conclusion of the temple visit, when his father became mildly insistent that he acknowledge acceptance of the orthodox Jewish beliefs, Jesus turned suddenly upon his parents and, looking appealingly into the eyes of his father, said: "My father, it cannot be true—the Father in heaven cannot so regard his erring children on earth. The heavenly Father cannot love his children less than you love me. And I well know, no matter what unwise thing I might do, you would never pour out wrath upon me nor vent anger against me. If you, my earthly father, possess such human reflections of the Divine, how much more must the heavenly Father be filled with goodness and overflowing with mercy. I refuse to believe that my Father in heaven loves me less than my father on earth."

125:0.7 (1378.2) When Joseph and Mary heard these words of their first-born son, they held their peace. And never again did they seek to change his mind about the love of God and the mercifulness of the Father in heaven.

Jesus Views the Temple

125:1.1 (1378.3) Everywhere Jesus went throughout the temple courts, he was shocked and sickened by the spirit of irreverence which he observed. He deemed the conduct of the temple throngs to be inconsistent with their presence in "his Father's house." But he received the shock of his young life when his father escorted him into the court of the gentiles with its noisy jargon, loud talking and cursing, mingled indiscriminately with the bleating of sheep and the babble of noises which betrayed the presence of the money-changers and the vendors of sacrificial animals and sundry other commercial commodities.

125:1.2 (1378.4) But most of all was his sense of propriety outraged by the sight of the frivolous courtesans parading about within this precinct of the temple, just such painted women as he had so recently seen when on a visit to Sepphoris. This profanation of the temple fully aroused all his youthful indignation, and he did not hesitate to express himself freely to Joseph.

125:1.3 (1378.5) Jesus admired the sentiment and service of the temple, but he was shocked by the spiritual ugliness which he beheld on the faces of so many of the unthinking worshipers.

125:1.4 (1378.6) They now passed down to the priests' court beneath the rock ledge in front of the temple, where the altar stood, to observe the killing of the droves of animals and the washing away of the blood from the hands of the officiating slaughter priests at the bronze fountain. The blood-stained pavement, the gory hands of the priests, and the sounds of the dying animals were more than this nature-loving lad could stand. The terrible sight sickened this boy of Nazareth; he clutched his father's arm and begged to be taken away. They walked back through the court of the gentiles, and even the coarse laughter and profane jesting which he there heard were a relief from the sights he had just beheld.

125:1.5 (1379.1) Joseph saw how his son had sickened at the sight of the temple rites and wisely led him around to view the "Gate Beautiful," the artistic gate made of Corinthian bronze. But Jesus had had enough for his first visit at the temple. They returned to the upper court for Mary and walked about in the open air and away from the crowds for an hour, viewing the Asmonean palace, the stately home of Herod, and the tower of the Roman guards. During this stroll Joseph explained to Jesus that only the inhabitants of Jerusalem were permitted to witness the daily sacrifices in the temple, and that the dwellers in Galilee came up only three times a year to participate in the temple worship: at the Passover,

at the feast of Pentecost (seven weeks after Passover), and at the feast of tabernacles in October. These feasts were established by Moses. They then discussed the two later established feasts of the dedication and of Purim.

Afterward they went to their lodgings and made ready for the celebration of the Passover.

Jesus and the Passover

125:2.1 (1379.2) Five Nazareth families were guests of, or associates with, the family of Simon of Bethany in the celebration of the Passover, Simon having purchased the paschal lamb for the company. It was the slaughter of these lambs in such enormous numbers that had so affected Jesus on his temple visit. It had been the plan to eat the Passover with Mary's relatives, but Jesus persuaded his parents to accept the invitation to go to Bethany.

125:2.2 (1379.3) That night they assembled for the Passover rites, eating the roasted flesh with unleavened bread and bitter herbs. Jesus, being a new son of the covenant, was asked to recount the origin of the Passover, and this he well did, but he somewhat disconcerted his parents by the inclusion of numerous remarks mildly reflecting the impressions made on his youthful but thoughtful mind by the things which he had so recently seen and heard. This was the beginning of the seven-day ceremonies of the feast of the Passover.

125:2.3 (1379.4) Even at this early date, though he said nothing about such matters to his parents, Jesus had begun to turn over in his mind the propriety of celebrating the Passover without the slaughtered lamb. He felt assured in his own mind that the Father in heaven was not pleased with this spectacle of sacrificial offerings, and as the years passed, he became increasingly determined someday to establish the celebration of a bloodless Passover.

125:2.4 (1379.5) Jesus slept very little that night. His rest was greatly disturbed by revolting dreams of slaughter and suffering. His mind was distraught and his heart torn by the inconsistencies and absurdities of the theology of the whole Jewish ceremonial system. His parents likewise slept little. They were greatly disconcerted by the events of the day just ended. They were completely upset in their own hearts by the lad's, to them, strange and determined attitude. Mary became nervously agitated during the fore part of the night, but Joseph remained calm, though he was equally puzzled. Both of them feared to talk frankly with the lad about these problems, though Jesus would gladly have talked with his parents if they had dared to encourage him.

125:2.5 (1379.6) The next day's services at the temple were more acceptable to Jesus and did much to relieve the unpleasant memories of the previous day. The following morning young Lazarus took Jesus in hand, and they began a systematic exploration of Jerusalem and its environs. Before the day was over, Jesus discovered the various places about the temple where teaching and question conferences were in progress; and aside from a few visits to the holy of holies to gaze in wonder as to what really was behind the veil of separation, he spent most of his time about the temple at these teaching conferences.

125:2.6 (1380.1) Throughout the Passover week, Jesus kept his place among the new sons of the commandment, and this meant that he must seat himself outside the rail which segregated all persons who were not full citizens of Israel. Being thus made conscious of his youth, he refrained from asking the many questions which surged back and forth in his mind; at least he refrained until the Passover celebration had ended and these restrictions on the newly consecrated youths were lifted.

125:2.7 (1380.2) On Wednesday of the Passover week, Jesus was permitted to go home with Lazarus to spend the night at Bethany. This evening, Lazarus, Martha, and Mary heard Jesus discuss things temporal and eternal, human and divine, and

from that night on they all three loved him as if he had been their own brother.

125:2.8 (1380.3) By the end of the week, Jesus saw less of Lazarus since he was not eligible for admission to even the outer circle of the temple discussions, though he attended some of the public talks delivered in the outer courts. Lazarus was the same age as Jesus, but in Jerusalem youths were seldom admitted to the consecration of sons of the law until they were a full thirteen years of age.

125:2.9 (1380.4) Again and again, during the Passover week, his parents would find Jesus sitting off by himself with his youthful head in his hands, profoundly thinking. They had never seen him behave like this, and not knowing how much he was confused in mind and troubled in spirit by the experience through which he was passing, they were sorely perplexed; they did not know what to do. They welcomed the passing of the days of the Passover week and longed to have their strangely acting son safely back in Nazareth.

125:2.10 (1380.5) Day by day Jesus was thinking through his problems. By the end of the week he had made many adjustments; but when the time came to return to Nazareth, his youthful mind was still swarming with perplexities and beset by a host of unanswered questions and unsolved problems.

125:2.11 (1380.6) Before Joseph and Mary left Jerusalem, in company with Jesus' Nazareth teacher they made definite arrangements for Jesus to return when he reached the age of fifteen to begin his long course of study in one of the best- known academies of the rabbis. Jesus accompanied his parents and teacher on their visits to the school, but they were all distressed to observe how indifferent he seemed to all they said and did. Mary was deeply pained at his reactions to the Jerusalem visit, and Joseph was profoundly perplexed at the lad's strange remarks and unusual conduct.

125:2.12 (1380.7) After all, Passover

week had been a great event in Jesus' life. He had enjoyed the opportunity of meeting scores of boys about his own age, fellow candidates for the consecration, and he utilized such contacts as a means of learning how people lived in Mesopotamia, Turkestan, and Parthia, as well as in the Far-Western provinces of Rome. He was already fairly conversant with the way in which the youth of Egypt and other regions near Palestine grew up. There were thousands of young people in Jerusalem at this time, and the Nazareth lad personally met, and more or less extensively interviewed, more than one hundred and fifty. He was particularly interested in those who hailed from the Far-Eastern and the remote Western countries. As a result of these contacts the lad began to entertain a desire to travel about the world for the purpose of learning how the various groups of his fellow men toiled for their livelihood.

Departure of Joseph and Mary

125:3.1 (1381.1) It had been arranged that the Nazareth party should gather in the region of the temple at midforenoon on the first day of the week after the Passover festival had ended. This they did and started out on the return journey to Nazareth. Jesus had gone into the temple to listen to the discussions while his parents awaited the assembly of their fellow travelers. Presently the company prepared to depart, the men going in one group and the women in another as was their custom in journeying to and from the Jerusalem festivals. Jesus had gone up to Jerusalem in company with his mother and the women. Being now a young man of the consecration, he was supposed to journey back to Nazareth in company with his father and the men. But as the Nazareth party moved on toward Bethany, Jesus was completely absorbed in the discussion of angels, in the temple, being wholly unmindful of the passing of the time for the departure of his parents. And he did not realize that he had been left behind until the noontime adjournment of the temple conferences.

125:3.2 (1381.2) The Nazareth travelers did not miss Jesus because Mary surmised he journeyed with the men, while Joseph thought he traveled with the women since he had gone up to Jerusalem with the women, leading Mary's donkey. They did not discover his absence until they reached Jericho and prepared to tarry for the night. After making inquiry of the last of the party to reach Jericho and learning that none of them had seen their son, they spent a sleepless night, turning over in their minds what might have happened to him, recounting many of his unusual reactions to the events of Passover week, and mildly chiding each other for not seeing to it that he was in the group before they left Jerusalem.

First and Second Days in the Temple

125:4.1 (1381.3) In the meantime, Jesus had remained in the temple throughout the afternoon, listening to the discussions and enjoying the more quiet and decorous atmosphere, the great crowds of Passover week having about disappeared. At the conclusion of the afternoon discussions, in none of which Jesus participated, he betook himself to Bethany, arriving just as Simon's family made ready to partake of their evening meal. The three youngsters were overjoyed to greet Jesus, and he remained in Simon's house for the night. He visited very little during the evening, spending much of the time alone in the garden meditating.

125:4.2 (1381.4) Early next day Jesus was up and on his way to the temple. On the brow of Olivet he paused and wept over the sight his eyes beheld—a spiritually impoverished people, tradition bound and living under the surveillance of the Roman legions. Early forenoon found him in the temple with his mind made up to take part in the discussions.

Meanwhile, Joseph and Mary also had arisen with the early dawn with the intention of retracing their steps to Jerusalem. First, they hastened to the house of their relatives, where they had lodged as a family during the Passover week, but inquiry elicited the fact that no one had seen Jesus. After searching all day and finding no trace of him, they returned to their relatives for the night.

125:4.3 (1382.1) At the second conference Jesus had made bold to ask questions, and in a very amazing way he participated in the temple discussions but always in a manner consistent with his youth. Sometimes his pointed questions were somewhat embarrassing to the learned teachers of the Jewish law, but he evinced such a spirit of candid fairness, coupled with an evident hunger for knowledge, that the majority of the temple teachers were disposed to treat him with every consideration. But when he presumed to question the justice of putting to death a drunken gentile who had wandered outside the court of the gentiles and unwittingly entered the forbidden and reputedly sacred precincts of the temple, one of the more intolerant teachers grew impatient with the lad's implied criticisms and, glowering down

upon him, asked how old he was. Jesus replied, "thirteen years lacking a trifle more than four months." "Then," rejoined the now irate teacher, "why are you here, since you are not of age as a son of the law?" And when Jesus explained that he had received consecration during the Passover, and that he was a finished student of the Nazareth schools, the teachers with one accord derisively replied, "We might have known; he is from Nazareth." But the leader insisted that Jesus was not to be blamed if the rulers of the synagogue at Nazareth had graduated him, technically, when he was twelve instead of thirteen; and notwithstanding that several of his detractors got up and left, it was ruled that the lad might continue undisturbed as a pupil of the temple discussions.

125:4.4 (1382.2) When this, his second day in the temple, was finished, again he went to Bethany for the night. And again he went out in the garden to meditate and pray. It was apparent that his mind was concerned with the contemplation of weighty problems.

The Third Day in the Temple

125:5.1 (1382.3) Jesus' third day with the scribes and teachers in the temple witnessed the gathering of many spectators who, having heard of this youth from Galilee, came to enjoy the experience of seeing a lad confuse the wise men of the law. Simon also came down from Bethany to see what the boy was up to. Throughout this day Joseph and Mary continued their anxious search for Jesus, even going several times into the temple but never thinking to scrutinize the several discussion groups, although they once came almost within hearing distance of his fascinating voice.

125:5.2 (1382.4) Before the day had ended, the entire attention of the chief discussion group of the temple had become focused upon the questions being asked by Jesus. Among his many questions were:

125:5.3 (1382.5) 1. What really exists in the holy of holies, behind the veil?

125:5.4 (1382.6) 2. Why should mothers in Israel be segregated from the male temple worshipers?

125:5.5 (1382.7) 3. If God is a father who loves his children, why all this slaughter of animals to gain divine favor—has the teaching of Moses been misunderstood?

125:5.6 (1382.8) 4. Since the temple is dedicated to the worship of the Father in heaven, is it consistent to permit the presence of those who engage in secular barter and trade?

125:5.7 (1382.9) 5. Is the expected Messiah to become a temporal prince to sit on the throne of David, or is he to function as the light of life in the establishment of a spiritual kingdom?

125:5.8 (1383.1) And all the day through, those who listened marveled at these questions, and none was more astonished than Simon. For more than four hours this Nazareth youth plied these Jewish teachers with thought-provoking and heart-searching questions. He made few comments on the remarks of his elders. He conveyed his teaching by the questions he would ask. By the deft and subtle phrasing of a question he would at one and the same time challenge their teaching and suggest his own. In the manner of his asking a question there was an appealing combination of sagacity

and humor which endeared him even to those who more or less resented his youthfulness. He was always eminently fair and considerate in the asking of these penetrating questions. On this eventful afternoon in the temple he exhibited that same reluctance to take unfair advantage of an opponent which characterized his entire subsequent public ministry. As a youth, and later on as a man, he seemed to be utterly free from all egoistic desire to win an argument merely to experience logical triumph over his fellows, being interested supremely in just one thing: to proclaim everlasting truth and thus effect a fuller revelation of the eternal God.

125:5.9 (1383.2) When the day was over, Simon and Jesus wended their way back to Bethany. For most of the distance both the man and the boy were silent. Again Jesus paused on the brow of Olivet, but as he viewed the city and its temple, he did not weep; he only bowed his head in silent devotion.

125:5.10 (1383.3) After the evening meal at Bethany he again declined to join the merry circle but instead went to the garden, where he lingered long into the night, vainly endeavoring to think out some definite plan of approach to the problem of his lifework and to decide how best he might labor to reveal to his spiritually blinded countrymen a more beautiful concept of the heavenly Father and so set them free from their terrible bondage to law, ritual, ceremonial, and musty tradition. But the clear light did not come to the truth-seeking lad.

The Fourth Day in the Temple

125:6.1 (1383.4) Jesus was strangely unmindful of his earthly parents; even at breakfast, when Lazarus's mother remarked that his parents must be about home by that time, Jesus did not seem to comprehend that they would be somewhat worried about his having lingered behind.

125:6.2 (1383.5) Again he journeyed to the temple, but he did not pause to meditate at the brow of Olivet. In the course of the morning's discussions much time was devoted to the law and the prophets, and the teachers were astonished that Jesus was so familiar with the Scriptures, in Hebrew as well as Greek. But they were amazed not so much by his knowledge of truth as by his youth.

125:6.3 (1383.6) At the afternoon conference they had hardly begun to answer his question relating to the purpose of prayer when the leader invited the lad to come forward and, sitting beside him, bade him state his own views regarding prayer and worship.

125:6.4 (1383.7) The evening before, Jesus' parents had heard about this strange youth who so deftly sparred with the expounders of the law, but it had not occurred to them that this lad was their son. They had about decided to journey out to the home of Zacharias as they thought Jesus might have gone thither to see Elizabeth and John. Thinking Zacharias might perhaps be at the temple, they stopped there on their way to the City of Judah. As they strolled through the courts of the temple, imagine their surprise and amazement when they recognized the voice of the missing lad and beheld him seated among the temple teachers.

125:6.5 (1384.1) Joseph was speechless, but Mary gave vent to her long-pent-up fear and anxiety when, rushing up to the lad, now standing to greet his astonished parents, she said: "My child, why have you treated us like this? It is now more than three days that your father and I have searched for you sorrowing. Whatever possessed you to desert us?" It was a tense moment. All eyes were turned on Jesus to hear what he would say. His father looked reprovingly at him but said nothing.

125:6.6 (1384.2) It should be remembered that Jesus was supposed to be a young man. He had finished the regular schooling of a child, had been recognized as a son of the law, and had received consecration as a citizen of Israel. And yet his mother more than mildly upbraided him before all the people assembled, right in the midst of the most serious and sublime effort of his young life, thus bringing to an inglorious termination one of the greatest opportunities ever to be granted him to function as a teacher of truth, a preacher of righteousness, a revealer of the loving character of his Father in heaven.

125:6.7 (1384.3) But the lad was equal to the occasion. When you take into fair consideration all the factors which combined to make up this situation, you will be better prepared to fathom the wisdom of the boy's reply to his mother's unintended rebuke. After a moment's thought, Jesus answered his mother, saying: "Why is it that you have so long sought me? Would you not expect to find me in my Father's house since the time has come when I should be about my Father's business?"

125:6.8 (1384.4) Everyone was astonished at the lad's manner of speaking. Silently they all withdrew and left him standing alone with his parents. Presently the young man relieved the embarrassment of all three when he quietly said: "Come, my parents, none has done aught but that which he thought best. Our Father in heaven has ordained these things; let us depart for home."

125:6.9 (1384.5) In silence they started out, arriving at Jericho for the night. Only once did they pause, and that on the brow of Olivet, when the lad raised his staff aloft

and, quivering from head to foot under the surging of intense emotion, said: "O Jerusalem, Jerusalem, and the people thereof, what slaves you are—subservient to the Roman yoke and victims of your own traditions—but I will return to cleanse yonder temple and deliver my people from this bondage!"

125:6.10 (1384.6) On the three days' journey to Nazareth Jesus said little; neither did his parents say much in his presence. They were truly at a loss to understand the conduct of their first-born son, but they did treasure in their hearts his sayings, even though they could not fully comprehend their meanings.

125:6.11 (1384.7) Upon reaching home, Jesus made a brief statement to his parents, assuring them of his affection and implying that they need not fear he would again give any occasion for their suffering anxiety because of his conduct. He concluded this momentous statement by saying: "While I must do the will of my Father in heaven, I will also be obedient to my father on earth. I will await my hour."

125:6.12 (1384.8) Though Jesus, in his mind, would many times refuse to consent to the well-intentioned but misguided efforts of his parents to dictate the course of his thinking or to establish the plan of his work on earth, still, in every manner consistent with his dedication to the doing of his Paradise Father's will, he did most gracefully conform to the desires of his earthly father and to the usages of his family in the flesh. Even when he could not consent, he would do everything possible to conform. He was an artist in the matter of adjusting his dedication to duty to his obligations of family loyalty and social service.

125:6.13 (1385.1) Joseph was puzzled, but Mary, as she reflected on these experiences, gained comfort, eventually viewing his utterance on Olivet as prophetic of the Messianic mission of her son as Israel's deliverer. She set to work with renewed energy to mold his thoughts into patriotic and nationalistic channels and enlisted the efforts of her brother, Jesus' favorite uncle; and in every other way did the mother of Jesus address herself to the task of preparing her first- born son to assume the leadership of those who would restore the throne of David and forever cast off the gentile yoke of political bondage.

Paper 126

The Two Crucial Years

126:0.1 (1386.1) OF ALL Jesus' earth-life experiences, the fourteenth and fifteenth years were the most crucial. These two years, after he began to be self-conscious of divinity and destiny, and before he achieved a large measure of communication with his indwelling Adjuster, were the most trying of his eventful life on Urantia. It is this period of two years which should be called the great test, the real temptation. No human youth, in passing through the early confusions and adjustment problems of adolescence, ever experienced a more crucial testing than that which Jesus passed through during his transition from childhood to young manhood.

126:0.2 (1386.2) This important period in Jesus' youthful development began with the conclusion of the Jerusalem visit and with his return to Nazareth. At first Mary was happy in the thought that she had her boy back once more, that Jesus had returned home to be a dutiful son—not that he was ever anything else—and that he would henceforth be more responsive to her plans for his future life. But she was not for long to bask in this sunshine of maternal delusion and unrecognized family pride; very soon she was to be more completely disillusioned. More and more the boy was in the company of his father; less and less did he come to her with his problems, while increasingly both his parents failed to comprehend his frequent alternation between the affairs of

this world and the contemplation of his relation to his Father's business. Frankly, they did not understand him, but they did truly love him.

126:0.3 (1386.3) As he grew older, Jesus' pity and love for the Jewish people deepened, but with the passing years, there developed in his mind a growing righteous resentment of the presence in the Father's temple of the politically appointed priests. Jesus had great respect for the sincere Pharisees and the honest scribes, but he held the hypocritical Pharisees and the dishonest theologians in great contempt; he looked with disdain upon all those religious leaders who were not sincere. When he scrutinized the leadership of Israel, he was sometimes tempted to look with favor on the possibility of his becoming the Messiah of Jewish expectation, but he never yielded to such a temptation.

126:0.4 (1386.4) The story of his exploits among the wise men of the temple in Jerusalem was gratifying to all Nazareth, especially to his former teachers in the synagogue school. For a time his praise was on everybody's lips. All the village recounted his childhood wisdom and praiseworthy conduct and predicted that he was destined to become a great leader in Israel; at last a really great teacher was to come out of Nazareth in Galilee. And they all looked forward to the time when he would be fifteen years of age so that he might be permitted regularly to read the Scriptures in the synagogue on the Sabbath day.

1   His Fourteenth Year (A.D. 8)

126:1.1 (1387.1) This is the calendar year of his fourteenth birthday. He had become a good yoke maker and worked well with both canvas and leather. He was also rapidly developing into an expert carpenter and cabinetmaker. This summer he made frequent trips to the top of the hill to the northwest of Nazareth for prayer and meditation. He was gradually becoming more self-conscious of the nature of his bestowal on earth.

126:1.2 (1387.2) This hill, a little more than one hundred years previously, had been the "high place of Baal," and now it was the site of the tomb of Simeon, a reputed holy man of Israel. From the summit of this hill of Simeon, Jesus looked out over Nazareth and the surrounding country. He would gaze upon Megiddo and recall the story of the Egyptian army winning its first great victory in Asia; and how, later on, another such army defeated the Judean king Josiah. Not far away he could look upon Taanach, where Deborah and Barak defeated Sisera. In the distance he could view the hills of Dothan, where he had been taught Joseph's brethren sold him into Egyptian slavery. He then would shift his gaze over to Ebal and Gerizim and recount to himself the traditions of Abraham, Jacob, and Abimelech. And thus he recalled and turned over in his mind the historic and traditional events of his father Joseph's people. *

126:1.3 (1387.3) He continued to carry on his advanced courses of reading under the synagogue teachers, and he also continued with the home education of his brothers and sisters as they grew up to suitable ages.

126:1.4 (1387.4) Early this year Joseph arranged to set aside the income from his Nazareth and Capernaum property to pay for Jesus' long course of study at Jerusalem, it having been planned that he should go to Jerusalem in August of the following year when he would be fifteen years of age.

126:1.5 (1387.5) By the beginning of this year both Joseph and Mary entertained frequent doubts about the destiny of their first-born son. He was indeed a brilliant and lovable child, but he was so difficult to understand, so hard to fathom, and again, nothing extraordinary or miraculous ever happened. Scores of times had his proud mother stood in breathless anticipation, expecting to see her son engage in some superhuman or miraculous performance, but always were her hopes dashed down in

cruel disappointment. And all this was discouraging, even disheartening. The devout people of those days truly believed that prophets and men of promise always demonstrated their calling and established their divine authority by performing miracles and working wonders. But Jesus did none of these things; wherefore was the confusion of his parents steadily increased as they contemplated his future.

126:1.6 (1387.6) The improved economic condition of the Nazareth family was reflected in many ways about the home and especially in the increased number of smooth white boards which were used as writing slates, the writing being done with charcoal. Jesus was also permitted to resume his music lessons; he was very fond of playing the harp.

126:1.7 (1387.7) Throughout this year it can truly be said that Jesus "grew in favor with man and with God." The prospects of the family seemed good; the future was bright.

2 The Death of Joseph

126:2.1 (1388.1) All did go well until that fateful day of Tuesday, September 25, when a runner from Sepphoris brought to this Nazareth home the tragic news that Joseph had been severely injured by the falling of a derrick while at work on the governor's residence. The messenger from Sepphoris had stopped at the shop on the way to Joseph's home, informing Jesus of his father's accident, and they went together to the house to break the sad news to Mary. Jesus desired to go immediately to his father, but Mary would hear to nothing but that she must hasten to her husband's side. She directed that James, then ten years of age, should accompany her to Sepphoris while Jesus remained home with the younger children until she should return, as she did not know how seriously Joseph had been injured. But Joseph died of his injuries before Mary arrived. They brought him to Nazareth, and on the following day he was laid to rest with his fathers.

126:2.2 (1388.2) Just at the time when prospects were good and the future looked bright, an apparently cruel hand struck down the head of this Nazareth household, the affairs of this home were disrupted, and every plan for Jesus and his future education was demolished. This carpenter lad, now just past fourteen years of age, awakened to the realization that he had not only to fulfill the commission of his heavenly Father to reveal the divine nature on earth and in the flesh, but that his young human nature must also shoulder the responsibility of caring for his widowed mother and seven brothers and sisters—and another yet to be born. This lad of Nazareth now became the sole support and comfort of this so suddenly bereaved family. Thus were permitted those occurrences of the natural order of events on Urantia which would force this young man of destiny so early to assume these heavy but highly educational and disciplinary responsibilities attendant upon becoming the head of a human family, of becoming father to his own brothers and sisters, of supporting and protecting his mother, of functioning as guardian of his father's home, the only home he was to know while on this world.

126:2.3 (1388.3) Jesus cheerfully accepted the responsibilities so suddenly thrust upon him, and he carried them faithfully to the end. At least one great problem and anticipated difficulty in his life had been tragically solved—he would not now be expected to go to Jerusalem to study under the rabbis. It remained always true that Jesus "sat at no man's feet." He was ever willing to learn from even the humblest of little children, but he never derived authority to teach truth from human sources.

126:2.4 (1388.4) Still he knew nothing of the Gabriel visit to his mother before his birth; he only learned of this from John on the day of his baptism, at the beginning of his public ministry.

126:2.5 (1388.5) As the years passed, this young carpenter of Nazareth increasingly measured every institution of society and every usage of religion by the unvarying test: What does it do for the human soul? does it bring God to man? does it bring man to God? While this youth did not wholly neglect the recreational and social aspects of life, more and more he devoted his time and energies to just two purposes: the care of his family and the preparation to do his Father's heavenly will on earth.

126:2.6 (1389.1) This year it became the custom for the neighbors to drop in during the winter evenings to hear Jesus play upon the harp, to listen to his stories (for the lad was a master storyteller), and to hear him read from the Greek scriptures.

126:2.7 (1389.2) The economic affairs of the family continued to run fairly smoothly as there was quite a sum of money on hand at the time of Joseph's death. Jesus early demonstrated the possession of keen business judgment and financial sagacity. He was liberal but frugal; he was saving but generous. He proved to be a wise and efficient administrator of his father's estate.

126:2.8 (1389.3) But in spite of all that Jesus and the Nazareth neighbors could do to bring cheer into the home, Mary, and even the children, were overcast with sadness. Joseph was gone. Joseph was an unusual husband and father, and they all missed him. And it seemed all the more tragic to think that he died ere they could speak to him or hear his farewell blessing.

3   The Fifteenth Year (A.D. 9)

126:3.1 (1389.4) By the middle of this fifteenth year—and we are reckoning time in accordance with the twentieth-century calendar, not by the Jewish year—Jesus had taken a firm grasp upon the management of his family. Before this year had passed, their savings had about disappeared, and they were face to face with the necessity of disposing of one of the Nazareth houses which

Joseph and his neighbor Jacob owned in partnership.

126:3.2 (1389.5) On Wednesday evening, April 17, A.D. 9, Ruth, the baby of the family, was born, and to the best of his ability Jesus endeavored to take the place of his father in comforting and ministering to his mother during this trying and peculiarly sad ordeal. For almost a score of years (until he began his public ministry) no father could have loved and nurtured his daughter any more affectionately and faithfully than Jesus cared for little Ruth. And he was an equally good father to all the other members of his family.

126:3.3 (1389.6) During this year Jesus first formulated the prayer which he subsequently taught to his apostles, and which to many has become known as "The Lord's Prayer." In a way it was an evolution of the family altar; they had many forms of praise and several formal prayers. After his father's death Jesus tried to teach the older children to express themselves individually in prayer—much as he so enjoyed doing— but they could not grasp his thought and would invariably fall back upon their memorized prayer forms. It was in this effort to stimulate his older brothers and sisters to say individual prayers that Jesus would endeavor to lead them along by suggestive phrases, and presently, without intention on his part, it developed that they were all using a form of prayer which was largely built up from these suggestive lines which Jesus had taught them.

126:3.4 (1389.7) At last Jesus gave up the idea of having each member of the family formulate spontaneous prayers, and one evening in October he sat down by the little squat lamp on the low stone table, and, on a piece of smooth cedar board about eighteen inches square, with a piece of charcoal he wrote out the prayer which became from that time on the standard family petition.

126:3.5 (1389.8) This year Jesus was much troubled with confused thinking. Family responsibility had quite effectively removed all thought of immediately carrying out any plan for responding to the Jerusalem visitation directing him to "be about his Father's business." Jesus rightly reasoned that the watchcare of his earthly father's family must take precedence of all duties; that the support of his family must become his first obligation.

126:3.6 (1390.1) In the course of this year Jesus found a passage in the so-called Book of Enoch which influenced him in the later adoption of the term "Son of Man" as a designation for his bestowal mission on Urantia. He had thoroughly considered the idea of the Jewish Messiah and was firmly convinced that he was not to be that Messiah. He longed to help his father's people, but he never expected to lead Jewish armies in overthrowing the foreign domination of Palestine. He knew he would never sit on the throne of David at Jerusalem. Neither did he believe that his mission was that of a spiritual deliverer or moral teacher solely to the Jewish people. In no sense, therefore, could his life mission be the fulfillment of the intense longings and supposed Messianic prophecies of the Hebrew scriptures; at least, not as the Jews understood these predictions of the prophets. Likewise he was certain he was never to appear as the Son of Man depicted by the Prophet Daniel.

126:3.7 (1390.2) But when the time came for him to go forth as a world teacher, what would he call himself? What claim should he make concerning his mission? By what name would he be called by the people who would become believers in his teachings?

126:3.8 (1390.3) While turning all these problems over in his mind, he found in the synagogue library at Nazareth, among the apocalyptic books which he had been studying, this manuscript called "The Book of Enoch"; and though he was certain that it had not been written by Enoch of old, it proved very intriguing to him, and he read and reread it many times. There was one passage which particularly impressed him, a passage in which this term "Son of Man" appeared. The writer of this so-called Book of Enoch went on to tell about this

Son of Man, describing the work he would do on earth and explaining that this Son of Man, before coming down on this earth to bring salvation to mankind, had walked through the courts of heavenly glory with his Father, the Father of all; and that he had turned his back upon all this grandeur and glory to come down on earth to proclaim salvation to needy mortals. As Jesus would read these passages (well understanding that much of the Eastern mysticism which had become admixed with these teachings was erroneous), he responded in his heart and recognized in his mind that of all the Messianic predictions of the Hebrew scriptures and of all the theories about the Jewish deliverer, none was so near the truth as this story tucked away in this only partially accredited Book of Enoch; and he then and there decided to adopt as his inaugural title "the Son of Man." And this he did when he subsequently began his public work. Jesus had an unerring ability for the recognition of truth, and truth he never hesitated to embrace, no matter from what source it appeared to emanate.

126:3.9 (1390.4) By this time he had quite thoroughly settled many things about his forthcoming work for the world, but he said nothing of these matters to his mother, who still held stoutly to the idea of his being the Jewish Messiah.

126:3.10 (1390.5) The great confusion of Jesus' younger days now arose. Having settled something about the nature of his mission on earth, "to be about his Father's business"—to show forth his Father's loving nature to all mankind—he began to ponder anew the many statements in the Scriptures referring to the coming of a national deliverer, a Jewish teacher or king. To what event did these prophecies refer? Was not he a Jew? or was he? Was he or was he not of the house of David? His mother averred he was; his father had ruled that he was not. He decided he was not. But had the prophets confused the nature and mission of the Messiah?

126:3.11 (1391.1) After all, could it be possible that his mother was right? In most matters, when differences of opinion had arisen in the past, she had been right. If he were a new teacher and not the Messiah, then how should he recognize the Jewish Messiah if such a one should appear in Jerusalem during the time of his earth mission; and, further, what should be his relation to this Jewish Messiah? And what should be his relation, after embarking on his life mission, to his family? to the Jewish commonwealth and religion? to the Roman Empire? to the gentiles and their religions? Each of these momentous problems this young Galilean turned over in his mind and seriously pondered while he continued to work at the carpenter's bench, laboriously making a living for himself, his mother, and eight other hungry mouths.

126:3.12 (1391.2) Before the end of this year Mary saw the family funds diminishing. She turned the sale of doves over to James. Presently they bought a second cow, and with the aid of Miriam they began the sale of milk to their Nazareth neighbors.

126:3.13 (1391.3) His profound periods of meditation, his frequent journeys to the hilltop for prayer, and the many strange ideas which Jesus advanced from time to time, thoroughly alarmed his mother. Sometimes she thought the lad was beside himself, and then she would steady her fears, remembering that he was, after all, a child of promise and in some manner different from other youths.

126:3.14 (1391.4) But Jesus was learning not to speak of all his thoughts, not to present all his ideas to the world, not even to his own mother. From this year on, Jesus' disclosures about what was going on in his mind steadily diminished; that is, he talked less about those things which an average person could not grasp, and which would lead to his being regarded as peculiar or different from ordinary folks. To all appearances he became commonplace and conventional, though he did long for someone who could understand his problems. He craved a trustworthy and confidential friend, but his problems were too complex for his human associates to comprehend.

The uniqueness of the unusual situation compelled him to bear his burdens alone.

4 First Sermon in the Synagogue

126:4.1 (1391.5) With the coming of his fifteenth birthday, Jesus could officially occupy the synagogue pulpit on the Sabbath day. Many times before, in the absence of speakers, Jesus had been asked to read the Scriptures, but now the day had come when, according to law, he could conduct the service. Therefore on the first Sabbath after his fifteenth birthday the chazan arranged for Jesus to conduct the morning service of the synagogue. And when all the faithful in Nazareth had assembled, the young man, having made his selection of Scriptures, stood up and began to read:

126:4.2 (1391.6) "The spirit of the Lord God is upon me, for the Lord has anointed me; he has sent me to bring good news to the meek, to bind up the brokenhearted, to proclaim liberty to the captives, and to set the spiritual prisoners free; to proclaim the year of God's favor and the day of our God's reckoning; to comfort all mourners, to give them beauty for ashes, the oil of joy in the place of mourning, a song of praise instead of the spirit of sorrow, that they may be called trees of righteousness, the planting of the Lord, wherewith he may be glorified.

126:4.3 (1392.1) "Seek good and not evil that you may live, and so the Lord, the God of hosts, shall be with you. Hate the evil and love the good; establish judgment in the gate. Perhaps the Lord God will be gracious to the remnant of Joseph.

126:4.4 (1392.2) "Wash yourselves, make yourselves clean; put away the evil of your doings from before my eyes; cease to do evil and learn to do good; seek justice, relieve the oppressed. Defend the fatherless and plead for the widow.

126:4.5 (1392.3) "Wherewith shall I come before the Lord, to bow myself before the Lord of all the earth? Shall I come before him with burnt offerings, with calves a year old? Will the Lord be pleased with thousands of rams, ten thousands of sheep, or with rivers of oil? Shall I give my first-born for my transgression, the fruit of my body for the sin of my soul? No! for the Lord has showed us, O men, what is good. And what does the Lord require of you but to deal justly, love mercy, and walk humbly with your God?

126:4.6 (1392.4) "To whom, then, will you liken God who sits upon the circle of the earth? Lift up your eyes and behold who has created all these worlds, who brings forth their host by number and calls them all by their names. He does all these things by the greatness of his might, and because he is strong in power, not one fails. He gives power to the weak, and to those who are weary he increases strength. Fear not, for I am with you; be not dismayed, for I am your God. I will strengthen you and I will help you; yes, I will uphold you with the right hand of my righteousness, for I am the Lord your God. And I will hold your right hand, saying to you, fear not, for I will help you.

126:4.7 (1392.5) "And you are my witness, says the Lord, and my servant whom I have chosen that all may know and believe me and understand that I am the Eternal. I, even I, am the Lord, and beside me there is no savior."

126:4.8 (1392.6) And when he had thus read, he sat down, and the people went to their homes, pondering over the words which he had so graciously read to them. Never had his townspeople seen him so magnificently solemn; never had they heard his voice so earnest and so sincere; never had they observed him so manly and decisive, so authoritative.

126:4.9 (1392.7) This Sabbath afternoon Jesus climbed the Nazareth hill with James and, when they returned home, wrote out the Ten Commandments in Greek on two smooth boards in charcoal. Subsequently Martha colored and decorated these boards, and for long they hung on the wall over James's small workbench.

5   *The Financial Struggle*

126:5.1 (1392.8) Gradually Jesus and his family returned to the simple life of their earlier years. Their clothes and even their food became simpler. They had plenty of milk, butter, and cheese. In season they enjoyed the produce of their garden, but each passing month necessitated the practice of greater frugality. Their breakfasts were very plain; they saved their best food for the evening meal. However, among these Jews lack of wealth did not imply social inferiority.

126:5.2 (1392.9) Already had this youth well-nigh encompassed the comprehension of how men lived in his day. And how well he understood life in the home, field, and workshop is shown by his subsequent teachings, which so repletely reveal his intimate contact with all phases of human experience.

126:5.3 (1392.10) The Nazareth chazan continued to cling to the belief that Jesus was to become a great teacher, probably the successor of the renowned Gamaliel at Jerusalem.

126:5.4 (1393.1) Apparently all Jesus' plans for a career were thwarted. The future did not look bright as matters now developed. But he did not falter; he was not discouraged. He lived on, day by day, doing well the present duty and faithfully discharging the immediate responsibilities of his station in life. Jesus' life is the everlasting comfort of all disappointed idealists.

126:5.5 (1393.2) The pay of a common day-laboring carpenter was slowly diminishing. By the end of this year Jesus could earn, by working early and late, only the equivalent of about twenty-five cents a day. By the next year they found it difficult to pay the civil taxes, not to mention the synagogue assessments and the temple tax of one-half shekel. During this year the tax collector tried to squeeze extra revenue out of Jesus, even threatening to take his harp.

126:5.6 (1393.3) Fearing that the copy of the Greek scriptures might be discovered and confiscated by the tax collectors, Jesus, on his fifteenth birthday, presented it to the Nazareth synagogue library as his maturity offering to the Lord.

126:5.7 (1393.4) The great shock of his fifteenth year came when Jesus went over to Sepphoris to receive the decision of Herod regarding the appeal taken to him in the dispute about the amount of money due Joseph at the time of his accidental death. Jesus and Mary had hoped for the receipt of a considerable sum of money when the treasurer at Sepphoris had offered them a paltry amount. Joseph's brothers had taken an appeal to Herod himself, and now Jesus stood in the palace and heard Herod decree that his father had nothing due him at the time of his death. And for such an unjust decision Jesus never again trusted Herod Antipas. It is not surprising that he once alluded to Herod as "that fox."

126:5.8 (1393.5) The close work at the carpenter's bench during this and subsequent years deprived Jesus of the opportunity of mingling with the caravan passengers. The family supply shop had already been taken over by his uncle, and Jesus worked altogether in the home shop, where he was near to help Mary with the family. About this time he began sending James up to the camel lot to gather information about world events, and thus he sought to keep in touch with the news of the day.

126:5.9 (1393.6) As he grew up to manhood, he passed through all those conflicts and confusions which the average young persons of previous and subsequent ages have undergone. And the rigorous experience of supporting his family was a sure safeguard against his having overmuch time for idle meditation or the indulgence of mystic tendencies.

126:5.10 (1393.7) This was the year that Jesus rented a considerable piece of land just to the north of their home, which was divided up as a family garden plot. Each of the older children had an individual garden, and they entered into keen competition in their agricultural efforts. Their eldest brother spent some time with them in the garden each day during the season of vegetable cultivation. As Jesus worked with his younger brothers and sisters in the garden, he many times entertained the wish that they were all located on a farm out in the country where they could enjoy the liberty and freedom of an unhampered life. But they did not find themselves growing up in the country; and Jesus, being a thoroughly practical youth as well as an idealist, intelligently and vigorously attacked his problem just as he found it, and did everything within his power to adjust himself and his family to the realities of their situation and to adapt their condition to the highest possible satisfaction of their individual and collective longings.

126:5.11 (1393.8) At one time Jesus faintly hoped that he might be able to gather up sufficient means, provided they could collect the considerable sum of money due his father for work on Herod's palace, to warrant undertaking the purchase of a small farm. He had really given serious thought to this plan of moving his family out into the country. But when Herod refused to pay them any of the funds due Joseph, they gave up the ambition of owning a home in the country. As it was, they contrived to enjoy much of the experience of farm life as they now had three cows, four sheep, a flock of chickens, a donkey, and a dog, in addition to the doves. Even the little tots had their regular duties to perform in the well-regulated scheme of management which characterized the home life of this Nazareth family.

126:5.12 (1394.1) With the close of this fifteenth year Jesus completed the traversal of that dangerous and difficult period in human existence, that time of transition between the more complacent years of childhood and the consciousness of approaching manhood with its increased responsibilities and opportunities for the acquirement of advanced experience in the development of a noble character. The growth period for mind and body had ended, and now began the real career of this young man of Nazareth.

Paper 127

The Adolescent Years

127:0.1 (1395.1) AS JESUS entered upon his adolescent years, he found himself the head and sole support of a large family. Within a few years after his father's death all their property was gone. As time passed, he became increasingly conscious of his pre-existence; at the same time he began more fully to realize that he was present on earth and in the flesh for the express purpose of revealing his Paradise Father to the children of men.

127:0.2 (1395.2) No adolescent youth who has lived or ever will live on this world or any other world has had or ever will have more weighty problems to resolve or more intricate difficulties to untangle. No youth of Urantia will ever be called upon to pass through more testing conflicts or more trying situations than Jesus himself endured during those strenuous years from fifteen to twenty.

127:0.3 (1395.3) Having thus tasted the actual experience of living these adolescent years on a world beset by evil and distraught by sin, the Son of Man became possessed of full knowledge about the life experience of the youth of all the realms of Nebadon, and thus forever he became the understanding refuge for the distressed and perplexed adolescents of all ages and on all worlds throughout the local universe.

127:0.4 (1395.4) Slowly, but certainly and by actual experience, this divine Son is earning the right to become sovereign of his universe, the unquestioned and supreme ruler of all created intelligences on all local universe worlds, the understanding refuge of the beings of all ages and of all degrees of personal endowment and experience.

1 The Sixteenth Year (A.D. 10)

127:1.1 (1395.5) The incarnated Son passed through infancy and experienced an uneventful childhood. Then he emerged from that testing and trying transition stage between childhood and young manhood— he became the adolescent Jesus.

127:1.2 (1395.6) This year he attained his full physical growth. He was a virile and comely youth. He became increasingly sober and serious, but he was kind and sympathetic. His eye was kind but searching; his smile was always engaging and reassuring. His voice was musical but authoritative; his greeting cordial but unaffected. Always, even in the most commonplace of contacts, there seemed to be in evidence the touch of a twofold nature, the human and the divine. Ever he displayed this combination of the sympathizing friend and the authoritative teacher. And these personality traits began early to become manifest, even in these adolescent years.

127:1.3 (1395.7) This physically strong and robust youth also acquired the full growth of his human intellect, not the full experience of human thinking but the fullness of capacity for such intellectual development. He possessed a healthy and well-proportioned body, a keen and analytical mind, a kind and sympathetic disposition, a somewhat fluctuating but aggressive temperament, all of which were becoming organized into a strong, striking, and attractive personality.

127:1.4 (1396.1) As time went on, it became more difficult for his mother and his brothers and sisters to understand him; they stumbled over his sayings and misinterpreted his doings. They were all unfitted to comprehend their eldest brother's life because their mother had given them to understand that he was destined to become the deliverer of the Jewish people. After they had received from Mary such intimations as family secrets, imagine their confusion when Jesus would make frank denials of all such ideas and intentions.

127:1.5 (1396.2) This year Simon started to school, and they were compelled to sell another house. James now took charge of the teaching of his three sisters, two of whom were old enough to begin serious study. As soon as Ruth grew up, she was taken in hand by Miriam and Martha. Ordinarily the girls of Jewish families received little education, but Jesus maintained (and his mother agreed) that girls should go to school the same as boys, and since the synagogue school would not receive them, there was nothing to do but conduct a home school especially for them.

127:1.6 (1396.3) Throughout this year Jesus was closely confined to the workbench. Fortunately he had plenty of work; his was of such a superior grade that he was never idle no matter how slack work might be in that region. At times he had so much to do that James would help him.

127:1.7 (1396.4) By the end of this year he had just about made up his mind that he would, after rearing his family and seeing them married, enter publicly upon his work as a teacher of truth and as a revealer of the heavenly Father to the world. He knew he was not to become the expected Jewish Messiah, and he concluded that it was next to useless to discuss these matters with his mother; he decided to allow her to entertain whatever ideas she might choose since all he had said in the past had made little or no impression upon her and he recalled that his father had never been able to say anything that would change her mind. From this year on he talked less and less with his mother, or anyone else, about these problems. His was such a peculiar mission that no one living on earth could give him advice concerning its prosecution.

127:1.8 (1396.5) He was a real though youthful father to the family; he spent every possible hour with the youngsters, and they truly loved him. His mother grieved to see him work so hard; she sorrowed that he was day by day toiling at the carpenter's bench earning a living for the family instead of being, as they had so fondly planned, at Jerusalem studying with the rabbis. While there was much about her son that Mary could not understand, she did love him, and she most thoroughly appreciated the willing manner in which he shouldered the responsibility of the home.

2   *The Seventeenth Year (A.D. 11)*

127:2.1 (1396.6) At about this time there was considerable agitation, especially at Jerusalem and in Judea, in favor of rebellion against the payment of taxes to Rome. There was coming into existence a strong nationalist party, presently to be called the Zealots. The Zealots, unlike the Pharisees, were not willing to await the coming of the Messiah. They proposed to bring things to a head through political revolt.

127:2.2 (1396.7) A group of organizers from Jerusalem arrived in Galilee and were making good headway until they reached Nazareth. When they came to see Jesus, he listened carefully to them and asked many questions but refused to join the party. He declined fully to disclose his reasons for not enlisting, and his refusal had the effect of keeping out many of his youthful fellows in Nazareth.

127:2.3 (1397.1) Mary did her best to induce him to enlist, but she could not budge him. She went so far as to intimate that his refusal to espouse the nationalist cause at her behest was insubordination, a violation of his pledge made upon their return from Jerusalem that he would be subject to his parents; but in answer to this insinuation he only laid a kindly hand on her shoulder and, looking into her face, said: "My mother, how could you?" And Mary withdrew her statement.

127:2.4 (1397.2) One of Jesus' uncles (Mary's brother Simon) had already joined this group, subsequently becoming an officer in the Galilean division. And for several years there was something of an estrangement between Jesus and his uncle.

127:2.5 (1397.3) But trouble began to brew in Nazareth. Jesus' attitude in these matters had resulted in creating a division among the Jewish youths of the city. About half had joined the nationalist organization, and the other half began the formation of an opposing group of more moderate patriots, expecting Jesus to assume the leadership. They were amazed when he refused the honor offered him, pleading as an excuse his heavy family responsibilities, which they all allowed. But the situation was still further complicated when, presently, a wealthy Jew, Isaac, a moneylender to the gentiles, came forward agreeing to support Jesus' family if he would lay down his tools and assume leadership of these Nazareth patriots.

127:2.6 (1397.4) Jesus, then scarcely seventeen years of age, was confronted with one of the most delicate and difficult situations of his early life. Patriotic issues, especially when complicated by tax-gathering foreign oppressors, are always difficult for spiritual leaders to relate themselves to, and it was doubly so in this case since the Jewish religion was involved in all this agitation against Rome.

127:2.7 (1397.5) Jesus' position was made more difficult because his mother and uncle, and even his younger brother James, all urged him to join the nationalist cause. All the better Jews of Nazareth had enlisted, and those young men who had not joined the movement would all enlist the moment Jesus changed his mind. He had but one wise counselor in all Nazareth, his old teacher, the chazan, who counseled him about his reply to the citizens' committee of Nazareth when they came to ask for his answer to the public appeal which had been made. In all Jesus' young life this was the very first time he had consciously resorted to public strategy. Theretofore, always had he depended upon a frank statement of truth to clarify the situation, but now he could not declare the full truth. He could not intimate that he was more than a man; he could not disclose his idea of the mission which awaited his attainment of a riper manhood. Despite these limitations his religious fealty and national loyalty were directly challenged. His family was in a turmoil, his youthful friends in division, and the entire Jewish contingent of the town in a hubbub. And to think that he was to blame for it all! And how innocent he had been of all intention to make trouble of any kind, much less a disturbance of this sort.

127:2.8 (1397.6) Something had to be done. He must state his position, and this he did bravely and diplomatically to the satisfaction of many, but not all. He adhered to the terms of his original plea, maintaining that his first duty was to his family, that a widowed mother and eight brothers and sisters needed something more than mere money could buy—the physical necessities of life—that they were entitled to a father's watchcare and guidance, and that he could not in clear conscience release himself from the obligation which a cruel accident had thrust upon him. He paid compliment to his mother and eldest brother for being willing to release him but reiterated that loyalty to a dead father forbade his leaving the family no matter how much money was forthcoming for their material support, making his never-to-be-forgotten statement that "money cannot love." In the course of this address Jesus made several veiled references to his "life mission" but explained that, regardless of whether or not it might be inconsistent with the military idea, it, along with everything else in his life, had been given up in order that he might be able to discharge faithfully his obligation to his family. Everyone in Nazareth well knew he was a good father to his family, and this was a matter so near the heart of every noble Jew that Jesus' plea found an appreciative response in the hearts of many of his hearers; and some of those who were not thus minded were disarmed by a speech made by James, which, while not on the program, was delivered at this time. That very day the chazan had

rehearsed James in his speech, but that was their secret.

127:2.9 (1398.1) James stated that he was sure Jesus would help to liberate his people if he (James) were only old enough to assume responsibility for the family, and that, if they would only consent to allow Jesus to remain "with us, to be our father and teacher, then you will have not just one leader from Joseph's family, but presently you will have five loyal nationalists, for are there not five of us boys to grow up and come forth from our brother-father's guidance to serve our nation?" And thus did the lad bring to a fairly happy ending a very tense and threatening situation.

127:2.10 (1398.2) The crisis for the time being was over, but never was this incident forgotten in Nazareth. The agitation persisted; not again was Jesus in universal favor; the division of sentiment was never fully overcome. And this, augmented by other and subsequent occurrences, was one of the chief reasons why he moved to Capernaum in later years. Henceforth Nazareth maintained a division of sentiment regarding the Son of Man.

127:2.11 (1398.3) James graduated at school this year and began full-time work at home in the carpenter shop. He had become a clever worker with tools and now took over the making of yokes and plows while Jesus began to do more house finishing and expert cabinet work.

127:2.12 (1398.4) This year Jesus made great progress in the organization of his mind. Gradually he had brought his divine and human natures together, and he accomplished all this organization of intellect by the force of his own decisions and with only the aid of his indwelling Monitor, just such a Monitor as all normal mortals on all postbestowal-Son worlds have within their minds. So far, nothing supernatural had happened in this young man's career except the visit of a messenger, dispatched by his elder brother Immanuel, who once appeared to him during the night at Jerusalem.

3   The Eighteenth Year (A.D. 12)

127:3.1 (1398.5) In the course of this year all the family property, except the home and garden, was disposed of. The last piece of Capernaum property (except an equity in one other), already mortgaged, was sold. The proceeds were used for taxes, to buy some new tools for James, and to make a payment on the old family supply and repair shop near the caravan lot, which Jesus now proposed to buy back since James was old enough to work at the house shop and help Mary about the home. With the financial pressure thus eased for the time being, Jesus decided to take James to the Passover. They went up to Jerusalem a day early, to be alone, going by way of Samaria. They walked, and Jesus told James about the historic places en route as his father had taught him on a similar journey five years before.

127:3.2 (1399.1) In passing through Samaria, they saw many strange sights. On this journey they talked over many of their problems, personal, family, and national. James was a very religious type of lad, and while he did not fully agree with his mother regarding the little he knew of the plans concerning Jesus' lifework, he did look forward to the time when he would be able to assume responsibility for the family so that Jesus could begin his mission. He was very appreciative of Jesus' taking him up to the Passover, and they talked over the future more fully than ever before.

127:3.3 (1399.2) Jesus did much thinking as they journeyed through Samaria, particularly at Bethel and when drinking from Jacob's well. He and his brother discussed the traditions of Abraham, Isaac, and Jacob. He did much to prepare James for what he was about to witness at Jerusalem, thus seeking to lessen the shock such as he himself had experienced on his first visit to the temple. But James was not so sensitive to some of these sights. He commented on the perfunctory and heartless manner in which some of the priests performed their duties but on the whole greatly enjoyed his sojourn at Jerusalem.

127:3.4 (1399.3) Jesus took James to Bethany for the Passover supper. Simon had been laid to rest with his fathers, and Jesus presided over this household as the head of the Passover family, having brought the paschal lamb from the temple.

127:3.5 (1399.4) After the Passover supper Mary sat down to talk with James while Martha, Lazarus, and Jesus talked together far into the night. The next day they attended the temple services, and James was received into the commonwealth of Israel. That morning, as they paused on the brow of Olivet to view the temple, while James exclaimed in wonder, Jesus gazed on Jerusalem in silence. James could not comprehend his brother's demeanor. That night they again returned to Bethany and would have departed for home the next day, but James was insistent on their going back to visit the temple, explaining that he wanted to hear the teachers. And while this was true, secretly in his heart he wanted to hear Jesus participate in the discussions, as he had heard his mother tell about. Accordingly, they went to the temple and heard the discussions, but Jesus asked no questions. It all seemed so puerile and insignificant to this awakening mind of man and God—he could only pity them. James was disappointed that Jesus said nothing. To his inquiries Jesus only made reply, "My hour has not yet come."

127:3.6 (1399.5) The next day they journeyed home by Jericho and the Jordan valley, and Jesus recounted many things by the way, including his former trip over this road when he was thirteen years old.

127:3.7 (1399.6) Upon returning to Nazareth, Jesus began work in the old family repair shop and was greatly cheered by being able to meet so many people each day from all parts of the country and surrounding districts. Jesus truly loved people—just common folks. Each month he made his payments on the shop and, with James's help, continued to provide for the family.

127:3.8 (1399.7) Several times a year, when visitors were not present thus to function, Jesus continued to read the Sabbath scriptures at the synagogue and many times offered comments on the lesson, but usually he so selected the passages that comment was unnecessary. He was skillful, so arranging the order of the reading of the various passages that the one would illuminate the other. He never failed, weather permitting, to take his brothers and sisters out on Sabbath afternoons for their nature strolls.

127:3.9 (1400.1) About this time the chazan inaugurated a young men's club for philosophic discussion which met at the homes of different members and often at his own home, and Jesus became a prominent member of this group. By this means he was enabled to regain some of the local prestige which he had lost at the time of the recent nationalistic controversies.

127:3.10 (1400.2) His social life, while restricted, was not wholly neglected. He had many warm friends and stanch admirers among both the young men and the young women of Nazareth.

127:3.11 (1400.3) In September, Elizabeth and John came to visit the Nazareth family. John, having lost his father, intended to return to the Judean hills to engage in agriculture and sheep raising unless Jesus advised him to remain in Nazareth to take up carpentry or some other line of work. They did not know that the Nazareth family was practically penniless. The more Mary and Elizabeth talked about their sons, the more they became convinced that it would be good for the two young men to work together and see more of each other.

127:3.12 (1400.4) Jesus and John had many talks together; and they talked over some very intimate and personal matters. When they had finished this visit, they decided not again to see each other until they should meet in their public service after "the heavenly Father should call"

them to their work. John was tremendously impressed by what he saw at Nazareth that he should return home and labor for the support of his mother. He became convinced that he was to be a part of Jesus' life mission, but he saw that Jesus was to occupy many years with the rearing of his family; so he was much more content to return to his home and settle down to the care of their little farm and to minister to the needs of his mother. And never again did John and Jesus see each other until that day by the Jordan when the Son of Man presented himself for baptism.

127:3.13 (1400.5) On Saturday afternoon, December 3, of this year, death for the second time struck at this Nazareth family. Little Amos, their baby brother, died after a week's illness with a high fever. After passing through this time of sorrow with her first-born son as her only support, Mary at last and in the fullest sense recognized Jesus as the real head of the family; and he was truly a worthy head.

127:3.14 (1400.6) For four years their standard of living had steadily declined; year by year they felt the pinch of increasing poverty. By the close of this year they faced one of the most difficult experiences of all their uphill struggles. James had not yet begun to earn much, and the expenses of a funeral on top of everything else staggered them. But Jesus would only say to his anxious and grieving mother: "Mother-Mary, sorrow will not help us; we are all doing our best, and mother's smile, perchance, might even inspire us to do better. Day by day we are strengthened for these tasks by our hope of better days ahead." His sturdy and practical optimism was truly contagious; all the children lived in an atmosphere of anticipation of better times and better things. And this hopeful courage contributed mightily to the development of strong and noble characters, in spite of the depressiveness of their poverty.

127:3.15 (1400.7) Jesus possessed the ability effectively to mobilize all his powers of mind, soul, and body on the task immediately in hand. He could concentrate his deep-thinking mind on the one problem which he wished to solve, and this, in connection with his untiring patience, enabled him serenely to endure the trials of a difficult mortal existence— to live as if he were "seeing Him who is invisible."

4   The Nineteenth Year (A.D. 13)

127:4.1 (1401.1) By this time Jesus and Mary were getting along much better. She regarded him less as a son; he had become to her more a father to her children. Each day's life swarmed with practical and immediate difficulties. Less frequently they spoke of his lifework, for, as time passed, all their thought was mutually devoted to the support and upbringing of their family of four boys and three girls.

127:4.2 (1401.2) By the beginning of this year Jesus had fully won his mother to the acceptance of his methods of child training—the positive injunction to do good in the place of the older Jewish method of forbidding to do evil. In his home and throughout his public-teaching career Jesus invariably employed the positive form of exhortation. Always and everywhere did he say, "You shall do this—you ought to do that." Never did he employ the negative mode of teaching derived from the ancient taboos. He refrained from placing emphasis on evil by forbidding it, while he exalted the good by commanding its performance. Prayer time in this household was the occasion for discussing anything and everything relating to the welfare of the family.

127:4.3 (1401.3) Jesus began wise discipline upon his brothers and sisters at such an early age that little or no punishment was ever required to secure their prompt and wholehearted obedience. The only exception was Jude, upon whom on sundry occasions Jesus found it necessary to impose penalties for his infractions of the rules of the home. On three occasions when it was deemed wise to punish Jude for self-confessed and deliberate violations of the family rules of conduct, his punishment was fixed by the unanimous decree of the older children and was assented to by Jude himself before it was inflicted.

127:4.4 (1401.4) While Jesus was most methodical and systematic in everything he did, there was also in all his administrative rulings a refreshing elasticity of interpretation and an individuality of adaptation that greatly impressed all the children with the spirit of justice which actuated their father-brother. He never arbitrarily disciplined his brothers and sisters, and such uniform fairness and personal consideration greatly endeared Jesus to all his family.

127:4.5 (1401.5) James and Simon grew up trying to follow Jesus' plan of placating their bellicose and sometimes irate playmates by persuasion and nonresistance, and they were fairly successful; but Joseph and Jude, while assenting to such teachings at home, made haste to defend themselves when assailed by their comrades; in particular was Jude guilty of violating the spirit of these teachings. But nonresistance was not a rule of the family. No penalty was attached to the violation of personal teachings.

127:4.6 (1401.6) In general, all of the children, particularly the girls, would consult Jesus about their childhood troubles and confide in him just as they would have in an affectionate father.

127:4.7 (1401.7) James was growing up to be a well-balanced and even-tempered youth, but he was not so spiritually inclined as Jesus. He was a much better student than Joseph, who, while a faithful worker, was even less spiritually minded. Joseph was a plodder and not up to the intellectual level of the other children. Simon was a well-meaning boy but too much of a dreamer. He was slow in getting settled down in life and was the cause of considerable anxiety to Jesus and Mary. But he was always a good and well-intentioned lad. Jude was a firebrand. He had the highest of ideals, but he was unstable in temperament. He had all and more of his mother's determination and aggressiveness, but he lacked much of her sense of proportion and discretion.

127:4.8 (1402.1) Miriam was a well-balanced and level-headed daughter with a keen appreciation of things noble and spiritual. Martha was slow in thought and action but a very dependable and efficient child. Baby Ruth was the sunshine of the home; though thoughtless of speech, she was most sincere of heart. She just about worshiped her big brother and father. But they did not spoil her. She was a beautiful child but not quite so comely as Miriam, who was the belle of the family, if not of the city.

127:4.9 (1402.2) As time passed, Jesus did much to liberalize and modify the family teachings and practices related to Sabbath observance and many other phases of religion, and to all these changes Mary gave hearty assent. By this time Jesus had become the unquestioned head of the house.

127:4.10 (1402.3) This year Jude started to school, and it was necessary for Jesus to sell his harp in order to defray these expenses. Thus disappeared the last of his recreational pleasures. He much loved to play the harp when tired in mind and weary in body, but he comforted himself with the thought that at least the harp was safe from seizure by the tax collector.

5   Rebecca, the Daughter of Ezra

127:5.1 (1402.4) Although Jesus was poor, his social standing in Nazareth was in no way impaired. He was one of the foremost young men of the city and very highly regarded by most of the young women. Since Jesus was such a splendid specimen of robust and intellectual manhood, and considering his reputation as a spiritual leader, it was not strange that Rebecca, the eldest daughter of Ezra, a wealthy merchant and trader of Nazareth, should discover that she was slowly falling in love with this son of

Joseph. She first confided her affection to Miriam, Jesus' sister, and Miriam in turn talked all this over with her mother. Mary was intensely aroused. Was she about to lose her son, now become the indispensable head of the family? Would troubles never cease? What next could happen? And then she paused to contemplate what effect marriage would have upon Jesus' future career; not often, but at least sometimes, did she recall the fact that Jesus was a "child of promise." After she and Miriam had talked this matter over, they decided to make an effort to stop it before Jesus learned about it, by going direct to Rebecca, laying the whole story before her, and honestly telling her about their belief that Jesus was a son of destiny; that he was to become a great religious leader, perhaps the Messiah.

127:5.2 (1402.5) Rebecca listened intently; she was thrilled with the recital and more than ever determined to cast her lot with this man of her choice and to share his career of leadership. She argued (to herself) that such a man would all the more need a faithful and efficient wife. She interpreted Mary's efforts to dissuade her as a natural reaction to the dread of losing the head and sole support of her family; but knowing that her father approved of her attraction for the carpenter's son, she rightly reckoned that he would gladly supply the family with sufficient income fully to compensate for the loss of Jesus' earnings. When her father agreed to such a plan, Rebecca had further conferences with Mary and Miriam, and when she failed to win their support, she made bold to go directly to Jesus. This she did with the co-operation of her father, who invited Jesus to their home for the celebration of Rebecca's seventeenth birthday.

127:5.3 (1403.1) Jesus listened attentively and sympathetically to the recital of these things, first by the father, then by Rebecca herself. He made kindly reply to the effect that no amount of money could take the place of his obligation personally to rear his father's family, to "fulfill the most sacred of all human trusts—loyalty to one's own flesh and blood." Rebecca's father was deeply touched by Jesus' words of family devotion and retired from the conference. His only remark to Mary, his wife, was: "We can't have him for a son; he is too noble for us."

127:5.4 (1403.2) Then began that eventful talk with Rebecca. Thus far in his life, Jesus had made little distinction in his association with boys and girls, with young men and young women. His mind had been altogether too much occupied with the pressing problems of practical earthly affairs and the intriguing contemplation of his eventual career "about his Father's business" ever to have given serious consideration to the consummation of personal love in human marriage.

But now he was face to face with another of those problems which every average human being must confront and decide. Indeed was he "tested in all points like as you are."

127:5.5 (1403.3) After listening attentively, he sincerely thanked Rebecca for her expressed admiration, adding, "it shall cheer and comfort me all the days of my life." He explained that he was not free to enter into relations with any woman other than those of simple brotherly regard and pure friendship. He made it clear that his first and paramount duty was the rearing of his father's family, that he could not consider marriage until that was accomplished; and then he added: "If I am a son of destiny, I must not assume obligations of lifelong duration until such a time as my destiny shall be made manifest."

127:5.6 (1403.4) Rebecca was heartbroken. She refused to be comforted and importuned her father to leave Nazareth until he finally consented to move to Sepphoris. In after years, to the many men who sought her hand in marriage, Rebecca had but one answer. She lived for only one purpose—to await the hour when this, to her, the greatest man who ever lived would begin his career as a teacher of living truth. And she followed him devotedly through his eventful years of public labor, being present (unobserved by Jesus) that day

when he rode triumphantly into Jerusalem; and she stood "among the other women" by the side of Mary on that fateful and tragic afternoon when the Son of Man hung upon the cross, to her, as well as to countless worlds on high, "the one altogether lovely and the greatest among ten thousand."

6   His Twentieth Year (A.D. 14)

127:6.1 (1403.5) The story of Rebecca's love for Jesus was whispered about Nazareth and later on at Capernaum, so that, while in the years to follow many women loved Jesus even as men loved him, not again did he have to reject the personal proffer of another good woman's devotion. From this time on human affection for Jesus partook more of the nature of worshipful and adoring regard. Both men and women loved him devotedly and for what he was, not with any tinge of self-satisfaction or desire for affectionate possession. But for many years, whenever the story of Jesus' human personality was recited, the devotion of Rebecca was recounted.

127:6.2 (1404.1) Miriam, knowing fully about the affair of Rebecca and knowing how her brother had forsaken even the love of a beautiful maiden (not realizing the factor of his future career of destiny), came to idealize Jesus and to love him with a touching and profound affection as for a father as well as for a brother.

127:6.3 (1404.2) Although they could hardly afford it, Jesus had a strange longing to go up to Jerusalem for the Passover. His mother, knowing of his recent experience with Rebecca, wisely urged him to make the journey. He was not markedly conscious of it, but what he most wanted was an opportunity to talk with Lazarus and to visit with Martha and Mary. Next to his own family he loved these three most of all.

127:6.4 (1404.3) In making this trip to Jerusalem, he went by way of Megiddo, Antipatris, and Lydda, in part covering the same route traversed when he was brought back to Nazareth on the return from Egypt. He spent four days going up to the Passover and thought much about the past events which had transpired in and around Megiddo, the international battlefield of Palestine.

127:6.5 (1404.4) Jesus passed on through Jerusalem, only pausing to look upon the temple and the gathering throngs of visitors. He had a strange and increasing aversion to this Herod-built temple with its politically appointed priesthood. He wanted most of all to see Lazarus, Martha, and Mary. Lazarus was the same age as Jesus and now head of the house; by the time of this visit Lazarus's mother had also been laid to rest. Martha was a little over one year older than Jesus, while Mary was two years younger. And Jesus was the idolized ideal of all three of them.

127:6.6 (1404.5) On this visit occurred one of those periodic outbreaks of rebellion against tradition—the expression of resentment for those ceremonial practices which Jesus deemed misrepresentative of his Father in heaven. Not knowing Jesus was coming, Lazarus had arranged to celebrate the Passover with friends in an adjoining village down the Jericho road. Jesus now proposed that they celebrate the feast where they were, at Lazarus's house. "But," said Lazarus, "we have no paschal lamb." And then Jesus entered upon a prolonged and convincing dissertation to the effect that the Father in heaven was not truly concerned with such childlike and meaningless rituals. After solemn and fervent prayer they rose, and Jesus said: "Let the childlike and darkened minds of my people serve their God as Moses directed; it is better that they do, but let us who have seen the light of life no longer approach our Father by the darkness of death. Let us be free in the knowledge of the truth of our Father's eternal love."

127:6.7 (1404.6) That evening about twilight these four sat down and partook of the first Passover feast ever to be celebrated by devout Jews without the paschal lamb. The unleavened bread and the wine had been made ready for this Passover, and these emblems, which Jesus termed "the bread of life" and "the water of life," he served to his companions, and they ate in solemn conformity with the teachings just imparted. It was his custom to engage in this sacramental ritual whenever he paid subsequent visits to Bethany. When he returned home, he told all this to his mother. She was shocked at first but came gradually to see his viewpoint; nevertheless, she was greatly relieved when Jesus assured her that he did not intend to introduce this new idea of the Passover in their family. At home with the children he continued, year by year, to eat the Passover "according to the law of Moses."

127:6.8 (1404.7) It was during this year that Mary had a long talk with Jesus about marriage. She frankly asked him if he would get married if he were free from his family responsibilities. Jesus explained to her that, since immediate duty forbade his marriage, he had given the subject little thought. He expressed himself as doubting that he would ever enter the marriage state; he said that all such things must await "my hour," the time when "my Father's work must begin." Having settled already in his mind that he was not to become the father of children in the flesh, he gave very little thought to the subject of human marriage.

127:6.9 (1405.1) This year he began anew the task of further weaving his mortal and divine natures into a simple and effective human individuality. And he continued to grow in moral status and spiritual understanding.

127:6.10 (1405.2) Although all their Nazareth property (except their home) was gone, this year they received a little financial help from the sale of an equity in a piece of property in Capernaum. This was the last of Joseph's entire estate. This real estate deal in Capernaum was with a boatbuilder named Zebedee.

127:6.11 (1405.3) Joseph graduated at the synagogue school this year and prepared to begin work at the small bench in the home carpenter shop. Although the estate of their father was exhausted, there were prospects that they would successfully fight off poverty since three of them were now regularly at work.

127:6.12 (1405.4) Jesus is rapidly becoming a man, not just a young man but an adult. He has learned well to bear responsibility. He knows how to carry on in the face of disappointment. He bears up bravely when his plans are thwarted and his purposes temporarily defeated. He has learned how to be fair and just even in the face of injustice. He is learning how to adjust his ideals of spiritual living to the practical demands of earthly existence. He is learning how to plan for the achievement of a higher and distant goal of idealism while he toils earnestly for the attainment of a nearer and immediate goal of necessity. He is steadily acquiring the art of adjusting his aspirations to the commonplace demands of the human occasion. He has very nearly mastered the technique of utilizing the energy of the spiritual drive to turn the mechanism of material achievement. He is slowly learning how to live the heavenly life while he continues on with the earthly existence. More and more he depends upon the ultimate guidance of his heavenly Father while he assumes the fatherly role of guiding and directing the children of his earth family. He is becoming experienced in the skillful wresting of victory from the very jaws of defeat; he is learning how to transform the difficulties of time into the triumphs of eternity.

127:6.13 (1405.5) And so, as the years pass, this young man of Nazareth continues to experience life as it is lived in mortal flesh on the worlds of time and space. He lives a full, representative, and replete life on Urantia. He left this world ripe in the experience which his creatures pass through during the short and strenuous years of their first life, the life in the flesh. And all this human experience is an eternal possession of the Universe Sovereign. He is our understanding brother, sympathetic friend, experienced sovereign, and merciful father.

127:6.14 (1405.6) As a child he accumulated a vast body of knowledge; as a youth he sorted, classified, and correlated this information; and now as a man of the realm he begins to organize these mental possessions preparatory to utilization in his subsequent teaching, ministry, and service in behalf of his fellow mortals on this world and on all other spheres of habitation throughout the entire universe of Nebadon.

127:6.15 (1405.7) Born into the world a babe of the realm, he has lived his childhood life and passed through the successive stages of youth and young manhood; he now stands on the threshold of full manhood, rich in the experience of human living, replete in the understanding of human nature, and full of sympathy for the frailties of human nature. He is becoming expert in the divine art of revealing his Paradise Father to all ages and stages of mortal creatures.

127:6.16 (1406.1) And now as a full-grown man—an adult of the realm—he prepares to continue his supreme mission of revealing God to men and leading men to God.

Paper 128

Jesus' Early Manhood

128:0.1 (1407.1) AS JESUS of Nazareth entered upon the early years of his adult life, he had lived, and continued to live, a normal and average human life on earth. Jesus came into this world just as other children come; he had nothing to do with selecting his parents. He did choose this particular world as the planet whereon to carry out his seventh and final bestowal, his incarnation in the likeness of mortal flesh, but otherwise he entered the world in a natural manner, growing up as a child of the realm and wrestling with the vicissitudes of his environment just as do other mortals on this and on similar worlds.

128:0.2 (1407.2) Always be mindful of the twofold purpose of Michael's bestowal on Urantia:

128:0.3 (1407.3) 1. The mastering of the experience of living the full life of a human creature in mortal flesh, the completion of his sovereignty in Nebadon.

128:0.4 (1407.4) 2. The revelation of the Universal Father to the mortal dwellers on the worlds of time and space and the more effective leading of these same mortals to a better understanding of the Universal Father.

128:0.5 (1407.5) All other creature benefits and universe advantages were incidental and secondary to these major purposes of the mortal bestowal.

1   The Twenty-First Year (A.D. 15)

128:1.1 (1407.6) With the attainment of adult years Jesus began in earnest and with full self-consciousness the task of completing the experience of mastering the knowledge of the life of his lowest form of intelligent creatures, thereby finally and fully earning the right of unqualified rulership of his self-created universe. He entered upon this stupendous task fully realizing his dual nature. But he had already effectively combined these two natures into one—Jesus of Nazareth.

128:1.2 (1407.7) Joshua ben Joseph knew full well that he was a man, a mortal man, born of woman. This is shown in the selection of his first title, the Son of Man. He was truly a partaker of flesh and blood, and even now, as he presides in sovereign authority over the destinies of a universe, he still bears among his numerous well-earned titles that of Son of Man. It is literally true that the creative Word—the Creator Son—of the Universal Father was "made flesh and dwelt as a man of the realm on Urantia." He labored, grew weary, rested, and slept. He hungered and satisfied such cravings with food; he thirsted and quenched his thirst with water. He experienced the full gamut of human feelings and emotions; he was "in all things tested, even as you are," and he suffered and died.

128:1.3 (1407.8) He obtained knowledge, gained experience, and combined these into wisdom, just as do other mortals of the realm. Until after his baptism he availed himself of no supernatural power. He employed no agency not a part of his human endowment as a son of Joseph and Mary.

128:1.4 (1408.1) As to the attributes of his prehuman existence, he emptied himself. Prior to the beginning of his public work his knowledge of men and events was wholly self-limited. He was a true man among men.

128:1.5 (1408.2) It is forever and gloriously true: "We have a high ruler who can be touched with the feeling of our infirmities. We have a Sovereign who was in all points tested and tempted like as we are, yet without sin." And since he himself has suffered, being tested and tried, he is abundantly able to understand and minister to those who are confused and distressed.

128:1.6 (1408.3) The Nazareth carpenter now fully understood the work before him, but he chose to live his human life in the channel of its natural flowing. And in some of these matters he is indeed an example to his mortal creatures, even as it is recorded: "Let this mind be in you which was also in Christ Jesus, who, being of the nature of God, thought it not strange to be equal with God. But he made himself to be of little import and, taking upon himself the form of a creature, was born in the likeness of mankind. And being thus fashioned as a man, he humbled himself and became obedient to death, even the death of the cross."

128:1.7 (1408.4) He lived his mortal life just as all others of the human family may live theirs, "who in the days of the flesh so frequently offered up prayers and supplications, even with strong feelings and tears, to Him who is able to save from all evil, and his prayers were effective because he believed." Wherefore it behooved him in every respect to be made like his brethren that he might become a merciful and understanding sovereign ruler over them.

128:1.8 (1408.5) Of his human nature he was never in doubt; it was self-evident and always present in his consciousness. But of his divine nature there was always room for doubt and conjecture, at least this was true right up to the event of his baptism. The self-realization of divinity was a slow and, from the human standpoint, a natural evolutionary revelation. This revelation and self-realization of divinity began in Jerusalem when he was not quite thirteen years old with the first supernatural occurrence of his human existence; and this experience of effecting the self-realization of his divine nature was completed at the time of his second supernatural experience while in the flesh, the episode attendant upon his baptism by John in the Jordan, which event marked the beginning of his public career of ministry and teaching.

128:1.9 (1408.6) Between these two celestial visitations, one in his thirteenth year and the other at his baptism, there occurred nothing supernatural or superhuman in the life of this incarnated Creator Son. Notwithstanding this, the babe of Bethlehem, the lad, youth, and man of Nazareth, was in reality the incarnated Creator of a universe; but he never once used aught of this power, nor did he utilize the guidance of celestial personalities, aside from that of his guardian seraphim, in the living of his human life up to the day of his baptism by John. And we who thus testify know whereof we speak.

128:1.10 (1408.7) And yet, throughout all these years of his life in the flesh he was truly divine. He was actually a Creator Son of the Paradise Father. When once he had espoused his public career, subsequent to the technical completion of his purely mortal experience of sovereignty acquirement, he did not hesitate publicly to admit that he was the Son of God. He did not hesitate to declare, "I am Alpha and Omega, the beginning and the end, the first and the last." He made no protest in later years when he was called Lord of Glory, Ruler of a Universe, the Lord God of all creation, the Holy One of Israel, the Lord of all, our Lord and our God, God with us, having a name above every name and on all worlds, the Omnipotence of a universe, the Universe Mind of this creation, the One in whom are hid all treasures of wisdom and knowledge, the fullness of Him who fills all things, the eternal Word of the eternal God, the One who was before all things and in whom all things consist, the Creator of the heavens and the earth, the Upholder of a universe, the Judge of all the earth, the Giver of life eternal, the True Shepherd, the Deliverer of the worlds, and the Captain of our salvation.

128:1.11 (1409.1) He never objected to any of these titles as they were applied to him subsequent to the emergence from his purely human life into the later years of his self-consciousness of the ministry of divinity in humanity, and for humanity, and to humanity on this world and for all other worlds. Jesus objected to but one title as applied to him: When he was once called Immanuel, he merely replied, "Not I, that is my elder brother."

128:1.12 (1409.2) Always, even after his emergence into the larger life on earth, Jesus was submissively subject to the will of the Father in heaven.

128:1.13 (1409.3) After his baptism he thought nothing of permitting his sincere believers and grateful followers to worship him. Even while he wrestled with poverty and toiled with his hands to provide the necessities of life for his family, his awareness that he was a Son of God was growing; he knew that he was the maker of the heavens and this very earth whereon he was now living out his human existence. And the hosts of celestial beings throughout the great and onlooking universe likewise knew that this man of Nazareth was their beloved Sovereign and Creator-father. A profound suspense pervaded the universe of Nebadon throughout these years; all celestial eyes were continuously focused on Urantia—on Palestine.

128:1.14 (1409.4) This year Jesus went up to Jerusalem with Joseph to celebrate the Passover. Having taken James to the temple for consecration, he deemed it his duty to take Joseph. Jesus never exhibited any degree of partiality in dealing with his family. He went with Joseph to Jerusalem by the usual Jordan valley route, but he returned to Nazareth by the east Jordan way, which led through Amathus. Going down the Jordan, Jesus narrated Jewish history to Joseph and on the return trip told him about the experiences of the reputed tribes of Ruben, Gad, and Gilead that traditionally had dwelt in these regions east of the river.

128:1.15 (1409.5) Joseph asked Jesus many leading questions concerning his life mission, but to most of these inquiries Jesus would only reply, "My hour has not yet come." However, in these intimate discussions many words were dropped which Joseph remembered during the stirring events of subsequent years. Jesus, with Joseph, spent this Passover with his three friends at Bethany, as was his custom when in Jerusalem attending these festival commemorations.

2   The Twenty-Second Year (A.D. 16)

128:2.1 (1409.6) This was one of several years during which Jesus' brothers and sisters were facing the trials and tribulations peculiar to the problems and readjustments of adolescence. Jesus now had brothers and sisters ranging in ages from seven to eighteen, and he was kept busy helping them to adjust themselves to the new awakenings of their intellectual and emotional lives. He had thus to grapple with the problems of adolescence as they became manifest in the lives of his younger brothers and sisters.

128:2.2 (1410.1) This year Simon graduated from school and began work with Jesus' old boyhood playmate and ever-ready defender, Jacob the stone mason. As a result of several family conferences it was decided that it was unwise for all the boys to take up carpentry. It was thought that by diversifying their trades they would be prepared to take contracts for putting up entire buildings. Again, they had not all kept busy since three of them had been working as full- time carpenters.

128:2.3 (1410.2) Jesus continued this year at house finishing and cabinetwork but spent most of his time at the caravan repair shop. James was beginning to alternate with him in attendance at the shop. The latter part of this year, when carpenter work was slack about Nazareth, Jesus left James in charge of the repair shop and Joseph at the home bench while he went over to Sepphoris to work with a smith. He worked six months with metals and acquired considerable skill at the anvil.

128:2.4 (1410.3) Before taking up his new employment at Sepphoris, Jesus held one of his periodic family conferences and solemnly installed James, then just past eighteen years old, as acting head of the family. He promised his brother hearty support and full co-operation and exacted formal promises of obedience to James from each member of the family.

From this day James assumed full financial responsibility for the family, Jesus making his weekly payments to his brother. Never again did Jesus take the reins out of James's hands. While working at Sepphoris he could have walked home every night if necessary, but he purposely remained away, assigning weather and other reasons, but his true motive was to train James and Joseph in the bearing of the family responsibility. He had begun the slow process of weaning his family. Each Sabbath Jesus returned to Nazareth, and sometimes during the week when occasion required, to observe the working of the new plan, to give advice and offer helpful suggestions.

128:2.5 (1410.4) Living much of the

time in Sepphoris for six months afforded Jesus a new opportunity to become better acquainted with the gentile viewpoint of life. He worked with gentiles, lived with gentiles, and in every possible manner did he make a close and painstaking study of their habits of living and of the gentile mind.

128:2.6 (1410.5) The moral standards of this home city of Herod Antipas were so far below those of even the caravan city of Nazareth that after six months' sojourn at Sepphoris Jesus was not averse to finding an excuse for returning to Nazareth. The group he worked for were to become engaged on public work in both Sepphoris and the new city of Tiberias, and Jesus was disinclined to have anything to do with any sort of employment under the supervision of Herod Antipas. And there were still other reasons which made it wise, in the opinion of Jesus, for him to go back to Nazareth. When he returned to the repair shop, he did not again assume the personal direction of family affairs. He worked in association with James at the shop and as far as possible permitted him to continue oversight of the home. James's management of family expenditures and his administration of the home budget were undisturbed.

128:2.7 (1410.6) It was by just such wise and thoughtful planning that Jesus prepared the way for his eventual withdrawal from active participation in the affairs of his family. When James had had two years' experience as acting head of the family—and two full years before he (James) was to be married—Joseph was placed in charge of the household funds and intrusted with the general management of the home.

3   The Twenty-Third Year (A.D. 17)

128:3.1 (1411.1) This year the financial pressure was slightly relaxed as four were at work. Miriam earned considerable by the sale of milk and butter; Martha had become an expert weaver. The purchase price of the repair shop was over one third paid. The situation was such that Jesus stopped work for three weeks to take Simon to Jerusalem for the Passover, and this was the longest period away from daily toil he had enjoyed since the death of his father.

128:3.2 (1411.2) They journeyed to Jerusalem by way of the Decapolis and through Pella, Gerasa, Philadelphia, Heshbon, and Jericho. They returned to Nazareth by the coast route, touching Lydda, Joppa, Caesarea, thence around Mount Carmel to Ptolemais and Nazareth. This trip fairly well acquainted Jesus with the whole of Palestine north of the Jerusalem district.

128:3.3 (1411.3) At Philadelphia Jesus and Simon became acquainted with a merchant from Damascus who developed such a great liking for the Nazareth couple that he insisted they stop with him at his Jerusalem headquarters. While Simon gave attendance at the temple, Jesus spent much of his time talking with this well-educated and much-traveled man of world affairs. This merchant owned over four thousand caravan camels; he had interests all over the Roman world and was now on his way to Rome. He proposed that Jesus come to Damascus to enter his Oriental import business, but Jesus explained that he did not feel justified in going so far away from his family just then. But on the way back home he thought much about these distant cities and the even more remote countries of the Far West and the Far East, countries he had so frequently heard spoken of by the caravan passengers and conductors.

128:3.4 (1411.4) Simon greatly enjoyed his visit to Jerusalem. He was duly received into the commonwealth of Israel at the Passover consecration of the new sons of the commandment. While Simon attended the Passover ceremonies, Jesus mingled with the throngs of visitors and engaged in many interesting personal conferences with numerous gentile proselytes.

128:3.5 (1411.5) Perhaps the most notable of all these contacts was the one with a young Hellenist named Stephen. This young man was on his first visit to Jerusalem and chanced to meet Jesus on Thursday afternoon of Passover week.

While they both strolled about viewing the Asmonean palace, Jesus began the casual conversation that resulted in their becoming interested in each other, and which led to a four-hour discussion of the way of life and the true God and his worship. Stephen was tremendously impressed with what Jesus said; he never forgot his words.

128:3.6 (1411.6) And this was the same Stephen who subsequently became a believer in the teachings of Jesus, and whose boldness in preaching this early gospel resulted in his being stoned to death by irate Jews. Some of Stephen's extraordinary boldness in proclaiming his view of the new gospel was the direct result of this earlier interview with Jesus. But Stephen never even faintly surmised that the Galilean he had talked with some fifteen years previously was the very same person whom he later proclaimed the world's Savior, and for whom he was so soon to die, thus becoming the first martyr of the newly evolving Christian faith. When Stephen yielded up his life as the price of his attack upon the Jewish temple and its traditional practices, there stood by one named Saul, a citizen of Tarsus. And when Saul saw how this Greek could die for his faith, there were aroused in his heart those emotions which eventually led him to espouse the cause for which Stephen died; later on he became the aggressive and indomitable Paul, the philosopher, if not the sole founder, of the Christian religion.

128:3.7 (1412.1) On the Sunday after Passover week Simon and Jesus started on their way back to Nazareth. Simon never forgot what Jesus taught him on this trip. He had always loved Jesus, but now he felt that he had begun to know his father-brother. They had many heart-to-heart talks as they journeyed through the country and prepared their meals by the wayside. They arrived home Thursday noon, and Simon kept the family up late

that night relating his experiences.

128:3.8 (1412.2) Mary was much upset by Simon's report that Jesus spent most of the time when in Jerusalem "visiting with the strangers, especially those from the far countries." Jesus' family never could comprehend his great interest in people, his urge to visit with them, to learn about their way of living, and to find out what they were thinking about.

128:3.9 (1412.3) More and more the Nazareth family became engrossed with their immediate and human problems; not often was mention made of the future mission of Jesus, and very seldom did he himself speak of his future career. His mother rarely thought about his being a child of promise. She was slowly giving up the idea that Jesus was to fulfill any divine mission on earth, yet at times her faith was revived when she paused to recall the Gabriel visitation before the child was born.

4   The Damascus Episode

128:4.1 (1412.4) The last four months of this year Jesus spent in Damascus as the guest of the merchant whom he first met at Philadelphia when on his way to Jerusalem. A representative of this merchant had sought out Jesus when passing through Nazareth and escorted him to Damascus. This part-Jewish merchant proposed to devote an extraordinary sum of money to the establishment of a school of religious philosophy at Damascus. He planned to create a center of learning which would out-rival Alexandria. And he proposed that Jesus should immediately begin a long tour of the world's educational centers preparatory to becoming the head of this new project. This was one of the greatest temptations that Jesus ever faced in the course of his purely human career.

128:4.2 (1412.5) Presently this merchant brought before Jesus a group of twelve merchants and bankers who agreed to support this newly projected school. Jesus manifested deep interest in the proposed school, helped them plan for its organization, but always expressed the fear that his other and unstated but prior obligations would prevent his accepting the direction of such a pretentious enterprise. His would-be benefactor was persistent, and he profitably employed Jesus at his home doing some translating while he, his wife, and their sons and daughters sought to prevail upon Jesus to accept the proffered honor. But he would not consent. He well knew that his mission on earth was not to be supported by institutions of learning; he knew that he must not obligate himself in the least to be directed by the "councils of men," no matter how well-intentioned.

128:4.3 (1412.6) He who was rejected by the Jerusalem religious leaders, even after he had demonstrated his leadership, was recognized and hailed as a master teacher by the businessmen and bankers of Damascus, and all this when he was an obscure and unknown carpenter of Nazareth.

128:4.4 (1412.7) He never spoke about this offer to his family, and the end of this year found him back in Nazareth going about his daily duties just as if he had never been tempted by the flattering propositions of his Damascus friends.

Neither did these men of Damascus ever associate the later citizen of Capernaum who turned all Jewry upside down with the former carpenter of Nazareth who had dared to refuse the honor which their combined wealth might have procured.

128:4.5 (1413.1) Jesus most cleverly and intentionally contrived to detach various episodes of his life so that they never became, in the eyes of the world, associated together as the doings of a single individual. Many times in subsequent years he listened to the recital of this very story of the strange Galilean who declined the opportunity of founding a school in Damascus to compete with Alexandria.

128:4.6 (1413.2) One purpose which Jesus had in mind, when he sought to segregate certain features of his earthly experience, was to prevent the building up of such a versatile and spectacular career as would cause subsequent generations to venerate the teacher in place of obeying the truth which he had lived and taught. Jesus did not want to build up such a human record of achievement as would attract attention from his teaching. Very early he recognized that his followers would be tempted to formulate a religion about him which might become a competitor of the gospel of the kingdom that he intended to proclaim to the world. Accordingly, he consistently sought to suppress everything during his eventful career which he thought might be made to serve this natural human tendency to exalt the teacher in place of proclaiming his teachings.

128:4.7 (1413.3) This same motive also explains why he permitted himself to be known by different titles during various epochs of his diversified life on earth. Again, he did not want to bring any undue influence to bear upon his family or others which would lead them to believe in him against their honest convictions. He always refused to take undue or unfair advantage of the human mind. He did not want men to believe in him unless their hearts were responsive to the spiritual realities revealed in his teachings.

128:4.8 (1413.4) By the end of this year the Nazareth home was running fairly smoothly. The children were growing up, and Mary was becoming accustomed to Jesus' being away from home. He continued to turn over his earnings to James for the support of the family, retaining only a small portion for his immediate personal expenses.

128:4.9 (1413.5) As the years passed, it became more difficult to realize that this man was a Son of God on earth. He seemed to become quite like an individual of the realm, just another man among men. And it was ordained by the Father in heaven that the bestowal should unfold in this very way.

5   The Twenty-Fourth Year (A.D. 18)

128:5.1 (1413.6) This was Jesus' first year of comparative freedom from family responsibility. James was very successful in managing the home with Jesus' help in counsel and finances.

128:5.2 (1413.7) The week following the Passover of this year a young man from Alexandria came down to Nazareth to arrange for a meeting, later in the year, between Jesus and a group of Alexandrian Jews at some point on the Palestinian coast. This conference was set for the middle of June, and Jesus went over to Caesarea to meet with five prominent Jews of Alexandria, who besought him to establish himself in their city as a religious teacher, offering as an inducement to begin with, the position of assistant to the chazan in their chief synagogue.

128:5.3 (1414.1) The spokesmen for this committee explained to Jesus that Alexandria was destined to become the headquarters of Jewish culture for the entire world; that the Hellenistic trend of Jewish affairs had virtually outdistanced the Babylonian school of thought. They reminded Jesus of the ominous rumblings of rebellion in Jerusalem and throughout Palestine and assured him that any uprising of the Palestinian Jews would be equivalent to national suicide, that the iron hand of Rome would crush the rebellion in three months, and that Jerusalem would be destroyed and the temple demolished, that not one stone would be left upon another.

128:5.4 (1414.2) Jesus listened to all they had to say, thanked them for their confidence, and, in declining to go to Alexandria, in substance said, "My hour has not yet come." They were nonplused by his apparent indifference to the honor they had sought to confer upon him. Before taking leave of Jesus, they presented him with a purse in token of the esteem of his Alexandrian friends and in compensation for the time and expense of coming over to Caesarea to confer with them. But he likewise refused the money, saying: "The house of Joseph has never received alms, and we cannot eat another's bread as long as I have strong arms and my brothers can labor."

128:5.5 (1414.3) His friends from Egypt set sail for home, and in subsequent years, when they heard rumors of the Capernaum boatbuilder who was creating such a commotion in Palestine, few of them surmised that he was the babe of Bethlehem grown up and the same strange-acting Galilean who had so unceremoniously declined the invitation to become a great teacher in Alexandria.

128:5.6 (1414.4) Jesus returned to Nazareth. The remainder of this year was the most uneventful six months of his whole career. He enjoyed this temporary respite from the usual program of problems to solve and difficulties to surmount. He communed much with his Father in heaven and made tremendous progress in the mastery of his human mind.

128:5.7 (1414.5) But human affairs on the worlds of time and space do not run smoothly for long. In December James had a private talk with Jesus, explaining that he was much in love with Esta, a young woman of Nazareth, and that they would sometime like to be married if it could be arranged. He called attention to the fact that Joseph would soon be eighteen years old, and that it would be a good experience for him to have a chance to serve as the acting head of the family. Jesus gave consent for James's marriage two years later, provided he had, during the intervening time, properly trained Joseph to assume direction of the home.

128:5.8 (1414.6) And now things began to happen—marriage was in the air. James's success in gaining Jesus' assent to his marriage emboldened Miriam to approach her brother-father with her plans. Jacob, the younger stone mason, onetime self-appointed champion of Jesus, now business associate of James and Joseph, had long sought to gain Miriam's hand in marriage. After Miriam had laid her plans before Jesus, he directed that Jacob should come to him making formal request for her and promised his blessing for the marriage just as soon as she felt that Martha was competent to assume her duties as eldest daughter.

128:5.9 (1414.7) When at home, he continued to teach the evening school three times a week, read the Scriptures often in the synagogue on the Sabbath, visited with his mother, taught the children, and in general conducted himself as a worthy and respected citizen of Nazareth in the commonwealth of Israel.

6 The Twenty-Fifth Year (A.D. 19)

128:6.1 (1415.1) This year began with the Nazareth family all in good health and witnessed the finishing of the regular schooling of all the children with the exception of certain work which Martha must do for Ruth.

128:6.2 (1415.2) Jesus was one of the most robust and refined specimens of manhood to appear on earth since the days of Adam. His physical development was superb. His mind was active, keen, and penetrating—compared with the average mentality of his contemporaries, it had developed gigantic proportions—and his spirit was indeed humanly divine.

128:6.3 (1415.3) The family finances were in the best condition since the disappearance of Joseph's estate. The final payments had been made on the caravan repair shop; they owed no man and for the first time in years had some funds ahead. This being true, and since he had taken his other brothers to Jerusalem for their first Passover ceremonies, Jesus decided to accompany Jude (who had just graduated from the synagogue school) on his first visit to the temple.

128:6.4 (1415.4) They went up to Jerusalem and returned by the same route, the Jordan valley, as Jesus feared trouble if he took his young brother through Samaria. Already at Nazareth Jude had got into slight trouble several times because of his hasty disposition, coupled with his strong patriotic sentiments.

128:6.5 (1415.5) They arrived at Jerusalem in due time and were on their way for a first visit to the temple, the very sight of which had stirred and thrilled Jude to the very depths of his soul, when they chanced to meet Lazarus of Bethany.

While Jesus talked with Lazarus and sought to arrange for their joint celebration of the Passover, Jude started up real trouble for them all. Close at hand stood a Roman guard who made some improper remarks regarding a Jewish girl who was passing. Jude flushed with fiery indignation and was not slow in expressing his resentment of such an impropriety directly to and within hearing of the soldier. Now the Roman legionnaires were very sensitive to anything bordering on Jewish disrespect; so the guard promptly placed Jude under arrest. This was too much for the young patriot, and before Jesus could caution him by a warning glance, he had delivered himself of a voluble denunciation of pent-up anti-Roman feelings, all of which only made a bad matter worse. Jude, with Jesus by his side, was taken at once to the military prison.

128:6.6 (1415.6) Jesus endeavored to obtain either an immediate hearing for Jude or else his release in time for the Passover celebration that evening, but he failed in these attempts. Since the next day was a "holy convocation" in Jerusalem, even the Romans would not presume to hear charges against a Jew. Accordingly, Jude remained in confinement until the morning of the second day after his arrest, and Jesus stayed at the prison with him. They were not present in the temple at the ceremony of receiving the sons of the law into the full citizenship of Israel. Jude did not pass through this formal ceremony for several years, until he was next in Jerusalem at a Passover and in connection with his propaganda work in behalf of the Zealots, the patriotic organization to which he belonged and in which he was very active.

128:6.7 (1415.7) The morning following their second day in prison Jesus appeared before the military magistrate in behalf of Jude. By making apologies for his brother's youth and by a further explanatory but judicious statement with reference to the provocative nature of the episode which had led up to the arrest of his brother, Jesus so handled the case that the magistrate expressed the opinion that the young Jew might have had some possible excuse for his violent outburst. After warning Jude not to allow himself again to be guilty of such rashness, he said to Jesus in dismissing them: "You had better keep your eye on the lad; he's liable to make a lot of trouble for all of you." And the Roman judge spoke the truth. Jude did make considerable trouble for Jesus, and always was the trouble of this same nature—clashes with the civil authorities because of his thoughtless and unwise patriotic outbursts.

128:6.8 (1416.1) Jesus and Jude walked over to Bethany for the night, explaining why they had failed to keep their appointment for the Passover supper, and set out for Nazareth the following day. Jesus did not tell the family about his young brother's arrest at Jerusalem, but he had a long talk with Jude about this episode some three weeks after their return. After this talk with Jesus Jude himself told the family. He never forgot the patience and forbearance his brother-father manifested throughout the whole of this trying experience.

128:6.9 (1416.2) This was the last Passover Jesus attended with any member of his own family. Increasingly the Son of Man was to become separated from close association with his own flesh and blood.

128:6.10 (1416.3) This year his seasons of deep meditation were often broken into by Ruth and her playmates. And always was Jesus ready to postpone the contemplation of his future work for the world and the universe that he might share in the childish joy and youthful gladness of these youngsters, who never tired of listening to Jesus relate the experiences of his various trips to Jerusalem. They also greatly enjoyed his stories about animals and nature.

128:6.11 (1416.4) The children were always welcome at the repair shop. Jesus provided sand, blocks, and stones by the side of the shop, and bevies of youngsters flocked there to amuse themselves. When they tired of their play, the more intrepid ones would peek into the shop, and if its keeper were not busy, they would make bold to go in and say, "Uncle Joshua, come out and tell us a big story." Then they would lead him out by tugging at his hands until he was seated on the favorite rock by the corner of the shop, with the children on the ground in a semicircle before him. And how the little folks did enjoy their Uncle Joshua. They were learning to laugh, and to laugh heartily. It was customary for one or two of the smallest of the children to climb upon his knees and sit there, looking up in wonderment at his expressive features as he told his stories. The children loved Jesus, and Jesus loved the children.

128:6.12 (1416.5) It was difficult for his friends to comprehend the range of his intellectual activities, how he could so suddenly and so completely swing from the profound discussion of politics, philosophy, or religion to the lighthearted and joyous playfulness of these tots of from five to ten years of age. As his own brothers and sisters grew up, as he gained more leisure, and before the grandchildren arrived, he paid a great deal of attention to these little ones. But he did not live on earth long enough to enjoy the grandchildren very much.

7   The Twenty-Sixth Year (A.D. 20)

128:7.1 (1416.6) As this year began, Jesus of Nazareth became strongly conscious that he possessed a wide range of potential power. But he was likewise fully persuaded that this power was not to be employed by his personality as the Son of Man, at least not until his hour should come.

128:7.2 (1417.1) At this time he thought much but said little about the relation of himself to his Father in heaven. And the conclusion of all this thinking was expressed once in his prayer on the hilltop, when he said: "Regardless of who I am and what power I may or may not wield, I always have been, and always will be, subject to the will of my Paradise Father." And yet, as this man walked about Nazareth to and from his work, it was literally true—as concerned a vast universe—that "in him were hidden all the treasures of wisdom and knowledge."

128:7.3 (1417.2) All this year the family affairs ran smoothly except for Jude. For years James had trouble with his youngest brother, who was not inclined to settle down to work nor was he to be depended upon for his share of the home expenses. While he would live at home, he was not conscientious about earning his share of the family upkeep.

128:7.4 (1417.3) Jesus was a man of peace, and ever and anon was he embarrassed by Jude's belligerent exploits and numerous patriotic outbursts. James and Joseph were in favor of casting him out, but Jesus would not consent. When their patience would be severely tried, Jesus would only counsel: "Be patient. Be wise in your counsel and eloquent in your lives, that your young brother may first know the better way and then be constrained to follow you in it." The wise and loving counsel of Jesus prevented a break in the family; they remained together. But Jude never was brought to his sober senses until after his marriage.

128:7.5 (1417.4) Mary seldom spoke of Jesus' future mission. Whenever this subject was referred to, Jesus only replied, "My hour has not yet come." Jesus had about completed the difficult task of weaning his family from dependence on the immediate presence of his personality. He was rapidly preparing for the day when he could consistently leave this Nazareth home to begin the more active prelude to his real ministry for men.

128:7.6 (1417.5) Never lose sight of the fact that the prime mission of Jesus in his seventh bestowal was the acquirement of creature experience, the achievement of the sovereignty of Nebadon. And in the gathering of this very experience he made the supreme revelation of the Paradise Father to Urantia and to his entire local universe. Incidental to these purposes he also undertook to untangle the complicated affairs of this planet as they were related to the Lucifer rebellion.

128:7.7 (1417.6) This year Jesus enjoyed more than usual leisure, and he devoted much time to training James in the management of the repair shop and Joseph in the direction of home affairs. Mary sensed that he was making ready to leave them. Leave them to go where? To do what? She had about given up the thought that Jesus was the Messiah. She could not understand him; she simply could not fathom her first-born son.

128:7.8 (1417.7) Jesus spent a great deal of time this year with the individual members of his family. He would take them for long and frequent strolls up the hill and through the countryside. Before harvest he took Jude to the farmer uncle south of Nazareth, but Jude did not remain long after the harvest. He ran away, and Simon later found him with the fishermen at the lake. When Simon brought him back home, Jesus talked things over with the runaway lad and, since he wanted to be a fisherman, went over to Magdala with him and put him in the care of a relative, a fisherman; and Jude worked fairly well and regularly from that time on until his marriage, and he continued as a fisherman after his marriage.

128:7.9 (1418.1) At last the day had come when all Jesus' brothers had chosen, and were established in, their lifework. The stage was being set for Jesus' departure from home.

128:7.10 (1418.2) In November a double wedding occurred. James and Esta, and Miriam and Jacob were married. It was truly a joyous occasion. Even Mary was once more happy except every now and then when she realized that Jesus was preparing to go away. She suffered under the burden of a great uncertainty: If Jesus would only sit down and talk it all over freely with her as he had done when he was a boy, but he was consistently uncommunicative; he was profoundly silent about the future.

128:7.11 (1418.3) James and his bride, Esta, moved into a neat little home on the west side of town, the gift of her father. While James continued his support of his mother's home, his quota was cut in half because of his marriage, and Joseph was formally installed by Jesus as head of the family. Jude was now very faithfully sending his share of funds home

each month. The weddings of James and Miriam had a very beneficial influence on Jude, and when he left for the fishing grounds, the day after the double wedding, he assured Joseph that he could depend on him "to do my full duty, and more if it is needed." And he kept his promise.

128:7.12 (1418.4) Miriam lived next door to Mary in the home of Jacob, Jacob the elder having been laid to rest with his fathers. Martha took Miriam's place in the home, and the new organization was working smoothly before the year ended.

128:7.13 (1418.5) The day after this double wedding Jesus held an important conference with James. He told James, confidentially, that he was preparing to leave home. He presented full title to the repair shop to James, formally and solemnly abdicated as head of Joseph's house, and most touchingly established his brother James as "head and protector of my father's house." He drew up, and they both signed, a secret compact in which it was stipulated that, in return for the gift of the repair shop, James

would henceforth assume full financial responsibility for the family, thus releasing Jesus from all further obligations in these matters. After the contract was signed, after the budget was so arranged that the actual expenses of the family would be met without any contribution from Jesus, Jesus said to James: "But, my son, I will continue to send you something each month until my hour shall have come, but what I send shall be used by you as the occasion demands. Apply my funds to the family necessities or pleasures as you see fit. Use them in case of sickness or apply them to meet the unexpected emergencies which may befall any individual member of the family."

128:7.14 (1418.6) And thus did Jesus make ready to enter upon the second and home-detached phase of his adult life before the public entrance upon his Father's business.

Paper 129

The Later Adult Life of Jesus

129:0.1 (1419.1) JESUS had fully and finally separated himself from the management of the domestic affairs of the Nazareth family and from the immediate direction of its individuals. He continued, right up to the event of his baptism, to contribute to the family finances and to take a keen personal interest in the spiritual welfare of every one of his brothers and sisters. And always was he ready to do everything humanly possible for the comfort and happiness of his widowed mother.

129:0.2 (1419.2) The Son of Man had now made every preparation for detaching himself permanently from the Nazareth home; and this was not easy for him to do. Jesus naturally loved his people; he loved his family, and this natural affection had been tremendously augmented by his extraordinary devotion to them. The more fully we bestow ourselves upon our fellows, the more we come to love them; and since Jesus had given himself so fully to his family, he loved them with a great and fervent affection.

129:0.3 (1419.3) All the family had slowly awakened to the realization that Jesus was making ready to leave them. The sadness of the anticipated separation was only tempered by this graduated method of preparing them for the announcement of his intended departure. For more than four years they discerned that he was planning for this eventual separation.

1 The Twenty-Seventh Year (A.D. 21)

129:1.1 (1419.4) In January of this year, A.D. 21, on a rainy Sunday morning, Jesus took unceremonious leave of his family, only explaining that he was going over to Tiberias and then on a visit to other cities about the Sea of Galilee. And thus he left them, never again to be a regular member of that household.

129:1.2 (1419.5) He spent one week at Tiberias, the new city which was soon to succeed Sepphoris as the capital of Galilee; and finding little to interest him, he passed on successively through Magdala and Bethsaida to Capernaum, where he stopped to pay a visit to his father's friend Zebedee. Zebedee's sons were fishermen; he himself was a boatbuilder. Jesus of Nazareth was an expert in both designing and building; he was a master at working with wood; and Zebedee had long known of the skill of the Nazareth craftsman. For a long time Zebedee had contemplated making improved boats; he now laid his plans before Jesus and invited the visiting carpenter to join him in the enterprise, and Jesus readily consented.

129:1.3 (1419.6) Jesus worked with Zebedee only a little more than one year, but during that time he created a new style of boat and established entirely new methods of boatmaking. By superior technique and greatly improved methods of steaming the boards, Jesus and Zebedee began to build boats of a very superior type, craft which were far more safe for sailing the lake than were the older types. For several years Zebedee had more work, turning out these new-style boats, than his small establishment could handle; in less than five years practically all the craft on the lake had been built in the shop of Zebedee at Capernaum. Jesus became well known to the Galilean fisherfolk as the designer of the new boats.

129:1.4 (1420.1) Zebedee was a moderately well-to-do man; his boatbuilding shops were on the lake to the south of Capernaum, and his home was situated down the lake shore near the fishing headquarters of Bethsaida. Jesus lived in the home of Zebedee during the year and more he remained at Capernaum. He had long worked alone in the world, that is, without a father, and greatly enjoyed this period of working with a father-partner.

129:1.5 (1420.2) Zebedee's wife, Salome, was a relative of Annas, onetime high priest at Jerusalem and still the most influential of the Sadducean group, having been deposed only eight years previously. Salome became a great admirer of Jesus. She loved him as she loved her own sons, James, John, and David, while her four daughters looked upon Jesus as their elder brother. Jesus often went out fishing with James, John, and David, and they learned that he was an experienced fisherman as well as an expert boatbuilder.

129:1.6 (1420.3) All this year Jesus sent money each month to James. He returned to Nazareth in October to attend Martha's wedding, and he was not again in Nazareth for over two years, when he returned shortly before the double wedding of Simon and Jude.

129:1.7 (1420.4) Throughout this year Jesus built boats and continued to observe how men lived on earth. Frequently he would go down to visit at the caravan station, Capernaum being on the direct travel route from Damascus to the south. Capernaum was a strong Roman military post, and the garrison's commanding officer was a gentile believer in Yahweh, "a devout man," as the Jews were wont to designate such proselytes. This officer belonged to a wealthy Roman family, and he took it upon himself to build a beautiful synagogue in Capernaum, which had been presented to the Jews a short time before Jesus came to live with Zebedee. Jesus conducted the services in this new synagogue more than half the time this year, and some of the caravan people who chanced to attend remembered him as the carpenter from Nazareth.

129:1.8 (1420.5) When it came to the payment of taxes, Jesus registered himself as a "skilled craftsman of Capernaum." From this day on to the end of his earth life he was known as a resident of Capernaum. He never claimed any other legal residence, although he did, for various reasons, permit others to assign his residence to Damascus, Bethany, Nazareth, and even Alexandria.

129:1.9 (1420.6) At the Capernaum synagogue he found many new books in the library chests, and he spent at least five evenings a week at intense study. One evening he devoted to social life with the older folks, and one evening he spent with the young people. There was something gracious and inspiring about the personality of Jesus which invariably attracted young people. He always made them feel at ease in his presence. Perhaps his great secret in getting along with them consisted in the twofold fact that he was always interested in what they were doing, while he seldom offered them advice unless they asked for it.

129:1.10 (1420.7) The Zebedee family almost worshiped Jesus, and they never failed to attend the conferences of questions and answers which he conducted each evening after supper before he departed for the synagogue to study. The youthful neighbors also came in frequently to attend these after-supper meetings. To these little gatherings Jesus gave varied and advanced instruction, just as advanced as they could comprehend. He talked quite freely with them, expressing his ideas and ideals about politics, sociology, science, and philosophy,

but never presumed to speak with authoritative finality except when discussing religion—the relation of man to God.

129:1.11 (1421.1) Once a week Jesus held a meeting with the entire household, shop, and shore helpers, for Zebedee had many employees. And it was among these workers that Jesus was first called "the Master." They all loved him. He enjoyed his labors with Zebedee in Capernaum, but he missed the children playing out by the side of the Nazareth carpenter shop.

129:1.12 (1421.2) Of the sons of Zebedee, James was the most interested in Jesus as a teacher, as a philosopher. John cared most for his religious teaching and opinions. David respected him as a mechanic but took little stock in his religious views and philosophic teachings.

129:1.13 (1421.3) Frequently Jude came over on the Sabbath to hear Jesus talk in the synagogue and would tarry to visit with him. And the more Jude saw of his eldest brother, the more he became convinced that Jesus was a truly great man.

129:1.14 (1421.4) This year Jesus made great advances in the ascendant mastery of his human mind and attained new and high levels of conscious contact with his indwelling Thought Adjuster.

129:1.15 (1421.5) This was the last year of his settled life. Never again did Jesus spend a whole year in one place or at one undertaking. The days of his earth pilgrimages were rapidly approaching. Periods of intense activity were not far in the future, but there were now about to intervene between his simple but intensely active life of the past and his still more intense and strenuous public ministry, a few years of extensive travel and highly diversified personal activity. His training as a man of the realm had to be completed before he could enter upon his career of teaching and preaching as the perfected God-man of the divine and posthuman phases of his Urantia bestowal.

2 The Twenty-Eighth Year (A.D. 22)

129:2.1 (1421.6) In March, A.D. 22, Jesus took leave of Zebedee and of Capernaum. He asked for a small sum of money to defray his expenses to Jerusalem. While working with Zebedee he had drawn only small sums of money, which each month he would send to the family at Nazareth. One month Joseph would come down to Capernaum for the money; the next month Jude would come over to Capernaum, get the money from Jesus, and take it up to Nazareth. Jude's fishing headquarters was only a few miles south of Capernaum.

129:2.2 (1421.7) When Jesus took leave of Zebedee's family, he agreed to remain in Jerusalem until Passover time, and they all promised to be present for that event. They even arranged to celebrate the Passover supper together. They all sorrowed when Jesus left them, especially the daughters of Zebedee.

129:2.3 (1421.8) Before leaving Capernaum, Jesus had a long talk with his new-found friend and close companion, John Zebedee. He told John that he contemplated traveling extensively until "my hour shall come" and asked John to act in his stead in the matter of sending some money to the family at Nazareth each month until the funds due him should be exhausted. And John made him this promise: "My Teacher, go about your business, do your work in the world; I will act for you in this or any other matter, and I will watch over your family even as I would foster my own mother and care for my own brothers and sisters. I will disburse your funds which my father holds as you have directed and as they may be needed, and when your money has been expended, if I do not receive more from you, and if your mother is in need, then will I share my own earnings with her. Go your way in peace. I will act in your stead in all these matters."

129:2.4 (1422.1) Therefore, after Jesus had departed for Jerusalem, John consulted with his father, Zebedee, regarding the money due Jesus, and he was surprised that it was such a large sum. As Jesus had left the matter so entirely in their hands, they agreed that it would be the better plan to invest these funds in property and use the income for assisting the family at Nazareth; and since Zebedee knew of a little house in Capernaum which carried a mortgage and was for sale, he directed John to buy this house with Jesus' money and hold the title in trust for his friend. And John did as his father advised him. For two years the rent of this house was applied on the mortgage, and this, augmented by a certain large fund which Jesus presently sent up to John to be used as needed by the family, almost equaled the amount of this obligation; and Zebedee supplied the difference, so that John paid up the remainder of the mortgage when it fell due, thereby securing clear title to this two-room house. In this way Jesus became the owner of a house in Capernaum, but he had not been told about it.

129:2.5 (1422.2) When the family at Nazareth heard that Jesus had departed from Capernaum, they, not knowing of this financial arrangement with John, believed the time had come for them to get along without any further help from Jesus. James remembered his contract with Jesus and, with the help of his brothers, forthwith assumed full responsibility for the care of the family.

129:2.6 (1422.3) But let us go back to observe Jesus in Jerusalem. For almost two months he spent the greater part of his time listening to the temple discussions with occasional visits to the various schools of the rabbis. Most of the Sabbath days he spent at Bethany.

129:2.7 (1422.4) Jesus had carried with him to Jerusalem a letter from Salome, Zebedee's wife, introducing him to the former high priest, Annas, as "one, the same as my own son." Annas spent much time with him, personally taking him to visit the many academies of the Jerusalem religious teachers. While Jesus thoroughly inspected these schools and carefully observed their methods of teaching, he never so much as asked a single question in public. Although Annas looked upon Jesus as a great man, he was puzzled as to how to advise him. He recognized the foolishness of suggesting that he enter any of the schools of Jerusalem as a student, and yet he well knew Jesus would never be accorded the status of a regular teacher inasmuch as he had never been trained in these schools.

129:2.8 (1422.5) Presently the time of the Passover drew near, and along with the throngs from every quarter there arrived at Jerusalem from Capernaum, Zebedee and his entire family. They all stopped at the spacious home of Annas, where they celebrated the Passover as one happy family.

129:2.9 (1422.6) Before the end of this Passover week, by apparent chance, Jesus met a wealthy traveler and his son, a young man about seventeen years of age. These travelers hailed from India, and being on their way to visit Rome and various other points on the Mediterranean, they had arranged to arrive in Jerusalem during the Passover, hoping to find someone whom they could engage as interpreter for both and tutor for the son. The father was insistent that Jesus consent to travel with them. Jesus told him about his family and that it was hardly fair to go away for almost two years, during which time they might find themselves in need. Whereupon, this traveler from the Orient proposed to advance to Jesus the wages of one year so that he could intrust such funds to his friends for the safeguarding of his family against want. And Jesus agreed to make the trip.

129:2.10 (1423.1) Jesus turned this large sum over to John the son of Zebedee. And you have been told how John applied this money toward the liquidation of the mortgage on the Capernaum property. Jesus took Zebedee fully into his confidence regarding this Mediterranean journey, but he enjoined him to tell no man, not even his own flesh and blood, and Zebedee never did disclose his knowledge of Jesus'

whereabouts during this long period of almost two years.

Before Jesus' return from this trip the family at Nazareth had just about given him up as dead. Only the assurances of Zebedee, who went up to Nazareth with his son John on several occasions, kept hope alive in Mary's heart.

129:2.11 (1423.2) During this time the Nazareth family got along very well; Jude had considerably increased his quota and kept up this extra contribution until he was married. Notwithstanding that they required little assistance, it was the practice of John Zebedee to take presents each month to Mary and Ruth, as Jesus had instructed him.

3   The Twenty-Ninth Year (A.D. 23)

129:3.1 (1423.3) The whole of Jesus' twenty-ninth year was spent finishing up the tour of the Mediterranean world. The main events, as far as we have permission to reveal these experiences, constitute the subjects of the narratives which immediately follow this paper.

129:3.2 (1423.4) Throughout this tour of the Roman world, for many reasons, Jesus was known as the Damascus scribe. At Corinth and other stops on the return trip he was, however, known as the Jewish tutor.

129:3.3 (1423.5) This was an eventful period in Jesus' life. While on this journey he made many contacts with his fellow men, but this experience is a phase of his life which he never revealed to any member of his family nor to any of the apostles. Jesus lived out his life in the flesh and departed from this world without anyone (save Zebedee of Bethsaida) knowing that he had made this extensive trip. Some of his friends thought he had returned to Damascus; others thought he had gone to India. His own family inclined to the belief that he was in Alexandria, as they knew that he had once been invited to go there for the purpose of becoming an assistant chazan.

129:3.4 (1423.6) When Jesus returned to Palestine, he did nothing to change the opinion of his family that he had gone from Jerusalem to Alexandria; he permitted them to continue in the belief that all the time he had been absent from Palestine had been spent in that city of learning and culture. Only Zebedee the boatbuilder of Bethsaida knew the facts about these matters, and Zebedee told no one.

129:3.5 (1423.7) In all your efforts to decipher the meaning of Jesus' life on Urantia, you must be mindful of the motivation of the Michael bestowal. If you would comprehend the meaning of many of his apparently strange doings, you must discern the purpose of his sojourn on your world. He was consistently careful not to build up an overattractive and attention-consuming personal career. He wanted to make no unusual or overpowering appeals to his fellow men. He was dedicated to the work of revealing the heavenly Father to his fellow mortals and at the same time was consecrated to the sublime task of living his mortal earth life all the while subject to the will of the same Paradise Father.

129:3.6 (1424.1) It will also always be helpful in understanding Jesus' life on earth if all mortal students of this divine bestowal will remember that, while he lived this life of incarnation on Urantia, he lived it for his entire universe. There was something special and inspiring associated with the life he lived in the flesh of mortal nature for every single inhabited sphere throughout all the universe of Nebadon. The same is also true of all those worlds which have become habitable since the eventful times of his sojourn on Urantia. And it will likewise be equally true of all worlds which may become inhabited by will creatures in all the future history of this local universe.

129:3.7 (1424.2) The Son of Man, during the time and through the experiences of this tour of the Roman world, practically completed his educational contact-training with the diversified peoples of the world of his day and generation. By the time of his return to Nazareth, through the medium of this travel-training he had just about learned how man lived and wrought out his existence on Urantia.

129:3.8 (1424.3) The real purpose of his trip around the Mediterranean basin was to know men. He came very close to hundreds of humankind on this journey. He met and loved all manner of men, rich and poor, high and low, black and white, educated and uneducated, cultured and uncultured, animalistic and spiritual, religious and irreligious, moral and immoral.

129:3.9 (1424.4) On this Mediterranean journey Jesus made great advances in his human task of mastering the material and mortal mind, and his indwelling Adjuster made great progress in the ascension and spiritual conquest of this same human intellect. By the end of this tour Jesus virtually knew—with all human certainty—that he was a Son of God, a Creator Son of the Universal Father. The Adjuster more and more was able to bring up in the mind of the Son of Man shadowy memories of his Paradise experience in association with his divine Father ere he ever came to organize and administer this local universe of Nebadon. Thus did the Adjuster, little by little, bring to Jesus' human consciousness those necessary memories of his former and divine existence in the various epochs of the well-nigh eternal past. The last episode of his prehuman experience to be brought forth by the Adjuster was his farewell conference with Immanuel of Salvington just before his surrender of conscious personality to embark upon the Urantia incarnation. And this final memory picture of prehuman existence was made clear in Jesus' consciousness on the very day of his baptism by John in the Jordan.

4 The Human Jesus

129:4.1 (1424.5) To the onlooking celestial intelligences of the local universe, this Mediterranean trip was the most enthralling of all Jesus' earth experiences, at least of all his career right up to the event of his crucifixion and mortal death. This was the fascinating period of his personal ministry in contrast with the soon-following epoch of public ministry. This unique episode was all the more engrossing because he was at this time still the carpenter of Nazareth, the boatbuilder of Capernaum, the scribe of Damascus; he was still the Son of Man. He had not yet achieved the complete mastery of his human mind; the Adjuster had not fully mastered and counterparted the mortal identity. He was still a man among men.

129:4.2 (1425.1) The purely human religious experience—the personal spiritual growth—of the Son of Man well-nigh reached the apex of attainment during this, the twenty-ninth year. This experience of spiritual development was a consistently gradual growth from the moment of the arrival of his Thought Adjuster until the day of the completion and confirmation of that natural and normal human relationship between the material mind of man and the mind-endowment of the spirit—the phenomenon of the making of these two minds one, the experience which the Son of Man attained in completion and finality, as an incarnated mortal of the realm, on the day of his baptism in the Jordan.

129:4.3 (1425.2) Throughout these years, while he did not appear to engage in so many seasons of formal communion with his Father in heaven, he perfected increasingly effective methods of personal communication with the indwelling spirit presence of the Paradise Father. He lived a real life, a full life, and a truly normal, natural, and average life in the flesh. He knows from personal experience the equivalent of the actuality of the entire sum and substance of the living of the life of human beings on the material worlds of time and space.

129:4.4 (1425.3) The Son of Man experienced those wide ranges of human emotion which reach from superb joy to profound sorrow. He was a child of joy

and a being of rare good humor; likewise was he a "man of sorrows and acquainted with grief." In a spiritual sense, he did live through the mortal life from the bottom to the top, from the beginning to the end. From a material point of view, he might appear to have escaped living through both social extremes of human existence, but intellectually he became wholly familiar with the entire and complete experience of humankind.

129:4.5 (1425.4) Jesus knows about the thoughts and feelings, the urges and impulses, of the evolutionary and ascendant mortals of the realms, from birth to death. He has lived the human life from the beginnings of physical, intellectual, and spiritual selfhood up through infancy, childhood, youth, and adulthood—even to the human experience of death. He not only passed through these usual and familiar human periods of intellectual and spiritual advancement, but he also fully experienced those higher and more advanced phases of human and Adjuster reconciliation which so few Urantia mortals ever attain. And thus he experienced the full life of mortal man, not only as it is lived on your world, but also as it is lived on all other evolutionary worlds of time and space, even on the highest and most advanced of all the worlds settled in light and life.

129:4.6 (1425.5) Although this perfect life which he lived in the likeness of mortal flesh may not have received the unqualified and universal approval of his fellow mortals, those who chanced to be his contemporaries on earth, still, the life which Jesus of Nazareth lived in the flesh and on Urantia did receive full and unqualified acceptance by the Universal Father as constituting at one and the same time, and in one and the same personality-life, the fullness of the revelation of the eternal God to mortal man and the presentation of perfected human personality to the satisfaction of the Infinite Creator.

129:4.7 (1425.6) And this was his true and supreme purpose. He did not come down to live on Urantia as the perfect and detailed example for any child or adult, any man or woman, in that age or any other. True it is, indeed, that in his full, rich, beautiful, and noble life we may all find much that is exquisitely exemplary, divinely inspiring, but this is because he lived a true and genuinely human life. Jesus did not live his life on earth in order to set an example for all other human beings to copy. He lived this life in the flesh by the same mercy ministry that you all may live your lives on earth; and as he lived his mortal life in his day and as he was, so did he thereby set the example for all of us thus to live our lives in our day and as we are. You may not aspire to live his life, but you can resolve to live your lives even as, and by the same means that, he lived his. Jesus may not be the technical and detailed example for all the mortals of all ages on all the realms of this local universe, but he is everlastingly the inspiration and guide of all Paradise pilgrims from the worlds of initial ascension up through a universe of universes and on through Havona to Paradise. Jesus is the new and living way from man to God, from the partial to the perfect, from the earthly to the heavenly, from time to eternity.

129:4.8 (1426.1) By the end of the twenty-ninth year Jesus of Nazareth had virtually finished the living of the life required of mortals as sojourners in the flesh. He came on earth the fullness of God to be manifest to man; he had now become well-nigh the perfection of man awaiting the occasion to become manifest to God. And he did all of this before he was thirty years of age.

Paper 130

On the Way to Rome

130:0.1 (1427.1) THE tour of the Roman world consumed most of the twenty-eighth and the entire twenty-ninth year of Jesus' life on earth. Jesus and the two natives from India—Gonod and his son Ganid—left Jerusalem on a Sunday morning, April 26, A.D. 22. They made their journey according to schedule, and Jesus said good-bye to the father and son in the city of Charax on the Persian Gulf on the tenth day of December the following year, A.D. 23.

130:0.2 (1427.2) From Jerusalem they went to Caesarea by way of Joppa. At Caesarea they took a boat for Alexandria. From Alexandria they sailed for Lasea in Crete. From Crete they sailed for Carthage, touching at Cyrene. At Carthage they took a boat for Naples, stopping at Malta, Syracuse, and Messina. From Naples they went to Capua, whence they traveled by the Appian Way to Rome.

130:0.3 (1427.3) After their stay in Rome they went overland to Tarentum, where they set sail for Athens in Greece, stopping at Nicopolis and Corinth. From Athens they went to Ephesus by way of Troas. From Ephesus they sailed for Cyprus, putting in at Rhodes on the way. They spent considerable time visiting and resting on Cyprus and then sailed for Antioch in Syria. From Antioch they journeyed south to Sidon and then went over to Damascus. From there they traveled by caravan to Mesopotamia, passing through Thapsacus and Larissa. They spent some time in Babylon, visited Ur and other places, and then went to Susa. From Susa they journeyed to Charax, from which place Gonod and Ganid embarked for India.

130:0.4 (1427.4) It was while working four months at Damascus that Jesus had picked up the rudiments of the language spoken by Gonod and Ganid. While there he had labored much of the time on translations from Greek into one of the languages of India, being assisted by a native of Gonod's home district.

130:0.5 (1427.5) On this Mediterranean tour Jesus spent about half of each day teaching Ganid and acting as interpreter during Gonod's business conferences and social contacts. The remainder of each day, which was at his disposal, he devoted to making those close personal contacts with his fellow men, those intimate associations with the mortals of the realm, which so characterized his activities during these years that just preceded his public ministry.

130:0.6 (1427.6) From firsthand observation and actual contact Jesus acquainted himself with the higher material and intellectual civilization of the Occident and the Levant; from Gonod and his brilliant son he learned a great deal about the civilization and culture of India and China, for Gonod, himself a citizen of India, had made three extensive trips to the empire of the yellow race.

130:0.7 (1427.7) Ganid, the young man, learned much from Jesus during this long and intimate association. They developed a great affection for each other, and the lad's father many times tried to persuade Jesus to return with them to India, but Jesus always declined, pleading the necessity for returning to his family in Palestine.

At Joppa—
Discourse on Jonah

130:1.1 (1428.1) During their stay in Joppa, Jesus met Gadiah, a Philistine interpreter who worked for one Simon a tanner. Gonod's agents in Mesopotamia had transacted much business with this Simon; so Gonod and his son desired to pay him a visit on their way to Caesarea. While they tarried at Joppa, Jesus and Gadiah became warm friends. This young Philistine was a truth seeker. Jesus was a truth giver; he was the truth for that generation on Urantia. When a great truth seeker and a great truth giver meet, the result is a great and liberating enlightenment born of the experience of new truth.

130:1.2 (1428.2) One day after the evening meal Jesus and the young Philistine strolled down by the sea, and Gadiah, not knowing that this "scribe of Damascus" was so well versed in the Hebrew traditions, pointed out to Jesus the ship landing from which it was reputed that Jonah

had embarked on his ill-fated voyage to Tarshish. And when he had concluded his remarks, he asked Jesus this question: "But do you suppose the big fish really did swallow Jonah?" Jesus perceived that this young man's life had been tremendously influenced by this tradition, and that its contemplation had impressed upon him the folly of trying to run away from duty; Jesus therefore said nothing that would suddenly destroy the foundations of Gadiah's present motivation for practical living. In answering this question, Jesus said: "My friend, we are all Jonahs with lives to live in accordance with the will of God, and at all times when we seek to escape the present duty of living by running away to far-off enticements, we thereby put ourselves in the immediate control of those influences which are not directed by the powers of truth and the forces of righteousness. The flight from duty is the sacrifice of truth. The escape from the service of light and life can only result in those distressing conflicts with the difficult whales of selfishness which lead eventually to darkness and death unless such God-forsaking Jonahs shall turn their hearts, even when in the very depths of despair, to seek after God and his goodness. And when such disheartened souls sincerely seek for God—hunger for truth and thirst for righteousness—there is nothing that can hold them in further captivity. No matter into what great depths they may have fallen, when they seek the light with a whole heart, the spirit of the Lord God of heaven will deliver them from their captivity; the evil circumstances of life will spew them out upon the dry land of fresh opportunities for renewed service and wiser living."

130:1.3 (1428.3) Gadiah was mightily moved by Jesus' teaching, and they talked long into the night by the seaside, and before they went to their lodgings, they prayed together and for each other. This was the same Gadiah who listened to the later preaching of Peter, became a profound believer in Jesus of Nazareth, and held a memorable argument with Peter one evening at the home of Dorcas. And Gadiah had very much to do with the final decision of Simon, the wealthy leather merchant, to embrace Christianity.

130:1.4 (1428.4) (In this narrative of the personal work of Jesus with his fellow mortals on this tour of the Mediterranean, we shall, in accordance with our permission, freely translate his words into modern phraseology current on Urantia at the time of this presentation.)

130:1.5 (1429.1) Jesus' last visit with Gadiah had to do with a discussion of good and evil. This young Philistine was much troubled by a feeling of injustice because of the presence of evil in the world alongside the good. He said: "How can God, if he is infinitely good, permit us to suffer the sorrows of evil; after all, who creates evil?" It was still believed by many in those days that God creates both good and evil, but Jesus never taught such error. In answering this question, Jesus said: "My brother, God is love; therefore he must be good, and his goodness is so great and real that it cannot contain the small and unreal things of evil. God is so positively good that there is absolutely no place in him for negative evil. Evil is the immature choosing and the unthinking misstep of those who are resistant to goodness, rejectful of beauty, and disloyal to truth. Evil is only the mis-adaptation of immaturity or the disruptive and distorting influence of ignorance. Evil is the inevitable darkness which follows upon the heels of the unwise rejection of light. Evil is that which is dark and untrue, and which, when consciously embraced and willfully endorsed, becomes sin.

130:1.6 (1429.2) "Your Father in heaven, by endowing you with the power to choose between truth and error, created the potential negative of the positive way of light and life; but such errors of evil are really nonexistent until such a time as an intelligent creature wills their existence by mischoosing the way of life. And then are such evils later exalted into sin by the knowing and deliberate choice of such a willful and rebellious creature. This is why our Father in heaven permits the good and the evil to go along together until the end of life, just as nature allows the wheat and the tares to grow side by side until the harvest." Gadiah was fully satisfied with Jesus' answer to his question after their subsequent discussion had made clear to his mind the real meaning of these momentous statements.

At Caesarea

130:2.1 (1429.3) Jesus and his friends tarried in Caesarea beyond the time expected because one of the huge steering paddles of the vessel on which they intended to embark was discovered to be in danger of cleaving. The captain decided to remain in port while a new one was being made. There was a shortage of skilled woodworkers for this task, so Jesus volunteered to assist. During the evenings Jesus and his friends strolled about on the beautiful wall which served as a promenade around the port. Ganid greatly enjoyed Jesus' explanation of the water system of the city and the technique whereby the tides were utilized to flush the city's streets and sewers. This youth of India was much impressed with the temple of Augustus, situated upon an elevation and surmounted by a colossal statue of the Roman emperor. The second afternoon of their stay the three of them attended a performance in the enormous amphitheater which could seat twenty thousand persons, and that night they went to a Greek play at the theater. These were the first exhibitions of this sort Ganid had ever witnessed, and he asked Jesus many questions about them. On the morning of the third day they paid a formal visit to the governor's palace, for Caesarea was the capital of Palestine and the residence of the Roman procurator.

130:2.2 (1429.4) At their inn there also lodged a merchant from Mongolia, and since this Far-Easterner talked Greek fairly well, Jesus had several long visits with him. This man was much impressed with Jesus' philosophy of life and never forgot his words of wisdom regarding "the living of the heavenly life while on earth by means of daily submission to the will of the heavenly Father." This merchant was a Taoist, and he had thereby become a strong believer in the doctrine of a universal Deity. When he returned to Mongolia, he began to teach these advanced truths to his neighbors and to his business associates, and as a direct result of such activities, his eldest son decided to become a Taoist priest. This young man exerted a great influence in behalf of advanced truth throughout his lifetime and was followed by a son and a grandson who likewise were devotedly loyal to the doctrine of the One God—the Supreme Ruler of Heaven.

130:2.3 (1430.1) While the eastern branch of the early Christian church, having its headquarters at Philadelphia, held more faithfully to the teachings of Jesus than did the Jerusalem brethren, it was regrettable that there was no one like Peter to go into China, or like Paul to enter India, where the spiritual soil was then so favorable for planting the seed of the new gospel of the kingdom. These very teachings of Jesus, as they were held by the Philadelphians, would have made just such an immediate and effective appeal to the minds of the spiritually hungry Asiatic peoples as did the preaching of Peter and Paul in the West.

130:2.4 (1430.2) One of the young men who worked with Jesus one day on the steering paddle became much interested in the words which he dropped from hour to hour as they toiled in the shipyard. When Jesus intimated that the Father in heaven was interested in the welfare of his children on earth, this young Greek, Anaxand, said: "If the Gods are interested in me, then why do they not remove the cruel and unjust foreman of this workshop?" He was startled when Jesus replied, "Since you know the ways of kindness and value justice, perhaps the Gods have brought this erring man near that you may lead him into this better way. Maybe you are the salt which is to make this brother more agreeable to all other men; that is, if you have not lost your savor. As it is, this man is your master in that his evil ways unfavorably influence you. Why not assert your mastery of evil by

virtue of the power of goodness and thus become the master of all relations between the two of you? I predict that the good in you could overcome the evil in him if you gave it a fair and living chance. There is no adventure in the course of mortal existence more enthralling than to enjoy the exhilaration of becoming the material life partner with spiritual energy and divine truth in one of their triumphant struggles with error and evil. It is a marvelous and transforming experience to become the living channel of spiritual light to the mortal who sits in spiritual darkness. If you are more blessed with truth than is this man, his need should challenge you. Surely you are not the coward who could stand by on the seashore and watch a fellow man who could not swim perish! How much more of value is this man's soul floundering in darkness compared to his body drowning in water!"

130:2.5 (1430.3) Anaxand was mightily moved by Jesus' words. Presently he told his superior what Jesus had said, and that night they both sought Jesus' advice as to the welfare of their souls. And later on, after the Christian message had been proclaimed in Caesarea, both of these men, one a Greek and the other a Roman, believed Philip's preaching and became prominent members of the church which he founded. Later this young Greek was appointed the steward of a Roman centurion, Cornelius, who became a believer through Peter's ministry. Anaxand continued to minister light to those who sat in darkness until the days of Paul's imprisonment at Caesarea, when he perished, by accident, in the great slaughter of twenty thousand Jews while he ministered to the suffering and dying.

130:2.6 (1431.1) Ganid was, by this time, beginning to learn how his tutor spent his leisure in this unusual personal ministry to his fellow men, and the young Indian set about to find out the motive for these incessant activities. He asked, "Why do you occupy yourself so continuously with these visits with strangers?" And Jesus answered: "Ganid, no man is
a stranger to one who knows God. In the experience of finding the Father in

heaven you discover that all men are your brothers, and does it seem strange that one should enjoy the exhilaration of meeting a newly discovered brother? To become acquainted with one's brothers and sisters, to know their problems and to learn to love them, is the supreme experience of living."

130:2.7 (1431.2) This was a conference which lasted well into the night, in the course of which the young man requested Jesus to tell him the difference between the will of God and that human mind act of choosing which is also called will. In substance Jesus said: The will of God is the way of God, partnership with the choice of God in the face of any potential alternative. To do the will of God, therefore, is the progressive experience of becoming more and more like God, and God is the source and destiny of all that is good and beautiful and true. The will of man is the way of man, the sum and substance of that which the mortal chooses to be and do. Will is the deliberate choice of a self-conscious being which leads to decision-conduct based on intelligent reflection.

130:2.8 (1431.3) That afternoon Jesus and Ganid had both enjoyed playing with a very intelligent shepherd dog, and Ganid wanted to know whether the dog had a soul, whether it had a will, and in response to his questions Jesus said: "The dog has a mind which can know material man, his master, but cannot know God, who is spirit; therefore the dog does not possess a spiritual nature and cannot enjoy a spiritual experience. The dog may have a will derived from nature and augmented by training, but such a power of mind is not a spiritual force, neither is it comparable to the human will, inasmuch as it is not reflective—it is not the result of discriminating higher and moral meanings or choosing spiritual and eternal values. It is the possession of such powers of spiritual discrimination and truth choosing that makes mortal man a moral being, a creature endowed with the attributes of spiritual responsibility and the potential of eternal survival." Jesus went on to explain that it is the absence of such mental powers in the animal which makes

it forever impossible for the animal world to develop language in time or to experience anything equivalent to personality survival in eternity. As a result of this day's instruction Ganid never again entertained belief in the transmigration of the souls of men into the bodies of animals.

130:2.9 (1431.4) The next day Ganid talked all this over with his father, and it was in answer to Gonod's question that Jesus explained that "human wills which are fully occupied with passing only upon temporal decisions having to do with the material problems of animal existence are doomed to perish in time. Those who make wholehearted moral decisions and unqualified spiritual choices are thus progressively identified with the indwelling and divine spirit, and thereby are they increasingly transformed into the values of eternal survival—unending progression of divine service."

130:2.10 (1431.5) It was on this same day that we first heard that momentous truth which, stated in modern terms, would signify: "Will is that manifestation of the human mind which enables the subjective consciousness to express itself objectively and to experience the phenomenon of aspiring to be Godlike." And it is in this same sense that every reflective and spiritually minded human being can become creative.

At Alexandria

130:3.1 (1432.1) It had been an eventful visit at Caesarea, and when the boat was ready, Jesus and his two friends departed at noon one day for Alexandria in Egypt.

130:3.2 (1432.2) The three enjoyed a most pleasant passage to Alexandria. Ganid was delighted with the voyage and kept Jesus busy answering questions. As they approached the city's harbor, the young man was thrilled by the great lighthouse of Pharos, located on the island which Alexander had joined by a mole to the mainland, thus creating two magnificent harbors and thereby making Alexandria the maritime commercial crossroads of Africa, Asia, and Europe. This great lighthouse was one of the seven wonders of the world and was the forerunner of all subsequent lighthouses. They arose early in the morning to view this splendid lifesaving device of man, and amidst the exclamations of Ganid Jesus said: "And you, my son, will be like this lighthouse when you return to India, even after your father is laid to rest; you will become like the light of life to those who sit about you in darkness, showing all who so desire the way to reach the harbor of salvation in safety." And as Ganid squeezed Jesus' hand, he said, "I will."

130:3.3 (1432.3) And again we remark that the early teachers of the Christian religion made a great mistake when they so exclusively turned their attention to the western civilization of the Roman world. The teachings of Jesus, as they were held by the Mesopotamian believers of the first century, would have been readily received by the various groups of Asiatic religionists.

130:3.4 (1432.4) By the fourth hour after landing they were settled near the eastern end of the long and broad avenue, one hundred feet wide and five miles long, which stretched on out to the western limits of this city of one million people. After the first survey of the city's chief attractions—university (museum), library, the royal mausoleum of Alexander, the palace, temple of Neptune, theater, and gymnasium—Gonod addressed himself to business while Jesus and Ganid went to the library, the greatest in the world. Here were assembled nearly a million manuscripts from all the civilized world: Greece, Rome, Palestine, Parthia, India, China, and even Japan. In this library Ganid saw the largest collection of Indian literature in all the world; and they spent some time here each day throughout their stay in Alexandria. Jesus told Ganid about the translation of the Hebrew scriptures into Greek at this place. And they discussed again and again all the religions of the world, Jesus endeavoring to point out to this young mind the truth in each, always adding: "But Yahweh

is the God developed from the revelations of Melchizedek and the covenant of Abraham. The Jews were the offspring of Abraham and subsequently occupied the very land wherein Melchizedek had lived and taught, and from which he sent teachers to all the world; and their religion eventually portrayed a clearer recognition of the Lord God of Israel as the Universal Father in heaven than any other world religion."

130:3.5 (1432.5) Under Jesus' direction Ganid made a collection of the teachings of all those religions of the world which recognized a Universal Deity, even though they might also give more or less recognition to subordinate deities. After much discussion Jesus and Ganid decided that the Romans had no real God in their religion, that their religion was hardly more than emperor worship. The Greeks, they concluded, had a philosophy but hardly a religion with a personal God. The mystery cults they discarded because of the confusion of their multiplicity, and because their varied concepts of Deity seemed to be derived from other and older religions.

130:3.6 (1433.1) Although these translations were made at Alexandria, Ganid did not finally arrange these selections and add his own personal conclusions until near the end of their sojourn in Rome. He was much surprised to discover that the best of the authors of the world's sacred literature all more or less clearly recognized the existence of an eternal God and were much in agreement with regard to his character and his relationship with mortal man.

130:3.7 (1433.2) Jesus and Ganid spent much time in the museum during their stay in Alexandria. This museum was not a collection of rare objects but rather a university of fine art, science, and literature. Learned professors here gave daily lectures, and in those times this was the intellectual center of the Occidental world. Day by day Jesus interpreted the lectures to Ganid; one day during the second week the young man exclaimed: "Teacher Joshua, you know more than these professors; you should stand up and tell them the great things you have told me; they are befogged by much thinking. I shall speak to my father and have him arrange it." Jesus smiled, saying: "You are an admiring pupil, but these teachers are not minded that you and I should instruct them. The pride of unspiritualized learning is a treacherous thing in human experience. The true teacher maintains his intellectual integrity by ever remaining a learner."

130:3.8 (1433.3) Alexandria was the city of the blended culture of the Occident and next to Rome the largest and most magnificent in the world. Here was located the largest Jewish synagogue in the world, the seat of government of the Alexandria Sanhedrin, the seventy ruling elders.

130:3.9 (1433.4) Among the many men with whom Gonod transacted business was a certain Jewish banker, Alexander, whose brother, Philo, was a famous religious philosopher of that time. Philo was engaged in the laudable but exceedingly difficult task of harmonizing Greek philosophy and Hebrew theology. Ganid and Jesus talked much about Philo's teachings and expected to attend some of his lectures, but throughout their stay at Alexandria this famous Hellenistic Jew lay sick abed.

130:3.10 (1433.5) Jesus commended to Ganid much in the Greek philosophy and the Stoic doctrines, but he impressed upon the lad the truth that these systems of belief, like the indefinite teachings of some of his own people, were religions only in the sense that they led men to find God and enjoy a living experience in knowing the Eternal.

Discourse on Reality

130:4.1 (1433.6) The night before they left Alexandria Ganid and Jesus had a long visit with one of the government professors at the university who lectured on the teachings of Plato. Jesus interpreted for the learned Greek teacher but injected no teaching of his own in refutation of the Greek philosophy. Gonod was away on business that evening; so, after the professor had departed, the teacher and his pupil had a long and heart-to-heart talk about Plato's doctrines.

While Jesus gave qualified approval of some of the Greek teachings which had to do with the theory that the material things of the world are shadowy reflections of invisible but more substantial spiritual realities, he sought to lay a more trustworthy foundation for the lad's thinking; so he began a long dissertation concerning the nature of reality in the universe. In substance and in modern phraseology Jesus said to Ganid:

130:4.2 (1434.1) The source of universe reality is the Infinite. The material things of finite creation are the time-space repercussions of the Paradise Pattern and the Universal Mind of the eternal God. Causation in the physical world, self-consciousness in the intellectual world, and progressing selfhood in the spirit world— these realities, projected on a universal scale, combined in eternal relatedness, and experienced with perfection of quality and divinity of value— constitute the reality of the Supreme. But in an ever-changing universe the Original Personality of causation, intelligence, and spirit experience is changeless, absolute. All things, even in an eternal universe of limitless values and divine qualities, may, and oftentimes do, change except the Absolutes and that which has attained the physical status, intellectual embrace, or spiritual identity which is absolute.

130:4.3 (1434.2) The highest level to which a finite creature can progress is the recognition of the Universal Father and the knowing of the Supreme. And even then such beings of finality destiny go on experiencing change in the motions of the physical world and in its material phenomena. Likewise do they remain aware of selfhood progression in their continuing ascension of the spiritual universe and of growing consciousness in their deepening appreciation of, and response to, the intellectual cosmos. Only in the perfection, harmony, and unanimity of will can the creature become as one with the Creator; and such a state of divinity is attained and maintained only by the creature's continuing to live in time and eternity by consistently conforming his finite personal will to the divine will of the Creator. Always must the desire to do the Father's will be supreme in the soul and dominant over the mind of an ascending son of God.

130:4.4 (1434.3) A one-eyed person can never hope to visualize depth of perspective. Neither can single-eyed material scientists nor single-eyed spiritual mystics and allegorists correctly visualize and adequately comprehend the true depths of universe reality. All true values of creature experience are concealed in depth of recognition.

130:4.5 (1434.4) Mindless causation cannot evolve the refined and complex from the crude and the simple, neither can spiritless experience evolve the divine characters of eternal survival from the material minds of the mortals of time. The one attribute of the universe which so exclusively characterizes the infinite Deity is this unending creative bestowal of personality which can survive in progressive Deity attainment.

130:4.6 (1434.5) Personality is that cosmic endowment, that phase of universal reality, which can coexist with unlimited change and at the same time retain its identity in the very presence of all such changes, and forever afterward.

130:4.7 (1434.6) Life is an adaptation of the original cosmic causation to the demands and possibilities of universe situations, and it comes into being by the action of the Universal Mind and the activation of the spirit spark of the God who is spirit. The meaning of life is its adaptability; the value of life is its progressability—even to the heights of God- consciousness.

130:4.8 (1434.7) Misadaptation of self-conscious life to the universe results

in cosmic disharmony. Final divergence of personality will from the trend of the universes terminates in intellectual isolation, personality segregation. Loss of the indwelling spirit pilot supervenes in spiritual cessation of existence. Intelligent and progressing life becomes then, in and of itself, an incontrovertible proof of the existence of a purposeful universe expressing the will of a divine Creator. And this life, in the aggregate, struggles toward higher values, having for its final goal the Universal Father.

130:4.9 (1435.1) Only in degree does man possess mind above the animal level aside from the higher and quasi-spiritual ministrations of intellect. Therefore animals (not having worship and wisdom) cannot experience superconsciousness, consciousness of consciousness. The animal mind is only conscious of the objective universe.

130:4.10 (1435.2) Knowledge is the sphere of the material or fact-discerning mind. Truth is the domain of the spiritually endowed intellect that is conscious of knowing God. Knowledge is demonstrable; truth is experienced. Knowledge is a possession of the mind; truth an experience of the soul, the progressing self. Knowledge is a function of the nonspiritual level; truth is a phase of the mind-spirit level of the universes. The eye of the material mind perceives a world of factual knowledge; the eye of the spiritualized intellect discerns a world of true values. These two views, synchronized and harmonized, reveal the world of reality, wherein wisdom interprets the phenomena of the universe in terms of progressive personal experience.

130:4.11 (1435.3) Error (evil) is the penalty of imperfection. The qualities of imperfection or facts of misadaptation are disclosed on the material level by critical observation and by scientific analysis; on the moral level, by human experience. The presence of evil constitutes proof of the inaccuracies of mind and the immaturity of the evolving self. Evil is, therefore, also a measure of imperfection in universe interpretation. The possibility of making mistakes is inherent in the acquisition of wisdom, the scheme of progressing from the partial and temporal to the complete and eternal, from the relative and imperfect to the final and perfected. Error is the shadow of relative incompleteness which must of necessity fall across man's ascending universe path to Paradise perfection. Error (evil) is not an actual universe quality; it is simply the observation of a relativity in the relatedness of the imperfection of the incomplete finite to the ascending levels of the Supreme and Ultimate.

130:4.12 (1435.4) Although Jesus told all this to the lad in language best suited to his comprehension, at the end of the discussion Ganid was heavy of eye and was soon lost in slumber. They rose early the next morning to go aboard the boat bound for Lasea on the island of Crete. But before they embarked, the lad had still further questions to ask about evil, to which Jesus replied:

130:4.13 (1435.5) Evil is a relativity concept. It arises out of the observation of the imperfections which appear in the shadow cast by a finite universe of things and beings as such a cosmos obscures the living light of the universal expression of the eternal realities of the Infinite One.

130:4.14 (1435.6) Potential evil is inherent in the necessary incompleteness of the revelation of God as a time-space-limited expression of infinity and eternity. The fact of the partial in the presence of the complete constitutes relativity of reality, creates necessity for intellectual choosing, and establishes value levels of spirit recognition and response. The incomplete and finite concept of the Infinite which is held by the temporal and limited creature mind is, in and of itself, potential evil. But the augmenting error of unjustified deficiency in reasonable spiritual rectification of these originally inherent intellectual disharmonies and spiritual insufficiencies, is equivalent to the realization of actual evil.

130:4.15 (1436.1) All static, dead, concepts are potentially evil. The finite shadow of relative and living truth is continually moving. Static concepts invariably retard science, politics, society, and religion. Static concepts may represent a certain knowledge, but they are deficient in wisdom and devoid of truth. But do not permit the concept of relativity so to mislead you that you fail to recognize the co-ordination of the universe under the guidance of the cosmic mind, and its stabilized control by the energy and spirit of the Supreme.

On the Island of Crete

130:5.1 (1436.2) The travelers had but one purpose in going to Crete, and that was to play, to walk about over the island, and to climb the mountains. The Cretans of that time did not enjoy an enviable reputation among the surrounding peoples. Nevertheless, Jesus and Ganid won many souls to higher levels of thinking and living and thus laid the foundation for the quick reception of the later gospel teachings when the first preachers from Jerusalem arrived. Jesus loved these Cretans, notwithstanding the harsh words which Paul later spoke concerning them when he subsequently sent Titus to the island to reorganize their churches.

130:5.2 (1436.3) On the mountainside in Crete Jesus had his first long talk with Gonod regarding religion. And the father was much impressed, saying: "No wonder the boy believes everything you tell him, but I never knew they had such a religion even in Jerusalem, much less in Damascus." It was during the island sojourn that Gonod first proposed to Jesus that he go back to India with them, and Ganid was delighted with the thought that Jesus might consent to such an arrangement.

130:5.3 (1436.4) One day when Ganid asked Jesus why he had not devoted himself to the work of a public teacher, he said: "My son, everything must await the coming of its time. You are born into the world, but no amount of anxiety and no manifestation of impatience will help you to grow up. You must, in all such matters, wait upon time. Time alone will ripen the green fruit upon the tree. Season follows season and sundown follows sunrise only with the passing of time. I am now on the way to Rome with you and your father, and that is sufficient for today. My tomorrow is wholly in the hands of my Father in heaven." And then he told Ganid the story of Moses and the forty years of watchful waiting and continued preparation.

130:5.4 (1436.5) One thing happened on a visit to Fair Havens which Ganid never forgot; the memory of this episode always caused him to wish he might do something to change the caste system of his native India. A drunken degenerate was attacking a slave girl on the public highway. When Jesus saw the plight of the girl, he rushed forward and drew the maiden away from the assault of the madman. While the frightened child clung to him, he held the infuriated man at a safe distance by his powerful extended right arm until the poor fellow had exhausted himself beating the air with his angry blows. Ganid felt a strong impulse to help Jesus handle the affair, but his father forbade him. Though they could not speak the girl's language, she could understand their act of mercy and gave token of her heartfelt appreciation as they all three escorted her home. This was probably as near a personal encounter with his fellows as Jesus ever had throughout his entire life in the flesh. But he had a difficult task that evening trying to explain to Ganid why he did not smite the drunken man. Ganid thought this man should have been struck at least as many times as he had struck the girl.

The Young Man Who Was Afraid

130:6.1 (1437.1) While they were up in the mountains, Jesus had a long talk with a young man who was fearful and downcast. Failing to derive comfort and courage from association with his fellows, this youth had sought the solitude of the hills; he had grown up with a feeling of helplessness and inferiority. These natural tendencies had been augmented by numerous difficult circumstances which the lad had encountered as he grew up, notably, the loss of his father when he was twelve years of age. As they met, Jesus said: "Greetings, my friend! why so downcast on such a beautiful day? If something has happened to distress you, perhaps I can in some manner assist you. At any rate it affords me real pleasure to proffer my services."

130:6.2 (1437.2) The young man was disinclined to talk, and so Jesus made a second approach to his soul, saying: "I understand you come up in these hills to get away from folks; so, of course, you do not want to talk with me, but I would like to know whether you are familiar with these hills; do you know the direction of the trails? and, perchance, could you inform me as to the best route to Phenix?" Now this youth was very familiar with these mountains, and he really became much interested in telling Jesus the way to Phenix, so much so that he marked out all the trails on the ground and fully explained every detail. But he was startled and made curious when Jesus, after saying good-bye and making as if he were taking leave, suddenly turned to him, saying: "I well know you wish to be left alone with your disconsolation; but it would be neither kind nor fair for me to receive such generous help from you as to how best to find my way to Phenix and then unthinkingly to go away from you without making the least effort to answer your appealing request for help and guidance regarding the best route to the goal of destiny which you seek in your heart while you tarry here on the mountainside. As you so well know the trails to Phenix, having traversed them many times, so do I well know the way to the city of your disappointed hopes and thwarted ambitions. And since you have asked me for help, I will not disappoint you." The youth was almost overcome, but he managed to stammer out, "But—I did not ask you for anything—" And Jesus, laying a gentle hand on his shoulder, said: "No, son, not with words but with longing looks did you appeal to my heart. My boy, to one who loves his fellows there is an eloquent appeal for help in your countenance of discouragement and despair. Sit down with me while I tell you of the service trails and happiness highways which lead from the sorrows of self to the joys of loving activities in the brotherhood of men and in the service of the God of heaven."

130:6.3 (1437.3) By this time the young man very much desired to talk with Jesus, and he knelt at his feet imploring Jesus to help him, to show him the way of escape from his world of personal sorrow and defeat. Said Jesus: "My friend, arise! Stand up like a man! You may be surrounded with small enemies and be retarded by many obstacles, but the big things and the real things of this world and the universe are on your side. The sun rises every morning to salute you just as it does the most powerful and prosperous man on earth. Look—you have a strong body and powerful muscles—your physical equipment is better than the average. Of course, it is just about useless while you sit out here on the mountainside and grieve over your misfortunes, real and fancied. But you could do great things with your body if you would hasten off to where great things are waiting to be done. You are trying to run away from your unhappy self, but it cannot be done. You and your problems of living are real; you cannot escape them as long as you live. But look again, your mind is clear and capable. Your strong body has an intelligent mind to direct it. Set your mind at work to solve its problems; teach your intellect to work for you; refuse longer to be dominated by fear like an unthinking animal. Your mind should be your courageous ally in the solution of your life problems rather than your being, as you have been, its abject fear-slave and the bond servant of depression and defeat. But most valuable of all, your potential of real achievement is the spirit which lives within you, and which will stimulate and inspire your mind to control itself and activate the body if you will release it from the fetters of fear and thus enable your spiritual nature to begin your deliverance from the evils of inaction by the power-presence of living faith. And then, forthwith, will this faith vanquish fear of men by the compelling presence of that new and all-dominating

love of your fellows which will so soon fill your soul to overflowing because of the consciousness which has been born in your heart that you are a child of God. *

130:6.4 (1438.1) "This day, my son, you are to be reborn, re-established as a man of faith, courage, and devoted service to man, for God's sake. And when you become so readjusted to life within yourself, you become likewise readjusted to the universe; you have been born again—born of the spirit—and henceforth will your whole life become one of victorious accomplishment. Trouble will invigorate you; disappointment will spur you on; difficulties will challenge you; and obstacles will stimulate you. Arise, young man! Say farewell to the life of cringing fear and fleeing cowardice. Hasten back to duty and live your life in the flesh as a son of God, a mortal dedicated to the ennobling service of man on earth and destined to the superb and eternal service of God in eternity."

130:6.5 (1438.2) And this youth, Fortune, subsequently became the leader of the Christians in Crete and the close associate of Titus in his labors for the uplift of the Cretan believers.

130:6.6 (1438.3) The travelers were truly rested and refreshed when they made ready about noon one day to sail for Carthage in northern Africa, stopping for two days at Cyrene. It was here that Jesus and Ganid gave first aid to a lad named Rufus, who had been injured by the breakdown of a loaded oxcart. They carried him home to his mother, and his father, Simon, little dreamed that the man whose cross he subsequently bore by orders of a Roman soldier was the stranger who once befriended his son.

At Carthage—Discourse on Time and Space

130:7.1 (1438.4) Most of the time en route to Carthage Jesus talked with his fellow travelers about things social, political, and commercial; hardly a word was said about religion. For the first time Gonod and Ganid discovered that Jesus was a good storyteller, and they kept him busy telling tales about his early life in Galilee. They also learned that he was reared in Galilee and not in either Jerusalem or Damascus.

130:7.2 (1438.5) When Ganid inquired what one could do to make friends, having noticed that the majority of persons whom they chanced to meet were attracted to Jesus, his teacher said: "Become interested in your fellows; learn how to love them and watch for the opportunity to do something for them which you are sure they want done," and then he quoted the olden Jewish proverb—"A man who would have friends must show himself friendly."

130:7.3 (1439.1) At Carthage Jesus had a long and memorable talk with a Mithraic priest about immortality, about time and eternity. This Persian had been educated at Alexandria, and he really desired to learn from Jesus. Put into the words of today, in substance Jesus said in answer to his many questions:

130:7.4 (1439.2) Time is the stream of flowing temporal events perceived by creature consciousness. Time is a name given to the succession-arrangement whereby events are recognized and segregated. The universe of space is a time-related phenomenon as it is viewed from any interior position outside of the fixed abode of Paradise. The motion of time is only revealed in relation to something which does not move in space as a time phenomenon. In the universe of universes Paradise and its Deities transcend both time and space. On the inhabited worlds, human personality (in dwelt and oriented by the Paradise Father's spirit) is the only physically related reality which can transcend the material sequence of temporal events.

130:7.5 (1439.3) Animals do not sense time as does man, and even to man, because of his sectional and circumscribed view, time appears as a succession of events; but as man ascends, as he progresses inward, the enlarging view of this event proces-

sion is such that it is discerned more and more in its wholeness. That which formerly appeared as a succession of events then will be viewed as a whole and perfectly related cycle; in this way will circular simultaneity increasingly displace the onetime consciousness of the linear sequence of events.

130:7.6 (1439.4) There are seven different conceptions of space as it is conditioned by time. Space is measured by time, not time by space. The confusion of the scientist grows out of failure to recognize the reality of space. Space is not merely an intellectual concept of the variation in relatedness of universe objects. Space is not empty, and the only thing man knows which can even partially transcend space is mind. Mind can function independently of the concept of the space-relatedness of material objects. Space is relatively and comparatively finite to all beings of creature status. The nearer consciousness approaches the awareness of seven cosmic dimensions, the more does the concept of potential space approach ultimacy. But the space potential is truly ultimate only on the absolute level.

130:7.7 (1439.5) It must be apparent that universal reality has an expanding and always relative meaning on the ascending and perfecting levels of the cosmos. Ultimately, surviving mortals achieve identity in a seven-dimensional universe.

130:7.8 (1439.6) The time-space concept of a mind of material origin is destined to undergo successive enlargements as the conscious and conceiving personality ascends the levels of the universes. When man attains the mind intervening between the material and the spiritual planes of existence, his ideas of time-space will be enormously expanded both as to quality of perception and quantity of experience. The enlarging cosmic conceptions of an advancing spirit personality are due to augmentations of both depth of insight and scope of consciousness. And as personality passes on, upward and inward, to the transcendental levels of Deity-likeness, the time-space concept will increasingly approximate the timeless and spaceless concepts of the Absolutes. Relatively, and in accordance with transcendental attainment, these concepts of the absolute level are to be envisioned by the children of ultimate destiny.

On the Way to Naples and Rome

130:8.1 (1440.1) The first stop on the way to Italy was at the island of Malta. Here Jesus had a long talk with a downhearted and discouraged young man named Claudus. This fellow had contemplated taking his life, but when he had finished talking with the scribe of Damascus, he said: "I will face life like a man; I am through playing the coward. I will go back to my people and begin all over again." Shortly he became an enthusiastic preacher of the Cynics, and still later on he joined hands with Peter in proclaiming Christianity in Rome and Naples, and after the death of Peter he went on to Spain preaching the gospel. But he never knew that the man who inspired him in Malta was the Jesus whom he subsequently proclaimed the world's Deliverer.

130:8.2 (1440.2) At Syracuse they spent a full week. The notable event of their stop here was the rehabilitation of Ezra, the backslidden Jew, who kept the tavern where Jesus and his companions stopped. Ezra was charmed by Jesus' approach and asked him to help him come back to the faith of Israel. He expressed his hopelessness by saying, "I want to be a true son of Abraham, but I cannot find God." Said Jesus: "If you truly want to find God, that desire is in itself evidence that you have already found him. Your trouble is not that you cannot find God, for the Father has already found you; your trouble is simply that you do not know God. Have you not read in the Prophet Jeremiah, 'You shall seek me and find me when you shall search for me with all your heart'? And again, does not this same prophet say: 'And I will give you a heart to know me, that I am the Lord, and you shall belong to my people, and I will be your God'? And have you

not also read in the Scriptures where it says: 'He looks down upon men, and if any will say: I have sinned and perverted that which was right, and it profited me not, then will God deliver that man's soul from darkness, and he shall see the light'?" And Ezra found God and to the satisfaction of his soul. Later, this Jew, in association with a well-to-do Greek proselyte, built the first Christian church in Syracuse.

130:8.3 (1440.3) At Messina they stopped for only one day, but that was long enough to change the life of a small boy, a fruit vendor, of whom Jesus bought fruit and in turn fed with the bread of life. The lad never forgot the words of Jesus and the kindly look which went with them when, placing his hand on the boy's shoulder, he said: "Farewell, my lad, be of good courage as you grow up to manhood and after you have fed the body learn how also to feed the soul. And my Father in heaven will be with you and go before you." The lad became a devotee of the Mithraic religion and later on turned to the Christian faith.

130:8.4 (1440.4) At last they reached Naples and felt they were not far from their destination, Rome. Gonod had much business to transact in Naples, and aside from the time Jesus was required as interpreter, he and Ganid spent their leisure visiting and exploring the city. Ganid was becoming adept at sighting those who appeared to be in need. They found much poverty in this city and distributed many alms. But Ganid never understood the meaning of Jesus' words when, after he had given a coin to a street beggar, he refused to pause and speak comfortingly to the man. Said Jesus: "Why waste words upon one who cannot perceive the meaning of what you say? The spirit of the Father cannot teach and save one who has no capacity for sonship." What Jesus meant was that the man was not of normal mind; that he lacked the ability to respond to spirit leading.

130:8.5 (1441.1) There was no outstanding experience in Naples; Jesus and the young man thoroughly canvassed the city and spread good cheer with many smiles upon hundreds of men, women, and children.

130:8.6 (1441.2) From here they went by way of Capua to Rome, making a stop of three days at Capua. By the Appian Way they journeyed on beside their pack animals toward Rome, all three being anxious to see this mistress of empire and the greatest city in all the world.

Paper 131

The World's Religions

131:0.1 (1442.1) DURING the Alexandrian sojourn of Jesus, Gonod, and Ganid, the young man spent much of his time and no small sum of his father's money making a collection of the teachings of the world's religions about God and his relations with mortal man. Ganid employed more than threescore learned translators in the making of this abstract of the religious doctrines of the world concerning the Deities. And it should be made plain in this record that all these teachings portraying monotheism were largely derived, directly or indirectly, from the preachments of the missionaries of Machiventa Melchizedek, who went forth from their Salem headquarters to spread the doctrine of one God—the Most High—to the ends of the earth.

131:0.2 (1442.2) There is presented herewith an abstract of Ganid's manuscript, which he prepared at Alexandria and Rome, and which was preserved in India for hundreds of years after his death. He collected this material under ten heads, as follows:

Cynicism

131:1.1 (1442.3) The residual teachings of the disciples of Melchizedek, excepting those which persisted in the Jewish religion, were best preserved in the doctrines of the Cynics. Ganid's selection embraced the following:

131:1.2 (1442.4) "God is supreme; he is the Most High of heaven and earth. God is the perfected circle of eternity, and he rules the universe of universes. He is the sole maker of the heavens and the earth. When he decrees a thing, that thing is. Our God is one God, and he is compassionate and merciful. Everything that is high, holy, true, and beautiful is like our God. The Most High is the light of heaven and earth; he is the God of the east, the west, the north, and the south.

131:1.3 (1442.5) "Even if the earth should pass away, the resplendent face of the Supreme would abide in majesty and glory. The Most High is the first and the last, the beginning and the end of everything. There is but this one God, and his name is Truth. God is self-existent, and he is devoid of all anger and enmity; he is immortal and infinite. Our God is omnipotent and bounteous. While he has many manifestations, we worship only God himself. God knows all—our secrets and our proclamations; he also knows what each of us deserves. His might is equal to all things.

131:1.4 (1442.6) "God is a peace giver and a faithful protector of all who fear and trust him. He gives salvation to all who serve him. All creation exists in the power of the Most High. His divine love springs forth from the holiness of his power, and affection is born of the might of his greatness. The Most High has decreed the union of body and soul and has endowed man with his own spirit. What man does must come to an end, but what the Creator does goes on forever. We gain knowledge from the experience of man, but we derive wisdom from the contemplation of the Most High.

131:1.5 (1443.1) "God pours rain upon the earth, he causes the sun to shine upon the sprouting grain, and he gives us the abundant harvest of the good things of this life and eternal salvation in the world to come. Our God enjoys great authority; his name is Excellent and his nature is unfathomable. When you are sick, it is the Most High who heals you. God is full of goodness toward all men; we have no friend like the Most High. His mercy fills all places and his goodness encompasses all souls. The Most High is changeless; and he is our helper in every time of need. Wherever you turn to pray, there is the face of the Most High and the open ear of our God. You may hide yourself from men, but not from God. God is not a great distance from us; he is omnipresent. God fills all places and lives in the heart of the man who fears his holy name. Creation is in the Creator and the Creator in his creation. We search for the Most High and then find him in our hearts. You go in quest of a dear friend, and then you discover him within your soul.

131:1.6 (1443.2) "The man who knows God looks upon all men as equal; they are his brethren. Those who are selfish, those who ignore their brothers in the flesh, have only weariness as their reward. Those who love their fellows and who have pure hearts shall see God. God never forgets sincerity. He will guide the honest of heart into the truth, for God is truth.

131:1.7 (1443.3) "In your lives overthrow error and overcome evil by the love of the living truth. In all your relations with men do good for evil. The Lord God is merciful and loving; he is forgiving. Let us love God, for he first loved us. By God's love and through his mercy we shall be saved. Poor men and rich men are brothers. God is their Father. The evil you would not have done you, do not to others.

131:1.8 (1443.4) "At all times call upon his name, and as you believe in his name, so shall your prayer be heard. What a great honor it is to worship the Most High! All the worlds and the universes worship the Most High. And with all your prayers give thanks—ascend to worship. Prayerful worship shuns evil and forbids sin. At all times let us praise the name of the Most High. The man who takes shelter in the Most High conceals his defects from the universe. When you stand before God with a clean heart, you become fearless of

all creation. The Most High is like a loving father and mother; he really loves us, his children on earth. Our God will forgive us and guide our footsteps into the ways of salvation. He will take us by the hand and lead us to himself. God saves those who trust him; he does not compel man to serve his name.

131:1.9 (1443.5) "If the faith of the Most High has entered your heart, then shall you abide free from fear throughout all the days of your life. Fret not yourself because of the prosperity of the ungodly; fear not those who plot evil; let the soul turn away from sin and put your whole trust in the God of salvation. The weary soul of the wandering mortal finds eternal rest in the arms of the Most High; the wise man hungers for the divine embrace; the earth child longs for the security of the arms of the Universal Father. The noble man seeks for that high estate wherein the soul of the mortal blends with the spirit of the Supreme. God is just: What fruit we receive not from our plantings in this world we shall receive in the next."

Judaism

131:2.1 (1444.1) The Kenites of Palestine salvaged much of the teaching of Melchizedek, and from these records, as preserved and modified by the Jews, Jesus and Ganid made the following selection:

131:2.2 (1444.2) "In the beginning God created the heavens and the earth and all things therein. And, behold, all he created was very good. The Lord, he is God; there is none beside him in heaven above or upon the earth beneath. Therefore shall you love the Lord your God with all your heart and with all your soul and with all your might. The earth shall be full of the knowledge of the Lord as the waters cover the sea. The heavens declare the glory of God, and the firmament shows his handiwork. Day after day utters speech; night after night shows knowledge. There is no speech or language where their voice is not heard. The Lord's work is great, and in wisdom has he made all things; the greatness of the Lord is unsearchable. He knows the number of the stars; he calls them all by their names.

131:2.3 (1444.3) "The power of the Lord is great and his understanding infinite. Says the Lord: 'As the heavens are higher than the earth, so are my ways higher than your ways, and my thoughts higher than your thoughts.' God reveals the deep and secret things because the light dwells with him. The Lord is merciful and gracious; he is long-suffering and abundant in goodness and truth. The Lord is good and upright; the meek will he guide in judgment. Taste and see that the Lord is good! Blessed is the man who trusts God. God is our refuge and strength, a very present help in trouble.

131:2.4 (1444.4) "The mercy of the Lord is from everlasting to everlasting upon those who fear him and his righteousness even to our children's children. The Lord is gracious and full of compassion. The Lord is good to all, and his tender mercies are over all his creation; he heals the brokenhearted and binds up their wounds. Whither shall I go from God's spirit? whither shall I flee from the divine presence? Thus says the High and Lofty One who inhabits eternity, whose name is Holy: 'I dwell in the high and holy place; also with him who is of a contrite heart and a humble spirit!' None can hide himself from our God, for he fills heaven and earth. Let the heavens be glad and let the earth rejoice. Let all nations say: The Lord reigns! Give thanks to God, for his mercy endures forever.

131:2.5 (1444.5) "The heavens declare God's righteousness, and all the people have seen his glory. It is God who has made us, and not we ourselves; we are his people, the sheep of his pasture. His mercy is everlasting, and his truth endures to all generations. Our God is governor among the nations. Let the earth be filled with his glory! O that men would praise the Lord for his goodness and for his wonderful gifts to the children of men!

131:2.6 (1444.6) "God has made man

a little less than divine and has crowned him with love and mercy. The Lord knows the way of the righteous, but the way of the ungodly shall perish. The fear of the Lord is the beginning of wisdom; the knowledge of the Supreme is understanding. Says the Almighty God: 'Walk before me and be perfect.' Forget not that pride goes before destruction and a haughty spirit before a fall. He who rules his own spirit is mightier than he who takes a city. Says the Lord God, the Holy One: 'In returning to your spiritual rest shall you be saved; in quietness and confidence shall be your strength.' They who wait upon the Lord shall renew their strength; they shall mount up with wings like eagles. They shall run and not be weary; they shall walk and not be faint. The Lord shall give you rest from your fear. Says the Lord: 'Fear not, for I am with you. Be not dismayed, for I am your God. I will strengthen you; I will help you; yes, I will uphold you with the right hand of my righteousness.'

131:2.7 (1445.1) "God is our Father; the Lord is our redeemer. God has created the universal hosts, and he preserves them all. His righteousness is like the mountains and his judgment like the great deep. He causes us to drink of the river of his pleasures, and in his light we shall see light. It is good to give thanks to the Lord and to sing praises to the Most High; to show forth loving-kindness in the morning and the divine faithfulness every night. God's kingdom is an everlasting kingdom, and his dominion endures throughout all generations. The Lord is my shepherd; I shall not want. He makes me to lie down in green pastures; he leads me beside still waters. He restores my soul. He leads me in the paths of righteousness. Yes, even though I walk through the valley of the shadow of death, I will fear no evil, for God is with me. Surely goodness and mercy shall follow me all the days of my life, and I shall dwell in the house of the Lord forever.

131:2.8 (1445.2) "Yahweh is the God of my salvation; therefore in the divine name will I put my trust. I will trust in the Lord with all my heart; I will lean not upon my own understanding. In all my ways I will acknowledge him, and he shall direct my paths. The Lord is faithful; he keeps his word with those who serve him; the just shall live by his faith. If you do not well, it is because sin lies at the door; men reap the evil they plough and the sin they sow. Fret not yourself because of evildoers. If you regard iniquity in your heart, the Lord will not hear you; if you sin against God, you also wrong your own soul. God will bring every man's work to judgment with every secret thing, whether it be good or evil. As a man thinks in his heart, so is he.

131:2.9 (1445.3) "The Lord is near all who call upon him in sincerity and in truth. Weeping may endure for a night, but joy comes in the morning. A merry heart does good like a medicine. No good thing will God withhold from those who walk uprightly. Fear God and keep his commandments, for this is the whole duty of man. Thus says the Lord who created the heavens and who formed the earth: 'There is no God beside me, a just God and a savior. Look to me and be saved, all the ends of the earth. If you seek me, you shall find me if you search for me with all your heart.' The meek shall inherit the earth and shall delight themselves in the abundance of peace. Whoever sows iniquity shall reap calamity; they who sow the wind shall reap the whirlwind.

131:2.10 (1445.4) "'Come now, let us reason together,' says the Lord, 'Though your sins be as scarlet, they shall be as white as snow. Though they be red like crimson, they shall be as wool.' But there is no peace for the wicked; it is your own sins which have withheld the good things from you. God is the health of my countenance and the joy of my soul. The eternal God is my strength; he is our dwelling place, and underneath are the everlasting arms. The Lord is near to those who are brokenhearted; he saves all who have a childlike spirit. Many are the afflictions of the righteous man, but the Lord delivers him out of them all. Commit your way to the Lord—trust him—and he will bring it to pass. He who dwells in the secret place

of the Most High shall abide under the shadow of the Almighty. *

131:2.11 (1445.5) "Love your neighbor as yourself; bear a grudge against no man. Whatsoever you hate do to no man. Love your brother, for the Lord has said: 'I will love my children freely.' The path of the just is as a shining light which shines more and more until the perfect day. They who are wise shall shine as the brightness of the firmament and they

who turn many to righteousness as the stars forever and ever. Let the wicked forsake his evil way and the unrighteous man his rebellious thoughts. Says the Lord: 'Let them return to me, and I will have mercy on them; I will abundantly pardon.'

131:2.12 (1446.1) "Says God, the creator of heaven and earth: 'Great peace have they who love my law. My commandments are: You shall love me with all your heart; you shall have no gods before me; you shall not take my name in vain; remember the Sabbath day to keep it holy; honor your father and mother; you shall not kill; you shall not commit adultery; you shall not steal; you shall not bear false witness; you shall not covet.'

131:2.13 (1446.2) "And to all who love the Lord supremely and their neighbors like themselves, the God of heaven says: 'I will ransom you from the grave; I will redeem you from death. I will be merciful to your children, as well as just. Have I not said of my creatures on earth, you are the sons of the living God? And have I not loved you with an everlasting love? Have I not called you to become like me and to dwell forever with me in Paradise?'"

Buddhism

131:3.1 (1446.3) Ganid was shocked to discover how near Buddhism came to being a great and beautiful religion without God, without a personal and universal Deity. However, he did find some record of certain earlier beliefs which reflected something of the influence of the teachings of the Melchizedek missionaries who continued their work in India even to the times of Buddha. Jesus and Ganid collected the following statements from the Buddhist literature:

131:3.2 (1446.4) "Out of a pure heart shall gladness spring forth to the Infinite; all my being shall be at peace with this supermortal rejoicing. My soul is filled with content, and my heart overflows with the bliss of peaceful trust. I have no fear; I am free from anxiety. I dwell in security, and my enemies cannot alarm me. I am satisfied with the fruits of my confidence. I have found the approach to the Immortal easy of access. I pray for faith to sustain me on the long journey; I know that faith from beyond will not fail me. I know my brethren will prosper if they become imbued with the faith of the Immortal, even the faith that creates modesty, uprightness, wisdom, courage, knowledge, and perseverance. Let us forsake sorrow and disown fear. By faith let us lay hold upon true righteousness and genuine manliness. Let us learn to meditate on justice and mercy. Faith is man's true wealth; it is the endowment of virtue and glory.

131:3.3 (1446.5) "Unrighteousness is contemptible; sin is despicable. Evil is degrading, whether held in thought or wrought out in deeds. Pain and sorrow follow in the path of evil as the dust follows the wind. Happiness and peace of mind follow pure thinking and virtuous living as the shadow follows the substance of material things. Evil is the fruit of wrongly directed thinking. It is evil to see sin where there is no sin; to see no sin where there is sin. Evil is the path of false doctrines. Those who avoid evil by seeing things as they are gain joy by thus embracing the truth. Make an end of your misery by loathing sin. When you look up to the Noble One, turn away from sin with a whole heart. Make no apology for evil; make no excuse for sin. By your efforts to make amends for past sins you acquire strength to resist future tendencies thereto. Restraint is born of repentance. Leave no fault unconfessed to the Noble One.

131:3.4 (1447.1) "Cheerfulness and gladness are the rewards of deeds well done and to the glory of the Immortal. No man can rob you of the liberty of your own mind. When the faith of your religion has emancipated your heart, when the mind, like a mountain, is settled and immovable, then shall the peace of the soul flow tranquilly like a river of waters. Those who are sure of salvation are forever free from lust, envy, hatred, and the delusions of wealth. While faith is the energy of the better life, nevertheless, must you work out your own salvation with perseverance. If you would be certain of your final salvation, then make sure that you sincerely seek to fulfill all righteousness. Cultivate the assurance of the heart which springs from within and thus come to enjoy the ecstasy of eternal salvation.

131:3.5 (1447.2) "No religionist may hope to attain the enlightenment of immortal wisdom who persists in being slothful, indolent, feeble, idle, shameless, and selfish. But whoso is thoughtful, prudent, reflective, fervent, and earnest—even while he yet lives on earth—may attain the supreme enlightenment of the peace and liberty of divine wisdom.

Remember, every act shall receive its reward. Evil results in sorrow and sin ends in pain. Joy and happiness are the outcome of a good life. Even the evildoer enjoys a season of grace before the time of the full ripening of his evil deeds, but inevitably there must come the full harvest of evil-doing. Let no man think lightly of sin, saying in his heart: 'The penalty of wrongdoing shall not come near me.' What you do shall be done to you, in the judgment of wisdom. Injustice done to your fellows shall come back upon you. The creature cannot escape the destiny of his deeds.

131:3.6 (1447.3) "The fool has said in his heart, 'Evil shall not overtake me'; but safety is found only when the soul craves reproof and the mind seeks wisdom. The wise man is a noble soul who is friendly in the midst of his enemies, tranquil among the turbulent, and generous among the grasping. Love of self is like weeds in a goodly field. Selfishness leads to grief; perpetual care kills. The tamed mind yields happiness. He is the greatest of warriors who overcomes and subdues himself. Restraint in all things is good. He alone is a superior person who esteems virtue and is observant of his duty.

Let not anger and hate master you. Speak harshly of no one. Contentment is the greatest wealth. What is given wisely is well saved. Do not to others those things you would not wish done to you. Pay good for evil; overcome evil with the good.

131:3.7 (1447.4) "A righteous soul is more to be desired than the sovereignty of all the earth. Immortality is the goal of sincerity; death, the end of thoughtless living. Those who are earnest die not; the thoughtless are dead already. Blessed are they who have insight into the deathless state. Those who torture the living will hardly find happiness after death. The unselfish go to heaven, where they rejoice in the bliss of infinite liberality and continue to increase in noble generosity. Every mortal who thinks righteously, speaks nobly, and acts unselfishly shall not only enjoy virtue here during this brief life but shall also, after the dissolution of the body, continue to enjoy the delights of heaven."

Hinduism

131:4.1 (1447.5) The missionaries of Melchizedek carried the teachings of the one God with them wherever they journeyed. Much of this monotheistic doctrine, together with other and previous concepts, became embodied in the subsequent teachings of Hinduism. Jesus and Ganid made the following excerpts:

131:4.2 (1448.1) "He is the great God, in every way supreme. He is the Lord who encompasses all things. He is the creator and controller of the universe of universes. God is one God; he is alone and by himself; he is the only one. And this one God is our Maker and the last destiny of the soul. The Supreme One is brilliant beyond description; he is the Light of Lights. Every heart and every world is illuminated by this divine light. God is our protector—he stands by the side of his creatures—and those who learn to know him become immortal. God is the great source of energy; he is the Great Soul. He exercises universal lordship over all. This one God is loving, glorious, and adorable. Our God is supreme in power and abides in the supreme abode. This true Person is eternal and divine; he is the primal Lord of heaven. All the prophets have hailed him, and he has revealed himself to us. We worship him. O Supreme Person, source of beings, Lord of creation, and ruler of the universe, reveal to us, your creatures, the power whereby you abide immanent! God has made the sun and the stars; he is bright, pure, and self-existent. His eternal knowledge is divinely wise. The Eternal is unpenetrated by evil. Inasmuch as the universe sprang from God, he does rule it appropriately. He is the cause of creation, and hence are all things established in him.

131:4.3 (1448.2) "God is the sure refuge of every good man when in need; the Immortal One cares for all mankind. God's salvation is strong and his kindness is gracious. He is a loving protector, a blessed defender. Says the Lord: 'I dwell within their own souls as a lamp of wisdom. I am the splendor of the splendid and the goodness of the good. Where two or three gather together, there am I also.' The creature cannot escape the presence of the Creator. The Lord even counts the ceaseless winking of every mortal's eyes; and we worship this divine Being as our inseparable companion. He is all-prevailing, bountiful, omnipresent, and infinitely kind. The Lord is our ruler, shelter, and supreme controller, and his primeval spirit dwells within the mortal soul. The Eternal Witness to vice and virtue dwells within man's heart. Let us long meditate on the adorable and divine Vivifier; let his spirit fully direct our thoughts. From this unreal world lead us to the real! From darkness lead us to the light! From death guide us to immortality!

131:4.4 (1448.3) "With our hearts purged of all hate, let us worship the Eternal. Our God is the Lord of prayer; he hears the cry of his children. Let all men submit their wills to him, the Resolute. Let us delight in the liberality of the Lord of prayer. Make prayer your inmost friend and worship your soul's support. 'If you will but worship me in love,' says the Eternal, 'I will give you the wisdom to attain me, for my worship is the virtue common to all creatures.' God is the illuminator of the gloomy and the power of those who are faint. Since God is our strong friend, we have no more fear. We praise the name of the never-conquered Conqueror. We worship him because he is man's faithful and eternal helper. God is our sure leader and unfailing guide. He is the great parent of heaven and earth, possessed of unlimited energy and infinite wisdom. His splendor is sublime and his beauty divine. He is the supreme refuge of the universe and the changeless guardian of everlasting law. Our God is the Lord of life and the Comforter of all men; he is the lover of mankind and the helper of those who are distressed. He is our life giver and the Good Shepherd of the human flocks.

God is our father, brother, and friend. And we long to know this God in our inner being.

131:4.5 (1448.4) "We have learned to win faith by the yearning of our hearts. We have attained wisdom by the restraint of our senses, and by wisdom we have experienced peace in the Supreme. He who is full of faith worships truly when his inner self is intent upon God. Our God wears the heavens as a mantle; he also inhabits the other six wide-spreading universes. He is supreme over all and in all. We crave forgiveness from the Lord for all of our trespasses against our fellows; and we would release our friend from the wrong he has done us. Our spirit loathes all evil; therefore, O Lord, free us from all taint of sin. We pray to God as a comforter, protector, and savior—one who loves us.

131:4.6 (1449.1) "The spirit of the Universe Keeper enters the soul of the simple creature. That man is wise who worships the One God. Those who strive for perfection must indeed know the Lord Supreme. He never fears who knows the blissful security of the Supreme, for the Supreme says to those who serve him, 'Fear not, for I am with you.' The God of providence is our Father. God is truth. And it is the desire of God that his creatures should understand him—come fully to know the truth. Truth is eternal; it sustains the universe. Our supreme desire shall be union with the Supreme. The Great Controller is the generator of all things—all evolves from him. And this is the sum of duty: Let no man do to another what would be repugnant to himself; cherish no malice, smite not him who smites you, conquer anger with mercy, and vanquish hate by benevolence. And all this we should do because God is a kind friend and a gracious father who remits all our earthly offenses.

131:4.7 (1449.2) "God is our Father, the earth our mother, and the universe our birthplace. Without God the soul is a prisoner; to know God releases the soul. By meditation on God, by union with him, there comes deliverance from the illusions of evil and ultimate salvation from all material fetters. When man shall roll up space as a piece of leather, then will come the end of evil because man has found God. O God, save us from the threefold ruin of hell—lust, wrath, and avarice! O soul, gird yourself for the spirit struggle of immortality! When the end of mortal life comes, hesitate not to forsake this body for a more fit and beautiful form and to awake in the realms of the Supreme and Immortal, where there is no fear, sorrow, hunger, thirst, or death. To know God is to cut the cords of death. The God-knowing soul rises in the universe like the cream appears on top of the milk. We worship God, the all-worker, the Great Soul, who is ever seated in the heart of his creatures. And they who know that God is enthroned in the human heart are destined to become like him—immortal. Evil must be left behind in this world, but virtue follows the soul to heaven.

131:4.8 (1449.3) "It is only the wicked

who say: The universe has neither truth nor a ruler; it was only designed for our lusts. Such souls are deluded by the smallness of their intellects. They thus abandon themselves to the enjoyment of their lusts and deprive their souls of the joys of virtue and the pleasures of righteousness. What can be greater than to experience salvation from sin? The man who has seen the Supreme is immortal. Man's friends of the flesh cannot survive death; virtue alone walks by man's side as he journeys ever onward toward the gladsome and sunlit fields of Paradise."

Zoroastrianism

131:5.1 (1449.4) Zoroaster was himself directly in contact with the descendants of the earlier Melchizedek missionaries, and their doctrine of the one God became a central teaching in the religion which he founded in Persia. Aside from Judaism, no religion of that day contained more of these Salem teachings. From the records of this religion Ganid made the following excerpts:

131:5.2 (1450.1) "All things come from, and belong to, the One God—all-wise, good, righteous, holy, resplendent, and glorious. This, our God, is the source of all luminosity. He is the Creator, the God of all good purposes, and the protector of the justice of the universe. The wise course in life is to act in consonance with the spirit of truth. God is all- seeing, and he beholds both the evil deeds of the wicked and the good works of the righteous; our God observes all things with a flashing eye. His touch is the touch of healing. The Lord is an all-powerful benefactor. God stretches out his beneficent hand to both the righteous and the wicked. God established the world and ordained the rewards for good and for evil. The all-wise God has promised immortality to the pious souls who think purely and act righteously. As you supremely desire, so shall you be. The light of the sun is as wisdom to those who discern God in the universe.

131:5.3 (1450.2) "Praise God by seeking the pleasure of the Wise One. Worship the God of light by joyfully walking in the paths ordained by his revealed religion. There is but one Supreme God, the Lord of Lights. We worship him who made the waters, plants, animals, the earth, and the heavens. Our God is Lord, most beneficent. We worship the most beauteous, the bountiful Immortal, endowed with eternal light. God is farthest from us and at the same time nearest to us in that he dwells within our souls. Our God is the divine and holiest Spirit of Paradise, and yet he is more friendly to man than the most friendly of all creatures. God is most helpful to us in this greatest of all businesses, the knowing of himself. God is our most adorable and righteous friend; he is our wisdom, life, and vigor of soul and body. Through our good thinking the wise Creator will enable us to do his will, thereby attaining the realization of all that is divinely perfect.

131:5.4 (1450.3) "Lord, teach us how to live this life in the flesh while preparing for the next life of the spirit. Speak to us, Lord, and we will do your bidding. Teach us the good paths, and we will go right. Grant us that we may attain union with you. We know that the religion is right which leads to union with righteousness. God is our wise nature, best thought, and righteous act. May God grant us unity with the divine spirit and immortality in himself!

131:5.5 (1450.4) "This religion of the Wise One cleanses the believer from every evil thought and sinful deed. I bow before the God of heaven in repentance if I have offended in thought, word, or act—intentionally or unintentionally—and I offer prayers for mercy and praise for forgiveness. I know when I make confession, if I purpose not to do again the evil thing, that sin will be removed from my soul. I know that forgiveness takes away the bonds of sin. Those who do evil shall receive punishment, but those who follow truth shall enjoy the bliss of an eternal salvation. Through grace lay hold upon us and minister saving power to our souls. We claim mercy because we aspire to attain perfection; we would be like God."

Suduanism (Jainism)

131:6.1 (1450.5) The third group of religious believers who preserved the doctrine of one God in India—the survival of the Melchizedek teaching—were known in those days as the Suduanists. Latterly these believers have become known as followers of Jainism. They taught:

131:6.2 (1450.6) "The Lord of Heaven is supreme. Those who commit sin will not ascend on high, but those who walk in the paths of righteousness shall find a place in heaven. We are assured of the life hereafter if we know truth. The soul of man may ascend to the highest heaven, there to develop its true spiritual nature, to attain perfection. The estate of heaven delivers man from the bondage of sin and introduces him to the final beatitudes; the righteous man has already experienced an end of sin and all its associated miseries. Self is man's invincible foe, and self is manifested as man's four greatest passions: anger, pride, deceit, and greed. Man's greatest victory is the conquest of himself. When man looks to God for forgiveness, and when he makes bold to enjoy such liberty, he is thereby delivered from fear. Man should journey through life treating his fellow creatures as he would like to be treated."

Shinto

131:7.1 (1451.1) Only recently had the manuscripts of this Far-Eastern religion been lodged in the Alexandrian library. It was the one world religion of which Ganid had never heard. This belief also contained remnants of the earlier Melchizedek teachings as is shown by the following abstracts:

131:7.2 (1451.2) "Says the Lord: 'You are all recipients of my divine power; all men enjoy my ministry of mercy. I derive
great pleasure in the multiplication of righteous men throughout the land. In both the beauties of nature and the virtues of men does the Prince of Heaven seek to reveal himself and to show forth his righteous nature. Since the olden people did not know my name, I manifested myself by being born into the world as a visible existence and endured such abasement even that man should not forget my name. I am the maker of heaven and earth; the sun and the moon and all the stars obey my will. I am the ruler of all creatures on land and in the four seas. Although I am great and supreme, still I have regard for the prayer of the poorest man. If any creature will worship me, I will hear his prayer and grant the desire of his heart.'

131:7.3 (1451.3) "'Every time man yields to anxiety, he takes one step away from the leading of the spirit of his heart.' Pride obscures God. If you would obtain heavenly help, put away your pride; every hair of pride shuts off saving light, as it were, by a great cloud. If you are not right on the inside, it is useless to pray for that which is on the outside. 'If I hear your prayers, it is because you come before me with a clean heart, free from falsehood and hypocrisy, with a soul which reflects truth like a mirror. If you would gain immortality, forsake the world and come to me.'"

Taoism

131:8.1 (1451.4) The messengers of Melchizedek penetrated far into China, and the doctrine of one God became a part of the earlier teachings of several Chinese religions; the one persisting the longest and containing most of the monotheistic truth was Taoism, and Ganid collected the following from the teachings of its founder:

131:8.2 (1451.5) "How pure and tranquil is the Supreme One and yet how powerful and mighty, how deep and unfathomable! This God of heaven is the honored ancestor of all things. If you know the Eternal, you are enlightened and wise. If you know not the Eternal, then does ignorance manifest itself as evil, and thus do the passions of sin arise. This wondrous Being existed before the heavens and the earth were. He is truly spiritual; he stands alone and changes not. He is indeed the world's mother, and all creation moves around him. This Great One imparts himself to men and thereby enables them to excel and to survive. Even if one has but a little knowledge, he can still walk in the ways of the Supreme; he can conform to the will of heaven.

131:8.3 (1452.1) "All good works of true service come from the Supreme. All things depend on the Great Source for life. The Great Supreme seeks no credit for his bestowals. He is supreme in power, yet he remains hidden from our gaze. He unceasingly transmutes his attributes while perfecting his creatures. The heavenly Reason is slow and patient in his designs but sure of his accomplishments. The Supreme overspreads the universe and sustains it all. How great and mighty are his overflowing influence and drawing power! True goodness is like water in that it blesses everything and harms nothing. And like water, true goodness seeks the lowest places, even those levels which others avoid, and that is because it is akin to the Supreme. The Supreme creates all things, in nature nourishing them and in spirit perfecting them. And it is a mystery how the Supreme fosters, protects, and perfects the creature without compelling him. He guides and directs, but without self-assertion. He ministers progression, but without domination.

131:8.4 (1452.2) "The wise man universalizes his heart. A little knowledge is a dangerous thing. Those who aspire to greatness must learn to humble themselves. In creation the Supreme became the world's mother. To know one's mother is to recognize one's sonship. He is a wise man who regards all parts from the point of view of the whole. Relate yourself to every man as if you were in his place. Recompense injury with kindness. If you love people, they will draw near you—you will have no difficulty in winning them.

131:8.5 (1452.3) "The Great Supreme is all-pervading; he is on the left hand and on the right; he supports all creation and indwells all true beings. You cannot find the Supreme, neither can you go to a place

where he is not. If a man recognizes the evil of his ways and repents of sin from the heart, then may he seek forgiveness; he may escape the penalty; he may change calamity into blessing. The Supreme is the secure refuge for all creation; he is the guardian and savior of mankind. If you seek for him daily, you shall find him. Since he can forgive sins, he is indeed most precious to all men. Always remember that God does not reward man for what he does but for what he is; therefore should you extend help to your fellows without the thought of rewards. Do good without thought of benefit to the self.

131:8.6 (1452.4) "They who know the laws of the Eternal are wise. Ignorance of the divine law is misery and disaster.

They who know the laws of God are liberal minded. If you know the Eternal, even though your body perish, your soul shall survive in spirit service. You are truly wise when you recognize your insignificance. If you abide in the light of the Eternal, you shall enjoy the enlightenment of the Supreme. Those who dedicate their persons to the service of the Supreme are joyous in this pursuit of the Eternal. When man dies, the spirit begins to wing its long flight on the great home journey."

Confucianism

131:9.1 (1452.5) Even the least God-recognizing of the world's great religions acknowledged the monotheism of the Melchizedek missionaries and their persistent successors. Ganid's summary of Confucianism was:

131:9.2 (1452.6) "What Heaven appoints is without error. Truth is real and divine. Everything originates in Heaven, and the Great Heaven makes no mistakes. Heaven has appointed many subordinates to assist in the instruction and uplifting of the inferior creatures. Great, very great, is the One God who rules man from on high. God is majestic in power and awful in judgment. But this Great God has conferred a moral sense even on many inferior people.

Heaven's bounty never stops. Benevolence is Heaven's choicest gift to men. Heaven has bestowed its nobility upon the soul of man; the virtues of man are the fruit of this endowment of Heaven's nobility. The Great Heaven is all-discerning and goes with man in all his doings. And we do well when we call the Great Heaven our Father and our Mother. If we are thus servants of our divine ancestors, then may we in confidence pray to Heaven. At all times and in everything let us stand in awe of the majesty of Heaven. We acknowledge, O God, the Most High and sovereign Potentate, that judgment rests with you, and that all mercy proceeds from the divine heart.

131:9.3 (1453.1) "God is with us; therefore we have no fear in our hearts. If there be found any virtue in me, it is the manifestation of Heaven who abides with me. But this Heaven within me often makes hard demands on my faith. If God is with me, I have determined to have no doubt in my heart. Faith must be very near the truth of things, and I do not see how a man can live without this good faith. Good and evil do not befall men without cause. Heaven deals with man's soul in accordance with its purpose. When you find yourself in the wrong, do not hesitate to confess your error and be quick to make amends.

131:9.4 (1453.2) "A wise man is occupied with the search for truth, not in seeking for a mere living. To attain the perfection of Heaven is the goal of man. The superior man is given to self-adjustment, and he is free from anxiety and fear. God is with you; have no doubt in your heart. Every good deed has its recompense. The superior man murmurs not against Heaven nor holds a grudge against men. What you do not like when done to yourself, do not to others. Let compassion be a part of all punishment; in every way endeavor to make punishment a blessing. Such is the way of Great Heaven. While all creatures must die and return to the earth, the spirit of the noble man goes forth to be displayed on high and to ascend to the glorious light of final brightness."

"Our Religion"

131:10.1 (1453.3) After the arduous labor of effecting this compilation of the teachings of the world religions concerning the Paradise Father, Ganid set himself to the task of formulating what he deemed to be a summary of the belief he had arrived at regarding God as a result of Jesus' teaching. This young man was in the habit of referring to such beliefs as "our religion." This was his record:

131:10.2 (1453.4) "The Lord our God is one Lord, and you should love him with all your mind and heart while you do your very best to love all his children as you love yourself. This one God is our heavenly Father, in whom all things consist, and who dwells, by his spirit, in every sincere human soul. And we who are the children of God should learn how to commit the keeping of our souls to him as to a faithful Creator. With our heavenly Father all things are possible. Since he is the Creator, having made all things and all beings, it could not be otherwise. Though we cannot see God, we can know him. And by daily living the will of the Father in heaven, we can reveal him to our fellow men.

131:10.3 (1453.5) "The divine riches of God's character must be infinitely deep and eternally wise. We cannot search out God by knowledge, but we can know him in our hearts by personal experience. While his justice may be past finding out, his mercy may be received by the humblest being on earth. While the Father fills the universe, he also lives in our hearts. The mind of man is human, mortal, but the spirit of man is divine, immortal. God is not only all-powerful but also all-wise. If our earth parents, being of evil tendency, know how to love their children and bestow good gifts on them, how much more must the good Father in heaven know how wisely to love his children on earth and to bestow suitable blessings upon them.

131:10.4 (1454.1) "The Father in heaven will not suffer a single child on earth to perish if that child has a desire to find the Father and truly longs to be like him. Our Father even loves the wicked and is always kind to the ungrateful. If more human beings could only know about the goodness of God, they would certainly be led to repent of their evil ways and forsake all known sin. All good things come down from the Father of light, in whom there is no variableness neither shadow of changing. The spirit of the true God is in man's heart. He intends that all men should be brothers. When men begin to feel after God, that is evidence that God has found them, and that they are in quest of knowledge about him.

We live in God and God dwells in us.

131:10.5 (1454.2) "I will no longer be satisfied to believe that God is the Father of all my people; I will henceforth believe that he is also my Father. Always will I try to worship God with the help of the Spirit of Truth, which is my helper when I have become really God-knowing. But first of all I am going to practice worshiping God by learning how to do the will of God on earth; that is, I am going to do my best to treat each of my fellow mortals just as I think God would like to have him treated. And when we live this sort of a life in the flesh, we may ask many things of God, and he will give us the desire of our hearts that we may be the better prepared to serve our fellows. And all of this loving service of the children of God enlarges our capacity to receive and experience the joys of heaven, the high pleasures of the ministry of the spirit of heaven.

131:10.6 (1454.3) "I will every day thank God for his unspeakable gifts; I will praise him for his wonderful works to the children of men. To me he is the Almighty, the Creator, the Power, and the Mercy, but best of all, he is my spirit Father, and as his earth child I am sometime going forth to see him. And my tutor has said that by searching for him I shall become like him. By faith in God I have attained peace with him. This new religion of ours is very full of joy, and it generates an enduring happiness. I am confident that I shall be faithful even to death, and that I will surely receive the crown of eternal life.

131:10.7 (1454.4) "I am learning to prove all things and adhere to that which is good. Whatsoever I would that men should do to me, that I will do to my fellows. By this new faith I know that man may become the son of God, but it sometimes terrifies me when I stop to think that all men are my brothers, but it must be true. I do not see how I can rejoice in the fatherhood of God while I refuse to accept the brotherhood of man. Whosoever calls upon the name of the Lord shall be saved. If that is true, then all men must be my brothers.

131:10.8 (1454.5) "Henceforth will I do my good deeds in secret; I will also pray most when by myself. I will judge not that I may not be unfair to my fellows. I am going to learn to love my enemies; I have not truly mastered this practice of being Godlike. Though I see God in these other religions, I find him in 'our religion' as being more beautiful, loving, merciful, personal, and positive. But most of all, this great and glorious Being is my spiritual Father; I am his child. And by no other means than my honest desire to be like him, I am eventually to find him and eternally to serve him. At last I have a religion with a God, a marvelous God, and he is a God of eternal salvation."

Paper 132

The Sojourn at Rome

132:0.1 (1455.1) SINCE Gonod carried greetings from the princes of India to Tiberius, the Roman ruler, on the third day after their arrival in Rome the two Indians and Jesus appeared before him. The morose emperor was unusually cheerful on this day and chatted long with the trio. And when they had gone from his presence, the emperor, referring to Jesus, remarked to the aide standing on his right, "If I had that fellow's kingly bearing and gracious manner, I would be a real emperor, eh?"

132:0.2 (1455.2) While at Rome, Ganid had regular hours for study and for visiting places of interest about the city. His father had much business to transact, and desiring that his son grow up to become a worthy successor in the management of his vast commercial interests, he thought the time had come to introduce the boy to the business world. There were many citizens of India in Rome, and often one of Gonod's own employees would accompany him as interpreter so that Jesus would have whole days to himself; this gave him time in which to become thoroughly acquainted with this city of two million inhabitants. He was frequently to be found in the forum, the center of political, legal, and business life. He often went up to the Capitolium and pondered the bondage of ignorance in which these Romans were held as he beheld this magnificent temple dedicated to Jupiter, Juno, and Minerva. He also spent much time on Palatine hill, where were located the emperor's residence, the temple of Apollo, and the Greek and Latin libraries.

132:0.3 (1455.3) At this time the Roman Empire included all of southern Europe, Asia Minor, Syria, Egypt, and northwest Africa; and its inhabitants embraced the citizens of every country of the Eastern Hemisphere. His desire to study and mingle with this cosmopolitan aggregation of Urantia mortals was the chief reason why Jesus consented to make this journey.

132:0.4 (1455.4) Jesus learned much about men while in Rome, but the most valuable of all the manifold experiences of his six months' sojourn in that city was his contact with, and influence upon, the religious leaders of the empire's capital.

Before the end of the first week in Rome Jesus had sought out, and had made the acquaintance of, the worth-while leaders of the Cynics, the Stoics, and the mystery cults, in particular the Mithraic group. Whether or not it was apparent to Jesus that the Jews were going to reject his mission, he most certainly foresaw that his mes-

sengers were presently coming to Rome to proclaim the kingdom of heaven; and he therefore set about, in the most amazing manner, to prepare the way for the better and more certain reception of their message. He selected five of the leading Stoics, eleven of the Cynics, and sixteen of the mystery-cult leaders and spent much of his spare time for almost six months in intimate association with these religious teachers. And this was his method of instruction: Never once did he attack their errors or even mention the flaws in their teachings. In each case he would select the truth in what they taught and then proceed so to embellish and illuminate this truth in their minds that in a very short time this enhancement of the truth effectively crowded out the associated error; and thus were these Jesus-taught men and women prepared for the subsequent recognition of additional and similar truths in the teachings of the early Christian missionaries. It was this early acceptance of the teachings of the gospel preachers which gave that powerful impetus to the rapid spread of Christianity in Rome and from there throughout the empire.

132:0.5 (1456.1) The significance of this remarkable doing can the better be understood when we record the fact that, out of this group of thirty-two Jesus-taught religious leaders in Rome, only two were unfruitful; the thirty became pivotal individuals in the establishment of Christianity in Rome, and certain of them also aided in turning the chief Mithraic temple into the first Christian church of that city. We who view human activities from behind the scenes and in the light of nineteen centuries of time recognize just three factors of paramount value in the early setting of the stage for the rapid spread of Christianity throughout Europe, and they are:

132:0.6 (1456.2) 1. The choosing and holding of Simon Peter as an apostle.

132:0.7 (1456.3) 2. The talk in Jerusalem with Stephen, whose death led to the winning of Saul of Tarsus.

132:0.8 (1456.4) 3. The preliminary preparation of these thirty Romans for the subsequent leadership of the new religion in Rome and throughout the empire.

132:0.9 (1456.5) Through all their experiences, neither Stephen nor the thirty chosen ones ever realized that they had once talked with the man whose name became the subject of their religious teaching. Jesus' work in behalf of the original thirty-two was entirely personal. In his labors for these individuals the scribe of Damascus never met more than three of them at one time, seldom more than two, while most often he taught them singly. And he could do this great work of religious training because these men and women were not tradition bound; they were not victims of a settled preconception as to all future religious developments.

132:0.10 (1456.6) Many were the times in the years so soon to follow that Peter, Paul, and the other Christian teachers in Rome heard about this scribe of Damascus who had preceded them, and who had so obviously (and as they supposed unwittingly) prepared the way for their coming with the new gospel. Though Paul never really surmised the identity of this scribe of Damascus, he did, a short time before his death, because of the similarity of personal descriptions, reach the conclusion that the "tentmaker of Antioch" was also the "scribe of Damascus." On one occasion, while preaching in Rome, Simon Peter, on listening to a description of the Damascus scribe, surmised that this individual might have been Jesus but quickly dismissed the idea, knowing full well (so he thought) that the Master had never been in Rome.

True Values

132:1.1 (1456.7) It was with Angamon, the leader of the Stoics, that Jesus had an all-night talk early during his sojourn in Rome. This man subsequently became a great friend of Paul and proved to be one of the strong supporters of the Christian church at Rome. In substance, and restated in modern phraseology, Jesus taught Angamon:

132:1.2 (1457.1) The standard of true values must be looked for in the spiritual world and on divine levels of eternal reality. To an ascending mortal all lower and material standards must be recognized as transient, partial, and inferior. The scientist, as such, is limited to the discovery of the relatedness of material facts. Technically, he has no right to assert that he is either materialist or idealist, for in so doing he has assumed to forsake the attitude of a true scientist since any and all such assertions of attitude are the very essence of philosophy.

132:1.3 (1457.2) Unless the moral insight and the spiritual attainment of mankind are proportionately augmented, the unlimited advancement of a purely materialistic culture may eventually become a menace to civilization. A purely materialistic science harbors within itself the potential seed of the destruction of all scientific striving, for this very attitude presages the ultimate collapse of a civilization which has abandoned its sense of moral values and has repudiated its spiritual goal of attainment.

132:1.4 (1457.3) The materialistic scientist and the extreme idealist are destined always to be at loggerheads. This is not true of those scientists and idealists who are in possession of a common standard of high moral values and spiritual test levels. In every age scientists and religionists must recognize that they are on trial before the bar of human need. They must eschew all warfare between themselves while they strive valiantly to justify their continued survival by enhanced devotion to the service of human progress. If the so-called science or religion of any age is false, then must it either purify its activities or pass away before the emergence of a material science or spiritual religion of a truer and more worthy order.

Good and Evil

132:2.1 (1457.4) Mardus was the acknowledged leader of the Cynics of Rome, and he became a great friend of the scribe of Damascus. Day after day he conversed with Jesus, and night upon night he listened to his supernal teaching. Among the more important discussions with Mardus was the one designed to answer this sincere Cynic's question about good and evil. In substance, and in twentieth-century phraseology, Jesus said:

132:2.2 (1457.5) My brother, good and evil are merely words symbolizing relative levels of human comprehension of the observable universe. If you are ethically lazy and socially indifferent, you can take as your standard of good the current social usages. If you are spiritually indolent and morally unprogressive, you may take as your standards of good the religious practices and traditions of your contemporaries. But the soul that survives time and emerges into eternity must make a living and personal choice between good and evil as they are determined by the true values of the spiritual standards established by the divine spirit which the Father in heaven has sent to dwell within the heart of man. This indwelling spirit is the standard of personality survival.

132:2.3 (1457.6) Goodness, like truth, is always relative and unfailingly evil-contrasted. It is the perception of these qualities of goodness and truth that enables the evolving souls of men to make those personal decisions of choice which are essential to eternal survival.

132:2.4 (1458.1) The spiritually blind individual who logically follows scientific dictation, social usage, and religious dogma stands in grave danger of sacrificing his moral freedom and losing his spiritual liberty. Such a soul is destined to become an intellectual parrot, a social automaton, and a slave to religious authority.

132:2.5 (1458.2) Goodness is always growing toward new levels of the increasing liberty of moral self-realization and spiritual personality attainment—the discovery of, and identification with, the indwelling Adjuster. An experience is good when it heightens the appreciation of beauty, augments the moral will, enhances the discernment of truth, enlarges the capacity to love and serve one's fellows, exalts the spiritual ideals, and unifies the supreme human motives of time with the eternal plans of the indwelling Adjuster, all of which lead directly to an increased desire to do the Father's will, thereby fostering the divine passion to find God and to be more like him.

132:2.6 (1458.3) As you ascend the universe scale of creature development, you will find increasing goodness and diminishing evil in perfect accordance with your capacity for goodness-experience and truth-discernment. The ability to entertain error or experience evil will not be fully lost until the ascending human soul achieves final spirit levels.

132:2.7 (1458.4) Goodness is living, relative, always progressing, invariably a personal experience, and everlastingly correlated with the discernment of truth and beauty. Goodness is found in the recognition of the positive truth-values of the spiritual level, which must, in human experience, be contrasted with the negative counterpart—the shadows of potential evil.

132:2.8 (1458.5) Until you attain Paradise levels, goodness will always be more of a quest than a possession, more of a goal than an experience of attainment. But even as you hunger and thirst for righteousness, you experience increasing satisfaction in the partial attainment of goodness. The presence of goodness and evil in the world is in itself positive proof of the existence and reality of man's moral will, the personality, which thus identifies these values and is also able to choose between them.

132:2.9 (1458.6) By the time of the attainment of Paradise the ascending mortal's capacity for identifying the self with true spirit values has become so enlarged as to result in the attainment of the perfection of the possession of the light of life. Such a perfected spirit personality becomes so wholly, divinely, and spiritually unified with the positive and supreme qualities of goodness, beauty, and truth that there remains no possibility that such a righteous spirit would cast any negative shadow of potential evil when exposed to the searching luminosity of the divine light of the infinite Rulers of Paradise. In all such spirit personalities, goodness is no longer partial, contrastive, and comparative; it has become divinely complete and spiritually replete; it approaches the purity and perfection of the Supreme.

132:2.10 (1458.7) The possibility of evil is necessary to moral choosing, but not the actuality thereof. A shadow is only relatively real. Actual evil is not necessary as a personal experience. Potential evil acts equally well as a decision stimulus in the realms of moral progress on the lower levels of spiritual development. Evil becomes a reality of personal experience only when a moral mind makes evil its choice.

Truth and Faith

132:3.1 (1459.1) Nabon was a Greek Jew and foremost among the leaders of the chief mystery cult in Rome, the Mithraic. While this high priest of Mithraism held many conferences with the Damascus scribe, he was most permanently influenced by their discussion of truth and faith one evening. Nabon had thought to make a convert of Jesus and had even suggested that he return to Palestine as a Mithraic teacher. He little realized that Jesus was preparing him to become one of the early converts to the gospel of the kingdom. Restated in modern phraseology, the substance of Jesus' teaching was:

132:3.2 (1459.2) Truth cannot be defined with words, only by living. Truth is always more than knowledge. Knowledge pertains to things observed, but truth transcends such purely material levels in that it consorts with wisdom and embraces such imponderables as human experience, even spiritual and living realities. Knowledge originates in science; wisdom, in true philosophy; truth, in the religious experience of spiritual living. Knowledge deals with facts; wisdom, with relationships; truth, with reality values.

132:3.3 (1459.3) Man tends to crystallize science, formulate philosophy, and dogmatize truth because he is mentally lazy in adjusting to the progressive struggles of living, while he is also terribly afraid of the unknown. Natural man is slow to initiate changes in his habits of thinking and in his techniques of living.

132:3.4 (1459.4) Revealed truth, personally discovered truth, is the supreme delight of the human soul; it is the joint creation of the material mind and the indwelling spirit. The eternal salvation of this truth-discerning and beauty-loving soul is assured by that hunger and thirst for goodness which leads this mortal to develop a singleness of purpose to do the Father's will, to find God and to become like him. There is never conflict between true knowledge and truth. There may be conflict between knowledge and human beliefs, beliefs colored with prejudice, distorted by fear, and dominated by the dread of facing new facts of material discovery or spiritual progress.

132:3.5 (1459.5) But truth can never become man's possession without the exercise of faith. This is true because man's thoughts, wisdom, ethics, and ideals will never rise higher than his faith, his sublime hope. And all such true faith is predicated on profound reflection, sincere self-criticism, and uncompromising moral consciousness. Faith is the inspiration of the spiritized creative imagination.

132:3.6 (1459.6) Faith acts to release the superhuman activities of the divine spark, the immortal germ, that lives within the mind of man, and which is the potential of eternal survival. Plants and animals survive in time by the technique of passing on from one generation to another identical particles of themselves. The human soul (personality) of man survives mortal death by identity association with this indwelling spark of divinity, which is immortal, and which functions to perpetuate the human personality upon a continuing and higher level of progressive universe existence. The concealed seed of the human soul is an immortal spirit. The second generation of the soul is the first of a succession of personality manifestations of spiritual and progressing existences, terminating only when this divine entity attains the source of its existence, the personal source of all existence, God, the Universal Father.

132:3.7 (1459.7) Human life continues—survives—because it has a universe function, the task of finding God. The faith-activated soul of man cannot stop short of the attainment of this goal of destiny; and when it does once achieve this divine goal, it can never end because it has become like God—eternal.

132:3.8 (1460.1) Spiritual evolution is an experience of the increasing and voluntary choice of goodness attended by an equal and progressive diminution of the possibility of evil. With the attainment of finality of choice for goodness and of completed capacity for truth appreciation, there comes into existence a perfection of beauty and holiness whose righteousness eternally inhibits the possibility of the emergence of even the concept of potential evil. Such a God- knowing soul casts no shadow of doubting evil when functioning on such a high spirit level of divine goodness.

132:3.9 (1460.2) The presence of the Paradise spirit in the mind of man constitutes the revelation promise and the faith pledge of an eternal existence of divine progression for every soul seeking to achieve identity with this immortal and indwelling spirit fragment of the Universal Father.

132:3.10 (1460.3) Universe progress is characterized by increasing personality freedom because it is associated with the progressive attainment of higher and higher levels of self-understanding and consequent voluntary self-restraint. The attainment of perfection of spiritual self-restraint equals completeness of universe freedom and personal liberty. Faith fosters and maintains man's soul in the midst of the confusion of his early orientation in such a vast universe, whereas prayer becomes the great unifier of the various inspirations of the creative imagination and the faith urges of a soul trying to identify itself with the spirit ideals of the indwelling and associated divine presence.

132:3.11 (1460.4) Nabon was greatly impressed by these words, as he was by each of his talks with Jesus. These truths continued to burn within his heart, and he was of great assistance to the later arriving preachers of Jesus' gospel.

Personal Ministry

132:4.1 (1460.5) Jesus did not devote all his leisure while in Rome to this work of preparing men and women to become future disciples in the oncoming kingdom. He spent much time gaining an intimate knowledge of all races and classes of men who lived in this, the largest and most cosmopolitan city of the world. In each of these numerous human contacts Jesus had a double purpose: He desired to learn their reactions to the life they were living in the flesh, and he was also minded to say or do something to make that life richer and more worth while. His religious teachings during these weeks were no different than those which characterized his later life as teacher of the twelve and preacher to the multitudes.

132:4.2 (1460.6) Always the burden of his message was: the fact of the heavenly Father's love and the truth of his mercy, coupled with the good news that man is a faith-son of this same God of love. Jesus' usual technique of social contact was to draw people out and into talking with him by asking them questions. The interview would usually begin by his asking them questions and end by their asking him questions. He was equally adept in teaching by either asking or answering questions. As a rule, to those he taught the most, he said the least. Those who derived most benefit from his personal ministry were overburdened, anxious, and dejected mortals who gained much relief because of the opportunity to unburden their souls to a sympathetic and understanding listener, and he was all that and more. And when these maladjusted human beings had told Jesus about their troubles, always was he able to offer practical and immediately helpful suggestions looking toward the correction of their real difficulties, albeit he did not neglect to speak words of present comfort and immediate consolation. And invariably would he tell these distressed mortals about the love of God and impart the information, by various and sundry methods, that they were the children of this loving Father in heaven.

132:4.3 (1461.1) In this manner, during the sojourn in Rome, Jesus personally came into affectionate and uplifting contact with upward of five hundred mortals of the realm. He thus gained a knowledge of the different races of mankind which he could never have acquired in Jerusalem and hardly even in Alexandria. He always regarded this six months as one of the richest and most informative of any like period of his earth life.

132:4.4 (1461.2) As might have been expected, such a versatile and aggressive man could not thus function for six months in the world's metropolis without being approached by numerous persons who desired to secure his services in connection with some business or, more often, for some project of teaching, social reform, or religious movement. More than a dozen such proffers were made, and he utilized each one as an opportunity for imparting some thought of spiritual ennoblement by well-chosen words or by some obliging service. Jesus was very fond of doing things—even little things—for all sorts of people.

132:4.5 (1461.3) He talked with a Roman senator on politics and statesmanship, and this one contact with Jesus made such an impression on this legislator that he spent the rest of his life vainly trying to induce his colleagues to change the course of the ruling policy from the idea of the government supporting and feeding the people to that of the people supporting the government. Jesus spent one evening with a wealthy slaveholder, talked about man as a son of God, and the next day this man, Claudius, gave freedom to one hundred and seventeen slaves. He visited at dinner with a Greek physician, telling him that his patients had minds and souls as well as bodies, and thus led this able doctor to attempt a more far-reaching ministry to his fellow men. He talked with all sorts of people in every walk of life. The only place in Rome he did not visit was the public baths. He refused to accompany his friends to the baths because of the sex promiscuity which there prevailed.

132:4.6 (1461.4) To a Roman soldier, as they walked along the Tiber, he said: "Be brave of heart as well as of hand. Dare to do justice and be big enough to show mercy. Compel your lower nature to obey your higher nature as you obey your superiors. Revere goodness and exalt truth. Choose the beautiful in place of the ugly. Love your fellows and reach out for God with a whole heart, for God is your Father in heaven."

132:4.7 (1461.5) To the speaker at the forum he said: "Your eloquence is pleasing, your logic is admirable, your voice is pleasant, but your teaching is hardly true. If you could only enjoy the inspiring satisfaction of knowing God as your spiritual Father, then you might employ your powers of speech to liberate your fellows from the bondage of darkness and from the slavery of ignorance." This was the Marcus who heard Peter preach in Rome and became his successor. When they crucified Simon Peter, it was this man who defied the Roman persecutors and boldly continued to preach the new gospel.

132:4.8 (1462.1) Meeting a poor man who had been falsely accused, Jesus went with him before the magistrate and, having been granted special permission to appear in his behalf, made that superb address in the course of which he said: "Justice makes a nation great, and the greater a nation the more solicitous will it be to see that injustice shall not befall even its most humble citizen. Woe upon any nation when only those who possess money and influence can secure ready justice before its courts! It is the sacred duty of a magistrate to acquit the innocent as well as to punish the guilty. Upon the impartiality, fairness, and integrity of its courts the endurance of a nation depends. Civil government is founded on justice, even as true religion is founded on mercy." The judge reopened the case, and when the evidence had been sifted, he discharged the prisoner. Of all Jesus' activities during these days of personal ministry, this came the nearest to being a public appearance.

Counseling the Rich Man

132:5.1 (1462.2) A certain rich man, a Roman citizen and a Stoic, became greatly interested in Jesus' teaching, having been introduced by Angamon. After many intimate conferences this wealthy citizen asked Jesus what he would do with wealth if he had it, and Jesus answered him: "I would bestow material wealth for the enhancement of material life, even as I would minister knowledge, wisdom, and spiritual service for the enrichment of the intellectual life, the ennoblement of the social life, and the advancement of the spiritual life. I would administer material wealth as a wise and effective trustee of the resources of one generation for the benefit and ennoblement of the next and succeeding generations."

132:5.2 (1462.3) But the rich man was not fully satisfied with Jesus' answer. He made bold to ask again: "But what do you think a man in my position should do with his wealth? Should I keep it, or should I give it away?" And when Jesus perceived that he really desired to know more of the truth about his loyalty to God and his duty to men, he further answered: "My good friend, I discern that you are a sincere seeker after wisdom and an honest lover of truth; therefore am I minded to lay before you my view of the solution of your

problems having to do with the responsibilities of wealth. I do this because you have asked for my counsel, and in giving you this advice, I am not concerned with the wealth of any other rich man; I am offering advice only to you and for your personal guidance. If you honestly desire to regard your wealth as a trust, if you really wish to become a wise and efficient steward of your accumulated wealth, then would I counsel you to make the following analysis of the sources of your riches: Ask yourself, and do your best to find the honest answer, whence came this wealth? And as a help in the study of the sources of your great fortune, I would suggest that you bear in mind the following ten different methods of amassing material wealth:

132:5.3 (1462.4) "1. Inherited wealth—riches derived from parents and other ancestors.

132:5.4 (1462.5) "2. Discovered wealth—riches derived from the uncultivated resources of mother earth.

132:5.5 (1462.6) "3. Trade wealth—riches obtained as a fair profit in the exchange and barter of material goods.

132:5.6 (1462.7) "4. Unfair wealth—riches derived from the unfair exploitation or the enslavement of one's fellows.

132:5.7 (1463.1) "5. Interest wealth—income derived from the fair and just earning possibilities of invested capital.

132:5.8 (1463.2) "6. Genius wealth—riches accruing from the rewards of the creative and inventive endowments of the human mind.

132:5.9 (1463.3) "7. Accidental wealth—riches derived from the generosity of one's fellows or taking origin in the circumstances of life.

132:5.10 (1463.4) "8. Stolen wealth—riches secured by unfairness, dishonesty, theft, or fraud.

132:5.11 (1463.5) "9. Trust funds—wealth lodged in your hands by your fellows for some specific use, now or in the future.

132:5.12 (1463.6) "10. Earned wealth—riches derived directly from your own personal labor, the fair and just reward of your own daily efforts of mind and body.

132:5.13 (1463.7) "And so, my friend, if you would be a faithful and just steward of your large fortune, before God and in service to men, you must approximately divide your wealth into these ten grand divisions, and then proceed to administer each portion in accordance with the wise and honest interpretation of the laws of justice, equity, fairness, and true efficiency; albeit, the God of heaven would not condemn you if sometimes you erred, in doubtful situations, on the side of merciful and unselfish regard for the distress of the suffering victims of the unfortunate circumstances of mortal life. When in honest doubt about the equity and justice of material situations, let your decisions favor those who are in need, favor those who suffer the misfortune of undeserved hardships."

132:5.14 (1463.8) After discussing these matters for several hours and in response to the rich man's request for further and more detailed instruction, Jesus went on to amplify his advice, in substance saying: "While I offer further suggestions concerning your attitude toward wealth, I would admonish you to receive my counsel as given only to you and for your personal guidance. I speak only for myself and to you as an inquiring friend. I adjure you not to become a dictator as to how other rich men shall regard their wealth. I would advise you:

132:5.15 (1463.9) "1. As steward of inherited wealth you should consider its sources. You are under moral obligation to represent the past generation in the honest transmittal of legitimate wealth to succeeding generations after subtracting a fair toll for the benefit of the present generation. But you are not obligated to perpetuate any dishonesty or injustice involved in the unfair accumulation of wealth by

your ancestors. Any portion of your inherited wealth which turns out to have been derived through fraud or unfairness, you may disburse in accordance with your convictions of justice, generosity, and restitution. The remainder of your legitimate inherited wealth you may use in equity and transmit in security as the trustee of one generation for another. Wise discrimination and sound judgment should dictate your decisions regarding the bequest of riches to your successors.

132:5.16 (1463.10) "2. Everyone who enjoys wealth as a result of discovery should remember that one individual can live on earth but a short season and should, therefore, make adequate provision for the sharing of these discoveries in helpful ways by the largest possible number of his fellow men. While the discoverer should not be denied all reward for efforts of discovery, neither should he selfishly presume to lay claim to all of the advantages and blessings to be derived from the uncovering of nature's hoarded resources.

132:5.17 (1464.1) "3. As long as men choose to conduct the world's business by trade and barter, they are entitled to a fair and legitimate profit. Every tradesman deserves wages for his services; the merchant is entitled to his hire. The fairness of trade and the honest treatment accorded one's fellows in the organized business of the world create many different sorts of profit wealth, and all these sources of wealth must be judged by the highest principles of justice, honesty, and fairness. The honest trader should not hesitate to take the same profit which he would gladly accord his fellow trader in a similar transaction. While this sort of wealth is not identical with individually earned income when business dealings are conducted on a large scale, at the same time, such honestly accumulated wealth endows its possessor with a considerable equity as regards a voice in its subsequent distribution.

132:5.18 (1464.2) "4. No mortal who knows God and seeks to do the divine will can stoop to engage in the oppressions of wealth. No noble man will strive to accumulate riches and amass wealth-power by the enslavement or unfair exploitation of his brothers in the flesh. Riches are a moral curse and a spiritual stigma when they are derived from the sweat of oppressed mortal man. All such wealth should be restored to those who have thus been robbed or to their children and their children's children. An enduring civilization cannot be built upon the practice of defrauding the laborer of his hire.

132:5.19 (1464.3) "5. Honest wealth is entitled to interest. As long as men borrow and lend, that which is fair interest may be collected provided the capital lent was legitimate wealth. First cleanse your capital before you lay claim to the interest. Do not become so small and grasping that you would stoop to the practice of usury. Never permit yourself to be so selfish as to employ money-power to gain unfair advantage over your struggling fellows. Yield not to the temptation to take usury from your brother in financial distress.

132:5.20 (1464.4) "6. If you chance to secure wealth by flights of genius, if your riches are derived from the rewards of inventive endowment, do not lay claim to an unfair portion of such rewards. The genius owes something to both his ancestors and his progeny; likewise is he under obligation to the race, nation, and circumstances of his inventive discoveries; he should also remember that it was as man among men that he labored and wrought out his inventions. It would be equally unjust to deprive the genius of all his increment of wealth. And it will ever be impossible for men to establish rules and regulations applicable equally to all these problems of the equitable distribution of wealth. You must first recognize man as your brother, and if you honestly desire to do by him as you would have him do by you, the commonplace dictates of justice, honesty, and fairness will guide you in the just and impartial settlement of every recurring problem of economic rewards and social justice.

132:5.21 (1464.5) "7. Except for the just and legitimate fees earned in administration, no man should lay personal claim to that wealth which time and chance may cause to fall into his hands. Accidental riches should be regarded somewhat in the light of a trust to be expended for the benefit of one's social or economic group. The possessors of such wealth should be accorded the major voice in the determination of the wise and effective distribution of such unearned resources. Civilized man will not always look upon all that he controls as his personal and private possession.

132:5.22 (1465.1) "8. If any portion of your fortune has been knowingly derived from fraud; if aught of your wealth has been accumulated by dishonest practices or unfair methods; if your riches are the product of unjust dealings with your fellows, make haste to restore all these ill-gotten gains to the rightful owners.

Make full amends and thus cleanse your fortune of all dishonest riches.

132:5.23 (1465.2) "9. The trusteeship of the wealth of one person for the benefit of others is a solemn and sacred responsibility. Do not hazard or jeopardize such a trust. Take for yourself of any trust only that which all honest men would allow.

132:5.24 (1465.3) "10. That part of your fortune which represents the earnings of your own mental and

physical efforts—if your work has been done in fairness and equity—is truly your own. No man can gainsay your right to hold and use such wealth as you may see fit provided your exercise of this right does not work harm upon your fellows."

132:5.25 (1465.4) When Jesus had finished counseling him, this wealthy Roman arose from his couch and, in saying farewell for the night, delivered himself of this promise: "My good friend, I perceive you are a man of great wisdom and goodness, and tomorrow I will begin the administration of all my wealth in accordance with your counsel."

Social Ministry

132:6.1 (1465.5) Here in Rome also occurred that touching incident in which the Creator of a universe spent several hours restoring a lost child to his anxious mother. This little boy had wandered away from his home, and Jesus found him crying in distress. He and Ganid were on their way to the libraries, but they devoted themselves to getting the child back home. Ganid never forgot Jesus' comment: "You know, Ganid, most human beings are like the lost child. They spend much of their time crying in fear and suffering in sorrow when, in very truth, they are but a short distance from safety and security, even as this child was only a little way from home. And all those who know the way of truth and enjoy the assurance of knowing God should esteem it a privilege, not a duty, to offer guidance to their fellows in their efforts to find the satisfactions of living. Did we not supremely enjoy this ministry of restoring the child to his mother? So do those who lead men to God experience the supreme satisfaction of human service." And from that day forward, for the remainder of his natural life, Ganid was continually on the lookout for lost children whom he might restore to their homes.

132:6.2 (1465.6) There was the widow with five children whose husband had been accidentally killed. Jesus told Ganid about the loss of his own father by an accident, and they went repeatedly to comfort this mother and her children, while Ganid sought money from his father to provide food and clothing. They did not cease their efforts until they had found a position for the eldest boy so that he could help in the care of the family.

132:6.3 (1465.7) That night, as Gonod listened to the recital of these experiences, he said to Jesus, good-naturedly: "I propose to make a scholar or a businessman of my son, and now you start out to make a philosopher or philanthropist of him." And Jesus smilingly replied: "Perhaps we will make him all four; then can he enjoy a four-fold satisfaction in life as his ear for the recognition of human melody will be able to recognize four tones instead of one." Then said Gonod: "I perceive that you really are a philosopher. You must write a book for future generations." And Jesus replied: "Not a book—my mission is to live a life in this generation and for all generations. I —" but he stopped, saying to Ganid, "My son, it is time to retire."

Trips About Rome

132:7.1 (1466.1) Jesus, Gonod, and Ganid made five trips away from Rome to points of interest in the surrounding territory. On their visit to the northern Italian lakes Jesus had the long talk with Ganid concerning the impossibility of teaching a man about God if the man does not desire to know God. They had casually met a thoughtless pagan while on their journey up to the lakes, and Ganid was surprised that Jesus did not follow out his usual practice of enlisting the man in conversation which would naturally lead up to the discussion of spiritual questions. When Ganid asked his teacher why he evinced so little interest in this pagan, Jesus answered:

132:7.2 (1466.2) "Ganid, the man was not hungry for truth. He was not dissatisfied with himself. He was not ready to ask for help, and the eyes of his mind were not open to receive light for the soul. That man was not ripe for the harvest of salvation; he must be allowed more time for the trials and difficulties of life to prepare him for the reception of wisdom and higher learning. Or, if we could have him live with us, we might by our lives show him the Father in heaven, and thus would he become so attracted by our lives as sons of God that he would be constrained to inquire about our Father. You cannot reveal God to those who do not seek for him; you cannot lead unwilling souls into the joys of salvation.

Man must become hungry for truth as a result of the experiences of living, or he must desire to know God as the result of contact with the lives of those who are acquainted with the divine Father before another human being can act as the means of leading such a fellow mortal to the Father in heaven. If we know God, our real business on earth is so to live as to permit the Father to reveal himself in our lives, and thus will all God-seeking persons see the Father and ask for our help in finding out more about the God who in this manner finds expression in our lives."

132:7.3 (1466.3) It was on the visit to Switzerland, up in the mountains, that Jesus had an all-day talk with both father and son about Buddhism. Many times Ganid had asked Jesus direct questions about Buddha, but he had always received more or less evasive replies. Now, in the presence of the son, the father asked Jesus a direct question about Buddha, and he received a direct reply. Said Gonod: "I would really like to know what you think of Buddha." And Jesus answered:

132:7.4 (1466.4) "Your Buddha was much better than your Buddhism. Buddha was a great man, even a prophet to his people, but he was an orphan prophet; by that I mean he early lost sight of his spiritual Father, the Father in heaven. His experience was tragic. He tried to live and teach as a messenger of God, but without God. Buddha guided his ship of salvation right up to the safe harbor, right up to the entrance to the haven of mortal salvation, and there, because of faulty charts of navigation, the good ship ran aground. There it has rested these many generations, motionless and almost hopelessly stranded. And thereon have many of your people remained all these years. They live within hailing distance of the safe waters of rest, but they refuse to enter because the noble craft of the good Buddha met the misfortune of grounding just outside the harbor. And the Buddhist peoples never will enter this harbor unless they abandon the philosophic craft of their prophet and seize upon his noble spirit. Had your people remained true to the spirit of Buddha, you would have long since entered your haven of spirit tranquillity, soul rest, and assurance of salvation.

132:7.5 (1467.1) "You see, Gonod, Buddha knew God in spirit but failed clearly to discover him in mind; the Jews discovered God in mind but largely failed to know him in spirit. Today, the Buddhists flounder about in a philosophy without God, while my people are piteously enslaved to the fear of a God without a saving philosophy of life and liberty. You have a philosophy without a God; the Jews have a God but are largely without a philosophy of living as related thereto. Buddha, failing to envision God as a spirit and as a Father, failed to provide in his teaching the moral energy and the spiritual driving power which a religion must possess if it is to change a race and exalt a nation."

132:7.6 (1467.2) Then exclaimed Ganid: "Teacher, let's you and I make a new religion, one good enough for India and big enough for Rome, and maybe we can trade it to the Jews for Yahweh." And Jesus replied: "Ganid, religions are not made. The religions of men grow up over long periods of time, while the revelations of God flash upon earth in the lives of the men who reveal God to their fellows." But they did not comprehend the meaning of these prophetic words.

132:7.7 (1467.3) That night after they had retired, Ganid could not sleep. He talked a long time with his father and finally said, "You know, father, I sometimes think Joshua is a prophet." And his father only sleepily replied, "My son, there are others —"

132:7.8 (1467.4) From this day, for the remainder of his natural life, Ganid continued to evolve a religion of his own. He was mightily moved in his own mind by Jesus' broadmindedness, fairness, and tolerance. In all their discussions of philosophy and religion this youth never experienced feelings of resentment or reactions of antagonism.

132:7.9 (1467.5) What a scene for the celestial intelligences to behold, this spectacle of the Indian lad proposing to the Creator of a universe that they make a new religion! And though the young man did not know it, they were making a new and everlasting religion right then and there—this new way of salvation, the revelation of God to man through, and in, Jesus. That which the lad wanted most to do he was unconsciously actually doing. And it was, and is, ever thus. That which the enlightened and reflective human imagination of spiritual teaching and leading wholeheartedly and unselfishly wants to do and be, becomes measurably creative in accordance with the degree of mortal dedication to the divine doing of the Father's will. When man goes in partnership with God, great things may, and do, happen.

The Return from Rome

133:0.1 (1468.1) WHEN preparing to leave Rome, Jesus said good-bye to none of his friends. The scribe of Damascus appeared in Rome without announcement and disappeared in like manner. It was a full year before those who knew and loved him gave up hope of seeing him again. Before the end of the second year small groups of those who had known him found themselves drawn together by their common interest in his teachings and through mutual memory of their good times with him. And these small groups of Stoics, Cynics, and mystery cultists continued to hold these irregular and informal meetings right up to the time of the appearance in Rome of the first preachers of the Christian religion.

133:0.2 (1468.2) Gonod and Ganid had purchased so many things in Alexandria and Rome that they sent all their belongings on ahead by pack train to Tarentum, while the three travelers walked leisurely across Italy over the great Appian Way. On this journey they encountered all sorts of human beings. Many noble Roman citizens and Greek colonists lived along this road, but already the progeny of great numbers of inferior slaves were beginning to make their appearance.

133:0.3 (1468.3) One day while resting at lunch, about halfway to Tarentum, Ganid asked Jesus a direct question as to what he thought of India's caste system. Said Jesus: "Though human beings differ in many ways, the one from another, before God and in the spiritual world all mortals stand on an equal footing. There are only two groups of mortals in the eyes of God: those who desire to do his will and those who do not. As the universe looks upon an inhabited world, it likewise discerns two great classes: those who know God and those who do not. Those who cannot know God are reckoned among the animals of any given realm. Mankind can appropriately be divided into many classes in accordance with differing qualifications, as they may be viewed physically, mentally, socially, vocationally, or morally, but as these different classes of mortals appear before the judgment bar of God, they stand on an equal footing; God is truly no respecter of persons. Although you cannot escape the recognition of differential human abilities and endowments in matters intellectual, social, and moral, you should make no such distinctions in the spiritual brotherhood of men when assembled for worship in the presence of God."

1. Mercy and Justice

133:1.1 (1468.4) A very interesting incident occurred one afternoon by the roadside as they neared Tarentum. They observed a rough and bullying youth brutally attacking a smaller lad. Jesus hastened to the assistance of the assaulted youth, and when he had rescued him, he tightly held on to the offender until the smaller lad had made his escape. The moment Jesus released the little bully, Ganid pounced upon the boy and began soundly to thrash him, and to Ganid's astonishment Jesus promptly interfered. After he had restrained Ganid and permitted the frightened boy to escape, the young man, as soon as he got his breath, excitedly exclaimed: "I cannot understand you, Teacher. If mercy requires that you rescue the smaller lad, does not justice demand the punishment of the larger and offending youth?" In answering, Jesus said:

133:1.2 (1469.1) "Ganid, it is true, you do not understand. Mercy ministry is always the work of the individual, but justice punishment is the function of the social, governmental, or universe administrative groups. As an individual I am beholden to show mercy; I must go to the rescue of the assaulted lad, and in all consistency I may employ sufficient force to restrain the aggressor. And that is just what I did. I achieved the deliverance of the assaulted lad; that was the end of mercy ministry. Then I forcibly detained the aggressor a sufficient length of time to enable the weaker party to the dispute to make his escape, after which I withdrew from the affair. I did not proceed to sit in judgment on the aggressor, thus to pass upon his motive—to adjudicate all that entered into his attack upon his fellow—and then undertake to execute the punishment which my mind might dictate as just recompense for his wrongdoing. Ganid, mercy may be lavish, but justice is precise. Cannot you discern that no two persons are likely to agree as to the punishment which would satisfy the demands of justice? One would impose forty lashes, another twenty, while still another would advise solitary confinement as a just punishment. Can you not see that on this world such responsibilities had better rest upon the group or be administered by chosen representatives of the group? In the universe, judgment is vested in those who fully know the antecedents of all wrongdoing as well as its motivation. In civilized society and in an organized universe the administration of justice presupposes the passing of just sentence consequent upon fair judgment, and such prerogatives are vested in the juridical groups of the worlds and in the all-knowing administrators of the higher universes of all creation."

133:1.3 (1469.2) For days they talked about this problem of manifesting mercy and administering justice. And Ganid, at least to some extent, understood why Jesus would not engage in personal combat. But Ganid asked one last question, to which he never received a fully satisfactory answer; and that question was: "But, Teacher, if a stronger and ill-tempered creature should attack you and threaten to destroy you, what would you do? Would you make no effort to defend yourself?" Although Jesus could not fully and satisfactorily answer the lad's question, inasmuch as he was not willing to disclose to him that he (Jesus) was living on earth as the exemplification of the Paradise Father's love to an onlooking universe, he did say this much:

133:1.4 (1469.3) "Ganid, I can well understand how some of these problems perplex you, and I will endeavor to answer your question. First, in all attacks which might be made upon my person, I would determine whether or not the aggressor was a son of God—my brother in the flesh—and if I thought such a creature did not possess moral judgment and spiritual reason, I would unhesitatingly defend myself to the full capacity of my powers of resistance, regardless of consequences to the attacker. But I would not thus assault a fellow man of sonship status, even in self-defense. That is, I would not punish him in advance and without judgment for his assault upon me. I would by every possible artifice seek to prevent and dissuade him from making such an attack and to mitigate it in case of my failure to abort it. Ganid, I have absolute confidence in my heavenly Father's overcare; I am consecrated to doing the will of my Father in heaven. I do not believe that real harm can befall me; I do not believe that my lifework can really be jeopardized by anything my enemies might wish to visit upon me, and surely we have no violence to fear from our friends. I am absolutely assured that the entire universe is friendly to me—this all-powerful truth I insist on believing with a wholehearted trust in spite of all appearances to the contrary."

133:1.5 (1470.1) But Ganid was not fully satisfied. Many times they talked over these matters, and Jesus told him some of his boyhood experiences and also about Jacob the stone mason's son. On learning how Jacob appointed himself to defend

Jesus, Ganid said: "Oh, I begin to see! In the first place very seldom would any normal human being want to attack such a kindly person as you, and even if anyone should be so unthinking as to do such a thing, there is pretty sure to be near at hand some other mortal who will fly to your assistance, even as you always go to the rescue of any person you observe to be in distress. In my heart, Teacher, I agree with you, but in my head I still think that if I had been Jacob, I would have enjoyed punishing those rude fellows who presumed to attack you just because they thought you would not defend yourself. I presume you are fairly safe in your journey through life since you spend much of your time helping others and ministering to your fellows in distress—well, most likely there'll always be someone on hand to defend you." And Jesus replied: "That test has not yet come, Ganid, and when it does, we will have to abide by the Father's will." And that was about all the lad could get his teacher to say on this difficult subject of self-defense and nonresistance. On another occasion he did draw from Jesus the opinion that organized society had every right to employ force in the execution of its just mandates. *

2.   Embarking at Tarentum

133:2.1 (1470.2) While tarrying at the ship landing, waiting for the boat to unload cargo, the travelers observed a man mistreating his wife. As was his custom, Jesus intervened in behalf of the person subjected to attack. He stepped up behind the irate husband and, tapping him gently on the shoulder, said: "My friend, may I speak with you in private for a moment?" The angry man was nonplused by such an approach and, after a moment of embarrassing hesitation, stammered out—"er—why—yes, what do you want with me?" When Jesus had led him to one side, he said: "My friend, I perceive that something terrible must have happened to you; I very much desire that you tell me what could happen to such a strong man to lead him to attack his wife, the mother of his children,

and that right out here before all eyes. I am sure you must feel that you have some good reason for this assault. What did the woman do to deserve such treatment from her husband? As I look upon you, I think I discern in your face the love of justice if not the desire to show mercy. I venture to say that, if you found me out by the wayside, attacked by robbers, you would unhesitatingly rush to my rescue. I dare say you have done many such brave things in the course of your life. Now, my friend, tell me what is the matter? Did the woman do something wrong, or did you foolishly lose your head and thoughtlessly assault her?" It was not so much what he said that touched this man's heart as the kindly look and the sympathetic smile which Jesus bestowed upon him at the conclusion of his remarks. Said the man: "I perceive you are a priest of the Cynics, and I am thankful you restrained me. My wife has done no great wrong; she is a good woman, but she irritates me by the manner in which she picks on me in public, and I lose my temper. I am sorry for my lack of self-control, and I promise to try to live up to my former pledge to one of your brothers who taught me the better way many years ago. I promise you." *

133:2.2 (1471.1) And then, in bidding him farewell, Jesus said: "My brother, always remember that man has no rightful authority over woman unless the woman has willingly and voluntarily given him such authority. Your wife has engaged to go through life with you, to help you fight its battles, and to assume the far greater share of the burden of bearing and rearing your children; and in return for this special service it is only fair that she receive from you that special protection which man can give to woman as the partner who must carry, bear, and nurture the children. The loving care and consideration which a man is willing to bestow upon his wife and their children are the measure of that man's attainment of the higher levels of creative and spiritual self-consciousness. Do you not know that men and women are partners with God in that they co-operate to create beings who grow up to possess themselves of the potential of immortal souls? The Father in heaven treats the Spirit Mother of the children of the universe as one equal to himself. It is Godlike to share your life and all that relates thereto on equal terms with the mother partner who so fully shares with you that divine experience of reproducing yourselves in the lives of your children. If you can only love your children as God loves you, you will love and cherish your wife as the Father in heaven honors and exalts the Infinite Spirit, the mother of all the spirit children of a vast universe."

133:2.3 (1471.2) As they went on board the boat, they looked back upon the scene of the teary-eyed couple standing in silent embrace. Having heard the latter half of Jesus' message to the man, Gonod was all day occupied with meditations thereon, and he resolved to reorganize his home when he returned to India.

133:2.4 (1471.3) The journey to Nicopolis was pleasant but slow as the wind was not favorable. The three spent many hours recounting their experiences in Rome and reminiscing about all that had happened to them since they first met in Jerusalem. Ganid was becoming imbued with the spirit of personal ministry. He began work on the steward of the ship, but on the second day, when he got into deep religious water, he called on Joshua to help him out.

133:2.5 (1471.4) They spent several days at Nicopolis, the city which Augustus had founded some fifty years before as the "city of victory" in commemoration of the battle of Actium, this site being the land whereon he camped with his army before the battle. They lodged in the home of one Jeramy, a Greek proselyte of the Jewish faith, whom they had met on shipboard. The Apostle Paul spent all winter with the son of Jeramy in the same house in the course of his third missionary journey. From Nicopolis they sailed on the same boat for Corinth, the capital of the Roman province of Achaia.

3.   *At Corinth*

133:3.1 (1471.5) By the time they reached Corinth, Ganid was becoming very much interested in the Jewish religion, and so it was not strange that, one day as they passed the synagogue and saw the people going in, he requested Jesus to take him to the service. That day they heard a learned rabbi discourse on the "Destiny of Israel," and after the service they met one Crispus, the chief ruler of this synagogue. Many times they went back to the synagogue services, but chiefly to meet Crispus. Ganid grew to be very fond of Crispus, his wife, and their family of five children. He much enjoyed observing how a Jew conducted his family life.

133:3.2 (1472.1) While Ganid studied family life, Jesus was teaching Crispus the better ways of religious living. Jesus held more than twenty sessions with this forward-looking Jew; and it is not surprising, years afterward, when Paul was preaching in this very synagogue, and when the Jews had rejected his message and had voted to forbid his further preaching in the synagogue, and when he then went to the gentiles, that Crispus with his entire family embraced the new religion, and that he became one of the chief supports of the Christian church which Paul subsequently organized at Corinth.

133:3.3 (1472.2) During the eighteen months Paul preached in Corinth, being later joined by Silas and Timothy, he met many others who had been taught by the "Jewish tutor of the son of an Indian merchant."

133:3.4 (1472.3) At Corinth they met people of every race hailing from three continents. Next to Alexandria and Rome, it was the most cosmopolitan city of the Mediterranean empire. There was much to attract one's attention in this city, and Ganid never grew weary of visiting the citadel which stood almost two thousand feet above the sea. He also spent a great deal of his spare time about the synagogue and in the home of Crispus. He was at first shocked, and later on charmed, by the status of woman in the Jewish home; it was a revelation to this young Indian.

133:3.5 (1472.4) Jesus and Ganid were often guests in another Jewish home, that of Justus, a devout merchant, who lived alongside the synagogue. And many times, subsequently, when the Apostle Paul sojourned in this home, did he listen to the recounting of these visits with the Indian lad and his Jewish tutor, while both Paul and Justus wondered whatever became of such a wise and brilliant Hebrew teacher.

133:3.6 (1472.5) When in Rome, Ganid observed that Jesus refused to accompany them to the public baths. Several times afterward the young man sought to induce Jesus further to express himself in regard to the relations of the sexes.

Though he would answer the lad's questions, he never seemed disposed to discuss these subjects at great length. One evening as they strolled about Corinth out near where the wall of the citadel ran down to the sea, they were accosted by two public women. Ganid had imbibed the idea, and rightly, that Jesus was a man of high ideals, and that he abhorred everything which partook of uncleanness or savored of evil; accordingly he spoke sharply to these women and rudely motioned them away. When Jesus saw this, he said to Ganid: "You mean well, but you should not presume thus to speak to the children of God, even though they chance to be his erring children. Who are we that we should sit in judgment on these women? Do you happen to know all of the circumstances which led them to resort to such methods of obtaining a livelihood? Stop here with me while we talk about these matters." The courtesans were astonished at what he said even more than was Ganid.

133:3.7 (1472.6) As they stood there in the moonlight, Jesus went on to say: "There lives within every human mind a divine spirit, the gift of the Father in heaven. This good spirit ever strives to lead us to God, to help us to find God

and to know God; but also within mortals there are many natural physical tendencies which the Creator put there to serve the well-being of the individual and the race. Now, oftentimes, men and women become confused in their efforts to understand themselves and to grapple with the manifold difficulties of making a living in a world so largely dominated by selfishness and sin. I perceive, Ganid, that neither of these women is willfully wicked. I can tell by their faces that they have experienced much sorrow; they have suffered much at the hands of an apparently cruel fate; they have not intentionally chosen this sort of life; they have, in discouragement bordering on despair, surrendered to the pressure of the hour and accepted this distasteful means of obtaining a livelihood as the best way out of a situation that to them appeared hopeless. Ganid, some people are really wicked at heart; they deliberately choose to do mean things, but, tell me, as you look into these now tear-stained faces, do you see anything bad or wicked?" And as Jesus paused for his reply, Ganid's voice choked up as he stammered out his answer: "No, Teacher, I do not. And I apologize for my rudeness to them—I crave their forgiveness." Then said Jesus: "And I bespeak for them that they have forgiven you as I speak for my Father in heaven that he has forgiven them. Now all of you come with me to a friend's house where we will seek refreshment and plan for the new and better life ahead." Up to this time the amazed women had not uttered a word; they looked at each other and silently followed as the men led the way.

133:3.8 (1473.1) Imagine the surprise of Justus' wife when, at this late hour, Jesus appeared with Ganid and these two strangers, saying: "You will forgive us for coming at this hour, but Ganid and I desire a bite to eat, and we would share it with these our new-found friends, who are also in need of nourishment; and besides all this, we come to you with the thought that you will be interested in counseling with us as to the best way to help these women get a new start in life. They can tell you their story, but I surmise they have had much trouble, and their very presence here in your house testifies how earnestly they crave to know good people, and how willingly they will embrace the opportunity to show all the world—and even the angels of heaven—what brave and noble women they can become."

133:3.9 (1473.2) When Martha, Justus' wife, had spread the food on the table, Jesus, taking unexpected leave of them, said: "As it is getting late, and since the young man's father will be awaiting us, we pray to be excused while we leave you here together—three women—the beloved children of the Most High. And I will pray for your spiritual guidance while you make plans for a new and better life on earth and eternal life in the great beyond."

133:3.10 (1473.3) Thus did Jesus and Ganid take leave of the women. So far the two courtesans had said nothing; likewise was Ganid speechless. And for a few moments so was Martha, but presently she rose to the occasion and did everything for these strangers that Jesus had hoped for. The elder of these two women died a short time thereafter, with bright hopes of eternal survival, and the younger woman worked at Justus' place of business and later became a lifelong member of the first Christian church in Corinth.

133:3.11 (1473.4) Several times in the home of Crispus, Jesus and Ganid met one Gaius, who subsequently became a loyal supporter of Paul. During these two months in Corinth they held intimate conversations with scores of worth-while individuals, and as a result of all these apparently casual contacts more than half of the individuals so affected became members of the subsequent Christian community.

133:3.12 (1473.5) When Paul first went to Corinth, he had not intended to make a prolonged visit. But he did not know how well the Jewish tutor had prepared the way for his labors. And further, he discovered that great interest had already been aroused by Aquila and Priscilla, Aquila being one of the Cynics with whom Jesus

had come in contact when in Rome. This couple were Jewish refugees from Rome, and they quickly embraced Paul's teachings. He lived with them and worked with them, for they were also tentmakers. It was because of these circumstances that Paul prolonged his stay in Corinth.

4   *Personal Work in Corinth*

133:4.1 (1474.1) Jesus and Ganid had many more interesting experiences in Corinth. They had close converse with a great number of persons who greatly profited by the instruction received from Jesus.

133:4.2 (1474.2) The miller he taught about grinding up the grains of truth in the mill of living experience so as to render the difficult things of divine life readily receivable by even the weak and feeble among one's fellow mortals. Said Jesus: "Give the milk of truth to those who are babes in spiritual perception. In your living and loving ministry serve spiritual food in attractive form and suited to the capacity of receptivity of each of your inquirers."

133:4.3 (1474.3) To the Roman centurion he said: "Render unto Caesar the things which are Caesar's and unto God the things which are God's. The sincere service of God and the loyal service of Caesar do not conflict unless Caesar should presume to arrogate to himself that homage which alone can be claimed by Deity. Loyalty to God, if you should come to know him, would render you all the more loyal and faithful in your devotion to a worthy emperor."

133:4.4 (1474.4) To the earnest leader of the Mithraic cult he said: "You do well to seek for a religion of eternal salvation, but you err to go in quest of such a glorious truth among man-made mysteries and human philosophies. Know you not that the mystery of eternal salvation dwells within your own soul? Do you not know that the God of heaven has sent his spirit to live within you, and that this spirit will lead all truth-loving and God-serving mortals out of this life and through the portals of death up to the eternal heights of light where God waits to receive his children? And never forget: You who know God are the sons of God if you truly yearn to be like him."

133:4.5 (1474.5) To the Epicurean teacher he said: "You do well to choose the best and esteem the good, but are you wise when you fail to discern the greater things of mortal life which are embodied in the spirit realms derived from the realization of the presence of God in the human heart? The great thing in all human experience is the realization of knowing the God whose spirit lives within you and seeks to lead you forth on that long and almost endless journey of attaining the personal presence of our common Father, the God of all creation, the Lord of universes."

133:4.6 (1474.6) To the Greek contractor and builder he said: "My friend, as you build the material structures of men, grow a spiritual character in the similitude of the divine spirit within your soul. Do not let your achievement as a temporal builder outrun your attainment as a spiritual son of the kingdom of heaven. While you build the mansions of time for another, neglect not to secure your title to the mansions of eternity for yourself. Ever remember, there is a city whose foundations are righteousness and truth, and whose builder and maker is God."

133:4.7 (1474.7) To the Roman judge he said: "As you judge men, remember that you yourself will also some day come to judgment before the bar of the Rulers of a universe. Judge justly, even mercifully, even as you shall some day thus crave merciful consideration at the hands of the Supreme Arbiter. Judge as you would be judged under similar circumstances, thus being guided by the spirit of the law as well as by its letter. And even as you accord justice dominated by fairness in the light of the need of those who are brought before you, so shall you have the right to expect justice tempered by mercy when you sometime stand before the Judge of all the earth."

133:4.8 (1475.1) To the mistress of the Greek inn he said: "Minister your hospitality as one who entertains the children of the Most High. Elevate the drudgery of your daily toil to the high levels of a fine art through the increasing realization that you minister to God in the persons whom he indwells by his spirit which has descended to live within the hearts of men, thereby seeking to transform their minds and lead their souls to the knowledge of the Paradise Father of all these bestowed gifts of the divine spirit."

133:4.9 (1475.2) Jesus had many visits with a Chinese merchant. In saying good-bye, he admonished him: "Worship only God, who is your true spirit ancestor. Remember that the Father's spirit ever lives within you and always points your soul-direction heavenward. If you follow the unconscious leadings of this immortal spirit, you are certain to continue on in the uplifted way of finding God. And when you do attain the Father in heaven, it will be because by seeking him you have become more and more like him. And so farewell, Chang, but only for a season, for we shall meet again in the worlds of light where the Father of spirit souls has provided many delightful stopping-places for those who are Paradise- bound."

133:4.10 (1475.3) To the traveler from Britain he said: "My brother, I perceive you are seeking for truth, and I suggest that the spirit of the Father of all truth may chance to dwell within you. Did you ever sincerely endeavor to talk with the spirit of your own soul? Such a thing is indeed difficult and seldom yields consciousness of success; but every honest attempt of the material mind to communicate with its indwelling spirit meets with certain success, notwithstanding that the majority of all such magnificent human experiences must long remain as superconscious registrations in the souls of such God-knowing mortals."

133:4.11 (1475.4) To the runaway lad Jesus said: "Remember, there are two things you cannot run away from—God and yourself. Wherever you may go, you take with you yourself and the spirit of the heavenly Father which lives within your heart. My son, stop trying to deceive yourself; settle down to the courageous practice of facing the facts of life; lay firm hold on the assurances of sonship with God and the certainty of eternal life, as I have instructed you. From this day on purpose to be a real man, a man determined to face life bravely and intelligently."

133:4.12 (1475.5) To the condemned criminal he said at the last hour: "My brother, you have fallen on evil times. You lost your way; you became entangled in the meshes of crime. From talking to you, I well know you did not plan to do the thing which is about to cost you your temporal life. But you did do this evil, and your fellows have adjudged you guilty; they have determined that you shall die. You or I may not deny the state this right of self-defense in the manner of its own choosing. There seems to be no way of humanly escaping the penalty of your wrongdoing. Your fellows must judge you by what you did, but there is a Judge to whom you may appeal for forgiveness, and who will judge you by your real motives and better intentions. You need not fear to meet the judgment of God if your repentance is genuine and your faith sincere. The fact that your error carries with it the death penalty imposed by man does not prejudice the chance of your soul to obtain justice and enjoy mercy before the heavenly courts."

133:4.13 (1476.1) Jesus enjoyed many intimate talks with a large number of hungry souls, too many to find a place in this record. The three travelers enjoyed their sojourn in Corinth. Excepting Athens, which was more renowned as an educational center, Corinth was the most important city in Greece during these Roman times, and their two months' stay in this thriving commercial center afforded opportunity for all three of them to gain much valuable experience. Their sojourn in this city was one of the most interesting of all their stops on the way back from Rome.

133:4.14 (1476.2) Gonod had many interests in Corinth, but finally his business was finished, and they prepared to sail for Athens. They traveled on a small boat which could be carried overland on a land track from one of Corinth's harbors to the other, a distance of ten miles.

5.   At Athens—
Discourse on Science

133:5.1 (1476.3) They shortly arrived at the olden center of Greek science and learning, and Ganid was thrilled with the thought of being in Athens, of being in Greece, the cultural center of the onetime Alexandrian empire, which had extended its borders even to his own land of India. There was little business to transact; so Gonod spent most of his time with Jesus and Ganid, visiting the many points of interest and listening to the interesting discussions of the lad and his versatile teacher.

133:5.2 (1476.4) A great university still thrived in Athens, and the trio made frequent visits to its halls of learning. Jesus and Ganid had thoroughly discussed the teachings of Plato when they attended the lectures in the museum at Alexandria. They all enjoyed the art of Greece, examples of which were still to be found here and there about the city.

133:5.3 (1476.5) Both the father and the son greatly enjoyed the discussion on science which Jesus had at their inn one evening with a Greek philosopher. After this pedant had talked for almost three hours, and when he had finished his discourse, Jesus, in terms of modern thought, said:

133:5.4 (1476.6) Scientists may some day measure the energy, or force manifestations, of gravitation, light, and electricity, but these same scientists can never (scientifically) tell you what these universe phenomena are. Science deals with physical-energy activities; religion deals with eternal values. True philosophy grows out of the wisdom which does its best to correlate these quantitative and qualitative observations. There always exists the danger that the purely physical scientist may become afflicted with mathematical pride and statistical egotism, not to mention spiritual blindness.

133:5.5 (1476.7) Logic is valid in the material world, and mathematics is reliable when limited in its application to physical things; but neither is to be regarded as wholly dependable or infallible when applied to life problems. Life embraces phenomena which are not wholly material. Arithmetic says that, if one man could shear a sheep in ten minutes, ten men could shear it in one minute. That is sound mathematics, but it is not true, for the ten men could not so do it; they would get in one another's way so badly that the work would be greatly delayed.

133:5.6 (1477.1) Mathematics asserts that, if one person stands for a certain unit of intellectual and moral value, ten persons would stand for ten times this value. But in dealing with human personality it would be nearer the truth to say that such a personality association is a sum equal to the square of the number of personalities concerned in the equation rather than the simple arithmetical sum. A social group of human beings in co-ordinated working harmony stands for a force far greater than the simple sum of its parts.

133:5.7 (1477.2) Quantity may be identified as a fact, thus becoming a scientific uniformity. Quality, being a matter of mind interpretation, represents an estimate of values, and must, therefore, remain an experience of the individual. When both science and religion become less dogmatic and more tolerant of criticism, philosophy will then begin to achieve unity in the intelligent comprehension of the universe.

133:5.8 (1477.3) There is unity in the cosmic universe if you could only discern its workings in actuality. The real universe is friendly to every child of the eternal God. The real problem is: How can the finite mind of man achieve a logical, true, and corresponding unity of thought? This universe-knowing state of mind can be had only by conceiving that the quantitative fact and the qualitative value have a common causation in the Paradise Father. Such a conception of reality yields a broader insight into the purposeful unity of universe phenomena; it even reveals a spiritual goal of progressive personality achievement. And this is a concept of unity which can sense the unchanging background of a living universe of continually changing impersonal relations and evolving personal relationships.

133:5.9 (1477.4) Matter and spirit and the state intervening between them are three interrelated and interassociated levels of the true unity of the real universe. Regardless of how divergent the universe phenomena of fact and value may appear to be, they are, after all, unified in the Supreme.

133:5.10 (1477.5) Reality of material existence attaches to unrecognized energy as well as to visible matter. When the energies of the universe are so slowed down that they acquire the requisite degree of motion, then, under favorable conditions, these same energies become mass. And forget not, the mind which can alone perceive the presence of apparent realities is itself also real. And the fundamental cause of this universe of energy-mass, mind, and spirit, is eternal—it exists and consists in the nature and reactions of the Universal Father and his absolute co-ordinates.

133:5.11 (1477.6) They were all more than astounded at the words of Jesus, and when the Greek took leave of them, he said: "At last my eyes have beheld a Jew who thinks something besides racial superiority and talks something besides religion." And they retired for the night.

133:5.12 (1477.7) The sojourn in Athens was pleasant and profitable, but it was not particularly fruitful in its human contacts. Too many of the Athenians of that day were either intellectually proud of their reputation of another day or mentally stupid and ignorant, being the offspring of the inferior slaves of those earlier periods when there was glory in Greece and wisdom in the minds of its people. Even then, there were still many keen minds to be found among the citizens of Athens.

6   *At Ephesus—*
Discourse on the Soul

133:6.1 (1477.8) On leaving Athens, the travelers went by way of Troas to Ephesus, the capital of the Roman province of Asia. They made many trips out to the famous temple of Artemis of the Ephesians, about two miles from the city.

Artemis was the most famous goddess of all Asia Minor and a perpetuation of the still earlier mother goddess of ancient Anatolian times. The crude idol exhibited in the enormous temple dedicated to her worship was reputed to have fallen from heaven. Not all of Ganid's early training to respect images as symbols of divinity had been eradicated, and he thought it best to purchase a little silver shrine in honor of this fertility goddess of Asia Minor. That night they talked at great length about the worship of things made with human hands.

133:6.2 (1478.1) On the third day of their stay they walked down by the river to observe the dredging of the harbor's mouth. At noon they talked with a young Phoenician who was homesick and much discouraged; but most of all he was envious of a certain young man who had received promotion over his head. Jesus spoke comforting words to him and quoted the olden Hebrew proverb: "A man's gift makes room for him and brings him before great men."

133:6.3 (1478.2) Of all the large cities they visited on this tour of the Mediterranean, they here accomplished the least of value to the subsequent work of the Christian missionaries. Christianity secured its start in Ephesus largely through the efforts of Paul, who resided here more than two years, making tents for a living and con-

ducting lectures on religion and philosophy each night in the main audience chamber of the school of Tyrannus.

133:6.4 (1478.3) There was a progressive thinker connected with this local school of philosophy, and Jesus had several profitable sessions with him. In the course of these talks Jesus had repeatedly used the word "soul." This learned Greek finally asked him what he meant by "soul," and he replied:

133:6.5 (1478.4) "The soul is the self-reflective, truth-discerning, and spirit-perceiving part of man which forever elevates the human being above the level of the animal world. Self-consciousness, in and of itself, is not the soul. Moral self- consciousness is true human self-realization and constitutes the foundation of the human soul, and the soul is that part of man which represents the potential survival value of human experience. Moral choice and spiritual attainment, the ability to know God and the urge to be like him, are the characteristics of the soul. The soul of man cannot exist apart from moral thinking and spiritual activity. A stagnant soul is a dying soul. But the soul of man is distinct from the divine spirit which dwells within the mind. The divine spirit arrives simultaneously with the first moral activity of the human mind, and that is the occasion of the birth of the soul.

133:6.6 (1478.5) "The saving or losing of a soul has to do with whether or not the moral consciousness attains survival status through eternal alliance with its associated immortal spirit endowment. Salvation is the spiritualization of the self- realization of the moral consciousness, which thereby becomes possessed of survival value. All forms of soul conflict consist in the lack of harmony between the moral, or spiritual, self-consciousness and the purely intellectual self- consciousness.

133:6.7 (1478.6) "The human soul, when matured, ennobled, and spiritualized, approaches the heavenly status in that it comes near to being an entity intervening between the material and the spiritual, the material self and the divine spirit. The evolving soul of a human being is difficult of description and more difficult of demonstration because it is not discoverable by the methods of either material investigation or spiritual proving. Material science cannot demonstrate the existence of a soul, neither can pure spirit-testing. Notwithstanding the failure of both material science and spiritual standards to discover the existence of the human soul, every morally conscious mortal knows of the existence of his soul as a real and actual personal experience."

7.   The Sojourn at Cyprus—Discourse on Mind

133:7.1 (1479.1) Shortly the travelers set sail for Cyprus, stopping at Rhodes. They enjoyed the long water voyage and arrived at their island destination much rested in body and refreshed in spirit.

133:7.2 (1479.2) It was their plan to enjoy a period of real rest and play on this visit to Cyprus as their tour of the Mediterranean was drawing to a close. They landed at Paphos and at once began the assembly of supplies for their sojourn of several weeks in the near-by mountains. On the third day after their arrival they started for the hills with their well-loaded pack animals.

133:7.3 (1479.3) For two weeks the trio greatly enjoyed themselves, and then, without warning, young Ganid was suddenly taken grievously ill. For two weeks he suffered from a raging fever, oftentimes becoming delirious; both Jesus and Gonod were kept busy attending the sick boy. Jesus skillfully and tenderly cared for the lad, and the father was amazed by both the gentleness and adeptness manifested in all his ministry to the afflicted youth. They were far from human habitations, and the boy was too ill to be moved; so they prepared as best they could to nurse him back to health right there in the mountains.

133:7.4 (1479.4) During Ganid's con-valescence of three weeks Jesus told him many interesting things about nature and her various moods. And what fun they had as they wandered over the mountains, the boy asking questions, Jesus answering them, and the father marveling at the whole performance.

133:7.5 (1479.5) The last week of their sojourn in the mountains Jesus and Ganid had a long talk on the functions of the human mind. After several hours of discussion the lad asked this question: "But, Teacher, what do you mean when you say that man experiences a higher form of self-consciousness than do the higher animals?" And as restated in modern phraseology, Jesus answered:

133:7.6 (1479.6) My son, I have already told you much about the mind of man and the divine spirit that lives therein, but now let me emphasize that self-consciousness is a reality. When any animal becomes self-conscious, it becomes a primitive man. Such an attainment results from a co-ordination of function between impersonal energy and spirit- conceiving mind, and it is this phenomenon which warrants the bestowal of an absolute focal point for the human personality, the spirit of the Father in heaven.

133:7.7 (1479.7) Ideas are not simply a record of sensations; ideas are sensations plus the reflective interpretations of the personal self; and the self is more than the sum of one's sensations. There begins to be something of an approach to unity in an evolving selfhood, and that unity is derived from the indwelling presence of a part of absolute unity which spiritually activates such a self-conscious animal-origin mind.

133:7.8 (1479.8) No mere animal could possess a time self-consciousness. Animals possess a physiological co-ordination of associated sensation-recognition and memory thereof, but none experience a meaningful recognition of sensation or exhibit a purposeful association of these combined physical experiences such as is manifested in the conclusions of intelligent and reflective human interpretations. And this fact of self-conscious existence, associated with the reality of his subsequent spiritual experience, constitutes man a potential son of the universe and foreshadows his eventual attainment of the Supreme Unity of the universe.

133:7.9 (1480.1) Neither is the human self merely the sum of the successive states of consciousness. Without the effective functioning of a consciousness sorter and associator there would not exist sufficient unity to warrant the designation of a selfhood. Such an ununified mind could hardly attain conscious levels of human status. If the associations of consciousness were just an accident, the minds of all men would then exhibit the uncontrolled and random associations of certain phases of mental madness. *

133:7.10 (1480.2) A human mind, built up solely out of the consciousness of physical sensations, could never attain spiritual levels; this kind of material mind would be utterly lacking in a sense of moral values and would be without a guiding sense of spiritual dominance which is so essential to achieving harmonious personality unity in time, and which is inseparable from personality survival in eternity.

133:7.11 (1480.3) The human mind early begins to manifest qualities which are supermaterial; the truly reflective human intellect is not altogether bound by the limits of time. That individuals so differ in their life performances indicates, not only the varying endowments of heredity and the different influences of the environment, but also the degree of unification with the indwelling spirit of the Father which has been achieved by the self, the measure of the identification of the one with the other.

133:7.12 (1480.4) The human mind does not well stand the conflict of double allegiance. It is a severe strain on the soul to undergo the experience of an effort to serve both good and evil. The supremely happy and efficiently unified mind is the one wholly dedicated to the doing of the will of the Father in heaven. Unresolved conflicts destroy unity and may terminate in mind disruption. But the survival character of a soul is not fostered by attempting to secure peace of mind at any price, by the surrender of noble aspirations, and by the compromise of spiritual ideals; rather is such peace attained by the stalwart assertion of the triumph of that which is true, and this victory is achieved in the overcoming of evil with the potent force of good.

133:7.13 (1480.5) The next day they departed for Salamis, where they embarked for Antioch on the Syrian coast.

8   At Antioch

133:8.1 (1480.6) Antioch was the capital of the Roman province of Syria, and here the imperial governor had his residence. Antioch had half a million inhabitants; it was the third city of the empire in size and the first in wickedness and flagrant immorality. Gonod had considerable business to transact; so Jesus and Ganid were much by themselves. They visited everything about this polyglot city except the grove of Daphne. Gonod and Ganid visited this notorious shrine of shame, but Jesus declined to accompany them. Such scenes were not so shocking to Indians, but they were repellent to an idealistic Hebrew.

133:8.2 (1480.7) Jesus became sober and reflective as he drew nearer Palestine and the end of their journey. He visited with few people in Antioch; he seldom went about in the city. After much questioning as to why his teacher manifested so little interest in Antioch, Ganid finally induced Jesus to say: "This city is not far from Palestine; maybe I shall come back here sometime."

133:8.3 (1481.1) Ganid had a very interesting experience in Antioch. This young man had proved himself an apt pupil and already had begun to make practical use of some of Jesus' teachings. There was a certain Indian connected with his father's business in Antioch who had become so unpleasant and disgruntled that his dismissal had been considered.

When Ganid heard this, he betook himself to his father's place of business and held a long conference with his fellow countryman. This man felt he had been put at the wrong job. Ganid told him about the Father in heaven and in many ways expanded his views of religion. But of all that Ganid said, the quotation of a Hebrew proverb did the most good, and that word of wisdom was: "Whatsoever your hand finds to do, do that with all your might."

133:8.4 (1481.2) After preparing their luggage for the camel caravan, they passed on down to Sidon and thence over to Damascus, and after three days they made ready for the long trek across the desert sands.

9   *In Mesopotamia*

133:9.1 (1481.3) The caravan trip across the desert was not a new experience for these much-traveled men. After Ganid had watched his teacher help with the loading of their twenty camels and observed him volunteer to drive their own animal, he exclaimed, "Teacher, is there anything that you cannot do?" Jesus only smiled, saying, "The teacher surely is not without honor in the eyes of a diligent pupil." And so they set forth for the ancient city of Ur.

133:9.2 (1481.4) Jesus was much interested in the early history of Ur, the birthplace of Abraham, and he was equally fascinated with the ruins and traditions of Susa, so much so that Gonod and Ganid extended their stay in these parts three weeks in order to afford Jesus more time to conduct his investigations and also to provide the better opportunity to persuade him to go back to India with them.

133:9.3 (1481.5) It was at Ur that Ganid had a long talk with Jesus regarding the difference between knowledge, wisdom, and truth. And he was greatly charmed with the saying of the Hebrew wise man: "Wisdom is the principal thing; therefore get wisdom. With all your quest for knowledge, get understanding. Exalt wisdom and she will promote you. She will bring you to honor if you will but embrace her."

133:9.4 (1481.6) At last the day came for the separation. They were all brave, especially the lad, but it was a trying ordeal. They were tearful of eye but courageous of heart. In bidding his teacher farewell, Ganid said: "Farewell, Teacher, but not forever. When I come again to Damascus, I will look for you. I love you, for I think the Father in heaven must be something like you; at least I know you are much like what you have told me about him. I will remember your teaching, but most of all, I will never forget you." Said the father, "Farewell to a great teacher, one who has made us better and helped us to know God." And Jesus replied, "Peace be upon you, and may the blessing of the Father in heaven ever abide with you." And Jesus stood on the shore and watched as the small boat carried them out to their anchored ship.

Thus the Master left his friends from India at Charax, never to see them again in this world; nor were they, in this world, ever to know that the man who later appeared as Jesus of Nazareth was this same friend they had just taken leave of— Joshua their teacher.

133:9.5 (1481.7) In India, Ganid grew up to become an influential man, a worthy successor of his eminent father, and he spread abroad many of the noble truths which he had learned from Jesus, his beloved teacher. Later on in life, when Ganid heard of the strange teacher in Palestine who terminated his career on a cross, though he recognized the similarity between the gospel of this Son of Man and the teachings of his Jewish tutor, it never occurred to him that these two were actually the same person.

133:9.6 (1482.1) Thus ended that chapter in the life of the Son of Man which might be termed: The mission of Joshua the teacher.

Paper 134

The Transition Years

134:0.1 (1483.1) DURING the Mediterranean journey Jesus had carefully studied the people he met and the countries through which he passed, and at about this time he reached his final decision as to the remainder of his life on earth. He had fully considered and now finally approved the plan which provided that he be born of Jewish parents in Palestine, and he therefore deliberately returned to Galilee to await the beginning of his lifework as a public teacher of truth; he began to lay plans for a public career in the land of his father Joseph's people, and he did this of his own free will.

134:0.2 (1483.2) Jesus had found out through personal and human experience that Palestine was the best place in all the Roman world wherein to set forth the closing chapters, and to enact the final scenes, of his life on earth. For the first time he became fully satisfied with the program of openly manifesting his true nature and of revealing his divine identity among the Jews and gentiles of his native Palestine. He definitely decided to finish his life on earth and to complete his career of mortal existence in the same land in which he entered the human experience as a helpless babe. His Urantia career began among the Jews in Palestine, and he chose to terminate his life in Palestine and among the Jews.

1   The Thirtieth Year (A.D. 24)

134:1.1 (1483.3) After taking leave of Gonod and Ganid at Charax (in December of A.D. 23), Jesus returned by way of Ur to Babylon, where he joined a desert caravan that was on its way to Damascus. From Damascus he went to Nazareth, stopping only a few hours at Capernaum, where he paused to call on Zebedee's family. There he met his brother James, who had sometime previously come over to work in his place in Zebedee's boatshop. After talking with James and Jude (who also chanced to be in Capernaum) and after turning over to his brother James the little house which John Zebedee had managed to buy, Jesus went on to Nazareth.

134:1.2 (1483.4) At the end of his Mediterranean journey Jesus had received sufficient money to meet his living expenses almost up to the time of the beginning of his public ministry. But aside from Zebedee of Capernaum and the people whom he met on this extraordinary trip, the world never knew that he made this journey. His family always believed that he spent this time in study at Alexandria. Jesus never confirmed these beliefs, neither did he make open denial of such misunderstandings.

134:1.3 (1483.5) During his stay of a few weeks at Nazareth, Jesus visited with his family and friends, spent some time at the repair shop with his brother Joseph, but devoted most of his attention to Mary and Ruth. Ruth was then nearly fifteen years old, and this was Jesus' first opportunity to have long talks with her since she had become a young woman.

134:1.4 (1484.1) Both Simon and Jude had for some time wanted to get married, but they had disliked to do this without Jesus' consent; accordingly they had postponed these events, hoping for their eldest brother's return. Though they all regarded James as the head of the family in most matters, when it came to getting married, they wanted the blessing of Jesus. So Simon and Jude were married at a double wedding in early March of this year, A.D. 24. All the older children were now married; only Ruth, the youngest, remained at home with Mary.

134:1.5 (1484.2) Jesus visited with the individual members of his family quite normally and naturally, but when they were all together, he had so little to say that they remarked about it among themselves. Mary especially was disconcerted by this unusually peculiar behavior of her first-born son.

134:1.6 (1484.3) About the time Jesus was preparing to leave Nazareth, the conductor of a large caravan which was passing through the city was taken violently ill, and Jesus, being a linguist, volunteered to take his place. Since this trip would necessitate his absence for a year, and inasmuch as all his brothers were married and his mother was living at home with Ruth, Jesus called a family conference at which he proposed that his mother and Ruth go to Capernaum to live in the home which he had so recently given to James. Accordingly, a few days after Jesus left with the caravan, Mary and Ruth moved to Capernaum, where they lived for the rest of Mary's life in the home that Jesus had provided. Joseph and his family moved into the old Nazareth home.

134:1.7 (1484.4) This was one of the more unusual years in the inner experience of the Son of Man; great progress was made in effecting working harmony between his human mind and the indwelling Adjuster. The Adjuster had been actively engaged in reorganizing the thinking and in rehearsing the mind for the great events which were in the not then distant future. The personality of Jesus was preparing for his great change in attitude toward the world. These were the in-between times, the transition stage of that being who began life as God appearing as man, and who was now making ready to complete his earth career as man appearing as God.

2   The Caravan Trip to the Caspian

134:2.1 (1484.5) It was the first of April, A.D. 24, when Jesus left Nazareth on the caravan trip to the Caspian Sea region. The caravan which Jesus joined as its conductor was going from Jerusalem by way of Damascus and Lake Urmia through Assyria, Media, and Parthia to the southeastern Caspian Sea region. It was a full year before he returned from this journey.

134:2.2 (1484.6) For Jesus this caravan trip was another adventure of exploration and personal ministry. He had an interesting experience with his caravan family—passengers, guards, and camel drivers. Scores of men, women, and children residing along the route followed by the caravan lived richer lives as a result of their contact with Jesus, to them, the extraordinary conductor of a commonplace caravan. Not all who enjoyed these occasions of his personal ministry profited thereby, but the vast majority of those who met and talked with him were made better for the remainder of their natural lives.

134:2.3 (1484.7) Of all his world travels this Caspian Sea trip carried Jesus nearest to the Orient and enabled him to gain a better understanding of the Far-Eastern peoples. He made intimate and personal contact with every one of the surviving races of Urantia excepting the red. He equally enjoyed his personal ministry to each of these varied races and blended peoples, and all of them were receptive to the living truth which he brought them. The Europeans from the Far West and the Asiatics from the Far East alike gave attention to his words of hope and eternal life and were equally influenced by the life of loving service and spiritual ministry which he so graciously lived among them.

134:2.4 (1485.1) The caravan trip was successful in every way. This was a most interesting episode in the human life of Jesus, for he functioned during this year in an executive capacity, being responsible for the material intrusted to his charge and for the safe conduct of the travelers making up the caravan party. And he most faithfully, efficiently, and wisely discharged his multiple duties.

134:2.5 (1485.2) On the return from the Caspian region, Jesus gave up the direction of the caravan at Lake Urmia, where he tarried for slightly over two weeks. He returned as a passenger with a later caravan to Damascus, where the owners of the camels besought him to remain in their service. Declining this offer, he journeyed on with the caravan train to Capernaum, arriving the first of April, A.D. 25. No longer did he regard Nazareth as his home. Capernaum had become the home of Jesus, James, Mary, and Ruth. But Jesus never again lived with his family; when in Capernaum he made his home with the Zebedees.

3   *The Urmia Lectures*

134:3.1 (1485.3) On the way to the Caspian Sea, Jesus had stopped several days for rest and recuperation at the old Persian city of Urmia on the western shores of Lake Urmia. On the largest of a group of islands situated a short distance offshore near Urmia was located a large building—a lecture amphitheater—dedicated to the "spirit of religion." This structure was really a temple of the philosophy of religions.

134:3.2 (1485.4) This temple of religion had been built by a wealthy merchant citizen of Urmia and his three sons. This man was Cymboyton, and he numbered among his ancestors many diverse peoples.

134:3.3 (1485.5) The lectures and discussions in this school of religion began at ten o'clock every morning in the week. The afternoon sessions started at three o'clock, and the evening debates opened at eight o'clock. Cymboyton or one of his three sons always presided at these sessions of teaching, discussion, and debate. The founder of this unique school of religions lived and died without ever revealing his personal religious beliefs. *

134:3.4 (1485.6) On several occasions Jesus participated in these discussions, and before he left Urmia, Cymboyton arranged with Jesus to sojourn with them for two weeks on his return trip and give twenty-four lectures on "The Brotherhood of Men," and to conduct twelve evening sessions of questions, discussions, and debates on his lectures in particular and on the brotherhood of men in general.

134:3.5 (1485.7) In accordance with this arrangement, Jesus stopped off on the return trip and delivered these lectures. This was the most systematic and formal of all the Master's teaching on Urantia. Never before or after did he say so much on one subject as was contained in these lectures and discussions on the brotherhood of men. In reality these lectures were on the "Kingdom of God" and the "Kingdoms of Men."

134:3.6 (1486.1) More than thirty religions and religious cults were represented on the faculty of this temple of religious philosophy. These teachers were chosen, supported, and fully accredited by their respective religious groups. At this time there were about seventy-five teachers on the faculty, and they lived in cottages each accommodating about a dozen persons. Every new moon these groups were changed by the casting of lots. Intolerance, a contentious spirit, or any other disposition to interfere with the smooth running of the community would bring about the prompt and summary dismissal of the offending teacher. He would be unceremoniously dismissed, and his alternate in waiting would be immediately installed in his place.

134:3.7 (1486.2) These teachers of the various religions made a great effort to show how similar their religions were in regard to the fundamental things of this life and the next. There was but one doctrine which had to be accepted in order to gain a seat on this faculty—every teacher must represent a religion which recognized God—some sort of supreme Deity. There were five independent teachers on the faculty who did not represent any organized religion, and it was as such an independent teacher that Jesus appeared before them.

134:3.8 (1486.3) [When we, the midwayers, first prepared the summary of Jesus' teachings at Urmia, there arose a disagreement between the seraphim of the churches and the seraphim of progress as to the wisdom of including these teachings in the Urantia Revelation. Conditions of the twentieth century, prevailing in both religion and human governments, are so different from those prevailing in Jesus' day that it was indeed difficult to adapt the Master's teachings at Urmia to the problems of the kingdom of God and the kingdoms of men as these world functions are existent in the twentieth century. We were never able to formulate a statement of the Master's teachings which was acceptable to both groups of these seraphim of planetary government. Finally, the Melchizedek chairman of the revelatory commission appointed a commission of three of our number to prepare our view of the Master's Urmia teachings as adapted to twentieth-century religious and political conditions on Urantia. Accordingly, we three secondary midwayers completed such an adaptation of Jesus' teachings, restating his pronouncements as we would apply them to present-day world conditions, and we now present these statements as they stand after having been edited by the Melchizedek chairman of the revelatory commission.]

4 Sovereignty— Divine and Human

134:4.1 (1486.4) The brotherhood of men is founded on the fatherhood of God. The family of God is derived from the love of God—God is love. God the Father divinely loves his children, all of them.

134:4.2 (1486.5) The kingdom of heaven, the divine government, is founded on the fact of divine sovereignty—God is spirit. Since God is spirit, this kingdom is spiritual. The kingdom of heaven is neither material nor merely intellectual; it is a spiritual relationship between God and man.

134:4.3 (1486.6) If different religions recognize the spirit sovereignty of God the Father, then will all such religions remain at peace. Only when one religion assumes that it is in some way superior to all others, and that it possesses exclusive authority over other religions, will such a religion presume to be intolerant of other religions or dare to persecute other religious believers.

134:4.4 (1487.1) Religious peace—brotherhood—can never exist unless all religions are willing to completely divest themselves of all ecclesiastical authority and fully surrender all concept of spiritual sovereignty. God alone is spirit sovereign.

134:4.5 (1487.2) You cannot have equality among religions (religious liberty) without having religious wars unless all religions consent to the transfer of all religious sovereignty to some superhuman level, to God himself.

134:4.6 (1487.3) The kingdom of heaven in the hearts of men will create religious unity (not necessarily uniformity) because any and all religious groups composed of such religious believers will be free from all notions of ecclesiastical authority—religious sovereignty.

134:4.7 (1487.4) God is spirit, and God gives a fragment of his spirit self to dwell in the heart of man. Spiritually, all men are equal. The kingdom of heaven is free from castes, classes, social levels, and economic groups. You are all brethren.

134:4.8 (1487.5) But the moment you lose sight of the spirit sovereignty of God the Father, some one religion will begin to assert its superiority over other religions; and then, instead of peace on earth and good will among men, there will start dissensions, recriminations, even religious wars, at least wars among religionists.

134:4.9 (1487.6) Freewill beings who regard themselves as equals, unless they mutually acknowledge themselves as subject to some supersovereignty, some authority over and above themselves, sooner or later are tempted to try out their ability to gain power and authority over other persons and groups. The concept of equality never brings peace except in the mutual recognition of some overcontrolling influence of supersovereignty.

134:4.10 (1487.7) The Urmia religionists lived together in comparative peace and tranquillity because they had fully surrendered all their notions of religious sovereignty. Spiritually, they all believed in a sovereign God; socially, full and unchallengeable authority rested in their presiding head—Cymboyton. They well knew what would happen to any teacher who assumed to lord it over his fellow teachers. There can be no lasting religious peace on Urantia until all religious groups freely surrender all their notions of divine favor, chosen people, and religious sovereignty. Only when God the Father becomes supreme will men become religious brothers and live together in religious peace on earth.

5   *Political Sovereignty*

134:5.1 (1487.8) [While the Master's teaching concerning the sovereignty of God is a truth—only complicated by the subsequent appearance of the religion about him among the world's religions—his presentations concerning political sovereignty are vastly complicated by the political evolution of nation life during the last nineteen hundred years and more. In the times of Jesus there were only two great world powers—the Roman Empire in the West and the Han Empire in the East—and these were widely separated by the Parthian kingdom and other intervening lands of the Caspian and Turkestan regions. We have, therefore, in the following presentation departed more widely from the substance of the Master's teachings at Urmia concerning political sovereignty, at the same time attempting to depict the import of such teachings as they are applicable to the peculiarly critical stage of the evolution of political sovereignty in the twentieth century after Christ.]

134:5.2 (1487.9) War on Urantia will never end so long as nations cling to the illusive notions of unlimited national sovereignty. There are only two levels of relative sovereignty on an inhabited world: the spiritual free will of the individual mortal and the collective sovereignty of mankind as a whole. Between the level of the individual human being and the level of the total of mankind, all groupings and associations are relative, transitory, and of value only in so far as they enhance the welfare, well-being, and progress of the individual and the planetary grand total—man and mankind.

134:5.3 (1488.1) Religious teachers must always remember that the spiritual sovereignty of God overrides all intervening and intermediate spiritual loyalties. Someday civil rulers will learn that the Most Highs rule in the kingdoms of men.

134:5.4 (1488.2) This rule of the Most Highs in the kingdoms of men is not for the especial benefit of any especially favored group of mortals. There is no such thing as a "chosen people." The rule of the Most Highs, the overcontrollers of political evolution, is a rule designed to foster the greatest good to the greatest number of all men and for the greatest length of time.

134:5.5 (1488.3) Sovereignty is power and it grows by organization. This growth of the organization of political power is good and proper, for it tends to encompass ever-widening segments of the total of mankind. But this same growth of political organizations creates a problem at every intervening stage between the initial and natural organization of political power— the family—and the final consummation of political growth—the government of all mankind, by all mankind, and for all mankind.

134:5.6 (1488.4) Starting out with parental power in the family group, political sovereignty evolves by organization as families overlap into consanguineous clans which become united, for various reasons, into tribal units— superconsanguineous political groupings. And then, by trade, commerce, and conquest, tribes become unified as a nation, while nations themselves sometimes become unified by empire.

134:5.7 (1488.5) As sovereignty passes from smaller groups to larger groups, wars are lessened. That is, minor wars between smaller nations are lessened, but the potential for greater wars is increased as the nations wielding sovereignty become larger and larger. Presently, when all the world has been explored and occupied, when nations are few, strong, and powerful, when these great and supposedly sovereign nations come to touch borders, when only oceans separate them, then will the stage be set for major wars, world-wide conflicts. So-called sovereign nations cannot rub elbows without generating conflicts and eventuating wars.

134:5.8 (1488.6) The difficulty in the evolution of political sovereignty from the family to all mankind, lies in the inertia-resistance exhibited on all intervening levels. Families have, on occasion, defied their clan, while clans and tribes have often been subversive of the sovereignty of the territorial state. Each new and forward evolution of political sovereignty is (and has always been) embarrassed and hampered by the "scaffolding stages" of the previous developments in political organization. And this is true because human loyalties, once mobilized, are hard to change. The same loyalty which makes possible the evolution of the tribe, makes difficult the evolution of the supertribe—the territorial state. And the same loyalty (patriotism) which makes possible the evolution of the territorial state, vastly complicates the evolutionary development of the government of all mankind.

134:5.9 (1488.7) Political sovereignty is created out of the surrender of self-determinism, first by the individual within the family and then by the families and clans in relation to the tribe and larger groupings. This progressive transfer of self-determination from the smaller to ever larger political organizations has generally proceeded unabated in the East since the establishment of the Ming and the Mogul dynasties. In the West it obtained for more than a thousand years right on down to the end of the World War, when an unfortunate retrograde movement temporarily reversed this normal trend by re-establishing the submerged political sovereignty of numerous small groups in Europe.

134:5.10 (1489.1) Urantia will not enjoy lasting peace until the so-called sovereign nations intelligently and fully surrender their sovereign powers into the hands of the brotherhood of men—mankind government. Internationalism—Leagues of Nations—can never bring permanent peace to mankind. World-wide confederations of nations will effectively prevent minor wars and acceptably control the smaller nations, but they will not prevent world wars nor control the three, four, or five most powerful governments. In the face of real conflicts, one of these world powers will withdraw from the League and declare war. You cannot prevent nations going to war as long as they remain infected with the delusional virus of national sovereignty. Internationalism is a step in the right direction. An international police force will prevent many minor wars, but it will not be effective in preventing major wars, conflicts between the great military governments of earth.

134:5.11 (1489.2) As the number of truly sovereign nations (great powers) decreases, so do both opportunity and need for mankind government increase. When there are only a few really sovereign (great) powers, either they must embark on the life and death struggle for national (imperial) supremacy, or else, by voluntary surrender of certain prerogatives of sovereignty, they must create the essential nucleus of supernational power which will serve as the beginning of the real sovereignty of all mankind.

134:5.12 (1489.3) Peace will not come to Urantia until every so-called sovereign nation surrenders its power to make war into the hands of a representative government of all mankind. Political sovereignty is innate with the peoples of the world. When all the peoples of Urantia create a world government, they have the right and the power to make such a government SOVEREIGN; and when such a representative or democratic world power controls the world's land, air, and naval forces, peace on earth and good will among men can prevail—but not until then.

134:5.13 (1489.4) To use an important nineteenth- and twentieth-century illustration: The forty-eight states of the American Federal Union have long enjoyed peace. They have no more wars among themselves. They have surrendered their sovereignty to the federal government, and through the arbitrament of war, they have abandoned all claims to the delusions of self-determination. While each state regulates its internal affairs, it is not concerned with foreign relations, tariffs, immigration, military affairs, or interstate commerce. Neither do the individual states concern themselves with matters of citizenship. The forty-eight states suffer the ravages of war only when the federal government's sovereignty is in some way jeopardized.

134:5.14 (1489.5) These forty-eight states, having abandoned the twin sophistries of sovereignty and self-determination, enjoy interstate peace and tranquillity. So will the nations of Urantia begin to enjoy peace when they freely surrender their respective sovereignties into the hands of a global government—the sovereignty of the brotherhood of men. In this world state the small nations will be as powerful as the great, even as the small state of Rhode Island has its two senators in the American Congress just the same as the populous state of New York or the large state of Texas.

134:5.15 (1490.1) The limited (state) sovereignty of these forty-eight states was created by men and for men. The superstate (national) sovereignty of the American Federal Union was created by the original thirteen of these states for their own benefit and for the benefit of men. Sometime the supernational sovereignty of the planetary government of mankind will be similarly created by nations for their own benefit and for the benefit of all men.

134:5.16 (1490.2) Citizens are not born for the benefit of governments; governments are organizations created and devised for the benefit of men. There can be no end to the evolution of political sovereignty short of the appearance of the government of the sovereignty of all men. All other sovereignties are relative in value, intermediate in meaning, and subordinate in status.

134:5.17 (1490.3) With scientific progress, wars are going to become more and more devastating until they become almost racially suicidal. How many world wars must be fought and how many leagues of nations must fail before men will be willing to establish the government of mankind and begin to enjoy the blessings of permanent peace and thrive on the tranquillity of good will—world-wide good will—among men?

6   Law, Liberty, and Sovereignty

134:6.1 (1490.4) If one man craves freedom—liberty—he must remember that all other men long for the same freedom. Groups of such liberty-loving mortals cannot live together in peace without becoming subservient to such laws, rules, and regulations as will grant each person the same degree of freedom while at the same time safeguarding an equal degree of freedom for all of his fellow mortals. If one man is to be absolutely free, then another must become an absolute slave. And the relative nature of freedom is true socially, economically, and politically. Freedom is the gift of civilization made possible by the enforcement of LAW.

134:6.2 (1490.5) Religion makes it spiritually possible to realize the brotherhood of men, but it will require mankind government to regulate the social, economic, and political problems associated with such a goal of human happiness and efficiency.

134:6.3 (1490.6) There shall be wars and rumors of wars—nation will rise against nation—just as long as the world's political sovereignty is divided up and unjustly held by a group of nation-states. England, Scotland, and Wales were always fighting each other until they gave up their respective sovereignties, reposing them in the United Kingdom.

134:6.4 (1490.7) Another world war will teach the so-called sovereign nations to form some sort of federation, thus creating the machinery for preventing small wars, wars between the lesser nations. But global wars will go on until the government of mankind is created. Global sovereignty will prevent global wars—nothing else can.

134:6.5 (1490.8) The forty-eight American free states live together in peace. There are among the citizens of these forty-eight states all of the various nationalities and races that live in the ever-warring nations of Europe. These Americans represent almost all the religions and religious sects and cults of the whole wide world, and yet here in North America they live together in peace. And all this is made possible because these forty-eight states have surrendered their sovereignty and have abandoned all notions of the supposed rights of self-determination.

134:6.6 (1490.9) It is not a question of armaments or disarmament. Neither does the question of conscription or voluntary military service enter into these problems of maintaining world-wide peace. If you take every form of modern mechanical armaments and all types of explosives away from strong nations, they will fight with fists, stones, and clubs as long as they cling to their delusions of the divine right of national sovereignty.

134:6.7 (1491.1) War is not man's great and terrible disease; war is a symptom, a result. The real disease is the virus of national sovereignty.

134:6.8 (1491.2) Urantia nations have not possessed real sovereignty; they never have had a sovereignty which could protect them from the ravages and devastations of world wars. In the creation of the global government of mankind, the nations are not giving up sovereignty so much as they are actually creating a real, bona fide, and lasting world sovereignty which will henceforth be fully able to protect them from all war. Local affairs will be handled by local governments; national affairs, by national governments; international affairs will be administered by global government.

134:6.9 (1491.3) World peace cannot be maintained by treaties, diplomacy, foreign policies, alliances, balances of power, or any other type of makeshift juggling with the sovereignties of nationalism. World law must come into being and must be enforced by world government—the sovereignty of all mankind.

134:6.10 (1491.4) The individual will enjoy far more liberty under world government. Today, the citizens of the great powers are taxed, regulated, and controlled almost oppressively, and much of this present interference with individual liberties will vanish when the national governments are willing to trustee their sovereignty as regards international affairs into the hands of global government.

134:6.11 (1491.5) Under global government the national groups will be afforded a real opportunity to realize and enjoy the personal liberties of genuine democracy. The fallacy of self-determination will be ended. With global regulation of money and trade will come the new era of world-wide peace. Soon may a global language evolve, and there will be at least some hope of sometime having a global religion—or religions with a global viewpoint.

134:6.12 (1491.6) Collective security will never afford peace until the collectivity includes all mankind.

134:6.13 (1491.7) The political sovereignty of representative mankind government will bring lasting peace on earth, and the spiritual brotherhood of man will forever insure good will among all men. And there is no other way whereby peace on earth and good will among men can be realized.

~ ~ ~ ~ ~ *

134:6.15 (1491.8) After the death of Cymboyton, his sons encountered great difficulties in maintaining a peaceful faculty. The repercussions of Jesus' teachings would have been much greater if the later Christian teachers who joined the Urmia faculty had exhibited more wisdom and exercised more tolerance.

134:6.16 (1491.9) Cymboyton's eldest son had appealed to Abner at Philadelphia for help, but Abner's choice of teachers was most unfortunate in that they turned out to be unyielding and uncompromising. These teachers sought to make their religion dominant over the other beliefs. They never suspected that the oft-referred-to lectures of the caravan conductor had been delivered by Jesus himself.

134:6.17 (1491.10) As confusion increased in the faculty, the three brothers withdrew their financial support, and after five years the school closed. Later it was reopened as a Mithraic temple and eventually burned down in connection with one of their orgiastic celebrations.

7   *The Thirty-First Year (A.D. 25)*

134:7.1 (1492.1) When Jesus returned from the journey to the Caspian Sea, he knew that his world travels were about finished. He made only one more trip outside of Palestine, and that was into Syria. After a brief visit to Capernaum, he went to Nazareth, stopping over a few days to visit. In the middle of April he left Nazareth for Tyre. From there he journeyed on north, tarrying for a few days at Sidon, but his destination was Antioch.

134:7.2 (1492.2) This is the year of Jesus' solitary wanderings through Palestine and Syria. Throughout this year of travel he was known by various names in different parts of the country: the carpenter of Nazareth, the boatbuilder of Capernaum, the scribe of Damascus, and the teacher of Alexandria.

134:7.3 (1492.3) At Antioch the Son of Man lived for over two months, working, observing, studying, visiting, ministering, and all the while learning how man lives, how he thinks, feels, and reacts to the environment of human existence. For three weeks of this period he worked as a tentmaker. He remained longer in Antioch than at any other place he visited on this trip. Ten years later, when the Apostle Paul was preaching in Antioch and heard his followers speak of the doctrines of the Damascus scribe, he little knew that his pupils had heard the voice, and listened to the teachings, of the Master himself.

134:7.4 (1492.4) From Antioch Jesus journeyed south along the coast to Caesarea, where he tarried for a few weeks, continuing down the coast to Joppa. From Joppa he traveled inland to Jamnia, Ashdod, and Gaza. From Gaza he took the inland trail to Beersheba, where he remained for a week.

134:7.5 (1492.5) Jesus then started on his final tour, as a private individual, through the heart of Palestine, going from Beersheba in the south to Dan in the north. On this journey northward he stopped at Hebron, Bethlehem (where he saw his birthplace), Jerusalem (he did not visit Bethany), Beeroth, Lebonah, Sychar, Shechem, Samaria, Geba, En-Gannim, Endor, Madon; passing through Magdala and Capernaum, he journeyed on north; and passing east of the Waters of Merom, he went by Karahta to Dan, or Caesarea-Philippi. *

134:7.6 (1492.6) The indwelling Thought Adjuster now led Jesus to forsake the dwelling places of men and betake himself up to Mount Hermon that he might finish his work of mastering his human mind and complete the task of effecting his full consecration to the remainder of his lifework on earth.

134:7.7 (1492.7) This was one of those

unusual and extraordinary epochs in the Master's earth life on Urantia. Another and very similar one was the experience he passed through when alone in the hills near Pella just subsequent to his baptism.

This period of isolation on Mount Hermon marked the termination of his purely human career, that is, the technical termination of the mortal bestowal, while the later isolation marked the beginning of the more divine phase of the bestowal. And Jesus lived alone with God for six weeks on the slopes of Mount Hermon.

8 The Sojourn on Mount Hermon

134:8.1 (1492.8) After spending some time in the vicinity of Caesarea-Philippi, Jesus made ready his supplies, and securing a beast of burden and a lad named Tiglath, he proceeded along the Damascus road to a village sometime known as Beit Jenn in the foothills of Mount Hermon. Here, near the middle of August, A.D. 25, he established his headquarters, and leaving his supplies in the custody of Tiglath, he ascended the lonely slopes of the mountain. Tiglath accompanied Jesus this first day up the mountain to a designated point about 6,000 feet above sea level, where they built a stone container in which Tiglath was to deposit food twice a week. *

134:8.2 (1493.1) The first day, after he had left Tiglath, Jesus had ascended the mountain only a short way when he paused to pray. Among other things he asked his Father to send back the guardian seraphim to "be with Tiglath." He requested that he be permitted to go up to his last struggle with the realities of mortal existence alone. And his request was granted. He went into the great test with only his indwelling Adjuster to guide and sustain him.

134:8.3 (1493.2) Jesus ate frugally while on the mountain; he abstained from all food only a day or two at a time. The superhuman beings who confronted him on this mountain, and with whom he wrestled in spirit, and whom he defeated

in power, were real; they were his archenemies in the system of Satania; they were not phantasms of the imagination evolved out of the intellectual vagaries of a weakened and starving mortal who could not distinguish reality from the visions of a disordered mind.

134:8.4 (1493.3) Jesus spent the last three weeks of August and the first three weeks of September on Mount Hermon. During these weeks he finished the mortal task of achieving the circles of mind-understanding and personality-control. Throughout this period of communion with his heavenly Father the indwelling Adjuster also completed the assigned services. The mortal goal of this earth creature was there attained. Only the final phase of mind and Adjuster attunement remained to be consummated.

134:8.5 (1493.4) After more than five weeks of unbroken communion with his Paradise Father, Jesus became absolutely assured of his nature and of the certainty of his triumph over the material levels of time-space personality manifestation. He fully believed in, and did not hesitate to assert, the ascendancy of his divine nature over his human nature.

134:8.6 (1493.5) Near the end of the mountain sojourn Jesus asked his Father if he might be permitted to hold conference with his Satania enemies as the Son of Man, as Joshua ben Joseph. This request was granted. During the last week on Mount Hermon the great temptation, the universe trial, occurred. Satan (representing Lucifer) and the rebellious Planetary Prince, Caligastia, were present with Jesus and were made fully visible to him. And this "temptation," this final trial of human loyalty in the face of the misrepresentations of rebel personalities, had not to do with food, temple pinnacles, or presumptuous acts. It had not to do with the kingdoms of this world but with the sovereignty of a mighty and glorious universe. The symbolism of your records was intended for the backward ages of the world's childlike thought. And subsequent generations should understand what a great struggle the Son of Man passed through that eventful day on Mount Hermon.

134:8.7 (1493.6) To the many proposals and counterproposals of the emissaries of Lucifer, Jesus only made reply: "May the will of my Paradise Father prevail, and you, my rebellious son, may the Ancients of Days judge you divinely. I am your Creator-father; I can hardly judge you justly, and my mercy you have already spurned. I commit you to the adjudication of the Judges of a greater universe."

134:8.8 (1494.1) To all the Lucifer-suggested compromises and makeshifts, to all such specious proposals about the incarnation bestowal, Jesus only made reply, "The will of my Father in Paradise be done." And when the trying ordeal was finished, the detached guardian seraphim returned to Jesus' side and ministered to him.

134:8.9 (1494.2) On an afternoon in late summer, amid the trees and in the silence of nature, Michael of Nebadon won the unquestioned sovereignty of his universe. On that day he completed the task set for Creator Sons to live to the full the incarnated life in the likeness of mortal flesh on the evolutionary worlds of time and space. The universe announcement of this momentous achievement was not made until the day of his baptism, months afterward, but it all really took place that day on the mountain. And when Jesus came down from his sojourn on Mount Hermon, the Lucifer rebellion in Satania and the Caligastia secession on Urantia were virtually settled. Jesus had paid the last price required of him to attain the sovereignty of his universe, which in itself regulates the status of all rebels and determines that all such future upheavals (if they ever occur) may be dealt with summarily and effectively. Accordingly, it may be seen that the so-called "great temptation" of Jesus took place sometime before his baptism and not just after that event. *

134:8.10 (1494.3) At the end of this sojourn on the mountain, as Jesus was making his descent, he met Tiglath coming up to the rendezvous with food. Turning him back, he said only: "The period of rest is over; I must return to my Father's business." He was a silent and much changed man as they journeyed back to Dan, where he took leave of the lad, giving him the donkey. He then proceeded south by the same way he had come, to Capernaum.

9   The Time of Waiting

134:9.1 (1494.4) It was now near the end of the summer, about the time of the day of atonement and the feast of tabernacles. Jesus had a family meeting in Capernaum over the Sabbath and the next day started for Jerusalem with John the son of Zebedee, going to the east of the lake and by Gerasa and on down the Jordan valley. While he visited some with his companion on the way, John noted a great change in Jesus.

134:9.2 (1494.5) Jesus and John stopped overnight at Bethany with Lazarus and his sisters, going early the next morning to Jerusalem. They spent almost three weeks in and around the city, at least John did. Many days John went into Jerusalem alone while Jesus walked about over the near-by hills and engaged in many seasons of spiritual communion with his Father in heaven.

134:9.3 (1494.6) Both of them were present at the solemn services of the day of atonement. John was much impressed by the ceremonies of this day of all days in the Jewish religious ritual, but Jesus remained a thoughtful and silent spectator. To the Son of Man this performance was pitiful and pathetic. He viewed it all as misrepresentative of the character and attributes of his Father in heaven. He looked upon the doings of this day as a travesty upon the facts of divine justice and the truths of infinite mercy. He burned to give vent to the declaration of the real truth about his Father's loving character and merciful conduct in the universe, but his faithful Monitor admonished him that his hour had not yet come. But that night, at Bethany, Jesus did drop numerous remarks which greatly disturbed John; and John never fully understood the real significance of what Jesus said in their hearing that evening.

134:9.4 (1495.1) Jesus planned to remain throughout the week of the feast of tabernacles with John. This feast was the annual holiday of all Palestine; it was the Jewish vacation time. Although Jesus did not participate in the merriment of the occasion, it was evident that he derived pleasure and experienced satisfaction as he beheld the lighthearted and joyous abandon of the young and the old.

134:9.5 (1495.2) In the midst of the week of celebration and ere the festivities were finished, Jesus took leave of John, saying that he desired to retire to the hills where he might the better commune with his Paradise Father. John would have gone with him, but Jesus insisted that he stay through the festivities, saying: "It is not required of you to bear the burden of the Son of Man; only the watchman must keep vigil while the city sleeps in peace." Jesus did not return to Jerusalem. After almost a week alone in the hills near Bethany, he departed for Capernaum. On the way home he spent a day and a night alone on the slopes of Gilboa, near where King Saul had taken his life; and when he arrived at Capernaum, he seemed more cheerful than when he had left John in Jerusalem.

134:9.6 (1495.3) The next morning Jesus went to the chest containing his personal effects, which had remained in Zebedee's workshop, put on his apron, and presented himself for work, saying, "It behooves me to keep busy while I wait for my hour to come." And he worked several months, until January of the following year, in the boatshop, by the side of his brother James. After this period of working with Jesus, no matter what doubts came up to becloud James's understanding of the lifework of the Son of Man, he never again really and wholly gave up his faith in the mission of Jesus.

134:9.7 (1495.4) During this final period of Jesus' work at the boatshop, he spent most of his time on the interior finishing of some of the larger craft. He took great pains with all his handiwork and seemed to experience the satisfaction of human achievement when he had completed a commendable piece of work. Though he wasted little time upon trifles, he was a painstaking workman when it came to the essentials of any given undertaking.

134:9.8 (1495.5) As time passed, rumors came to Capernaum of one John who was preaching while baptizing penitents in the Jordan, and John preached: "The kingdom of heaven is at hand; repent and be baptized." Jesus listened to these reports as John slowly worked his way up the Jordan valley from the ford of the river nearest to Jerusalem. But Jesus worked on, making boats, until John had journeyed up the river to a point near Pella in the month of January of the next year, A.D. 26, when he laid down his tools, declaring, "My hour has come," and presently presented himself to John for baptism.

134:9.9 (1495.6) But a great change had been coming over Jesus. Few of the people who had enjoyed his visits and ministrations as he had gone up and down in the land ever subsequently recognized in the public teacher the same person they had known and loved as a private individual in former years. And there was a reason for this failure of his early beneficiaries to recognize him in his later role of public and authoritative teacher. For long years this transformation of mind and spirit had been in progress, and it was finished during the eventful sojourn on Mount Hermon.

Paper 135

John the Baptist

135:0.1 (1496.1) JOHN the Baptist was born March 25, 7 B.C., in accordance with the promise that Gabriel made to Elizabeth in June of the previous year. For five months Elizabeth kept secret Gabriel's visitation; and when she told her husband, Zacharias, he was greatly troubled and fully believed her narrative only after he had an unusual dream about six weeks before the birth of John. Excepting the visit of Gabriel to Elizabeth and the dream of Zacharias, there was nothing unusual or supernatural connected with the birth of John the Baptist.

135:0.2 (1496.2) On the eighth day John was circumcised according to the Jewish custom. He grew up as an ordinary child, day by day and year by year, in the small village known in those days as the City of Judah, about four miles west of Jerusalem.

135:0.3 (1496.3) The most eventful occurrence in John's early childhood was the visit, in company with his parents, to Jesus and the Nazareth family. This visit occurred in the month of June, 1 B.C., when he was a little over six years of age.

135:0.4 (1496.4) After their return from Nazareth John's parents began the systematic education of the lad. There was no synagogue school in this little village; however, as he was a priest, Zacharias was fairly well educated, and Elizabeth was far better educated than the average Judean woman; she was also of the priesthood, being a descendant of the "daughters of Aaron." Since John was an only child, they spent a great deal of time on his mental and spiritual training. Zacharias had only short periods of service at the temple in Jerusalem so that he devoted much of his time to teaching his son.

135:0.5 (1496.5) Zacharias and Elizabeth had a small farm on which they raised sheep. They hardly made a living on this land, but Zacharias received a regular allowance from the temple funds dedicated to the priesthood.

1   John Becomes a Nazarite

135:1.1 (1496.6) John had no school from which to graduate at the age of fourteen, but his parents had selected this as the appropriate year for him to take the formal Nazarite vow. Accordingly, Zacharias and Elizabeth took their son to Engedi, down by the Dead Sea. This was the southern headquarters of the Nazarite brotherhood, and there the lad was duly and solemnly inducted into this order for life. After these ceremonies and the making of the vows to abstain from all intoxicating drinks, to let the hair grow, and to refrain from touching the dead, the family proceeded to Jerusalem, where, before the temple, John completed the making of the offerings which were required of those taking Nazarite vows.

135:1.2 (1496.7) John took the same life vows that had been administered to his illustrious predecessors, Samson and the prophet Samuel. A life Nazarite was looked upon as a sanctified and holy personality. The Jews regarded a Nazarite with almost the respect and veneration accorded the high priest, and this was not strange since Nazarites of lifelong consecration were the only persons, except high priests, who were ever permitted to enter the holy of holies in the temple.

135:1.3 (1497.1) John returned home from Jerusalem to tend his father's sheep and grew up to be a strong man with a noble character.

135:1.4 (1497.2) When sixteen years old, John, as a result of reading about Elijah, became greatly impressed with the prophet of Mount Carmel and decided to adopt his style of dress. From that day on John always wore a hairy garment with a leather girdle. At sixteen he was more than six feet tall and almost full grown. With his flowing hair and peculiar mode of dress he was indeed a picturesque youth. And his parents expected great things of this their only son, a child of promise and a Nazarite for life.

2 The Death of Zacharias

135:2.1 (1497.3) After an illness of several months Zacharias died in July, A.D. 12, when John was just past eighteen years of age. This was a time of great embarrassment to John since the Nazarite vow forbade contact with the dead, even in one's own family. Although John had endeavored to comply with the restrictions of his vow regarding contamination by the dead, he doubted that he had been wholly obedient to the requirements of the Nazarite order; therefore, after his father's burial he went to Jerusalem, where, in the Nazarite corner of the women's court, he offered the sacrifices required for his cleansing.

135:2.2 (1497.4) In September of this year Elizabeth and John made a journey to Nazareth to visit Mary and Jesus. John had just about made up his mind to launch out in his lifework, but he was admonished, not only by Jesus' words but also by his example, to return home, take care of his mother, and await the "coming of the Father's hour." After bidding Jesus and Mary good-bye at the end of this enjoyable visit, John did not again see Jesus until the event of his baptism in the Jordan.

135:2.3 (1497.5) John and Elizabeth returned to their home and began to lay plans for the future. Since John refused to accept the priest's allowance due him from the temple funds, by the end of two years they had all but lost their home; so they decided to go south with the sheep herd. Accordingly, the summer that John was twenty years of age witnessed their removal to Hebron. In the so-called "wilderness of Judea" John tended his sheep along a brook that was tributary to a larger stream which entered the Dead Sea at Engedi. The Engedi colony included not only Nazarites of lifelong and time-period consecration but numerous other ascetic herdsmen who congregated in this region with their herds and fraternized with the Nazarite brotherhood. They supported themselves by sheep raising and from gifts which wealthy Jews made to the order.

135:2.4 (1497.6) As time passed, John returned less often to Hebron, while he made more frequent visits to Engedi. He was so entirely different from the majority of the Nazarites that he found it very difficult fully to fraternize with the brotherhood. But he was very fond of Abner, the acknowledged leader and head of the Engedi colony.

3 The Life of a Shepherd

135:3.1 (1497.7) Along the valley of this little brook John built no less than a dozen stone shelters and night corrals, consisting of piled-up stones, wherein he could watch over and safeguard his herds of sheep and goats. John's life as a shepherd afforded him a great deal of time for thought. He talked much with Ezda, an orphan lad of Beth-zur, whom he had in a way adopted, and who cared for the herds when he made trips to Hebron to see his mother and to sell sheep, as well as when he went down to Engedi for Sabbath services. John and the lad lived very simply, subsisting on mutton, goat's milk, wild honey, and the edible locusts of that region. This, their regular diet, was supplemented by provisions brought from Hebron and Engedi from time to time.

135:3.2 (1498.1) Elizabeth kept John posted about Palestinian and world affairs, and his conviction grew deeper and deeper that the time was fast approaching when the old order was to end; that he was to become the herald of the approach of a new age, "the kingdom of heaven." This rugged shepherd was very partial to the writings of the Prophet Daniel. He read a thousand times Daniel's description of the great image, which Zacharias had told him represented the history of the great kingdoms of the world, beginning with Babylon, then Persia, Greece, and finally Rome. John perceived that already was Rome composed of such polyglot peoples and races that it could never become a strongly cemented and firmly consolidated empire. He believed that Rome was even then divided, as Syria, Egypt, Palestine, and other provinces; and then he further read "in the days of these kings shall the God of heaven set up a kingdom which shall never be destroyed. And this kingdom shall not be left to other people but shall break in pieces and consume all these kingdoms, and it shall stand forever." "And there was given him dominion and glory and a kingdom that all peoples, nations, and languages should serve him. His dominion is an everlasting dominion, which shall not pass away, and his kingdom never shall be destroyed." "And the kingdom and dominion and the greatness of the kingdom under the whole heaven shall be given to the people of the saints of the Most High, whose kingdom is an everlasting kingdom, and all dominions shall serve and obey him."

135:3.3 (1498.2) John was never able completely to rise above the confusion produced by what he had heard from his parents concerning Jesus and by these passages which he read in the Scriptures. In Daniel he read: "I saw in the night visions, and, behold, one like the Son of Man came with the clouds of heaven, and there was given him dominion and glory and a kingdom." But these words of the prophet did not harmonize with what his parents had taught him. Neither did his talk with Jesus, at the time of his visit when he was eighteen years old, correspond with these statements of the Scriptures. Notwithstanding this confusion, throughout all of his perplexity his mother assured him that his distant cousin, Jesus of Nazareth, was the true Messiah, that he had come to sit on the throne of David, and that he (John) was to become his advance herald and chief support.

135:3.4 (1498.3) From all John heard of the vice and wickedness of Rome and the dissoluteness and moral barrenness of the empire, from what he knew of the evil doings of Herod Antipas and the governors of Judea, he was minded to believe that the end of the age was impending. It seemed to this rugged and noble child of nature that the world was ripe for the end of the age of man and the dawn of the new and divine age—the kingdom of heaven. The feeling grew in John's heart that he was to be the last of the old prophets and the first of the new. And he fairly vibrated with the mounting impulse to go forth and proclaim to all men: "Repent! Get right with God! Get ready for the end; prepare yourselves for the appearance of the new and eternal order of earth affairs, the kingdom of heaven."

4   *The Death of Elizabeth*

135:4.1 (1499.1) On August 17, A.D. 22, when John was twenty-eight years of age, his mother suddenly passed away. Elizabeth's friends, knowing of the Nazarite restrictions regarding contact with the dead, even in one's own family, made all arrangements for the burial of Elizabeth before sending for John. When he received word of the death of his mother, he directed Ezda to drive his herds to Engedi and started for Hebron.

135:4.2 (1499.2) On returning to Engedi from his mother's funeral, he presented his flocks to the brotherhood and for a season detached himself from the outside world while he fasted and prayed. John knew only of the old methods of approach to divinity; he knew only of the records of such as Elijah, Samuel, and Daniel. Elijah was his ideal of a prophet. Elijah was the first of the teachers of Israel to be regarded as a prophet, and John truly believed that he was to be the last of this long and illustrious line of the messengers of heaven.

135:4.3 (1499.3) For two and a half years John lived at Engedi, and he persuaded most of the brotherhood that "the end of the age was at hand"; that "the kingdom of heaven was about to appear." And all his early teaching was based upon the current Jewish idea and concept of the Messiah as the promised deliverer of the Jewish nation from the domination of their gentile rulers.

135:4.4 (1499.4) Throughout this period John read much in the sacred writings which he found at the Engedi home of the Nazarites. He was especially impressed by Isaiah and by Malachi, the last of the prophets up to that time. He read and reread the last five chapters of Isaiah, and he believed these prophecies. Then he would read in Malachi: "Behold, I will send you Elijah the prophet before the coming of the great and dreadful day of the Lord; and he shall turn the hearts of the fathers toward the children and the hearts of the children toward their fathers, lest I come and smite the earth with a curse." And it was only this promise of Malachi that Elijah would return that deterred John from going forth to preach about the coming kingdom and to exhort his fellow Jews to flee from the wrath to come. John was ripe for the proclamation of the message of the coming kingdom, but this expectation of the coming of Elijah held him back for more than two years. He knew he was not Elijah. What did Malachi mean? Was the prophecy literal or figurative? How could he know the truth? He finally dared to think that, since the first of the prophets was called Elijah, so the last should be known, eventually, by the same name. Nevertheless, he had doubts, doubts sufficient to prevent his ever calling himself Elijah.

135:4.5 (1499.5) It was the influence of Elijah that caused John to adopt his methods of direct and blunt assault upon the sins and vices of his contemporaries. He sought to dress like Elijah, and he endeavored to talk like Elijah; in every outward aspect he was like the olden prophet. He was just such a stalwart and picturesque child of nature, just such a fearless and daring preacher of righteousness. John was not illiterate, he did well know the Jewish sacred writings, but he was hardly cultured. He was a clear thinker, a powerful speaker, and a fiery denunciator. He was hardly an example to his age, but he was an eloquent rebuke.

135:4.6 (1499.6) At last he thought out the method of proclaiming the new age, the kingdom of God; he settled that he was to become the herald of the Messiah; he swept aside all doubts and departed from Engedi one day in March of A.D. 25 to begin his short but brilliant career as a public preacher.

5   The Kingdom of God

135:5.1 (1500.1) In order to understand John's message, account should be taken of the status of the Jewish people at the time he appeared upon the stage of action. For almost one hundred years all Israel had been in a quandary; they were at a loss to explain their continuous subjugation to gentile overlords. Had not Moses taught that righteousness was always rewarded with prosperity and power? Were they not God's chosen people? Why was the throne of David desolate and vacant? In the light of the Mosaic doctrines and the precepts of the prophets the Jews found it difficult to explain their long-continued national desolation.

135:5.2 (1500.2) About one hundred years before the days of Jesus and John a new school of religious teachers arose in Palestine, the apocalyptists. These new teachers evolved a system of belief that accounted for the sufferings and humiliation of the Jews on the ground that they were paying the penalty for the nation's sins. They fell back onto the well-known reasons assigned to explain the Babylonian and other captivities of former times. But, so taught the apocalyptists, Israel should take heart; the days of their affliction were almost over; the discipline of God's chosen people was about finished; God's patience with the gentile foreigners was about exhausted. The end of Roman rule was synonymous with the end of the age and, in a certain sense, with the end of the world. These new teachers leaned heavily on the predictions of Daniel, and they consistently taught that creation was about to pass into its final stage; the kingdoms of this world were about to become the kingdom of God. To the Jewish mind of that day this was the meaning of that phrase—the kingdom of heaven—which runs throughout the teachings of both John and Jesus. To the Jews of Palestine the phrase "kingdom of heaven" had but one meaning: an absolutely righteous state in which God (the Messiah) would rule the nations of earth in perfection of power just as he ruled in heaven—"Your will be done on earth as in heaven."

135:5.3 (1500.3) In the days of John all Jews were expectantly asking, "How soon will the kingdom come?" There was a general feeling that the end of the rule of the gentile nations was drawing near. There was present throughout all Jewry a lively hope and a keen expectation that the consummation of the desire of the ages would occur during the lifetime of that generation.

135:5.4 (1500.4) While the Jews differed greatly in their estimates of the nature of the coming kingdom, they were alike in their belief that the event was impending, near at hand, even at the door. Many who read the Old Testament literally looked expectantly for a new king in Palestine, for a regenerated Jewish nation delivered from its enemies and presided over by the successor of King David, the Messiah who would quickly be acknowledged as the rightful and righteous ruler of all the world. Another, though smaller, group of devout Jews held a vastly different view of this kingdom of God. They taught that the coming kingdom was not of this world, that the world was approaching its certain end, and that "a new heaven and a new earth" were to usher in the establishment of the kingdom of God; that this kingdom was to be an everlasting dominion, that sin was to be ended, and that the citizens of the new kingdom were to become immortal in their enjoyment of this endless bliss.

135:5.5 (1500.5) All were agreed that some drastic purging or purifying discipline would of necessity precede the establishment of the new kingdom on earth. The literalists taught that a world-wide war would ensue which would destroy all unbelievers, while the faithful would sweep on to universal and eternal victory. The spiritists taught that the kingdom would be ushered in by the great judgment of God which would relegate the unrighteous to their well-deserved judgment of punishment and final destruction, at the same time elevating the believing saints of the chosen people to high seats of honor and authority with the Son of Man, who would rule over the redeemed nations in God's name. And this latter group even believed that many devout gentiles might be admitted to the fellowship of the new kingdom.

135:5.6 (1501.1) Some of the Jews held to the opinion that God might possibly establish this new kingdom by direct and divine intervention, but the vast majority believed that he would interpose some representative intermediary, the Messiah. And that was the only possible meaning the term Messiah could have had in the minds of the Jews of the generation of John and Jesus. Messiah could not possibly refer to one who merely taught God's will or proclaimed the necessity for righteous living. To all such holy persons the Jews gave the title of prophet. The Messiah was to be more than a prophet; the Messiah was to bring in the establishment of the new kingdom, the kingdom of God. No one who failed to do this could be the Messiah in the traditional Jewish sense.

135:5.7 (1501.2) Who would this Messiah be? Again the Jewish teachers differed. The older ones clung to the doctrine of the son of David. The newer taught that, since the new kingdom was a heavenly kingdom, the new ruler might also be a divine personality, one who had long sat at God's right hand in heaven. And strange as it may appear, those who thus conceived of the ruler of the new kingdom looked upon him not as a human Messiah, not as a mere man, but as "the Son of Man"—a Son of God—a heavenly Prince, long held in waiting thus to assume the rulership of the earth made new.

Such was the religious background of the Jewish world when John went forth proclaiming: "Repent, for the kingdom of heaven is at hand!"

135:5.8 (1501.3) It becomes apparent, therefore, that John's announcement of the coming kingdom had not less than half a dozen different meanings in the minds of those who listened to his impassioned preaching. But no matter what significance they attached to the phrases which John employed, each of these various groups of Jewish-kingdom expectants was intrigued by the proclamations of this sincere, enthusiastic, rough-and-ready preacher of righteousness and repentance, who so solemnly exhorted his hearers to "flee from the wrath to come."

6   *John Begins to Preach*

135:6.1 (1501.4) Early in the month of March, A.D. 25, John journeyed around the western coast of the Dead Sea and up the river Jordan to opposite Jericho, the ancient ford over which Joshua and the children of Israel passed when they first entered the promised land; and crossing over to the other side of the river, he established himself near the entrance to the ford and began to preach to the people who passed by on their way back and forth across the river. This was the most frequented of all the Jordan crossings.

135:6.2 (1501.5) It was apparent to all who heard John that he was more than a preacher. The great majority of those who listened to this strange man who had come up from the Judean wilderness went away believing that they had heard the voice of a prophet. No wonder the souls of these weary and expectant Jews were deeply stirred by such a phenomenon. Never in all Jewish history had the devout children of Abraham so longed for the "consolation of Israel" or more ardently anticipated "the restoration of the kingdom." Never in all Jewish history could John's message, "the

kingdom of heaven is at hand," have made such a deep and universal appeal as at the very time he so mysteriously appeared on the bank of this southern crossing of the Jordan.

135:6.3 (1502.1) He came from the herdsmen, like Amos. He was dressed like Elijah of old, and he thundered his admonitions and poured forth his warnings in the "spirit and power of Elijah." It is not surprising that this strange preacher created a mighty stir throughout all Palestine as the travelers carried abroad the news of his preaching along the Jordan.

135:6.4 (1502.2) There was still another and a new feature about the work of this Nazarite preacher: He baptized every one of his believers in the Jordan "for the remission of sins." Although baptism was not a new ceremony among the Jews, they had never seen it employed as John now made use of it. It had long been the practice thus to baptize the gentile proselytes into the fellowship of the outer court of the temple, but never had the Jews themselves been asked to submit to the baptism of repentance. Only fifteen months intervened between the time John began to preach and baptize and his arrest and imprisonment at the instigation of Herod Antipas, but in this short time he baptized considerably over one hundred thousand penitents.

135:6.5 (1502.3) John preached four months at Bethany ford before starting north up the Jordan. Tens of thousands of listeners, some curious but many earnest and serious, came to hear him from all parts of Judea, Perea, and Samaria. Even a few came from Galilee.

135:6.6 (1502.4) In May of this year, while he still lingered at Bethany ford, the priests and Levites sent a delegation out to inquire of John whether he claimed to be the Messiah, and by whose authority he preached. John answered these questioners by saying: "Go tell your masters that you have heard 'the voice of one crying in the wilderness,' as spoken by the prophet, saying, 'make ready the way of the Lord, make straight a highway for our God. Every valley shall be filled, and every mountain and hill shall be brought low; the uneven ground shall become a plain, while the rough places shall become a smooth valley; and all flesh shall see the salvation of God.'"

135:6.7 (1502.5) John was a heroic but tactless preacher. One day when he was preaching and baptizing on the west bank of the Jordan, a group of Pharisees and a number of Sadducees came forward and presented themselves for baptism.

Before leading them down into the water, John, addressing them as a group said: "Who warned you to flee, as vipers before the fire, from the wrath to come? I will baptize you, but I warn you to bring forth fruit worthy of sincere repentance if you would receive the remission of your sins. Tell me not that Abraham is your father. I declare that God is able of these twelve stones here before you to raise up worthy children for Abraham. And even now is the ax laid to the very roots of the trees. Every tree that brings not forth good fruit is destined to be cut down and cast into the fire." (The twelve stones to which he referred were the reputed memorial stones set up by Joshua to commemorate the crossing of the "twelve tribes" at this very point when they first entered the promised land.)

135:6.8 (1502.6) John conducted classes for his disciples, in the course of which he instructed them in the details of their new life and endeavored to answer their many questions. He counseled the teachers to instruct in the spirit as well as the letter of the law. He instructed the rich to feed the poor; to the tax gatherers he said: "Extort no more than that which is assigned you." To the soldiers he said: "Do no violence and exact nothing wrongfully—be content with your wages." While he counseled all: "Make ready for the end of the age—the kingdom of heaven is at hand."

7   *John Journeys North*

135:7.1 (1503.1) John still had confused ideas about the coming kingdom and its king. The longer he preached the more confused he became, but never did this intellectual uncertainty concerning the nature of the coming kingdom in the least lessen his conviction of the certainty of the kingdom's immediate appearance. In mind John might be confused, but in spirit never. He was in no doubt about the coming kingdom, but he was far from certain as to whether or not Jesus was to be the ruler of that kingdom. As long as John held to the idea of the restoration of the throne of David, the teachings of his parents that Jesus, born in the City of David, was to be the long-expected deliverer, seemed consistent; but at those times when he leaned more toward the doctrine of a spiritual kingdom and the end of the temporal age on earth, he was sorely in doubt as to the part Jesus would play in such events. Sometimes he questioned everything, but not for long. He really wished he might talk it all over with his cousin, but that was contrary to their expressed agreement.

135:7.2 (1503.2) As John journeyed north, he thought much about Jesus. He paused at more than a dozen places as he traveled up the Jordan. It was at Adam that he first made reference to "another one who is to come after me" in answer to the direct question which his disciples asked him, "Are you the Messiah?" And he went on to say: "There will come after me one who is greater than I, whose sandal straps I am not worthy to stoop down and unloose. I baptize you with water, but he will baptize you with the Holy Spirit. And his shovel is in his hand thoroughly to cleanse his threshing floor; he will gather the wheat into his garner, but the chaff will he burn up with the judgment fire."

135:7.3 (1503.3) In response to the

questions of his disciples John continued to expand his teachings, from day to day adding more that was helpful and comforting compared with his early and cryptic message: "Repent and be baptized." By this time throngs were arriving from Galilee and the Decapolis. Scores of earnest believers lingered with their adored teacher day after day.

8   Meeting of Jesus and John

135:8.1 (1503.4) By December of A.D. 25, when John reached the neighborhood of Pella in his journey up the Jordan, his fame had extended throughout all Palestine, and his work had become the chief topic of conversation in all the towns about the lake of Galilee. Jesus had spoken favorably of John's message, and this had caused many from Capernaum to join John's cult of repentance and baptism. James and John the fishermen sons of Zebedee had gone down in December, soon after John took up his preaching position near Pella, and had offered themselves for baptism. They went to see John once a week and brought back to Jesus fresh, firsthand reports of the evangelist's work. *

135:8.2 (1503.5) Jesus' brothers James and Jude had talked about going down to John for baptism; and now that Jude had come over to Capernaum for the Sabbath services, both he and James, after listening to Jesus' discourse in the synagogue, decided to take counsel with him concerning their plans. This was on Saturday night, January 12, A.D. 26. Jesus requested that they postpone the discussion until the following day, when he would give them his answer. He slept very little that night, being in close communion with the Father in heaven. He had arranged to have noontime lunch with his brothers and to advise them concerning baptism by John. That Sunday morning Jesus was working as usual in the boatshop. James and Jude had arrived with the lunch and were waiting in the lumber room for him, as it was not yet time for the midday recess, and they knew that Jesus

was very regular about such matters.

135:8.3 (1504.1) Just before the noon rest, Jesus laid down his tools, removed his work apron, and merely announced to the three workmen in the room with him, "My hour has come." He went out to his brothers James and Jude, repeating, "My hour has come—let us go to John." And they started immediately for Pella, eating their lunch as they journeyed. This was on Sunday, January 13. They tarried for the night in the Jordan valley and arrived on the scene of John's baptizing about noon of the next day.

135:8.4 (1504.2) John had just begun baptizing the candidates for the day. Scores of repentants were standing in line awaiting their turn when Jesus and his two brothers took up their positions in this line of earnest men and women who had become believers in John's preaching of the coming kingdom. John had been inquiring about Jesus of Zebedee's sons. He had heard of Jesus' remarks concerning his preaching, and he was day by day expecting to see him arrive on the scene, but he had not expected to greet him in the line of baptismal candidates.

135:8.5 (1504.3) Being engrossed with the details of rapidly baptizing such a large number of converts, John did not look up to see Jesus until the Son of Man stood in his immediate presence. When John recognized Jesus, the ceremonies were halted for a moment while he greeted his cousin in the flesh and asked, "But why do you come down into the water to greet me?" And Jesus answered, "To be subject to your baptism." John replied: "But I have need to be baptized by you. Why do you come to me?" And Jesus whispered to John: "Bear with me now, for it becomes us to set this example for my brothers standing here with me, and that the people may know that my hour has come."

135:8.6 (1504.4) There was a tone of finality and authority in Jesus' voice. John was atremble with emotion as he made ready to baptize Jesus of Nazareth in the

Jordan at noon on Monday, January 14, A.D. 26. Thus did John baptize Jesus and his two brothers James and Jude. And when John had baptized these three, he dismissed the others for the day, announcing that he would resume baptisms at noon the next day. As the people were departing, the four men still standing in the water heard a strange sound, and presently there appeared for a moment an apparition immediately over the head of Jesus, and they heard a voice saying, "This is my beloved Son in whom I am well pleased." A great change came over the countenance of Jesus, and coming up out of the water in silence he took leave of them, going toward the hills to the east. And no man saw Jesus again for forty days.

135:8.7 (1504.5) John followed Jesus a sufficient distance to tell him the story of Gabriel's visit to his mother ere either had been born, as he had heard it so many times from his mother's lips. He allowed Jesus to continue on his way after he had said, "Now I know of a certainty that you are the Deliverer." But Jesus made no reply.

9   *Forty Days of Preaching*

135:9.1 (1505.1) When John returned to his disciples (he now had some twenty-five or thirty who abode with him constantly), he found them in earnest conference, discussing what had just happened in connection with Jesus' baptism. They were all the more astonished when John now made known to them the story of the Gabriel visitation to Mary before Jesus was born, and also that Jesus spoke no word to him even after he had told him about this. There was no rain that evening, and this group of thirty or more talked long into the starlit night. They wondered where Jesus had gone, and when they would see him again.

135:9.2 (1505.2) After the experience of this day the preaching of John took on new and certain notes of proclamation concerning the coming kingdom and the expected Messiah. It was a tense time, these forty days of tarrying, waiting for the return of Jesus. But John continued to preach with great power, and his disciples began at about this time to preach to the overflowing throngs which gathered around John at the Jordan.

135:9.3 (1505.3) In the course of these forty days of waiting, many rumors spread about the countryside and even to Tiberias and Jerusalem. Thousands came over to see the new attraction in John's camp, the reputed Messiah, but Jesus was not to be seen. When the disciples of John asserted that the strange man of God had gone to the hills, many doubted the entire story.

135:9.4 (1505.4) About three weeks after Jesus had left them, there arrived on the scene at Pella a new deputation from the priests and Pharisees at Jerusalem. They asked John directly if he was Elijah or the prophet that Moses promised; and when John said, "I am not," they made bold to ask, "Are you the Messiah?" and John answered, "I am not." Then said these men from Jerusalem: "If you are not Elijah, nor the prophet, nor the Messiah, then why do you baptize the people and create all this stir?" And John replied: "It should be for those who have heard me and received my baptism to say who I am, but I declare to you that, while I baptize with water, there has been among us one who will return to baptize you with the Holy Spirit."

135:9.5 (1505.5) These forty days were a difficult period for John and his disciples. What was to be the relation of John to Jesus? A hundred questions came up for discussion. Politics and selfish preferment began to make their appearance.

Intense discussions grew up around the various ideas and concepts of the Messiah. Would he become a military leader and a Davidic king? Would he smite the Roman armies as Joshua had the Canaanites? Or would he come to establish a spiritual kingdom? John rather decided, with the minority, that Jesus had come to establish the kingdom of heaven, although he was not altogether clear in his own mind as to just what was to be embraced within this mission of the establishment of the kingdom of heaven.

135:9.6 (1505.6) These were strenuous days in John's experience, and he prayed for the return of Jesus. Some of John's disciples organized scouting parties to go in search of Jesus, but John forbade, saying: "Our times are in the hands of the God of heaven; he will direct his chosen Son."

135:9.7 (1505.7) It was early on the morning of Sabbath, February 23, that the company of John, engaged in eating their morning meal, looked up toward the north and beheld Jesus coming to them. As he approached them, John stood upon a large rock and, lifting up his sonorous voice, said: "Behold the Son of God, the deliverer of the world! This is he of whom I have said, 'After me there will come one who is preferred before me because he was before me.' For this cause came I out of the wilderness to preach repentance and to baptize with water, proclaiming that the kingdom of heaven is at hand. And now comes one who shall baptize you with the Holy Spirit. And I beheld the divine spirit descending upon this man, and I heard the voice of God declare, 'This is my beloved Son in whom I am well pleased.'"

135:9.8 (1506.1) Jesus bade them return to their food while he sat down to eat with John, his brothers James and Jude having returned to Capernaum.

135:9.9 (1506.2) Early in the morning of the next day he took leave of John and his disciples, going back to Galilee. He gave them no word as to when they would again see him. To John's inquiries about his own preaching and mission Jesus only said, "My Father will guide you now and in the future as he has in the past." And these two great men separated that morning on the banks of the Jordan, never again to greet each other in the flesh.

John Journeys South

135:10.1 (1506.3) Since Jesus had gone north into Galilee, John felt led to retrace his steps southward. Accordingly, on Sunday morning, March 3, John and the remainder of his disciples began their journey south. About one quarter of John's immediate followers had meantime departed for Galilee in quest of Jesus. There was a sadness of confusion about John. He never again preached as he had before baptizing Jesus. He somehow felt that the responsibility of the coming kingdom was no longer on his shoulders. He felt that his work was almost finished; he was disconsolate and lonely. But he preached, baptized, and journeyed on southward.

135:10.2 (1506.4) Near the village of Adam, John tarried for several weeks, and it was here that he made the memorable attack upon Herod Antipas for unlawfully taking the wife of another man. By June of this year (A.D. 26) John was back at the Bethany ford of the Jordan, where he had begun his preaching of the coming kingdom more than a year previously. In the weeks following the baptism of Jesus the character of John's preaching gradually changed into a proclamation of mercy for the common people, while he denounced with renewed vehemence the corrupt political and religious rulers.

135:10.3 (1506.5) Herod Antipas, in whose territory John had been preaching, became alarmed lest he and his disciples should start a rebellion. Herod also resented John's public criticisms of his domestic affairs. In view of all this, Herod decided to put John in prison. Accordingly, very early in the morning of June 12, before the multitude arrived to hear the preaching and witness the baptizing, the agents of Herod placed John under arrest. As weeks passed and he was not released, his disciples scattered over all Palestine, many of them going into Galilee to join the followers of Jesus.

John in Prison

135:11.1 (1506.6) John had a lonely and somewhat bitter experience in prison. Few of his followers were permitted to see him. He longed to see Jesus but had to be content with hearing of his work through those of his followers who had become believers in the Son of Man. He was often tempted to doubt Jesus and his divine mission. If Jesus were the Messiah, why did he do nothing to deliver him from this unbearable imprisonment? For more than a year and a half this rugged man of God's outdoors languished in that despicable prison. And this experience was a great test of his faith in, and loyalty to, Jesus. Indeed, this whole experience was a great test of John's faith even in God. Many times was he tempted to doubt even the genuineness of his own mission and experience.

135:11.2 (1507.1) After he had been in prison several months, a group of his disciples came to him and, after reporting concerning the public activities of Jesus, said: "So you see, Teacher, that he who was with you at the upper Jordan prospers and receives all who come to him. He even feasts with publicans and sinners. You bore courageous witness to him, and yet he does nothing to effect your deliverance." But John answered his friends: "This man can do nothing unless it has been given him by his Father in heaven. You well remember that I said, 'I am not the Messiah, but I am one sent on before to prepare the way for him.' And that I did. He who has the bride is the bridegroom, but the friend of the bridegroom who stands near by and hears him rejoices greatly because of the bridegroom's voice. This, my joy, therefore is fulfilled. He must increase but I must decrease. I am of this earth and have declared my message. Jesus of Nazareth comes down to the earth from heaven and is above us all. The Son of Man has descended from God, and the words of God he will declare to you. For the Father in heaven gives not the spirit by measure to his own Son. The Father loves his Son and will presently put all things in the hands of this Son. He who believes in the Son has eternal life. And these words which I speak are true and abiding." *

135:11.3 (1507.2) These disciples were amazed at John's pronouncement, so much so that they departed in silence. John was also much agitated, for he perceived that he had uttered a prophecy. Never again did he wholly doubt the mission and divinity of Jesus. But it was a sore disappointment to John that Jesus sent him no word, that he came not to see him, and that he exercised none of his great power to deliver him from prison. But Jesus knew all about this. He had great love for John, but being now cognizant of his divine nature and knowing fully the great things in preparation for John when he departed from this world and also knowing that John's work on earth was finished, he constrained himself not to interfere in the natural outworking of the great preacher-prophet's career.

135:11.4 (1507.3) This long suspense in prison was humanly unbearable. Just a few days before his death John again sent trusted messengers to Jesus, inquiring: "Is my work done? Why do I languish in prison? Are you truly the Messiah, or shall we look for another?" And when these two disciples gave this message to Jesus, the Son of Man replied: "Go back to John and tell him that I have not forgotten but to suffer me also this, for it becomes us to fulfill all righteousness. Tell John what you have seen and heard—that the poor have good tidings preached to them—and, finally, tell the beloved herald of my earth mission that he shall be abundantly blessed in the age to come if he finds no occasion to doubt and stumble over me." And this was the last word John received from Jesus. This message greatly comforted him and did much to stabilize his faith and prepare him for the tragic end of his life in the flesh which followed so soon upon the heels of this memorable occasion.

Death of John the Baptist

135:12.1 (1508.1) As John was working in southern Perea when arrested, he was taken immediately to the prison of the fortress of Machaerus, where he was incarcerated until his execution. Herod ruled over Perea as well as Galilee, and he maintained residence at this time at both Julias and Machaerus in Perea. In Galilee the official residence had been moved from Sepphoris to the new capital at Tiberias.

135:12.2 (1508.2) Herod feared to release John lest he instigate rebellion. He feared to put him to death lest the multitude riot in the capital, for thousands of Pereans believed that John was a holy man, a prophet. Therefore Herod kept the Nazarite preacher in prison, not knowing what else to do with him. Several times John had been before Herod, but never would he agree either to leave the domains of Herod or to refrain from all public activities if he were released. And this new agitation concerning Jesus of Nazareth, which was steadily increasing, admonished Herod that it was no time to turn John loose. Besides, John was also a victim of the intense and bitter hatred of Herodias, Herod's unlawful wife.

135:12.3 (1508.3) On numerous occasions Herod talked with John about the kingdom of heaven, and while sometimes seriously impressed with his message, he was afraid to release him from prison.

135:12.4 (1508.4) Since much building was still going on at Tiberias, Herod spent considerable time at his Perean residences, and he was partial to the fortress of Machaerus. It was a matter of several years before all the public buildings and the official residence at Tiberias were fully completed.

135:12.5 (1508.5) In celebration of his birthday Herod made a great feast in the Machaerian palace for his chief officers and other men high in the councils of the government of Galilee and Perea. Since Herodias had failed to bring about John's death by direct appeal to Herod, she now set herself to the task of having John put to death by cunning planning.

135:12.6 (1508.6) In the course of the evening's festivities and entertainment, Herodias presented her daughter to dance before the banqueters. Herod was very much pleased with the damsel's performance and, calling her before him, said: "You are charming. I am much pleased with you. Ask me on this my birthday for whatever you desire, and I will give it to you, even to the half of my kingdom." And Herod did all this while well under the influence of his many wines. The young lady drew aside and inquired of her mother what she should ask of Herod. Herodias said, "Go to Herod and ask for the head of John the Baptist." And the young woman, returning to the banquet table, said to Herod, "I request that you forthwith give me the head of John the Baptist on a platter."

135:12.7 (1508.7) Herod was filled with fear and sorrow, but because of his oath and because of all those who sat at meat with him, he would not deny the request. And Herod Antipas sent a soldier, commanding him to bring the head of John. So was John that night beheaded in the prison, the soldier bringing the head of the prophet on a platter and presenting it to the young woman at the rear of the banquet hall. And the damsel gave the platter to her mother. When John's disciples heard of this, they came to the prison for the body of John, and after laying it in a tomb, they went and told Jesus.

Paper 136

Baptism and the Forty Days

136:0.1 (1509.1) JESUS began his public work at the height of the popular interest in John's preaching and at a time when the Jewish people of Palestine were eagerly looking for the appearance of the Messiah. There was a great contrast between John and Jesus. John was an eager and earnest worker, but Jesus was a calm and happy laborer; only a few times in his entire life was he ever in a hurry. Jesus was a comforting consolation to the world and somewhat of an example; John was hardly a comfort or an example. He preached the kingdom of heaven but hardly entered into the happiness thereof. Though Jesus spoke of John as the greatest of the prophets of the old order, he also said that the least of those who saw the great light of the new way and entered thereby into the kingdom of heaven was indeed greater than John.

136:0.2 (1509.2) When John preached the coming kingdom, the burden of his message was: Repent! flee from the wrath to come. When Jesus began to preach, there remained the exhortation to repentance, but such a message was always followed by the gospel, the good tidings of the joy and liberty of the new kingdom.

1   Concepts of the Expected Messiah

136:1.1 (1509.3) The Jews entertained many ideas about the expected deliverer, and each of these different schools of Messianic teaching was able to point to statements in the Hebrew scriptures as proof of their contentions. In a general way, the Jews regarded their national history as beginning with Abraham and culminating in the Messiah and the new age of the kingdom of God. In earlier times they had envisaged this deliverer as "the servant of the Lord," then as "the Son of Man," while latterly some even went so far as to refer to the Messiah as the "Son of God." But no matter whether he was called the "seed of Abraham" or "the son of David," all were agreed that he was to be the Messiah, the "anointed one." Thus did the concept evolve from the "servant of the Lord" to the "son of David," "Son of Man," and "Son of God."

136:1.2 (1509.4) In the days of John and Jesus the more learned Jews had developed an idea of the coming Messiah as the perfected and representative Israelite, combining in himself as the "servant of the Lord" the threefold office of prophet, priest, and king.

136:1.3 (1509.5) The Jews devoutly believed that, as Moses had delivered their fathers from Egyptian bondage by miraculous wonders, so would the coming Messiah deliver the Jewish people from Roman domination by even greater miracles of power and marvels of racial triumph. The rabbis had gathered together almost five hundred passages from the Scriptures which, notwithstanding their apparent contradictions, they averred were prophetic of the coming Messiah. And amidst all these details of time, technique, and function, they almost completely lost sight of the personality of the promised Messiah. They were looking for a restoration of Jewish national glory—Israel's temporal exaltation—rather than for the salvation of the world. It therefore becomes evident that Jesus of Nazareth could never satisfy this materialistic Messianic concept of the Jewish mind. Many of their reputed Messianic predictions, had they but viewed these prophetic utterances in a different light, would have very naturally prepared their minds for a recognition of Jesus as the terminator of one age and the inaugurator of a new and better dispensation of mercy and salvation for all nations.

136:1.4 (1510.1) The Jews had been brought up to believe in the doctrine of the Shekinah. But this reputed symbol of the Divine Presence was not to be seen in the temple. They believed that the coming of the Messiah would effect its restoration. They held confusing ideas about racial sin and the supposed evil nature of man. Some taught that Adam's sin had cursed the human race, and that the Messiah would remove this curse and restore man to divine favor. Others taught that God, in creating man, had put into his being both good and evil natures; that when he observed the outworking of this arrangement, he was greatly disappointed, and that "He repented that he had thus made man." And those who taught this believed that the Messiah was to come in order to redeem man from this inherent evil nature.

136:1.5 (1510.2) The majority of the Jews believed that they continued to languish under Roman rule because of their national sins and because of the halfheartedness of the gentile proselytes. The Jewish nation had not wholeheartedly repented; therefore did the Messiah delay his coming. There was much talk about repentance; wherefore the mighty and immediate appeal of John's preaching, "Repent and be baptized, for the kingdom of heaven is at hand." And the kingdom of heaven could mean only one thing to any devout Jew: The coming of the Messiah.

136:1.6 (1510.3) There was one feature of the bestowal of Michael which was utterly foreign to the Jewish conception of the Messiah, and that was the union of the two natures, the human and the divine. The Jews had variously conceived of the Messiah as perfected human, superhuman, and even as divine, but they never entertained the concept of the union of the human and the divine. And this was the great stumbling block of Jesus' early disciples. They grasped the human concept of the Messiah as the son of David, as presented by the earlier prophets; as the Son of Man, the superhuman idea of Daniel and some of the later prophets; and even as the Son of God, as depicted by the author of the Book of Enoch and by certain of his contemporaries; but never had they for a single moment entertained the true concept of the union in one earth personality of the two natures, the human and the divine. The incarnation of the Creator in the form of the creature had not been revealed beforehand. It was revealed only in Jesus; the world knew nothing of such things until the Creator Son was made flesh and dwelt among the mortals of the realm.

2   The Baptism of Jesus

136:2.1 (1510.4) Jesus was baptized at the very height of John's preaching when Palestine was aflame with the expectancy of his message—"the kingdom of God is at hand"—when all Jewry was engaged in serious and solemn self-examination. The Jewish sense of racial solidarity was very profound. The Jews not only believed that the sins of the father might afflict his children, but they firmly believed that the sin of one individual might curse the nation.

Accordingly, not all who submitted to John's baptism regarded themselves as being guilty of the specific sins which John denounced. Many devout souls were baptized by John for the good of Israel. They feared lest some sin of ignorance on their part might delay the coming of the Messiah. They felt themselves to belong to a guilty and sin-cursed nation, and they presented themselves for baptism that they might by so doing manifest fruits of race penitence. It is therefore evident that Jesus in no sense received John's baptism as a rite of repentance or for the remission of sins. In accepting baptism at the hands of John, Jesus was only following the example of many pious Israelites.

136:2.2 (1511.1) When Jesus of Nazareth went down into the Jordan to be baptized, he was a mortal of the realm who had attained the pinnacle of human evolutionary ascension in all matters related to the conquest of mind and to self-identification with the spirit. He stood in the Jordan that day a perfected mortal of the evolutionary worlds of time and space. Perfect synchrony and full communication had become established between the mortal mind of Jesus and the indwelling spirit Adjuster, the divine gift of his Father in Paradise. And just such an Adjuster indwells all normal beings living on Urantia since the ascension of Michael to the headship of his universe, except that Jesus' Adjuster had been previously prepared for this special mission by similarly indwelling another superhuman incarnated in the likeness of mortal flesh, Machiventa Melchizedek.

136:2.3 (1511.2) Ordinarily, when a mortal of the realm attains such high levels of personality perfection, there occur those preliminary phenomena of spiritual elevation which terminate in eventual fusion of the matured soul of the mortal with its associated divine Adjuster. And such a change was apparently due to take place in the personality experience of Jesus of Nazareth on that very day when he went down into the Jordan with his two brothers to be baptized by John.

This ceremony was the final act of his purely human life on Urantia, and many superhuman observers expected to witness the fusion of the Adjuster with its indwelt mind, but they were all destined to suffer disappointment. Something new and even greater occurred. As John laid his hands upon Jesus to baptize him, the indwelling Adjuster took final leave of the perfected human soul of Joshua ben Joseph. And in a few moments this divine entity returned from Divinington as a Personalized Adjuster and chief of his kind throughout the entire local universe of Nebadon. Thus did Jesus observe his own former divine spirit descending on its return to him in personalized form. And he heard this same spirit of Paradise origin now speak, saying, "This is my beloved Son in whom I am well pleased." And John, with Jesus' two brothers, also heard these words. John's disciples, standing by the water's edge, did not hear these words, neither did they see the apparition of the Personalized Adjuster. Only the eyes of Jesus beheld the Personalized Adjuster.

136:2.4 (1511.3) When the returned and now exalted Personalized Adjuster had thus spoken, all was silence. And while the four of them tarried in the water, Jesus, looking up to the near-by Adjuster, prayed: "My Father who reigns in heaven, hallowed be your name. Your kingdom come! Your will be done on earth, even as it is in heaven." When he had prayed, the "heavens were opened," and the Son of Man saw the vision, presented by the now Personalized Adjuster, of himself as a Son of God as he was before he came to earth in the likeness of mortal flesh, and as he would be when the incarnated life should be finished. This heavenly vision was seen only by Jesus.

136:2.5 (1512.1) It was the voice of the Personalized Adjuster that John and Jesus heard, speaking in behalf of the Universal Father, for the Adjuster is of, and as, the Paradise Father. Throughout the remainder of Jesus' earth life this Personalized Adjuster was associated with him in all his labors; Jesus was in constant communion with this exalted Adjuster.

136:2.6 (1512.2) When Jesus was baptized, he repented of no misdeeds; he made no confession of sin. His was the baptism of consecration to the performance of the will of the heavenly Father. At his baptism he heard the unmistakable call of his Father, the final summons to be about his Father's business, and he went away into private seclusion for forty days to think over these manifold problems. In thus retiring for a season from active personality contact with his earthly associates, Jesus, as he was and on Urantia, was following the very procedure that obtains on the morontia worlds whenever an ascending mortal fuses with the inner presence of the Universal Father.

136:2.7 (1512.3) This day of baptism ended the purely human life of Jesus. The divine Son has found his Father, the Universal Father has found his incarnated Son, and they speak the one to the other.

136:2.8 (1512.4) (Jesus was almost thirty-one and one-half years old when he was baptized. While Luke says that Jesus was baptized in the fifteenth year of the reign of Tiberius Caesar, which would be A.D. 29 since Augustus died in A.D. 14, it should be recalled that Tiberius was coemperor with Augustus for two and one-half years before the death of Augustus, having had coins struck in his honor in October, A.D. 11. The fifteenth year of his actual rule was, therefore, this very year of A.D. 26, that of Jesus' baptism. And this was also the year that Pontius Pilate began his rule as governor of Judea.)

3   *The Forty Days*

136:3.1 (1512.5) Jesus had endured the great temptation of his mortal bestowal before his baptism when he had been wet with the dews of Mount Hermon for six weeks. There on Mount Hermon, as an unaided mortal of the realm, he had met and defeated the Urantia pretender, Caligastia, the prince of this world. That eventful day, on the universe records, Jesus of Nazareth had become the Planetary Prince of Urantia. And this Prince of Urantia, so soon to be proclaimed supreme Sovereign of Nebadon, now went into forty days of retirement to formulate the plans and determine upon the technique of proclaiming the new kingdom of God in the hearts of men.

136:3.2 (1512.6) After his baptism he entered upon the forty days of adjusting himself to the changed relationships of the world and the universe occasioned by the personalization of his Adjuster. During this isolation in the Perean hills he determined upon the policy to be pursued and the methods to be employed in the new and changed phase of earth life which he was about to inaugurate.

136:3.3 (1512.7) Jesus did not go into retirement for the purpose of fasting and for the affliction of his soul. He was not an ascetic, and he came forever to destroy all such notions regarding the approach to God. His reasons for seeking this retirement were entirely different from those which had actuated Moses and Elijah, and even John the Baptist. Jesus was then wholly self-conscious concerning his relation to the universe of his making and also to the universe of universes, supervised by the Paradise Father, his Father in heaven.

He now fully recalled the bestowal charge and its instructions administered by his elder brother, Immanuel, ere he entered upon his Urantia incarnation. He now clearly and fully comprehended all these far-flung relationships, and he desired to be away for a season of quiet meditation so that he could think out the plans and decide upon the procedures for the prosecution of his public labors in behalf of this world and for all other worlds in his local universe.

136:3.4 (1513.1) While wandering about in the hills, seeking a suitable shelter, Jesus encountered his universe chief executive, Gabriel, the Bright and Morning Star of Nebadon. Gabriel now re-established personal communication with the Creator Son of the universe; they met directly for the first time since Michael took leave of his associates on Salvington when he went to Edentia preparatory to entering upon the Urantia bestowal. Gabriel, by direction of Immanuel and on authority of the Uversa Ancients of Days, now laid before Jesus information indicating that his bestowal experience on Urantia was practically finished so far as concerned the earning of the perfected sovereignty of his universe and the termination of the Lucifer rebellion. The former was achieved on the day of his baptism when the personalization of his Adjuster demonstrated the perfection and completion of his bestowal in the likeness of mortal flesh, and the latter was a fact of history on that day when he came down from Mount Hermon to join the waiting lad, Tiglath. Jesus was now informed, upon the highest authority of the local universe and the superuniverse, that his bestowal work was finished in so far as it affected his personal status in relation to sovereignty and rebellion. He had already had this assurance direct from Paradise in the baptismal vision and in the phenomenon of the personalization of his indwelling Thought Adjuster.

136:3.5 (1513.2) While he tarried on the mountain, talking with Gabriel, the Constellation Father of Edentia appeared to Jesus and Gabriel in person, saying: "The records are completed. The sovereignty of Michael number 611,121 over his universe of Nebadon rests in completion at the right hand of the Universal Father. I bring to you the bestowal release of Immanuel, your sponsor-brother for the Urantia incarnation. You are at liberty now or at any subsequent time, in the manner of your own choosing, to terminate your incarnation bestowal, ascend to the right hand of your Father, receive your sovereignty, and assume your well-earned unconditional rulership of all Nebadon. I also testify to the completion of the records of the superuniverse, by authorization of the Ancients of Days, having to do with the termination of all sin-rebellion in your universe and endowing you with full and unlimited authority to deal with any and all such possible upheavals in the future. Technically, your work on Urantia and in the flesh of the mortal creature is finished. Your course from now on is a matter of your own choosing."

136:3.6 (1513.3) When the Most High Father of Edentia had taken leave, Jesus held long converse with Gabriel regarding the welfare of the universe and, sending greetings to Immanuel, proffered his assurance that, in the work which he was about to undertake on Urantia, he would be ever mindful of the counsel he had received in connection with the prebestowal charge administered on Salvington.

136:3.7 (1514.1) Throughout all of these forty days of isolation James and John the sons of Zebedee were engaged in searching for Jesus. Many times they were not far from his abiding place, but never did they find him.

4   *Plans for Public Work*

136:4.1 (1514.2) Day by day, up in the hills, Jesus formulated the plans for the remainder of his Urantia bestowal. He first decided not to teach contemporaneously with John. He planned to remain in comparative retirement until the work of John achieved its purpose, or until John was suddenly stopped by imprisonment. Jesus well knew that John's fearless and tactless preaching would presently arouse the fears and enmity of the civil rulers. In view of John's precarious situation, Jesus began definitely to plan his program of public labors in behalf of his people and the world, in behalf of every inhabited world throughout his vast universe. Michael's mortal bestowal was on Urantia but for all worlds of Nebadon.

136:4.2 (1514.3) The first thing Jesus did, after thinking through the general plan of co-ordinating his program with John's movement, was to review in his mind the instructions of Immanuel. Carefully he thought over the advice given him concerning his methods of labor, and that he was to leave no permanent writing on the planet. Never again did Jesus write on anything except sand. On his next visit to Nazareth, much to the sorrow of his brother Joseph, Jesus destroyed all of his writing that was preserved on the boards about the carpenter shop, and which hung upon the walls of the old home. And Jesus pondered well over Immanuel's advice pertaining to his economic, social, and political attitude toward the world as he should find it.

136:4.3 (1514.4) Jesus did not fast during this forty days' isolation. The longest period he went without food was his first two days in the hills when he was so engrossed with his thinking that he forgot all about eating. But on the third day he went in search of food. Neither was he tempted during this time by any evil spirits or rebel personalities of station on this world or from any other world.

136:4.4 (1514.5) These forty days were the occasion of the final conference between the human and the divine minds, or rather the first real functioning of these two minds as now made one. The results of this momentous season of meditation demonstrated conclusively that the divine mind has triumphantly and spiritually dominated the human intellect. The mind of man has become the mind of God from this time on, and though the selfhood of the mind of man is ever present, always does this spiritualized human mind say, "Not my will but yours be done."

136:4.5 (1514.6) The transactions of this eventful time were not the fantastic visions of a starved and weakened mind, neither were they the confused and puerile symbolisms which afterward gained record as the "temptations of Jesus in the wilderness." Rather was this a season for thinking over the whole eventful and varied career of the Urantia bestowal and for the careful laying of those plans for further ministry which would best serve this world while also contributing something to the betterment of all other rebellion-isolated spheres. Jesus thought over the whole span of human life on Urantia, from the days of Andon and Fonta, down through Adam's default, and on to the ministry of the Melchizedek of Salem.

136:4.6 (1514.7) Gabriel had reminded Jesus that there were two ways in which he might manifest himself to the world in case he should choose to tarry on Urantia for a time. And it was made clear to Jesus that his choice in this matter would have nothing to do with either his universe sovereignty or the termination of the Lucifer rebellion. These two ways of world ministry were:

136:4.7 (1515.1) 1. His own way— the way that might seem most pleasant and profitable from the standpoint of the immediate needs of this world and the present edification of his own universe.

136:4.8 (1515.2) 2. The Father's way— the exemplification of a farseeing ideal of creature life visualized by the high personalities of the Paradise administration of the universe of universes.

136:4.9 (1515.3) It was thus made clear to Jesus that there were two ways in which he could order the remainder of his earth life. Each of these ways had something to be said in its favor as it might be regarded in the light of the immediate situation. The Son of Man clearly saw that his choice between these two modes of conduct would have nothing to do with his reception of universe sovereignty; that was a matter already settled and sealed on the records of the universe of universes and only awaited his demand in person. But it was indicated to Jesus that it would afford his Paradise brother, Immanuel, great satisfaction if he, Jesus, should see fit to finish up his earth career of incarnation as he had so nobly begun it, always subject to the Father's will. On the third day of this isolation Jesus promised himself he would go back to the world to finish his earth career, and that in a situation involving any two ways he would always choose the Father's will. And he lived out the remainder of his earth life always true to that resolve. Even to the bitter end he invariably subordinated his sovereign will to that of his heavenly Father.

136:4.10 (1515.4) The forty days in the mountain wilderness were not a period of great temptation but rather the period of the Master's great decisions. During these days of lone communion with himself and his Father's immediate presence— the Personalized Adjuster (he no longer had a personal seraphic guardian)—he arrived, one by one, at the great decisions which were to control his policies and conduct for the remainder of his earth career. Subsequently the tradition of a great temptation became attached to this period of isolation through confusion with the fragmentary narratives of the Mount Hermon struggles, and further because it was the custom to have all great prophets and human leaders begin their public careers by undergoing these supposed seasons of fasting and prayer. It had always been Jesus' practice, when facing any new or serious decisions, to withdraw for communion with his own spirit that he might seek to know the will of God.

136:4.11 (1515.5) In all this planning for the remainder of his earth life, Jesus was always torn in his human heart by two opposing courses of conduct:

136:4.12 (1515.6) 1. He entertained a

strong desire to win his people—and the whole world—to believe in him and to accept his new spiritual kingdom. And he well knew their ideas concerning the coming Messiah.

136:4.13 (1515.7) 2. To live and work as he knew his Father would approve, to conduct his work in behalf of other worlds in need, and to continue, in the establishment of the kingdom, to reveal the Father and show forth his divine character of love.

136:4.14 (1515.8) Throughout these eventful days Jesus lived in an ancient rock cavern, a shelter in the side of the hills near a village sometime called Beit Adis. He drank from the small spring which came from the side of the hill near this rock shelter.

5   *The First Great Decision*

136:5.1 (1516.1) On the third day after beginning this conference with himself and his Personalized Adjuster, Jesus was presented with the vision of the assembled celestial hosts of Nebadon sent by their commanders to wait upon the will of their beloved Sovereign. This mighty host embraced twelve legions of seraphim and proportionate numbers of every order of universe intelligence. And the first great decision of Jesus' isolation had to do with whether or not he would make use of these mighty personalities in connection with the ensuing program of his public work on Urantia.

136:5.2 (1516.2) Jesus decided that he would not utilize a single personality of this vast assemblage unless it should become evident that this was his Father's will. Notwithstanding this general decision, this vast host remained with him throughout the balance of his earth life, always in readiness to obey the least expression of their Sovereign's will.

Although Jesus did not constantly behold these attendant personalities with his human eyes, his associated Personalized

Adjuster did constantly behold, and could communicate with, all of them.

136:5.3 (1516.3) Before coming down from the forty days' retreat in the hills, Jesus assigned the immediate command of this attendant host of universe personalities to his recently Personalized Adjuster, and for more than four years of Urantia time did these selected personalities from every division of universe intelligences obediently and respectfully function under the wise guidance of this exalted and experienced Personalized Mystery Monitor. In assuming command of this mighty assembly, the Adjuster, being a onetime part and essence of the Paradise Father, assured Jesus that in no case would these superhuman agencies be permitted to serve, or manifest themselves in connection with, or in behalf of, his earth career unless it should develop that the Father willed such intervention. Thus by one great decision Jesus voluntarily deprived himself of all superhuman cooperation in all matters having to do with the remainder of his mortal career unless the Father might independently choose to participate in some certain act or episode of the Son's earth labors.

136:5.4 (1516.4) In accepting this command of the universe hosts in attendance upon Christ Michael, the Personalized Adjuster took great pains to point out to Jesus that, while such an assembly of universe creatures could be limited in their space activities by the delegated authority of their Creator, such limitations were not operative in connection with their function in time. And this limitation was dependent on the fact that Adjusters are nontime beings when once they are personalized. Accordingly was Jesus admonished that, while the Adjuster's control of the living intelligences placed under his command would be complete and perfect as to all matters involving space, there could be no such perfect limitations imposed regarding time. Said the Adjuster: "I will, as you have directed, enjoin the employment of this attendant host of universe intelligences in any manner in connection with your earth career except in those cases where the Paradise Father directs me to release such agencies in order that his divine will of your choosing may be accomplished, and in those instances where you may engage in any choice or act of your divine-human will which shall only involve departures from the natural earth order as to time. In all such events I am powerless, and your creatures here assembled in perfection and unity of power are likewise helpless. If your united natures once entertain such desires, these mandates of your choice will be forthwith executed. Your wish in all such matters will constitute the abridgment

of time, and the thing projected is existent. Under my command this constitutes the fullest possible limitation which can be imposed upon your potential sovereignty. In my self-consciousness time is nonexistent, and therefore I cannot limit your creatures in anything related thereto."

136:5.5 (1517.1) Thus did Jesus become apprised of the working out of his decision to go on living as a man among men. He had by a single decision excluded all of his attendant universe hosts of varied intelligences from participating in his ensuing public ministry except in such matters as concerned time only. It therefore becomes evident that any possible supernatural or supposedly superhuman accompaniments of Jesus' ministry pertained wholly to the elimination of time unless the Father in heaven specifically ruled otherwise. No miracle, ministry of mercy, or any other possible event occurring in connection with Jesus' remaining earth labors could possibly be of the nature or character of an act transcending the natural laws established and regularly working in the affairs of man as he lives on Urantia except in this expressly stated matter of time. No limits, of course, could be placed upon the manifestations of "the Father's will." The elimination of time in connection with the expressed desire of this potential Sovereign of a universe could only be avoided by the direct and explicit act of the will of this God-man to the effect that time, as related to the act or event in question, should not be shortened or eliminated. In order to prevent the appearance of

apparent time miracles, it was necessary for Jesus to remain constantly time conscious. Any lapse of time consciousness on his part, in connection with the entertainment of definite desire, was equivalent to the enactment of the thing conceived in the mind of this Creator Son, and without the intervention of time.

136:5.6 (1517.2) Through the supervising control of his associated and Personalized Adjuster it was possible for Michael perfectly to limit his personal earth activities with reference to space, but it was not possible for the Son of Man thus to limit his new earth status as potential Sovereign of Nebadon as regards time. And this was the actual status of Jesus of Nazareth as he went forth to begin his public ministry on Urantia.

6   The Second Decision

136:6.1 (1517.3) Having settled his policy concerning all personalities of all classes of his created intelligences, so far as this could be determined in view of the inherent potential of his new status of divinity, Jesus now turned his thoughts toward himself. What would he, now the fully self-conscious creator of all things and beings existent in this universe, do with these creator prerogatives in the recurring life situations which would immediately confront him when he returned to Galilee to resume his work among men? In fact, already, and right where he was in these lonely hills, had this problem forcibly presented itself in the matter of obtaining food. By the third day of his solitary meditations the human body grew hungry. Should he go in quest of food as any ordinary man would, or should he merely exercise his normal creative powers and produce suitable bodily nourishment ready at hand? And this great decision of the Master has been portrayed to you as a temptation—as a challenge by supposed enemies that he "command that these stones become loaves of bread."

136:6.2 (1518.1) Jesus thus settled upon another and consistent policy for the remainder of his earth labors. As far as his personal necessities were concerned, and in general even in his relations with other personalities, he now deliberately chose to pursue the path of normal earthly existence; he definitely decided against a policy which would transcend, violate, or outrage his own established natural laws. But he could not promise himself, as he had already been warned by his Personalized Adjuster, that these natural laws might not, in certain conceivable circumstances, be greatly accelerated. In principle, Jesus decided that his lifework should be organized and prosecuted in accordance with natural law and in harmony with the existing social organization. The Master thereby chose a program of living which was the equivalent of deciding against miracles and wonders. Again he decided in favor of "the Father's will"; again he surrendered everything into the hands of his Paradise Father.

136:6.3 (1518.2) Jesus' human nature dictated that the first duty was self-preservation; that is the normal attitude of the natural man on the worlds of time and space, and it is, therefore, a legitimate reaction of a Urantia mortal. But Jesus was not concerned merely with this world and its creatures; he was living a life designed to instruct and inspire the manifold creatures of a far-flung universe.

136:6.4 (1518.3) Before his baptismal illumination he had lived in perfect submission to the will and guidance of his heavenly Father. He emphatically decided to continue on in just such implicit mortal dependence on the Father's will. He purposed to follow the unnatural course— he decided not to seek self-preservation. He chose to go on pursuing the policy of refusing to defend himself. He formulated his conclusions in the words of Scripture familiar to his human mind: "Man shall not live by bread alone but by every word that proceeds from the mouth of God." In reaching this conclusion in regard to the appetite of the physical nature as expressed in hunger for food, the Son of Man made his final declaration concerning all other urges of the flesh and the natural impulses of human nature.

136:6.5 (1518.4) His superhuman power he might possibly use for others, but for himself, never. And he pursued this policy consistently to the very end, when it was jeeringly said of him: "He saved others; himself he cannot save"— because he would not.

136:6.6 (1518.5) The Jews were expecting a Messiah who would do even greater wonders than Moses, who was reputed to have brought forth water from the rock in a desert place and to have fed their forefathers with manna in the wilderness. Jesus knew the sort of Messiah his compatriots expected, and he had all the powers and prerogatives to measure up to their most sanguine expectations, but he decided against such a magnificent program of power and glory. Jesus looked upon such a course of expected miracle working as a harking back to the olden days of ignorant magic and the degraded practices of the savage medicine men. Possibly, for the salvation of his creatures, he might accelerate natural law, but to transcend his own laws, either for the benefit of himself or the overawing of his fellow men, that he would not do. And the Master's decision was final.

136:6.7 (1518.6) Jesus sorrowed for his people; he fully understood how they had been led up to the expectation of the coming Messiah, the time when "the earth will yield its fruits ten thousandfold, and on one vine there will be a thousand branches, and each branch will produce a thousand clusters, and each cluster will produce a thousand grapes, and each grape will produce a gallon of wine." The Jews believed the Messiah would usher in an era of miraculous plenty. The Hebrews had long been nurtured on traditions of miracles and legends of wonders.

136:6.8 (1519.1) He was not a Messiah coming to multiply bread and wine. He came not to minister to temporal needs only; he came to reveal his Father in heaven to his children on earth, while he sought to lead his earth children to join him in a sincere effort so to live as to do the will of the Father in heaven.

136:6.9 (1519.2) In this decision Jesus of Nazareth portrayed to an onlooking universe the folly and sin of prostituting divine talents and God-given abilities for personal aggrandizement or for purely selfish gain and glorification. That was the sin of Lucifer and Caligastia.

136:6.10 (1519.3) This great decision of Jesus portrays dramatically the truth that selfish satisfaction and sensuous gratification, alone and of themselves, are not able to confer happiness upon evolving human beings. There are higher values in mortal existence—intellectual mastery and spiritual achievement—which far transcend the necessary gratification of man's purely physical appetites and urges. Man's natural endowment of talent and ability should be chiefly devoted to the development and ennoblement of his higher powers of mind and spirit.

136:6.11 (1519.4) Jesus thus revealed to the creatures of his universe the technique of the new and better way, the higher moral values of living and the deeper spiritual satisfactions of evolutionary human existence on the worlds of space.

7   The Third Decision

136:7.1 (1519.5) Having made his decisions regarding such matters as food and physical ministration to the needs of his material body, the care of the health of himself and his associates, there remained yet other problems to solve. What would be his attitude when confronted by personal danger? He decided to exercise normal watchcare over his human safety and to take reasonable precaution to prevent the untimely termination of his career in the flesh but to refrain from all superhuman intervention when the crisis of his life in the flesh should come. As he was formulating this decision, Jesus was seated under the shade of a tree on an overhanging ledge of rock with a precipice right there before him. He fully realized that he could cast himself off the ledge and out into space, and that nothing could happen to harm him provided he would rescind his first great decision not to invoke the interposition of his celestial intelligences in the prosecution of his lifework on Urantia, and provided he would abrogate his second decision concerning his attitude toward self-preservation.

136:7.2 (1519.6) Jesus knew his fellow countrymen were expecting a Messiah who would be above natural law. Well had he been taught that Scripture: "There shall no evil befall you, neither shall any plague come near your dwelling. For he shall give his angels charge over you, to keep you in all your ways. They shall bear you up in their hands lest you dash your foot against a stone." Would this sort of presumption, this defiance of his Father's laws of gravity, be justified in order to protect himself from possible harm or, perchance, to win the confidence of his mistaught and distracted people? But such a course, however gratifying to the sign-seeking Jews, would be, not a revelation of his Father, but a questionable trifling with the established laws of the universe of universes.

136:7.3 (1519.7) Understanding all of this and knowing that the Master refused to work in defiance of his established laws of nature in so far as his personal conduct was concerned, you know of a certainty that he never walked on the water nor did anything else which was an outrage to his material order of administering the world; always, of course, bearing in mind that there had, as yet, been found no way whereby he could be wholly delivered from the lack of control over the element of time in connection with those matters put under the jurisdiction of the Personalized Adjuster.

136:7.4 (1520.1) Throughout his entire earth life Jesus was consistently loyal to this decision. No matter whether the Pharisees taunted him for a sign, or the watchers at Calvary dared him to come down from the cross, he steadfastly adhered to the decision of this hour on the hillside.

8   *The Fourth Decision*

136:8.1 (1520.2) The next great problem with which this God-man wrestled and which he presently decided in accordance with the will of the Father in heaven, concerned the question as to whether or not any of his superhuman powers should be employed for the purpose of attracting the attention and winning the adherence of his fellow men. Should he in any manner lend his universe powers to the gratification of the Jewish hankering for the spectacular and the marvelous? He decided that he should not. He settled upon a policy of procedure which eliminated all such practices as the method of bringing his mission to the notice of men. And he consistently lived up to this great decision. Even when he permitted the manifestation of numerous time-shortening ministrations of mercy, he almost invariably admonished the recipients of his healing ministry to tell no man about the benefits they had received. And always did he refuse the taunting challenge of his enemies to "show us a sign" in proof and demonstration of his divinity.

136:8.2 (1520.3) Jesus very wisely foresaw that the working of miracles and the execution of wonders would call forth only outward allegiance by overawing the material mind; such performances would not reveal God nor save men. He refused to become a mere wonder-worker. He resolved to become occupied with but a single task—the establishment of the kingdom of heaven.

136:8.3 (1520.4) Throughout all this momentous dialogue of Jesus' communing with himself, there was present the human element of questioning and near-doubting, for Jesus was man as well as God. It was evident he would never be received by the Jews as the Messiah if he did not work wonders.

Besides, if he would consent to do just one unnatural thing, the human mind would know of a certainty that it was in subservience to a truly divine mind. Would it be consistent with "the Father's will" for the divine mind to make this concession to the doubting nature of the human mind? Jesus decided that it would not and cited the presence of the Personalized Adjuster as sufficient proof of divinity in partnership with humanity.

136:8.4 (1520.5) Jesus had traveled much; he recalled Rome, Alexandria, and Damascus. He knew the methods of the world—how people gained their ends in politics and commerce by compromise and diplomacy. Would he utilize this knowledge in the furtherance of his mission on earth? No! He likewise decided against all compromise with the wisdom of the world and the influence of riches in the establishment of the kingdom. He again chose to depend exclusively on the Father's will.

136:8.5 (1520.6) Jesus was fully aware of the short cuts open to one of his powers. He knew many ways in which the attention of the nation, and the whole world, could be immediately focused upon himself. Soon the Passover would be celebrated at Jerusalem; the city would be thronged with visitors. He could ascend the pinnacle of the temple and before the bewildered multitude walk out on the air; that would be the kind of a Messiah they were looking for. But he would subsequently disappoint them since he had not come to re-establish David's throne. And he knew the futility of the Caligastia method of trying to get ahead of the natural, slow, and sure way of accomplishing the divine purpose. Again the Son of Man bowed obediently to the Father's way, the Father's will.

136:8.6 (1521.1) Jesus chose to establish the kingdom of heaven in the hearts of mankind by natural, ordinary, difficult, and trying methods, just such procedures as his earth children must subsequently follow in their work of enlarging and extending that heavenly kingdom. For well did the Son of Man know that it would be "through much tribulation that many of the children of all ages would enter into the kingdom." Jesus was now passing through the great test of civilized man, to have power and steadfastly refuse to use it for purely selfish or personal purposes.

136:8.7 (1521.2) In your consideration of the life and experience of the Son of Man, it should be ever borne in mind that the Son of God was incarnate in the mind of a first-century human being, not in the mind of a twentieth-century or other-century mortal. By this we mean to convey the idea that the human endowments of Jesus were of natural acquirement. He was the product of the hereditary and environmental factors of his time, plus the influence of his training and education. His humanity was genuine, natural, wholly derived from the antecedents of, and fostered by, the actual intellectual status and social and economic conditions of that day and generation. While in the experience of this God-man there was always the possibility that the divine mind would transcend the human intellect, nonetheless, when, and as, his human mind functioned, it did perform as would a true mortal mind under the conditions of the human environment of that day.

136:8.8 (1521.3) Jesus portrayed to all the worlds of his vast universe the folly of creating artificial situations for the purpose of exhibiting arbitrary authority or of indulging exceptional power for the purpose of enhancing moral values or accelerating spiritual progress. Jesus decided that he would not lend his mission on earth to a repetition of the disappointment of the reign of the Maccabees. He refused to prostitute his divine attributes for the purpose of acquiring unearned popularity or for gaining political prestige. He would not countenance the transmutation of divine and creative energy into national power or international prestige. Jesus of Nazareth refused to compromise with evil, much less to consort with sin. The Master triumphantly put loyalty to his Father's will above every other earthly and temporal consideration.

9   The Fifth Decision

136:9.1 (1521.4) Having settled such questions of policy as pertained to his individual relations to natural law and spiritual power, he turned his attention to the choice of methods to be employed in the proclamation and establishment of the kingdom of God. John had already begun this work; how might he continue the message? How should he take over John's mission? How should he organize his followers for effective effort and intelligent co-operation? Jesus was now reaching the final decision which would forbid that he further regard himself as the Jewish Messiah, at least as the Messiah was popularly conceived in that day.

136:9.2 (1522.1) The Jews envisaged a deliverer who would come in miraculous power to cast down Israel's enemies and establish the Jews as world rulers, free from want and oppression. Jesus knew that this hope would never be realized. He knew that the kingdom of heaven had to do with the overthrow of evil in the hearts of men, and that it was purely a matter of spiritual concern. He thought out the advisability of inaugurating the spiritual kingdom with a brilliant and dazzling display of power—and such a course would have been permissible and wholly within the jurisdiction of Michael—but he fully decided against such a plan. He would not compromise with the revolutionary techniques of Caligastia. He had won the world in potential by submission to the Father's will, and he proposed to finish his work as he had begun it, and as the Son of Man.

136:9.3 (1522.2) You can hardly imagine what would have happened on Urantia had this God-man, now in potential possession of all power in heaven and on earth, once decided to unfurl the banner of sovereignty, to marshal his wonder-working battalions in militant array! But he would not compromise. He would not serve evil that the worship of God might presumably be derived therefrom. He would abide by the Father's will. He would proclaim to an onlooking universe, "You shall worship the Lord your God and him only shall you serve."

136:9.4 (1522.3) As the days passed, with ever-increasing clearness Jesus perceived what kind of a truth-revealer he was to become. He discerned that God's way was not going to be the easy way. He began to realize that the cup of the remainder of his human experience might possibly be bitter, but he decided to drink it.

136:9.5 (1522.4) Even his human mind is saying good-bye to the throne of David. Step by step this human mind follows in the path of the divine. The human mind still asks questions but unfailingly accepts the divine answers as final rulings in this combined life of living as a man in the world while all the time submitting unqualifiedly to the doing of the Father's eternal and divine will.

136:9.6 (1522.5) Rome was mistress of the Western world. The Son of Man, now in isolation and achieving these momentous decisions, with the hosts of heaven at his command, represented the last chance of the Jews to attain world dominion; but this earthborn Jew, who possessed such tremendous wisdom and power, declined to use his universe endowments either for the aggrandizement of himself or for the enthronement of his people. He saw, as it were, "the kingdoms of this world," and he possessed the power to take them. The Most Highs of Edentia had resigned all these powers into his hands, but he did not want them. The kingdoms of earth were paltry things to interest the Creator and Ruler of a universe. He had only one objective, the further revelation of God to man, the establishment of the kingdom, the rule of the heavenly Father in the hearts of mankind.

136:9.7 (1522.6) The idea of battle, contention, and slaughter was repugnant to Jesus; he would have none of it. He would appear on earth as the Prince of Peace to reveal a God of love. Before his baptism he

had again refused the offer of the Zealots to lead them in rebellion against the Roman oppressors. And now he made his final decision regarding those Scriptures which his mother had taught him, such as: "The Lord has said to me, 'You are my Son; this day have I begotten you. Ask of me, and I will give you the heathen for your inheritance and the uttermost parts of the earth for your possession. You shall break them with a rod of iron; you shall dash them in pieces like a potter's vessel.'"

136:9.8 (1522.7) Jesus of Nazareth reached the conclusion that such utterances did not refer to him. At last, and finally, the human mind of the Son of Man made a clean sweep of all these Messianic difficulties and contradictions—Hebrew scriptures, parental training, chazan teaching, Jewish expectations, and human ambitious longings; once and for all he decided upon his course. He would return to Galilee and quietly begin the proclamation of the kingdom and trust his Father (the Personalized Adjuster) to work out the details of procedure day by day.

136:9.9 (1523.1) By these decisions Jesus set a worthy example for every person on every world throughout a vast universe when he refused to apply material tests to prove spiritual problems, when he refused presumptuously to defy natural laws. And he set an inspiring example of universe loyalty and moral nobility when he refused to grasp temporal power as the prelude to spiritual glory.

136:9.10 (1523.2) If the Son of Man had any doubts about his mission and its nature when he went up in the hills after his baptism, he had none when he came back to his fellows following the forty days of isolation and decisions.

136:9.11 (1523.3) Jesus has formulated a program for the establishment of the Father's kingdom. He will not cater to the physical gratification of the people. He will not deal out bread to the multitudes as he has so recently seen it being done in Rome. He will not attract attention to himself by wonder-working, even though the Jews are expecting just that sort of a deliverer. Neither will he seek to win acceptance of a spiritual message by a show of political authority or temporal power.

136:9.12 (1523.4) In rejecting these methods of enhancing the coming kingdom in the eyes of the expectant Jews, Jesus made sure that these same Jews would certainly and finally reject all of his claims to authority and divinity. Knowing all this, Jesus long sought to prevent his early followers alluding to him as the Messiah.

136:9.13 (1523.5) Throughout his public ministry he was confronted with the necessity of dealing with three constantly recurring situations: the clamor to be fed, the insistence on miracles, and the final request that he allow his followers to make him king. But Jesus never departed from the decisions which he made during these days of his isolation in the Perean hills.

10   The Sixth Decision

136:10.1 (1523.6) On the last day of this memorable isolation, before starting down the mountain to join John and his disciples, the Son of Man made his final decision. And this decision he communicated to the Personalized Adjuster in these words, "And in all other matters, as in these now of decision-record, I pledge you I will be subject to the will of my Father." And when he had thus spoken, he journeyed down the mountain. And his face shone with the glory of spiritual victory and moral achievement.

Paper 137

Tarrying Time in Galilee

137:0.1 (1524.1) EARLY on Saturday morning, February 23, A.D. 26, Jesus came down from the hills to rejoin John's company encamped at Pella. All that day Jesus mingled with the multitude. He ministered to a lad who had injured himself in a fall and journeyed to the near-by village of Pella to deliver the boy safely into the hands of his parents.

1   Choosing the First Four Apostles

137:1.1 (1524.2) During this Sabbath two of John's leading disciples spent much time with Jesus. Of all John's followers one named Andrew was the most profoundly impressed with Jesus; he accompanied him on the trip to Pella with the injured boy. On the way back to John's rendezvous he asked Jesus many questions, and just before reaching their destination, the two paused for a short talk, during which Andrew said: "I have observed you ever since you came to Capernaum, and I believe you are the new Teacher, and though I do not understand all your teaching, I have fully made up my mind to follow you; I would sit at your feet and learn the whole truth about the new kingdom." And Jesus, with hearty assurance, welcomed Andrew as the first of his apostles, that group of twelve who were to labor with him in the work of establishing the new kingdom of God in the hearts of men.

137:1.2 (1524.3) Andrew was a silent observer of, and sincere believer in, John's work, and he had a very able and enthusiastic brother, named Simon, who was one of John's foremost disciples. It would not be amiss to say that Simon was one of John's chief supporters.

137:1.3 (1524.4) Soon after Jesus and Andrew returned to the camp, Andrew sought out his brother, Simon, and taking him aside, informed him that he had settled in his own mind that Jesus was the great Teacher, and that he had pledged himself as a disciple. He went on to say that Jesus had accepted his proffer of service and suggested that he (Simon) likewise go to Jesus and offer himself for fellowship in the service of the new kingdom. Said Simon: "Ever since this man came to work in Zebedee's shop, I have believed he was sent by God, but what about John? Are we to forsake him? Is this the right thing to do?" Whereupon they agreed to go at once to consult John. John was saddened by the thought of losing two of his able advisers and most promising disciples, but he bravely answered their inquiries, saying: "This is but the beginning; presently will my work end, and we shall all become his disciples." Then Andrew beckoned to Jesus to draw aside while he announced that his brother desired to join himself to the service of the new kingdom. And in welcoming Simon as his second apostle, Jesus said: "Simon, your enthusiasm is commendable, but it is dangerous to the work of the kingdom. I admonish you to become more thoughtful in your speech. I would change your name to Peter."

137:1.4 (1525.1) The parents of the injured lad who lived at Pella had besought Jesus to spend the night with them, to make their house his home, and he had promised. Before leaving Andrew and his brother, Jesus said, "Early on the morrow we go into Galilee."

137:1.5 (1525.2) After Jesus had returned to Pella for the night, and while Andrew and Simon were yet discussing the nature of their service in the establishment of the forthcoming kingdom, James and John the sons of Zebedee arrived upon the scene, having just returned from their long and futile searching in the hills for Jesus. When they heard Simon Peter tell how he and his brother, Andrew, had become the first accepted counselors of the new kingdom, and that they were to leave with their new Master on the morrow for Galilee, both James and John were sad. They had known Jesus for some time, and they loved him. They had searched for him many days in the hills, and now they returned to learn that others had been preferred before them. They inquired where Jesus had gone and made haste to find him.

137:1.6 (1525.3) Jesus was asleep when they reached his abode, but they awakened

him, saying: "How is it that, while we who have so long lived with you are searching in the hills for you, you prefer others before us and choose Andrew and Simon as your first associates in the new kingdom?" Jesus answered them, "Be calm in your hearts and ask yourselves, 'who directed that you should search for the Son of Man when he was about his Father's business?'" After they had recited the details of their long search in the hills, Jesus further instructed them: "You should learn to search for the secret of the new kingdom in your hearts and not in the hills. That which you sought was already present in your souls. You are indeed my brethren—you needed not to be received by me—already were you of the kingdom, and you should be of good cheer, making ready also to go with us tomorrow into Galilee." John then made bold to ask, "But, Master, will James and I be associates with you in the new kingdom, even as Andrew and Simon?" And Jesus, laying a hand on the shoulder of each of them, said: "My brethren, you were already with me in the spirit of the kingdom, even before these others made request to be received. You, my brethren, have no need to make request for entrance into the kingdom; you have been with me in the kingdom from the beginning. Before men, others may take precedence over you, but in my heart did I also number you in the councils of the kingdom, even before you thought to make this request of me. And even so might you have been first before men had you not been absent engaged in a well-intentioned but self-appointed task of seeking for one who was not lost. In the coming kingdom, be not mindful of those things which foster your anxiety but rather at all times concern yourselves only with doing the will of the Father who is in heaven."

137:1.7 (1525.4) James and John received the rebuke in good grace; never more were they envious of Andrew and Simon. And they made ready, with their two associate apostles, to depart for Galilee the next morning. From this day on the term apostle was employed to distinguish the chosen family of Jesus' advisers from the vast multitude of believing disciples who subsequently followed him.

137:1.8 (1525.5) Late that evening, James, John, Andrew, and Simon held converse with John the Baptist, and with tearful eye but steady voice the stalwart Judean prophet surrendered two of his leading disciples to become the apostles of the Galilean Prince of the coming kingdom.

2   Choosing Philip and Nathaniel

137:2.1 (1526.1) Sunday morning, February 24, A.D. 26, Jesus took leave of John the Baptist by the river near Pella, never again to see him in the flesh.

137:2.2 (1526.2) That day, as Jesus and his four disciple-apostles departed for Galilee, there was a great tumult in the camp of John's followers. The first great division was about to take place. The day before, John had made his positive pronouncement to Andrew and Ezra that Jesus was the Deliverer. Andrew decided to follow Jesus, but Ezra rejected the mild-mannered carpenter of Nazareth, proclaiming to his associates: "The Prophet Daniel declares that the Son of Man will come with the clouds of heaven, in power and great glory. This Galilean carpenter, this Capernaum boatbuilder, cannot be the Deliverer. Can such a gift of God come out of Nazareth? This Jesus is a relative of John, and through much kindness of heart has our teacher been deceived. Let us remain aloof from this false Messiah." When John rebuked Ezra for these utterances, he drew away with many disciples and hastened south. And this group continued to baptize in John's name and eventually founded a sect of those who believed in John but refused to accept Jesus. A remnant of this group persists in Mesopotamia even to this day.

137:2.3 (1526.3) While this trouble was brewing among John's followers, Jesus and his four disciple-apostles were well on their way toward Galilee. Before they crossed the Jordan, to go by way of Nain to Nazareth, Jesus, looking ahead and up the road, saw one Philip of Bethsaida with a friend coming toward them. Jesus had known Philip aforetime, and he was also well known to all four of the new apostles. He was on his way with his friend Nathaniel to visit John at Pella to learn more about the reported coming of the kingdom of God, and he was delighted to greet Jesus. Philip had been an admirer of Jesus ever since he first came to Capernaum. But Nathaniel, who lived at Cana of Galilee, did not know Jesus. Philip went forward to greet his friends while Nathaniel rested under the shade of a tree by the roadside.

137:2.4 (1526.4) Peter took Philip to one side and proceeded to explain that they, referring to himself, Andrew, James, and John, had all become associates of Jesus in the new kingdom and strongly urged Philip to volunteer for service. Philip was in a quandary. What should he do? Here, without a moment's warning—on the roadside near the Jordan—there had come up for immediate decision the most momentous question of a lifetime. By this time he was in earnest converse with Peter, Andrew, and John while Jesus was outlining to James the trip through Galilee and on to Capernaum. Finally, Andrew suggested to Philip, "Why not ask the Teacher?"

137:2.5 (1526.5) It suddenly dawned on Philip that Jesus was a really great man, possibly the Messiah, and he decided to abide by Jesus' decision in this matter; and he went straight to him, asking, "Teacher, shall I go down to John or shall I join my friends who follow you?" And Jesus answered, "Follow me." Philip was thrilled with the assurance that he had found the Deliverer.

137:2.6 (1526.6) Philip now motioned to the group to remain where they were while he hurried back to break the news of his decision to his friend Nathaniel, who still tarried behind under the mulberry tree, turning over in his mind the many things which he had heard concerning John the Baptist, the coming kingdom, and the expected Messiah. Philip broke in upon these meditations, exclaiming, "I have found the Deliverer, him of whom Moses and the prophets wrote and whom John has proclaimed." Nathaniel, looking up, inquired, "Whence comes this teacher?" And Philip replied, "He is Jesus of Nazareth, the son of Joseph, the carpenter, more recently residing at Capernaum." And then, somewhat shocked, Nathaniel asked, "Can any such good thing come out of Nazareth?" But Philip, taking him by the arm, said, "Come and see."

137:2.7 (1527.1) Philip led Nathaniel to Jesus, who, looking benignly into the face of the sincere doubter, said: "Behold a genuine Israelite, in whom there is no deceit. Follow me." And Nathaniel, turning to Philip, said: "You are right. He is indeed a master of men. I will also follow, if I am worthy." And Jesus nodded to Nathaniel, again saying, "Follow me."

137:2.8 (1527.2) Jesus had now assembled one half of his future corps of intimate associates, five who had for some time known him and one stranger, Nathaniel. Without further delay they crossed the Jordan and, going by the village of Nain, reached Nazareth late that evening.

137:2.9 (1527.3) They all remained overnight with Joseph in Jesus' boyhood home. The associates of Jesus little understood why their new-found teacher was so concerned with completely destroying every vestige of his writing which remained about the home in the form of the ten commandments and other mottoes and sayings. But this proceeding, together with the fact that they never saw him subsequently write—except upon the dust or in the sand— made a deep impression upon their minds. *

3   The Visit to Capernaum

137:3.1 (1527.4) The next day Jesus sent his apostles on to Cana, since all of them were invited to the wedding of a prominent young woman of that town,

while he prepared to pay a hurried visit to his mother at Capernaum, stopping at Magdala to see his brother Jude.

137:3.2 (1527.5) Before leaving Nazareth, the new associates of Jesus told Joseph and other members of Jesus' family about the wonderful events of the then recent past and gave free expression to their belief that Jesus was the long- expected deliverer. And these members of Jesus' family talked all this over, and Joseph said: "Maybe, after all, Mother was right—maybe our strange brother is the coming king."

137:3.3 (1527.6) Jude was present at Jesus' baptism and, with his brother James, had become a firm believer in Jesus' mission on earth. Although both James and Jude were much perplexed as to the nature of their brother's mission, their mother had resurrected all her early hopes of Jesus as the Messiah, the son of David, and she encouraged her sons to have faith in their brother as the deliverer of Israel.

137:3.4 (1527.7) Jesus arrived in Capernaum Monday night, but he did not go to his own home, where lived James and his mother; he went directly to the home of Zebedee. All his friends at Capernaum saw a great and pleasant change in him. Once more he seemed to be comparatively cheerful and more like himself as he was during the earlier years at Nazareth. For years previous to his baptism and the isolation periods just before and just after, he had grown increasingly serious and self-contained. Now he seemed quite like his old self to all of them. There was about him something of majestic import and exalted aspect, but he was once again lighthearted and joyful.

137:3.5 (1528.1) Mary was thrilled with expectation. She anticipated that the promise of Gabriel was nearing fulfillment. She expected all Palestine soon to be startled and stunned by the miraculous revelation of her son as the supernatural king of the Jews. But to all of the many questions which his mother, James, Jude, and Zebedee asked, Jesus only smilingly replied: "It is better that I tarry here for a while; I must do the will of my Father who is in heaven."

137:3.6 (1528.2) On the next day, Tuesday, they all journeyed over to Cana for the wedding of Naomi, which was to take place on the following day. And in spite of Jesus' repeated warnings that they tell no man about him "until the Father's hour shall come," they insisted on quietly spreading the news abroad that they had found the Deliverer. They each confidently expected that Jesus would inaugurate his assumption of Messianic authority at the forthcoming wedding at Cana, and that he would do so with great power and sublime grandeur. They remembered what had been told them about the phenomena attendant upon his baptism, and they believed that his future course on earth would be marked by increasing manifestations of supernatural wonders and miraculous demonstrations. Accordingly, the entire countryside was preparing to gather together at Cana for the wedding feast of Naomi and Johab the son of Nathan.

137:3.7 (1528.3) Mary had not been so joyous in years. She journeyed to Cana in the spirit of the queen mother on the way to witness the coronation of her son. Not since he was thirteen years old had Jesus' family and friends seen him so carefree and happy, so thoughtful and understanding of the wishes and desires of his associates, so touchingly sympathetic. And so they all whispered among themselves, in small groups, wondering what was going to happen. What would this strange person do next? How would he usher in the glory of the coming kingdom? And they were all thrilled with the thought that they were to be present to see the revelation of the might and power of Israel's God.

4   The Wedding at Cana

137:4.1 (1528.4) By noon on Wednesday almost a thousand guests had arrived in Cana, more than four times the number bidden to the wedding feast. It was a Jewish custom to celebrate weddings on Wednesday, and the invitations had been sent abroad for the wedding one month previously. In the forenoon and early afternoon it appeared more like a public reception for Jesus than a wedding. Everybody wanted to greet this near-famous Galilean, and he was most cordial to all, young and old, Jew and gentile. And everybody rejoiced when Jesus consented to lead the preliminary wedding procession.

137:4.2 (1528.5) Jesus was now thoroughly self-conscious regarding his human existence, his divine pre-existence, and the status of his combined, or fused, human and divine natures. With perfect poise he could at one moment enact the human role or immediately assume the personality prerogatives of the divine nature.

137:4.3 (1528.6) As the day wore on, Jesus became increasingly conscious that the people were expecting him to perform some wonder; more especially he recognized that his family and his six disciple-apostles were looking for him appropriately to announce his forthcoming kingdom by some startling and supernatural manifestation.

137:4.4 (1529.1) Early in the afternoon Mary summoned James, and together they made bold to approach Jesus to inquire if he would admit them to his confidence to the extent of informing them at what hour and at what point in connection with the wedding ceremonies he had planned to manifest himself as the "supernatural one." No sooner had they spoken of these matters to Jesus than they saw they had aroused his characteristic indignation. He said only: "If you love me, then be willing to tarry with me while I wait upon the will of my Father who is in heaven." But the eloquence of his rebuke lay in the expression of his face.

137:4.5 (1529.2) This move of his mother was a great disappointment to the human Jesus, and he was much sobered by his reaction to her suggestive proposal that he permit himself to indulge in some outward demonstration of his divinity.

That was one of the very things he had decided not to do when so recently isolated in the hills. For several hours Mary was much depressed. She said to James: "I cannot understand him; what can it all mean? Is there no end to his strange conduct?" James and Jude tried to comfort their mother, while Jesus withdrew for an hour's solitude. But he returned to the gathering and was once more lighthearted and joyous.

137:4.6 (1529.3) The wedding proceeded with a hush of expectancy, but the entire ceremony was finished and not a move, not a word, from the honored guest. Then it was whispered about that the carpenter and boatbuilder, announced by John as "the Deliverer," would show his hand during the evening festivities, perhaps at the wedding supper. But all expectance of such a demonstration was effectually removed from the minds of his six disciple-apostles when he called them together just before the wedding supper and, in great earnestness, said: "Think not that I have come to this place to work some wonder for the gratification of the curious or for the conviction of those who doubt. Rather are we here to wait upon the will of our Father who is in heaven." But when Mary and the others saw him in consultation with his associates, they were fully persuaded in their own minds that something extraordinary was about to happen. And they all sat down to enjoy the wedding supper and the evening of festive good fellowship.

137:4.7 (1529.4) The father of the bridegroom had provided plenty of wine for all the guests bidden to the marriage feast, but how was he to know that the marriage of his son was to become an event so closely associated with the expected manifestation of Jesus as the Messianic deliverer? He was delighted to have the honor of numbering the celebrated Galilean among his guests, but before the wedding supper was over, the servants brought him the disconcerting news that the wine was running short. By the time the formal supper had ended and the guests were strolling about

in the garden, the mother of the bridegroom confided to Mary that the supply of wine was exhausted. And Mary confidently said: "Have no worry—I will speak to my son. He will help us." And thus did she presume to speak, notwithstanding the rebuke of but a few hours before.

137:4.8 (1529.5) Throughout a period of many years, Mary had always turned to Jesus for help in every crisis of their home life at Nazareth so that it was only natural for her to think of him at this time. But this ambitious mother had still other motives for appealing to her eldest son on this occasion. As Jesus was standing alone in a corner of the garden, his mother approached him, saying, "My son, they have no wine." And Jesus answered, "My good woman, what have I to do with that?" Said Mary, "But I believe your hour has come; cannot you help us?" Jesus replied: "Again I declare that I have not come to do things in this wise. Why do you trouble me again with these matters?" And then, breaking down in tears, Mary entreated him, "But, my son, I promised them that you would help us; won't you please do something for me?" And then spoke Jesus: "Woman, what have you to do with making such promises? See that you do it not again.

We must in all things wait upon the will of the Father in heaven."

137:4.9 (1530.1) Mary the mother of Jesus was crushed; she was stunned! As she stood there before him motionless, with the tears streaming down her face, the human heart of Jesus was overcome with compassion for the woman who had borne him in the flesh; and bending forward, he laid his hand tenderly upon her head, saying: "Now, now, Mother Mary, grieve not over my apparently hard sayings, for have I not many times told you that I have come only to do the will of my heavenly Father? Most gladly would I do what you ask of me if it were a part of the Father's will—" and Jesus stopped short, he hesitated. Mary seemed to sense that something was happening. Leaping up, she threw her arms around Jesus' neck, kissed him, and rushed off to the servants' quarters, saying, "Whatever my son says, that do." But Jesus said nothing. He now realized that he had already said—or rather desirefully thought—too much.

137:4.10 (1530.2) Mary was dancing with glee. She did not know how the wine would be produced, but she confidently believed that she had finally persuaded her first-born son to assert his authority, to dare to step forth and claim his position and exhibit his Messianic power. And, because of the presence and association of certain universe powers and personalities, of which all those present were wholly ignorant, she was not to be disappointed. The wine Mary desired and which Jesus, the God-man, humanly and sympathetically wished for, was forthcoming.

137:4.11 (1530.3) Near at hand stood six waterpots of stone, filled with water, holding about twenty gallons apiece. This water was intended for subsequent use in the final purification ceremonies of the wedding celebration. The commotion of the servants about these huge stone vessels, under the busy direction of his mother, attracted Jesus' attention, and going over, he observed that they were drawing wine out of them by the pitcherful.

137:4.12 (1530.4) It was gradually dawning upon Jesus what had happened. Of all persons present at the marriage feast of Cana, Jesus was the most surprised. Others had expected him to work a wonder, but that was just what he had purposed not to do. And then the Son of Man recalled the admonition of his Personalized Thought Adjuster in the hills. He recounted how the Adjuster had warned him about the inability of any power or personality to deprive him of the creator prerogative of independence of time. On this occasion power transformers, midwayers, and all other required personalities were assembled near the water and other necessary elements, and in the face of the expressed wish of the Universe Creator Sovereign, there was no escaping the instantaneous appearance of wine. And this occurrence was made doubly certain since the Personalized Adjuster had signified that the execution of the Son's desire was in no way a contravention of the Father's will.

137:4.13 (1530.5) But this was in no sense a miracle. No law of nature was modified, abrogated, or even transcended. Nothing happened but the abrogation of time in association with the celestial assembly of the chemical elements requisite for the elaboration of the wine. At Cana on this occasion the agents of the Creator made wine just as they do by the ordinary natural processes except that they did it independently of time and with the intervention of superhuman agencies in the matter of the space assembly of the necessary chemical ingredients.

137:4.14 (1531.1) Furthermore it was evident that the enactment of this so-called miracle was not contrary to the will of the Paradise Father, else it would not have transpired, since Jesus had already subjected himself in all things to the Father's will.

137:4.15 (1531.2) When the servants drew this new wine and carried it to the best man, the "ruler of the feast," and when he had tasted it, he called to the bridegroom, saying: "It is the custom to set out first the good wine and, when the guests have well drunk, to bring forth the inferior fruit of the vine; but you have kept the best of the wine until the last of the feast."

137:4.16 (1531.3) Mary and the disciples of Jesus were greatly rejoiced at the supposed miracle which they thought Jesus had intentionally performed, but Jesus withdrew to a sheltered nook of the garden and engaged in serious thought for a few brief moments. He finally decided that the episode was beyond his personal control under the circumstances and, not being adverse to his Father's will, was inevitable. When he returned to the people, they regarded him with awe; they all believed in him as the Messiah. But Jesus was sorely perplexed, knowing that they believed in him only because of the unusual occurrence which they had just inadvertently beheld. Again Jesus retired for a season to the housetop that he might think it all over.

137:4.17 (1531.4) Jesus now fully comprehended that he must constantly be on guard lest his indulgence of sympathy and pity become responsible for repeated episodes of this sort. Nevertheless, many similar events occurred before the Son of Man took final leave of his mortal life in the flesh.

5   *Back in Capernaum*

137:5.1 (1531.5) Though many of the guests remained for the full week of wedding festivities, Jesus, with his newly chosen disciple-apostles—James, John, Andrew, Peter, Philip, and Nathaniel—departed very early the next morning for Capernaum, going away without taking leave of anyone. Jesus' family and all his friends in Cana were much distressed because he so suddenly left them, and Jude, Jesus' youngest brother, set out in search of him. Jesus and his apostles went directly to the home of Zebedee at Bethsaida. On this journey Jesus talked over many things of importance to the coming kingdom with his newly chosen associates and especially warned them to make no mention of the turning of the water into wine. He also advised them to avoid the cities of Sepphoris and Tiberias in their future work.

137:5.2 (1531.6) After supper that evening, in this home of Zebedee and Salome, there was held one of the most important conferences of all Jesus' earthly career. Only the six apostles were present at this meeting; Jude arrived as they were about to separate. These six chosen men had journeyed from Cana to Bethsaida with Jesus, walking, as it were, on air. They were alive with expectancy and thrilled with the thought of having been selected as close associates of the Son of Man. But when Jesus set out to make clear to them who he was and what was to be his mission on earth and how it might possibly end, they were stunned. They could not grasp what he was telling

them. They were speechless; even Peter was crushed beyond expression. Only the deep-thinking Andrew dared to make reply to Jesus' words of counsel.

When Jesus perceived that they did not comprehend his message, when he saw that their ideas of the Jewish Messiah were so completely crystallized, he sent them to their rest while he walked and talked with his brother Jude. And before Jude took leave of Jesus, he said with much feeling: "My father-brother, I never have understood you. I do not know of a certainty whether you are what my mother has taught us, and I do not fully comprehend the coming kingdom, but I do know you are a mighty man of God. I heard the voice at the Jordan, and I am a believer in you, no matter who you are." And when he had spoken, he departed, going to his own home at Magdala.

137:5.3 (1532.1) That night Jesus did not sleep. Donning his evening wraps, he sat out on the lake shore thinking, thinking until the dawn of the next day. In the long hours of that night of meditation Jesus came clearly to comprehend that he never would be able to make his followers see him in any other light than as the long-expected Messiah. At last he recognized that there was no way to launch his message of the kingdom except as the fulfillment of John's prediction and as the one for whom the Jews were looking. After all, though he was not the Davidic type of Messiah, he was truly the fulfillment of the prophetic utterances of the more spiritually minded of the olden seers. Never again did he wholly deny that he was the Messiah. He decided to leave the final untangling of this complicated situation to the outworking of the Father's will.

137:5.4 (1532.2) The next morning Jesus joined his friends at breakfast, but they were a cheerless group. He visited with them and at the end of the meal gathered them about him, saying: "It is my Father's will that we tarry hereabouts for a season. You have heard John say that he came to prepare the way for the kingdom; therefore it behooves us to await the completion of

John's preaching. When the forerunner of the Son of Man shall have finished his work, we will begin the proclamation of the good tidings of the kingdom." He directed his apostles to return to their nets while he made ready to go with Zebedee to the boatshop, promising to see them the next day at the synagogue, where he was to speak, and appointing a conference with them that Sabbath afternoon.

6   The Events of a Sabbath Day

137:6.1 (1532.3) Jesus' first public appearance following his baptism was in the Capernaum synagogue on Sabbath, March 2, A.D. 26. The synagogue was crowded to overflowing. The story of the baptism in the Jordan was now augmented by the fresh news from Cana about the water and the wine. Jesus gave seats of honor to his six apostles, and seated with them were his brothers in the flesh James and Jude. His mother, having returned to Capernaum with James the evening before, was also present, being seated in the women's section of the synagogue. The entire audience was on edge; they expected to behold some extraordinary manifestation of supernatural power which would be a fitting testimony to the nature and authority of him who was that day to speak to them. But they were destined to disappointment.

137:6.2 (1532.4) When Jesus stood up, the ruler of the synagogue handed him the Scripture roll, and he read from the Prophet Isaiah: "Thus says the Lord: 'The heaven is my throne, and the earth is my footstool. Where is the house that you built for me? And where is the place of my dwelling? All these things have my hands made,' says the Lord. 'But to this man will I look, even to him who is poor and of a contrite spirit, and who trembles at my word.' Hear the word of the Lord, you who tremble and fear: 'Your brethren hated you and cast you out for my name's sake.' But let the Lord be glorified. He shall appear to you in joy, and all others shall be ashamed. A voice from the city, a voice from the temple, a voice

from the Lord says: 'Before she travailed, she brought forth; before her pain came, she was delivered of a man child.' Who has heard such a thing? Shall the earth be made to bring forth in one day? Or can a nation be born at once? But thus says the Lord: 'Behold I will extend peace like a river, and the glory of even the gentiles shall be like a flowing stream. As one whom his mother comforts, so will I comfort you. And you shall be comforted even in Jerusalem. And when you see these things, your heart shall rejoice.'"

137:6.3 (1533.1) When he had finished this reading, Jesus handed the roll back to its keeper. Before sitting down, he simply said: "Be patient and you shall see the glory of God; even so shall it be with all those who tarry with me and thus learn to do the will of my Father who is in heaven." And the people went to their homes, wondering what was the meaning of all this.

137:6.4 (1533.2) That afternoon Jesus and his apostles, with James and Jude, entered a boat and pulled down the shore a little way, where they anchored while he talked to them about the coming kingdom. And they understood more than they had on Thursday night.

137:6.5 (1533.3) Jesus instructed them to take up their regular duties until "the hour of the kingdom comes." And to encourage them, he set an example by going back regularly to work in the boatshop. In explaining that they should spend three hours every evening in study and preparation for their future work, Jesus further said: "We will all remain hereabout until the Father bids me call you. Each of you must now return to his accustomed work just as if nothing had happened. Tell no man about me and remember that my kingdom is not to come with noise and glamor, but rather must it come through the great change which my Father will have wrought in your hearts and in the hearts of those who shall be called to join you in the councils of the kingdom. You are now my friends; I trust you and I love you; you are soon to become my personal associates.

Be patient, be gentle. Be ever obedient to the Father's will. Make yourselves ready for the call of the kingdom. While you will experience great joy in the service of my Father, you should also be prepared for trouble, for I warn you that it will be only through much tribulation that many will enter the kingdom. But those who have found the kingdom, their joy will be full, and they shall be called the blest of all the earth. But do not entertain false hope; the world will stumble at my words. Even you, my friends, do not fully perceive what I am unfolding to your confused minds. Make no mistake; we go forth to labor for a generation of sign seekers. They will demand wonder- working as the proof that I am sent by my Father, and they will be slow to recognize in the revelation of my Father's love the credentials of my mission."

137:6.6 (1533.4) That evening, when they had returned to the land, before they went their way, Jesus, standing by the water's edge, prayed: "My Father, I thank you for these little ones who, in spite of their doubts, even now believe. And for their sakes have I set myself apart to do your will. And now may they learn to be one, even as we are one."

7   *Four Months of Training*

137:7.1 (1533.5) For four long months—March, April, May, and June—this tarrying time continued; Jesus held over one hundred long and earnest, though cheerful and joyous, sessions with these six associates and his own brother James. Owing to sickness in his family, Jude seldom was able to attend these classes. James, Jesus' brother, did not lose faith in him, but during these months of delay and inaction Mary nearly despaired of her son. Her faith, raised to such heights at Cana, now sank to new low levels. She could only fall back on her so oft-repeated exclamation: "I cannot understand him. I cannot figure out what it all means." But James's wife did much to bolster Mary's courage.

137:7.2 (1534.1) Throughout these four months these seven believers, one his own brother in the flesh, were getting acquainted with Jesus; they were getting used to the idea of living with this God-man. Though they called him Rabbi, they were learning not to be afraid of him. Jesus possessed that matchless grace of personality which enabled him so to live among them that they were not dismayed by his divinity. They found it really easy to be "friends with God," God incarnate in the likeness of mortal flesh. This time of waiting severely tested the entire group of believers. Nothing, absolutely nothing, miraculous happened. Day by day they went about their ordinary work, while night after night they sat at Jesus' feet. And they were held together by his matchless personality and by the gracious words which he spoke to them evening upon evening.

137:7.3 (1534.2) This period of waiting and teaching was especially hard on Simon Peter. He repeatedly sought to persuade Jesus to launch forth with the preaching of the kingdom in Galilee while John continued to preach in Judea. But Jesus' reply to Peter ever was: "Be patient, Simon. Make progress. We shall be none too ready when the Father calls." And Andrew would calm Peter now and then with his more seasoned and philosophic counsel. Andrew was tremendously impressed with the human naturalness of Jesus. He never grew weary of contemplating how one who could live so near God could be so friendly and considerate of men.

137:7.4 (1534.3) Throughout this entire period Jesus spoke in the synagogue but twice. By the end of these many weeks of waiting the reports about his baptism and the wine of Cana had begun to quiet down. And Jesus saw to it that no more apparent miracles happened during this time. But even though they lived so quietly at Bethsaida, reports of the strange doings of Jesus had been carried to Herod Antipas, who in turn sent spies to ascertain what he was about. But Herod was more concerned about the preaching of John. He decided not to molest Jesus, whose work continued along so quietly at Capernaum.

137:7.5 (1534.4) In this time of waiting Jesus endeavored to teach his associates what their attitude should be toward the various religious groups and the political parties of Palestine. Jesus' words always were, "We are seeking to win all of them, but we are not of any of them."

137:7.6 (1534.5) The scribes and rabbis, taken together, were called Pharisees. They referred to themselves as the "associates." In many ways they were the progressive group among the Jews, having adopted many teachings not clearly found in the Hebrew scriptures, such as belief in the resurrection of the dead, a doctrine only mentioned by a later prophet, Daniel.

137:7.7 (1534.6) The Sadducees consisted of the priesthood and certain wealthy Jews. They were not such sticklers for the details of law enforcement. The Pharisees and Sadducees were really religious parties, rather than sects.

137:7.8 (1534.7) The Essenes were a true religious sect, originating during the Maccabean revolt, whose requirements were in some respects more exacting than those of the Pharisees. They had adopted many Persian beliefs and practices, lived as a brotherhood in monasteries, refrained from marriage, and had all things in common. They specialized in teachings about angels.

137:7.9 (1535.1) The Zealots were a group of intense Jewish patriots. They advocated that any and all methods were justified in the struggle to escape the bondage of the Roman yoke.

137:7.10 (1535.2) The Herodians were a purely political party that advocated emancipation from the direct Roman rule by a restoration of the Herodian dynasty.

137:7.11 (1535.3) In the very midst of Palestine there lived the Samaritans, with whom "the Jews had no dealings," notwithstanding that they held many views similar to the Jewish teachings.

137:7.12 (1535.4) All of these parties and sects, including the smaller Nazarite brotherhood, believed in the sometime coming of the Messiah. They all looked for a national deliverer. But Jesus was very positive in making it clear that he and his disciples would not become allied to any of these schools of thought or practice. The Son of Man was to be neither a Nazarite nor an Essene.

137:7.13 (1535.5) While Jesus later directed that the apostles should go forth, as John had, preaching the gospel and instructing believers, he laid emphasis on the proclamation of the "good tidings of the kingdom of heaven." He unfailingly impressed upon his associates that they must "show forth love, compassion, and sympathy." He early taught his followers that the kingdom of heaven was a spiritual experience having to do with the enthronement of God in the hearts of men.

137:7.14 (1535.6) As they thus tarried before embarking on their active public preaching, Jesus and the seven spent two evenings each week at the synagogue in the study of the Hebrew scriptures. In later years after seasons of intense public work, the apostles looked back upon these four months as the most precious and profitable of all their association with the Master. Jesus taught these men all they could assimilate. He did not make the mistake of over teaching them. He did not precipitate confusion by the presentation of truth too far beyond their capacity to comprehend.

8   Sermon on the Kingdom

137:8.1 (1535.7) On Sabbath, June 22, shortly before they went out on their first preaching tour and about ten days after John's imprisonment, Jesus occupied the synagogue pulpit for the second time since bringing his apostles to Capernaum.

137:8.2 (1535.8) A few days before the

preaching of this sermon on "The King-dom," as Jesus was at work in the boatshop,

Peter brought him the news of John's arrest. Jesus laid down his tools once more, removed his apron, and said to Peter: "The Father's hour has come. Let us make ready to proclaim the gospel of the kingdom."

137:8.3 (1535.9) Jesus did his last work at the carpenter bench on this Tuesday, June 18, A.D. 26. Peter rushed out of the shop and by midafternoon had rounded up all of his associates, and leaving them in a grove by the shore, he went in quest of Jesus. But he could not find him, for the Master had gone to a different grove to pray. And they did not see him until late that evening when he returned to Zebedee's house and asked for food. The next day he sent his brother James to ask for the privilege of speaking in the synagogue the coming Sabbath day. And the ruler of the synagogue was much pleased that Jesus was again willing to conduct the service.

137:8.4 (1536.1) Before Jesus preached this memorable sermon on the kingdom of God, the first pretentious effort of his public career, he read from the Scriptures these passages: "You shall be to me a king-dom of priests, a holy people.

Yahweh is our judge, Yahweh is our lawgiver, Yahweh is our king; he will save us. Yahweh is my king and my God. He is a great king over all the earth. Loving-kindness is upon Israel in this kingdom. Blessed be the glory of the Lord for he is our King."

137:8.5 (1536.2) When he had finished reading, Jesus said:

137:8.6 (1536.3) "I have come to proclaim the establishment of the Father's kingdom. And this kingdom shall include the worshiping souls of Jew and gentile, rich and poor, free and bond, for my Father is no respecter of persons; his love and his mercy are over all.

137:8.7 (1536.4) "The Father in heaven sends his spirit to indwell the minds of men, and when I shall have finished my work on earth, likewise shall the Spirit of Truth be poured out upon all flesh. And the spirit of my Father and the Spirit of Truth shall establish you in the coming kingdom of spiritual understanding and divine righteousness. My kingdom is not of this world. The Son of Man will not lead forth armies in battle for the establishment of a throne of power or a kingdom of worldly glory. When my kingdom shall have come, you shall know the Son of Man as the Prince of Peace, the revelation of the everlasting Father. The children of this world fight for the establishment and enlargement of the kingdoms of this world, but my disciples shall enter the kingdom of heaven by their moral decisions and by their spirit victories; and when they once enter therein, they shall find joy, righteousness, and eternal life.

137:8.8 (1536.5) "Those who first seek to enter the kingdom, thus beginning to strive for a nobility of character like that of my Father, shall presently possess all else that is needful. But I say to you in all sincerity: Unless you seek entrance into the kingdom with the faith and trusting dependence of a little child, you shall in no wise gain admission.

137:8.9 (1536.6) "Be not deceived by those who come saying here is the kingdom or there is the kingdom, for my Father's kingdom concerns not things visible and material. And this kingdom is even now among you, for where the spirit of God teaches and leads the soul of man, there in reality is the kingdom of heaven. And this kingdom of God is righteousness, peace, and joy in the Holy Spirit.

137:8.10 (1536.7) "John did indeed baptize you in token of repentance and for the remission of your sins, but when you enter the heavenly kingdom, you will be baptized with the Holy Spirit.

137:8.11 (1536.8) "In my Father's kingdom there shall be neither Jew nor gentile, only those who seek perfection through service, for I declare that he who would be great in my Father's kingdom must first become server of all. If you are willing to serve your fellows, you shall sit down with me in my kingdom, even as, by serving in the similitude of the creature, I shall presently sit down with my Father in his kingdom.

137:8.12 (1536.9) "This new kingdom is like a seed growing in the good soil of a field. It does not attain full fruit quickly. There is an interval of time between the establishment of the kingdom in the soul of man and that hour when the kingdom ripens into the full fruit of everlasting righteousness and eternal salvation.

137:8.13 (1536.10) "And this kingdom which I declare to you is not a reign of power and plenty. The kingdom of heaven is not a matter of meat and drink but rather a life of progressive righteousness and increasing joy in the perfecting service of my Father who is in heaven. For has not the Father said of his children of the world, 'It is my will that they should eventually be perfect, even as I am perfect.'

137:8.14 (1537.1) "I have come to preach the glad tidings of the kingdom. I have not come to add to the heavy burdens of those who would enter this kingdom. I proclaim the new and better way, and those who are able to enter the coming kingdom shall enjoy the divine rest. And whatever it shall cost you in the things of the world, no matter what price you may pay to enter the kingdom of heaven, you shall receive manifold more of joy and spiritual progress in this world, and in the age to come eternal life.

137:8.15 (1537.2) "Entrance into the Father's kingdom waits not upon marching armies, upon overturned kingdoms of this world, nor upon the breaking of captive yokes. The kingdom of heaven is at hand, and all who enter therein shall find abundant liberty and joyous salvation.

137:8.16 (1537.3) "This kingdom is an everlasting dominion. Those who enter the kingdom shall ascend to my Father; they will certainly attain the right hand of his glory in Paradise. And all who enter the kingdom of heaven shall become the sons of God, and in the age to come so shall they ascend to the Father. And I have not come to call the would-be righteous but sinners and all who hunger and thirst for the righteousness of divine perfection.

137:8.17 (1537.4) "John came preaching repentance to prepare you for the kingdom; now have I come proclaiming faith, the gift of God, as the price of entrance into the kingdom of heaven. If you would but believe that my Father loves you with an infinite love, then you are in the kingdom of God."

137:8.18 (1537.5) When he had thus spoken, he sat down. All who heard him were astonished at his words. His disciples marveled. But the people were not prepared to receive the good news from the lips of this God-man. About one third who heard him believed the message even though they could not fully comprehend it; about one third prepared in their hearts to reject such a purely spiritual concept of the expected kingdom, while the remaining one third could not grasp his teaching, many truly believing that he "was beside himself."

Paper 138

Training the Kingdom's Messengers

138:0.1 (1538.1) AFTER preaching the sermon on "The Kingdom," Jesus called the six apostles together that afternoon and began to disclose his plans for visiting the cities around and about the Sea of Galilee. His brothers James and Jude were very much hurt because they were not called to this conference. Up to this time they had regarded themselves as belonging to Jesus' inner circle of associates. But Jesus planned to have no close relatives as members of this corps of apostolic directors of the kingdom. This failure to include James and Jude among the chosen few, together with his apparent aloofness from his mother ever since the experience at Cana, was the starting point of an ever-widening gulf between Jesus and his family. This situation continued throughout his public ministry—they very nearly rejected him— and these differences were not fully removed until after his death and resurrection. His mother constantly wavered between attitudes of fluctuating faith and hope, and increasing emotions of disappointment, humiliation, and despair.

Only Ruth, the youngest, remained unswervingly loyal to her father-brother.

138:0.2 (1538.2) Until after the resurrection, Jesus' entire family had very little to do with his ministry. If a prophet is not without honor save in his own country, he is not without understanding appreciation save in his own family.

Final Instructions

138:1.1 (1538.3) The next day, Sunday, June 23, A.D. 26, Jesus imparted his final instructions to the six. He directed them to go forth, two and two, to teach the glad tidings of the kingdom. He forbade them to baptize and advised against public preaching. He went on to explain that later he would permit them to preach in public, but that for a season, and for many reasons, he desired them to acquire practical experience in dealing personally with their fellow men. Jesus purposed to make their first tour entirely one of personal work. Although this announcement was something of a disappointment to the apostles, still they saw, at least in part, Jesus' reason for thus beginning the proclamation of the kingdom, and they started out in good heart and with confident enthusiasm. He sent them forth by twos, James and John going to Kheresa, Andrew and Peter to Capernaum, while Philip and Nathaniel went to Tarichea.

138:1.2 (1538.4) Before they began this first two weeks of service, Jesus announced to them that he desired to ordain twelve apostles to continue the work of the kingdom after his departure and authorized each of them to choose one man from among his early converts for membership in the projected corps of apostles. John spoke up, asking: "But, Master, will these six men come into our midst and share all things equally with us who have been with you since the Jordan and have heard all your teaching in preparation for this, our first labor for the kingdom?" And Jesus replied: "Yes, John, the men you choose shall become one with us, and you will teach them all that pertains to the kingdom, even as I have taught you." After thus speaking, Jesus left them.

138:1.3 (1539.1) The six did not separate to go to their work until they had exchanged many words in discussion of Jesus' instruction that each of them should choose a new apostle. Andrew's counsel finally prevailed, and they went forth to their labors. In substance Andrew said: "The Master is right; we are too few to encompass this work. There is need for more teachers, and the Master has manifested great confidence in us inasmuch as he has intrusted us with the choosing of these six new apostles." This morning, as they separated to go to their work, there was a bit of concealed depression in each heart. They knew they were going to miss Jesus, and besides their fear and timidity, this was not the way they had pictured the kingdom of heaven being inaugurated.

138:1.4 (1539.2) It had been arranged that the six were to labor for two weeks, after which they were to return to the home of Zebedee for a conference. Meantime Jesus went over to Nazareth to visit with Joseph and Simon and other members of his family living in that vicinity. Jesus did everything humanly possible, consistent with his dedication to the doing of his Father's will, to retain the confidence and affection of his family. In this matter he did his full duty and more.

138:1.5 (1539.3) While the apostles were out on this mission, Jesus thought much about John, now in prison. It was a great temptation to use his potential powers to release him, but once more he resigned himself to "wait upon the Father's will."

Choosing the Six

138:2.1 (1539.4) This first missionary tour of the six was eminently successful. They all discovered the great value of direct and personal contact with men. They returned to Jesus more fully realizing that, after all, religion is purely and wholly a matter of personal experience. They began to sense how hungry were the common people to hear words of religious comfort and spiritual good cheer. When they assembled about Jesus, they all wanted to talk at once, but Andrew assumed charge, and as he called upon them one by one, they made their formal reports to the Master and presented their nominations for the six new apostles.

138:2.2 (1539.5) Jesus, after each man had presented his selection for the new apostleships, asked all the others to vote upon the nomination; thus all six of the new apostles were formally accepted by all of the older six. Then Jesus announced that they would all visit these candidates and give them the call to service.

138:2.3 (1539.6) The newly selected apostles were:

138:2.4 (1539.7) 1. Matthew Levi, the customs collector of Capernaum, who had his office just to the east of the city, near the borders of Batanea. He was selected by Andrew.

138:2.5 (1539.8) 2. Thomas Didymus, a fisherman of Tarichea and onetime carpenter and stone mason of Gadara. He was selected by Philip.

138:2.6 (1539.9) 3. James Alpheus, a fisherman and farmer of Kheresa, was selected by James Zebedee.

138:2.7 (1539.10) 4. Judas Alpheus, the twin brother of James Alpheus, also a fisherman, was selected by John Zebedee.

138:2.8 (1540.1) 5. Simon Zelotes was a high officer in the patriotic organization of the Zealots, a position which he gave up to join Jesus' apostles. Before joining the Zealots, Simon had been a merchant. He was selected by Peter.

138:2.9 (1540.2) 6. Judas Iscariot was an only son of wealthy Jewish parents living in Jericho. He had become attached to John the Baptist, and his Sadducee parents had disowned him. He was looking for employment in these regions when Jesus' apostles found him, and chiefly because of his experience with finances, Nathaniel invited him to join their ranks. Judas Iscariot was the only Judean among the twelve apostles.

138:2.10 (1540.3) Jesus spent a full day with the six, answering their questions and listening to the details of their reports, for they had many interesting and profitable experiences to relate. They now saw the wisdom of the Master's plan of sending them out to labor in a quiet and personal manner before the launching of their more pretentious public efforts.

The Call of Matthew and Simon

138:3.1 (1540.4) The next day Jesus and the six went to call upon Matthew, the customs collector. Matthew was awaiting them, having balanced his books and made ready to turn the affairs of his office over to his brother. As they approached the toll house, Andrew stepped forward with Jesus, who, looking into Matthew's face, said, "Follow me." And he arose and went to his house with Jesus and the apostles.

138:3.2 (1540.5) Matthew told Jesus of the banquet he had arranged for that evening, at least that he wished to give such a dinner to his family and friends if Jesus would approve and consent to be the guest of honor. And Jesus nodded his consent. Peter then took Matthew aside and explained that he had invited one Simon to join the apostles and secured his consent that Simon be also bidden to this feast.

138:3.3 (1540.6) After a noontide luncheon at Matthew's house they all went with Peter to call upon Simon the Zealot, whom they found at his old place of business, which was now being conducted by his nephew. When Peter led Jesus up to Simon, the Master greeted the fiery patriot and only said, "Follow me."

138:3.4 (1540.7) They all returned to Matthew's home, where they talked much about politics and religion until the hour of the evening meal. The Levi family had long been engaged in business and tax gathering; therefore many of the guests bidden to this banquet by Matthew would have been denominated "publicans and sinners" by the Pharisees.

138:3.5 (1540.8) In those days, when a reception-banquet of this sort was tendered a prominent individual, it was the custom for all interested persons to linger about the banquet room to observe the guests at meat and to listen to the conversation and speeches of the men of honor. Accordingly, most of the Capernaum Pharisees were present on this occasion to observe Jesus' conduct at this unusual social gathering.

138:3.6 (1540.9) As the dinner progressed, the joy of the diners mounted to heights of good cheer, and everybody was having such a splendid time that the onlooking Pharisees began, in their hearts, to criticize Jesus for his participation in such a lighthearted and carefree affair. Later in the evening, when they were making speeches, one of the more malignant of the Pharisees went so far as to criticize Jesus' conduct to Peter, saying: "How dare you to teach that this man is righteous when he eats with publicans and sinners and thus lends his presence to such scenes of careless pleasure making." Peter whispered this criticism to Jesus before he spoke the parting blessing upon those assembled. When Jesus began to speak, he said: "In coming here tonight to welcome Matthew and Simon to our fellowship, I am glad to witness your lightheartedness and social good cheer, but you should rejoice still more because many of you will find entrance into the coming kingdom of the spirit, wherein you shall more abundantly enjoy the good things of the kingdom of heaven. And to you who stand about criticizing me in your hearts because I have come here to make merry with these friends, let me say that I have come to proclaim joy to the socially downtrodden and spiritual liberty to the moral captives. Need I remind you that they who are whole need not a physician, but rather those who are sick? I have come, not to call the righteous, but sinners."

138:3.7 (1541.1) And truly this was a strange sight in all Jewry: to see a man of righteous character and noble sentiments mingling freely and joyously with the common people, even with an irreligious and pleasure-seeking throng of publicans and reputed sinners. Simon Zelotes desired to make a speech at this gathering in Matthew's house, but Andrew, knowing that Jesus did not want the coming kingdom to become confused with the Zealots' movement, prevailed upon him to refrain from making any public remarks.

138:3.8 (1541.2) Jesus and the apostles remained that night in Matthew's house, and as the people went to their homes, they spoke of but one thing: the goodness and friendliness of Jesus.

The Call of the Twins

138:4.1 (1541.3) On the morrow all nine of them went by boat over to Kheresa to execute the formal calling of the next two apostles, James and Judas the twin sons of Alpheus, the nominees of James and John Zebedee. The fisherman twins were expecting Jesus and his apostles and were therefore awaiting them on the shore. James Zebedee presented the Master to the Kheresa fishermen, and Jesus, gazing on them, nodded and said, "Follow me."

138:4.2 (1541.4) That afternoon, which they spent together, Jesus fully instructed them concerning attendance upon festive gatherings, concluding his remarks by saying: "All men are my brothers. My Father in heaven does not despise any creature of our making. The kingdom of heaven is open to all men and women. No man may close the door of mercy in the face of any hungry soul who may seek to gain an entrance thereto. We will sit at meat with all who desire to hear of the kingdom. As our Father in heaven looks down upon men, they are all alike. Refuse not therefore to break bread with Pharisee or sinner, Sadducee or publican, Roman or Jew, rich or poor, free or bond. The door of the kingdom is wide open for all who desire to know the truth and to find God."

138:4.3 (1541.5) That night at a simple supper at the Alpheus home, the twin brothers were received into the apostolic family. Later in the evening Jesus gave his apostles their first lesson dealing with the origin, nature, and destiny of unclean spirits, but they could not comprehend the import of what he told them. They found it very easy to love and admire Jesus but very difficult to understand many of his teachings.

138:4.4 (1542.1) After a night of rest the entire party, now numbering eleven, went by boat over to Tarichea.

The Call of Thomas and Judas

138:5.1 (1542.2) Thomas the fisherman and Judas the wanderer met Jesus and the apostles at the fisher-boat landing at Tarichea, and Thomas led the party to his near-by home. Philip now presented Thomas as his nominee for apostleship and Nathaniel presented Judas Iscariot, the Judean, for similar honors. Jesus looked upon Thomas and said: "Thomas, you lack faith; nevertheless, I receive you. Follow me." To Judas Iscariot the Master said: "Judas, we are all of one flesh, and as I receive you into our midst, I pray that you will always be loyal to your Galilean brethren. Follow me."

138:5.2 (1542.3) When they had refreshed themselves, Jesus took the twelve apart for a season to pray with them and to instruct them in the nature and work of the Holy Spirit, but again did they largely fail to comprehend the meaning of those wonderful truths which he endeavored to teach them. One would grasp one point and one would comprehend another, but none of them could encompass the whole of his teaching. Always would they make the mistake of trying to fit Jesus' new gospel into their old forms of religious belief. They could not grasp the idea that Jesus had come to proclaim a new gospel of salvation and to establish a new way of finding God; they did not perceive that he was a new revelation of the Father in heaven.

138:5.3 (1542.4) The next day Jesus left his twelve apostles quite alone; he wanted them to become acquainted and desired that they be alone to talk over what he had taught them. The Master returned for the evening meal, and during the after-supper hours he talked to them about the ministry of seraphim, and some of the apostles comprehended his teaching.

They rested for a night and the next day departed by boat for Capernaum.

138:5.4 (1542.5) Zebedee and Salome had gone to live with their son David so that their large home could be turned over to Jesus and his twelve apostles. Here Jesus spent a quiet Sabbath with his chosen messengers; he carefully outlined the plans for proclaiming the kingdom and fully explained the importance of avoiding any clash with the civil authorities, saying: "If the civil rulers are to be rebuked, leave that task to me. See that you make no denunciations of Caesar or his servants." It was this same evening that Judas Iscariot took Jesus aside to inquire why nothing was done to get John out of prison. And Judas was not wholly satisfied with Jesus' attitude.

The Week of Intensive Training

138:6.1 (1542.6) The next week was devoted to a program of intense training. Each day the six new apostles were put in the hands of their respective nominators for a thoroughgoing review of all they had learned and experienced in preparation for the work of the kingdom. The older apostles carefully reviewed, for the benefit of the younger six, Jesus' teachings up to that hour. Evenings they all assembled in Zebedee's garden to receive Jesus' instruction.

138:6.2 (1542.7) It was at this time that Jesus established the mid-week holiday for rest and recreation. And they pursued this plan of relaxation for one day each week throughout the remainder of his material life. As a general rule, they never prosecuted their regular activities on Wednesday. On this weekly holiday Jesus would usually take himself away from them, saying: "My children, go for a day of play. Rest yourselves from the arduous labors of the kingdom and enjoy the refreshment that comes from reverting to your former vocations or from discovering new sorts of recreational activity." While Jesus, at this period of his earth life, did not actually require this day of rest, he conformed to this plan because he knew it was best for his human associates. Jesus was the teacher—the Master; his associates were his pupils—disciples.

138:6.3 (1543.1) Jesus endeavored to make clear to his apostles the difference between his teachings and his life among them and the teachings which might subsequently spring up about him. Said Jesus: "My kingdom and the gospel related thereto shall be the burden of your message. Be not sidetracked into preaching about me and about my teachings.
Proclaim the gospel of the kingdom and portray my revelation of the Father in heaven but do not be misled into the bypaths of creating legends and building up a cult having to do with beliefs and teachings about my beliefs and teachings." But again they did not understand why he thus spoke, and no man dared to ask why he so taught them.

138:6.4 (1543.2) In these early teachings Jesus sought to avoid controversies with his apostles as far as possible except-

ing those involving wrong concepts of his Father in heaven. In all such matters he never hesitated to correct erroneous beliefs. There was just one motive in Jesus' post-baptismal life on Urantia, and that was a better and truer revelation of his Paradise Father; he was the pioneer of the new and better way to God, the way of faith and love. Ever his exhortation to the apostles was: "Go seek for the sinners; find the down-hearted and comfort the anxious."

138:6.5 (1543.3) Jesus had a perfect grasp of the situation; he possessed unlimited power, which might have been utilized in the furtherance of his mission, but he was wholly content with means and personalities which most people would have regarded as inadequate and would have looked upon as insignificant. He was engaged in a mission of enormous dramatic possibilities, but he insisted on going about his Father's business in the most quiet and undramatic manner; he studiously avoided all display of power. And he now planned to work quietly, at least for several months, with his twelve apostles around about the Sea of Galilee.

Another Disappointment

138:7.1 (1543.4) Jesus had planned for a quiet missionary campaign of five months' personal work. He did not tell the apostles how long this was to last; they worked from week to week. And early on this first day of the week, just as he was about to announce this to his twelve apostles, Simon Peter, James Zebedee, and Judas Iscariot came to have private converse with him. Taking Jesus aside, Peter made bold to say: "Master, we come at the behest of our associates to inquire whether the time is not now ripe to enter into the kingdom. And will you proclaim the kingdom at Capernaum, or are we to move on to Jerusalem? And when shall we learn, each of us, the positions we are to occupy with you in the establishment of the kingdom—" and Peter would have gone on asking further questions, but Jesus raised an admonitory hand and stopped him. And beckoning the other apostles standing near by to join them, Jesus said: "My little children, how long shall I bear with you! Have I not made it plain to you that my kingdom is not of this world? I have told you many times that I have not come to sit on David's throne, and now how is it that you are inquiring which place each of you will occupy in the Father's kingdom? Can you not perceive that I have called you as ambassadors of a spiritual kingdom? Do you not understand that soon, very soon, you are to represent me in the world and in the proclamation of the kingdom, even as I now represent my Father who is in heaven? Can it be that I have chosen you and instructed you as messengers of the kingdom, and yet you do not comprehend the nature and significance of this coming kingdom of divine pre-eminence in the hearts of men? My friends, hear me once more. Banish from your minds this idea that my kingdom is a rule of power or a reign of glory. Indeed, all power in heaven and on earth will presently be given into my hands, but it is not the Father's will that we use this divine endowment to glorify ourselves during this age. In another age you shall indeed sit with me in power and glory, but it behooves us now to submit to the will of the Father and to go forth in humble obedience to execute his bidding on earth."

138:7.2 (1544.1) Once more were his associates shocked, stunned. Jesus sent them away two and two to pray, asking them to return to him at noontime. On this crucial forenoon they each sought to find God, and each endeavored to cheer and strengthen the other, and they returned to Jesus as he had bidden them.

138:7.3 (1544.2) Jesus now recounted for them the coming of John, the baptism in the Jordan, the marriage feast at Cana, the recent choosing of the six, and the withdrawal from them of his own brothers in the flesh, and warned them that the enemy of the kingdom would seek also to draw them away. After this short but earnest talk the apostles all arose, under Peter's leadership, to declare their undying devotion to their Master and to pledge their unswerving loyalty to the kingdom, as Thomas expressed it, "To this coming kingdom, no matter what it is and even if I do not fully understand it." They all truly believed in Jesus, even though they did not fully comprehend his teaching.

138:7.4 (1544.3) Jesus now asked them how much money they had among them; he also inquired as to what provision had been made for their families. When it developed that they had hardly sufficient funds to maintain themselves for two weeks, he said: "It is not the will of my Father that we begin our work in this way. We will remain here by the sea two weeks and fish or do whatever our hands find to do; and in the meantime, under the guidance of Andrew, the first chosen apostle, you shall so organize yourselves as to provide for everything needful in your future work, both for the present personal ministry and also when I shall subsequently ordain you to preach the gospel and instruct believers." They were all greatly cheered by these words; this was their first clear-cut and positive intimation that Jesus designed later on to enter upon more aggressive and pretentious public efforts. *

138:7.5 (1544.4) The apostles spent the remainder of the day perfecting their organization and completing arrangements for boats and nets for embarking on the morrow's fishing as they had all decided to devote themselves to fishing; most of them had been fishermen, even Jesus was an experienced boatman and fisherman. Many of the boats which they used the next few years had been built by Jesus' own hands. And they were good and trustworthy boats.

138:7.6 (1544.5) Jesus enjoined them to devote themselves to fishing for two weeks, adding, "And then will you go forth to become fishers of men." They fished in three groups, Jesus going out with a different group each night. And they all so much enjoyed Jesus! He was a good fisherman, a cheerful companion, and an inspiring friend; the more they worked with him, the more they loved him. Said Matthew one day: "The more you understand some people, the less you admire them, but of this man, even the less I comprehend him, the more I love him."

138:7.7 (1545.1) This plan of fishing two weeks and going out to do personal work in behalf of the kingdom for two weeks was followed for more than five months, even to the end of this year of A.D. 26, until after the cessation of those special persecutions which had been directed against John's disciples subsequent to his imprisonment.

First Work of the Twelve

138:8.1 (1545.2) After disposing of the fish catches of two weeks, Judas Iscariot, the one chosen to act as treasurer of the twelve, divided the apostolic funds into six equal portions, funds for the care of dependent families having been already provided. And then near the middle of August, in the year A.D. 26, they went forth two and two to the fields of work assigned by Andrew. The first two weeks Jesus went out with Andrew and Peter, the second two weeks with James and John, and so on with the other couples in the order of their choosing. In this way he was able to go out at least once with each couple before he called them together for the beginning of their public ministry.

138:8.2 (1545.3) Jesus taught them to preach the forgiveness of sin through faith in God without penance or sacrifice, and that the Father in heaven loves all his children with the same eternal love. He enjoined his apostles to refrain from discussing:

138:8.3 (1545.4) 1. The work and imprisonment of John the Baptist.

138:8.4 (1545.5) 2. The voice at the baptism. Said Jesus: "Only those who heard the voice may refer to it. Speak only that which you have heard from me; speak not hearsay."

138:8.5 (1545.6) 3. The turning of the water into wine at Cana. Jesus seriously charged them, saying, "Tell no man about the water and the wine."

138:8.6 (1545.7) They had wonderful times throughout these five or six months during which they worked as fishermen every alternate two weeks, thereby earning enough money to support themselves in the field for each succeeding two weeks of missionary work for the kingdom.

138:8.7 (1545.8) The common people marveled at the teaching and ministry of Jesus and his apostles. The rabbis had long taught the Jews that the ignorant could not be pious or righteous. But Jesus' apostles were both pious and righteous; yet they were cheerfully ignorant of much of the learning of the rabbis and the wisdom of the world.

138:8.8 (1545.9) Jesus made plain to his apostles the difference between the repentance of so-called good works as taught by the Jews and the change of mind by faith—the new birth—which he required as the price of admission to the kingdom. He taught his apostles that faith was the only requisite to entering the Father's kingdom. John had taught them "repentance—to flee from the wrath to come." Jesus taught, "Faith is the open door for entering into the present, perfect, and eternal love of God." Jesus did not speak like a prophet, one who comes to declare the word of God. He seemed to speak of himself as one having authority. Jesus sought to divert their minds from miracle seeking to the finding of a real and personal experience in the satisfaction and assurance of the indwelling of God's spirit of love and saving grace.

138:8.9 (1545.10) The disciples early learned that the Master had a profound respect and sympathetic regard for every human being he met, and they were tremendously impressed by this uniform and unvarying consideration which he so consistently gave to all sorts of men, women, and children. He would pause in the midst of a profound discourse that he might go out in the road to speak good cheer to a passing woman laden with her burden of body and soul. He would interrupt a serious conference with his apostles to fraternize with an intruding child. Nothing ever seemed so important to Jesus as the individual human who chanced to be in his immediate presence. He was master and teacher, but he was more—he was also a friend and neighbor, an understanding comrade.

138:8.10 (1546.1) Though Jesus' public teaching mainly consisted in parables and short discourses, he invariably taught his apostles by questions and answers. He would always pause to answer sincere questions during his later public discourses.

138:8.11 (1546.2) The apostles were at first shocked by, but early became accustomed to, Jesus' treatment of women; he made it very clear to them that women were to be accorded equal rights with men in the kingdom.

Five Months of Testing

138:9.1 (1546.3) This somewhat monotonous period of alternate fishing and personal work proved to be a grueling experience for the twelve apostles, but they endured the test. With all of their grumblings, doubts, and transient dissatisfactions they remained true to their vows of devotion and loyalty to the Master. It was their personal association with Jesus during these months of testing that so endeared him to them that they all (save Judas Iscariot) remained loyal and true to him even in the dark hours of the trial and crucifixion. Real men simply could not actually desert a revered teacher who had lived so close to them and had been so devoted to them as had Jesus. Through the dark hours of the Master's death, in the hearts of these apostles all reason, judgment, and logic were set aside in deference to just one extraordinary human emotion—the supreme sentiment of friendship-loyalty. These five months of

work with Jesus led these apostles, each one of them, to regard him as the best friend he had in all the world. And it was this human sentiment, and not his superb teachings or marvelous doings, that held them together until after the resurrection and the renewal of the proclamation of the gospel of the kingdom.

138:9.2 (1546.4) Not only were these months of quiet work a great test to the apostles, a test which they survived, but this season of public inactivity was a great trial to Jesus' family. By the time Jesus was prepared to launch forth on his public work, his entire family (except Ruth) had practically deserted him. On only a few occasions did they attempt to make subsequent contact with him, and then it was to persuade him to return home with them, for they came near to believing that he was beside himself. They simply could not fathom his philosophy nor grasp his teaching; it was all too much for those of his own flesh and blood.

138:9.3 (1546.5) The apostles carried on their personal work in Capernaum, Bethsaida-Julias, Chorazin, Gerasa, Hippos, Magdala, Cana, Bethlehem of Galilee, Jotapata, Ramah, Safed, Gischala, Gadara, and Abila. Besides these towns they labored in many villages as well as in the countryside. By the end of this period the twelve had worked out fairly satisfactory plans for the care of their respective families. Most of the apostles were married, some had several children, but they had made such arrangements for the support of their home folks that, with some little assistance from the apostolic funds, they could devote their entire energies to the Master's work without having to worry about the financial welfare of their families.

Organization of the Twelve

138:10.1 (1547.1) The apostles early organized themselves in the following manner:

138:10.2 (1547.2) 1. Andrew, the first chosen apostle, was designated chairman and director general of the twelve.

138:10.3 (1547.3) 2. Peter, James, and John were appointed personal companions of Jesus. They were to attend him day and night, to minister to his physical and sundry needs, and to accompany him on those night vigils of prayer and mysterious communion with the Father in heaven.

138:10.4 (1547.4) 3. Philip was made steward of the group. It was his duty to provide food and to see that visitors, and even the multitude of listeners at times, had something to eat.

138:10.5 (1547.5) 4. Nathaniel watched over the needs of the families of the twelve. He received regular reports as to the requirements of each apostle's family and, making requisition on Judas, the treasurer, would send funds each week to those in need.

138:10.6 (1547.6) 5. Matthew was the fiscal agent of the apostolic corps. It was his duty to see that the budget was balanced, the treasury replenished. If the funds for mutual support were not forthcoming, if donations sufficient to maintain the party were not received, Matthew was empowered to order the twelve back to their nets for a season. But this was never necessary after they began their public work; he always had sufficient funds in the treasurer's hands to finance their activities.

138:10.7 (1547.7) 6. Thomas was manager of the itinerary. It devolved upon him to arrange lodgings and in a general way select places for teaching and preaching, thereby insuring a smooth and expeditious travel schedule.

138:10.8 (1547.8) 7. James and Judas the twin sons of Alpheus were assigned to the management of the multitudes. It was their task to deputize a sufficient number of assistant ushers to enable them to maintain order among the crowds during the preaching.

138:10.9 (1547.9) 8. Simon Zelotes was given charge of recreation and play. He managed the Wednesday programs and also sought to provide for a few hours of relaxation and diversion each day.

138:10.10 (1547.10) 9. Judas Iscariot was appointed treasurer. He carried the bag. He paid all expenses and kept the books. He made budget estimates for Matthew from week to week and also made weekly reports to Andrew. Judas paid out funds on Andrew's authorization.

138:10.11 (1547.11) In this way the twelve functioned from their early organization up to the time of the reorganization made necessary by the desertion of Judas, the betrayer. The Master and his disciple-apostles went on in this simple manner until Sunday, January 12, A.D. 27, when he called them together and formally ordained them as ambassadors of the kingdom and preachers of its glad tidings. And soon thereafter they prepared to start for Jerusalem and Judea on their first public preaching tour.

Paper 139

The Twelve Apostles

139:0.1 (1548.1) IT IS an eloquent testimony to the charm and righteousness of Jesus' earth life that, although he repeatedly dashed to pieces the hopes of his apostles and tore to shreds their every ambition for personal exaltation, only one deserted him.

139:0.2 (1548.2) The apostles learned from Jesus about the kingdom of heaven, and Jesus learned much from them about the kingdom of men, human nature as it lives on Urantia and on the other evolutionary worlds of time and space. These twelve men represented many different types of human temperament, and they had not been made alike by schooling. Many of these Galilean fishermen carried heavy strains of gentile blood as a result of the forcible conversion of the gentile population of Galilee one hundred years previously.

139:0.3 (1548.3) Do not make the mistake of regarding the apostles as being altogether ignorant and unlearned. All of them, except the Alpheus twins, were graduates of the synagogue schools, having been thoroughly trained in the Hebrew scriptures and in much of the current knowledge of that day. Seven were graduates of the Capernaum synagogue schools, and there were no better Jewish schools in all Galilee.

139:0.4 (1548.4) When your records refer to these messengers of the kingdom as being "ignorant and unlearned," it was intended to convey the idea that they were laymen, unlearned in the lore of the rabbis and untrained in the methods of rabbinical interpretation of the Scriptures. They were lacking in so-called higher education. In modern times they would certainly be considered uneducated, and in some circles of society even uncultured. One thing is certain: They had not all been put through the same rigid and stereotyped educational curriculum. From adolescence on they had enjoyed separate experiences of learning how to live.

Andrew, the First Chosen

139:1.1 (1548.5) Andrew, chairman of the apostolic corps of the kingdom, was born in Capernaum. He was the oldest child in a family of five—himself, his brother Simon, and three sisters. His father, now dead, had been a partner of Zebedee in the fish-drying business at Bethsaida, the fishing harbor of Capernaum. When he became an apostle, Andrew was unmarried but made his home with his married brother, Simon Peter. Both were fishermen and partners of James and John the sons of Zebedee.

139:1.2 (1548.6) In A.D. 26, the year he was chosen as an apostle, Andrew was 33, a full year older than Jesus and the oldest of the apostles. He sprang from an excellent line of ancestors and was the ablest man of the twelve. Excepting oratory, he was the peer of his associates in almost every imaginable ability. Jesus never gave Andrew a nickname, a fraternal designation. But even as the apostles soon began to call Jesus Master, so they also designated Andrew by a term the equivalent of Chief.

139:1.3 (1549.1) Andrew was a good organizer but a better administrator. He was one of the inner circle of four apostles, but his appointment by Jesus as the head of the apostolic group made it necessary for him to remain on duty with his brethren while the other three enjoyed very close communion with the Master. To the very end Andrew remained dean of the apostolic corps.

139:1.4 (1549.2) Although Andrew was never an effective preacher, he was an efficient personal worker, being the pioneer missionary of the kingdom in that, as the first chosen apostle, he immediately brought to Jesus his brother, Simon, who subsequently became one of the greatest preachers of the kingdom. Andrew was the chief supporter of Jesus' policy of utilizing the program of personal work as a means of training the twelve as messengers of the kingdom.

139:1.5 (1549.3) Whether Jesus privately taught the apostles or preached to the multitude, Andrew was usually conversant with what was going on; he was an understanding executive and an efficient administrator. He rendered a prompt decision on every matter brought to his notice unless he deemed the problem one beyond the domain of his authority, in which event he would take it straight to Jesus.

139:1.6 (1549.4) Andrew and Peter were very unlike in character and temperament, but it must be recorded everlastingly to their credit that they got along together splendidly. Andrew was never jealous of Peter's oratorical ability. Not often will an older man of Andrew's type be observed exerting such a profound influence over a younger and talented brother.

Andrew and Peter never seemed to be in the least jealous of each other's abilities or achievements. Late on the evening of the day of Pentecost, when, largely through the energetic and inspiring preaching of Peter, two thousand souls were added to the kingdom, Andrew said to his brother: "I could not do that, but I am glad I have a brother who could." To which Peter replied: "And but for your bringing me to the Master and by your steadfastness keeping me with him, I should not have been here to do this." Andrew and Peter were the exceptions to the rule, proving that even brothers can live together peaceably and work together effectively.

139:1.7 (1549.5) After Pentecost Peter was famous, but it never irritated the older Andrew to spend the rest of his life being introduced as "Simon Peter's brother."

139:1.8 (1549.6) Of all the apostles, Andrew was the best judge of men. He knew that trouble was brewing in the heart of Judas Iscariot even when none of the others suspected that anything was wrong with their treasurer; but he told none of them his fears. Andrew's great service to the kingdom was in advising Peter, James, and John concerning the choice of the first missionaries who were sent out to proclaim the gospel, and also in counseling these early leaders about the organization of the administrative affairs of the kingdom. Andrew had a great gift for discovering the hidden resources and latent talents of young people.

139:1.9 (1549.7) Very soon after Jesus' ascension on high, Andrew began the writing of a personal record of many of the sayings and doings of his departed Master. After Andrew's death other copies of this private record were made and circulated freely among the early teachers of the Christian church. These informal notes of Andrew's were subsequently edited, amended, altered, and added to until they made up a fairly consecutive narrative of the Master's life on earth.

The last of these few altered and amended copies was destroyed by fire at Alexandria about one hundred years after the original was written by the first chosen of the twelve apostles.

139:1.10 (1550.1) Andrew was a man of clear insight, logical thought, and firm decision, whose great strength of character consisted in his superb stability. His temperamental handicap was his lack of enthusiasm; he many times failed to encourage his associates by judicious commendation. And this reticence to praise the worthy accomplishments of his friends grew out of his abhorrence of flattery and insincerity. Andrew was one of those all-round, even-tempered, self-made, and successful men of modest affairs.

139:1.11 (1550.2) Every one of the apostles loved Jesus, but it remains true that each of the twelve was drawn toward him because of some certain trait of personality which made a special appeal to the individual apostle. Andrew admired Jesus because of his consistent sincerity, his unaffected dignity. When men once knew Jesus, they were possessed with the urge to share him with their friends; they really wanted all the world to know him.

139:1.12 (1550.3) When the later persecutions finally scattered the apostles from Jerusalem, Andrew journeyed through Armenia, Asia Minor, and Macedonia and, after bringing many thousands into the kingdom, was finally apprehended and crucified in Patrae in Achaia. It was two full days before this robust man expired on the cross, and throughout these tragic hours he continued effectively to proclaim the glad tidings of the salvation of the kingdom of heaven.

Simon Peter

139:2.1 (1550.4) When Simon joined the apostles, he was thirty years of age. He was married, had three children, and lived at Bethsaida, near Capernaum. His brother, Andrew, and his wife's mother lived with him. Both Peter and Andrew were fisher partners of the sons of Zebedee.

139:2.2 (1550.5) The Master had known Simon for some time before Andrew presented him as the second of the apostles. When Jesus gave Simon the name Peter, he did it with a smile; it was to be a sort of nickname. Simon was well known to all his friends as an erratic and impulsive fellow. True, later on, Jesus did attach a new and significant import to this lightly bestowed nickname.

139:2.3 (1550.6) Simon Peter was a man of impulse, an optimist. He had grown up permitting himself freely to indulge strong feelings; he was constantly getting into difficulties because he persisted in speaking without thinking. This sort of thoughtlessness also made incessant trouble for all of his friends and associates and was the cause of his receiving many mild rebukes from his Master. The only reason Peter did not get into more trouble because of his thoughtless speaking was that he very early learned to talk over many of his plans and schemes with his brother, Andrew, before he ventured to make public proposals.

139:2.4 (1550.7) Peter was a fluent speaker, eloquent and dramatic. He was also a natural and inspirational leader of men, a quick thinker but not a deep reasoner. He asked many questions, more than all the apostles put together, and while the majority of these questions were good and relevant, many of them were thoughtless and foolish. Peter did not have a deep mind, but he knew his mind fairly well. He was therefore a man of quick decision and sudden action. While others talked in their astonishment at seeing Jesus on the beach, Peter jumped in and swam ashore to meet the Master.

139:2.5 (1551.1) The one trait which Peter most admired in Jesus was his supernal tenderness. Peter never grew weary of contemplating Jesus' forbearance. He never forgot the lesson about forgiving the wrongdoer, not only seven times but seventy times and seven. He thought much about these impressions of the Master's forgiving character during those dark and dismal days immediately following his thoughtless and unintended denial of Jesus in the high priest's courtyard.

139:2.6 (1551.2) Simon Peter was distressingly vacillating; he would suddenly swing from one extreme to the other. First he refused to let Jesus wash his feet and then, on hearing the Master's reply, begged to be washed all over. But, after all, Jesus knew that Peter's faults were of the head and not of the heart. He was one of the most inexplicable combinations of courage and cowardice that ever lived on earth. His great strength of character was loyalty, friendship. Peter really and truly loved Jesus. And yet despite this towering strength of devotion he was so unstable and inconstant that he permitted a servant girl to tease him into denying his Lord and Master. Peter could withstand persecution and any other form of direct assault, but he withered and shrank before ridicule. He was a brave soldier when facing a frontal attack, but he was a fear-cringing coward when surprised with an assault from the rear.

139:2.7 (1551.3) Peter was the first of Jesus' apostles to come forward to defend the work of Philip among the Samaritans and Paul among the gentiles; yet later on at Antioch he reversed himself when confronted by ridiculing Judaizers, temporarily withdrawing from the gentiles only to bring down upon his head the fearless denunciation of Paul.

139:2.8 (1551.4) He was the first one of the apostles to make wholehearted confession of Jesus' combined humanity and divinity and the first—save Judas—to deny him. Peter was not so much of a dreamer, but he disliked to descend from the clouds of ecstasy and the enthusiasm of dramatic indulgence to the plain and matter-of-fact world of reality.

139:2.9 (1551.5) In following Jesus, literally and figuratively, he was either leading the procession or else trailing behind —"following afar off." But he was the outstanding preacher of the twelve; he did more than any other one man, aside from Paul, to establish the kingdom and send its messengers to the four corners of the earth in one generation.

139:2.10 (1551.6) After his rash denials of the Master he found himself, and with Andrew's sympathetic and understanding guidance he again led the way back to the fish nets while the apostles tarried to find out what was to happen after the crucifixion. When he was fully assured that Jesus had forgiven him and knew he had been received back into the Master's fold, the fires of the kingdom burned so brightly within his soul that he became a great and saving light to thousands who sat in darkness.

139:2.11 (1551.7) After leaving Jerusalem and before Paul became the leading spirit among the gentile Christian churches, Peter traveled extensively, visiting all the churches from Babylon to Corinth. He even visited and ministered to many of the churches which had been raised up by Paul. Although Peter and Paul differed much in temperament and education, even in theology, they worked together harmoniously for the upbuilding of the churches during their later years.

139:2.12 (1552.1) Something of Peter's style and teaching is shown in the sermons partially recorded by Luke and in the Gospel of Mark. His vigorous style was better shown in his letter known as the First Epistle of Peter; at least this was true before it was subsequently altered by a disciple of Paul.

139:2.13 (1552.2) But Peter persisted in making the mistake of trying to convince the Jews that Jesus was, after all, really and truly the Jewish Messiah. Right up to the day of his death, Simon Peter continued to suffer confusion in his mind between the concepts of Jesus as the Jewish Messiah, Christ as the world's redeemer, and the Son of Man as the revelation of God, the loving Father of all mankind.

139:2.14 (1552.3) Peter's wife was a very able woman. For years she labored acceptably as a member of the women's corps, and when Peter was driven out of Jerusalem, she accompanied him upon all his journeys to the churches as well as on all his missionary excursions. And the day her illustrious husband yielded up his life, she was thrown to the wild beasts in the arena at Rome.

139:2.15 (1552.4) And so this man Peter, an intimate of Jesus, one of the inner circle, went forth from Jerusalem proclaiming the glad tidings of the kingdom with power and glory until the fullness of his ministry had been accomplished; and he regarded himself as the recipient of high honors when his captors informed him that he must die as his Master had died—on the cross. And thus was Simon Peter crucified in Rome.

James Zebedee

139:3.1 (1552.5) James, the older of the two apostle sons of Zebedee, whom Jesus nicknamed "sons of thunder," was thirty years old when he became an apostle. He was married, had four children, and lived near his parents in the outskirts of Capernaum, Bethsaida. He was a fisherman, plying his calling in company with his younger brother John and in association with Andrew and Simon. James and his brother John enjoyed the advantage of having known Jesus longer than any of the other apostles.

139:3.2 (1552.6) This able apostle was a temperamental contradiction; he seemed really to possess two natures, both of which were actuated by strong feelings. He was particularly vehement when his indignation was once fully aroused. He had a fiery temper when once it was adequately provoked, and when the storm was over, he was always wont to justify and excuse his anger under the pretense that it was wholly a manifestation of righteous indignation. Except for these periodic upheavals of wrath, James's personality was much like that of Andrew. He did not have Andrew's discretion or insight into human nature, but he was a much better public speaker. Next to Peter, unless it was Matthew, James was the best public orator among the twelve.

139:3.3 (1552.7) Though James was in no sense moody, he could be quiet and taciturn one day and a very good talker and storyteller the next. He usually talked freely with Jesus, but among the twelve, for days at a time he was the silent man. His one great weakness was these spells of unaccountable silence.

139:3.4 (1552.8) The outstanding feature of James's personality was his ability to see all sides of a proposition. Of all the twelve, he came the nearest to grasping the real import and significance of Jesus' teaching. He, too, was slow at first to comprehend the Master's meaning, but ere they had finished their training, he had acquired a superior concept of Jesus' message. James was able to understand a wide range of human nature; he got along well with the versatile Andrew, the impetuous Peter, and his self-contained brother John.

139:3.5 (1553.1) Though James and John had their troubles trying to work together, it was inspiring to observe how well they got along. They did not succeed quite so well as Andrew and Peter, but they did much better than would ordinarily be expected of two brothers, especially such headstrong and determined brothers. But, strange as it may seem, these two sons of Zebedee were much more tolerant of each other than they were of strangers. They had great affection for one another; they had always been happy playmates. It was these "sons of thunder" who wanted to call fire down from heaven to destroy the Samaritans who presumed to show disrespect for their Master. But the untimely death of James greatly modified the vehement temperament of his younger brother John.

139:3.6 (1553.2) That characteristic of Jesus which James most admired was

the Master's sympathetic affection. Jesus' understanding interest in the small and the great, the rich and the poor, made a great appeal to him.

139:3.7 (1553.3) James Zebedee was a well-balanced thinker and planner. Along with Andrew, he was one of the more level-headed of the apostolic group. He was a vigorous individual but was never in a hurry. He was an excellent balance wheel for Peter.

139:3.8 (1553.4) He was modest and undramatic, a daily server, an unpretentious worker, seeking no special reward when he once grasped something of the real meaning of the kingdom. And even in the story about the mother of James and John, who asked that her sons be granted places on the right hand and the left hand of Jesus, it should be remembered that it was the mother who made this request. And when they signified that they were ready to assume such responsibilities, it should be recognized that they were cognizant of the dangers accompanying the Master's supposed revolt against the Roman power, and that they were also willing to pay the price. When Jesus asked if they were ready to drink the cup, they replied that they were. And as concerns James, it was literally true—he did drink the cup with the Master, seeing that he was the first of the apostles to experience martyrdom, being early put to death with the sword by Herod Agrippa. James was thus the first of the twelve to sacrifice his life upon the new battle line of the kingdom.

Herod Agrippa feared James above all the other apostles. He was indeed often quiet and silent, but he was brave and determined when his convictions were aroused and challenged.

139:3.9 (1553.5) James lived his life to the full, and when the end came, he bore himself with such grace and fortitude that even his accuser and informer, who attended his trial and execution, was so touched that he rushed away from the scene of James's death to join himself to the disciples of Jesus.

John Zebedee

139:4.1 (1553.6) When he became an apostle, John was twenty-four years old and was the youngest of the twelve. He was unmarried and lived with his parents at Bethsaida; he was a fisherman and worked with his brother James in partnership with Andrew and Peter. Both before and after becoming an apostle, John functioned as the personal agent of Jesus in dealing with the Master's family, and he continued to bear this responsibility as long as Mary the mother of Jesus lived.

139:4.2 (1553.7) Since John was the youngest of the twelve and so closely asso- ciated with Jesus in his family affairs, he was very dear to the Master, but it cannot be truthfully said that he was "the disciple whom Jesus loved." You would hardly sus- pect such a magnanimous personality as Jesus to be guilty of showing favoritism, of loving one of his apostles more than the others. The fact that John was one of the three personal aides of Jesus lent further color to this mistaken idea, not to mention that John, along with his brother James, had known Jesus longer than the others.

139:4.3 (1554.1) Peter, James, and John were assigned as personal aides to Jesus soon after they became apostles. Shortly after the selection of the twelve and at the time Jesus appointed Andrew to act as director of the group, he said to him: "And now I desire that you assign two or three of your associates to be with me and to remain by my side, to comfort me and to minister to my daily needs." And Andrew thought best to select for this special duty the next three first- chosen apostles. He would have liked to volunteer for such a blessed service himself, but the Master had already given him his commission; so he immediately directed that Peter, James, and John attach themselves to Jesus.

139:4.4 (1554.2) John Zebedee had many lovely traits of character, but one which was not so lovely was his inordinate but usually well-concealed conceit. His long association with Jesus made many and great changes in his character. This conceit was greatly lessened, but after growing old and becoming more or less childish, this self-esteem reappeared to a certain extent, so that, when engaged in directing Nathan in the writing of the Gospel which now bears his name, the aged apostle did not hesitate repeatedly to refer to himself as the "disciple whom Jesus loved." In view of the fact that John came nearer to being the chum of Jesus than any other earth mortal, that he was his chosen personal representative in so many matters, it is not strange that he should have come to regard himself as the "disciple whom Jesus loved" since he most certainly knew he was the disciple whom Jesus so frequently trusted.

139:4.5 (1554.3) The strongest trait in John's character was his dependability; he was prompt and courageous, faithful and devoted. His greatest weakness was this characteristic conceit. He was the young- est member of his father's family and the youngest of the apostolic group. Perhaps he was just a bit spoiled; maybe he had been humored slightly too much. But the John of after years was a very different type of person than the self-admiring and arbitrary young man who joined the ranks of Jesus' apostles when he was twenty-four.

139:4.6 (1554.4) Those characteris- tics of Jesus which John most appreciated were the Master's love and unselfishness; these traits made such an impression on him that his whole subsequent life became dominated by the sentiment of love and brotherly devotion. He talked about love and wrote about love. This "son of thunder" became the "apostle of love"; and at Ephe- sus, when the aged bishop was no longer able to stand in the pulpit and preach but had to be carried to church in a chair, and when at the close of the service he was asked to say a few words to the believers, for years his only utterance was, "My little children, love one another."

139:4.7 (1554.5) John was a man of few words except when his temper was aroused. He thought much but said little.

As he grew older, his temper became more subdued, better controlled, but he never overcame his disinclination to talk; he never fully mastered this reticence. But he was gifted with a remarkable and creative imagination.

139:4.8 (1555.1) There was another side to John that one would not expect to find in this quiet and introspective type. He was somewhat bigoted and inordinately intolerant. In this respect he and James were much alike—they both wanted to call down fire from heaven on the heads of the disrespectful Samaritans. When John encountered some strangers teaching in Jesus' name, he promptly forbade them. But he was not the only one of the twelve who was tainted with this kind of self-esteem and superiority consciousness.

139:4.9 (1555.2) John's life was tremendously influenced by the sight of Jesus' going about without a home as he knew how faithfully he had made provision for the care of his mother and family. John also deeply sympathized with Jesus because of his family's failure to understand him, being aware that they were gradually withdrawing from him. This entire situation, together with Jesus' ever deferring his slightest wish to the will of the Father in heaven and his daily life of implicit trust, made such a profound impression on John that it produced marked and permanent changes in his character, changes which manifested themselves throughout his entire subsequent life.

139:4.10 (1555.3) John had a cool and daring courage which few of the other apostles possessed. He was the one apostle who followed right along with Jesus the night of his arrest and dared to accompany his Master into the very jaws of death. He was present and near at hand right up to the last earthly hour and was found faithfully carrying out his trust with regard to Jesus' mother and ready to receive such additional instructions as might be given during the last moments of the Master's mortal existence. One thing is certain, John was thoroughly dependable. John usually sat on Jesus' right hand when the twelve were at meat. He was the first of the twelve really and fully to believe in the resurrection, and he was the first to recognize the Master when he came to them on the seashore after his resurrection.

139:4.11 (1555.4) This son of Zebedee was very closely associated with Peter in the early activities of the Christian movement, becoming one of the chief supporters of the Jerusalem church. He was the right-hand support of Peter on the day of Pentecost.

139:4.12 (1555.5) Several years after the martyrdom of James, John married his brother's widow. The last twenty years of his life he was cared for by a loving granddaughter.

139:4.13 (1555.6) John was in prison several times and was banished to the Isle of Patmos for a period of four years until another emperor came to power in Rome. Had not John been tactful and sagacious, he would undoubtedly have been killed as was his more outspoken brother James. As the years passed, John, together with James the Lord's brother, learned to practice wise conciliation when they appeared before the civil magistrates. They found that a "soft answer turns away wrath." They also learned to represent the church as a "spiritual brotherhood devoted to the social service of mankind" rather than as "the kingdom of heaven." They taught loving service rather than ruling power—kingdom and king.

139:4.14 (1555.7) When in temporary exile on Patmos, John wrote the Book of Revelation, which you now have in greatly abridged and distorted form. This Book of Revelation contains the surviving fragments of a great revelation, large portions of which were lost, other portions of which were removed, subsequent to John's writing. It is preserved in only fragmentary and adulterated form.

139:4.15 (1555.8) John traveled much, labored incessantly, and after becoming bishop of the Asia churches, settled down at Ephesus. He directed his associate, Nathan, in the writing of the so-called "Gospel according to John," at Ephesus, when he was ninety-nine years old. Of all the twelve apostles, John Zebedee eventually became the outstanding theologian.

He died a natural death at Ephesus in A.D. 103 when he was one hundred and one years of age.

Philip the Curious

139:5.1 (1556.1) Philip was the fifth apostle to be chosen, being called when Jesus and his first four apostles were on their way from John's rendezvous on the Jordan to Cana of Galilee. Since he lived at Bethsaida, Philip had for some time known of Jesus, but it had not occurred to him that Jesus was a really great man until that day in the Jordan valley when he said, "Follow me." Philip was also somewhat influenced by the fact that Andrew, Peter, James, and John had accepted Jesus as the Deliverer.

139:5.2 (1556.2) Philip was twenty-seven years of age when he joined the apostles; he had recently been married, but he had no children at this time. The nickname which the apostles gave him signified "curiosity." Philip was always wanting to be shown. He never seemed to see very far into any proposition. He was not necessarily dull, but he lacked imagination. This lack of imagination was the great weakness of his character. He was a commonplace and matter-of- fact individual.

139:5.3 (1556.3) When the apostles were organized for service, Philip was made steward; it was his duty to see that they were at all times supplied with provisions. And he was a good steward. His strongest characteristic was his methodical thoroughness; he was both mathematical and systematic.

139:5.4 (1556.4) Philip came from a family of seven, three boys and four girls. He was next to the oldest, and after the resurrection he baptized his entire family into the kingdom. Philip's people were fisherfolk. His father was a very able man, a

deep thinker, but his mother was of a very mediocre family. Philip was not a man who could be expected to do big things, but he was a man who could do little things in a big way, do them well and acceptably. Only a few times in four years did he fail to have food on hand to satisfy the needs of all. Even the many emergency demands attendant upon the life they lived seldom found him unprepared. The commissary department of the apostolic family was intelligently and efficiently managed.

139:5.5 (1556.5) The strong point about Philip was his methodical reliability; the weak point in his make-up was his utter lack of imagination, the absence of the ability to put two and two together to obtain four. He was mathematical in the abstract but not constructive in his imagination. He was almost entirely lacking in certain types of imagination. He was the typical everyday and commonplace average man. There were a great many such men and women among the multitudes who came to hear Jesus teach and preach, and they derived great comfort from observing one like themselves elevated to an honored position in the councils of the Master; they derived courage from the fact that one like themselves had already found a high place in the affairs of the kingdom. And Jesus learned much about the way some human minds function as he so patiently listened to Philip's foolish questions and so many times complied with his steward's request to "be shown."

139:5.6 (1556.6) The one quality about Jesus which Philip so continuously admired was the Master's unfailing generosity. Never could Philip find anything in Jesus which was small, niggardly, or stingy, and he worshiped this ever-present and unfailing liberality.

139:5.7 (1557.1) There was little about Philip's personality that was impressive. He was often spoken of as "Philip of Bethsaida, the town where Andrew and Peter live." He was almost without discerning vision; he was unable to grasp the dramatic possibilities of a given situation. He was not pessimistic; he was simply prosaic. He was also greatly lacking in spiritual insight. He would not hesitate to interrupt Jesus in the midst of one of the Master's most profound discourses to ask an apparently foolish question. But Jesus never reprimanded him for such thoughtlessness; he was patient with him and considerate of his inability to grasp the deeper meanings of the teaching. Jesus well knew that, if he once rebuked Philip for asking these annoying questions, he would not only wound this honest soul, but such a reprimand would so hurt Philip that he would never again feel free to ask questions. Jesus knew that on his worlds of space there were untold billions of similar slow-thinking mortals, and he wanted to encourage them all to look to him and always to feel free to come to him with their questions and problems. After all, Jesus was really more interested in Philip's foolish questions than in the sermon he might be preaching. Jesus was supremely interested in men, all kinds of men.

139:5.8 (1557.2) The apostolic steward was not a good public speaker, but he was a very persuasive and successful personal worker. He was not easily discouraged; he was a plodder and very tenacious in anything he undertook. He had that great and rare gift of saying, "Come." When his first convert, Nathaniel, wanted to argue about the merits and demerits of Jesus and Nazareth, Philip's effective reply was, "Come and see." He was not a dogmatic preacher who exhorted his hearers to "Go"—do this and do that. He met all situations as they arose in his work with "Come"—"come with me; I will show you the way." And that is always the effective technique in all forms and phases of teaching. Even parents may learn from Philip the better way of saying to their children not "Go do this and go do that," but rather, "Come with us while we show and share with you the better way."

139:5.9 (1557.3) The inability of Philip to adapt himself to a new situation was well shown when the Greeks came to him at Jerusalem, saying: "Sir, we desire to see Jesus." Now Philip would have said to any Jew asking such a question, "Come." But these men were foreigners, and Philip could remember no instructions from his superiors regarding such matters; so the only thing he could think to do was to consult the chief, Andrew, and then they both escorted the inquiring Greeks to Jesus. Likewise, when he went into Samaria preaching and baptizing believers, as he had been instructed by his Master, he refrained from laying hands on his converts in token of their having received the Spirit of Truth. This was done by Peter and John, who presently came down from Jerusalem to observe his work in behalf of the mother church.

139:5.10 (1557.4) Philip went on through the trying times of the Master's death, participated in the reorganization of the twelve, and was the first to go forth to win souls for the kingdom outside of the immediate Jewish ranks, being most successful in his work for the Samaritans and in all his subsequent labors in behalf of the gospel.

139:5.11 (1557.5) Philip's wife, who was an efficient member of the women's corps, became actively associated with her husband in his evangelistic work after their flight from the Jerusalem persecutions. His wife was a fearless woman. She stood at the foot of Philip's cross encouraging him to proclaim the glad tidings even to his murderers, and when his strength failed, she began the recital of the story of salvation by faith in Jesus and was silenced only when the irate Jews rushed upon her and stoned her to death. Their eldest daughter, Leah, continued their work, later on becoming the renowned prophetess of Hierapolis.

139:5.12 (1558.1) Philip, the onetime steward of the twelve, was a mighty man in the kingdom, winning souls wherever he went; and he was finally crucified for his faith and buried at Hierapolis.

Honest Nathaniel

139:6.1 (1558.2) Nathaniel, the sixth and last of the apostles to be chosen by the

Master himself, was brought to Jesus by his friend Philip. He had been associated in several business enterprises with Philip and, with him, was on the way down to see John the Baptist when they encountered Jesus.

139:6.2 (1558.3) When Nathaniel joined the apostles, he was twenty-five years old and was the next to the youngest of the group. He was the youngest of a family of seven, was unmarried, and the only support of aged and infirm parents, with whom he lived at Cana; his brothers and sister were either married or deceased, and none lived there. Nathaniel and Judas Iscariot were the two best educated men among the twelve. Nathaniel had thought to become a merchant.

139:6.3 (1558.4) Jesus did not himself give Nathaniel a nickname, but the twelve soon began to speak of him in terms that signified honesty, sincerity. He was "without guile." And this was his great virtue; he was both honest and sincere. The weakness of his character was his pride; he was very proud of his family, his city, his reputation, and his nation, all of which is commendable if it is not carried too far. But Nathaniel was inclined to go to extremes with his personal prejudices. He was disposed to prejudge individuals in accordance with his personal opinions. He was not slow to ask the question, even before he had met Jesus, "Can any good thing come out of Nazareth?" But Nathaniel was not obstinate, even if he was proud. He was quick to reverse himself when he once looked into Jesus' face.

139:6.4 (1558.5) In many respects Nathaniel was the odd genius of the twelve. He was the apostolic philosopher and dreamer, but he was a very practical sort of dreamer. He alternated between seasons of profound philosophy and periods of rare and droll humor; when in the proper mood, he was probably the best storyteller among the twelve. Jesus greatly enjoyed hearing Nathaniel discourse on things both serious and frivolous. Nathaniel progressively took Jesus and the kingdom more seriously, but never did he take himself seriously.

139:6.5 (1558.6) The apostles all loved and respected Nathaniel, and he got along with them splendidly, excepting Judas Iscariot. Judas did not think Nathaniel took his apostleship sufficiently seriously and once had the temerity to go secretly to Jesus and lodge complaint against him. Said Jesus: "Judas, watch carefully your steps; do not over magnify your office. Who of us is competent to judge his brother? It is not the Father's will that his children should partake only of the serious things of life. Let me repeat: I have come that my brethren in the flesh may have joy, gladness, and life more abundantly. Go then, Judas, and do well that which has been intrusted to you but leave Nathaniel, your brother, to give account of himself to God." And the memory of this, with that of many similar experiences, long lived in the self-deceiving heart of Judas Iscariot.

139:6.6 (1559.1) Many times, when Jesus was away on the mountain with Peter, James, and John, and things were becoming tense and tangled among the apostles, when even Andrew was in doubt about what to say to his disconsolate brethren, Nathaniel would relieve the tension by a bit of philosophy or a flash of humor; good humor, too.

139:6.7 (1559.2) Nathaniel's duty was to look after the families of the twelve. He was often absent from the apostolic councils, for when he heard that sickness or anything out of the ordinary had happened to one of his charges, he lost no time in getting to that home. The twelve rested securely in the knowledge that their families' welfare was safe in the hands of Nathaniel.

139:6.8 (1559.3) Nathaniel most revered Jesus for his tolerance. He never grew weary of contemplating the broad mindedness and generous sympathy of the Son of Man.

139:6.9 (1559.4) Nathaniel's father (Bartholomew) died shortly after Pentecost, after which this apostle went into Mesopotamia and India proclaiming the glad tidings of the kingdom and baptizing believers. His brethren never knew what became of their onetime philosopher, poet, and humorist. But he also was a great man in the kingdom and did much to spread his Master's teachings, even though he did not participate in the organization of the subsequent Christian church. Nathaniel died in India.

Matthew Levi

139:7.1 (1559.5) Matthew, the seventh apostle, was chosen by Andrew. Matthew belonged to a family of tax gatherers, or publicans, but was himself a customs collector in Capernaum, where he lived. He was thirty-one years old and married and had four children. He was a man of moderate wealth, the only one of any means belonging to the apostolic corps. He was a good business man, a good social mixer, and was gifted with the ability to make friends and to get along smoothly with a great variety of people.

139:7.2 (1559.6) Andrew appointed Matthew the financial representative of the apostles. In a way he was the fiscal agent and publicity spokesman for the apostolic organization. He was a keen judge of human nature and a very efficient propagandist. His is a personality difficult to visualize, but he was a very earnest disciple and an increasing believer in the mission of Jesus and in the certainty of the kingdom. Jesus never gave Levi a nickname, but his fellow apostles commonly referred to him as the "money-getter."

139:7.3 (1559.7) Levi's strong point was his wholehearted devotion to the cause. That he, a publican, had been taken in by Jesus and his apostles was the cause for overwhelming gratitude on the part of the former revenue collector. However, it required some little time for the rest of the apostles, especially Simon Zelotes and Judas Iscariot, to become reconciled to the publican's presence in their midst. Mat-

thew's weakness was his shortsighted and materialistic viewpoint of life.

But in all these matters he made great progress as the months went by. He, of course, had to be absent from many of the most precious seasons of instruction as it was his duty to keep the treasury replenished.

139:7.4 (1559.8) It was the Master's forgiving disposition which Matthew most appreciated. He would never cease to recount that faith only was necessary in the business of finding God. He always liked to speak of the kingdom as "this business of finding God."

139:7.5 (1560.1) Though Matthew was a man with a past, he gave an excellent account of himself, and as time went on, his associates became proud of the publican's performances. He was one of the apostles who made extensive notes on the sayings of Jesus, and these notes were used as the basis of Isador's subsequent narrative of the sayings and doings of Jesus, which has become known as the Gospel according to Matthew.

139:7.6 (1560.2) The great and useful life of Matthew, the business man and customs collector of Capernaum, has been the means of leading thousands upon thousands of other business men, public officials, and politicians, down through the subsequent ages, also to hear that engaging voice of the Master saying, "Follow me." Matthew really was a shrewd politician, but he was intensely loyal to Jesus and supremely devoted to the task of seeing that the messengers of the coming kingdom were adequately financed.

139:7.7 (1560.3) The presence of Matthew among the twelve was the means of keeping the doors of the kingdom wide open to hosts of downhearted and outcast souls who had regarded themselves as long since without the bounds of religious consolation. Outcast and despairing men and women flocked to hear Jesus, and he never turned one away.

139:7.8 (1560.4) Matthew received freely tendered offerings from believing disciples and the immediate auditors of the Master's teachings, but he never openly solicited funds from the multitudes. He did all his financial work in a quiet and personal way and raised most of the money among the more substantial class of interested believers. He gave practically the whole of his modest fortune to the work of the Master and his apostles, but they never knew of this generosity, save Jesus, who knew all about it. Matthew hesitated openly to contribute to the apostolic funds for fear that Jesus and his associates might regard his money as being tainted; so he gave much in the names of other believers. During the earlier months, when Matthew knew his presence among them was more or less of a trial, he was strongly tempted to let them know that his funds often supplied them with their daily bread, but he did not yield. When evidence of the disdain of the publican would become manifest, Levi would burn to reveal to them his generosity, but always he managed to keep still.

139:7.9 (1560.5) When the funds for the week were short of the estimated requirements, Levi would often draw heavily upon his own personal resources. Also, sometimes when he became greatly interested in Jesus' teaching, he preferred to remain and hear the instruction, even though he knew he must personally make up for his failure to solicit the necessary funds. But Levi did so wish that Jesus might know that much of the money came from his pocket! He little realized that the Master knew all about it. The apostles all died without knowing that Matthew was their benefactor to such an extent that, when he went forth to proclaim the gospel of the kingdom after the beginning of the persecutions, he was practically penniless.

139:7.10 (1560.6) When these persecutions caused the believers to forsake Jerusalem, Matthew journeyed north, preaching the gospel of the kingdom and baptizing believers. He was lost to the knowledge of his former apostolic associates, but on he went, preaching and baptizing, through Syria, Cappadocia, Galatia, Bithynia, and Thrace. And it was in Thrace, at Lysimachia, that certain unbelieving Jews conspired with the Roman soldiers to encompass his death. And this regenerated publican died triumphant in the faith of a salvation he had so surely learned from the teachings of the Master during his recent sojourn on earth.

Thomas Didymus

139:8.1 (1561.1) Thomas was the eighth apostle, and he was chosen by Philip. In later times he has become known as "doubting Thomas," but his fellow apostles hardly looked upon him as a chronic doubter. True, his was a logical, skeptical type of mind, but he had a form of courageous loyalty which forbade those who knew him intimately to regard him as a trifling skeptic.

139:8.2 (1561.2) When Thomas joined the apostles, he was twenty-nine years old, was married, and had four children. Formerly he had been a carpenter and stone mason, but latterly he had become a fisherman and resided at Tarichea, situated on the west bank of the Jordan where it flows out of the Sea of Galilee, and he was regarded as the leading citizen of this little village. He had little education, but he possessed a keen, reasoning mind and was the son of excellent parents, who lived at Tiberias. Thomas had the one truly analytical mind of the twelve; he was the real scientist of the apostolic group.

139:8.3 (1561.3) The early home life of Thomas had been unfortunate; his parents were not altogether happy in their married life, and this was reflected in Thomas's adult experience. He grew up having a very disagreeable and quarrelsome disposition. Even his wife was glad to see him join the apostles; she was relieved by the thought that her pessimistic husband would be away from home most of the time. Thomas also had a streak of suspicion which made it very difficult to get along peaceably with him. Peter was very much upset by Thomas at first, complaining to his brother, Andrew, that Thomas was "mean, ugly, and always suspicious." But the better his associates knew Thomas, the more they liked him. They found he was superbly honest and unflinchingly loyal. He was perfectly sincere and unquestionably truthful, but he was a natural-born faultfinder and had grown up to become a real pessimist. His analytical mind had become cursed with suspicion. He was rapidly losing faith in his fellow men when he became associated with the twelve and thus came in contact with the noble character of Jesus. This association with the Master began at once to transform Thomas's whole disposition and to effect great changes in his mental reactions to his fellow men.

139:8.4 (1561.4) Thomas's great strength was his superb analytical mind coupled with his unflinching courage—when he had once made up his mind. His great weakness was his suspicious doubting, which he never fully overcame throughout his whole lifetime in the flesh.

139:8.5 (1561.5) In the organization of the twelve Thomas was assigned to arrange and manage the itinerary, and he was an able director of the work and movements of the apostolic corps. He was a good executive, an excellent businessman, but he was handicapped by his many moods; he was one man one day and another man the next. He was inclined toward melancholic brooding when he joined the apostles, but contact with Jesus and the apostles largely cured him of this morbid introspection.

139:8.6 (1561.6) Jesus enjoyed Thomas very much and had many long, personal talks with him. His presence among the apostles was a great comfort to all honest doubters and encouraged many troubled minds to come into the kingdom, even if they could not wholly understand everything about the spiritual and philosophic phases of the teachings of Jesus. Thomas's membership in the twelve was a standing declaration that Jesus loved even honest doubters.

139:8.7 (1562.1) The other apostles held Jesus in reverence because of some special and outstanding trait of his replete personality, but Thomas revered his Master because of his superbly balanced character. Increasingly Thomas admired and honored one who was so lovingly merciful yet so inflexibly just and fair; so firm but never obstinate; so calm but never indifferent; so helpful and so sympathetic but never meddlesome or dictatorial; so strong but at the same time so gentle; so positive but never rough or rude; so tender but never vacillating; so pure and innocent but at the same time so virile, aggressive, and forceful; so truly courageous but never rash or foolhardy; such a lover of nature but so free from all tendency to revere nature; so humorous and so playful, but so free from levity and frivolity. It was this matchless symmetry of personality that so charmed Thomas. He probably enjoyed the highest intellectual understanding and personality appreciation of Jesus of any of the twelve.

139:8.8 (1562.2) In the councils of the twelve Thomas was always cautious, advocating a policy of safety first, but if his conservatism was voted down or overruled, he was always the first fearlessly to move out in execution of the program decided upon. Again and again would he stand out against some project as being foolhardy and presumptuous; he would debate to the bitter end, but when Andrew would put the proposition to a vote, and after the twelve would elect to do that which he had so strenuously opposed, Thomas was the first to say, "Let's go!" He was a good loser. He did not hold grudges nor nurse wounded feelings. Time and again did he oppose letting Jesus expose himself to danger, but when the Master would decide to take such risks, always was it Thomas who rallied the apostles with his courageous words, "Come on, comrades, let's go and die with him."

139:8.9 (1562.3) Thomas was in some respects like Philip; he also wanted "to be shown," but his outward expressions of doubt were based on entirely different intellectual operations. Thomas was analytical, not merely skeptical. As far as personal physical courage was concerned, he was one of the bravest among the twelve.

139:8.10 (1562.4) Thomas had some very bad days; he was blue and downcast at times. The loss of his twin sister when he was nine years old had occasioned him much youthful sorrow and had added to his temperamental problems of later life. When Thomas would become despondent, sometimes it was Nathaniel who helped him to recover, sometimes Peter, and not infrequently one of the Alpheus twins. When he was most depressed, unfortunately he always tried to avoid coming in direct contact with Jesus. But the Master knew all about this and had an understanding sympathy for his apostle when he was thus afflicted with depression and harassed by doubts.

139:8.11 (1562.5) Sometimes Thomas would get permission from Andrew to go off by himself for a day or two. But he soon learned that such a course was not wise; he early found that it was best, when he was downhearted, to stick close to his work and to remain near his associates. But no matter what happened in his emotional life, he kept right on being an apostle. When the time actually came to move forward, it was always Thomas who said, "Let's go!"

139:8.12 (1562.6) Thomas is the great example of a human being who has doubts, faces them, and wins. He had a great mind; he was no carping critic. He was a logical thinker; he was the acid test of Jesus and his fellow apostles. If Jesus and his work had not been genuine, it could not have held a man like Thomas from the start to the finish. He had a keen and sure sense of fact. At the first appearance of fraud or deception Thomas would have forsaken them all. Scientists may not fully understand all about Jesus and his work on earth, but there lived and worked with the Master and his human associates a man whose mind was that of a true scientist—Thomas Didymus—and he believed in Jesus of Nazareth.

139:8.13 (1563.1) Thomas had a trying time during the days of the trial and crucifixion. He was for a season in the depths of despair, but he rallied his courage, stuck to the apostles, and was present with them to welcome Jesus on the Sea of Galilee. For a while he succumbed to his doubting depression but eventually rallied his faith and courage. He gave wise counsel to the apostles after Pentecost and, when persecution scattered the believers, went to Cyprus, Crete, the North African coast, and Sicily, preaching the glad tidings of the kingdom and baptizing believers. And Thomas continued preaching and baptizing until he was apprehended by the agents of the Roman government and was put to death in Malta. Just a few weeks before his death he had begun the writing of the life and teachings of Jesus.

James and Judas Alpheus

1.   139:10.1 (1563.2) James and Judas the sons of Alpheus, the twin fishermen living near Kheresa, were the ninth and tenth apostles and were chosen by James and John Zebedee. They were twenty-six years old and married, James having three children, Judas two.

139:10.2 (1563.3) There is not much to be said about these two commonplace fisher folk. They loved their Master and Jesus loved them, but they never interrupted his discourses with questions. They understood very little about the philosophical discussions or the theological debates of their fellow apostles, but they rejoiced to find themselves numbered among such a group of mighty men. These two men were almost identical in personal appearance, mental characteristics, and extent of spiritual perception. What may be said of one should be recorded of the other.

139:10.3 (1563.4) Andrew assigned them to the work of policing the multitudes. They were the chief ushers of the preaching hours and, in fact, the general servants and errand boys of the twelve. They helped Philip with the supplies, they carried money to the families for Nathaniel, and always were they ready to lend a helping hand to any one of the apostles.

139:10.4 (1563.5) The multitudes of the common people were greatly encouraged to find two like themselves honored with places among the apostles. By their very acceptance as apostles these mediocre twins were the means of bringing a host of fainthearted believers into the kingdom. And, too, the common people took more kindly to the idea of being directed and managed by official ushers who were very much like themselves.

139:10.5 (1563.6) James and Judas, who were also called Thaddeus and Lebbeus, had neither strong points nor weak points. The nicknames given them by the disciples were good-natured designations of mediocrity. They were "the least of all the apostles"; they knew it and felt cheerful about it.

139:10.6 (1563.7) James Alpheus especially loved Jesus because of the Master's simplicity. These twins could not comprehend the mind of Jesus, but they did grasp the sympathetic bond between themselves and the heart of their Master. Their minds were not of a high order; they might even reverently be called stupid, but they had a real experience in their spiritual natures. They believed in Jesus; they were sons of God and fellows of the kingdom.

139:10.7 (1564.1) Judas Alpheus was drawn toward Jesus because of the Master's unostentatious humility. Such humility linked with such personal dignity made a great appeal to Judas. The fact that Jesus would always enjoin silence regarding his unusual acts made a great impression on this simple child of nature.

139:10.8 (1564.2) The twins were good-natured, simple-minded helpers, and everybody loved them. Jesus welcomed these young men of one talent to positions of honor on his personal staff in the kingdom because there are untold millions of other such simple and fear-ridden souls on the worlds of space whom he likewise wishes to welcome into active and believing fellowship with himself and his outpoured Spirit of Truth. Jesus does not look down upon littleness, only upon evil and sin. James and Judas were little, but they were also faithful. They were simple and ignorant, but they were also big-hearted, kind, and generous. *

139:10.9 (1564.3) And how gratefully proud were these humble men on that day when the Master refused to accept a certain rich man as an evangelist unless he would sell his goods and help the poor. When the people heard this and beheld the twins among his counselors, they knew of a certainty that Jesus was no respecter of persons. But only a divine institution—the kingdom of heaven—could ever have been built upon such a mediocre human foundation!

139:10.10 (1564.4) Only once or twice in all their association with Jesus did the twins venture to ask questions in public. Judas was once intrigued into asking Jesus a question when the Master had talked about revealing himself openly to the world. He felt a little disappointed that there were to be no more secrets among the twelve, and he made bold to ask: "But, Master, when you do thus declare yourself to the world, how will you favor us with special manifestations of your goodness?"

139:10.11 (1564.5) The twins served faithfully until the end, until the dark days of trial, crucifixion, and despair. They never lost their heart faith in Jesus, and (save John) they were the first to believe in his resurrection. But they could not comprehend the establishment of the kingdom. Soon after their Master was crucified, they returned to their families and nets; their work was done. They had not the ability to go on in the more complex battles of the kingdom. But they lived and died conscious of having been honored and blessed with four years of close and personal association with a Son of God, the sovereign maker of a universe.

Simon the Zealot

139:11.1 (1564.6) Simon Zelotes, the eleventh apostle, was chosen by Simon Peter. He was an able man of good ancestry and lived with his family at Capernaum. He was twenty-eight years old when he became attached to the apostles. He was a fiery agitator and was also a man who spoke much without thinking. He had been a merchant in Capernaum before he turned his entire attention to the patriotic organization of the Zealots.

139:11.2 (1564.7) Simon Zelotes was given charge of the diversions and relaxation of the apostolic group, and he was a very efficient organizer of the play life and recreational activities of the twelve.

139:11.3 (1564.8) Simon's strength was his inspirational loyalty. When the apostles found a man or woman who floundered in indecision about entering the kingdom, they would send for Simon. It usually required only about fifteen minutes for this enthusiastic advocate of salvation through faith in God to settle all doubts and remove all indecision, to see a new soul born into the "liberty of faith and the joy of salvation."

139:11.4 (1565.1) Simon's great weakness was his material-mindedness. He could not quickly change himself from a Jewish nationalist to a spiritually minded internationalist. Four years was too short a time in which to make such an intellectual and emotional transformation, but Jesus was always patient with him.

139:11.5 (1565.2) The one thing about Jesus which Simon so much admired was the Master's calmness, his assurance, poise, and inexplicable composure.

139:11.6 (1565.3) Although Simon was a rabid revolutionist, a fearless firebrand of agitation, he gradually subdued his fiery nature until he became a powerful and effective preacher of "Peace on earth and good will among men." Simon was a great debater; he did like to argue. And when it came to dealing with the legalistic minds of the educated Jews or the intellectual quibblings of the Greeks, the task was always assigned to Simon.

139:11.7 (1565.4) He was a rebel by nature and an iconoclast by training, but Jesus won him for the higher concepts of the kingdom of heaven. He had always identified himself with the party of protest, but he now joined the party of progress, unlimited and eternal progression of spirit and truth. Simon was a man of intense loyalties and warm personal devotions, and he did profoundly love Jesus.

139:11.8 (1565.5) Jesus was not afraid to identify himself with business men, laboring men, optimists, pessimists, philosophers, skeptics, publicans, politicians, and patriots.

139:11.9 (1565.6) The Master had many talks with Simon, but he never fully succeeded in making an internationalist out of this ardent Jewish nationalist. Jesus often told Simon that it was proper to want to see the social, economic, and political orders improved, but he would always add: "That is not the business of the kingdom of heaven. We must be dedicated to the doing of the Father's will. Our business is to be ambassadors of a spiritual government on high, and we must not immediately concern ourselves with aught but the representation of the will and character of the divine Father who stands at the head of the government whose credentials we bear." It was all difficult for Simon to comprehend, but gradually he began to grasp something of the meaning of the Master's teaching.

139:11.10 (1565.7) After the dispersion because of the Jerusalem persecutions, Simon went into temporary retirement. He was literally crushed. As a nationalist patriot he had surrendered in deference to Jesus' teachings; now all was lost. He was in despair, but in a few years he rallied his hopes and went forth to proclaim the gospel of the kingdom.

139:11.11 (1565.8) He went to Alexandria and, after working up the Nile, penetrated into the heart of Africa, everywhere preaching the gospel of Jesus and baptizing believers. Thus he labored until he was an old man and feeble. And he died and was buried in the heart of Africa.

Judas Iscariot

139:12.1 (1565.9) Judas Iscariot, the twelfth apostle, was chosen by Nathaniel. He was born in Kerioth, a small town in southern Judea. When he was a lad, his parents moved to Jericho, where he lived and had been employed in his father's various business enterprises until he became interested in the preaching and work of John the Baptist. Judas's parents were Sadducees, and when their son joined John's disciples, they disowned him.

139:12.2 (1566.1) When Nathaniel met Judas at Tarichea, he was seeking employment with a fish-drying enterprise at the lower end of the Sea of Galilee. He was thirty years of age and unmarried when he joined the apostles. He was probably the best-educated man among the twelve and the only Judean in the Master's apostolic family. Judas had no outstanding trait of personal strength, though he had many outwardly appearing traits of culture and habits of training. He was a good thinker but not always a truly honest thinker. Judas did not really understand himself; he was not really sincere in dealing with himself.

139:12.3 (1566.2) Andrew appointed Judas treasurer of the twelve, a position which he was eminently fitted to hold, and up to the time of the betrayal of his Master he discharged the responsibilities of his office honestly, faithfully, and most efficiently.

139:12.4 (1566.3) There was no special trait about Jesus which Judas admired above the generally attractive and exquisitely charming personality of the Master. Judas was never able to rise above his Judean prejudices against his Galilean associates; he would even criticize in his mind many things about Jesus. Him whom eleven of the apostles looked upon as the perfect man, as the "one altogether lovely and the chiefest among ten thousand," this self-satisfied Judean often dared to criticize in his own heart. He really entertained the notion that Jesus was timid and somewhat afraid to assert his own power and authority.

139:12.5 (1566.4) Judas was a good business man. It required tact, ability, and patience, as well as painstaking devotion, to manage the financial affairs of such an idealist as Jesus, to say nothing of wrestling with the helter-skelter business methods of some of his apostles. Judas really was a great executive, a farseeing and able financier. And he was a stickler for organization. None of the twelve ever criticized Judas. As far as they could see, Judas Iscariot was a matchless treasurer, a learned man, a loyal (though sometimes critical) apostle, and in every sense of the word a great success. The apostles loved Judas; he was really one of them. He must have believed in Jesus, but we doubt whether he really loved the Master with a whole heart. The case of Judas illustrates the truthfulness of that saying: "There is a way that seems right to a man, but the end thereof is death." It is altogether possible to fall victim to the peaceful deception of pleasant adjustment to the paths of sin and death. Be assured that Judas was always financially loyal to his Master and his fellow apostles. Money could never have been the motive for his betrayal of the Master.

139:12.6 (1566.5) Judas was an only son of unwise parents. When very young, he was pampered and petted; he was a spoiled child. As he grew up, he had exaggerated ideas about his self-importance. He was a poor loser. He had loose and distorted ideas about fairness; he was given to the indulgence of hate and suspicion. He was an expert at misinterpretation of the words and acts of his friends. All through his life Judas had cultivated the habit of getting even with those whom he fancied had mistreated him. His sense of values and loyalties was defective.

139:12.7 (1566.6) To Jesus, Judas was a faith adventure. From the beginning the Master fully understood the weakness of this apostle and well knew the dangers of admitting him to fellowship. But it is the nature of the Sons of God to give every created being a full and equal chance for salvation and survival. Jesus wanted not only the mortals of this world but the onlookers of innumerable other worlds to know that, when doubts exist as to the sincerity and wholeheartedness of a creature's devotion to the kingdom, it is the invariable practice of the Judges of men fully to receive the doubtful candidate. The door of eternal life is wide open to all; "whosoever will may come"; there are no restrictions or qualifications save the faith of the one who comes.

139:12.8 (1567.1) This is just the reason why Jesus permitted Judas to go on to the very end, always doing everything possible to transform and save this weak and confused apostle. But when light is not honestly received and lived up to, it tends to become darkness within the soul. Judas grew intellectually regarding Jesus' teachings about the kingdom, but he did not make progress in the acquirement of spiritual character as did the other apostles. He failed to make satisfactory personal progress in spiritual experience.

139:12.9 (1567.2) Judas became increasingly a brooder over personal disappointment, and finally he became a victim of resentment. His feelings had been many times hurt, and he grew abnormally suspicious of his best friends, even of the Master. Presently he became obsessed with the idea of getting even, anything to avenge himself, yes, even betrayal of his associates and his Master.

139:12.10 (1567.3) But these wicked and dangerous ideas did not take definite shape until the day when a grateful woman broke an expensive box of incense at Jesus' feet. This seemed wasteful to Judas, and when his public protest was so sweepingly disallowed by Jesus right there in the hearing of all, it was too much. That event determined the mobilization of all the accumulated hate, hurt, malice, prejudice, jealousy, and revenge of a lifetime, and he made up his mind to get even with he knew not whom; but he crystallized all the evil of his nature upon the one innocent person in all the sordid drama of his unfortunate life just because Jesus happened to be the chief actor in the episode which marked his passing from the progressive kingdom of light into that self-chosen domain of darkness.

139:12.11 (1567.4) The Master many times, both privately and publicly, had warned Judas that he was slipping, but divine warnings are usually useless in dealing with embittered human nature. Jesus did everything possible, consistent with man's moral freedom, to prevent Judas's choosing to go the wrong way. The great test finally came. The son of resentment failed; he yielded to the sour and sordid dictates of a proud and vengeful mind of exaggerated self- importance and swiftly plunged on down into confusion, despair, and depravity.

139:12.12 (1567.5) Judas then entered into the base and shameful intrigue to betray his Lord and Master and quickly carried the nefarious scheme into effect. During the outworking of his anger-conceived plans of traitorous betrayal, he experienced moments of regret and shame, and in these lucid intervals he faintheartedly conceived, as a defense in his own mind, the idea that Jesus might possibly exert his power and deliver himself at the last moment. *

139:12.13 (1567.6) When the sordid and sinful business was all over, this renegade mortal, who thought lightly of selling his friend for thirty pieces of silver to satisfy his long-nursed craving for revenge, rushed out and committed the final act in the drama of fleeing from the realities of mortal existence—suicide.

139:12.14 (1567.7) The eleven apostles were horrified, stunned. Jesus regarded the betrayer only with pity. The worlds have found it difficult to forgive Judas, and his name has become eschewed throughout a far-flung universe.

Paper 140

The Ordination of the Twelve

140:0.1 (1568.1) JUST before noon on Sunday, January 12, A.D. 27, Jesus called the apostles together for their ordination as public preachers of the gospel of the kingdom. The twelve were expecting to be called almost any day; so this morning they did not go out far from the shore to fish. Several of them were lingering near the shore repairing their nets and tinkering with their fishing paraphernalia.

140:0.2 (1568.2) As Jesus started down the seashore calling the apostles, he first hailed Andrew and Peter, who were fishing near the shore; next he signaled to James and John, who were in a boat near by, visiting with their father, Zebedee, and mending their nets. Two by two he gathered up the other apostles, and when he had assembled all twelve, he journeyed with them to the highlands north of Capernaum, where he proceeded to instruct them in preparation for their formal ordination.

140:0.3 (1568.3) For once all twelve of the apostles were silent; even Peter was in a reflective mood. At last the long- waited-for hour had come! They were going apart with the Master to participate in some sort of solemn ceremony of personal consecration and collective dedication to the sacred work of representing their Master in the proclamation of the coming of his Father's kingdom.

Preliminary Instruction

140:1.1 (1568.4) Before the formal ordination service Jesus spoke to the twelve as they were seated about him: "My brethren, this hour of the kingdom has come. I have brought you apart here with me to present you to the Father as ambassadors of the kingdom. Some of you heard me speak of this kingdom in the synagogue when you first were called. Each of you has learned more about the Father's kingdom since you have been with me working in the cities around about the Sea of Galilee. But just now I have something more to tell you concerning this kingdom.

140:1.2 (1568.5) "The new kingdom which my Father is about to set up in the hearts of his earth children is to be an everlasting dominion. There shall be no end of this rule of my Father in the hearts of those who desire to do his divine will. I declare to you that my Father is not the God of Jew or gentile. Many shall come from the east and from the west to sit down with us in the Father's kingdom, while many of the children of Abraham will refuse to enter this new brotherhood of the rule of the Father's spirit in the hearts of the children of men.

140:1.3 (1568.6) "The power of this kingdom shall consist, not in the strength of armies nor in the might of riches, but rather in the glory of the divine spirit that shall come to teach the minds and rule the hearts of the reborn citizens of this heavenly kingdom, the sons of God. This is the brotherhood of love wherein righteousness reigns, and whose battle cry shall be: Peace on earth and good will to all men. This kingdom, which you are so soon to go forth proclaiming, is the desire of the good men of all ages, the hope of all the earth, and the fulfillment of the wise promises of all the prophets.

140:1.4 (1569.1) "But for you, my children, and for all others who would follow you into this kingdom, there is set a severe test. Faith alone will pass you through its portals, but you must bring forth the fruits of my Father's spirit if you would continue to ascend in the progressive life of the divine fellowship. Verily, verily, I say to you, not every one who says, 'Lord, Lord,' shall enter the kingdom of heaven; but rather he who does the will of my Father who is in heaven.

140:1.5 (1569.2) "Your message to the world shall be: Seek first the kingdom of God and his righteousness, and in finding these, all other things essential to eternal survival shall be secured therewith. And now would I make it plain to you that this kingdom of my Father will not come with an outward show of power or with unseemly demonstration. You are not to go hence in the proclamation of the kingdom, saying, 'it is here' or 'it is there,' for this kingdom of which you preach is God within you.

140:1.6 (1569.3) "Whosoever would become great in my Father's kingdom shall become a minister to all; and whosoever would be first among you, let him become the server of his brethren. But when you are once truly received as citizens in the heavenly kingdom, you are no longer servants but sons, sons of the living God. And so shall this kingdom progress in the world until it shall break down every barrier and bring all men to know my Father and believe in the saving truth which I have come to declare. Even now is the kingdom at hand, and some of you will not die until you have seen the reign of God come in great power.

140:1.7 (1569.4) "And this which your eyes now behold, this small beginning of twelve commonplace men, shall multiply and grow until eventually the whole earth shall be filled with the praise of my Father. And it will not be so much by the words you speak as by the lives you live that men will know you have been with me and have learned of the realities of the kingdom. And while I would lay no grievous burdens upon your minds, I am about to put upon your souls the solemn responsibility of representing me in the world when I shall presently leave you as I now represent my Father in this life which I am living in the flesh." And when he had finished speaking, he stood up.

The Ordination

140:2.1 (1569.5) Jesus now instructed the twelve mortals who had just listened to his declaration concerning the kingdom to kneel in a circle about him. Then the Master placed his hands upon the head of each apostle, beginning with Judas Iscariot and ending with Andrew. When he had blessed them, he extended his hands and prayed:

140:2.2 (1569.6) "My Father, I now bring to you these men, my messengers. From among our children on earth I have chosen these twelve to go forth to represent me as I came forth to represent you. Love them and be with them as you have loved and been with me. And now, my Father, give these men wisdom as I place all the affairs of the coming kingdom in their hands. And I would, if it is your will, tarry on earth a time to help them in their labors for the kingdom. And again, my Father, I thank you for these men, and I commit them to your keeping while I go on to finish the work you have given me to do."

140:2.3 (1570.1) When Jesus had finished praying, the apostles remained each man bowed in his place. And it was many minutes before even Peter dared lift up his eyes to look upon the Master. One by one they embraced Jesus, but no man said aught. A great silence pervaded the place while a host of celestial beings looked down upon this solemn and sacred scene—the Creator of a universe placing the affairs of the divine brotherhood of man under the direction of human minds.

The Ordination Sermon

140:3.1 (1570.2) Then Jesus spoke, saying: "Now that you are ambassadors of my Father's kingdom, you have thereby become a class of men separate and distinct from all other men on earth. You are not now as men among men but as the enlightened citizens of another and heavenly country among the ignorant creatures of this dark world. It is not enough that you live as you were before this hour, but henceforth must you live as those who have tasted the glories of a better life and have been sent back to earth as ambassadors of the Sovereign of that new and better world. Of the teacher more is expected than of the pupil; of the master more is exacted than of the servant. Of the citizens of the heavenly kingdom more is required than of the citizens of the earthly rule. Some of the things which I am about to say to you may seem hard, but you have elected to represent me in the world even as I now represent the Father; and as my agents on earth you will be obligated to abide by those teachings and practices which are reflective of my ideals of mortal living on the worlds of space, and which I exemplify in my earth life of revealing the Father who is in heaven.

140:3.2 (1570.3) "I send you forth to proclaim liberty to the spiritual captives, joy to those in the bondage of fear, and to heal the sick in accordance with the will of my Father in heaven. When you find my children in distress, speak encouragingly to them, saying:

140:3.3 (1570.4) "Happy are the poor in spirit, the humble, for theirs are the treasures of the kingdom of heaven.

140:3.4 (1570.5) "Happy are they who hunger and thirst for righteousness, for they shall be filled.

140:3.5 (1570.6) "Happy are the meek, for they shall inherit the earth.

140:3.6 (1570.7) "Happy are the pure in heart, for they shall see God.

140:3.7 (1570.8) "And even so speak to my children these further words of spiritual comfort and promise:

140:3.8 (1570.9) "Happy are they who mourn, for they shall be comforted. Happy are they who weep, for they shall receive the spirit of rejoicing.

140:3.9 (1570.10) "Happy are the merciful, for they shall obtain mercy.

140:3.10 (1570.11) "Happy are the peacemakers, for they shall be called the sons of God.

140:3.11 (1570.12) "Happy are they who are persecuted for righteousness' sake, for theirs is the kingdom of heaven. Happy are you when men shall revile you and persecute you and shall say all manner of evil against you falsely. Rejoice and be exceedingly glad, for great is your reward in heaven.

140:3.12 (1570.13) "My brethren, as I send you forth, you are the salt of the earth, salt with a saving savor. But if this salt has lost its savor, wherewith shall it be salted? It is henceforth good for nothing but to be cast out and trodden under foot of men.

140:3.13 (1570.14) "You are the light of the world. A city set upon a hill cannot be hid. Neither do men light a candle and put it under a bushel, but on a candlestick; and it gives light to all who are in the house. Let your light so shine before men that they may see your good works and be led to glorify your Father who is in heaven.

140:3.14 (1571.1) "I am sending you out into the world to represent me and to act as ambassadors of my Father's kingdom, and as you go forth to proclaim the glad tidings, put your trust in the Father whose messengers you are. Do not forcibly resist injustice; put not your trust in the arm of the flesh. If your neighbor smites you on the right cheek, turn to him the other also. Be willing to suffer injustice rather than to go to law among yourselves. In kindness and with mercy minister to all who are in distress and in need.

140:3.15 (1571.2) "I say to you: Love your enemies, do good to those who hate you, bless those who curse you, and pray for those who despitefully use you. And whatsoever you believe that I would do to men, do you also to them.

140:3.16 (1571.3) "Your Father in heaven makes the sun to shine on the evil as well as upon the good; likewise he sends rain on the just and the unjust. You are the sons of God; even more, you are now the ambassadors of my Father's kingdom. Be merciful, even as God is merciful, and in the eternal future of the kingdom you shall be perfect, even as your heavenly Father is perfect.

140:3.17 (1571.4) "You are commissioned to save men, not to judge them. At the end of your earth life you will all expect mercy; therefore do I require of you during your mortal life that you show mercy to all of your brethren in the flesh. Make not the mistake of trying to pluck a mote out of your brother's eye when there is a beam in your own eye. Having first cast the beam out of your own eye, you can the better see to cast the mote out of your brother's eye.

140:3.18 (1571.5) "Discern the truth clearly; live the righteous life fearlessly; and so shall you be my apostles and my Father's ambassadors. You have heard it said: 'If the blind lead the blind, they both shall fall into the pit.' If you would guide others into the kingdom, you must yourselves walk in the clear light of living truth. In all the business of the kingdom I exhort you to show just judgment and keen wisdom. Present not that which is holy to dogs, neither cast your pearls before swine, lest they trample your gems under foot and turn to rend you.

140:3.19 (1571.6) "I warn you against false prophets who will come to you in sheep's clothing, while on the inside they are as ravening wolves. By their fruits you shall know them. Do men gather grapes from thorns or figs from thistles? Even so, every good tree brings forth good fruit, but the corrupt tree bears evil fruit. A good tree cannot yield evil fruit, neither can a corrupt tree produce good fruit. Every tree that does not bring forth good fruit is presently hewn down and cast into the fire. In gaining an entrance into the kingdom of heaven, it is the motive that counts. My Father looks into the hearts of men and judges by their inner longings and their sincere intentions.

140:3.20 (1571.7) "In the great day of the kingdom judgment, many will say to me, 'Did we not prophesy in your name and by your name do many wonderful works?' But I will be compelled to say to them, 'I never knew you; depart from me you who are false teachers.' But every one who hears this charge and sincerely executes his commission to represent me before men even as I have represented my Father to you, shall find an abundant entrance into my service and into the kingdom of the heavenly Father."

140:3.21 (1571.8) Never before had the apostles heard Jesus speak in this way, for he had talked to them as one having supreme authority. They came down from the mountain about sundown, but no man asked Jesus a question.

You Are the Salt of the Earth

140:4.1 (1572.1) The so-called "Sermon on the Mount" is not the gospel of Jesus. It does contain much helpful instruction, but it was Jesus' ordination charge to the twelve apostles. It was the Master's personal commission to those who were to go on preaching the gospel and aspiring to represent him in the world of men even as he was so eloquently and perfectly representative of his Father.

140:4.2 (1572.2) "You are the salt of the earth, salt with a saving savor. But if this salt has lost its savor, wherewith shall it be salted? It is henceforth good for nothing but to be cast out and trodden under foot of men."

140:4.3 (1572.3) In Jesus' time salt was precious. It was even used for money. The modern word "salary" is derived from salt. Salt not only flavors food, but it is also a preservative. It makes other things more tasty, and thus it serves by being spent.

140:4.4 (1572.4) "You are the light of the world. A city set on a hill cannot be hid. Neither do men light a candle and put it under a bushel, but on a candlestick; and it gives light to all who are in the house. Let your light so shine before men that they may see your good works and be led to glorify your Father who is in heaven."

140:4.5 (1572.5) While light dispels darkness, it can also be so "blinding" as to confuse and frustrate. We are admonished to let our light so shine that our fellows will be guided into new and godly paths of enhanced living. Our light should so shine as not to attract attention to self. Even one's vocation can be utilized as an effective "reflector" for the dissemination of this light of life.

140:4.6 (1572.6) Strong characters are not derived from not doing wrong but rather from actually doing right. Unselfishness is the badge of human greatness. The highest levels of self-realization are attained by worship and service. The happy and effective person is motivated, not by fear of wrongdoing, but by love of right doing.

140:4.7 (1572.7) "By their fruits you shall know them." Personality is basically changeless; that which changes—grows—is the moral character. The major error of modern religions is negativism. The tree which bears no fruit is "hewn down and cast into the fire." Moral worth cannot be derived from mere repression—obeying the injunction "Thou shalt not." Fear and shame are unworthy motivations for religious living. Religion is valid only when it reveals the fatherhood of God and enhances the brotherhood of men.

140:4.8 (1572.8) An effective philosophy of living is formed by a combination of cosmic insight and the total of one's emotional reactions to the social and economic environment. Remember: While inherited urges cannot be fundamentally modified, emotional responses to such urges can be changed; therefore the moral nature can be modified, character can be improved. In the strong character emotional responses are integrated and co-ordinated, and thus is produced a unified personality. Deficient unification weakens the moral nature and engenders unhappiness.

140:4.9 (1572.9) Without a worthy goal, life becomes aimless and unprofitable, and much unhappiness results. Jesus' discourse at the ordination of the twelve constitutes a master philosophy of life. Jesus exhorted his followers to exercise experiential faith. He admonished them not to depend on mere intellectual assent, credulity, and established authority.

140:4.10 (1573.1) Education should be a technique of learning (discovering) the better methods of gratifying our natural and inherited urges, and happiness is the resulting total of these enhanced techniques of emotional satisfactions.

Happiness is little dependent on environment, though pleasing surroundings may greatly contribute thereto.

140:4.11 (1573.2) Every mortal really craves to be a complete person, to be perfect even as the Father in heaven is perfect, and such attainment is possible because in the last analysis the "universe is truly fatherly."

Fatherly and Brotherly Love

140:5.1 (1573.3) From the Sermon on the Mount to the discourse of the Last Supper, Jesus taught his followers to manifest fatherly love rather than brotherly love. Brotherly love would love your neighbor as you love yourself, and that would be adequate fulfillment of the "golden rule." But fatherly affection would require that you should love your fellow mortals as Jesus loves you.

140:5.2 (1573.4) Jesus loves mankind with a dual affection. He lived on earth as a twofold personality—human and divine. As the Son of God he loves man with a fatherly love—he is man's Creator, his universe Father. As the Son of Man, Jesus loves mortals as a brother—he was truly a man among men.

140:5.3 (1573.5) Jesus did not expect his followers to achieve an impossible manifestation of brotherly love, but he did expect them to so strive to be like God—to be perfect even as the Father in heaven is perfect—that they could begin to look upon man as God looks upon his creatures and therefore could begin to love men as God loves them—to show forth the beginnings of a fatherly affection. In the course of these exhortations to the twelve apostles, Jesus sought to reveal this new concept of fatherly love as it is related to certain emotional attitudes concerned in making numerous environmental social adjustments.

140:5.4 (1573.6) The Master introduced this momentous discourse by calling attention to four faith attitudes as the prelude to the subsequent portrayal of his four transcendent and supreme reactions of fatherly love in contrast to the limitations of mere brotherly love.

140:5.5 (1573.7) He first talked about those who were poor in spirit, hungered after righteousness, endured meekness, and who were pure in heart. Such spirit-discerning mortals could be expected to attain such levels of divine selflessness as to be able to attempt the amazing exercise of fatherly affection; that even as mourners they would be empowered to show mercy, promote peace, and endure persecutions, and throughout all of these trying situations to love even unlovely mankind with a fatherly love. A father's affection can attain levels of devotion that immeasurably transcend a brother's affection.

140:5.6 (1573.8) The faith and the love of these beatitudes strengthen moral character and create happiness. Fear and anger weaken character and destroy happiness. This momentous sermon started out upon the note of happiness.

140:5.7 (1573.9) 1. "Happy are the poor in spirit—the humble." To a child, happiness is the satisfaction of immediate pleasure craving. The adult is willing to sow seeds of self-denial in order to reap subsequent harvests of augmented happiness. In Jesus' times and since, happiness has all too often been associated with the idea of the possession of wealth. In the story of the Pharisee and the publican praying in the temple, the one felt rich in spirit—egotistical; the other felt "poor in spirit"—humble. One was self-sufficient; the other was teachable and truth-seeking.

The poor in spirit seek for goals of spiritual wealth—for God. And such seekers after truth do not have to wait for rewards in a distant future; they are rewarded now. They find the kingdom of heaven within their own hearts, and they experience such happiness now.

140:5.8 (1574.1) 2. "Happy are they who hunger and thirst for righteousness, for they shall be filled." Only those who feel poor in spirit will ever hunger for righteousness. Only the humble seek for divine strength and crave spiritual power. But it is most dangerous to knowingly engage in spiritual fasting in order to improve one's appetite for spiritual endowments. Physical fasting becomes dangerous after four or five days; one is apt to lose all desire for food. Prolonged fasting, either physical or spiritual, tends to destroy hunger.

140:5.9 (1574.2) Experiential righteousness is a pleasure, not a duty. Jesus' righteousness is a dynamic love—fatherly-brotherly affection. It is not the negative or thou-shalt-not type of righteousness. How could one ever hunger for something negative—something "not to do"?

140:5.10 (1574.3) It is not so easy to teach a child mind these first two of the beatitudes, but the mature mind should grasp their significance.

140:5.11 (1574.4) 3. "Happy are the meek, for they shall inherit the earth." Genuine meekness has no relation to fear. It is rather an attitude of man co-operating with God—"Your will be done." It embraces patience and forbearance and is motivated by an unshakable faith in a lawful and friendly universe. It masters all temptations to rebel against the divine leading. Jesus was the ideal meek man of Urantia, and he inherited a vast universe.

140:5.12 (1574.5) 4. "Happy are the pure in heart, for they shall see God." Spiritual purity is not a negative quality, except that it does lack suspicion and revenge. In discussing purity, Jesus did not intend to deal exclusively with human sex attitudes.

He referred more to that faith which man should have in his fellow man; that faith which a parent has in his child, and which enables him to love his fellows even as a father would love them. A father's love need not pamper, and it does not condone evil, but it is always anticynical. Fatherly love has singleness of purpose, and it always looks for the best in man; that is the attitude of a true parent.

140:5.13 (1574.6) To see God—by faith—means to acquire true spiritual insight. And spiritual insight enhances Adjuster guidance, and these in the end augment God-consciousness. And when you know the Father, you are confirmed in the assurance of divine sonship, and you can increasingly love each of your brothers in the flesh, not only as a brother— with brotherly love—but also as a father—with fatherly affection.

140:5.14 (1574.7) It is easy to teach this admonition even to a child. Children are naturally trustful, and parents should see to it that they do not lose that simple faith. In dealing with children, avoid all deception and refrain from suggesting suspicion. Wisely help them to choose their heroes and select their lifework.

140:5.15 (1574.8) And then Jesus went on to instruct his followers in the realization of the chief purpose of all human struggling—perfection—even divine attainment. Always he admonished them: "Be you perfect, even as your Father in heaven is perfect." He did not exhort the twelve to love their neighbors as they loved themselves. That would have been a worthy achievement; it would have indicated the achievement of brotherly love. He rather admonished his apostles to love men as he had loved them—to love with a fatherly as well as a brotherly affection. And he illustrated this by pointing out four supreme reactions of fatherly love:

140:5.16 (1575.1) 1. "Happy are they who mourn, for they shall be comforted." So-called common sense or the best of logic would never suggest that happiness could be derived from mourning. But Jesus did not refer to outward or ostentatious mourning. He alluded to an emotional attitude of tenderheartedness. It is a great error to teach boys and young men that it is unmanly to show tenderness or otherwise to give evidence of emotional feeling or physical suffering. Sympathy is a worthy attribute of the male as well as the female. It is not necessary to be calloused in order to be manly. This is the wrong way to create courageous men.

The world's great men have not been afraid to mourn. Moses, the mourner, was a greater man than either Samson or Goliath. Moses was a superb leader, but he was also a man of meekness. Being sensitive and responsive to human need creates genuine and lasting happiness, while such kindly attitudes safeguard the soul from the destructive influences of anger, hate, and suspicion.

140:5.17 (1575.2) 2. "Happy are the merciful, for they shall obtain mercy." Mercy here denotes the height and depth and breadth of the truest friendship—loving-kindness. Mercy sometimes may be passive, but here it is active and dynamic—supreme fatherliness. A loving parent experiences little difficulty in forgiving his child, even many times. And in an unspoiled child the urge to relieve suffering is natural. Children are normally kind and sympathetic when old enough to appreciate actual conditions.

140:5.18 (1575.3) 3. "Happy are the peacemakers, for they shall be called the sons of God." Jesus' hearers were longing for military deliverance, not for peacemakers. But Jesus' peace is not of the pacific and negative kind. In the face of trials and persecutions he said, "My peace I leave with you." "Let not your heart be troubled, neither let it be afraid." This is the peace that prevents ruinous conflicts. Personal peace integrates personality. Social peace prevents fear, greed, and anger. Political peace prevents race antagonisms, national suspicions, and war. Peacemaking is the cure of distrust and suspicion.

140:5.19 (1575.4) Children can easily be taught to function as peacemakers. They enjoy team activities; they like to play together. Said the Master at another time: "Whosoever will save his life shall lose it, but whosoever will lose his life shall find it."

140:5.20 (1575.5) 4. "Happy are they who are persecuted for righteousness' sake, for theirs is the kingdom of heaven. Happy are you when men shall revile you and persecute you and shall say all manner of evil against you falsely. Rejoice and be exceedingly glad, for great is your reward in heaven."

140:5.21 (1575.6) So often persecution does follow peace. But young people and brave adults never shun difficulty or danger. "Greater love has no man than to lay down his life for his friends." And a fatherly love can freely do all these things—things which brotherly love can hardly encompass. And progress has always been the final harvest of persecution.

140:5.22 (1575.7) Children always respond to the challenge of courage. Youth is ever willing to "take a dare." And every child should early learn to sacrifice.

140:5.23 (1575.8) And so it is revealed that the beatitudes of the Sermon on the Mount are based on faith and love and not on law—ethics and duty.

140:5.24 (1575.9) Fatherly love delights in returning good for evil—doing good in retaliation for injustice.

The Evening of the Ordination

140:6.1 (1576.1) Sunday evening, on reaching the home of Zebedee from the highlands north of Capernaum, Jesus and the twelve partook of a simple meal. Afterward, while Jesus went for a walk along the beach, the twelve talked among themselves. After a brief conference, while the twins built a small fire to give them warmth and more light, Andrew went out to find

Jesus, and when he had overtaken him, he said: "Master, my brethren are unable to comprehend what you have said about the kingdom. We do not feel able to begin this work until you have given us further instruction. I have come to ask you to join us in the garden and help us to understand the meaning of your words." And Jesus went with Andrew to meet with the apostles.

140:6.2 (1576.2) When he had entered the garden, he gathered the apostles around him and taught them further, saying: "You find it difficult to receive my message because you would build the new teaching directly upon the old, but I declare that you must be reborn. You must start out afresh as little children and be willing to trust my teaching and believe in God. The new gospel of the kingdom cannot be made to conform to that which is. You have wrong ideas of the Son of Man and his mission on earth. But do not make the mistake of thinking that I have come to set aside the law and the prophets; I have not come to destroy but to fulfill, to enlarge and illuminate. I come not to transgress the law but rather to write these new commandments on the tablets of your hearts.

140:6.3 (1576.3) "I demand of you a righteousness that shall exceed the righteousness of those who seek to obtain the Father's favor by almsgiving, prayer, and fasting. If you would enter the kingdom, you must have a righteousness that consists in love, mercy, and truth—the sincere desire to do the will of my Father in heaven."

140:6.4 (1576.4) Then said Simon Peter: "Master, if you have a new commandment, we would hear it. Reveal the new way to us." Jesus answered Peter: "You have heard it said by those who teach the law: 'You shall not kill; that whosoever kills shall be subject to judgment.' But I look beyond the act to uncover the motive. I declare to you that every one who is angry with his brother is in danger of condemnation. He who nurses hatred in his heart and plans vengeance in his mind stands in danger of judgment. You must judge your fellows by their deeds; the Father in heaven judges by the intent.

140:6.5 (1576.5) "You have heard the teachers of the law say, 'You shall not commit adultery.' But I say to you that every man who looks upon a woman with intent to lust after her has already committed adultery with her in his heart. You can only judge men by their acts, but my Father looks into the hearts of his children and in mercy adjudges them in accordance with their intents and real desires."

140:6.6 (1576.6) Jesus was minded to go on discussing the other commandments when James Zebedee interrupted him, asking: "Master, what shall we teach the people regarding divorcement? Shall we allow a man to divorce his wife as Moses has directed?" And when Jesus heard this question, he said: "I have not come to legislate but to enlighten. I have come not to reform the kingdoms of this world but rather to establish the kingdom of heaven. It is not the will of the Father that I should yield to the temptation to teach you rules of government, trade, or social behavior, which, while they might be good for today, would be far from suitable for the society of another age. I am on earth solely to comfort the minds, liberate the spirits, and save the souls of men. But I will say, concerning this question of divorcement, that, while Moses looked with favor upon such things, it was not so in the days of Adam and in the Garden."

140:6.7 (1577.1) After the apostles had talked among themselves for a short time, Jesus went on to say: "Always must you recognize the two viewpoints of all mortal conduct—the human and the divine; the ways of the flesh and the way of the spirit; the estimate of time and the viewpoint of eternity." And though the twelve could not comprehend all that he taught them, they were truly helped by this instruction.

140:6.8 (1577.2) And then said Jesus: "But you will stumble over my teaching because you are wont to interpret my message literally; you are slow to discern the spirit of my teaching. Again must you remember that you are my messengers; you are beholden to live your lives as I have in spirit lived mine. You are my personal representatives; but do not err in expecting all men to live as you do in every particular. Also must you remember that I have sheep not of this flock, and that I am beholden to them also, to the end that I must provide for them the pattern of doing the will of God while living the life of the mortal nature."

140:6.9 (1577.3) Then asked Nathaniel: "Master, shall we give no place to justice? The law of Moses says, 'An eye for an eye, and a tooth for a tooth.' What shall we say?" And Jesus answered: "You shall return good for evil. My messengers must not strive with men, but be gentle toward all. Measure for measure shall not be your rule. The rulers of men may have such laws, but not so in the kingdom; mercy always shall determine your judgments and love your conduct. And if these are hard sayings, you can even now turn back. If you find the requirements of apostleship too hard, you may return to the less rigorous pathway of discipleship."

140:6.10 (1577.4) On hearing these startling words, the apostles drew apart by themselves for a while, but they soon returned, and Peter said: "Master, we would go on with you; not one of us would turn back. We are fully prepared to pay the extra price; we will drink the cup. We would be apostles, not merely disciples."

140:6.11 (1577.5) When Jesus heard this, he said: "Be willing, then, to take up your responsibilities and follow me. Do your good deeds in secret; when you give alms, let not the left hand know what the right hand does. And when you pray, go apart by yourselves and use not vain repetitions and meaningless phrases. Always remember that the Father knows what you need even before you ask him. And be not given to fasting with a sad countenance to be seen by men. As my chosen apostles, now set apart for the service of the kingdom, lay not up for yourselves treasures on earth, but by your unselfish service lay up for yourselves treasures in heaven, for where your treasures are, there will your hearts be also.

140:6.12 (1577.6) "The lamp of the body is the eye; if, therefore, your eye is generous, your whole body will be full of light. But if your eye is selfish, the whole body will be filled with darkness. If the very light which is in you is turned to darkness, how great is that darkness!"

140:6.13 (1577.7) And then Thomas asked Jesus if they should "continue having everything in common." Said the Master: "Yes, my brethren, I would that we should live together as one understanding family. You are intrusted with a great work, and I crave your undivided service. You know that it has been well said: 'No man can serve two masters.' You cannot sincerely worship God and at the same time wholeheartedly serve mammon. Having now enlisted unreservedly in the work of the kingdom, be not anxious for your lives; much less be concerned with what you shall eat or what you shall drink; nor yet for your bodies, what clothing you shall wear. Already have you learned that willing hands and earnest hearts shall not go hungry. And now, when you prepare to devote all of your energies to the work of the kingdom, be assured that the Father will not be unmindful of your needs. Seek first the kingdom of God, and when you have found entrance thereto, all things needful shall be added to you. Be not, therefore, unduly anxious for the morrow. Sufficient for the day is the trouble thereof."

140:6.14 (1578.1) When Jesus saw they were disposed to stay up all night to ask questions, he said to them: "My brethren, you are earthen vessels; it is best for you to go to your rest so as to be ready for the morrow's work." But sleep had departed from their eyes. Peter ventured to request of his Master that "I have just a little private talk with you. Not that I would have secrets from my brethren, but I have a troubled spirit, and if, perchance, I should deserve a rebuke from my master, I could the better endure it alone with you." And Jesus said,

"Come with me, Peter"—leading the way into the house. When Peter returned from the presence of his Master much cheered and greatly encouraged, James decided to go in to talk with Jesus. And so on through the early hours of the morning, the other apostles went in one by one to talk with the Master. When they had all held personal conferences with him save the twins, who had fallen asleep, Andrew went in to Jesus and said: "Master, the twins have fallen asleep in the garden by the fire; shall I arouse them to inquire if they would also talk with you?" And Jesus smilingly said to Andrew, "They do well—trouble them not." And now the night was passing; the light of another day was dawning.

The Week Following the Ordination

140:7.1 (1578.2) After a few hours' sleep, when the twelve were assembled for a late breakfast with Jesus, he said: "Now must you begin your work of preaching the glad tidings and instructing believers. Make ready to go to Jerusalem." After Jesus had spoken, Thomas mustered up courage to say: "I know, Master, that we should now be ready to enter upon the work, but I fear we are not yet able to accomplish this great undertaking. Would you consent for us to stay hereabouts for just a few days more before we begin the work of the kingdom?" And when Jesus saw that all of his apostles were possessed by this same fear, he said: "It shall be as you have requested; we will remain here over the Sabbath day."

140:7.2 (1578.3) For weeks and weeks small groups of earnest truth seekers, together with curious spectators, had been coming to Bethsaida to see Jesus. Already word about him had spread over the countryside; inquiring groups had come from cities as far away as Tyre, Sidon, Damascus, Caesarea, and Jerusalem. Heretofore, Jesus had greeted these people and taught them concerning the kingdom, but the Master now turned this work over to the twelve. Andrew would select one of the apostles and assign him to a group of visitors, and sometimes all twelve of them were so engaged.

140:7.3 (1578.4) For two days they worked, teaching by day and holding private conferences late into the night. On the third day Jesus visited with Zebedee and Salome while he sent his apostles off to "go fishing, seek carefree change, or perchance visit your families." On Thursday they returned for three more days of teaching.

140:7.4 (1578.5) During this week of rehearsing, Jesus many times repeated to his apostles the two great motives of his post baptismal mission on earth:

140:7.5 (1578.6) 1. To reveal the Father to man.

140:7.6 (1578.7) 2. To lead men to become son-conscious—to faith-realize that they are the children of the Most High.

140:7.7 (1579.1) One week of this varied experience did much for the twelve; some even became over self-confident. At the last conference, the night after the Sabbath, Peter and James came to Jesus, saying, "We are ready—let us now go forth to take the kingdom." To which Jesus replied, "May your wisdom equal your zeal and your courage atone for your ignorance."

140:7.8 (1579.2) Though the apostles failed to comprehend much of his teaching, they did not fail to grasp the significance of the charmingly beautiful life he lived with them.

Thursday Afternoon on the Lake

140:8.1 (1579.3) Jesus well knew that his apostles were not fully assimilating his teachings. He decided to give some special instruction to Peter, James, and John, hoping they would be able to clarify the ideas of their associates. He saw that, while some features of the idea of a spiritual kingdom were being grasped by the twelve, they steadfastly persisted in attaching these new spiritual teachings directly onto their old and entrenched literal concepts of the kingdom of heaven as a restoration of David's throne and the re-establishment of Israel as a temporal power on earth. Accordingly, on Thursday afternoon Jesus went out from the shore in a boat with Peter, James, and John to talk over the affairs of the kingdom. This was a four hours' teaching conference, embracing scores of questions and answers, and may most profitably be put in this record by reorganizing the summary of this momentous afternoon as it was given by Simon Peter to his brother, Andrew, the following morning:

140:8.2 (1579.4) 1. Doing the Father's will. Jesus' teaching to trust in the over care of the heavenly Father was not a blind and passive fatalism. He quoted with approval, on this afternoon, an old Hebrew saying: "He who will not work shall not eat." He pointed to his own experience as sufficient commentary on his teachings. His precepts about trusting the Father must not be adjudged by the social or economic conditions of modern times or any other age. His instruction embraces the ideal principles of living near God in all ages and on all worlds.

140:8.3 (1579.5) Jesus made clear to the three the difference between the requirements of apostleship and discipleship. And even then he did not forbid the exercise of prudence and foresight by the twelve. What he preached against was not forethought but anxiety, worry. He taught the active and alert submission to God's will. In answer to many of their questions regarding frugality and thriftiness, he simply called attention to his life as carpenter, boatmaker, and fisherman, and to his careful organization of the twelve. He sought to make it clear that the world is not to be regarded as an enemy; that the circumstances of life constitute a divine dispensation working along with the children of God.

140:8.4 (1579.6) Jesus had great difficulty in getting them to understand his personal practice of nonresistance. He absolutely refused to defend himself, and it appeared to the apostles that he would be pleased if they would pursue the same policy. He taught them not to resist evil, not to combat injustice or injury, but he did not teach passive tolerance of wrongdoing. And he made it plain on this afternoon that he approved of the social punishment of evildoers and criminals, and that the civil government must sometimes employ force for the maintenance of social order and in the execution of justice.

140:8.5 (1579.7) He never ceased to warn his disciples against the evil practice of retaliation; he made no allowance for revenge, the idea of getting even. He deplored the holding of grudges. He disallowed the idea of an eye for an eye and a tooth for a tooth. He discountenanced the whole concept of private and personal revenge, assigning these matters to civil government, on the one hand, and to the judgment of God, on the other. He made it clear to the three that his teachings applied to the individual, not the state. He summarized his instructions up to that time regarding these matters, as:

140:8.6 (1580.1) Love your enemies—remember the moral claims of human brotherhood.

140:8.7 (1580.2) The futility of evil: A wrong is not righted by vengeance. Do not make the mistake of fighting evil with its own weapons.

140:8.8 (1580.3) Have faith—confidence in the eventual triumph of divine justice and eternal goodness.

140:8.9 (1580.4) 2. Political attitude. He cautioned his apostles to be discreet in their remarks concerning the strained relations then existing between the Jewish people and the Roman government; he forbade them to become in any way embroiled in these difficulties. He was always careful to avoid the political snares of his enemies, ever making reply, "Render to Caesar the things which are Caesar's and to God the things which are God's." He refused to have his attention diverted from his mission of establishing a new way of salvation; he would not permit himself to be concerned about anything else. In his personal life he was always duly observant of all civil laws and regulations; in all his public teachings he ignored the civic, social, and economic realms. He told the three apostles that he was concerned only with the principles of man's inner and personal spiritual life.

140:8.10 (1580.5) Jesus was not, therefore, a political reformer. He did not come to reorganize the world; even if he had done this, it would have been applicable only to that day and generation. Nevertheless, he did show man the best way of living, and no generation is exempt from the labor of discovering how best to adapt Jesus' life to its own problems. But never make the mistake of identifying Jesus' teachings with any political or economic theory, with any social or industrial system.

140:8.11 (1580.6) 3. Social attitude. The Jewish rabbis had long debated the question: Who is my neighbor? Jesus came presenting the idea of active and spontaneous kindness, a love of one's fellow men so genuine that it expanded the neighborhood to include the whole world, thereby making all men one's neighbors. But with all this, Jesus was interested only in the individual, not the mass. Jesus was not a sociologist, but he did labor to break down all forms of selfish isolation. He taught pure sympathy, compassion. Michael of Nebadon is a mercy-dominated Son; compassion is his very nature.

140:8.12 (1580.7) The Master did not say that men should never entertain their friends at meat, but he did say that his followers should make feasts for the poor and the unfortunate. Jesus had a firm sense of justice, but it was always tempered with mercy. He did not teach his apostles that they were to be imposed upon by social parasites or professional alms-seekers. The nearest he came to making sociological pronouncements was to say, "Judge not, that you be not judged."

140:8.13 (1580.8) He made it clear that indiscriminate kindness may be blamed for many social evils. The following day Jesus definitely instructed Judas that no apostolic funds were to be given out as alms except upon his request or upon the joint petition of two of the apostles. In all these matters it was the practice of Jesus always to say, "Be as wise as serpents but as harmless as doves." It seemed to be his purpose in all social situations to teach patience, tolerance, and forgiveness.

140:8.14 (1581.1) The family occupied the very center of Jesus' philosophy of life—here and hereafter. He based his teachings about God on the family, while he sought to correct the Jewish tendency to over honor ancestors. He exalted family life as the highest human duty but made it plain that family relationships must not interfere with religious obligations. He called attention to the fact that the family is a temporal institution; that it does not survive death. Jesus did not hesitate to give up his family when the family ran counter to the Father's will. He taught the new and larger brotherhood of man—the sons of God. In Jesus' time divorce practices were lax in Palestine and throughout the Roman Empire. He repeatedly refused to lay down laws regarding marriage and divorce, but many of Jesus' early followers had strong opinions on divorce and did not hesitate to attribute them to him. All of the New Testament writers held to these more stringent and advanced ideas about divorce except John Mark.

140:8.15 (1581.2) 4. Economic attitude. Jesus worked, lived, and traded in the world as he found it. He was not an economic reformer, although he did frequently call attention to the injustice of the unequal distribution of wealth. But he did not offer any suggestions by way of remedy. He made it plain to the three that, while his apostles were not to hold property, he was not preaching against wealth and property, merely its unequal and unfair distribution. He recognized the need for social justice and industrial fairness, but he offered no rules for their attainment.

140:8.16 (1581.3) He never taught his followers to avoid earthly possessions, only his twelve apostles. Luke, the physician,

was a strong believer in social equality, and he did much to interpret Jesus' sayings in harmony with his personal beliefs. Jesus never personally directed his followers to adopt a communal mode of life; he made no pronouncement of any sort regarding such matters.

140:8.17 (1581.4) Jesus frequently warned his listeners against covetousness, declaring that "a man's happiness consists not in the abundance of his material possessions." He constantly reiterated, "What shall it profit a man if he gain the whole world and lose his own soul?" He made no direct attack on the possession of property, but he did insist that it is eternally essential that spiritual values come first. In his later teachings he sought to correct many erroneous Urantia views of life by narrating numerous parables which he presented in the course of his public ministry. Jesus never intended to formulate economic theories; he well knew that each age must evolve its own remedies for existing troubles. And if Jesus were on earth today, living his life in the flesh, he would be a great disappointment to the majority of good men and women for the simple reason that he would not take sides in present-day political, social, or economic disputes. He would remain grandly aloof while teaching you how to perfect your inner spiritual life so as to render you manifold more competent to attack the solution of your purely human problems.

140:8.18 (1581.5) Jesus would make all men Godlike and then stand by sympathetically while these sons of God solve their own political, social, and economic problems. It was not wealth that he denounced, but what wealth does to the majority of its devotees. On this Thursday afternoon Jesus first told his associates that "it is more blessed to give than to receive."

140:8.19 (1581.6) 5. Personal religion. You, as did his apostles, should the better understand Jesus' teachings by his life. He lived a perfected life on Urantia, and his unique teachings can only be understood when that life is visualized in its immediate background. It is his life, and not his lessons to the twelve or his sermons to the multitudes, that will assist most in revealing the Father's divine character and loving personality.

140:8.20 (1582.1) Jesus did not attack the teachings of the Hebrew prophets or the Greek moralists. The Master recognized the many good things which these great teachers stood for, but he had come down to earth to teach something additional, "the voluntary conformity of man's will to God's will." Jesus did not want simply to produce a religious man, a mortal wholly occupied with religious feelings and actuated only by spiritual impulses. Could you have had but one look at him, you would have known that Jesus was a real man of great experience in the things of this world. The teachings of Jesus in this respect have been grossly perverted and much misrepresented all down through the centuries of the Christian era; you have also held perverted ideas about the Master's meekness and humility. What he aimed at in his life appears to have been a superb self-respect. He only advised man to humble himself that he might become truly exalted; what he really aimed at was true humility toward God. He placed great value upon sincerity—a pure heart. Fidelity was a cardinal virtue in his estimate of character, while courage was the very heart of his teachings. "Fear not" was his watchword, and patient endurance his ideal of strength of character. The teachings of Jesus constitute a religion of valor, courage, and heroism. And this is just why he chose as his personal representatives twelve commonplace men, the majority of whom were rugged, virile, and manly fishermen.

140:8.21 (1582.2) Jesus had little to say about the social vices of his day; seldom did he make reference to moral delinquency. He was a positive teacher of true virtue. He studiously avoided the negative method of imparting instruction; he refused to advertise evil. He was not even a moral reformer. He well knew, and so taught his apostles, that the sensual urges of mankind are not suppressed by either religious rebuke or legal prohibitions. His few denunciations were largely directed against pride, cruelty, oppression, and hypocrisy.

140:8.22 (1582.3) Jesus did not vehemently denounce even the Pharisees, as did John. He knew many of the scribes and Pharisees were honest of heart; he understood their enslaving bondage to religious traditions. Jesus laid great emphasis on "first making the tree good." He impressed the three that he valued the whole life, not just a certain few special virtues.

140:8.23 (1582.4) The one thing which John gained from this day's teaching was that the heart of Jesus' religion consisted in the acquirement of a compassionate character coupled with a personality motivated to do the will of the Father in heaven.

140:8.24 (1582.5) Peter grasped the idea that the gospel they were about to proclaim was really a fresh beginning for the whole human race. He conveyed this impression subsequently to Paul, who formulated therefrom his doctrine of Christ as "the second Adam."

140:8.25 (1582.6) James grasped the thrilling truth that Jesus wanted his children on earth to live as though they were already citizens of the completed heavenly kingdom.

140:8.26 (1582.7) Jesus knew men were different, and he so taught his apostles. He constantly exhorted them to refrain from trying to mold the disciples and believers according to some set pattern. He sought to allow each soul to develop in its own way, a perfecting and separate individual before God. In answer to one of Peter's many questions, the Master said: "I want to set men free so that they can start out afresh as little children upon the new and better life." Jesus always insisted that true goodness must be unconscious, in bestowing charity not allowing the left hand to know what the right hand does.

140:8.27 (1583.1) The three apostles were shocked this afternoon when they realized that their Master's religion made no provision for spiritual self-examination. All religions before and after the times of Jesus, even Christianity, carefully provide for conscientious self-examination. But not so with the religion of Jesus of Nazareth. Jesus' philosophy of life is without religious introspection. The carpenter's son never taught character building; he taught character growth, declaring that the kingdom of heaven is like a mustard seed. But Jesus said nothing which would proscribe self-analysis as a prevention of conceited egotism.

140:8.28 (1583.2) The right to enter the kingdom is conditioned by faith, personal belief. The cost of remaining in the progressive ascent of the kingdom is the pearl of great price, in order to possess which a man sells all that he has.

140:8.29 (1583.3) The teaching of Jesus is a religion for everybody, not alone for weaklings and slaves. His religion never became crystallized (during his day) into creeds and theological laws; he left not a line of writing behind him. His life and teachings were bequeathed the universe as an inspirational and idealistic inheritance suitable for the spiritual guidance and moral instruction of all ages on all worlds. And even today, Jesus' teaching stands apart from all religions, as such, albeit it is the living hope of every one of them.

140:8.30 (1583.4) Jesus did not teach his apostles that religion is man's only earthly pursuit; that was the Jewish idea of serving God. But he did insist that religion was the exclusive business of the twelve. Jesus taught nothing to deter his believers from the pursuit of genuine culture; he only detracted from the tradition-bound religious schools of Jerusalem. He was liberal, big-hearted, learned, and tolerant. Self-conscious piety had no place in his philosophy of righteous living. *

140:8.31 (1583.5) The Master offered no solutions for the nonreligious problems of his own age nor for any subsequent age. Jesus wished to develop spiritual insight into eternal realities and to stimulate initiative in the originality of living; he concerned himself exclusively with the underlying and permanent spiritual needs of the human race. He revealed a goodness equal to God. He exalted love—truth, beauty, and goodness—as the divine ideal and the eternal reality.

140:8.32 (1583.6) The Master came to create in man a new spirit, a new will—to impart a new capacity for knowing the truth, experiencing compassion, and choosing goodness—the will to be in harmony with God's will, coupled with the eternal urge to become perfect, even as the Father in heaven is perfect.

The Day of Consecration

140:9.1 (1583.7) The next Sabbath day Jesus devoted to his apostles, journeying back to the highland where he had ordained them; and there, after a long and beautifully touching personal message of encouragement, he engaged in the solemn act of the consecration of the twelve. This Sabbath afternoon Jesus assembled the apostles around him on the hillside and gave them into the hands of his heavenly Father in preparation for the day when he would be compelled to leave them alone in the world. There was no new teaching on this occasion, just visiting and communion.

140:9.2 (1584.1) Jesus reviewed many features of the ordination sermon, delivered on this same spot, and then, calling them before him one by one, he commissioned them to go forth in the world as his representatives. The Master's consecration charge was: "Go into all the world and preach the glad tidings of the kingdom. Liberate spiritual captives, comfort the oppressed, and minister to the afflicted. Freely you have received, freely give."

140:9.3 (1584.2) Jesus advised them to take neither money nor extra clothing, saying, "The laborer is worthy of his hire." And finally he said: "Behold I send you forth as sheep in the midst of wolves; be you therefore as wise as serpents and as harmless as doves. But take heed, for your enemies will bring you up before their councils, while in their synagogues they will castigate you. Before governors and rulers you will be brought because you believe this gospel, and your very testimony shall be a witness for me to them. And when they lead you to judgment, be not anxious about what you shall say, for the spirit of my Father indwells you and will at such a time speak through you. Some of you will be put to death, and before you establish the kingdom on earth, you will be hated by many peoples because of this gospel; but fear not; I will be with you, and my spirit shall go before you into all the world. And my Father's presence will abide with you while you go first to the Jews, then to the gentiles."

140:9.4 (1584.3) And when they came down from the mountain, they journeyed back to their home in Zebedee's house.

The Evening After the Consecration

140:10.1 (1584.4) That evening while teaching in the house, for it had begun to rain, Jesus talked at great length, trying to show the twelve what they must be, not what they must do. They knew only a religion that imposed the doing of certain things as the means of attaining righteousness—salvation. But Jesus would reiterate, "In the kingdom you must be righteous in order to do the work." Many times did he repeat, "Be you therefore perfect, even as your Father in heaven is perfect." All the while was the Master explaining to his bewildered apostles that the salvation which he had come to bring to the world was to be had only by believing, by simple and sincere faith. Said Jesus: "John preached a baptism of repentance, sorrow for the old way of living. You are to proclaim the baptism of fellowship with God. Preach repentance to those who stand in need of such teaching, but to those already seeking sincere entrance to the kingdom,

open the doors wide and bid them enter into the joyous fellowship of the sons of God." But it was a difficult task to persuade these Galilean fishermen that, in the kingdom, being righteous, by faith, must precede doing righteousness in the daily life of the mortals of earth.

140:10.2 (1584.5) Another great handicap in this work of teaching the twelve was their tendency to take highly idealistic and spiritual principles of religious truth and remake them into concrete rules of personal conduct. Jesus would present to them the beautiful spirit of the soul's attitude, but they insisted on translating such teachings into rules of personal behavior. Many times, when they did make sure to remember what the Master said, they were almost certain to forget what he did not say. But they slowly assimilated his teaching because Jesus was all that he taught. What they could not gain from his verbal instruction, they gradually acquired by living with him.

140:10.3 (1585.1) It was not apparent to the apostles that their Master was engaged in living a life of spiritual inspiration for every person of every age on every world of a far-flung universe. Notwithstanding what Jesus told them from time to time, the apostles did not grasp the idea that he was doing a work on this world but for all other worlds in his vast creation. Jesus lived his earth life on Urantia, not to set a personal example of mortal living for the men and women of this world, but rather to create a high spiritual and inspirational ideal for all mortal beings on all worlds.

140:10.4 (1585.2) This same evening Thomas asked Jesus: "Master, you say that we must become as little children before we can gain entrance to the Father's kingdom, and yet you have warned us not to be deceived by false prophets nor to become guilty of casting our pearls before swine. Now, I am honestly puzzled. I cannot understand your teaching." Jesus replied to Thomas: "How long shall I bear with you! Ever you insist on making literal all that I teach. When I asked you to become as little children as the price of entering the kingdom, I referred not to ease of deception, mere willingness to believe, nor to quickness to trust pleasing strangers. What I did desire that you should gather from the illustration was the child-father relationship. You are the child, and it is your Father's kingdom you seek to enter. There is present that natural affection between every normal child and its father which insures an understanding and loving relationship, and which forever precludes all disposition to bargain for the Father's love and mercy. And the gospel you are going forth to preach has to do with a salvation growing out of the faith-realization of this very and eternal child- father relationship."

140:10.5 (1585.3) The one characteristic of Jesus' teaching was that the morality of his philosophy originated in the personal relation of the individual to God—this very child-father relationship. Jesus placed emphasis on the individual, not on the race or nation. While eating supper, Jesus had the talk with Matthew in which he explained that the morality of any act is determined by the individual's motive. Jesus' morality was always positive. The golden rule as restated by Jesus demands active social contact; the older negative rule could be obeyed in isolation. Jesus stripped morality of all rules and ceremonies and elevated it to majestic levels of spiritual thinking and truly righteous living.

140:10.6 (1585.4) This new religion of Jesus was not without its practical implications, but whatever of practical political, social, or economic value there is to be found in his teaching is the natural outworking of this inner experience of the soul as it manifests the fruits of the spirit in the spontaneous daily ministry of genuine personal religious experience.

140:10.7 (1585.5) After Jesus and Matthew had finished talking, Simon Zelotes asked, "But, Master, are all men the sons of God?" And Jesus answered: "Yes, Simon, all men are the sons of God, and that is the good news you are going to proclaim." But the apostles could not grasp such a doc-trine; it was a new, strange, and startling announcement. And it was because of his desire to impress this truth upon them that Jesus taught his followers to treat all men as their brothers.

140:10.8 (1585.6) In response to a question asked by Andrew, the Master made it clear that the morality of his teaching was inseparable from the religion of his living. He taught morality, not from the nature of man, but from the relation of man to God.

140:10.9 (1585.7) John asked Jesus, "Master, what is the kingdom of heaven?" And Jesus answered: "The kingdom of heaven consists in these three essentials: first, recognition of the fact of the sovereignty of God; second, belief in the truth of sonship with God; and third, faith in the effectiveness of the supreme human desire to do the will of God—to be like God. And this is the good news of the gospel: that by faith every mortal may have all these essentials of salvation."

140:10.10 (1586.1) And now the week of waiting was over, and they prepared to depart on the morrow for Jerusalem.

Paper 141

Beginning the Public Work

141:0.1 (1587.1) ON THE first day of the week, January 19, A.D. 27, Jesus and the twelve apostles made ready to depart from their headquarters in Bethsaida. The twelve knew nothing of their Master's plans except that they were going up to Jerusalem to attend the Passover feast in April, and that it was the intention to journey by way of the Jordan valley.

They did not get away from Zebedee's house until near noon because the families of the apostles and others of the disciples had come to say good-bye and wish them well in the new work they were about to begin.

141:0.2 (1587.2) Just before leaving, the apostles missed the Master, and Andrew went out to find him. After a brief search he found Jesus sitting in a boat down the beach, and he was weeping. The twelve had often seen their Master when he seemed to grieve, and they had beheld his brief seasons of serious preoccupation of mind, but none of them had ever seen him weep. Andrew was somewhat startled to see the Master thus affected on the eve of their departure for Jerusalem, and he ventured to approach Jesus and ask: "On this great day, Master, when we are to depart for Jerusalem to proclaim the Father's kingdom, why is it that you weep? Which of us has offended you?" And Jesus, going back with Andrew to join the twelve, answered him: "No one of you has grieved me. I am saddened only because none of my father Joseph's family have remembered to come over to bid us Godspeed." At this time Ruth was on a visit to her brother Joseph at Nazareth. Other members of his family were kept away by pride, disappointment, misunderstanding, and petty resentment indulged as a result of hurt feelings.

Leaving Galilee

141:1.1 (1587.3) Capernaum was not far from Tiberias, and the fame of Jesus had begun to spread well over all of Galilee and even to parts beyond. Jesus knew that Herod would soon begin to take notice of his work; so he thought best to journey south and into Judea with his apostles. A company of over one hundred believers desired to go with them, but Jesus spoke to them and besought them not to accompany the apostolic group on their way down the Jordan. Though they consented to remain behind, many of them followed after the Master within a few days.

141:1.2 (1587.4) The first day Jesus and the apostles only journeyed as far as Tarichea, where they rested for the night. The next day they traveled to a point on the Jordan near Pella where John had preached about one year before, and where Jesus had received baptism. Here they tarried for

more than two weeks, teaching and preaching. By the end of the first week several hundred people had assembled in a camp near where Jesus and the twelve dwelt, and they had come from Galilee, Phoenicia, Syria, the Decapolis, Perea, and Judea.

141:1.3 (1588.1) Jesus did no public preaching. Andrew divided the multitude and assigned the preachers for the forenoon and afternoon assemblies; after the evening meal Jesus talked with the twelve. He taught them nothing new but reviewed his former teaching and answered their many questions. On one of these evenings he told the twelve something about the forty days which he spent in the hills near this place.

141:1.4 (1588.2) Many of those who came from Perea and Judea had been baptized by John and were interested in finding out more about Jesus' teachings. The apostles made much progress in teaching the disciples of John inasmuch as they did not in any way detract from John's preaching, and since they did not at this time even baptize their new disciples.

But it was always a stumbling stone to John's followers that Jesus, if he were all that John had announced, did nothing to get him out of prison. John's disciples never could understand why Jesus did not prevent the cruel death of their beloved leader.

141:1.5 (1588.3) From night to night Andrew carefully instructed his fellow apostles in the delicate and difficult task of getting along smoothly with the followers of John the Baptist. During this first year of Jesus' public ministry more than three fourths of his followers had previously followed John and had received his baptism. This entire year of A.D. 27 was spent in quietly taking over John's work in Perea and Judea.

God's Law and the Father's Will

141:2.1 (1588.4) The night before they left Pella, Jesus gave the apostles some further instruction with regard to the new kingdom. Said the Master: "You have been taught to look for the coming of the kingdom of God, and now I come announcing that this long-looked-for kingdom is near at hand, even that it is already here and in our midst. In every kingdom there must be a king seated upon his throne and decreeing the laws of the realm. And so have you developed a concept of the kingdom of heaven as a glorified rule of the Jewish people over all the peoples of the earth with Messiah sitting on David's throne and from this place of miraculous power promulgating the laws of all the world. But, my children, you see not with the eye of faith, and you hear not with the understanding of the spirit. I declare that the kingdom of heaven is the realization and acknowledgment of God's rule within the hearts of men. True, there is a King in this kingdom, and that King is my Father and your Father. We are indeed his loyal subjects, but far transcending that fact is the transforming truth that we are his sons. In my life this truth is to become manifest to all. Our Father also sits upon a throne, but not one made with hands. The throne of the Infinite is the eternal dwelling place of the Father in the heaven of heavens; he fills all things and proclaims his laws to universes upon universes. And the Father also rules within the hearts of his children on earth by the spirit which he has sent to live within the souls of mortal men.

141:2.2 (1588.5) "When you are the subjects of this kingdom, you indeed are made to hear the law of the Universe Ruler; but when, because of the gospel of the kingdom which I have come to declare, you faith-discover yourselves as sons, you henceforth look not upon yourselves as law-subject creatures of an all-powerful king but as privileged sons of a loving and divine Father. Verily, verily, I say to you, when the Father's will is your law, you are hardly in the kingdom. But when the Father's will becomes truly your will, then are you in very truth in the kingdom because the kingdom has thereby become an established experience in you. When God's will is your law, you are noble slave

subjects; but when you believe in this new gospel of divine sonship, my Father's will becomes your will, and you are elevated to the high position of the free children of God, liberated sons of the kingdom."

141:2.3 (1589.1) Some of the apostles grasped something of this teaching, but none of them comprehended the full significance of this tremendous announcement, unless it was James Zebedee. But these words sank into their hearts and came forth to gladden their ministry during later years of service.

The Sojourn at Amathus

141:3.1 (1589.2) The Master and his apostles remained near Amathus for almost three weeks. The apostles continued to preach twice daily to the multitude, and Jesus preached each Sabbath afternoon. It became impossible to continue the Wednesday playtime; so Andrew arranged that two apostles should rest each day of the six days in the week, while all were on duty during the Sabbath services.

141:3.2 (1589.3) Peter, James, and John did most of the public preaching. Philip, Nathaniel, Thomas, and Simon did much of the personal work and conducted classes for special groups of inquirers; the twins continued their general police supervision, while Andrew, Matthew, and Judas developed into a general managerial committee of three, although each of these three also did considerable religious work.

141:3.3 (1589.4) Andrew was much occupied with the task of adjusting the constantly recurring misunderstandings and disagreements between the disciples of John and the newer disciples of Jesus. Serious situations would arise every few days, but Andrew, with the assistance of his apostolic associates, managed to induce the contending parties to come to some sort of agreement, at least temporarily. Jesus refused to participate in any of these conferences; neither would he give any advice about the proper adjustment of these difficulties. He never once offered a suggestion as to how the apostles should solve these perplexing problems. When Andrew came to Jesus with these questions, he would always say: "It is not wise for the host to participate in the family troubles of his guests; a wise parent never takes sides in the petty quarrels of his own children."

141:3.4 (1589.5) The Master displayed great wisdom and manifested perfect fairness in all of his dealings with his apostles and with all of his disciples. Jesus was truly a master of men; he exercised great influence over his fellow men because of the combined charm and force of his personality. There was a subtle commanding influence in his rugged, nomadic, and homeless life. There was intellectual attractiveness and spiritual drawing power in his authoritative manner of teaching, in his lucid logic, his strength of reasoning, his sagacious insight, his alertness of mind, his matchless poise, and his sublime tolerance. He was simple, manly, honest, and fearless. With all of this physical and intellectual influence manifest in the Master's presence, there were also all those spiritual charms of being which have become associated with his personality—patience, tenderness, meekness, gentleness, and humility.

141:3.5 (1589.6) Jesus of Nazareth was indeed a strong and forceful personality; he was an intellectual power and a spiritual stronghold. His personality not only appealed to the spiritually minded women among his followers, but also to the educated and intellectual Nicodemus and to the hardy Roman soldier, the captain stationed on guard at the cross, who, when he had finished watching the Master die, said, "Truly, this was a Son of God." And red-blooded, rugged Galilean fishermen called him Master.

141:3.6 (1590.1) The pictures of Jesus have been most unfortunate. These paintings of the Christ have exerted a deleterious influence on youth; the temple merchants would hardly have fled before Jesus if he had been such a man as your artists usually have depicted. His was a dignified manhood; he was good, but natural. Jesus did not pose as a mild, sweet, gentle, and kindly mystic. His teaching was thrillingly dynamic. He not only meant well, but he went about actually doing good.

141:3.7 (1590.2) The Master never said, "Come to me all you who are indolent and all who are dreamers." But he did many times say, "Come to me all you who labor, and I will give you rest—spiritual strength." The Master's yoke is, indeed, easy, but even so, he never imposes it; every individual must take this yoke of his own free will.

141:3.8 (1590.3) Jesus portrayed conquest by sacrifice, the sacrifice of pride and selfishness. By showing mercy, he meant to portray spiritual deliverance from all grudges, grievances, anger, and the lust for selfish power and revenge. And when he said, "Resist not evil," he later explained that he did not mean to condone sin or to counsel fraternity with iniquity. He intended the more to teach forgiveness, to "resist not evil treatment of one's personality, evil injury to one's feelings of personal dignity."

Teaching About the Father

141:4.1 (1590.4) While sojourning at Amathus, Jesus spent much time with the apostles instructing them in the new concept of God; again and again did he impress upon them that God is a Father, not a great and supreme bookkeeper who is chiefly engaged in making damaging entries against his erring children on earth, recordings of sin and evil to be used against them when he subsequently sits in judgment upon them as the just Judge of all creation. The Jews had long conceived of God as a king over all, even as a Father of the nation, but never before had large numbers of mortal men held the idea of God as a loving Father of the individual.

141:4.2 (1590.5) In answer to Thomas's question, "Who is this God of the kingdom?" Jesus replied: "God is your Father, and religion—my gospel—is nothing more nor less than the believing recognition of the truth that you are his son. And I am here among you in the flesh to make clear both of these ideas in my life and teachings."

141:4.3 (1590.6) Jesus also sought to free the minds of his apostles from the idea of offering animal sacrifices as a religious duty. But these men, trained in the religion of the daily sacrifice, were slow to comprehend what he meant.

Nevertheless, the Master did not grow weary in his teaching. When he failed to reach the minds of all of the apostles by means of one illustration, he would restate his message and employ another type of parable for purposes of illumination.

141:4.4 (1590.7) At this same time Jesus began to teach the twelve more fully concerning their mission "to comfort the afflicted and minister to the sick." The Master taught them much about the whole man—the union of body, mind, and spirit to form the individual man or woman. Jesus told his associates about the three forms of affliction they would meet and went on to explain how they should minister to all who suffer the sorrows of human sickness. He taught them to recognize:

141:4.5 (1591.1) 1. Diseases of the flesh—those afflictions commonly regarded as physical sickness.

141:4.6 (1591.2) 2. Troubled minds—those nonphysical afflictions which were subsequently looked upon as emotional and mental difficulties and disturbances.

141:4.7 (1591.3) 3. The possession of evil spirits.

141:4.8 (1591.4) Jesus explained to his apostles on several occasions the nature, and something concerning the origin, of these evil spirits, in that day often also called unclean spirits. The Master well knew the difference between the possession of evil spirits and insanity, but the apostles did not. Neither was it possible, in view of their limited knowledge of the early

history of Urantia, for Jesus to undertake to make this matter fully understandable. But he many times said to them, alluding to these evil spirits: "They shall no more molest men when I shall have ascended to my Father in heaven, and after I shall have poured out my spirit upon all flesh in those times when the kingdom will come in great power and spiritual glory."

141:4.9 (1591.5) From week to week and from month to month, throughout this entire year, the apostles paid more and more attention to the healing ministry of the sick.

Spiritual Unity

141:5.1 (1591.6) One of the most eventful of all the evening conferences at Amathus was the session having to do with the discussion of spiritual unity. James Zebedee had asked, "Master, how shall we learn to see alike and thereby enjoy more harmony among ourselves?" When Jesus heard this question, he was stirred within his spirit, so much so that he replied: "James, James, when did I teach you that you should all see alike? I have come into the world to proclaim spiritual liberty to the end that mortals may be empowered to live individual lives of originality and freedom before God. I do not desire that social harmony and fraternal peace shall be purchased by the sacrifice of free personality and spiritual originality. What I require of you, my apostles, is spirit unity—and that you can experience in the joy of your united dedication to the wholehearted doing of the will of my Father in heaven. You do not have to see alike or feel alike or even think alike in order spiritually to be alike. Spiritual unity is derived from the consciousness that each of you is indwelt, and increasingly dominated, by the spirit gift of the heavenly Father. Your apostolic harmony must grow out of the fact that the spirit hope of each of you is identical in origin, nature, and destiny.

141:5.2 (1591.7) "In this way you may experience a perfected unity of spirit purpose and spirit understanding growing out of the mutual consciousness of the identity of each of your indwelling Paradise spirits; and you may enjoy all of this profound spiritual unity in the very face of the utmost diversity of your individual attitudes of intellectual thinking, temperamental feeling, and social conduct. Your personalities may be refreshingly diverse and markedly different, while your spiritual natures and spirit fruits of divine worship and brotherly love may be so unified that all who behold your lives will of a surety take cognizance of this spirit identity and soul unity; they will recognize that you have been with me and have thereby learned, and acceptably, how to do the will of the Father in heaven. You can achieve the unity of the service of God even while you render such service in accordance with the technique of your own original endowments of mind, body, and soul.

141:5.3 (1592.1) "Your spirit unity implies two things, which always will be found to harmonize in the lives of individual believers: First, you are possessed with a common motive for life service; you all desire above everything to do the will of the Father in heaven. Second, you all have a common goal of existence; you all purpose to find the Father in heaven, thereby proving to the universe that you have become like him."

141:5.4 (1592.2) Many times during the training of the twelve Jesus reverted to this theme. Repeatedly he told them it was not his desire that those who believed in him should become dogmatized and standardized in accordance with the religious interpretations of even good men. Again and again he warned his apostles against the formulation of creeds and the establishment of traditions as a means of guiding and controlling believers in the gospel of the kingdom.

Last Week at Amathus

141:6.1 (1592.3) Near the end of the last week at Amathus, Simon Zelotes brought to Jesus one Teherma, a Persian doing business at Damascus. Teherma had heard of Jesus and had come to Capernaum to see him, and there learning that Jesus had gone with his apostles down the Jordan on the way to Jerusalem, he set out to find him. Andrew had presented Teherma to Simon for instruction. Simon looked upon the Persian as a "fire worshiper," although Teherma took great pains to explain that fire was only the visible symbol of the Pure and Holy One. After talking with Jesus, the Persian signified his intention of remaining for several days to hear the teaching and listen to the preaching.

141:6.2 (1592.4) When Simon Zelotes and Jesus were alone, Simon asked the Master: "Why is it that I could not persuade him? Why did he so resist me and so readily lend an ear to you?" Jesus answered: "Simon, Simon, how many times have I instructed you to refrain from all efforts to take something out of the hearts of those who seek salvation? How often have I told you to labor only to put something into these hungry souls? Lead men into the kingdom, and the great and living truths of the kingdom will presently drive out all serious error. When you have presented to mortal man the good news that God is his Father, you can the easier persuade him that he is in reality a son of God. And having done that, you have brought the light of salvation to the one who sits in darkness. Simon, when the Son of Man came first to you, did he come denouncing Moses and the prophets and proclaiming a new and better way of life? No. I came not to take away that which you had from your forefathers but to show you the perfected vision of that which your fathers saw only in part. Go then, Simon, teaching and preaching the kingdom, and when you have a man safely and securely within the kingdom, then is the time, when such a one shall come to you with inquiries, to impart instruction having to do with the progressive advancement of the soul within the divine kingdom."

141:6.3 (1592.5) Simon was astonished at these words, but he did as Jesus had instructed him, and Teherma, the Persian, was numbered among those who entered the kingdom.

141:6.4 (1592.6) That night Jesus discoursed to the apostles on the new life in the kingdom. He said in part: "When you enter the kingdom, you are reborn. You cannot teach the deep things of the spirit to those who have been born only of the flesh; first see that men are born of the spirit before you seek to instruct them in the advanced ways of the spirit. Do not undertake to show men the beauties of the temple until you have first taken them into the temple. Introduce men to God and as the sons of God before you discourse on the doctrines of the fatherhood of God and the sonship of men. Do not strive with men—always be patient. It is not your kingdom; you are only ambassadors. Simply go forth proclaiming: This is the kingdom of heaven—God is your Father and you are his sons, and this good news, if you wholeheartedly believe it, is your eternal salvation."

141:6.5 (1593.1) The apostles made great progress during the sojourn at Amathus. But they were very much disappointed that Jesus would give them no suggestions about dealing with John's disciples. Even in the important matter of baptism, all that Jesus said was: "John did indeed baptize with water, but when you enter the kingdom of heaven, you shall be baptized with the Spirit."

At *Bethany Beyond Jordan*

141:7.1 (1593.2) On February 26, Jesus, his apostles, and a large group of followers journeyed down the Jordan to the ford near Bethany in Perea, the place where John first made proclamation of the coming kingdom. Jesus with his apostles remained here, teaching and preaching, for four weeks before they went on up to Jerusalem.

141:7.2 (1593.3) The second week of the sojourn at Bethany beyond Jordan, Jesus took Peter, James, and John into the hills across the river and south of Jericho for a three days' rest. The Master taught these three many new and advanced truths about the kingdom of heaven. For the purpose of this record we will reorganize and classify these teachings as follows:

141:7.3 (1593.4) Jesus endeavored to make clear that he desired his disciples, having tasted of the good spirit realities of the kingdom, so to live in the world that men, by seeing their lives, would become kingdom conscious and hence be led to inquire of believers concerning the ways of the kingdom. All such sincere seekers for the truth are always glad to hear the glad tidings of the faith gift which insures admission to the kingdom with its eternal and divine spirit realities.

141:7.4 (1593.5) The Master sought to impress upon all teachers of the gospel of the kingdom that their only business was to reveal God to the individual man as his Father—to lead this individual man to become son-conscious; then to present this same man to God as his faith son. Both of these essential revelations are accomplished in Jesus. He became, indeed, "the way, the truth, and the life." The religion of Jesus was wholly based on the living of his bestowal life on earth.

When Jesus departed from this world, he left behind no books, laws, or other forms of human organization affecting the religious life of the individual.

141:7.5 (1593.6) Jesus made it plain that he had come to establish personal and eternal relations with men which should forever take precedence over all other human relationships. And he emphasized that this intimate spiritual fellowship was to be extended to all men of all ages and of all social conditions among all peoples. The only reward which he held out for his children was: in this world—spiritual joy and divine communion; in the next world—eternal life in the progress of the divine spirit realities of the Paradise Father.

141:7.6 (1593.7) Jesus laid great emphasis upon what he called the two truths of first import in the teachings of the kingdom, and they are: the attainment of salvation by faith, and faith alone, associated with the revolutionary teaching of the attainment of human liberty through the sincere recognition of truth, "You shall know the truth, and the truth shall make you free." Jesus was the truth made manifest in the flesh, and he promised to send his Spirit of Truth into the hearts of all his children after his return to the Father in heaven.

141:7.7 (1594.1) The Master was teaching these apostles the essentials of truth for an entire age on earth. They often listened to his teachings when in reality what he said was intended for the inspiration and edification of other worlds. He exemplified a new and original plan of life. From the human standpoint he was indeed a Jew, but he lived his life for all the world as a mortal of the realm.

141:7.8 (1594.2) To insure the recognition of his Father in the unfolding of the plan of the kingdom, Jesus explained that he had purposely ignored the "great men of earth." He began his work with the poor, the very class which had been so neglected by most of the evolutionary religions of preceding times. He despised no man; his plan was world-wide, even universal. He was so bold and emphatic in these announcements that even Peter, James, and John were tempted to think he might possibly be beside himself.

141:7.9 (1594.3) He sought mildly to impart to these apostles the truth that he had come on this bestowal mission, not to set an example for a few earth creatures, but to establish and demonstrate a standard of human life for all peoples upon all worlds throughout his entire universe. And this standard approached the highest perfection, even the final goodness of the Universal Father. But the apostles could not grasp the meaning of his words.

141:7.10 (1594.4) He announced that he had come to function as a teacher, a teacher sent from heaven to present spiritual truth to the material mind. And this is exactly what he did; he was a teacher, not a preacher. From the human viewpoint Peter was a much more effective preacher than Jesus. Jesus' preaching was so effective because of his unique personality, not so much because of compelling oratory or emotional appeal. Jesus spoke directly to men's souls. He was a teacher of man's spirit, but through the mind. He lived with men.

141:7.11 (1594.5) It was on this occasion that Jesus intimated to Peter, James, and John that his work on earth was in some respects to be limited by the commission of his "associate on high," referring to the prebestowal instructions of his Paradise brother, Immanuel. He told them that he had come to do his Father's will and only his Father's will. Being thus motivated by a wholehearted singleness of purpose, he was not anxiously bothered by the evil in the world.

141:7.12 (1594.6) The apostles were beginning to recognize the unaffected friendliness of Jesus. Though the Master was easy of approach, he always lived independent of, and above, all human beings. Not for one moment was he ever dominated by any purely mortal influence or subject to frail human judgment. He paid no attention to public opinion, and he was uninfluenced by praise. He seldom paused to correct misunderstandings or to resent misrepresentation. He never asked any man for advice; he never made requests for prayers.

141:7.13 (1594.7) James was astonished at how Jesus seemed to see the end from the beginning. The Master rarely appeared to be surprised. He was never excited, vexed, or disconcerted. He never apologized to any man. He was at times saddened, but never discouraged.

141:7.14 (1594.8) More clearly John recognized that, notwithstanding all of his divine endowments, after all, he was human. Jesus lived as a man among men and understood, loved, and knew how to manage men. In his personal life he was so human, and yet so faultless. And he was always unselfish.

141:7.15 (1595.1) Although Peter, James, and John could not understand very much of what Jesus said on this occasion, his gracious words lingered in their hearts, and after the crucifixion and resurrection they came forth greatly to enrich and gladden their subsequent ministry. No wonder these apostles did not fully comprehend the Master's words, for he was projecting to them the plan of a new age.

Working in Jericho

141:8.1 (1595.2) Throughout the four weeks' sojourn at Bethany beyond Jordan, several times each week Andrew would assign apostolic couples to go up to Jericho for a day or two. John had many believers in Jericho, and the majority of them welcomed the more advanced teachings of Jesus and his apostles. On these Jericho visits the apostles began more specifically to carry out Jesus' instructions to minister to the sick; they visited every house in the city and sought to comfort every afflicted person.

141:8.2 (1595.3) The apostles did some public work in Jericho, but their efforts were chiefly of a more quiet and personal nature. They now made the discovery that the good news of the kingdom was very comforting to the sick; that their message carried healing for the afflicted. And it was in Jericho that Jesus' commission to the twelve to preach the glad tidings of the kingdom and minister to the afflicted was first fully carried into effect.

141:8.3 (1595.4) They stopped in Jericho on the way up to Jerusalem and were overtaken by a delegation from Mesopotamia that had come to confer with Jesus. The apostles had planned to spend but a day here, but when these truth seekers from the East arrived, Jesus spent three days with them, and they returned to their various homes along the Euphrates happy in the knowledge of the new truths of the kingdom of heaven.

Departing for Jerusalem

141:9.1 (1595.5) On Monday, the last day of March, Jesus and the apostles began their journey up the hills toward Jerusalem. Lazarus of Bethany had been down to the Jordan twice to see Jesus, and every arrangement had been made for the Master and his apostles to make their headquarters with Lazarus and his sisters at Bethany as long as they might desire to stay in Jerusalem.

141:9.2 (1595.6) The disciples of John remained at Bethany beyond the Jordan, teaching and baptizing the multitudes, so that Jesus was accompanied only by the twelve when he arrived at Lazarus's home. Here Jesus and the apostles tarried for five days, resting and refreshing themselves before going on to Jerusalem for the Passover. It was a great event in the lives of Martha and Mary to have the Master and his apostles in the home of their brother, where they could minister to their needs.

141:9.3 (1595.7) On Sunday morning, April 6, Jesus and the apostles went down to Jerusalem; and this was the first time the Master and all of the twelve had been there together.

Paper 142

The Passover at Jerusalem

142:0.1 (1596.1) THE month of April Jesus and the apostles worked in Jerusalem, going out of the city each evening to spend the night at Bethany. Jesus himself spent one or two nights each week in Jerusalem at the home of Flavius, a Greek Jew, where many prominent Jews came in secret to interview him.

142:0.2 (1596.2) The first day in Jerusalem Jesus called upon his friend of former years, Annas, the onetime high priest and relative of Salome, Zebedee's wife. Annas had been hearing about Jesus and his teachings, and when Jesus called at the high priest's home, he was received with much reserve. When Jesus perceived Annas's coldness, he took immediate leave, saying as he departed: "Fear is man's chief enslaver and pride his great weakness; will you betray yourself into bondage to both of these destroyers of joy and liberty?" But Annas made no reply. The Master did not again see Annas until the time when he sat with his son-in-law in judgment on the Son of Man.

1   Teaching in the Temple

142:1.1 (1596.3) Throughout this month Jesus or one of the apostles taught daily in the temple. When the Passover crowds were too great to find entrance to the temple teaching, the apostles conducted many teaching groups outside the sacred precincts. The burden of their message was:

142:1.2 (1596.4) 1. The kingdom of heaven is at hand.

142:1.3 (1596.5) 2. By faith in the fatherhood of God you may enter the kingdom of heaven, thus becoming the sons of God.

142:1.4 (1596.6) 3. Love is the rule of living within the kingdom—supreme devotion to God while loving your neighbor as yourself.

142:1.5 (1596.7) 4. Obedience to the will of the Father, yielding the fruits of the spirit in one's personal life, is the law of the kingdom.

142:1.6 (1596.8) The multitudes who came to celebrate the Passover heard this teaching of Jesus, and hundreds of them rejoiced in the good news. The chief priests and rulers of the Jews became much con-cerned about Jesus and his apostles and debated among themselves as to what should be done with them.

142:1.7 (1596.9) Besides teaching in and about the temple, the apostles and other believers were engaged in doing much personal work among the Passover throngs. These interested men and women carried the news of Jesus' message from this Passover celebration to the uttermost parts of the Roman Empire and also to the East. This was the beginning of the spread of the gospel of the kingdom to the outside world. No longer was the work of Jesus to be confined to Palestine.

2   God's Wrath

142:2.1 (1597.1) There was in Jerusalem in attendance upon the Passover festivities one Jacob, a wealthy Jewish trader from Crete, and he came to Andrew making request to see Jesus privately. Andrew arranged this secret meeting with Jesus at Flavius's home the evening of the next day. This man could not comprehend the Master's teachings, and he came because he desired to inquire more fully about the kingdom of God. Said Jacob to Jesus: "But, Rabbi, Moses and the olden prophets tell us that Yahweh is a jealous God, a God of great wrath and fierce anger. The prophets say he hates evildoers and takes vengeance on those who obey not his law. You and your disciples teach us that God is a kind and compassionate Father who so loves all men that he would welcome them into this new kingdom of heaven, which you proclaim is so near at hand."

142:2.2 (1597.2) When Jacob finished speaking, Jesus replied: "Jacob, you have well stated the teachings of the olden prophets who taught the children of their generation in accordance with the light of their day. Our Father in Paradise is changeless. But the concept of his nature has enlarged and grown from the days of Moses down through the times of Amos and even to the generation of the prophet Isaiah. And now have I come in the flesh to reveal the Father in new glory and to show forth his love and mercy to all men on all worlds. As the gospel of this kingdom shall spread over the world with its message of good cheer and good will to all men, there will grow up improved and better relations among the families of all nations. As time passes, fathers and their children will love each other more, and thus will be brought about a better understanding of the love of the Father in heaven for his children on earth. Remember, Jacob, that a good and true father not only loves his family as a whole—as a family—but he also truly loves and affectionately cares for each individual member."

142:2.3 (1597.3) After considerable discussion of the heavenly Father's character, Jesus paused to say: "You, Jacob, being a father of many, know well the truth of my words." And Jacob said: "But, Master, who told you I was the father of six children? How did you know this about me?" And the Master replied: "Suffice it to say that the Father and the Son know all things, for indeed they see all. Loving your children as a father on earth, you must now accept as a reality the love of the heavenly Father for you—not just for all the children of Abraham, but for you, your individual soul."

142:2.4 (1597.4) Then Jesus went on to say: "When your children are very young and immature, and when you must chastise them, they may reflect that their father is angry and filled with resentful wrath. Their immaturity cannot penetrate beyond the punishment to discern the father's farseeing and corrective affection. But when these same children become grown-up men and women, would it not be folly for them to cling to these earlier and misconceived notions regarding their father? As men and women they should now discern their father's love in all these early disciplines. And should not mankind, as the centuries pass, come the better to understand the true nature and loving character of the Father in heaven? What profit have you from successive generations of spiritual illumination if you persist in viewing God as Moses and the prophets saw him? I say

to you, Jacob, under the bright light of this hour you should see the Father as none of those who have gone before ever beheld him. And thus seeing him, you should rejoice to enter the kingdom wherein such a merciful Father rules, and you should seek to have his will of love dominate your life henceforth."

142:2.5 (1598.1) And Jacob answered: "Rabbi, I believe; I desire that you lead me into the Father's kingdom."

3 The Concept of God

142:3.1 (1598.2) The twelve apostles, most of whom had listened to this discussion of the character of God, that night asked Jesus many questions about the Father in heaven. The Master's answers to these questions can best be presented by the following summary in modern phraseology:

142:3.2 (1598.3) Jesus mildly upbraided the twelve, in substance saying: Do you not know the traditions of Israel relating to the growth of the idea of Yahweh, and are you ignorant of the teaching of the Scriptures concerning the doctrine of God? And then did the Master proceed to instruct the apostles about the evolution of the concept of Deity throughout the course of the development of the Jewish people. He called attention to the following phases of the growth of the God idea:

142:3.3 (1598.4) 1. Yahweh—the god of the Sinai clans. This was the primitive concept of Deity which Moses exalted to the higher level of the Lord God of Israel. The Father in heaven never fails to accept the sincere worship of his children on earth, no matter how crude their concept of Deity or by what name they symbolize his divine nature.

142:3.4 (1598.5) 2. The Most High. This concept of the Father in heaven was proclaimed by Melchizedek to Abraham and was carried far from Salem by those who subsequently believed in this enlarged and expanded idea of Deity. Abraham and his brother left Ur because of the establishment of sun worship, and they became believers in Melchizedek's teaching of El Elyon—the Most High God. Theirs was a composite concept of God, consisting in a blending of their older Mesopotamian ideas and the Most High doctrine.

142:3.5 (1598.6) 3. El Shaddai. During these early days many of the Hebrews worshiped El Shaddai, the Egyptian concept of the God of heaven, which they learned about during their captivity in the land of the Nile. Long after the times of Melchizedek all three of these concepts of God became joined together to form the doctrine of the creator Deity, the Lord God of Israel.

142:3.6 (1598.7) 4. Elohim. From the times of Adam the teaching of the Paradise Trinity has persisted. Do you not recall how the Scriptures begin by asserting that "In the beginning the Gods created the heavens and the earth"? This indicates that when that record was made the Trinity concept of three Gods in one had found lodgment in the religion of our forebears.

142:3.7 (1598.8) 5. The Supreme Yahweh. By the times of Isaiah these beliefs about God had expanded into the concept of a Universal Creator who was simultaneously all-powerful and all-merciful. And this evolving and enlarging concept of God virtually supplanted all previous ideas of Deity in our fathers' religion.

142:3.8 (1598.9) 6. The Father in heaven. And now do we know God as our Father in heaven. Our teaching provides a religion wherein the believer is a son of God. That is the good news of the gospel of the kingdom of heaven. Coexistent with the Father are the Son and the Spirit, and the revelation of the nature and ministry of these Paradise Deities will continue to enlarge and brighten throughout the endless ages of the eternal spiritual progression of the ascending sons of God. At all times and during all ages the true worship of any human being—as concerns individual spiritual progress—is recognized by the indwelling spirit as homage rendered to the Father in heaven.

142:3.9 (1599.1) Never before had the apostles been so shocked as they were upon hearing this recounting of the growth of the concept of God in the Jewish minds of previous generations; they were too bewildered to ask questions. As they sat before Jesus in silence, the Master continued: "And you would have known these truths had you read the Scriptures.

Have you not read in Samuel where it says: 'And the anger of the Lord was kindled against Israel, so much so that he moved David against them, saying, go number Israel and Judah'? And this was not strange because in the days of Samuel the children of Abraham really believed that Yahweh created both good and evil. But when a later writer narrated these events, subsequent to the enlargement of the Jewish concept of the nature of God, he did not dare attribute evil to Yahweh; therefore he said: 'And Satan stood up against Israel and provoked David to number Israel.' Cannot you discern that such records in the Scriptures clearly show how the concept of the nature of God continued to grow from one generation to another?

142:3.10 (1599.2) "Again should you have discerned the growth of the understanding of divine law in perfect keeping with these enlarging concepts of divinity. When the children of Israel came out of Egypt in the days before the enlarged revelation of Yahweh, they had ten commandments which served as their law right up to the times when they were encamped before Sinai. And these ten commandments were:

142:3.11 (1599.3) "1. You shall worship no other god, for the Lord is a jealous God.

142:3.12 (1599.4) "2. You shall not make molten gods.

142:3.13 (1599.5) "3. You shall not neglect to keep the feast of unleavened bread.

142:3.14 (1599.6) "4. Of all the males of men or cattle, the first-born are mine, says the Lord.

142:3.15 (1599.7) "5. Six days you may work, but on the seventh day you shall rest.

142:3.16 (1599.8) "6. You shall not fail to observe the feast of the first fruits and the feast of the ingathering at the end of the year.

142:3.17 (1599.9) "7. You shall not offer the blood of any sacrifice with leavened bread.

142:3.18 (1599.10) "8. The sacrifice of the feast of the Passover shall not be left until morning.

142:3.19 (1599.11) "9. The first of the first fruits of the ground you shall bring to the house of the Lord your God.

142:3.20 (1599.12) "10. You shall not seethe a kid in its mother's milk.

142:3.21 (1599.13) "And then, amidst the thunders and lightnings of Sinai, Moses gave them the new ten commandments, which you will all allow are more worthy utterances to accompany the enlarging Yahweh concepts of Deity. And did you never take notice of these commandments as twice recorded in the Scriptures, that in the first case deliverance from Egypt is assigned as the reason for Sabbath keeping, while in a later record the advancing religious beliefs of our forefathers demanded that this be changed to the recognition of the fact of creation as the reason for Sabbath observance? *

142:3.22 (1599.14) "And then will you remember that once again—in the greater spiritual enlightenment of Isaiah's day—these ten negative commandments were changed into the great and positive law of love, the injunction to love God supremely and your neighbor as yourself. And it is this supreme law of love for God and for man that I also declare to you as constituting the whole duty of man."

142:3.23 (1600.1) And when he had finished speaking, no man asked him a question. They went, each one to his sleep.

4   Flavius and Greek Culture

142:4.1 (1600.2) Flavius, the Greek Jew, was a proselyte of the gate, having been neither circumcised nor baptized; and since he was a great lover of the beautiful in art and sculpture, the house which he occupied when sojourning in Jerusalem was a beautiful edifice. This home was exquisitely adorned with priceless treasures which he had gathered up here and there on his world travels. When he first thought of inviting Jesus to his home, he feared that the Master might take offense at the sight of these so-called images. But Flavius was agreeably surprised when Jesus entered the home that, instead of rebuking him for having these supposedly idolatrous objects scattered about the house, he manifested great interest in the entire collection and asked many appreciative questions about each object as Flavius escorted him from room to room, showing him all of his favorite statues.

142:4.2 (1600.3) The Master saw that his host was bewildered at his friendly attitude toward art; therefore, when they had finished the survey of the entire collection, Jesus said: "Because you appreciate the beauty of things created by my Father and fashioned by the artistic hands of man, why should you expect to be rebuked? Because Moses onetime sought to combat idolatry and the worship of false gods, why should all men frown upon the reproduction of grace and beauty? I say to you, Flavius, Moses' children have misunderstood him, and now do they make false gods of even his prohibitions of images and the likeness of things in heaven and on earth. But even if Moses taught such restrictions to the darkened minds of those days, what has that to do with this day when the Father in heaven is revealed as the universal Spirit Ruler over all? And, Flavius, I declare that in the coming kingdom they shall no longer teach, 'Do not worship this and do not worship that'; no longer shall they concern themselves with commands to refrain from this and take care not to do that, but rather shall all be concerned with one supreme duty. And this duty of man is expressed in two great privileges: sincere worship of the infinite Creator, the Paradise Father, and loving service bestowed upon one's fellow men. If you love your neighbor as you love yourself, you really know that you are a son of God.

142:4.3 (1600.4) "In an age when my Father was not well understood, Moses was justified in his attempts to withstand idolatry, but in the coming age the Father will have been revealed in the life of the Son; and this new revelation of God will make it forever unnecessary to confuse the Creator Father with idols of stone or images of gold and silver.

Henceforth, intelligent men may enjoy the treasures of art without confusing such material appreciation of beauty with the worship and service of the Father in Paradise, the God of all things and all beings."

142:4.4 (1600.5) Flavius believed all that Jesus taught him. The next day he went to Bethany beyond the Jordan and was baptized by the disciples of John. And this he did because the apostles of Jesus did not yet baptize believers. When Flavius returned to Jerusalem, he made a great feast for Jesus and invited sixty of his friends. And many of these guests also became believers in the message of the coming kingdom.

5   The Discourse on Assurance

142:5.1 (1601.1) One of the great sermons which Jesus preached in the temple this Passover week was in answer to a question asked by one of his hearers, a man from Damascus. This man asked Jesus: "But, Rabbi, how shall we know of a certainty that you are sent by God, and that we may truly enter into this kingdom which you and your disciples declare is near at hand?" And Jesus answered:

142:5.2 (1601.2) "As to my message and the teaching of my disciples, you should judge them by their fruits. If we proclaim to you the truths of the spirit, the spirit will witness in your hearts that our message is genuine. Concerning the kingdom and your assurance of acceptance by the heavenly Father, let me ask what father among you who is a worthy and kindhearted father would keep his son in anxiety or suspense regarding his status in the family or his place of security in the affections of his father's heart? Do you earth fathers take pleasure in torturing your children with uncertainty about their place of abiding love in your human hearts? Neither does your Father in heaven leave his faith children of the spirit in doubtful uncertainty as to their position in the kingdom. If you receive God as your Father, then indeed and in truth are you the sons of God. And if you are sons, then are you secure in the position and standing of all that concerns eternal and divine sonship. If you believe my words, you thereby believe in Him who sent me, and by thus believing in the Father, you have made your status in heavenly citizenship sure. If you do the will of the Father in heaven, you shall never fail in the attainment of the eternal life of progress in the divine kingdom.

142:5.3 (1601.3) "The Supreme Spirit shall bear witness with your spirits that you are truly the children of God. And if you are the sons of God, then have you been born of the spirit of God; and whosoever has been born of the spirit has in himself the power to overcome all doubt, and this is the victory that overcomes all uncertainty, even your faith.

142:5.4 (1601.4) "Said the Prophet Isaiah, speaking of these times: 'When the spirit is poured upon us from on high, then shall the work of righteousness become peace, quietness, and assurance forever.' And for all who truly believe this gospel, I will become surety for their reception into the eternal mercies and the everlasting life of my Father's kingdom. You, then, who hear this message and believe this gospel of the kingdom are the sons of God, and you have life everlasting; and the evidence to all the world that you have been born of the spirit is that you sincerely love one another."

142:5.5 (1601.5) The throng of listeners remained many hours with Jesus, asking him questions and listening attentively to his comforting answers. Even the apostles were emboldened by Jesus' teaching to preach the gospel of the kingdom with more power and assurance. This experience at Jerusalem was a great inspiration to the twelve. It was their first contact with such enormous crowds, and they learned many valuable lessons which proved of great assistance in their later work.

6   The Visit with Nicodemus

142:6.1 (1601.6) One evening at the home of Flavius there came to see Jesus one Nicodemus, a wealthy and elderly member of the Jewish Sanhedrin. He had heard much about the teachings of this Galilean, and so he went one afternoon to hear him as he taught in the temple courts. He would have gone often to hear Jesus teach, but he feared to be seen by the people in attendance upon his teaching, for already were the rulers of the Jews so at variance with Jesus that no member of the Sanhedrin would want to be identified in any open manner with him. Accordingly, Nicodemus had arranged with Andrew to see Jesus privately and after nightfall on this particular evening. Peter, James, and John were in Flavius's garden when the interview began, but later they all went into the house where the discourse continued.

142:6.2 (1602.1) In receiving Nicodemus, Jesus showed no particular deference; in talking with him, there was no compromise or undue persuasiveness. The Master made no attempt to repulse his secretive caller, nor did he employ sarcasm. In all his dealings with the distinguished visitor, Jesus was calm, earnest, and dignified. Nicodemus was not an official delegate of the Sanhedrin; he came to see Jesus wholly because of his personal and sincere interest in the Master's teachings.

142:6.3 (1602.2) Upon being presented by Flavius, Nicodemus said: "Rabbi, we know that you are a teacher sent by God, for no mere man could so teach unless God were with him. And I am desirous of knowing more about your teachings regarding the coming kingdom."

142:6.4 (1602.3) Jesus answered Nicodemus: "Verily, verily, I say to you, Nicodemus, except a man be born from above, he cannot see the kingdom of God." Then replied Nicodemus: "But how can a man be born again when he is old? He cannot enter a second time into his mother's womb to be born."

142:6.5 (1602.4) Jesus said: "Nevertheless, I declare to you, except a man be born of the spirit, he cannot enter into the kingdom of God. That which is born of the flesh is flesh, and that which is born of the spirit is spirit. But you should not marvel that I said you must be born from above. When the wind blows, you hear the rustle of the leaves, but you do not see the wind—whence it comes or whither it goes—and so it is with everyone born of the spirit. With the eyes of the flesh you can behold the manifestations of the spirit, but you cannot actually discern the spirit."

142:6.6 (1602.5) Nicodemus replied: "But I do not understand—how can that be?" Said Jesus: "Can it be that you are a teacher in Israel and yet ignorant of all this? It becomes, then, the duty of those who know about the realities of the spirit to reveal these things to those who discern only the manifestations of the material world. But will you believe us if we tell you of the heavenly truths? Do you have the courage, Nicodemus, to believe in one who has descended from heaven, even the Son of Man?"

142:6.7 (1602.6) And Nicodemus said: "But how can I begin to lay hold upon this spirit which is to remake me in preparation for entering into the kingdom?" Jesus answered: "Already does the spirit of the

Father in heaven indwell you. If you would be led by this spirit from above, very soon would you begin to see with the eyes of the spirit, and then by the wholehearted choice of spirit guidance would you be born of the spirit since your only purpose in living would be to do the will of your Father who is in heaven. And so finding yourself born of the spirit and happily in the kingdom of God, you would begin to bear in your daily life the abundant fruits of the spirit."

142:6.8 (1602.7) Nicodemus was thoroughly sincere. He was deeply impressed but went away bewildered. Nicodemus was accomplished in self-development, in self-restraint, and even in high moral qualities. He was refined, egoistic, and altruistic; but he did not know how to submit his will to the will of the divine Father as a little child is willing to submit to the guidance and leading of a wise and loving earthly father, thereby becoming in reality a son of God, a progressive heir of the eternal kingdom.

142:6.9 (1603.1) But Nicodemus did summon faith enough to lay hold of the kingdom. He faintly protested when his colleagues of the Sanhedrin sought to condemn Jesus without a hearing; and with Joseph of Arimathea, he later boldly acknowledged his faith and claimed the body of Jesus, even when most of the disciples had fled in fear from the scenes of their Master's final suffering and death.

7   *The Lesson on the Family*

142:7.1 (1603.2) After the busy period of teaching and personal work of Passover week in Jerusalem, Jesus spent the next Wednesday at Bethany with his apostles, resting. That afternoon, Thomas asked a question which elicited a long and instructive answer. Said Thomas: "Master, on the day we were set apart as ambassadors of the kingdom, you told us many things, instructed us regarding our personal mode of life, but what shall we teach the multitude? How are these people to live after the kingdom more fully comes?

Shall your disciples own slaves? Shall your believers court poverty and shun property? Shall mercy alone prevail so that we shall have no more law and justice?" Jesus and the twelve spent all afternoon and all that evening, after supper, discussing Thomas's questions. For the purposes of this record we present the following summary of the Master's instruction:

142:7.2 (1603.3) Jesus sought first to make plain to his apostles that he himself was on earth living a unique life in the flesh, and that they, the twelve, had been called to participate in this bestowal experience of the Son of Man; and as such coworkers, they, too, must share in many of the special restrictions and obligations of the entire bestowal experience.

There was a veiled intimation that the Son of Man was the only person who had ever lived on earth who could simultaneously see into the very heart of God and into the very depths of man's soul.

142:7.3 (1603.4) Very plainly Jesus explained that the kingdom of heaven was an evolutionary experience, beginning here on earth and progressing up through successive life stations to Paradise. In the course of the evening he definitely stated that at some future stage of kingdom development he would revisit this world in spiritual power and divine glory.

142:7.4 (1603.5) He next explained that the "kingdom idea" was not the best way to illustrate man's relation to God; that he employed such figures of speech because the Jewish people were expecting the kingdom, and because John had preached in terms of the coming kingdom. Jesus said: "The people of another age will better understand the gospel of the kingdom when it is presented in terms expressive of the family relationship—when man understands religion as the teaching of the fatherhood of God and the brotherhood of man, sonship with God." Then the Master discoursed at some length on the earthly family as an illustration of the heavenly family, restating the two fundamental laws of living: the first commandment of love for the father, the head of the family, and the second commandment of mutual love among the children, to love your brother as yourself. And then he explained that such a quality of brotherly affection would invariably manifest itself in unselfish and loving social service.

142:7.5 (1603.6) Following that, came the memorable discussion of the fundamental characteristics of family life and their application to the relationship existing between God and man. Jesus stated that a true family is founded on the following seven facts:

142:7.6 (1604.1) 1. The fact of existence. The relationships of nature and the phenomena of mortal likenesses are bound up in the family: Children inherit certain parental traits. The children take origin in the parents; personality existence depends on the act of the parent. The relationship of father and child is inherent in all nature and pervades all living existences.

142:7.7 (1604.2) 2. Security and pleasure. True fathers take great pleasure in providing for the needs of their children. Many fathers are not content with supplying the mere wants of their children but enjoy making provision for their pleasures also.

142:7.8 (1604.3) 3. Education and training. Wise fathers carefully plan for the education and adequate training of their sons and daughters. When young they are prepared for the greater responsibilities of later life.

142:7.9 (1604.4) 4. Discipline and restraint. Farseeing fathers also make provision for the necessary discipline, guidance, correction, and sometimes restraint of their young and immature offspring.

142:7.10 (1604.5) 5. Companionship and loyalty. The affectionate father holds intimate and loving intercourse with his children. Always is his ear open to their petitions; he is ever ready to share their hardships and assist them over their dif-

ficulties. The father is supremely interested in the progressive welfare of his progeny.

142:7.11 (1604.6) 6. Love and mercy. A compassionate father is freely forgiving; fathers do not hold vengeful memories against their children. Fathers are not like judges, enemies, or creditors. Real families are built upon tolerance, patience, and forgiveness.

142:7.12 (1604.7) 7. Provision for the future. Temporal fathers like to leave an inheritance for their sons. The family continues from one generation to another. Death only ends one generation to mark the beginning of another. Death terminates an individual life but not necessarily the family.

142:7.13 (1604.8) For hours the Master discussed the application of these features of family life to the relations of man, the earth child, to God, the Paradise Father. And this was his conclusion: "This entire relationship of a son to the Father, I know in perfection, for all that you must attain of sonship in the eternal future I have now already attained. The Son of Man is prepared to ascend to the right hand of the Father, so that in me is the way now open still wider for all of you to see God and, ere you have finished the glorious progression, to become perfect, even as your Father in heaven is perfect."

142:7.14 (1604.9) When the apostles heard these startling words, they recalled the pronouncements which John made at the time of Jesus' baptism, and they also vividly recalled this experience in connection with their preaching and teaching subsequent to the Master's death and resurrection.

142:7.15 (1604.10) Jesus is a divine Son, one in the Universal Father's full confidence. He had been with the Father and comprehended him fully. He had now lived his earth life to the full satisfaction of the Father, and this incarnation in the flesh had enabled him fully to comprehend man. Jesus was the perfection of man; he had attained just such perfection as all true believers are destined to attain in him and through him. Jesus revealed a God of perfection to man and presented in himself the perfected son of the realms to God.

142:7.16 (1605.1) Although Jesus discoursed for several hours, Thomas was not yet satisfied, for he said: "But, Master, we do not find that the Father in heaven always deals kindly and mercifully with us. Many times we grievously suffer on earth, and not always are our prayers answered. Where do we fail to grasp the meaning of your teaching?"

142:7.17 (1605.2) Jesus replied: "Thomas, Thomas, how long before you will acquire the ability to listen with the ear of the spirit? How long will it be before you discern that this kingdom is a spiritual kingdom, and that my Father is also a spiritual being? Do you not understand that I am teaching you as spiritual children in the spirit family of heaven, of which the fatherhead is an infinite and eternal spirit? Will you not allow me to use the earth family as an illustration of divine relationships without so literally applying my teaching to material affairs? In your minds cannot you separate the spiritual realities of the kingdom from the material, social, economic, and political problems of the age? When I speak the language of the spirit, why do you insist on translating my meaning into the language of the flesh just because I presume to employ commonplace and literal relationships for purposes of illustration? My children, I implore that you cease to apply the teaching of the kingdom of the spirit to the sordid affairs of slavery, poverty, houses, and lands, and to the material problems of human equity and justice. These temporal matters are the concern of the men of this world, and while in a way they affect all men, you have been called to represent me in the world, even as I represent my Father. You are spiritual ambassadors of a spiritual kingdom, special representatives of the spirit Father. By this time it should be possible for me to instruct you as full-grown men of the spirit kingdom. Must I ever address you only as

children?

Will you never grow up in spirit perception? Nevertheless, I love you and will bear with you, even to the very end of our association in the flesh. And even then shall my spirit go before you into all the world."

8   In Southern Judea

142:8.1 (1605.3) By the end of April the opposition to Jesus among the Pharisees and Sadducees had become so pronounced that the Master and his apostles decided to leave Jerusalem for a while, going south to work in Bethlehem and Hebron. The entire month of May was spent in doing personal work in these cities and among the people of the surrounding villages. No public preaching was done on this trip, only house-to-house visitation. A part of this time, while the apostles taught the gospel and ministered to the sick, Jesus and Abner spent at Engedi, visiting the Nazarite colony. John the Baptist had gone forth from this place, and Abner had been head of this group. Many of the Nazarite brotherhood became believers in Jesus, but the majority of these ascetic and eccentric men refused to accept him as a teacher sent from heaven because he did not teach fasting and other forms of self-denial.

142:8.2 (1605.4) The people living in this region did not know that Jesus had been born in Bethlehem. They always supposed the Master had been born at Nazareth, as did the vast majority of his disciples, but the twelve knew the facts.

142:8.3 (1605.5) This sojourn in the south of Judea was a restful and fruitful season of labor; many souls were added to the kingdom. By the first days of June the agitation against Jesus had so quieted down in Jerusalem that the Master and the apostles returned to instruct and comfort believers.

142:8.4 (1606.1) Although Jesus and the apostles spent the entire month of June in or near Jerusalem, they did no public teaching during this period. They lived for the most part in tents, which they pitched in a shaded park, or garden, known in that day as Gethsemane. This park was situated on the western slope of the Mount of Olives not far from the brook Kidron. The Sabbath weekends they usually spent with Lazarus and his sisters at Bethany. Jesus entered within the walls of Jerusalem only a few times, but a large number of interested inquirers came out to Gethsemane to visit with him. One Friday evening Nicodemus and one Joseph of Arimathea ventured out to see Jesus but turned back through fear even after they were standing before the entrance to the Master's tent. And, of course, they did not perceive that Jesus knew all about their doings. *

142:8.5 (1606.2) When the rulers of the Jews learned that Jesus had returned to Jerusalem, they prepared to arrest him; but when they observed that he did no public preaching, they concluded that he had become frightened by their previous agitation and decided to allow him to carry on his teaching in this private manner without further molestation. And thus affairs moved along quietly until the last days of June, when one Simon, a member of the Sanhedrin, publicly espoused the teachings of Jesus, after so declaring himself before the rulers of the Jews. Immediately a new agitation for Jesus' apprehension sprang up and grew so strong that the Master decided to retire into the cities of Samaria and the Decapolis.

Paper 143

Going Through Samaria

143:0.1 (1607.1) AT THE end of June, A.D. 27, because of the increasing opposition of the Jewish religious rulers, Jesus and the twelve departed from Jerusalem, after sending their tents and meager personal effects to be stored at the home of Lazarus at Bethany. Going north into Samaria, they tarried over the Sabbath at Bethel. Here

they preached for several days to the people who came from Gophna and Ephraim. A group of citizens from Arimathea and Thamna came over to invite Jesus to visit their villages. The Master and his apostles spent more than two weeks teaching the Jews and Samaritans of this region, many of whom came from as far as Antipatris to hear the good news of the kingdom.

143:0.2 (1607.2) The people of southern Samaria heard Jesus gladly, and the apostles, with the exception of Judas Iscariot, succeeded in overcoming much of their prejudice against the Samaritans. It was very difficult for Judas to love these Samaritans. The last week of July Jesus and his associates made ready to depart for the new Greek cities of Phasaelis and Archelais near the Jordan.

Preaching at Archelais

143:1.1 (1607.3) The first half of the month of August the apostolic party made its headquarters at the Greek cities of Archelais and Phasaelis, where they had their first experience preaching to well-nigh exclusive gatherings of gentiles—Greeks, Romans, and Syrians—for few Jews dwelt in these two Greek towns. In contacting with these Roman citizens, the apostles encountered new difficulties in the proclamation of the message of the coming kingdom, and they met with new objections to the teachings of Jesus. At one of the many evening conferences with his apostles, Jesus listened attentively to these objections to the gospel of the kingdom as the twelve repeated their experiences with the subjects of their personal labors.

143:1.2 (1607.4) A question asked by Philip was typical of their difficulties. Said Philip: "Master, these Greeks and Romans make light of our message, saying that such teachings are fit for only weaklings and slaves. They assert that the religion of the heathen is superior to our teaching because it inspires to the acquirement of a strong, robust, and aggressive character.

They affirm that we would convert all men into enfeebled specimens of passive non-resisters who would soon perish from the face of the earth. They like you, Master, and freely admit that your teaching is heavenly and ideal, but they will not take us seriously. They assert that your religion is not for this world; that men cannot live as you teach. And now, Master, what shall we say to these gentiles?"

143:1.3 (1607.5) After Jesus had heard similar objections to the gospel of the kingdom presented by Thomas, Nathaniel, Simon Zelotes, and Matthew, he said to the twelve:

143:1.4 (1608.1) "I have come into this world to do the will of my Father and to reveal his loving character to all mankind. That, my brethren, is my mission. And this one thing I will do, regardless of the misunderstanding of my teachings by Jews or gentiles of this day or of another generation. But you should not overlook the fact that even divine love has its severe disciplines. A father's love for his son oftentimes impels the father to restrain the unwise acts of his thoughtless offspring. The child does not always comprehend the wise and loving motives of the father's restraining discipline. But I declare to you that my Father in Paradise does rule a universe of universes by the compelling power of his love. Love is the greatest of all spirit realities. Truth is a liberating revelation, but love is the supreme relationship. And no matter what blunders your fellow men make in their world management of today, in an age to come the gospel which I declare to you will rule this very world. The ultimate goal of human progress is the reverent recognition of the fatherhood of God and the loving materialization of the brotherhood of man.

143:1.5 (1608.2) "But who told you that my gospel was intended only for slaves and weaklings? Do you, my chosen apostles, resemble weaklings? Did John look like a weakling? Do you observe that I am enslaved by fear? True, the poor and oppressed of this generation have the gospel preached to them. The religions of this world have neglected the poor, but my

Father is no respecter of persons. Besides, the poor of this day are the first to heed the call to repentance and acceptance of sonship. The gospel of the kingdom is to be preached to all men—Jew and gentile, Greek and Roman, rich and poor, free and bond—and equally to young and old, male and female.

143:1.6 (1608.3) "Because my Father is a God of love and delights in the practice of mercy, do not imbibe the idea that the service of the kingdom is to be one of monotonous ease. The Paradise ascent is the supreme adventure of all time, the rugged achievement of eternity. The service of the kingdom on earth will call for all the courageous manhood that you and your coworkers can muster. Many of you will be put to death for your loyalty to the gospel of this kingdom. It is easy to die in the line of physical battle when your courage is strengthened by the presence of your fighting comrades, but it requires a higher and more profound form of human courage and devotion calmly and all alone to lay down your life for the love of a truth enshrined in your mortal heart.

143:1.7 (1608.4) "Today, the unbelievers may taunt you with preaching a gospel of nonresistance and with living lives of nonviolence, but you are the first volunteers of a long line of sincere believers in the gospel of this kingdom who will astonish all mankind by their heroic devotion to these teachings. No armies of the world have ever displayed more courage and bravery than will be portrayed by you and your loyal successors who shall go forth to all the world proclaiming the good news—the fatherhood of God and the brotherhood of men. The courage of the flesh is the lowest form of bravery. Mind bravery is a higher type of human courage, but the highest and supreme is uncompromising loyalty to the enlightened convictions of profound spiritual realities. And such courage constitutes the heroism of the God-knowing man. And you are all God-knowing men; you are in very truth the personal associates of the Son of Man."

143:1.8 (1608.5) This was not all that Jesus said on that occasion, but it is the introduction of his address, and he went on at great length in amplification and in illustration of this pronouncement. This was one of the most impassioned addresses which Jesus ever delivered to the twelve. Seldom did the Master speak to his apostles with evident strong feeling, but this was one of those few occasions when he spoke with manifest earnestness, accompanied by marked emotion.

143:1.9 (1609.1) The result upon the public preaching and personal ministry of the apostles was immediate; from that very day their message took on a new note of courageous dominance. The twelve continued to acquire the spirit of positive aggression in the new gospel of the kingdom. From this day forward they did not occupy themselves so much with the preaching of the negative virtues and the passive injunctions of their Master's many-sided teaching.

Lesson on Self-Mastery

143:2.1 (1609.2) The Master was a perfected specimen of human self-control. When he was reviled, he reviled not; when he suffered, he uttered no threats against his tormentors; when he was denounced by his enemies, he simply committed himself to the righteous judgment of the Father in heaven.

143:2.2 (1609.3) At one of the evening conferences, Andrew asked Jesus: "Master, are we to practice self-denial as John taught us, or are we to strive for the self-control of your teaching? Wherein does your teaching differ from that of John?" Jesus answered: "John indeed taught you the way of righteousness in accordance with the light and laws of his fathers, and that was the religion of self-examination and self-denial. But I come with a new message of self- forgetfulness and self-control. I show to you the way of life as revealed to me by my Father in heaven.

143:2.3 (1609.4) "Verily, verily, I say to you, he who rules his own self is greater than he who captures a city. Self-mastery is the measure of man's moral nature and the indicator of his spiritual development. In the old order you fasted and prayed; as the new creature of the rebirth of the spirit, you are taught to believe and rejoice. In the Father's kingdom you are to become new creatures; old things are to pass away; behold I show you how all things are to become new. And by your love for one another you are to convince the world that you have passed from bondage to liberty, from death into life everlasting.

143:2.4 (1609.5) "By the old way you seek to suppress, obey, and conform to the rules of living; by the new way you are first transformed by the Spirit of Truth and thereby strengthened in your inner soul by the constant spiritual renewing of your mind, and so are you endowed with the power of the certain and joyous performance of the gracious, acceptable, and perfect will of God. Forget not—it is your personal faith in the exceedingly great and precious promises of God that ensures your becoming partakers of the divine nature. Thus by your faith and the spirit's transformation, you become in reality the temples of God, and his spirit actually dwells within you. If, then, the spirit dwells within you, you are no longer bondslaves of the flesh but free and liberated sons of the spirit. The new law of the spirit endows you with the liberty of self-mastery in place of the old law of the fear of self-bondage and the slavery of self-denial.

143:2.5 (1609.6) "Many times, when you have done evil, you have thought to charge up your acts to the influence of the evil one when in reality you have but been led astray by your own natural tendencies. Did not the Prophet Jeremiah long ago tell you that the human heart is deceitful above all things and sometimes even desperately wicked? How easy for you to become self-deceived and thereby fall into foolish fears, divers lusts, enslaving pleasures, malice, envy, and even vengeful hatred!

143:2.6 (1610.1) "Salvation is by the regeneration of the spirit and not by the self-righteous deeds of the flesh. You are justified by faith and fellowshipped by grace, not by fear and the self-denial of the flesh, albeit the Father's children who have been born of the spirit are ever and always masters of the self and all that pertains to the desires of the flesh. When you know that you are saved by faith, you have real peace with God. And all who follow in the way of this heavenly peace are destined to be sanctified to the eternal service of the ever-advancing sons of the eternal God.

Henceforth, it is not a duty but rather your exalted privilege to cleanse yourselves from all evils of mind and body while you seek for perfection in the love of God.

143:2.7 (1610.2) "Your sonship is grounded in faith, and you are to remain unmoved by fear. Your joy is born of trust in the divine word, and you shall not therefore be led to doubt the reality of the Father's love and mercy. It is the very goodness of God that leads men into true and genuine repentance. Your secret of the mastery of self is bound up with your faith in the indwelling spirit, which ever works by love. Even this saving faith you have not of yourselves; it also is the gift of God. And if you are the children of this living faith, you are no longer the bond slaves of self but rather the triumphant masters of yourselves, the liberated sons of God.

143:2.8 (1610.3) "If, then, my children, you are born of the spirit, you are forever delivered from the self-conscious bondage of a life of self-denial and watch-care over the desires of the flesh, and you are translated into the joyous kingdom of the spirit, whence you spontaneously show forth the fruits of the spirit in your daily lives; and the fruits of the spirit are the essence of the highest type of enjoyable and ennobling self-control, even the heights of terrestrial mortal attainment—true self-mastery."

Diversion and Relaxation

143:3.1 (1610.4) About this time a state of great nervous and emotional tension developed among the apostles and their immediate disciple associates. They had hardly become accustomed to living and working together. They were experiencing increasing difficulties in maintaining harmonious relations with John's disciples. The contact with the gentiles and the Samaritans was a great trial to these Jews. And besides all this, the recent utterances of Jesus had augmented their disturbed state of mind. Andrew was almost beside himself; he did not know what next to do, and so he went to the Master with his problems and perplexities. When Jesus had listened to the apostolic chief relate his troubles, he said: "Andrew, you cannot talk men out of their perplexities when they reach such a stage of involvement, and when so many persons with strong feelings are concerned. I cannot do what you ask of me—I will not participate in these personal social difficulties—but I will join you in the enjoyment of a three-day period of rest and relaxation. Go to your brethren and announce that all of you are to go with me up on Mount Sartaba, where I desire to rest for a day or two.

143:3.2 (1610.5) "Now you should go to each of your eleven brethren and talk with him privately, saying: 'The Master desires that we go apart with him for a season to rest and relax. Since we all have recently experienced much vexation of spirit and stress of mind, I suggest that no mention be made of our trials and troubles while on this holiday. Can I depend upon you to co-operate with me in this matter?' In this way privately and personally approach each of your brethren." And Andrew did as the Master had instructed him.

143:3.3 (1611.1) This was a marvelous occasion in the experience of each of them; they never forgot the day going up the mountain. Throughout the entire trip hardly a word was said about their troubles. Upon reaching the top of the mountain, Jesus seated them about him while he said: "My brethren, you must all learn the value of rest and the efficacy of relaxation. You must realize that the best method of solving some entangled problems is to forsake them for a time.

Then when you go back fresh from your rest or worship, you are able to attack your troubles with a clearer head and a steadier hand, not to mention a more resolute heart. Again, many times your problem is found to have shrunk in size and proportions while you have been resting your mind and body."

143:3.4 (1611.2) The next day Jesus assigned to each of the twelve a topic for discussion. The whole day was devoted to reminiscences and to talking over matters not related to their religious work. They were momentarily shocked when Jesus even neglected to give thanks—verbally—when he broke bread for their noontide lunch. This was the first time they had ever observed him to neglect such formalities.

143:3.5 (1611.3) When they went up the mountain, Andrew's head was full of problems. John was inordinately perplexed in his heart. James was grievously troubled in his soul. Matthew was hard pressed for funds inasmuch as they had been sojourning among the gentiles. Peter was overwrought and had recently been more temperamental than usual. Judas was suffering from a periodic attack of sensitiveness and selfishness. Simon was unusually upset in his efforts to reconcile his patriotism with the love of the brotherhood of man. Philip was more and more nonplused by the way things were going. Nathaniel had been less humorous since they had come in contact with the gentile populations, and Thomas was in the midst of a severe season of depression. Only the twins were normal and unperturbed. All of them were exceedingly perplexed about how to get along peaceably with John's disciples.

143:3.6 (1611.4) The third day when they started down the mountain and back to their camp, a great change had come over them. They had made the important discovery that many human perplexities are in reality nonexistent, that many pressing troubles are the creations of exaggerated fear and the offspring of augmented apprehension. They had learned that all such perplexities are best handled by being forsaken; by going off they had left such problems to solve themselves.

143:3.7 (1611.5) Their return from this holiday marked the beginning of a period of greatly improved relations with the followers of John. Many of the twelve really gave way to mirth when they noted the changed state of everybody's mind and observed the freedom from nervous irritability which had come to them as a result of their three days' vacation from the routine duties of life. There is always danger that monotony of human contact will greatly multiply perplexities and magnify difficulties.

143:3.8 (1611.6) Not many of the gentiles in the two Greek cities of Archelais and Phasaelis believed in the gospel, but the twelve apostles gained a valuable experience in this their first extensive work with exclusively gentile populations. On a Monday morning, about the middle of the month, Jesus said to Andrew: "We go into Samaria." And they set out at once for the city of Sychar, near Jacob's well.

The Jews and the Samaritans

143:4.1 (1612.1) For more than six hundred years the Jews of Judea, and later on those of Galilee also, had been at enmity with the Samaritans. This ill feeling between the Jews and the Samaritans came about in this way: About seven hundred years B.C., Sargon, king of Assyria, in subduing a revolt in central Palestine, carried away and into captivity over twenty-five thousand Jews of the northern kingdom of Israel and installed in their place an almost equal number of the descendants of the Cuthites, Sepharvites, and the Hamathites. Later on, Ashurbanipal sent still other colonies to dwell in Samaria.

143:4.2 (1612.2) The religious enmity between the Jews and the Samaritans dated from the return of the former from the Babylonian captivity, when the Samaritans worked to prevent the rebuilding of Jerusalem. Later they offended the Jews by extending friendly assistance to the armies of Alexander. In return for their friendship Alexander gave the Samaritans permission to build a temple on Mount Gerizim, where they worshiped Yahweh and their tribal gods and offered sacrifices much after the order of the temple services at Jerusalem. At least they continued this worship up to the time of the Maccabees, when John Hyrcanus destroyed their temple on Mount Gerizim. The Apostle Philip, in his labors for the Samaritans after the death of Jesus, held many meetings on the site of this old Samaritan temple.

143:4.3 (1612.3) The antagonisms between the Jews and the Samaritans were time-honored and historic; increasingly since the days of Alexander they had had no dealings with each other. The twelve apostles were not averse to preaching in the Greek and other gentile cities of the Decapolis and Syria, but it was a severe test of their loyalty to the Master when he said, "Let us go into Samaria." But in the year and more they had been with Jesus, they had developed a form of personal loyalty which transcended even their faith in his teachings and their prejudices against the Samaritans.

The Woman of Sychar

143:5.1 (1612.4) When the Master and the twelve arrived at Jacob's well, Jesus, being weary from the journey, tarried by the well while Philip took the apostles with him to assist in bringing food and tents from Sychar, for they were disposed to stay in this vicinity for a while. Peter and the Zebedee sons would have remained with Jesus, but he requested that they go with their brethren, saying: "Have no fear for me; these Samaritans will be friendly; only our brethren, the Jews, seek to harm us." And it was almost six o'clock on this summer's evening when Jesus sat down by the well to await the return of the apostles.

143:5.2 (1612.5) The water of Jacob's well was less mineral than that from the wells of Sychar and was therefore much valued for drinking purposes. Jesus was thirsty, but there was no way of getting water from the well. When, therefore, a woman of Sychar came up with her water pitcher and prepared to draw from the well, Jesus said to her, "Give me a drink." This woman of Samaria knew Jesus was a Jew by his appearance and dress, and she surmised that he was a Galilean Jew from his accent. Her name was Nalda and she was a comely creature. She was much surprised to have a Jewish man thus speak to her at the well and ask for water, for it was not deemed proper in those days for a self- respecting man to speak to a woman in public, much less for a Jew to converse with a Samaritan. Therefore Nalda asked Jesus, "How is it that you, being a Jew, ask for a drink of me, a Samaritan woman?" Jesus answered: "I have indeed asked you for a drink, but if you could only understand, you would ask me for a draught of the living water." Then said Nalda: "But, Sir, you have nothing to draw with, and the well is deep; whence, then, have you this living water? Are you greater than our father Jacob who gave us this well, and who drank thereof himself and his sons and his cattle also?"

143:5.3 (1613.1) Jesus replied: "Everyone who drinks of this water will thirst again, but whosoever drinks of the water of the living spirit shall never thirst. And this living water shall become in him a well of refreshment springing up even to eternal life." Nalda then said: "Give me this water that I thirst not, neither come all the way hither to draw. Besides, anything which a Samaritan woman could receive from such a commendable Jew would be a pleasure." *

143:5.4 (1613.2) Nalda did not know how to take Jesus' willingness to talk with her. She beheld in the Master's face the countenance of an upright and holy man, but she mistook friendliness for commonplace familiarity, and she misinterpreted his figure of speech as a form of making advances to her. And being a woman of lax morals, she was minded openly to become flirtatious, when Jesus, looking straight into her eyes, with a commanding voice said, "Woman, go get your husband and bring him hither." This command brought Nalda to her senses. She saw that she had misjudged the Master's kindness; she perceived that she had misconstrued his manner of speech. She was frightened; she began to realize that she stood in the presence of an unusual person, and groping about in her mind for a suitable reply, in great confusion, she said, "But, Sir, I cannot call my husband, for I have no husband." Then said Jesus: "You have spoken the truth, for, while you may have once had a husband, he with whom you are now living is not your husband. Better it would be if you would cease to trifle with my words and seek for the living water which I have this day offered you."

143:5.5 (1613.3) By this time Nalda was sobered, and her better self was awakened. She was not an immoral woman wholly by choice. She had been ruthlessly and unjustly cast aside by her husband and in dire straits had consented to live with a certain Greek as his wife, but without marriage. Nalda now felt greatly ashamed that she had so unthinkingly spoken to Jesus, and she most penitently addressed the Master, saying: "My Lord, I repent of my manner of speaking to you, for I perceive that you are a holy man or maybe a prophet." And she was just about to seek direct and personal help from the Master when she did what so many have done before and since—dodged the issue of personal salvation by turning to the discussion of theology and philosophy. She quickly turned the conversation from her own needs to a theological controversy. Pointing over to Mount Gerizim, she continued: "Our fathers worshiped on this mountain, and yet you would say that in Jerusalem is the place where men ought to worship; which, then, is the right place to worship God?"

143:5.6 (1613.4) Jesus perceived the attempt of the woman's soul to avoid direct and searching contact with its Maker, but he also saw that there was present in her soul a desire to know the better way of life. After all, there was in Nalda's heart a true thirst for the living water; therefore he dealt patiently with her, saying: "Woman, let me say to you that the day is soon coming when neither on this mountain nor in Jerusalem will you worship the Father. But now you worship that which you know not, a mixture of the religion of many pagan gods and gentile philosophies. The Jews at least know whom they worship; they have removed all confusion by concentrating their worship upon one God, Yahweh. But you should believe me when I say that the hour will soon come—even now is—when all sincere worshipers will worship the Father in spirit and in truth, for it is just such worshipers the Father seeks. God is spirit, and they who worship him must worship him in spirit and in truth. Your salvation comes not from knowing how others should worship or where but by receiving into your own heart this living water which I am offering you even now."

143:5.7 (1614.1) But Nalda would make one more effort to avoid the discussion of the embarrassing question of her personal life on earth and the status of her soul before God. Once more she resorted to questions of general religion, saying: "Yes, I know, Sir, that John has preached about the coming of the Converter, he who will be called the Deliverer, and that, when he shall come, he will declare to us all things"—and Jesus, interrupting Nalda, said with startling assurance, "I who speak to you am he."

143:5.8 (1614.2) This was the first direct, positive, and undisguised pronouncement of his divine nature and sonship which Jesus had made on earth; and it was made to a woman, a Samaritan woman, and a woman of questionable character in the eyes of men up to this moment, but a woman whom the divine eye beheld as having been sinned against more than as sinning of her own desire and as now being a human soul who desired salvation, desired it sincerely and wholeheartedly, and that was enough.

143:5.9 (1614.3) As Nalda was about to voice her real and personal longing for better things and a more noble way of living, just as she was ready to speak the real desire of her heart, the twelve apostles returned from Sychar, and coming upon this scene of Jesus' talking so intimately with this woman—this Samaritan woman, and alone—they were more than astonished. They quickly deposited their supplies and drew aside, no man daring to reprove him, while Jesus said to Nalda: "Woman, go your way; God has forgiven you. Henceforth you will live a new life. You have received the living water, and a new joy will spring up within your soul, and you shall become a daughter of the Most High." And the woman, perceiving the disapproval of the apostles, left her waterpot and fled to the city.

143:5.10 (1614.4) As she entered the city, she proclaimed to everyone she met: "Go out to Jacob's well and go quickly, for there you will see a man who told me all I ever did. Can this be the Converter?" And ere the sun went down, a great crowd had assembled at Jacob's well to hear Jesus. And the Master talked to them more about the water of life, the gift of the indwelling spirit.

143:5.11 (1614.5) The apostles never ceased to be shocked by Jesus' willingness to talk with women, women of questionable character, even immoral women. It was very difficult for Jesus to teach his apostles that women, even so- called immoral women, have souls which can choose God as their Father, thereby becoming daughters of God and candidates for life everlasting. Even nineteen centuries later many show the same unwillingness to grasp the Master's teachings. Even the Christian religion has been persistently built up around the fact of the death of Christ instead of around the truth of his life. The world should be more concerned with his happy and God-revealing life than with his tragic and sorrowful death.

143:5.12 (1614.6) Nalda told this entire story to the Apostle John the next day, but he never revealed it fully to the other apostles, and Jesus did not speak of it in detail to the twelve.

143:5.13 (1615.1) Nalda told John that Jesus had told her "all I ever did." John many times wanted to ask Jesus about this visit with Nalda, but he never did. Jesus told her only one thing about herself, but his look into her eyes and the manner of his dealing with her had so brought all of her checkered life in panoramic review before her mind in a moment of time that she associated all of this self-revelation of her past life with the look and the word of the Master. Jesus never told her she had had five husbands. She had lived with four different men since her husband cast her aside, and this, with all her past, came up so vividly in her mind at the moment when she realized Jesus was a man of God that she subsequently repeated to John that Jesus had really told her all about herself.

The Samaritan Revival

143:6.1 (1615.2) On the evening that Nalda drew the crowd out from Sychar to see Jesus, the twelve had just returned with food, and they besought Jesus to eat with them instead of talking to the people, for they had been without food all day and were hungry. But Jesus knew that darkness would soon be upon them; so he persisted in his determination to talk to the people before he sent them away. When Andrew sought to persuade him to eat a bite before speaking to the crowd, Jesus said, "I have meat to eat that you do not know about." When the apostles heard this, they said among themselves: "Has any man brought him aught to eat? Can it be that the woman gave him food as well as drink?" When Jesus heard them talking among themselves, before he spoke to the people, he turned aside and said to the twelve: "My meat is to do the will of Him who sent me and to accomplish His work. You should no longer say it is such and such a time until the harvest. Behold these people coming out from a Samaritan city to hear us; I tell you the fields are already white for the harvest. He who reaps receives wages and gathers this fruit to eternal life; consequently the sowers and the reapers rejoice together. For herein is the saying true: 'One sows and another reaps.' I am now sending you to reap that whereon you have not labored; others have labored, and you are about to enter into their labor." This he said in reference to the preaching of John the Baptist.

143:6.2 (1615.3) Jesus and the apostles went into Sychar and preached two days before they established their camp on Mount Gerizim. And many of the dwellers in Sychar believed the gospel and made request for baptism, but the apostles of Jesus did not yet baptize.

143:6.3 (1615.4) The first night of the camp on Mount Gerizim the apostles expected that Jesus would rebuke them for their attitude toward the woman at Jacob's well, but he made no reference to the matter. Instead he gave them that memorable talk on "The realities which are central in the kingdom of God." In any religion it is very easy to allow values to become disproportionate and to permit facts to occupy the place of truth in one's theology. The fact of the cross became the very center of subsequent Christianity; but it is not the central truth of the religion which may be derived from the life and teachings of Jesus of Nazareth.

143:6.4 (1615.5) The theme of Jesus' teaching on Mount Gerizim was: That he wants all men to see God as a Father-friend just as he (Jesus) is a brother-friend. And again and again he impressed upon them that love is the greatest relationship in the world—in the universe—just as truth is the greatest pronouncement of the observation of these divine relationships.

143:6.5 (1616.1) Jesus declared himself so fully to the Samaritans because he could safely do so, and because he knew that he would not again visit the heart of Samaria to preach the gospel of the kingdom.

143:6.6 (1616.2) Jesus and the twelve camped on Mount Gerizim until the end of August. They preached the good news of the kingdom—the fatherhood of God—to the Samaritans in the cities by day and spent the nights at the camp. The work which Jesus and the twelve did in these Samaritan cities yielded many souls for the kingdom and did much to prepare the way for the marvelous work of Philip in these regions after Jesus' death and resurrection, subsequent to the dispersion of the apostles to the ends of the earth by the bitter persecution of believers at Jerusalem.

Teachings About Prayer and Worship

143:7.1 (1616.3) At the evening conferences on Mount Gerizim, Jesus taught many great truths, and in particular he laid emphasis on the following:

143:7.2 (1616.4) True religion is the act of an individual soul in its self-conscious relations with the Creator; organized religion is man's attempt to socialize the worship of individual religionists.

143:7.3 (1616.5) Worship—contemplation of the spiritual—must alternate with service, contact with material reality. Work should alternate with play; religion should be balanced by humor. Profound philosophy should be relieved by rhythmic poetry. The strain of living—the time tension of personality—should be relaxed by the restfulness of worship. The feelings of insecurity arising from the fear of personality isolation in the universe should be antidoted by the faith contemplation of the Father and by the attempted realization of the Supreme.

143:7.4 (1616.6) Prayer is designed to make man less thinking but more realizing; it is not designed to increase knowledge but rather to expand insight.

143:7.5 (1616.7) Worship is intended to anticipate the better life ahead and then to reflect these new spiritual significances back onto the life which now is. Prayer is spiritually sustaining, but worship is divinely creative.

143:7.6 (1616.8) Worship is the technique of looking to the One for the inspiration of service to the many. Worship is the yardstick which measures the extent of the soul's detachment from the material universe and its simultaneous and secure attachment to the spiritual realities of all creation.

143:7.7 (1616.9) Prayer is self-reminding—sublime thinking; worship is self-forgetting—superthinking. Worship is effortless attention, true and ideal soul rest, a form of restful spiritual exertion.

143:7.8 (1616.10) Worship is the act of a part identifying itself with the Whole; the finite with the Infinite; the son with the Father; time in the act of striking step with eternity. Worship is the act of the son's personal communion with the divine Father, the assumption of refreshing, creative, fraternal, and romantic attitudes by the human soul-spirit.

143:7.9 (1616.11) Although the apostles grasped only a few of his teachings at the camp, other worlds did, and other generations on earth will.

Paper 144

At Gilboa and in the Decapolis

144:0.1 (1617.1) SEPTEMBER and October were spent in retirement at a secluded camp upon the slopes of Mount Gilboa. The month of September Jesus spent here alone with his apostles, teaching and instructing them in the truths of the kingdom.

144:0.2 (1617.2) There were a number of reasons why Jesus and his apostles were in retirement at this time on the borders of Samaria and the Decapolis. The Jerusalem religious rulers were very antagonistic; Herod Antipas still held John in prison,

fearing either to release or execute him, while he continued to entertain suspicions that John and Jesus were in some way associated. These conditions made it unwise to plan for aggressive work in either Judea or Galilee. There was a third reason: the slowly augmenting tension between the leaders of John's disciples and the apostles of Jesus, which grew worse with the increasing number of believers.

144:0.3 (1617.3) Jesus knew that the days of the preliminary work of teaching and preaching were about over, that the next move involved the beginning of the full and final effort of his life on earth, and he did not wish the launching of this undertaking to be in any manner either trying or embarrassing to John the Baptist. Jesus had therefore decided to spend some time in retirement rehearsing his apostles and then to do some quiet work in the cities of the Decapolis until John should be either executed or released to join them in a united effort.

The Gilboa Encampment

144:1.1 (1617.4) As time passed, the twelve became more devoted to Jesus and increasingly committed to the work of the kingdom. Their devotion was in large part a matter of personal loyalty. They did not grasp his many-sided teaching; they did not fully comprehend the nature of Jesus or the significance of his bestowal on earth.

144:1.2 (1617.5) Jesus made it plain to his apostles that they were in retirement for three reasons: 144:1.3 (1617.6) 1. To confirm their understanding of, and faith in, the gospel of the kingdom. 144:1.4 (1617.7) 2. To allow opposition to their work in both Judea and Galilee to quiet down. 144:1.5 (1617.8) 3. To await the fate of John the Baptist.

144:1.6 (1617.9) While tarrying on Gilboa, Jesus told the twelve much about his early life and his experiences on Mount Hermon; he also revealed something of what happened in the hills during the forty days immediately after his baptism. And he directly charged them that they should tell no man about these experiences until after he had returned to the Father.

144:1.7 (1618.1) During these September weeks they rested, visited, recounted their experiences since Jesus first called them to service, and engaged in an earnest effort to co-ordinate what the Master had so far taught them. In a measure they all sensed that this would be their last opportunity for prolonged rest. They realized that their next public effort in either Judea or Galilee would mark the beginning of the final proclamation of the coming kingdom, but they had little or no settled idea as to what the kingdom would be when it came. John and Andrew thought the kingdom had already come; Peter and James believed that it was yet to come; Nathaniel and Thomas frankly confessed they were puzzled; Matthew, Philip, and Simon Zelotes were uncertain and confused; the twins were blissfully ignorant of the controversy; and Judas Iscariot was silent, noncommittal.

144:1.8 (1618.2) Much of this time Jesus was alone on the mountain near the camp. Occasionally he took with him Peter, James, or John, but more often he went off to pray or commune alone. Subsequent to the baptism of Jesus and the forty days in the Perean hills, it is hardly proper to speak of these seasons of communion with his Father as prayer, nor is it consistent to speak of Jesus as worshiping, but it is altogether correct to allude to these seasons as personal communion with his Father.

144:1.9 (1618.3) The central theme of the discussions throughout the entire month of September was prayer and worship. After they had discussed worship for some days, Jesus finally delivered his memorable discourse on prayer in answer to Thomas's request: "Master, teach us how to pray."

144:1.10 (1618.4) John had taught his disciples a prayer, a prayer for salvation in the coming kingdom. Although Jesus never forbade his followers to use

John's form of prayer, the apostles very early perceived that their Master did not fully approve of the practice of uttering set and formal prayers. Nevertheless, believers constantly requested to be taught how to pray. The twelve longed to know what form of petition Jesus would approve. And it was chiefly because of this need for some simple petition for the common people that Jesus at this time consented, in answer to Thomas's request, to teach them a suggestive form of prayer. Jesus gave this lesson one afternoon in the third week of their sojourn on Mount Gilboa.

The Discourse on Prayer

144:2.1 (1618.5) "John indeed taught you a simple form of prayer: 'O Father, cleanse us from sin, show us your glory, reveal your love, and let your spirit sanctify our hearts forevermore, Amen!' He taught this prayer that you might have something to teach the multitude. He did not intend that you should use such a set and formal petition as the expression of your own souls in prayer.

144:2.2 (1618.6) "Prayer is entirely a personal and spontaneous expression of the attitude of the soul toward the spirit; prayer should be the communion of sonship and the expression of fellowship. Prayer, when indited by the spirit, leads to co-operative spiritual progress. The ideal prayer is a form of spiritual communion which leads to intelligent worship.

True praying is the sincere attitude of reaching heavenward for the attainment of your ideals.

144:2.3 (1619.1) "Prayer is the breath of the soul and should lead you to be persistent in your attempt to ascertain the Father's will. If any one of you has a neighbor, and you go to him at midnight and say: 'Friend, lend me three loaves, for a friend of mine on a journey has come to see me, and I have nothing to set before him'; and if your neighbor answers, 'Trouble me not, for the door is now shut and the children and I are in bed; therefore I cannot rise and give you bread,' you will persist, explaining that your friend hungers, and that you have no food to offer him. I say to you, though your neighbor will not rise and give you bread because he is your friend, yet because of your importunity he will get up and give you as many loaves as you need. If, then, persistence will win favors even from mortal man, how much more will your persistence in the spirit win the bread of life for you from the willing hands of the Father in heaven. Again I say to you: Ask and it shall be given you; seek and you shall find; knock and it shall be opened to you. For every one who asks receives; he who seeks finds; and to him who knocks the door of salvation will be opened.

144:2.4 (1619.2) "Which of you who is a father, if his son asks unwisely, would hesitate to give in accordance with parental wisdom rather than in the terms of the son's faulty petition? If the child needs a loaf, will you give him a stone just because he unwisely asks for it? If your son needs a fish, will you give him a watersnake just because it may chance to come up in the net with the fish and the child foolishly asks for the serpent? If you, then, being mortal and finite, know how to answer prayer and give good and appropriate gifts to your children, how much more shall your heavenly Father give the spirit and many additional blessings to those who ask him? Men ought always to pray and not become discouraged.

144:2.5 (1619.3) "Let me tell you the story of a certain judge who lived in a wicked city. This judge feared not God nor had respect for man. Now there was a needy widow in that city who came repeatedly to this unjust judge, saying, 'Protect me from my adversary.' For some time he would not give ear to her, but presently he said to himself: 'Though I fear not God nor have regard for man, yet because this widow ceases not to trouble me, I will vindicate her lest she wear me out by her continual coming.' These stories I tell you to encourage you to persist in praying and not to intimate that your petitions will change the just and righteous Father above.

Your persistence, however, is not to win favor with God but to change your earth attitude and to enlarge your soul's capacity for spirit receptivity.

144:2.6 (1619.4) "But when you pray, you exercise so little faith. Genuine faith will remove mountains of material difficulty which may chance to lie in the path of soul expansion and spiritual progress."

The Believer's Prayer

144:3.1 (1619.5) But the apostles were not yet satisfied; they desired Jesus to give them a model prayer which they could teach the new disciples. After listening to this discourse on prayer, James Zebedee said: "Very good, Master, but we do not desire a form of prayer for ourselves so much as for the newer believers who so frequently beseech us, 'Teach us how acceptably to pray to the Father in heaven.'"

144:3.2 (1619.6) When James had finished speaking, Jesus said: "If, then, you still desire such a prayer, I would present the one which I taught my brothers and sisters in Nazareth":

144:3.3 (1620.1) Our Father who is in heaven,
144:3.4 (1620.2) Hallowed be your name.
144:3.5 (1620.3) Your kingdom come; your will be done
144:3.6 (1620.4) On earth as it is in heaven.
144:3.7 (1620.5) Give us this day our bread for tomorrow; 144:3.8 (1620.6) Refresh our souls with the water of life. 144:3.9 (1620.7) And forgive us every one our debts * 144:3.10 (1620.8) As we also have forgiven our debtors. 144:3.11 (1620.9) Save us in temptation, deliver us from evil,
144:3.12 (1620.10) And increasingly make us perfect like yourself.
144:3.13 (1620.11) It is not strange that the apostles desired Jesus to teach them a model prayer for believers. John the Baptist had taught his followers several

prayers; all great teachers had formulated prayers for their pupils. The religious teachers of the Jews had some twenty-five or thirty set prayers which they recited in the synagogues and even on the street corners. Jesus was particularly averse to praying in public. Up to this time the twelve had heard him pray only a few times. They observed him spending entire nights at prayer or worship, and they were very curious to know the manner or form of his petitions. They were really hard pressed to know what to answer the multitudes when they asked to be taught how to pray as John had taught his disciples.

144:3.14 (1620.12) Jesus taught the twelve always to pray in secret; to go off by themselves amidst the quiet surroundings of nature or to go in their rooms and shut the doors when they engaged in prayer.

144:3.15 (1620.13) After Jesus' death and ascension to the Father it became the practice of many believers to finish this so- called Lord's prayer by the addition of—"In the name of the Lord Jesus Christ." Still later on, two lines were lost in copying, and there was added to this prayer an extra clause, reading: "For yours is the kingdom and the power and the glory, forevermore."

144:3.16 (1620.14) Jesus gave the apostles the prayer in collective form as they had prayed it in the Nazareth home. He never taught a formal personal prayer, only group, family, or social petitions. And he never volunteered to do that.

144:3.17 (1620.15) Jesus taught that effective prayer must be:
144:3.18 (1620.16) 1. Unselfish—not alone for oneself.
144:3.19 (1620.17) 2. Believing—according to faith.
144:3.20 (1620.18) 3. Sincere—honest of heart.
144:3.21 (1620.19) 4. Intelligent—according to light.
144:3.22 (1620.20) 5. Trustful—in submission to the Father's all-wise will.
144:3.23 (1620.21) When Jesus spent whole nights on the mountain in prayer, it was mainly for his disciples, particularly for the twelve. The Master prayed very little for himself, although he engaged in much worship of the nature of understanding communion with his Paradise Father.

More About Prayer

144:4.1 (1620.22) For days after the discourse on prayer the apostles continued to ask the Master questions regarding this all-important and worshipful practice. Jesus' instruction to the apostles during these days, regarding prayer and worship, may be summarized and restated in modern phraseology as follows:

144:4.2 (1621.1) The earnest and longing repetition of any petition, when such a prayer is the sincere expression of a child of God and is uttered in faith, no matter how ill-advised or impossible of direct answer, never fails to expand the soul's capacity for spiritual receptivity.

144:4.3 (1621.2) In all praying, remember that sonship is a gift. No child has aught to do with earning the status of son or daughter. The earth child comes into being by the will of its parents. Even so, the child of God comes into grace and the new life of the spirit by the will of the Father in heaven. Therefore must the kingdom of heaven—divine sonship—be received as by a little child. You earn righteousness—progressive character development—but you receive sonship by grace and through faith.

144:4.4 (1621.3) Prayer led Jesus up to the super communion of his soul with the Supreme Rulers of the universe of universes. Prayer will lead the mortals of earth up to the communion of true worship. The soul's spiritual capacity for receptivity determines the quantity of heavenly blessings which can be personally appropriated and consciously realized as an answer to prayer.

144:4.5 (1621.4) Prayer and its associated worship is a technique of detachment from the daily routine of life, from the monotonous grind of material existence. It is an avenue of approach to spiritualized self-realization and individuality of intellectual and religious attainment.

144:4.6 (1621.5) Prayer is an antidote for harmful introspection. At least, prayer as the Master taught it is such a beneficent ministry to the soul. Jesus consistently employed the beneficial influence of praying for one's fellows. The Master usually prayed in the plural, not in the singular. Only in the great crises of his earth life did Jesus ever pray for himself.

144:4.7 (1621.6) Prayer is the breath of the spirit life in the midst of the material civilization of the races of mankind.

Worship is salvation for the pleasure-seeking generations of mortals.

144:4.8 (1621.7) As prayer may be likened to recharging the spiritual batteries of the soul, so worship may be compared to the act of tuning in the soul to catch the universe broadcasts of the infinite spirit of the Universal Father.

144:4.9 (1621.8) Prayer is the sincere and longing look of the child to its spirit Father; it is a psychologic process of exchanging the human will for the divine will. Prayer is a part of the divine plan for making over that which is into that which ought to be.

144:4.10 (1621.9) One of the reasons why Peter, James, and John, who so often accompanied Jesus on his long night vigils, never heard Jesus pray, was because their Master so rarely uttered his prayers as spoken words. Practically all of Jesus' praying was done in the spirit and in the heart—silently.

144:4.11 (1621.10) Of all the apostles, Peter and James came the nearest to comprehending the Master's teaching about prayer and worship.

Other Forms of Prayer

144:5.1 (1621.11) From time to time, during the remainder of Jesus' sojourn on earth, he brought to the notice of the apostles several additional forms of prayer, but he did this only in illustration of other matters, and he enjoined that these "parable prayers" should not be taught to the multitudes. Many of them were from other inhabited planets, but this fact Jesus did not reveal to the twelve. Among these prayers were the following:

144:5.2 (1622.1) Our Father in whom consist the universe realms,
144:5.3 (1622.2) Uplifted be your name and all-glorious your character. 144:5.4 (1622.3) Your presence encompasses us, and your glory is manifested 144:5.5 (1622.4) Imperfectly through us as it is in perfection shown on high. 144:5.6 (1622.5) Give us this day the vivifying forces of light,
144:5.7 (1622.6) And let us not stray into the evil bypaths of our imagination, 144:5.8 (1622.7) For yours is the glorious indwelling, the everlasting power, 144:5.9 (1622.8) And to us, the eternal gift of the infinite love of your Son.
144:5.10 (1622.9) Even so, and everlastingly true.

~ ~ ~ ~ ~ *

144:5.12 (1622.10) Our creative Parent, who is in the center of the universe, 144:5.13 (1622.11) Bestow upon us your nature and give to us your character. 144:5.14 (1622.12) Make us sons and daughters of yours by grace
144:5.15 (1622.13) And glorify your name through our eternal achievement.
144:5.16 (1622.14) Your adjusting and controlling spirit give to live and dwell within us 144:5.17 (1622.15) That we may do your will on this sphere as angels do your bidding in light. 144:5.18 (1622.16) Sustain us this day in our progress along the path of truth.
144:5.19 (1622.17) Deliver us from inertia, evil, and all sinful transgression.

144:5.20 (1622.18) Be patient with us as we show loving-kindness to our fellows. 144:5.21 (1622.19) Shed abroad the spirit of your mercy in our creature hearts.

144:5.22 (1622.20) Lead us by your own hand, step by step, through the uncertain maze of life, 144:5.23 (1622.21) And when our end shall come, receive into your own bosom our faithful spirits. 144:5.24 (1622.22) Even so, not our desires but your will be done.

~ ~ ~ ~ ~ *

144:5.26 (1622.23) Our perfect and righteous heavenly Father,

144:5.27 (1622.24) This day guide and direct our journey.

144:5.28 (1622.25) Sanctify our steps and co-ordinate our thoughts.

144:5.29 (1622.26) Ever lead us in the ways of eternal progress. 144:5.30 (1622.27) Fill us with wisdom to the fullness of power 144:5.31 (1622.28) And vitalize us with your infinite energy.

144:5.32 (1622.29) Inspire us with the divine consciousness of 144:5.33 (1622.30) The presence and guidance of the seraphic hosts. 144:5.34 (1622.31) Guide us ever upward in the pathway of light; 144:5.35 (1622.32) Justify us fully in the day of the great judgment. 144:5.36 (1622.33) Make us like yourself in eternal glory

144:5.37 (1622.34) And receive us into your endless service on high.

~ ~ ~ ~ ~ *

144:5.39 (1622.35) Our Father who is in the mystery,

144:5.40 (1622.36) Reveal to us your holy character.

144:5.41 (1622.37) Give your children on earth this day 144:5.42 (1622.38) To see the way, the light, and the truth. 144:5.43 (1622.39) Show us the pathway of eternal progress 144:5.441 (1622.40) And give us the will to walk therein.

144:5.45 (1622.41) Establish within us your divine kingship

144:5.46 (1622.42) And thereby bestow upon us the full mastery of self. 144:5.47 (1622.43) Let us not stray into paths of darkness and death; 144:5.48

(1622.44) Lead us everlastingly beside the waters of life.

144:5.49 (1622.45) Hear these our prayers for your own sake;

144:5.50 (1622.46) Be pleased to make us more and more like yourself.

144:5.51 (1623.1) At the end, for the sake of the divine Son,

144:5.52 (1623.2) Receive us into the eternal arms.

144:5.53 (1623.3) Even so, not our will but yours be done.

~ ~ ~ ~ ~ *

144:5.55 (1623.4) Glorious Father and Mother, in one parent combined,

144:5.56 (1623.5) Loyal would we be to your divine nature. 144:5.57 (1623.6) Your own self to live again in and through us 144:5.58 (1623.7) By the gift and bestowal of your divine spirit, 144:5.59 (1623.8) Thus reproducing you imperfectly in this sphere

144:5.60 (1623.9) As you are perfectly and majestically shown on high.

144:5.61 (1623.10) Give us day by day your sweet ministry of brotherhood

144:5.62 (1623.11) And lead us moment by moment in the pathway of loving service.

144:5.63 (1623.12) Be you ever and unfailingly patient with us

144:5.64 (1623.13) Even as we show forth your patience to our children. 144:5.65 (1623.14) Give us the divine wisdom that does all things well 144:5.66 (1623.15)

And the infinite love that is gracious to every creature.

144:5.67 (1623.16) Bestow upon us your patience and loving-kindness

144:5.68 (1623.17) That our charity may enfold the weak of the realm.

144:5.69 (1623.18) And when our career is finished, make it an honor to your name,

144:5.70 (1623.19) A pleasure to your good spirit, and a satisfaction to our soul helpers.

144:5.71 (1623.20) Not as we wish, our loving Father, but as you desire the eternal good of your mortal children,

144:5.72 (1623.21) Even so may it be.

~ ~ ~ ~ ~ *

144:5.74 (1623.22) Our all-faithful Source and all-powerful Center,

144:5.75 (1623.23) Reverent and holy be the name of your all-gracious Son.

144:5.76 (1623.24) Your bounties and your blessings have descended upon us,

144:5.77 (1623.25) Thus empowering us to perform your will and execute your bidding. 144:5.78 (1623.26) Give us moment by moment the sustenance of the tree of life; 144:5.79 (1623.27) Refresh us day by day with the living waters of the river thereof.

144:5.80 (1623.28) Step by step lead us out of darkness and into the divine light. 144:5.81 (1623.29) Renew our minds by the transformations of the indwelling spirit, 144:5.82 (1623.30) And when the mortal end shall finally come upon us,

144:5.83 (1623.31) Receive us to yourself and send us forth in eternity.

144:5.84 (1623.32) Crown us with celestial diadems of fruitful service,

144:5.85 (1623.33) And we shall glorify the Father, the Son, and the Holy Influence.

144:5.86 (1623.34) Even so, throughout a universe without end.

~ ~ ~ ~ ~ *

144:5.88 (1623.35) Our Father who dwells in the secret places of the universe,

144:5.89 (1623.36) Honored be your name, reverenced your mercy, and respected your judgment.

144:5.90 (1623.37) Let the sun of righteousness shine upon us at noontime,

144:5.91 (1623.38) While we beseech you to guide our wayward steps in the twilight.

144:5.92 (1623.39) Lead us by the hand in the ways of your own choosing

144:5.93 (1623.40) And forsake us not when the path is hard and the hours are dark.

144:5.94 (1623.41) Forget us not as we so often neglect and forget you. 144:5.95 (1623.42) But be you merciful and love us as we desire to love you. 144:5.96 (1623.43) Look down upon us in kindness and forgive us in mercy 144:5.97 (1623.44) As we in justice forgive those who distress and injure us. 144:5.98 (1624.1) May the love, devotion, and bestowal of the majestic Son

144:5.99 (1624.2) Make available life everlasting with your endless mercy and love. 144:5.100 (1624.3) May the God of universes bestow upon us the full measure of his spirit; 144:5.101 (1624.4) Give us grace to yield to the leading of this spirit.

144:5.102 (1624.5) By the loving ministry of devoted seraphic hosts 144:5.103 (1624.6) May the Son guide and lead us to the end of the age. 144:5.104 (1624.7) Make us ever and increasingly like yourself

144:5.105 (1624.8) And at our end receive us into the eternal Paradise embrace.

144:5.106 (1624.9) Even so, in the name of the bestowal Son

144:5.107 (1624.10) And for the honor and glory of the Supreme Father.

144:5.108 (1624.11) Though the apostles were not at liberty to present these prayer lessons in their public teachings, they profited much from all of these revelations in their personal religious experiences. Jesus utilized these and other prayer models as illustrations in connection with the intimate instruction of the twelve, and specific permission has been granted for transcribing these seven specimen prayers into this record.

Conference with John's Apostles

144:6.1 (1624.12) Around the first of October, Philip and some of his fellow apostles were in a near-by village buying food when they met some of the apostles of John the Baptist. As a result of this chance meeting in the market place there came about a three weeks' conference at the Gilboa camp between the apostles of Jesus and the apostles of John, for John had recently appointed twelve of his leaders to be apostles, following the precedent of Jesus. John had done this in response to the urging of Abner, the chief of his loyal supporters. Jesus was present at the Gilboa camp throughout the first week of this joint conference but absented himself the last two weeks.

144:6.2 (1624.13) By the beginning of the second week of this month, Abner had assembled all of his associates at the Gilboa camp and was prepared to go into council with the apostles of Jesus. For three weeks these twenty-four men were in session three times a day and for six days each week. The first week Jesus mingled with them between their forenoon, afternoon, and evening sessions. They wanted the Master to meet with them and preside over their joint deliberations, but he steadfastly refused to participate in their discussions, though he did consent to speak to them on three occasions. These talks by Jesus to the twenty-four were on sympathy, co-operation, and tolerance.

144:6.3 (1624.14) Andrew and Abner alternated in presiding over these joint meetings of the two apostolic groups. These men had many difficulties to discuss and numerous problems to solve. Again and again would they take their troubles to Jesus, only to hear him say: "I am concerned only with your personal and purely religious problems. I am the representative of the Father to the individual, not to the group. If you are in personal difficulty in your relations with God, come to me, and I will hear you and counsel you in the solution of your problem. But when you enter upon the co- ordination of divergent human interpretations of religious questions and upon the socialization of religion, you are destined to solve all such problems by your own decisions. Albeit, I am ever sympathetic and always interested, and when you arrive at your conclusions touching these matters of nonspiritual import, provided you are all agreed, then I pledge in advance my full approval and hearty co-operation. And now, in order to leave you unhampered in your deliberations, I am leaving you for two weeks. Be not anxious about me, for I will return to you. I will be about my Father's business, for we have other realms besides this one."

144:6.4 (1625.1) After thus speaking, Jesus went down the mountainside, and they saw him no more for two full weeks. And they never knew where he went or what he did during these days. It was some time before the twenty-four could settle down to the serious consideration of their problems, they were so disconcerted by the absence of the Master.

However, within a week they were again in the heart of their discussions, and they could not go to Jesus for help.

144:6.5 (1625.2) The first item the group agreed upon was the adoption of the prayer which Jesus had so recently taught them. It was unanimously voted to accept this prayer as the one to be taught believers by both groups of apostles.

144:6.6 (1625.3) They next decided that, as long as John lived, whether in prison or out, both groups of twelve apostles would go on with their work, and that joint meetings for one week would be held every three months at places to be agreed upon from time to time.

144:6.7 (1625.4) But the most serious of all their problems was the question of baptism. Their difficulties were all the more aggravated because Jesus had refused to make any pronouncement upon the subject. They finally agreed: As long as John lived, or until they might jointly modify this decision, only the apostles of John would baptize believers, and only the apostles of Jesus would finally instruct the new disciples. Accordingly, from that time until after the death of John, two of the apostles of John accompanied Jesus and his apostles to baptize believers, for the joint council had unanimously voted that baptism was to become the initial step in the outward alliance with the affairs of the kingdom.

144:6.8 (1625.5) It was next agreed, in case of the death of John, that the apostles of John would present themselves to Jesus and become subject to his direction, and that they would baptize no more unless authorized by Jesus or his apostles.

144:6.9 (1625.6) And then was it voted that, in case of John's death, the apostles of Jesus would begin to baptize with water as the emblem of the baptism of the divine Spirit. As to whether or not repentance should be attached to the preaching of baptism was left optional; no decision was made binding upon the group. John's apostles preached, "Repent and be baptized." Jesus' apostles proclaimed, "Believe and be baptized."

144:6.10 (1625.7) And this is the story of the first attempt of Jesus' followers to co-ordinate divergent efforts, compose differences of opinion, organize group undertakings, legislate on outward observances, and socialize personal religious practices.

144:6.11 (1625.8) Many other minor matters were considered and their solutions unanimously agreed upon. These twenty- four men had a truly remarkable experience these two weeks when they were compelled to face problems and compose difficulties without Jesus. They learned to differ, to debate, to contend, to pray, and to compromise, and throughout it all to remain sympathetic with the other person's viewpoint and to maintain at least some degree of tolerance for his honest opinions.

144:6.12 (1625.9) On the afternoon of their final discussion of financial questions, Jesus returned, heard of their deliberations, listened to their decisions, and said: "These, then, are your conclusions, and I shall help you each to carry out the spirit of your united decisions."

144:6.13 (1626.1) Two months and a half from this time John was executed, and throughout this period the apostles of John remained with Jesus and the twelve. They all worked together and baptized believers during this season of labor in the cities of the Decapolis. The Gilboa camp was broken up on November 2, A.D. 27.

In the Decapolis Cities

144:7.1 (1626.2) Throughout the months of November and December, Jesus and the twenty-four worked quietly in the Greek cities of the Decapolis, chiefly in Scythopolis, Gerasa, Abila, and Gadara. This was really the end of that preliminary period of taking over John's work and organization. Always does the socialized religion of a new revelation pay the price of compromise with the established forms and usages of the preceding religion which it seeks to salvage. Baptism was the price which the followers of Jesus paid in order to carry with them, as a socialized religious group, the followers of John the Baptist. John's followers, in joining Jesus' followers, gave up just about everything except water baptism.

144:7.2 (1626.3) Jesus did little public teaching on this mission to the cities of the Decapolis. He spent considerable time teaching the twenty-four and had many special sessions with John's twelve apostles. In time they became more understanding as to why Jesus did not go to visit John in prison, and why he made no effort to secure his release. But they never could understand why Jesus did no marvelous works, why he refused to produce outward signs of his divine authority. Before coming to the Gilboa camp, they had believed in Jesus mostly because of John's testimony, but soon they were beginning to believe as a result of their own contact with the Master and his teachings.

144:7.3 (1626.4) For these two months the group worked most of the time in pairs, one of Jesus' apostles going out with one of John's. The apostle of John baptized, the apostle of Jesus instructed, while they both preached the gospel of the kingdom as they understood it. And they won many souls among these gentiles and apostate Jews.

144:7.4 (1626.5) Abner, the chief of John's apostles, became a devout believer in Jesus and was later on made the head of a group of seventy teachers whom the

Master commissioned to preach the gospel.

In Camp Near Pella

144:8.1 (1626.6) The latter part of December they all went over near the Jordan, close by Pella, where they again began to teach and preach. Both Jews and gentiles came to this camp to hear the gospel. It was while Jesus was teaching the multitude one afternoon that some of John's special friends brought the Master the last message which he ever had from the Baptist.

144:8.2 (1626.7) John had now been in prison a year and a half, and most of this time Jesus had labored very quietly; so it was not strange that John should be led to wonder about the kingdom. John's friends interrupted Jesus' teaching to say to him: "John the Baptist has sent us to ask—are you truly the Deliverer, or shall we look for another?"

144:8.3 (1626.8) Jesus paused to say to John's friends: "Go back and tell John that he is not forgotten. Tell him what you have seen and heard, that the poor have good tidings preached to them." And when Jesus had spoken further to the messengers of John, he turned again to the multitude and said: "Do not think that John doubts the gospel of the kingdom. He makes inquiry only to assure his disciples who are also my disciples. John is no weakling. Let me ask you who heard John preach before Herod put him in prison: What did you behold in John—a reed shaken with the wind? A man of changeable moods and clothed in soft raiment? As a rule they who are gorgeously apparelled and who live delicately are in kings' courts and in the mansions of the rich. But what did you see when you beheld John? A prophet? Yes, I say to you, and much more than a prophet. Of John it was written: 'Behold, I send my messenger before your face; he shall prepare the way before you.'

144:8.4 (1627.1) "Verily, verily, I say to you, among those born of women there has not arisen a greater than John the Baptist; yet he who is but small in the kingdom of heaven is greater because he has been born of the spirit and knows that he has become a son of God."

144:8.5 (1627.2) Many who heard Jesus that day submitted themselves to John's baptism, thereby publicly professing entrance into the kingdom. And the apostles of John were firmly knit to Jesus from that day forward. This occurrence marked the real union of John's and Jesus' followers.

144:8.6 (1627.3) After the messengers had conversed with Abner, they departed for Machaerus to tell all this to John. He was greatly comforted, and his faith was strengthened by the words of Jesus and the message of Abner.

144:8.7 (1627.4) On this afternoon Jesus continued to teach, saying: "But to what shall I liken this generation? Many of you will receive neither John's message nor my teaching. You are like the children playing in the market place who call to their fellows and say: 'We piped for you and you did not dance; we wailed and you did not mourn.' And so with some of you. John came neither eating nor drinking, and they said he had a devil. The Son of Man comes eating and drinking, and these same people say: 'Behold, a gluttonous man and a winebibber, a friend of publicans and sinners!' Truly, wisdom is justified by her children.

144:8.8 (1627.5) "It would appear that the Father in heaven has hidden some of these truths from the wise and haughty, while he has revealed them to babes. But the Father does all things well; the Father reveals himself to the universe by the methods of his own choosing. Come, therefore, all you who labor and are heavy laden, and you shall find rest for your souls. Take upon you the divine yoke, and you will experience the peace of God, which passes all understanding."

Death of John the Baptist

144:9.1 (1627.6) John the Baptist was executed by order of Herod Antipas on the evening of January 10, A.D. 28. The next day a few of John's disciples who had gone to Machaerus heard of his execution and, going to Herod, made request for his body, which they put in a tomb, later giving it burial at Sebaste, the home of Abner. The following day, January 12, they started north to the camp of John's and Jesus' apostles near Pella, and they told Jesus about the death of John.

When Jesus heard their report, he dismissed the multitude and, calling the twenty-four together, said: "John is dead. Herod has beheaded him. Tonight go into joint council and arrange your affairs accordingly. There shall be delay no longer. The hour has come to proclaim the kingdom openly and with power. Tomorrow we go into Galilee."

144:9.2 (1627.7) Accordingly, early on the morning of January 13, A.D. 28, Jesus and the apostles, accompanied by some twenty-five disciples, made their way to Capernaum and lodged that night in Zebedee's house.

Paper 145

Four Eventful Days at Capernaum

145:0.1 (1628.1) JESUS and the apostles arrived in Capernaum the evening of Tuesday, January 13. As usual, they made their headquarters at the home of Zebedee in Bethsaida. Now that John the Baptist had been sent to his death, Jesus prepared to launch out in the first open and public preaching tour of Galilee. The news that Jesus had returned rapidly spread throughout the city, and early the next day, Mary the mother of Jesus hastened away, going over to Nazareth to visit her son Joseph.

145:0.2 (1628.2) Wednesday, Thursday, and Friday Jesus spent at the Zebedee house instructing his apostles preparatory to their first extensive public preaching tour. He also received and taught many earnest inquirers, both singly and in groups. Through Andrew, he arranged to speak in the synagogue on the coming Sabbath day.

145:0.3 (1628.3) Late on Friday evening Jesus' baby sister, Ruth, secretly paid him a visit. They spent almost an hour together in a boat anchored a short distance from the shore. No human being, save John Zebedee, ever knew of this visit, and he was admonished to tell no man. Ruth was the only member of Jesus' family who consistently and unwaveringly believed in the divinity of his earth mission from the times of her earliest spiritual consciousness right on down through his eventful ministry, death, resurrection, and ascension; and she finally passed on to the worlds beyond never having doubted the supernatural character of her father-brother's mission in the flesh. Baby Ruth was the chief comfort of Jesus, as regards his earth family, throughout the trying ordeal of his trial, rejection, and crucifixion.

The Draught of Fishes

145:1.1 (1628.4) On Friday morning of this same week, when Jesus was teaching by the seaside, the people crowded him so near the water's edge that he signaled to some fishermen occupying a near-by boat to come to his rescue. Entering the boat, he continued to teach the assembled multitude for more than two hours. This boat was named "Simon"; it was the former fishing vessel of Simon Peter and had been built by Jesus' own hands. On this particular morning the boat was being used by David Zebedee and two associates, who had just come in near shore from a fruitless night of fishing on the lake. They were cleaning and mending their nets when Jesus requested them to come to his assistance.

145:1.2 (1628.5) After Jesus had finished teaching the people, he said to David: "As you were delayed by coming to my help, now let me work with you. Let us go fishing; put out into yonder deep and let down your nets for a draught." But Simon, one of David's assistants, answered: "Master, it is useless. We toiled all night and took nothing; however, at your bidding we will put out and let down the nets." And Simon consented to follow Jesus' directions because of a gesture made by his master, David. When they had proceeded to the place designated by Jesus, they let down their nets and enclosed such a multitude of fish that they feared the nets would break, so much so that they signaled to their associates on the shore to come to their assistance. When they had filled all three boats with fish, almost to sinking, this Simon fell down at Jesus' knees, saying, "Depart from me, Master, for I am a sinful man." Simon and all who were concerned in this episode were amazed at the draught of fishes. From that day David Zebedee, this Simon, and their associates forsook their nets and followed Jesus.

145:1.3 (1629.1) But this was in no sense a miraculous draught of fishes. Jesus was a close student of nature; he was an experienced fisherman and knew the habits of the fish in the Sea of Galilee. On this occasion he merely directed these men to the place where the fish were usually to be found at this time of day. But Jesus' followers always regarded this as a miracle.

Afternoon at the Synagogue

1.   145:2.1 (1629.2) The next Sabbath, at the afternoon service in the synagogue, Jesus preached his sermon on "The Will of the Father in Heaven." In the morning Simon Peter had preached on "The Kingdom." At the Thursday evening meeting of the synagogue Andrew had taught, his subject being "The New Way." At this particular time more people believed in Jesus in Capernaum than in any other one city on earth.

145:2.2 (1629.3) As Jesus taught in the synagogue this Sabbath afternoon, according to custom he took the first text from the law, reading from the Book of Exodus: "And you shall serve the Lord, your God, and he shall bless your bread and your water, and all sickness shall be taken away from you." He chose the second text from the Prophets, reading from Isaiah: "Arise and shine, for your light has come, and the glory of the Lord has risen upon you. Darkness may cover the earth and gross darkness the people, but the spirit of the Lord shall arise upon you, and the divine glory shall be seen with you. Even the gentiles shall come to this light, and many great minds shall surrender to the brightness of this light."

145:2.3 (1629.4) This sermon was an effort on Jesus' part to make clear the fact that religion is a personal experience.

Among other things, the Master said:

145:2.4 (1629.5) "You well know that, while a kindhearted father loves his family as a whole, he so regards them as a group because of his strong affection for each individual member of that family. No longer must you approach the Father in heaven as a child of Israel but as a child of God. As a group, you are indeed the children of Israel, but as individuals, each one of you is a child of God. I have come, not to reveal the Father to the children of Israel, but rather to bring this knowledge of God and the revelation of his love and mercy to the individual believer as a genuine personal experience. The prophets have all taught you that Yahweh cares for his people, that God loves Israel. But I have come among you to proclaim a greater truth, one which many of the later prophets also grasped, that God loves you—every one of you—as individuals. All these generations have you had a national or racial religion; now have I come to give you a personal religion.

145:2.5 (1630.1) "But even this is not a new idea. Many of the spiritually minded among you have known this truth, inasmuch as some of the prophets have so instructed you. Have you not read in the Scriptures where the Prophet Jeremiah says: 'In those days they shall no more say, the fathers have eaten sour grapes and the children's teeth are set on edge. Every man shall die for his own iniquity; every man who eats sour grapes, his teeth shall be set on edge.

Behold, the days shall come when I will make a new covenant with my people, not according to the covenant which I made with their fathers when I brought them out of the land of Egypt, but according to the new way. I will even write my law in their hearts. I will be their God, and they shall be my people. In that day they shall not say, one man to his neighbor, do you know the Lord? Nay! For they shall all know me personally, from the least to the greatest.'

145:2.6 (1630.2) "Have you not read these promises? Do you not believe the Scriptures? Do you not understand that the prophet's words are fulfilled in what you behold this very day? And did not Jeremiah exhort you to make religion an affair of the heart, to relate yourselves to God as individuals? Did not the prophet tell you that the God of heaven would search your individual hearts? And were you not warned that the natural human heart is deceitful above all things and oftentimes desperately wicked?

145:2.7 (1630.3) "Have you not read also where Ezekiel taught even your fathers that religion must become a reality in your individual experiences? No more shall you use the proverb which says, 'The fathers have eaten sour grapes and the children's teeth are set on edge.' 'As I live,' says the Lord God, 'behold all souls are mine; as the soul of the father, so also the soul of the son. Only the soul that sins shall die.' And then Ezekiel foresaw even this day when he spoke in behalf of God, saying: 'A new heart also will I give you, and a new spirit will I put within you.'

145:2.8 (1630.4) "No more should you fear that God will punish a nation for the sin of an individual; neither will the Father in heaven punish one of his believing children for the sins of a nation, albeit the individual member of any family must often suffer the material consequences of family mistakes and group transgressions. Do you not realize that the hope of a better nation—or a better world—is bound up in the progress and enlightenment of the individual?"

145:2.9 (1630.5) Then the Master portrayed that the Father in heaven, after man discerns this spiritual freedom, wills that his children on earth should begin that eternal ascent of the Paradise career which consists in the creature's conscious response to the divine urge of the indwelling spirit to find the Creator, to know God and to seek to become like him.

145:2.10 (1630.6) The apostles were greatly helped by this sermon. All of them realized more fully that the gospel of the kingdom is a message directed to the individual, not to the nation.

145:2.11 (1630.7) Even though the people of Capernaum were familiar with Jesus' teaching, they were astonished at his sermon on this Sabbath day. He taught, indeed, as one having authority and not as the scribes.

145:2.12 (1630.8) Just as Jesus finished speaking, a young man in the congregation who had been much agitated by his words was seized with a violent epileptic attack and loudly cried out. At the end of the seizure, when recovering consciousness, he spoke in a dreamy state, saying: "What have we to do with you, Jesus of Nazareth? You are the holy one of God; have you come to destroy us?" Jesus bade the people be quiet and, taking the young man by the hand, said, "Come out of it"—and he was immediately awakened.

145:2.13 (1631.1) This young man was not possessed of an unclean spirit or demon; he was a victim of ordinary epilepsy. But he had been taught that his affliction was due to possession by an evil spirit. He believed this teaching and behaved accordingly in all that he thought or said concerning his ailment. The people all believed that such phenomena were directly caused by the presence of unclean spirits. Accordingly they believed that Jesus had cast a demon out of this man. But Jesus did not at that time cure his epilepsy. Not until later on that day, after sundown, was this man really healed. Long after the day of Pentecost the Apostle John, who was the last to write of Jesus' doings, avoided all reference to these so-called acts of "casting out devils," and this he did in view of the fact that such cases of demon possession never occurred after Pentecost.

145:2.14 (1631.2) As a result of this commonplace incident the report was rapidly spread through Capernaum that Jesus had cast a demon out of a man and miraculously healed him in the synagogue at the conclusion of his afternoon sermon. The Sabbath was just the time for the rapid and effective spreading of such a startling rumor. This report was also carried to all the smaller settlements around Capernaum, and many of the people believed it.

145:2.15 (1631.3) The cooking and the housework at the large Zebedee home, where Jesus and the twelve made their headquarters, was for the most part done by Simon Peter's wife and her mother. Peter's home was near that of Zebedee; and Jesus and his friends stopped there on the way from the synagogue because Peter's wife's mother had for several days been sick with chills and fever. Now it chanced that, at about the time Jesus stood over this sick woman, holding her hand, smoothing her brow, and speaking words of comfort and encouragement, the fever left her. Jesus had not yet had time to explain to his apostles that no miracle had been wrought at the synagogue; and with this incident so fresh and vivid in their minds, and recalling the water and the wine at Cana, they seized upon this coincidence as another miracle, and some of them rushed out to spread the news abroad throughout the city.

145:2.16 (1631.4) Amatha, Peter's mother-in-law, was suffering from malarial fever. She was not miraculously healed by Jesus at this time. Not until several hours later, after sundown, was her cure effected in connection with the extraordinary event which occurred in the front yard of the Zebedee home.

145:2.17 (1631.5) And these cases are typical of the manner in which a wonder-seeking generation and a miracle-minded people unfailingly seized upon all such coincidences as the pretext for proclaiming that another miracle had been wrought by Jesus.

The Healing at Sundown

145:3.1 (1631.6) By the time Jesus and his apostles had made ready to partake of their evening meal near the end of this eventful Sabbath day, all Capernaum and its environs were agog over these reputed miracles of healing; and all who were sick or afflicted began preparations to go to Jesus or to have themselves carried there by their friends just as soon as the sun went down. According to Jewish teaching it was not permissible even to go in quest of health during the sacred hours of the Sabbath.

145:3.2 (1632.1) Therefore, as soon as the sun sank beneath the horizon, scores of afflicted men, women, and children began to make their way toward the Zebedee home in Bethsaida. One man started out with his paralyzed daughter just as soon as the sun sank behind his neighbor's house.

145:3.3 (1632.2) The whole day's events had set the stage for this extraordinary sundown scene. Even the text Jesus had used for his afternoon sermon had intimated that sickness should be banished; and he had spoken with such unprecedented power and authority! His message was so compelling! While he made no appeal to human authority, he did speak directly to the consciences and souls of men. Though he did not resort to logic, legal quibbles, or clever sayings, he did make a powerful, direct, clear, and personal appeal to the hearts of his hearers.

145:3.4 (1632.3) That Sabbath was a great day in the earth life of Jesus, yes, in the life of a universe. To all local universe intents and purposes the little Jewish city of Capernaum was the real capital of Nebadon. The handful of Jews in the Capernaum synagogue were not the only beings to hear that momentous closing statement of Jesus' sermon: "Hate is the shadow of fear; revenge the mask of cowardice." Neither could his hearers forget his blessed words, declaring, "Man is the son of God, not a child of the devil."

145:3.5 (1632.4) Soon after the setting of the sun, as Jesus and the apostles still lingered about the supper table, Peter's wife heard voices in the front yard and, on going to the door, saw a large company of sick folks assembling, and that the road from Capernaum was crowded by those who were on their way to seek healing at Jesus' hands. On seeing this sight, she went at once and informed her husband, who told Jesus.

145:3.6 (1632.5) When the Master stepped out of the front entrance of Zebedee's house, his eyes met an array of stricken and afflicted humanity. He gazed upon almost one thousand sick and ailing human beings; at least that was the number of persons gathered together before him. Not all present were afflicted; some had come assisting their loved ones in this effort to secure healing.

145:3.7 (1632.6) The sight of these afflicted mortals, men, women, and children, suffering in large measure as a result of the mistakes and misdeeds of his own trusted Sons of universe administration, peculiarly touched the human heart of Jesus and challenged the divine mercy of this benevolent Creator Son. But Jesus well knew he could never build an enduring spiritual movement upon the foundation of purely material wonders. It had been his consistent policy to refrain from exhibiting his creator prerogatives. Not since Cana had the supernatural or miraculous

attended his teaching; still, this afflicted multitude touched his sympathetic heart and mightily appealed to his understanding affection.

145:3.8 (1632.7) A voice from the front yard exclaimed: "Master, speak the word, restore our health, heal our diseases, and save our souls." No sooner had these words been uttered than a vast retinue of seraphim, physical controllers, Life Carriers, and midwayers, such as always attended this incarnated Creator of a universe, made themselves ready to act with creative power should their Sovereign give the signal. This was one of those moments in the earth career of Jesus in which divine wisdom and human compassion were so interlocked in the judgment of the Son of Man that he sought refuge in appeal to his Father's will.

145:3.9 (1632.8) When Peter implored the Master to heed their cry for help, Jesus, looking down upon the afflicted throng, answered: "I have come into the world to reveal the Father and establish his kingdom. For this purpose have I lived my life to this hour. If, therefore, it should be the will of Him who sent me and not inconsistent with my dedication to the proclamation of the gospel of the kingdom of heaven, I would desire to see my children made whole—and —" but the further words of Jesus were lost in the tumult.

145:3.10 (1633.1) Jesus had passed the responsibility of this healing decision to the ruling of his Father. Evidently the Father's will interposed no objection, for the words of the Master had scarcely been uttered when the assembly of celestial personalities serving under the command of Jesus' Personalized Thought Adjuster was mightily astir. The vast retinue descended into the midst of this motley throng of afflicted mortals, and in a moment of time 683 men, women, and children were made whole, were perfectly healed of all their physical diseases and other material disorders. Such a scene was never witnessed on earth before that day, nor since. And for those of us who were present to behold this creative wave of healing, it was indeed a thrilling spectacle.

145:3.11 (1633.2) But of all the beings who were astonished at this sudden and unexpected outbreak of supernatural healing, Jesus was the most surprised. In a moment when his human interests and sympathies were focused upon the scene of suffering and affliction there spread out before him, he neglected to bear in his human mind the admonitory warnings of his Personalized Adjuster regarding the impossibility of limiting the time element of the creator prerogatives of a Creator Son under certain conditions and in certain circumstances. Jesus desired to see these suffering mortals made whole if his Father's will would not thereby be violated. The Personalized Adjuster of Jesus instantly ruled that such an act of creative energy at that time would not transgress the will of the Paradise Father, and by such a decision—in view of Jesus' preceding expression of healing desire—the creative act was. What a Creator Son desires and his Father wills IS. Not in all of Jesus' subsequent earth life did another such en masse physical healing of mortals take place.

145:3.12 (1633.3) As might have been expected, the fame of this sundown healing at Bethsaida in Capernaum spread throughout all Galilee and Judea and to the regions beyond. Once more were the fears of Herod aroused, and he sent watchers to report on the work and teachings of Jesus and to ascertain if he was the former carpenter of Nazareth or John the Baptist risen from the dead.

145:3.13 (1633.4) Chiefly because of this unintended demonstration of physical healing, henceforth, throughout the remainder of his earth career, Jesus became as much a physician as a preacher. True, he continued his teaching, but his personal work consisted mostly in ministering to the sick and the distressed, while his apostles did the work of public preaching and baptizing believers.

145:3.14 (1633.5) But the majority of those who were recipients of supernatural or creative physical healing at this sundown demonstration of divine energy were not permanently spiritually benefited by this extraordinary manifestation of mercy. A small number were truly edified by this physical ministry, but the spiritual kingdom was not advanced in the hearts of men by this amazing eruption of timeless creative healing.

145:3.15 (1633.6) The healing wonders which every now and then attended Jesus' mission on earth were not a part of his plan of proclaiming the kingdom. They were incidentally inherent in having on earth a divine being of well-nigh unlimited creator prerogatives in association with an unprecedented combination of divine mercy and human sympathy. But such so-called miracles gave Jesus much trouble in that they provided prejudice-raising publicity and afforded much unsought notoriety.

The Evening After

145:4.1 (1634.1) Throughout the evening following this great outburst of healing, the rejoicing and happy throng overran Zebedee's home, and the apostles of Jesus were keyed up to the highest pitch of emotional enthusiasm. From a human standpoint, this was probably the greatest day of all the great days of their association with Jesus. At no time before or after did their hopes surge to such heights of confident expectation. Jesus had told them only a few days before, and when they were yet within the borders of Samaria, that the hour had come when the kingdom was to be proclaimed in power, and now their eyes had seen what they supposed was the fulfillment of that promise. They were thrilled by the vision of what was to come if this amazing manifestation of healing power was just the beginning. Their lingering doubts of Jesus' divinity were banished. They were literally intoxicated with the ecstasy of their bewildered enchantment.

145:4.2 (1634.2) But when they sought for Jesus, they could not find him.

The Master was much perturbed by what had happened. These men, women, and children who had been healed of diverse diseases lingered late into the evening, hoping for Jesus' return that they might thank him. The apostles could not understand the Master's conduct as the hours passed and he remained in seclusion; their joy would have been full and perfect but for his continued absence. When Jesus did return to their midst, the hour was late, and practically all of the beneficiaries of the healing episode had gone to their homes. Jesus refused the congratulations and adoration of the twelve and the others who had lingered to greet him, only saying: "Rejoice not that my Father is powerful to heal the body, but rather that he is mighty to save the soul. Let us go to our rest, for tomorrow we must be about the Father's business."

145:4.3 (1634.3) And again did twelve disappointed, perplexed, and heart-sorrowing men go to their rest; few of them, except the twins, slept much that night. No sooner would the Master do something to cheer the souls and gladden the hearts of his apostles, than he seemed immediately to dash their hopes in pieces and utterly to demolish the foundations of their courage and enthusiasm. As these bewildered fishermen looked into each other's eyes, there was but one thought: "We cannot understand him. What does all this mean?"

Early Sunday Morning

145:5.1 (1634.4) Neither did Jesus sleep much that Saturday night. He realized that the world was filled with physical distress and overrun with material difficulties, and he contemplated the great danger of being compelled to devote so much of his time to the care of the sick and afflicted that his mission of establishing the spiritual kingdom in the hearts of men would be interfered with or at least subordinated to the ministry of things physical. Because of these and similar thoughts which occupied the mortal mind of Jesus during the night, he arose that Sunday morning long before daybreak and went all alone to one of his

favorite places for communion with the Father. The theme of Jesus' prayer on this early morning was for wisdom and judgment that he might not allow his human sympathy, joined with his divine mercy, to make such an appeal to him in the presence of mortal suffering that all of his time would be occupied with physical ministry to the neglect of the spiritual. Though he did not wish altogether to avoid ministering to the sick, he knew that he must also do the more important work of spiritual teaching and religious training.

145:5.2 (1635.1) Jesus went out in the hills to pray so many times because there were no private rooms suitable for his personal devotions.

145:5.3 (1635.2) Peter could not sleep that night; so, very early, shortly after Jesus had gone out to pray, he aroused James and John, and the three went to find their Master. After more than an hour's search they found Jesus and besought him to tell them the reason for his strange conduct. They desired to know why he appeared to be troubled by the mighty outpouring of the spirit of healing when all the people were overjoyed and his apostles so much rejoiced.

145:5.4 (1635.3) For more than four hours Jesus endeavored to explain to these three apostles what had happened. He taught them about what had transpired and explained the dangers of such manifestations. Jesus confided to them the reason for his coming forth to pray. He sought to make plain to his personal associates the real reasons why the kingdom of the Father could not be built upon wonder-working and physical healing. But they could not comprehend his teaching.

145:5.5 (1635.4) Meanwhile, early Sunday morning, other crowds of afflicted souls and many curiosity seekers began to gather about the house of Zebedee. They clamored to see Jesus. Andrew and the apostles were so perplexed that, while Simon Zelotes talked to the assembly, Andrew, with several of his associates, went to find Jesus. When Andrew had located Jesus in company with the three, he said: "Master, why do you leave us alone with the multitude? Behold, all men seek you; never before have so many sought after your teaching. Even now the house is surrounded by those who have come from near and far because of your mighty works. Will you not return with us to minister to them?"

145:5.6 (1635.5) When Jesus heard this, he answered: "Andrew, have I not taught you and these others that my mission on earth is the revelation of the Father, and my message the proclamation of the kingdom of heaven? How is it, then, that you would have me turn aside from my work for the gratification of the curious and for the satisfaction of those who seek for signs and wonders? Have we not been among these people all these months, and have they flocked in multitudes to hear the good news of the kingdom? Why have they now come to besiege us? Is it not because of the healing of their physical bodies rather than as a result of the reception of spiritual truth for the salvation of their souls? When men are attracted to us because of extraordinary manifestations, many of them come seeking not for truth and salvation but rather in quest of healing for their physical ailments and to secure deliverance from their material difficulties.

145:5.7 (1635.6) "All this time I have been in Capernaum, and both in the synagogue and by the seaside have I proclaimed the good news of the kingdom to all who had ears to hear and hearts to receive the truth. It is not the will of my Father that I should return with you to cater to these curious ones and to become occupied with the ministry of things physical to the exclusion of the spiritual. I have ordained you to preach the gospel and minister to the sick, but I must not become engrossed in healing to the exclusion of my teaching. No, Andrew, I will not return with you. Go and tell the people to believe in that which we have taught them and to rejoice in the liberty of the sons of God, and make ready for our departure for the other cities of Galilee, where the way has already been prepared for the preaching of the good tidings of the kingdom. It was for this purpose that I came forth from the Father. Go, then, and prepare for our immediate departure while I here await your return."

145:5.8 (1636.1) When Jesus had spoken, Andrew and his fellow apostles sorrowfully made their way back to Zebedee's house, dismissed the assembled multitude, and quickly made ready for the journey as Jesus had directed. And so, on the afternoon of Sunday, January 18, A.D. 28, Jesus and the apostles started out upon their first really public and open preaching tour of the cities of Galilee. On this first tour they preached the gospel of the kingdom in many cities, but they did not visit Nazareth.

145:5.9 (1636.2) That Sunday afternoon, shortly after Jesus and his apostles had left for Rimmon, his brothers James and Jude came to see him, calling at Zebedee's house. About noon of that day Jude had sought out his brother James and insisted that they go to Jesus. By the time James consented to go with Jude, Jesus had already departed.

145:5.10 (1636.3) The apostles were loath to leave the great interest which had been aroused at Capernaum. Peter calculated that no less than one thousand believers could have been baptized into the kingdom. Jesus listened to them patiently, but he would not consent to return. Silence prevailed for a season, and then Thomas addressed his fellow apostles, saying: "Let's go! The Master has spoken. No matter if we cannot fully comprehend the mysteries of the kingdom of heaven, of one thing we are certain: We follow a teacher who seeks no glory for himself." And reluctantly they went forth to preach the good tidings in the cities of Galilee.

Paper 146

First Preaching Tour of Galilee

146:0.1 (1637.1) THE first public preaching tour of Galilee began on Sunday, January 18, A.D. 28, and continued for about two months, ending with the return to Capernaum on March 17. On this tour Jesus and the twelve apostles, assisted by the former apostles of John, preached the gospel and baptized believers in Rimmon, Jotapata, Ramah, Zebulun, Iron, Gischala, Chorazin, Madon, Cana, Nain, and Endor. In these cities they tarried and taught, while in many other smaller towns they proclaimed the gospel of the kingdom as they passed through.

146:0.2 (1637.2) This was the first time Jesus permitted his associates to preach without restraint. On this tour he cautioned them on only three occasions; he admonished them to remain away from Nazareth and to be discreet when passing through Capernaum and Tiberias. It was a source of great satisfaction to the apostles at last to feel they were at liberty to preach and teach without restriction, and they threw themselves into the work of preaching the gospel, ministering to the sick, and baptizing believers, with great earnestness and joy.

1   Preaching at Rimmon

146:1.1 (1637.3) The small city of Rimmon had once been dedicated to the worship of a Babylonian god of the air, Ramman. Many of the earlier Babylonian and later Zoroastrian teachings were still embraced in the beliefs of the Rimmonites; therefore did Jesus and the twenty-four devote much of their time to the task of making plain the difference between these older beliefs and the new gospel of the kingdom. Peter here preached one of the great sermons of his early career on "Aaron and the Golden Calf."

146:1.2 (1637.4) Although many of the citizens of Rimmon became believers in Jesus' teachings, they made great trouble for their brethren in later years. It is difficult to convert nature worshipers to the full fellowship of the adoration of a spiritual ideal during the short space of a single lifetime.

146:1.3 (1637.5) Many of the better of the Babylonian and Persian ideas of light and darkness, good and evil, time and eternity, were later incorporated in the doctrines of so-called Christianity, and their inclusion rendered the Christian teachings more immediately acceptable to the peoples of the Near East. In like manner, the inclusion of many of Plato's theories of the ideal spirit or invisible patterns of all things visible and material, as later adapted by Philo to the Hebrew theology, made Paul's Christian teachings more easy of acceptance by the western Greeks.

146:1.4 (1637.6) It was at Rimmon that Todan first heard the gospel of the kingdom, and he later carried this message into Mesopotamia and far beyond. He was among the first to preach the good news to those who dwelt beyond the Euphrates.

2   At Jotapata

146:2.1 (1638.1) While the common people of Jotapata heard Jesus and his apostles gladly and many accepted the gospel of the kingdom, it was the discourse of Jesus to the twenty-four on the second evening of their sojourn in this small town that distinguishes the Jotapata mission. Nathaniel was confused in his mind about the Master's teachings concerning prayer, thanksgiving, and worship, and in response to his question Jesus spoke at great length in further explanation of his teaching. Summarized in modern phraseology, this discourse may be presented as emphasizing the following points:

146:2.2 (1638.2) 1. The conscious and persistent regard for iniquity in the heart of man gradually destroys the prayer connection of the human soul with the spirit circuits of communication between man and his Maker. Naturally God hears the petition of his child, but when the human heart deliberately and persistently harbors the concepts of iniquity, there gradually ensues the loss of personal communion between the earth child and his heavenly Father.

146:2.3 (1638.3) 2. That prayer which is inconsistent with the known and established laws of God is an abomination to the Paradise Deities. If man will not listen to the Gods as they speak to their creation in the laws of spirit, mind, and matter, the very act of such deliberate and conscious disdain by the creature turns the ears of spirit personalities away from hearing the personal petitions of such lawless and disobedient mortals. Jesus quoted to his apostles from the Prophet Zechariah: "But they refused to hearken and pulled away the shoulder and stopped their ears that they should not hear. Yes, they made their hearts adamant like a stone, lest they should hear my law and the words which I sent by my spirit through the prophets; therefore did the results of their evil thinking come as a great wrath upon their guilty heads. And so it came to pass that they cried for mercy, but there was no ear open to hear." And then Jesus quoted the proverb of the wise man who said: "He who turns away his ear from hearing the divine law, even his prayer shall be an abomination."

146:2.4 (1638.4) 3. By opening the human end of the channel of the God-man communication, mortals make immediately available the ever-flowing stream of divine ministry to the creatures of the worlds. When man hears God's spirit speak within the human heart, inherent in such an experience is the fact that God simultaneously hears that man's prayer. Even the forgiveness of sin operates in this same unerring fashion. The Father in heaven has forgiven you even before you have thought to ask him, but such forgiveness is not available in your personal religious experience until such a time as you forgive your fellow men. God's forgiveness in fact is not conditioned upon your forgiving your fellows, but in experience it is exactly so conditioned. And this fact of the synchrony of divine and human forgiveness was thus recognized and linked together in the prayer which Jesus taught the apostles.

146:2.5 (1638.5) 4. There is a basic law of justice in the universe which mercy is powerless to circumvent. The unselfish glories of Paradise are not possible of reception by a thoroughly selfish creature of the realms of time and space. Even the infinite love of God cannot force the salvation of eternal survival upon any mortal creature who does not choose to survive. Mercy has great latitude of bestowal, but, after all, there are mandates of justice which even love combined with mercy cannot effectively abrogate. Again Jesus quoted from the Hebrew scriptures: "I have called and you refused to hear; I stretched out my hand, but no man regarded. You have set at naught all my counsel, and you have rejected my reproof, and because of this rebellious attitude it becomes inevitable that you shall call upon me and fail to receive an answer. Having rejected the way of life, you may seek me diligently in your times of suffering, but you will not find me."

146:2.6 (1639.1) 5. They who would receive mercy must show mercy; judge not that you be not judged. With the spirit with which you judge others you also shall be judged. Mercy does not wholly abrogate universe fairness. In the end it will prove true: "Whoso stops his ears to the cry of the poor, he also shall some day cry for help, and no one will hear him." The sincerity of any prayer is the assurance of its being heard; the spiritual wisdom and universe consistency of any petition is the determiner of the time, manner, and degree of the answer. A wise father does not literally answer the foolish prayers of his ignorant and inexperienced children, albeit the children may derive much pleasure and real soul satisfaction from the making of such absurd petitions.

146:2.7 (1639.2) 6. When you have

become wholly dedicated to the doing of the will of the Father in heaven, the answer to all your petitions will be forthcoming because your prayers will be in full accordance with the Father's will, and the Father's will is ever manifest throughout his vast universe. What the true son desires and the infinite Father wills IS. Such a prayer cannot remain unanswered, and no other sort of petition can possibly be fully answered.

146:2.8 (1639.3) 7. The cry of the righteous is the faith act of the child of God which opens the door of the Father's storehouse of goodness, truth, and mercy, and these good gifts have long been in waiting for the son's approach and personal appropriation. Prayer does not change the divine attitude toward man, but it does change man's attitude toward the changeless Father. The motive of the prayer gives it right of way to the divine ear, not the social, economic, or outward religious status of the one who prays.

146:2.9 (1639.4) 8. Prayer may not be employed to avoid the delays of time or to transcend the handicaps of space. Prayer is not designed as a technique for aggrandizing self or for gaining unfair advantage over one's fellows. A thoroughly selfish soul cannot pray in the true sense of the word. Said Jesus: "Let your supreme delight be in the character of God, and he shall surely give you the sincere desires of your heart." "Commit your way to the Lord; trust in him, and he will act." "For the Lord hears the cry of the needy, and he will regard the prayer of the destitute."

146:2.10 (1639.5) 9. "I have come forth from the Father; if, therefore, you are ever in doubt as to what you would ask of the Father, ask in my name, and I will present your petition in accordance with your real needs and desires and in accordance with my Father's will." Guard against the great danger of becoming self-centered in your prayers. Avoid praying much for yourself; pray more for the spiritual progress of your brethren. Avoid materialistic praying; pray in the spirit and for the abundance of the gifts of the spirit.

146:2.11 (1639.6) 10. When you pray for the sick and afflicted, do not expect that your petitions will take the place of loving and intelligent ministry to the necessities of these afflicted ones. Pray for the welfare of your families, friends, and fellows, but especially pray for those who curse you, and make loving petitions for those who persecute you. "But when to pray, I will not say. Only the spirit that dwells within you may move you to the utterance of those petitions which are expressive of your inner relationship with the Father of spirits."

146:2.12 (1640.1) 11. Many resort to prayer only when in trouble. Such a practice is thoughtless and misleading. True, you do well to pray when harassed, but you should also be mindful to speak as a son to your Father even when all goes well with your soul. Let your real petitions always be in secret. Do not let men hear your personal prayers. Prayers of thanksgiving are appropriate for groups of worshipers, but the prayer of the soul is a personal matter. There is but one form of prayer which is appropriate for all God's children, and that is: "Nevertheless, your will be done."

146:2.13 (1640.2) 12. All believers in this gospel should pray sincerely for the extension of the kingdom of heaven. Of all the prayers of the Hebrew scriptures he commented most approvingly on the petition of the Psalmist: "Create in me a clean heart, O God, and renew a right spirit within me. Purge me from secret sins and keep back your servant from presumptuous transgression." Jesus commented at great length on the relation of prayer to careless and offending speech, quoting: "Set a watch, O Lord, before my mouth; keep the door of my lips." "The human tongue," said Jesus, "is a member which few men can tame, but the spirit within can transform this unruly member into a kindly voice of tolerance and an inspiring minister of mercy."

146:2.14 (1640.3) 13. Jesus taught that the prayer for divine guidance over the pathway of earthly life was next in importance to the petition for a knowledge of the Father's will. In reality this means a prayer for divine wisdom. Jesus never taught that human knowledge and special skill could be gained by prayer. But he did teach that prayer is a factor in the enlargement of one's capacity to receive the presence of the divine spirit. When Jesus taught his associates to pray in the spirit and in truth, he explained that he referred to praying sincerely and in accordance with one's enlightenment, to praying wholeheartedly and intelligently, earnestly and steadfastly.

146:2.15 (1640.4) 14. Jesus warned his followers against thinking that their prayers would be rendered more efficacious by ornate repetitions, eloquent phraseology, fasting, penance, or sacrifices. But he did exhort his believers to employ prayer as a means of leading up through thanksgiving to true worship. Jesus deplored that so little of the spirit of thanksgiving was to be found in the prayers and worship of his followers. He quoted from the Scriptures on this occasion, saying: "It is a good thing to give thanks to the Lord and to sing praises to the name of the Most High, to acknowledge his loving-kindness every morning and his faithfulness every night, for God has made me glad through his work. In everything I will give thanks according to the will of God."

146:2.16 (1640.5) 15. And then Jesus said: "Be not constantly overanxious about your common needs. Be not apprehensive concerning the problems of your earthly existence, but in all these things by prayer and supplication, with the spirit of sincere thanksgiving, let your needs be spread out before your Father who is in heaven." Then he quoted from the Scriptures: "I will praise the name of God with a song and will magnify him with thanksgiving. And this will please the Lord better than the sacrifice of an ox or bullock with horns and hoofs."

146:2.17 (1641.1) 16. Jesus taught his followers that, when they had made their prayers to the Father, they should remain for a time in silent receptivity to afford the indwelling spirit the better opportunity to speak to the listening soul. The spirit of the Father speaks best to man when the human mind is in an attitude of true worship. We worship God by the aid of the Father's indwelling spirit and by the illumination of the human mind through the ministry of truth. Worship, taught Jesus, makes one increasingly like the being who is worshiped. Worship is a transforming experience whereby the finite gradually approaches and ultimately attains the presence of the Infinite.

146:2.18 (1641.2) And many other truths did Jesus tell his apostles about man's communion with God, but not many of them could fully encompass his teaching.

3   The Stop at Ramah

146:3.1 (1641.3) At Ramah Jesus had the memorable discussion with the aged Greek philosopher who taught that science and philosophy were sufficient to satisfy the needs of human experience. Jesus listened with patience and sympathy to this Greek teacher, allowing the truth of many things he said but pointing out that, when he was through, he had failed in his discussion of human existence to explain "whence, why, and whither," and added: "Where you leave off, we begin. Religion is a revelation to man's soul dealing with spiritual realities which the mind alone could never discover or fully fathom. Intellectual strivings may reveal the facts of life, but the gospel of the kingdom unfolds the truths of being. You have discussed the material shadows of truth; will you now listen while I tell you about the eternal and spiritual realities which cast these transient time shadows of the material facts of mortal existence?" For more than an hour Jesus taught this Greek the saving truths of the gospel of the kingdom. The old philosopher was susceptible to the Master's mode of approach, and being sincerely honest of heart, he quickly believed this gospel of salvation.

146:3.2 (1641.4) The apostles were a

bit disconcerted by the open manner of Jesus' assent to many of the Greek's propositions, but Jesus afterward privately said to them: "My children, marvel not that I was tolerant of the Greek's philosophy. True and genuine inward certainty does not in the least fear outward analysis, nor does truth resent honest criticism. You should never forget that intolerance is the mask covering up the entertainment of secret doubts as to the trueness of one's belief. No man is at any time disturbed by his neighbor's attitude when he has perfect confidence in the truth of that which he wholeheartedly believes. Courage is the confidence of thoroughgoing honesty about those things which one professes to believe. Sincere men are unafraid of the critical examination of their true convictions and noble ideals."

146:3.3 (1641.5) On the second evening at Ramah, Thomas asked Jesus this question: "Master, how can a new believer in your teaching really know, really be certain, about the truth of this gospel of the kingdom?"

146:3.4 (1641.6) And Jesus said to Thomas: "Your assurance that you have entered into the kingdom family of the Father, and that you will eternally survive with the children of the kingdom, is wholly a matter of personal experience—faith in the word of truth. Spiritual assurance is the equivalent of your personal religious experience in the eternal realities of divine truth and is otherwise equal to your intelligent understanding of truth realities plus your spiritual faith and minus your honest doubts.

146:3.5 (1642.1) "The Son is naturally endowed with the life of the Father. Having been endowed with the living spirit of the Father, you are therefore sons of God. You survive your life in the material world of the flesh because you are identified with the Father's living spirit, the gift of eternal life. Many, indeed, had this life before I came forth from the Father, and many more have received this spirit because they believed my word; but I declare that, when I return to the Father, he will send his spirit into the hearts of all men.

146:3.6 (1642.2) "While you cannot observe the divine spirit at work in your minds, there is a practical method of discovering the degree to which you have yielded the control of your soul powers to the teaching and guidance of this indwelling spirit of the heavenly Father, and that is the degree of your love for your fellow men. This spirit of the Father partakes of the love of the Father, and as it dominates man, it unfailingly leads in the directions of divine worship and loving regard for one's fellows. At first you believe that you are sons of God because my teaching has made you more conscious of the inner leadings of our Father's indwelling presence; but presently the Spirit of Truth shall be poured out upon all flesh, and it will live among men and teach all men, even as I now live among you and speak to you the words of truth. And this Spirit of Truth, speaking for the spiritual endowments of your souls, will help you to know that you are the sons of God. It will unfailingly bear witness with the Father's indwelling presence, your spirit, then dwelling in all men as it now dwells in some, telling you that you are in reality the sons of God.

146:3.7 (1642.3) "Every earth child who follows the leading of this spirit shall eventually know the will of God, and he who surrenders to the will of my Father shall abide forever. The way from the earth life to the eternal estate has not been made plain to you, but there is a way, there always has been, and I have come to make that way new and living. He who enters the kingdom has eternal life already—he shall never perish. But much of this you will the better understand when I shall have returned to the Father and you are able to view your present experiences in retrospect."

146:3.8 (1642.4) And all who heard these blessed words were greatly cheered. The Jewish teachings had been confused and uncertain regarding the survival of the righteous, and it was refreshing and inspiring for Jesus' followers to hear these very definite and positive words of assurance about the eternal survival of all true believers.

146:3.9 (1642.5) The apostles continued to preach and baptize believers, while they kept up the practice of visiting from house to house, comforting the downcast and ministering to the sick and afflicted. The apostolic organization was expanded in that each of Jesus' apostles now had one of John's as an associate; Abner was the associate of Andrew; and this plan prevailed until they went down to Jerusalem for the next Passover.

146:3.10 (1642.6) The special instruction given by Jesus during their stay at Zebulun had chiefly to do with further discussions of the mutual obligations of the kingdom and embraced teaching designed to make clear the differences between personal religious experience and the amities of social religious obligations. This was one of the few times the Master ever discussed the social aspects of religion. Throughout his entire earth life Jesus gave his followers very little instruction regarding the socialization of religion.

146:3.11 (1643.1) In Zebulun the people were of a mixed race, hardly Jew or gentile, and few of them really believed in Jesus, notwithstanding they had heard of the healing of the sick at Capernaum.

4   The Gospel at Iron

146:4.1 (1643.2) At Iron, as in many of even the smaller cities of Galilee and Judea, there was a synagogue, and during the earlier times of Jesus' ministry it was his custom to speak in these synagogues on the Sabbath day. Sometimes he would speak at the morning service, and Peter or one of the other apostles would preach at the afternoon hour. Jesus and the apostles would also often teach and preach at the weekday evening assemblies at the synagogue. Although the religious leaders at Jerusalem became increasingly antagonistic toward Jesus, they exercised no direct control over the synagogues outside of that city. It was not until later in Jesus' public ministry that they were able to create such a widespread sentiment against him as to bring about the almost universal closing of the synagogues to his teaching. At this time all the synagogues of Galilee and Judea were open to him. *

146:4.2 (1643.3) Iron was the site of extensive mineral mines for those days, and since Jesus had never shared the life of the miner, he spent most of his time, while sojourning at Iron, in the mines. While the apostles visited the homes and preached in the public places, Jesus worked in the mines with these underground laborers. The fame of Jesus as a healer had spread even to this remote village, and many sick and afflicted sought help at his hands, and many were greatly benefited by his healing ministry. But in none of these cases did the Master perform a so-called miracle of healing save in that of the leper.

146:4.3 (1643.4) Late on the afternoon of the third day at Iron, as Jesus was returning from the mines, he chanced to pass through a narrow side street on his way to his lodging place. As he drew near the squalid hovel of a certain leprous man, the afflicted one, having heard of his fame as a healer, made bold to accost him as he passed his door, saying as he knelt before him: "Lord, if only you would, you could make me clean. I have heard the message of your teachers, and I would enter the kingdom if I could be made clean." And the leper spoke in this way because among the Jews lepers were forbidden even to attend the synagogue or otherwise engage in public worship. This man really believed that he could not be received into the coming kingdom unless he could find a cure for his leprosy. And when Jesus saw him in his affliction and heard his words of clinging faith, his human heart was touched, and the divine mind was moved with compassion. As Jesus looked upon him, the man fell upon his face and worshiped. Then the Master stretched forth his hand and, touching him, said: "I will—be clean." And immediately he was healed; the leprosy no longer afflicted him.

146:4.4 (1643.5) When Jesus had lifted the man upon his feet, he charged him: "See that you tell no man about your healing but rather go quietly about your business, showing yourself to the priest and offering those sacrifices commanded by Moses in testimony of your cleansing." But this man did not do as Jesus had instructed him. Instead, he began to publish abroad throughout the town that Jesus had cured his leprosy, and since he was known to all the village, the people could plainly see that he had been cleansed of his disease. He did not go to the priests as Jesus had admonished him. As a result of his spreading abroad the news that Jesus had healed him, the Master was so thronged by the sick that he was forced to rise early the next day and leave the village. Although Jesus did not again enter the town, he remained two days in the outskirts near the mines, continuing to instruct the believing miners further regarding the gospel of the kingdom.

146:4.5 (1644.1) This cleansing of the leper was the first so-called miracle which Jesus had intentionally and deliberately performed up to this time. And this was a case of real leprosy.

146:4.6 (1644.2) From Iron they went to Gischala, spending two days proclaiming the gospel, and then departed for Chorazin, where they spent almost a week preaching the good news; but they were unable to win many believers for the kingdom in Chorazin. In no place where Jesus had taught had he met with such a general rejection of his message. The sojourn at Chorazin was very depressing to most of the apostles, and Andrew and Abner had much difficulty in upholding the courage of their associates. And so, passing quietly through Capernaum, they went on to the village of Madon, where they fared little better. There prevailed in the minds of most of the apostles the idea that their failure to meet with success in these towns so recently visited was due to Jesus' insistence that they refrain, in their teaching and preaching, from referring to him as a healer. How they wished he would cleanse another leper or in some other manner so manifest his power as to attract the attention of the people! But the Master was unmoved by their earnest urging.

5   Back in Cana

146:5.1 (1644.3) The apostolic party was greatly cheered when Jesus announced, "Tomorrow we go to Cana." They knew they would have a sympathetic hearing at Cana, for Jesus was well known there. They were doing well with their work of bringing people into the kingdom when, on the third day, there arrived in Cana a certain prominent citizen of Capernaum, Titus, who was a partial believer, and whose son was critically ill. He heard that Jesus was at Cana; so he hastened over to see him. The believers at Capernaum thought Jesus could heal any sickness.

146:5.2 (1644.4) When this nobleman had located Jesus in Cana, he besought him to hurry over to Capernaum and heal his afflicted son. While the apostles stood by in breathless expectancy, Jesus, looking at the father of the sick boy, said: "How long shall I bear with you? The power of God is in your midst, but except you see signs and behold wonders, you refuse to believe." But the nobleman pleaded with Jesus, saying: "My Lord, I do believe, but come ere my child perishes, for when I left him he was even then at the point of death." And when Jesus had bowed his head a moment in silent meditation, he suddenly spoke, "Return to your home; your son will live." Titus believed the word of Jesus and hastened back to Capernaum. And as he was returning, his servants came out to meet him, saying, "Rejoice, for your son is improved—he lives." Then Titus inquired of them at what hour the boy began to mend, and when the servants answered "yesterday about the seventh hour the fever left him," the father recalled that it was about that hour when Jesus had said, "Your son will live." And Titus henceforth believed with a whole heart, and all his family also believed. This son became a mighty minister of the kingdom and later yielded up his life with those who suffered in Rome.

Though the entire household of Titus, their friends, and even the apostles regarded this episode as a miracle, it was not. At least this was not a miracle of curing physical disease. It was merely a case of preknowledge concerning the course of natural law, just such knowledge as Jesus frequently resorted to subsequent to his baptism.

146:5.3 (1645.1) Again was Jesus compelled to hasten away from Cana because of the undue attention attracted by the second episode of this sort to attend his ministry in this village. The townspeople remembered the water and the wine, and now that he was supposed to have healed the nobleman's son at so great a distance, they came to him, not only bringing the sick and afflicted but also sending messengers requesting that he heal sufferers at a distance. And when Jesus saw that the whole countryside was aroused, he said, "Let us go to Nain."

6 Nain and the Widow's Son

146:6.1 (1645.2) These people believed in signs; they were a wonder-seeking generation. By this time the people of central and southern Galilee had become miracle minded regarding Jesus and his personal ministry. Scores, hundreds, of honest persons suffering from purely nervous disorders and afflicted with emotional disturbances came into Jesus' presence and then returned home to their friends announcing that Jesus had healed them. And such cases of mental healing these ignorant and simple-minded people regarded as physical healing, miraculous cures.

146:6.2 (1645.3) When Jesus sought to leave Cana and go to Nain, a great multitude of believers and many curious people followed after him. They were bent on beholding miracles and wonders, and they were not to be disappointed. As Jesus and his apostles drew near the gate of the city, they met a funeral procession on its way to the near-by cemetery, carrying the only son of a widowed mother of Nain. This woman was much respected, and half of the village followed the bearers of the bier of this supposedly dead boy. When the funeral procession had come up to Jesus and his followers, the widow and her friends recognized the Master and besought him to bring the son back to life. Their miracle expectancy was aroused to such a high pitch they thought Jesus could cure any human disease, and why could not such a healer even raise the dead? Jesus, while being thus importuned, stepped forward and, raising the covering of the bier, examined the boy. Discovering that the young man was not really dead, he perceived the tragedy which his presence could avert; so, turning to the mother, he said: "Weep not. Your son is not dead; he sleeps. He will be restored to you." And then, taking the young man by the hand, he said, "Awake and arise." And the youth who was supposed to be dead presently sat up and began to speak, and Jesus sent them back to their homes.

146:6.3 (1645.4) Jesus endeavored to calm the multitude and vainly tried to explain that the lad was not really dead, that he had not brought him back from the grave, but it was useless. The multitude which followed him, and the whole village of Nain, were aroused to the highest pitch of emotional frenzy. Fear seized many, panic others, while still others fell to praying and wailing over their sins. And it was not until long after nightfall that the clamoring multitude could be dispersed. And, of course, notwithstanding Jesus' statement that the boy was not dead, everyone insisted that a miracle had been wrought, even the dead raised. Although Jesus told them the boy was merely in a deep sleep, they explained that that was the manner of his speaking and called attention to the fact that he always in great modesty tried to hide his miracles.

146:6.4 (1646.1) So the word went abroad throughout Galilee and into Judea that Jesus had raised the widow's son from the dead, and many who heard this report believed it. Never was Jesus able to make even all his apostles fully understand that the widow's son was not really dead when he bade him awake and arise. But he did impress them sufficiently to keep it out of all subsequent records except that of Luke, who recorded it as the episode had been related to him. And again was Jesus so besieged as a physician that he departed early the next day for Endor.

7   *At Endor*

146:7.1 (1646.2) At Endor Jesus escaped for a few days from the clamoring multitudes in quest of physical healing. During their sojourn at this place the Master recounted for the instruction of the apostles the story of King Saul and the witch of Endor. Jesus plainly told his apostles that the stray and rebellious midwayers who had oftentimes impersonated the supposed spirits of the dead would soon be brought under control so that they could no more do these strange things. He told his followers that, after he returned to the Father, and after they had poured out their spirit upon all flesh, no more could such semispirit beings—so-called unclean spirits—possess the feeble- and evil-minded among mortals.

146:7.2 (1646.3) Jesus further explained to his apostles that the spirits of departed human beings do not come back to the world of their origin to communicate with their living fellows. Only after the passing of a dispensational age would it be possible for the advancing spirit of mortal man to return to earth and then only in exceptional cases and as a part of the spiritual administration of the planet.

146:7.3 (1646.4) When they had rested two days, Jesus said to his apostles: "On the morrow let us return to Capernaum to tarry and teach while the countryside quiets down. At home they will have by this time partly recovered from this sort of excitement."

Paper 147

The Interlude Visit to Jerusalem

147:0.1 (1647.1) JESUS and the apostles arrived in Capernaum on Wednesday, March 17, and spent two weeks at the Bethsaida headquarters before they departed for Jerusalem. These two weeks the apostles taught the people by the seaside while Jesus spent much time alone in the hills about his Father's business. During this period Jesus, accompanied by James and John Zebedee, made two secret trips to Tiberias, where they met with the believers and instructed them in the gospel of the kingdom.

147:0.2 (1647.2) Many of the household of Herod believed in Jesus and attended these meetings. It was the influence of these believers among Herod's official family that had helped to lessen that ruler's enmity toward Jesus. These believers at Tiberias had fully explained to Herod that the "kingdom" which Jesus proclaimed was spiritual in nature and not a political venture. Herod rather believed these members of his own household and therefore did not permit himself to become unduly alarmed by the spreading abroad of the reports concerning Jesus' teaching and healing. He had no objections to Jesus' work as a healer or religious teacher. Notwithstanding the favorable attitude of many of Herod's advisers, and even of Herod himself, there existed a group of his subordinates who were so influenced by the religious leaders at Jerusalem that they remained bitter and threatening enemies of Jesus and the apostles and, later on, did much to hamper their public activities. The greatest danger to Jesus lay in the Jerusalem religious leaders and not in Herod.

And it was for this very reason that Jesus and the apostles spent so much time and did most of their public preaching in Galilee rather than at Jerusalem and in Judea.

1 The Centurion's Servant

147:1.1 (1647.3) On the day before they made ready to go to Jerusalem for the feast of the Passover, Mangus, a centurion, or captain, of the Roman guard stationed at Capernaum, came to the rulers of the synagogue, saying: "My faithful orderly is sick and at the point of death. Would you, therefore, go to Jesus in my behalf and beseech him to heal my servant?" The Roman captain did this because he thought the Jewish leaders would have more influence with Jesus. So the elders went to see Jesus and their spokesman said: "Teacher, we earnestly request you to go over to Capernaum and save the favorite servant of the Roman centurion, who is worthy of your notice because he loves our nation and even built us the very synagogue wherein you have so many times spoken."

147:1.2 (1647.4) And when Jesus had heard them, he said, "I will go with you." And as he went with them over to the centurion's house, and before they had entered his yard, the Roman soldier sent his friends out to greet Jesus, instructing them to say: "Lord, trouble not yourself to enter my house, for I am not worthy that you should come under my roof.

Neither did I think myself worthy to come to you; wherefore I sent the elders of your own people. But I know that you can speak the word where you stand and my servant will be healed. For I am myself under the orders of others, and I have soldiers under me, and I say to this one go, and he goes; to another come, and he comes, and to my servants do this or do that, and they do it."

147:1.3 (1648.1) And when Jesus heard these words, he turned and said to his apostles and those who were with them: "I marvel at the belief of the gentile. Verily, verily, I say to you, I have not found so great faith, no, not in Israel." Jesus, turning from the house, said, "Let us go hence." And the friends of the centurion went into the house and told Mangus what Jesus had said.

And from that hour the servant began to mend and was eventually restored to his normal health and usefulness.

147:1.4 (1648.2) But we never knew just what happened on this occasion. This is simply the record, and as to whether or not invisible beings ministered healing to the centurion's servant, was not revealed to those who accompanied Jesus. We only know of the fact of the servant's complete recovery.

2 The Journey to Jerusalem

147:2.1 (1648.3) Early on the morning of Tuesday, March 30, Jesus and the apostolic party started on their journey to Jerusalem for the Passover, going by the route of the Jordan valley. They arrived on the afternoon of Friday, April 2, and established their headquarters, as usual, at Bethany. Passing through Jericho, they paused to rest while Judas made a deposit of some of their common funds in the bank of a friend of his family. This was the first time Judas had carried a surplus of money, and this deposit was left undisturbed until they passed through Jericho again when on that last and eventful journey to Jerusalem just before the trial and death of Jesus.

147:2.2 (1648.4) The party had an uneventful trip to Jerusalem, but they had hardly got themselves settled at Bethany when from near and far those seeking healing for their bodies, comfort for troubled minds, and salvation for their souls, began to congregate, so much so that Jesus had little time for rest. Therefore they pitched tents at Gethsemane, and the Master would go back and forth from Bethany to Gethsemane to avoid the crowds which so constantly thronged him. The apostolic party spent almost three weeks at Jerusalem, but Jesus enjoined them to do no public preaching, only private teaching and personal work.

147:2.3 (1648.5) At Bethany they quietly celebrated the Passover. And this was the first time that Jesus and all of the twelve partook of the bloodless Passover feast. The apostles of John did not eat the Passover with Jesus and his apostles; they celebrated the feast with Abner and many of the early believers in John's preaching. This was the second Passover Jesus had observed with his apostles in Jerusalem.

147:2.4 (1648.6) When Jesus and the twelve departed for Capernaum, the apostles of John did not return with them. Under the direction of Abner they remained in Jerusalem and the surrounding country, quietly laboring for the extension of the kingdom, while Jesus and the twelve returned to work in Galilee. Never again were the twenty-four all together until a short time before the commissioning and sending forth of the seventy evangelists. But the two groups were co-operative, and notwithstanding their differences of opinion, the best of feelings prevailed.

3　　　*At the Pool of Bethesda*

147:3.1 (1649.1) The afternoon of the second Sabbath in Jerusalem, as the Master and the apostles were about to participate in the temple services, John said to Jesus, "Come with me, I would show you something." John conducted Jesus out through one of the Jerusalem gates to a pool of water called Bethesda. Surrounding this pool was a structure of five porches under which a large group of sufferers lingered in quest of healing. This was a hot spring whose reddish- tinged water would bubble up at irregular intervals because of gas accumulations in the rock caverns underneath the pool. This periodic disturbance of the warm waters was believed by many to be due to supernatural influences, and it was a popular belief that the first person who entered the water after such a disturbance would be healed of whatever infirmity he had.

147:3.2 (1649.2) The apostles were somewhat restless under the restrictions imposed by Jesus, and John, the youngest of the twelve, was especially restive under this restraint. He had brought Jesus to the pool thinking that the sight of the assembled sufferers would make such an appeal to the Master's compassion that he would be moved to perform a miracle of healing, and thereby would all Jerusalem be astounded and presently be won to believe in the gospel of the kingdom. Said John to Jesus: "Master, see all of these suffering ones; is there nothing we can do for them?" And Jesus replied: "John, why would you tempt me to turn aside from the way I have chosen? Why do you go on desiring to substitute the working of wonders and the healing of the sick for the proclamation of the gospel of eternal truth? My son, I may not do that which you desire, but gather together these sick and afflicted that I may speak words of good cheer and eternal comfort to them."

147:3.3 (1649.3) In speaking to those assembled, Jesus said: "Many of you are here, sick and afflicted, because of your many years of wrong living. Some suffer from the accidents of time, others as a result of the mistakes of their forebears, while some of you struggle under the handicaps of the imperfect conditions of your temporal existence. But my Father works, and I would work, to improve your earthly state but more especially to insure your eternal estate. None of us can do much to change the difficulties of life unless we discover the Father in heaven so wills. After all, we are all beholden to do the will of the Eternal. If you could all be healed of your physical afflictions, you would indeed marvel, but it is even greater that you should be cleansed of all spiritual disease and find yourselves healed of all moral infirmities. You are all God's children; you are the sons of the heavenly Father. The bonds of time may seem to afflict you, but the God of eternity loves you. And when the time of judgment shall come, fear not, you shall all find, not only justice, but an abundance of mercy. Verily, verily, I say to you: He who hears the gospel of the kingdom and believes in this teaching of sonship with God, has eternal life; already are such believers passing from judgment and death to light and life. And the hour is coming in which even those who are in the tombs shall hear the voice of the resurrection."

147:3.4 (1649.4) And many of those who heard believed the gospel of the kingdom. Some of the afflicted were so inspired and spiritually revivified that they went about proclaiming that they had also been cured of their physical ailments.

147:3.5 (1649.5) One man who had been many years downcast and grievously afflicted by the infirmities of his troubled mind, rejoiced at Jesus' words and, picking up his bed, went forth to his home, even though it was the Sabbath day. This afflicted man had waited all these years for somebody to help him; he was such a victim of the feeling of his own helplessness that he had never once entertained the idea of helping himself which proved to be the one thing he had to do in order to effect recovery—take up his bed and walk.

147:3.6 (1650.1) Then said Jesus to John: "Let us depart ere the chief priests and the scribes come upon us and take offense that we spoke words of life to these afflicted ones." And they returned to the temple to join their companions, and presently all of them departed to spend the night at Bethany. But John never told the other apostles of this visit of himself and Jesus to the pool of Bethesda on this Sabbath afternoon.

4   The Rule of Living

147:4.1 (1650.2) On the evening of this same Sabbath day, at Bethany, while Jesus, the twelve, and a group of believers were assembled about the fire in Lazarus's garden, Nathaniel asked Jesus this question: "Master, although you have taught us the positive version of the old rule of life, instructing us that we should do to others as we wish them to do to us, I do not fully discern how we can always abide by such an injunction. Let me illustrate my contention by citing the example of a lustful man

who thus wickedly looks upon his intended consort in sin. How can we teach that this evil- intending man should do to others as he would they should do to him?"

147:4.2 (1650.3) When Jesus heard Nathaniel's question, he immediately stood upon his feet and, pointing his finger at the apostle, said: "Nathaniel, Nathaniel! What manner of thinking is going on in your heart? Do you not receive my teachings as one who has been born of the spirit? Do you not hear the truth as men of wisdom and spiritual understanding? When I admonished you to do to others as you would have them do to you, I spoke to men of high ideals, not to those who would be tempted to distort my teaching into a license for the encouragement of evil-doing."

147:4.3 (1650.4) When the Master had spoken, Nathaniel stood up and said: "But, Master, you should not think that I approve of such an interpretation of your teaching. I asked the question because I conjectured that many such men might thus misjudge your admonition, and I hoped you would give us further instruction regarding these matters." And then when Nathaniel had sat down, Jesus continued speaking: "I well know, Nathaniel, that no such idea of evil is approved in your mind, but I am disappointed in that you all so often fail to put a genuinely spiritual interpretation upon my commonplace teachings, instruction which must be given you in human language and as men must speak. Let me now teach you concerning the differing levels of meaning attached to the interpretation of this rule of living, this admonition to 'do to others that which you desire others to do to you':

147:4.4 (1650.5) "1. The level of the flesh. Such a purely selfish and lustful interpretation would be well exemplified by the supposition of your question.

147:4.5 (1650.6) "2. The level of the feelings. This plane is one level higher than that of the flesh and implies that sympathy and pity would enhance one's interpretation of this rule of living.

147:4.6 (1650.7) "3. The level of mind. Now come into action the reason of mind and the intelligence of experience. Good judgment dictates that such a rule of living should be interpreted in consonance with the highest idealism embodied in the nobility of profound self-respect.

147:4.7 (1651.1) "4. The level of brotherly love. Still higher is discovered the level of unselfish devotion to the welfare of one's fellows. On this higher plane of wholehearted social service growing out of the consciousness of the fatherhood of God and the consequent recognition of the brotherhood of man, there is discovered a new and far more beautiful interpretation of this basic rule of life.

147:4.8 (1651.2) "5. The moral level. And then when you attain true philosophic levels of interpretation, when you have real insight into the rightness and wrongness of things, when you perceive the eternal fitness of human relationships, you will begin to view such a problem of interpretation as you would imagine a high-minded, idealistic, wise, and impartial third person would so view and interpret such an injunction as applied to your personal problems of adjustment to your life situations.

147:4.9 (1651.3) "6. The spiritual level. And then last, but greatest of all, we attain the level of spirit insight and spiritual interpretation which impels us to recognize in this rule of life the divine command to treat all men as we conceive God would treat them. That is the universe ideal of human relationships. And this is your attitude toward all such problems when your supreme desire is ever to do the Father's will. I would, therefore, that you should do to all men that which you know I would do to them in like circumstances."

147:4.10 (1651.4) Nothing Jesus had said to the apostles up to this time had ever more astonished them. They continued to discuss the Master's words long after he had retired. While Nathaniel was slow to recover from his supposition that Jesus had misunderstood the spirit of his question, the others were more than thankful that their philosophic fellow apostle had had the courage to ask such a thought-provoking question.

5   Visiting Simon the Pharisee

147:5.1 (1651.5) Though Simon was not a member of the Jewish Sanhedrin, he was an influential Pharisee of Jerusalem. He was a halfhearted believer, and notwithstanding that he might be severely criticized therefor, he dared to invite Jesus and his personal associates, Peter, James, and John, to his home for a social meal. Simon had long observed the Master and was much impressed with his teachings and even more so with his personality. *

147:5.2 (1651.6) The wealthy Pharisees were devoted to almsgiving, and they did not shun publicity regarding their philanthropy. Sometimes they would even blow a trumpet as they were about to bestow charity upon some beggar. It was the custom of these Pharisees, when they provided a banquet for distinguished guests, to leave the doors of the house open so that even the street beggars might come in and, standing around the walls of the room behind the couches of the diners, be in position to receive portions of food which might be tossed to them by the banqueters.

147:5.3 (1651.7) On this particular occasion at Simon's house, among those who came in off the street was a woman of unsavory reputation who had recently become a believer in the good news of the gospel of the kingdom. This woman was well known throughout all Jerusalem as the former keeper of one of the so-called high-class brothels located hard by the temple court of the gentiles. She had, on accepting the teachings of Jesus, closed up her nefarious place of business and had induced the majority of the women associated with her to accept the gospel and change their mode of living; notwithstanding this, she was still held in great disdain by the Pharisees and was compelled to wear her hair down—the badge of harlotry. This unnamed woman had brought with her a large flask of perfumed anointing lotion and, standing behind Jesus as he reclined at meat, began to anoint his feet while she also wet his feet with her tears of gratitude, wiping them with the hair of her head. And when she had finished this anointing, she continued weeping and kissing his feet.

147:5.4 (1652.1) When Simon saw all this, he said to himself: "This man, if he were a prophet, would have perceived who and what manner of woman this is who thus touches him; that she is a notorious sinner." And Jesus, knowing what was going on in Simon's mind, spoke up, saying: "Simon, I have something which I would like to say to you." Simon answered, "Teacher, say on." Then said Jesus: "A certain wealthy moneylender had two debtors. The one owed him five hundred denarii and the other fifty. Now, when neither of them had wherewith to pay, he forgave them both. Which of them do you think, Simon, would love him most?" Simon answered, "He, I suppose, whom he forgave the most." And Jesus said, "You have rightly judged," and pointing to the woman, he continued: "Simon, take a good look at this woman. I entered your house as an invited guest, yet you gave me no water for my feet. This grateful woman has washed my feet with tears and wiped them with the hair of her head. You gave me no kiss of friendly greeting, but this woman, ever since she came in, has not ceased to kiss my feet. My head with oil you neglected to anoint, but she has anointed my feet with precious lotions. And what is the meaning of all this? Simply that her many sins have been forgiven, and this has led her to love much. But those who have received but little forgiveness sometimes love but little." And turning around toward the woman, he took her by the hand and, lifting her up, said: "You have indeed repented of your sins, and they are forgiven. Be not discouraged by the thoughtless and unkind attitude of your fellows; go on in the joy and liberty of the kingdom of heaven."

147:5.5 (1652.2) When Simon and his friends who sat at meat with him heard these words, they were the more astonished, and they began to whisper among themselves, "Who is this man that he even dares to forgive sins?" And when Jesus heard them thus murmuring, he turned to dismiss the woman, saying, "Woman, go in peace; your faith has saved you."

147:5.6 (1652.3) As Jesus arose with his friends to leave, he turned to Simon and said: "I know your heart, Simon, how you are torn betwixt faith and doubts, how you are distraught by fear and troubled by pride; but I pray for you that you may yield to the light and may experience in your station in life just such mighty transformations of mind and spirit as may be comparable to the tremendous changes which the gospel of the kingdom has already wrought in the heart of your unbidden and unwelcome guest. And I declare to all of you that the Father has opened the doors of the heavenly kingdom to all who have the faith to enter, and no man or association of men can close those doors even to the most humble soul or supposedly most flagrant sinner on earth if such sincerely seek an entrance." And Jesus, with Peter, James, and John, took leave of their host and went to join the rest of the apostles at the camp in the garden of Gethsemane.

147:5.7 (1653.1) That same evening Jesus made the long-to-be-remembered address to the apostles regarding the relative value of status with God and progress in the eternal ascent to Paradise. Said Jesus: "My children, if there exists a true and living connection between the child and the Father, the child is certain to progress continuously toward the Father's ideals. True, the child may at first make slow progress, but the progress is none the less sure. The important thing is not the rapidity of your progress but rather its certainty. Your actual achievement is not so important as the fact that the direction of your progress is Godward. What you are becoming day by day is of infinitely more importance than what you are today.

147:5.8 (1653.2) "This transformed woman whom some of you saw at Simon's house today is, at this moment, living on a level which is vastly below that of Simon and his well-meaning associates; but while these Pharisees are occupied with the false progress of the illusion of traversing deceptive circles of meaningless ceremonial services, this woman has, in dead earnest, started out on the long and eventful search for God, and her path toward heaven is not blocked by spiritual pride and moral self-satisfaction. The woman is, humanly speaking, much farther away from God than Simon, but her soul is in progressive motion; she is on the way toward an eternal goal. There are present in this woman tremendous spiritual possibilities for the future. Some of you may not stand high in actual levels of soul and spirit, but you are making daily progress on the living way opened up, through faith, to God. There are tremendous possibilities in each of you for the future. Better by far to have a small but living and growing faith than to be possessed of a great intellect with its dead stores of worldly wisdom and spiritual unbelief."

147:5.9 (1653.3) But Jesus earnestly warned his apostles against the foolishness of the child of God who presumes upon the Father's love. He declared that the heavenly Father is not a lax, loose, or foolishly indulgent parent who is ever ready to condone sin and forgive recklessness. He cautioned his hearers not mistakenly to apply his illustrations of father and son so as to make it appear that God is like some overindulgent and unwise parents who conspire with the foolish of earth to encompass the moral undoing of their thoughtless children, and who are thereby certainly and directly contributing to the delinquency and early demoralization of their own offspring. Said Jesus: "My Father does not indulgently condone those acts and practices of his children which are self-destructive and suicidal to all moral growth and spiritual progress. Such sinful practices are an abomination in the sight of God."

147:5.10 (1653.4) Many other semi-private meetings and banquets did Jesus attend with the high and the low, the rich and the poor, of Jerusalem before he and his apostles finally departed for Capernaum. And many, indeed, became believers in the gospel of the kingdom and were subsequently baptized by Abner and his associates, who remained behind to foster the interests of the kingdom in Jerusalem and thereabouts.

6 Returning to Capernaum

147:6.1 (1653.5) The last week of April, Jesus and the twelve departed from their Bethany headquarters near Jerusalem and began their journey back to Capernaum by way of Jericho and the Jordan.

147:6.2 (1654.1) The chief priests and the religious leaders of the Jews held many secret meetings for the purpose of deciding what to do with Jesus. They were all agreed that something should be done to put a stop to his teaching, but they could not agree on the method. They had hoped that the civil authorities would dispose of him as Herod had put an end to John, but they discovered that Jesus was so conducting his work that the Roman officials were not much alarmed by his preaching. Accordingly, at a meeting which was held the day before Jesus' departure for Capernaum, it was decided that he would have to be apprehended on a religious charge and be tried by the Sanhedrin. Therefore a commission of six secret spies was appointed to follow Jesus, to observe his words and acts, and when they had amassed sufficient evidence of lawbreaking and blasphemy, to return to Jerusalem with their report. These six Jews caught up with the apostolic party, numbering about thirty, at Jericho and, under the pretense of desiring to become disciples, attached themselves to Jesus' family of followers, remaining with the group up to the time of the beginning of the second preaching tour in Galilee; whereupon three of them returned to Jerusalem to submit their report to the chief priests and the Sanhedrin.

147:6.3 (1654.2) Peter preached to the assembled multitude at the crossing of the Jordan, and the following morning they moved up the river toward Amathus. They wanted to proceed straight on to Capernaum, but such a crowd gathered here they remained three days, preaching, teaching, and baptizing. They did not move toward home until early Sabbath morning, the first day of May. The Jerusalem spies were sure they would now secure their first charge against Jesus— that of Sabbath breaking—since he had presumed to start his journey on the Sabbath day. But they were doomed to disappointment because, just before their departure, Jesus called Andrew into his presence and before them all instructed him to proceed for a distance of only one thousand yards, the legal Jewish Sabbath day's journey.

147:6.4 (1654.3) But the spies did not have long to wait for their opportunity to accuse Jesus and his associates of Sabbath breaking. As the company passed along the narrow road, the waving wheat, which was just then ripening, was near at hand on either side, and some of the apostles, being hungry, plucked the ripe grain and ate it. It was customary for travelers to help themselves to grain as they passed along the road, and therefore no thought of wrongdoing was attached to such conduct. But the spies seized upon this as a pretext for assailing Jesus. When they saw Andrew rub the grain in his hand, they went up to him and said: "Do you not know that it is unlawful to pluck and rub the grain on the Sabbath day?" And Andrew answered: "But we are hungry and rub only sufficient for our needs; and since when did it become sinful to eat grain on the Sabbath day?" But the Pharisees answered: "You do no wrong in eating, but you do break the law in plucking and rubbing out the grain between your hands; surely your Master would not approve of such acts." Then said Andrew: "But if it is not wrong to eat the grain, surely the rubbing out between our hands is hardly more work than the chewing of the grain, which you allow; wherefore do you quibble over such

trifles?" When Andrew intimated that they were quibblers, they were indignant, and rushing back to where Jesus walked along, talking to Matthew, they protested, saying: "Behold, Teacher, your apostles do that which is unlawful on the Sabbath day; they pluck, rub, and eat the grain. We are sure you will command them to cease." And then said Jesus to the accusers: "You are indeed zealous for the law, and you do well to remember the Sabbath day to keep it holy; but did you never read in the Scripture that, one day when David was hungry, he and they who were with him entered the house of God and ate the showbread, which it was not lawful for anyone to eat save the priests? and David also gave this bread to those who

were with him. And have you not read in our law that it is lawful to do many needful things on the Sabbath day? And shall I not, before the day is finished, see you eat that which you have brought along for the needs of this day? My good men, you do well to be zealous for the Sabbath, but you would do better to guard the health and well-being of your fellows. I declare that the Sabbath was made for man and not man for the Sabbath. And if you are here present with us to watch my words, then will I openly proclaim that the Son of Man is lord even of the Sabbath."

147:6.5 (1655.1) The Pharisees were astonished and confounded by his words of discernment and wisdom. For the remainder of the day they kept by themselves and dared not ask any more questions.

147:6.6 (1655.2) Jesus' antagonism to the Jewish traditions and slavish ceremonials was always positive. It consisted in what he did and in what he affirmed. The Master spent little time in negative denunciations. He taught that those who know God can enjoy the liberty of living without deceiving themselves by the licenses of sinning. Said Jesus to the apostles: "Men, if you are enlightened by the truth and really know what you are doing, you are blessed; but if you know not the divine way, you are unfortunate and already breakers of the law."

7 Back in Capernaum

147:7.1 (1655.3) It was around noon on Monday, May 3, when Jesus and the twelve came to Bethsaida by boat from Tarichea. They traveled by boat in order to escape those who journeyed with them. But by the next day the others, including the official spies from Jerusalem, had again found Jesus.

147:7.2 (1655.4) On Tuesday evening Jesus was conducting one of his customary classes of questions and answers when the leader of the six spies said to him: "I was today talking with one of John's disciples who is here attending upon your teaching, and we were at a loss to understand why you never command your disciples to fast and pray as we Pharisees fast and as John bade his followers." And Jesus, referring to a statement by John, answered this questioner: "Do the sons of the bridechamber fast while the bridegroom is with them? As long as the bridegroom remains with them, they can hardly fast. But the time is coming when the bridegroom shall be taken away, and during those times the children of the bride chamber undoubtedly will fast and pray. To pray is natural for the children of light, but fasting is not a part of the gospel of the kingdom of heaven. Be reminded that a wise tailor does not sew a piece of new and un-shrunk cloth upon an old garment, lest, when it is wet, it shrink and produce a worse rent. Neither do men put new wine into old wine skins, lest the new wine burst the skins so that both the wine and the skins perish. The wise man puts the new wine into fresh wine skins. Therefore do my disciples show wisdom in that they do not bring too much of the old order over into the new teaching of the gospel of the kingdom. You who have lost your teacher may be justified in fasting for a time.

Fasting may be an appropriate part of the law of Moses, but in the coming kingdom the sons of God shall experience freedom from fear and joy in the divine spirit." And when they heard these words, the disciples of John were comforted while the Pharisees themselves were the more confounded.

147:7.3 (1656.1) Then the Master proceeded to warn his hearers against entertaining the notion that all olden teaching should be replaced entirely by new doctrines. Said Jesus: "That which is old and also true must abide. Likewise, that which is new but false must be rejected. But that which is new and also true, have the faith and courage to accept.

Remember it is written: 'Forsake not an old friend, for the new is not comparable to him. As new wine, so is a new friend; if it becomes old, you shall drink it with gladness.'"

8 The Feast of Spiritual Goodness

147:8.1 (1656.2) That night, long after the usual listeners had retired, Jesus continued to teach his apostles. He began this special instruction by quoting from the Prophet Isaiah:

147:8.2 (1656.3) "'Why have you fasted? For what reason do you afflict your souls while you continue to find pleasure in oppression and to take delight in injustice? Behold, you fast for the sake of strife and contention and to smite with the fist of wickedness. But you shall not fast in this way to make your voices heard on high.

147:8.3 (1656.4) "'Is it such a fast that I have chosen—a day for a man to afflict his soul? Is it to bow down his head like a bulrush, to grovel in sackcloth and ashes? Will you dare to call this a fast and an acceptable day in the sight of the Lord? Is not this the fast I should choose: to loose the bonds of wickedness, to undo the knots of heavy burdens, to let the oppressed go free, and to break every yoke? Is it not to share my bread with the hungry and to bring those who are homeless and poor to my house? And when I see those who are naked, I will clothe them.

147:8.4 (1656.5) "'Then shall your light break forth as the morning while your health springs forth speedily. Your righteousness shall go before you while the glory of the Lord shall be your rear guard. Then will you call upon the Lord, and he shall answer; you will cry out, and he shall say—Here am I. And all this he will do if you refrain from oppression, condemnation, and vanity. The Father rather desires that you draw out your heart to the hungry, and that you minister to the afflicted souls; then shall your light shine in obscurity, and even your darkness shall be as the noonday.

Then shall the Lord guide you continually, satisfying your soul and renewing your strength. You shall become like a watered garden, like a spring whose waters fail not. And they who do these things shall restore the wasted glories; they shall raise up the foundations of many generations; they shall be called the rebuilders of broken walls, the restorers of safe paths in which to dwell.'"

147:8.5 (1656.6) And then long into the night Jesus propounded to his apostles the truth that it was their faith that made them secure in the kingdom of the present and the future, and not their affliction of soul nor fasting of body. He exhorted the apostles at least to live up to the ideas of the prophet of old and expressed the hope that they would progress far beyond even the ideals of Isaiah and the older prophets. His last words that night were: "Grow in grace by means of that living faith which grasps the fact that you are the sons of God while at the same time it recognizes every man as a brother."

147:8.6 (1656.7) It was after two o'clock in the morning when Jesus ceased speaking and every man went to his place for sleep.

Paper 148

Training Evangelists at Bethsaida

148:0.1 (1657.1) FROM May 3 to October 3, A.D. 28, Jesus and the apostolic party were in residence at the Zebedee home at Bethsaida. Throughout this five months' period of the dry season an enormous camp was maintained by the seaside near the Zebedee residence, which had been greatly enlarged to accommodate the growing family of Jesus. This seaside camp, occupied by an ever-changing population of truth seekers, healing candidates, and curiosity devotees, numbered from five hundred to fifteen hundred. This tented city was under the general supervision of David Zebedee, assisted by the Alpheus twins. The encampment was a model in order and sanitation as well as in its general administration. The sick of different types were segregated and were under the supervision of a believer physician, a Syrian named Elman.

148:0.2 (1657.2) Throughout this period the apostles would go fishing at least one day a week, selling their catch to David for consumption by the seaside encampment. The funds thus received were turned over to the group treasury. The twelve were permitted to spend one week out of each month with their families or friends.

148:0.3 (1657.3) While Andrew continued in general charge of the apostolic activities, Peter was in full charge of the school of the evangelists. The apostles all did their share in teaching groups of evangelists each forenoon, and both teachers and pupils taught the people during the afternoons. After the evening meal, five nights a week, the apostles conducted question classes for the benefit of the evangelists. Once a week Jesus presided at this question hour, answering the holdover questions from previous sessions.

148:0.4 (1657.4) In five months several thousand came and went at this encampment. Interested persons from every part of the Roman Empire and from the lands east of the Euphrates were in frequent attendance. This was the longest settled and well-organized period of the Master's teaching. Jesus' immediate family spent most of this time at either Nazareth or Cana.

148:0.5 (1657.5) The encampment was not conducted as a community of common interests, as was the apostolic family. David Zebedee managed this large tent city so that it became a self-sustaining enterprise, notwithstanding that no one was ever turned away. This ever-changing camp was an indispensable feature of Peter's evangelistic training school.

A New School of the Prophets

148:1.1 (1657.6) Peter, James, and Andrew were the committee designated by Jesus to pass upon applicants for admission to the school of evangelists. All the races and nationalities of the Roman world and the East, as far as India, were represented among the students in this new school of the prophets. This school was conducted on the plan of learning and doing. What the students learned during the forenoon they taught to the assembly by the seaside during the afternoon. After supper they informally discussed both the learning of the forenoon and the teaching of the afternoon.

148:1.2 (1658.1) Each of the apostolic teachers taught his own view of the gospel of the kingdom. They made no effort to teach just alike; there was no standardized or dogmatic formulation of theologic doctrines. Though they all taught the same truth, each apostle presented his own personal interpretation of the Master's teaching. And Jesus upheld this presentation of the diversity of personal experience in the things of the kingdom, unfailingly harmonizing and co- ordinating these many and divergent views of the gospel at his weekly question hours. Notwithstanding this great degree of personal liberty in matters of teaching, Simon Peter tended to dominate the theology of the school of evangelists.

Next to Peter, James Zebedee exerted the greatest personal influence.

148:1.3 (1658.2) The one hundred and more evangelists trained during this five months by the seaside represented the material from which (excepting Abner and John's apostles) the later seventy gospel teachers and preachers were drawn. The school of evangelists did not have everything in common to the same degree as did the twelve.

148:1.4 (1658.3) These evangelists, though they taught and preached the gospel, did not baptize believers until after they were later ordained and commissioned by Jesus as the seventy messengers of the kingdom. Only seven of the large number healed at the sundown scene at this place were to be found among these evangelistic students. The nobleman's son of Capernaum was one of those trained for gospel service in Peter's school.

The Bethsaida Hospital

148:2.1 (1658.4) In connection with the seaside encampment, Elman, the Syrian physician, with the assistance of a corps of twenty-five young women and twelve men, organized and conducted for four months what should be regarded as the kingdom's first hospital. At this infirmary, located a short distance to the south of the main tented city, they treated the sick in accordance with all known material methods as well as by the spiritual practices of prayer and faith encouragement. Jesus visited the sick of this encampment not less than three times a week and made personal contact with each sufferer. As far as we know, no so-called miracles of supernatural healing occurred among the one thousand afflicted and ailing persons who went away from this infirmary improved or cured. However, the vast majority of these benefited individuals ceased not to proclaim that Jesus had healed them.

148:2.2 (1658.5) Many of the cures effected by Jesus in connection with his ministry in behalf of Elman's patients did, indeed, appear to resemble the working of miracles, but we were instructed that they were only just such transformations of mind and spirit as may occur in the experience of expectant and faith-dominated persons who are under the immediate and inspirational influence of a strong, positive, and beneficent personality whose ministry banishes fear and destroys anxiety.

148:2.3 (1658.6) Elman and his associates endeavored to teach the truth to these sick ones concerning the "possession of evil spirits," but they met with little success. The belief that physical sickness and mental derangement could be caused by the dwelling of a so-called unclean spirit in the mind or body of the afflicted person was well-nigh universal.

148:2.4 (1659.1) In all his contact with the sick and afflicted, when it came to the technique of treatment or the revelation of the unknown causes of disease, Jesus did not disregard the instructions of his Paradise brother, Immanuel, given ere he embarked upon the venture of the Urantia incarnation. Notwithstanding this, those who ministered to the sick learned many helpful lessons by observing the manner in which Jesus inspired the faith and confidence of the sick and suffering.

148:2.5 (1659.2) The camp disbanded a short time before the season for the increase in chills and fever drew on.

The Father's Business

148:3.1 (1659.3) Throughout this period Jesus conducted public services at the encampment less than a dozen times and spoke only once in the Capernaum synagogue, the second Sabbath before their departure with the newly trained evangelists upon their second public preaching tour of Galilee.

148:3.2 (1659.4) Not since his baptism had the Master been so much alone as during this period of the evangelists' training encampment at Bethsaida. Whenever any one of the apostles ventured to ask Jesus why he was absent so much from their midst, he would invariably answer that he was "about the Father's business."

148:3.3 (1659.5) During these periods of absence, Jesus was accompanied by only two of the apostles. He had released Peter, James, and John temporarily from their assignment as his personal companions that they might also participate in the work of training the new evangelistic candidates, numbering more than one hundred. When the Master desired to go to the hills about the Father's business, he would summon to accompany him any two of the apostles who might be at liberty. In this way each of the twelve enjoyed an opportunity for close association and intimate contact with Jesus.

148:3.4 (1659.6) It has not been revealed for the purposes of this record, but we have been led to infer that the Master, during many of these solitary seasons in the hills, was in direct and executive association with many of his chief directors of universe affairs. Ever since about the time of his baptism this incarnated Sovereign of our universe had become increasingly and consciously active in the direction of certain phases of universe administration. And we have always held the opinion that, in some way not revealed to his immediate associates, during these weeks of decreased participation in the affairs of earth he was engaged in the direction of those high spirit intelligences who were charged with the running of a vast universe, and that the human Jesus chose to designate such activities on his part as being "about his Father's business."

148:3.5 (1659.7) Many times, when Jesus was alone for hours, but when two of his apostles were near by, they observed his features undergo rapid and multitudinous changes, although they heard him speak no words. Neither did they observe any visible manifestation of celestial beings who might have been in communication with their Master, such as some of them did witness on a subsequent occasion.

Evil, Sin, and Iniquity

148:4.1 (1659.8) It was the habit of Jesus two evenings each week to hold special converse with individuals who desired to talk with him, in a certain secluded and sheltered corner of the Zebedee garden. At one of these evening conversations in private Thomas asked the Master this question: "Why is it necessary for men to be born of the spirit in order to enter the kingdom? Is rebirth necessary to escape the control of the evil one? Master, what is evil?" When Jesus heard these questions, he said to Thomas:

148:4.2 (1660.1) "Do not make the mistake of confusing evil with the evil one, more correctly the iniquitous one. He whom you call the evil one is the son of self-love, the high administrator who knowingly went into deliberate rebellion against the rule of my Father and his loyal Sons. But I have already vanquished these sinful rebels. Make clear in your mind these different attitudes toward the Father and his universe. Never forget these laws of relation to the Father's will:

148:4.3 (1660.2) "Evil is the unconscious or unintended transgression of the divine law, the Father's will. Evil is likewise the measure of the imperfectness of obedience to the Father's will.

148:4.4 (1660.3) "Sin is the conscious, knowing, and deliberate transgression of the divine law, the Father's will. Sin is the measure of unwillingness to be divinely led and spiritually directed.

148:4.5 (1660.4) "Iniquity is the willful, determined, and persistent transgression of the divine law, the Father's will. Iniquity is the measure of the continued rejection of the Father's loving plan of personality survival and the Sons' merciful ministry of salvation.

148:4.6 (1660.5) "By nature, before the rebirth of the spirit, mortal man is subject to inherent evil tendencies, but such natural imperfections of behavior are neither sin nor iniquity. Mortal man is just beginning his long ascent to the perfection of the Father in Paradise. To be imperfect or partial in natural endowment is not sinful. Man is indeed subject to evil, but he is in no sense the child of the evil one unless he has knowingly and deliberately chosen the paths of sin and the life of iniquity. Evil is inherent in the natural order of this world, but sin is an attitude of conscious rebellion which was brought to this world by those who fell from spiritual light into gross darkness.

148:4.7 (1660.6) "You are confused, Thomas, by the doctrines of the Greeks and the errors of the Persians. You do not understand the relationships of evil and sin because you view mankind as beginning on earth with a perfect Adam and rapidly degenerating, through sin, to man's present deplorable estate. But why do you refuse to comprehend the meaning of the record which discloses how Cain, the son of Adam, went over into the land of Nod and there got himself a wife? And why do you refuse to interpret the meaning of the record which portrays the sons of God finding wives for themselves among the daughters of men?

148:4.8 (1660.7) "Men are, indeed, by nature evil, but not necessarily sinful. The new birth—the baptism of the spirit—is essential to deliverance from evil and necessary for entrance into the kingdom of heaven, but none of this detracts from the fact that man is the son of God. Neither does this inherent presence of potential evil mean that man is in some mysterious way estranged from the Father in heaven so that, as an alien, foreigner, or stepchild, he must in some manner seek for legal adoption by the Father. All such notions are born, first, of your misunderstanding of the Father and, second, of your ignorance of the origin, nature, and destiny of man.

148:4.9 (1660.8) "The Greeks

and others have taught you that man is descending from godly perfection steadily down toward oblivion or destruction; I have come to show that man, by entrance into the kingdom, is ascending certainly and surely up to God and divine perfection. Any being who in any manner falls short of the divine and spiritual ideals of the eternal Father's will is potentially evil, but such beings are in no sense sinful, much less iniquitous.

148:4.10 (1661.1) "Thomas, have you not read about this in the Scriptures, where it is written: 'You are the children of the Lord your God.' 'I will be his Father and he shall be my son.' 'I have chosen him to be my son—I will be his Father.' 'Bring my sons from far and my daughters from the ends of the earth; even every one who is called by my name, for I have created them for my glory.' 'You are the sons of the living God.' 'They who have the spirit of God are indeed the sons of God.' While there is a material part of the human father in the natural child, there is a spiritual part of the heavenly Father in every faith son of the kingdom."

148:4.11 (1661.2) All this and much more Jesus said to Thomas, and much of it the apostle comprehended, although Jesus admonished him to "speak not to the others concerning these matters until after I shall have returned to the Father." And Thomas did not mention this interview until after the Master had departed from this world.

The Purpose of Affliction

148:5.1 (1661.3) At another of these private interviews in the garden Nathaniel asked Jesus: "Master, though I am beginning to understand why you refuse to practice healing indiscriminately, I am still at a loss to understand why the loving Father in heaven permits so many of his children on earth to suffer so many afflictions." The Master answered Nathaniel, saying:

148:5.2 (1661.4) "Nathaniel, you and many others are thus perplexed because you do not comprehend how the natural order of this world has been so many times upset by the sinful adventures of certain rebellious traitors to the Father's will. And I have come to make a beginning of setting these things in order. But many ages will be required to restore this part of the universe to former paths and thus release the children of men from the extra burdens of sin and rebellion. The presence of evil alone is sufficient test for the ascension of man—sin is not essential to survival.

148:5.3 (1661.5) "But, my son, you should know that the Father does not purposely afflict his children. Man brings down upon himself unnecessary affliction as a result of his persistent refusal to walk in the better ways of the divine will.

Affliction is potential in evil, but much of it has been produced by sin and iniquity. Many unusual events have transpired on this world, and it is not strange that all thinking men should be perplexed by the scenes of suffering and affliction which they witness. But of one thing you may be sure: The Father does not send affliction as an arbitrary punishment for wrongdoing. The imperfections and handicaps of evil are inherent; the penalties of sin are inevitable; the destroying consequences of iniquity are inexorable. Man should not blame God for those afflictions which are the natural result of the life which he chooses to live; neither should man complain of those experiences which are a part of life as it is lived on this world. It is the Father's will that mortal man should work persistently and consistently toward the betterment of his estate on earth. Intelligent application would enable man to overcome much of his earthly misery.

148:5.4 (1662.1) "Nathaniel, it is our mission to help men solve their spiritual problems and in this way to quicken their minds so that they may be the better prepared and inspired to go about solving their manifold material problems. I know of your confusion as you have read the Scriptures. All too often there has prevailed a tendency to ascribe to God the responsibility for everything which ignorant man fails to understand. The Father is not personally responsible for all you may fail to comprehend. Do not doubt the love of the Father just because some just and wise law of his ordaining chances to afflict you because you have innocently or deliberately transgressed such a divine ordinance.

148:5.5 (1662.2) "But, Nathaniel, there is much in the Scriptures which would have instructed you if you had only read with discernment. Do you not remember that it is written: 'My son, despise not the chastening of the Lord; neither be weary of his correction, for whom the Lord loves he corrects, even as the father corrects the son in whom he takes delight.' 'The Lord does not afflict willingly.' 'Before I was afflicted, I went astray, but now do I keep the law. Affliction was good for me that I might thereby learn the divine statutes.' 'I know your sorrows. The eternal God is your refuge, while underneath are the everlasting arms.' 'The Lord also is a refuge for the oppressed, a haven of rest in times of trouble.' 'The Lord will strengthen him upon the bed of affliction; the Lord will not forget the sick.' 'As a father shows compassion for his children, so is the Lord compassionate to those who fear him. He knows your body; he remembers that you are dust.' 'He heals the brokenhearted and binds up their wounds.' 'He is the hope of the poor, the strength of the needy in his distress, a refuge from the storm, and a shadow from the devastating heat.' 'He gives power to the faint, and to them who have no might he increases strength.' 'A bruised reed shall he not break, and the smoking flax he will not quench.' 'When you pass through the waters of affliction, I will be with you, and when the rivers of adversity overflow you, I will not forsake you.' 'He has sent me to bind up the brokenhearted, to proclaim liberty to the captives, and to comfort all who mourn.' 'There is correction in suffering; affliction does not spring forth from the dust.'"

The Misunderstanding of Suffering — Discourse on Job

148:6.1 (1662.3) It was this same evening at Bethsaida that John also asked Jesus why so many apparently innocent people suffered from so many diseases and experienced so many afflictions. In answering John's questions, among many other things, the Master said:

148:6.2 (1662.4) "My son, you do not comprehend the meaning of adversity or the mission of suffering. Have you not read that masterpiece of Semitic literature—the Scripture story of the afflictions of Job? Do you not recall how this wonderful parable begins with the recital of the material prosperity of the Lord's servant? You well remember that Job was blessed with children, wealth, dignity, position, health, and everything else which men value in this temporal life.

According to the time-honored teachings of the children of Abraham such material prosperity was all-sufficient evidence of divine favor. But such material possessions and such temporal prosperity do not indicate God's favor. My Father in heaven loves the poor just as much as the rich; he is no respecter of persons.

148:6.3 (1663.1) "Although transgression of divine law is sooner or later followed by the harvest of punishment, while men certainly eventually do reap what they sow, still you should know that human suffering is not always a punishment for antecedent sin. Both Job and his friends failed to find the true answer for their perplexities. And with the light you now enjoy you would hardly assign to either Satan or God the parts they play in this unique parable. While Job did not, through suffering, find the resolution of his intellectual troubles or the solution of his philosophical difficulties, he did achieve great victories; even in the very face of the breakdown of his theological defenses he ascended to those spiritual heights where he could sincerely say, 'I abhor myself'; then was there granted him the salvation of a vision of God. So even through misunderstood suffering, Job ascended to the superhuman plane of moral understanding and spiritual insight. When the suffering servant obtains a vision of God, there follows a soul peace which passes all human understanding.

148:6.4 (1663.2) "The first of Job's friends, Eliphaz, exhorted the sufferer to exhibit in his afflictions the same fortitude he had prescribed for others during the days of his prosperity. Said this false comforter: 'Trust in your religion, Job; remember that it is the wicked and not the righteous who suffer. You must deserve this punishment, else you would not be afflicted. You well know that no man can be righteous in God's sight. You know that the wicked never really prosper. Anyway, man seems predestined to trouble, and perhaps the Lord is only chastising you for your own good.' No wonder poor Job failed to get much comfort from such an interpretation of the problem of human suffering.

148:6.5 (1663.3) "But the counsel of his second friend, Bildad, was even more depressing, notwithstanding its soundness from the standpoint of the then accepted theology. Said Bildad: 'God cannot be unjust. Your children must have been sinners since they perished; you must be in error, else you would not be so afflicted. And if you are really righteous,

God will certainly deliver you from your afflictions. You should learn from the history of God's dealings with man that the Almighty destroys only the wicked.'

148:6.6 (1663.4) "And then you remember how Job replied to his friends, saying: 'I well know that God does not hear my cry for help. How can God be just and at the same time so utterly disregard my innocence? I am learning that I can get no satisfaction from appealing to the Almighty. Cannot you discern that God tolerates the persecution of the good by the wicked? And since man is so weak, what chance has he for consideration at the hands of an omnipotent God? God has made me as I am, and when he thus turns upon me, I am defenseless. And why did God ever create me just to suffer in this miserable fashion?'

148:6.7 (1663.5) "And who can challenge the attitude of Job in view of the counsel of his friends and the erroneous ideas of God which occupied his own mind? Do you not see that Job longed for a human God, that he hungered to commune with a divine Being who knows man's mortal estate and understands that the just must often suffer in innocence as a part of this first life of the long Paradise ascent? Wherefore has the Son of Man come forth from the Father to live such a life in the flesh that he will be able to comfort and succor all those who must henceforth be called upon to endure the afflictions of Job.

148:6.8 (1663.6) "Job's third friend, Zophar, then spoke still less comforting words when he said: 'You are foolish to claim to be righteous, seeing that you are thus afflicted. But I admit that it is impossible to comprehend God's ways. Perhaps there is some hidden purpose in all your miseries.' And when Job had listened to all three of his friends, he appealed directly to God for help, pleading the fact that 'man, born of woman, is few of days and full of trouble.'

148:6.9 (1664.1) "Then began the second session with his friends. Eliphaz grew more stern, accusing, and sarcastic. Bildad became indignant at Job's contempt for his friends. Zophar reiterated his melancholy advice. Job by this time had become disgusted with his friends and appealed again to God, and now he appealed to a just God against the God of injustice embodied in the philosophy of his friends and enshrined even in his own religious attitude. Next Job took refuge in the consolation of a future life in which the inequities of mortal existence may be more justly rectified. Failure to receive help from man drives Job to God. Then ensues the great struggle in his heart between faith and doubt. Finally, the human sufferer begins to see the light of life; his tortured soul ascends to new heights of hope and courage; he may suffer on and even die, but his enlightened soul now utters that cry of triumph, 'My Vindicator lives!'

148:6.10 (1664.2) "Job was altogether right when he challenged the doctrine that God afflicts children in order to punish their parents. Job was ever ready to admit that God is righteous, but he longed for some soul-satisfying revelation of the personal character of the Eternal. And that is our mission on earth. No more shall suffering mortals be denied the comfort of knowing the love of God and understanding the mercy of the Father in heaven. While the speech of God spoken from the whirlwind was a majestic concept for the day of its utterance, you have already learned that the Father does not thus reveal himself, but rather that he speaks within the human heart as a still, small voice, saying, 'This is the way; walk therein.' Do you not comprehend that God dwells within you, that he has become what you are that he may make you what he is!"

148:6.11 (1664.3) Then Jesus made this final statement: "The Father in heaven does not willingly afflict the children of men. Man suffers, first, from the accidents of time and the imperfections of the evil of an immature physical existence. Next, he suffers the inexorable consequences of sin—the transgression of the laws of life and light. And finally, man reaps the harvest of his own iniquitous persistence in rebellion against the righteous rule of heaven on earth. But man's miseries are not a personal visitation of divine judgment. Man can, and will, do much to lessen his temporal sufferings. But once and for all be delivered from the superstition that God afflicts man at the behest of the evil one. Study the Book of Job just to discover how many wrong ideas of God even good men may honestly entertain; and then note how even the painfully afflicted Job found the God of comfort and salvation in spite of such erroneous teachings. At last his faith pierced the clouds of suffering to discern the light of life pouring forth from the Father as healing mercy and everlasting righteousness."

148:6.12 (1664.4) John pondered these sayings in his heart for many days. His entire afterlife was markedly changed as a result of this conversation with the Master in the garden, and he did much, in later times, to cause the other apostles to change their viewpoints regarding the source, nature, and purpose of commonplace human afflictions. But John never spoke of this conference until after the Master had departed.

The Man with the Withered Hand

148:7.1 (1664.5) The second Sabbath before the departure of the apostles and the new corps of evangelists on the second preaching tour of Galilee, Jesus spoke in the Capernaum synagogue on the "Joys of Righteous Living." When Jesus had finished speaking, a large group of those who were maimed, halt, sick, and afflicted crowded up around him, seeking healing. Also in this group were the apostles, many of the new evangelists, and the Pharisaic spies from Jerusalem.

Everywhere that Jesus went (except when in the hills about the Father's business) the six Jerusalem spies were sure to follow.

148:7.2 (1665.1) The leader of the spying Pharisees, as Jesus stood talking to the people, induced a man with a withered hand to approach him and ask if it would be lawful to be healed on the Sabbath day or should he seek help on another day. When Jesus saw the man, heard his words, and perceived that he had been sent by the Pharisees, he said: "Come forward while I ask you a question. If you had a sheep and it should fall into a pit on the Sabbath day, would you reach down, lay hold on it, and lift it out? Is it lawful to do such things on the Sabbath day?" And the man answered: "Yes, Master, it would be lawful thus to do well on the Sabbath day." Then said Jesus, speaking to all of them: "I know wherefore you have sent this man into my presence. You would find cause for offense in me if you could tempt me to show mercy on the Sabbath day. In silence you all agreed that it was lawful to lift the unfortunate sheep out of the pit, even on the Sabbath, and I call you to witness that it is lawful to exhibit loving-kindness on the Sabbath day not only to animals but also to men. How much more valuable is a man than a sheep! I proclaim that it is lawful to do good to men on the Sabbath day." And as they all stood before him in silence, Jesus, addressing the man with the withered hand, said: "Stand up here by my side that all may see you. And now that you may know that it is my Father's will that you do good on the Sabbath day, if you have the faith to be healed, I bid you stretch out your hand."

148:7.3 (1665.2) And as this man stretched forth his withered hand, it was made whole. The people were minded to turn upon the Pharisees, but Jesus bade them be calm, saying: "I have just told you that it is lawful to do good on the Sabbath, to save life, but I did not instruct you to do harm and give way to the desire to kill." The angered Pharisees went away, and notwithstanding it was the Sabbath day, they hastened forthwith to Tiberias and took counsel with Herod, doing everything in their power to arouse his prejudice in order to secure the Herodians as allies against Jesus. But Herod refused to take action against Jesus, advising that they carry their complaints to Jerusalem.

148:7.4 (1665.3) This is the first case of a miracle to be wrought by Jesus in response to the challenge of his enemies. And the Master performed this so-called miracle, not as a demonstration of his healing power, but as an effective protest against making the Sabbath rest of religion a veritable bondage of meaningless restrictions upon all mankind. This man returned to his work as a stone mason, proving to be one of those whose healing was followed by a life of thanksgiving and righteousness.

Last Week at Bethsaida

148:8.1 (1665.4) The last week of the sojourn at Bethsaida the Jerusalem spies became much divided in their attitude toward Jesus and his teachings. Three of these Pharisees were tremendously impressed by what they had seen and heard. Meanwhile, at Jerusalem, Abraham, a young and influential member of the Sanhedrin, publicly espoused the teachings of Jesus and was baptized in the pool of Siloam by Abner. All Jerusalem was agog over this event, and messengers were immediately dispatched to Bethsaida recalling the six spying Pharisees.

148:8.2 (1666.1) The Greek philosopher who had been won for the kingdom on the previous tour of Galilee returned with certain wealthy Jews of Alexandria, and once more they invited Jesus to come to their city for the purpose of establishing a joint school of philosophy and religion as well as an infirmary for the sick. But Jesus courteously declined the invitation.

148:8.3 (1666.2) About this time there arrived at the Bethsaida encampment a trance prophet from Bagdad, one Kirmeth. This supposed prophet had peculiar visions when in trance and dreamed fantastic dreams when his sleep was disturbed. He created a considerable disturbance at the camp, and Simon Zelotes was in favor of dealing rather roughly with the self-deceived pretender, but Jesus intervened and allowed him entire freedom of action for a few days. All who heard his preaching soon recognized that his teaching was not sound as judged by the gospel of the kingdom. He shortly returned to Bagdad, taking with him only a half dozen unstable and erratic souls. But before Jesus interceded for the Bagdad prophet, David Zebedee, with the assistance of a self-appointed committee, had taken Kirmeth out into the lake and, after repeatedly plunging him into the water, had advised him to depart hence—to organize and build a camp of his own.

148:8.4 (1666.3) On this same day, Beth-Marion, a Phoenician woman, became so fanatical that she went out of her head and, after almost drowning from trying to walk on the water, was sent away by her friends.

148:8.5 (1666.4) The new Jerusalem convert, Abraham the Pharisee, gave all of his worldly goods to the apostolic treasury, and this contribution did much to make possible the immediate sending forth of the one hundred newly trained evangelists. Andrew had already announced the closing of the encampment, and everybody prepared either to go home or else to follow the evangelists into Galilee.

Healing the Paralytic

148:9.1 (1666.5) On Friday afternoon, October 1, when Jesus was holding his last meeting with the apostles, evangelists, and other leaders of the disbanding encampment, and with the six Pharisees from Jerusalem seated in the front row of this assembly in the spacious and enlarged front room of the Zebedee home, there occurred one of the strangest and most unique episodes of all Jesus' earth life. The Master was, at this time, speaking as he stood in this large room, which had been built to accommodate these gatherings during the rainy season. The house was entirely surrounded by a vast concourse of people who were straining their ears to catch some part of Jesus' discourse.

148:9.2 (1666.6) While the house was thus thronged with people and entirely surrounded by eager listeners, a man long afflicted with paralysis was carried down from Capernaum on a small couch by his friends. This paralytic had heard that Jesus was about to leave Bethsaida, and having talked with Aaron the stone mason, who had been so recently made whole, he resolved to be carried into Jesus' presence, where he could seek healing. His friends tried to gain entrance to Zebedee's house by both the front and back doors, but too many people were crowded together. But the paralytic refused to accept defeat; he directed his friends to procure ladders by which they ascended to the roof of the room in which Jesus was speaking, and after loosening the tiles, they boldly lowered the sick man on his couch by ropes until the afflicted one rested on the floor immediately in front of the Master. When Jesus saw what they had done, he ceased speaking, while those who were with him in the room marveled at the perseverance of the sick man and his friends. Said the paralytic: "Master, I would not disturb your teaching, but I am determined to be made whole. I am not like those who received healing and immediately forgot your teaching. I would be made whole that I might serve in the kingdom of heaven." Now, notwithstanding that this man's affliction had been brought upon him by his own misspent life, Jesus, seeing his faith, said to the paralytic: "Son, fear not; your sins are forgiven. Your faith shall save you."

148:9.3 (1667.1) When the Pharisees from Jerusalem, together with other scribes and lawyers who sat with them, heard this pronouncement by Jesus, they began to say to themselves: "How dare this man thus speak? Does he not understand that such words are blasphemy? Who can forgive sin but God?" Jesus, perceiving in his spirit that they thus reasoned within their own minds and among themselves, spoke to them, saying: "Why do you so reason in your hearts? Who are you that you sit in judgment over me? What is the difference whether I say to this paralytic, your sins are forgiven, or arise, take up your bed, and walk? But that you who witness all this may finally know that the Son of Man has authority and power on earth to forgive sins, I will say to this afflicted man, Arise, take up your bed, and go to your own house." And when Jesus had thus spoken, the paralytic arose, and as they made way for him, he walked out before them all. And those who saw these things were amazed. Peter dismissed the assemblage, while many prayed and glorified God, confessing that they had never before seen such strange happenings.

148:9.4 (1667.2) And it was about this time that the messengers of the Sanhedrin arrived to bid the six spies return to Jerusalem. When they heard this message, they fell to earnest debate among themselves; and after they had finished their discussions, the leader and two of his associates returned with the messengers to Jerusalem, while three of the spying Pharisees confessed faith in Jesus and, going immediately to the lake, were baptized by Peter and fellowshipped by the apostles as children of the kingdom.

Paper 149

The Second Preaching Tour

149:0.1 (1668.1) THE second public preaching tour of Galilee began on Sunday, October 3, A.D. 28, and continued for almost three months, ending on December 30. Participating in this effort were Jesus and his twelve apostles, assisted by the newly recruited corps of 117 evangelists and by numerous other interested persons. On this tour they visited Gadara, Ptolemais, Japhia, Dabaritta, Megiddo, Jezreel, Scythopolis, Tarichea, Hippos, Gamala, Bethsaida-Julias, and many other cities and villages.

149:0.2 (1668.2) Before the departure on this Sunday morning Andrew and Peter asked Jesus to give the final charge to the new evangelists, but the Master declined, saying that it was not his province to do those things which others could acceptably perform. After due deliberation it was decided that James Zebedee should administer the charge. At the conclusion of James's remarks Jesus said to the evangelists: "Go now forth to do the work as you have been charged, and later on, when you have shown yourselves competent and faithful, I will ordain you to preach the gospel of the kingdom."

149:0.3 (1668.3) On this tour only James and John traveled with Jesus. Peter and the other apostles each took with them about one dozen of the evangelists and maintained close contact with them while they carried on their work of preaching and teaching. As fast as believers were ready to enter the kingdom, the apostles would administer baptism. Jesus and his two companions traveled extensively during these three months, often visiting two cities in one day to observe the work of the evangelists and to encourage them in their efforts to establish the kingdom. This entire second preaching tour was principally an effort to afford practical experience for this corps of 117 newly trained evangelists.

149:0.4 (1668.4) Throughout this period and subsequently, up to the time of the final departure of Jesus and the twelve for Jerusalem, David Zebedee maintained a permanent headquarters for the work of the kingdom in his father's house at Bethsaida. This was the clearinghouse for Jesus' work on earth and the relay station for the messenger service which David carried on between the workers in various parts of Palestine and adjacent regions. He did all of this on his own initiative but with the approval of Andrew. David employed forty to fifty messengers in this intelligence division of the rapidly enlarging and extending work of the kingdom. While thus employed, he partially supported himself by spending some of his time at his old work of fishing.

1 The Widespread Fame of Jesus

149:1.1 (1668.5) By the time the camp at Bethsaida had been broken up, the fame of Jesus, particularly as a healer, had spread to all parts of Palestine and through all of Syria and the surrounding countries. For weeks after they left Bethsaida, the sick continued to arrive, and when they did not find the Master, on learning from David where he was, they would go in search of him. On this tour Jesus did not deliberately perform any so-called miracles of healing.

Nevertheless, scores of afflicted found restoration of health and happiness as a result of the reconstructive power of the intense faith which impelled them to seek for healing.

149:1.2 (1669.1) There began to appear about the time of this mission—and continued throughout the remainder of Jesus' life on earth—a peculiar and unexplained series of healing phenomena. In the course of this three months' tour more than one hundred men, women, and children from Judea, Idumea, Galilee, Syria, Tyre, and Sidon, and from beyond the Jordan were beneficiaries of this unconscious healing by Jesus and, returning to their homes, added to the enlargement of Jesus' fame. And they did this notwithstanding that Jesus would, every time he observed one of these cases of spontaneous healing, directly charge the beneficiary to "tell no man."

149:1.3 (1669.2) It was never revealed to us just what occurred in these cases of spontaneous or unconscious healing. The Master never explained to his apostles how these healings were effected, other than that on several occasions he merely said, "I perceive that power has gone forth from me." On one occasion he remarked when touched by an ailing child, "I perceive that life has gone forth from me."

149:1.4 (1669.3) In the absence of direct word from the Master regarding the nature of these cases of spontaneous healing, it would be presuming on our part to undertake to explain how they were accomplished, but it will be permissible to record our opinion of all such healing phenomena. We believe that many of these apparent miracles of healing, as they occurred in the course of Jesus' earth ministry, were the result of the coexistence of the following three powerful, potent, and associated influences:

149:1.5 (1669.4) 1. The presence of strong, dominant, and living faith in the heart of the human being who persistently sought healing, together with the fact that such healing was desired for its spiritual benefits rather than for purely physical restoration.

149:1.6 (1669.5) 2. The existence, concomitant with such human faith, of the great sympathy and compassion of the incarnated and mercy-dominated Creator Son of God, who actually possessed in his person almost unlimited and timeless creative healing powers and prerogatives.

149:1.7 (1669.6) 3. Along with the faith of the creature and the life of the Creator it should also be noted that this God-man was the personified expression of the Father's will. If, in the contact of the human need and the divine power to meet it, the Father did not will otherwise, the two became one, and the healing occurred unconsciously to the human Jesus but was immediately recognized by his divine nature. The explanation, then, of many of these cases of healing must be found in a great law which has long been known to us, namely, What the Creator Son desires and the eternal Father wills IS.

149:1.8 (1669.7) It is, then, our opinion that, in the personal presence of Jesus, certain forms of profound human faith were literally and truly compelling in the manifestation of healing by certain creative forces and personalities of the universe who were at that time so intimately associated with the Son of Man. It therefore becomes a fact of record that Jesus did frequently suffer men to heal themselves in his presence by their powerful, personal faith.

149:1.9 (1670.1) Many others sought healing for wholly selfish purposes. A rich widow of Tyre, with her retinue, came seeking to be healed of her infirmities, which were many; and as she followed Jesus about through Galilee, she continued to offer more and more money, as if the power of God were something to be purchased by the highest bidder. But never would she become interested in the gospel of the kingdom; it was only the cure of her physical ailments that she sought.

2 Attitude of the People

149:2.1 (1670.2) Jesus understood the minds of men. He knew what was in the heart of man, and had his teachings been left as he presented them, the only commentary being the inspired interpretation afforded by his earth life, all nations and all religions of the world would speedily have embraced the gospel of the kingdom. The well-meant efforts of Jesus' early followers to restate his teachings so as to make them the more acceptable to certain nations, races, and religions, only resulted in making such teachings the less acceptable to all other nations, races, and religions.

149:2.2 (1670.3) The Apostle Paul, in his efforts to bring the teachings of Jesus to the favorable notice of certain groups in his day, wrote many letters of instruction and admonition. Other teachers of Jesus' gospel did likewise, but none of them realized that some of these writings would subsequently be brought together by those who would set them forth as the embodiment of the teachings of Jesus. And so, while so-called Christianity does contain more of the Master's gospel than any other religion, it does also contain much that Jesus did not teach. Aside from the incorporation of many teachings from the Persian mysteries and much of the Greek philosophy into early Christianity, two great mistakes were made:

149:2.3 (1670.4) 1. The effort to connect the gospel teaching directly onto the Jewish theology, as illustrated by the Christian doctrines of the atonement—the teaching that Jesus was the sacrificed Son who would satisfy the Father's stern justice and appease the divine wrath. These teachings originated in a praiseworthy effort to make the gospel of the kingdom more acceptable to disbelieving Jews. Though these efforts failed as far as winning the Jews was concerned, they did not fail to confuse and alienate many honest souls in all subsequent generations.

149:2.4 (1670.5) 2. The second great blunder of the Master's early followers, and one which all subsequent generations have persisted in perpetuating, was to organize the Christian teaching so completely about the person of Jesus. This overemphasis of the personality of Jesus in the theology of Christianity has worked to obscure his teachings, and all of this has made it increasingly difficult for Jews, Mohammedans, Hindus, and other Eastern religionists to accept the teachings of Jesus. We would not belittle the place of the person of Jesus in a religion which might bear his name, but we would not permit such consideration to eclipse his inspired life or to supplant his saving message: the fatherhood of God and the brotherhood of man.

149:2.5 (1670.6) The teachers of the religion of Jesus should approach other religions with the recognition of the truths which are held in common (many of which come directly or indirectly from Jesus' message) while they refrain from placing so much emphasis on the differences.

149:2.6 (1671.1) While, at that particular time, the fame of Jesus rested chiefly upon his reputation as a healer, it does not follow that it continued so to rest. As time passed, more and more he was sought for spiritual help. But it was the physical cures that made the most direct and immediate appeal to the common people. Jesus was increasingly sought by the victims of moral enslavement and mental harassments, and he invariably taught them the way of deliverance.

Fathers sought his advice regarding the management of their sons, and mothers came for help in the guidance of their daughters. Those who sat in darkness came to him, and he revealed to them the light of life. His ear was ever open to the sorrows of mankind, and he always helped those who sought his ministry.

149:2.7 (1671.2) When the Creator himself was on earth, incarnated in the likeness of mortal flesh, it was inevitable that some extraordinary things should happen. But you should never approach Jesus through these so-called miraculous occurrences. Learn to approach the miracle through Jesus, but do not make the mistake of approaching Jesus through the miracle. And this admonition is warranted, notwithstanding that Jesus of Nazareth is the only founder of a religion who performed supermaterial acts on earth.

149:2.8 (1671.3) The most astonishing and the most revolutionary feature of Michael's mission on earth was his attitude toward women. In a day and generation when a man was not supposed to salute even his own wife in a public place, Jesus dared to take women along as teachers of the gospel in connection with his third tour of Galilee. And he had the consummate courage to do this in the face of the rabbinic teaching which declared that it was "better that the words of the law should be burned than delivered to women."

149:2.9 (1671.4) In one generation Jesus lifted women out of the disrespectful oblivion and the slavish drudgery of the ages. And it is the one shameful thing about the religion that presumed to take Jesus' name that it lacked the moral courage to follow this noble example in its subsequent attitude toward women.

149:2.10 (1671.5) As Jesus mingled with the people, they found him entirely free from the superstitions of that day. He was free from religious prejudices; he was never intolerant. He had nothing in his heart resembling social antagonism. While he complied with the good in the religion of his fathers, he did not hesitate to disregard man-made traditions of superstition and bondage. He dared to teach that catastrophes of nature, accidents of time, and other calamitous happenings are not visitations of divine judgments or mysterious dispensations of Providence. He denounced slavish devotion to meaningless ceremonials and exposed the fallacy of materialistic worship. He boldly proclaimed man's spiritual freedom and dared to teach that mortals of the flesh are indeed and in truth sons of the living God.

149:2.11 (1671.6) Jesus transcended all the teachings of his forebears when he boldly substituted clean hearts for clean hands as the mark of true religion. He put reality in the place of tradition and swept aside all pretensions of vanity and hypocrisy. And yet this fearless man of God did not give vent to destructive criticism or manifest an utter disregard of the religious, social, economic, and political usages of his day. He was not a militant revolutionist; he was a progressive evolutionist. He engaged in the destruction of that which was only when he simultaneously offered his fellows the superior thing which ought to be.

149:2.12 (1672.1) Jesus received the obedience of his followers without exacting it. Only three men who received his personal call refused to accept the invitation to discipleship. He exercised a peculiar drawing power over men, but he was not dictatorial. He commanded confidence, and no man ever resented his giving a command. He assumed absolute authority over his disciples, but no one ever objected. He permitted his followers to call him Master.

149:2.13 (1672.2) The Master was admired by all who met him except by those who entertained deep-seated religious prejudices or those who thought they discerned political dangers in his teachings. Men were astonished at the originality and authoritativeness of his teaching. They marveled at his patience in dealing with backward and troublesome inquirers. He inspired hope and confidence in the hearts of all who came under his ministry. Only those who had not met him feared him, and he was hated only by those who regarded him as the champion of that truth which was destined to overthrow the evil and error which they had determined to hold in their hearts at all cost.

149:2.14 (1672.3) On both friends and foes he exercised a strong and peculiarly fascinating influence. Multitudes would follow him for weeks, just to hear his gracious words and behold his simple life. Devoted men and women loved Jesus with a well-nigh superhuman affection. And the better they knew him the more they loved him. And all this is still true; even today and in all future ages, the more man comes to know this God-man, the more he will love and follow after him.

3 Hostility of the Religious Leaders

149:3.1 (1672.4) Notwithstanding the favorable reception of Jesus and his teachings by the common people, the religious leaders at Jerusalem became increasingly alarmed and antagonistic. The Pharisees had formulated a systematic and dogmatic theology. Jesus was a teacher who taught as the occasion served; he was not a systematic teacher. Jesus taught not so much from the law as from life, by parables. (And when he employed a parable for illustrating his message, he designed to utilize just one feature of the story for that purpose. Many wrong ideas concerning the teachings of Jesus may be secured by attempting to make allegories out of his parables.)

149:3.2 (1672.5) The religious leaders at Jerusalem were becoming well-nigh frantic as a result of the recent conversion of young Abraham and by the desertion of the three spies who had been baptized by Peter, and who were now out with the evangelists on this second preaching tour of Galilee. The Jewish leaders were increasingly blinded by fear and prejudice, while their hearts were hardened by the continued rejection of the appealing truths of the gospel of the kingdom. When men shut off the appeal to the spirit that dwells within them, there is little that can be done to modify their attitude.

149:3.3 (1672.6) When Jesus first met with the evangelists at the Bethsaida camp, in concluding his address, he said: "You should remember that in body and mind—emotionally—men react individually. The only uniform thing about men is the indwelling spirit. Though divine spirits may vary somewhat in the nature and extent of their experience, they react uniformly to all spiritual appeals. Only through, and by appeal to, this spirit can mankind ever

attain unity and brotherhood." But many of the leaders of the Jews had closed the doors of their hearts to the spiritual appeal of the gospel. From this day on they ceased not to plan and plot for the Master's destruction. They were convinced that Jesus must be apprehended, convicted, and executed as a religious offender, a violator of the cardinal teachings of the Jewish sacred law.

4 Progress of the Preaching Tour

149:4.1 (1673.1) Jesus did very little public work on this preaching tour, but he conducted many evening classes with the believers in most of the cities and villages where he chanced to sojourn with James and John. At one of these evening sessions one of the younger evangelists asked Jesus a question about anger, and the Master, among other things, said in reply: *

149:4.2 (1673.2) "Anger is a material manifestation which represents, in a general way, the measure of the failure of the spiritual nature to gain control of the combined intellectual and physical natures. Anger indicates your lack of tolerant brotherly love plus your lack of self-respect and self-control. Anger depletes the health, debases the mind, and handicaps the spirit teacher of man's soul. Have you not read in the Scriptures that 'wrath kills the foolish man,' and that man 'tears himself in his anger'? That 'he who is slow of wrath is of great understanding,' while 'he who is hasty of temper exalts folly'? You all know that 'a soft answer turns away wrath,' and how 'grievous words stir up anger.' 'Discretion defers anger,' while 'he who has no control over his own self is like a defenseless city without walls.' 'Wrath is cruel and anger is outrageous.' 'Angry men stir up strife, while the furious multiply their transgressions.' 'Be not hasty in spirit, for anger rests in the bosom of fools.'" Before Jesus ceased speaking, he said further: "Let your hearts be so dominated by love that your spirit guide will have little trouble in delivering you from the tendency to give vent to those outbursts of animal anger which are inconsistent with the status of divine sonship."

149:4.3 (1673.3) On this same occasion the Master talked to the group about the desirability of possessing well-balanced characters. He recognized that it was necessary for most men to devote themselves to the mastery of some vocation, but he deplored all tendency toward overspecialization, toward becoming narrow-minded and circumscribed in life's activities. He called attention to the fact that any virtue, if carried to extremes, may become a vice. Jesus always preached temperance and taught consistency—proportionate adjustment of life problems. He pointed out that overmuch sympathy and pity may degenerate into serious emotional instability; that enthusiasm may drive on into fanaticism. He discussed one of their former associates whose imagination had led him off into visionary and impractical undertakings. At the same time he warned them against the dangers of the dullness of overconservative mediocrity.

149:4.4 (1673.4) And then Jesus discoursed on the dangers of courage and faith, how they sometimes lead unthinking souls on to recklessness and presumption. He also showed how prudence and discretion, when carried too far, lead to cowardice and failure. He exhorted his hearers to strive for originality while they shunned all tendency toward eccentricity. He pleaded for sympathy without sentimentality, piety without sanctimoniousness. He taught reverence free from fear and superstition.

149:4.5 (1674.1) It was not so much what Jesus taught about the balanced character that impressed his associates as the fact that his own life was such an eloquent exemplification of his teaching. He lived in the midst of stress and storm, but he never wavered. His enemies continually laid snares for him, but they never entrapped him. The wise and learned endeavored to trip him, but he did not stumble. They sought to embroil him in debate, but his answers were always enlightening, dignified, and final. When he was interrupted in his discourses with multitudinous ques-

tions, his answers were always significant and conclusive. Never did he resort to ignoble tactics in meeting the continuous pressure of his enemies, who did not hesitate to employ every sort of false, unfair, and unrighteous mode of attack upon him.

149:4.6 (1674.2) While it is true that many men and women must assiduously apply themselves to some definite pursuit as a livelihood vocation, it is nevertheless wholly desirable that human beings should cultivate a wide range of cultural familiarity with life as it is lived on earth. Truly educated persons are not satisfied with remaining in ignorance of the lives and doings of their fellows.

5   *Lesson Regarding Contentment*

149:5.1 (1674.3) When Jesus was visiting the group of evangelists working under the supervision of Simon Zelotes, during their evening conference Simon asked the Master: "Why are some persons so much more happy and contented than others? Is contentment a matter of religious experience?" Among other things, Jesus said in answer to Simon's question:

149:5.2 (1674.4) "Simon, some persons are naturally more happy than others. Much, very much, depends upon the willingness of man to be led and directed by the Father's spirit which lives within him. Have you not read in the Scriptures the words of the wise man, 'The spirit of man is the candle of the Lord, searching all the inward parts'? And also that such spirit-led mortals say: 'The lines are fallen to me in pleasant places; yes, I have a goodly heritage.' 'A little that a righteous man has is better than the riches of many wicked,' for 'a good man shall be satisfied from within himself.' 'A merry heart makes a cheerful countenance and is a continual feast. Better is a little with the reverence of the Lord than great treasure and trouble therewith. Better is a dinner of herbs where love is than a fatted ox and hatred therewith. Better is a little with righteousness than great revenues without rectitude.' 'A merry heart does good like a medicine.' 'Better is a handful with composure than a superabundance with sorrow and vexation of spirit.'

149:5.3 (1674.5) "Much of man's sorrow is born of the disappointment of his ambitions and the wounding of his pride. Although men owe a duty to themselves to make the best of their lives on earth, having thus sincerely exerted themselves, they should cheerfully accept their lot and exercise ingenuity in making the most of that which has fallen to their hands. All too many of man's troubles take origin in the fear soil of his own natural heart. 'The wicked flee when no man pursues.' 'The wicked are like the troubled sea, for it cannot rest, but its waters cast up mire and dirt; there is no peace, says God, for the wicked.'

149:5.4 (1674.6) "Seek not, then, for false peace and transient joy but rather for the assurance of faith and the sureties of divine sonship which yield composure, contentment, and supreme joy in the spirit."

149:5.5 (1675.1) Jesus hardly regarded this world as a "vale of tears." He rather looked upon it as the birth sphere of the eternal and immortal spirits of Paradise ascension, the "vale of soul making."

6   The "Fear of the Lord"

149:6.1 (1675.2) It was at Gamala, during the evening conference, that Philip said to Jesus: "Master, why is it that the Scriptures instruct us to 'fear the Lord,' while you would have us look to the Father in heaven without fear? How are we to harmonize these teachings?" And Jesus replied to Philip, saying:

149:6.2 (1675.3) "My children, I am not surprised that you ask such questions. In the beginning it was only through fear that man could learn reverence, but I have come to reveal the Father's love so that you will be attracted to the worship of the Eternal by the drawing of a son's affectionate recognition and reciprocation of the Father's profound and perfect love. I would deliver you from the bondage of driving yourselves through slavish fear to the irksome service of a jealous and wrathful King-God. I would instruct you in the Father-son relationship of God and man so that you may be joyfully led into that sublime and supernal free worship of a loving, just, and merciful Father-God.

149:6.3 (1675.4) "The 'fear of the Lord' has had different meanings in the successive ages, coming up from fear, through anguish and dread, to awe and reverence. And now from reverence I would lead you up, through recognition, realization, and appreciation, to love. When man recognizes only the works of God, he is led to fear the Supreme; but when man begins to understand and experience the personality and character of the living God, he is led increasingly to love such a good and perfect, universal and eternal Father. And it is just this changing of the relation of man to God that constitutes the mission of the Son of Man on earth.

149:6.4 (1675.5) "Intelligent children do not fear their father in order that they may receive good gifts from his hand; but having already received the abundance of good things bestowed by the dictates of the father's affection for his sons and daughters, these much loved children are led to love their father in responsive recognition and appreciation of such munificent beneficence. The goodness of God leads to repentance; the beneficence of God leads to service; the mercy of God leads to salvation; while the love of God leads to intelligent and freehearted worship.

149:6.5 (1675.6) "Your forebears feared God because he was mighty and mysterious. You shall adore him because he is magnificent in love, plenteous in mercy, and glorious in truth. The power of God engenders fear in the heart of man, but the nobility and righteousness of his personality beget reverence, love, and willing worship. A dutiful and affectionate son does not fear or dread even a mighty and noble father. I have come into the world to put love in the place of fear, joy in the place of sorrow, confidence in the place of dread, loving service and appreciative worship in the place of slavish bondage and meaningless ceremonies. But it is still true of those who sit in darkness that 'the fear of the Lord is the beginning of wisdom.' But when the light has more fully come, the sons of God are led to praise the Infinite for what he is rather than to fear him for what he does.

149:6.6 (1675.7) "When children are young and unthinking, they must necessarily be admonished to honor their parents; but when they grow older and become somewhat more appreciative of the benefits of the parental ministry and protection, they are led up, through understanding respect and increasing affection, to that level of experience where they actually love their parents for what they are more than for what they have done. The father naturally loves his child, but the child must develop his love for the father from the fear of what the father can do, through awe, dread, dependence, and reverence, to the appreciative and affectionate regard of love.

149:6.7 (1676.1) "You have been taught that you should 'fear God and keep his commandments, for that is the whole duty of man.' But I have come to give you a new and higher commandment. I would teach you to 'love God and learn to do his will, for that is the highest privilege of the liberated sons of God.' Your fathers were taught to 'fear God—the Almighty King.' I teach you, 'Love God—the all-merciful Father.'

149:6.8 (1676.2) "In the kingdom of heaven, which I have come to declare, there is no high and mighty king; this kingdom is a divine family. The universally recognized and unreservedly worshiped center and head of this far-flung brotherhood of intelligent beings is my Father and your Father. I am his Son, and you are also his sons. Therefore it is eternally true that you and I are brethren in the heavenly estate, and all the more so since we have become brethren in the flesh of the earthly life. Cease, then, to fear God as a king or serve him as a master; learn to reverence him as the Creator; honor him as the Father of your spirit youth; love him as a merciful defender; and ultimately worship him as the loving and all- wise Father of your more mature spiritual realization and appreciation.

149:6.9 (1676.3) "Out of your wrong concepts of the Father in heaven grow your false ideas of humility and springs much of your hypocrisy. Man may be a worm of the dust by nature and origin, but when he becomes indwelt by my Father's spirit, that man becomes divine in his destiny. The bestowal spirit of my Father will surely return to the divine source and universe level of origin, and the human soul of mortal man which shall have become the reborn child of this indwelling spirit shall certainly ascend with the divine spirit to the very presence of the eternal Father.

149:6.10 (1676.4) "Humility, indeed, becomes mortal man who receives all these gifts from the Father in heaven, albeit there is a divine dignity attached to all such faith candidates for the eternal ascent of the heavenly kingdom. The meaningless and menial practices of an ostentatious and false humility are incompatible with the appreciation of the source of your salvation and the recognition of the destiny of your spirit-born souls. Humility before God is altogether appropriate in the depths of your hearts; meekness before men is commendable; but the hypocrisy of self-conscious and attention-craving humility is childish and unworthy of the enlightened sons of the kingdom.

149:6.11 (1676.5) "You do well to be meek before God and self-controlled before men, but let your meekness be of spiritual origin and not the self-deceptive display of a self-conscious sense of self-righteous superiority. The prophet spoke advisedly when he said, 'Walk humbly with God,' for, while the Father in heaven is the Infinite and the Eternal, he also dwells 'with him who is of a contrite mind and a humble spirit.' My Father disdains pride, loathes hypocrisy, and abhors iniquity. And it was to emphasize the value of sincerity and perfect trust in the loving support and faithful guidance of the heavenly Father that I have so often referred to the little child as illustrative of the attitude of mind and the response of spirit which are so essential to the entrance of mortal man into the spirit realities of the kingdom of heaven.

149:6.12 (1677.1) "Well did the Prophet Jeremiah describe many mortals when he said: 'You are near God in the mouth but far from him in the heart.' And have you not also read that direful warning of the prophet who said: 'The priests thereof teach for hire, and the prophets thereof divine for money. At the same time they profess piety and proclaim that the Lord is with them.' Have you not been well warned against those who 'speak peace to their neighbors when mischief is in their hearts,' those who 'flatter with the lips while the heart is given to double-dealing'? Of all the sorrows of a trusting man, none are so terrible as to be 'wounded in the house of a trusted friend.'" *

7   Returning to Bethsaida

149:7.1 (1677.2) Andrew, in consultation with Simon Peter and with the approval of Jesus, had instructed David at Bethsaida to dispatch messengers to the various preaching groups with instructions to terminate the tour and return to Bethsaida sometime on Thursday, December 30. By supper time on that rainy day all of the apostolic party and the teaching evangelists had arrived at the Zebedee home. *

149:7.2 (1677.3) The group remained together over the Sabbath day, being accommodated in the homes of Bethsaida and near-by Capernaum, after which the entire party was granted a two weeks' recess to go home to their families, visit their friends, or go fishing. The two or three days they were together in Bethsaida were, indeed, exhilarating and inspiring; even the

older teachers were edified by the young preachers as they narrated their experiences.

149:7.3 (1677.4) Of the 117 evangelists who participated in this second preaching tour of Galilee, only about seventy-five survived the test of actual experience and were on hand to be assigned to service at the end of the two weeks' recess.

Jesus, with Andrew, Peter, James, and John, remained at the Zebedee home and spent much time in conference regarding the welfare and extension of the kingdom.

Paper 150

The Third Preaching Tour

150:0.1 (1678.1) ON SUNDAY evening, January 16, A.D. 29, Abner, with the apostles of John, reached Bethsaida and went into joint conference with Andrew and the apostles of Jesus the next day. Abner and his associates made their headquarters at Hebron and were in the habit of coming up to Bethsaida periodically for these conferences.

150:0.2 (1678.2) Among the many matters considered by this joint conference was the practice of anointing the sick with certain forms of oil in connection with prayers for healing. Again did Jesus decline to participate in their discussions or to express himself regarding their conclusions. The apostles of John had always used the anointing oil in their ministry to the sick and afflicted, and they sought to establish this as a uniform practice for both groups, but the apostles of Jesus refused to bind themselves by such a regulation.

150:0.3 (1678.3) On Tuesday, January 18, the twenty-four were joined by the tested evangelists, about seventy-five in number, at the Zebedee house in Bethsaida preparatory to being sent forth on the third preaching tour of Galilee. This third mission continued for a period of seven weeks.

150:0.4 (1678.4) The evangelists were sent out in groups of five, while Jesus and the twelve traveled together most of the time, the apostles going out two and two to baptize believers as occasion required. For a period of almost three weeks Abner and his associates also worked with the evangelistic groups, advising them and baptizing believers. They visited Magdala, Tiberias, Nazareth, and all the principal cities and villages of central and southern Galilee, all the places previously visited and many others. This was their last message to Galilee, except to the northern portions.

1   The Women's Evangelistic Corps

150:1.1 (1678.5) Of all the daring things which Jesus did in connection with his earth career, the most amazing was his sudden announcement on the evening of January 16: "On the morrow we will set apart ten women for the ministering work of the kingdom." At the beginning of the two weeks' period during which the apostles and the evangelists were to be absent from Bethsaida on their furlough, Jesus requested David to summon his parents back to their home and to dispatch messengers calling to Bethsaida ten devout women who had served in the administration of the former encampment and the tented infirmary. These women had all listened to the instruction given the young evangelists, but it had never occurred to either themselves or their teachers that Jesus would dare to commission women to teach the gospel of the kingdom and minister to the sick. These ten women selected and commissioned by Jesus were: Susanna, the daughter of the former chazan of the Nazareth synagogue; Joanna, the wife of Chuza, the steward of Herod Antipas; Elizabeth, the daughter of a wealthy Jew of Tiberias and Sepphoris; Martha, the elder sister of Andrew and Peter; Rachel, the sister-in-law of Jude, the Master's brother in the flesh; Nasanta, the daughter of Elman, the Syrian physician; Milcha, a cousin of the Apostle Thomas; Ruth, the eldest daughter of Matthew Levi; Celta, the daughter of a Roman centurion; and Agaman, a widow of Damascus. Subsequently, Jesus added two other women to this group— Mary Magdalene and Rebecca, the daughter of Joseph of Arimathea.

150:1.2 (1679.1) Jesus authorized these women to effect their own organization and directed Judas to provide funds for their equipment and for pack animals. The ten elected Susanna as their chief and Joanna as their treasurer. From this time on they furnished their own funds; never again did they draw upon Judas for support.

150:1.3 (1679.2) It was most astounding in that day, when women were not even allowed on the main floor of the synagogue (being confined to the women's gallery), to behold them being recognized as authorized teachers of the new gospel of the kingdom. The charge which Jesus gave these ten women as he set them apart for gospel teaching and ministry was the emancipation proclamation which set free all women and for all time; no more was man to look upon woman as his spiritual inferior. This was a decided shock to even the twelve apostles. Notwithstanding they had many times heard the Master say that "in the kingdom of heaven there is neither rich nor poor, free nor bond, male nor female, all are equally the sons and daughters of God," they were literally stunned when he proposed formally to commission these ten women as religious teachers and even to permit their traveling about with them. The whole country was stirred up by this proceeding, the enemies of Jesus making great capital out of this move, but everywhere the women believers in the good news stood stanchly behind their chosen sisters and voiced no uncertain approval of this tardy acknowledgment of woman's place in religious work. And this liberation of women, giving them due recognition, was practiced by the apostles immediately after the Master's departure, albeit they fell back to the olden customs in subsequent generations. Throughout the early days of the Christian church women teachers and ministers were called deaconesses and were accorded general recognition. But Paul, despite the fact that he conceded all this in theory, never really incorporated it into his own attitude and personally found it difficult to carry out in practice.

2   The Stop at Magdala

150:2.1 (1679.3) As the apostolic party journeyed from Bethsaida, the women traveled in the rear. During the conference time they always sat in a group in front and to the right of the speaker. Increasingly, women had become believers in the gospel of the kingdom, and it had been a source of much difficulty and no end of embarrassment when they had desired to hold personal converse with Jesus or one of the apostles. Now all this was changed. When any of the women believers desired to see the Master or confer with the apostles, they went to Susanna, and in company with one of the twelve women evangelists, they would go at once into the presence of the Master or one of his apostles.

150:2.2 (1680.1) It was at Magdala that the women first demonstrated their usefulness and vindicated the wisdom of their choosing. Andrew had imposed rather strict rules upon his associates about doing personal work with women, especially with those of questionable character. When the party entered Magdala, these ten women evangelists were free to enter the evil resorts and preach the glad tidings directly to all their inmates. And when visiting the sick, these women were able to draw very close in their ministry to their afflicted sisters. As the result of the ministry of these ten women (afterward known as the twelve women) at this place, Mary Magdalene was won for the kingdom. Through a succession of misfortunes and in consequence of the attitude of reputable society toward women who commit such errors of judgment, this woman had found herself in one of the nefarious resorts of Magdala. It was Martha and Rachel who made plain to Mary that the doors of the kingdom were open to even such as she. Mary believed the good news and was baptized by Peter the next day.

150:2.3 (1680.2) Mary Magdalene became the most effective teacher of the gospel among this group of twelve women evangelists. She was set apart for such service, together with Rebecca, at Jotapata about four weeks subsequent to her conversion. Mary and Rebecca, with the others of this group, went on through the remainder of Jesus' life on earth, laboring faithfully and effectively for the enlightenment and uplifting of their downtrodden sisters; and when the last and tragic episode in the drama of Jesus' life was being enacted, notwithstanding the apostles all fled but one, these women were all present, and not one either denied or betrayed him.

3   Sabbath at Tiberias

150:3.1 (1680.3) The Sabbath services of the apostolic party had been put in the hands of the women by Andrew, upon instructions from Jesus. This meant, of course, that they could not be held in the new synagogue. The women selected Joanna to have charge of this occasion, and the meeting was held in the banquet room of Herod's new palace, Herod being away in residence at Julias in Perea. Joanna read from the Scriptures concerning woman's work in the religious life of Israel, making reference to Miriam, Deborah, Esther, and others.

150:3.2 (1680.4) Late that evening Jesus gave the united group a memorable talk on "Magic and Superstition." In those days the appearance of a bright and supposedly new star was regarded as a token indicating that a great man had been born on earth. Such a star having then recently been observed, Andrew asked Jesus if these beliefs were well founded. In the long answer to Andrew's question the Master entered upon a thoroughgoing discussion of the whole subject of human superstition. The statement which Jesus made at this time may be summarized in modern phraseology as follows:

150:3.3 (1680.5) 1. The courses of the stars in the heavens have nothing whatever to do with the events of human life on earth. Astronomy is a proper pursuit of science, but astrology is a mass of superstitious error which has no place in the gospel of the kingdom.

150:3.4 (1680.6) 2. The examination of the internal organs of an animal recently killed can reveal nothing about weather, future events, or the outcome of human affairs.

150:3.5 (1680.7) 3. The spirits of the dead do not come back to communicate with their families or their onetime friends among the living.

150:3.6 (1681.1) 4. Charms and relics are impotent to heal disease, ward off disaster, or influence evil spirits; the belief in all such material means of influencing the spiritual world is nothing but gross superstition.

150:3.7 (1681.2) 5. Casting lots, while it may be a convenient way of settling many minor difficulties, is not a method designed to disclose the divine will. Such outcomes are purely matters of material chance. The only means of communion with the spiritual world is embraced in the spirit endowment of mankind, the indwelling spirit of the Father, together with the outpoured spirit of the Son and the omnipresent influence of the Infinite Spirit.

150:3.8 (1681.3) 6. Divination, sorcery, and witchcraft are superstitions of ignorant minds, as also are the delusions of magic. The belief in magic numbers, omens of good luck, and harbingers of bad luck, is pure and unfounded superstition.

150:3.9 (1681.4) 7. The interpretation of dreams is largely a superstitious and groundless system of ignorant and fantastic speculation. The gospel of the kingdom

must have nothing in common with the soothsayer priests of primitive religion.

150:3.10 (1681.5) 8. The spirits of good or evil cannot dwell within material symbols of clay, wood, or metal; idols are nothing more than the material of which they are made.

150:3.11 (1681.6) 9. The practices of the enchanters, the wizards, the magicians, and the sorcerers, were derived from the superstitions of the Egyptians, the Assyrians, the Babylonians, and the ancient Canaanites. Amulets and all sorts of incantations are futile either to win the protection of good spirits or to ward off supposed evil spirits.

150:3.12 (1681.7) 10. He exposed and denounced their belief in spells, ordeals, bewitching, cursing, signs, mandrakes, knotted cords, and all other forms of ignorant and enslaving superstition.

4   Sending the Apostles Out Two and Two

150:4.1 (1681.8) The next evening, having gathered together the twelve apostles, the apostles of John, and the newly commissioned women's group, Jesus said: "You see for yourselves that the harvest is plenteous, but the laborers are few. Let us all, therefore, pray the Lord of the harvest that he send forth still more laborers into his fields. While I remain to comfort and instruct the younger teachers, I would send out the older ones two and two that they may pass quickly over all Galilee preaching the gospel of the kingdom while it is yet convenient and peaceful." Then he designated the pairs of apostles as he desired them to go forth, and they were: Andrew and Peter, James and John Zebedee, Philip and Nathaniel, Thomas and Matthew, James and Judas Alpheus, Simon Zelotes and Judas Iscariot.

150:4.2 (1681.9) Jesus arranged the date for meeting the twelve at Nazareth, and in parting, he said: "On this mission go not to any city of the gentiles, neither go into Samaria, but go instead to the lost sheep of the house of Israel. Preach the gospel of the kingdom and proclaim the saving truth that man is a son of God. Remember that the disciple is hardly above his master nor a servant greater than his lord. It is enough for the disciple to be equal with his master and the servant to become like his lord. If some people have dared to call the master of the house an associate of Beelzebub, how much more shall they so regard those of his household! But you should not fear these unbelieving enemies. I declare to you that there is nothing covered up that is not going to be revealed; there is nothing hidden that shall not be known. What I have taught you privately, that preach with wisdom in the open. What I have revealed to you in the inner chamber, that you are to proclaim in due season from the housetops. And I say to you, my friends and disciples, be not afraid of those who can kill the body, but who are not able to destroy the soul; rather put your trust in Him who is able to sustain the body and save the soul. *

150:4.3 (1682.1) "Are not two sparrows sold for a penny? And yet I declare that not one of them is forgotten in God's sight. Know you not that the very hairs of your head are all numbered? Fear not, therefore; you are of more value than a great many sparrows. Be not ashamed of my teaching; go forth proclaiming peace and good will, but be not deceived— peace will not always attend your preaching. I came to bring peace on earth, but when men reject my gift, division and turmoil result. When all of a family receive the gospel of the kingdom, truly peace abides in that house; but when some of the family enter the kingdom and others reject the gospel, such division can produce only sorrow and sadness. Labor earnestly to save the whole family lest a man's foes become those of his own household. But, when you have done your utmost for all of every family, I declare to you that he who loves father or mother more than this gospel is not worthy of the kingdom."

150:4.4 (1682.2) When the twelve had heard these words, they made ready to depart. And they did not again come together until the time of their assembling at Nazareth to meet with Jesus and the other disciples as the Master had arranged.

5   *What Must I Do to Be Saved?*

150:5.1 (1682.3) One evening at Shunem, after John's apostles had returned to Hebron, and after Jesus' apostles had been sent out two and two, when the Master was engaged in teaching a group of twelve of the younger evangelists who were laboring under the direction of Jacob, together with the twelve women, Rachel asked Jesus this question: "Master, what shall we answer when women ask us, What shall I do to be saved?" When Jesus heard this question, he answered:

150:5.2 (1682.4) "When men and women ask what shall we do to be saved, you shall answer, Believe this gospel of the kingdom; accept divine forgiveness. By faith recognize the indwelling spirit of God, whose acceptance makes you a son of God. Have you not read in the Scriptures where it says, 'In the Lord have I righteousness and strength.' Also where the Father says, 'My righteousness is near; my salvation has gone forth, and my arms shall enfold my people.' 'My soul shall be joyful in the love of my God, for he has clothed me with the garments of salvation and has covered me with the robe of his righteousness.' Have you not also read of the Father that his name 'shall be called the Lord our righteousness.' 'Take away the filthy rags of self-righteousness and clothe my son with the robe of divine righteousness and eternal salvation.' It is forever true, 'the just shall live by faith.' Entrance into the Father's kingdom is wholly free, but progress—growth in grace—is essential to continuance therein.

150:5.3 (1682.5) "Salvation is the gift of the Father and is revealed by his Sons. Acceptance by faith on your part makes you a partaker of the divine nature, a son or a daughter of God. By faith you are justified; by faith are you saved; and by this same faith are you eternally advanced in the way of progressive and divine perfection. By faith was Abraham justified and made aware of salvation by the teachings of Melchizedek. All down through the ages has this same faith saved the sons of men, but now has a Son come forth from the Father to make salvation more real and acceptable."

150:5.4 (1683.1) When Jesus had left off speaking, there was great rejoicing among those who had heard these gracious words, and they all went on in the days that followed proclaiming the gospel of the kingdom with new power and with renewed energy and enthusiasm. And the women rejoiced all the more to know they were included in these plans for the establishment of the kingdom on earth.

150:5.5 (1683.2) In summing up his final statement, Jesus said: "You cannot buy salvation; you cannot earn righteousness. Salvation is the gift of God, and righteousness is the natural fruit of the spirit-born life of sonship in the kingdom. You are not to be saved because you live a righteous life; rather is it that you live a righteous life because you have already been saved, have recognized sonship as the gift of God and service in the kingdom as the supreme delight of life on earth. When men believe this gospel, which is a revelation of the goodness of God, they will be led to voluntary repentance of all known sin. Realization of sonship is incompatible with the desire to sin. Kingdom believers hunger for righteousness and thirst for divine perfection."

6   The Evening Lessons

150:6.1 (1683.3) At the evening discussions Jesus talked upon many subjects. During the remainder of this tour—before they all reunited at Nazareth—he discussed "The Love of God," "Dreams and Visions,"

"Malice," "Humility and Meekness," "Courage and Loyalty," "Music and Worship," "Service and Obedience," "Pride and Presumption," "Forgiveness in Relation to Repentance," "Peace and Perfection," "Evil Speaking and Envy," "Evil, Sin, and Temptation," "Doubts and Unbelief," "Wisdom and Worship." With the older apostles away, these younger groups of both men and women more freely entered into these discussions with the Master.

150:6.2 (1683.4) After spending two or three days with one group of twelve evangelists, Jesus would move on to join another group, being informed as to the whereabouts and movements of all these workers by David's messengers. This being their first tour, the women remained much of the time with Jesus. Through the messenger service each of these groups was kept fully informed concerning the progress of the tour, and the receipt of news from other groups was always a source of encouragement to these scattered and separated workers.

150:6.3 (1683.5) Before their separation it had been arranged that the twelve apostles, together with the evangelists and the women's corps, should assemble at Nazareth to meet the Master on Friday, March 4. Accordingly, about this time, from all parts of central and southern Galilee these various groups of apostles and evangelists began moving toward Nazareth. By midafternoon, Andrew and Peter, the last to arrive, had reached the encampment prepared by the early arrivals and situated on the highlands to the north of the city. And this was the first time Jesus had visited Nazareth since the beginning of his public ministry.

7   The Sojourn at Nazareth

150:7.1 (1683.6) This Friday afternoon Jesus walked about Nazareth quite unobserved and wholly unrecognized. He passed by the home of his childhood and the carpenter shop and spent a half hour on the hill which he so much enjoyed when a lad. Not since the day of his baptism by John in the Jordan had the Son of Man had such a flood of human emotion stirred up within his soul. While coming down from the mount, he heard the familiar sounds of the trumpet blast announcing the going down of the sun, just as he had so many, many times heard it when a boy growing up in Nazareth. Before returning to the encampment, he walked down by the synagogue where he had gone to school and indulged his mind in many reminiscences of his childhood days. Earlier in the day Jesus had sent Thomas to arrange with the ruler of the synagogue for his preaching at the Sabbath morning service.

150:7.2 (1684.1) The people of Nazareth were never reputed for piety and righteous living. As the years passed, this village became increasingly contaminated by the low moral standards of near-by Sepphoris. Throughout Jesus' youth and young manhood there had been a division of opinion in Nazareth regarding him; there was much resentment when he moved to Capernaum. While the inhabitants of Nazareth had heard much about the doings of their former carpenter, they were offended that he had never included his native village in any of his earlier preaching tours. They had indeed heard of Jesus' fame, but the majority of the citizens were angry because he had done none of his great works in the city of his youth. For months the people of Nazareth had discussed Jesus much, but their opinions were, on the whole, unfavorable to him.

150:7.3 (1684.2) Thus did the Master find himself in the midst of, not a welcome homecoming, but a decidedly hostile and hypercritical atmosphere. But this was not all. His enemies, knowing that he was to spend this Sabbath day in Nazareth and supposing that he would speak in the synagogue, had hired numerous rough and uncouth men to harass him and in every way possible make trouble.

150:7.4 (1684.3) Most of the older of Jesus' friends, including the doting chazan teacher of his youth, were dead or had left Nazareth, and the younger generation was prone to resent his fame with strong jealousy. They failed to remember his early devotion to his father's family, and they were bitter in their criticism of his neglect to visit his brother and his married sisters living in Nazareth. The attitude of Jesus' family toward him had also tended to increase this unkind feeling of the citizenry. The orthodox among the Jews even presumed to criticize Jesus because he walked too fast on the way to the synagogue this Sabbath morning.

8   The Sabbath Service

150:8.1 (1684.4) This Sabbath was a beautiful day, and all Nazareth, friends and foes, turned out to hear this former citizen of their town discourse in the synagogue. Many of the apostolic retinue had to remain without the synagogue; there was not room for all who had come to hear him. As a young man Jesus had often spoken in this place of worship, and this morning, when the ruler of the synagogue handed him the roll of sacred writings from which to read the Scripture lesson, none present seemed to recall that this was the very manuscript which he had presented to this synagogue.

150:8.2 (1684.5) The services on this day were conducted just as when Jesus had attended them as a boy. He ascended the speaking platform with the ruler of the synagogue, and the service was begun by the recital of two prayers: "Blessed is the Lord, King of the world, who forms the light and creates the darkness, who makes peace and creates everything; who, in mercy, gives light to the earth and to those who dwell upon it and in goodness, day by day and every day, renews the works of creation. Blessed is the Lord our God for the glory of his handiworks and for the light-giving lights which he has made for his praise. Selah. Blessed is the Lord our God, who has formed the lights."

150:8.3 (1685.1) After a moment's

pause they again prayed: "With great love has the Lord our God loved us, and with much overflowing pity has he pitied us, our Father and our King, for the sake of our fathers who trusted in him. You taught them the statutes of life; have mercy upon us and teach us. Enlighten our eyes in the law; cause our hearts to cleave to your commandments; unite our hearts to love and fear your name, and we shall not be put to shame, world without end. For you are a God who prepares salvation, and us have you chosen from among all nations and tongues, and in truth have you brought us near your great name—selah—that we may lovingly praise your unity. Blessed is the Lord, who in love chose his people Israel."

150:8.4 (1685.2) The congregation then recited the Shema, the Jewish creed of faith. This ritual consisted in repeating numerous passages from the law and indicated that the worshipers took upon themselves the yoke of the kingdom of heaven, also the yoke of the commandments as applied to the day and the night.

150:8.5 (1685.3) And then followed the third prayer: "True it is that you are Yahweh, our God and the God of our fathers; our King and the King of our fathers; our Savior and the Savior of our fathers; our Creator and the rock of our salvation; our help and our deliverer. Your name is from everlasting, and there is no God beside you. A new song did they that were delivered sing to your name by the seashore; together did all praise and own you King and say, Yahweh shall reign, world without end. Blessed is the Lord who saves Israel."

150:8.6 (1685.4) The ruler of the synagogue then took his place before the ark, or chest, containing the sacred writings and began the recitation of the nineteen prayer eulogies, or benedictions. But on this occasion it was desirable to shorten the service in order that the distinguished guest might have more time for his discourse; accordingly, only the first and last of the benedictions were recited. The first was: "Blessed is the Lord our God, and the God of our fathers, the God of Abraham, and the God of Isaac, and the God of Jacob; the great, the mighty, and the terrible God, who shows mercy and kindness, who creates all things, who remembers the gracious promises to the fathers and brings a savior to their children's children for his own name's sake, in love. O King, helper, savior, and shield! Blessed are you, O Yahweh, the shield of Abraham."

150:8.7 (1685.5) Then followed the last benediction: "O bestow on your people Israel great peace forever, for you are King and the Lord of all peace. And it is good in your eyes to bless Israel at all times and at every hour with peace. Blessed are you, Yahweh, who blesses his people Israel with peace." The congregation looked not at the ruler as he recited the benedictions. Following the benedictions he offered an informal prayer suitable for the occasion, and when this was concluded, all the congregation joined in saying amen.

150:8.8 (1685.6) Then the chazan went over to the ark and brought out a roll, which he presented to Jesus that he might read the Scripture lesson. It was customary to call upon seven persons to read not less than three verses of the law, but this practice was waived on this occasion that the visitor might read the lesson of his own selection. Jesus, taking the roll, stood up and began to read from Deuteronomy: "For this commandment which I give you this day is not hidden from you, neither is it far off. It is not in heaven, that you should say, who shall go up for us to heaven and bring it down to us that we may hear and do it? Neither is it beyond the sea, that you should say, who will go over the sea for us to bring the commandment to us that we may hear and do it? No, the word of life is very near to you, even in your presence and in your heart, that you may know and obey it."

150:8.9 (1686.1) And when he had ceased reading from the law, he turned to Isaiah and began to read: "The spirit of the Lord is upon me because he has anointed me to preach good tidings to the poor. He has sent me to proclaim release to the captives and the recovering of sight to the blind, to set at liberty those who are bruised and to proclaim the acceptable year of the Lord."

150:8.10 (1686.2) Jesus closed the book and, after handing it back to the ruler of the synagogue, sat down and began to discourse to the people. He began by saying: "Today are these Scriptures fulfilled." And then Jesus spoke for almost fifteen minutes on "The Sons and Daughters of God." Many of the people were pleased with the discourse, and they marveled at his graciousness and wisdom.

150:8.11 (1686.3) It was customary in the synagogue, after the conclusion of the formal service, for the speaker to remain so that those who might be interested could ask him questions. Accordingly, on this Sabbath morning Jesus stepped down into the crowd which pressed forward to ask questions. In this group were many turbulent individuals whose minds were bent on mischief, while about the fringe of this crowd there circulated those debased men who had been hired to make trouble for Jesus. Many of the disciples and evangelists who had remained without now pressed into the synagogue and were not slow to recognize that trouble was brewing. They sought to lead the Master away, but he would not go with them.

9   The Nazareth Rejection

150:9.1 (1686.4) Jesus found himself surrounded in the synagogue by a great throng of his enemies and a sprinkling of his own followers, and in reply to their rude questions and sinister banterings he half humorously remarked: "Yes, I am Joseph's son; I am the carpenter, and I am not surprised that you remind me of the proverb, 'Physician heal yourself,' and that you challenge me to do in Nazareth what you have heard I did at Capernaum; but I call you to witness that even the Scriptures declare that 'a prophet is not without honor save in his own country and among his own people.'"

150:9.2 (1686.5) But they jostled him and, pointing accusing fingers at him, said: "You think you are better than the people of Nazareth; you moved away from us, but your brother is a common workman, and your sisters still live among us. We know your mother, Mary. Where are they today? We hear big things about you, but we notice that you do no wonders when you come back." Jesus answered them: "I love the people who dwell in the city where I grew up, and I would rejoice to see you all enter the kingdom of heaven, but the doing of the works of God is not for me to determine. The transformations of grace are wrought in response to the living faith of those who are the beneficiaries."

150:9.3 (1686.6) Jesus would have good-naturedly managed the crowd and effectively disarmed even his violent enemies had it not been for the tactical blunder of one of his own apostles, Simon Zelotes, who, with the help of Nahor, one of the younger evangelists, had meanwhile gathered together a group of Jesus' friends from among the crowd and, assuming a belligerent attitude, had served notice on the enemies of the Master to go hence. Jesus had long taught the apostles that a soft answer turns away wrath, but his followers were not accustomed to seeing their beloved teacher, whom they so willingly called Master, treated with such discourtesy and disdain. It was too much for them, and they found themselves giving expression to passionate and vehement resentment, all of which only tended to arouse the mob spirit in this ungodly and uncouth assembly. And so, under the leadership of hirelings, these ruffians laid hold upon Jesus and rushed him out of the synagogue to the brow of a near-by precipitous hill, where they were minded to shove him over the edge to his death below. But just as they were about to push him over the edge of the cliff, Jesus turned suddenly upon his captors and, facing them, quietly folded his arms. He said nothing, but his friends were more than astonished when, as he started to walk forward, the mob parted and permitted him to pass on unmolested.

150:9.4 (1687.1) Jesus, followed by his disciples, proceeded to their encampment, where all this was recounted. And they made ready that evening to go back to Capernaum early the next day, as Jesus had directed. This turbulent ending of the third public preaching tour had a sobering effect upon all of Jesus' followers. They were beginning to realize the meaning of some of the Master's teachings; they were awaking to the fact that the kingdom would come only through much sorrow and bitter disappointment.

150:9.5 (1687.2) They left Nazareth this Sunday morning, and traveling by different routes, they all finally assembled at Bethsaida by noon on Thursday, March 10. They came together as a sober and serious group of disillusioned preachers of the gospel of truth and not as an enthusiastic and all-conquering band of triumphant crusaders.

Paper 151

Tarrying and Teaching by the Seaside

151:0.1 (1688.1) BY MARCH 10 all of the preaching and teaching groups had forgathered at Bethsaida. Thursday night and Friday many of them went out to fish, while on the Sabbath day they attended the synagogue to hear an aged Jew of Damascus discourse on the glory of father Abraham. Jesus spent most of this Sabbath day alone in the hills. That Saturday night the Master talked for more than an hour to the assembled groups on "The mission of adversity and the spiritual value of disappointment." This was a memorable occasion, and his hearers never forgot the lesson he imparted.

151:0.2 (1688.2) Jesus had not fully recovered from the sorrow of his recent rejection at Nazareth; the apostles were aware of a peculiar sadness mingled with his usual cheerful demeanor. James and John were with him much of the time, Peter being more than occupied with the many responsibilities having to do with the welfare and direction of the new corps of evangelists. This time of waiting before starting for the Passover at Jerusalem, the women spent in visiting from house to house, teaching the gospel, and ministering to the sick in Capernaum and the surrounding cities and villages.

The Parable of the Sower

151:1.1 (1688.3) About this time Jesus first began to employ the parable method of teaching the multitudes that so frequently gathered about him. Since Jesus had talked with the apostles and others long into the night, on this Sunday morning very few of the group were up for breakfast; so he went out by the seaside and sat alone in the boat, the old fishing boat of Andrew and Peter, which was always kept at his disposal, and meditated on the next move to be made in the work of extending the kingdom. But the Master was not to be alone for long. Very soon the people from Capernaum and near-by villages began to arrive, and by ten o'clock that morning almost one thousand were assembled on shore near Jesus' boat and were clamoring for attention. Peter was now up and, making his way to the boat, said to Jesus, "Master, shall I talk to them?" But Jesus answered, "No, Peter, I will tell them a story." And then Jesus began the recital of the parable of the sower, one of the first of a long series of such parables which he taught the throngs that followed after him. This boat had an elevated seat on which he sat (for it was the custom to sit when teaching) while he talked to the crowd assembled along the shore. After Peter had spoken a few words, Jesus said:

151:1.2 (1688.4) "A sower went forth to sow, and it came to pass as he sowed that some seed fell by the wayside to be trodden underfoot and devoured by the birds of heaven. Other seed fell upon the rocky places where there was little earth, and immediately it sprang up because there was no depth to the soil, but as soon as the sun shone, it withered because it had no root whereby to secure moisture. Other seed fell among the thorns, and as the thorns grew up, it was choked so that it yielded no grain. Still other seed fell upon good ground and, growing, yielded, some thirtyfold, some sixtyfold, and some a hundredfold." And when he had finished speaking this parable, he said to the multitude, "He who has ears to hear, let him hear."

151:1.3 (1689.1) The apostles and those who were with them, when they heard Jesus teach the people in this manner, were greatly perplexed; and after much talking among themselves, that evening in the Zebedee garden Matthew said to Jesus: "Master, what is the meaning of the dark sayings which you present to the multitude? Why do you speak in parables to those who seek the truth?" And Jesus answered:

151:1.4 (1689.2) "In patience have I instructed you all this time. To you it is given to know the mysteries of the kingdom of heaven, but to the undiscerning multitudes and to those who seek our destruction, from now on, the mysteries of the kingdom shall be presented in parables. And this we will do so that those who really desire to enter the kingdom may discern the meaning of the teaching and thus find salvation, while those who listen only to ensnare us may be the more confounded in that they will see without seeing and will hear without hearing. My children, do you not perceive the law of the spirit which decrees that to him who has shall be given so that he shall have an abundance; but from him who has not shall be taken away even that which he has. Therefore will I henceforth speak to the people much in parables to the end that our friends and those who desire to know the truth may find that which they seek, while our enemies and those who love not the truth may hear without understanding. Many of these people follow not in the way of the truth. The prophet did, indeed, describe all such

undiscerning souls when he said: 'For this people's heart has waxed gross, and their ears are dull of hearing, and their eyes they have closed lest they should discern the truth and understand it in their hearts.'"

151:1.5 (1689.3) The apostles did not fully comprehend the significance of the Master's words. As Andrew and Thomas talked further with Jesus, Peter and the other apostles withdrew to another portion of the garden where they engaged in earnest and prolonged discussion.

Interpretation of the Parable

151:2.1 (1689.4) Peter and the group about him came to the conclusion that the parable of the sower was an allegory, that each feature had some hidden meaning, and so they decided to go to Jesus and ask for an explanation. Accordingly, Peter approached the Master, saying: "We are not able to penetrate the meaning of this parable, and we desire that you explain it to us since you say it is given us to know the mysteries of the kingdom." And when Jesus heard this, he said to Peter: "My son, I desire to withhold nothing from you, but first suppose you tell me what you have been talking about; what is your interpretation of the parable?"

151:2.2 (1689.5) After a moment of silence, Peter said: "Master, we have talked much concerning the parable, and this is the interpretation I have decided upon: The sower is the gospel preacher; the seed is the word of God. The seed which fell by the wayside represents those who do not understand the gospel teaching. The birds which snatched away the seed that fell upon the hardened ground represent Satan, or the evil one, who steals away that which has been sown in the hearts of these ignorant ones. The seed which fell upon the rocky places, and which sprang up so suddenly, represents those superficial and unthinking persons who, when they hear the glad tidings, receive the message with joy; but because the truth has no real root in their deeper understanding, their devotion is short-lived in the face of tribulation and persecution. When trouble comes, these believers stumble; they fall away when tempted. The seed which fell among thorns represents those who hear the word willingly, but who allow the cares of the world and the deceitfulness of riches to choke the word of truth so that it becomes unfruitful. Now the seed which fell on good ground and sprang up to bear, some thirty, some sixty, and some a hundredfold, represents those who, when they have heard the truth, receive it with varying degrees of appreciation—owing to their differing intellectual endowments—and hence manifest these varying degrees of religious experience."

151:2.3 (1690.1) Jesus, after listening to Peter's interpretation of the parable, asked the other apostles if they did not also have suggestions to offer. To this invitation only Nathaniel responded. Said he: "Master, while I recognize many good things about Simon Peter's interpretation of the parable, I do not fully agree with him. My idea of this parable would be: The seed represents the gospel of the kingdom, while the sower stands for the messengers of the kingdom. The seed which fell by the wayside on hardened ground represents those who have heard but little of the gospel, along with those who are indifferent to the message, and who have hardened their hearts. The birds of the sky that snatched away the seed which fell by the wayside represent one's habits of life, the temptation of evil, and the desires of the flesh. The seed which fell among the rocks stands for those emotional souls who are quick to receive new teaching and equally quick to give up the truth when confronted with the difficulties and realities of living up to this truth; they lack spiritual perception. The seed which fell among the thorns represents those who are attracted to the truths of the gospel; they are minded to follow its teachings, but they are prevented by the pride of life, jealousy, envy, and the anxieties of human existence. The seed which fell on good soil, springing up to bear, some thirty, some sixty, and some a hundredfold, represents the natural and varying degrees of ability to comprehend

truth and respond to its spiritual teachings by men and women who possess diverse endowments of spirit illumination."

151:2.4 (1690.2) When Nathaniel had finished speaking, the apostles and their associates fell into serious discussion and engaged in earnest debate, some contending for the correctness of Peter's interpretation, while almost an equal number sought to defend Nathaniel's explanation of the parable. Meanwhile Peter and Nathaniel had withdrawn to the house, where they were involved in a vigorous and determined effort the one to convince and change the mind of the other.

151:2.5 (1690.3) The Master permitted this confusion to pass the point of most intense expression; then he clapped his hands and called them about him. When they had all gathered around him once more, he said, "Before I tell you about this parable, do any of you have aught to say?" Following a moment of silence, Thomas spoke up: "Yes, Master, I wish to say a few words. I remember that you once told us to beware of this very thing. You instructed us that, when using illustrations for our preaching, we should employ true stories, not fables, and that we should select a story best suited to the illustration of the one central and vital truth which we wished to teach the people, and that, having so used the story, we should not attempt to make a spiritual application of all the minor details involved in the telling of the story. I hold that Peter and Nathaniel are both wrong in their attempts to interpret this parable. I admire their ability to do these things, but I am equally sure that all such attempts to make a natural parable yield spiritual analogies in all its features can only result in confusion and serious misconception of the true purpose of such a parable. That I am right is fully proved by the fact that, whereas we were all of one mind an hour ago, now are we divided into two separate groups who hold different opinions concerning this parable and hold such opinions so earnestly as to interfere, in my opinion, with our ability fully to grasp the great truth which you had in mind when you presented this parable to the multitude and subsequently asked us to make comment upon it."

151:2.6 (1691.1) The words which Thomas spoke had a quieting effect on all of them. He caused them to recall what Jesus had taught them on former occasions, and before Jesus resumed speaking, Andrew arose, saying: "I am persuaded that Thomas is right, and I would like to have him tell us what meaning he attaches to the parable of the sower." After Jesus had beckoned Thomas to speak, he said: "My brethren, I did not wish to prolong this discussion, but if you so desire, I will say that I think this parable was spoken to teach us one great truth. And that is that our teaching of the gospel of the kingdom, no matter how faithfully and efficiently we execute our divine commissions, is going to be attended by varying degrees of success; and that all such differences in results are directly due to conditions inherent in the circumstances of our ministry, conditions over which we have little or no control."

151:2.7 (1691.2) When Thomas had finished speaking, the majority of his fellow preachers were about ready to agree with him, even Peter and Nathaniel were on their way over to speak with him, when Jesus arose and said: "Well done, Thomas; you have discerned the true meaning of parables; but both Peter and Nathaniel have done you all equal good in that they have so fully shown the danger of undertaking to make an allegory out of my parables. In your own hearts you may often profitably engage in such flights of the speculative imagination, but you make a mistake when you seek to offer such conclusions as a part of your public teaching."

151:2.8 (1691.3) Now that the tension was over, Peter and Nathaniel congratulated each other on their interpretations, and with the exception of the Alpheus twins, each of the apostles ventured to make an interpretation of the parable of the sower before they retired for the night. Even Judas Iscariot offered a very plausible interpretation. The twelve would often, among themselves, attempt to figure out the Master's parables as they would an allegory, but never again did they regard such speculations seriously. This was a very profitable session for the apostles and their associates, especially so since from this time on Jesus more and more employed parables in connection with his public teaching.

More About Parables

151:3.1 (1691.4) The apostles were parable-minded, so much so that the whole of the next evening was devoted to the further discussion of parables. Jesus introduced the evening's conference by saying: "My beloved, you must always make a difference in teaching so as to suit your presentation of truth to the minds and hearts before you. When you stand before a multitude of varying intellects and temperaments, you cannot speak different words for each class of hearers, but you can tell a story to convey your teaching; and each group, even each individual, will be able to make his own interpretation of your parable in accordance with his own intellectual and spiritual endowments. You are to let your light shine but do so with wisdom and discretion. No man, when he lights a lamp, covers it up with a vessel or puts it under the bed; he puts his lamp on a stand where all can behold the light. Let me tell you that nothing is hid in the kingdom of heaven which shall not be made manifest; neither are there any secrets which shall not ultimately be made known.

Eventually, all these things shall come to light. Think not only of the multitudes and how they hear the truth; take heed also to yourselves how you hear. Remember that I have many times told you: To him who has shall be given more, while from him who has not shall be taken away even that which he thinks he has."

151:3.2 (1692.1) The continued discussion of parables and further instruction as to their interpretation may be summarized and expressed in modern phraseology as follows:

151:3.3 (1692.2) 1. Jesus advised against the use of either fables or allegories in teaching the truths of the gospel. He did recommend the free use of parables, especially nature parables. He emphasized the value of utilizing the analogy existing between the natural and the spiritual worlds as a means of teaching truth. He frequently alluded to the natural as "the unreal and fleeting shadow of spirit realities."

151:3.4 (1692.3) 2. Jesus narrated three or four parables from the Hebrew scriptures, calling attention to the fact that this method of teaching was not wholly new. However, it became almost a new method of teaching as he employed it from this time onward.

151:3.5 (1692.4) 3. In teaching the apostles the value of parables, Jesus called attention to the following points:

151:3.6 (1692.5) The parable provides for a simultaneous appeal to vastly different levels of mind and spirit. The parable stimulates the imagination, challenges the discrimination, and provokes critical thinking; it promotes sympathy without arousing antagonism.

151:3.7 (1692.6) The parable proceeds from the things which are known to the discernment of the unknown. The parable utilizes the material and natural as a means of introducing the spiritual and the supermaterial.

151:3.8 (1692.7) Parables favor the making of impartial moral decisions. The parable evades much prejudice and puts new truth gracefully into the mind and does all this with the arousal of a minimum of the self-defense of personal resentment.

151:3.9 (1692.8) To reject the truth contained in parabolical analogy requires conscious intellectual action which is directly in contempt of one's honest judgment and fair decision. The parable conduces to the forcing of thought through the sense of hearing.

151:3.10 (1692.9) The use of the par-able form of teaching enables the teacher to present new and even startling truths while at the same time he largely avoids all controversy and outward clashing with tradition and established authority.

151:3.11 (1693.1) The parable also possesses the advantage of stimulating the memory of the truth taught when the same familiar scenes are subsequently encountered.

151:3.12 (1693.2) In this way Jesus sought to acquaint his followers with many of the reasons underlying his practice of increasingly using parables in his public teaching.

151:3.13 (1693.3) Toward the close of the evening's lesson Jesus made his first comment on the parable of the sower. He said the parable referred to two things: First, it was a review of his own ministry up to that time and a forecast of what lay ahead of him for the remainder of his life on earth. And second, it was also a hint as to what the apostles and other messengers of the kingdom might expect in their ministry from generation to generation as time passed.

151:3.14 (1693.4) Jesus also resorted to the use of parables as the best possible refutation of the studied effort of the religious leaders at Jerusalem to teach that all of his work was done by the assistance of demons and the prince of devils. The appeal to nature was in contravention of such teaching since the people of that day looked upon all natural phenomena as the product of the direct act of spiritual beings and supernatural forces. He also determined upon this method of teaching because it enabled him to proclaim vital truths to those who desired to know the better way while at the same time affording his enemies less opportunity to find cause for offense and for accusations against him.

151:3.15 (1693.5) Before he dismissed the group for the night, Jesus said: "Now will I tell you the last of the parable of the sower. I would test you to know how you will receive this: The kingdom of heaven is also like a man who cast good seed upon the earth; and while he slept by night and went about his business by day, the seed sprang up and grew, and although he knew not how it came about, the plant came to fruit. First there was the blade, then the ear, then the full grain in the ear. And then when the grain was ripe, he put forth the sickle, and the harvest was finished. He who has an ear to hear, let him hear."

151:3.16 (1693.6) Many times did the apostles turn this saying over in their minds, but the Master never made further mention of this addition to the parable of the sower.

More Parables by the Sea

151:4.1 (1693.7) The next day Jesus again taught the people from the boat, saying: "The kingdom of heaven is like a man who sowed good seed in his field; but while he slept, his enemy came and sowed weeds among the wheat and hastened away. And so when the young blades sprang up and later were about to bring forth fruit, there appeared also the weeds. Then the servants of this householder came and said to him: 'Sir, did you not sow good seed in your field? Whence then come these weeds?' And he replied to his servants, 'An enemy has done this.' The servants then asked their master, 'Would you have us go out and pluck up these weeds?' But he answered them and said: 'No, lest while you are gathering them up, you uproot the wheat also. Rather let them both grow together until the time of the harvest, when I will say to the reapers, Gather up first the weeds and bind them in bundles to burn and then gather up the wheat to be stored in my barn.'"

151:4.2 (1693.8) After the people had asked a few questions, Jesus spoke another parable: "The kingdom of heaven is like a grain of mustard seed which a man sowed in his field. Now a mustard seed is the least of seeds, but when it is full grown, it becomes the greatest of all herbs and is like a tree so that the birds of heaven are able to come and rest in the branches thereof."

151:4.3 (1694.1) "The kingdom of heaven is also like leaven which a woman took and hid in three measures of meal, and in this way it came about that all of the meal was leavened."

151:4.4 (1694.2) "The kingdom of heaven is also like a treasure hidden in a field, which a man discovered. In his joy he went forth to sell all he had that he might have the money to buy the field."

151:4.5 (1694.3) "The kingdom of heaven is also like a merchant seeking goodly pearls; and having found one pearl of great price, he went out and sold everything he possessed that he might be able to buy the extraordinary pearl."

151:4.6 (1694.4) "Again, the kingdom of heaven is like a sweep net which was cast into the sea, and it gathered up every kind of fish. Now, when the net was filled, the fishermen drew it up on the beach, where they sat down and sorted out the fish, gathering the good into vessels while the bad they threw away."

151:4.7 (1694.5) Many other parables spoke Jesus to the multitudes. In fact, from this time forward he seldom taught the masses except by this means. After speaking to a public audience in parables, he would, during the evening classes, more fully and explicitly expound his teachings to the apostles and the evangelists.

The Visit to Kheresa

151:5.1 (1694.6) The multitude continued to increase throughout the week. On Sabbath Jesus hastened away to the hills, but when Sunday morning came, the crowds returned. Jesus spoke to them in the early afternoon after the preaching of Peter, and when he had finished, he said to his apostles: "I am weary of the throngs; let us cross over to the other side that we may rest for a day."

151:5.2 (1694.7) On the way across the lake they encountered one of those violent and sudden windstorms which are characteristic of the Sea of Galilee, especially at this season of the year. This body of water is almost seven hundred feet below the level of the sea and is surrounded by high banks, especially on the west. There are steep gorges leading up from the lake into the hills, and as the heated air rises in a pocket over the lake during the day, there is a tendency after sunset for the cooling air of the gorges to rush down upon the lake. These gales come on quickly and sometimes go away just as suddenly.

151:5.3 (1694.8) It was just such an evening gale that caught the boat carrying Jesus over to the other side on this Sunday evening. Three other boats containing some of the younger evangelists were trailing after. This tempest was severe, notwithstanding that it was being confined to this region of the lake, there being no evidence of a storm on the western shore. The wind was so strong that the waves began to wash over the boat. The high wind had torn the sail away before the apostles could furl it, and they were now entirely dependent on their oars as they laboriously pulled for the shore, a little more than a mile and a half distant.

151:5.4 (1694.9) Meanwhile Jesus lay asleep in the stern of the boat under a small overhead shelter. The Master was weary when they left Bethsaida, and it was to secure rest that he had directed them to sail him across to the other side. These ex-fishermen were strong and experienced oarsmen, but this was one of the worst gales they had ever encountered.

Although the wind and the waves tossed their boat about as though it were a toy ship, Jesus slumbered on undisturbed. Peter was at the right-hand oar near the stern. When the boat began to fill with water, he dropped his oar and, rushing over to Jesus, shook him vigorously in order to awaken him, and when he was aroused, Peter said: "Master, don't you know we are in a violent storm? If you do not save us, we will all perish."

151:5.5 (1695.1) As Jesus came out in the rain, he looked first at Peter, and then peering into the darkness at the struggling oarsmen, he turned his glance back upon Simon Peter, who, in his agitation, had not yet returned to his oar, and said: "Why are all of you so filled with fear? Where is your faith? Peace, be quiet." Jesus had hardly uttered this rebuke to Peter and the other apostles, he had hardly bidden Peter seek peace wherewith to quiet his troubled soul, when the disturbed atmosphere, having established its equilibrium, settled down into a great calm. The angry waves almost immediately subsided, while the dark clouds, having spent themselves in a short shower, vanished, and the stars of heaven shone overhead. All this was purely coincidental as far as we can judge; but the apostles, particularly Simon Peter, never ceased to regard the episode as a nature miracle. It was especially easy for the men of that day to believe in nature miracles inasmuch as they firmly believed that all nature was a phenomenon directly under the control of spirit forces and supernatural beings.

151:5.6 (1695.2) Jesus plainly explained to the twelve that he had spoken to their troubled spirits and had addressed himself to their fear-tossed minds, that he had not commanded the elements to obey his word, but it was of no avail. The Master's followers always persisted in placing their own interpretation on all such coincidental occurrences. From this day on they insisted on regarding the Master as having absolute power over the natural elements. Peter never grew weary of reciting how "even the winds and the waves obey him."

151:5.7 (1695.3) It was late in the evening when Jesus and his associates reached the shore, and since it was a calm and beautiful night, they all rested in the boats, not going ashore until shortly after sunrise the next morning. When they were gathered together, about forty in all, Jesus said: "Let us go up into yonder hills and tarry for a few days while we ponder over the problems of the Father's kingdom."

The Kheresa Lunatic

151:6.1 (1695.4) Although most of the near-by eastern shore of the lake sloped up gently to the highlands beyond, at this particular spot there was a steep hillside, the shore in some places dropping sheer down into the lake. Pointing up to the side of the near-by hill, Jesus said: "Let us go up on this hillside for our breakfast and under some of the shelters rest and talk."

151:6.2 (1695.5) This entire hillside was covered with caverns which had been hewn out of the rock. Many of these niches were ancient sepulchres. About halfway up the hillside on a small, relatively level spot was the cemetery of the little village of Kheresa. As Jesus and his associates passed near this burial ground, a lunatic who lived in these hillside caverns rushed up to them. This demented man was well known about these parts, having onetime been bound with fetters and chains and confined in one of the grottoes. Long since he had broken his shackles and now roamed at will among the tombs and abandoned sepulchres. *

151:6.3 (1696.1) This man, whose name was Amos, was afflicted with a periodic form of insanity. There were considerable spells when he would find some clothing and deport himself fairly well among his fellows. During one of these lucid intervals he had gone over to Bethsaida, where he heard the preaching of Jesus and the apostles, and at that time had become a halfhearted believer in the gospel of the kingdom. But soon a stormy phase of his trouble appeared, and he fled to the tombs, where he moaned, cried out aloud, and so conducted himself as to terrorize all who chanced to meet him.

151:6.4 (1696.2) When Amos recognized Jesus, he fell down at his feet and exclaimed: "I know you, Jesus, but I am possessed of many devils, and I beseech that you will not torment me." This man truly believed that his periodic mental affliction was due to the fact that, at such times, evil or unclean spirits entered into him and dominated his mind and body. His troubles were mostly emotional—his brain was not grossly diseased.

151:6.5 (1696.3) Jesus, looking down upon the man crouching like an animal at his feet, reached down and, taking him by the hand, stood him up and said to him: "Amos, you are not possessed of a devil; you have already heard the good news that you are a son of God. I command you to come out of this spell." And when Amos heard Jesus speak these words, there occurred such a transformation in his intellect that he was immediately restored to his right mind and the normal control of his emotions. By this time a considerable crowd had assembled from the near-by village, and these people, augmented by the swine herders from the highland above them, were astonished to see the lunatic sitting with Jesus and his followers, in possession of his right mind and freely conversing with them.

151:6.6 (1696.4) As the swine herders rushed into the village to spread the news of the taming of the lunatic, the dogs charged upon a small and untended herd of about thirty swine and drove most of them over a precipice into the sea. And it was this incidental occurrence, in connection with the presence of Jesus and the supposed miraculous curing of the lunatic, that gave origin to the legend that Jesus had cured Amos by casting a legion of devils out of him, and that these devils had entered into the herd of swine, causing them forthwith to rush headlong to their destruction in the sea below. Before the day was over, this episode was published abroad by the swine tenders, and the whole village believed it.

Amos most certainly believed this story; he saw the swine tumbling over the brow of the hill shortly after his troubled mind had quieted down, and he always believed that they carried with them the very evil spirits which had so long tormented and afflicted him. And this had a good deal to do with the permanency of his cure. It is equally true that all of Jesus' apostles (save Thomas) believed that the episode of the swine was directly connected with the cure of Amos.

151:6.7 (1696.5) Jesus did not obtain the rest he was looking for. Most of that day he was thronged by those who came in response to the word that Amos had been cured, and who were attracted by the story that the demons had gone out of the lunatic into the herd of swine. And so, after only one night of rest, early Tuesday morning Jesus and his friends were awakened by a delegation of these swine-raising gentiles who had come to urge that he depart from their midst. Said their spokesman to Peter and Andrew: "Fishermen of Galilee, depart from us and take your prophet with you. We know he is a holy man, but the gods of our country do not know him, and we stand in danger of losing many swine. The fear of you has descended upon us, so that we pray you to go hence." And when Jesus heard them, he said to Andrew, "Let us return to our place."

151:6.8 (1697.1) As they were about to depart, Amos besought Jesus to permit him to go back with them, but the Master would not consent. Said Jesus to Amos: "Forget not that you are a son of God. Return to your own people and show them what great things God has done for you." And Amos went about publishing that Jesus had cast a legion of devils out of his troubled soul, and that these evil spirits had entered into a herd of swine, driving them to quick destruction. And he did not stop until he had gone into all the cities of the Decapolis, declaring what great things Jesus had done for him.

Paper 152

Events Leading up to the Capernaum Crisis

152:0.1 (1698.1) THE story of the cure of Amos, the Kheresa lunatic, had already reached Bethsaida and Capernaum, so that a great crowd was waiting for Jesus when his boat landed that Tuesday forenoon. Among this throng were the new observers from the Jerusalem Sanhedrin who had come down to Capernaum to find cause for the Master's apprehension and conviction. As Jesus spoke with those who had assembled to greet him, Jairus, one of the rulers of the synagogue, made his way through the crowd and, falling down at his feet, took him by the hand and besought that he would hasten away with him, saying: "Master, my little daughter, an only child, lies in my home at the point of death. I pray that you will come and heal her." When Jesus heard the request of this father, he said: "I will go with you."

152:0.2 (1698.2) As Jesus went along with Jairus, the large crowd which had heard the father's request followed on to see what would happen. Shortly before they reached the ruler's house, as they hastened through a narrow street and as the throng jostled him, Jesus suddenly stopped, exclaiming, "Someone touched me." And when those who were near him denied that they had touched him, Peter spoke up: "Master, you can see that this crowd presses you, threatening to crush us, and yet you say 'someone has touched me.' What do you mean?" Then Jesus said: "I asked who touched me, for I perceived that living energy had gone forth from me." As Jesus looked about him, his eyes fell upon a near-by woman, who, coming forward, knelt at his feet and said: "For years I have been afflicted with a scourging hemorrhage. I have suffered many things from many physicians; I have spent all my substance, but none could cure me. Then I heard of you, and I thought if I may but touch the hem of his garment, I shall certainly be made whole. And so I pressed forward with the crowd as it moved along until, standing near you, Master, I touched the border of your garment, and I was made whole; I know that I have been healed of my affliction."

152:0.3 (1698.3) When Jesus heard this, he took the woman by the hand and, lifting her up, said: "Daughter, your faith has made you whole; go in peace." It was her faith and not her touch that made her whole. And this case is a good illustration of many apparently miraculous cures which attended upon Jesus' earth career, but which he in no sense consciously willed. The passing of time demonstrated that this woman was really cured of her malady. Her faith was of the sort that laid direct hold upon the creative power resident in the Master's person. With the faith she had, it was only necessary to approach the Master's person. It was not at all necessary to touch his garment; that was merely the superstitious part of her belief. Jesus called this woman, Veronica of Caesarea-Philippi, into his presence to correct two errors which might have lingered in her mind, or which might have persisted in the minds of those who witnessed this healing: He did not want Veronica to go away thinking that her fear in attempting to steal her cure had been honored, or that her superstition in associating the touch of his garment with her healing had been effective. He desired all to know that it was her pure and living faith that had wrought the cure.

At Jairus's House

152:1.1 (1699.1) Jairus was, of course, terribly impatient of this delay in reaching his home; so they now hastened on at quickened pace. Even before they entered the ruler's yard, one of his servants came out, saying: "Trouble not the Master; your daughter is dead." But Jesus seemed not to heed the servant's words, for, taking with him Peter, James, and John, he turned and said to the grief-stricken father: "Fear not;

only believe." When he entered the house, he found the flute-players already there with the mourners, who were making an unseemly tumult; already were the relatives engaged in weeping and wailing. And when he had put all the mourners out of the room, he went in with the father and mother and his three apostles. He had told the mourners that the damsel was not dead, but they laughed him to scorn.

Jesus now turned to the mother, saying: "Your daughter is not dead; she is only asleep." And when the house had quieted down, Jesus, going up to where the child lay, took her by the hand and said, "Daughter, I say to you, awake and arise!" And when the girl heard these words, she immediately rose up and walked across the room. And presently, after she had recovered from her daze, Jesus directed that they should give her something to eat, for she had been a long time without food.

152:1.2 (1699.2) Since there was much agitation in Capernaum against Jesus, he called the family together and explained that the maiden had been in a state of coma following a long fever, and that he had merely aroused her, that he had not raised her from the dead. He likewise explained all this to his apostles, but it was futile; they all believed he had raised the little girl from the dead. What Jesus said in explanation of many of these apparent miracles had little effect on his followers. They were miracle-minded and lost no opportunity to ascribe another wonder to Jesus. Jesus and the apostles returned to Bethsaida after he had specifically charged all of them that they should tell no man.

152:1.3 (1699.3) When he came out of Jairus's house, two blind men led by a dumb boy followed him and cried out for healing. About this time Jesus' reputation as a healer was at its very height. Everywhere he went the sick and the afflicted were waiting for him. The Master now looked much worn, and all of his friends were becoming concerned lest he continue his work of teaching and healing to the point of actual collapse.

152:1.4 (1699.4) Jesus' apostles, let alone the common people, could not understand the nature and attributes of this God- man. Neither has any subsequent generation been able to evaluate what took place on earth in the person of Jesus of Nazareth. And there can never occur an opportunity for either science or religion to check up on these remarkable events for the simple reason that such an extraordinary situation can never again occur, either on this world or on any other world in Nebadon. Never again, on any world in this entire universe, will a being appear in the likeness of mortal flesh, at the same time embodying all the attributes of creative energy combined with spiritual endowments which transcend time and most other material limitations.

152:1.5 (1700.1) Never before Jesus was on earth, nor since, has it been possible so directly and graphically to secure the results attendant upon the strong and living faith of mortal men and women. To repeat these phenomena, we would have to go into the immediate presence of Michael, the Creator, and find him as he was in those days—the Son of Man.

Likewise, today, while his absence prevents such material manifestations, you should refrain from placing any sort of limitation on the possible exhibition of his spiritual power. Though the Master is absent as a material being, he is present as a spiritual influence in the hearts of men. By going away from the world, Jesus made it possible for his spirit to live alongside that of his Father which indwells the minds of all mankind.

Feeding the Five Thousand

152:2.1 (1700.2) Jesus continued to teach the people by day while he instructed the apostles and evangelists at night. On Friday he declared a furlough of one week that all his followers might go home or to their friends for a few days before preparing to go up to Jerusalem for the Passover. But more than one half of his disciples

refused to leave him, and the multitude was daily increasing in size, so much so that David Zebedee desired to establish a new encampment, but Jesus refused consent. The Master had so little rest over the Sabbath that on Sunday morning, March 27, he sought to get away from the people. Some of the evangelists were left to talk to the multitude while Jesus and the twelve planned to escape, unnoticed, to the opposite shore of the lake, where they proposed to obtain much needed rest in a beautiful park south of Bethsaida-Julias. This region was a favorite resorting place for Capernaum folks; they were all familiar with these parks on the eastern shore.

152:2.2 (1700.3) But the people would not have it so. They saw the direction taken by Jesus' boat, and hiring every craft available, they started out in pursuit. Those who could not obtain boats fared forth on foot to walk around the upper end of the lake.

152:2.3 (1700.4) By late afternoon more than a thousand persons had located the Master in one of the parks, and he spoke to them briefly, being followed by Peter. Many of these people had brought food with them, and after eating the evening meal, they gathered about in small groups while Jesus' apostles and disciples taught them.

152:2.4 (1700.5) Monday afternoon the multitude had increased to more than three thousand. And still—way into the evening—the people continued to flock in, bringing all manner of sick folks with them. Hundreds of interested persons had made their plans to stop over at Capernaum to see and hear Jesus on their way to the Passover, and they simply refused to be disappointed. By Wednesday noon about five thousand men, women, and children were assembled here in this park to the south of Bethsaida-Julias. The weather was pleasant, it being near the end of the rainy season in this locality.

152:2.5 (1700.6) Philip had provided a three days' supply of food for Jesus and the twelve, which was in the custody of the

Mark lad, their boy of all chores. By afternoon of this, the third day for almost half of this multitude, the food the people had brought with them was nearly exhausted. David Zebedee had no tented city here to feed and accommodate the crowds. Neither had Philip made food provision for such a multitude. But the people, even though they were hungry, would not go away. It was being quietly whispered about that Jesus, desiring to avoid trouble with both Herod and the Jerusalem leaders, had chosen this quiet spot outside the jurisdiction of all his enemies as the proper place to be crowned king. The enthusiasm of the people was rising every hour. Not a word was said to Jesus, though, of course, he knew all that was going on. Even the twelve apostles were still tainted with such notions, and especially the younger evangelists. The apostles who favored this attempt to proclaim Jesus king were Peter, John, Simon Zelotes, and Judas Iscariot. Those opposing the plan were Andrew, James, Nathaniel, and Thomas. Matthew, Philip, and the Alpheus twins were noncommittal. The ringleader of this plot to make him king was Joab, one of the young evangelists.

152:2.6 (1701.1) This was the stage setting about five o'clock on Wednesday afternoon, when Jesus asked James Alpheus to summon Andrew and Philip. Said Jesus: "What shall we do with the multitude? They have been with us now three days, and many of them are hungry. They have no food." Philip and Andrew exchanged glances, and then Philip answered: "Master, you should send these people away so that they may go to the villages around about and buy themselves food." And Andrew, fearing the materialization of the king plot, quickly joined with Philip, saying: "Yes, Master, I think it best that you dismiss the multitude so that they may go their way and buy food while you secure rest for a season." By this time others of the twelve had joined the conference. Then said Jesus: "But I do not desire to send them away hungry; can you not feed them?" This was too much for Philip, and he spoke right up: "Master, in this country place where can we buy bread for this multitude? Two hundred denarii worth would not be enough for lunch."

152:2.7 (1701.2) Before the apostles had an opportunity to express themselves, Jesus turned to Andrew and Philip, saying: "I do not want to send these people away. Here they are, like sheep without a shepherd. I would like to feed them. What food have we with us?" While Philip was conversing with Matthew and Judas, Andrew sought out the Mark lad to ascertain how much was left of their store of provisions. He returned to Jesus, saying: "The lad has left only five barley loaves and two dried fishes"—and Peter promptly added, "We have yet to eat this evening."

152:2.8 (1701.3) For a moment Jesus stood in silence. There was a faraway look in his eyes. The apostles said nothing. Jesus turned suddenly to Andrew and said, "Bring me the loaves and fishes." And when Andrew had brought the basket to Jesus, the Master said: "Direct the people to sit down on the grass in companies of one hundred and appoint a leader over each group while you bring all of the evangelists here with us."

152:2.9 (1701.4) Jesus took up the loaves in his hands, and after he had given thanks, he broke the bread and gave to his apostles, who passed it on to their associates, who in turn carried it to the multitude. Jesus in like manner broke and distributed the fishes. And this multitude did eat and were filled. And when they had finished eating, Jesus said to the disciples: "Gather up the broken pieces that remain over so that nothing will be lost." And when they had finished gathering up the fragments, they had twelve basketfuls. They who ate of this extraordinary feast numbered about five thousand men, women, and children.

152:2.10 (1702.1) And this is the first and only nature miracle which Jesus performed as a result of his conscious pre planning. It is true that his disciples were disposed to call many things miracles which were not, but this was a genuine supernatural ministration. In this case, so we were taught, Michael multiplied food elements as he always does except for the elimination of the time factor and the visible life channel.

The King-Making Episode

1. 152:3.1 (1702.2) The feeding of the five thousand by supernatural energy was another of those cases where human pity plus creative power equaled that which happened. Now that the multitude had been fed to the full, and since Jesus' fame was then and there augmented by this stupendous wonder, the project to seize the Master and proclaim him king required no further personal direction. The idea seemed to spread through the crowd like a contagion. The reaction of the multitude to this sudden and spectacular supplying of their physical needs was profound and overwhelming. For a long time the Jews had been taught that the Messiah, the son of David, when he should come, would cause the land again to flow with milk and honey, and that the bread of life would be bestowed upon them as manna from heaven was supposed to have fallen upon their forefathers in the wilderness. And was not all of this expectation now fulfilled right before their eyes? When this hungry, undernourished multitude had finished gorging itself with the wonder-food, there was but one unanimous reaction: "Here is our king." The wonder-working deliverer of Israel had come. In the eyes of these simple-minded people the power to feed carried with it the right to rule. No wonder, then, that the multitude, when it had finished feasting, rose as one man and shouted, "Make him king!"

152:3.2 (1702.3) This mighty shout enthused Peter and those of the apostles who still retained the hope of seeing Jesus assert his right to rule. But these false hopes were not to live for long. This mighty shout of the multitude had hardly ceased to reverberate from the near-by rocks when Jesus stepped upon a huge stone and, lifting up his right hand to command their attention, said: "My children, you mean well, but you are shortsighted and material-minded." There was a brief pause; this stalwart Galilean was there majestically posed in the enchanting glow of that eastern twilight. Every inch he looked a king as he continued to speak to this breathless multitude: "You would make me king, not because your souls have been lighted with a great truth, but because your stomachs have been filled with bread. How many times have I told you that my kingdom is not of this world? This kingdom of heaven which we proclaim is a spiritual brotherhood, and no man rules over it seated upon a material throne. My Father in heaven is the all-wise and the all-powerful Ruler over this spiritual brotherhood of the sons of God on earth. Have I so failed in revealing to you the Father of spirits that you would make a king of his Son in the flesh! Now all of you go hence to your own homes. If you must have a king, let the Father of lights be enthroned in the heart of each of you as the spirit Ruler of all things."

152:3.3 (1702.4) These words of Jesus sent the multitude away stunned and disheartened. Many who had believed in him turned back and followed him no more from that day. The apostles were speechless; they stood in silence gathered about the twelve baskets of the fragments of food; only the chore boy, the Mark lad, spoke, "And he refused to be our king." Jesus, before going off to be alone in the hills, turned to Andrew and said: "Take your brethren back to Zebedee's house and pray with them, especially for your brother, Simon Peter."

Simon Peter's Night Vision

152:4.1 (1703.1) The apostles, without their Master—sent off by themselves—entered the boat and in silence began to row toward Bethsaida on the western shore of the lake. None of the twelve was so crushed and downcast as Simon Peter.

Hardly a word was spoken; they were all thinking of the Master alone in the hills. Had he forsaken them? He had never before sent them all away and refused to go with them. What could all this mean?

152:4.2 (1703.2) Darkness descended upon them, for there had arisen a strong and contrary wind which made progress almost impossible. As the hours of darkness and hard rowing passed, Peter grew weary and fell into a deep sleep of exhaustion. Andrew and James put him to rest on the cushioned seat in the stern of the boat. While the other apostles toiled against the wind and the waves, Peter dreamed a dream; he saw a vision of Jesus coming to them walking on the sea. When the Master seemed to walk on by the boat, Peter cried out, "Save us, Master, save us." And those who were in the rear of the boat heard him say some of these words. As this apparition of the night season continued in Peter's mind, he dreamed that he heard Jesus say: "Be of good cheer; it is I; be not afraid." This was like the balm of Gilead to Peter's disturbed soul; it soothed his troubled spirit, so that (in his dream) he cried out to the Master: "Lord, if it really is you, bid me come and walk with you on the water." And when Peter started to walk upon the water, the boisterous waves frightened him, and as he was about to sink, he cried out, "Lord, save me!" And many of the twelve heard him utter this cry. Then Peter dreamed that Jesus came to the rescue and, stretching forth his hand, took hold and lifted him up, saying: "O, you of little faith, wherefore did you doubt?"

152:4.3 (1703.3) In connection with the latter part of his dream Peter arose from the seat whereon he slept and actually stepped overboard and into the water. And he awakened from his dream as Andrew, James, and John reached down and pulled him out of the sea.

152:4.4 (1703.4) To Peter this experience was always real. He sincerely believed that Jesus came to them that night. He only partially convinced John Mark, which explains why Mark left a portion of the story out of his narrative. Luke, the physician, who made careful search into these matters, concluded that the episode was a vision of Peter's and therefore refused to give place to this story in the preparation of his narrative.

Back in Bethsaida

152:5.1 (1703.5) Thursday morning, before daylight, they anchored their boat offshore near Zebedee's house and sought sleep until about noontime. Andrew was first up and, going for a walk by the sea, found Jesus, in company with their chore boy, sitting on a stone by the water's edge. Notwithstanding that many of the multitude and the young evangelists searched all night and much of the next day about the eastern hills for Jesus, shortly after midnight he and the Mark lad had started to walk around the lake and across the river, back to Bethsaida.

152:5.2 (1704.1) Of the five thousand who were miraculously fed, and who, when their stomachs were full and their hearts empty, would have made him king, only about five hundred persisted in following after him. But before these received word that he was back in Bethsaida, Jesus asked Andrew to assemble the twelve apostles and their associates, including the women, saying, "I desire to speak with them." And when all were ready, Jesus said:

152:5.3 (1704.2) "How long shall I bear with you? Are you all slow of spiritual comprehension and deficient in living faith? All these months have I taught you the truths of the kingdom, and yet are you dominated by material motives instead of spiritual considerations. Have you not even read in the Scriptures where Moses exhorted the unbelieving children of Israel, saying: 'Fear not, stand still and see the salvation of the Lord'? Said the singer: 'Put your trust in the Lord.' 'Be patient, wait upon the Lord and be of good courage. He shall strengthen your heart.' 'Cast your burden on the Lord, and he shall sustain you. Trust him at all times and pour out your heart to him, for God is your refuge.' 'He who dwells in the secret place of the Most High shall abide under the shadow of the Almighty.' 'It is better to trust the Lord than to put confidence in human princes.'

152:5.4 (1704.3) "And now do you all see that the working of miracles and the performance of material wonders will not win souls for the spiritual kingdom? We fed the multitude, but it did not lead them to hunger for the bread of life neither to thirst for the waters of spiritual righteousness. When their hunger was satisfied, they sought not entrance into the kingdom of heaven but rather sought to proclaim the Son of Man king after the manner of the kings of this world, only that they might continue to eat bread without having to toil therefor. And all this, in which many of you did more or less participate, does nothing to reveal the heavenly Father or to advance his kingdom on earth. Have we not sufficient enemies among the religious leaders of the land without doing that which is likely to estrange also the civil rulers? I pray that the Father will anoint your eyes that you may see and open your ears that you may hear, to the end that you may have full faith in the gospel which I have taught you."

152:5.5 (1704.4) Jesus then announced that he wished to withdraw for a few days of rest with his apostles before they made ready to go up to Jerusalem for the Passover, and he forbade any of the disciples or the multitude to follow him.

Accordingly they went by boat to the region of Gennesaret for two or three days of rest and sleep. Jesus was preparing for a great crisis of his life on earth, and he therefore spent much time in communion with the Father in heaven.

152:5.6 (1704.5) The news of the feeding of the five thousand and the attempt to make Jesus king aroused widespread curiosity and stirred up the fears of both the religious leaders and the civil rulers throughout all Galilee and Judea. While this great miracle did nothing to further the gospel of the kingdom in the souls of material-minded and halfhearted believers, it did serve the purpose of bringing to a head the miracle-seeking and king-craving proclivities of Jesus' immediate family of apostles and close disciples. This spectacular episode brought an end to the early era of teaching, training, and healing, thereby preparing the way for the inauguration of this last year of proclaiming the higher and more spiritual phases of the new gospel of the kingdom—divine sonship, spiritual liberty, and eternal salvation.

At Gennesaret

152:6.1 (1705.1) While resting at the home of a wealthy believer in the Gennesaret region, Jesus held informal conferences with the twelve every afternoon. The ambassadors of the kingdom were a serious, sober, and chastened group of disillusioned men. But even after all that had happened, and as subsequent events disclosed, these twelve men were not yet fully delivered from their inbred and long-cherished notions about the coming of the Jewish Messiah. Events of the preceding few weeks had moved too swiftly for these astonished fishermen to grasp their full significance. It requires time for men and women to effect radical and extensive changes in their basic and fundamental concepts of social conduct, philosophic attitudes, and religious convictions.

152:6.2 (1705.2) While Jesus and the twelve were resting at Gennesaret, the multitudes dispersed, some going to their homes, others going on up to Jerusalem for the Passover. In less than one month's time the enthusiastic and open followers of Jesus, who numbered more than fifty thousand in Galilee alone, shrank to less than five hundred. Jesus desired to give his apostles such an experience with the fickleness of popular acclaim that they would not be tempted to rely on such manifestations of transient religious hysteria after he should leave them alone in the work of the kingdom, but he was only partially successful in this effort.

152:6.3 (1705.3) The second night of their sojourn at Gennesaret the Master again told the apostles the parable of the sower and added these words: "You see, my children, the appeal to human feelings is transitory and utterly disappointing; the exclusive appeal to the intellect of man is likewise empty and barren; it is only by making your appeal to the spirit which lives within the human mind that you can hope to achieve lasting success and accomplish those marvelous transformations of human character that are presently shown in the abundant yielding of the genuine fruits of the spirit in the daily lives of all who are thus delivered from the darkness of doubt by the birth of the spirit into the light of faith—the kingdom of heaven."

152:6.4 (1705.4) Jesus taught the appeal to the emotions as the technique of arresting and focusing the intellectual attention. He designated the mind thus aroused and quickened as the gateway to the soul, where there resides that spiritual nature of man which must recognize truth and respond to the spiritual appeal of the gospel in order to afford the permanent results of true character transformations.

152:6.5 (1705.5) Jesus thus endeavored to prepare the apostles for the impending shock—the crisis in the public attitude toward him which was only a few days distant. He explained to the twelve that the religious rulers of Jerusalem would conspire with Herod Antipas to effect their destruction. The twelve began to realize more fully (though not finally) that Jesus was not going to sit on David's throne. They saw more fully that spiritual truth was not to be advanced by material wonders. They began to realize that the feeding of the five thousand and the popular movement to make Jesus king was the apex of the miracle-seeking, wonder-working expectance of the people and the height of Jesus' acclaim by the populace. They vaguely discerned and dimly foresaw the approaching times of spiritual sifting and cruel adversity.

These twelve men were slowly awaking to the realization of the real nature of their task as ambassadors of the kingdom, and they began to gird themselves for the trying and testing ordeals of the last year of the Master's ministry on earth.

152:6.6 (1706.1) Before they left Gen-nesaret, Jesus instructed them regarding the miraculous feeding of the five thousand, telling them just why he engaged in this extraordinary manifestation of creative power and also assuring them that he did not thus yield to his sympathy for the multitude until he had ascertained that it was "according to the Father's will."

At Jerusalem

152:7.1 (1706.2) Sunday, April 3, Jesus, accompanied only by the twelve apostles, started from Bethsaida on the journey to Jerusalem. To avoid the multitudes and to attract as little attention as possible, they journeyed by way of Gerasa and Philadelphia. He forbade them to do any public teaching on this trip; neither did he permit them to teach or preach while sojourning in Jerusalem. They arrived at Bethany, near Jerusalem, late on Wednesday evening, April 6. For this one night they stopped at the home of Lazarus, Martha, and Mary, but the next day they separated. Jesus, with John, stayed at the home of a believer named Simon, near the house of Lazarus in Bethany. Judas Iscariot and Simon Zelotes stopped with friends in Jerusalem, while the rest of the apostles sojourned, two and two, in different homes.

152:7.2 (1706.3) Jesus entered Jerusalem only once during this Passover, and that was on the great day of the feast. Many of the Jerusalem believers were brought out by Abner to meet Jesus at Bethany. During this sojourn at Jerusalem the twelve learned how bitter the feeling was becoming toward their Master. They departed from Jerusalem all believing that a crisis was impending.

152:7.3 (1706.4) On Sunday, April 24, Jesus and the apostles left Jerusalem for Bethsaida, going by way of the coast cities of Joppa, Caesarea, and Ptolemais. Thence, overland they went by Ramah and Chorazin to Bethsaida, arriving on Friday, April 29. Immediately on reaching home, Jesus dispatched Andrew to ask of the ruler of the synagogue permission to speak the next day, that being the Sabbath, at the afternoon service. And Jesus well knew that that would be the last time he would ever be permitted to speak in the Capernaum synagogue.

Paper 153

The Crisis at Capernaum

153:0.1 (1707.1) ON FRIDAY evening, the day of their arrival at Bethsaida, and on Sabbath morning, the apostles noticed that Jesus was seriously occupied with some momentous problem; they were cognizant that the Master was giving unusual thought to some important matter. He ate no breakfast and but little at noontide. All of Sabbath morning and the evening before, the twelve and their associates were gathered together in small groups about the house, in the garden, and along the seashore. There was a tension of uncertainty and a suspense of apprehension resting upon all of them.

Jesus had said little to them since they left Jerusalem.

153:0.2 (1707.2) Not in months had they seen the Master so preoccupied and uncommunicative. Even Simon Peter was depressed, if not downcast. Andrew was at a loss to know what to do for his dejected associates. Nathaniel said they were in the midst of the "lull before the storm." Thomas expressed the opinion that "something out of the ordinary is about to happen." Philip advised David Zebedee to "forget about plans for feeding and lodging the multitude until we know what the Master is thinking about." Matthew was putting forth renewed efforts to replenish the treasury. James and John talked over the forthcoming sermon in the synagogue and speculated much as to its probable nature and scope. Simon Zelotes expressed the belief, in reality a hope, that "the Father in heaven may be about to intervene in some unexpected manner for the vindication and support

of his Son," while Judas Iscariot dared to indulge the thought that possibly Jesus was oppressed with regrets that "he did not have the courage and daring to permit the five thousand to proclaim him king of the Jews."

153:0.3 (1707.3) It was from among such a group of depressed and disconsolate followers that Jesus went forth on this beautiful Sabbath afternoon to preach his epoch-making sermon in the Capernaum synagogue. The only word of cheerful greeting or well-wishing from any of his immediate followers came from one of the unsuspecting Alpheus twins, who, as Jesus left the house on his way to the synagogue, saluted him cheerily and said: "We pray the Father will help you, and that we may have bigger multitudes than ever."

The Setting of the Stage

153:1.1 (1707.4) A distinguished congregation greeted Jesus at three o'clock on this exquisite Sabbath afternoon in the new Capernaum synagogue. Jairus presided and handed Jesus the Scriptures to read. The day before, fifty-three Pharisees and Sadducees had arrived from Jerusalem; more than thirty of the leaders and rulers of the neighboring synagogues were also present. These Jewish religious leaders were acting directly under orders from the Sanhedrin at Jerusalem, and they constituted the orthodox vanguard which had come to inaugurate open warfare on Jesus and his disciples. Sitting by the side of these Jewish leaders, in the synagogue seats of honor, were the official observers of Herod Antipas, who had been directed to ascertain the truth concerning the disturbing reports that an attempt had been made by the populace to proclaim Jesus the king of the Jews, over in the domains of his brother Philip.

153:1.2 (1708.1) Jesus comprehended that he faced the immediate declaration of avowed and open warfare by his increasing enemies, and he elected boldly to assume the offensive. At the feeding of the five thousand he had challenged their ideas of the material Messiah; now he chose again openly to attack their concept of the Jewish deliverer. This crisis, which began with the feeding of the five thousand, and which terminated with this Sabbath afternoon sermon, was the outward turning of the tide of popular fame and acclaim. Henceforth, the work of the kingdom was to be increasingly concerned with the more important task of winning lasting spiritual converts for the truly religious brotherhood of mankind. This sermon marks the crisis in the transition from the period of discussion, controversy, and decision to that of open warfare and final acceptance or final rejection.

153:1.3 (1708.2) The Master well knew that many of his followers were slowly but surely preparing their minds finally to reject him. He likewise knew that many of his disciples were slowly but certainly passing through that training of mind and that discipline of soul which would enable them to triumph over doubt and courageously to assert their full-fledged faith in the gospel of the kingdom. Jesus fully understood how men prepare themselves for the decisions of a crisis and the performance of sudden deeds of courageous choosing by the slow process of the reiterated choosing between the recurring situations of good and evil. He subjected his chosen messengers to repeated rehearsals in disappointment and provided them with frequent and testing opportunities for choosing between the right and the wrong way of meeting spiritual trials. He knew he could depend on his followers, when they met the final test, to make their vital decisions in accordance with prior and habitual mental attitudes and spirit reactions.

153:1.4 (1708.3) This crisis in Jesus' earth life began with the feeding of the five thousand and ended with this sermon in the synagogue; the crisis in the lives of the apostles began with this sermon in the synagogue and continued for a whole year, ending only with the Master's trial and crucifixion.

153:1.5 (1708.4) As they sat there in the synagogue that afternoon before Jesus began to speak, there was just one great mystery, just one supreme question, in the minds of all. Both his friends and his foes pondered just one thought, and that was: "Why did he himself so deliberately and effectively turn back the tide of popular enthusiasm?" And it was immediately before and immediately after this sermon that the doubts and disappointments of his disgruntled adherents grew into unconscious opposition and eventually turned into actual hatred. It was after this sermon in the synagogue that Judas Iscariot entertained his first conscious thought of deserting. But he did, for the time being, effectively master all such inclinations.

153:1.6 (1708.5) Everyone was in a state of perplexity. Jesus had left them dumfounded and confounded. He had recently engaged in the greatest demonstration of supernatural power to characterize his whole career. The feeding of the five thousand was the one event of his earth life which made the greatest appeal to the Jewish concept of the expected Messiah. But this extraordinary advantage was immediately and unexplainedly offset by his prompt and unequivocal refusal to be made king.

153:1.7 (1709.1) On Friday evening, and again on Sabbath morning, the Jerusalem leaders had labored long and earnestly with Jairus to prevent Jesus' speaking in the synagogue, but it was of no avail. Jairus's only reply to all this pleading was: "I have granted this request, and I will not violate my word."

The Epochal Sermon

153:2.1 (1709.2) Jesus introduced this sermon by reading from the law as found in Deuteronomy: "But it shall come to pass, if this people will not hearken to the voice of God, that the curses of transgression shall surely overtake them. The Lord shall cause you to be smitten by your enemies;

you shall be removed into all the kingdoms of the earth. And the Lord shall bring you and the king you have set up over you into the hands of a strange nation. You shall become an astonishment, a proverb, and a byword among all nations. Your sons and your daughters shall go into captivity. The strangers among you shall rise high in authority while you are brought very low. And these things shall be upon you and your seed forever because you would not hearken to the word of the Lord. Therefore shall you serve your enemies who shall come against you. You shall endure hunger and thirst and wear this alien yoke of iron. The Lord shall bring against you a nation from afar, from the end of the earth, a nation whose tongue you shall not understand, a nation of fierce countenance, a nation which will have little regard for you. And they shall besiege you in all your towns until the high fortified walls wherein you have trusted come down; and all the land shall fall into their hands. And it shall come to pass that you will be driven to eat the fruit of your own bodies, the flesh of your sons and daughters, during this time of siege, because of the straitness wherewith your enemies shall press you."

153:2.2 (1709.3) And when Jesus had finished this reading, he turned to the Prophets and read from Jeremiah: "'If you will not hearken to the words of my servants the prophets whom I have sent you, then will I make this house like Shiloh, and I will make this city a curse to all the nations of the earth.' And the priests and the teachers heard Jeremiah speak these words in the house of the Lord. And it came to pass that, when Jeremiah had made an end of speaking all that the Lord had commanded him to speak to all the people, the priests and teachers laid hold of him, saying, 'You shall surely die.'

And all the people crowded around Jeremiah in the house of the Lord. And when the princes of Judah heard these things, they sat in judgment on Jeremiah. Then spoke the priests and the teachers to the princes and to all the people, saying: 'This man is worthy to die, for he has prophesied against our city, and you

have heard him with your own ears.' Then spoke Jeremiah to all the princes and to all the people: 'The Lord sent me to prophesy against this house and against this city all the words which you have heard. Now, therefore, amend your ways and reform your doings and obey the voice of the Lord your God that you may escape the evil which has been pronounced against you. As for me, behold I am in your hands. Do with me as seems good and right in your eyes. But know you for certain that, if you put me to death, you shall bring innocent blood upon yourselves and upon this people, for of a truth the Lord has sent me to speak all these words in your ears.'

153:2.3 (1710.1) "The priests and teachers of that day sought to kill Jeremiah, but the judges would not consent, albeit, for his words of warning, they did let him down by cords in a filthy dungeon until he sank in mire up to his armpits. That is what this people did to the Prophet Jeremiah when he obeyed the Lord's command to warn his brethren of their impending political downfall. Today, I desire to ask you: What will the chief priests and religious leaders of this people do with the man who dares to warn them of the day of their spiritual doom? Will you also seek to put to death the teacher who dares to proclaim the word of the Lord, and who fears not to point out wherein you refuse to walk in the way of light which leads to the entrance to the kingdom of heaven?

153:2.4 (1710.2) "What is it you seek as evidence of my mission on earth? We have left you undisturbed in your positions of influence and power while we preached glad tidings to the poor and the outcast. We have made no hostile attack upon that which you hold in reverence but have rather proclaimed new liberty for man's fear-ridden soul. I came into the world to reveal my Father and to establish on earth the spiritual brotherhood of the sons of God, the kingdom of heaven. And notwithstanding that I have so many times reminded you that my kingdom is not of this world, still has my Father granted you many manifestations of material wonders in addition to more evidential spiritual transformations and regenerations.

153:2.5 (1710.3) "What new sign is it that you seek at my hands? I declare that you already have sufficient evidence to enable you to make your decision. Verily, verily, I say to many who sit before me this day, you are confronted with the necessity of choosing which way you will go; and I say to you, as Joshua said to your forefathers, 'choose you this day whom you will serve.' Today, many of you stand at the parting of the ways.

153:2.6 (1710.4) "Some of you, when you could not find me after the feasting of the multitude on the other side, hired the Tiberias fishing fleet, which a week before had taken shelter near by during a storm, to go in pursuit of me, and what for? Not for truth and righteousness or that you might the better know how to serve and minister to your fellow men! No, but rather that you might have more bread for which you had not labored. It was not to fill your souls with the word of life, but only that you might fill the belly with the bread of ease. And long have you been taught that the Messiah, when he should come, would work those wonders which would make life pleasant and easy for all the chosen people. It is not strange, then, that you who have been thus taught should long for the loaves and the fishes. But I declare to you that such is not the mission of the Son of Man. I have come to proclaim spiritual liberty, teach eternal truth, and foster living faith.

153:2.7 (1710.5) "My brethren, hanker not after the meat which perishes but rather seek for the spiritual food that nourishes even to eternal life; and this is the bread of life which the Son gives to all who will take it and eat, for the Father has given the Son this life without measure. And when you asked me, 'What must we do to perform the works of God?' I plainly told you: 'This is the work of God, that you believe him whom he has sent.'"

153:2.8 (1710.6) And then said Jesus, pointing up to the device of a pot of manna which decorated the lintel of this new synagogue, and which was embellished with grape clusters: "You have thought that your forefathers in the wilderness ate manna—the bread of heaven—but I say to you that this was the bread of earth. While Moses did not give your fathers bread from heaven, my Father now stands ready to give you the true bread of life. The bread of heaven is that which comes down from God and gives eternal life to the men of the world. And when you say to me, Give us this living bread, I will answer: I am this bread of life. He who comes to me shall not hunger, while he who believes me shall never thirst. You have seen me, lived with me, and beheld my works, yet you believe not that I came forth from the Father. But to those who do believe—fear not. All those led of the Father shall come to me, and he who comes to me shall in nowise be cast out.

153:2.9 (1711.1) "And now let me declare to you, once and for all time, that I have come down upon the earth, not to do my own will, but the will of Him who sent me. And this is the final will of Him who sent me, that of all those he has given me I should not lose one. And this is the will of the Father: That every one who beholds the Son and who believes him shall have eternal life. Only yesterday did I feed you with bread for your bodies; today I offer you the bread of life for your hungry souls. Will you now take the bread of the spirit as you then so willingly ate the bread of this world?"

153:2.10 (1711.2) As Jesus paused for a moment to look over the congregation, one of the teachers from Jerusalem (a member of the Sanhedrin) rose up and asked: "Do I understand you to say that you are the bread which comes down from heaven, and that the manna which Moses gave to our fathers in the wilderness did not?" And Jesus answered the Pharisee, "You understood aright." Then said the Pharisee: "But are you not Jesus of Nazareth, the son of Joseph, the carpenter? Are not your father and mother, as well as your brothers and sisters, well known to many of us? How then is it that you appear here in God's house and declare that you have come down from heaven?"

153:2.11 (1711.3) By this time there was much murmuring in the synagogue, and such a tumult was threatened that Jesus stood up and said: "Let us be patient; the truth never suffers from honest examination. I am all that you say but more. The Father and I are one; the Son does only that which the Father teaches him, while all those who are given to the Son by the Father, the Son will receive to himself. You have read where it is written in the Prophets, 'You shall all be taught by God,' and that 'Those whom the Father teaches will hear also his Son.' Every one who yields to the teaching of the Father's indwelling spirit will eventually come to me. Not that any man has seen the Father, but the Father's spirit does live within man. And the Son who came down from heaven, he has surely seen the Father. And those who truly believe this Son already have eternal life.

153:2.12 (1711.4) "I am this bread of life. Your fathers ate manna in the wilderness and are dead. But this bread which comes down from God, if a man eats thereof, he shall never die in spirit. I repeat, I am this living bread, and every soul who attains the realization of this united nature of God and man shall live forever. And this bread of life which I give to all who will receive is my own living and combined nature. The Father in the Son and the Son one with the Father—that is my life-giving revelation to the world and my saving gift to all nations."

153:2.13 (1711.5) When Jesus had finished speaking, the ruler of the synagogue dismissed the congregation, but they would not depart. They crowded up around Jesus to ask more questions while others murmured and disputed among themselves. And this state of affairs continued for more than three hours. It was well past seven o'clock before the audience finally dispersed.

The After Meeting

153:3.1 (1712.1) Many were the questions asked Jesus during this after meeting. Some were asked by his perplexed disciples, but more were asked by caviling unbelievers who sought only to embarrass and entrap him.

153:3.2 (1712.2) One of the visiting Pharisees, mounting a lampstand, shouted out this question: "You tell us that you are the bread of life. How can you give us your flesh to eat or your blood to drink? What avail is your teaching if it cannot be carried out?" And Jesus answered this question, saying: "I did not teach you that my flesh is the bread of life nor that my blood is the water thereof. But I did say that my life in the flesh is a bestowal of the bread of heaven. The fact of the Word of God bestowed in the flesh and the phenomenon of the Son of Man subject to the will of God, constitute a reality of experience which is equivalent to the divine sustenance. You cannot eat my flesh nor can you drink my blood, but you can become one in spirit with me even as I am one in spirit with the Father. You can be nourished by the eternal word of God, which is indeed the bread of life, and which has been bestowed in the likeness of mortal flesh; and you can be watered in soul by the divine spirit, which is truly the water of life. The Father has sent me into the world to show how he desires to indwell and direct all men; and I have so lived this life in the flesh as to inspire all men likewise ever to seek to know and do the will of the indwelling heavenly Father."

153:3.3 (1712.3) Then one of the Jerusalem spies who had been observing Jesus and his apostles, said: "We notice that neither you nor your apostles wash your hands properly before you eat bread. You must well know that such a practice as eating with defiled and unwashed hands is a transgression of the law of the elders. Neither do you properly wash your drinking cups and eating vessels. Why is it that you show such disrespect for the traditions of the fathers and the laws of our elders?" And when

Jesus heard him speak, he answered: "Why is it that you transgress the commandments of God by the laws of your tradition? The commandment says, 'Honor your father and your mother,' and directs that you share with them your substance if necessary; but you enact a law of tradition which permits undutiful children to say that the money wherewith the parents might have been assisted has been 'given to God.' The law of the elders thus relieves such crafty children of their responsibility, notwithstanding that the children subsequently use all such monies for their own comfort. Why is it that you in this way make void the commandment by your own tradition? Well did Isaiah prophesy of you hypocrites, saying: 'This people honors me with their lips, but their heart is far from me. In vain do they worship me, teaching as their doctrines the precepts of men.'

153:3.4 (1712.4) "You can see how it is that you desert the commandment while you hold fast to the tradition of men. Altogether willing are you to reject the word of God while you maintain your own traditions. And in many other ways do you dare to set up your own teachings above the law and the prophets."

153:3.5 (1712.5) Jesus then directed his remarks to all present. He said: "But hearken to me, all of you. It is not that which enters into the mouth that spiritually defiles the man, but rather that which proceeds out of the mouth and from the heart." But even the apostles failed fully to grasp the meaning of his words, for Simon Peter also asked him: "Lest some of your hearers be unnecessarily offended, would you explain to us the meaning of these words?" And then said Jesus to Peter: "Are you also hard of understanding? Know you not that every plant which my heavenly Father has not planted shall be rooted up? Turn now your attention to those who would know the truth. You cannot compel men to love the truth. Many of these teachers are blind guides. And you know that, if the blind lead the blind, both shall fall into the pit. But hearken while I tell you the truth concerning those things which morally defile and spiritually contaminate men. I declare it is not that which enters the body by the mouth or gains access to the mind through the eyes and ears, that defiles the man. Man is only defiled by that evil which may originate within the heart, and which finds expression in the words and deeds of such unholy persons. Do you not know it is from the heart that there come forth evil thoughts, wicked projects of murder, theft, and adulteries, together with jealousy, pride, anger, revenge, railings, and false witness? And it is just such things that defile men, and not that they eat bread with ceremonially unclean hands."

153:3.6 (1713.1) The Pharisaic commissioners of the Jerusalem Sanhedrin were now almost convinced that Jesus must be apprehended on a charge of blasphemy or on one of flouting the sacred law of the Jews; wherefore their efforts to involve him in the discussion of, and possible attack upon, some of the traditions of the elders, or so-called oral laws of the nation. No matter how scarce water might be, these traditionally enslaved Jews would never fail to go through with the required ceremonial washing of the hands before every meal. It was their belief that "it is better to die than to transgress the commandments of the elders." The spies asked this question because it had been reported that Jesus had said, "Salvation is a matter of clean hearts rather than of clean hands." But such beliefs, when they once become a part of one's religion, are hard to get away from. Even many years after this day the Apostle Peter was still held in the bondage of fear to many of these traditions about things clean and unclean, only being finally delivered by experiencing an extraordinary and vivid dream. All of this can the better be understood when it is recalled that these Jews looked upon eating with unwashed hands in the same light as commerce with a harlot, and both were equally punishable by excommunication.

153:3.7 (1713.2) Thus did the Master elect to discuss and expose the folly of the whole rabbinic system of rules and regulations which was represented by the oral law—the traditions of the elders, all of which were regarded as more sacred and more binding upon the Jews than even the teachings of the Scriptures. And Jesus spoke out with less reserve because he knew the hour had come when he could do nothing more to prevent an open rupture of relations with these religious leaders.

Last Words in the Synagogue

153:4.1 (1713.3) In the midst of the discussions of this after meeting, one of the Pharisees from Jerusalem brought to Jesus a distraught youth who was possessed of an unruly and rebellious spirit. Leading this demented lad up to Jesus, he said: "What can you do for such affliction as this? Can you cast out devils?" And when the Master looked upon the youth, he was moved with compassion and, beckoning for the lad to come to him, took him by the hand and said: "You know who I am; come out of him; and I charge one of your loyal fellows to see that you do not return." And immediately the lad was normal and in his right mind. And this is the first case where Jesus really cast an "evil spirit" out of a human being. All of the previous cases were only supposed possession of the devil; but this was a genuine case of demoniac possession, even such as sometimes occurred in those days and right up to the day of Pentecost, when the Master's spirit was poured out upon all flesh, making it forever impossible for these few celestial rebels to take such advantage of certain unstable types of human beings.

153:4.2 (1714.1) When the people marveled, one of the Pharisees stood up and charged that Jesus could do these things because he was in league with devils; that he admitted in the language which he employed in casting out this devil that they were known to each other; and he went on to state that the religious teachers and leaders at Jerusalem had decided that Jesus did all his so-called miracles by the power of Beelzebub, the prince of devils. Said the Pharisee: "Have nothing to do with this man; he is in partnership with Satan."

153:4.3 (1714.2) Then said Jesus: "How can Satan cast out Satan? A kingdom divided against itself cannot stand; if a house be divided against itself, it is soon brought to desolation. Can a city withstand a siege if it is not united? If Satan casts out Satan, he is divided against himself; how then shall his kingdom stand? But you should know that no one can enter into the house of a strong man and despoil his goods except he first overpower and bind that strong man. And so, if I by the power of Beelzebub cast out devils, by whom do your sons cast them out? Therefore shall they be your judges. But if I, by the spirit of God, cast out devils, then has the kingdom of God truly come upon you. If you were not blinded by prejudice and misled by fear and pride, you would easily perceive that one who is greater than devils stands in your midst. You compel me to declare that he who is not with me is against me, while he who gathers not with me scatters abroad. Let me utter a solemn warning to you who would presume, with your eyes open and with premeditated malice, knowingly to ascribe the works of God to the doings of devils! Verily, verily, I say to you, all your sins shall be forgiven, even all of your blasphemies, but whosoever shall blaspheme against God with deliberation and wicked intention shall never obtain forgiveness. Since such persistent workers of iniquity will never seek nor receive forgiveness, they are guilty of the sin of eternally rejecting divine forgiveness.

153:4.4 (1714.3) "Many of you have this day come to the parting of the ways; you have come to a beginning of the making of the inevitable choice between the will of the Father and the self-chosen ways of darkness. And as you now choose, so shall you eventually be. You must either make the tree good and its fruit good, or else will the tree become corrupt and its fruit corrupt. I declare that in my Father's eternal kingdom the tree is known by its fruits. But some of you who are as vipers, how can you, having already chosen evil, bring forth good fruits? After all, out of the abundance of the evil in your hearts your mouths speak."

153:4.5 (1714.4) Then stood up another Pharisee, who said: "Teacher, we would have you give us a predetermined sign which we will agree upon as establishing your authority and right to teach. Will you agree to such an arrangement?" And when Jesus heard this, he said: "This faithless and sign-seeking generation seeks a token, but no sign shall be given you other than that which you already have, and that which you shall see when the Son of Man departs from among you."

153:4.6 (1714.5) And when he had finished speaking, his apostles surrounded him and led him from the synagogue. In silence they journeyed home with him to Bethsaida. They were all amazed and somewhat terror-stricken by the sudden change in the Master's teaching tactics. They were wholly unaccustomed to seeing him perform in such a militant manner.

The Saturday Evening

153:5.1 (1715.1) Time and again had Jesus dashed to pieces the hopes of his apostles, repeatedly had he crushed their fondest expectations, but no time of disappointment or season of sorrow had ever equaled that which now overtook them. And, too, there was now admixed with their depression a real fear for their safety. They were all surprisingly startled by the suddenness and completeness of the desertion of the populace. They were also somewhat frightened and disconcerted by the unexpected boldness and assertive determination exhibited by the Pharisees who had come down from Jerusalem. But most of all they were bewildered by Jesus' sudden change of tactics. Under ordinary circumstances they would have welcomed the appearance of this more militant attitude, but coming as it did, along with so much that was unexpected, it startled them.

153:5.2 (1715.2) And now, on top of all of these worries, when they reached home, Jesus refused to eat. For hours he isolated himself in one of the upper rooms. It was almost midnight when Joab, the leader of the evangelists, returned and reported that about one third of his associates had deserted the cause. All through the evening loyal disciples had come and gone, reporting that the revulsion of feeling toward the Master was general in Capernaum. The leaders from Jerusalem were not slow to feed this feeling of disaffection and in every way possible to seek to promote the movement away from Jesus and his teachings. During these trying hours the twelve women were in session over at Peter's house.

They were tremendously upset, but none of them deserted.

153:5.3 (1715.3) It was a little after midnight when Jesus came down from the upper chamber and stood among the twelve and their associates, numbering about thirty in all. He said: "I recognize that this sifting of the kingdom distresses you, but it is unavoidable. Still, after all the training you have had, was there any good reason why you should stumble at my words? Why is it that you are filled with fear and consternation when you see the kingdom being divested of these lukewarm multitudes and these halfhearted disciples? Why do you grieve when the new day is dawning for the shining forth in new glory of the spiritual teachings of the kingdom of heaven? If you find it difficult to endure this test, what, then, will you do when the Son of Man must return to the Father? When and how will you prepare yourselves for the time when I ascend to the place whence I came to this world?

153:5.4 (1715.4) "My beloved, you must remember that it is the spirit that quickens; the flesh and all that pertains thereto is of little profit. The words which I have spoken to you are spirit and life. Be of good cheer! I have not deserted you.

Many shall be offended by the plain speaking of these days. Already you have heard that many of my disciples have turned back; they walk no more with me.

From the beginning I knew that these half-hearted believers would fall out by the way. Did I not choose you twelve men and set you apart as ambassadors of the kingdom? And now at such a time as this would you also desert? Let each of you look to his own faith, for one of you stands in grave danger." And when Jesus had finished speaking, Simon Peter said: "Yes, Lord, we are sad and perplexed, but we will never forsake you.

You have taught us the words of eternal life. We have believed in you and followed with you all this time. We will not turn back, for we know that you are sent by God." And as Peter ceased speaking, they all with one accord nodded their approval of his pledge of loyalty.

153:5.5 (1716.1) Then said Jesus: "Go to your rest, for busy times are upon us; active days are just ahead."

Paper 154

Last Days at Capernaum

154:0.1 (1717.1) ON THE eventful Saturday night of April 30, as Jesus was speaking words of comfort and courage to his downcast and bewildered disciples, at Tiberias a council was being held between Herod Antipas and a group of special commissioners representing the Jerusalem Sanhedrin. These scribes and Pharisees urged Herod to arrest Jesus; they did their best to convince him that Jesus was stirring up the populace to dissension and even to rebellion. But Herod refused to take action against him as a political offender. Herod's advisers had correctly reported the episode across the lake when the people sought to proclaim Jesus king and how he rejected the proposal.

154:0.2 (1717.2) One of Herod's official family, Chuza, whose wife belonged to the women's ministering corps, had informed him that Jesus did not propose to meddle with the affairs of earthly rule;

that he was only concerned with the establishment of the spiritual brotherhood of his believers, which brotherhood he called the kingdom of heaven. Herod had confidence in Chuza's reports, so much so that he refused to interfere with Jesus' activities. Herod was also influenced at this time, in his attitude toward Jesus, by his superstitious fear of John the Baptist. Herod was one of those apostate Jews who, while he believed nothing, feared everything. He had a bad conscience for having put John to death, and he did not want to become entangled in these intrigues against Jesus. He knew of many cases of sickness which had been apparently healed by Jesus, and he regarded him as either a prophet or a relatively harmless religious fanatic.

154:0.3 (1717.3) When the Jews threatened to report to Caesar that he was shielding a traitorous subject, Herod ordered them out of his council chamber. Thus matters rested for one week, during which time Jesus prepared his followers for the impending dispersion.

A Week of Counsel

154:1.1 (1717.4) From May 1 to May 7 Jesus held intimate counsel with his followers at the Zebedee house. Only the tried and trusted disciples were admitted to these conferences. At this time there were only about one hundred disciples who had the moral courage to brave the opposition of the Pharisees and openly declare their adherence to Jesus. With this group he held sessions morning, afternoon, and evening. Small companies of inquirers assembled each afternoon by the seaside, where some of the evangelists or apostles discoursed to them. These groups seldom numbered more than fifty.

154:1.2 (1717.5) On Friday of this week official action was taken by the rulers of the Capernaum synagogue closing the house of God to Jesus and all his followers. This action was taken at the instigation of the Jerusalem Pharisees. Jairus resigned as chief ruler and openly aligned himself with Jesus.

154:1.3 (1718.1) The last of the seaside meetings was held on Sabbath afternoon, May 7. Jesus talked to less than one hundred and fifty who had assembled at that time. This Saturday night marked the time of the lowest ebb in the tide of popular regard for Jesus and his teachings. From then on there was a steady, slow, but more healthful and dependable growth in favorable sentiment; a new following was built up which was better grounded in spiritual faith and true religious experience. The more or less composite and compromising transition stage between the materialistic concepts of the kingdom held by the Master's followers and those more idealistic and spiritual concepts taught by Jesus, had now definitely ended. From now on there was a more open proclamation of the gospel of the kingdom in its larger scope and in its far-flung spiritual implications.

A Week of Rest

154:2.1 (1718.2) Sunday, May 8, A.D. 29, at Jerusalem, the Sanhedrin passed a decree closing all the synagogues of Palestine to Jesus and his followers. This was a new and unprecedented usurpation of authority by the Jerusalem Sanhedrin. Theretofore each synagogue had existed and functioned as an independent congregation of worshipers and was under the rule and direction of its own board of governors. Only the synagogues of Jerusalem had been subject to the authority of the Sanhedrin. This summary action of the Sanhedrin was followed by the resignation of five of its members. One hundred messengers were immediately dispatched to convey and enforce this decree. Within the short space of two weeks every synagogue in Palestine had bowed to this manifesto of the Sanhedrin except the synagogue at Hebron. The rulers of the Hebron synagogue refused to acknowledge the right of the Sanhedrin to exercise such jurisdiction over their assembly. This refusal to accede to the Jerusalem decree was based on their contention of congregational autonomy rather than on sympathy with Jesus' cause. Shortly thereafter the Hebron synagogue was destroyed by fire.

154:2.2 (1718.3) This same Sunday morning, Jesus declared a week's holiday, urging all of his disciples to return to their homes or friends to rest their troubled souls and speak words of encouragement to their loved ones. He said: "Go to your several places to play or fish while you pray for the extension of the kingdom."

154:2.3 (1718.4) This week of rest enabled Jesus to visit many families and groups about the seaside. He also went fishing with David Zebedee on several occasions, and while he went about alone much of the time, there always lurked near by two or three of David's most trusted messengers, who had no uncertain orders from their chief respecting the safeguarding of Jesus. There was no public teaching of any sort during this week of rest.

154:2.4 (1718.5) This was the week that Nathaniel and James Zebedee suffered from more than a slight illness. For three days and nights they were acutely afflicted with a painful digestive disturbance. On the third night Jesus sent Salome, James's mother, to her rest, while he ministered to his suffering apostles. Of course Jesus could have instantly healed these two men, but that is not the method of either the Son or the Father in dealing with these commonplace difficulties and afflictions of the children of men on the evolutionary worlds of time and space. Never once, throughout all of his eventful life in the flesh, did Jesus engage in any sort of supernatural ministration to any member of his earth family or in behalf of any one of his immediate followers.

154:2.5 (1719.1) Universe difficulties must be met and planetary obstacles must be encountered as a part of the experience training provided for the growth and development, the progressive perfection, of the evolving souls of mortal creatures. The spiritualization of the human soul requires intimate experience with the educational solving of a wide range of real universe problems. The animal nature and the lower forms of will creatures do not progress favorably in environmental ease. Problematic situations, coupled with exertion stimuli, conspire to produce those activities of mind, soul, and spirit which contribute mightily to the achievement of worthy goals of mortal progression and to the attainment of higher levels of spirit destiny.

The Second Tiberias Conference

154:3.1 (1719.2) On May 16 the second conference at Tiberias between the authorities at Jerusalem and Herod Antipas was convened. Both the religious and the political leaders from Jerusalem were in attendance. The Jewish leaders were able to report to Herod that practically all the synagogues in both Galilee and Judea were closed to Jesus' teachings. A new effort was made to have Herod place Jesus under arrest, but he refused to do their bidding. On May 18, however, Herod did agree to the plan of permitting the Sanhedrin authorities to seize Jesus and carry him to Jerusalem to be tried on religious charges, provided the Roman ruler of Judea concurred in such an arrangement. Meanwhile, Jesus' enemies were industriously spreading the rumor throughout Galilee that Herod had become hostile to Jesus, and that he meant to exterminate all who believed in his teachings.

154:3.2 (1719.3) On Saturday night, May 21, word reached Tiberias that the civil authorities at Jerusalem had no objection to the agreement between Herod and the Pharisees that Jesus be seized and carried to Jerusalem for trial before the Sanhedrin on charges of flouting the sacred laws of the Jewish nation. Accordingly, just before midnight of this day, Herod signed the decree which authorized the officers of the Sanhedrin to seize Jesus within Herod's domains and forcibly to carry him to Jerusalem for trial. Strong pressure from many sides was brought to bear upon Herod before he consented to grant this permission, and he well knew that Jesus could not expect a fair trial before his bitter enemies at Jerusalem.

Saturday Night in Capernaum

154:4.1 (1719.4) On this same Saturday night, in Capernaum a group of fifty leading citizens met at the synagogue to discuss the momentous question: "What shall we do with Jesus?" They talked and debated until after midnight, but they could not find any common ground for agreement. Aside from a few persons who inclined to the belief that Jesus might be the Messiah, at least a holy man, or perhaps a prophet, the meeting was divided into four nearly equal groups who held, respectively, the following views of Jesus:

154:4.2 (1719.5) 1. That he was a deluded and harmless religious fanatic.

154:4.3 (1719.6) 2. That he was a dangerous and designing agitator who might stir up rebellion. 154:4.4 (1720.1) 3. That he was in league with devils, that he might even be a prince of devils. 154:4.5 (1720.2) 4. That he was beside himself, that he was mad, mentally unbalanced.

154:4.6 (1720.3) There was much talk about Jesus' preaching doctrines which were upsetting for the common people; his enemies maintained that his teachings were impractical, that everything would go to pieces if everybody made an honest effort to live in accordance with his ideas. And the men of many subsequent generations have said the same things.

Many intelligent and well-meaning men, even in the more enlightened age of these revelations, maintain that modern civilization could not have been built upon the teachings of Jesus—and they are partially right. But all such doubters forget that a much better civilization could have been built upon his teachings, and sometime will be. This world has never seriously tried to carry out the teachings of Jesus on a large scale, notwithstanding that halfhearted attempts have often been made to follow the doctrines of so-called Christianity.

The Eventful Sunday Morning

154:5.1 (1720.4) May 22 was an eventful day in the life of Jesus. On this Sunday morning, before daybreak, one of David's messengers arrived in great haste from Tiberias, bringing the word that Herod had authorized, or was about to authorize, the arrest of Jesus by the officers of the Sanhedrin. The receipt of the news of this impending danger caused David Zebedee to arouse his messengers and send them out to all the local groups of disciples, summoning them for an emergency council at seven o'clock that morning. When the sister-in-law of Jude (Jesus' brother) heard this alarming report, she hastened word to all of Jesus' family who dwelt near by, summoning them forthwith to assemble at Zebedee's house. And in response to this hasty call, presently there were assembled Mary, James, Joseph, Jude, and Ruth.

154:5.2 (1720.5) At this early morning meeting Jesus imparted his farewell instructions to the assembled disciples; that is, he bade them farewell for the time being, knowing well that they would soon be dispersed from Capernaum. He directed them all to seek God for guidance and to carry on the work of the kingdom regardless of consequences. The evangelists were to labor as they saw fit until such time as they might be called. He selected twelve of the evangelists to accompany him; the twelve apostles he directed to remain with him no matter what happened. The twelve women he instructed to remain at the Zebedee house and at Peter's house until he should send for them.

154:5.3 (1720.6) Jesus consented to David Zebedee's continuing his countrywide messenger service, and in bidding the Master farewell presently, David said: "Go forth to your work, Master. Don't let the bigots catch you, and never doubt that the messengers will follow after you. My men will never lose contact with you, and through them you shall know of the kingdom in other parts, and by them we will all know about you. Nothing that might happen to me will interfere with this service, for I have appointed first and second leaders, even a third. I am neither a teacher nor a preacher, but it is in my heart to do this, and none can stop me."

154:5.4 (1720.7) About 7:30 this morning Jesus began his parting address to almost one hundred believers who had crowded indoors to hear him. This was a solemn occasion for all present, but Jesus seemed unusually cheerful; he was once more like his normal self. The seriousness of weeks had gone, and he inspired all of them with his words of faith, hope, and courage.

Jesus' Family Arrives

154:6.1 (1721.1) It was about eight o'clock on this Sunday morning when five members of Jesus' earth family arrived on the scene in response to the urgent summons of Jude's sister-in-law. Of all his family in the flesh, only one, Ruth, believed wholeheartedly and continuously in the divinity of his mission on earth. Jude and James, and even Joseph, still retained much of their faith in Jesus, but they had permitted pride to interfere with their better judgment and real spiritual inclinations. Mary was likewise torn between love and fear, between mother love and family pride. Though she was harassed by doubts, she could never quite forget the visit of Gabriel ere Jesus was born. The Pharisees had been laboring to persuade Mary that Jesus was beside himself, demented. They urged her to go with her sons and seek to dissuade him from further efforts at public teaching. They assured Mary that soon Jesus' health would break, and that only dishonor and disgrace could come upon the entire family as a result of allowing him to go on. And so, when the word came from Jude's sister-in-law, all five of them started at once for Zebedee's house, having been together at Mary's home, where they had met with the Pharisees the evening before. They had talked with the Jerusalem leaders long into the night, and all were more or less convinced that Jesus was acting strangely, that he had acted strangely for some time. While Ruth could not explain all of his conduct, she insisted that he had always treated his family fairly and refused to agree to the program of trying to dissuade him from further work.

154:6.2 (1721.2) On the way to Zebedee's house they talked these things over and agreed among themselves to try to persuade Jesus to come home with them, for, said Mary: "I know I could influence my son if he would only come home and listen to me." James and Jude had heard rumors concerning the plans to arrest Jesus and take him to Jerusalem for trial. They also feared for their own safety. As long as Jesus was a popular figure in the public eye, his family allowed matters to drift along, but now that the people of Capernaum and the leaders at Jerusalem had suddenly turned against him, they began keenly to feel the pressure of the supposed disgrace of their embarrassing position.

154:6.3 (1721.3) They had expected to meet Jesus, take him aside, and urge him to go home with them. They had thought to assure him that they would forget his neglect of them—they would forgive and forget—if he would only give up the foolishness of trying to preach a new religion which could bring only trouble to himself and dishonor upon his family. To all of this Ruth would say only: "I will tell my brother that I think he is a man of God, and that I hope he would be willing to die before he would allow these wicked Pharisees to stop his preaching." Joseph promised to keep Ruth quiet while the others labored with Jesus.

154:6.4 (1721.4) When they reached the Zebedee house, Jesus was in the very midst of delivering his parting address to the disciples. They sought to gain entrance to the house, but it was crowded to overflowing. Finally they established themselves on the back porch and had word passed in to Jesus, from person to person, so that it finally was whispered to him by Simon Peter, who interrupted his talking for the purpose, and who said: "Behold, your mother and your brothers are outside, and they are very anxious to speak with you." Now it did not occur to his mother how important was the giving of this parting message to his followers, neither did she know that his address was likely to be terminated any moment by the arrival of his apprehenders. She really thought, after so long an apparent estrangement, in view of the fact that she and his brothers had shown the grace actually to come to him, that Jesus would cease speaking and come to them the moment he received word they were waiting.

154:6.5 (1722.1) It was just another of those instances in which his earth family could not comprehend that he must be about his Father's business. And so Mary and his brothers were deeply hurt when, notwithstanding that he paused in his speaking to receive the message, instead of his rushing out to greet them, they heard his musical voice speak with increased volume: "Say to my mother and my brothers that they should have no fear for me. The Father who sent me into the world will not forsake me; neither shall any harm come upon my family. Bid them be of good courage and put their trust in the Father of the kingdom. But, after all, who is my mother and who are my brothers?" And stretching forth his hands toward all of his disciples assembled in the room, he said: "I have no mother; I have no brothers. Behold my mother and behold my brethren! For whosoever does the will of my Father who is in heaven, the same is my mother, my brother, and my sister."

154:6.6 (1722.2) And when Mary heard these words, she collapsed in Jude's arms. They carried her out in the garden to revive her while Jesus spoke the concluding words of his parting message. He would then have gone out to confer with his mother and his brothers, but a messenger arrived in haste from Tiberias bringing word that the officers of the Sanhedrin were on their way with authority to arrest Jesus and carry him to Jerusalem. Andrew received this message and, interrupting Jesus, told it to him.

154:6.7 (1722.3) Andrew did not recall that David had posted some twenty-five sentinels about the Zebedee house, and that no one could take them by surprise; so he asked Jesus what should be done. The Master stood there in silence while his mother, having heard the words, "I have no mother," was recovering from the shock in the garden. It was at just this time that a woman in the room stood up and exclaimed, "Blessed is the womb that bore you and blessed are the breasts that nursed you." Jesus turned aside a moment from his conversation with Andrew to answer this woman by saying, "No, rather is the one blessed who hears the word of God and dares to obey it."

154:6.8 (1722.4) Mary and Jesus' brothers thought that Jesus did not understand them, that he had lost interest in them, little realizing that it was they who failed to understand Jesus. Jesus fully understood how difficult it is for men to break with their past. He knew how human beings are swayed by the preacher's eloquence, and how the conscience responds to emotional appeal as the mind does to logic and reason, but he also knew how far more difficult it is to persuade men to disown the past.

154:6.9 (1722.5) It is forever true that all who may think they are misunderstood or not appreciated have in Jesus a sympathizing friend and an understanding counselor. He had warned his apostles that a man's foes may be they of his own household, but he had hardly realized how near this prediction would come to apply to his own experience. Jesus did not forsake his earth family to do his Father's work— they forsook him. Later on, after the Master's death and resurrection, when James became connected with the early Christian movement, he suffered immeasurably as a result of his failure to enjoy this earlier association with Jesus and his disciples.

154:6.10 (1723.1) In passing through these events, Jesus chose to be guided by the limited knowledge of his human mind. He desired to undergo the experience with his associates as a mere man. And it was in the human mind of Jesus to see his family before he left. He did not wish to stop in the midst of his discourse and thus render their first meeting after so long a separation such a public affair. He had intended to finish his address and then have a visit with them before leaving, but this plan was thwarted by the conspiracy of events which immediately followed.

154:6.11 (1723.2) The haste of their flight was augmented by the arrival of a party of David's messengers at the rear entrance of the Zebedee home. The commotion produced by these men frightened the apostles into thinking that these new arrivals might be their apprehenders, and in fear of immediate arrest, they hastened through the front entrance to the waiting boat. And all of this explains why Jesus did not see his family waiting on the back porch.

154:6.12 (1723.3) But he did say to David Zebedee as he entered the boat in hasty flight: "Tell my mother and my brothers that I appreciate their coming, and that I intended to see them. Admonish them to find no offense in me but rather to seek for a knowledge of the will of God and for grace and courage to do that will."

The Hasty Flight

154:7.1 (1723.4) And so it was on this Sunday morning, the twenty-second of May, in the year A.D. 29, that Jesus, with his twelve apostles and the twelve evangelists, engaged in this hasty flight from the Sanhedrin officers who were on their way to Bethsaida with authority from Herod Antipas to arrest him and take him to Jerusalem for trial on charges of blasphemy and other violations of the sacred laws of the Jews. It was almost half past eight this beautiful morning when this company of twenty-five manned the oars and pulled for the eastern shore of the Sea of Galilee.

154:7.2 (1723.5) Following the Master's boat was another and smaller craft, containing six of David's messengers, who had instructions to maintain contact with Jesus and his associates and to see that information of their whereabouts and safety was regularly transmitted to the home of Zebedee in Bethsaida, which had served as headquarters for the work of the kingdom for some time. But Jesus was never again to make his home at the house of Zebedee. From now on, throughout the remainder of his earth life, the Master truly "had not where to lay his head." No more did he have even the semblance of a settled abode.

154:7.3 (1723.6) They rowed over to near the village of Kheresa, put their boat in the custody of friends, and began the wanderings of this eventful last year of the Master's life on earth. For a time they remained in the domains of Philip, going from Kheresa up to Caesarea-Philippi, thence making their way over to the coast of Phoenicia. *

154:7.4 (1723.7) The crowd lingered about the home of Zebedee watching these two boats make their way over the lake toward the eastern shore, and they were well started when the Jerusalem officers hurried up and began their search for Jesus. They refused to believe he had escaped them, and while Jesus and his party were journeying northward through Batanea, the Pharisees and their assistants spent almost a full week vainly searching for him in the neighborhood of Capernaum.

154:7.5 (1724.1) Jesus' family returned to their home in Capernaum and spent almost a week in talking, debating, and praying. They were filled with confusion and consternation. They enjoyed no peace of mind until Thursday afternoon, when Ruth returned from a visit to the Zebedee house, where she learned from David that her father-brother was safe and in good health and making his way toward the Phoenician coast.

Paper 155

Fleeing Through Northern Galilee

155:0.1 (1725.1) SOON after landing near Kheresa on this eventful Sunday, Jesus and the twenty-four went a little way to the north, where they spent the night in a beautiful park south of Bethsaida-Julias. They were familiar with this camping place, having stopped there in days gone by. Before retiring for the night, the Master called his followers around him and discussed with them the plans for their projected tour through Batanea and northern Galilee to the Phoenician coast.

Why Do the Heathen Rage?

155:1.1 (1725.2) Said Jesus: "You should all recall how the Psalmist spoke of these times, saying, 'Why do the heathen rage and the peoples plot in vain? The kings of the earth set themselves, and the rulers of the people take counsel together, against the Lord and against his anointed, saying, Let us break the bonds of mercy asunder and let us cast away the cords of love.'

155:1.2 (1725.3) "Today you see this fulfilled before your eyes. But you shall not see the remainder of the Psalmist's prophecy fulfilled, for he entertained erroneous ideas about the Son of Man and his mission on earth. My kingdom is founded on love, proclaimed in mercy, and established by unselfish service. My Father does not sit in heaven laughing in derision at the heathen. He is not wrathful in his great displeasure. True is the promise that the Son shall have these so-called heathen (in reality his ignorant and untaught brethren) for an inheritance. And I will receive these gentiles with open arms of mercy and affection. All this loving-kindness shall be shown the so-called heathen, notwithstanding the unfortunate declaration of the record which intimates that the triumphant Son 'shall break them with a rod of iron and dash them to pieces like a potter's vessel.' The Psalmist exhorted you to 'serve the Lord with fear'—I bid you enter into the exalted privileges of divine sonship by faith; he commands you to rejoice with trembling; I bid you rejoice with assurance. He says, 'Kiss the Son, lest he be angry, and you perish when his wrath is kindled.' But you who have lived with me well know that anger and wrath are not a part of the establishment of the kingdom of heaven in the hearts of men. But the Psalmist did glimpse the true light when, in finishing this exhortation, he said: 'Blessed are they who put their trust in this Son.'"

155:1.3 (1725.4) Jesus continued to teach the twenty-four, saying: "The heathen are not without excuse when they rage at us. Because their outlook is small and narrow, they are able to concentrate their energies enthusiastically. Their goal is near and more or less visible; wherefore do they strive with valiant and effective execution. You who have professed entrance into the kingdom of heaven are altogether too vacillating and indefinite in your teaching conduct. The heathen strike directly for their objectives; you are guilty of too much chronic yearning. If you desire to enter the kingdom, why do you not take it by spiritual assault even as the heathen take a city they lay siege to? You are hardly worthy of the kingdom when your service consists so largely in an attitude of regretting the past, whining over the present, and vainly hoping for the future. Why do the heathen rage? Because they know not the truth. Why do you languish in futile yearning? Because you obey not the truth. Cease your useless yearning and go forth bravely doing that which concerns the establishment of the kingdom.

155:1.4 (1726.1) "In all that you do, become not one-sided and overspecialized. The Pharisees who seek our destruction verily think they are doing God's service. They have become so narrowed by tradition that they are blinded by prejudice and hardened by fear. Consider the Greeks, who have a science without religion, while the Jews have a religion without science. And when men become thus misled into accepting a narrow and confused disintegration of truth, their only hope of salvation is to become truth-co-ordinated—converted."

155:1.5 (1726.2) "Let me emphatically state this eternal truth: If you, by truth co-ordination, learn to exemplify in your lives this beautiful wholeness of righteousness, your fellow men will then seek after you that they may gain what you have so acquired. The measure wherewith truth seekers are drawn to you represents the measure of your truth endowment, your righteousness. The extent to which you have to go with your message to the people is, in a way, the measure of your failure to live the whole or righteous life, the truth-co-ordinated life."

155:1.6 (1726.3) And many other things the Master taught his apostles and the evangelists before they bade him good night and sought rest upon their pillows.

The Evangelists in Chorazin

155:2.1 (1726.4) On Monday morning, May 23, Jesus directed Peter to go over to Chorazin with the twelve evangelists while he, with the eleven, departed for Caesarea-Philippi, going by way of the Jordan to the Damascus-Capernaum road, thence northeast to the junction with the road to Caesarea-Philippi, and then on into that city, where they tarried and taught for two weeks. They arrived during the afternoon of Tuesday, May 24.

155:2.2 (1726.5) Peter and the evangelists sojourned in Chorazin for two weeks, preaching the gospel of the kingdom to a small but earnest company of believers. But they were not able to win many new converts. No city of all Galilee yielded so few souls for the kingdom as Chorazin. In accordance with Peter's instructions the twelve evangelists had less to say about healing—things physical—while they preached and taught with increased vigor the spiritual truths of the heavenly kingdom. These two weeks at Chorazin constituted a veritable baptism of adversity for the twelve evangelists in that it was the most difficult and unproductive period in their careers up to this time. Being thus deprived of the satisfaction of winning souls for the kingdom, each of them the more earnestly and honestly took stock of his own soul and its progress in the spiritual paths of the new life.

155:2.3 (1726.6) When it appeared that no more people were minded to seek entrance into the kingdom, Peter, on Tuesday, June 7, called his associates together and departed for Caesarea-Philippi to join Jesus and the apostles. They arrived about noontime on Wednesday and spent the entire evening in rehearsing their experiences among the unbelievers of Chorazin. During the discussions of this evening Jesus made further reference to the parable of the sower and taught them much about the meaning of the apparent failure of life undertakings.

At Caesarea-Philippi

155:3.1 (1727.1) Although Jesus did no public work during this two weeks' sojourn near Caesarea-Philippi, the apostles held numerous quiet evening meetings in the city, and many of the believers came out to the camp to talk with the Master. Very few were added to the group of believers as a result of this visit. Jesus talked with the apostles each day, and they more clearly discerned that a new phase of the work of preaching the kingdom of heaven was now beginning. They were commencing to comprehend that the "kingdom of heaven is not meat and drink but the realization of the spiritual joy of the acceptance of divine sonship."

155:3.2 (1727.2) The sojourn at Caesarea-Philippi was a real test to the eleven apostles; it was a difficult two weeks for them to live through. They were well-nigh

depressed, and they missed the periodic stimulation of Peter's enthusiastic personality. In these times it was truly a great and testing adventure to believe in Jesus and go forth to follow after him. Though they made few converts during these two weeks, they did learn much that was highly profitable from their daily conferences with the Master.

155:3.3 (1727.3) The apostles learned that the Jews were spiritually stagnant and dying because they had crystallized truth into a creed; that when truth becomes formulated as a boundary line of self-righteous exclusiveness instead of serving as signposts of spiritual guidance and progress, such teachings lose their creative and life-giving power and ultimately become merely preservative and fossilizing.

155:3.4 (1727.4) Increasingly they learned from Jesus to look upon human personalities in terms of their possibilities in time and in eternity. They learned that many souls can best be led to love the unseen God by being first taught to love their brethren whom they can see. And it was in this connection that new meaning became attached to the Master's pronouncement concerning unselfish service for one's fellows: "Inasmuch as you did it to one of the least of my brethren, you did it to me."

155:3.5 (1727.5) One of the great lessons of this sojourn at Caesarea had to do with the origin of religious traditions, with the grave danger of allowing a sense of sacredness to become attached to nonsacred things, common ideas, or everyday events. From one conference they emerged with the teaching that true religion was man's heartfelt loyalty to his highest and truest convictions.

155:3.6 (1727.6) Jesus warned his believers that, if their religious longings were only material, increasing knowledge of nature would, by progressive displacement of the supposed supernatural origin of things, ultimately deprive them of their faith in God. But that, if their religion were spiritual, never could the progress of physical science disturb their faith in eternal realities and divine values.

155:3.7 (1727.7) They learned that, when religion is wholly spiritual in motive, it makes all life more worth while, filling it with high purposes, dignifying it with transcendent values, inspiring it with superb motives, all the while comforting the human soul with a sublime and sustaining hope. True religion is designed to lessen the strain of existence; it releases faith and courage for daily living and unselfish serving. Faith promotes spiritual vitality and righteous fruitfulness.

155:3.8 (1727.8) Jesus repeatedly taught his apostles that no civilization could long survive the loss of the best in its religion. And he never grew weary of pointing out to the twelve the great danger of accepting religious symbols and ceremonies in the place of religious experience. His whole earth life was consistently devoted to the mission of thawing out the frozen forms of religion into the liquid liberties of enlightened sonship.

On the Way to Phoenicia

155:4.1 (1728.1) On Thursday morning, June 9, after receiving word regarding the progress of the kingdom brought by the messengers of David from Bethsaida, this group of twenty-five teachers of truth left Caesarea-Philippi to begin their journey to the Phoenician coast. They passed around the marsh country, by way of Luz, to the point of junction with the Magdala-Mount Lebanon trail road, thence to the crossing with the road leading to Sidon, arriving there Friday afternoon.

155:4.2 (1728.2) While pausing for lunch under the shadow of an overhanging ledge of rock, near Luz, Jesus delivered one of the most remarkable addresses which his apostles ever listened to throughout all their years of association with him. No sooner had they seated themselves to break bread than Simon Peter asked Jesus: "Master, since the Father in heaven knows all things, and since his spirit is our support in the establishment of the kingdom of heaven on earth, why is it that we flee from the threats of our enemies? Why do we refuse to confront the foes of truth?" But before Jesus had begun to answer Peter's question, Thomas broke in, asking: "Master, I should really like to know just what is wrong with the religion of our enemies at Jerusalem. What is the real difference between their religion and ours? Why is it we are at such diversity of belief when we all profess to serve the same God?" And when Thomas had finished, Jesus said: "While I would not ignore Peter's question, knowing full well how easy it would be to misunderstand my reasons for avoiding an open clash with the rulers of the Jews at just this time, still it will prove more helpful to all of you if I choose rather to answer Thomas's question. And that I will proceed to do when you have finished your lunch."

The Discourse on True Religion

155:5.1 (1728.3) This memorable discourse on religion, summarized and restated in modern phraseology, gave expression to the following truths:

155:5.2 (1728.4) While the religions of the world have a double origin—natural and revelatory—at any one time and among any one people there are to be found three distinct forms of religious devotion. And these three manifestations of the religious urge are:

155:5.3 (1728.5) 1. Primitive religion. The seminatural and instinctive urge to fear mysterious energies and worship superior forces, chiefly a religion of the physical nature, the religion of fear.

155:5.4 (1728.6) 2. The religion of civilization. The advancing religious concepts and practices of the civilizing races—the religion of the mind—the intellectual theology of the authority of established religious tradition.

155:5.5 (1728.7) 3. True religion—the religion of revelation. The revelation of supernatural values, a partial insight into eternal realities, a glimpse of the goodness and beauty of the infinite character of the Father in heaven—the religion of the spirit as demonstrated in human experience.

155:5.6 (1729.1) The religion of the physical senses and the superstitious fears of natural man, the Master refused to belittle, though he deplored the fact that so much of this primitive form of worship should persist in the religious forms of the more intelligent races of mankind. Jesus made it clear that the great difference between the religion of the mind and the religion of the spirit is that, while the former is upheld by ecclesiastical authority, the latter is wholly based on human experience.

155:5.7 (1729.2) And then the Master, in his hour of teaching, went on to make clear these truths:

155:5.8 (1729.3) Until the races become highly intelligent and more fully civilized, there will persist many of those childlike and superstitious ceremonies which are so characteristic of the evolutionary religious practices of primitive and backward peoples. Until the human race progresses to the level of a higher and more general recognition of the realities of spiritual experience, large numbers of men and women will continue to show a personal preference for those religions of authority which require only intellectual assent, in contrast to the religion of the spirit, which entails active participation of mind and soul in the faith adventure of grappling with the rigorous realities of progressive human experience.

155:5.9 (1729.4) The acceptance of the traditional religions of authority presents the easy way out for man's urge to seek satisfaction for the longings of his spiritual nature. The settled, crystallized, and established religions of authority afford a ready refuge to which the distracted and distraught soul of man may flee when harassed by fear and tormented by uncertainty. Such a religion requires of its devotees, as the price to be paid for its satisfactions and assurances, only a passive and purely intellectual assent.

155:5.10 (1729.5) And for a long time there will live on earth those timid, fearful, and hesitant individuals who will prefer thus to secure their religious consolations, even though, in so casting their lot with the religions of authority, they compromise the sovereignty of personality, debase the dignity of self-respect, and utterly surrender the right to participate in that most thrilling and inspiring of all possible human experiences: the personal quest for truth, the exhilaration of facing the perils of intellectual discovery, the determination to explore the realities of personal religious experience, the supreme satisfaction of experiencing the personal triumph of the actual realization of the victory of spiritual faith over intellectual doubt as it is honestly won in the supreme adventure of all human existence—man seeking God, for himself and as himself, and finding him.

155:5.11 (1729.6) The religion of the spirit means effort, struggle, conflict, faith, determination, love, loyalty, and progress. The religion of the mind—the theology of authority—requires little or none of these exertions from its formal believers. Tradition is a safe refuge and an easy path for those fearful and halfhearted souls who instinctively shun the spirit struggles and mental uncertainties associated with those faith voyages of daring adventure out upon the high seas of unexplored truth in search for the farther shores of spiritual realities as they may be discovered by the progressive human mind and experienced by the evolving human soul.

155:5.12 (1729.7) And Jesus went on to say: "At Jerusalem the religious leaders have formulated the various doctrines of their traditional teachers and the prophets of other days into an established system of intellectual beliefs, a religion of authority. The appeal of all such religions is largely to the mind. And now are we about to enter upon a deadly conflict with such a religion since we will so shortly begin the bold proclamation of a new religion—a religion which is not a religion in the present-day meaning of that word, a religion that makes its chief appeal to the divine spirit of my Father which resides in the mind of man; a religion which shall derive its authority from the fruits of its acceptance that will so certainly appear in the personal experience of all who really and truly become believers in the truths of this higher spiritual communion."

155:5.13 (1730.1) Pointing out each of the twenty-four and calling them by name, Jesus said: "And now, which one of you would prefer to take this easy path of conformity to an established and fossilized religion, as defended by the Pharisees at Jerusalem, rather than to suffer the difficulties and persecutions attendant upon the mission of proclaiming a better way of salvation to men while you realize the satisfaction of discovering for yourselves the beauties of the realities of a living and personal experience in the eternal truths and supreme grandeurs of the kingdom of heaven? Are you fearful, soft, and ease-seeking? Are you afraid to trust your future in the hands of the God of truth, whose sons you are? Are you distrustful of the Father, whose children you are? Will you go back to the easy path of the certainty and intellectual settledness of the religion of traditional authority, or will you gird yourselves to go forward with me into that uncertain and troublous future of proclaiming the new truths of the religion of the spirit, the kingdom of heaven in the hearts of men?"

155:5.14 (1730.2) All twenty-four of his hearers rose to their feet, intending to signify their united and loyal response to this, one of the few emotional appeals which Jesus ever made to them, but he raised his hand and stopped them, saying: "Go now apart by yourselves, each man alone with the Father, and there find the unemotional answer to my question, and having found such a true and sincere attitude of soul, speak that answer freely and boldly to my Father and your Father, whose infinite life of love is the very spirit of the religion we proclaim."

155:5.15 (1730.3) The evangelists and apostles went apart by themselves for a short time. Their spirits were uplifted, their minds were inspired, and their emotions mightily stirred by what Jesus had said. But when Andrew called them together, the Master said only: "Let us resume our journey. We go into Phoenicia to tarry for a season, and all of you should pray the Father to transform your emotions of mind and body into the higher loyalties of mind and the more satisfying experiences of the spirit."

155:5.16 (1730.4) As they journeyed on down the road, the twenty-four were silent, but presently they began to talk one with another, and by three o'clock that afternoon they could not go farther; they came to a halt, and Peter, going up to Jesus, said: "Master, you have spoken to us the words of life and truth. We would hear more; we beseech you to speak to us further concerning these matters."

The Second Discourse on Religion

155:6.1 (1730.5) And so, while they paused in the shade of the hillside, Jesus continued to teach them regarding the religion of the spirit, in substance saying:

155:6.2 (1730.6) You have come out from among those of your fellows who choose to remain satisfied with a religion of mind, who crave security and prefer conformity. You have elected to exchange your feelings of authoritative certainty for the assurances of the spirit of adventurous and progressive faith. You have dared to protest against the grueling bondage of institutional religion and to reject the authority of the traditions of record which are now regarded as the word of God. Our Father did indeed speak through Moses, Elijah, Isaiah, Amos, and Hosea, but he did not cease to minister words of truth to the world when these prophets of old made an end of their utterances. My Father is no respecter of races or generations in that the word of truth is vouchsafed one age and withheld from another. Commit not the folly of calling that divine which is wholly human, and fail not to discern the words of truth which come not through the traditional oracles of supposed inspiration.

155:6.3 (1731.1) I have called upon you to be born again, to be born of the spirit. I have called you out of the darkness of authority and the lethargy of tradition into the transcendent light of the realization of the possibility of making for yourselves the greatest discovery possible for the human soul to make—the supernal experience of finding God for yourself, in yourself, and of yourself, and of doing all this as a fact in your own personal experience. And so may you pass from death to life, from the authority of tradition to the experience of knowing God; thus will you pass from darkness to light, from a racial faith inherited to a personal faith achieved by actual experience; and thereby will you progress from a theology of mind handed down by your ancestors to a true religion of spirit which shall be built up in your souls as an eternal endowment.

155:6.4 (1731.2) Your religion shall change from the mere intellectual belief in traditional authority to the actual experience of that living faith which is able to grasp the reality of God and all that relates to the divine spirit of the Father. The religion of the mind ties you hopelessly to the past; the religion of the spirit consists in progressive revelation and ever beckons you on toward higher and holier achievements in spiritual ideals and eternal realities.

155:6.5 (1731.3) While the religion of authority may impart a present feeling of settled security, you pay for such a transient satisfaction the price of the loss of your spiritual freedom and religious liberty. My Father does not require of you as the price of entering the kingdom of heaven that you should force yourself to subscribe to a belief in things which are spiritually repugnant, unholy, and untruthful. It is not required of you that your own sense of mercy, justice, and truth should be outraged by submission to an outworn system of religious forms and ceremonies. The religion of the spirit leaves you forever free to follow the truth wherever the leadings of the spirit may take you. And who can judge— perhaps this spirit may have something to impart to this generation which other generations have refused to hear?

155:6.6 (1731.4) Shame on those false religious teachers who would drag hungry souls back into the dim and distant past and there leave them! And so are these unfortunate persons doomed to become frightened by every new discovery, while they are discomfited by every new revelation of truth. The prophet who said, "He will be kept in perfect peace whose mind is stayed on God," was not a mere intellectual believer in authoritative theology. This truth-knowing human had discovered God; he was not merely talking about God.

155:6.7 (1731.5) I admonish you to give up the practice of always quoting the prophets of old and praising the heroes of Israel, and instead aspire to become living prophets of the Most High and spiritual heroes of the coming kingdom. To honor the God-knowing leaders of the past may indeed be worth while, but why, in so doing, should you sacrifice the supreme experience of human existence: finding God for yourselves and knowing him in your own souls?

155:6.8 (1732.1) Every race of mankind has its own mental outlook upon human existence; therefore must the religion of the mind ever run true to these various racial viewpoints. Never can the religions of authority come to unification.

Human unity and mortal brotherhood can be achieved only by and through the super endowment of the religion of the spirit. Racial minds may differ, but all mankind is indwelt by the same divine and eternal spirit. The hope of human brotherhood can only be realized when, and as, the divergent mind religions of authority become impregnated with, and overshadowed by, the unifying and ennobling religion of the spirit—the religion of personal spiritual experience.

155:6.9 (1732.2) The religions of authority can only divide men and set them in conscientious array against each other; the religion of the spirit will progressively draw men together and cause them to become understandingly sympathetic with one another. The religions of authority require of men uniformity in belief, but this is impossible of realization in the present state of the world. The religion of the spirit requires only unity of experience—uniformity of destiny—making full allowance for diversity of belief. The religion of the spirit requires only uniformity of insight, not uniformity of viewpoint and outlook. The religion of the spirit does not demand uniformity of intellectual views, only unity of spirit feeling. The religions of authority crystallize into lifeless creeds; the religion of the spirit grows into the increasing joy and liberty of ennobling deeds of loving service and merciful ministration.

155:6.10 (1732.3) But watch, lest any of you look with disdain upon the children of Abraham because they have fallen on these evil days of traditional barrenness. Our forefathers gave themselves up to the persistent and passionate search for God, and they found him as no other whole race of men have ever known him since the times of Adam, who knew much of this as he was himself a Son of God. My Father has not failed to mark the long and untiring struggle of Israel, ever since the days of Moses, to find God and to know God. For weary generations the Jews have not ceased to toil, sweat, groan, travail, and endure the sufferings and experience the sorrows of a misunderstood and despised people, all in order that they might come a little nearer the discovery of the truth about God. And, notwithstanding all the failures and falterings of Israel, our fathers progressively, from Moses to the times of Amos and Hosea, did reveal increasingly to the whole world an ever clearer and more truthful picture of the eternal God. And so was the way prepared for the still greater revelation of the Father which you have been called to share.

155:6.11 (1732.4) Never forget there is only one adventure which is more satisfying and thrilling than the attempt to discover the will of the living God, and that is the supreme experience of honestly trying to do that divine will. And fail not to remember that the will of God can be done in any earthly occupation. Some callings are not holy and others secular. All things are sacred in the lives of those who are spirit led; that is, subordinated to truth, ennobled by love, dominated by mercy, and restrained by fairness—justice. The spirit which my Father and I shall send into the world is not only the Spirit of Truth but also the spirit of idealistic beauty.

155:6.12 (1732.5) You must cease to seek for the word of God only on the pages of the olden records of theologic authority. Those who are born of the spirit of God shall henceforth discern the word of God regardless of whence it appears to take origin. Divine truth must not be discounted because the channel of its bestowal is apparently human. Many of your brethren have minds which accept the theory of God while they spiritually fail to realize the presence of God. And that is just the reason why I have so often taught you that the kingdom of heaven can best be realized by acquiring the spiritual attitude of a sincere child. It is not the mental immaturity of the child that I commend to you but rather the spiritual simplicity of such an easy-believing and fully-trusting little one. It is not so important that you should know about the fact of God as that you should increasingly grow in the ability to feel the presence of God.

155:6.13 (1733.1) When you once begin to find God in your soul, presently you will begin to discover him in other men's souls and eventually in all the creatures and creations of a mighty universe. But what chance does the Father have to appear as a God of supreme loyalties and divine ideals in the souls of men who give little or no time to the thoughtful contemplation of such eternal realities? While the mind is not the seat of the spiritual nature, it is indeed the gateway thereto.

155:6.14 (1733.2) But do not make the mistake of trying to prove to other men that you have found God; you cannot consciously produce such valid proof, albeit there are two positive and powerful demonstrations of the fact that you are God-knowing, and they are:

155:6.15 (1733.3) 1. The fruits of the spirit of God showing forth in your daily routine life.

155:6.16 (1733.4) 2. The fact that your entire life plan furnishes positive proof that you have unreservedly risked everything you are and have on the adventure of survival after death in the pursuit of the hope of finding the God of eternity, whose presence you have foretasted in time.

155:6.17 (1733.5) Now, mistake not, my Father will ever respond to the faintest flicker of faith. He takes note of the physical and superstitious emotions of the primitive man. And with those honest but fearful souls whose faith is so weak that it amounts to little more than an intellectual conformity to a passive attitude of assent to religions of authority, the Father is ever alert to honor and foster even all such feeble attempts to reach out for him. But you who have been called out of darkness into the light are expected to believe with a whole heart; your faith shall dominate the combined attitudes of body, mind, and spirit.

155:6.18 (1733.6) You are my apostles, and to you religion shall not become a theologic shelter to which you may flee in fear of facing the rugged realities of spiritual progress and idealistic adventure; but rather shall your religion become the fact of real experience which testifies that God has found you, idealized, ennobled, and spiritualized you, and that you have enlisted in the eternal adventure of finding the God who has thus found and sonshipped you.

155:6.19 (1733.7) And when Jesus had finished speaking, he beckoned to Andrew and, pointing to the west toward Phoenicia, said: "Let us be on our way."

Paper 156

The Sojourn at Tyre and Sidon

156:0.1 (1734.1) ON FRIDAY afternoon, June 10, Jesus and his associates arrived in the environs of Sidon, where they stopped at the home of a well-to-do woman who had been a patient in the Bethsaida hospital during the times when Jesus was at the height of his popular favor. The evangelists and the apostles were lodged with her friends in the immediate neighborhood, and they rested over the Sabbath day amid these refreshing surroundings. They spent almost two and one-half weeks in Sidon and vicinity before they prepared to visit the coast cities to the north.

156:0.2 (1734.2) This June Sabbath day was one of great quiet. The evangelists and apostles were altogether absorbed in their meditations regarding the discourses of the Master on religion to which they had listened en route to Sidon. They were all able to appreciate something of what he had told them, but none of them fully grasped the import of his teaching.

The Syrian Woman

156:1.1 (1734.3) There lived near the home of Karuska, where the Master lodged, a Syrian woman who had heard much of Jesus as a great healer and teacher, and on this Sabbath afternoon she came over, bringing her little daughter. The child, about twelve years old, was afflicted with a grievous nervous disorder characterized by convulsions and other distressing manifestations.

156:1.2 (1734.4) Jesus had charged his associates to tell no one of his presence at the home of Karuska, explaining that he desired to have a rest. While they had obeyed their Master's instructions, the servant of Karuska had gone over to the house of this Syrian woman, Norana, to inform her that Jesus lodged at the home of her mistress and had urged this anxious mother to bring her afflicted daughter for healing. This mother, of course, believed that her child was possessed by a demon, an unclean spirit.

156:1.3 (1734.5) When Norana arrived with her daughter, the Alpheus twins explained through an interpreter that the Master was resting and could not be disturbed; whereupon Norana replied that she and the child would remain right there until the Master had finished his rest. Peter also endeavored to reason with her and to persuade her to go home. He explained that Jesus was weary with much teaching and healing, and that he had come to Phoenicia for a period of quiet and rest. But it was futile; Norana would not leave. To Peter's entreaties she replied only: "I will not depart until I have seen your Master. I know he can cast the demon out of my child, and I will not go until the healer has looked upon my daughter."

156:1.4 (1734.6) Then Thomas sought to send the woman away but met only with failure. To him she said: "I have faith that your Master can cast out this demon which torments my child. I have heard of his mighty works in Galilee, and I believe in him. What has happened to you, his disciples, that you would send away those who come seeking your Master's help?" And when she had thus spoken, Thomas withdrew.

156:1.5 (1735.1) Then came forward Simon Zelotes to remonstrate with Norana. Said Simon: "Woman, you are a Greek-speaking gentile. It is not right that you should expect the Master to take the bread intended for the children of the favored household and cast it to the dogs." But Norana refused to take offense at Simon's thrust. She replied only: "Yes, teacher, I understand your words. I am only a dog in the eyes of the Jews, but as concerns your Master, I am a believing dog. I am determined that he shall see my daughter, for I am persuaded that, if he shall but look upon her, he will heal her. And even you, my good man, would not dare to deprive the dogs of the privilege of obtaining the crumbs which chance to fall from the children's table."

156:1.6 (1735.2) At just this time the little girl was seized with a violent convulsion before them all, and the mother cried out: "There, you can see that my child is possessed by an evil spirit. If our need does not impress you, it would appeal to your Master, who I have been told loves all men and dares even to heal the gentiles when they believe. You are not worthy to be his disciples. I will not go until my child has been cured."

156:1.7 (1735.3) Jesus, who had heard all of this conversation through an open window, now came outside, much to their surprise, and said: "O woman, great is your faith, so great that I cannot withhold that which you desire; go your way in peace. Your daughter already has been made whole." And the little girl was well from that hour. As Norana and the child took leave, Jesus entreated them to tell no one of this occurrence; and while his associates did comply with this request, the mother and the child ceased not to proclaim the fact of the little girl's healing throughout all the countryside and even in Sidon, so much so that Jesus found it advisable to change his lodgings within a few days.

156:1.8 (1735.4) The next day, as Jesus taught his apostles, commenting on the cure of the daughter of the Syrian woman, he said: "And so it has been all the way along; you see for yourselves how the gentiles are able to exercise saving faith in the teachings of the gospel of the kingdom of heaven. Verily, verily, I tell you that the Father's kingdom shall be taken by the gentiles if the children of Abraham are not minded to show faith enough to enter therein."

Teaching in
Sidon

156:2.1 (1735.5) In entering Sidon, Jesus and his associates passed over a bridge, the first one many of them had ever seen. As they walked over this bridge, Jesus, among other things, said: "This world is only a bridge; you may pass over it, but you should not think to build a dwelling place upon it."

156:2.2 (1735.6) As the twenty-four began their labors in Sidon, Jesus went to stay in a home just north of the city, the house of Justa and her mother, Bernice. Jesus taught the twenty-four each morning at the home of Justa, and they went abroad in Sidon to teach and preach during the afternoons and evenings.

156:2.3 (1735.7) The apostles and the evangelists were greatly cheered by the manner in which the gentiles of Sidon received their message; during their short sojourn many were added to the kingdom. This period of about six weeks in Phoenicia was a very fruitful time in the work of winning souls, but the later Jewish writers of the Gospels were wont lightly to pass over the record of this warm reception of Jesus' teachings by these gentiles at this very time when such a large number of his own people were in hostile array against him.

156:2.4 (1736.1) In many ways these gentile believers appreciated Jesus' teachings more fully than the Jews. Many of these Greek-speaking Syrophoenicians came to know not only that Jesus was like God but also that God was like Jesus. These so-called heathen achieved a good understanding of the Master's teachings about the uniformity of the laws of this world and the entire universe. They grasped the teaching that God is no respecter of persons, races, or nations; that there is no favoritism with the Universal Father; that the universe is wholly and ever law-abiding and unfailingly dependable. These gentiles were not afraid of Jesus; they dared to accept his message. All down through the ages men have not been unable to comprehend Jesus; they have been afraid to.

156:2.5 (1736.2) Jesus made it clear to the twenty-four that he had not fled from Galilee because he lacked courage to confront his enemies. They comprehended that he was not yet ready for an open clash with established religion, and that he did not seek to become a martyr. It was during one of these conferences at the home of Justa that the Master first told his disciples that "even though heaven and earth shall pass away, my words of truth shall not."

156:2.6 (1736.3) The theme of Jesus' instructions during the sojourn at Sidon was spiritual progression. He told them they could not stand still; they must go forward in righteousness or retrogress into evil and sin. He admonished them to "forget those things which are in the past while you push forward to embrace the greater realities of the kingdom." He besought them not to be content with their childhood in the gospel but to strive for the attainment of the full stature of divine sonship in the communion of the spirit and in the fellowship of believers.

156:2.7 (1736.4) Said Jesus: "My disciples must not only cease to do evil but learn to do well; you must not only be cleansed from all conscious sin, but you must refuse to harbor even the feelings of guilt. If you confess your sins, they are forgiven; therefore must you maintain a conscience void of offense."

156:2.8 (1736.5) Jesus greatly enjoyed the keen sense of humor which these gentiles exhibited. It was the sense of humor displayed by Norana, the Syrian woman, as well as her great and persistent faith, that so touched the Master's heart and appealed to his mercy. Jesus greatly regretted that his people—the Jews—were so lacking in humor. He once said to Thomas: "My people take themselves too seriously; they are just about devoid of an appreciation of humor. The burdensome religion of the Pharisees could never have had origin among a people with a sense of humor. They also lack consistency; they strain at gnats and swallow camels."

The Journey up the Coast

156:3.1 (1736.6) On Tuesday, June 28, the Master and his associates left Sidon, going up the coast to Porphyreon and Heldua. They were well received by the gentiles, and many were added to the kingdom during this week of teaching and preaching. The apostles preached in Porphyreon and the evangelists taught in Heldua. While the twenty-four were thus engaged in their work, Jesus left them for a period of three or four days, paying a visit to the coast city of Beirut, where he visited with a Syrian named Malach, who was a believer, and who had been at Bethsaida the year before.

156:3.2 (1737.1) On Wednesday, July 6, they all returned to Sidon and tarried at the home of Justa until Sunday morning, when they departed for Tyre, going south along the coast by way of Sarepta, arriving at Tyre on Monday, July 11. By this time the apostles and the evangelists were becoming accustomed to working among these so-called gentiles, who were in reality mainly descended from the earlier Canaanite tribes of still earlier Semitic origin. All of these peoples spoke the Greek language. It was a great surprise to the apostles and evangelists to observe the eagerness of these gentiles to hear the gospel and to note the readiness with which many of them believed.

At Tyre

156:4.1 (1737.2) From July 11 to July 24 they taught in Tyre. Each of the apostles took with him one of the evangelists, and thus two and two they taught and preached in all parts of Tyre and its environs. The polyglot population of this busy seaport heard them gladly, and many were baptized into the outward fellowship of the kingdom. Jesus maintained his headquarters at the home of a Jew named Joseph, a believer, who lived three or four miles south of Tyre,

not far from the tomb of Hiram who had been king of the city-state of Tyre during the times of David and Solomon.

156:4.2 (1737.3) Daily, for this period of two weeks, the apostles and evangelists entered Tyre by way of Alexander's mole to conduct small meetings, and each night most of them would return to the encampment at Joseph's house south of the city. Every day believers came out from the city to talk with Jesus at his resting place. The Master spoke in Tyre only once, on the afternoon of July 20, when he taught the believers concerning the Father's love for all mankind and about the mission of the Son to reveal the Father to all races of men. There was such an interest in the gospel of the kingdom among these gentiles that, on this occasion, the doors of the Melkarth temple were opened to him, and it is interesting to record that in subsequent years a Christian church was built on the very site of this ancient temple.

156:4.3 (1737.4) Many of the leaders in the manufacture of Tyrian purple, the dye that made Tyre and Sidon famous the world over, and which contributed so much to their world-wide commerce and consequent enrichment, believed in the kingdom. When, shortly thereafter, the supply of the sea animals which were the source of this dye began to diminish, these dye makers went forth in search of new habitats of these shellfish. And thus migrating to the ends of the earth, they carried with them the message of the fatherhood of God and the brotherhood of man—the gospel of the kingdom.

Jesus' Teaching at Tyre

156:5.1 (1737.5) On this Wednesday afternoon, in the course of his address, Jesus first told his followers the story of the white lily which rears its pure and snowy head high into the sunshine while its roots are grounded in the slime and muck of the darkened soil beneath. "Likewise," said he, "mortal man, while he has his roots of origin and being in the animal soil of human nature, can by faith raise his spiritual nature up into the sunlight of heavenly truth and actually bear the noble fruits of the spirit."

156:5.2 (1738.1) It was during this same sermon that Jesus made use of his first and only parable having to do with his own trade—carpentry. In the course of his admonition to "Build well the foundations for the growth of a noble character of spiritual endowments," he said: "In order to yield the fruits of the spirit, you must be born of the spirit. You must be taught by the spirit and be led by the spirit if you would live the spirit-filled life among your fellows. But do not make the mistake of the foolish carpenter who wastes valuable time squaring, measuring, and smoothing his worm-eaten and inwardly rotting timber and then, when he has thus bestowed all of his labor upon the unsound beam, must reject it as unfit to enter into the foundations of the building which he would construct to withstand the assaults of time and storm. Let every man make sure that the intellectual and moral foundations of character are such as will adequately support the superstructure of the enlarging and ennobling spiritual nature, which is thus to transform the mortal mind and then, in association with that re-created mind, is to achieve the evolvement of the soul of immortal destiny. Your spirit nature— the jointly created soul—is a living growth, but the mind and morals of the individual are the soil from which these higher manifestations of human development and divine destiny must spring. The soil of the evolving soul is human and material, but the destiny of this combined creature of mind and spirit is spiritual and divine."

156:5.3 (1738.2) On the evening of this same day Nathaniel asked Jesus: "Master, why do we pray that God will lead us not into temptation when we well know from your revelation of the Father that he never does such things?" Jesus answered Nathaniel:

156:5.4 (1738.3) "It is not strange that you ask such questions seeing that you are beginning to know the Father as I know him, and not as the early Hebrew prophets so dimly saw him. You well know how our forefathers were disposed to see God in almost everything that happened. They looked for the hand of God in all natural occurrences and in every unusual episode of human experience. They connected God with both good and evil. They thought he softened the heart of Moses and hardened the heart of Pharaoh. When man had a strong urge to do something, good or evil, he was in the habit of accounting for these unusual emotions by remarking: 'The Lord spoke to me saying, do thus and so, or go here and there.' Accordingly, since men so often and so violently ran into temptation, it became the habit of our forefathers to believe that God led them thither for testing, punishing, or strengthening. But you, indeed, now know better. You know that men are all too often led into temptation by the urge of their own selfishness and by the impulses of their animal natures. When you are in this way tempted, I admonish you that, while you recognize temptation honestly and sincerely for just what it is, you intelligently redirect the energies of spirit, mind, and body, which are seeking expression, into higher channels and toward more idealistic goals. In this way may you transform your temptations into the highest types of uplifting mortal ministry while you almost wholly avoid these wasteful and weakening conflicts between the animal and spiritual natures.

156:5.5 (1738.4) "But let me warn you against the folly of undertaking to surmount temptation by the effort of supplanting one desire by another and supposedly superior desire through the mere force of the human will. If you would be truly triumphant over the temptations of the lesser and lower nature, you must come to that place of spiritual advantage where you have really and truly developed an actual interest in, and love for, those higher and more idealistic forms of conduct which your mind is desirous of substituting for these lower and less idealistic habits of behavior that you recognize as temptation. You will in this way be delivered through spiritual transformation rather than be increasingly overburdened with the deceptive suppression of mortal desires. The old and the inferior will be forgotten in the love for the new and the superior. Beauty is always triumphant over ugliness in the hearts of all who are illuminated by the love of truth.

There is mighty power in the expulsive energy of a new and sincere spiritual affection. And again I say to you, be not overcome by evil but rather overcome evil with good."

156:5.6 (1739.1) Long into the night the apostles and evangelists continued to ask questions, and from the many answers we would present the following thoughts, restated in modern phraseology:

156:5.7 (1739.2) Forceful ambition, intelligent judgment, and seasoned wisdom are the essentials of material success.

Leadership is dependent on natural ability, discretion, will power, and determination. Spiritual destiny is dependent on faith, love, and devotion to truth—hunger and thirst for righteousness—the wholehearted desire to find God and to be like him.

156:5.8 (1739.3) Do not become discouraged by the discovery that you are human. Human nature may tend toward evil, but it is not inherently sinful. Be not downcast by your failure wholly to forget some of your regrettable experiences. The mistakes which you fail to forget in time will be forgotten in eternity. Lighten your burdens of soul by speedily acquiring a long-distance view of your destiny, a universe expansion of your career.

156:5.9 (1739.4) Make not the mistake of estimating the soul's worth by the imperfections of the mind or by the appetites of the body. Judge not the soul nor evaluate its destiny by the standard of a single unfortunate human episode. Your spiritual destiny is conditioned only by your spiritual longings and purposes.

156:5.10 (1739.5) Religion is the exclusively spiritual experience of the evolving immortal soul of the God-knowing man, but moral power and spiritual energy are mighty forces which may be utilized in dealing with difficult social situations and in solving intricate economic problems. These moral and spiritual endowments make all levels of human living richer and more meaningful.

156:5.11 (1739.6) You are destined to live a narrow and mean life if you learn to love only those who love you. Human love may indeed be reciprocal, but divine love is outgoing in all its satisfaction-seeking. The less of love in any creature's nature, the greater the love need, and the more does divine love seek to satisfy such need. Love is never self-seeking, and it cannot be self-bestowed. Divine love cannot be self-contained; it must be unselfishly bestowed.

156:5.12 (1739.7) Kingdom believers should possess an implicit faith, a whole-souled belief, in the certain triumph of righteousness. Kingdom builders must be undoubting of the truth of the gospel of eternal salvation. Believers must increasingly learn how to step aside from the rush of life—escape the harassments of material existence—while they refresh the soul, inspire the mind, and renew the spirit by worshipful communion.

156:5.13 (1739.8) God-knowing individuals are not discouraged by misfortune or downcast by disappointment. Believers are immune to the depression consequent upon purely material upheavals; spirit livers are not perturbed by the episodes of the material world. Candidates for eternal life are practitioners of an invigorating and constructive technique for meeting all of the vicissitudes and harassments of mortal living. Every day a true believer lives, he finds it easier to do the right thing.

156:5.14 (1740.1) Spiritual living mightily increases true self-respect. But self-respect is not self-admiration. Self-respect is always co-ordinate with the love and service of one's fellows. It is not possible to respect yourself more than you love your neighbor; the one is the measure of the capacity for the other.

156:5.15 (1740.2) As the days pass, every true believer becomes more skillful in alluring his fellows into the love of eternal truth. Are you more resourceful in revealing goodness to humanity today than you were yesterday? Are you a better righteousness recommender this year than you were last year? Are you becoming increasingly artistic in your technique of leading hungry souls into the spiritual kingdom?

156:5.16 (1740.3) Are your ideals sufficiently high to insure your eternal salvation while your ideas are so practical as to render you a useful citizen to function on earth in association with your mortal fellows? In the spirit, your citizenship is in heaven; in the flesh, you are still citizens of the earth kingdoms. Render to the Caesars the things which are material and to God those which are spiritual.

156:5.17 (1740.4) The measure of the spiritual capacity of the evolving soul is your faith in truth and your love for man, but the measure of your human strength of character is your ability to resist the holding of grudges and your capacity to withstand brooding in the face of deep sorrow. Defeat is the true mirror in which you may honestly view your real self.

156:5.18 (1740.5) As you grow older in years and more experienced in the affairs of the kingdom, are you becoming more tactful in dealing with troublesome mortals and more tolerant in living with stubborn associates? Tact is the fulcrum of social leverage, and tolerance is the earmark of a great soul. If you possess these rare and charming gifts, as the days pass you will become more alert and expert in your worthy efforts to avoid all unnecessary social misunderstandings. Such wise souls are able to avoid much of the trouble which is certain to be the portion of all who suffer from lack of emotional adjustment, those who refuse to grow up, and those who refuse to grow old gracefully.

156:5.19 (1740.6) Avoid dishonesty and unfairness in all your efforts to preach truth and proclaim the gospel. Seek no unearned recognition and crave no undeserved sympathy. Love, freely receive from both divine and human sources regardless of your deserts, and love freely in return. But in all other things related to honor and adulation seek only that which honestly belongs to you.

156:5.20 (1740.7) The God-conscious mortal is certain of salvation; he is unafraid of life; he is honest and consistent. He knows how bravely to endure unavoidable suffering; he is uncomplaining when faced by inescapable hardship.

156:5.21 (1740.8) The true believer does not grow weary in well-doing just because he is thwarted. Difficulty whets the ardor of the truth lover, while obstacles only challenge the exertions of the undaunted kingdom builder.

156:5.22 (1740.9) And many other things Jesus taught them before they made ready to depart from Tyre.

156:5.23 (1740.10) The day before Jesus left Tyre for the return to the region of the Sea of Galilee, he called his associates together and directed the twelve evangelists to go back by a route different from that which he and the twelve apostles were to take. And after the evangelists here left Jesus, they were never again so intimately associated with him.

The Return from Phoenicia

156:6.1 (1741.1) About noon on Sunday, July 24, Jesus and the twelve left the home of Joseph, south of Tyre, going down the coast to Ptolemais. Here they tarried for a day, speaking words of comfort to the company of believers resident there. Peter preached to them on the evening of July 25.

156:6.2 (1741.2) On Tuesday they left Ptolemais, going east inland to near Jotapata by way of the Tiberias road. Wednesday they stopped at Jotapata and instructed the believers further in the things of the kingdom. Thursday they left Jotapata, going north on the Nazareth-Mount Lebanon trail to the village of Zebulun, by way of Ramah. They held meetings at Ramah on Friday and remained over the Sabbath. They reached Zebulun on Sunday, the 31st, holding a meeting that evening and departing the next morning.

156:6.3 (1741.3) Leaving Zebulun, they journeyed over to the junction with the Magdala-Sidon road near Gischala, and thence they made their way to Gennesaret on the western shores of the lake of Galilee, south of Capernaum, where they had appointed to meet with David Zebedee, and where they intended to take counsel as to the next move to be made in the work of preaching the gospel of the kingdom.

156:6.4 (1741.4) During a brief conference with David they learned that many leaders were then gathered together on the opposite side of the lake near Kheresa, and accordingly, that very evening a boat took them across. For one day they rested quietly in the hills, going on the next day to the park, near by, where the Master once fed the five thousand. Here they rested for three days and held daily conferences, which were attended by about fifty men and women, the remnants of the once numerous company of believers resident in Capernaum and its environs.

156:6.5 (1741.5) While Jesus was absent from Capernaum and Galilee, the period of the Phoenician sojourn, his enemies reckoned that the whole movement had been broken up and concluded that Jesus' haste in withdrawing indicated he was so thoroughly frightened that he would not likely ever return to bother them. All active opposition to his teachings had about subsided. The believers were beginning to hold public meetings once more, and there was occurring a gradual but effective consolidation of the tried and true survivors of the great sifting through which the gospel believers had just passed.

156:6.6 (1741.6) Philip, the brother of Herod, had become a halfhearted believer in Jesus and sent word that the Master was free to live and work in his domains.

156:6.7 (1741.7) The mandate to close the synagogues of all Jewry to the teachings of Jesus and all his followers had worked adversely upon the scribes and Pharisees. Immediately upon Jesus' removing himself as an object of controversy, there occurred a reaction among the entire Jewish people; there was general resentment against the Pharisees and the Sanhedrin leaders at Jerusalem. Many of the rulers of the synagogues began surreptitiously to open their synagogues to Abner and his associates, claiming that these teachers were followers of John and not disciples of Jesus.

156:6.8 (1741.8) Even Herod Antipas experienced a change of heart and, on learning that Jesus was sojourning across the lake in the territory of his brother Philip, sent word to him that, while he had signed warrants for his arrest in Galilee, he had not so authorized his apprehension in Perea, thus indicating that Jesus would not be molested if he remained outside of Galilee; and he communicated this same ruling to the Jews at Jerusalem.

156:6.9 (1742.1) And that was the situation about the first of August, A.D. 29, when the Master returned from the Phoenician mission and began the reorganization of his scattered, tested, and depleted forces for this last and eventful year of his mission on earth.

156:6.10 (1742.2) The issues of battle are clearly drawn as the Master and his associates prepare to begin the proclamation of a new religion, the religion of the spirit of the living God who dwells in the minds of men.

Paper 157

At Caesarea-Philippi

1   The Temple-Tax Collector

157:0.1 (1743.1) BEFORE Jesus took the twelve for a short sojourn in the vicinity of Caesarea-Philippi, he arranged through the messengers of David to go over to Capernaum on Sunday, August 7, for the purpose of meeting his family. By prearrangement this visit was to occur at the Zebedee boatshop. David Zebedee had arranged with Jude, Jesus' brother, for the presence of the entire Nazareth family—Mary and all of Jesus' brothers and sisters—and Jesus went with Andrew and Peter to keep this appointment. It was certainly the intention of Mary and the children to keep this engagement, but it so happened that a group of the Pharisees, knowing that Jesus was on the opposite side of the lake in Philip's domains, decided to call upon Mary to learn what they could of his whereabouts. The arrival of these Jerusalem emissaries greatly perturbed Mary, and noting the tension and nervousness of the entire family, they concluded that Jesus must have been expected to pay them a visit. Accordingly they installed themselves in Mary's home and, after summoning reinforcements, waited patiently for Jesus' arrival. And this, of course, effectively prevented any of the family from attempting to keep their appointment with Jesus. Several times during the day both Jude and Ruth endeavored to elude the vigilance of the Pharisees in their efforts to send word to Jesus, but it was of no avail.

157:0.2 (1743.2) Early in the afternoon David's messengers brought Jesus word that the Pharisees were encamped on the doorstep of his mother's house, and therefore he made no attempt to visit his family. And so again, through no fault of either, Jesus and his earth family failed to make contact.

157:1.1 (1743.3) As Jesus, with Andrew and Peter, tarried by the lake near the boatshop, a temple-tax collector came upon them and, recognizing Jesus, called Peter to one side and said: "Does not your Master pay the temple tax?" Peter was inclined to show indignation at the suggestion that Jesus should be expected to contribute to the maintenance of the religious activities of his sworn enemies, but, noting a peculiar expression on the face of the tax collector, he rightly surmised that it was the purpose to entrap them in the act of refusing to pay the customary half shekel for the support of the temple services at Jerusalem. Accordingly, Peter replied: "Why of course the Master pays the temple tax. You wait by the gate, and I will presently return with the tax."

157:1.2 (1743.4) Now Peter had spoken hastily. Judas carried their funds, and he was across the lake. Neither he, his brother, nor Jesus had brought along any money. And knowing that the Pharisees were looking for them, they could not well go to Bethsaida to obtain money. When Peter told Jesus about the collector and that he had promised him the money, Jesus said: "If you have promised, then should you pay. But wherewith will you redeem your promise? Will you again become a fisherman that you may honor your word? Nevertheless, Peter, it is well in the circumstances that we pay the tax. Let us give these men no occasion for offense at our attitude. We will wait here while you go with the boat and cast for the fish, and when you have sold them at yonder market, pay the collector for all three of us."

157:1.3 (1744.1) All of this had been overheard by the secret messenger of David who stood near by, and who then signaled to an associate, fishing near the shore, to come in quickly. When Peter made ready to go out in the boat for a catch, this messenger and his fisherman friend presented him with several large baskets of fish and assisted him in carrying them to the fish merchant near by, who purchased the catch, paying sufficient, with what was added by the messenger of David, to meet the temple tax for the three. The collector accepted the tax, forgoing the penalty for tardy payment because they had been for some time absent from Galilee.

157:1.4 (1744.2) It is not strange that you have a record of Peter's catching a fish with a shekel in its mouth. In those days there were current many stories about finding treasures in the mouths of fishes; such tales of near miracles were commonplace. So, as Peter left them to go toward the boat, Jesus remarked, half-humorously: "Strange that the sons of the king must pay tribute; usually it is the stranger who is taxed for the upkeep of the court, but it behooves us to afford no stumbling block for the authorities. Go hence! maybe you will catch the fish with the shekel in its mouth." Jesus having thus spoken, and Peter so soon appearing with the temple tax, it is not surprising that the episode became later expanded into a miracle as recorded by the writer of Matthew's Gospel.

157:1.5 (1744.3) Jesus, with Andrew and Peter, waited by the seashore until nearly sundown. Messengers brought them word that Mary's house was still under surveillance; therefore, when it grew dark, the three waiting men entered their boat and slowly rowed away toward the eastern shore of the Sea of Galilee.

2   At Bethsaida-Julias

157:2.1 (1744.4) On Monday, August 8, while Jesus and the twelve apostles were encamped in Magadan Park, near Bethsaida-Julias, more than one hundred believers, the evangelists, the women's corps, and others interested in the establishment of the kingdom, came over from Capernaum for a conference. And many of the Pharisees, learning that Jesus was here, came also. By this time some of the Sadducees were united with the Pharisees in their effort to entrap Jesus. Before going into the closed conference with the believers, Jesus held a public meeting at which the Pharisees were present, and they heckled the Master and otherwise sought to disturb the assembly. Said the leader of the disturbers: "Teacher, we would like you to give us a sign of your authority to teach, and then, when the same shall come to pass, all men will know that you have been sent by God." And Jesus answered them: "When it is evening, you say it will be fair weather, for the heaven is red; in the morning it will be foul weather, for the heaven is red and lowering.

When you see a cloud rising in the west, you say showers will come; when the wind blows from the south, you say scorching heat will come. How is it that you so well know how to discern the face of the heavens but are so utterly unable to discern the signs of the times? To those who would know the truth, already has a sign been given; but to an evil-minded and hypocritical generation no sign shall be given."

157:2.2 (1745.1) When Jesus had thus spoken, he withdrew and prepared for the evening conference with his followers. At this conference it was decided to undertake a united mission throughout all the cities and villages of the Decapolis as soon as Jesus and the twelve should return from their proposed visit to Caesarea-Philippi. The Master participated in planning for the Decapolis mission and, in dismissing the company, said: "I say to you, beware of the leaven of the Pharisees and the Sadducees. Be not deceived by their show of much learning and by their profound loyalty to the forms of religion. Be only concerned with the spirit of living truth and the power of true religion. It is not the fear of a dead religion that will save you but rather your faith in a living experience in the spiritual realities of the kingdom. Do not allow yourselves to become blinded by prejudice and paralyzed by fear. Neither permit reverence for the traditions so to pervert your understanding that your eyes see not and your ears hear not. It is not the purpose of true religion merely to bring peace but rather to insure progress. And there can be no peace in the heart or progress in the mind unless you fall wholeheartedly in love with truth, the ideals of eternal realities. The issues of life and death are being set before you— the sinful pleasures of time against the righteous realities of eternity. Even now you should begin to find deliverance from the bondage of fear and doubt as you enter upon the living of the new life of faith and hope. And when the feelings of service for your fellow men arise within your soul, do not stifle them; when the emotions of love for your neighbor well up within your heart, give expression to such urges of affection in intelligent ministry to the real needs of your fellows."

3   Peter's Confession

157:3.1 (1745.2) Early Tuesday morning Jesus and the twelve apostles left Magadan Park for Caesarea-Philippi, the capital of the Tetrarch Philip's domain. Caesarea-Philippi was situated in a region of wondrous beauty. It nestled in a charming valley between scenic hills where the Jordan poured forth from an underground cave. The heights of Mount Hermon were in full view to the north, while from the hills just to the south a magnificent view was had of the upper Jordan and the Sea of Galilee.

157:3.2 (1745.3) Jesus had gone to Mount Hermon in his early experience with the affairs of the kingdom, and now that he was entering upon the final epoch of his work, he desired to return to this mount of trial and triumph, where he hoped the apostles might gain a new vision of their responsibilities and acquire new strength for the trying times just ahead. As they journeyed along the way, about the time of passing south of the Waters of Merom, the apostles fell to talking among themselves about their recent experiences in Phoenicia and elsewhere and to recounting how their message had been received, and how the different peoples regarded their Master.

157:3.3 (1745.4) As they paused for lunch, Jesus suddenly confronted the twelve with the first question he had ever addressed to them concerning himself. He asked this surprising question, "Who do men say that I am?"

157:3.4 (1746.1) Jesus had spent long months in training these apostles as to the nature and character of the kingdom of heaven, and he well knew the time had come when he must begin to teach them more about his own nature and his personal relationship to the kingdom. And now, as they were seated under the mulberry trees, the Master made ready to hold one of the most momentous sessions of his long association with the chosen apostles.

157:3.5 (1746.2) More than half the apostles participated in answering Jesus' question. They told him that he was regarded as a prophet or as an extraordinary man by all who knew him; that even his enemies greatly feared him, accounting for his powers by the indictment that he was in league with the prince of devils. They told him that some in Judea and Samaria who had not met him personally believed he was John the Baptist risen from the dead. Peter explained that he had been, at sundry times and by various persons, compared with Moses, Elijah, Isaiah, and Jeremiah. When Jesus had listened to this report, he drew himself upon his feet, and looking down upon the twelve sitting about him in a semicircle, with startling emphasis he pointed to them with a sweeping gesture of his hand and asked, "But who say you that I am?" There was a moment of tense silence. The twelve never took their eyes off the Master, and then Simon Peter, springing to his feet, exclaimed: "You are the Deliverer, the Son of the living God." And the eleven sitting apostles arose to their feet with one accord, thereby indicating that Peter had spoken for all of them.

157:3.6 (1746.3) When Jesus had beckoned them again to be seated, and while still standing before them, he said:

"This has been revealed to you by my Father. The hour has come when you should know the truth about me. But for the time being I charge you that you tell this to no man. Let us go hence."

157:3.7 (1746.4) And so they resumed their journey to Caesarea-Philippi, arriving late that evening and stopping at the home of Celsus, who was expecting them. The apostles slept little that night; they seemed to sense that a great event in their lives and in the work of the kingdom had transpired.

4   *The Talk About the Kingdom*

157:4.1 (1746.5) Since the occasions of Jesus' baptism by John and the turning of the water into wine at Cana, the apostles had, at various times, virtually accepted him as the Messiah. For short periods some of them had truly believed that he was the expected Deliverer. But hardly would such hopes spring up in their hearts than the Master would dash them to pieces by some crushing word or disappointing deed. They had long been in a state of turmoil due to conflict between the concepts of the expected Messiah which they held in their minds and the experience of their extraordinary association with this extraordinary man which they held in their hearts.

157:4.2 (1746.6) It was late forenoon on this Wednesday when the apostles assembled in Celsus' garden for their noontime meal. During most of the night and since they had arisen that morning, Simon Peter and Simon Zelotes had been earnestly laboring with their brethren to bring them all to the point of the wholehearted acceptance of the Master, not merely as the Messiah, but also as the divine Son of the living God. The two Simons were well-nigh agreed in their estimate of Jesus, and they labored diligently to bring their brethren around to the full acceptance of their views. While Andrew continued as the director-general of the apostolic corps, his brother, Simon Peter, was becoming, increasingly and by common consent, the spokesman for the twelve.

157:4.3 (1747.1) They were all seated in the garden at just about noon when the Master appeared. They wore expressions of dignified solemnity, and all arose to their feet as he approached them. Jesus relieved the tension by that friendly and fraternal smile which was so characteristic of him when his followers took themselves, or some happening related to themselves, too seriously. With a commanding gesture he indicated that they should be seated. Never again did the twelve greet their Master by arising when he came into their presence. They saw that he did not approve of such an outward show of respect.

157:4.4 (1747.2) After they had partaken of their meal and were engaged in discussing plans for the forthcoming tour of the Decapolis, Jesus suddenly looked up into their faces and said: "Now that a full day has passed since you assented to Simon Peter's declaration regarding the identity of the Son of Man, I would ask if you still hold to your decision?" On hearing this, the twelve stood upon their feet, and Simon Peter, stepping a few paces forward toward Jesus, said: "Yes, Master, we do. We believe that you are the Son of the living God." And Peter sat down with his brethren.

157:4.5 (1747.3) Jesus, still standing, then said to the twelve: "You are my chosen ambassadors, but I know that, in the circumstances, you could not entertain this belief as a result of mere human knowledge. This is a revelation of the spirit of my Father to your inmost souls. And when, therefore, you make this confession by the insight of the spirit of my Father which dwells within you, I am led to declare that upon this foundation will I build the brotherhood of the kingdom of heaven. Upon this rock of spiritual reality will I build the living temple of spiritual fellowship in the eternal realities of my Father's kingdom. All the forces of evil and the hosts of sin shall not prevail against this human fraternity of the divine spirit. And while my Father's spirit shall ever be the divine guide and mentor of all who enter the bonds of this spirit fellowship, to you and your successors I now deliver the keys of the outward kingdom—the authority over things temporal—the social and economic features of this association of men and women as fellows of the kingdom." And again he charged them, for the time being, that they should tell no man that he was the Son of God.

157:4.6 (1747.4) Jesus was beginning to have faith in the loyalty and integrity of his apostles. The Master conceived that a faith which could stand what his chosen representatives had recently passed through would undoubtedly endure the fiery trials which were just ahead and emerge from the apparent wreckage of all their hopes into the new light of a new dispensation and thereby be able to go forth to enlighten a world sitting in darkness. On this day the Master began to believe in the faith of his apostles, save one.

157:4.7 (1747.5) And ever since that day this same Jesus has been building that living temple upon that same eternal foundation of his divine sonship, and those who thereby become self-conscious sons of God are the human stones which constitute this living temple of sonship erecting to the glory and honor of the wisdom and love of the eternal Father of spirits.

157:4.8 (1747.6) And when Jesus had thus spoken, he directed the twelve to go apart by themselves in the hills to seek wisdom, strength, and spiritual guidance until the time of the evening meal. And they did as the Master admonished them.

5   The New Concept

157:5.1 (1748.1) The new and vital feature of Peter's confession was the clear-cut recognition that Jesus was the Son of God, of his unquestioned divinity. Ever since his baptism and the wedding at Cana these apostles had variously regarded him as the Messiah, but it was not a part of the Jewish concept of the national deliverer that he should be divine. The Jews had not taught that the Messiah would spring from divinity; he was to be the "anointed one," but hardly had they contemplated him as being "the Son of God." In the second confession more emphasis was placed upon the combined nature, the supernal fact that he was the Son of Man and the Son of God, and it was upon this great truth of the union of the human nature with the divine nature that Jesus declared he would build the kingdom of heaven.

157:5.2 (1748.2) Jesus had sought to live his life on earth and complete his bestowal mission as the Son of Man. His followers were disposed to regard him as the expected Messiah. Knowing that he could never fulfill their Messianic expectations, he endeavored to effect such a modification of their concept of the Messiah as would enable him partially to meet their expectations. But he now recognized that such a plan could hardly be carried through successfully. He therefore elected boldly to disclose the third plan—openly to announce his divinity, acknowledge the truthfulness of
Peter's confession, and directly proclaim to the twelve that he was a Son of God.

157:5.3 (1748.3) For three years Jesus had been proclaiming that he was the "Son of Man," while for these same three years the apostles had been increasingly insistent that he was the expected Jewish Messiah. He now disclosed that he was the Son of God, and upon the concept of the combined nature of the Son of Man and the Son of God, he determined to build the kingdom of heaven. He had decided to refrain from further efforts to convince them that he was not the Messiah. He now proposed boldly to reveal to them what he is, and then to ignore their determination to persist in regarding him as the Messiah.

6   The Next Afternoon

157:6.1 (1748.4) Jesus and the apostles remained another day at the home of Celsus, waiting for messengers to arrive from David Zebedee with funds. Following the collapse of the popularity of Jesus with the masses there occurred a great falling off in revenue. When they reached Caesarea-Philippi, the treasury was empty. Matthew was loath to leave Jesus and his brethren at such a time, and he had no ready funds of his own to hand over to Judas as he had so many times done in the past. However, David Zebedee had foreseen this probable diminution of revenue and had accordingly instructed his messengers that, as they made their way through Judea, Samaria, and Galilee, they should act as collectors of money to be forwarded to the exiled apostles and their Master. And so, by evening of this day, these messengers arrived from Bethsaida bringing funds sufficient to sustain the apostles until their return to embark upon the Decapolis tour. Matthew expected to have money from the sale of his last piece of property in Capernaum by that time, having arranged that these funds should be anonymously turned over to Judas.

157:6.2 (1749.1) Neither Peter nor the other apostles had a very adequate conception of Jesus' divinity. They little realized that this was the beginning of a new epoch in their Master's career on earth, the time when the teacher-healer was becoming the newly conceived Messiah—the Son of God. From this time on a new note appeared in the Master's message. Henceforth his one ideal of living was the revelation of the Father, while his one idea in teaching was to present to his universe the personification of that supreme wisdom which can only be comprehended by living it. He came that we all might have life and have it more abundantly.

157:6.3 (1749.2) Jesus now entered upon the fourth and last stage of his human life in the flesh. The first stage was that of his childhood, the years when he was only dimly conscious of his origin, nature, and destiny as a human being. The second stage was the increasingly self-conscious years of youth and advancing manhood, during which he came more clearly to comprehend his divine nature and human

mission. This second stage ended with the experiences and revelations associated with his baptism. The third stage of the Master's earth experience extended from the baptism through the years of his ministry as teacher and healer and up to this momentous hour of Peter's confession at Caesarea- Philippi. This third period of his earth life embraced the times when his apostles and his immediate followers knew him as the Son of Man and regarded him as the Messiah. The fourth and last period of his earth career began here at Caesarea-Philippi and extended on to the crucifixion. This stage of his ministry was characterized by his acknowledgment of divinity and embraced the labors of his last year in the flesh. During the fourth period, while the majority of his followers still regarded him as the Messiah, he became known to the apostles as the Son of God. Peter's confession marked the beginning of the new period of the more complete realization of the truth of his supreme ministry as a bestowal Son on Urantia and for an entire universe, and the recognition of that fact, at least hazily, by his chosen ambassadors.

157:6.4 (1749.3) Thus did Jesus exemplify in his life what he taught in his religion: the growth of the spiritual nature by the technique of living progress. He did not place emphasis, as did his later followers, upon the incessant struggle between the soul and the body. He rather taught that the spirit was easy victor over both and effective in the profitable reconciliation of much of this intellectual and instinctual warfare.

157:6.5 (1749.4) A new significance attaches to all of Jesus' teachings from this point on. Before Caesarea-Philippi he presented the gospel of the kingdom as its master teacher. After Caesarea-Philippi he appeared not merely as a teacher but as the divine representative of the eternal Father, who is the center and circumference of this spiritual kingdom, and it was required that he do all this as a human being, the Son of Man.

157:6.6 (1749.5) Jesus had sincerely endeavored to lead his followers into the spiritual kingdom as a teacher, then as a teacher-healer, but they would not have it so. He well knew that his earth mission could not possibly fulfill the Messianic expectations of the Jewish people; the olden prophets had portrayed a Messiah which he could never be. He sought to establish the Father's kingdom as the Son of Man, but his followers would not go forward in the adventure. Jesus, seeing this, then elected to meet his believers part way and in so doing prepared openly to assume the role of the bestowal Son of God.

157:6.7 (1750.1) Accordingly, the apostles heard much that was new as Jesus talked to them this day in the garden. And some of these pronouncements sounded strange even to them. Among other startling announcements they listened to such as the following:

157:6.8 (1750.2) "From this time on, if any man would have fellowship with us, let him assume the obligations of sonship and follow me. And when I am no more with you, think not that the world will treat you better than it did your Master. If you love me, prepare to prove this affection by your willingness to make the supreme sacrifice."

157:6.9 (1750.3) "And mark well my words: I have not come to call the righteous, but sinners. The Son of Man came not to be ministered to, but to minister and to bestow his life as the gift for all. I declare to you that I have come to seek and to save those who are lost."

157:6.10 (1750.4) "No man in this world now sees the Father except the Son who came forth from the Father. But if the Son be lifted up, he will draw all men to himself, and whosoever believes this truth of the combined nature of the Son shall be endowed with life that is more than age-abiding."

157:6.11 (1750.5) "We may not yet proclaim openly that the Son of Man is the Son of God, but it has been revealed to you; wherefore do I speak boldly to you concerning these mysteries. Though I stand before you in this physical presence, I came

forth from God the Father. Before Abraham was, I am. I did come forth from the Father into this world as you have known me, and I declare to you that I must presently leave this world and return to the work of my Father."

157:6.12 (1750.6) "And now can your faith comprehend the truth of these declarations in the face of my warning you that the Son of Man will not meet the expectations of your fathers as they conceived the Messiah? My kingdom is not of this world. Can you believe the truth about me in the face of the fact that, though the foxes have holes and the birds of heaven have nests, I have not where to lay my head?"

157:6.13 (1750.7) "Nevertheless, I tell you that the Father and I are one. He who has seen me has seen the Father. My Father is working with me in all these things, and he will never leave me alone in my mission, even as I will never forsake you when you presently go forth to proclaim this gospel throughout the world."

157:6.14 (1750.8) "And now have I brought you apart with me and by yourselves for a little while that you may comprehend the glory, and grasp the grandeur, of the life to which I have called you: the faith-adventure of the establishment of my Father's kingdom in the hearts of mankind, the building of my fellowship of living association with the souls of all who believe this gospel."

157:6.15 (1750.9) The apostles listened to these bold and startling statements in silence; they were stunned. And they dispersed in small groups to discuss and ponder the Master's words. They had confessed that he was the Son of God, but they could not grasp the full meaning of what they had been led to do.

7   Andrew's Conference

157:7.1 (1750.10) That evening Andrew took it upon himself to hold a personal and searching conference with each of his brethren, and he had profitable and heartening talks with all of his associates except Judas Iscariot. Andrew had never enjoyed such intimate personal association with Judas as with the other apostles and therefore had not thought it of serious account that Judas never had freely and confidentially related himself to the head of the apostolic corps. But Andrew was now so worried by Judas's attitude that, later on that night, after all the apostles were fast asleep, he sought out Jesus and presented his cause for anxiety to the Master. Said Jesus: "It is not amiss, Andrew, that you have come to me with this matter, but there is nothing more that we can do; only go on placing the utmost confidence in this apostle. And say nothing to his brethren concerning this talk with me."

157:7.2 (1751.1) And that was all Andrew could elicit from Jesus. Always had there been some strangeness between this Judean and his Galilean brethren. Judas had been shocked by the death of John the Baptist, severely hurt by the Master's rebukes on several occasions, disappointed when Jesus refused to be made king, humiliated when he fled from the Pharisees, chagrined when he refused to accept the challenge of the Pharisees for a sign, bewildered by the refusal of his Master to resort to manifestations of power, and now, more recently, depressed and sometimes dejected by an empty treasury. And Judas missed the stimulus of the multitudes.

157:7.3 (1751.2) Each of the other apostles was, in some and varying measure, likewise affected by these selfsame trials and tribulations, but they loved Jesus. At least they must have loved the Master more than did Judas, for they went through with him to the bitter end.

157:7.4 (1751.3) Being from Judea, Judas took personal offense at Jesus' recent warning to the apostles to "beware the leaven of the Pharisees"; he was disposed to regard this statement as a veiled reference to himself. But the great mistake of Judas was: Time and again, when Jesus would send his apostles off by themselves to pray, Judas, instead of engaging in sincere communion with the spiritual forces of the universe, indulged in thoughts of human fear while he persisted in the entertainment of subtle doubts about the mission of Jesus as well as giving in to his unfortunate tendency to harbor feelings of revenge.

157:7.5 (1751.4) And now Jesus would take his apostles along with him to Mount Hermon, where he had appointed to inaugurate his fourth phase of earth ministry as the Son of God. Some of them were present at his baptism in the Jordan and had witnessed the beginning of his career as the Son of Man, and he desired that some of them should also be present to hear his authority for the assumption of the new and public role of a Son of God. Accordingly, on the morning of Friday, August 12, Jesus said to the twelve: "Lay in provisions and prepare yourselves for a journey to yonder mountain, where the spirit bids me go to be endowed for the finish of my work on earth. And I would take my brethren along that they may also be strengthened for the trying times of going with me through this experience."

Paper 158

The Mount of Transfiguration

158:0.1 (1752.1) IT WAS near sundown on Friday afternoon, August 12, A.D. 29, when Jesus and his associates reached the foot of Mount Hermon, near the very place where the lad Tiglath once waited while the Master ascended the mountain alone to settle the spiritual destinies of Urantia and technically to terminate the Lucifer rebellion. And here they sojourned for two days in spiritual preparation for the events so soon to follow.

158:0.2 (1752.2) In a general way, Jesus knew beforehand what was to transpire on the mountain, and he much desired that all his apostles might share this experience. It was to fit them for this revelation of himself that he tarried with them at the foot of the mountain. But they could not attain those spiritual levels which would justify their exposure to the full experience of the visitation of the celestial beings so soon to appear on earth. And since he could not take all of his associates with him, he decided to take only the three who were in the habit of accompanying him on such special vigils. Accordingly, only Peter, James, and John shared even a part of this unique experience with the Master.

1   *The Transfiguration*

158:1.1 (1752.3) Early on the morning of Monday, August 15, Jesus and the three apostles began the ascent of Mount Hermon, and this was six days after the memorable noontide confession of Peter by the roadside under the mulberry trees.

158:1.2 (1752.4) Jesus had been summoned to go up on the mountain, apart by himself, for the transaction of important matters having to do with the progress of his bestowal in the flesh as this experience was related to the universe of his own creation. It is significant that this extraordinary event was timed to occur while Jesus and the apostles were in the lands of the gentiles, and that it actually transpired on a mountain of the gentiles.

158:1.3 (1752.5) They reached their destination, about halfway up the mountain, shortly before noon, and while eating lunch, Jesus told the three apostles something of his experience in the hills to the east of Jordan shortly after his baptism and also some more of his experience on Mount Hermon in connection with his former visit to this lonely retreat.

158:1.4 (1752.6) When a boy, Jesus used to ascend the hill near his home and dream of the battles which had been fought by the armies of empires on the plain of Esdraelon; now he ascended Mount Hermon to receive the endowment which

was to prepare him to descend upon the plains of the Jordan to enact the closing scenes of the drama of his bestowal on Urantia. The Master could have relinquished the struggle this day on Mount Hermon and returned to his rule of the universe domains, but he not only chose to meet the requirements of his order of divine sonship embraced in the mandate of the Eternal Son on Paradise, but he also elected to meet the last and full measure of the present will of his Paradise Father. On this day in August three of his apostles saw him decline to be invested with full universe authority. They looked on in amazement as the celestial messengers departed, leaving him alone to finish out his earth life as the Son of Man and the Son of God.

158:1.5 (1753.1) The faith of the apostles was at a high point at the time of the feeding of the five thousand, and then it rapidly fell almost to zero. Now, as a result of the Master's admission of his divinity, the lagging faith of the twelve arose in the next few weeks to its highest pitch, only to undergo a progressive decline. The third revival of their faith did not occur until after the Master's resurrection.

158:1.6 (1753.2) It was about three o'clock on this beautiful afternoon that Jesus took leave of the three apostles, saying: "I go apart by myself for a season to commune with the Father and his messengers; I bid you tarry here and, while awaiting my return, pray that the Father's will may be done in all your experience in connection with the further bestowal mission of the Son of Man." And after saying this to them, Jesus withdrew for a long conference with Gabriel and the Father Melchizedek, not returning until about six o'clock. When Jesus saw their anxiety over his prolonged absence, he said: "Why were you afraid? You well know I must be about my Father's business; wherefore do you doubt when I am not with you? I now declare that the Son of Man has chosen to go through his full life in your midst and as one of you. Be of good cheer; I will not leave you until my work is finished."

158:1.7 (1753.3) As they partook of their meager evening meal, Peter asked the Master, "How long do we remain on this mountain away from our brethren?" And Jesus answered: "Until you shall see the glory of the Son of Man and know that whatsoever I have declared to you is true." And they talked over the affairs of the Lucifer rebellion while seated about the glowing embers of their fire until darkness drew on and the apostles' eyes grew heavy, for they had begun their journey very early that morning.

158:1.8 (1753.4) When the three had been fast asleep for about half an hour, they were suddenly awakened by a near-by crackling sound, and much to their amazement and consternation, on looking about them, they beheld Jesus in intimate converse with two brilliant beings clothed in the habiliments of the light of the celestial world. And Jesus' face and form shone with the luminosity of a heavenly light. These three conversed in a strange language, but from certain things said, Peter erroneously conjectured that the beings with Jesus were Moses and Elijah; in reality, they were Gabriel and the Father Melchizedek. The physical controllers had arranged for the apostles to witness this scene because of Jesus' request.

158:1.9 (1753.5) The three apostles were so badly frightened that they were slow in collecting their wits, but Peter, who was first to recover himself, said, as the dazzling vision faded from before them and they observed Jesus standing alone: "Jesus, Master, it is good to have been here. We rejoice to see this glory. We are loath to go back down to the inglorious world. If you are willing, let us abide here, and we will erect three tents, one for you, one for Moses, and one for Elijah." And Peter said this because of his confusion, and because nothing else came into his mind at just that moment.

158:1.10 (1753.6) While Peter was yet speaking, a silvery cloud drew near and overshadowed the four of them. The apostles now became greatly frightened, and as they fell down on their faces to worship, they heard a voice, the same that had spoken on the occasion of Jesus' baptism, say: "This is my beloved Son; give heed to him." And when the cloud vanished, again was Jesus alone with the three, and he reached down and touched them, saying: "Arise and be not afraid; you shall see greater things than this." But the apostles were truly afraid; they were a silent and thoughtful trio as they made ready to descend the mountain shortly before midnight.

2   Coming Down the Mountain

158:2.1 (1754.1) For about half the distance down the mountain not a word was spoken. Jesus then began the conversation by remarking: "Make certain that you tell no man, not even your brethren, what you have seen and heard on this mountain until the Son of Man has risen from the dead." The three apostles were shocked and bewildered by the Master's words, "until the Son of Man has risen from the dead." They had so recently reaffirmed their faith in him as the Deliverer, the Son of God, and they had just beheld him transfigured in glory before their very eyes, and now he began to talk about "rising from the dead"!

158:2.2 (1754.2) Peter shuddered at the thought of the Master's dying—it was too disagreeable an idea to entertain—and fearing that James or John might ask some question relative to this statement, he thought best to start up a diverting conversation and, not knowing what else to talk about, gave expression to the first thought coming into his mind, which was: "Master, why is it that the scribes say that Elijah must first come before the Messiah shall appear?" And Jesus, knowing that Peter sought to avoid reference to his death and resurrection, answered: "Elijah indeed comes first to prepare the way for the Son of Man, who must suffer many things and finally be rejected. But I tell you that Elijah has already come, and they received him not but did to him whatsoever they willed." And then did the three apostles perceive that he referred to John the Baptist as Elijah. Jesus knew that, if they insisted on regarding him as the Messiah, then must John be the Elijah of the prophecy.

158:2.3 (1754.3) Jesus enjoined silence about their observation of the foretaste of his postresurrection glory because he did not want to foster the notion that, being now received as the Messiah, he would in any degree fulfill their erroneous concepts of a wonder-working deliverer. Although Peter, James, and John pondered all this in their minds, they spoke not of it to any man until after the Master's resurrection.

158:2.4 (1754.4) As they continued to descend the mountain, Jesus said to them: "You would not receive me as the Son of Man; therefore have I consented to be received in accordance with your settled determination, but, mistake not, the will of my Father must prevail. If you thus choose to follow the inclination of your own wills, you must prepare to suffer many disappointments and experience many trials, but the training which I have given you should suffice to bring you triumphantly through even these sorrows of your own choosing."

158:2.5 (1754.5) Jesus did not take Peter, James, and John with him up to the mount of the transfiguration because they were in any sense better prepared than the other apostles to witness what happened, or because they were spiritually more fit to enjoy such a rare privilege. Not at all. He well knew that none of the twelve were spiritually qualified for this experience; therefore did he take with him only the three apostles who were assigned to accompany him at those times when he desired to be alone to enjoy solitary communion.

3   Meaning of the Transfiguration

158:3.1 (1755.1) That which Peter, James, and John witnessed on the mount of transfiguration was a fleeting glimpse of a celestial pageant which transpired that eventful day on Mount Hermon. The transfiguration was the occasion of:

158:3.2 (1755.2) 1. The acceptance of the fullness of the bestowal of the incarnated life of Michael on Urantia by the Eternal Mother-Son of Paradise. As far as concerned the requirements of the Eternal Son, Jesus had now received assurance of their fulfillment. And Gabriel brought Jesus that assurance.

158:3.3 (1755.3) 2. The testimony of the satisfaction of the Infinite Spirit as to the fullness of the Urantia bestowal in the likeness of mortal flesh. The universe representative of the Infinite Spirit, the immediate associate of Michael on Salvington and his ever-present coworker, on this occasion spoke through the Father Melchizedek.

158:3.4 (1755.4) Jesus welcomed this testimony regarding the success of his earth mission presented by the messengers of the Eternal Son and the Infinite Spirit, but he noted that his Father did not indicate that the Urantia bestowal was finished; only did the unseen presence of the Father bear witness through Jesus' Personalized Adjuster, saying, "This is my beloved Son; give heed to him." And this was spoken in words to be heard also by the three apostles.

158:3.5 (1755.5) After this celestial visitation Jesus sought to know his Father's will and decided to pursue the mortal bestowal to its natural end. This was the significance of the transfiguration to Jesus. To the three apostles it was an event marking the entrance of the Master upon the final phase of his earth career as the Son of God and the Son of Man.

158:3.6 (1755.6) After the formal visitation of Gabriel and the Father Melchizedek, Jesus held informal converse with these, his Sons of ministry, and communed with them concerning the affairs of the universe.

4   The Epileptic Boy

158:4.1 (1755.7) It was shortly before breakfast time on this Tuesday morning when Jesus and his companions arrived at the apostolic camp. As they drew near, they discerned a considerable crowd gathered around the apostles and soon began to hear the loud words of argument and disputation of this group of about fifty persons, embracing the nine apostles and a gathering equally divided between Jerusalem scribes and believing disciples who had tracked Jesus and his associates in their journey from Magadan.

158:4.2 (1755.8) Although the crowd engaged in numerous arguments, the chief controversy was about a certain citizen of Tiberias who had arrived the preceding day in quest of Jesus. This man, James of Safed, had a son about fourteen years old, an only child, who was severely afflicted with epilepsy. In addition to this nervous malady this lad had become possessed by one of those wandering, mischievous, and rebellious midwayers who were then present on earth and uncontrolled, so that the youth was both epileptic and demon-possessed.

158:4.3 (1755.9) For almost two weeks this anxious father, a minor official of Herod Antipas, had wandered about through the western borders of Philip's domains, seeking Jesus that he might entreat him to cure this afflicted son. And he did not catch up with the apostolic party until about noon of this day when Jesus was up on the mountain with the three apostles.

158:4.4 (1756.1) The nine apostles were much surprised and considerably perturbed when this man, accompanied by almost forty other persons who were looking for Jesus, suddenly came upon them. At the time of the arrival of this group the nine apostles, at least the majority of them, had succumbed to their old temptation—that of discussing who should be greatest in the coming kingdom; they were busily arguing about the probable positions which would be assigned the individual apostles. They simply could not free themselves entirely from the long-cherished idea of the material mission of the Messiah. And now that Jesus himself had accepted their confession that he was indeed the Deliverer—at least he had admitted the fact of his divinity—what was more natural than that, during this period of separation from the Master, they should fall to talking about those hopes and ambitions which were uppermost in their hearts. And they were engaged in these discussions when James of Safed and his fellow seekers after Jesus came upon them.

158:4.5 (1756.2) Andrew stepped up to greet this father and his son, saying, "Whom do you seek?" Said James: "My good man, I search for your Master. I seek healing for my afflicted son. I would have Jesus cast out this devil that possesses my child." And then the father proceeded to relate to the apostles how his son was so afflicted that he had many times almost lost his life as a result of these malignant seizures.

158:4.6 (1756.3) As the apostles listened, Simon Zelotes and Judas Iscariot stepped into the presence of the father, saying: "We can heal him; you need not wait for the Master's return. We are ambassadors of the kingdom; no longer do we hold these things in secret. Jesus is the Deliverer, and the keys of the kingdom have been delivered to us." By this time Andrew and Thomas were in consultation at one side. Nathaniel and the others looked on in amazement; they were all aghast at the sudden boldness, if not presumption, of Simon and Judas. Then said the father: "If it has been given you to do these works, I pray that you will speak those words which will deliver my child from this bondage." Then Simon stepped forward and, placing his hand on the head of the child, looked directly into his eyes and commanded: "Come out of him, you unclean spirit; in the name of Jesus obey me." But the lad had only a more violent fit, while the scribes mocked the apostles in derision, and the disappointed believers suffered the taunts of these unfriendly critics. *

158:4.7 (1756.4) Andrew was deeply chagrined at this ill-advised effort and its dismal failure. He called the apostles aside for conference and prayer. After this season of meditation, feeling keenly the sting of their defeat and sensing the humiliation resting upon all of them, Andrew sought, in a second attempt, to cast out the demon, but only failure crowned his efforts. Andrew frankly confessed defeat and requested the father to remain with them overnight or until Jesus' return, saying: "Perhaps this sort goes not out except by the Master's personal command."

158:4.8 (1756.5) And so, while Jesus was descending the mountain with the exuberant and ecstatic Peter, James, and John, their nine brethren likewise were sleepless in their confusion and downcast humiliation. They were a dejected and chastened group. But James of Safed would not give up. Although they could give him no idea as to when Jesus might return, he decided to stay on until the Master came back.

5   *Jesus Heals the Boy*

158:5.1 (1757.1) As Jesus drew near, the nine apostles were more than relieved to welcome him, and they were greatly encouraged to behold the good cheer and unusual enthusiasm which marked the countenances of Peter, James, and John.
They all rushed forward to greet Jesus and their three brethren. As they exchanged greetings, the crowd came up, and Jesus asked, "What were you disputing about as we drew near?" But before the disconcerted and humiliated apostles could reply to the Master's question, the anxious father of the afflicted lad stepped forward and, kneeling at Jesus' feet, said: "Master, I have a son, an only child, who is possessed by an evil spirit. Not only does he cry out in terror, foam at the mouth, and fall like

a dead person at the time of seizure, but oftentimes this evil spirit which possesses him rends him in convulsions and sometimes has cast him into the water and even into the fire. With much grinding of teeth and as a result of many bruises, my child wastes away. His life is worse than death; his mother and I are of a sad heart and a broken spirit. About noon yesterday, seeking for you, I caught up with your disciples, and while we were waiting, your apostles sought to cast out this demon, but they could not do it. And now, Master, will you do this for us, will you heal my son?"

158:5.2 (1757.2) When Jesus had listened to this recital, he touched the kneeling father and bade him rise while he gave the near-by apostles a searching survey. Then said Jesus to all those who stood before him: "O faithless and perverse generation, how long shall I bear with you? How long shall I be with you? How long ere you learn that the works of faith come not forth at the bidding of doubting unbelief?" And then, pointing to the bewildered father, Jesus said, "Bring hither your son." And when James had brought the lad before Jesus, he asked, "How long has the boy been afflicted in this way?" The father answered, "Since he was a very young child." And as they talked, the youth was seized with a violent attack and fell in their midst, gnashing his teeth and foaming at the mouth. After a succession of violent convulsions he lay there before them as one dead. Now did the father again kneel at Jesus' feet while he implored the Master, saying: "If you can cure him, I beseech you to have compassion on us and deliver us from this affliction." And when Jesus heard these words, he looked down into the father's anxious face, saying: "Question not my Father's power of love, only the sincerity and reach of your faith. All things are possible to him who really believes." And then James of Safed spoke those long-to-be-remembered words of commingled faith and doubt, "Lord, I believe. I pray you help my unbelief."

158:5.3 (1757.3) When Jesus heard these words, he stepped forward and, taking the lad by the hand, said: "I will do this in accordance with my Father's will and in honor of living faith. My son, arise! Come out of him, disobedient spirit, and go not back into him." And placing the hand of the lad in the hand of the father, Jesus said: "Go your way. The Father has granted the desire of your soul." And all who were present, even the enemies of Jesus, were astonished at what they saw.

158:5.4 (1757.4) It was indeed a disillusionment for the three apostles who had so recently enjoyed the spiritual ecstasy of the scenes and experiences of the transfiguration, so soon to return to this scene of the defeat and discomfiture of their fellow apostles. But it was ever so with these twelve ambassadors of the kingdom. They never failed to alternate between exaltation and humiliation in their life experiences.

158:5.5 (1758.1) This was a true healing of a double affliction, a physical ailment and a spirit malady. And the lad was permanently cured from that hour. When James had departed with his restored son, Jesus said: "We go now to Caesarea- Philippi; make ready at once." And they were a quiet group as they journeyed southward while the crowd followed on behind. *

6   In Celsus' Garden

158:6.1 (1758.2) They remained overnight with Celsus, and that evening in the garden, after they had eaten and rested, the twelve gathered about Jesus, and Thomas said: "Master, while we who tarried behind still remain ignorant of what transpired up on the mountain, and which so greatly cheered our brethren who were with you, we crave to have you talk with us concerning our defeat and instruct us in these matters, seeing that those things which happened on the mountain cannot be disclosed at this time."

158:6.2 (1758.3) And Jesus answered Thomas, saying: "Everything which your brethren heard on the mountain shall be revealed to you in due season. But I will now show you the cause of your defeat in that which you so unwisely attempted. While your Master and his companions, your brethren, ascended yonder mountain yesterday to seek for a larger knowledge of the Father's will and to ask for a richer endowment of wisdom effectively to do that divine will,

you who remained on watch here with instructions to strive to acquire the mind of spiritual insight and to pray with us for a fuller revelation of the Father's will, failed to exercise the faith at your command but, instead, yielded to the temptation and fell into your old evil tendencies to seek for yourselves preferred places in the kingdom of heaven—the material and temporal kingdom which you persist in contemplating. And you cling to these erroneous concepts in spite of the reiterated declaration that my kingdom is not of this world.

158:6.3 (1758.4) "No sooner does your faith grasp the identity of the Son of Man than your selfish desire for worldly preferment creeps back upon you, and you fall to discussing among yourselves as to who should be greatest in the kingdom of heaven, a kingdom which, as you persist in conceiving it, does not exist, nor ever shall. Have not I told you that he who would be greatest in the kingdom of my Father's spiritual brotherhood must become little in his own eyes and thus become the server of his brethren? Spiritual greatness consists in an understanding love that is Godlike and not in an enjoyment of the exercise of material power for the exaltation of self. In what you attempted, in which you so completely failed, your purpose was not pure. Your motive was not divine. Your ideal was not spiritual. Your ambition was not altruistic. Your procedure was not based on love, and your goal of attainment was not the will of the Father in heaven.

158:6.4 (1758.5) "How long will it take you to learn that you cannot time-shorten the course of established natural phenomena except when such things are in accordance with the Father's will? nor can you do spiritual work in the absence of spiritual power. And you can do neither of these, even when their potential is present, without the existence of that third and essential human factor, the personal experience of the possession of living faith. Must you always have material manifestations as an attraction for the spiritual realities of the kingdom? Can you not grasp the spirit significance of my mission without the visible exhibition of unusual works? When can you be depended upon to adhere to the higher and spiritual realities of the kingdom regardless of the outward appearance of all material manifestations?"

158:6.5 (1759.1) When Jesus had thus spoken to the twelve, he added: "And now go to your rest, for on the morrow we return to Magadan and there take counsel concerning our mission to the cities and villages of the Decapolis. And in the conclusion of this day's experience, let me declare to each of you that which I spoke to your brethren on the mountain, and let these words find a deep lodgment in your hearts: The Son of Man now enters upon the last phase of the bestowal. We are about to begin those labors which shall presently lead to the great and final testing of your faith and devotion when I shall be delivered into the hands of the men who seek my destruction. And remember what I am saying to you: The Son of Man will be put to death, but he shall rise again."

158:6.6 (1759.2) They retired for the night, sorrowful. They were bewildered; they could not comprehend these words. And while they were afraid to ask aught concerning what he had said, they did recall all of it subsequent to his resurrection.

7   *Peter's Protest*

158:7.1 (1759.3) Early this Wednesday morning Jesus and the twelve departed from Caesarea-Philippi for Magadan Park near Bethsaida-Julias. The apostles had slept very little that night, so they were up early and ready to go. Even the stolid

Alpheus twins had been shocked by this talk about the death of Jesus. As they journeyed south, just beyond the Waters of Merom they came to the Damascus road, and desiring to avoid the scribes and others whom Jesus knew would presently be coming along after them, he directed that they go on to Capernaum by the Damascus road which passes through Galilee. And he did this because he knew that those who followed after him would go on down over the east Jordan road since they reckoned that Jesus and the apostles would fear to pass through the territory of Herod Antipas.

Jesus sought to elude his critics and the crowd which followed him that he might be alone with his apostles this day. *

158:7.2 (1759.4) They traveled on through Galilee until well past the time for their lunch, when they stopped in the shade to refresh themselves. And after they had partaken of food, Andrew, speaking to Jesus, said: "Master, my brethren do not comprehend your deep sayings. We have come fully to believe that you are the Son of God, and now we hear these strange words about leaving us, about dying. We do not understand your teaching. Are you speaking to us in parables? We pray you to speak to us directly and in undisguised form."

158:7.3 (1759.5) In answer to Andrew, Jesus said: "My brethren, it is because you have confessed that I am the Son of God that I am constrained to begin to unfold to you the truth about the end of the bestowal of the Son of Man on earth. You insist on clinging to the belief that I am the Messiah, and you will not abandon the idea that the Messiah must sit upon a throne in Jerusalem; wherefore do I persist in telling you that the Son of Man must presently go to Jerusalem, suffer many things, be rejected by the scribes, the elders, and the chief priests, and after all this be killed and raised from the dead. And I speak not a parable to you; I speak the truth to you that you may be prepared for these events when they suddenly come upon us." And while he was yet speaking, Simon Peter, rushing impetuously toward him, laid his hand upon the Master's shoulder and said:

"Master, be it far from us to contend with you, but I declare that these things shall never happen to you."

158:7.4 (1760.1) Peter spoke thus because he loved Jesus; but the Master's human nature recognized in these words of well-meant affection the subtle suggestion of temptation that he change his policy of pursuing to the end his earth bestowal in accordance with the will of his Paradise Father. And it was because he detected the danger of permitting the suggestions of even his affectionate and loyal friends to dissuade him, that he turned upon Peter and the other apostles, saying: "Get you behind me. You savor of the spirit of the adversary, the tempter. When you talk in this manner, you are not on my side but rather on the side of our enemy. In this way do you make your love for me a stumbling block to my doing the Father's will. Mind not the ways of men but rather the will of God."

158:7.5 (1760.2) After they had recovered from the first shock of Jesus' stinging rebuke, and before they resumed their journey, the Master spoke further: "If any man would come after me, let him disregard himself, take up his responsibilities daily, and follow me. For whosoever would save his life selfishly, shall lose it, but whosoever loses his life for my sake and the gospel's, shall save it. What does it profit a man to gain the whole world and lose his own soul? What would a man give in exchange for eternal life? Be not ashamed of me and my words in this sinful and hypocritical generation, even as I will not be ashamed to acknowledge you when in glory I appear before my Father in the presence of all the celestial hosts. Nevertheless, many of you now standing before me shall not taste death till you see this kingdom of God come with power."

158:7.6 (1760.3) And thus did Jesus make plain to the twelve the painful and conflicting path which they must tread if they would follow him. What a shock these words were to these Galilean fishermen who persisted in dreaming of an earthly kingdom with positions of honor for themselves! But their loyal hearts were stirred by this courageous appeal, and not one of them was minded to forsake him. Jesus was not sending them alone into the conflict; he was leading them. He asked only that they bravely follow.

158:7.7 (1760.4) Slowly the twelve were grasping the idea that Jesus was telling them something about the possibility of his dying. They only vaguely comprehended what he said about his death, while his statement about rising from the dead utterly failed to register in their minds. As the days passed, Peter, James, and John, recalling their experience upon the mount of the transfiguration, arrived at a fuller understanding of certain of these matters.

158:7.8 (1760.5) In all the association of the twelve with their Master, only a few times did they see that flashing eye and hear such swift words of rebuke as were administered to Peter and the rest of them on this occasion. Jesus had always been patient with their human shortcomings, but not so when faced by an impending threat against the program of implicitly carrying out his Father's will regarding the remainder of his earth career. The apostles were literally stunned; they were amazed and horrified. They could not find words to express their sorrow. Slowly they began to realize what the Master must endure, and that they must go through these experiences with him, but they did not awaken to the reality of these coming events until long after these early hints of the impending tragedy of his latter days.

158:7.9 (1761.1) In silence Jesus and the twelve started for their camp at Magadan Park, going by way of Capernaum. As the afternoon wore on, though they did not converse with Jesus, they talked much among themselves while Andrew talked with the Master.

ished speaking, they entered the boat and sailed across to Magadan.

8   *At Peter's House*

158:8.1 (1761.2) Entering Capernaum at twilight, they went by unfrequented thoroughfares directly to the home of Simon Peter for their evening meal. While David Zebedee made ready to take them across the lake, they lingered at Simon's house, and Jesus, looking up at Peter and the other apostles, asked: "As you walked along together this afternoon, what was it that you talked about so earnestly among yourselves?" The apostles held their peace because many of them had continued the discussion begun at Mount Hermon as to what positions they were to have in the coming kingdom; who should be the greatest, and so on. Jesus, knowing what it was that occupied their thoughts that day, beckoned to one of Peter's little ones and, setting the child down among them, said: "Verily, verily, I say to you, except you turn about and become more like this child, you will make little progress in the kingdom of heaven. Whosoever shall humble himself and become as this little one, the same shall become greatest in the kingdom of heaven. And whoso receives such a little one receives me. And they who receive me receive also Him who sent me. If you would be first in the kingdom, seek to minister these good truths to your brethren in the flesh. But whosoever causes one of these little ones to stumble, it would be better for him if a millstone were hanged about his neck and he were cast into the sea. If the things you do with your hands, or the things you see with your eyes give offense in the progress of the kingdom, sacrifice these cherished idols, for it is better to enter the kingdom minus many of the beloved things of life rather than to cling to these idols and find yourself shut out of the kingdom. But most of all, see that you despise not one of these little ones, for their angels do always behold the faces of the heavenly hosts."

158:8.2 (1761.3) When Jesus had fin-

Paper 159

The Decapolis Tour

159:0.1 (1762.1) WHEN Jesus and the twelve arrived at Magadan Park, they found awaiting them a group of almost one hundred evangelists and disciples, including the women's corps, and they were ready immediately to begin the teaching and preaching tour of the cities of the Decapolis.

159:0.2 (1762.2) On this Thursday morning, August 18, the Master called his followers together and directed that each of the apostles should associate himself with one of the twelve evangelists, and that with others of the evangelists they should go out in twelve groups to labor in the cities and villages of the Decapolis. The women's corps and others of the disciples he directed to remain with him. Jesus allotted four weeks to this tour, instructing his followers to return to Magadan not later than Friday, September 16. He promised to visit them often during this time. In the course of this month these twelve groups labored in Gerasa, Gamala, Hippos, Zaphon, Gadara, Abila, Edrei, Philadelphia, Heshbon, Dium, Scythopolis, and many other cities. Throughout this tour no miracles of healing or other extraordinary events occurred.

1   *The Sermon on Forgiveness*

159:1.1 (1762.3) One evening at Hippos, in answer to a disciple's question, Jesus taught the lesson on forgiveness. Said the Master:

159:1.2 (1762.4) "If a kindhearted man has a hundred sheep and one of them goes astray, does he not immediately leave the ninety and nine and go out in search of the one that has gone astray? And if he is a good shepherd, will he not keep up his quest for the lost sheep until he finds it? And then, when the shepherd has found his lost sheep, he lays it over his shoulder and, going home rejoicing, calls to his friends and neighbors, 'Rejoice with me, for I have found my sheep that was lost.' I declare that there is more joy in heaven over one sinner who repents than over ninety and nine righteous persons who need no repentance. Even so, it is not the will of my Father in heaven that one of these little ones should go astray, much less that they should perish. In your religion God may receive repentant sinners; in the gospel of the kingdom the Father goes forth to find them even before they have seriously thought of repentance.

159:1.3 (1762.5) "The Father in heaven loves his children, and therefore should you learn to love one another; the Father in heaven forgives you your sins; therefore should you learn to forgive one another. If your brother sins against you, go to him and with tact and patience show him his fault. And do all this between you and him alone. If he will listen to you, then have you won your brother. But if your brother will not hear you, if he persists in the error of his way, go again to him, taking with you one or two mutual friends that you may thus have two or even three witnesses to confirm your testimony and establish the fact that you have dealt justly and mercifully with your offending brother. Now if he refuses to hear your brethren, you may tell the whole story to the congregation, and then, if he refuses to hear the brotherhood, let them take such action as they deem wise; let such an unruly member become an outcast from the kingdom. While you cannot pretend to sit in judgment on the souls of your fellows, and while you may not forgive sins or otherwise presume to usurp the prerogatives of the supervisors of the heavenly hosts, at the same time, it has been committed to your hands that you should maintain temporal order in the kingdom on earth. While you may not meddle with the divine decrees concerning eternal life, you shall determine the issues

of conduct as they concern the temporal welfare of the brotherhood on earth. And so, in all these matters connected with the discipline of the brotherhood, whatsoever you shall decree on earth, shall be recognized in heaven. Although you cannot determine the eternal fate of the individual, you may legislate regarding the conduct of the group, for, where two or three of you agree concerning any of these things and ask of me, it shall be done for you if your petition is not inconsistent with the will of my Father in heaven.

And all this is ever true, for, where two or three believers are gathered together, there am I in the midst of them."

159:1.4 (1763.1) Simon Peter was the apostle in charge of the workers at Hippos, and when he heard Jesus thus speak, he asked: "Lord, how often shall my brother sin against me, and I forgive him? Until seven times?" And Jesus answered Peter: "Not only seven times but even to seventy times and seven. Therefore may the kingdom of heaven be likened to a certain king who ordered a financial reckoning with his stewards. And when they had begun to conduct this examination of accounts, one of his chief retainers was brought before him confessing that he owed his king ten thousand talents.

Now this officer of the king's court pleaded that hard times had come upon him, and that he did not have wherewith to pay this obligation. And so the king commanded that his property be confiscated, and that his children be sold to pay his debt. When this chief steward heard this stern decree, he fell down on his face before the king and implored him to have mercy and grant him more time, saying, 'Lord, have a little more patience with me, and I will pay you all.' And when the king looked upon this negligent servant and his family, he was moved with compassion. He ordered that he should be released, and that the loan should be wholly forgiven.

159:1.5 (1763.2) "And this chief steward, having thus received mercy and forgiveness at the hands of the king, went about his business, and finding one of his subordinate stewards who owed him a mere hundred denarii, he laid hold upon him and, taking him by the throat, said, 'Pay me all you owe.' And then did this fellow steward fall down before the chief steward and, beseeching him, said: 'Only have patience with me, and I will presently be able to pay you.' But the chief steward would not show mercy to his fellow steward but rather had him cast in prison until he should pay his debt.

When his fellow servants saw what had happened, they were so distressed that they went and told their lord and master, the king. When the king heard of the doings of his chief steward, he called this ungrateful and unforgiving man before him and said: 'You are a wicked and unworthy steward. When you sought for compassion, I freely forgave you your entire debt. Why did you not also show mercy to your fellow steward, even as I showed mercy to you?' And the king was so very angry that he delivered his ungrateful chief steward to the jailers that they might hold him until he had paid all that was due. And even so shall my heavenly Father show the more abundant mercy to those who freely show mercy to their fellows. How can you come to God asking consideration for your shortcomings when you are wont to chastise your brethren for being guilty of these same human frailties? I say to all of you: Freely you have received the good things of the kingdom; therefore freely give to your fellows on earth."

159:1.6 (1764.1) Thus did Jesus teach the dangers and illustrate the unfairness of sitting in personal judgment upon one's fellows. Discipline must be maintained, justice must be administered, but in all these matters the wisdom of the brotherhood should prevail. Jesus invested legislative and judicial authority in the group, not in the individual. Even this investment of authority in the group must not be exercised as personal authority. There is always danger that the verdict of an individual may be warped by prejudice or distorted by passion. Group judgment is more likely to remove the dangers and eliminate the unfairness of personal bias. Jesus sought always to minimize the elements of unfair-

ness, retaliation, and vengeance.

159:1.7 (1764.2) [The use of the term seventy-seven as an illustration of mercy and forbearance was derived from the Scriptures referring to Lamech's exultation because of the metal weapons of his son Tubal-Cain, who, comparing these superior instruments with those of his enemies, exclaimed: "If Cain, with no weapon in his hand, was avenged seven times, I shall now be avenged seventy-seven."]

2   The Strange Preacher

159:2.1 (1764.3) Jesus went over to Gamala to visit John and those who worked with him at that place. That evening, after the session of questions and answers, John said to Jesus: "Master, yesterday I went over to Ashtaroth to see a man who was teaching in your name and even claiming to be able to cast out devils. Now this fellow had never been with us, neither does he follow after us; therefore I forbade him to do such things." Then said Jesus: "Forbid him not. Do you not perceive that this gospel of the kingdom shall presently be proclaimed in all the world? How can you expect that all who will believe the gospel shall be subject to your direction? Rejoice that already our teaching has begun to manifest itself beyond the bounds of our personal influence. Do you not see, John, that those who profess to do great works in my name must eventually support our cause? They certainly will not be quick to speak evil of me. My son, in matters of this sort it would be better for you to reckon that he who is not against us is for us. In the generations to come many who are not wholly worthy will do many strange things in my name, but I will not forbid them. I tell you that, even when a cup of cold water is given to a thirsty soul, the Father's messengers shall ever make record of such a service of love."

159:2.2 (1764.4) This instruction greatly perplexed John. Had he not heard the Master say, "He who is not with me is against me"? And he did not perceive that in this case Jesus was referring to man's personal relation to the spiritual teachings of the kingdom, while in the other case reference was made to the outward and far-flung social relations of believers regarding the questions of administrative control and the jurisdiction of one group of believers over the work of other groups which would eventually compose the forthcoming world-wide brotherhood.

159:2.3 (1765.1) But John oftentimes recounted this experience in connection with his subsequent labors in behalf of the kingdom. Nevertheless, many times did the apostles take offense at those who made bold to teach in the Master's name. To them it always seemed inappropriate that those who had never sat at Jesus' feet should dare to teach in his name.

159:2.4 (1765.2) This man whom John forbade to teach and work in Jesus' name did not heed the apostle's injunction. He went right on with his efforts and raised up a considerable company of believers at Kanata before going on into Mesopotamia. This man, Aden, had been led to believe in Jesus through the testimony of the demented man whom Jesus healed near Kheresa, and who so confidently believed that the supposed evil spirits which the Master cast out of him entered the herd of swine and rushed them headlong over the cliff to their destruction.

3   Instruction for Teachers and Believers

159:3.1 (1765.3) At Edrei, where Thomas and his associates labored, Jesus spent a day and a night and, in the course of the evening's discussion, gave expression to the principles which should guide those who preach truth, and which should activate all who teach the gospel of the kingdom. Summarized and restated in modern phraseology, Jesus taught:

159:3.2 (1765.4) Always respect the personality of man. Never should a righteous cause be promoted by force; spiritual victories can be won only by spiritual power. This injunction against the employment of material influences refers to psychic force as well as to physical force. Overpowering arguments and mental superiority are not to be employed to coerce men and women into the kingdom. Man's mind is not to be crushed by the mere weight of logic or overawed by shrewd eloquence. While emotion as a factor in human decisions cannot be wholly eliminated, it should not be directly appealed to in the teachings of those who would advance the cause of the kingdom. Make your appeals directly to the divine spirit that dwells within the minds of men. Do not appeal to fear, pity, or mere sentiment. In appealing to men, be fair; exercise self-control and exhibit due restraint; show proper respect for the personalities of your pupils. Remember that I have said: "Behold, I stand at the door and knock, and if any man will open, I will come in."

159:3.3 (1765.5) In bringing men into the kingdom, do not lessen or destroy their self-respect. While overmuch self-respect may destroy proper humility and end in pride, conceit, and arrogance, the loss of self-respect often ends in paralysis of the will. It is the purpose of this gospel to restore self-respect to those who have lost it and to restrain it in those who have it. Make not the mistake of only condemning the wrongs in the lives of your pupils; remember also to accord generous recognition for the most praiseworthy things in their lives. Forget not that I will stop at nothing to restore self- respect to those who have lost it, and who really desire to regain it.

159:3.4 (1765.6) Take care that you do not wound the self-respect of timid and fearful souls. Do not indulge in sarcasm at the expense of my simple-minded brethren. Be not cynical with my fear-ridden children. Idleness is destructive of self-respect; therefore, admonish your brethren ever to keep busy at their chosen tasks, and put forth every effort to secure work for those who find themselves without employment.

159:3.5 (1766.1) Never be guilty of such unworthy tactics as endeavoring to frighten men and women into the kingdom. A loving father does not frighten his children into yielding obedience to his just requirements.

159:3.6 (1766.2) Sometime the children of the kingdom will realize that strong feelings of emotion are not equivalent to the leadings of the divine spirit. To be strongly and strangely impressed to do something or to go to a certain place, does not necessarily mean that such impulses are the leadings of the indwelling spirit.

159:3.7 (1766.3) Forewarn all believers regarding the fringe of conflict which must be traversed by all who pass from the life as it is lived in the flesh to the higher life as it is lived in the spirit. To those who live quite wholly within either realm, there is little conflict or confusion, but all are doomed to experience more or less uncertainty during the times of transition between the two levels of living. In entering the kingdom, you cannot escape its responsibilities or avoid its obligations, but remember: The gospel yoke is easy and the burden of truth is light.

159:3.8 (1766.4) The world is filled with hungry souls who famish in the very presence of the bread of life; men die searching for the very God who lives within them. Men seek for the treasures of the kingdom with yearning hearts and weary feet when they are all within the immediate grasp of living faith. Faith is to religion what sails are to a ship; it is an addition of power, not an added burden of life. There is but one struggle for those who enter the kingdom, and that is to fight the good fight of faith. The believer has only one battle, and that is against doubt—unbelief.

159:3.9 (1766.5) In preaching the gospel of the kingdom, you are simply teaching friendship with God. And this fellowship will appeal alike to men and women in that both will find that which most truly satisfies their characteristic longings and ideals. Tell my children that I am not only tender of their feelings and

patient with their frailties, but that I am also ruthless with sin and intolerant of iniquity. I am indeed meek and humble in the presence of my Father, but I am equally and relentlessly inexorable where there is deliberate evil-doing and sinful rebellion against the will of my Father in heaven.

159:3.10 (1766.6) You shall not portray your teacher as a man of sorrows. Future generations shall know also the radiance of our joy, the buoyance of our good will, and the inspiration of our good humor. We proclaim a message of good news which is infectious in its transforming power. Our religion is throbbing with new life and new meanings. Those who accept this teaching are filled with joy and in their hearts are constrained to rejoice evermore. Increasing happiness is always the experience of all who are certain about God.

159:3.11 (1766.7) Teach all believers to avoid leaning upon the insecure props of false sympathy. You cannot develop strong characters out of the indulgence of self-pity; honestly endeavor to avoid the deceptive influence of mere fellowship in misery. Extend sympathy to the brave and courageous while you withhold overmuch pity from those cowardly souls who only halfheartedly stand up before the trials of living. Offer not consolation to those who lie down before their troubles without a struggle. Sympathize not with your fellows merely that they may sympathize with you in return.

159:3.12 (1766.8) When my children once become self-conscious of the assurance of the divine presence, such a faith will expand the mind, ennoble the soul, reinforce the personality, augment the happiness, deepen the spirit perception, and enhance the power to love and be loved.

159:3.13 (1767.1) Teach all believers that those who enter the kingdom are not thereby rendered immune to the accidents of time or to the ordinary catastrophes of nature. Believing the gospel will not prevent getting into trouble, but it will insure that you shall be unafraid when trouble does overtake you. If you dare to believe in me and wholeheartedly proceed to follow after me, you shall most certainly by so doing enter upon the sure pathway to trouble. I do not promise to deliver you from the waters of adversity, but I do promise to go with you through all of them.

159:3.14 (1767.2) And much more did Jesus teach this group of believers before they made ready for the night's sleep. And they who heard these sayings treasured them in their hearts and did often recite them for the edification of the apostles and disciples who were not present when they were spoken.

4   The Talk with Nathaniel

159:4.1 (1767.3) And then went Jesus over to Abila, where Nathaniel and his associates labored. Nathaniel was much bothered by some of Jesus' pronouncements which seemed to detract from the authority of the recognized Hebrew scriptures. Accordingly, on this night, after the usual period of questions and answers, Nathaniel took Jesus away from the others and asked: "Master, could you trust me to know the truth about the Scriptures? I observe that you teach us only a portion of the sacred writings—the best as I view it—and I infer that you reject the teachings of the rabbis to the effect that the words of the law are the very words of God, having been with God in heaven even before the times of Abraham and Moses. What is the truth about the Scriptures?" When Jesus heard the question of his bewildered apostle, he answered:

159:4.2 (1767.4) "Nathaniel, you have rightly judged; I do not regard the Scriptures as do the rabbis. I will talk with you about this matter on condition that you do not relate these things to your brethren, who are not all prepared to receive this teaching. The words of the law of Moses and the teachings of the Scriptures were not in existence before Abraham. Only in recent times have the Scriptures been gathered together as we now have them. While they contain the best of the higher thoughts and longings of the Jewish people, they also contain much that is far from being representative of the character and teachings of the Father in heaven; wherefore must I choose from among the better teachings those truths which are to be gleaned for the gospel of the kingdom.

159:4.3 (1767.5) "These writings are the work of men, some of them holy men, others not so holy. The teachings of these books represent the views and extent of enlightenment of the times in which they had their origin. As a revelation of truth, the last are more dependable than the first. The Scriptures are faulty and altogether human in origin, but mistake not, they do constitute the best collection of religious wisdom and spiritual truth to be found in all the world at this time.

159:4.4 (1767.6) "Many of these books were not written by the persons whose names they bear, but that in no way detracts from the value of the truths which they contain. If the story of Jonah should not be a fact, even if Jonah had never lived, still would the profound truth of this narrative, the love of God for Nineveh and the so-called heathen, be none the less precious in the eyes of all those who love their fellow men. The Scriptures are sacred because they present the thoughts and acts of men who were searching for God, and who in these writings left on record their highest concepts of righteousness, truth, and holiness. The Scriptures contain much that is true, very much, but in the light of your present teaching, you know that these writings also contain much that is misrepresentative of the Father in heaven, the loving God I have come to reveal to all the worlds.

159:4.5 (1768.1) "Nathaniel, never permit yourself for one moment to believe the Scripture records which tell you that the God of love directed your forefathers to go forth in battle to slay all their enemies— men, women, and children. Such records are the words of men, not very holy men, and they are not the word of God. The Scriptures always have, and always will, reflect the intellectual, moral, and spiritual status of those who create them. Have you not noted that the concepts of Yahweh grow in beauty and glory as the prophets make their records from Samuel to Isaiah? And you should remember that the Scriptures are intended for religious instruction and spiritual guidance. They are not the works of either historians or philosophers.

159:4.6 (1768.2) "The thing most deplorable is not merely this erroneous idea of the absolute perfection of the Scripture record and the infallibility of its teachings, but rather the confusing misinterpretation of these sacred writings by the tradition-enslaved scribes and Pharisees at Jerusalem. And now will they employ both the doctrine of the inspiration of the Scriptures and their misinterpretations thereof in their determined effort to withstand these newer teachings of the gospel of the kingdom. Nathaniel, never forget, the Father does not limit the revelation of truth to any one generation or to any one people. Many earnest seekers after the truth have been, and will continue to be, confused and disheartened by these doctrines of the perfection of the Scriptures.

159:4.7 (1768.3) "The authority of truth is the very spirit that indwells its living manifestations, and not the dead words of the less illuminated and supposedly inspired men of another generation. And even if these holy men of old lived inspired and spirit-filled lives, that does not mean that their words were similarly spiritually inspired. Today we make no record of the teachings of this gospel of the kingdom lest, when I have gone, you speedily become divided up into sundry groups of truth contenders as a result of the diversity of your interpretation of my teachings. For this generation it is best that we live these truths while we shun the making of records.

159:4.8 (1768.4) "Mark you well my words, Nathaniel, nothing which human nature has touched can be regarded as infallible. Through the mind of man divine truth may indeed shine forth, but always of relative purity and partial divinity. The creature may crave infallibility, but only the Creators possess it.

159:4.9 (1768.5) "But the greatest error of the teaching about the Scriptures is the doctrine of their being sealed books of mystery and wisdom which only the wise minds of the nation dare to interpret. The revelations of divine truth are not sealed except by human ignorance, bigotry, and narrow-minded intolerance. The light of the Scriptures is only dimmed by prejudice and darkened by superstition. A false fear of sacredness has prevented religion from being safeguarded by common sense. The fear of the authority of the sacred writings of the past effectively prevents the honest souls of today from accepting the new light of the gospel, the light which these very God-knowing men of another generation so intensely longed to see.

159:4.10 (1769.1) "But the saddest feature of all is the fact that some of the teachers of the sanctity of this traditionalism know this very truth. They more or less fully understand these limitations of Scripture, but they are moral cowards, intellectually dishonest. They know the truth regarding the sacred writings, but they prefer to withhold such disturbing facts from the people. And thus do they pervert and distort the Scriptures, making them the guide to slavish details of the daily life and an authority in things nonspiritual instead of appealing to the sacred writings as the repository of the moral wisdom, religious inspiration, and the spiritual teaching of the God-knowing men of other generations."

159:4.11 (1769.2) Nathaniel was enlightened, and shocked, by the Master's pronouncement. He long pondered this talk in the depths of his soul, but he told no man concerning this conference until after Jesus' ascension; and even then he feared to impart the full story of the Master's instruction.

5   The Positive
Nature of Jesus' Religion

159:5.1 (1769.3) At Philadelphia, where James was working, Jesus taught the disciples about the positive nature of the gospel of the kingdom. When, in the course of his remarks, he intimated that some parts of the Scripture were more truth-containing than others and admonished his hearers to feed their souls upon the best of the spiritual food, James interrupted the Master, asking: "Would you be good enough, Master, to suggest to us how we may choose the better passages from the Scriptures for our personal edification?" And Jesus replied: "Yes, James, when you read the Scriptures look for those eternally true and divinely beautiful teachings, such as:

159:5.2 (1769.4) "Create in me a clean heart, O Lord.

159:5.3 (1769.5) "The Lord is my shepherd; I shall not want.

159:5.4 (1769.6) "You should love your neighbor as yourself.

159:5.5 (1769.7) "For I, the Lord your God, will hold your right hand, saying, fear not; I will help you.

159:5.6 (1769.8) "Neither shall the nations learn war any more."

159:5.7 (1769.9) And this is illustrative of the way Jesus, day by day, appropriated the cream of the Hebrew scriptures for the instruction of his followers and for inclusion in the teachings of the new gospel of the kingdom. Other religions had suggested the thought of the nearness of God to man, but Jesus made the care of God for man like the solicitude of a loving father for the welfare of his dependent children and then made this teaching the cornerstone of his religion. And thus did the doctrine of the fatherhood of God make imperative the practice of the brotherhood of man. The worship of God and the service of man became the sum and substance of his religion. Jesus took the best of the Jewish religion and translated it to a worthy setting in the new teachings of the gospel of the kingdom.

159:5.8 (1769.10) Jesus put the spirit of positive action into the passive doctrines of the Jewish religion. In the place of negative compliance with ceremonial requirements, Jesus enjoined the positive doing of that which his new religion required of those who accepted it. Jesus' religion consisted not merely in believing, but in actually doing, those things which the gospel required. He did not teach that the essence of his religion consisted in social service, but rather that social service was one of the certain effects of the possession of the spirit of true religion.

159:5.9 (1770.1) Jesus did not hesitate to appropriate the better half of a Scripture while he repudiated the lesser portion. His great exhortation, "Love your neighbor as yourself," he took from the Scripture which reads: "You shall not take vengeance against the children of your people, but you shall love your neighbor as yourself." Jesus appropriated the positive portion of this Scripture while rejecting the negative part. He even opposed negative or purely passive nonresistance. Said he: "When an enemy smites you on one cheek, do not stand there dumb and passive but in positive attitude turn the other; that is, do the best thing possible actively to lead your brother in error away from the evil paths into the better ways of righteous living." Jesus required his followers to react positively and aggressively to every life situation. The turning of the other cheek, or whatever act that may typify, demands initiative, necessitates vigorous, active, and courageous expression of the believer's personality.

159:5.10 (1770.2) Jesus did not advocate the practice of negative submission to the indignities of those who might purposely seek to impose upon the practitioners of nonresistance to evil, but rather that his followers should be wise and alert in the quick and positive reaction of good to evil to the end that they might effectively overcome evil with good.

Forget not, the truly good is invariably more powerful than the most malignant evil. The Master taught a positive standard of righteousness: "Whosoever wishes to be my disciple, let him disregard himself and take up the full measure of his responsibilities daily to follow me." And he so lived himself in that "he went about doing good." And this aspect of the gospel was well illustrated by many parables which he later spoke to his followers. He never exhorted his followers patiently to bear their obligations but rather with energy and enthusiasm to live up to the full measure of their human responsibilities and divine privileges in the kingdom of God.

159:5.11 (1770.3) When Jesus instructed his apostles that they should, when one unjustly took away the coat, offer the other garment, he referred not so much to a literal second coat as to the idea of doing something positive to save the wrongdoer in the place of the olden advice to retaliate—"an eye for an eye" and so on. Jesus abhorred the idea either of retaliation or of becoming just a passive sufferer or victim of injustice. On this occasion he taught them the three ways of contending with, and resisting, evil:

159:5.12 (1770.4) 1. To return evil for evil—the positive but unrighteous method.
159:5.13 (1770.5) 2. To suffer evil without complaint and without resistance—the purely negative method.
159:5.14 (1770.6) 3. To return good for evil, to assert the will so as to become master of the situation, to overcome evil with good—the positive and righteous method.

159:5.15 (1770.7) One of the apostles once asked: "Master, what should I do if a stranger forced me to carry his pack for a mile?" Jesus answered: "Do not sit down and sigh for relief while you berate the stranger under your breath.
Righteousness comes not from such passive attitudes. If you can think of nothing more effectively positive to do, you can at least carry the pack a second mile. That will of a certainty challenge the unrighteous and ungodly stranger."

159:5.16 (1770.8) The Jews had heard of a God who would forgive repentant sin-ners and try to forget their misdeeds, but not until Jesus came, did men hear about a God who went in search of lost sheep, who took the initiative in looking for sinners, and who rejoiced when he found them willing to return to the Father's house. This positive note in religion Jesus extended even to his prayers. And he converted the negative golden rule into a positive admonition of human fairness.

159:5.17 (1771.1) In all his teaching Jesus unfailingly avoided distracting details. He shunned flowery language and avoided the mere poetic imagery of a play upon words. He habitually put large meanings into small expressions. For purposes of illustration Jesus reversed the current meanings of many terms, such as salt, leaven, fishing, and little children. He most effectively employed the antithesis, comparing the minute to the infinite and so on. His pictures were striking, such as, "The blind leading the blind." But the greatest strength to be found in his illustrative teaching was its naturalness. Jesus brought the philosophy of religion from heaven down to earth. He portrayed the elemental needs of the soul with a new insight and a new bestowal of affection.

6   The Return to Magadan

159:6.1 (1771.2) The mission of four weeks in the Decapolis was moderately successful. Hundreds of souls were received into the kingdom, and the apostles and evangelists had a valuable experience in carrying on their work without the inspiration of the immediate personal presence of Jesus.

159:6.2 (1771.3) On Friday, September 16, the entire corps of workers assembled by prearrangement at Magadan Park. On the Sabbath day a council of more than one hundred believers was held at which the future plans for extending the work of the kingdom were fully considered. The messengers of David were present and made reports concerning the welfare of the believers throughout Judea, Samaria, Galilee, and adjoining districts.

159:6.3 (1771.4) Few of Jesus' followers at this time fully appreciated the great value of the services of the messenger corps. Not only did the messengers keep the believers throughout Palestine in touch with each other and with Jesus and the apostles, but during these dark days they also served as collectors of funds, not only for the sustenance of Jesus and his associates, but also for the support of the families of the twelve apostles and the twelve evangelists.

159:6.4 (1771.5) About this time Abner moved his base of operations from Hebron to Bethlehem, and this latter place was also the headquarters in Judea for David's messengers. David maintained an overnight relay messenger service between Jerusalem and Bethsaida. These runners left Jerusalem each evening, relaying at Sychar and Scythopolis, arriving in Bethsaida by breakfast time the next morning.

159:6.5 (1771.6) Jesus and his associates now prepared to take a week's rest before they made ready to start upon the last epoch of their labors in behalf of the kingdom. This was their last rest, for the Perean mission developed into a campaign of preaching and teaching which extended right on down to the time of their arrival at Jerusalem and of the enactment of the closing episodes of Jesus' earth career.

Paper 160

Rodan of Alexandria

160:0.1 (1772.1) ON SUNDAY morning, September 18, Andrew announced that no work would be planned for the coming week. All of the apostles, except Nathaniel and Thomas, went home to visit their families or to sojourn with friends. This week Jesus enjoyed a period of almost complete rest, but Nathaniel and Thomas were very busy with their discussions with a certain Greek philosopher from Alexandria named Rodan. This Greek had recently become a disciple of Jesus through the teaching of one of Abner's associates who had conducted a mission at Alexandria. Rodan was now earnestly engaged in the task of harmonizing his philosophy of life with Jesus' new religious teachings, and he had come to Magadan hoping that the Master would talk these problems over with him. He also desired to secure a firsthand and authoritative version of the gospel from either Jesus or one of his apostles. Though the Master declined to enter into such a conference with Rodan, he did receive him graciously and immediately directed that Nathaniel and Thomas should listen to all he had to say and tell him about the gospel in return.

1 Rodan's Greek Philosophy

160:1.1 (1772.2) Early Monday morning, Rodan began a series of ten addresses to Nathaniel, Thomas, and a group of some two dozen believers who chanced to be at Magadan. These talks, condensed, combined, and restated in modern phraseology, present the following thoughts for consideration:

160:1.2 (1772.3) Human life consists in three great drives—urges, desires, and lures. Strong character, commanding personality, is only acquired by converting the natural urge of life into the social art of living, by transforming present desires into those higher longings which are capable of lasting attainment, while the commonplace lure of existence must be transferred from one's conventional and established ideas to the higher realms of unexplored ideas and undiscovered ideals.

160:1.3 (1772.4) The more complex civilization becomes, the more difficult will become the art of living. The more rapid the changes in social usage, the more complicated will become the task of character development. Every ten generations mankind must learn anew the art of living if progress is to continue. And if man becomes so ingenious that he more rapidly adds to the complexities of society, the art of living will need to be remastered in less time, perhaps every single generation. If the evolution of the art of living fails to keep pace with the technique of existence, humanity will quickly revert to the simple urge of living—the attainment of the satisfaction of present desires. Thus will humanity remain immature; society will fail in growing up to full maturity.

160:1.4 (1773.1) Social maturity is equivalent to the degree to which man is willing to surrender the gratification of mere transient and present desires for the entertainment of those superior longings the striving for whose attainment affords the more abundant satisfactions of progressive advancement toward permanent goals. But the true badge of social maturity is the willingness of a people to surrender the right to live peaceably and contentedly under the ease-promoting standards of the lure of established beliefs and conventional ideas for the disquieting and energy-requiring lure of the pursuit of the unexplored possibilities of the attainment of undiscovered goals of idealistic spiritual realities.

160:1.5 (1773.2) Animals respond nobly to the urge of life, but only man can attain the art of living, albeit the majority of mankind only experience the animal urge to live. Animals know only this blind and instinctive urge; man is capable of transcending this urge to natural function. Man may elect to live upon the high plane of intelligent art, even that of celestial joy and spiritual ecstasy. Animals make no inquiry into the purposes of life; therefore they never worry, neither do they commit suicide. Suicide among men testifies that such beings have emerged from the purely animal stage of existence, and to the further fact that the exploratory efforts of such human beings have failed to attain the artistic levels of mortal experience. Animals know not the meaning of life; man not only possesses capacity for the recognition of values and the comprehension of meanings, but he also is conscious of the meaning of meanings—he is self-conscious of insight.

160:1.6 (1773.3) When men dare to forsake a life of natural craving for one of adventurous art and uncertain logic, they must expect to suffer the consequent hazards of emotional casualties—conflicts, unhappiness, and uncertainties—at least until the time of their attainment of some degree of intellectual and emotional maturity. Discouragement, worry, and indolence are positive evidence of moral immaturity. Human society is confronted with two problems: attainment of the maturity of the individual and attainment of the maturity of the race. The mature human being soon begins to look upon all other mortals with feelings of tenderness and with emotions of tolerance. Mature men view immature folks with the love and consideration that parents bear their children.

160:1.7 (1773.4) Successful living is nothing more or less than the art of the mastery of dependable techniques for solving common problems. The first step in the solution of any problem is to locate the difficulty, to isolate the problem, and frankly to recognize its nature and gravity. The great mistake is that, when life problems excite our profound fears, we refuse to recognize them. Likewise, when the acknowledgment of our difficulties entails the reduction of our long- cherished conceit, the admission of envy, or the abandonment of deep-seated prejudices, the average person prefers to cling to the old illusions of safety and to the long-cherished false feelings of security. Only a brave person is willing honestly to admit, and fearlessly to face, what a sincere and logical mind discovers.

160:1.8 (1773.5) The wise and effective solution of any problem demands that the mind shall be free from bias, passion, and all other purely personal prejudices which might interfere with the disinterested survey of the actual factors that go to make up the problem presenting itself for solution. The solution of life problems requires courage and sincerity. Only honest and brave individuals are able to follow valiantly through the perplexing and confusing maze of living to where the logic of a fearless mind may lead. And this emancipation of the mind and soul can never be effected without the driving power of an intelligent enthusiasm which borders on religious zeal. It requires the lure of a great ideal to drive man on in the pursuit of a goal which is beset with difficult material problems and manifold intellectual hazards.

160:1.9 (1774.1) Even though you are effectively armed to meet the difficult situations of life, you can hardly expect success unless you are equipped with that wisdom of mind and charm of personality which enable you to win the hearty support and co-operation of your fellows. You cannot hope for a large measure of success in either secular or religious work unless you can learn how to persuade your fellows, to prevail with men. You simply must have tact and tolerance.

160:1.10 (1774.2) But the greatest of all methods of problem solving I have learned from Jesus, your Master. I refer to that which he so consistently practices, and which he has so faithfully taught you, the isolation of worshipful meditation. In this habit of Jesus' going off so frequently by himself to commune with the Father in heaven is to be found the technique, not only of gathering strength and wisdom for the ordinary conflicts of living, but also of appropriating the energy for the solution of the higher problems of a moral and spiritual nature. But even correct methods of solving problems will not compensate for inherent defects of personality or atone for the absence of the hunger and thirst for true righteousness.

160:1.11 (1774.3) I am deeply impressed with the custom of Jesus in going apart by himself to engage in these seasons of solitary survey of the problems of living; to seek for new stores of wisdom and energy for meeting the manifold demands of social service; to quicken and deepen the supreme purpose of living by actually subjecting the total personality to the consciousness of contacting with divinity; to grasp for possession of new and better methods of adjusting oneself to the ever-changing situations of living existence; to effect those vital reconstructions and readjustments of one's personal attitudes which are so essential to enhanced insight into everything worth while and real; and to do all of this with an eye single to the glory of God—to breathe in sincerity your Master's favorite prayer, "Not my will, but yours, be done."

160:1.12 (1774.4) This worshipful practice of your Master brings that relaxation which renews the mind; that illumination which inspires the soul; that courage which enables one bravely to face one's problems; that self-understanding which obliterates debilitating fear; and that consciousness of union with divinity which equips man with the assurance that

enables him to dare to be Godlike. The relaxation of worship, or spiritual communion as practiced by the Master, relieves tension, removes conflicts, and mightily augments the total resources of the personality. And all this philosophy, plus the gospel of the kingdom, constitutes the new religion as I understand it.

160:1.13 (1774.5) Prejudice blinds the soul to the recognition of truth, and prejudice can be removed only by the sincere devotion of the soul to the adoration of a cause that is all-embracing and all-inclusive of one's fellow men. Prejudice is inseparably linked to selfishness. Prejudice can be eliminated only by the abandonment of self-seeking and by substituting therefor the quest of the satisfaction of the service of a cause that is not only greater than self, but one that is even greater than all humanity—the search for God, the attainment of divinity. The evidence of maturity of personality consists in the transformation of human desire so that it constantly seeks for the realization of those values which are highest and most divinely real.

160:1.14 (1774.6) In a continually

changing world, in the midst of an evolving social order, it is impossible to maintain settled and established goals of destiny. Stability of personality can be experienced only by those who have discovered and embraced the living God as the eternal goal of infinite attainment. And thus to transfer one's goal from time to eternity, from earth to Paradise, from the human to the divine, requires that man shall become regenerated, converted, be born again; that he shall become the re-created child of the divine spirit; that he shall gain entrance into the brotherhood of the kingdom of heaven. All philosophies and religions which fall short of these ideals are immature. The philosophy which I teach, linked with the gospel which you preach, represents the new religion of maturity, the ideal of all future generations. And this is true because our ideal is final, infallible, eternal, universal, absolute, and infinite.

160:1.15 (1775.1) My philosophy gave me the urge to search for the realities of true attainment, the goal of maturity. But my urge was impotent; my search lacked driving power; my quest suffered from the absence of certainty of directionization. And these deficiencies have been abundantly supplied by this new gospel of Jesus, with its enhancement of insights, elevation of ideals, and settledness of goals. Without doubts and misgivings I can now whole-heartedly enter upon the eternal venture.

2   The Art of Living

160:2.1 (1775.2) There are just two ways in which mortals may live together: the material or animal way and the spiritual or human way. By the use of signals and sounds animals are able to communicate with each other in a limited way. But such forms of communication do not convey meanings, values, or ideas. The one distinction between man and the animal is that man can communicate with his fellows by means of symbols which most certainly designate and identify meanings, values, ideas, and even ideals.

160:2.2 (1775.3) Since animals cannot communicate ideas to each other, they cannot develop personality. Man develops personality because he can thus communicate with his fellows concerning both ideas and ideals.

160:2.3 (1775.4) It is this ability to communicate and share meanings that constitutes human culture and enables man, through social associations, to build civilizations. Knowledge and wisdom become cumulative because of man's ability to communicate these possessions to succeeding generations. And thereby arise the cultural activities of the race: art, science, religion, and philosophy.

160:2.4 (1775.5) Symbolic communication between human beings predetermines the bringing into existence of social groups. The most effective of all social groups is the family, more particularly the two parents. Personal affection is the spiritual bond which holds together these material associations. Such an effective relationship is also possible between two persons of the same sex, as is so abundantly illustrated in the devotions of genuine friendships.

160:2.5 (1775.6) These associations of friendship and mutual affection are socializing and ennobling because they encourage and facilitate the following essential factors of the higher levels of the art of living:

160:2.6 (1775.7) 1. Mutual self-expression and self-understanding. Many noble human impulses die because there is no one to hear their expression. Truly, it is not good for man to be alone. Some degree of recognition and a certain amount of appreciation are essential to the development of human character. Without the genuine love of a home, no child can achieve the full development of normal character. Character is something more than mere mind and morals. Of all social relations calculated to develop character, the most effective and ideal is the affectionate and understanding friendship of man and woman in the mutual embrace of intelligent wedlock. Marriage, with its manifold relations, is best designed to draw forth those precious impulses and those higher motives which are indispensable to the development of a strong character. I do not hesitate thus to glorify family life, for your Master has wisely chosen the father- child relationship as the very cornerstone of this new gospel of the kingdom. And such a matchless community of relationship, man and woman in the fond embrace of the highest ideals of time, is so valuable and satisfying an experience that it is worth any price, any sacrifice, requisite for its possession.

160:2.7 (1776.1) 2. Union of souls—the mobilization of wisdom. Every human being sooner or later acquires a certain concept of this world and a certain vision of the next. Now it is possible, through personality association, to unite these views of temporal existence and eternal prospects. Thus does the mind of one augment its spiritual values by gaining much of the insight of the other. In this way men enrich the soul by pooling their respective spiritual possessions. Likewise, in this same way, man is enabled to avoid that ever-present tendency to fall victim to distortion of vision, prejudice of viewpoint, and narrowness of judgment. Fear, envy, and conceit can be prevented only by intimate contact with other minds. I call your attention to the fact that the Master never sends you out alone to labor for the extension of the kingdom; he always sends you out two and two. And since wisdom is super knowledge, it follows that, in the union of wisdom, the social group, small or large, mutually shares all knowledge.

160:2.8 (1776.2) 3. The enthusiasm for living. Isolation tends to exhaust the energy charge of the soul. Association with one's fellows is essential to the renewal of the zest for life and is indispensable to the maintenance of the courage to fight those battles consequent upon the ascent to the higher levels of human living. Friendship enhances the joys and glorifies the triumphs of life. Loving and intimate human associations tend to rob suffering of its sorrow and hardship of much of its bitterness. The presence of a friend enhances all beauty and exalts every goodness. By intelligent symbols man is able to quicken and enlarge the appreciative capacities of his friends. One of the crowning glories of human friendship is this power and possibility of the mutual stimulation of the imagination. Great spiritual power is inherent in the consciousness of wholehearted devotion to a common cause, mutual loyalty to a cosmic Deity.

160:2.9 (1776.3) 4. The enhanced defense against all evil. Personality association and mutual affection is an efficient insurance against evil. Difficulties, sorrow, disappointment, and defeat are more painful and disheartening when borne alone. Association does not transmute evil into righteousness, but it does aid in greatly lessening the sting. Said your Master, "Happy are they who mourn"—if a friend is at hand to comfort. There is positive strength in the knowledge that you live for the welfare of others, and that these others likewise live for your welfare and advancement. Man languishes in isolation. Human beings unfailingly become discouraged when they view only the transitory transactions of time. The present, when divorced from the past and the future, becomes exasperatingly trivial. Only a glimpse of the circle of eternity can inspire man to do his best and can challenge the best in him to do its utmost. And when man is thus at his best, he lives most unselfishly for the good of others, his fellow sojourners in time and eternity.

160:2.10 (1777.1) I repeat, such inspiring and ennobling association finds its ideal possibilities in the human marriage relation. True, much is attained out of marriage, and many, many marriages utterly fail to produce these moral and spiritual fruits. Too many times marriage is entered by those who seek other values which are lower than these superior accompaniments of human maturity. Ideal marriage must be founded on something more stable than the fluctuations of sentiment and the fickleness of mere sex attraction; it must be based on genuine and mutual personal devotion. And thus, if you can build up such trustworthy and effective small units of human association, when these are assembled in the aggregate, the world will behold a great and glorified social structure, the civilization of mortal maturity. Such a race might begin to realize something of your Master's ideal of "peace on earth and good will among men." While such a society would not be perfect or entirely free from evil, it would at least approach the stabilization of maturity.

3   *The Lures of Maturity*

160:3.1 (1777.2) The effort toward maturity necessitates work, and work requires energy. Whence the power to accomplish all this? The physical things can be taken for granted, but the Master has well said, "Man cannot live by bread alone." Granted the possession of a normal body and reasonably good health, we must next look for those lures which will act as a stimulus to call forth man's slumbering spiritual forces. Jesus has taught us that God lives in man; then how can we induce man to release these soul-bound powers of divinity and infinity? How shall we induce men to let go of God that he may spring forth to the refreshment of our own souls while in transit outward and then to serve the purpose of enlightening, uplifting, and blessing countless other souls? How best can I awaken these latent powers for good which lie dormant in your souls? One thing I am sure of: Emotional excitement is not the ideal spiritual stimulus. Excitement does not augment energy; it rather exhausts the powers of both mind and body. Whence then comes the energy to do these great things? Look to your Master. Even now he is out in the hills taking in power while we are here giving out energy. The secret of all this problem is wrapped up in spiritual communion, in worship. From the human standpoint it is a question of combined meditation and relaxation. Meditation makes the contact of mind with spirit; relaxation determines the capacity for spiritual receptivity. And this interchange of strength for weakness, courage for fear, the will of God for the mind of self, constitutes worship. At least, that is the way the philosopher views it.

160:3.2 (1777.3) When these experiences are frequently repeated, they crystallize into habits, strength-giving and worshipful habits, and such habits eventually formulate themselves into a spiritual character, and such a character is finally recognized by one's fellows as a mature personality. These practices are difficult and time-consuming at first, but when they become habitual, they are at once restful and timesaving. The more complex society becomes, and the more the lures of civilization multiply, the more urgent will become the necessity for God-knowing individuals to form such protective habitual practices designed to conserve and augment their spiritual energies. *

160:3.3 (1778.1) Another requirement for the attainment of maturity is the cooperative adjustment of social groups to an ever-changing environment. The immature individual arouses the antagonisms of his fellows; the mature man wins the hearty co-operation of his associates, thereby many times multiplying the fruits of his life efforts.

160:3.4 (1778.2) My philosophy tells me that there are times when I must fight, if need be, for the defense of my concept of righteousness, but I doubt not that the Master, with a more mature type of personality, would easily and gracefully gain an equal victory by his superior and winsome technique of tact and tolerance. All too often, when we battle for the right, it turns out that both the victor and the vanquished have sustained defeat. I heard the Master say only yesterday that the "wise man, when seeking entrance through the locked door, would not destroy the door but rather would seek for the key wherewith to unlock it." Too often we engage in a fight merely to convince ourselves that we are not afraid.

160:3.5 (1778.3) This new gospel of the kingdom renders a great service to the art of living in that it supplies a new and richer incentive for higher living. It presents a new and exalted goal of destiny, a supreme life purpose. And these new concepts of the eternal and divine goal of existence are in themselves transcendent stimuli, calling forth the reaction of the very best that is resident in man's higher nature. On every mountaintop of intellectual thought are to be found relaxation for the mind, strength for the soul, and communion for the spirit. From such vantage points of high living, man is able to transcend the material irritations of the lower levels of thinking—worry, jealousy, envy, revenge, and the pride of immature personality. These high-climbing souls deliver themselves from a multitude of the crosscurrent conflicts of the trifles of living, thus becoming free to attain consciousness of the higher currents of spirit concept and celestial communication. But the life purpose must be jealously guarded from the temptation to seek for easy and transient attainment; likewise must it be so fostered as to become immune to the disastrous threats of fanaticism.

4   The Balance of Maturity

160:4.1 (1778.4) While you have an eye single to the attainment of eternal realities, you must also make provision for the necessities of temporal living. While the spirit is our goal, the flesh is a fact. Occasionally the necessities of living may fall into our hands by accident, but in general, we must intelligently work for them. The two major problems of life are: making a temporal living and the achievement of eternal survival. And even the problem of making a living requires religion for its ideal solution. These are both highly personal problems. True religion, in fact, does not function apart from the individual.

160:4.2 (1778.5) The essentials of the temporal life, as I see them, are:

160:4.3 (1778.6) 1. Good physical health.

160:4.4 (1778.7) 2. Clear and clean thinking.

160:4.5 (1778.8) 3. Ability and skill.

160:4.6 (1778.9) 4. Wealth—the goods of life.

160:4.7 (1778.10) 5. Ability to withstand defeat.

160:4.8 (1778.11) 6. Culture—education and wisdom.

160:4.9 (1779.1) Even the physical problems of bodily health and efficiency are best solved when they are viewed from the religious standpoint of our Master's teaching: That the body and mind of man are the dwelling place of the gift of the Gods, the spirit of God becoming the spirit of man. The mind of man thus becomes the mediator between material things and spiritual realities.

160:4.10 (1779.2) It requires intelligence to secure one's share of the desirable things of life. It is wholly erroneous to suppose that faithfulness in doing one's daily work will insure the rewards of wealth. Barring the occasional and accidental acquirement of wealth, the material rewards of the temporal life are found to flow in certain well-organized channels, and only those who have access to these channels may expect to be well rewarded for their temporal efforts. Poverty must ever be the lot of all men who seek for wealth in isolated and individual channels. Wise planning, therefore, becomes the one thing essential to worldly prosperity. Success requires not only devotion to one's work but also that one should function as a part of some one of the channels of material wealth. If you are unwise, you can bestow a devoted life upon your generation without material reward; if you are an accidental beneficiary of the flow of wealth, you may roll in luxury even though you have done nothing worth while for your fellow men.

160:4.11 (1779.3) Ability is that which you inherit, while skill is what you acquire. Life is not real to one who cannot do some one thing well, expertly. Skill is one of the real sources of the satisfaction of living. Ability implies the gift of foresight, farseeing vision. Be not deceived by the tempting rewards of dishonest achievement; be willing to toil for the later returns inherent in honest endeavor. The wise man is able to distinguish between means and ends; otherwise, sometimes over planning for the future defeats its own high purpose. As a pleasure seeker you should aim always to be a producer as well as a consumer.

160:4.12 (1779.4) Train your memory to hold in sacred trust the strength-giving and worth-while episodes of life, which you can recall at will for your pleasure and edification. Thus build up for yourself and in yourself reserve galleries of beauty, goodness, and artistic grandeur. But the noblest of all memories are the treasured recollections of the great moments of a superb friendship. And all of these memory treasures radiate their most precious and exalting influences under the releasing touch of spiritual worship.

160:4.13 (1779.5) But life will become a burden of existence unless you learn how to fail gracefully. There is an art in defeat which noble souls always acquire; you must know how to lose cheerfully; you must be fearless of disappointment. Never hesitate to admit failure. Make no attempt to hide failure under deceptive smiles and beaming optimism. It sounds well always to claim success, but the end results are appalling. Such a technique leads directly to the creation of a world of unreality and to the inevitable crash of ultimate disillusionment.

160:4.14 (1779.6) Success may generate courage and promote confidence, but wisdom comes only from the experiences of adjustment to the results of one's failures. Men who prefer optimistic illusions to reality can never become wise. Only those who face facts and adjust them to ideals can achieve wisdom. Wisdom embraces both the fact and the ideal and therefore saves its devotees from both of those barren extremes of philosophy—the man whose idealism excludes facts and the materialist who is devoid of spiritual outlook. Those timid souls who can only

keep up the struggle of life by the aid of continuous false illusions of success are doomed to suffer failure and experience defeat as they ultimately awaken from the dream world of their own imaginations.

160:4.15 (1780.1) And it is in this business of facing failure and adjusting to defeat that the far-reaching vision of religion exerts its supreme influence. Failure is simply an educational episode—a cultural experiment in the acquirement of wisdom—in the experience of the God-seeking man who has embarked on the eternal adventure of the exploration of a universe. To such men defeat is but a new tool for the achievement of higher levels of universe reality.

160:4.16 (1780.2) The career of a God-seeking man may prove to be a great success in the light of eternity, even though the whole temporal-life enterprise may appear as an overwhelming failure, provided each life failure yielded the culture of wisdom and spirit achievement. Do not make the mistake of confusing knowledge, culture, and wisdom. They are related in life, but they represent vastly differing spirit values; wisdom ever dominates knowledge and always glorifies culture.

5   The Religion of the Ideal

160:5.1 (1780.3) You have told me that your Master regards genuine human religion as the individual's experience with spiritual realities. I have regarded religion as man's experience of reacting to something which he regards as being worthy of the homage and devotion of all mankind. In this sense, religion symbolizes our supreme devotion to that which represents our highest concept of the ideals of reality and the farthest reach of our minds toward eternal possibilities of spiritual attainment.

160:5.2 (1780.4) When men react to religion in the tribal, national, or racial sense, it is because they look upon those without their group as not being truly human. We always look upon the object of our religious loyalty as being worthy of the reverence of all men. Religion can never be a matter of mere intellectual belief or philosophic reasoning; religion is always and forever a mode of reacting to the situations of life; it is a species of conduct. Religion embraces thinking, feeling, and acting reverently toward some reality which we deem worthy of universal adoration.

160:5.3 (1780.5) If something has become a religion in your experience, it is self-evident that you already have become an active evangel of that religion since you deem the supreme concept of your religion as being worthy of the worship of all mankind, all universe intelligences. If you are not a positive and missionary evangel of your religion, you are self- deceived in that what you call a religion is only a traditional belief or a mere system of intellectual philosophy. If your religion is a spiritual experience, your object of worship must be the universal spirit reality and ideal of all your spiritualized concepts. All religions based on fear, emotion, tradition, and philosophy I term the intellectual religions, while those based on true spirit experience I would term the true religions. The object of religious devotion may be material or spiritual, true or false, real or unreal, human or divine. Religions can therefore be either good or evil.

160:5.4 (1780.6) Morality and religion are not necessarily the same. A system of morals, by grasping an object of worship, may become a religion. A religion, by losing its universal appeal to loyalty and supreme devotion, may evolve into a system of philosophy or a code of morals. This thing, being, state, or order of existence, or possibility of attainment which constitutes the supreme ideal of religious loyalty, and which is the recipient of the religious devotion of those who worship, is God. Regardless of the name applied to this ideal of spirit reality, it is God.

160:5.5 (1781.1) The social characteristics of a true religion consist in the fact that it invariably seeks to convert the indi- vidual and to transform the world. Religion implies the existence of undiscovered ideals which far transcend the known standards of ethics and morality embodied in even the highest social usages of the most mature institutions of civilization. Religion reaches out for undiscovered ideals, unexplored realities, superhuman values, divine wisdom, and true spirit attainment. True religion does all of this; all other beliefs are not worthy of the name. You cannot have a genuine spiritual religion without the supreme and supernal ideal of an eternal God. A religion without this God is an invention of man, a human institution of lifeless intellectual beliefs and meaningless emotional ceremonies. A religion might claim as the object of its devotion a great ideal. But such ideals of unreality are not attainable; such a concept is illusionary. The only ideals susceptible of human attainment are the divine realities of the infinite values resident in the spiritual fact of the eternal God.

160:5.6 (1781.2) The word God, the idea of God as contrasted with the ideal of God, can become a part of any religion, no matter how puerile or false that religion may chance to be. And this idea of God can become anything which those who entertain it may choose to make it. The lower religions shape their ideas of God to meet the natural state of the human heart; the higher religions demand that the human heart shall be changed to meet the demands of the ideals of true religion.

160:5.7 (1781.3) The religion of Jesus transcends all our former concepts of the idea of worship in that he not only portrays his Father as the ideal of infinite reality but positively declares that this divine source of values and the eternal center of the universe is truly and personally attainable by every mortal creature who chooses to enter the kingdom of heaven on earth, thereby acknowledging the acceptance of sonship with God and brotherhood with man. That, I submit, is the highest concept of religion the world has ever known, and I pronounce that there can never be a higher since this gospel embraces the infinity of realities, the divinity of values, and the eternity of universal attainments. Such a concept constitutes the achievement of the experience of the idealism of the supreme and the ultimate.

160:5.8 (1781.4) I am not only intrigued by the consummate ideals of this religion of your Master, but I am mightily moved to profess my belief in his announcement that these ideals of spirit realities are attainable; that you and I can enter upon this long and eternal adventure with his assurance of the certainty of our ultimate arrival at the portals of Paradise. My brethren, I am a believer, I have embarked; I am on my way with you in this eternal venture. The Master says he came from the Father, and that he will show us the way. I am fully persuaded he speaks the truth. I am finally convinced that there are no attainable ideals of reality or values of perfection apart from the eternal and Universal Father.

160:5.9 (1781.5) I come, then, to worship, not merely the God of existences, but the God of the possibility of all future existences. Therefore must your devotion to a supreme ideal, if that ideal is real, be devotion to this God of past, present, and future universes of things and beings. And there is no other God, for there cannot possibly be any other God. All other gods are figments of the imagination, illusions of mortal mind, distortions of false logic, and the self- deceptive idols of those who create them. Yes, you can have a religion without this God, but it does not mean anything. And if you seek to substitute the word God for the reality of this ideal of the living God, you have only deluded yourself by putting an idea in the place of an ideal, a divine reality. Such beliefs are merely religions of wishful fancy.

160:5.10 (1782.1) I see in the teachings of Jesus, religion at its best. This gospel enables us to seek for the true God and to find him. But are we willing to pay the price of this entrance into the kingdom of heaven? Are we willing to be born again? to be remade? Are we willing to be subject to this terrible and testing process of self-destruction and soul reconstruction? Has not the Master said: "Whoso would save his life must lose it. Think not that I have come to bring peace but rather a soul struggle"? True, after we pay the price of dedication to the Father's will, we do experience great peace provided we continue to walk in these spiritual paths of consecrated living.

160:5.11 (1782.2) Now are we truly forsaking the lures of the known order of existence while we unreservedly dedicate our quest to the lures of the unknown and unexplored order of the existence of a future life of adventure in the spirit worlds of the higher idealism of divine reality. And we seek for those symbols of meaning wherewith to convey to our fellow men these concepts of the reality of the idealism of the religion of Jesus, and we will not cease to pray for that day when all mankind shall be thrilled by the communal vision of this supreme truth. Just now, our focalized concept of the Father, as held in our hearts, is that God is spirit; as conveyed to our fellows, that God is love.

160:5.12 (1782.3) The religion of Jesus demands living and spiritual experience. Other religions may consist in traditional beliefs, emotional feelings, philosophic consciousness, and all of that, but the teaching of the Master requires the attainment of actual levels of real spirit progression.

160:5.13 (1782.4) The consciousness of the impulse to be like God is not true religion. The feelings of the emotion to worship God are not true religion. The knowledge of the conviction to forsake self and serve God is not true religion. The wisdom of the reasoning that this religion is the best of all is not religion as a personal and spiritual experience. True religion has reference to destiny and reality of attainment as well as to the reality and idealism of that which is wholeheartedly faith-accepted. And all of this must be made personal to us by the revelation of the Spirit of Truth.

160:5.14 (1782.5) And thus ended the dissertations of the Greek philosopher, one of the greatest of his race, who had become a believer in the gospel of Jesus.

Paper 161

Further Discussions with Rodan

161:0.1 (1783.1) ON SUNDAY, September 25, A.D. 29, the apostles and the evangelists assembled at Magadan. After a long conference that evening with his associates, Jesus surprised all by announcing that early the next day he and the twelve apostles would start for Jerusalem to attend the feast of tabernacles. He directed that the evangelists visit the believers in Galilee, and that the women's corps return for a while to Bethsaida.

161:0.2 (1783.2) When the hour came to leave for Jerusalem, Nathaniel and Thomas were still in the midst of their discussions with Rodan of Alexandria, and they secured the Master's permission to remain at Magadan for a few days. And so, while Jesus and the ten were on their way to Jerusalem, Nathaniel and Thomas were engaged in earnest debate with Rodan. The week prior, in which Rodan had expounded his philosophy, Thomas and Nathaniel had alternated in presenting the gospel of the kingdom to the Greek philosopher. Rodan discovered that he had been well instructed in Jesus' teachings by one of the former apostles of John the Baptist who had been his teacher at Alexandria.

1   The Personality of God

161:1.1 (1783.3) There was one matter on which Rodan and the two apostles did not see alike, and that was the personality of God. Rodan readily accepted all that was presented to him regarding the attributes of God, but he contended that the Father in heaven is not, cannot be, a person as man conceives personality. While the apostles found themselves in difficulty trying to prove that God is a person, Rodan found it still more difficult to prove he is not a person.

161:1.2 (1783.4) Rodan contended that the fact of personality consists in the coexistent fact of full and mutual communication between beings of equality, beings who are capable of sympathetic understanding. Said Rodan: "In order to be a person, God must have symbols of spirit communication which would enable him to become fully understood by those who make contact with him. But since God is infinite and eternal, the Creator of all other beings, it follows that, as regards beings of equality, God is alone in the universe. There are none equal to him; there are none with whom he can communicate as an equal. God indeed may be the source of all personality, but as such he is transcendent to personality, even as the Creator is above and beyond the creature."

161:1.3 (1783.5) This contention greatly troubled Thomas and Nathaniel, and they had asked Jesus to come to their rescue, but the Master refused to enter into their discussions. He did say to Thomas: "It matters little what idea of the Father you may entertain as long as you are spiritually acquainted with the ideal of his infinite and eternal nature."

161:1.4 (1784.1) Thomas contended that God does communicate with man, and therefore that the Father is a person, even within the definition of Rodan. This the Greek rejected on the ground that God does not reveal himself personally; that he is still a mystery. Then Nathaniel appealed to his own personal experience with God, and that Rodan allowed, affirming that he had recently had similar experiences, but these experiences, he contended, proved only the reality of God, not his personality.

161:1.5 (1784.2) By Monday night Thomas gave up. But by Tuesday night Nathaniel had won Rodan to believe in the personality of the Father, and he effected this change in the Greek's views by the following steps of reasoning:

161:1.6 (1784.3) 1. The Father in Paradise does enjoy equality of communication with at least two other beings who are fully equal to himself and wholly like himself—the Eternal Son and the Infinite Spirit. In view of the doctrine of the Trinity, the Greek was compelled to concede the personality possibility of the Universal Father. (It was the later consideration of these discussions which led to the enlarged conception of the Trinity in the minds of the twelve apostles. Of course, it was the general belief that Jesus was the Eternal Son.)

161:1.7 (1784.4) 2. Since Jesus was equal with the Father, and since this Son had achieved the manifestation of personality to his earth children, such a phenomenon constituted proof of the fact, and demonstration of the possibility, of the possession of personality by all three of the Godheads and forever settled the question regarding the ability of God to communicate with man and the possibility of man's communicating with God.

161:1.8 (1784.5) 3. That Jesus was on terms of mutual association and perfect communication with man; that Jesus was the Son of God. That the relation of Son and Father presupposes equality of communication and mutuality of sympathetic understanding; that Jesus and the Father were one. That Jesus maintained at one and the same time understanding communication with both God and man, and that, since both God and man comprehended the meaning of the symbols of Jesus' communication, both God and man possessed the attributes of personality in so far as the requirements of the ability of intercommunication were concerned. That the personality of Jesus demonstrated the personality of God, while it proved conclusively the presence of God in man. That two things which are related to the same thing are related to each other.

161:1.9 (1784.6) 4. That personality represents man's highest concept of human reality and divine values; that God also represents man's highest concept of divine reality and infinite values; therefore, that God must be a divine and infinite personality, a personality in reality although infinitely and eternally transcending man's concept and definition of personality, but nevertheless always and universally a personality.

161:1.10 (1784.7) 5. That God must be a personality since he is the Creator of all personality and the destiny of all personality. Rodan had been tremendously influenced by the teaching of Jesus, "Be you therefore perfect, even as your Father in heaven is perfect."

161:1.11 (1784.8) When Rodan heard these arguments, he said: "I am convinced. I will confess God as a person if you will permit me to qualify my confession of such a belief by attaching to the meaning of personality a group of extended values, such as superhuman, transcendent, supreme, infinite, eternal, final, and universal. I am now convinced that, while God must be infinitely more than a personality, he cannot be anything less. I am satisfied to end the argument and to accept Jesus as the personal revelation of the Father and the satisfaction of all unsatisfied factors in logic, reason, and philosophy."

2   The Divine Nature of Jesus

161:2.1 (1785.1) Since Nathaniel and Thomas had so fully approved Rodan's views of the gospel of the kingdom, there remained only one more point to consider, the teaching dealing with the divine nature of Jesus, a doctrine only so recently publicly announced. Nathaniel and Thomas jointly presented their views of the divine nature of the Master, and the following narrative is a condensed, rearranged, and restated presentation of their teaching:

161:2.2 (1785.2) 1. Jesus has admitted his divinity, and we believe him. Many remarkable things have happened in connection with his ministry which we can understand only by believing that he is the Son of God as well as the Son of Man.

161:2.3 (1785.3) 2. His life association with us exemplifies the ideal of human friendship; only a divine being could possibly be such a human friend. He is the most truly unselfish person we have ever known. He is the friend even of sinners; he dares to love his enemies. He is very loyal to us. While he does not hesitate to reprove us, it is plain to all that he truly loves us. The better you know him, the more you will love him.

You will be charmed by his unswerving devotion. Through all these years of our failure to comprehend his mission, he has been a faithful friend. While he makes no use of flattery, he does treat us all with equal kindness; he is invariably tender and compassionate. He has shared his life and everything else with us. We are a happy community; we share all things in common. We do not believe that a mere human could live such a blameless life under such trying circumstances.

161:2.4 (1785.4) 3. We think Jesus is divine because he never does wrong; he makes no mistakes. His wisdom is extraordinary; his piety superb. He lives day by day in perfect accord with the Father's will. He never repents of misdeeds because he transgresses none of the Father's laws. He prays for us and with us, but he never asks us to pray for him. We believe that he is consistently sinless. We do not think that one who is only human ever professed to live such a life. He claims to live a perfect life, and we acknowledge that he does. Our piety springs from repentance, but his piety springs from righteousness. He even professes to forgive sins and does heal diseases. No mere man would sanely profess to forgive sin; that is a divine prerogative. And he has seemed to be thus perfect in his righteousness from the times of our first contact with him. We grow in grace and in the knowledge of the truth, but our Master exhibits maturity of righteousness to start with. All men, good and evil, recognize these elements of goodness in Jesus. And yet never is his piety obtrusive or ostentatious. He is both meek and fearless. He seems to approve of our belief in his divinity. He is either what he professes to be, or else he is the greatest hypocrite and fraud the world has ever known. We are persuaded that he is just what he claims to be.

161:2.5 (1785.5) 4. The uniqueness of his character and the perfection of his emotional control convince us that he is a combination of humanity and divinity. He unfailingly responds to the spectacle of human need; suffering never fails to appeal to him. His compassion is moved alike by physical suffering, mental anguish, or spiritual sorrow. He is quick to recognize and generous to acknowledge the presence of faith or any other grace in his fellow men. He is so just and fair and at the same time so merciful and considerate. He grieves over the spiritual obstinacy of the people and rejoices when they consent to see the light of truth.

161:2.6 (1786.1) 5. He seems to know the thoughts of men's minds and to understand the longings of their hearts. And he is always sympathetic with our troubled spirits. He seems to possess all our human emotions, but they are magnificently glorified. He strongly loves goodness and equally hates sin. He possesses a superhuman consciousness of the presence of Deity. He prays like a man but performs like a God. He seems to foreknow things; he even now dares to speak about his death, some mystic reference to his future glorification. While he is kind, he is also brave and courageous. He never falters in doing his duty.

161:2.7 (1786.2) 6. We are constantly impressed by the phenomenon of his superhuman knowledge. Hardly does a day pass but something transpires to disclose that the Master knows what is going on away from his immediate presence. He also seems to know about the thoughts of his associates. He undoubtedly has communion with celestial personalities; he unquestionably lives on a spiritual plane far above the rest of us. Everything seems to be open to his unique understanding.

He asks us questions to draw us out, not to gain information.

161:2.8 (1786.3) 7. Recently the Master does not hesitate to assert his super-humanity. From the day of our ordination as apostles right on down to recent times, he has never denied that he came from the Father above. He speaks with the authority of a divine teacher. The Master does not hesitate to refute the religious teachings of today and to declare the new gospel with positive authority. He is assertive, positive, and authoritative. Even John the Baptist, when he heard Jesus speak, declared that he was the Son of God. He seems to be so sufficient within himself. He craves not the support of the multitude; he is indifferent to the opinions of men. He is brave and yet so free from pride.

161:2.9 (1786.4) 8. He constantly talks about God as an ever-present associate in all that he does. He goes about doing good, for God seems to be in him. He makes the most astounding assertions about himself and his mission on earth, statements which would be absurd if he were not divine. He once declared, "Before Abraham was, I am." He has definitely claimed divinity; he professes to be in partnership with God. He well-nigh exhausts the possibilities of language in the reiteration of his claims of intimate association with the heavenly Father. He even dares to assert that he and the Father are one. He says that anyone who has

seen him has seen the Father. And he says and does all these tremendous things with such childlike naturalness. He alludes to his association with the Father in the same manner that he refers to his association with us. He seems to be so sure about God and speaks of these relations in such a matter-of-fact way. *

161:2.10 (1786.5) 9. In his prayer life he appears to communicate directly with his Father. We have heard few of his prayers, but these few would indicate that he talks with God, as it were, face to face. He seems to know the future as well as the past. He simply could not be all of this and do all of these extraordinary things unless he were something more than human. We know he is human, we are sure of that, but we are almost equally sure that he is also divine. We believe that he is divine. We are convinced that he is the Son of Man and the Son of God.

161:2.11 (1787.1) When Nathaniel and Thomas had concluded their conferences with Rodan, they hurried on toward Jerusalem to join their fellow apostles, arriving on Friday of that week. This had been a great experience in the lives of all three of these believers, and the other apostles learned much from the recounting of these experiences by Nathaniel and Thomas.

161:2.12 (1787.2) Rodan made his way back to Alexandria, where he long taught his philosophy in the school of Meganta. He became a mighty man in the later affairs of the kingdom of heaven; he was a faithful believer to the end of his earth days, yielding up his life in Greece with others when the persecutions were at their height.

3　　*Jesus' Human and Divine Minds*

161:3.1 (1787.3) Consciousness of divinity was a gradual growth in the mind of Jesus up to the occasion of his baptism. After he became fully self-conscious of his divine nature, prehuman existence, and universe prerogatives, he seems to have possessed the power of variously limiting his human consciousness of his divinity. It appears to us that from his baptism until the crucifixion it was entirely optional with Jesus whether to depend only on the human mind or to utilize the knowledge of both the human and the divine minds. At times he appeared to avail himself of only that information which was resident in the human intellect. On other occasions he appeared to act with such full-ness of knowledge and wisdom as could be afforded only by the utilization of the superhuman content of his divine consciousness.

161:3.2 (1787.4) We can understand his unique performances only by accepting the theory that he could, at will, self-limit his divinity consciousness. We are fully cognizant that he frequently withheld from his associates his foreknowledge of events, and that he was aware of the nature of their thinking and planning. We understand that he did not wish his followers to know too fully that he was able to discern their thoughts and to penetrate their plans. He did not desire too far to transcend the concept of the human as it was held in the minds of his apostles and disciples.

161:3.3 (1787.5) We are utterly at a loss to differentiate between his practice of self-limiting his divine consciousness and his technique of concealing his preknowledge and thought discernment from his human associates. We are convinced that he used both of these techniques, but we are not always able, in a given instance, to specify which method he may have employed. We frequently observed him acting with only the human content of consciousness; then would we behold him in conference with the directors of the celestial hosts of the universe and discern the undoubted functioning of the divine mind. And then on almost numberless occasions did we witness the working of this combined personality of man and God as it was activated by the apparent perfect union of the human and the divine minds. This is the limit of our knowledge of such phenomena; we really do not actually know the full truth about this mystery.

Paper 162

At the Feast of Tabernacles

162:0.1 (1788.1) WHEN Jesus started up to Jerusalem with the ten apostles, he planned to go through Samaria, that being the shorter route. Accordingly, they passed down the eastern shore of the lake and, by way of Scythopolis, entered the borders of Samaria. Near nightfall Jesus sent Philip and Matthew over to a village on the eastern slopes of Mount Gilboa to secure lodging for the company. It so happened that these villagers were greatly prejudiced against the Jews, even more so than the average Samaritans, and these feelings were heightened at this particular time as so many were on their way to the feast of tabernacles. These people knew very little about Jesus, and they refused him lodging because he and his associates were Jews. When Matthew and Philip manifested indignation and informed these Samaritans that they were declining to entertain the Holy One of Israel, the infuriated villagers chased them out of the little town with sticks and stones.

162:0.2 (1788.2) After Philip and Matthew had returned to their fellows and reported how they had been driven out of the village, James and John stepped up to Jesus and said: "Master, we pray you to give us permission to bid fire come down from heaven to devour these insolent and impenitent Samaritans." But when Jesus heard these words of vengeance, he turned upon the sons of Zebedee and severely rebuked them: "You know not what manner of attitude you manifest.

Vengeance savors not of the outlook of the kingdom of heaven. Rather than dispute, let us journey over to the little village by the Jordan ford." Thus because of sectarian prejudice these Samaritans denied themselves the honor of showing hospitality to the Creator Son of a universe.

162:0.3 (1788.3) Jesus and the ten stopped for the night at the village near the Jordan ford. Early the next day they crossed the river and continued on to Jerusalem by way of the east Jordan highway, arriving at Bethany late Wednesday evening. Thomas and Nathaniel arrived on Friday, having been delayed by their conferences with Rodan.

162:0.4 (1788.4) Jesus and the twelve remained in the vicinity of Jerusalem until the end of the following month (October), about four and one-half weeks. Jesus himself went into the city only a few times, and these brief visits were made during the days of the feast of tabernacles. He spent a considerable portion of October with Abner and his associates at Bethlehem.

1   The Dangers of the Visit to Jerusalem

162:1.1 (1788.5) Long before they fled from Galilee, the followers of Jesus had implored him to go to Jerusalem to proclaim the gospel of the kingdom in order that his message might have the prestige of having been preached at the center of Jewish culture and learning; but now that he had actually come to Jerusalem to teach, they were afraid for his life. Knowing that the Sanhedrin had sought to bring Jesus to Jerusalem for trial and recalling the Master's recently reiterated declarations that he must be subject to death, the apostles had been literally stunned by his sudden decision to attend the feast of tabernacles. To all their previous entreaties that he go to Jerusalem he had replied, "The hour has not yet come." Now, to their protests of fear he answered only, "But the hour has come."

162:1.2 (1789.1) During the feast of tabernacles Jesus went boldly into Jerusalem on several occasions and publicly taught in the temple. This he did in spite of the efforts of his apostles to dissuade him. Though they had long urged him to proclaim his message in Jerusalem, they now feared to see him enter the city at this time, knowing full well that the scribes and Pharisees were bent on bringing about his death.

162:1.3 (1789.2) Jesus' bold appearance in Jerusalem more than ever confused his followers. Many of his disciples, and even Judas Iscariot, the apostle, had dared to think that Jesus had fled in haste into Phoenicia because he feared the Jewish leaders and Herod Antipas. They failed to comprehend the significance of the Master's movements. His presence in Jerusalem

at the feast of tabernacles, even in opposition to the advice of his followers, sufficed forever to put an end to all whisperings about fear and cowardice.

162:1.4 (1789.3) During the feast of tabernacles, thousands of believers from all parts of the Roman Empire saw Jesus, heard him teach, and many even journeyed out to Bethany to confer with him regarding the progress of the kingdom in their home districts.

162:1.5 (1789.4) There were many reasons why Jesus was able publicly to preach in the temple courts throughout the days of the feast, and chief of these was the fear that had come over the officers of the Sanhedrin as a result of the secret division of sentiment in their own ranks. It was a fact that many of the members of the Sanhedrin either secretly believed in Jesus or else were decidedly averse to arresting him during the feast, when such large numbers of people were present in Jerusalem, many of whom either believed in him or were at least friendly to the spiritual movement which he sponsored.

162:1.6 (1789.5) The efforts of Abner and his associates throughout Judea had also done much to consolidate sentiment favorable to the kingdom, so much so that the enemies of Jesus dared not be too outspoken in their opposition. This was one of the reasons why Jesus could publicly visit Jerusalem and live to go away. One or two months before this he would certainly have been put to death.

162:1.7 (1789.6) But the audacious boldness of Jesus in publicly appearing in Jerusalem overawed his enemies; they were not prepared for such a daring challenge. Several times during this month the Sanhedrin made feeble attempts to place the Master under arrest, but nothing came of these efforts. His enemies were so taken aback by Jesus' unexpected public appearance in Jerusalem that they conjectured he must have been promised protection by the Roman authorities.

Knowing that Philip (Herod Antipas's

brother) was almost a follower of Jesus, the members of the Sanhedrin speculated that Philip had secured for Jesus promises of protection against his enemies. Jesus had departed from their jurisdiction before they awakened to the realization that they had been mistaken in the belief that his sudden and bold appearance in Jerusalem had been due to a secret understanding with the Roman officials.

162:1.8 (1789.7) Only the twelve apostles had known that Jesus intended to attend the feast of tabernacles when they had departed from Magadan. The other followers of the Master were greatly astonished when he appeared in the temple courts and began publicly to teach, and the Jewish authorities were surprised beyond expression when it was reported that he was teaching in the temple.

162:1.9 (1790.1) Although his disciples had not expected Jesus to attend the feast, the vast majority of the pilgrims from afar who had heard of him entertained the hope that they might see him at Jerusalem. And they were not disappointed, for on several occasions he taught in Solomon's Porch and elsewhere in the temple courts. These teachings were really the official or formal announcement of the divinity of Jesus to the Jewish people and to the whole world.

162:1.10 (1790.2) The multitudes who listened to the Master's teachings were divided in their opinions. Some said he was a good man; some a prophet; some that he was truly the Messiah; others said he was a mischievous meddler, that he was leading the people astray with his strange doctrines. His enemies hesitated to denounce him openly for fear of his friendly believers, while his friends feared to acknowledge him openly for fear of the Jewish leaders, knowing that the Sanhedrin was determined to put him to death. But even his enemies marveled at his teaching, knowing that he had not been instructed in the schools of the rabbis.

162:1.11 (1790.3) Every time Jesus went to Jerusalem, his apostles were filled with terror. They were the more afraid as, from day to day, they listened to his increasingly bold pronouncements regarding the nature of his mission on earth. They were unaccustomed to hearing Jesus make such positive claims and such amazing assertions even when preaching among his friends.

2 The First Temple Talk

1. 162:2.1 (1790.4) The first afternoon that Jesus taught in the temple, a considerable company sat listening to his words depicting the liberty of the new gospel and the joy of those who believe the good news, when a curious listener interrupted him to ask: "Teacher, how is it you can quote the Scriptures and teach the people so fluently when I am told that you are untaught in the learning of the rabbis?" Jesus replied: "No man has taught me the truths which I declare to you. And this teaching is not mine but His who sent me. If any man really desires to do my Father's will, he shall certainly know about my teaching, whether it be God's or whether I speak for myself. He who speaks for himself seeks his own glory, but when I declare the words of the Father, I thereby seek the glory of him who sent me. But before you try to enter into the new light, should you not rather follow the light you already have? Moses gave you the law, yet how many of you honestly seek to fulfill its demands? Moses in this law enjoins you, saying, 'You shall not kill'; notwithstanding this command some of you seek to kill the Son of Man."

162:2.2 (1790.5) When the crowd heard these words, they fell to wrangling among themselves. Some said he was mad; some that he had a devil. Others said this was indeed the prophet of Galilee whom the scribes and Pharisees had long sought to kill. Some said the religious authorities were afraid to molest him; others thought that they laid not hands upon him because they had become believers in him. After considerable debate one of the crowd stepped forward and asked Jesus, "Why do the rulers seek to kill you?" And he replied: "The rulers seek to kill me because they resent my teaching about the good news of the kingdom, a gospel that sets men free from the burdensome traditions of a formal religion of ceremonies which these teachers are determined to uphold at any cost. They circumcise in accordance with the law on the Sabbath day, but they would kill me because I once on the Sabbath day set free a man held in the bondage of affliction. They follow after me on the Sabbath to spy on me but would kill me because on another occasion I chose to make a grievously stricken man completely whole on the Sabbath day. They seek to kill me because they well know that, if you honestly believe and dare to accept my teaching, their system of traditional religion will be overthrown, forever destroyed. Thus will they be deprived of authority over that to which they have devoted their lives since they steadfastly refuse to accept this new and more glorious gospel of the kingdom of God. And now do I appeal to every one of you: Judge not according to outward appearances but rather judge by the true spirit of these teachings; judge righteously."

162:2.3 (1791.1) Then said another inquirer: "Yes, Teacher, we do look for the Messiah, but when he comes, we know that his appearance will be in mystery. We know whence you are. You have been among your brethren from the beginning. The deliverer will come in power to restore the throne of David's kingdom. Do you really claim to be the Messiah?" And Jesus replied: "You claim to know me and to know whence I am. I wish your claims were true, for indeed then would you find abundant life in that knowledge. But I declare that I have not come to you for myself; I have been sent by the Father, and he who sent me is true and faithful. By refusing to hear me, you are refusing to receive Him who sends me. You, if you will receive this gospel, shall come to know Him who sent me. I know the Father, for I have come from the Father to declare and reveal him to you." *

162:2.4 (1791.2) The agents of the scribes wanted to lay hands upon him, but they feared the multitude, for many believed in him. Jesus' work since his baptism had become well known to all Jewry, and as many of these people recounted these things, they said among themselves: "Even though this teacher is from Galilee, and even though he does not meet all of our expectations of the Messiah, we wonder if the deliverer, when he does come, will really do anything more wonderful than this Jesus of Nazareth has already done."

162:2.5 (1791.3) When the Pharisees and their agents heard the people talking this way, they took counsel with their leaders and decided that something should be done forthwith to put a stop to these public appearances of Jesus in the temple courts. The leaders of the Jews, in general, were disposed to avoid a clash with Jesus, believing that the Roman authorities had promised him immunity. They could not otherwise account for his boldness in coming at this time to Jerusalem; but the officers of the Sanhedrin did not wholly believe this rumor. They reasoned that the Roman rulers would not do such a thing secretly and without the knowledge of the highest governing body of the Jewish nation.

162:2.6 (1791.4) Accordingly, Eber, the proper officer of the Sanhedrin, with two assistants was dispatched to arrest Jesus. As Eber made his way toward Jesus, the Master said: "Fear not to approach me. Draw near while you listen to my teaching. I know you have been sent to apprehend me, but you should understand that nothing will befall the Son of Man until his hour comes. You are not arrayed against me; you come only to do the bidding of your masters, and even these rulers of the Jews verily think they are doing God's service when they secretly seek my destruction.

162:2.7 (1792.1) "I bear none of you ill will. The Father loves you, and therefore do I long for your deliverance from the bondage of prejudice and the darkness of tradition. I offer you the liberty of life and the joy of salvation. I proclaim the new and living way, the deliverance from evil and the breaking of the bondage of sin. I have come that you might have life, and have it eternally. You seek to be rid of me and my disquieting teachings. If you could only realize that I am to be with you only a little while! In just a short time I go to Him who sent me into this world. And then will many of you diligently seek me, but you shall not discover my presence, for where I am about to go you cannot come. But all who truly seek to find me shall sometime attain the life that leads to my Father's presence."

162:2.8 (1792.2) Some of the scoffers said among themselves: "Where will this man go that we cannot find him? Will he go to live among the Greeks? Will he destroy himself? What can he mean when he declares that soon he will depart from us, and that we cannot go where he goes?"

162:2.9 (1792.3) Eber and his assistants refused to arrest Jesus; they returned to their meeting place without him. When, therefore, the chief priests and the Pharisees upbraided Eber and his assistants because they had not brought Jesus with them, Eber only replied: "We feared to arrest him in the midst of the multitude because many believe in him. Besides, we never heard a man speak like this man. There is something out of the ordinary about this teacher. You would all do well to go over to hear him." And when the chief rulers heard these words, they were astonished and spoke tauntingly to Eber: "Are you also led astray? Are you about to believe in this deceiver? Have you heard that any of our learned men or any of the rulers have believed in him? Have any of the scribes or the Pharisees been deceived by his clever teachings? How does it come that you are influenced by the behavior of this ignorant multitude who know not the law or the prophets? Do you not know that such untaught people are accursed?" And then answered Eber: "Even so, my masters, but this man speaks to the multitude words of mercy and hope. He cheers the downhearted, and his words were comforting even to our souls. What can there be wrong in these teachings even though he

may not be the Messiah of the Scriptures? And even then does not our law require fairness? Do we condemn a man before we hear him?" And the chief of the Sanhedrin was wroth with Eber and, turning upon him, said: "Have you gone mad? Are you by any chance also from Galilee? Search the Scriptures, and you will discover that out of Galilee arises no prophet, much less the Messiah."

162:2.10 (1792.4) The Sanhedrin disbanded in confusion, and Jesus withdrew to Bethany for the night.

3   The Woman Taken in Adultery

162:3.1 (1792.5) It was during this visit to Jerusalem that Jesus dealt with a certain woman of evil repute who was brought into his presence by her accusers and his enemies. The distorted record you have of this episode would suggest that this woman had been brought before Jesus by the scribes and Pharisees, and that Jesus so dealt with them as to indicate that these religious leaders of the Jews might themselves have been guilty of immorality. Jesus well knew that, while these scribes and Pharisees were spiritually blind and intellectually prejudiced by their loyalty to tradition, they were to be numbered among the most thoroughly moral men of that day and generation.

162:3.2 (1793.1) What really happened was this: Early the third morning of the feast, as Jesus approached the temple, he was met by a group of the hired agents of the Sanhedrin who were dragging a woman along with them. As they came near, the spokesman said: "Master, this woman was taken in adultery—in the very act. Now, the law of Moses commands that we should stone such a woman. What do you say should be done with her?"

162:3.3 (1793.2) It was the plan of Jesus' enemies, if he upheld the law of Moses requiring that the self-confessed transgressor be stoned, to involve him in difficulty with the Roman rulers, who had denied the Jews the right to inflict the death penalty without the approval of a Roman tribunal. If he forbade stoning the woman, they would accuse him before the Sanhedrin of setting himself up above Moses and the Jewish law. If he remained silent, they would accuse him of cowardice. But the Master so managed the situation that the whole plot fell to pieces of its own sordid weight.

162:3.4 (1793.3) This woman, once comely, was the wife of an inferior citizen of Nazareth, a man who had been a troublemaker for Jesus throughout his youthful days. The man, having married this woman, did most shamefully force her to earn their living by making commerce of her body. He had come up to the feast at Jerusalem that his wife might thus prostitute her physical charms for financial gain. He had entered into a bargain with the hirelings of the Jewish rulers thus to betray his own wife in her commercialized vice. And so they came with the woman and her companion in transgression for the purpose of ensnaring Jesus into making some statement which could be used against him in case of his arrest.

162:3.5 (1793.4) Jesus, looking over the crowd, saw her husband standing behind the others. He knew what sort of man he was and perceived that he was a party to the despicable transaction. Jesus first walked around to near where this degenerate husband stood and wrote upon the sand a few words which caused him to depart in haste. Then he came back before the woman and wrote again upon the ground for the benefit of her would-be accusers; and when they read his words, they, too, went away, one by one. And when the Master had written in the sand the third time, the woman's companion in evil took his departure, so that, when the Master raised himself up from this writing, he beheld the woman standing alone before him. Jesus said: "Woman, where are your accusers? did no man remain to stone you?" And the woman, lifting up her eyes, answered, "No man, Lord." And then said Jesus: "I know about you; neither do I condemn you. Go your way in peace." And this woman, Hildana, forsook her wicked husband and joined herself to the disciples of the kingdom.

4   *The Feast of Tabernacles*

162:4.1 (1793.5) The presence of people from all of the known world, from Spain to India, made the feast of tabernacles an ideal occasion for Jesus for the first time publicly to proclaim his full gospel in Jerusalem. At this feast the people lived much in the open air, in leafy booths. It was the feast of the harvest ingathering, and coming, as it did, in the cool of the autumn months, it was more generally attended by the Jews of the world than was the Passover at the end of the winter or Pentecost at the beginning of summer. The apostles at last beheld their Master making the bold announcement of his mission on earth before all the world, as it were.

162:4.2 (1794.1) This was the feast of feasts, since any sacrifice not made at the other festivals could be made at this time. This was the occasion of the reception of the temple offerings; it was a combination of vacation pleasures with the solemn rites of religious worship. Here was a time of racial rejoicing, mingled with sacrifices, Levitical chants, and the solemn blasts of the silvery trumpets of the priests. At night the impressive spectacle of the temple and its pilgrim throngs was brilliantly illuminated by the great candelabras which burned brightly in the court of the women as well as by the glare of scores of torches standing about the temple courts. The entire city was gaily decorated except the Roman castle of Antonia, which looked down in grim contrast upon this festive and worshipful scene. And how the Jews did hate this ever-present reminder of the Roman yoke!

162:4.3 (1794.2) Seventy bullocks were sacrificed during the feast, the symbol of the seventy nations of heathendom. The ceremony of the outpouring of the water symbolized the outpouring of the divine spirit. This ceremony of the water followed the sunrise procession of the priests and Levites. The worshipers passed down the steps leading from the court of Israel to the court of the women while successive blasts were blown upon the silvery trumpets. And then the faithful marched on toward the Beautiful Gate, which opened upon the court of the gentiles. Here they turned about to face westward, to repeat their chants, and to continue their march for the symbolic water.

162:4.4 (1794.3) On the last day of the feast almost four hundred and fifty priests with a corresponding number of Levites officiated. At daybreak the pilgrims assembled from all parts of the city, each carrying in the right hand a sheaf of myrtle, willow, and palm branches, while in the left hand each one carried a branch of the paradise apple—the citron, or the "forbidden fruit." These pilgrims divided into three groups for this early morning ceremony. One band remained at the temple to attend the morning sacrifices; another group marched down below Jerusalem to near Maza to cut the willow branches for the adornment of the sacrificial altar, while the third group formed a procession to march from the temple behind the water priest, who, to the sound of the silvery trumpets, bore the golden pitcher which was to contain the symbolic water, out through Ophel to near Siloam, where was located the fountain gate. After the golden pitcher had been filled at the pool of Siloam, the procession marched back to the temple, entering by way of the water gate and going directly to the court of the priests, where the priest bearing the water pitcher was joined by the priest bearing the wine for the drink offering. These two priests then repaired to the silver funnels leading to the base of the altar and poured the contents of the pitchers therein. The execution of this rite of pouring the wine and the water was the signal for the assembled pilgrims to begin the chanting of the Psalms from 113 to 118 inclusive, in alternation with the Levites. And as they repeated these lines, they would wave their sheaves at the altar. Then followed the sacrifices for the day, associated with the repeating of the Psalm for the day, the Psalm for the last day of the feast being the eighty-second, beginning with the fifth verse.

5 Sermon on the Light of the World

162:5.1 (1794.4) On the evening of the next to the last day of the feast, when the scene was brilliantly illuminated by the lights of the candelabras and the torches, Jesus stood up in the midst of the assembled throng and said:

162:5.2 (1795.1) "I am the light of the world. He who follows me shall not walk in darkness but shall have the light of life. Presuming to place me on trial and assuming to sit as my judges, you declare that, if I bear witness of myself, my witness cannot be true. But never can the creature sit in judgment on the Creator. Even if I do bear witness about myself, my witness is everlastingly true, for I know whence I came, who I am, and whither I go. You who would kill the Son of Man know not whence I came, who I am, or whither I go. You only judge by the appearances of the flesh; you do not perceive the realities of the spirit. I judge no man, not even my archenemy. But if I should choose to judge, my judgment would be true and righteous, for I would judge not alone but in association with my Father, who sent me into the world, and who is the source of all true judgment. You even allow that the witness of two reliable persons may be accepted—well, then, I bear witness of these truths; so also does my Father in heaven. And when I told you this yesterday, in your darkness you asked me, 'Where is your Father?' Truly, you know neither me nor my Father, for if you had known me, you would also have known the Father. *

162:5.3 (1795.2) "I have already told you that I am going away, and that you will seek me and not find me, for where I am going you cannot come. You who would reject this light are from beneath; I am from above. You who prefer to sit in darkness are of this world; I am not of this world, and I live in the eternal light of the Father of lights. You all have had abundant opportunity to learn who I am, but you shall have still other evidence confirming the identity of the Son of Man. I am the light of life, and every one who deliberately and with understanding rejects this saving light shall die in his sins. Much I have to tell you, but you are unable to receive my words. However, he who sent me is true and faithful; my Father loves even his erring children. And all that my Father has spoken I also proclaim to the world.

162:5.4 (1795.3) "When the Son of Man is lifted up, then shall you all know that I am he, and that I have done nothing of myself but only as the Father has taught me. I speak these words to you and to your children. And he who sent me is even now with me; he has not left me alone, for I do always that which is pleasing in his sight."

162:5.5 (1795.4) As Jesus thus taught the pilgrims in the temple courts, many believed. And no man dared to lay hands upon him.

6   *Discourse on the Water of Life*

162:6.1 (1795.5) On the last day, the great day of the feast, as the procession from the pool of Siloam passed through the temple courts, and just after the water and the wine had been poured down upon the altar by the priests, Jesus, standing among the pilgrims, said: "If any man thirst, let him come to me and drink. From the Father above I bring to this world the water of life. He who believes me shall be filled with the spirit which this water represents, for even the Scriptures have said, 'Out of him shall flow rivers of living waters.' When the Son of Man has finished his work on earth, there shall be poured out upon all flesh the living Spirit of Truth. Those who receive this spirit shall never know spiritual thirst."

162:6.2 (1795.6) Jesus did not interrupt the service to speak these words. He addressed the worshipers immediately after the chanting of the Hallel, the responsive reading of the Psalms accompanied by waving of the branches before the altar.

Just here was a pause while the sacrifices were being prepared, and it was at this time that the pilgrims heard the fascinating voice of the Master declare that he was the giver of living water to every spirit-thirsting soul.

162:6.3 (1796.1) At the conclusion of this early morning service Jesus continued to teach the multitude, saying: "Have you not read in the Scripture: 'Behold, as the waters are poured out upon the dry ground and spread over the parched soil, so will I give the spirit of holiness to be poured out upon your children for a blessing even to your children's children'?

Why will you thirst for the ministry of the spirit while you seek to water your souls with the traditions of men, poured from the broken pitchers of ceremonial service? That which you see going on about this temple is the way in which your fathers sought to symbolize the bestowal of the divine spirit upon the children of faith, and you have done well to perpetuate these symbols, even down to this day. But now has come to this generation the revelation of the Father of spirits through the bestowal of his Son, and all of this will certainly be followed by the bestowal of the spirit of the Father and the Son upon the children of men. To every one who has faith shall this bestowal of the spirit become the true teacher of the way which leads to life everlasting, to the true waters of life in the kingdom of heaven on earth and in the Father's Paradise over there."

162:6.4 (1796.2) And Jesus continued to answer the questions of both the multitude and the Pharisees. Some thought he was a prophet; some believed him to be the Messiah; others said he could not be the Christ, seeing that he came from Galilee, and that the Messiah must restore David's throne. Still they dared not arrest him.

7   *The Discourse on Spiritual Freedom*

162:7.1 (1796.3) On the afternoon of the last day of the feast and after the apostles had failed in their efforts to persuade him to flee from Jerusalem, Jesus again went into the temple to teach. Finding a large company of believers assembled in Solomon's Porch, he spoke to them, saying:

162:7.2 (1796.4) "If my words abide in you and you are minded to do the will of my Father, then are you truly my disciples. You shall know the truth, and the truth shall make you free. I know how you will answer me: We are the children of Abraham, and we are in bondage to none; how then shall we be made free? Even so, I do not speak of outward subjection to another's rule; I refer to the liberties of the soul. Verily, verily, I say to you, everyone who commits sin is the bond servant of sin. And you know that the bond servant is not likely to abide forever in the master's house. You also know that the son does remain in his father's house. If, therefore, the Son shall make you free, shall make you sons, you shall be free indeed. *

162:7.3 (1796.5) "I know that you are Abraham's seed, yet your leaders seek to kill me because my word has not been allowed to have its transforming influence in their hearts. Their souls are sealed by prejudice and blinded by the pride of revenge. I declare to you the truth which the eternal Father shows me, while these deluded teachers seek to do the things which they have learned only from their temporal fathers. And when you reply that Abraham is your father, then do I tell you that, if you were the children of Abraham, you would do the works of Abraham. Some of you believe my teaching, but others seek to destroy me because I have told you the truth which I received from God. But Abraham did not so treat the truth of God. I perceive that some among you are determined to do the works of the evil one. If God were

your Father, you would know me and love the truth which I reveal. Will you not see that I come forth from the Father, that I am sent by God, that I am not doing this work of myself? Why do you not understand my words? Is it because you have chosen to become the children of evil? If you are the children of darkness, you will hardly walk in the light of the truth which I reveal. The children of evil follow only in the ways of their father, who was a deceiver and stood not for the truth because there came to be no truth in him. But now comes the Son of Man speaking and living the truth, and many of you refuse to believe.

162:7.4 (1797.1) "Which of you convicts me of sin? If I, then, proclaim and live the truth shown me by the Father, why do you not believe? He who is of God hears gladly the words of God; for this cause many of you hear not my words, because you are not of God. Your teachers have even presumed to say that I do my works by the power of the prince of devils. One near by has just said that I have a devil, that I am a child of the devil. But all of you who deal honestly with your own souls know full well that I am not a devil. You know that I honor the Father even while you would dishonor me. I seek not my own glory, only the glory of my Paradise Father. And I do not judge you, for there is one who judges for me.

162:7.5 (1797.2) "Verily, verily, I say to you who believe the gospel that, if a man will keep this word of truth alive in his heart, he shall never taste death. And now just at my side a scribe says this statement proves that I have a devil, seeing that Abraham is dead, also the prophets. And he asks: 'Are you so much greater than Abraham and the prophets that you dare to stand here and say that whoso keeps your word shall not taste death? Who do you claim to be that you dare to utter such blasphemies?' And I say to all such that, if I glorify myself, my glory is as nothing. But it is the Father who shall glorify me, even the same Father whom you call God. But you have failed to know this your God and my Father, and I have come to bring you together; to show you how to become truly the sons of God. Though you know not the Father, I truly know him. Even Abraham rejoiced to see my day, and by faith he saw it and was glad."

162:7.6 (1797.3) When the unbelieving Jews and the agents of the Sanhedrin who had gathered about by this time heard these words, they raised a tumult, shouting: "You are not fifty years of age, and yet you talk about seeing Abraham; you are a child of the devil!" Jesus was unable to continue the discourse. He only said as he departed, "Verily, verily, I say to you, before Abraham was, I am." Many of the unbelievers rushed forth for stones to cast at him, and the agents of the Sanhedrin sought to place him under arrest, but the Master quickly made his way through the temple corridors and escaped to a secret meeting place near Bethany where Martha, Mary, and Lazarus awaited him.

8   The Visit with Martha and Mary

162:8.1 (1797.4) It had been arranged that Jesus should lodge with Lazarus and his sisters at a friend's house, while the apostles were scattered here and there in small groups, these precautions being taken because the Jewish authorities were again becoming bold with their plans to arrest him.

162:8.2 (1797.5) For years it had been the custom for these three to drop everything and listen to Jesus' teaching whenever he chanced to visit them. With the loss of their parents, Martha had assumed the responsibilities of the home life, and so on this occasion, while Lazarus and Mary sat at Jesus' feet drinking in his refreshing teaching, Martha made ready to serve the evening meal. It should be explained that Martha was unnecessarily distracted by numerous needless tasks, and that she was cumbered by many trivial cares; that was her disposition.

162:8.3 (1798.1) As Martha busied herself with all these supposed duties, she was perturbed because Mary did nothing to help. Therefore she went to Jesus and said: "Master, do you not care that my sister has left me alone to do all of the serving? Will you not bid her to come and help me?" Jesus answered: "Martha, Martha, why are you always anxious about so many things and troubled by so many trifles? Only one thing is really worth while, and since Mary has chosen this good and needful part, I shall not take it away from her. But when will both of you learn to live as I have taught you: both serving in co-operation and both refreshing your souls in unison? Can you not learn that there is a time for everything—that the lesser matters of life should give way before the greater things of the heavenly kingdom?"

9   At Bethlehem with Abner

162:9.1 (1798.2) Throughout the week that followed the feast of tabernacles, scores of believers forgathered at Bethany and received instruction from the twelve apostles. The Sanhedrin made no effort to molest these gatherings since Jesus was not present; he was throughout this time working with Abner and his associates in Bethlehem. The day following the close of the feast, Jesus had departed for Bethany, and he did not again teach in the temple during this visit to Jerusalem.

162:9.2 (1798.3) At this time, Abner was making his headquarters at Bethlehem, and from that center many workers had been sent to the cities of Judea and southern Samaria and even to Alexandria. Within a few days of his arrival, Jesus and Abner completed the arrangements for the consolidation of the work of the two groups of apostles.

162:9.3 (1798.4) Throughout his visit to the feast of tabernacles, Jesus had divided his time about equally between Bethany and Bethlehem. At Bethany he spent considerable time with his apostles; at Bethlehem he gave much instruction to Abner and the other former apostles of John. And it was this intimate contact that finally led them to believe in him. These former apostles of John the Baptist were influenced by the courage he displayed in his public teaching in Jerusalem as well as by the sympathetic understanding they experienced in his private teaching at Bethlehem. These influences finally and fully won over each of Abner's associates to a wholehearted acceptance of the kingdom and all that such a step implied.

162:9.4 (1798.5) Before leaving Bethlehem for the last time, the Master made arrangements for them all to join him in the united effort which was to precede the ending of his earth career in the flesh. It was agreed that Abner and his associates were to join Jesus and the twelve in the near future at Magadan Park.

162:9.5 (1798.6) In accordance with this understanding, early in November Abner and his eleven fellows cast their lot with Jesus and the twelve and labored with them as one organization right on down to the crucifixion.

162:9.6 (1798.7) In the latter part of October Jesus and the twelve withdrew from the immediate vicinity of Jerusalem. On Sunday, October 30, Jesus and his associates left the city of Ephraim, where he had been resting in seclusion for a few days, and, going by the west Jordan highway directly to Magadan Park, arrived late on the afternoon of Wednesday, November 2.

162:9.7 (1799.1) The apostles were greatly relieved to have the Master back on friendly soil; no more did they urge him to go up to Jerusalem to proclaim the gospel of the kingdom.

Paper 163

Ordination of the Seventy at Magadan

163:0.1 (1800.1) A FEW days after the return of Jesus and the twelve to Magadan from Jerusalem, Abner and a group of some fifty disciples arrived from Bethlehem. At this time there were also assembled at Magadan Camp the evangelistic corps, the women's corps, and about one hundred and fifty other true and tried disciples from all parts of Palestine.

After devoting a few days to visiting and the reorganization of the camp, Jesus and the twelve began a course of intensive training for this special group of believers, and from this well-trained and experienced aggregation of disciples the Master subsequently chose the seventy teachers and sent them forth to proclaim the gospel of the kingdom. This regular instruction began on Friday, November 4, and continued until Sabbath, November 19.

163:0.2 (1800.2) Jesus gave a talk to this company each morning. Peter taught methods of public preaching; Nathaniel instructed them in the art of teaching; Thomas explained how to answer questions; while Matthew directed the organization of their group finances. The other apostles also participated in this training in accordance with their special experience and natural talents.

Ordination of the Seventy

163:1.1 (1800.3) The seventy were ordained by Jesus on Sabbath afternoon, November 19, at the Magadan Camp, and Abner was placed at the head of these gospel preachers and teachers. This corps of seventy consisted of Abner and ten of the former apostles of John, fifty-one of the earlier evangelists, and eight other disciples who had distinguished themselves in the service of the kingdom.

163:1.2 (1800.4) About two o'clock on this Sabbath afternoon, between showers of rain, a company of believers, augmented by the arrival of David and the majority of his messenger corps and numbering over four hundred, assembled on the shore of the lake of Galilee to witness the ordination of the seventy.

163:1.3 (1800.5) Before Jesus laid his hands upon the heads of the seventy to set them apart as gospel messengers, addressing them, he said: "The harvest is indeed plenteous, but the laborers are few; therefore I exhort all of you to pray that the Lord of the harvest will send still other laborers into his harvest. I am about to set you apart as messengers of the kingdom; I am about to send you to Jew and gentile as lambs among wolves. As you go your ways, two and two, I instruct you to carry neither purse nor extra clothing, for you go forth on this first mission for only a short season. Salute no man by the way, attend only to your work. Whenever you go to stay at a home, first say: Peace be to this household. If those who love peace live therein, you shall abide there; if not, then shall you depart. And having selected this home, remain there for your stay in that city, eating and drinking whatever is set before you. And you do this because the laborer is worthy of his sustenance. Move not from house to house because a better lodging may be offered. Remember, as you go forth proclaiming peace on earth and good will among men, you must contend with bitter and self-deceived enemies; therefore be as wise as serpents while you are also as harmless as doves.

163:1.4 (1801.1) "And everywhere you go, preach, saying, 'The kingdom of heaven is at hand,' and minister to all who may be sick in either mind or body. Freely you have received of the good things of the kingdom; freely give. If the people of any city receive you, they shall find an abundant entrance into the Father's kingdom; but if the people of any city refuse to receive this gospel, still shall you proclaim your message as you depart from that unbelieving community, saying, even as you leave, to those who reject your teaching: 'Notwithstanding you reject the truth, it remains that the kingdom of God has come near you.' He who hears you hears me. And he who hears me hears Him who sent me. He who rejects your gospel message rejects me. And he who rejects me rejects Him who sent me."

163:1.5 (1801.2) When Jesus had thus spoken to the seventy, he began with Abner and, as they knelt in a circle about him, laid his hands upon the head of every man.

163:1.6 (1801.3) Early the next morning Abner sent the seventy messengers into all the cities of Galilee, Samaria, and Judea. And these thirty-five couples went forth preaching and teaching for about six weeks, all of them returning to the new camp near Pella, in Perea, on Friday, December 30.

The Rich Young Man and Others

163:2.1 (1801.4) Over fifty disciples who sought ordination and appointment to membership in the seventy were rejected by the committee appointed by Jesus to select these candidates. This committee consisted of Andrew, Abner, and the acting head of the evangelistic corps. In all cases where this committee of three were not unanimous in agreement, they brought the candidate to Jesus, and while the Master never rejected a single person who craved ordination as a gospel messenger, there were more than a dozen who, when they had talked with Jesus, no more desired to become gospel messengers.

163:2.2 (1801.5) One earnest disciple came to Jesus, saying: "Master, I would be one of your new apostles, but my father is very old and near death; could I be permitted to return home to bury him?" To this man Jesus said: "My son, the foxes have holes, and the birds of heaven have nests, but the Son of Man has nowhere to lay his head. You are a faithful disciple, and you can remain such while you return home to minister to your loved ones, but not so with my gospel messengers. They have forsaken all to follow me and proclaim the kingdom. If you would be an ordained teacher, you must let others bury the dead while you go forth to publish the good news." And this man went away in great disappointment.

163:2.3 (1801.6) Another disciple came to the Master and said: "I would become an ordained messenger, but I would like to go to my home for a short while to comfort my family." And Jesus replied: "If you would be ordained, you must be willing to forsake all. The gospel messengers cannot have divided affections. No man, having put his hand to the plough, if he turns back, is worthy to become a messenger of the kingdom."

163:2.4 (1801.7) Then Andrew brought to Jesus a certain rich young man who was a devout believer, and who desired to receive ordination. This young man, Matadormus, was a member of the Jerusalem Sanhedrin; he had heard Jesus teach and had been subsequently instructed in the gospel of the kingdom by Peter and the other apostles. Jesus talked with Matadormus concerning the requirements of ordination and requested that he defer decision until after he had thought more fully about the matter. Early the next morning, as Jesus was going for a walk, this young man accosted him and said: "Master, I would know from you the assurances of eternal life. Seeing that I have observed all the commandments from my youth, I would like to know what more I must do to gain eternal life?" In answer to this question Jesus said: "If you keep all the commandments—do not commit adultery, do not kill, do not steal, do not bear false witness, do not defraud, honor your parents—you do well, but salvation is the reward of faith, not merely of works. Do you believe this gospel of the kingdom?" And Matadormus answered: "Yes, Master, I do believe everything you and your apostles have taught me." And Jesus said, "Then are you indeed my disciple and a child of the kingdom."

163:2.5 (1802.1) Then said the young man: "But, Master, I am not content to be your disciple; I would be one of your new messengers." When Jesus heard this, he looked down upon him with a great love and said: "I will have you to be one of my messengers if you are willing to pay the price, if you will supply the one thing which you lack." Matadormus replied: "Master, I will do anything if I may be allowed to follow you." Jesus, kissing the kneeling young man on the forehead, said: "If you would be my messenger, go and sell all that you have and, when you have bestowed the proceeds upon the poor or upon your brethren, come and follow me, and you shall have treasure in the kingdom of heaven."

163:2.6 (1802.2) When Matadormus heard this, his countenance fell. He arose and went away sorrowful, for he had great possessions. This wealthy young Pharisee had been raised to believe that wealth was the token of God's favor. Jesus knew that he was not free from the love of himself and his riches. The Master wanted to deliver him from the love of wealth, not necessarily from the wealth. While the disciples of Jesus did not part with all their worldly goods, the apostles and the seventy did. Matadormus desired to be one of the seventy new messengers, and that was the reason for Jesus' requiring him to part with all of his temporal possessions.

163:2.7 (1802.3) Almost every human being has some one thing which is held on to as a pet evil, and which the entrance into the kingdom of heaven requires as a part of the price of admission. If Matadormus had parted with his wealth, it probably would have been put right back into his hands for administration as treasurer of the seventy. For later on, after the establishment of the church at Jerusalem, he did obey the Master's injunction, although it was then too late to enjoy membership in the seventy, and he became the treasurer of the Jerusalem church, of which James the Lord's brother in the flesh was the head.

163:2.8 (1802.4) Thus always it was and forever will be: Men must arrive at their own decisions. There is a certain range of the freedom of choice which mortals may exercise. The forces of the spiritual world will not coerce man; they allow him to go the way of his own choosing.

163:2.9 (1802.5) Jesus foresaw that Matadormus, with his riches, could not possibly become an ordained associate of men who had forsaken all for the gospel; at the same time, he saw that, without his riches, he would become the ultimate leader of all of them. But, like Jesus' own brethren, he never became great in the kingdom because he deprived himself of that intimate and personal association with the Master which might have been his experience had he been willing to do at this time the very thing which Jesus asked, and which, several years subsequently, he actually did.

163:2.10 (1803.1) Riches have nothing directly to do with entrance into the kingdom of heaven, but the love of wealth does. The spiritual loyalties of the kingdom are incompatible with servility to materialistic mammon. Man may not share his supreme loyalty to a spiritual ideal with a material devotion.

163:2.11 (1803.2) Jesus never taught that it was wrong to have wealth. He required only the twelve and the seventy to dedicate all of their worldly possessions to the common cause. Even then, he provided for the profitable liquidation of their property, as in the case of the Apostle Matthew. Jesus many times advised his well-to-do disciples as he taught the rich man of Rome. The Master regarded the wise investment of excess earnings as a legitimate form of insurance against future and unavoidable adversity. When the apostolic treasury was overflowing, Judas put funds on deposit to be used subsequently when they might suffer greatly from a diminution of income. This Judas did after consultation with Andrew. Jesus never personally had anything to do with the apostolic finances except in the disbursement of alms. But there was one economic abuse which he many times condemned, and that was the unfair exploitation of the weak, unlearned, and less fortunate of men by their strong, keen, and more intelligent fellows. Jesus declared that such inhuman treatment of men, women, and children was incompatible with the ideals of the brotherhood of the kingdom of heaven.

The Discussion About Wealth

163:3.1 (1803.3) By the time Jesus had finished talking with Matadormus, Peter and a number of the apostles had gathered about him, and as the rich young man was departing, Jesus turned around to face the apostles and said: "You see how difficult it is for those who have riches to enter fully into the kingdom of God! Spiritual worship cannot be shared with material devotions; no man can serve two masters. You have a saying that it is 'easier for a camel to go through the eye of a needle than for the heathen to inherit eternal life.' And I declare that it is as easy for this camel to go through the needle's eye as for these self-satisfied rich ones to enter the kingdom of heaven."

163:3.2 (1803.4) When Peter and the apostles heard these words, they were astonished exceedingly, so much so that Peter said: "Who then, Lord, can be saved? Shall all who have riches be kept out of the kingdom?" And Jesus replied: "No, Peter, but all who put their trust in riches shall hardly enter into the spiritual life that leads to eternal progress. But even then, much which is impossible to man is not beyond the reach of the Father in heaven; rather should we recognize that with God all things are possible."

163:3.3 (1803.5) As they went off by themselves, Jesus was grieved that Matadormus did not remain with them, for he greatly loved him. And when they had walked down by the lake, they sat there beside the water, and Peter, speaking for the twelve (who were all present by this time), said: "We are troubled by your words to the rich young man. Shall we require those who would follow you to give up all their worldly goods?" And Jesus said: "No, Peter, only those who would become apostles, and who desire to live with me as you do and as one family. But the Father requires that the affections of his children be pure and undivided. Whatever thing or person comes between you and the love of the truths of the kingdom, must be surrendered. If one's wealth does not invade the precincts of the soul, it is of no consequence in the spiritual life of those who would enter the kingdom."

163:3.4 (1804.1) And then said Peter, "But, Master, we have left everything to follow you, what then shall we have?" And Jesus spoke to all of the twelve: "Verily, verily, I say to you, there is no man who has left wealth, home, wife, brethren, parents, or children for my sake and for the sake of the kingdom of heaven who shall not receive manifold more in this world, perhaps with some persecutions, and in the world to come eternal life. But many who are first shall be last, while the last shall often be first. The Father deals with his creatures in accordance with their needs and in obedience to his just laws of merciful and loving consideration for the welfare of a universe.

163:3.5 (1804.2) "The kingdom of heaven is like a householder who was a large employer of men, and who went out early in the morning to hire laborers to work in his vineyard. When he had agreed with the laborers to pay them a denarius a day, he sent them into the vineyard. Then he went out about nine o'clock, and seeing others standing in the market place idle, he said to them: 'Go you also to work in my vineyard, and whatsoever is right I will pay you.' And they went at once to work. Again he went out about twelve and about three and did likewise. And going to the market place about five in the afternoon, he found still others standing idle, and he inquired of them, 'Why do you stand here idle all the day?' And the men answered, 'Because nobody has hired us.' Then said the householder: 'Go you also to work in my vineyard, and whatever is right I will pay you.'

163:3.6 (1804.3) "When evening came, this owner of the vineyard said to his steward: 'Call the laborers and pay them their wages, beginning with the last hired and ending with the first.' When those who were hired about five o'clock came, they received a denarius each, and so it was with each of the other laborers. When the men who were hired at the beginning of the day saw how the later comers were paid, they expected to receive more than the amount agreed upon. But like the others every man received only a denarius. And when each had received his pay, they complained to the householder, saying: 'These men who were hired last worked only one hour, and yet you have paid them the same as us who have borne the burden of the day in the scorching sun.'

163:3.7 (1804.4) "Then answered the householder: 'My friends, I do you no wrong. Did not each of you agree to work for a denarius a day? Take now that which is yours and go your way, for it is my desire to give to those who came last as much as I have given to you. Is it not lawful for me to do what I will with my own? or do you begrudge my generosity because I desire to be good and to show mercy?'"

Farewell to the Seventy

163:4.1 (1804.5) It was a stirring time about the Magadan Camp the day the seventy went forth on their first mission. Early that morning, in his last talk with the seventy, Jesus placed emphasis on the following:

163:4.2 (1804.6) 1. The gospel of the kingdom must be proclaimed to all the world, to gentile as well as to Jew.

163:4.3 (1804.7) 2. While ministering to the sick, refrain from teaching the expectation of miracles.

163:4.4 (1805.1) 3. Proclaim a spiritual brotherhood of the sons of God, not an outward kingdom of worldly power and material glory.

163:4.5 (1805.2) 4. Avoid loss of time through overmuch social visiting and other trivialities which might detract from wholehearted devotion to preaching the gospel.

163:4.6 (1805.3) 5. If the first house to be selected for a headquarters proves to be a worthy home, abide there throughout the sojourn in that city.

163:4.7 (1805.4) 6. Make clear to all faithful believers that the time for an open break with the religious leaders of the Jews at Jerusalem has now come.

163:4.8 (1805.5) 7. Teach that man's whole duty is summed up in this one commandment: Love the Lord your God with all your mind and soul and your neighbor as yourself. (This they were to teach as man's whole duty in place of the 613 rules of living expounded by the Pharisees.)

163:4.9 (1805.6) When Jesus had talked thus to the seventy in the presence of all the apostles and disciples, Simon Peter took them off by themselves and preached to them their ordination sermon, which was an elaboration of the Master's charge given at the time he laid his hands upon them and set them apart as messengers of the kingdom. Peter exhorted the seventy to cherish in their experience the following virtues:

163:4.10 (1805.7) 1. Consecrated devotion. To pray always for more laborers to be sent forth into the gospel harvest. He explained that, when one so prays, he will the more likely say, "Here am I; send me." He admonished them to neglect not their daily worship.

163:4.11 (1805.8) 2. True courage. He warned them that they would encounter hostility and be certain to meet with persecution. Peter told them their mission was no undertaking for cowards and advised those who were afraid to step out before they started. But none withdrew.

163:4.12 (1805.9) 3. Faith and trust.

They must go forth on this short mission wholly unprovided for; they must trust the Father for food and shelter and all other things needful.

163:4.13 (1805.10) 4. Zeal and initiative. They must be possessed with zeal and intelligent enthusiasm; they must attend strictly to their Master's business. Oriental salutation was a lengthy and elaborate ceremony; therefore had they been instructed to "salute no man by the way," which was a common method of exhorting one to go about his business without the waste of time. It had nothing to do with the matter of friendly greeting.

163:4.14 (1805.11) 5. Kindness and courtesy. The Master had instructed them to avoid unnecessary waste of time in social ceremonies, but he enjoined courtesy toward all with whom they should come in contact. They were to show every kindness to those who might entertain them in their homes. They were strictly warned against leaving a modest home to be entertained in a more comfortable or influential one.

163:4.15 (1805.12) 6. Ministry to the sick. The seventy were charged by Peter to search out the sick in mind and body and to do everything in their power to bring about the alleviation or cure of their maladies.

163:4.16 (1805.13) And when they had been thus charged and instructed, they started out, two and two, on their mission in Galilee, Samaria, and Judea.

163:4.17 (1806.1) Although the Jews had a peculiar regard for the number seventy, sometimes considering the nations of heathendom as being seventy in number, and although these seventy messengers were to go with the gospel to all peoples, still as far as we can discern, it was only coincidental that this group happened to number just seventy. Certain it was that Jesus would have accepted no less than half a dozen others, but they were unwilling to pay the price of forsaking wealth and families.

Moving the Camp to Pella

163:5.1 (1806.2) Jesus and the twelve now prepared to establish their last headquarters in Perea, near Pella, where the Master was baptized in the Jordan. The last ten days of November were spent in council at Magadan, and on Tuesday, December 6, the entire company of almost three hundred started out at daybreak with all their effects to lodge that night near Pella by the river. This was the same site, by the spring, that John the Baptist had occupied with his camp several years before.

163:5.2 (1806.3) After the breaking up of the Magadan Camp, David Zebedee returned to Bethsaida and began immediately to curtail the messenger service. The kingdom was taking on a new phase. Daily, pilgrims arrived from all parts of Palestine and even from remote regions of the Roman Empire. Believers occasionally came from Mesopotamia and from the lands east of the Tigris. Accordingly, on Sunday, December 18, David, with the help of his messenger corps, loaded on to the pack animals the camp equipage, then stored in his father's house, with which he had formerly conducted the camp of Bethsaida by the lake. Bidding farewell to Bethsaida for the time being, he proceeded down the lake shore and along the Jordan to a point about one-half mile north of the apostolic camp; and in less than a week he was prepared to offer hospitality to almost fifteen hundred pilgrim visitors. The apostolic camp could accommodate about five hundred. This was the rainy season in Palestine, and these accommodations were required to take care of the ever-increasing number of inquirers, mostly earnest, who came into Perea to see Jesus and to hear his teaching.

163:5.3 (1806.4) David did all this on his own initiative, though he had taken counsel with Philip and Matthew at Magadan. He employed the larger part of his former messenger corps as his helpers in conducting this camp; he now used less than twenty men on regular messenger duty. Near the end of December and before the return of the seventy, almost eight hundred visitors were gathered about the Master, and they found lodging in David's camp.

The Return of the Seventy

163:6.1 (1806.5) On Friday, December 30, while Jesus was away in the near-by hills with Peter, James, and John, the seventy messengers were arriving by couples, accompanied by numerous believers, at the Pella headquarters. All seventy were assembled at the teaching site about five o'clock when Jesus returned to the camp. The evening meal was delayed for more than an hour while these enthusiasts for the gospel of the kingdom related their experiences. David's messengers had brought much of this news to the apostles during previous weeks, but it was truly inspiring to hear these newly ordained teachers of the gospel personally tell how their message had been received by hungry Jews and gentiles. At last Jesus was able to see men going out to spread the good news without his personal presence. The Master now knew that he could leave this world without seriously hindering the progress of the kingdom.

163:6.2 (1807.1) When the seventy related how "even the devils were subject" to them, they referred to the wonderful cures they had wrought in the cases of victims of nervous disorders. Nevertheless, there had been a few cases of real spirit possession relieved by these ministers, and referring to these, Jesus said: "It is not strange that these disobedient minor spirits should be subject to you, seeing that I beheld Satan falling as lightning from heaven. But rejoice not so much over this, for I declare to you that, as soon as I return to my Father, we will send forth our spirits into the very minds of men so that no more can these few lost spirits enter the minds of unfortunate mortals. I rejoice with you that you have power with men, but be not lifted up because of this experience but the rather rejoice that your names are written on the rolls of heaven, and that you are thus to go forward in an endless career of spiritual conquest." *

163:6.3 (1807.2) And it was at this time, just before partaking of the evening meal, that Jesus experienced one of those rare moments of emotional ecstasy which his followers had occasionally witnessed. He said: "I thank you, my Father, Lord of heaven and earth, that, while this wonderful gospel was hidden from the wise and self-righteous, the spirit has revealed these spiritual glories to these children of the kingdom. Yes, my Father, it must have been pleasing in your sight to do this, and I rejoice to know that the good news will spread to all the world even after I shall have returned to you and the work which you have given me to perform. I am mightily moved as I realize you are about to deliver all authority into my hands, that only you really know who I am, and that only I really know you, and those to whom I have revealed you. And when I have finished this revelation to my brethren in the flesh, I will continue the revelation to your creatures on high."

163:6.4 (1807.3) When Jesus had thus spoken to the Father, he turned aside to speak to his apostles and ministers: "Blessed are the eyes which see and the ears which hear these things. Let me say to you that many prophets and many of the great men of the past ages have desired to behold what you now see, but it was not granted them. And many generations of the children of light yet to come will, when they hear of these things, envy you who have heard and seen them."

163:6.5 (1807.4) Then, speaking to all the disciples, he said: "You have heard how many cities and villages have received the good news of the kingdom, and how my ministers and teachers have been received by both the Jew and the gentile. And blessed indeed are these communities which have elected to believe the gospel of the kingdom. But woe upon the light-rejecting inhabitants of Chorazin, Bethsaida-Julias, and Capernaum, the cities which did not well receive these messengers. I declare that, if the mighty works done in these places had been done in Tyre and Sidon, the people of these so-called heathen cities would have long since repented in sackcloth and ashes. It shall indeed be more tolerable for Tyre and Sidon in the day of judgment."

163:6.6 (1807.5) The next day being the Sabbath, Jesus went apart with the seventy and said to them: "I did indeed rejoice with you when you came back bearing the good tidings of the reception of the gospel of the kingdom by so many people scattered throughout Galilee, Samaria, and Judea. But why were you so surprisingly elated? Did you not expect that your message would manifest power in its delivery? Did you go forth with so little faith in this gospel that you come back in surprise at its effectiveness? And now, while I would not quench your spirit of rejoicing, I would sternly warn you against the subtleties of pride, spiritual pride. If you could understand the downfall of Lucifer, the iniquitous one, you would solemnly shun all forms of spiritual pride.

163:6.7 (1808.1) "You have entered upon this great work of teaching mortal man that he is a son of God. I have shown you the way; go forth to do your duty and be not weary in well doing. To you and to all who shall follow in your steps down through the ages, let me say: I always stand near, and my invitation-call is, and ever shall be, Come to me all you who labor and are heavy laden, and I will give you rest. Take my yoke upon you and learn of me, for I am true and loyal, and you shall find spiritual rest for your souls."

163:6.8 (1808.2) And they found the Master's words to be true when they put his promises to the test. And since that day countless thousands also have tested and proved the surety of these same promises.

Preparation for the Last Mission

163:7.1 (1808.3) The next few days were busy times in the Pella camp; preparations for the Perean mission were being completed. Jesus and his associates were about to enter upon their last mission, the three months' tour of all Perea, which terminated only upon the Master's entering Jerusalem for his final labors on earth. Throughout this period the headquarters of Jesus and the twelve apostles was maintained here at the Pella camp.

163:7.2 (1808.4) It was no longer necessary for Jesus to go abroad to teach the people. They now came to him in increasing numbers each week and from all parts, not only from Palestine but from the whole Roman world and from the Near East. Although the Master participated with the seventy in the tour of Perea, he spent much of his time at the Pella camp, teaching the multitude and instructing the twelve. Throughout this three months' period at least ten of the apostles remained with Jesus.

163:7.3 (1808.5) The women's corps also prepared to go out, two and two, with the seventy to labor in the larger cities of Perea. This original group of twelve women had recently trained a larger corps of fifty women in the work of home visitation and in the art of ministering to the sick and the afflicted. Perpetua, Simon Peter's wife, became a member of this new division of the women's corps and was intrusted with the leadership of the enlarged women's work under Abner. After Pentecost she remained with her illustrious husband, accompanying him on all of his missionary tours; and on the day Peter was crucified in Rome, she was fed to the wild beasts in the arena. This new women's corps also had as members the wives of Philip and Matthew and the mother of James and John.

163:7.4 (1808.6) The work of the kingdom now prepared to enter upon its terminal phase under the personal leadership of Jesus. And this present phase was one of spiritual depth in contrast with the miracle-minded and wonder-seeking multitudes who followed after the Master during the former days of popularity in Galilee. However, there were still any number of his followers who were material-minded, and who failed to grasp the truth that the kingdom of heaven is the spiritual brotherhood of man founded on the eternal fact of the universal fatherhood of God.

Paper 164

At the Feast of Dedication

164:0.1 (1809.1) AS THE camp at Pella was being established, Jesus, taking with him Nathaniel and Thomas, secretly went up to Jerusalem to attend the feast of the dedication. Not until they passed over the Jordan at the Bethany ford, did the two apostles become aware that their Master was going on to Jerusalem. When they perceived that he really intended to be present at the feast of dedication, they remonstrated with him most earnestly, and using every sort of argument, they sought to dissuade him. But their efforts were of no avail; Jesus was determined to visit Jerusalem. To all their entreaties and to all their warnings emphasizing the folly and danger of placing himself in the hands of the Sanhedrin, he would reply only, "I would give these teachers in Israel another opportunity to see the light, before my hour comes."

164:0.2 (1809.2) On they went toward Jerusalem, the two apostles continuing to express their feelings of fear and to voice their doubts about the wisdom of such an apparently presumptuous undertaking. They reached Jericho about half past four and prepared to lodge there for the night.

Story of the Good Samaritan

164:1.1 (1809.3) That evening a considerable company gathered about Jesus and the two apostles to ask questions, many of which the apostles answered, while others the Master discussed. In the course of the evening a certain lawyer, seeking to entangle Jesus in a compromising disputation, said: "Teacher, I would like to ask you just what I should do to inherit eternal life?" Jesus answered, "What is written in the law and the prophets; how do you read the Scriptures?" The lawyer, knowing the teachings of both Jesus and the Pharisees, answered: "To love the Lord God with all your heart, soul, mind, and strength, and your neighbor as yourself." Then said Jesus: "You have answered right; this, if you really do, will lead to life everlasting."

164:1.2 (1809.4) But the lawyer was not wholly sincere in asking this question, and desiring to justify himself while also hoping to embarrass Jesus, he ventured to ask still another question. Drawing a little closer to the Master, he said, "But, Teacher, I should like you to tell me just who is my neighbor?" The lawyer asked this question hoping to entrap Jesus into making some statement that would contravene the Jewish law which defined one's neighbor as "the children of one's people." The Jews looked upon all others as "gentile dogs." This lawyer was somewhat familiar with Jesus' teachings and therefore well knew that the Master thought differently; thus he hoped to lead him into saying something which could be construed as an attack upon the sacred law.

164:1.3 (1810.1) But Jesus discerned the lawyer's motive, and instead of falling into the trap, he proceeded to tell his hearers a story, a story which would be fully appreciated by any Jericho audience. Said Jesus: "A certain man was going down from Jerusalem to Jericho, and he fell into the hands of cruel brigands, who robbed him, stripped him and beat him, and departing, left him half dead. Very soon, by chance, a certain priest was going down that way, and when he came upon the wounded man, seeing his sorry plight, he passed by on the other side of the road. And in like manner a Levite also, when he came along and saw the man, passed by on the other side. Now, about this time, a certain Samaritan, as he journeyed down to Jericho, came across this wounded man; and when he saw how he had been robbed and beaten, he was moved with compassion, and going over to him, he bound up his wounds, pouring on oil and wine, and setting the man upon his own beast, brought him here to the inn and took care of him. And on the morrow he took out some money and, giving it to the host, said: 'Take good care of my friend, and if the expense is more, when I come back again, I will repay you.' Now let me ask you: Which of these three turned out to be the neighbor of him who fell among the robbers?" And when the lawyer perceived that he had fallen into his own snare, he answered, "He who showed mercy on him." And Jesus said, "Go and do likewise."

164:1.4 (1810.2) The lawyer answered, "He who showed mercy," that he might refrain from even speaking that odious word, Samaritan. The lawyer was forced to give the very answer to the question, "Who is my neighbor?" which Jesus wished given, and which, if Jesus had so stated, would have directly involved him in the charge of heresy. Jesus not only confounded the dishonest lawyer, but he told his hearers a story which was at the same time a beautiful admonition to all his followers and a stunning rebuke to all Jews regarding their attitude toward the Samaritans. And this story has continued to promote brotherly love among all who have subsequently believed the gospel of Jesus.

At Jerusalem

164:2.1 (1810.3) Jesus had attended the feast of tabernacles that he might proclaim the gospel to the pilgrims from all parts of the empire; he now went up to the feast of the dedication for just one purpose: to give the Sanhedrin and the Jewish leaders another chance to see the light. The principal event of these few days in Jerusalem occurred on Friday night at the home of Nicodemus. Here were gathered together some twenty-five Jewish leaders who believed Jesus' teaching.

Among this group were fourteen men who were then, or had recently been, members of the Sanhedrin. This meeting was attended by Eber, Matadormus, and Joseph of Arimathea.

164:2.2 (1810.4) On this occasion Jesus' hearers were all learned men, and both they and his two apostles were amazed at the breadth and depth of the remarks which the Master made to this distinguished group. Not since the times when he had taught in Alexandria, Rome, and in the islands of the Mediterranean, had he exhibited such learning and shown such a grasp of the affairs of men, both secular and religious.

164:2.3 (1810.5) When this little meeting broke up, all went away mystified by the Master's personality, charmed by his gracious manner, and in love with the man. They had sought to advise Jesus concerning his desire to win the remaining members of the Sanhedrin. The Master listened attentively, but silently, to all their proposals. He well knew none of their plans would work. He surmised that the majority of the Jewish leaders never would accept the gospel of the kingdom; nevertheless, he gave them all this one more chance to choose. But when he went forth that night, with Nathaniel and Thomas, to lodge on the Mount of Olives, he had not yet decided upon the method he would pursue in bringing his work once more to the notice of the Sanhedrin.

164:2.4 (1811.1) That night Nathaniel and Thomas slept little; they were too much amazed by what they had heard at Nicodemus's house. They thought much over the final remark of Jesus regarding the offer of the former and present members of the Sanhedrin to go with him before the seventy. The Master said: "No, my brethren, it would be to no purpose. You would multiply the wrath to be visited upon your own heads, but you would not in the least mitigate the hatred which they bear me. Go, each of you, about the Father's business as the spirit leads you while I once more bring the kingdom to their notice in the manner which my Father may direct."

Healing the Blind Beggar

164:3.1 (1811.2) The next morning the three went over to Martha's home at Bethany for breakfast and then went immediately into Jerusalem. This Sabbath morning, as Jesus and his two apostles drew near the temple, they encountered a well-known beggar, a man who had been born blind, sitting at his usual place. Although these mendicants did not solicit or receive alms on the Sabbath day, they were permitted thus to sit in their usual places. Jesus paused and looked upon the beggar. As he gazed upon this man who had been born blind, the idea came into his mind as to how he would once more bring his mission on earth to the notice of the Sanhedrin and the other Jewish leaders and religious teachers.

164:3.2 (1811.3) As the Master stood there before the blind man, engrossed in deep thought, Nathaniel, pondering the possible cause of this man's blindness, asked: "Master, who did sin, this man or his parents, that he should be born blind?"

164:3.3 (1811.4) The rabbis taught that all such cases of blindness from birth were caused by sin. Not only were children conceived and born in sin, but a child could be born blind as a punishment for some specific sin committed by its father.

They even taught that a child itself might sin before it was born into the world. They also taught that such defects could be caused by some sin or other indulgence of the mother while carrying the child.

164:3.4 (1811.5) There was, throughout all these regions, a lingering belief in reincarnation. The older Jewish teachers, together with Plato, Philo, and many of the Essenes, tolerated the theory that men may reap in one incarnation what they have sown in a previous existence; thus in one life they were believed to be expiating the sins committed in preceding lives. The Master found it difficult to make men believe that their souls had not had previous existences.

164:3.5 (1811.6) However, inconsistent as it seems, while such blindness was supposed to be the result of sin, the Jews held that it was meritorious in a high degree to give alms to these blind beggars. It was the custom of these blind men constantly to chant to the passers-by, "O tenderhearted, gain merit by assisting the blind."

164:3.6 (1811.7) Jesus entered into the discussion of this case with Nathaniel and Thomas, not only because he had already decided to use this blind man as the means of that day bringing his mission once more prominently to the notice of the Jewish leaders, but also because he always encouraged his apostles to seek for the true causes of all phenomena, natural or spiritual. He had often warned them to avoid the common tendency to assign spiritual causes to commonplace physical events.

164:3.7 (1812.1) Jesus decided to use this beggar in his plans for that day's work, but before doing anything for the blind man, Josiah by name, he proceeded to answer Nathaniel's question. Said the Master: "Neither did this man sin nor his parents that the works of God might be manifest in him. This blindness has come upon him in the natural course of events, but we must now do the works of Him who sent me, while it is still day, for the night will certainly come when it will be impossible to do the work we are about to perform. When I am in the world, I am the light of the world, but in only a little while I will not be with you."

164:3.8 (1812.2) When Jesus had spoken, he said to Nathaniel and Thomas:

"Let us create the sight of this blind man on this Sabbath day that the scribes and Pharisees may have the full occasion which they seek for accusing the Son of Man." Then, stooping over, he spat on the ground and mixed the clay with the spittle, and speaking of all this so that the blind man could hear, he went up to Josiah and put the clay over his sightless eyes, saying: "Go, my son, wash away this clay in the pool of Siloam, and immediately you shall receive your sight." And when Josiah had so washed in the pool of Siloam, he returned to his friends and family, seeing.

164:3.9 (1812.3) Having always been a beggar, he knew nothing else; so, when the first excitement of the creation of his sight had passed, he returned to his usual place of alms-seeking. His friends, neighbors, and all who had known him aforetime, when they observed that he could see, all said, "Is this not Josiah the blind beggar?" Some said it was he, while others said, "No, it is one like him, but this man can see." But when they asked the man himself, he answered, "I am he."

164:3.10 (1812.4) When they began to inquire of him how he was able to see, he answered them: "A man called Jesus came by this way, and when talking about me with his friends, he made clay with spittle, anointed my eyes, and directed that I should go and wash in the pool of Siloam. I did what this man told me, and immediately I received my sight. And that is only a few hours ago. I do not yet know the meaning of much that I see." And when the people who began to gather about him asked where they could find the strange man who had healed him, Josiah could answer only that he did not know.

164:3.11 (1812.5) This is one of the strangest of all the Master's miracles. This man did not ask for healing. He did not know that the Jesus who had directed him to wash at Siloam, and who had promised him vision, was the prophet of Galilee who had preached in Jerusalem during the feast of tabernacles. This man had little faith that he would receive his sight, but the people of that day had great faith in the efficacy of the spittle of a great or holy man; and from Jesus' conversation with Nathaniel and Thomas, Josiah had concluded that his would-be benefactor was a great man, a learned teacher or a holy prophet; accordingly he did as Jesus directed him.

164:3.12 (1812.6) Jesus made use of the clay and the spittle and directed him to wash in the symbolic pool of Siloam for three reasons:

164:3.13 (1812.7) 1. This was not a miracle response to the individual's faith. This was a wonder which Jesus chose to perform for a purpose of his own, but which he so arranged that this man might derive lasting benefit therefrom.

164:3.14 (1813.1) 2. As the blind man had not asked for healing, and since the faith he had was slight, these material acts were suggested for the purpose of encouraging him. He did believe in the superstition of the efficacy of spittle, and he knew the pool of Siloam was a semisacred place. But he would hardly have gone there had it not been necessary to wash away the clay of his anointing. There was just enough ceremony about the transaction to induce him to act.

164:3.15 (1813.2) 3. But Jesus had a third reason for resorting to these material means in connection with this unique transaction: This was a miracle wrought purely in obedience to his own choosing, and thereby he desired to teach his followers of that day and all subsequent ages to refrain from despising or neglecting material means in the healing of the sick. He wanted to teach them that they must cease to regard miracles as the only method of curing human diseases.

164:3.16 (1813.3) Jesus gave this man his sight by miraculous working, on this Sabbath morning and in Jerusalem near the temple, for the prime purpose of making this act an open challenge to the Sanhedrin and all the Jewish teachers and religious leaders. This was his way of proclaiming an open break with the Pharisees. He was always positive in everything he did. And it was for the purpose of bringing these matters before the Sanhedrin that Jesus brought his two apostles to this man early in the afternoon of this Sabbath day and deliberately provoked those discussions which compelled the Pharisees to take notice of the miracle.

Josiah Before the Sanhedrin

164:4.1 (1813.4) By mid-afternoon the healing of Josiah had raised such a discussion around the temple that the leaders of the Sanhedrin decided to convene the council in its usual temple meeting place. And they did this in violation of a standing rule which forbade the meeting of the Sanhedrin on the Sabbath day. Jesus knew that Sabbath breaking would be one of the chief charges to be brought against him when the final test came, and he desired to be brought before the Sanhedrin for adjudication of the charge of having healed a blind man on the Sabbath day, when the very session of the high Jewish court sitting in judgment on him for this act of mercy would be deliberating on these matters on the Sabbath day and in direct violation of their own self-imposed laws.

164:4.2 (1813.5) But they did not call Jesus before them; they feared to. Instead, they sent forthwith for Josiah. After some preliminary questioning, the spokesman for the Sanhedrin (about fifty members being present) directed Josiah to tell them what had happened to him. Since his healing that morning Josiah had learned from Thomas, Nathaniel, and others that the Pharisees were angry about his healing on the Sabbath, and that they were likely to make trouble for all concerned; but Josiah did not yet perceive that Jesus was he who was called the Deliverer. So, when the Pharisees questioned him, he said: "This man came along, put clay upon my eyes, told me to go wash in Siloam, and I do now see."

164:4.3 (1813.6) One of the older

Pharisees, after making a lengthy speech, said: "This man cannot be from God because you can see that he does not observe the Sabbath. He violates the law, first, in making the clay, then, in sending this beggar to wash in Siloam on the Sabbath day. Such a man cannot be a teacher sent from God."

164:4.4 (1813.7) Then one of the younger men who secretly believed in Jesus, said: "If this man is not sent by God, how can he do these things? We know that one who is a common sinner cannot perform such miracles. We all know this beggar and that he was born blind; now he sees. Will you still say that this prophet does all these wonders by the power of the prince of devils?" And for every Pharisee who dared to accuse and denounce Jesus one would arise to ask entangling and embarrassing questions, so that a serious division arose among them. The presiding officer saw whither they were drifting, and in order to allay the discussion, he prepared further to question the man himself. Turning to Josiah, he said: "What do you have to say about this man, this Jesus, whom you claim opened your eyes?" And Josiah answered, "I think he is a prophet."

164:4.5 (1814.1) The leaders were greatly troubled and, knowing not what else to do, decided to send for Josiah's parents to learn whether he had actually been born blind. They were loath to believe that the beggar had been healed.

164:4.6 (1814.2) It was well known about Jerusalem, not only that Jesus was denied entrance into all synagogues, but that all who believed in his teaching were likewise cast out of the synagogue, excommunicated from the congregation of Israel; and this meant denial of all rights and privileges of every sort throughout all Jewry except the right to buy the necessaries of life.

164:4.7 (1814.3) When, therefore, Josiah's parents, poor and fear-burdened souls, appeared before the august Sanhedrin, they were afraid to speak freely. Said

the spokesman of the court: "Is this your son? and do we understand aright that he was born blind? If this is true, how is it that he can now see?" And then Josiah's father, seconded by his mother, answered: "We know that this is our son and that he was born blind, but how it is that he has come to see, or who it was that opened his eyes, we know not. Ask him; he is of age; let him speak for himself."

164:4.8 (1814.4) They now called Josiah up before them a second time. They were not getting along well with their scheme of holding a formal trial, and some were beginning to feel strange about doing this on the Sabbath; accordingly, when they recalled Josiah, they attempted to ensnare him by a different mode of attack. The officer of the court spoke to the former blind man, saying: "Why do you not give God the glory for this? why do you not tell us the whole truth about what happened? We all know that this man is a sinner. Why do you refuse to discern the truth? You know that both you and this man stand convicted of Sabbath breaking. Will you not atone for your sin by acknowledging God as your healer, if you still claim that your eyes have this day been opened?"

164:4.9 (1814.5) But Josiah was neither dumb nor lacking in humor; so he replied to the officer of the court: "Whether this man is a sinner, I know not; but one thing I do know—that, whereas I was blind, now I see." And since they could not entrap Josiah, they sought further to question him, asking: "Just how did he open your eyes? what did he actually do to you? what did he say to you? did he ask you to believe in him?"

164:4.10 (1814.6) Josiah replied, somewhat impatiently: "I have told you exactly how it all happened, and if you did not believe my testimony, why would you hear it again? Would you by any chance also become his disciples?" When Josiah had thus spoken, the Sanhedrin broke up in confusion, almost violence, for the leaders rushed upon Josiah, angrily exclaiming: "You may talk about being this man's disciple, but we are disciples of Moses, and we are the teachers of the laws of God. We know that God spoke through Moses, but as for this man Jesus, we know not whence he is."

164:4.11 (1814.7) Then Josiah, standing upon a stool, shouted abroad to all who could hear, saying: "Hearken, you who claim to be the teachers of all Israel, while I declare to you that herein is a great marvel since you confess that you know not whence this man is, and yet you know of a certainty, from the testimony which you have heard, that he opened my eyes. We all know that God does not perform such works for the ungodly; that God would do such a thing only at the request of a true worshiper—for one who is holy and righteous. You know that not since the beginning of the world have you ever heard of the opening of the eyes of one who was born blind. Look, then, all of you, upon me and realize what has been done this day in Jerusalem! I tell you, if this man were not from God, he could not do this." And as the Sanhedrists departed in anger and confusion, they shouted to him: "You were altogether born in sin, and do you now presume to teach us? Maybe you were not really born blind, and even if your eyes were opened on the Sabbath day, this was done by the power of the prince of devils." And they went at once to the synagogue to cast out Josiah.

164:4.12 (1815.1) Josiah entered this trial with meager ideas about Jesus and the nature of his healing. Most of the daring testimony which he so cleverly and courageously bore before this supreme tribunal of all Israel developed in his mind as the trial proceeded along such unfair and unjust lines.

Teaching in Solomon's Porch

164:5.1 (1815.2) All of the time this Sabbath-breaking session of the Sanhedrin was in progress in one of the temple chambers, Jesus was walking about near at hand, teaching the people in Solomon's Porch, hoping that he would be summoned before the Sanhedrin where he could tell them the good news of the liberty and joy of divine sonship in the kingdom of God. But they were afraid to send for him. They were always disconcerted by these sudden and public appearances of Jesus in Jerusalem. The very occasion they had so ardently sought, Jesus now gave them, but they feared to bring him before the Sanhedrin even as a witness, and even more they feared to arrest him.

164:5.2 (1815.3) This was midwinter in Jerusalem, and the people sought the partial shelter of Solomon's Porch; and as Jesus lingered, the crowds asked him many questions, and he taught them for more than two hours. Some of the Jewish teachers sought to entrap him by publicly asking him: "How long will you hold us in suspense? If you are the Messiah, why do you not plainly tell us?" Said Jesus: "I have told you about myself and my Father many times, but you will not believe me. Can you not see that the works I do in my Father's name bear witness for me? But many of you believe not because you belong not to my fold. The teacher of truth attracts only those who hunger for the truth and who thirst for righteousness. My sheep hear my voice and I know them and they follow me. And to all who follow my teaching I give eternal life; they shall never perish, and no one shall snatch them out of my hand. My Father, who has given me these children, is greater than all, so that no one is able to pluck them out of my Father's hand. The Father and I are one." Some of the unbelieving Jews rushed over to where they were still building the temple to pick up stones to cast at Jesus, but the believers restrained them.

164:5.3 (1815.4) Jesus continued his teaching: "Many loving works have I shown you from the Father, so that now would I inquire for which one of these good works do you think to stone me?" And then answered one of the Pharisees: "For no good work would we stone you but for blasphemy, inasmuch as you, being a man, dare to make yourself equal with God." And Jesus answered: "You charge the Son of Man with blasphemy because you refused to believe me when I declared to you that I was sent by God. If I do not the works of God, believe me not, but if I do the works of God, even though you believe not in me, I should think you would believe the works. But that you may be certain of what I proclaim, let me again assert that the Father is in me and I in the Father, and that, as the Father dwells in me, so will I dwell in every one who believes this gospel." And when the people heard these words, many of them rushed out to lay hands upon the stones to cast at him, but he passed out through the temple precincts; and meeting Nathaniel and Thomas, who had been in attendance upon the session of the Sanhedrin, he waited with them near the temple until Josiah came from the council chamber.

164:5.4 (1816.1) Jesus and the two apostles did not go in search of Josiah at his home until they heard he had been cast out of the synagogue. When they came to his house, Thomas called him out in the yard, and Jesus, speaking to him, said: "Josiah, do you believe in the Son of God?" And Josiah answered, "Tell me who he is that I may believe in him." And Jesus said: "You have both seen and heard him, and it is he who now speaks to you." And Josiah said, "Lord, I believe," and falling down, he worshiped.

164:5.5 (1816.2) When Josiah learned that he had been cast out of the synagogue, he was at first greatly downcast, but he was much encouraged when Jesus directed that he should immediately prepare to go with them to the camp at Pella.
This simple-minded man of Jerusalem had indeed been cast out of a Jewish synagogue, but behold the Creator of a universe leading him forth to become associated with the spiritual nobility of that day and generation.

164:5.6 (1816.3) And now Jesus left Jerusalem, not again to return until near the time when he prepared to leave this world. With the two apostles and Josiah

the Master went back to Pella. And Josiah proved to be one of the recipients of the Master's miraculous ministry who turned out fruitfully, for he became a lifelong preacher of the gospel of the kingdom.

Paper 165

The Perean Mission Begins

165:0.1 (1817.1) ON TUESDAY, January 3, A.D. 30, Abner, the former chief of the twelve apostles of John the Baptist, a Nazarite and onetime head of the Nazarite school at Engedi, now chief of the seventy messengers of the kingdom, called his associates together and gave them final instructions before sending them on a mission to all of the cities and villages of Perea. This Perean mission continued for almost three months and was the last ministry of the Master. From these labors Jesus went directly to Jerusalem to pass through his final experiences in the flesh. The seventy, supplemented by the periodic labors of Jesus and the twelve apostles, worked in the following cities and towns and some fifty additional villages: Zaphon, Gadara, Macad, Arbela, Ramath, Edrei, Bosora, Caspin, Mispeh, Gerasa, Ragaba, Succoth, Amathus, Adam, Penuel, Capitolias, Dion, Hatita, Gadda, Philadelphia, Jogbehah, Gilead, Beth-Nimrah, Tyrus, Elealah, Livias, Heshbon, Callirrhoe, Beth-Peor, Shittim, Sibmah, Medeba, Beth-Meon, Areopolis, and Aroer.

165:0.2 (1817.2) Throughout this tour of Perea the women's corps, now numbering sixty-two, took over most of the work of ministration to the sick. This was the final period of the development of the higher spiritual aspects of the gospel of the kingdom, and there was, accordingly, an absence of miracle working. No other part of Palestine was so thoroughly worked by the apostles and disciples of Jesus, and in no other region did the better classes of citizens so generally accept the Master's teaching. *

165:0.3 (1817.3) Perea at this time was about equally gentile and Jewish, the Jews having been generally removed from these regions during the times of Judas Maccabee. Perea was the most beautiful and picturesque province of all Palestine. It was generally referred to by the Jews as "the land beyond the Jordan." *

165:0.4 (1817.4) Throughout this period Jesus divided his time between the camp at Pella and trips with the twelve to assist the seventy in the various cities where they taught and preached. Under Abner's instructions the seventy baptized all believers, although Jesus had not so charged them.

At the Pella Camp

165:1.1 (1817.5) By the middle of January more than twelve hundred persons were gathered together at Pella, and Jesus taught this multitude at least once each day when he was in residence at the camp, usually speaking at nine o'clock in the morning if not prevented by rain. Peter and the other apostles taught each afternoon. The evenings Jesus reserved for the usual sessions of questions and answers with the twelve and other advanced disciples. The evening groups averaged about fifty.

165:1.2 (1817.6) By the middle of March, the time when Jesus began his journey toward Jerusalem, over four thousand persons composed the large audience which heard Jesus or Peter preach each morning. The Master chose to terminate his work on earth when the interest in his message had reached a high point, the highest point attained under this second or nonmiraculous phase of the progress of the kingdom. While three quarters of the multitude were truth seekers, there were also present a large number of Pharisees from Jerusalem and elsewhere, together with many doubters and cavilers.

165:1.3 (1818.1) Jesus and the twelve apostles devoted much of their time to the multitude assembled at the Pella camp. The twelve paid little or no attention to the field work, only going out with Jesus to visit Abner's associates from time to time. Abner was very familiar with the Perean district since this was the field in which his former master, John the Baptist, had done most of his work. After beginning the Perean mission, Abner and the seventy never returned to the Pella camp.

Sermon on the Good Shepherd

165:2.1 (1818.2) A company of over three hundred Jerusalemites, Pharisees and others, followed Jesus north to Pella when he hastened away from the jurisdiction of the Jewish rulers at the ending of the feast of the dedication; and it was in the presence of these Jewish teachers and leaders, as well as in the hearing of the twelve apostles, that Jesus preached the sermon on the "Good Shepherd." After half an hour of informal discussion, speaking to a group of about one hundred, Jesus said:

165:2.2 (1818.3) "On this night I have much to tell you, and since many of you are my disciples and some of you my bitter enemies, I will present my teaching in a parable, so that you may each take for yourself that which finds a reception in your heart.

165:2.3 (1818.4) "Tonight, here before me are men who would be willing to die for me and for this gospel of the kingdom, and some of them will so offer themselves in the years to come; and here also are some of you, slaves of tradition, who have followed me down from Jerusalem, and who, with your darkened and deluded leaders, seek to kill the Son of Man. The life which I now live in the flesh shall judge both of you, the true shepherds and the false shepherds. If the false shepherd were blind, he would have no sin, but you claim that you see; you profess to be teachers in Israel; therefore does your sin remain upon you.

165:2.4 (1818.5) "The true shepherd gathers his flock into the fold for the night in times of danger. And when the morning has come, he enters into the fold by the door, and when he calls, the sheep know his voice. Every shepherd who gains entrance to the sheepfold by any other means than by the door is a thief and a robber. The true shepherd enters the fold after the porter has opened the door for him, and his sheep, knowing his voice, come out at his word; and when they that are his are thus brought forth, the true shepherd goes before them; he leads the way and the sheep follow him. His sheep follow him because they know his voice; they will not follow a stranger. They will flee from the stranger because they know not his voice. This multitude which is gathered about us here are like sheep without a shepherd, but when we speak to them, they know the shepherd's voice, and they follow after us; at least, those who hunger for truth and thirst for righteousness do. Some of you are not of my fold; you know not my voice, and you do not follow me. And because you are false shepherds, the sheep know not your voice and will not follow you."

165:2.5 (1819.1) And when Jesus had spoken this parable, no one asked him a question. After a time he began again to speak and went on to discuss the parable:

165:2.6 (1819.2) "You who would be the undershepherds of my Father's flocks must not only be worthy leaders, but you must also feed the flock with good food; you are not true shepherds unless you lead your flocks into green pastures and beside still waters.

165:2.7 (1819.3) "And now, lest some of you too easily comprehend this parable, I will declare that I am both the door to the Father's sheepfold and at the same time the true shepherd of my Father's flocks. Every shepherd who seeks to enter the fold without me shall fail, and the sheep will not hear his voice. I, with those who minister with me, am the door.

Every soul who enters upon the eternal way by the means I have created and ordained shall be saved and will be able to go on to the attainment of the eternal pastures of Paradise.

165:2.8 (1819.4) "But I also am the true shepherd who is willing even to lay down his life for the sheep. The thief breaks into the fold only to steal, and to kill, and to destroy; but I have come that you all may have life and have it more abundantly. He who is a hireling, when danger arises, will flee and allow the sheep to be scattered and destroyed; but the true shepherd will not flee when the wolf comes; he will protect his flock and, if necessary, lay down his life for his sheep. Verily, verily, I say to you, friends and enemies, I am the true shepherd; I know my own and my own know me. I will not flee in the face of danger. I will finish this service of the completion of my Father's will, and I will not forsake the flock which the Father has intrusted to my keeping.

165:2.9 (1819.5) "But I have many other sheep not of this fold, and these words are true not only of this world. These other sheep also hear and know my voice, and I have promised the Father that they shall all be brought into one fold, one brotherhood of the sons of God. And then shall you all know the voice of one shepherd, the true shepherd, and shall all acknowledge the fatherhood of God.

165:2.10 (1819.6) "And so shall you know why the Father loves me and has put all of his flocks in this domain in my hands for keeping; it is because the Father knows that I will not falter in the safeguarding of the sheepfold, that I will not desert my sheep, and that, if it shall be required, I will not hesitate to lay down my life in the service of his manifold flocks. But, mind you, if I lay down my life, I will take it up again. No man nor any other creature can take away my life. I have the right and the power to lay down my life, and I have the same power and right to take it up again. You cannot understand this, but I received such authority from my Father even before this world was."

165:2.11 (1819.7) When they heard these words, his apostles were confused, his disciples were amazed, while the Pharisees from Jerusalem and around about went out into the night, saying, "He is either mad or has a devil." But even some of the Jerusalem teachers said: "He speaks like one having authority; besides, who ever saw one having a devil open the eyes of a man born blind and do all of the wonderful things which this man has done?"

165:2.12 (1819.8) On the morrow about half of these Jewish teachers professed belief in Jesus, and the other half in dismay returned to Jerusalem and their homes.

Sabbath Sermon at Pella

165:3.1 (1819.9) By the end of January the Sabbath-afternoon multitudes numbered almost three thousand. On Saturday, January 28, Jesus preached the memorable sermon on "Trust and Spiritual Preparedness." After preliminary remarks by Simon Peter, the Master said:

165:3.2 (1820.1) "What I have many times said to my apostles and to my disciples, I now declare to this multitude: Beware of the leaven of the Pharisees which is hypocrisy, born of prejudice and nurtured in traditional bondage, albeit many of these Pharisees are honest of heart and some of them abide here as my disciples. Presently all of you shall understand my teaching, for there is nothing now covered that shall not be revealed. That which is now hid from you shall all be made known when the Son of Man has completed his mission on earth and in the flesh.

165:3.3 (1820.2) "Soon, very soon, will the things which our enemies now plan in secrecy and in darkness be brought out into the light and be proclaimed from the housetops. But I say to you, my friends, when they seek to destroy the Son of Man, be not afraid of them. Fear not those who, although they may be able to kill the body, after that have no more power over you. I admonish you to fear none, in heaven or on earth, but to rejoice in the knowledge of Him who has power to deliver you from all unrighteousness and to present you blameless before the judgment seat of a universe. *

165:3.4 (1820.3) "Are not five sparrows sold for two pennies? And yet, when these birds flit about in quest of their sustenance, not one of them exists without the knowledge of the Father, the source of all life. To the seraphic guardians the very hairs of your head are numbered. And if all of this is true, why should you live in fear of the many trifles which come up in your daily lives? I say to you: Fear not; you are of much more value than many sparrows.

165:3.5 (1820.4) "All of you who have had the courage to confess faith in my gospel before men I will presently acknowledge before the angels of heaven; but he who shall knowingly deny the truth of my teachings before men shall be denied by his guardian of destiny even before the angels of heaven.

165:3.6 (1820.5) "Say what you will about the Son of Man, and it shall be forgiven you; but he who presumes to blaspheme against God shall hardly find forgiveness. When men go so far as knowingly to ascribe the doings of God to the forces of evil, such deliberate rebels will hardly seek forgiveness for their sins.

165:3.7 (1820.6) "And when our enemies bring you before the rulers of the synagogues and before other high authorities, be not concerned about what you should say and be not anxious as to how you should answer their questions, for the spirit that dwells within you shall certainly teach you in that very hour what you should say in honor of the gospel of the kingdom.

165:3.8 (1820.7) "How long will you tarry in the valley of decision? Why do you halt between two opinions? Why should Jew or gentile hesitate to accept the good news that he is a son of the eternal God? How long will it take us to persuade you to enter joyfully into your spiritual inheritance? I came into this world to reveal the Father to you and to lead you to the Father. The first I have done, but the last I may not do without your consent; the Father never compels any man to enter the kingdom. The invitation ever has been and always will be: Whosoever will, let him come and freely partake of the water of life."

165:3.9 (1820.8) When Jesus had finished speaking, many went forth to be baptized by the apostles in the Jordan while he listened to the questions of those who remained.

Dividing the Inheritance

165:4.1 (1821.1) As the apostles baptized believers, the Master talked with those who tarried. And a certain young man said to him: "Master, my father died leaving much property to me and my brother, but my brother refuses to give me that which is my own. Will you, then, bid my brother divide this inheritance with me?" Jesus was mildly indignant that this material-minded youth should bring up for discussion such a question of business; but he proceeded to use the occasion for the impartation of further instruction. Said Jesus: "Man, who made me a divider over you? Where did you get the idea that I give attention to the material affairs of this world?" And then, turning to all who were about him, he said: "Take heed and keep yourselves free from covetousness; a man's life consists not in the abundance of the things which he may possess. Happiness comes not from the power of wealth, and joy springs not from riches. Wealth, in itself, is not a curse, but the love of riches many times leads to such devotion to the things of this world that the soul becomes blinded to the beautiful attractions of the spiritual realities of the kingdom of God on earth and to the joys of eternal life in heaven.

165:4.2 (1821.2) "Let me tell you a story of a certain rich man whose ground brought forth plentifully; and when he had become very rich, he began to reason with himself, saying: 'What shall I do with all my riches? I now have so much that I have no place to store my wealth.' And when he had meditated on his problem, he said: 'This I will do; I will pull down my barns and build greater ones, and thus will I have abundant room in which to store my fruits and my goods.

Then can I say to my soul, soul, you have much wealth laid up for many years; take now your ease; eat, drink, and be merry, for you are rich and increased in goods.'

165:4.3 (1821.3) "But this rich man was also foolish. In providing for the material requirements of his mind and body, he had failed to lay up treasures in heaven for the satisfaction of the spirit and for the salvation of the soul. And even then he was not to enjoy the pleasure of consuming his hoarded wealth, for that very night was his soul required of him. That night there came the brigands who broke into his house to kill him, and after they had plundered his barns, they burned that which remained. And for the property which escaped the robbers his heirs fell to fighting among themselves. This man laid up treasures for himself on earth, but he was not rich toward God."

165:4.4 (1821.4) Jesus thus dealt with the young man and his inheritance because he knew that his trouble was covetousness. Even if this had not been the case, the Master would not have interfered, for he never meddled with the temporal affairs of even his apostles, much less his disciples.

165:4.5 (1821.5) When Jesus had finished his story, another man rose up and asked him: "Master, I know that your apostles have sold all their earthly possessions to follow you, and that they have all things in common as do the Essenes, but would you have all of us who are your disciples do likewise? Is it a sin to possess honest wealth?" And Jesus replied to this question: "My friend, it is not a sin to have honorable wealth; but it is a sin if you convert the wealth of material possessions into treasures which may absorb your interests and divert your affections from devotion to the spiritual pursuits of the kingdom. There is no sin in having honest possessions on earth provided your treasure is in heaven, for where your treasure is there will your heart be also. There is a great difference between wealth which leads to

covetousness and selfishness and that which is held and dispensed in the spirit of stewardship by those who have an abundance of this world's goods, and who so bountifully contribute to the support of those who devote all their energies to the work of the kingdom. Many of you who are here and without money are fed and lodged in yonder tented city because liberal men and women of means have given funds to your host, David Zebedee, for such purposes.

165:4.6 (1822.1) "But never forget that, after all, wealth is unenduring. The love of riches all too often obscures and even destroys the spiritual vision. Fail not to recognize the danger of wealth's becoming, not your servant, but your master."

165:4.7 (1822.2) Jesus did not teach nor countenance improvidence, idleness, indifference to providing the physical necessities for one's family, or dependence upon alms. But he did teach that the material and temporal must be subordinated to the welfare of the soul and the progress of the spiritual nature in the kingdom of heaven.

165:4.8 (1822.3) Then, as the people went down by the river to witness the baptizing, the first man came privately to Jesus about his inheritance inasmuch as he thought Jesus had dealt harshly with him; and when the Master had again heard him, he replied: "My son, why do you miss the opportunity to feed upon the bread of life on a day like this in order to indulge your covetous disposition? Do you not know that the Jewish laws of inheritance will be justly administered if you will go with your complaint to the court of the synagogue? Can you not see that my work has to do

with making sure that you know about your heavenly inheritance? Have you not read the Scripture: 'There is he who waxes rich by his wariness and much pinching, and this is the portion of his reward: Whereas he says, I have found rest and now shall be able to eat continually of my goods, yet he knows not what time shall bring upon him, and also that he must leave all these things to others when he dies.' Have you not read the commandment: 'You shall not covet.' And again, 'They have eaten and filled themselves and waxed fat, and then did they turn to other gods.' Have you read in the Psalms that 'the Lord abhors the covetous,' and that 'the little a righteous man has is better than the riches of many wicked.' 'If riches increase, set not your heart upon them.' Have you read where Jeremiah said, 'Let not the rich man glory in his riches'; and Ezekiel spoke truth when he said, 'With their mouths they make a show of love, but their hearts are set upon their own selfish gain.'" *

165:4.9 (1822.4) Jesus sent the young man away, saying to him, "My son, what shall it profit you if you gain the whole world and lose your own soul?"

165:4.10 (1822.5) To another standing near by who asked Jesus how the wealthy would stand in the day of judgment, he replied: "I have come to judge neither the rich nor the poor, but the lives men live will sit in judgment on all. Whatever else may concern the wealthy in the judgment, at least three questions must be answered by all who acquire great wealth, and these questions are:

165:4.11 (1822.6) "1. How much wealth did you accumulate?
165:4.12 (1822.7) "2. How did you get this wealth?
165:4.13 (1822.8) "3. How did you use your wealth?"
165:4.14 (1822.9) Then Jesus went into his tent to rest for a while before the evening meal. When the apostles had finished with the baptizing, they came also and would have talked with him about wealth on earth and treasure in heaven,

but he was asleep.

Talks to the Apostles on Wealth

165:5.1 (1823.1) That evening after supper, when Jesus and the twelve gathered together for their daily conference, Andrew asked: "Master, while we were baptizing the believers, you spoke many words to the lingering multitude which we did not hear. Would you be willing to repeat these words for our benefit?" And in response to Andrew's request, Jesus said:

165:5.2 (1823.2) "Yes, Andrew, I will speak to you about these matters of wealth and self-support, but my words to you, the apostles, must be somewhat different from those spoken to the disciples and the multitude since you have forsaken everything, not only to follow me, but to be ordained as ambassadors of the kingdom. Already have you had several years' experience, and you know that the Father whose kingdom you proclaim will not forsake you. You have dedicated your lives to the ministry of the kingdom; therefore be not anxious or worried about the things of the temporal life, what you shall eat, nor yet for your body, what you shall wear. The welfare of the soul is more than food and drink; the progress in the spirit is far above the need of raiment. When you are tempted to doubt the sureness of your bread, consider the ravens; they sow not neither reap, they have no storehouses or barns, and yet the Father provides food for every one of them that seeks it. And of how much more value are you than many birds! Besides, all of your anxiety or fretting doubts can do nothing to supply your material needs. Which of you by anxiety can add a handbreadth to your stature or a day to your life? Since such matters are not in your hands, why do you give anxious thought to any of these problems?

165:5.3 (1823.3) "Consider the lilies, how they grow; they toil not, neither do they spin; yet I say to you, even Solomon in all his glory was not arrayed like one of these. If God so clothes the grass of the field, which is alive today and tomorrow is cut down and cast into the fire, how much more shall he clothe you, the ambassadors of the heavenly kingdom. O you of little faith! When you wholeheartedly devote yourselves to the proclamation of the gospel of the kingdom, you should not be of doubtful minds concerning the support of yourselves or the families you have forsaken. If you give your lives truly to the gospel, you shall live by the gospel. If you are only believing disciples, you must earn your own bread and contribute to the sustenance of all who teach and preach and heal. If you are anxious about your bread and water, wherein are you different from the nations of the world who so diligently seek such necessities?

Devote yourselves to your work, believing that both the Father and I know that you have need of all these things. Let me assure you, once and for all, that, if you dedicate your lives to the work of the kingdom, all your real needs shall be supplied. Seek the greater thing, and the lesser will be found therein; ask for the heavenly, and the earthly shall be included. The shadow is certain to follow the substance.

165:5.4 (1823.4) "You are only a small group, but if you have faith, if you will not stumble in fear, I declare that it is my Father's good pleasure to give you this kingdom. You have laid up your treasures where the purse waxes not old, where no thief can despoil, and where no moth can destroy. And as I told the people, where your treasure is, there will your heart be also.

165:5.5 (1824.1) "But in the work which is just ahead of us, and in that which remains for you after I go to the Father, you will be grievously tried. You must all be on your watch against fear and doubts. Every one of you, gird up the loins of your minds and let your lamps be kept burning. Keep yourselves like men who are watching for their master to return from the marriage feast so that, when he comes and knocks, you may quickly open to him. Such watchful servants are blessed by the master who finds them faithful at such a great moment.

Then will the master make his servants sit down while he himself serves them. Verily, verily, I say to you that a crisis is just ahead in your lives, and it behooves you to watch and be ready.

165:5.6 (1824.2) "You well understand that no man would suffer his house to be broken into if he knew what hour the thief was to come. Be you also on watch for yourselves, for in an hour that you least suspect and in a manner you think not, shall the Son of Man depart."

165:5.7 (1824.3) For some minutes the twelve sat in silence. Some of these warnings they had heard before but not in the setting presented to them at this time.

Answer to Peter's Question

165:6.1 (1824.4) As they sat thinking, Simon Peter asked: "Do you speak this parable to us, your apostles, or is it for all the disciples?" And Jesus answered:

165:6.2 (1824.5) "In the time of testing, a man's soul is revealed; trial discloses what really is in the heart. When the servant is tested and proved, then may the lord of the house set such a servant over his household and safely trust this faithful steward to see that his children are fed and nurtured. Likewise, will I soon know who can be trusted with the welfare of my children when I shall have returned to the Father. As the lord of the household shall set the true and tried servant over the affairs of his family, so will I exalt those who endure the trials of this hour in the affairs of my kingdom.

165:6.3 (1824.6) "But if the servant is slothful and begins to say in his heart, 'My master delays his coming,' and begins to mistreat his fellow servants and to eat and drink with the drunken, then the lord of that servant will come at a time when he looks not for him and, finding him unfaithful, will cast him out in disgrace. Therefore you do well to prepare yourselves for that day when you will be visited suddenly and in an unexpected manner. Remember, much has been given to you; therefore will much be required of you. Fiery trials are drawing near you. I have a baptism to be baptized with, and I am on watch until this is accomplished. You preach peace on earth, but my mission will not bring peace in the material affairs of men—not for a time, at least. Division can only be the result where two members of a family believe in me and three members reject this gospel. Friends, relatives, and loved ones are destined to be set against each other by the gospel you preach. True, each of these believers shall have great and lasting peace in his own heart, but peace on earth will not come until all are willing to believe and enter into their glorious inheritance of sonship with God. Nevertheless, go into all the world proclaiming this gospel to all nations, to every man, woman, and child."

165:6.4 (1824.7) And this was the end of a full and busy Sabbath day. On the morrow Jesus and the twelve went into the cities of northern Perea to visit with the seventy, who were working in these regions under Abner's supervision.

Paper 166

Last Visit to Northern Perea

166:0.1 (1825.1) FROM February 11 to 20, Jesus and the twelve made a tour of all the cities and villages of northern Perea where the associates of Abner and the members of the women's corps were working. They found these messengers of the gospel meeting with success, and Jesus repeatedly called the attention of his apostles to the fact that the gospel of the kingdom could spread without the accompaniment of miracles and wonders.

166:0.2 (1825.2) This entire mission of three months in Perea was successfully carried on with little help from the twelve apostles, and the gospel from this time on reflected, not so much Jesus' personality, as his teachings. But his followers did not long follow his instructions, for soon after Jesus' death and resurrection they departed from his teachings and began to build the early church around the miraculous concepts and the glorified memories of his divine-human personality.

The Pharisees at Ragaba

166:1.1 (1825.3) On Sabbath, February 18, Jesus was at Ragaba, where there lived a wealthy Pharisee named Nathaniel; and since quite a number of his fellow Pharisees were following Jesus and the twelve around the country, he made a breakfast on this Sabbath morning for all of them, about twenty in number, and invited Jesus as the guest of honor.

166:1.2 (1825.4) By the time Jesus arrived at this breakfast, most of the Pharisees, with two or three lawyers, were already there and seated at the table. The Master immediately took his seat at the left of Nathaniel without going to the water basins to wash his hands. Many of the Pharisees, especially those favorable to Jesus' teachings, knew that he washed his hands only for purposes of cleanliness, that he abhorred these purely ceremonial performances; so they were not surprised at his coming directly to the table without having twice washed his hands. But Nathaniel was shocked by this failure of the Master to comply with the strict requirements of Pharisaic practice. Neither did Jesus wash his hands, as did the Pharisees, after each course of food nor at the end of the meal.

166:1.3 (1825.5) After considerable whispering between Nathaniel and an unfriendly Pharisee on his right and after much lifting of eyebrows and sneering curling of lips by those who sat opposite the Master, Jesus finally said: "I had thought that you invited me to this house to break bread with you and perchance to inquire of me concerning the proclamation of the new gospel of the kingdom of God; but I perceive that you have brought me here to witness an exhibition of ceremonial devotion to your own self-righteousness. That service you have now done me; what next will you honor me with as your guest on this occasion?"

166:1.4 (1826.1) When the Master had thus spoken, they cast their eyes upon the table and remained silent. And since no one spoke, Jesus continued: "Many of you Pharisees are here with me as friends, some are even my disciples, but the majority of the Pharisees are persistent in their refusal to see the light and acknowledge the truth, even when the work of the gospel is brought before them in great power. How carefully you cleanse the outside of the cups and the platters while the spiritual-food vessels are filthy and polluted! You make sure to present a pious and holy appearance to the people, but your inner souls are filled with self-righteousness, covetousness, extortion, and all manner of spiritual wickedness. Your leaders even dare to plot and plan the murder of the Son of Man. Do not you foolish men understand that the God of heaven looks at the inner motives of the soul as well as on your outer pretenses and your pious professions? Think not that the giving of alms and the paying of tithes will cleanse you from unrighteousness and enable you to stand clean in the presence of the Judge of all men. Woe upon you Pharisees who have persisted in rejecting the light of life! You are meticulous in tithing and ostentatious in almsgiving, but you knowingly spurn the visitation of God and reject the revelation of his love. Though it is all right for you to give attention to these minor duties, you should not have left these weightier requirements undone. Woe upon all who shun justice, spurn mercy, and reject truth! Woe upon all those who despise the revelation of the Father while they seek the chief seats in the synagogue and crave flattering salutations in the market places!"

166:1.5 (1826.2) When Jesus would have risen to depart, one of the lawyers who was at the table, addressing him, said: "But, Master, in some of your statements you reproach us also. Is there nothing good in the scribes, the Pharisees, or the lawyers?" And Jesus, standing, replied to the lawyer: "You, like the Pharisees, delight in the first places at the feasts and in wearing long robes while you put heavy burdens, grievous to be borne, on men's shoulders. And when the souls of men stagger under these heavy burdens, you will not so much as lift with one of your fingers. Woe upon you who take your greatest delight in building tombs for the prophets your fathers killed! And that you consent to what your fathers did is made manifest when you now plan to kill those who come in this day doing what the prophets did in their day— proclaiming the righteousness of God and revealing the mercy of the heavenly Father. But of all the generations that are past, the blood of the prophets and the apostles shall be required of this perverse and self-righteous generation. Woe upon all of you lawyers who have taken away the key of knowledge from the common people! You yourselves refuse to enter into the way of truth, and at the same time you would hinder all others who seek to enter therein. But you cannot thus shut up the doors of the kingdom of heaven; these we have opened to all who have the faith to enter, and these portals of mercy shall not be closed by the prejudice and arrogance of false teachers and untrue shepherds who are like whited sepulchres which, while outwardly they appear beautiful, are inwardly full of dead men's bones and all manner of spiritual uncleanness."

166:1.6 (1826.3) And when Jesus had finished speaking at Nathaniel's table, he went out of the house without partaking of food. And of the Pharisees who heard these words, some became believers in his teaching and entered into the kingdom, but the larger number persisted in the way of darkness, becoming all the more determined to lie in wait for him that they might catch some of his words which could be used to bring him to trial and judgment before the Sanhedrin at Jerusalem.

166:1.7 (1827.1) There were just three things to which the Pharisees paid particular attention:

166:1.8 (1827.2) 1. The practice of strict tithing.

166:1.9 (1827.3) 2. Scrupulous observance of the laws of purification.

166:1.10 (1827.4) 3. Avoidance of association with all non-Pharisees.

166:1.11 (1827.5) At this time Jesus sought to expose the spiritual barrenness of the first two practices, while he reserved his remarks designed to rebuke the Pharisees' refusal to engage in social intercourse with non-Pharisees for another and subsequent occasion when he would again be dining with many of these same men.

The Ten Lepers

166:2.1 (1827.6) The next day Jesus went with the twelve over to Amathus, near the border of Samaria, and as they approached the city, they encountered a group of ten lepers who sojourned near this place. Nine of this group were Jews, one a Samaritan. Ordinarily these Jews would have refrained from all association or contact with this Samaritan, but their common affliction was more than enough to overcome all religious prejudice. They had heard much of Jesus and his earlier miracles of healing, and since the seventy made a practice of announcing the time of Jesus' expected arrival when the Master was out with the twelve on these tours, the ten lepers had been made aware that he was expected to appear in this vicinity at about this time; and they were, accordingly, posted here on the outskirts of the city where they hoped to attract his attention and ask for healing. When the lepers saw Jesus drawing near them, not daring to approach him, they stood afar off and cried to him: "Master, have mercy on us; cleanse us from our affliction. Heal us as you have healed others."

166:2.2 (1827.7) Jesus had just been explaining to the twelve why the gentiles of Perea, together with the less orthodox Jews, were more willing to believe the gospel preached by the seventy than were the more orthodox and tradition-bound Jews of Judea. He had called their attention to the fact that their message had likewise been more readily received by the Galileans, and even by the Samaritans. But the twelve apostles were hardly yet willing to entertain kind feelings for the long-despised Samaritans.

166:2.3 (1827.8) Accordingly, when Simon Zelotes observed the Samaritan among the lepers, he sought to induce the Master to pass on into the city without even hesitating to exchange greetings with them. Said Jesus to Simon: "But what if the Samaritan loves God as well as the Jews? Should we sit in judgment on our fellow men? Who can tell? if we make these ten men whole, perhaps the Samaritan will prove more grateful even than the Jews. Do you feel certain about your opinions, Simon?" And Simon quickly replied, "If you cleanse them, you will soon find out." And Jesus replied: "So shall it be, Simon, and you will soon know the truth regarding the gratitude of men and the loving mercy of God."

166:2.4 (1827.9) Jesus, going near the lepers, said: "If you would be made whole, go forthwith and show yourselves to the priests as required by the law of Moses." And as they went, they were made whole. But when the Samaritan saw that he was being healed, he turned back and, going in quest of Jesus, began to glorify God with a loud voice. And when he had found the Master, he fell on his knees at his feet and gave thanks for his cleansing. The nine others, the Jews, had also discovered their healing, and while they also were grateful for their cleansing, they continued on their way to show themselves to the priests.

166:2.5 (1828.1) As the Samaritan remained kneeling at Jesus' feet, the Master, looking about at the twelve, especially at Simon Zelotes, said: "Were not ten cleansed? Where, then, are the other nine, the Jews? Only one, this alien, has returned to give glory to God." And then he said to the Samaritan, "Arise and go your way; your faith has made you whole."

166:2.6 (1828.2) Jesus looked again at his apostles as the stranger departed. And the apostles all looked at Jesus, save Simon Zelotes, whose eyes were downcast. The twelve said not a word. Neither did Jesus speak; it was not necessary that he should.

166:2.7 (1828.3) Though all ten of these men really believed they had leprosy, only four were thus afflicted. The other six were cured of a skin disease which had been mistaken for leprosy. But the Samaritan really had leprosy.

166:2.8 (1828.4) Jesus enjoined the twelve to say nothing about the cleansing of the lepers, and as they went on into Amathus, he remarked: "You see how it is that the children of the house, even when they are insubordinate to their Father's will, take their blessings for granted. They think it a small matter if they neglect to give thanks when the Father bestows healing upon them, but the strangers, when they receive gifts from the head of the house, are filled with wonder and are constrained to give thanks in recognition of the good things bestowed upon them." And still the apostles said nothing in reply to the Master's words.

The Sermon at Gerasa

166:3.1 (1828.5) As Jesus and the twelve visited with the messengers of the kingdom at Gerasa, one of the Pharisees who believed in him asked this question: "Lord, will there be few or many really saved?" And Jesus, answering, said:

166:3.2 (1828.6) "You have been taught that only the children of Abraham will be saved; that only the gentiles of adoption can hope for salvation. Some of you have reasoned that, since the Scriptures record that only Caleb and Joshua from among all the hosts that went out of Egypt lived to enter the promised land, only a comparatively few of those who seek the kingdom of heaven shall find entrance thereto.

166:3.3 (1828.7) "You also have another saying among you, and one that contains much truth: That the way which leads to eternal life is straight and narrow, that the door which leads thereto is likewise narrow so that, of those who seek salvation, few can find entrance through this door. You also have a teaching that the way which leads to destruction is broad, that the entrance thereto is wide, and that there are many who choose to go this way. And this proverb is not without its meaning. But I declare that salvation is first a matter of your personal choosing. Even if the door to the way of life is narrow, it is wide enough to admit all who sincerely seek to enter, for I am that door. And the Son will never refuse entrance to any child of the universe who, by faith, seeks to find the Father through the Son.

166:3.4 (1829.1) "But herein is the danger to all who would postpone their entrance into the kingdom while they continue to pursue the pleasures of immaturity and indulge the satisfactions of selfishness: Having refused to enter the kingdom as a spiritual experience, they may subsequently seek entrance thereto when the glory of the better way becomes revealed in the age to come. And when, therefore, those who spurned the kingdom when I came in the likeness of humanity seek to find an entrance when it is revealed in the likeness of divinity, then will I say to all such selfish ones: I know not whence you are. You had your chance to prepare for this heavenly citizenship, but you refused all such proffers of mercy; you rejected all invitations to come while the door was open. Now, to you who have refused salvation, the door is shut. This door is not open to those who would enter the kingdom for selfish glory. Salvation is not for those who are unwilling to pay the price of wholehearted dedication to doing my Father's will. When in spirit and soul you have turned your backs upon the Father's kingdom, it is useless in mind and body to stand before this door and knock, saying, 'Lord, open to us; we would also be great in the kingdom.' Then will I declare that you are not of my fold. I will not receive you to be among those who have fought the good fight of faith and won the reward of unselfish service in the kingdom on earth. And when you say, 'Did we not eat and drink with you, and did you not teach in our streets?' then shall I again declare that you are spiritual strangers; that we were not fellow servants in the Father's ministry of mercy on earth; that I do not know you; and then shall the Judge of all the earth say to you: 'Depart from us, all you who have taken delight in the works of iniquity.'

166:3.5 (1829.2) "But fear not; every one who sincerely desires to find eternal life by entrance into the kingdom of God shall certainly find such everlasting salvation. But you who refuse this salvation will some day see the prophets of the seed of Abraham sit down with the believers of the gentile nations in this glorified kingdom to partake of the bread of life and to refresh themselves with the water thereof. And they who shall thus take the kingdom in spiritual power and by the persistent assaults of living faith will come from the north and the south and from the east and the west. And, behold, many who are first will be last, and those who are last will many times be first."

166:3.6 (1829.3) This was indeed a new and strange version of the old and familiar proverb of the straight and narrow way.

166:3.7 (1829.4) Slowly the apostles and many of the disciples were learning the meaning of Jesus' early declaration: "Unless you are born again, born of the spirit, you cannot enter the kingdom of God." Nevertheless, to all who are honest of heart and sincere in faith, it remains eternally true: "Behold, I stand at the doors of men's hearts and knock, and if any man will open to me, I will come in and sup with him and will feed him with the bread of life; we shall be one in spirit and purpose, and so shall we ever be brethren in the long and fruitful service of the search for the Paradise Father." And so, whether few or many are to be saved altogether depends on whether few or many will heed the invitation: "I am the door, I am the new and living way, and whosoever wills may enter to embark upon the endless truth-search for eternal life."

166:3.8 (1829.5) Even the apostles were unable fully to comprehend his teaching as to the necessity for using spiritual force for the purpose of breaking through all material resistance and for surmounting every earthly obstacle which might chance to stand in the way of grasping the all-important spiritual values of the new life in the spirit as the liberated sons of God.

Teaching About Accidents

166:4.1 (1830.1) While most Palestinians ate only two meals a day, it was the custom of Jesus and the apostles, when on a journey, to pause at midday for rest and refreshment. And it was at such a noontide stop on the way to Philadelphia that Thomas asked Jesus: "Master, from hearing your remarks as we journeyed this morning, I would like to inquire whether spiritual beings are concerned in the production of strange and extraordinary events in the material world and, further, to ask whether the angels and other spirit beings are able to prevent accidents."

166:4.2 (1830.2) In answer to Thomas's inquiry, Jesus said: "Have I been so long with you, and yet you continue to ask me such questions? Have you failed to observe how the Son of Man lives as one with you and consistently refuses to employ the forces of heaven for his personal sustenance? Do we not all live by the same means whereby all men exist? Do you see the power of the spiritual world manifested in the material life of this world, save for the revelation of the Father and the sometime healing of his afflicted children?

166:4.3 (1830.3) "All too long have your fathers believed that prosperity was the token of divine approval; that adversity was the proof of God's displeasure. I declare that such beliefs are superstitions. Do you not observe that far greater numbers of the poor joyfully receive the gospel and immediately enter the kingdom? If riches evidence divine favor, why do the rich so many times refuse to believe this good news from heaven?

166:4.4 (1830.4) "The Father causes his rain to fall on the just and the unjust; the sun likewise shines on the righteous and the unrighteous. You know about those Galileans whose blood Pilate mingled with the sacrifices, but I tell you these Galileans were not in any manner sinners above all their fellows just because this happened to them. You also know about the eighteen men upon whom the tower of Siloam fell, killing them. Think not that these men who were thus destroyed were offenders above all their brethren in Jerusalem. These folks were simply innocent victims of one of the accidents of time.

166:4.5 (1830.5) "There are three groups of events which may occur in your lives:

166:4.6 (1830.6) "1. You may share in those normal happenings which are a part of the life you and your fellows live on the face of the earth.

166:4.7 (1830.7) "2. You may chance to fall victim to one of the accidents of nature, one of the mischances of men, knowing full well that such occurrences are in no way prearranged or otherwise produced by the spiritual forces of the realm.

166:4.8 (1830.8) "3. You may reap the harvest of your direct efforts to comply with the natural laws governing the world.

166:4.9 (1830.9) "There was a certain man who planted a fig tree in his yard, and when he had many times sought fruit thereon and found none, he called the vine-dressers before him and said: 'Here have I come these three seasons looking for fruit on this fig tree and have found none. Cut down this barren tree; why should it encumber the ground?' But the head gardener answered his master: 'Let it alone for one more year so that I may dig around it and put on fertilizer, and then, next year, if it bears no fruit, it shall be cut down.' And when they had thus complied with the laws of fruitfulness, since the tree was living and good, they were rewarded with an abundant yield.

166:4.10 (1831.1) "In the matter of sickness and health, you should know that these bodily states are the result of material causes; health is not the smile of heaven, neither is affliction the frown of God.

166:4.11 (1831.2) "The Father's human children have equal capacity for the reception of material blessings; therefore does he bestow things physical upon the children of men without discrimination. When it comes to the bestowal of spiritual gifts, the Father is limited by man's capacity for receiving these divine endowments. Although the Father is no respecter of persons, in the bestowal of spiritual gifts he is limited by man's faith and by his willingness always to abide by the Father's will."

166:4.12 (1831.3) As they journeyed on toward Philadelphia, Jesus continued to teach them and to answer their questions having to do with accidents, sickness, and miracles, but they were not able fully to comprehend this instruction. One hour of teaching will not wholly change the beliefs of a lifetime, and so Jesus found it necessary to reiterate his message, to tell again and again that which he wished them to understand; and even then they failed to grasp the meaning of his earth mission until after his death and resurrection.

The Congregation at Philadelphia

166:5.1 (1831.4) Jesus and the twelve were on their way to visit Abner and his associates, who were preaching and teaching in Philadelphia. Of all the cities of Perea, in Philadelphia the largest group of Jews and gentiles, rich and poor, learned and unlearned, embraced the teachings of the seventy, thereby entering into the kingdom of heaven. The synagogue of Philadelphia had never been subject to the supervision of the Sanhedrin at Jerusalem and therefore had never been closed to the teachings of Jesus and his associates. At this

very time, Abner was teaching three times a day in the Philadelphia synagogue.

166:5.2 (1831.5) This very synagogue later on became a Christian church and was the missionary headquarters for the promulgation of the gospel through the regions to the east. It was long a stronghold of the Master's teachings and stood alone in this region as a center of Christian learning for centuries.

166:5.3 (1831.6) The Jews at Jerusalem had always had trouble with the Jews of Philadelphia. And after the death and resurrection of Jesus the Jerusalem church, of which James the Lord's brother was head, began to have serious difficulties with the Philadelphia congregation of believers. Abner became the head of the Philadelphia church, continuing as such until his death. And this estrangement with Jerusalem explains why nothing is heard of Abner and his work in the Gospel records of the New Testament. This feud between Jerusalem and Philadelphia lasted throughout the lifetimes of James and Abner and continued for some time after the destruction of Jerusalem. Philadelphia was really the headquarters of the early church in the south and east as Antioch was in the north and west. *

166:5.4 (1831.7) It was the apparent misfortune of Abner to be at variance with all of the leaders of the early Christian church. He fell out with Peter and James (Jesus' brother) over questions of administration and the jurisdiction of the Jerusalem church; he parted company with Paul over differences of philosophy and theology. Abner was more Babylonian than Hellenic in his philosophy, and he stubbornly resisted all attempts of Paul to remake the teachings of Jesus so as to present less that was objectionable, first to the Jews, then to the Greco-Roman believers in the mysteries.

166:5.5 (1832.1) Thus was Abner compelled to live a life of isolation. He was head of a church which was without standing at Jerusalem. He had dared to defy James the

Lord's brother, who was subsequently supported by Peter. Such conduct effectively separated him from all his former associates. Then he dared to withstand Paul. Although he was wholly sympathetic with Paul in his mission to the gentiles, and though he supported him in his contentions with the church at Jerusalem, he bitterly opposed the version of Jesus' teachings which Paul elected to preach. In his last years Abner denounced Paul as the "clever corrupter of the life teachings of Jesus of Nazareth, the Son of the living God."

166:5.6 (1832.2) During the later years of Abner and for some time thereafter, the believers at Philadelphia held more strictly to the religion of Jesus, as he lived and taught, than any other group on earth.

166:5.7 (1832.3) Abner lived to be 89 years old, dying at Philadelphia on the 21st day of November, A.D. 74. And to the very end he was a faithful believer in, and teacher of, the gospel of the heavenly kingdom.

Paper 167

The Visit to Philadelphia

167:0.1 (1833.1) THROUGHOUT this period of the Perean ministry, when mention is made of Jesus and the apostles visiting the various localities where the seventy were at work, it should be recalled that, as a rule, only ten were with him since it was the practice to leave at least two of the apostles at Pella to instruct the multitude. As Jesus prepared to go on to Philadelphia, Simon Peter and his brother, Andrew, returned to the Pella encampment to teach the crowds there assembled. When the Master left the camp at Pella to visit about Perea, it was not uncommon for from three to five hundred of the campers to follow him. When he arrived at Philadelphia, he was accompanied by over six hundred followers.

167:0.2 (1833.2) No miracles had attended the recent preaching tour through the Decapolis, and, excepting the cleansing of the ten lepers, thus far there had been no miracles on this Perean mission. This was a period when the gospel was proclaimed with power, without miracles, and most of the time without the personal presence of Jesus or even of his apostles.

167:0.3 (1833.3) Jesus and the ten apostles arrived at Philadelphia on Wednesday, February 22, and spent Thursday and Friday resting from their recent travels and labors. That Friday night James spoke in the synagogue, and a general council was called for the following evening. They were much rejoiced over the progress of the gospel at Philadelphia and among the near-by villages. The messengers of David also brought word of the further advancement of the kingdom throughout Palestine, as well as good news from Alexandria and Damascus.

Breakfast with the Pharisees

167:1.1 (1833.4) There lived in Philadelphia a very wealthy and influential Pharisee who had accepted the teachings of Abner, and who invited Jesus to his house Sabbath morning for breakfast. It was known that Jesus was expected in Philadelphia at this time; so a large number of visitors, among them many Pharisees, had come over from Jerusalem and from elsewhere. Accordingly, about forty of these leading men and a few lawyers were bidden to this breakfast, which had been arranged in honor of the Master.

167:1.2 (1833.5) As Jesus lingered by the door, speaking with Abner, and after the host had seated himself, there came into the room one of the leading Pharisees of Jerusalem, a member of the Sanhedrin, and as was his habit, he made straight for the seat of honor at the left of the host. But since this place had been reserved for the

Master and that on the right for Abner, the host beckoned the Jerusalem Pharisee to sit four seats to the left, and this dignitary was much offended because he did not receive the seat of honor.

167:1.3 (1834.1) Soon they were all seated and enjoying the visiting among themselves since the majority of those present were disciples of Jesus or else were friendly to the gospel. Only his enemies took notice of the fact that he did not observe the ceremonial washing of his hands before he sat down to eat. Abner washed his hands at the beginning of the meal but not during the serving.

167:1.4 (1834.2) Near the end of the meal there came in from the street a man long afflicted with a chronic disease and now in a dropsical condition. This man was a believer, having recently been baptized by Abner's associates. He made no request of Jesus for healing, but the Master knew full well that this afflicted man came to this breakfast hoping thereby to escape the crowds which thronged him and thus be more likely to engage his attention. This man knew that few miracles were then being performed; however, he had reasoned in his heart that his sorry plight might possibly appeal to the Master's compassion. And he was not mistaken, for, when he entered the room, both Jesus and the self-righteous Pharisee from Jerusalem took notice of him. The Pharisee was not slow to voice his resentment that such a one should be permitted to enter the room. But Jesus looked upon the sick man and smiled so benignly that he drew near and sat down upon the floor. As the meal was ending, the Master looked over his fellow guests and then, after glancing significantly at the man with dropsy, said: "My friends, teachers in Israel and learned lawyers, I would like to ask you a question: Is it lawful to heal the sick and afflicted on the Sabbath day, or not?" But those who were there present knew Jesus too well; they held their peace; they answered not his question.

167:1.5 (1834.3) Then went Jesus over to where the sick man sat and, taking him by the hand, said: "Arise and go your way. You have not asked to be healed, but I know the desire of your heart and the faith of your soul." Before the man left the room, Jesus returned to his seat and, addressing those at the table, said: "Such works my Father does, not to tempt you into the kingdom, but to reveal himself to those who are already in the kingdom. You can perceive that it would be like the Father to do just such things because which one of you, having a favorite animal that fell in the well on the Sabbath day, would not go right out and draw him up?" And since no one would answer him, and inasmuch as his host evidently approved of what was going on, Jesus stood up and spoke to all present: "My brethren, when you are bidden to a marriage feast, sit not down in the chief seat, lest, perchance, a more honored man than you has been invited, and the host will have to come to you and request that you give your place to this other and honored guest. In this event, with shame you will be required to take a lower place at the table. When you are bidden to a feast, it would be the part of wisdom, on arriving at the festive table, to seek for the lowest place and take your seat therein, so that, when the host looks over the guests, he may say to you: 'My friend, why sit in the seat of the least? come up higher'; and thus will such a one have glory in the presence of his fellow guests. Forget not, every one who exalts himself shall be humbled, while he who truly humbles himself shall be exalted. Therefore, when you entertain at dinner or give a supper, invite not always your friends, your brethren, your kinsmen, or your rich neighbors that they in return may bid you to their feasts, and thus will you be recompensed. When you give a banquet, sometimes bid the poor, the maimed, and the blind. In this way you shall be blessed in your heart, for you well know that the lame and the halt cannot repay you for your loving ministry."

Parable of the Great Supper

167:2.1 (1835.1) As Jesus finished

speaking at the breakfast table of the Pharisee, one of the lawyers present, desiring to relieve the silence, thoughtlessly said: "Blessed is he who shall eat bread in the kingdom of God"—that being a common saying of those days. And then Jesus spoke a parable, which even his friendly host was compelled to take to heart. He said:

167:2.2 (1835.2) "A certain ruler gave a great supper, and having bidden many guests, he dispatched his servants at suppertime to say to those who were invited, 'Come, for everything is now ready.' And they all with one accord began to make excuses. The first said, 'I have just bought a farm, and I must needs go to prove it; I pray you have me excused.' Another said, 'I have bought five yoke of oxen, and I must go to receive them; I pray you have me excused.' And another said, 'I have just married a wife, and therefore I cannot come.' So the servants went back and reported this to their master. When the master of the house heard this, he was very angry, and turning to his servants, he said: 'I have made ready this marriage feast; the fatlings are killed, and all is in readiness for my guests, but they have spurned my invitation; they have gone every man after his lands and his merchandise, and they even show disrespect to my servants who bid them come to my feast. Go out quickly, therefore, into the streets and lanes of the city, out into the highways and the byways, and bring hither the poor and the outcast, the blind and the lame, that the marriage feast may have guests.' And the servants did as their lord commanded, and even then there was room for more guests. Then said the lord to his servants: 'Go now out into the roads and the countryside and constrain those who are there to come in that my house may be filled. I declare that none of those who were first bidden shall taste of my supper.' And the servants did as their master commanded, and the house was filled." *

167:2.3 (1835.3) And when they heard these words, they departed; every man went to his own place. At least one of the sneering Pharisees present that morning comprehended the meaning of this parable, for he was baptized that day and made public confession of his faith in the gospel of the kingdom. Abner preached on this parable that night at the general council of believers.

167:2.4 (1835.4) The next day all of the apostles engaged in the philosophic exercise of endeavoring to interpret the meaning of this parable of the great supper. Though Jesus listened with interest to all of these differing interpretations, he steadfastly refused to offer them further help in understanding the parable. He would only say, "Let every man find out the meaning for himself and in his own soul."

The Woman with the Spirit of Infirmity

167:3.1 (1835.5) Abner had arranged for the Master to teach in the synagogue on this Sabbath day, the first time Jesus had appeared in a synagogue since they had all been closed to his teachings by order of the Sanhedrin. At the conclusion of the service Jesus looked down before him upon an elderly woman who wore a downcast expression, and who was much bent in form. This woman had long been fear-ridden, and all joy had passed out of her life. As Jesus stepped down from the pulpit, he went over to her and, touching her bowed-over form on the shoulder, said: "Woman, if you would only believe, you could be wholly loosed from your spirit of infirmity." And this woman, who had been bowed down and bound up by the depressions of fear for more than eighteen years, believed the words of the Master and by faith straightened up immediately. When this woman saw that she had been made straight, she lifted up her voice and glorified God.

167:3.2 (1836.1) Notwithstanding that this woman's affliction was wholly mental, her bowed-over form being the result of her depressed mind, the people thought that Jesus had healed a real physical disorder. Although the congregation of the synagogue at Philadelphia was friendly toward the teachings of Jesus, the chief ruler of the synagogue was an unfriendly Pharisee. And as he shared the opinion of the congregation that Jesus had healed a physical disorder, and being indignant because Jesus had presumed to do such a thing on the Sabbath, he stood up before the congregation and said: "Are there not six days in which men should do all their work? In these working days come, therefore, and be healed, but not on the Sabbath day."

167:3.3 (1836.2) When the unfriendly ruler had thus spoken, Jesus returned to the speaker's platform and said: "Why play the part of hypocrites? Does not every one of you, on the Sabbath, loose his ox from the stall and lead him forth for watering? If such a service is permissible on the Sabbath day, should not this woman, a daughter of Abraham who has been bound down by evil these eighteen years, be loosed from this bondage and led forth to partake of the waters of liberty and life, even on this Sabbath day?" And as the woman continued to glorify God, his critic was put to shame, and the congregation rejoiced with her that she had been healed.

167:3.4 (1836.3) As a result of his public criticism of Jesus on this Sabbath the chief ruler of the synagogue was deposed, and a follower of Jesus was put in his place.

167:3.5 (1836.4) Jesus frequently delivered such victims of fear from their spirit of infirmity, from their depression of mind, and from their bondage of fear. But the people thought that all such afflictions were either physical disorders or possession of evil spirits.

167:3.6 (1836.5) Jesus taught again in the synagogue on Sunday, and many were baptized by Abner at noon on that day in the river which flowed south of the city. On the morrow Jesus and the ten apostles would have started back to the Pella encampment but for the arrival of one of David's messengers, who brought an urgent message to Jesus from his friends at Bethany, near Jerusalem.

The Message from Bethany

167:4.1 (1836.6) Very late on Sunday night, February 26, a runner from Bethany arrived at Philadelphia, bringing a message from Martha and Mary which said, "Lord, he whom you love is very sick." This message reached Jesus at the close of the evening conference and just as he was taking leave of the apostles for the night. At first Jesus made no reply. There occurred one of those strange interludes, a time when he appeared to be in communication with something outside of, and beyond, himself. And then, looking up, he addressed the messenger in the hearing of the apostles, saying: "This sickness is really not to the death. Doubt not that it may be used to glorify God and exalt the Son."

167:4.2 (1837.1) Jesus was very fond of Martha, Mary, and their brother, Lazarus; he loved them with a fervent affection. His first and human thought was to go to their assistance at once, but another idea came into his combined mind. He had almost given up hope that the Jewish leaders at Jerusalem would ever accept the kingdom, but he still loved his people, and there now occurred to him a plan whereby the scribes and Pharisees of Jerusalem might have one more chance to accept his teachings; and he decided, his Father willing, to make this last appeal to Jerusalem the most profound and stupendous outward working of his entire earth career. The Jews clung to the idea of a wonder-working deliverer. And though he refused to stoop to the performance of material wonders or to the enactment of temporal exhibitions of political power, he did now ask the Father's consent for the manifestation of his hitherto unexhibited power over life and death.

167:4.3 (1837.2) The Jews were in the habit of burying their dead on the day of their demise; this was a necessary practice in such a warm climate. It often happened that they put in the tomb one who was merely comatose, so that on the second or even the third day, such a one would come forth from the tomb. But it was the belief of the Jews that, while the spirit or soul might linger near the body for two or three days, it never tarried after the third day; that decay was well advanced by the fourth day, and that no one ever returned from the tomb after the lapse of such a period. And it was for these reasons that Jesus tarried yet two full days in Philadelphia before he made ready to start for Bethany. *

167:4.4 (1837.3) Accordingly, early on Wednesday morning he said to his apostles: "Let us prepare at once to go into Judea again." And when the apostles heard their Master say this, they drew off by themselves for a time to take counsel of one another. James assumed the direction of the conference, and they all agreed that it was only folly to allow Jesus to go again into Judea, and they came back as one man and so informed him. Said James: "Master, you were in Jerusalem a few weeks back, and the leaders sought your death, while the people were minded to stone you. At that time you gave these men their chance to receive the truth, and we will not permit you to go again into Judea."

167:4.5 (1837.4) Then said Jesus: "But do you not understand that there are twelve hours of the day in which work may safely be done? If a man walks in the day, he does not stumble inasmuch as he has light. If a man walks in the night, he is liable to stumble since he is without light. As long as my day lasts, I fear not to enter Judea. I would do one more mighty work for these Jews; I would give them one more chance to believe, even on their own terms—conditions of outward glory and the visible manifestation of the power of the Father and the love of the Son. Besides, do you not realize that our friend Lazarus has fallen asleep, and I would go to awake him out of this sleep!"

167:4.6 (1837.5) Then said one of the apostles: "Master, if Lazarus has fallen asleep, then will he the more surely recover." It was the custom of the Jews at that time to speak of death as a form of sleep, but as the apostles did not understand that Jesus meant that Lazarus had departed from this world, he now said plainly: "Lazarus is dead. And I am glad for your sakes, even if the others are not thereby saved, that I was not there, to the end that you shall now have new cause to believe in me; and by that which you will witness, you should all be strengthened in preparation for that day when I shall take leave of you and go to the Father."

167:4.7 (1838.1) When they could not persuade him to refrain from going into Judea, and when some of the apostles were loath even to accompany him, Thomas addressed his fellows, saying: "We have told the Master our fears, but he is determined to go to Bethany. I am satisfied it means the end; they will surely kill him, but if that is the Master's choice, then let us acquit ourselves like men of courage; let us go also that we may die with him." And it was ever so; in matters requiring deliberate and sustained courage, Thomas was always the mainstay of the twelve apostles.

On the Way to Bethany

167:5.1 (1838.2) On the way to Judea Jesus was followed by a company of almost fifty of his friends and enemies. At their noon lunchtime, on Wednesday, he talked to his apostles and this group of followers on the "Terms of Salvation," and at the end of this lesson told the parable of the Pharisee and the publican (a tax collector). Said Jesus: "You see, then, that the Father gives salvation to the children of men, and this salvation is a free gift to all who have the faith to receive sonship in the divine family. There is nothing man can do to earn this salvation. Works of self-righteousness cannot buy the favor of God, and much praying in public will not atone for lack of living faith in the heart. Men you may deceive

by your outward service, but God looks into your souls. What I am telling you is well illustrated by two men who went into the temple to pray, the one a Pharisee and the other a publican. The Pharisee stood and prayed to himself: 'O God, I thank you that I am not like the rest of men, extortioners, unlearned, unjust, adulterers, or even like this publican. I fast twice a week; I give tithes of all that I get.' But the publican, standing afar off, would not so much as lift his eyes to heaven but smote his breast, saying, 'God be merciful to me a sinner.' I tell you that the publican went home with God's approval rather than the Pharisee, for every one who exalts himself shall be humbled, but he who humbles himself shall be exalted."

167:5.2 (1838.3) That night, in Jericho, the unfriendly Pharisees sought to entrap the Master by inducing him to discuss marriage and divorce, as did their fellows one time in Galilee, but Jesus artfully avoided their efforts to bring him into conflict with their laws concerning divorce. As the publican and the Pharisee illustrated good and bad religion, their divorce practices served to contrast the better marriage laws of the Jewish code with the disgraceful laxity of the Pharisaic interpretations of these Mosaic divorce statutes. The Pharisee judged himself by the lowest standard; the publican squared himself by the highest ideal. Devotion, to the Pharisee, was a means of inducing self-righteous inactivity and the assurance of false spiritual security; devotion, to the publican, was a means of stirring up his soul to the realization of the need for repentance, confession, and the acceptance, by faith, of merciful forgiveness. The Pharisee sought justice; the publican sought mercy. The law of the universe is: Ask and you shall receive; seek and you shall find.

167:5.3 (1838.4) Though Jesus refused to be drawn into a controversy with the Pharisees concerning divorce, he did proclaim a positive teaching of the highest ideals regarding marriage. He exalted marriage as the most ideal and highest of all human relationships. Likewise, he intimated strong disapproval of the lax and unfair divorce practices of the Jerusalem Jews, who at that time permitted a man to divorce his wife for the most trifling of reasons, such as being a poor cook, a faulty housekeeper, or for no better reason than that he had become enamored of a better-looking woman. *

167:5.4 (1839.1) The Pharisees had even gone so far as to teach that divorce of this easy variety was a special dispensation granted the Jewish people, particularly the Pharisees. And so, while Jesus refused to make pronouncements dealing with marriage and divorce, he did most bitterly denounce these shameful floutings of the marriage relationship and pointed out their injustice to women and children. He never sanctioned any divorce practice which gave man any advantage over woman; the Master countenanced only those teachings which accorded women equality with men.

167:5.5 (1839.2) Although Jesus did not offer new mandates governing marriage and divorce, he did urge the Jews to live up to their own laws and higher teachings. He constantly appealed to the written Scriptures in his effort to improve their practices along these social lines. While thus upholding the high and ideal concepts of marriage, Jesus skillfully avoided clashing with his questioners about the social practices represented by either their written laws or their much-cherished divorce privileges.

167:5.6 (1839.3) It was very difficult for the apostles to understand the Master's reluctance to make positive pronouncements relative to scientific, social, economic, and political problems. They did not fully realize that his earth mission was exclusively concerned with revelations of spiritual and religious truths.

167:5.7 (1839.4) After Jesus had talked about marriage and divorce, later on that evening his apostles privately asked many additional questions, and his answers to these inquiries relieved their minds of many misconceptions. At the conclusion of this conference Jesus said: "Marriage is honorable and is to be desired by all men. The fact that the Son of Man pursues his earth mission alone is in no way a reflection on the desirability of marriage. That I should so work is the Father's will, but this same Father has directed the creation of male and female, and it is the divine will that men and women should find their highest service and consequent joy in the establishment of homes for the reception and training of children, in the creation of whom these parents become copartners with the Makers of heaven and earth. And for this cause shall a man leave his father and mother and shall cleave to his wife, and they two shall become as one."

167:5.8 (1839.5) And in this way Jesus relieved the minds of the apostles of many worries about marriage and cleared up many misunderstandings regarding divorce; at the same time he did much to exalt their ideals of social union and to augment their respect for women and children and for the home.

Blessing the Little Children

167:6.1 (1839.6) That evening Jesus' message regarding marriage and the blessedness of children spread all over Jericho, so that the next morning, long before Jesus and the apostles prepared to leave, even before breakfast time, scores of mothers came to where Jesus lodged, bringing their children in their arms and leading them by their hands, and desired that he bless the little ones. When the apostles went out to view this assemblage of mothers with their children, they endeavored to send them away, but these women refused to depart until the Master laid his hands on their children and blessed them. And when the apostles loudly rebuked these mothers, Jesus, hearing the tumult, came out and indignantly reproved them, saying: "Suffer little children to come to me; forbid them not, for of such is the kingdom of heaven. Verily, verily, I say to you, whosoever receives not the kingdom of God as a little child shall hardly enter therein to grow up to the full stature of spiritual manhood."

167:6.2 (1840.1) And when the Master had spoken to his apostles, he received all of the children, laying his hands on them, while he spoke words of courage and hope

to their mothers.

167:6.3 (1840.2) Jesus often talked to his apostles about the celestial mansions and taught that the advancing children of God must there grow up spiritually as children grow up physically on this world. And so does the sacred oftentimes appear to be the common, as on this day these children and their mothers little realized that the onlooking intelligences of Nebadon beheld the children of Jericho playing with the Creator of a universe.

167:6.4 (1840.3) Woman's status in Palestine was much improved by Jesus' teaching; and so it would have been throughout the world if his followers had not departed so far from that which he painstakingly taught them.

167:6.5 (1840.4) It was also at Jericho, in connection with the discussion of the early religious training of children in habits of divine worship, that Jesus impressed upon his apostles the great value of beauty as an influence leading to the urge to worship, especially with children. The Master by precept and example taught the value of worshiping the Creator in the midst of the natural surroundings of creation. He preferred to commune with the heavenly Father amidst the trees and among the lowly creatures of the natural world. He rejoiced to contemplate the Father through the inspiring spectacle of the starry realms of the Creator Sons.

167:6.6 (1840.5) When it is not possible to worship God in the tabernacles of nature, men should do their best to provide houses of beauty, sanctuaries of appealing simplicity and artistic embellishment, so that the highest of human emotions may be aroused in association with the intellectual approach to spiritual communion with God. Truth, beauty, and holiness are powerful and effective aids to true worship. But spirit communion is not promoted by mere massive ornateness and overmuch embellishment with man's elaborate and ostentatious art. Beauty is most religious when it is most simple and naturelike.

How unfortunate that little children should have their first introduction to concepts of public worship in cold and barren rooms so devoid of the beauty appeal and so empty of all suggestion of good cheer and inspiring holiness! The child should be introduced to worship in nature's outdoors and later accompany his parents to public houses of religious assembly which are at least as materially attractive and artistically beautiful as the home in which he is daily domiciled.

The Talk About Angels

167:7.1 (1840.6) As they journeyed up the hills from Jericho to Bethany, Nathaniel walked most of the way by the side of Jesus, and their discussion of children in relation to the kingdom of heaven led indirectly to the consideration of the ministry of angels. Nathaniel finally asked the Master this question: "Seeing that the high priest is a Sadducee, and since the Sadducees do not believe in angels, what shall we teach the people regarding the heavenly ministers?" Then, among other things, Jesus said:

167:7.2 (1841.1) "The angelic hosts are a separate order of created beings; they are entirely different from the material order of mortal creatures, and they function as a distinct group of universe intelligences. Angels are not of that group of creatures called 'the Sons of God' in the Scriptures; neither are they the glorified spirits of mortal men who have gone on to progress through the mansions on high. Angels are a direct creation, and they do not reproduce themselves. The angelic hosts have only a spiritual kinship with the human race. As man progresses in the journey to the Father in Paradise, he does traverse a state of being at one time analogous to the state of the angels, but mortal man never becomes an angel.

167:7.3 (1841.2) "The angels never die, as man does. The angels are immortal unless, perchance, they become involved in sin as did some of them with the deceptions of Lucifer. The angels are the spirit servants in heaven, and they are neither all-wise nor all-powerful. But all of the loyal angels are truly pure and holy.

167:7.4 (1841.3) "And do you not remember that I said to you once before that, if you had your spiritual eyes anointed, you would then see the heavens opened and behold the angels of God ascending and descending? It is by the ministry of the angels that one world may be kept in touch with other worlds, for have I not repeatedly told you that I have other sheep not of this fold? And these angels are not the spies of the spirit world who watch upon you and then go forth to tell the Father the thoughts of your heart and to report on the deeds of the flesh. The Father has no need of such service inasmuch as his own spirit lives within you. But these angelic spirits do function to keep one part of the heavenly creation informed concerning the doings of other and remote parts of the universe. And many of the angels, while functioning in the government of the Father and the universes of the Sons, are assigned to the service of the human races. When I taught you that many of these seraphim are ministering spirits, I spoke not in figurative language nor in poetic strains. And all this is true, regardless of your difficulty in comprehending such matters.

167:7.5 (1841.4) "Many of these angels are engaged in the work of saving men, for have I not told you of the seraphic joy when one soul elects to forsake sin and begin the search for God? I did even tell you of the joy in the presence of the angels of heaven over one sinner who repents, thereby indicating the existence of other and higher orders of celestial beings who are likewise concerned in the spiritual welfare and with the divine progress of mortal man.

167:7.6 (1841.5) "Also are these angels very much concerned with the means whereby man's spirit is released from the tabernacles of the flesh and his soul escorted to the mansions in heaven. Angels are the sure and heavenly guides of the soul of man during that uncharted and indefinite period of time which intervenes between the death of the flesh and the new life in the spirit abodes."

167:7.7 (1841.6) And he would have spoken further with Nathaniel regarding the ministry of angels, but he was interrupted by the approach of Martha, who had been informed that the Master was drawing near to Bethany by friends who had observed him ascending the hills to the east. And she now hastened to greet him.

Paper 168

The Resurrection of Lazarus

168:0.1 (1842.1) IT WAS shortly after noon when Martha started out to meet Jesus as he came over the brow of the hill near Bethany. Her brother, Lazarus, had been dead four days and had been laid away in their private tomb at the far end of the garden late on Sunday afternoon. The stone at the entrance of the tomb had been rolled in place on the morning of this day, Thursday.

168:0.2 (1842.2) When Martha and Mary sent word to Jesus concerning Lazarus's illness, they were confident the Master would do something about it. They knew that their brother was desperately sick, and though they hardly dared hope that Jesus would leave his work of teaching and preaching to come to their assistance, they had such confidence in his power to heal disease that they thought he would just speak the curative words, and Lazarus would immediately be made whole. And when Lazarus died a few hours after the messenger left Bethany for Philadelphia, they reasoned that it was because the Master did not learn of their brother's illness until it was too late, until he had already been dead for several hours.

168:0.3 (1842.3) But they, with all of their believing friends, were greatly puzzled by the message which the runner brought back Tuesday forenoon when he reached Bethany. The messenger insisted that he heard Jesus say, "...this sickness is really not to the death." Neither could they understand why he sent no word to them nor otherwise proffered assistance.

168:0.4 (1842.4) Many friends from near-by hamlets and others from Jerusalem came over to comfort the sorrow-stricken sisters. Lazarus and his sisters were the children of a well-to-do and honorable Jew, one who had been the leading resident of the little village of Bethany. And notwithstanding that all three had long been ardent followers of Jesus, they were highly respected by all who knew them. They had inherited extensive vineyards and olive orchards in this vicinity, and that they were wealthy was further attested by the fact that they could afford a private burial tomb on their own premises. Both of their parents had already been laid away in this tomb.

168:0.5 (1842.5) Mary had given up the thought of Jesus' coming and was abandoned to her grief, but Martha clung to the hope that Jesus would come, even up to the time on that very morning when they rolled the stone in front of the tomb and sealed the entrance. Even then she instructed a neighbor lad to keep watch down the Jericho road from the brow of the hill to the east of Bethany; and it was this lad who brought tidings to Martha that Jesus and his friends were approaching.

168:0.6 (1842.6) When Martha met Jesus, she fell at his feet, exclaiming, "Master, if you had been here, my brother would not have died!" Many fears were passing through Martha's mind, but she gave expression to no doubt, nor did she venture to criticize or question the Master's conduct as related to Lazarus's death. When she had spoken, Jesus reached down and, lifting her upon her feet, said, "Only have faith, Martha, and your brother shall rise again." Then answered Martha: "I know that he will rise again in the resurrection of the last day; and even now I believe that whatever you shall ask of God, our Father will give you."

168:0.7 (1843.1) Then said Jesus, looking straight into the eyes of Martha: "I am the resurrection and the life; he who believes in me, though he dies, yet shall he live. In truth, whosoever lives and believes in me shall never really die. Martha, do you believe this?" And Martha answered the Master: "Yes, I have long believed that you are the Deliverer, the Son of the living God, even he who should come to this world."

168:0.8 (1843.2) Jesus having inquired for Mary, Martha went at once into the house and, whispering to her sister, said, "The Master is here and has asked for you." And when Mary heard this, she rose up quickly and hastened out to meet Jesus, who still tarried at the place, some distance from the house, where Martha had first met him. The friends who were with Mary, seeking to comfort her, when they saw that she rose up quickly and went out, followed her, supposing that she was going to the tomb to weep.

168:0.9 (1843.3) Many of those present were Jesus' bitter enemies. That is why Martha had come out to meet him alone, and also why she went in secretly to inform Mary that he had asked for her. Martha, while craving to see Jesus, desired to avoid any possible unpleasantness which might be caused by his coming suddenly into the midst of a large group of his Jerusalem enemies. It had been Martha's intention to remain in the house with their friends while Mary went to greet Jesus, but in this she failed, for they all followed Mary and so found themselves unexpectedly in the presence of the Master.

168:0.10 (1843.4) Martha led Mary to Jesus, and when she saw him, she fell at his feet, exclaiming, "If you had only been here, my brother would not have died!" And when Jesus saw how they all grieved over the death of Lazarus, his soul was moved with compassion.

168:0.11 (1843.5) When the mourners saw that Mary had gone to greet Jesus, they withdrew for a short distance while both Martha and Mary talked with the Master and received further words of comfort and exhortation to maintain strong faith in the Father and complete resignation to the divine will.

168:0.12 (1843.6) The human mind of Jesus was mightily moved by the contention between his love for Lazarus and the bereaved sisters and his disdain and contempt for the outward show of affection manifested by some of these unbelieving and murderously intentioned Jews. Jesus indignantly resented the show of forced and outward mourning for Lazarus by some of these professed friends inasmuch as such false sorrow was associated in their hearts with so much bitter enmity toward himself. Some of these Jews, however, were sincere in their mourning, for they were real friends of the family.

At the Tomb of Lazarus

168:1.1 (1843.7) After Jesus had spent a few moments in comforting Martha and Mary, apart from the mourners, he asked them, "Where have you laid him?" Then Martha said, "Come and see." And as the Master followed on in silence with the two sorrowing sisters, he wept. When the friendly Jews who followed after them saw his tears, one of them said: "Behold how he loved him. Could not he who opened the eyes of the blind have kept this man from dying?" By this time they were standing before the family tomb, a small natural cave, or declivity, in the ledge of rock which rose up some thirty feet at the far end of the garden plot.

168:1.2 (1844.1) It is difficult to explain to human minds just why Jesus wept. While we have access to the registration of the combined human emotions and divine thoughts, as of record in the mind of the Personalized Adjuster, we are not altogether certain about the real cause of these emotional manifestations. We are inclined to believe that Jesus wept because of a number of thoughts and feelings which were going through his mind at this time, such as:

168:1.3 (1844.2) 1. He felt a genuine and sorrowful sympathy for Martha and Mary; he had a real and deep human affection for these sisters who had lost their brother.

168:1.4 (1844.3) 2. He was perturbed in his mind by the presence of the crowd of mourners, some sincere and some merely pretenders. He always resented these outward exhibitions of mourning. He knew the sisters loved their brother and had faith in the survival of believers. These conflicting emotions may possibly explain why he groaned as they came near the tomb.

168:1.5 (1844.4) 3. He truly hesitated about bringing Lazarus back to the mortal life. His sisters really needed him, but Jesus regretted having to summon his friend back to experience the bitter persecution which he well knew Lazarus would have to endure as a result of being the subject of the greatest of all demonstrations of the divine power of the Son of Man.

168:1.6 (1844.5) And now we may relate an interesting and instructive fact: Although this narrative unfolds as an apparently natural and normal event in human affairs, it has some very interesting side lights. While the messenger went to Jesus on Sunday, telling him of Lazarus's illness, and while Jesus sent word that it was "not to the death," at the same time he went in person up to Bethany and even asked the sisters, "Where have you laid him?" Even though all of this seems to indicate that the Master was proceeding after the manner of this life and in accordance with the limited knowledge of the human mind, nevertheless, the records of the universe reveal that Jesus' Personalized Adjuster issued orders for the indefinite detention of Lazarus's Thought Adjuster on the planet subsequent to Lazarus's death, and that this order was made of record just fifteen minutes before Lazarus breathed his last.

168:1.7 (1844.6) Did the divine mind of Jesus know, even before Lazarus died, that he would raise him from the dead? We do not know. We know only what we are herewith placing on record.

168:1.8 (1844.7) Many of Jesus' enemies were inclined to sneer at his manifestations of affection, and they said among themselves: "If he thought so much of this man, why did he tarry so long before coming to Bethany? If he is what they claim, why did he not save his dear friend? What is the good of healing strangers in Galilee if he cannot save those whom he loves?" And in many other ways they mocked and made light of the teachings and works of Jesus.

168:1.9 (1844.8) And so, on this Thursday afternoon at about half past two o'clock, was the stage all set in this little hamlet of Bethany for the enactment of the greatest of all works connected with the earth ministry of Michael of Nebadon, the greatest manifestation of divine power during his incarnation in the flesh, since his own resurrection occurred after he had been liberated from the bonds of mortal habitation.

168:1.10 (1845.1) The small group assembled before Lazarus's tomb little realized the presence near at hand of a vast concourse of all orders of celestial beings assembled under the leadership of Gabriel and now in waiting, by direction of the Personalized Adjuster of Jesus, vibrating with expectancy and ready to execute the bidding of their beloved Sovereign.

168:1.11 (1845.2) When Jesus spoke those words of command, "Take away the stone," the assembled celestial hosts made ready to enact the drama of the resurrection of Lazarus in the likeness of his mortal flesh. Such a form of resurrection involves difficulties of execution which far transcend the usual technique of the resurrection of mortal creatures in morontia form and requires far more celestial personalities and a far greater organization of universe facilities.

168:1.12 (1845.3) When Martha and

Mary heard this command of Jesus directing that the stone in front of the tomb be rolled away, they were filled with conflicting emotions. Mary hoped that Lazarus was to be raised from the dead, but Martha, while to some extent sharing her sister's faith, was more exercised by the fear that Lazarus would not be presentable, in his appearance, to Jesus, the apostles, and their friends. Said Martha: "Must we roll away the stone? My brother has now been dead four days, so that by this time decay of the body has begun." Martha also said this because she was not certain as to why the Master had requested that the stone be removed; she thought maybe Jesus wanted only to take one last look at Lazarus. She was not settled and constant in her attitude. As they hesitated to roll away the stone, Jesus said: "Did I not tell you at the first that this sickness was not to the death? Have I not come to fulfill my promise? And after I came to you, did I not say that, if you would only believe, you should see the glory of God? Wherefore do you doubt? How long before you will believe and obey?"

168:1.13 (1845.4) When Jesus had finished speaking, his apostles, with the assistance of willing neighbors, laid hold upon the stone and rolled it away from the entrance to the tomb.

168:1.14 (1845.5) It was the common belief of the Jews that the drop of gall on the point of the sword of the angel of death began to work by the end of the third day, so that it was taking full effect on the fourth day. They allowed that the soul of man might linger about the tomb until the end of the third day, seeking to reanimate the dead body; but they firmly believed that such a soul had gone on to the abode of departed spirits ere the fourth day had dawned.

168:1.15 (1845.6) These beliefs and opinions regarding the dead and the departure of the spirits of the dead served to make sure, in the minds of all who were now present at Lazarus's tomb and subsequently to all who might hear of what was about to occur, that this was really and truly a case of the raising of the dead by the personal working of one who declared he was "the resurrection and the life."

The Resurrection of Lazarus

168:2.1 (1845.7) As this company of some forty-five mortals stood before the tomb, they could dimly see the form of Lazarus, wrapped in linen bandages, resting on the right lower niche of the burial cave. While these earth creatures stood there in almost breathless silence, a vast host of celestial beings had swung into their places preparatory to answering the signal for action when it should be given by Gabriel, their commander.

168:2.2 (1846.1) Jesus lifted up his eyes and said: "Father, I am thankful that you heard and granted my request. I know that you always hear me, but because of those who stand here with me, I thus speak with you, that they may believe that you have sent me into the world, and that they may know that you are working with me in that which we are about to do." And when he had prayed, he cried with a loud voice, "Lazarus, come forth!"

168:2.3 (1846.2) Though these human observers remained motionless, the vast celestial host was all astir in unified action in obedience to the Creator's word. In just twelve seconds of earth time the hitherto lifeless form of Lazarus began to move and presently sat up on the edge of the stone shelf whereon it had rested. His body was bound about with grave cloths, and his face was covered with a napkin. And as he stood up before them—alive—Jesus said, "Loose him and let him go."

168:2.4 (1846.3) All, save the apostles, with Martha and Mary, fled to the house. They were pale with fright and overcome with astonishment. While some tarried, many hastened to their homes.

168:2.5 (1846.4) Lazarus greeted Jesus and the apostles and asked the meaning of the grave cloths and why he had awakened in the garden. Jesus and the apostles drew to one side while Martha told Lazarus of his death, burial, and resurrection. She had to explain to him that he had died on Sunday and was now brought back to life on Thursday, inasmuch as he had had no consciousness of time since falling asleep in death.

168:2.6 (1846.5) As Lazarus came out of the tomb, the Personalized Adjuster of Jesus, now chief of his kind in this local universe, gave command to the former Adjuster of Lazarus, now in waiting, to resume abode in the mind and soul of the resurrected man.

168:2.7 (1846.6) Then went Lazarus over to Jesus and, with his sisters, knelt at the Master's feet to give thanks and offer praise to God. Jesus, taking Lazarus by the hand, lifted him up, saying: "My son, what has happened to you will also be experienced by all who believe this gospel except that they shall be resurrected in a more glorious form. You shall be a living witness of the truth which I spoke—I am the resurrection and the life. But let us all now go into the house and partake of nourishment for these physical bodies."

168:2.8 (1846.7) As they walked toward the house, Gabriel dismissed the extra groups of the assembled heavenly host while he made record of the first instance on Urantia, and the last, where a mortal creature had been resurrected in the likeness of the physical body of death.

168:2.9 (1846.8) Lazarus could hardly comprehend what had occurred. He knew he had been very sick, but he could recall only that he had fallen asleep and been awakened. He was never able to tell anything about these four days in the tomb because he was wholly unconscious. Time is nonexistent to those who sleep the sleep of death.

168:2.10 (1846.9) Though many believed in Jesus as a result of this mighty work, others only hardened their hearts the more to reject him. By noon the next day this story had spread over all Jerusalem. Scores of men and women went to Bethany to look upon Lazarus and talk with him, and the alarmed and disconcerted Pharisees hastily called a meeting of the Sanhedrin that they might determine what should be done about these new developments.

Meeting of the Sanhedrin

168:3.1 (1847.1) Even though the testimony of this man raised from the dead did much to consolidate the faith of the mass of believers in the gospel of the kingdom, it had little or no influence on the attitude of the religious leaders and rulers at Jerusalem except to hasten their decision to destroy Jesus and stop his work.

168:3.2 (1847.2) At one o'clock the next day, Friday, the Sanhedrin met to deliberate further on the question, "What shall we do with Jesus of Nazareth?" After more than two hours of discussion and acrimonious debate, a certain Pharisee presented a resolution calling for Jesus' immediate death, proclaiming that he was a menace to all Israel and formally committing the Sanhedrin to the decision of death, without trial and in defiance of all precedent.

168:3.3 (1847.3) Time and again had this august body of Jewish leaders decreed that Jesus be apprehended and brought to trial on charges of blasphemy and numerous other accusations of flouting the Jewish sacred law. They had once before even gone so far as to declare he should die, but this was the first time the Sanhedrin had gone on record as desiring to decree his death in advance of a trial. But this resolution did not come to a vote since fourteen members of the Sanhedrin resigned in a body when such an unheard-of action was proposed. While these resignations were not formally acted upon for almost two weeks, this group of fourteen withdrew from the Sanhedrin on that day, never again to sit in the council. When these resignations were subsequently acted upon, five other members were thrown out because their associates believed they entertained friendly feelings toward Jesus. With the ejection of these nineteen men the Sanhedrin was in a position to try and to condemn Jesus with a solidarity bordering on unanimity.

168:3.4 (1847.4) The following week Lazarus and his sisters were summoned to appear before the Sanhedrin. When their testimony had been heard, no doubt could be entertained that Lazarus had been raised from the dead. Though the transactions of the Sanhedrin virtually admitted the resurrection of Lazarus, the record carried a resolution attributing this and all other wonders worked by Jesus to the power of the prince of devils, with whom Jesus was declared to be in league.

168:3.5 (1847.5) No matter what the source of his wonder-working power, these Jewish leaders were persuaded that, if he were not immediately stopped, very soon all the common people would believe in him; and further, that serious complications with the Roman authorities would arise since so many of his believers regarded him as the Messiah, Israel's deliverer.

168:3.6 (1847.6) It was at this same meeting of the Sanhedrin that Caiaphas the high priest first gave expression to that old Jewish adage, which he so many times repeated: "It is better that one man die, than that the community perish."

168:3.7 (1847.7) Although Jesus had received warning of the doings of the Sanhedrin on this dark Friday afternoon, he was not in the least perturbed and continued resting over the Sabbath with friends in Bethpage, a hamlet near Bethany. Early Sunday morning Jesus and the apostles assembled, by prearrangement, at the home of Lazarus, and taking leave of the Bethany family, they started on their journey back to the Pella encampment.

The Answer to Prayer

168:4.1 (1848.1) On the way from Bethany to Pella the apostles asked Jesus many questions, all of which the Master freely answered except those involving the details of the resurrection of the dead. Such problems were beyond the comprehension capacity of his apostles; therefore did the Master decline to discuss these questions with them. Since they had departed from Bethany in secret, they were alone. Jesus therefore embraced the opportunity to say many things to the ten which he thought would prepare them for the trying days just ahead.

168:4.2 (1848.2) The apostles were much stirred up in their minds and spent considerable time discussing their recent experiences as they were related to prayer and its answering. They all recalled Jesus' statement to the Bethany messenger at Philadelphia, when he said plainly, "This sickness is not really to the death." And yet, in spite of this promise, Lazarus actually died. All that day, again and again, they reverted to the discussion of this question of the answer to prayer.

168:4.3 (1848.3) Jesus' answers to their many questions may be summarized as follows:

168:4.4 (1848.4) 1. Prayer is an expression of the finite mind in an effort to approach the Infinite. The making of a prayer must, therefore, be limited by the knowledge, wisdom, and attributes of the finite; likewise must the answer be conditioned by the vision, aims, ideals, and prerogatives of the Infinite. There never can be observed an unbroken continuity of material phenomena between the making of a prayer and the reception of the full spiritual answer thereto.

168:4.5 (1848.5) 2. When a prayer is apparently unanswered, the delay often betokens a better answer, although one which is for some good reason greatly delayed. When Jesus said that Lazarus's sickness was really not to the death, he had already been dead eleven hours. No sincere prayer is denied an answer except when the superior viewpoint of the spiritual world has devised a better answer, an answer which meets the petition of the spirit of man as contrasted with the prayer of the mere mind of man.

168:4.6 (1848.6) 3. The prayers of time, when indited by the spirit and expressed in faith, are often so vast and all-encompassing that they can be answered only in eternity; the finite petition is sometimes so fraught with the grasp of the Infinite that the answer must long be postponed to await the creation of adequate capacity for receptivity; the prayer of faith may be so all-embracing that the answer can be received only on Paradise.

168:4.7 (1848.7) 4. The answers to the prayer of the mortal mind are often of such a nature that they can be received and recognized only after that same praying mind has attained the immortal state. The prayer of the material being can many times be answered only when such an individual has progressed to the spirit level.

168:4.8 (1848.8) 5. The prayer of a God-knowing person may be so distorted by ignorance and so deformed by superstition that the answer thereto would be highly undesirable. Then must the intervening spirit beings so translate such a prayer that, when the answer arrives, the petitioner wholly fails to recognize it as the answer to his prayer.

168:4.9 (1848.9) 6. All true prayers are addressed to spiritual beings, and all such petitions must be answered in spiritual terms, and all such answers must consist in spiritual realities. Spirit beings cannot bestow material answers to the spirit petitions of even material beings. Material beings can pray effectively only when they "pray in the spirit."

168:4.10 (1849.1) 7. No prayer can hope for an answer unless it is born of the spirit and nurtured by faith. Your sincere faith implies that you have in advance virtually granted your prayer hearers the full right to answer your petitions in accordance with that supreme wisdom and that divine love which your faith depicts as always actuating those beings to whom you pray.

168:4.11 (1849.2) 8. The child is always within his rights when he presumes to petition the parent; and the parent is always within his parental obligations to the immature child when his superior wisdom dictates that the answer to the child's prayer be delayed, modified, segregated, transcended, or postponed to another stage of spiritual ascension.

168:4.12 (1849.3) 9. Do not hesitate to pray the prayers of spirit longing; doubt not that you shall receive the answer to your petitions. These answers will be on deposit, awaiting your achievement of those future spiritual levels of actual cosmic attainment, on this world or on others, whereon it will become possible for you to recognize and appropriate the long-waiting answers to your earlier but ill-timed petitions.

168:4.13 (1849.4) 10. All genuine spirit-born petitions are certain of an answer. Ask and you shall receive. But you should remember that you are progressive creatures of time and space; therefore must you constantly reckon with the time-space factor in the experience of your personal reception of the full answers to your manifold prayers and petitions.

What Became of Lazarus

168:5.1 (1849.5) Lazarus remained at the Bethany home, being the center of great interest to many sincere believers and to numerous curious individuals, until the days of the crucifixion of Jesus, when he received warning that the Sanhedrin had decreed his death. The rulers of the Jews were determined to put a stop to the further spread of the teachings of Jesus, and they well judged that it would be useless to put Jesus to death if they permitted Lazarus, who represented the very peak of his wonder-working, to live and bear testimony to the fact that Jesus had raised him from the dead. Already had Lazarus suffered bitter persecution from them.

168:5.2 (1849.6) And so Lazarus took hasty leave of his sisters at Bethany, fleeing down through Jericho and across the Jordan, never permitting himself to rest long until he had reached Philadelphia. Lazarus knew Abner well, and here he felt safe from the murderous intrigues of the wicked Sanhedrin.

168:5.3 (1849.7) Soon after this Martha and Mary disposed of their lands at Bethany and joined their brother in Perea. Meantime, Lazarus had become the treasurer of the church at Philadelphia. He became a strong supporter of Abner in his controversy with Paul and the Jerusalem church and ultimately died, when 67 years old, of the same sickness that carried him off when he was a younger man at Bethany.

Paper 169

Last Teaching at Pella

169:0.1 (1850.1) LATE on Monday evening, March 6, Jesus and the ten apostles arrived at the Pella camp. This was the last week of Jesus' sojourn there, and he was very active in teaching the multitude and instructing the apostles. He preached every afternoon to the crowds and each night answered questions for the apostles and certain of the more advanced disciples residing at the camp.

169:0.2 (1850.2) Word regarding the resurrection of Lazarus had reached the encampment two days before the Master's arrival, and the entire assembly was agog. Not since the feeding of the five thousand had anything occurred which so aroused the imagination of the people. And thus it was at the very height of the second phase of the public ministry of the kingdom that Jesus planned to teach this one short week at Pella and then to begin the tour of southern Perea which led right up to the final and tragic experiences of the last week in Jerusalem.

169:0.3 (1850.3) The Pharisees and the chief priests had begun to formulate their charges and to crystallize their accusations. They objected to the Master's teachings on these grounds:

169:0.4 (1850.4) 1. He is a friend of publicans and sinners; he receives the ungodly and even eats with them.

169:0.5 (1850.5) 2. He is a blasphemer; he talks about God as being his Father and thinks he is equal with God.

169:0.6 (1850.6) 3. He is a lawbreaker. He heals disease on the Sabbath and in many other ways flouts the sacred law of Israel.

169:0.7 (1850.7) 4. He is in league with devils. He works wonders and does seeming miracles by the power of Beelzebub, the prince of devils.

Parable of the Lost Son

169:1.1 (1850.8) On Thursday afternoon Jesus talked to the multitude about the "Grace of Salvation." In the course of this sermon he retold the story of the lost sheep and the lost coin and then added his favorite parable of the prodigal son.
Said Jesus:

169:1.2 (1850.9) "You have been admonished by the prophets from Samuel to John that you should seek for God—search for truth. Always have they said, 'Seek the Lord while he may be found.' And all such teaching should be taken to heart. But I have come to show you that, while you are seeking to find God, God is likewise seeking to find you. Many times have I told you the story of the good shepherd who left the ninety and nine sheep in the fold while he went forth searching for the one that was lost, and how, when he had found the straying sheep, he laid it over his shoulder and tenderly carried it back to the fold. And when the lost sheep had been restored to the fold, you remember that the good shepherd called in his friends and bade them rejoice with him over the finding of the sheep that had been lost. Again I say there is more joy in heaven over one sinner who repents than over the ninety and nine just persons who need no repentance. The fact that souls are lost only increases the interest of the heavenly Father. I have come to this world to do my Father's bidding, and it has truly been said of the Son of Man that he is a friend of publicans and sinners.

169:1.3 (1851.1) "You have been taught that divine acceptance comes after your repentance and as a result of all your works of sacrifice and penitence, but I assure you that the Father accepts you even before you have repented and sends the Son and his associates to find you and bring you, with rejoicing, back to the fold, the kingdom of sonship and spiritual progress. You are all like sheep which have gone astray, and I have come to seek and to save those who are lost.

169:1.4 (1851.2) "And you should also remember the story of the woman who, having had ten pieces of silver made into a necklace of adornment, lost one piece, and how she lit the lamp and diligently swept the house and kept up the search until she found the lost piece of silver. And as soon as she found the coin that was lost, she called together her friends and neighbors, saying, 'Rejoice with me, for I have found the piece that was lost.' So again I say, there is always joy in the presence of the angels of heaven over one sinner who repents and returns to the Father's fold. And I tell you this story to impress upon you that the Father and his Son go forth to search for those who are lost, and in this search we employ all influences capable of rendering assistance in our diligent efforts to find those who are lost, those who stand in need of salvation. And so, while the Son of Man goes out in the wilderness to seek for the sheep gone

astray, he also searches for the coin which is lost in the house. The sheep wanders away, unintentionally; the coin is covered by the dust of time and obscured by the accumulation of the things of men.

169:1.5 (1851.3) "And now I would like to tell you the story of a thoughtless son of a well-to-do farmer who deliberately left his father's house and went off into a foreign land, where he fell into much tribulation. You recall that the sheep strayed away without intention, but this youth left his home with premeditation. It was like this:

169:1.6 (1851.4) "A certain man had two sons; one, the younger, was lighthearted and carefree, always seeking for a good time and shirking responsibility, while his older brother was serious, sober, hard-working, and willing to bear responsibility. Now these two brothers did not get along well together; they were always quarreling and bickering. The younger lad was cheerful and vivacious, but indolent and unreliable; the older son was steady and industrious, at the same time self-centered, surly, and conceited. The younger son enjoyed play but shunned work; the older devoted himself to work but seldom played. This association became so disagreeable that the younger son came to his father and said: 'Father, give me the third portion of your possessions which would fall to me and allow me to go out into the world to seek my own fortune.' And when the father heard this request, knowing how unhappy the young man was at home and with his older brother, he divided his property, giving the youth his share.

169:1.7 (1851.5) "Within a few weeks the young man gathered together all his funds and set out upon a journey to a far country, and finding nothing profitable to do which was also pleasurable, he soon wasted all his inheritance in riotous living. And when he had spent all, there arose a prolonged famine in that country, and he found himself in want. And so, when he suffered hunger and his distress was great, he found employment with one of the citizens of that country, who sent him into the fields to feed swine. And the young man would fain have filled himself with the husks which the swine ate, but no one would give him anything.

169:1.8 (1852.1) "One day, when he was very hungry, he came to himself and said: 'How many hired servants of my father have bread enough and to spare while I perish with hunger, feeding swine off here in a foreign country! I will arise and go to my father, and I will say to him: Father, I have sinned against heaven and against you. I am no more worthy to be called your son; only be willing to make me one of your hired servants.' And when the young man had reached this decision, he arose and started out for his father's house.

169:1.9 (1852.2) "Now this father had grieved much for his son; he had missed the cheerful, though thoughtless, lad. This father loved this son and was always on the lookout for his return, so that on the day he approached his home, even while he was yet afar off, the father saw him and, being moved with loving compassion, ran out to meet him, and with affectionate greeting he embraced and kissed him. And after they had thus met, the son looked up into his father's tearful face and said: 'Father, I have sinned against heaven and in your sight; I am no more worthy to be called a son'— but the lad did not find opportunity to complete his confession because the overjoyed father said to the servants who had by this time come running up: 'Bring quickly his best robe, the one I have saved, and put it on him and put the son's ring on his hand and fetch sandals for his feet.'

169:1.10 (1852.3) "And then, after the happy father had led the footsore and weary lad into the house, he called to his servants: 'Bring on the fatted calf and kill it, and let us eat and make merry, for this my son was dead and is alive again; he was lost and is found.' And they all gathered about the father to rejoice with him over the restoration of his son.

169:1.11 (1852.4) "About this time, while they were celebrating, the elder son came in from his day's work in the field, and as he drew near the house, he heard the music and the dancing. And when he came up to the back door, he called out one of the servants and inquired as to the meaning of all this festivity. And then said the servant: 'Your long-lost brother has come home, and your father has killed the fatted calf to rejoice over his son's safe return. Come in that you also may greet your brother and receive him back into your father's house.'

169:1.12 (1852.5) "But when the older brother heard this, he was so hurt and angry he would not go into the house. When his father heard of his resentment of the welcome of his younger brother, he went out to entreat him. But the older son would not yield to his father's persuasion. He answered his father, saying: 'Here these many years have I served you, never transgressing the least of your commands, and yet you never gave me even a kid that I might make merry with my friends. I have remained here to care for you all these years, and you never made rejoicing over my faithful service, but when this your son returns, having squandered your substance with harlots, you make haste to kill the fatted calf and make merry over him.'

169:1.13 (1852.6) "Since this father truly loved both of his sons, he tried to reason with this older one: 'But, my son, you have all the while been with me, and all this which I have is yours. You could have had a kid at any time you had made friends to share your merriment. But it is only proper that you should now join with me in being glad and merry because of your brother's return. Think of it, my son, your brother was lost and is found; he has returned alive to us!'"

169:1.14 (1853.1) This was one of the most touching and effective of all the parables which Jesus ever presented to impress upon his hearers the Father's willingness to receive all who seek entrance into the kingdom of heaven.

169:1.15 (1853.2) Jesus was very partial to telling these three stories at the same time. He presented the story of the lost sheep to show that, when men unintentionally stray away from the path of life, the Father is mindful of such lost ones and goes out, with his Sons, the true shepherds of the flock, to seek the lost sheep. He then would recite the story of the coin lost in the house to illustrate how thorough is the divine searching for all who are confused, confounded, or otherwise spiritually blinded by the material cares and accumulations of life. And then he would launch forth into the telling of this parable of the lost son, the reception of the returning prodigal, to show how complete is the restoration of the lost son into his Father's house and heart.

169:1.16 (1853.3) Many, many times during his years of teaching, Jesus told and retold this story of the prodigal son. This parable and the story of the good Samaritan were his favorite means of teaching the love of the Father and the neighborliness of man.

Parable of the Shrewd Steward

169:2.1 (1853.4) One evening Simon Zelotes, commenting on one of Jesus' statements, said: "Master, what did you mean when you said today that many of the children of the world are wiser in their generation than are the children of the kingdom since they are skillful in making friends with the mammon of unrighteousness?" Jesus answered:

169:2.2 (1853.5) "Some of you, before you entered the kingdom, were very shrewd in dealing with your business associates. If you were unjust and often unfair, you were nonetheless prudent and farseeing in that you transacted your business with an eye single to your present profit and future safety. Likewise should you now so order your lives in the kingdom as to provide for your present joy while you also make certain of your future enjoyment of treasures laid up in heaven. If you were so diligent in making gains for yourselves when in the service of self, why should you show less

diligence in gaining souls for the kingdom since you are now servants of the brotherhood of man and stewards of God?

169:2.3 (1853.6) "You may all learn a lesson from the story of a certain rich man who had a shrewd but unjust steward. This steward had not only oppressed his master's clients for his own selfish gain, but he had also directly wasted and squandered his master's funds. When all this finally came to the ears of his master, he called the steward before him and

asked the meaning of these rumors and required that he should give immediate accounting of his stewardship and prepare to turn his master's affairs over to another.

169:2.4 (1853.7) "Now this unfaithful steward began to say to himself: 'What shall I do since I am about to lose this stewardship? I have not the strength to dig; to beg I am ashamed. I know what I will do to make certain that, when I am put out of this stewardship, I will be welcomed into the houses of all who do business with my master.' And then, calling in each of his lord's debtors, he said to the first, 'How much do you owe my master?' He answered, 'A hundred measures of oil.' Then said the steward, 'Take your wax board bond, sit down quickly, and change it to fifty.' Then he said to another debtor, 'How much do you owe?' And he replied, 'A hundred measures of wheat.' Then said the steward, 'Take your bond and write fourscore.' And this he did with numerous other debtors. And so did this dishonest steward seek to make friends for himself after he would be discharged from his stewardship. Even his lord and master, when he subsequently found out about this, was compelled to admit that his unfaithful steward had at least shown sagacity in the manner in which he had sought to provide for future days of want and adversity.

169:2.5 (1854.1) "And it is in this way that the sons of this world sometimes show more wisdom in their preparation for the future than do the children of light. I say to you who profess to be acquiring treasure in heaven: Take lessons from those who make friends with the mammon of unrighteousness, and likewise so conduct your lives that you make eternal friendship with the forces of righteousness in order that, when all things earthly fail, you shall be joyfully received into the eternal habitations.

169:2.6 (1854.2) "I affirm that he who is faithful in little will also be faithful in much, while he who is unrighteous in little will also be unrighteous in much. If you have not shown foresight and integrity in the affairs of this world, how can you hope to be faithful and prudent when you are trusted with the stewardship of the true riches of the heavenly kingdom? If you are not good stewards and faithful bankers, if you have not been faithful in that which is another's, who will be foolish enough to give you great treasure in your own name?

169:2.7 (1854.3) "And again I assert that no man can serve two masters; either he will hate the one and love the other, or else he will hold to one while he despises the other. You cannot serve God and mammon."

169:2.8 (1854.4) When the Pharisees who were present heard this, they began to sneer and scoff since they were much given to the acquirement of riches. These unfriendly hearers sought to engage Jesus in unprofitable argumentation, but he refused to debate with his enemies. When the Pharisees fell to wrangling among themselves, their loud speaking attracted large numbers of the multitude encamped thereabouts; and when they began to dispute with each other, Jesus withdrew, going to his tent for the night.

The Rich Man and the Beggar

169:3.1 (1854.5) When the meeting became too noisy, Simon Peter, standing up, took charge, saying: "Men and brethren, it is not seemly thus to dispute among yourselves. The Master has spoken, and you do well to ponder his words. And this is no new doctrine which he proclaimed to you. Have you not also heard the allegory of the Nazarites concerning the rich man and the beggar? Some of us heard John the Baptist thunder this parable of warning to those who love riches and covet dishonest wealth. And while this olden parable is not according to the gospel we preach, you would all do well to heed its lessons until such a time as you comprehend the new light of the kingdom of heaven. The story as John told it was like this:

169:3.2 (1854.6) "There was a certain rich man named Dives, who, being clothed in purple and fine linen, lived in mirth and splendor every day. And there was a certain beggar named Lazarus, who was laid at this rich man's gate, covered with sores and desiring to be fed with the crumbs which fell from the rich man's table; yes, even the dogs came and licked his sores. And it came to pass that the beggar died and was carried away by the angels to rest in Abraham's bosom. And then, presently, this rich man also died and was buried with great pomp and regal splendor. When the rich man departed from this world, he waked up in Hades, and finding himself in torment, he lifted up his eyes and beheld Abraham afar off and Lazarus in his bosom. And then Dives cried aloud: 'Father Abraham, have mercy on me and send over Lazarus that he may dip the tip of his finger in water to cool my tongue, for I am in great anguish because of my punishment.' And then Abraham replied: 'My son, you should remember that in your lifetime you enjoyed the good things while Lazarus in like manner suffered the evil. But now all this is changed, seeing that Lazarus is comforted while you are tormented. And besides, between us and you there is a great gulf so that we cannot go to you, neither can you come over to us.' Then said Dives to Abraham: 'I pray you send Lazarus back to my father's house, inasmuch as I have five brothers, that he may so testify as to prevent my brothers from coming to this place of torment.' But Abraham said: 'My son, they have Moses and the prophets; let them hear them.' And then answered Dives: 'No, No, Father Abraham! but if one go to them from the dead, they will repent.' And then said Abraham: 'If they hear not

Moses and the prophets, neither will they be persuaded even if one were to rise from the dead.'" *

169:3.3 (1855.1) After Peter had recited this ancient parable of the Nazarite brotherhood, and since the crowd had quieted down, Andrew arose and dismissed them for the night. Although both the apostles and his disciples frequently asked Jesus questions about the parable of Dives and Lazarus, he never consented to make comment thereon.

The Father and His Kingdom

169:4.1 (1855.2) Jesus always had trouble trying to explain to the apostles that, while they proclaimed the establishment of the kingdom of God, the Father in heaven was not a king. At the time Jesus lived on earth and taught in the flesh, the people of Urantia knew mostly of kings and emperors in the governments of the nations, and the Jews had long contemplated the coming of the kingdom of God. For these and other reasons, the Master thought best to designate the spiritual brotherhood of man as the kingdom of heaven and the spirit head of this brotherhood as the Father in heaven. Never did Jesus refer to his Father as a king. In his intimate talks with the apostles he always referred to himself as the Son of Man and as their elder brother. He depicted all his followers as servants of mankind and messengers of the gospel of the kingdom.

169:4.2 (1855.3) Jesus never gave his apostles a systematic lesson concerning the personality and attributes of the Father in heaven. He never asked men to believe in his Father; he took it for granted they did. Jesus never belittled himself by offering arguments in proof of the reality of the Father. His teaching regarding the Father all centered in the declaration that he and the Father are one; that he who has seen the Son has seen the Father; that the Father, like the Son, knows all things; that only the Son really knows the Father, and he to whom

the Son will reveal him; that he who knows the Son knows also the Father; and that the Father sent him into the world to reveal their combined natures and to show forth their conjoint work. He never made other pronouncements about his Father except to the woman of Samaria at Jacob's well, when he declared, "God is spirit."

169:4.3 (1856.1) You learn about God from Jesus by observing the divinity of his life, not by depending on his teachings. From the life of the Master you may each assimilate that concept of God which represents the measure of your capacity to perceive realities spiritual and divine, truths real and eternal. The finite can never hope to comprehend the Infinite except as the Infinite was focalized in the time-space personality of the finite experience of the human life of Jesus of Nazareth.

169:4.4 (1856.2) Jesus well knew that God can be known only by the realities of experience; never can he be understood by the mere teaching of the mind. Jesus taught his apostles that, while they never could fully understand God, they could most certainly know him, even as they had known the Son of Man. You can know God, not by understanding what Jesus said, but by knowing what Jesus was. Jesus was a revelation of God.

169:4.5 (1856.3) Except when quoting the Hebrew scriptures, Jesus referred to Deity by only two names: God and Father. And when the Master made reference to his Father as God, he usually employed the Hebrew word signifying the plural God (the Trinity) and not the word Yahweh, which stood for the progressive conception of the tribal God of the Jews.

169:4.6 (1856.4) Jesus never called the Father a king, and he very much regretted that the Jewish hope for a restored kingdom and John's proclamation of a coming kingdom made it necessary for him to denominate his proposed spiritual brotherhood the kingdom of heaven. With the one exception—the declaration that "God is spirit"—Jesus never referred to Deity in any manner other than in terms descriptive of his own personal relationship with the First Source and Center of Paradise.

169:4.7 (1856.5) Jesus employed the word God to designate the idea of Deity and the word Father to designate the experience of knowing God. When the word Father is employed to denote God, it should be understood in its largest possible meaning. The word God cannot be defined and therefore stands for the infinite concept of the Father, while the term Father, being capable of partial definition, may be employed to represent the human concept of the divine Father as he is associated with man during the course of mortal existence.

169:4.8 (1856.6) To the Jews, Elohim was the God of gods, while Yahweh was the God of Israel. Jesus accepted the concept of Elohim and called this supreme group of beings God. In the place of the concept of Yahweh, the racial deity, he introduced the idea of the fatherhood of God and the world-wide brotherhood of man. He exalted the Yahweh concept of a deified racial Father to the idea of a Father of all the children of men, a divine Father of the individual believer. And he further taught that this God of universes and this Father of all men were one and the same Paradise Deity.

169:4.9 (1856.7) Jesus never claimed to be the manifestation of Elohim (God) in the flesh. He never declared that he was a revelation of Elohim (God) to the worlds. He never taught that he who had seen him had seen Elohim (God). But he did proclaim himself as the revelation of the Father in the flesh, and he did say that whoso had seen him had seen the Father. As the divine Son he claimed to represent only the Father.

169:4.10 (1857.1) He was, indeed, the Son of even the Elohim God; but in the likeness of mortal flesh and to the mortal sons of God, he chose to limit his life revelation to the portrayal of his Father's character in so far as such a revelation might be comprehensible to mortal man. As regards the character of the other persons of the Paradise Trinity, we shall have to be content with the teaching that they are altogether like the Father, who has been revealed in personal portraiture in the life of his incarnated Son, Jesus of Nazareth.

169:4.11 (1857.2) Although Jesus revealed the true nature of the heavenly Father in his earth life, he taught little about him. In fact, he taught only two things: that God in himself is spirit, and that, in all matters of relationship with his creatures, he is a Father. On this evening Jesus made the final pronouncement of his relationship with God when he declared: "I have come out from the Father, and I have come into the world; again, I will leave the world and go to the Father."

169:4.12 (1857.3) But mark you! never did Jesus say, "Whoso has heard me has heard God." But he did say, "He who has seen me has seen the Father." To hear Jesus' teaching is not equivalent to knowing God, but to see Jesus is an experience which in itself is a revelation of the Father to the soul. The God of universes rules the far-flung creation, but it is the Father in heaven who sends forth his spirit to dwell within your minds.

169:4.13 (1857.4) Jesus is the spiritual lens in human likeness which makes visible to the material creature Him who is invisible. He is your elder brother who, in the flesh, makes known to you a Being of infinite attributes whom not even the celestial hosts can presume fully to understand. But all of this must consist in the personal experience of the individual believer. God who is spirit can be known only as a spiritual experience. God can be revealed to the finite sons of the material worlds, by the divine Son of the spiritual realms, only as a Father. You can know the Eternal as a Father; you can worship him as the God of universes, the infinite Creator of all existences.

Paper 170

The Kingdom of Heaven

170:0.1 (1858.1) SATURDAY afternoon, March 11, Jesus preached his last sermon at Pella. This was among the notable addresses of his public ministry, embracing a full and complete discussion of the kingdom of heaven. He was aware of the confusion which existed in the minds of his apostles and disciples regarding the meaning and significance of the terms "kingdom of heaven" and "kingdom of God," which he used as interchangeable designations of his bestowal mission. Although the very term kingdom of heaven should have been enough to separate what it stood for from all connection with earthly kingdoms and temporal governments, it was not. The idea of a temporal king was too deep- rooted in the Jewish mind thus to be dislodged in a single generation. Therefore Jesus did not at first openly oppose this long-nourished concept of the kingdom.

170:0.2 (1858.2) This Sabbath afternoon the Master sought to clarify the teaching about the kingdom of heaven; he discussed the subject from every viewpoint and endeavored to make clear the many different senses in which the term had been used. In this narrative we will amplify the address by adding numerous statements made by Jesus on previous occasions and by including some remarks made only to the apostles during the evening discussions of this same day.

We will also make certain comments dealing with the subsequent outworking of the kingdom idea as it is related to the later Christian church.

Concepts of the Kingdom of Heaven

170:1.1 (1858.3) In connection with the recital of Jesus' sermon it should be noted that throughout the Hebrew scriptures there was a dual concept of the kingdom of heaven. The prophets presented the kingdom of God as:

170:1.2 (1858.4) 1. A present reality; and as

170:1.3 (1858.5) 2. A future hope— when the kingdom would be realized in fullness upon the appearance of the Messiah. This is the kingdom concept which John the Baptist taught.

170:1.4 (1858.6) From the very first Jesus and the apostles taught both of these concepts. There were two other ideas of the kingdom which should be borne in mind:

170:1.5 (1858.7) 3. The later Jewish concept of a world-wide and transcendental kingdom of supernatural origin and miraculous inauguration.

170:1.6 (1858.8) 4. The Persian teachings portraying the establishment of a divine kingdom as the achievement of the triumph of good over evil at the end of the world.

170:1.7 (1858.9) Just before the advent of Jesus on earth, the Jews combined and confused all of these ideas of the kingdom into their apocalyptic concept of the Messiah's coming to establish the age of the Jewish triumph, the eternal age of God's supreme rule on earth, the new world, the era in which all mankind would worship Yahweh. In choosing to utilize this concept of the kingdom of heaven, Jesus elected to appropriate the most vital and culminating heritage of both the Jewish and Persian religions.

170:1.8 (1859.1) The kingdom of heaven, as it has been understood and misunderstood down through the centuries of the Christian era, embraced four distinct groups of ideas:

170:1.9 (1859.2) 1. The concept of the Jews.

170:1.10 (1859.3) 2. The concept of the Persians.

170:1.11 (1859.4) 3. The personal-experience concept of Jesus—"the kingdom of heaven within you."

170:1.12 (1859.5) 4. The composite and confused concepts which the founders and promulgators of Christianity have sought to impress upon the world.

170:1.13 (1859.6) At different times and in varying circumstances it appears that Jesus may have presented numerous concepts of the "kingdom" in his public teachings, but to his apostles he always taught the kingdom as embracing man's personal experience in relation to his fellows on earth and to the Father in heaven. Concerning the kingdom, his last word always was, "The kingdom is within you."

170:1.14 (1859.7) Centuries of confusion regarding the meaning of the term "kingdom of heaven" have been due to three factors:

170:1.15 (1859.8) 1. The confusion occasioned by observing the idea of the "kingdom" as it passed through the various progressive phases of its recasting by Jesus and his apostles.

170:1.16 (1859.9) 2. The confusion which was inevitably associated with the transplantation of early Christianity from a Jewish to a gentile soil.

170:1.17 (1859.10) 3. The confusion which was inherent in the fact that Christianity became a religion which was organized about the central idea of Jesus' person; the gospel of the kingdom became more and more a religion about him.

Jesus' Concept of the Kingdom

170:2.1 (1859.11) The Master made it clear that the kingdom of heaven must begin with, and be centered in, the dual concept of the truth of the fatherhood of God and the correlated fact of the brotherhood of man. The acceptance of such a teaching, Jesus declared, would liberate man from the age-long bondage of animal fear and at the same time enrich human

living with the following endowments of the new life of spiritual liberty:

170:2.2 (1859.12) 1. The possession of new courage and augmented spiritual power. The gospel of the kingdom was to set man free and inspire him to dare to hope for eternal life.

170:2.3 (1859.13) 2. The gospel carried a message of new confidence and true consolation for all men, even for the poor.

170:2.4 (1859.14) 3. It was in itself a new standard of moral values, a new ethical yardstick wherewith to measure human conduct. It portrayed the ideal of a resultant new order of human society.

170:2.5 (1859.15) 4. It taught the preeminence of the spiritual compared with the material; it glorified spiritual realities and exalted superhuman ideals.

170:2.6 (1860.1) 5. This new gospel held up spiritual attainment as the true goal of living. Human life received a new endowment of moral value and divine dignity.

170:2.7 (1860.2) 6. Jesus taught that eternal realities were the result (reward) of righteous earthly striving. Man's mortal sojourn on earth acquired new meanings consequent upon the recognition of a noble destiny.

170:2.8 (1860.3) 7. The new gospel affirmed that human salvation is the revelation of a far-reaching divine purpose to be fulfilled and realized in the future destiny of the endless service of the salvaged sons of God.

170:2.9 (1860.4) These teachings cover the expanded idea of the kingdom which was taught by Jesus. This great concept was hardly embraced in the elementary and confused kingdom teachings of John the Baptist.

170:2.10 (1860.5) The apostles were unable to grasp the real meaning of the Master's utterances regarding the kingdom. The subsequent distortion of Jesus' teachings, as they are recorded in the New Testament, is because the concept of the gospel writers was colored by the belief that Jesus was then absent from the world for only a short time; that he would soon return to establish the kingdom in power and glory—just such an idea as they held while he was with them in the flesh. But Jesus did not connect the establishment of the kingdom with the idea of his return to this world. That centuries have passed with no signs of the appearance of the "New Age" is in no way out of harmony with Jesus' teaching.

170:2.11 (1860.6) The great effort embodied in this sermon was the attempt to translate the concept of the kingdom of heaven into the ideal of the idea of doing the will of God. Long had the Master taught his followers to pray: "Your kingdom come; your will be done"; and at this time he earnestly sought to induce them to abandon the use of the term kingdom of God in favor of the more practical equivalent, the will of God. But he did not succeed.

170:2.12 (1860.7) Jesus desired to substitute for the idea of the kingdom, king, and subjects, the concept of the heavenly family, the heavenly Father, and the liberated sons of God engaged in joyful and voluntary service for their fellow men and in the sublime and intelligent worship of God the Father.

170:2.13 (1860.8) Up to this time the apostles had acquired a double viewpoint of the kingdom; they regarded it as:
170:2.14 (1860.9) 1. A matter of personal experience then present in the hearts of true believers, and
170:2.15 (1860.10) 2. A question of racial or world phenomena; that the kingdom was in the future, something to look forward to.

170:2.16 (1860.11) They looked upon the coming of the kingdom in the hearts of men as a gradual development, like the leaven in the dough or like the growing of the mustard seed. They believed that the coming of the kingdom in the racial or world sense would be both sudden and spectacular. Jesus never tired of telling them that the kingdom of heaven was their personal experience of realizing the higher qualities of spiritual living; that these realities of the spirit experience are progressively translated to new and higher levels of divine certainty and eternal grandeur.

170:2.17 (1860.12) On this afternoon the Master distinctly taught a new concept of the double nature of the kingdom in that he portrayed the following two phases:

170:2.18 (1860.13) "First. The kingdom of God in this world, the supreme desire to do the will of God, the unselfish love of man which yields the good fruits of improved ethical and moral conduct.

170:2.19 (1861.1) "Second. The kingdom of God in heaven, the goal of mortal believers, the estate wherein the love for God is perfected, and wherein the will of God is done more divinely."

170:2.20 (1861.2) Jesus taught that, by faith, the believer enters the kingdom now. In the various discourses he taught that two things are essential to faith-entrance into the kingdom:

170:2.21 (1861.3) 1. Faith, sincerity. To come as a little child, to receive the bestowal of sonship as a gift; to submit to the doing of the Father's will without questioning and in the full confidence and genuine trustfulness of the Father's wisdom; to come into the kingdom free from prejudice and preconception; to be open-minded and teachable like an unspoiled child.
170:2.22 (1861.4) 2. Truth hunger. The thirst for righteousness, a change of mind, the acquirement of the motive to be like God and to find God.

170:2.23 (1861.5) Jesus taught that sin is not the child of a defective nature but rather the offspring of a knowing mind dominated by an unsubmissive will. Regarding sin, he taught that God has forgiven; that we make such forgiveness personally available by the act of forgiving our fellows. When you forgive your brother in the flesh, you thereby create the capacity in your own soul for the reception of the reality of God's forgiveness of your own misdeeds.

170:2.24 (1861.6) By the time the Apostle John began to write the story of Jesus' life and teachings, the early Christians had experienced so much trouble with the kingdom-of-God idea as a breeder of persecution that they had largely abandoned the use of the term. John talks much about the "eternal life." Jesus often spoke of it as the "kingdom of life." He also frequently referred to "the kingdom of God within you." He once spoke of such an experience as "family fellowship with God the Father." Jesus sought to substitute many terms for the kingdom but always without success.

Among others, he used: the family of God, the Father's will, the friends of God, the fellowship of believers, the brotherhood of man, the Father's fold, the children of God, the fellowship of the faithful, the Father's service, and the liberated sons of God.

170:2.25 (1861.7) But he could not escape the use of the kingdom idea. It was more than fifty years later, not until after the destruction of Jerusalem by the Roman armies, that this concept of the kingdom began to change into the cult of eternal life as its social and institutional aspects were taken over by the rapidly expanding and crystallizing Christian church.

In Relation to Righteousness

170:3.1 (1861.8) Jesus was always trying to impress upon his apostles and disciples that they must acquire, by faith, a righteousness which would exceed the righteousness of slavish works which some of the scribes and Pharisees paraded so vaingloriously before the world.

170:3.2 (1861.9) Though Jesus taught that faith, simple childlike belief, is the key to the door of the kingdom, he also taught that, having entered the door, there are the progressive steps of righteousness which every believing child must ascend in order to grow up to the full stature of the robust sons of God.

170:3.3 (1861.10) It is in the consideration of the technique of receiving God's forgiveness that the attainment of the righteousness of the kingdom is revealed. Faith is the price you pay for entrance into the family of God; but forgiveness is the act of God which accepts your faith as the price of admission. And the reception of the forgiveness of God by a kingdom believer involves a definite and actual experience and consists in the following four steps, the kingdom steps of inner righteousness:

170:3.4 (1862.1) 1. God's forgiveness is made actually available and is personally experienced by man just in so far as he forgives his fellows.

170:3.5 (1862.2) 2. Man will not truly forgive his fellows unless he loves them as himself.

170:3.6 (1862.3) 3. To thus love your neighbor as yourself is the highest ethics.

170:3.7 (1862.4) 4. Moral conduct, true righteousness, becomes, then, the natural result of such love.

170:3.8 (1862.5) It therefore is evident that the true and inner religion of the kingdom unfailingly and increasingly tends to manifest itself in practical avenues of social service. Jesus taught a living religion that impelled its believers to engage in the doing of loving service. But Jesus did not put ethics in the place of religion. He taught religion as a cause and ethics as a result.

170:3.9 (1862.6) The righteousness of any act must be measured by the motive; the highest forms of good are therefore unconscious. Jesus was never concerned with morals or ethics as such. He was wholly concerned with that inward and spiritual fellowship with God the Father which so certainly and directly manifests itself as outward and loving service for man. He taught that the religion of the kingdom is a genuine personal experience which no man can contain within himself; that the consciousness of being a member of the family of believers leads inevitably to the practice of the precepts of the family conduct, the service of one's brothers and sisters in the effort to enhance and enlarge the brotherhood.

170:3.10 (1862.7) The religion of the kingdom is personal, individual; the fruits, the results, are familial, social. Jesus never failed to exalt the sacredness of the individual as contrasted with the community. But he also recognized that man develops his character by unselfish service; that he unfolds his moral nature in loving relations with his fellows.

170:3.11 (1862.8) By teaching that the kingdom is within, by exalting the individual, Jesus struck the deathblow of the old society in that he ushered in the new dispensation of true social righteousness. This new order of society the world has little known because it has refused to practice the principles of the gospel of the kingdom of heaven. And when this kingdom of spiritual pre-eminence does come upon the earth, it will not be manifested in mere improved social and material conditions, but rather in the glories of those enhanced and enriched spiritual values which are characteristic of the approaching age of improved human relations and advancing spiritual attainments.

Jesus' Teaching About the Kingdom

170:4.1 (1862.9) Jesus never gave a precise definition of the kingdom. At one time he would discourse on one phase of the kingdom, and at another time he would discuss a different aspect of the brotherhood of God's reign in the hearts of men. In the course of this Sabbath afternoon's sermon Jesus noted no less than five phases, or epochs, of the kingdom, and they were:

170:4.2 (1862.10) 1. The personal and inward experience of the spiritual life of the fellowship of the individual believer with God the Father.

170:4.3 (1863.1) 2. The enlarging brotherhood of gospel believers, the social aspects of the enhanced morals and quickened ethics resulting from the reign of God's spirit in the hearts of individual believers.

170:4.4 (1863.2) 3. The supermortal brotherhood of invisible spiritual beings which prevails on earth and in heaven, the superhuman kingdom of God.

170:4.5 (1863.3) 4. The prospect of the more perfect fulfillment of the will of God, the advance toward the dawn of a new social order in connection with improved spiritual living—the next age of man.

170:4.6 (1863.4) 5. The kingdom in its fullness, the future spiritual age of light and life on earth.

170:4.7 (1863.5) Wherefore must we always examine the Master's teaching to ascertain which of these five phases he may have reference to when he makes use of the term kingdom of heaven. By this process of gradually changing man's will and thus affecting human decisions, Michael and his associates are likewise gradually but certainly changing the entire course of human evolution, social and otherwise.

170:4.8 (1863.6) The Master on this occasion placed emphasis on the following five points as representing the cardinal features of the gospel of the kingdom:

170:4.9 (1863.7) 1. The pre-eminence of the individual.

170:4.10 (1863.8) 2. The will as the determining factor in man's experience.

170:4.11 (1863.9) 3. Spiritual fellowship with God the Father.

170:4.12 (1863.10) 4. The supreme satisfactions of the loving service of man.

170:4.13 (1863.11) 5. The transcendency of the spiritual over the material in human personality.

170:4.14 (1863.12) This world has

never seriously or sincerely or honestly tried out these dynamic ideas and divine ideals of Jesus' doctrine of the kingdom of heaven. But you should not become discouraged by the apparently slow progress of the kingdom idea on Urantia. Remember that the order of progressive evolution is subjected to sudden and unexpected periodical changes in both the material and the spiritual worlds. The bestowal of Jesus as an incarnated Son was just such a strange and unexpected event in the spiritual life of the world. Neither make the fatal mistake, in looking for the age manifestation of the kingdom, of failing to effect its establishment within your own souls.

170:4.15 (1863.13) Although Jesus referred one phase of the kingdom to the future and did, on numerous occasions, intimate that such an event might appear as a part of a world crisis; and though he did likewise most certainly, on several occasions, definitely promise sometime to return to Urantia, it should be recorded that he never positively linked these two ideas together. He promised a new revelation of the kingdom on earth and at some future time; he also promised sometime to come back to this world in person; but he did not say that these two events were synonymous.

From all we know these promises may, or may not, refer to the same event.

170:4.16 (1863.14) His apostles and disciples most certainly linked these two teachings together. When the kingdom failed to materialize as they had expected, recalling the Master's teaching concerning a future kingdom and remembering his promise to come again, they jumped to the conclusion that these promises referred to an identical event; and therefore they lived in hope of his immediate second coming to establish the kingdom in its fullness and with power and glory.

And so have successive believing generations lived on earth entertaining the same inspiring but disappointing hope.

Later Ideas of the Kingdom

170:5.1 (1864.1) Having summarized the teachings of Jesus about the kingdom of heaven, we are permitted to narrate certain later ideas which became attached to the concept of the kingdom and to engage in a prophetic forecast of the kingdom as it may evolve in the age to come.

170:5.2 (1864.2) Throughout the first centuries of the Christian propaganda, the idea of the kingdom of heaven was tremendously influenced by the then rapidly spreading notions of Greek idealism, the idea of the natural as the shadow of the spiritual—the temporal as the time shadow of the eternal.

170:5.3 (1864.3) But the great step which marked the transplantation of the teachings of Jesus from a Jewish to a gentile soil was taken when the Messiah of the kingdom became the Redeemer of the church, a religious and social organization growing out of the activities of Paul and his successors and based on the teachings of Jesus as they were supplemented by the ideas of Philo and the Persian doctrines of good and evil.

170:5.4 (1864.4) The ideas and ideals of Jesus, embodied in the teaching of the gospel of the kingdom, nearly failed of realization as his followers progressively distorted his pronouncements. The Master's concept of the kingdom was notably modified by two great tendencies:

170:5.5 (1864.5) 1. The Jewish believers persisted in regarding him as the Messiah. They believed that Jesus would very soon return actually to establish the worldwide and more or less material kingdom.

170:5.6 (1864.6) 2. The gentile Christians began very early to accept the doctrines of Paul, which led increasingly to the general belief that Jesus was the Redeemer of the children of the church, the new and institutional successor of the earlier concept of the purely spiritual brotherhood of the kingdom.

170:5.7 (1864.7) The church, as a social outgrowth of the kingdom, would have been wholly natural and even desirable.

The evil of the church was not its existence, but rather that it almost completely supplanted the Jesus concept of the kingdom. Paul's institutionalized church became a virtual substitute for the kingdom of heaven which Jesus had proclaimed.

170:5.8 (1864.8) But doubt not, this same kingdom of heaven which the Master taught exists within the heart of the believer, will yet be proclaimed to this Christian church, even as to all other religions, races, and nations on earth—even to every individual.

170:5.9 (1864.9) The kingdom of Jesus' teaching, the spiritual ideal of individual righteousness and the concept of man's divine fellowship with God, became gradually submerged into the mystic conception of the person of Jesus as the Redeemer-Creator and spiritual head of a socialized religious community. In this way a formal and institutional church became the substitute for the individually spirit-led brotherhood of the kingdom.

170:5.10 (1864.10) The church was an inevitable and useful social result of Jesus' life and teachings; the tragedy consisted in the fact that this social reaction to the teachings of the kingdom so fully displaced the spiritual concept of the real kingdom as Jesus taught and lived it.

170:5.11 (1865.1) The kingdom, to the Jews, was the Israelite community; to the gentiles it became the Christian church. To Jesus the kingdom was the sum of those individuals who had confessed their faith in the fatherhood of God, thereby declaring their wholehearted dedication to the doing of the will of God, thus becoming members of the spiritual brotherhood of man.

170:5.12 (1865.2) The Master fully realized that certain social results would appear in the world as a consequence of the spread of the gospel of the kingdom; but he intended that all such desirable social manifestations should appear as unconscious and inevitable outgrowths, or natural fruits, of this inner personal experience of individual believers, this purely spiritual fellowship and communion with the divine spirit which indwells and activates all such believers.

170:5.13 (1865.3) Jesus foresaw that a social organization, or church, would follow the progress of the true spiritual kingdom, and that is why he never opposed the apostles' practicing the rite of John's baptism. He taught that the truth- loving soul, the one who hungers and thirsts for righteousness, for God, is admitted by faith to the spiritual kingdom; at the same time the apostles taught that such a believer is admitted to the social organization of disciples by the outward rite of baptism.

170:5.14 (1865.4) When Jesus' immediate followers recognized their partial failure to realize his ideal of the establishment of the kingdom in the hearts of men by the spirit's domination and guidance of the individual believer, they set about to save his teaching from being wholly lost by substituting for the Master's ideal of the kingdom the gradual creation of a visible social organization, the Christian church. And when they had accomplished this program of substitution, in order to maintain consistency and to provide for the recognition of the Master's teaching regarding the fact of the kingdom, they proceeded to set the kingdom off into the future. The church, just as soon as it was well established, began to teach that the kingdom was in reality to appear at the culmination of the Christian age, at the second coming of Christ.

170:5.15 (1865.5) In this manner the kingdom became the concept of an age, the idea of a future visitation, and the ideal of the final redemption of the saints of the

Most High. The early Christians (and all too many of the later ones) generally lost sight of the Father-and-son idea embodied in Jesus' teaching of the kingdom, while they substituted therefor the well-organized social fellowship of the church. The church thus became in the main a social brotherhood which effectively displaced Jesus' concept and ideal of a spiritual brotherhood.

170:5.16 (1865.6) Jesus' ideal concept largely failed, but upon the foundation of the Master's personal life and teachings, supplemented by the Greek and Persian concepts of eternal life and augmented by Philo's doctrine of the temporal contrasted with the spiritual, Paul went forth to build up one of the most progressive human societies which has ever existed on Urantia.

170:5.17 (1865.7) The concept of Jesus is still alive in the advanced religions of the world. Paul's Christian church is the socialized and humanized shadow of what Jesus intended the kingdom of heaven to be—and what it most certainly will yet become. Paul and his successors partly transferred the issues of eternal life from the individual to the church. Christ thus became the head of the church rather than the elder brother of each individual believer in the Father's family of the kingdom. Paul and his contemporaries applied all of Jesus' spiritual implications regarding himself and the individual believer to the church as a group of believers; and in doing this, they struck a deathblow to Jesus' concept of the divine kingdom in the heart of the individual believer.

170:5.18 (1866.1) And so, for centuries, the Christian church has labored under great embarrassment because it dared to lay claim to those mysterious powers and privileges of the kingdom, powers and privileges which can be exercised and experienced only between Jesus and his spiritual believer brothers. And thus it becomes apparent that membership in the church does not necessarily mean fellowship in the kingdom; one is spiritual, the other mainly social.

170:5.19 (1866.2) Sooner or later another and greater John the Baptist is due to arise proclaiming "the kingdom of God is at hand"—meaning a return to the high spiritual concept of Jesus, who proclaimed that the kingdom is the will of his heavenly Father dominant and transcendent in the heart of the believer—and doing all this without in any way referring either to the visible church on earth or to the anticipated second coming of Christ. There must come a revival of the actual teachings of Jesus, such a restatement as will undo the work of his early followers who went about to create a sociophilosophical system of belief regarding the fact of Michael's sojourn on earth. In a short time the teaching of this story about Jesus nearly supplanted the preaching of Jesus' gospel of the kingdom. In this way a historical religion displaced that teaching in which Jesus had blended man's highest moral ideas and spiritual ideals with man's most sublime hope for the future—eternal life. And that was the gospel of the kingdom.

170:5.20 (1866.3) It is just because the gospel of Jesus was so many-sided that within a few centuries students of the records of his teachings became divided up into so many cults and sects. This pitiful subdivision of Christian believers results from failure to discern in the Master's manifold teachings the divine oneness of his matchless life. But someday the true believers in Jesus will not be thus spiritually divided in their attitude before unbelievers. Always we may have diversity of intellectual comprehension and interpretation, even varying degrees of socialization, but lack of spiritual brotherhood is both inexcusable and reprehensible.

170:5.21 (1866.4) Mistake not! there is in the teachings of Jesus an eternal nature which will not permit them forever to remain unfruitful in the hearts of thinking men. The kingdom as Jesus conceived it has to a large extent failed on earth; for the time being, an outward church has taken its place; but you should comprehend that this church is only the larval stage of the thwarted spiritual kingdom, which will carry it through this material age and over into a more spiritual dispensation where the Master's teachings may enjoy a fuller opportunity for development. Thus does the so-called Christian church become the cocoon in which the kingdom of Jesus' concept now slumbers. The kingdom of the divine brotherhood is still alive and will eventually and certainly come forth from this long submergence, just as surely as the butterfly eventually emerges as the beautiful unfolding of its less attractive creature of metamorphic development.

Paper 171

On the Way to Jerusalem

171:0.1 (1867.1) THE day after the memorable sermon on "The Kingdom of Heaven," Jesus announced that on the following day he and the apostles would depart for the Passover at Jerusalem, visiting numerous cities in southern Perea on the way.

171:0.2 (1867.2) The address on the kingdom and the announcement that he was going to the Passover set all his followers to thinking that he was going up to Jerusalem to inaugurate the temporal kingdom of Jewish supremacy. No matter what Jesus said about the nonmaterial character of the kingdom, he could not wholly remove from the minds of his Jewish hearers the idea that the Messiah was to establish some kind of nationalistic government with headquarters at Jerusalem.

171:0.3 (1867.3) What Jesus said in his Sabbath sermon only tended to confuse the majority of his followers; very few were enlightened by the Master's discourse. The leaders understood something of his teachings regarding the inner kingdom, "the kingdom of heaven within you," but they also knew that he had spoken about another and future kingdom, and it was this kingdom they believed he was now

going up to Jerusalem to establish. When they were disappointed in this expectation, when he was rejected by the Jews, and later on, when Jerusalem was literally destroyed, they still clung to this hope, sincerely believing that the Master would soon return to the world in great power and majestic glory to establish the promised kingdom.

171:0.4 (1867.4) It was on this Sunday afternoon that Salome the mother of James and John Zebedee came to Jesus with her two apostle sons and, in the manner of approaching an Oriental potentate, sought to have Jesus promise in advance to grant whatever request she might make. But the Master would not promise; instead, he asked her, "What do you want me to do for you?" Then answered Salome: "Master, now that you are going up to Jerusalem to establish the kingdom, I would ask you in advance to promise me that these my sons shall have honor with you, the one to sit on your right hand and the other to sit on your left hand in your kingdom."

171:0.5 (1867.5) When Jesus heard Salome's request, he said: "Woman, you know not what you ask." And then, looking straight into the eyes of the two honor-seeking apostles, he said: "Because I have long known and loved you; because I have even lived in your mother's house; because Andrew has assigned you to be with me at all times; therefore do you permit your mother to come to me secretly, making this unseemly request. But let me ask you: Are you able to drink the cup I am about to drink?" And without a moment for thought, James and John answered, "Yes, Master, we are able." Said Jesus: "I am saddened that you know not why we go up to Jerusalem; I am grieved that you understand not the nature of my kingdom; I am disappointed that you bring your mother to make this request of me; but I know you love me in your hearts; therefore I declare that you shall indeed drink of my cup of bitterness and share in my humiliation, but to sit on my right hand and on my left hand is not mine to give. Such honors are reserved for those who have been designated by my Father."

171:0.6 (1868.1) By this time someone had carried word of this conference to Peter and the other apostles, and they were highly indignant that James and John would seek to be preferred before them, and that they would secretly go with their mother to make such a request. When they fell to arguing among themselves, Jesus called them all together and said: "You well understand how the rulers of the gentiles lord it over their subjects, and how those who are great exercise authority. But it shall not be so in the kingdom of heaven. Whosoever would be great among you, let him first become your servant. He who would be first in the kingdom, let him become your minister. I declare to you that the Son of Man came not to be ministered to but to minister; and I now go up to Jerusalem to lay down my life in the doing of the Father's will and in the service of my brethren." When the apostles heard these words, they withdrew by themselves to pray. That evening, in response to the labors of Peter, James and John made suitable apologies to the ten and were restored to the good graces of their brethren.

171:0.7 (1868.2) In asking for places on the right hand and on the left hand of Jesus at Jerusalem, the sons of Zebedee little realized that in less than one month their beloved teacher would be hanging on a Roman cross with a dying thief on one side and another transgressor on the other side. And their mother, who was present at the crucifixion, well remembered the foolish request she had made of Jesus at Pella regarding the honors she so unwisely sought for her apostle sons.

The Departure from Pella

171:1.1 (1868.3) On the forenoon of Monday, March 13, Jesus and his twelve apostles took final leave of the Pella encampment, starting south on their tour of the cities of southern Perea, where Abner's associates were at work. They spent more than two weeks visiting among the seventy and then went directly to Jerusalem for the Passover.

171:1.2 (1868.4) When the Master left Pella, the disciples encamped with the apostles, about one thousand in number, followed after him. About one half of this group left him at the Jordan ford on the road to Jericho when they learned he was going over to Heshbon, and after he had preached the sermon on "Counting the Cost." They went on up to Jerusalem, while the other half followed him for two weeks, visiting the towns in southern Perea.

171:1.3 (1868.5) In a general way, most of Jesus' immediate followers understood that the camp at Pella had been abandoned, but they really thought this indicated that their Master at last intended to go to Jerusalem and lay claim to David's throne. A large majority of his followers never were able to grasp any other concept of the kingdom of heaven; no matter what he taught them, they would not give up this Jewish idea of the kingdom.

171:1.4 (1868.6) Acting on the instructions of the Apostle Andrew, David Zebedee closed the visitors' camp at Pella on Wednesday, March 15. At this time almost four thousand visitors were in residence, and this does not include the one thousand and more persons who sojourned with the apostles at what was known as the teachers' camp, and who went south with Jesus and the twelve. Much as David disliked to do it, he sold the entire equipment to numerous buyers and proceeded with the funds to Jerusalem, subsequently turning the money over to Judas Iscariot.

171:1.5 (1869.1) David was present in Jerusalem during the tragic last week, taking his mother back with him to Bethsaida after the crucifixion. While awaiting Jesus and the apostles, David stopped with Lazarus at Bethany and became tremendously agitated by the manner in which the Pharisees had begun to persecute and harass him since his resurrection. Andrew had directed David to discontinue the messenger service; and this was construed by all as an indication of the early establishment of the kingdom at Jerusalem. David found himself without a job, and he had about decided to become the self-appointed defender of Lazarus when presently the object of his indignant solicitude fled in haste to Philadelphia. Accordingly, sometime after the resurrection and also after the death of his mother, David betook himself to Philadelphia, having first assisted Martha and Mary in disposing of their real estate; and there, in association with Abner and Lazarus, he spent the remainder of his life, becoming the financial overseer of all those large interests of the kingdom which had their center at Philadelphia during the lifetime of Abner.

171:1.6 (1869.2) Within a short time after the destruction of Jerusalem, Antioch became the headquarters of Pauline Christianity, while Philadelphia remained the center of the Abnerian kingdom of heaven. From Antioch the Pauline version of the teachings of Jesus spread about to all the Western world; from Philadelphia the missionaries of the Abnerian version of the kingdom of heaven spread throughout Mesopotamia and Arabia until the later times when these uncompromising emissaries of the teachings of Jesus were overwhelmed by the sudden rise of Islam.

On Counting the Cost

171:2.1 (1869.3) When Jesus and the company of almost one thousand followers arrived at the Bethany ford of the Jordan sometimes called Bethabara, his disciples began to realize that he was not going directly to Jerusalem. While they hesitated and debated among themselves, Jesus climbed upon a huge stone and delivered that discourse which has become known as "Counting the Cost." The Master said:

171:2.2 (1869.4) "You who would follow after me from this time on, must be willing to pay the price of wholehearted dedication to the doing of my Father's will. If you would be my disciples, you must be willing to forsake father, mother, wife,

children, brothers, and sisters. If any one of you would now be my disciple, you must be willing to give up even your life just as the Son of Man is about to offer up his life for the completion of the mission of doing the Father's will on earth and in the flesh.

171:2.3 (1869.5) "If you are not willing to pay the full price, you can hardly be my disciple. Before you go further, you should each sit down and count the cost of being my disciple. Which one of you would undertake to build a watchtower on your lands without first sitting down to count up the cost to see whether you had money enough to complete it? If you fail thus to reckon the cost, after you have laid the foundation, you may discover that you are unable to finish that which you have begun, and therefore will all your neighbors mock you, saying, 'Behold, this man began to build but was unable to finish his work.' Again, what king, when he prepares to make war upon another king, does not first sit down and take counsel as to whether he will be able, with ten thousand men, to meet him who comes against him with twenty thousand? If the king cannot afford to meet his enemy because he is unprepared, he sends an embassy to this other king, even when he is yet a great way off, asking for terms of peace.

171:2.4 (1870.1) "Now, then, must each of you sit down and count the cost of being my disciple. From now on you will not be able to follow after us, listening to the teaching and beholding the works; you will be required to face bitter persecutions and to bear witness for this gospel in the face of crushing disappointment. If you are unwilling to renounce all that you are and to dedicate all that you have, then are you unworthy to be my disciple. If you have already conquered yourself within your own heart, you need have no fear of that outward victory which you must presently gain when the Son of Man is rejected by the chief priests and the Sadducees and is given into the hands of mocking unbelievers.

171:2.5 (1870.2) "Now should you examine yourself to find out your motive for being my disciple. If you seek honor and glory, if you are worldly minded, you are like the salt when it has lost its savor. And when that which is valued for its saltiness has lost its savor, wherewith shall it be seasoned? Such a condiment is useless; it is fit only to be cast out among the refuse. Now have I warned you to turn back to your homes in peace if you are not willing to drink with me the cup which is being prepared. Again and again have I told you that my kingdom is not of this world, but you will not believe me. He who has ears to hear let him hear what I say."

171:2.6 (1870.3) Immediately after speaking these words, Jesus, leading the twelve, started off on the way to Heshbon, followed by about five hundred. After a brief delay the other half of the multitude went on up to Jerusalem. His apostles, together with the leading disciples, thought much about these words, but still they clung to the belief that, after this brief period of adversity and trial, the kingdom would certainly be set up somewhat in accordance with their long-cherished hopes.

The Perean Tour

171:3.1 (1870.4) For more than two weeks Jesus and the twelve, followed by a crowd of several hundred disciples, journeyed about in southern Perea, visiting all of the towns wherein the seventy labored. Many gentiles lived in this region, and since few were going up to the Passover feast at Jerusalem, the messengers of the kingdom went right on with their work of teaching and preaching.

171:3.2 (1870.5) Jesus met Abner at Heshbon, and Andrew directed that the labors of the seventy should not be interrupted by the Passover feast; Jesus advised that the messengers should go forward with their work in complete disregard of what was about to happen at Jerusalem. He also counseled Abner to permit the women's corps, at least such as desired, to go to Jerusalem for the Passover. And this was the last time Abner ever saw Jesus in the flesh. His

farewell to Abner was: "My son, I know you will be true to the kingdom, and I pray the Father to grant you wisdom that you may love and understand your brethren."

171:3.3 (1870.6) As they traveled from city to city, large numbers of their followers deserted to go on to Jerusalem so that, by the time Jesus started for the Passover, the number of those who followed along with him day by day had dwindled to less than two hundred.

171:3.4 (1871.1) The apostles understood that Jesus was going to Jerusalem for the Passover. They knew that the Sanhedrin had broadcast a message to all Israel that he had been condemned to die and directing that anyone knowing his whereabouts should inform the Sanhedrin; and yet, despite all this, they were not so alarmed as they had been when he had announced to them in Philadelphia that he was going to Bethany to see Lazarus. This change of attitude from that of intense fear to a state of hushed expectancy was mostly because of Lazarus's resurrection. They had reached the conclusion that Jesus might, in an emergency, assert his divine power and put to shame his enemies. This hope, coupled with their more profound and mature faith in the spiritual supremacy of their Master, accounted for the outward courage displayed by his immediate followers, who now made ready to follow him into Jerusalem in the very face of the open declaration of the Sanhedrin that he must die.

171:3.5 (1871.2) The majority of the apostles and many of his inner disciples did not believe it possible for Jesus to die; they, believing that he was "the resurrection and the life," regarded him as immortal and already triumphant over death.

Teaching at Livias

171:4.1 (1871.3) On Wednesday evening, March 29, Jesus and his followers encamped at Livias on their way to Jerusalem, after having completed their tour of the cities of southern Perea. It was during this night at Livias that Simon Zelotes and Simon Peter, having conspired to have delivered into their hands at this place more than one hundred swords, received and distributed these arms to all who would accept them and wear them concealed beneath their cloaks. Simon Peter was still wearing his sword on the night of the Master's betrayal in the garden.

171:4.2 (1871.4) Early on Thursday morning before the others were awake, Jesus called Andrew and said: "Awaken your brethren! I have something to say to them." Jesus knew about the swords and which of his apostles had received and were wearing these weapons, but he never disclosed to them that he knew such things. When Andrew had aroused his associates, and they had assembled off by themselves, Jesus said: "My children, you have been with me a long while, and I have taught you much that is needful for this time, but I would now warn you not to put your trust in the uncertainties of the flesh nor in the frailties of man's defense against the trials and testing which lie ahead of us. I have called you apart here by yourselves that I may once more plainly tell you that we are going up to Jerusalem, where you know the Son of Man has already been condemned to death. Again am I telling you that the Son of Man will be delivered into the hands of the chief priests and the religious rulers; that they will condemn him and then deliver him into the hands of the gentiles. And so will they mock the Son of Man, even spit upon him and scourge him, and they will deliver him up to death. And when they kill the Son of Man, be not dismayed, for I declare that on the third day he shall rise. Take heed to yourselves and remember that I have forewarned you."

171:4.3 (1871.5) Again were the apostles amazed, stunned; but they could not bring themselves to regard his words as literal; they could not comprehend that the Master meant just what he said. They were so blinded by their persistent belief in the temporal kingdom on earth, with headquarters at Jerusalem, that they simply could not—would not— permit themselves to accept Jesus' words as literal. They pondered all that day as to what the Master could mean by such strange pronouncements. But none of them dared to ask him a question concerning these statements. Not until after his death did these bewildered apostles wake up to the realization that the Master had spoken to them plainly and directly in anticipation of his crucifixion.

171:4.4 (1872.1) It was here at Livias, just after breakfast, that certain friendly Pharisees came to Jesus and said: "Flee in haste from these parts, for Herod, just as he sought John, now seeks to kill you. He fears an uprising of the people and has decided to kill you. We bring you this warning that you may escape."

171:4.5 (1872.2) And this was partly true. The resurrection of Lazarus frightened and alarmed Herod, and knowing that the Sanhedrin had dared to condemn Jesus, even in advance of a trial, Herod made up his mind either to kill Jesus or to drive him out of his domains. He really desired to do the latter since he so feared him that he hoped he would not be compelled to execute him.

171:4.6 (1872.3) When Jesus heard what the Pharisees had to say, he replied: "I well know about Herod and his fear of this gospel of the kingdom. But, mistake not, he would much prefer that the Son of Man go up to Jerusalem to suffer and die at the hands of the chief priests; he is not anxious, having stained his hands with the blood of John, to become responsible for the death of the Son of Man. Go you and tell that fox that the Son of Man preaches in Perea today, tomorrow goes into Judea, and after a few days, will be perfected in his mission on earth and prepared to ascend to the Father."

171:4.7 (1872.4) Then turning to his apostles, Jesus said: "From olden times the prophets have perished in Jerusalem, and it is only befitting that the Son of Man should go up to the city of the Father's house to be offered up as the price of human bigotry and as the result of religious prejudice and spiritual blindness. O Jerusalem, Jerusalem, which kills the prophets and stones the teachers of truth! How often would I have gathered your children together even as a hen gathers her own brood under her wings, but you would not let me do it! Behold, your house is about to be left to you desolate!

You will many times desire to see me, but you shall not. You will then seek but not find me." And when he had spoken, he turned to those around him and said: "Nevertheless, let us go up to Jerusalem to attend the Passover and do that which becomes us in fulfilling the will of the Father in heaven."

171:4.8 (1872.5) It was a confused and bewildered group of believers who this day followed Jesus into Jericho. The apostles could discern only the certain note of final triumph in Jesus' declarations regarding the kingdom; they just could not bring themselves to that place where they were willing to grasp the warnings of the impending setback. When Jesus spoke of "rising on the third day," they seized upon this statement as signifying a sure triumph of the kingdom immediately following an unpleasant preliminary skirmish with the Jewish religious leaders. The "third day" was a common Jewish expression signifying "presently" or "soon thereafter." When Jesus spoke of "rising," they thought he referred to the "rising of the kingdom."

171:4.9 (1872.6) Jesus had been accepted by these believers as the Messiah, and the Jews knew little or nothing about a suffering Messiah. They did not understand that Jesus was to accomplish many things by his death which could never have been achieved by his life. While it was the resurrection of Lazarus that nerved the apostles to enter Jerusalem, it was the memory of the transfiguration that sustained the Master at this trying period of his bestowal.

The Blind Man at Jericho

171:5.1 (1873.1) Late on the afternoon of Thursday, March 30, Jesus and his apostles, at the head of a band of about two hundred followers, approached the walls of Jericho. As they came near the gate of the city, they encountered a throng of beggars, among them one Bartimeus, an elderly man who had been blind from his youth. This blind beggar had heard much about Jesus and knew all about his healing of the blind Josiah at Jerusalem. He had not known of Jesus' last visit to Jericho until he had gone on to Bethany. Bartimeus had resolved that he would never again allow Jesus to visit Jericho without appealing to him for the restoration of his sight.

171:5.2 (1873.2) News of Jesus' approach had been heralded throughout Jericho, and hundreds of the inhabitants flocked forth to meet him. When this great crowd came back escorting the Master into the city, Bartimeus, hearing the heavy tramping of the multitude, knew that something unusual was happening, and so he asked those standing near him what was going on. And one of the beggars replied, "Jesus of Nazareth is passing by." When Bartimeus heard that Jesus was near, he lifted up his voice and began to cry aloud, "Jesus, Jesus, have mercy upon me!" And as he continued to cry louder and louder, some of those near to Jesus went over and rebuked him, requesting him to hold his peace; but it was of no avail; he cried only the more and the louder.

171:5.3 (1873.3) When Jesus heard the blind man crying out, he stood still. And when he saw him, he said to his friends, "Bring the man to me." And then they went over to Bartimeus, saying: "Be of good cheer; come with us, for the Master calls for you." When Bartimeus heard these words, he threw aside his cloak, springing forward toward the center of the road, while those near by guided him to Jesus. Addressing Bartimeus, Jesus said: "What do you want me to do for you?"

Then answered the blind man, "I would have my sight restored." And when Jesus heard this request and saw his faith, he said: "You shall receive your sight; go your way; your faith has made you whole." Immediately he received his sight, and he remained near Jesus, glorifying God, until the Master started on the next day for Jerusalem, and then he went before the multitude declaring to all how his sight had been restored in Jericho.

The Visit to Zaccheus

171:6.1 (1873.4) When the Master's procession entered Jericho, it was nearing sundown, and he was minded to abide there for the night. As Jesus passed by the customs house, Zaccheus the chief publican, or tax collector, happened to be present, and he much desired to see Jesus. This chief publican was very rich and had heard much about this prophet of Galilee. He had resolved that he would see what sort of a man Jesus was the next time he chanced to visit Jericho; accordingly, Zaccheus sought to press through the crowd, but it was too great, and being short of stature, he could not see over their heads. And so the chief publican followed on with the crowd until they came near the center of the city and not far from where he lived. When he saw that he would be unable to penetrate the crowd, and thinking that Jesus might be going right on through the city without stopping, he ran on ahead and climbed up into a sycamore tree whose spreading branches overhung the roadway. He knew that in this way he could obtain a good view of the Master as he passed by. And he was not disappointed, for, as Jesus passed by, he stopped and, looking up at Zaccheus, said: "Make haste, Zaccheus, and come down, for tonight I must abide at your house." And when Zaccheus heard these astonishing words, he almost fell out of the tree in his haste to get down, and going up to Jesus, he expressed great joy that the Master should be willing to stop at his house.

171:6.2 (1874.1) They went at once to the home of Zaccheus, and those who lived in Jericho were much surprised that Jesus would consent to abide with the chief publican. Even while the Master and his apostles lingered with Zaccheus before the door of his house, one of the Jericho Pharisees, standing near by, said: "You see how this man has gone to lodge with a sinner, an apostate son of Abraham who is an extortioner and a robber of his own people." And when Jesus heard this, he looked down at Zaccheus and smiled. Then Zaccheus stood upon a stool and said: "Men of Jericho, hear me! I may be a publican and a sinner, but the great Teacher has come to abide in my house; and before he goes in, I tell you that I am going to bestow one half of all my goods upon the poor, and beginning tomorrow, if I have wrongfully exacted aught from any man, I will restore fourfold. I am going to seek salvation with all my heart and learn to do righteousness in the sight of God."

171:6.3 (1874.2) When Zaccheus had ceased speaking, Jesus said: "Today has salvation come to this home, and you have become indeed a son of Abraham." And turning to the crowd assembled about them, Jesus said: "And marvel not at what I say nor take offense at what we do, for I have all along declared that the Son of Man has come to seek and to save that which is lost."

171:6.4 (1874.3) They lodged with Zaccheus for the night. On the morrow they arose and made their way up the "road of robbers" to Bethany on their way to the Passover at Jerusalem.

"As Jesus Passed By"

171:7.1 (1874.4) Jesus spread good cheer everywhere he went. He was full of grace and truth. His associates never ceased to wonder at the gracious words that proceeded out of his mouth. You can cultivate gracefulness, but graciousness is the aroma of friendliness which emanates from a love-saturated soul.

171:7.2 (1874.5) Goodness always compels respect, but when it is devoid of grace, it often repels affection. Goodness is universally attractive only when it is gracious. Goodness is effective only when it is attractive.

171:7.3 (1874.6) Jesus really understood men; therefore could he manifest genuine sympathy and show sincere compassion. But he seldom indulged in pity. While his compassion was boundless, his sympathy was practical, personal, and constructive. Never did his familiarity with suffering breed indifference, and he was able to minister to distressed souls without increasing their self-pity.

171:7.4 (1874.7) Jesus could help men so much because he loved them so sincerely. He truly loved each man, each woman, and each child. He could be such a true friend because of his remarkable insight—he knew so fully what was in the heart and in the mind of man. He was an interested and keen observer. He was an expert in the comprehension of human need, clever in detecting human longings.

171:7.5 (1874.8) Jesus was never in a hurry. He had time to comfort his fellow men "as he passed by." And he always made his friends feel at ease. He was a charming listener. He never engaged in the meddlesome probing of the souls of his associates. As he comforted hungry minds and ministered to thirsty souls, the recipients of his mercy did not so much feel that they were confessing to him as that they were conferring with him. They had unbounded confidence in him because they saw he had so much faith in them.

171:7.6 (1875.1) He never seemed to be curious about people, and he never manifested a desire to direct, manage, or follow them up. He inspired profound self-confidence and robust courage in all who enjoyed his association. When he smiled on a man, that mortal experienced increased capacity for solving his manifold problems.

171:7.7 (1875.2) Jesus loved men so much and so wisely that he never hesitated to be severe with them when the occasion demanded such discipline. He frequently set out to help a person by asking for help. In this way he elicited interest, appealed to the better things in human nature.

171:7.8 (1875.3) The Master could discern saving faith in the gross superstition of the woman who sought healing by touching the hem of his garment. He was always ready and willing to stop a sermon or detain a multitude while he ministered to the needs of a single person, even to a little child. Great things happened not only because people had faith in Jesus, but also because Jesus had so much faith in them.

171:7.9 (1875.4) Most of the really important things which Jesus said or did seemed to happen casually, "as he passed by." There was so little of the professional, the well-planned, or the premeditated in the Master's earthly ministry. He dispensed health and scattered happiness naturally and gracefully as he journeyed through life. It was literally true, "He went about doing good."

171:7.10 (1875.5) And it behooves the Master's followers in all ages to learn to minister as "they pass by"—to do unselfish good as they go about their daily duties.

Parable of the Pounds

171:8.1 (1875.6) They did not start from Jericho until near noon since they sat up late the night before while Jesus taught Zaccheus and his family the gospel of the kingdom. About halfway up the ascending road to Bethany the party paused for lunch while the multitude passed on to Jerusalem, not knowing that Jesus and the apostles were going to abide that night on the Mount of Olives.

171:8.2 (1875.7) The parable of the pounds, unlike the parable of the talents, which was intended for all the disciples, was spoken more exclusively to the apostles and was largely based on the experience of Archelaus and his futile attempt to gain the rule of the kingdom of Judea. This is one of the few parables of the Master to be founded on an actual historic character. It was not strange that they should have had Archelaus in mind inasmuch as the house of Zaccheus in Jericho was very near the ornate palace of Archelaus, and his aqueduct ran along the road by which they had departed from Jericho.

171:8.3 (1875.8) Said Jesus: "You think that the Son of Man goes up to Jerusalem to receive a kingdom, but I declare that you are doomed to disappointment. Do you not remember about a certain prince who went into a far country to receive for himself a kingdom, but even before he could return, the citizens of his province, who in their hearts had already rejected him, sent an embassy after him, saying, 'We will not have this man to reign over us'? As this king was rejected in the temporal rule, so is the Son of Man to be rejected in the spiritual rule. Again I declare that my kingdom is not of

this world; but if the Son of Man had been accorded the spiritual rule of his people, he would have accepted such a kingdom of men's souls and would have reigned over such a dominion of human hearts. Notwithstanding that they reject my spiritual rule over them, I will return again to receive from others such a kingdom of spirit as is now denied me. You will see the Son of Man rejected now, but in another age that which the children of Abraham now reject will be received and exalted.

171:8.4 (1876.1) "And now, as the rejected nobleman of this parable, I would call before me my twelve servants, special stewards, and giving into each of your hands the sum of one pound, I would admonish each to heed well my instructions that you trade diligently with your trust fund while I am away that you may have wherewith to justify your stewardship when I return, when a reckoning shall be required of you.

171:8.5 (1876.2) "And even if this rejected Son should not return, another Son will be sent to receive this kingdom, and this Son will then send for all of you to receive your report of stewardship and to be made glad by your gains.

171:8.6 (1876.3) "And when these stewards were subsequently called together for an accounting, the first came forward, saying, 'Lord, with your pound I have made ten pounds more.' And his master said to him: 'Well done; you are a good servant; because you have proved faithful in this matter, I will give you authority over ten cities.' And the second came, saying, 'Your pound left with me, Lord, has made five pounds.' And the master said, 'I will accordingly make you ruler over five cities.' And so on down through the others until the last of the servants, on being called to account, reported: 'Lord, behold, here is your pound, which I have kept safely done up in this napkin. And this I did because I feared you; I believed that you were unreasonable, seeing that you take up where you have not laid down, and that you seek to reap where you have not sown.' Then said his lord: 'You negligent and unfaithful servant, I will judge you out of your own mouth. You knew that I reap where I have apparently not sown; therefore you knew this reckoning would be required of you. Knowing this, you should have at least given my money to the banker that at my coming I might have had it with proper interest.'

171:8.7 (1876.4) "And then said this ruler to those who stood by: 'Take the money from this slothful servant and give it to him who has ten pounds.' And when they reminded the master that such a one already had ten pounds, he said: 'To every one who has shall be given more, but from him who has not, even that which he has shall be taken away from him.'"

171:8.8 (1876.5) And then the apostles sought to know the difference between the meaning of this parable and that of the former parable of the talents, but Jesus would only say, in answer to their many questions: "Ponder well these words in your hearts while each of you finds out their true meaning."

171:8.9 (1876.6) It was Nathaniel who so well taught the meaning of these two parables in the after years, summing up his teachings in these conclusions:

171:8.10 (1876.7) 1. Ability is the practical measure of life's opportunities.

You will never be held responsible for the accomplishment of that which is beyond your abilities.

171:8.11 (1876.8) 2. Faithfulness is the unerring measure of human trustworthiness. He who is faithful in little things is also likely to exhibit faithfulness in everything consistent with his endowments.

171:8.12 (1876.9) 3. The Master grants the lesser reward for lesser faithfulness when there is like opportunity.

171:8.13 (1877.1) 4. He grants a like reward for like faithfulness when there is lesser opportunity.

171:8.14 (1877.2) When they had finished their lunch, and after the multitude of followers had gone on toward Jerusalem, Jesus, standing there before the apostles in the shade of an overhanging rock by the roadside, with cheerful dignity and a gracious majesty pointed his finger westward, saying: "Come, my brethren, let us go on into Jerusalem, there to receive that which awaits us; thus shall we fulfill the will of the heavenly Father in all things."

171:8.15 (1877.3) And so Jesus and his apostles resumed this, the Master's last journey to Jerusalem in the likeness of the flesh of mortal man.

Paper 172

Going into Jerusalem

172:0.1 (1878.1) JESUS and the apostles arrived at Bethany shortly after four o'clock on Friday afternoon, March 31, A.D.

1. Lazarus, his sisters, and their friends were expecting them; and since so many people came every day to talk with Lazarus about his resurrection, Jesus was informed that arrangements had been made for him to stay with a neighboring believer, one Simon, the leading citizen of the little village since the death of Lazarus's father.

172:0.2 (1878.2) That evening, Jesus

received many visitors, and the common folks of Bethany and Bethpage did their best to make him feel welcome. Although many thought Jesus was now going into Jerusalem, in utter defiance of the Sanhedrin's decree of death, to proclaim himself king of the Jews, the Bethany family—Lazarus, Martha, and Mary— more fully realized that the Master was not that kind of a king; they dimly felt that this might be his last visit to Jerusalem and Bethany.

172:0.3 (1878.3) The chief priests were informed that Jesus lodged at Bethany, but they thought best not to attempt to seize him among his friends; they decided to await his coming on into Jerusalem. Jesus knew about all this, but he was majestically calm; his friends had never seen him more composed and congenial; even the apostles were astounded that he should be so unconcerned when the Sanhedrin had called upon all Jewry to deliver him into their hands. While the Master slept that night, the apostles watched over him by twos, and many of them were girded with swords. Early the next morning they were awakened by hundreds of pilgrims who came out from Jerusalem, even on the Sabbath day, to see Jesus and Lazarus, whom he had raised from the dead.

Sabbath at Bethany

172:1.1 (1878.4) Pilgrims from outside of Judea, as well as the Jewish authorities, had all been asking: "What do you think? will Jesus come up to the feast?" Therefore, when the people heard that Jesus was at Bethany, they were glad, but the chief priests and Pharisees were somewhat perplexed. They were pleased to have him under their jurisdiction, but they were a trifle disconcerted by his boldness; they remembered that on his previous visit to Bethany, Lazarus had been raised from the dead, and Lazarus was becoming a big problem to the enemies of Jesus.

172:1.2 (1878.5) Six days before the Passover, on the evening after the Sabbath, all Bethany and Bethpage joined in celebrating the arrival of Jesus by a public banquet at the home of Simon. This supper was in honor of both Jesus and Lazarus; it was tendered in defiance of the Sanhedrin. Martha directed the serving of the food; her sister Mary was among the women onlookers as it was against the custom of the Jews for a woman to sit at a public banquet. The agents of the Sanhedrin were present, but they feared to apprehend Jesus in the midst of his friends.

172:1.3 (1879.1) Jesus talked with Simon about Joshua of old, whose namesake he was, and recited how Joshua and the Israelites had come up to Jerusalem through Jericho. In commenting on the legend of the walls of Jericho falling down, Jesus said: "I am not concerned with such walls of brick and stone; but I would cause the walls of prejudice, self- righteousness, and hate to crumble before this preaching of the Father's love for all men."

172:1.4 (1879.2) The banquet went along in a very cheerful and normal manner except that all the apostles were unusually sober. Jesus was exceptionally cheerful and had been playing with the children up to the time of coming to the table.

172:1.5 (1879.3) Nothing out of the ordinary happened until near the close of the feasting when Mary the sister of Lazarus stepped forward from among the group of women onlookers and, going up to where Jesus reclined as the guest of honor, proceeded to open a large alabaster cruse of very rare and costly ointment; and after anointing the Master's head, she began to pour it upon his feet as she took down her hair and wiped them with it. The whole house became filled with the odor of the ointment, and everybody present was amazed at what Mary had done. Lazarus said nothing, but when some of the people murmured, showing indignation that so costly an ointment should be thus used, Judas Iscariot stepped over to where Andrew reclined and said: "Why was this ointment not sold and the money bestowed to feed the poor? You should speak to the Master that he rebuke such waste."

172:1.6 (1879.4) Jesus, knowing what they thought and hearing what they said, put his hand upon Mary's head as she knelt by his side and, with a kindly expression upon his face, said: "Let her alone, every one of you. Why do you trouble her about this, seeing that she has done a good thing in her heart? To you who murmur and say that this ointment should have been sold and the money given to the poor, let me say that you have the poor always with you so that you may minister to them at any time it seems good to you; but I shall not always be with you; I go soon to my Father. This woman has long saved this ointment for my body at its burial, and now that it has seemed good to her to make this anointing in anticipation of my death, she shall not be denied such satisfaction. In the doing of this, Mary has reproved all of you in that by this act she evinces faith in what I have said about my death and ascension to my Father in heaven. This woman shall not be reproved for that which she has this night done; rather do I say to you that in the ages to come, wherever this gospel shall be preached throughout the whole world, what she has done will be spoken of in memory of her."

172:1.7 (1879.5) It was because of this rebuke, which he took as a personal reproof, that Judas Iscariot finally made up his mind to seek revenge for his hurt feelings. Many times had he entertained such ideas subconsciously, but now he dared to think such wicked thoughts in his open and conscious mind. And many others encouraged him in this attitude since the cost of this ointment was a sum equal to the earnings of one man for one year— enough to provide bread for five thousand persons. But Mary loved Jesus; she had provided this precious ointment with which to embalm his body in death, for she believed his words when he forewarned them that he must die, and it was not to be denied her if she changed her mind and chose to bestow this offering upon the Master while he yet lived.

172:1.8 (1879.6) Both Lazarus and Martha knew that Mary had long saved the money wherewith to buy this cruse of spikenard, and they heartily approved of her doing as her heart desired in such a matter, for they were well-to-do and could easily afford to make such an offering.

172:1.9 (1880.1) When the chief priests heard of this dinner in Bethany for Jesus and Lazarus, they began to take counsel among themselves as to what should be done with Lazarus. And presently they decided that Lazarus must also die. They rightly concluded that it would be useless to put Jesus to death if they permitted Lazarus, whom he had raised from the dead, to live.

Sunday Morning with the Apostles

172:2.1 (1880.2) On this Sunday morning, in Simon's beautiful garden, the Master called his twelve apostles around him and gave them their final instructions preparatory to entering Jerusalem. He told them that he would probably deliver many addresses and teach many lessons before returning to the Father but advised the apostles to refrain from doing any public work during this Passover sojourn in Jerusalem. He instructed them to remain near him and to "watch and pray." Jesus knew that many of his apostles and immediate followers even then carried swords concealed on their persons, but he made no reference to this fact.

172:2.2 (1880.3) This morning's instructions embraced a brief review of their ministry from the day of their ordination near Capernaum down to this day when they were preparing to enter Jerusalem. The apostles listened in silence; they asked no questions.

172:2.3 (1880.4) Early that morning David Zebedee had turned over to Judas the funds realized from the sale of the equipment of the Pella encampment, and Judas, in turn, had placed the greater part of this money in the hands of Simon, their host, for safekeeping in anticipation of the exigencies of their entry into Jerusalem.

172:2.4 (1880.5) After the conference with the apostles Jesus held converse with Lazarus and instructed him to avoid the sacrifice of his life to the vengefulness of the Sanhedrin. It was in obedience to this admonition that Lazarus, a few days later, fled to Philadelphia when the officers of the Sanhedrin sent men to arrest him.

172:2.5 (1880.6) In a way, all of Jesus' followers sensed the impending crisis, but they were prevented from fully realizing its seriousness by the unusual cheerfulness and exceptional good humor of the Master.

The Start for Jerusalem

172:3.1 (1880.7) Bethany was about two miles from the temple, and it was half past one that Sunday afternoon when Jesus made ready to start for Jerusalem. He had feelings of profound affection for Bethany and its simple people. Nazareth, Capernaum, and Jerusalem had rejected him, but Bethany had accepted him, had believed in him. And it was in this small village, where almost every man, woman, and child were believers, that he chose to perform the mightiest work of his earth bestowal, the resurrection of Lazarus. He did not raise Lazarus that the villagers might believe, but rather because they already believed.

172:3.2 (1880.8) All morning Jesus had thought about his entry into Jerusalem. Heretofore he had always endeavored to suppress all public acclaim of him as the Messiah, but it was different now; he was nearing the end of his career in the flesh, his death had been decreed by the Sanhedrin, and no harm could come from allowing his disciples to give free expression to their feelings, just as might occur if he elected to make a formal and public entry into the city.

172:3.3 (1881.1) Jesus did not decide to make this public entrance into Jerusalem as a last bid for popular favor nor as a final grasp for power. Neither did he do it altogether to satisfy the human longings of his disciples and apostles. Jesus entertained none of the illusions of a fantastic dreamer; he well knew what was to be the outcome of this visit.

172:3.4 (1881.2) Having decided upon making a public entrance into Jerusalem, the Master was confronted with the necessity of choosing a proper method of executing such a resolve. Jesus thought over all of the many more or less contradictory so-called Messianic prophesies, but there seemed to be only one which was at all appropriate for him to follow. Most of these prophetic utterances depicted a king, the son and successor of David, a bold and aggressive temporal deliverer of all Israel from the yoke of foreign domination. But there was one Scripture that had sometimes been associated with the Messiah by those who held more to the spiritual concept of his mission, which Jesus thought might consistently be taken as a guide for his projected entry into Jerusalem. This Scripture was found in Zechariah, and it said: "Rejoice greatly, O daughter of Zion; shout, O daughter of Jerusalem. Behold, your king comes to you. He is just and he brings salvation. He comes as the lowly one, riding upon an ass, upon a colt, the foal of an ass."

172:3.5 (1881.3) A warrior king always entered a city riding upon a horse; a king on a mission of peace and friendship always entered riding upon an ass. Jesus would not enter Jerusalem as a man on horseback, but he was willing to enter peacefully and with good will as the Son of Man on a donkey.

172:3.6 (1881.4) Jesus had long tried by direct teaching to impress upon his apostles and his disciples that his kingdom was not of this world, that it was a purely spiritual matter; but he had not succeeded in this effort. Now, what he had failed to do by plain and personal teaching, he would attempt to accomplish by a symbolic appeal. Accordingly, right after the

noon lunch, Jesus called Peter and John, and after directing them to go over to Bethpage, a neighboring village a little off the main road and a short distance northwest of Bethany, he further said: "Go to Bethpage, and when you come to the junction of the roads, you will find the colt of an ass tied there. Loose the colt and bring it back with you. If anyone asks you why you do this, merely say, 'The Master has need of him.'" And when the two apostles had gone into Bethpage as the Master had directed, they found the colt tied near his mother in the open street and close to a house on the corner. As Peter began to untie the colt, the owner came over and asked why they did this, and when Peter answered him as Jesus had directed, the man said: "If your Master is Jesus from Galilee, let him have the colt." And so they returned bringing the colt with them. *

172:3.7 (1881.5) By this time several hundred pilgrims had gathered around Jesus and his apostles. Since mid-forenoon the visitors passing by on their way to the Passover had tarried. Meanwhile, David Zebedee and some of his former messenger associates took it upon themselves to hasten on down to Jerusalem, where they effectively spread the report among the throngs of visiting pilgrims about the temple that Jesus of Nazareth was making a triumphal entry into the city. Accordingly, several thousand of these visitors flocked forth to greet this much-talked-of prophet and wonder- worker, whom some believed to be the Messiah. This multitude, coming out from Jerusalem, met Jesus and the crowd going into the city just after they had passed over the brow of Olivet and had begun the descent into the city.

172:3.8 (1882.1) As the procession started out from Bethany, there was great enthusiasm among the festive crowd of disciples, believers, and visiting pilgrims, many hailing from Galilee and Perea. Just before they started, the twelve women of the original women's corps, accompanied by some of their associates, arrived on the scene and joined this unique procession as it moved on joyously toward the city.

172:3.9 (1882.2) Before they started, the Alpheus twins put their cloaks on the donkey and held him while the Master got on. As the procession moved toward the summit of Olivet, the festive crowd threw their garments on the ground and brought branches from the near-by trees in order to make a carpet of honor for the donkey bearing the royal Son, the promised Messiah. As the merry crowd moved on toward Jerusalem, they began to sing, or rather to shout in unison, the Psalm, "Hosanna to the son of David; blessed is he who comes in the name of the Lord. Hosanna in the highest. Blessed be the kingdom that comes down from heaven."

172:3.10 (1882.3) Jesus was light-hearted and cheerful as they moved along until he came to the brow of Olivet, where the city and the temple towers came into full view; there the Master stopped the procession, and a great silence came upon all as they beheld him weeping. Looking down upon the vast multitude coming forth from the city to greet him, the Master, with much emotion and with tearful voice, said: "O Jerusalem, if you had only known, even you, at least in this your day, the things which belong to your peace, and which you could so freely have had! But now are these glories about to be hid from your eyes. You are about to reject the Son of Peace and turn your backs upon the gospel of salvation. The days will soon come upon you wherein your enemies will cast a trench around about you and lay siege to you on every side; they shall utterly destroy you, insomuch that not one stone shall be left upon another. And all this shall befall you because you knew not the time of your divine visitation. You are about to reject the gift of God, and all men will reject you."

172:3.11 (1882.4) When he had finished speaking, they began the descent of Olivet, and presently were joined by the multitude of visitors who had come from Jerusalem waving palm branches, shouting hosannas, and otherwise expressing gleefulness and good fellowship. The Master had not planned that these crowds should come out from Jerusalem to meet them; that was the work of others. He never premeditated anything which was dramatic.

172:3.12 (1882.5) Along with the multitude which poured out to welcome the Master, there came also many of the Pharisees and his other enemies. They were so much perturbed by this sudden and unexpected outburst of popular acclaim that they feared to arrest him lest such action precipitate an open revolt of the populace. They greatly feared the attitude of the large numbers of visitors, who had heard much of Jesus, and who, many of them, believed in him.

172:3.13 (1882.6) As they neared Jerusalem, the crowd became more demonstrative, so much so that some of the Pharisees made their way up alongside Jesus and said: "Teacher, you should rebuke your disciples and exhort them to behave more seemly." Jesus answered: "It is only fitting that these children should welcome the Son of Peace, whom the chief priests have rejected. It would be useless to stop them lest in their stead these stones by the roadside cry out."

172:3.14 (1882.7) The Pharisees hastened on ahead of the procession to rejoin the Sanhedrin, which was then in session at the temple, and they reported to their associates: "Behold, all that we do is of no avail; we are confounded by this Galilean. The people have gone mad over him; if we do not stop these ignorant ones, all the world will go after him."

172:3.15 (1883.1) There really was no deep significance to be attached to this superficial and spontaneous outburst of popular enthusiasm. This welcome, although it was joyous and sincere, did not betoken any real or deep-seated conviction in the hearts of this festive multitude. These same crowds were equally as willing quickly to reject Jesus later on this week when the Sanhedrin once took a firm and decided stand against him, and when they became disillusioned—when they realized that Jesus was not going to establish the kingdom in accordance with their long-cherished expectations.

172:3.16 (1883.2) But the whole city was mightily stirred up, insomuch that everyone asked, "Who is this man?" And the multitude answered, "This is the prophet of Galilee, Jesus of Nazareth."

Visiting About the Temple

172:4.1 (1883.3) While the Alpheus twins returned the donkey to its owner, Jesus and the ten apostles detached themselves from their immediate associates and strolled about the temple, viewing the preparations for the Passover. No attempt was made to molest Jesus as the Sanhedrin greatly feared the people, and that was, after all, one of the reasons Jesus had for allowing the multitude thus to acclaim him. The apostles little understood that this was the only human procedure which could have been effective in preventing Jesus' immediate arrest upon entering the city. The Master desired to give the inhabitants of Jerusalem, high and low, as well as the tens of thousands of Passover visitors, this one more and last chance to hear the gospel and receive, if they would, the Son of Peace.

172:4.2 (1883.4) And now, as the evening drew on and the crowds went in quest of nourishment, Jesus and his immediate followers were left alone. What a strange day it had been! The apostles were thoughtful, but speechless. Never, in their years of association with Jesus, had they seen such a day. For a moment they sat down by the treasury, watching the people drop in their contributions: the rich putting much in the receiving box and all giving something in accordance with the extent of their possessions. At last there came along a poor widow, scantily attired, and they observed as she cast two mites (small coppers) into the trumpet. And then said Jesus, calling the attention of the apostles to the widow: "Heed well what you have just seen. This poor widow cast in more than all the others, for all these others, from their superfluity, cast in some trifle as a gift, but this poor woman, even though she is in want, gave all that she had, even her living."

172:4.3 (1883.5) As the evening drew on, they walked about the temple courts in silence, and after Jesus had surveyed these familiar scenes once more, recalling his emotions in connection with previous visits, not excepting the earlier ones, he said, "Let us go up to Bethany for our rest." Jesus, with Peter and John, went to the home of Simon, while the other apostles lodged among their friends in Bethany and Bethpage.

The Apostles' Attitude

172:5.1 (1883.6) This Sunday evening as they returned to Bethany, Jesus walked in front of the apostles. Not a word was spoken until they separated after arriving at Simon's house. No twelve human beings ever experienced such diverse and inexplicable emotions as now surged through the minds and souls of these ambassadors of the kingdom. These sturdy Galileans were confused and disconcerted; they did not know what to expect next; they were too surprised to be much afraid. They knew nothing of the Master's plans for the next day, and they asked no questions. They went to their lodgings, though they did not sleep much, save the twins. But they did not keep armed watch over Jesus at Simon's house.

172:5.2 (1884.1) Andrew was thoroughly bewildered, well-nigh confused. He was the one apostle who did not seriously undertake to evaluate the popular outburst of acclaim. He was too preoccupied with the thought of his responsibility as chief of the apostolic corps to give serious consideration to the meaning or significance of the loud hosannas of the multitude. Andrew was busy watching some of his associates who he feared might be led away by their emotions during the excitement, particularly Peter, James, John, and Simon Zelotes. Throughout this day and those which immediately followed, Andrew was troubled with serious doubts, but he never expressed any of these misgivings to his apostolic associates. He was concerned about the attitude of some of the twelve who he knew were armed with swords; but he did not know that his own brother, Peter, was carrying such a weapon. And so the procession into Jerusalem made a comparatively superficial impression upon Andrew; he was too busy with the responsibilities of his office to be otherwise affected. *

172:5.3 (1884.2) Simon Peter was at first almost swept off his feet by this popular manifestation of enthusiasm; but he was considerably sobered by the time they returned to Bethany that night. Peter simply could not figure out what the Master was about. He was terribly disappointed that Jesus did not follow up this wave of popular favor with some kind of a pronouncement. Peter could not understand why Jesus did not speak to the multitude when they arrived at the temple, or at least permit one of the apostles to address the crowd. Peter was a great preacher, and he disliked to see such a large, receptive, and enthusiastic audience go to waste. He would so much have liked to preach the gospel of the kingdom to that throng right there in the temple; but the Master had specifically charged them that they were to do no teaching or preaching while in Jerusalem this Passover week. The reaction from the spectacular procession into the city was disastrous to Simon Peter; by night he was sobered and inexpressibly saddened.

172:5.4 (1884.3) To James Zebedee, this Sunday was a day of perplexity and profound confusion; he could not grasp the purport of what was going on; he could not comprehend the Master's purpose in permitting this wild acclaim and then in refusing to say a word to the people when they arrived at the temple. As the procession moved down Olivet toward Jerusalem, more especially when they were met by the thousands of pilgrims who poured forth to welcome the Master, James was cruelly torn by his conflicting emotions of elation and gratification at what he saw and by his profound feeling of fear as to what would happen when they reached the temple. And then was he downcast and overcome by disappointment when Jesus climbed off the donkey and proceeded to walk leisurely about the temple courts. James could not understand the reason for throwing away such a magnificent opportunity to proclaim the kingdom. By night, his mind was held firmly in the grip of a distressing and dreadful uncertainty.

172:5.5 (1884.4) John Zebedee came somewhere near understanding why Jesus did this; at least he grasped in part the spiritual significance of this so-called triumphal entry into Jerusalem. As the multitude moved on toward the temple, and as John beheld his Master sitting there astride the colt, he recalled hearing Jesus onetime quote the passage of Scripture, the utterance of Zechariah, which described the coming of the Messiah as a man of peace and riding into Jerusalem on an ass. As John turned this Scripture over in his mind, he began to comprehend the symbolic significance of this Sunday-afternoon pageant. At least, he grasped enough of the meaning of this Scripture to enable him somewhat to enjoy the episode and to prevent his becoming overmuch depressed by the apparent purposeless ending of the triumphal procession. John had a type of mind which naturally tended to think and feel in symbols.

172:5.6 (1885.1) Philip was entirely unsettled by the suddenness and spontaneity of the outburst. He could not collect his thoughts sufficiently while on the way down Olivet to arrive at any settled notion as to what all the demonstration was about. In a way, he enjoyed the performance because his Master was being honored. By the time they reached the temple, he was perturbed by the thought that Jesus might possibly ask him to feed the multitude, so that the conduct of Jesus in turning leisurely away from the crowds, which so sorely disappointed the majority of the apostles, was a great relief to Philip. Multitudes had sometimes been a great trial to the steward of the twelve. After he was relieved of these personal fears regarding the material needs of the crowds, Philip joined with Peter in the expression of disappointment that nothing was done to teach the multitude. That night Philip got to thinking over these experiences and was tempted to doubt the whole idea of the kingdom; he honestly wondered what all these things could mean, but he expressed his doubts to no one; he loved Jesus too much. He had great personal faith in the Master.

172:5.7 (1885.2) Nathaniel, aside from the symbolic and prophetic aspects, came the nearest to understanding the Master's reason for enlisting the popular support of the Passover pilgrims. He reasoned it out, before they reached the temple, that without such a demonstrative entry into Jerusalem Jesus would have been arrested by the Sanhedrin officials and cast into prison the moment he presumed to enter the city. He was not, therefore, in the least surprised that the Master made no further use of the cheering crowds when he had once got inside the walls of the city and had thus so forcibly impressed the Jewish leaders that they would refrain from placing him under immediate arrest. Understanding the real reason for the Master's entering the city in this manner, Nathaniel naturally followed along with more poise and was less perturbed and disappointed by Jesus' subsequent conduct than were the other apostles. Nathaniel had great confidence in Jesus' understanding of men as well as in his sagacity and cleverness in handling difficult situations.

172:5.8 (1885.3) Matthew was at first nonplused by this pageant performance. He did not grasp the meaning of what his eyes were seeing until he also recalled the Scripture in Zechariah where the prophet had alluded to the rejoicing of Jerusalem because her king had come bringing salvation and riding upon the colt of an ass. As the procession moved in the direction of the city and then drew on toward the temple, Matthew became ecstatic; he was certain that something extraordinary would happen when the Master arrived at the temple at the head of this shouting multitude. When one of the Pharisees mocked Jesus, saying, "Look, everybody, see who comes here, the king of the Jews riding on an ass!" Matthew kept his hands off of him only by exercising great restraint. None of the twelve was more depressed on the way back to Bethany that evening. Next to Simon Peter and Simon Zelotes, he experienced the highest nervous tension and was in a state of exhaustion by night. But by morning Matthew was much cheered; he was, after all, a cheerful loser.

172:5.9 (1886.1) Thomas was the most bewildered and puzzled man of all the twelve. Most of the time he just followed along, gazing at the spectacle and honestly wondering what could be the Master's motive for participating in such a peculiar demonstration. Down deep in his heart he regarded the whole performance as a little childish, if not downright foolish. He had never seen Jesus do anything like this and was at a loss to account for his strange conduct on this Sunday afternoon. By the time they reached the temple, Thomas had deduced that the purpose of this popular demonstration was so to frighten the Sanhedrin that they would not dare immediately to arrest the Master. On the way back to Bethany Thomas thought much but said nothing. By bedtime the Master's cleverness in staging the tumultuous entry into Jerusalem had begun to make a somewhat humorous appeal, and he was much cheered up by this reaction.

172:5.10 (1886.2) This Sunday started off as a great day for Simon Zelotes. He saw visions of wonderful doings in Jerusalem the next few days, and in that he was right, but Simon dreamed of the establishment of the new national rule of the Jews, with Jesus on the throne of David. Simon saw the nationalists springing into action as soon as the kingdom was announced, and himself in supreme command of the assembling military forces of the new kingdom. On the way down Olivet he even envisaged the Sanhedrin and all of their sympathizers dead before sunset of that day. He really believed something great was going to happen. He was the noisiest man in the whole multitude. By five o'clock that afternoon he was a silent, crushed, and disillusioned apostle. He never fully recovered from the depression which settled down on him as a result of this day's shock; at least not until long after the Master's resurrection.

172:5.11 (1886.3) To the Alpheus twins this was a perfect day. They really enjoyed it all the way through, and not being present during the time of quiet visitation about the temple, they escaped much of the anticlimax of the popular upheaval. They could not possibly understand the downcast behavior of the apostles when they came back to Bethany that evening. In the memory of the twins this was always their day of being nearest heaven on earth. This day was the satisfying climax of their whole career as apostles. And the memory of the elation of this Sunday afternoon carried them on through all of the tragedy of this eventful week, right up to the hour of the crucifixion. It was the most befitting entry of the king the twins could conceive; they enjoyed every moment of the whole pageant. They fully approved of all they saw and long cherished the memory.

172:5.12 (1886.4) Of all the apostles, Judas Iscariot was the most adversely affected by this processional entry into Jerusalem. His mind was in a disagreeable ferment because of the Master's rebuke the preceding day in connection with Mary's anointing at the feast in Simon's house. Judas was disgusted with the whole spectacle. To him it seemed childish, if not indeed ridiculous. As this vengeful apostle looked upon the proceedings of this Sunday afternoon, Jesus seemed to him more to resemble a clown than a king. He heartily resented the whole performance. He shared the views of the Greeks and Romans, who looked down upon anyone who would consent to ride upon an ass or the colt of an ass. By the time the triumphal procession had entered the city, Judas had about made up his mind to abandon the whole idea of such a kingdom; he was almost resolved to forsake all such farcical attempts to establish the kingdom of

heaven. And then he thought of the resurrection of Lazarus, and many other things, and decided to stay on with the twelve, at least for another day. Besides, he carried the bag, and he would not desert with the apostolic funds in his possession. On the way back to Bethany that night his conduct did not seem strange since all of the apostles were equally downcast and silent.

172:5.13 (1887.1) Judas was tremendously influenced by the ridicule of his Sadducean friends. No other single factor exerted such a powerful influence on him, in his final determination to forsake Jesus and his fellow apostles, as a certain episode which occurred just as Jesus reached the gate of the city: A prominent Sadducee (a friend of Judas's family) rushed up to him in a spirit of gleeful ridicule and, slapping him on the back, said: "Why so troubled of countenance, my good friend; cheer up and join us all while we acclaim this Jesus of Nazareth the king of the Jews as he rides through the gates of Jerusalem seated on an ass." Judas had never shrunk from persecution, but he could not stand this sort of ridicule. With the long-nourished emotion of revenge there was now blended this fatal fear of ridicule, that terrible and fearful feeling of being ashamed of his Master and his fellow apostles. At heart, this ordained ambassador of the kingdom was already a deserter; it only remained for him to find some plausible excuse for an open break with the Master.

Paper 173

Monday in Jerusalem

173:0.1 (1888.1) EARLY on this Monday morning, by prearrangement, Jesus and the apostles assembled at the home of Simon in Bethany, and after a brief conference they set out for Jerusalem. The twelve were strangely silent as they journeyed on toward the temple; they had not recovered from the experience of the preceding day. They were expectant, fearful, and profoundly affected by a certain feeling of detachment growing out of the Master's sudden change of tactics, coupled with his instruction that they were to engage in no public teaching throughout this Passover week.

173:0.2 (1888.2) As this group journeyed down Mount Olivet, Jesus led the way, the apostles following closely behind in meditative silence. There was just one thought uppermost in the minds of all save Judas Iscariot, and that was: What will the Master do today? The one absorbing thought of Judas was: What shall I do? Shall I go on with Jesus and my associates, or shall I withdraw? And if I am going to quit, how shall I break off?

173:0.3 (1888.3) It was about nine o'clock on this beautiful morning when these men arrived at the temple. They went at once to the large court where Jesus so often taught, and after greeting the believers who were awaiting him, Jesus mounted one of the teaching platforms and began to address the gathering crowd. The apostles withdrew for a short distance and awaited developments.

Cleansing the Temple

173:1.1 (1888.4) A huge commercial traffic had grown up in association with the services and ceremonies of the temple worship. There was the business of providing suitable animals for the various sacrifices. Though it was permissible for a worshiper to provide his own sacrifice, the fact remained that this animal must be free from all "blemish" in the meaning of the Levitical law and as interpreted by official inspectors of the temple. Many a worshiper had experienced the humiliation of having his supposedly perfect animal rejected by the temple examiners. It therefore became the more general practice to purchase sacrificial animals at the temple, and although there were several stations on near-by Olivet where they could be bought, it had become the vogue to buy these animals directly from the temple pens. Gradually there had grown up this custom of selling all kinds of sacrificial animals in the temple courts. An extensive business, in which enormous profits were made, had thus been brought into existence. Part of these gains was reserved for the temple treasury, but the larger part went indirectly into the hands of the ruling high-priestly families.

173:1.2 (1888.5) This sale of animals in the temple prospered because, when the worshiper purchased such an animal, although the price might be somewhat high, no more fees had to be paid, and he could be sure the intended sacrifice would not be rejected on the ground of possessing real or technical blemishes. At one time or another systems of exorbitant overcharge were practiced upon the common people, especially during the great national feasts. At one time the greedy priests went so far as to demand the equivalent of the value of a week's labor for a pair of doves which should have been sold to the poor for a few pennies. The "sons of Annas" had already begun to establish their bazaars in the temple precincts, those very merchandise marts which persisted to the time of their final overthrow by a mob three years before the destruction of the temple itself.

173:1.3 (1889.1) But traffic in sacrificial animals and sundry merchandise was not the only way in which the courts of the temple were profaned. At this time there was fostered an extensive system of banking and commercial exchange which was carried on right within the temple precincts. And this all came about in the following manner: During the Asmonean dynasty the Jews coined their own silver money, and it had become the practice to require the temple dues of one-half shekel and all other temple fees to be paid with this Jewish coin. This regulation necessitated that money-changers be licensed to exchange the many sorts of currency in circulation throughout Palestine and other provinces of the Roman Empire for this orthodox shekel of Jewish coining. The temple head tax, payable by all except women, slaves, and minors, was one-half shekel, a coin about the size of a ten-cent piece but twice as thick. By the times of Jesus the priests had also been exempted from the payment of temple dues. Accordingly, from the 15th to the 25th of the month preceding the Passover, accredited money-changers erected their booths in the principal cities of Palestine for the purpose of providing the Jewish people with proper money to meet the temple dues after they had reached Jerusalem.

After this ten-day period these money-changers moved on to Jerusalem and proceeded to set up their exchange tables in the courts of the temple. They were permitted to charge the equivalent of from three to four cents commission for the exchange of a coin valued at about ten cents, and in case a coin of larger value was offered for exchange, they were allowed to collect double. Likewise did these temple bankers profit from the exchange of all money intended for the purchase of sacrificial animals and for the payment of vows and the making of offerings. *

173:1.4 (1889.2) These temple money-changers not only conducted a regular banking business for profit in the exchange of more than twenty sorts of money which the visiting pilgrims would periodically bring to Jerusalem, but they also engaged in all other kinds of transactions pertaining to the banking business. Both the temple treasury and the temple rulers profited tremendously from these commercial activities. It was not uncommon for the temple treasury to hold upwards of ten million dollars while the common people languished in poverty and continued to pay these unjust levies.

173:1.5 (1889.3) In the midst of this noisy aggregation of money-changers, merchandisers, and cattle sellers, Jesus, on this Monday morning, attempted to teach the gospel of the heavenly kingdom. He was not alone in resenting this profanation of the temple; the common people, especially the Jewish visitors from foreign provinces, also heartily resented this profiteering desecration of their national house of worship. At this time the Sanhedrin itself held its regular meetings in a chamber surrounded by all this babble and confusion of trade and barter.

173:1.6 (1890.1) As Jesus was about to begin his address, two things happened to arrest his attention. At the money table of a near-by exchanger a violent and heated argument had arisen over the alleged overcharging of a Jew from Alexandria, while at the same moment the air was rent by the bellowing of a drove of some one hundred bullocks which was being driven from one section of the animal pens to another. As Jesus paused, silently but thoughtfully contemplating this scene of commerce and confusion, close by he beheld a simple-minded Galilean, a man he had once talked with in Iron, being ridiculed and jostled about by supercilious and would-be superior Judeans; and all of this combined to produce one of those strange and periodic uprisings of indignant emotion in the soul of Jesus.

173:1.7 (1890.2) To the amazement of his apostles, standing near at hand, who refrained from participation in what so soon followed, Jesus stepped down from the teaching platform and, going over to the lad who was driving the cattle through the court, took from him his whip of cords and swiftly drove the animals from the temple. But that was not all; he strode majestically before the wondering gaze of the thousands assembled in the temple court to the farthest cattle pen and proceeded to open the gates of every stall and to drive out the imprisoned animals. By this time the assembled pilgrims were electrified, and with uproarious shouting they moved toward the bazaars and began to overturn the tables of the money-changers. In less than five minutes all commerce had been swept from the temple. By the time the near-by Roman guards had appeared on the scene, all was quiet, and the crowds had become orderly; Jesus, returning to the speaker's stand, spoke to the multitude: "You have this day witnessed that which is written in the Scriptures: 'My house shall be called a house of prayer for all nations, but you have made it a den of robbers.'"

173:1.8 (1890.3) But before he could

utter other words, the great assembly broke out in hosannas of praise, and presently a throng of youths stepped out from the crowd to sing grateful hymns of appreciation that the profane and profiteering merchandisers had been ejected from the sacred temple. By this time certain of the priests had arrived on the scene, and one of them said to Jesus, "Do you not hear what the children of the Levites say?" And the Master replied, "Have you never read, 'Out of the mouths of babes and sucklings has praise been perfected'?" And all the rest of that day while Jesus taught, guards set by the people stood watch at every archway, and they would not permit anyone to carry even an empty vessel across the temple courts.

173:1.9 (1890.4) When the chief priests and the scribes heard about these happenings, they were dumfounded. All the more they feared the Master, and all the more they determined to destroy him. But they were nonplused. They did not know how to accomplish his death, for they greatly feared the multitudes, who were now so outspoken in their approval of his overthrow of the profane profiteers. And all this day, a day of quiet and peace in the temple courts, the people heard Jesus' teaching and literally hung on his words.

173:1.10 (1890.5) This surprising act of Jesus was beyond the comprehension of his apostles. They were so taken aback by this sudden and unexpected move of their Master that they remained throughout the whole episode huddled together near the speaker's stand; they never lifted a hand to further this cleansing of the temple. If this spectacular event had occurred the day before, at the time of Jesus' triumphal arrival at the temple at the termination of his tumultuous procession through the gates of the city, all the while loudly acclaimed by the multitude, they would have been ready for it, but coming as it did, they were wholly unprepared to participate.

173:1.11 (1891.1) This cleansing of the temple discloses the Master's attitude toward commercializing the practices of religion as well as his detestation of all forms of unfairness and profiteering at the expense of the poor and the unlearned. This episode also demonstrates that Jesus did not look with approval upon the refusal to employ force to protect the majority of any given human group against the unfair and enslaving practices of unjust minorities who may be able to entrench themselves behind political, financial, or ecclesiastical power. Shrewd, wicked, and designing men are not to be permitted to organize themselves for the exploitation and oppression of those who, because of their idealism, are not disposed to resort to force for self-protection or for the furtherance of their laudable life projects.

Challenging the Master's Authority

173:2.1 (1891.2) On Sunday the triumphal entry into Jerusalem so overawed the Jewish leaders that they refrained from placing Jesus under arrest. Today, this spectacular cleansing of the temple likewise effectively postponed the Master's apprehension. Day by day the rulers of the Jews were becoming more and more determined to destroy him, but they were distraught by two fears, which conspired to delay the hour of striking. The chief priests and the scribes were unwilling to arrest Jesus in public for fear the multitude might turn upon them in a fury of resentment; they also dreaded the possibility of the Roman guards being called upon to quell a popular uprising.

173:2.2 (1891.3) At the noon session of the Sanhedrin it was unanimously agreed that Jesus must be speedily destroyed, inasmuch as no friend of the Master attended this meeting. But they could not agree as to when and how he should be taken into custody. Finally they agreed upon appointing five groups to go out among the people and seek to entangle him in his teaching or otherwise to discredit him in the sight of those who listened to his instruction. Accordingly, about two o'clock, when Jesus had just begun his discourse on "The Liberty of Sonship," a group of these elders of Israel made their way up near Jesus and, interrupting him in the customary manner, asked this question: "By what authority do you do these things? Who gave you this authority?"

173:2.3 (1891.4) It was altogether proper that the temple rulers and the officers of the Jewish Sanhedrin should ask this question of anyone who presumed to teach and perform in the extraordinary manner which had been characteristic of Jesus, especially as concerned his recent conduct in clearing the temple of all commerce. These traders and money- changers all operated by direct license from the highest rulers, and a percentage of their gains was supposed to go directly into the temple treasury. Do not forget that authority was the watchword of all Jewry. The prophets were always stirring up trouble because they so boldly presumed to teach without authority, without having been duly instructed in the rabbinic academies and subsequently regularly ordained by the Sanhedrin. Lack of this authority in pretentious public teaching was looked upon as indicating either ignorant presumption or open rebellion. At this time only the Sanhedrin could ordain an elder or teacher, and such a ceremony had to take place in the presence of at least three persons who had previously been so ordained. Such an ordination conferred the title of "rabbi" upon the teacher and also qualified him to act as a judge, "binding and loosing such matters as might be brought to him for adjudication."

173:2.4 (1892.1) The rulers of the temple came before Jesus at this afternoon hour challenging not only his teaching but his acts. Jesus well knew that these very men had long publicly taught that his authority for teaching was Satanic, and that all his mighty works had been wrought by the power of the prince of devils. Therefore did the Master begin his answer to their question by asking them a counter-question. Said Jesus: "I would also like to ask you one question which, if you will answer

me, I likewise will tell you by what authority I do these works. The baptism of John, whence was it? Did John get his authority from heaven or from men?"

173:2.5 (1892.2) And when his questioners heard this, they withdrew to one side to take counsel among themselves as to what answer they might give. They had thought to embarrass Jesus before the multitude, but now they found themselves much confused before all who were assembled at that time in the temple court. And their discomfiture was all the more apparent when they returned to Jesus, saying: "Concerning the baptism of John, we cannot answer; we do not know." And they so answered the Master because they had reasoned among themselves: If we shall say from heaven, then will he say, Why did you not believe him, and perchance will add that he received his authority from John; and if we shall say from men, then might the multitude turn upon us, for most of them hold that John was a prophet; and so they were compelled to come before Jesus and the people confessing that they, the religious teachers and leaders of Israel, could not (or would not) express an opinion about John's mission. And when they had spoken, Jesus, looking down upon them, said, "Neither will I tell you by what authority I do these things."

173:2.6 (1892.3) Jesus never intended to appeal to John for his authority; John had never been ordained by the Sanhedrin. Jesus' authority was in himself and in his Father's eternal supremacy.

173:2.7 (1892.4) In employing this method of dealing with his adversaries, Jesus did not mean to dodge the question. At first it may seem that he was guilty of a masterly evasion, but it was not so. Jesus was never disposed to take unfair advantage of even his enemies. In this apparent evasion he really supplied all his hearers with the answer to the Pharisees' question as to the authority behind his mission. They had asserted that he performed by authority of the prince of devils. Jesus had repeatedly asserted that all his teaching and works were by the power and authority of his Father in heaven. This the Jewish leaders refused to accept and were seeking to corner him into admitting that he was an irregular teacher since he had never been sanctioned by the Sanhedrin. In answering them as he did, while not claiming authority from John, he so satisfied the people with the inference that the effort of his enemies to ensnare him was effectively turned upon themselves and was much to their discredit in the eyes of all present.

173:2.8 (1892.5) And it was this genius of the Master for dealing with his adversaries that made them so afraid of him. They attempted no more questions that day; they retired to take further counsel among themselves. But the people were not slow to discern the dishonesty and insincerity in these questions asked by the Jewish rulers. Even the common folk could not fail to distinguish between the moral majesty of the Master and the designing hypocrisy of his enemies. But the cleansing of the temple had brought the Sadducees over to the side of the Pharisees in perfecting the plan to destroy Jesus. And the Sadducees now represented a majority of the Sanhedrin.

Parable of the Two Sons

173:3.1 (1893.1) As the caviling Pharisees stood there in silence before Jesus, he looked down on them and said: "Since you are in doubt about John's mission and arrayed in enmity against the teaching and the works of the Son of Man, give ear while I tell you a parable: A certain great and respected landholder had two sons, and desiring the help of his sons in the management of his large estates, he came to one of them, saying, 'Son, go work today in my vineyard.' And this unthinking son answered his father, saying, 'I will not go'; but afterward he repented and went. When he had found his older son, likewise he said to him, 'Son, go work in my vineyard.' And this hypocritical and unfaithful son answered, 'Yes, my father, I will go.' But when his father had departed, he went not. Let me ask you, which of these sons really did his father's will?"

173:3.2 (1893.2) And the people spoke with one accord, saying, "The first son." And then said Jesus: "Even so; and now do I declare that the publicans and harlots, even though they appear to refuse the call to repentance, shall see the error of their way and go on into the kingdom of God before you, who make great pretensions of serving the Father in heaven while you refuse to do the works of the Father. It was not you, the Pharisees and scribes, who believed John, but rather the publicans and sinners; neither do you believe my teaching, but the common people hear my words gladly."

173:3.3 (1893.3) Jesus did not despise the Pharisees and Sadducees personally. It was their systems of teaching and practice which he sought to discredit. He was hostile to no man, but here was occurring the inevitable clash between a new and living religion of the spirit and the older religion of ceremony, tradition, and authority.

173:3.4 (1893.4) All this time the twelve apostles stood near the Master, but they did not in any manner participate in these transactions. Each one of the twelve was reacting in his own peculiar way to the events of these closing days of Jesus' ministry in the flesh, and each one likewise remained obedient to the Master's injunction to refrain from all public teaching and preaching during this Passover week.

Parable of the Absent Landlord

173:4.1 (1893.5) When the chief Pharisees and the scribes who had sought to entangle Jesus with their questions had finished listening to the story of the two sons, they withdrew to take further counsel, and the Master, turning his attention to the listening multitude, told another parable:

173:4.2 (1893.6) "There was a good man who was a householder, and he planted a vineyard. He set a hedge about it, dug a pit for the wine press, and built a watchtower for the guards. Then he let this vineyard out to tenants while he went on a long journey into another country. And when the season of the fruits drew near, he sent servants to the tenants to receive his rental. But they took counsel among themselves and refused to give these servants the fruits due their master; instead, they fell upon his servants, beating one, stoning another, and sending the others away empty-handed. And when the householder heard about all this, he sent other and more trusted servants to deal with these wicked tenants, and these they wounded and also treated shamefully. And then the householder sent his favorite servant, his steward, and him they killed. And still, in patience and with forbearance, he dispatched many other servants, but none would they receive.

Some they beat, others they killed, and when the householder had been so dealt with, he decided to send his son to deal with these ungrateful tenants, saying to himself, 'They may mistreat my servants, but they will surely show respect for my beloved son.' But when these unrepentant and wicked tenants saw the son, they reasoned among themselves: 'This is the heir; come, let us kill him and then the inheritance will be ours.' So they laid hold on him, and after casting him out of the vineyard, they killed him. When the lord of that vineyard shall hear how they have rejected and killed his son, what will he do to those ungrateful and wicked tenants?"

173:4.3 (1894.1) And when the people heard this parable and the question Jesus asked, they answered, "He will destroy those miserable men and let out his vineyard to other and honest farmers who will render to him the fruits in their season." And when some of them who heard perceived that this parable referred to the Jewish nation and its treatment of the prophets and to the impending rejection of Jesus and the gospel of the kingdom, they said in sorrow, "God forbid that we should go on doing these things."

173:4.4 (1894.2) Jesus saw a group of the Sadducees and Pharisees making their way through the crowd, and he paused for a moment until they drew near him, when he said: "You know how your fathers rejected the prophets, and you well know that you are set in your hearts to reject the Son of Man." And then, looking with searching gaze upon those priests and elders who were standing near him, Jesus said: "Did you never read in the Scripture about the stone which the builders rejected, and which, when the people had discovered it, was made into the cornerstone? And so once more do I warn you that, if you continue to reject this gospel, presently will the kingdom of God be taken away from you and be given to a people willing to receive the good news and to bring forth the fruits of the spirit. And there is a mystery about this stone, seeing that whoso falls upon it, while he is thereby broken in pieces, shall be saved; but on whomsoever this stone falls, he will be ground to dust and his ashes scattered to the four winds."

173:4.5 (1894.3) When the Pharisees heard these words, they understood that Jesus referred to themselves and the other Jewish leaders. They greatly desired to lay hold on him then and there, but they feared the multitude. However, they were so angered by the Master's words that they withdrew and held further counsel among themselves as to how they might bring about his death. And that night both the Sadducees and the Pharisees joined hands in the plan to entrap him the next day.

Parable of the Marriage Feast

173:5.1 (1894.4) After the scribes and rulers had withdrawn, Jesus addressed himself again to the assembled crowd and spoke the parable of the wedding feast. He said:

173:5.2 (1894.5) "The kingdom of heaven may be likened to a certain king who made a marriage feast for his son and dispatched messengers to call those who had previously been invited to the feast to come, saying, 'Everything is ready for the marriage supper at the king's palace.' Now, many of those who had once promised to attend, at this time refused to come. When the king heard of these rejections of his invitation, he sent other servants and messengers, saying: 'Tell all those who were bidden, to come, for, behold, my dinner is ready. My oxen and my fatlings are killed, and all is in readiness for the celebration of the forthcoming marriage of my son.' But again did the thoughtless make light of this call of their king, and they went their ways, one to the farm, another to the pottery, and others to their merchandise. Still others were not content thus to slight the king's call, but in open rebellion they laid hands on the king's messengers and shamefully mistreated them, even killing some of them. And when the king perceived that his chosen guests, even those who had accepted his preliminary invitation and had promised to attend the wedding feast, had finally rejected his call and in rebellion had assaulted and slain his chosen messengers, he was exceedingly wroth. And then this insulted king ordered out his armies and the armies of his allies and instructed them to destroy these rebellious murderers and to burn down their city.

173:5.3 (1895.1) "And when he had punished those who spurned his invitation, he appointed yet another day for the wedding feast and said to his messengers: 'They who were first bidden to the wedding were not worthy; so go now into the parting of the ways and into the highways and even beyond the borders of the city, and as many as you shall find, bid even these strangers to come in and attend this wedding feast.' And then these servants went out into the highways and the out-of-the-way places, and they gathered together as many as they found, good and bad, rich and poor, so that at last the wedding chamber was filled with willing guests. When all was ready, the king came in to view his guests, and much to his surprise he saw there a man without a wedding garment. The king, since he had freely provided wedding garments for all his guests, addressing this man, said: 'Friend, how is it that you come into my guest chamber on this occasion without a wedding garment?' And this unprepared man was speechless. Then said the king

to his servants: 'Cast out this thoughtless guest from my house to share the lot of all the others who have spurned my hospitality and rejected my call. I will have none here except those who delight to accept my invitation, and who do me the honor to wear those guest garments so freely provided for all.'"

173:5.4 (1895.2) After speaking this parable, Jesus was about to dismiss the multitude when a sympathetic believer, making his way through the crowds toward him, asked: "But, Master, how shall we know about these things? how shall we be ready for the king's invitation? what sign will you give us whereby we shall know that you are the Son of God?" And when the Master heard this, he said, "Only one sign shall be given you." And then, pointing to his own body, he continued, "Destroy this temple, and in three days I will raise it up." But they did not understand him, and as they dispersed, they talked among themselves, saying, "Almost fifty years has this temple been in building, and yet he says he will destroy it and raise it up in three days." Even his own apostles did not comprehend the significance of this utterance, but subsequently, after his resurrection, they recalled what he had said.

173:5.5 (1895.3) About four o'clock this afternoon Jesus beckoned to his apostles and indicated that he desired to leave the temple and to go to Bethany for their evening meal and a night of rest. On the way up Olivet Jesus instructed Andrew, Philip, and Thomas that, on the morrow, they should establish a camp nearer the city which they could occupy during the remainder of the Passover week. In compliance with this instruction the following morning they pitched their tents in the hillside ravine overlooking the public camping park of Gethsemane, on a plot of ground belonging to Simon of Bethany.

173:5.6 (1896.1) Again it was a silent group of Jews who made their way up the western slope of Olivet on this Monday night. These twelve men, as never before, were beginning to sense that something tragic was about to happen. While the dramatic cleansing of the temple during the early morning had aroused their hopes of seeing the Master assert himself and manifest his mighty powers, the events of the entire afternoon only operated as an anticlimax in that they all pointed to the certain rejection of Jesus' teaching by the Jewish authorities. The apostles were gripped by suspense and were held in the firm grasp of a terrible uncertainty. They realized that only a few short days could intervene between the events of the day just passed and the crash of an impending doom. They all felt that something tremendous was about to happen, but they knew not what to expect. They went to their various places for rest, but they slept very little. Even the Alpheus twins were at last aroused to the realization that the events of the Master's life were moving swiftly toward their final culmination.

Paper 174

Tuesday Morning in the Temple

174:0.1 (1897.1) ABOUT seven o'clock on this Tuesday morning Jesus met the apostles, the women's corps, and some two dozen other prominent disciples at the home of Simon. At this meeting he said farewell to Lazarus, giving him that instruction which led him so soon to flee to Philadelphia in Perea, where he later became connected with the missionary movement having its headquarters in that city. Jesus also said good-bye to the aged Simon, and gave his parting advice to the women's corps, as he never again formally addressed them.

174:0.2 (1897.2) This morning he greeted each of the twelve with a personal salutation. To Andrew he said: "Be not dismayed by the events just ahead. Keep a firm hold on your brethren and see that they do not find you downcast." To Peter he said: "Put not your trust in the arm of flesh nor in weapons of steel. Establish yourself on the spiritual foundations of the eternal rocks." To James he said: "Falter not because of outward appearances. Remain firm in your faith, and you shall soon know of the reality of that which you believe." To John he said: "Be gentle; love even your enemies; be tolerant. And remember that I have trusted you with many things." To Nathaniel he said: "Judge not by appearances; remain firm in your faith when all appears to vanish; be true to your commission as an ambassador of the kingdom." To Philip he said: "Be unmoved by the events now impending. Remain unshaken, even when you cannot see the way. Be loyal to your oath of consecration." To Matthew he said: "Forget not the mercy that received you into the kingdom. Let no man cheat you of your eternal reward. As you have withstood the inclinations of the mortal nature, be willing to be steadfast." To Thomas he said: "No matter how difficult it may be, just now you must walk by faith and not by sight. Doubt not that I am able to finish the work I have begun, and that I shall eventually see all of my faithful ambassadors in the kingdom beyond." To the Alpheus twins he said: "Do not allow the things which you cannot understand to crush you. Be true to the affections of your hearts and put not your trust in either great men or the changing attitude of the people. Stand by your brethren." And to Simon Zelotes he said: "Simon, you may be crushed by disappointment, but your spirit shall rise above all that may come upon you. What you have failed to learn from me, my spirit will teach you. Seek the true realities of the spirit and cease to be attracted by unreal and material shadows." And to Judas Iscariot he said: "Judas, I have loved you and have prayed that you would love your brethren. Be not weary in well doing; and I would warn you to beware the slippery paths of flattery and the poison darts of ridicule."

174:0.3 (1897.3) And when he had concluded these greetings, he departed for Jerusalem with Andrew, Peter, James, and John as the other apostles set about the establishment of the Gethsemane camp, where they were to go that night, and where they made their headquarters for the remainder of the Master's life in the flesh. About halfway down the slope of Olivet Jesus paused and visited more than an hour with the four apostles.

Divine Forgiveness

174:1.1 (1898.1) For several days Peter and James had been engaged in discussing their differences of opinion about the Master's teaching regarding the forgiveness of sin. They had both agreed to lay the matter before Jesus, and Peter embraced this occasion as a fitting opportunity for securing the Master's counsel. Accordingly, Simon Peter broke in on the conversation dealing with the differences between praise and worship, by asking: "Master, James and I are not in accord regarding your teachings having to do with the forgiveness of sin. James claims you teach that the Father forgives us even before we ask him, and I maintain that repentance and confession must precede the forgiveness. Which of us is right? what do you say?"

174:1.2 (1898.2) After a short silence Jesus looked significantly at all four and answered: "My brethren, you err in your opinions because you do not comprehend the nature of those intimate and loving relations between the creature and the Creator, between man and God. You fail to grasp that understanding sympathy which the wise parent entertains for his immature and sometimes erring child. It is indeed doubtful whether intelligent and affectionate parents are ever called upon to forgive an average and normal child. Understanding relationships associated with attitudes of love effectively prevent all those estrangements which later necessitate the readjustment of repentance by the child with forgiveness by the parent.

174:1.3 (1898.3) "A part of every father lives in the child. The father enjoys priority and superiority of understanding in all matters connected with the child-parent relationship. The parent is able to view the immaturity of the child in the light of the more advanced parental maturity, the riper experience of the older partner. With the earthly child and the heavenly Father, the divine parent possesses infinity and divinity of sympathy and capacity for loving understanding. Divine forgiveness is inevitable; it is inherent and inalienable in God's infinite understanding, in his perfect knowledge of all that concerns the mistaken judgment and erroneous choosing of the child. Divine justice is so eternally fair that it unfailingly embodies understanding mercy.

174:1.4 (1898.4) "When a wise man understands the inner impulses of his fellows, he will love them. And when you love your brother, you have already forgiven him. This capacity to understand man's nature and forgive his apparent wrongdoing is Godlike. If you are wise parents, this is the way you will love and understand your children, even forgive them when transient misunderstanding has apparently separated you. The child, being immature and lacking in the fuller understanding of the depth of the child-father relationship, must frequently feel a sense of guilty separation from a father's full approval, but the true father is never conscious of any such separation. Sin is an experience of creature consciousness; it is not a part of God's consciousness.

174:1.5 (1898.5) "Your inability or unwillingness to forgive your fellows is the measure of your immaturity, your failure to attain adult sympathy, understanding, and love. You hold grudges and nurse vengefulness in direct proportion to your ignorance of the inner nature and true longings of your children and your fellow beings. Love is the outworking of the divine and inner urge of life. It is founded on understanding, nurtured by unselfish service, and perfected in wisdom."

Questions by the Jewish Rulers

174:2.1 (1899.1) On Monday evening

there had been held a council between the Sanhedrin and some fifty additional leaders selected from among the scribes, Pharisees, and the Sadducees. It was the consensus of this meeting that it would be dangerous to arrest Jesus in public because of his hold upon the affections of the common people. It was also the opinion of the majority that a determined effort should be made to discredit him in the eyes of the multitude before he should be arrested and brought to trial. Accordingly, several groups of learned men were designated to be on hand the next morning in the temple to undertake to entrap him with difficult questions and otherwise to seek to embarrass him before the people. At last, the Pharisees, Sadducees, and even the Herodians were all united in this effort to discredit Jesus in the eyes of the Passover multitudes.

174:2.2 (1899.2) Tuesday morning, when Jesus arrived in the temple court and began to teach, he had uttered but few words when a group of the younger students from the academies, who had been rehearsed for this purpose, came forward and by their spokesman addressed Jesus: "Master, we know you are a righteous teacher, and we know that you proclaim the ways of truth, and that you serve only God, for you fear no man, and that you are no respecter of persons. We are only students, and we would know the truth about a matter which troubles us; our difficulty is this: Is it lawful for us to give tribute to Caesar? Shall we give or shall we not give?" Jesus, perceiving their hypocrisy and craftiness, said to them: "Why do you thus come to tempt me? Show me the tribute money, and I will answer you." And when they handed him a denarius, he looked at it and said, "Whose image and superscription does this coin bear?" And when they answered him, "Caesar's," Jesus said, "Render to Caesar the things that are Caesar's and render to God the things that are God's."

174:2.3 (1899.3) When he had thus answered these young scribes and their Herodian accomplices, they withdrew from his presence, and the people, even the Sad-

ducees, enjoyed their discomfiture. Even the youths who had endeavored to entrap him marveled greatly at the unexpected sagacity of the Master's answer.

174:2.4 (1899.4) The previous day the rulers had sought to trip him before the multitude on matters of ecclesiastical authority, and having failed, they now sought to involve him in a damaging discussion of civil authority. Both Pilate and Herod were in Jerusalem at this time, and Jesus' enemies conjectured that, if he would dare to advise against the payment of tribute to Caesar, they could go at once before the Roman authorities and charge him with sedition. On the other hand, if he should advise the payment of tribute in so many words, they rightly calculated that such a pronouncement would greatly wound the national pride of his Jewish hearers, thereby alienating the good will and affection of the multitude.

174:2.5 (1899.5) In all this the enemies of Jesus were defeated since it was a well-known ruling of the Sanhedrin, made for the guidance of the Jews dispersed among the gentile nations, that the "right of coinage carried with it the right to levy taxes." In this manner Jesus avoided their trap. To have answered "No" to their question would have been equivalent to inciting rebellion; to have answered "Yes" would have shocked the deep-rooted nationalist sentiments of that day. The Master did not evade the question; he merely employed the wisdom of making a double reply. Jesus was never evasive, but he was always wise in his dealings with those who sought to harass and destroy him.

The Sadducees and the Resurrection

174:3.1 (1900.1) Before Jesus could get started with his teaching, another group came forward to question him, this time a company of the learned and crafty Sadducees. Their spokesman, drawing near to him, said: "Master, Moses said that if a married man should die, leaving no children, his brother should take the wife and raise up seed for the deceased brother. Now there occurred a case where a certain man who had six brothers died childless; his next brother took his wife but also soon died, leaving no children. Likewise did the second brother take the wife, but he also died leaving no offspring. And so on until all six of the brothers had had her, and all six of them passed on without leaving children. And then, after them all, the woman herself died. Now, what we would like to ask you is this: In the resurrection whose wife will she be since all seven of these brothers had her?"

174:3.2 (1900.2) Jesus knew, and so did the people, that these Sadducees were not sincere in asking this question because it was not likely that such a case would really occur; and besides, this practice of the brothers of a dead man seeking to beget children for him was practically a dead letter at this time among the Jews. Nevertheless, Jesus condescended to reply to their mischievous question. He said: "You all do err in asking such questions because you know neither the Scriptures nor the living power of God. You know that the sons of this world can marry and are given in marriage, but you do not seem to understand that they who are accounted worthy to attain the worlds to come, through the resurrection of the righteous, neither marry nor are given in marriage. Those who experience the resurrection from the dead are more like the angels of heaven, and they never die. These resurrected ones are eternally the sons of God; they are the children of light resurrected into the progress of eternal life. And even your Father Moses understood this, for, in connection with his experiences at the burning bush, he heard the Father say, 'I am the God of Abraham, the God of Isaac, and the God of Jacob.' And so, along with Moses, do I declare that my Father is not the God of the dead but of the living. In him you all do live, reproduce, and possess your mortal existence."

174:3.3 (1900.3) When Jesus had finished answering these questions, the Sadducees withdrew, and some of the Phari-

sees so far forgot themselves as to exclaim, "True, true, Master, you have well answered these unbelieving Sadducees." The Sadducees dared not ask him any more questions, and the common people marveled at the wisdom of his teaching.

174:3.4 (1900.4) Jesus appealed only to Moses in his encounter with the Sadducees because this religio-political sect acknowledged the validity of only the five so-called Books of Moses; they did not allow that the teachings of the prophets were admissible as a basis of doctrinal dogmas. The Master in his answer, though positively affirming the fact of the survival of mortal creatures by the technique of the resurrection, did not in any sense speak approvingly of the Pharisaic beliefs in the resurrection of the literal human body. The point Jesus wished to emphasize was: That the Father had said, "I am the God of Abraham, Isaac, and Jacob," not I was their God.

174:3.5 (1900.5) The Sadducees had thought to subject Jesus to the withering influence of ridicule, knowing full well that persecution in public would most certainly create further sympathy for him in the minds of the multitude.

The Great Commandment

174:4.1 (1901.1) Another group of Sadducees had been instructed to ask Jesus entangling questions about angels, but when they beheld the fate of their comrades who had sought to entrap him with questions concerning the resurrection, they very wisely decided to hold their peace; they retired without asking a question. It was the prearranged plan of the confederated Pharisees, scribes, Sadducees, and Herodians to fill up the entire day with these entangling questions, hoping thereby to discredit Jesus before the people and at the same time effectively to prevent his having any time for the proclamation of his disturbing teachings.

174:4.2 (1901.2) Then came forward

one of the groups of the Pharisees to ask harassing questions, and the spokesman, signaling to Jesus, said: "Master, I am a lawyer, and I would like to ask you which, in your opinion, is the greatest commandment?" Jesus answered: "There is but one commandment, and that one is the greatest of all, and that commandment is: 'Hear O Israel, the Lord our God, the Lord is one; and you shall love the Lord your God with all your heart and with all your soul, with all your mind and with all your strength.' This is the first and great commandment.

And the second commandment is like this first; indeed, it springs directly therefrom, and it is: 'You shall love your neighbor as yourself.' There is no other commandment greater than these; on these two commandments hang all the law and the prophets."

174:4.3 (1901.3) When the lawyer perceived that Jesus had answered not only in accordance with the highest concept of Jewish religion, but that he had also answered wisely in the sight of the assembled multitude, he thought it the better part of valor openly to commend the Master's reply. Accordingly, he said: "Of a truth, Master, you have well said that God is one and there is none beside him; and that to love him with all the heart, understanding, and strength, and also to love one's neighbor as one's self, is the first and great commandment; and we are agreed that this great commandment is much more to be regarded than all the burnt offerings and sacrifices." When the lawyer answered thus discreetly, Jesus looked down upon him and said, "My friend, I perceive that you are not far from the kingdom of God."

174:4.4 (1901.4) Jesus spoke the truth when he referred to this lawyer as being "not far from the kingdom," for that very night he went out to the Master's camp near Gethsemane, professed faith in the gospel of the kingdom, and was baptized by Josiah, one of the disciples of Abner.

174:4.5 (1901.5) Two or three other groups of the scribes and Pharisees were present and had intended to ask questions, but they were either disarmed by Jesus' answer to the lawyer, or they were deterred by the discomfiture of all who had undertaken to ensnare him. After this no man dared to ask him another question in public.

174:4.6 (1901.6) When no more questions were forthcoming, and as the noon hour was near, Jesus did not resume his teaching but was content merely to ask the Pharisees and their associates a question. Said Jesus: "Since you ask no more questions, I would like to ask you one. What do you think of the Deliverer? That is, whose son is he?" After a brief pause one of the scribes answered, "The Messiah is the son of David." And since Jesus knew that there had been much debate, even among his own disciples, as to whether or not he was the son of David, he asked this further question: "If the Deliverer is indeed the son of David, how is it that, in the Psalm which you accredit to David, he himself, speaking in the spirit, says, 'The Lord said to my lord, sit on my right hand until I make your enemies the footstool of your feet.' If David calls him Lord, how then can he be his son?" Although the rulers, the scribes, and the chief priests made no reply to this question, they likewise refrained from asking him any more questions in an effort to entangle him. They never answered this question which Jesus put to them, but after the Master's death they attempted to escape the difficulty by changing the interpretation of this Psalm so as to make it refer to Abraham instead of the Messiah. Others sought to escape the dilemma by disallowing that David was the author of this so-called Messianic Psalm.

174:4.7 (1902.1) A short time back the Pharisees had enjoyed the manner in which the Sadducees had been silenced by the Master; now the Sadducees were delighted by the failure of the Pharisees; but such rivalry was only momentary; they speedily forgot their time-honored differences in the united effort to stop Jesus' teachings and doings. But throughout all of these experiences the common people heard him gladly.

The Inquiring Greeks

174:5.1 (1902.2) About noontime, as Philip was purchasing supplies for the new camp which was that day being established near Gethsemane, he was accosted by a delegation of strangers, a group of believing Greeks from Alexandria, Athens, and Rome, whose spokesman said to the apostle: "You have been pointed out to us by those who know you; so we come to you, Sir, with the request to see Jesus, your Master." Philip was taken by surprise thus to meet these prominent and inquiring Greek gentiles in the market place, and, since Jesus had so explicitly charged all of the twelve not to engage in any public teaching during the Passover week, he was a bit perplexed as to the right way to handle this matter. He was also disconcerted because these men were foreign gentiles. If they had been Jews or near-by and familiar gentiles, he would not have hesitated so markedly. What he did was this: He asked these Greeks to remain right where they were. As he hastened away, they supposed that he went in search of Jesus, but in reality he hurried off to the home of Joseph, where he knew Andrew and the other apostles were at lunch; and calling Andrew out, he explained the purpose of his coming, and then, accompanied by Andrew, he returned to the waiting Greeks.

174:5.2 (1902.3) Since Philip had about finished the purchasing of supplies, he and Andrew returned with the Greeks to the home of Joseph, where Jesus received them; and they sat near while he spoke to his apostles and a number of leading disciples assembled at this luncheon. Said Jesus:

174:5.3 (1902.4) "My Father sent me to this world to reveal his loving-kindness to the children of men, but those to whom I first came have refused to receive me. True, indeed, many of you have believed my gospel for yourselves, but the children of Abraham and their leaders are about to reject me, and in so doing they will reject Him who sent me. I have freely proclaimed the gospel of salvation to this people; I have told them of sonship with joy, liberty, and life more abundant in the spirit. My Father has done many wonderful works among these fear-ridden sons of men. But truly did the Prophet Isaiah refer to this people when he wrote: 'Lord, who has believed our teachings? And to whom has the Lord been revealed?' Truly have the leaders of my people deliberately blinded their eyes that they see not, and hardened their hearts lest they believe and be saved. All these years have I sought to heal them of their unbelief that they might be recipients of the Father's eternal salvation. I know that not all have failed me; some of you have indeed believed my message. In this room now are a full score of men who were once members of the Sanhedrin, or who were high in the councils of the nation, albeit even some of you still shrink from open confession of the truth lest they cast you out of the synagogue. Some of you are tempted to love the glory of men more than the glory of God. But I am constrained to show forbearance since I fear for the safety and loyalty of even some of those who have been so long near me, and who have lived so close by my side.

174:5.4 (1903.1) "In this banquet chamber I perceive there are assembled Jews and gentiles in about equal numbers, and I would address you as the first and last of such a group that I may instruct in the affairs of the kingdom before I go to my Father."

174:5.5 (1903.2) These Greeks had been in faithful attendance upon Jesus' teaching in the temple. On Monday evening they had held a conference at the home of Nicodemus, which lasted until the dawn of day, and thirty of them had elected to enter the kingdom.

174:5.6 (1903.3) As Jesus stood before them at this time, he perceived the end of one dispensation and the beginning of another. Turning his attention to the Greeks, the Master said:

174:5.7 (1903.4) "He who believes this gospel, believes not merely in me but in Him who sent me. When you look upon me, you see not only the Son of Man but also Him who sent me. I am the light of the world, and whosoever will believe my teaching shall no longer abide in darkness. If you gentiles will hear me, you shall receive the words of life and shall enter forthwith into the joyous liberty of the truth of sonship with God. If my fellow countrymen, the Jews, choose to reject me and to refuse my teachings, I will not sit in judgment on them, for I came not to judge the world but to offer it salvation. Nevertheless, they who reject me and refuse to receive my teaching shall be brought to judgment in due season by my Father and those whom he has appointed to sit in judgment on such as reject the gift of mercy and the truths of salvation. Remember, all of you, that I speak not of myself, but that I have faithfully declared to you that which the Father commanded I should reveal to the children of men. And these words which the Father directed me to speak to the world are words of divine truth, everlasting mercy, and eternal life.

174:5.8 (1903.5) "But to both Jew and gentile I declare the hour has about come when the Son of Man will be glorified. You well know that, except a grain of wheat falls into the earth and dies, it abides alone; but if it dies in good soil, it springs up again to life and bears much fruit. He who selfishly loves his life stands in danger of losing it; but he who is willing to lay down his life for my sake and the gospel's shall enjoy a more abundant existence on earth and in heaven, life eternal. If you will truly follow me, even after I have gone to my Father, then shall you become my disciples and the sincere servants of your fellow mortals.

174:5.9 (1903.6) "I know my hour is approaching, and I am troubled. I perceive that my people are determined to spurn the kingdom, but I am rejoiced to receive these truth-seeking gentiles who come here today inquiring for the way of light.
Nevertheless, my heart aches for my people, and my soul is distraught by that which lies just before me. What shall I say as I look ahead and discern what is about to befall me? Shall I say, Father save me from

this awful hour? No! For this very purpose have I come into the world and even to this hour. Rather will I say, and pray that you will join me: Father, glorify your name; your will be done."

174:5.10 (1904.1) When Jesus had thus spoken, the Personalized Adjuster of his indwelling during prebaptismal times appeared before him, and as he paused noticeably, this now mighty spirit of the Father's representation spoke to Jesus of Nazareth, saying: "I have glorified my name in your bestowals many times, and I will glorify it once more."

174:5.11 (1904.2) While the Jews and gentiles here assembled heard no voice, they could not fail to discern that the Master had paused in his speaking while a message came to him from some superhuman source. They all said, every man to the one who was by him, "An angel has spoken to him."

174:5.12 (1904.3) Then Jesus continued to speak: "All this has not happened for my sake but for yours. I know of a certainty that the Father will receive me and accept my mission in your behalf, but it is needful that you be encouraged and be made ready for the fiery trial which is just ahead. Let me assure you that victory shall eventually crown our united efforts to enlighten the world and liberate mankind. The old order is bringing itself to judgment; the Prince of this world I have cast down; and all men shall become free by the light of the spirit which I will pour out upon all flesh after I have ascended to my Father in heaven.

174:5.13 (1904.4) "And now I declare to you that I, if I be lifted up on earth and in your lives, will draw all men to myself and into the fellowship of my Father. You have believed that the Deliverer would abide on earth forever, but I declare that the Son of Man will be rejected by men, and that he will go back to the Father. Only a little while will I be with you; only a little time will the living light be among this darkened generation. Walk while you have this light so that the oncoming darkness and confusion may not overtake you. He who walks in the darkness knows not where he goes; but if you will choose to walk in the light, you shall all indeed become liberated sons of God. And now, all of you, come with me while we go back to the temple and I speak farewell words to the chief priests, the scribes, the Pharisees, the Sadducees, the Herodians, and the benighted rulers of Israel."

174:5.14 (1904.5) Having thus spoken, Jesus led the way over the narrow streets of Jerusalem back to the temple. They had just heard the Master say that this was to be his farewell discourse in the temple, and they followed him in silence and in deep meditation.

Paper 175

The Last Temple Discourse

175:0.1 (1905.1) SHORTLY after two o'clock on this Tuesday afternoon, Jesus, accompanied by eleven apostles, Joseph of Arimathea, the thirty Greeks, and certain other disciples, arrived at the temple and began the delivery of his last address in the courts of the sacred edifice. This discourse was intended to be his last appeal to the Jewish people and the final indictment of his vehement enemies and would-be destroyers—the scribes, Pharisees, Sadducees, and the chief rulers of Israel. Throughout the forenoon the various groups had had an opportunity to question Jesus; this afternoon no one asked him a question.

175:0.2 (1905.2) As the Master began to speak, the temple court was quiet and orderly. The money-changers and the merchandisers had not dared again to enter the temple since Jesus and the aroused multitude had driven them out the previous day. Before beginning the discourse, Jesus tenderly looked down upon this audience which was so soon to hear his farewell public address of mercy to mankind cou-

pled with his last denunciation of the false teachers and the bigoted rulers of the Jews.

The Discourse

175:1.1 (1905.3) "This long time have I been with you, going up and down in the land proclaiming the Father's love for the children of men, and many have seen the light and, by faith, have entered into the kingdom of heaven. In connection with this teaching and preaching the Father has done many wonderful works, even to the resurrection of the dead. Many sick and afflicted have been made whole because they believed; but all of this proclamation of truth and healing of disease has not opened the eyes of those who refuse to see light, those who are determined to reject this gospel of the kingdom.

175:1.2 (1905.4) "In every manner consistent with doing my Father's will, I and my apostles have done our utmost to live in peace with our brethren, to conform with the reasonable requirements of the laws of Moses and the traditions of Israel. We have persistently sought peace, but the leaders of Israel will not have it. By rejecting the truth of God and the light of heaven, they are aligning themselves on the side of error and darkness. There cannot be peace between light and darkness, between life and death, between truth and error.

175:1.3 (1905.5) "Many of you have dared to believe my teachings and have already entered into the joy and liberty of the consciousness of sonship with God. And you will bear me witness that I have offered this same sonship with God to all the Jewish nation, even to these very men who now seek my destruction. And even now would my Father receive these blinded teachers and these hypocritical leaders if they would only turn to him and accept his mercy. Even now it is not too late for this people to receive the word of heaven and to welcome the Son of Man.

175:1.4 (1906.1) "My Father has long dealt in mercy with this people. Generation after generation have we sent our prophets to teach and warn them, and generation after generation have they killed these heaven-sent teachers. And now do your willful high priests and stubborn rulers go right on doing this same thing. As Herod brought about the death of John, you likewise now make ready to destroy the Son of Man.

175:1.5 (1906.2) "As long as there is a chance that the Jews will turn to my Father and seek salvation, the God of Abraham, Isaac, and Jacob will keep his hands of mercy outstretched toward you; but when you have once filled up your cup of impenitence, and when once you have finally rejected my Father's mercy, this nation will be left to its own counsels, and it shall speedily come to an inglorious end. This people was called to become the light of the world, to show forth the spiritual glory of a God-knowing race, but you have so far departed from the fulfillment of your divine privileges that your leaders are about to commit the supreme folly of all the ages in that they are on the verge of finally rejecting the gift of God to all men and for all ages—the revelation of the love of the Father in heaven for all his creatures on earth.

175:1.6 (1906.3) "And when you do once reject this revelation of God to man, the kingdom of heaven shall be given to other peoples, to those who will receive it with joy and gladness. In the name of the Father who sent me, I solemnly warn you that you are about to lose your position in the world as the standard-bearers of eternal truth and the custodians of the divine law. I am just now offering you your last chance to come forward and repent, to signify your intention to seek God with all your hearts and to enter, like little children and by sincere faith, into the security and salvation of the kingdom of heaven.

175:1.7 (1906.4) "My Father has long worked for your salvation, and I came down to live among you and personally show you the way. Many of both the Jews and the Samaritans, and even the gentiles, have believed the gospel of the kingdom, but those who should be first to come forward and accept the light of heaven have steadfastly refused to believe the revelation of the truth of God—God revealed in man and man uplifted to God.

175:1.8 (1906.5) "This afternoon my apostles stand here before you in silence, but you shall soon hear their voices ringing out with the call to salvation and with the urge to unite with the heavenly kingdom as the sons of the living God. And now I call to witness these, my disciples and believers in the gospel of the kingdom, as well as the unseen messengers by their sides, that I have once more offered Israel and her rulers deliverance and salvation. But you all behold how the Father's mercy is slighted and how the messengers of truth are rejected. Nevertheless, I admonish you that these scribes and Pharisees still sit in Moses' seat, and therefore, until the Most Highs who rule in the kingdoms of men shall finally overthrow this nation and destroy the place of these rulers, I bid you co-operate with these elders in Israel. You are not required to unite with them in their plans to destroy the Son of Man, but in everything related to the peace of Israel you are to be subject to them. In all these matters do whatsoever they bid you and observe the essentials of the law but do not pattern after their evil works. Remember, this is the sin of these rulers: They say that which is good, but they do it not. You well know how these leaders bind heavy burdens on your shoulders, burdens grievous to bear, and that they will not lift as much as one finger to help you bear these weighty burdens. They have oppressed you with ceremonies and enslaved you by traditions.

175:1.9 (1907.1) "Furthermore, these self-centered rulers delight in doing their good works so that they will be seen by men. They make broad their phylacteries and enlarge the borders of their official robes. They crave the chief places at the feasts and demand the chief seats in the synagogues. They covet laudatory salutations in the market places and desire to be called rabbi by all men. And even while they seek all this honor from men, they secretly lay hold of widows' houses and take profit from the services of the sacred temple. For a pretense these hypocrites make long prayers in public and give alms to attract the notice of their fellows.

175:1.10 (1907.2) "While you should honor your rulers and reverence your teachers, you should call no man Father in the spiritual sense, for there is one who is your Father, even God. Neither should you seek to lord it over your brethren in the kingdom. Remember, I have taught you that he who would be greatest among you should become the server of all. If you presume to exalt yourselves before God, you will certainly be humbled; but whoso truly humbles himself will surely be exalted. Seek in your daily lives, not self-glorification, but the glory of God. Intelligently subordinate your own wills to the will of the Father in heaven.

175:1.11 (1907.3) "Mistake not my words. I bear no malice toward these chief priests and rulers who even now seek my destruction; I have no ill will for these scribes and Pharisees who reject my teachings. I know that many of you believe in secret, and I know you will openly profess your allegiance to the kingdom when my hour comes. But how will your rabbis justify themselves since they profess to talk with God and then presume to reject and destroy him who comes to reveal the Father to the worlds?

175:1.12 (1907.4) "Woe upon you, scribes and Pharisees, hypocrites! You would shut the doors of the kingdom of heaven against sincere men because they happen to be unlearned in the ways of your teaching. You refuse to enter the kingdom and at the same time do everything within your power to prevent all others from entering. You stand with your backs to the doors of salvation and fight with all who would enter therein.

175:1.13 (1907.5) "Woe upon you, scribes and Pharisees, hypocrites that you are! for you do indeed encompass land and

sea to make one proselyte, and when you have succeeded, you are not content until you have made him twofold worse than he was as a child of the heathen.

175:1.14 (1907.6) "Woe upon you, chief priests and rulers who lay hold of the property of the poor and demand heavy dues of those who would serve God as they think Moses ordained! You who refuse to show mercy, can you hope for mercy in the worlds to come?

175:1.15 (1907.7) "Woe upon you, false teachers, blind guides! What can be expected of a nation when the blind lead the blind? They both shall stumble into the pit of destruction.

175:1.16 (1907.8) "Woe upon you who dissimulate when you take an oath! You are tricksters since you teach that a man may swear by the temple and break his oath, but that whoso swears by the gold in the temple must remain bound. You are all fools and blind. You are not even consistent in your dishonesty, for which is the greater, the gold or the temple which has supposedly sanctified the gold? You also teach that, if a man swears by the altar, it is nothing; but that, if one swears by the gift that is upon the altar, then shall he be held as a debtor. Again are you blind to the truth, for which is the greater, the gift or the altar which sanctifies the gift? How can you justify such hypocrisy and dishonesty in the sight of the God of heaven?

175:1.17 (1908.1) "Woe upon you, scribes and Pharisees and all other hypocrites who make sure that they tithe mint, anise, and cumin and at the same time disregard the weightier matters of the law—faith, mercy, and judgment! Within reason, the one you ought to have done but not to have left the other undone. You are truly blind guides and dumb teachers; you strain out the gnat and swallow the camel.

175:1.18 (1908.2) "Woe upon you, scribes, Pharisees, and hypocrites! for you are scrupulous to cleanse the outside of the cup and the platter, but within there remains the filth of extortion, excesses, and deception. You are spiritually blind. Do you not recognize how much better it would be first to cleanse the inside of the cup, and then that which spills over would of itself cleanse the outside? You wicked reprobates! you make the outward performances of your religion to conform with the letter of your interpretation of Moses' law while your souls are steeped in iniquity and filled with murder.

175:1.19 (1908.3) "Woe upon all of you who reject truth and spurn mercy! Many of you are like whited sepulchres, which outwardly appear beautiful but within are full of dead men's bones and all sorts of uncleanness. Even so do you who knowingly reject the counsel of God appear outwardly to men as holy and righteous, but inwardly your hearts are filled with hypocrisy and iniquity.

175:1.20 (1908.4) "Woe upon you, false guides of a nation! Over yonder have you built a monument to the martyred prophets of old, while you plot to destroy Him of whom they spoke. You garnish the tombs of the righteous and flatter yourselves that, had you lived in the days of your fathers, you would not have killed the prophets; and then in the face of such self-righteous thinking you make ready to slay him of whom the prophets spoke, the Son of Man. Inasmuch as you do these things, are you witness to yourselves that you are the wicked sons of them who slew the prophets. Go on, then, and fill up the cup of your condemnation to the full! *

175:1.21 (1908.5) "Woe upon you, children of evil! John did truly call you the offspring of vipers, and I ask how can you escape the judgment that John pronounced upon you?

175:1.22 (1908.6) "But even now I offer you in my Father's name mercy and forgiveness; even now I proffer the loving hand of eternal fellowship. My Father has sent you the wise men and the prophets; some you have persecuted and others you have killed. Then appeared John proclaim-ing the coming of the Son of Man, and him you destroyed after many had believed his teaching. And now you make ready to shed more innocent blood. Do you not compre-hend that a terrible day of reckoning will come when the Judge of all the earth shall require of this people an accounting for the way they have rejected, persecuted, and destroyed these messengers of heaven? Do you not understand that you must account for all of this righteous blood, from the first prophet killed down to the times of Zecha-riah, who was slain between the sanctuary and the altar? And if you go on in your evil ways, this accounting may be required of this very generation.

175:1.23 (1908.7) "O Jerusalem and the children of Abraham, you who have stoned the prophets and killed the teach-ers that were sent to you, even now would I gather your children together as a hen gathers her chickens under her wings, but you will not!

175:1.24 (1908.8) "And now I take leave of you. You have heard my message and have made your decision. Those who have believed my gospel are even now safe within the kingdom of God. To you who have chosen to reject the gift of God, I say that you will no more see me teaching in the temple. My work for you is done. Behold, I now go forth with my children, and your house is left to you desolate!"

175:1.25 (1908.9) And then the Master beckoned his followers to depart from the temple.

Status of Individual Jews

175:2.1 (1909.1) The fact that the spiritual leaders and the religious teach-ers of the Jewish nation onetime rejected the teachings of Jesus and conspired to bring about his cruel death, does not in any manner affect the status of any individual Jew in his standing before God. And it should not cause those who profess to be followers of the Christ to be prejudiced against the Jew as a fellow mortal. The Jews, as a nation, as a sociopolitical group, paid in full the terrible price of rejecting the Prince of Peace. Long since they ceased to be the spiritual torchbearers of divine truth to the races of mankind, but this constitutes no valid reason why the individual descendants of these long-ago Jews should be made to suffer the persecutions which have been visited upon them by intolerant, unworthy, and bigoted professed followers of Jesus of Nazareth, who was, himself, a Jew by natural birth.

175:2.2 (1909.2) Many times has this unreasoning and un-Christlike hatred and persecution of modern Jews terminated in the suffering and death of some innocent and unoffending Jewish individual whose very ancestors, in the times of Jesus, heartily accepted his gospel and presently died unflinchingly for that truth which they so wholeheartedly believed. What a shudder of horror passes over the onlooking celestial beings as they behold the professed followers of Jesus indulge themselves in persecuting, harassing, and even murdering the later-day descendants of Peter, Philip, Matthew, and others of the Palestinian Jews who so gloriously yielded up their lives as the first martyrs of the gospel of the heavenly kingdom!

175:2.3 (1909.3) How cruel and unreasoning to compel innocent children to suffer for the sins of their progenitors, misdeeds of which they are wholly ignorant, and for which they could in no way be responsible! And to do such wicked deeds in the name of one who taught his disciples to love even their enemies! It has become necessary, in this recital of the life of Jesus, to portray the manner in which certain of his fellow Jews rejected him and conspired to bring about his ignominious death; but we would warn all who read this narrative that the presentation of such a historical recital in no way justifies the unjust hatred, nor condones the unfair attitude of mind, which so many professed Christians have maintained toward individual Jews for many centuries. Kingdom believers, those

who follow the teachings of Jesus, must cease to mistreat the individual Jew as one who is guilty of the rejection and crucifixion of Jesus. The Father and his Creator Son have never ceased to love the Jews. God is no respecter of persons, and salvation is for the Jew as well as for the gentile.

The Fateful Sanhedrin Meeting

175:3.1 (1909.4) At eight o'clock on this Tuesday evening the fateful meeting of the Sanhedrin was called to order. On many previous occasions had this supreme court of the Jewish nation informally decreed the death of Jesus. Many times had this august ruling body determined to put a stop to his work, but never before had they resolved to place him under arrest and to bring about his death at any and all costs. It was just before midnight on this Tuesday, April 4, A.D. 30, that the Sanhedrin, as then constituted, officially and unanimously voted to impose the death sentence upon both Jesus and Lazarus. This was the answer to the Master's last appeal to the rulers of the Jews which he had made in the temple only a few hours before, and it represented their reaction of bitter resentment toward Jesus' last and vigorous indictment of these same chief priests and impenitent Sadducees and Pharisees. The passing of death sentence (even before his trial) upon the Son of God was the Sanhedrin's reply to the last offer of heavenly mercy ever to be extended to the Jewish nation, as such.

175:3.2 (1910.1) From this time on the Jews were left to finish their brief and short lease of national life wholly in accordance with their purely human status among the nations of Urantia. Israel had repudiated the Son of the God who made a covenant with Abraham, and the plan to make the children of Abraham the light-bearers of truth to the world had been shattered. The divine covenant had been abrogated, and the end of the Hebrew nation drew on apace.

175:3.3 (1910.2) The officers of the

Sanhedrin were given the orders for Jesus' arrest early the next morning, but with instructions that he must not be apprehended in public. They were told to plan to take him in secret, preferably suddenly and at night. Understanding that he might not return that day (Wednesday) to teach in the temple, they instructed these officers of the Sanhedrin to "bring him before the high Jewish court sometime before midnight on Thursday."

The Situation in Jerusalem

175:4.1 (1910.3) At the conclusion of Jesus' last discourse in the temple, the apostles once more were left in confusion and consternation. Before the Master began his terrible denunciation of the Jewish rulers, Judas had returned to the temple, so that all twelve heard this latter half of Jesus' last discourse in the temple. It is unfortunate that Judas Iscariot could not have heard the first and mercy-proffering half of this farewell address. He did not hear this last offer of mercy to the Jewish rulers because he was still in conference with a certain group of Saducean relatives and friends with whom he had lunched, and with whom he was conferring as to the most fitting manner of dissociating himself from Jesus and his fellow apostles. It was while listening to the Master's final indictment of the Jewish leaders and rulers that Judas finally and fully made up his mind to forsake the gospel movement and wash his hands of the whole enterprise. Nevertheless, he left the temple in company with the twelve, went with them to Mount Olivet, where, with his fellow apostles, he listened to that fateful discourse on the destruction of Jerusalem and the end of the Jewish nation, and remained with them that Tuesday night at the new camp near Gethsemane.

175:4.2 (1910.4) The multitude who heard Jesus swing from his merciful appeal to the Jewish leaders into that sudden and scathing rebuke which bordered on ruthless denunciation, were stunned and bewildered. That night, while the Sanhedrin sat in death judgment upon Jesus, and while the Master sat with his apostles and certain of his disciples out on the Mount of Olives foretelling the death of the Jewish nation, all Jerusalem was given over to the serious and suppressed discussion of just one question: "What will they do with Jesus?"

175:4.3 (1910.5) At the home of Nicodemus more than thirty prominent Jews who were secret believers in the kingdom met and debated what course they would pursue in case an open break with the Sanhedrin should come. All present agreed that they would make open acknowledgment of their allegiance to the Master in the very hour they should hear of his arrest. And that is just what they did.

175:4.4 (1911.1) The Sadducees, who now controlled and dominated the Sanhedrin, were desirous of making away with Jesus for the following reasons:

175:4.5 (1911.2) 1. They feared that the increased popular favor with which the multitude regarded him threatened to endanger the existence of the Jewish nation by possible involvement with the Roman authorities.

175:4.6 (1911.3) 2. His zeal for temple reform struck directly at their revenues; the cleansing of the temple affected their pocketbooks.

175:4.7 (1911.4) 3. They felt themselves responsible for the preservation of social order, and they feared the consequences of the further spread of Jesus' strange and new doctrine of the brotherhood of man.

175:4.8 (1911.5) The Pharisees had different motives for wanting to see Jesus put to death. They feared him because:
175:4.9 (1911.6) 1. He was arrayed in telling opposition to their traditional hold upon the people. The Pharisees were ultraconservative, and they bitterly resented these supposedly radical attacks upon their vested prestige as religious teachers.

175:4.10 (1911.7) 2. They held that Jesus was a lawbreaker; that he had shown utter disregard for the Sabbath and numerous other legal and ceremonial requirements.

175:4.11 (1911.8) 3. They charged him with blasphemy because he alluded to God as his Father.

175:4.12 (1911.9) 4. And now were they thoroughly angry with him because of his last discourse of bitter denunciation which he had this day delivered in the temple as the concluding portion of his farewell address.

175:4.13 (1911.10) The Sanhedrin, having formally decreed the death of Jesus and having issued orders for his arrest, adjourned on this Tuesday near midnight, after appointing to meet at ten o'clock the next morning at the home of Caiaphas the high priest for the purpose of formulating the charges on which Jesus should be brought to trial.

175:4.14 (1911.11) A small group of the Sadducees had actually proposed to dispose of Jesus by assassination, but the Pharisees utterly refused to countenance such a procedure.

175:4.15 (1911.12) And this was the situation in Jerusalem and among men on this eventful day while a vast concourse of celestial beings hovered over this momentous scene on earth, anxious to do something to assist their beloved Sovereign but powerless to act because they were effectively restrained by their commanding superiors.

Paper 176

Tuesday Evening on Mount Olivet

176:0.1 (1912.1) THIS Tuesday afternoon, as Jesus and the apostles passed out of the temple on their way to the Geth-semane camp, Matthew, calling attention to the temple construction, said: "Master, observe what manner of buildings these are. See the massive stones and the beautiful adornment; can it be that these buildings are to be destroyed?" As they went on toward Olivet, Jesus said: "You see these stones and this massive temple; verily, verily, I say to you: In the days soon to come there shall not be left one stone upon another. They shall all be thrown down." These remarks depicting the destruction of the sacred temple aroused the curiosity of the apostles as they walked along behind the Master; they could conceive of no event short of the end of the world which would occasion the destruction of the temple.

176:0.2 (1912.2) In order to avoid the crowds passing along the Kidron valley toward Gethsemane, Jesus and his associates were minded to climb up the western slope of Olivet for a short distance and then follow a trail over to their private camp near Gethsemane located a short distance above the public camping ground. As they turned to leave the road leading on to Bethany, they observed the temple, glorified by the rays of the setting sun; and while they tarried on the mount, they saw the lights of the city appear and beheld the beauty of the illuminated temple; and there, under the mellow light of the full moon, Jesus and the twelve sat down. The Master talked with them, and presently Nathaniel asked this question: "Tell us, Master, how shall we know when these events are about to come to pass?"

1   The Destruction of Jerusalem

176:1.1 (1912.3) In answering Nathaniel's question, Jesus said: "Yes, I will tell you about the times when this people shall have filled up the cup of their iniquity; when justice shall swiftly descend upon this city of our fathers. I am about to leave you; I go to the Father. After I leave you, take heed that no man deceive you, for many will come as deliverers and will lead many astray. When you hear of wars and rumors of wars, be not troubled, for though all these things will happen, the end of Jerusalem is not yet at hand. You should not be perturbed by famines or earthquakes; neither should you be concerned when you are delivered up to the civil authorities and are persecuted for the sake of the gospel. You will be thrown out of the synagogue and put in prison for my sake, and some of you will be killed. When you are brought up before governors and rulers, it shall be for a testimony of your faith and to show your steadfastness in the gospel of the kingdom. And when you stand before judges, be not anxious beforehand as to what you should say, for the spirit will teach you in that very hour what you should answer your adversaries. In these days of travail, even your own kinsfolk, under the leadership of those who have rejected the Son of Man, will deliver you up to prison and death. For a time you may be hated by all men for my sake, but even in these persecutions I will not forsake you; my spirit will not desert you. Be patient! doubt not that this gospel of the kingdom will triumph over all enemies and, eventually, be proclaimed to all nations."

176:1.2 (1913.1) Jesus paused while he looked down upon the city. The Master realized that the rejection of the spiritual concept of the Messiah, the determination to cling persistently and blindly to the material mission of the expected deliverer, would presently bring the Jews in direct conflict with the powerful Roman armies, and that such a contest could only result in the final and complete overthrow of the Jewish nation. When his people rejected his spiritual bestowal and refused to receive the light of heaven as it so mercifully shone upon them, they thereby sealed their doom as an independent people with a special spiritual mission on earth. Even the Jewish leaders subsequently recognized that it was this secular idea of the Messiah which directly led to the turbulence which eventually brought about their destruction.

176:1.3 (1913.2) Since Jerusalem was to become the cradle of the early gospel movement, Jesus did not want its teach-

ers and preachers to perish in the terrible overthrow of the Jewish people in connection with the destruction of Jerusalem; wherefore did he give these instructions to his followers. Jesus was much concerned lest some of his disciples become involved in these soon-coming revolts and so perish in the downfall of Jerusalem.

176:1.4 (1913.3) Then Andrew inquired: "But, Master, if the Holy City and the temple are to be destroyed, and if you are not here to direct us, when should we forsake Jerusalem?" Said Jesus: "You may remain in the city after I have gone, even through these times of travail and bitter persecution, but when you finally see Jerusalem being encompassed by the Roman armies after the revolt of the false prophets, then will you know that her desolation is at hand; then must you flee to the mountains. Let none who are in the city and around about tarry to save aught, neither let those who are outside dare to enter therein. There will be great tribulation, for these will be the days of gentile vengeance. And after you have deserted the city, this disobedient people will fall by the edge of the sword and will be led captive into all nations; and so shall Jerusalem be trodden down by the gentiles. In the meantime, I warn you, be not deceived. If any man comes to you, saying, 'Behold, here is the Deliverer,' or 'Behold, there is he,' believe it not, for many false teachers will arise and many will be led astray; but you should not be deceived, for I have told you all this beforehand."

176:1.5 (1913.4) The apostles sat in silence in the moonlight for a considerable time while these astounding predictions of the Master sank into their bewildered minds. And it was in conformity with this very warning that practically the entire group of believers and disciples fled from Jerusalem upon the first appearance of the Roman troops, finding a safe shelter in Pella to the north.

176:1.6 (1913.5) Even after this explicit warning, many of Jesus' followers interpreted these predictions as referring to the changes which would obviously occur in Jerusalem when the reappearing of the Messiah would result in the establishment of the New Jerusalem and in the enlargement of the city to become the world's capital. In their minds these Jews were determined to connect the destruction of the temple with the "end of the world." They believed this New Jerusalem would fill all Palestine; that the end of the world would be followed by the immediate appearance of the "new heavens and the new earth." And so it was not strange that Peter should say: "Master, we know that all things will pass away when the new heavens and the new earth appear, but how shall we know when you will return to bring all this about?"

176:1.7 (1914.1) When Jesus heard this, he was thoughtful for some time and then said: "You ever err since you always try to attach the new teaching to the old; you are determined to misunderstand all my teaching; you insist on interpreting the gospel in accordance with your established beliefs. Nevertheless, I will try to enlighten you."

2   The Master's Second Coming

176:2.1 (1914.2) On several occasions Jesus had made statements which led his hearers to infer that, while he intended presently to leave this world, he would most certainly return to consummate the work of the heavenly kingdom. As the conviction grew on his followers that he was going to leave them, and after he had departed from this world, it was only natural for all believers to lay fast hold upon these promises to return. The doctrine of the second coming of Christ thus became early incorporated into the teachings of the Christians, and almost every subsequent generation of disciples has devoutly believed this truth and has confidently looked forward to his sometime coming.

176:2.2 (1914.3) If they were to part with their Master and Teacher, how much more did these first disciples and the apostles grasp at this promise to return, and they lost no time in associating the predicted destruction of Jerusalem with this promised second coming. And they continued thus to interpret his words notwithstanding that, throughout this evening of instruction on Mount Olivet, the Master took particular pains to prevent just such a mistake.

176:2.3 (1914.4) In further answer to Peter's question, Jesus said: "Why do you still look for the Son of Man to sit upon the throne of David and expect that the material dreams of the Jews will be fulfilled? Have I not told you all these years that my kingdom is not of this world? The things which you now look down upon are coming to an end, but this will be a new beginning out of which the gospel of the kingdom will go to all the world and this salvation will spread to all peoples. And when the kingdom shall have come to its full fruition, be assured that the Father in heaven will not fail to visit you with an enlarged revelation of truth and an enhanced demonstration of righteousness, even as he has already bestowed upon this world him who became the prince of darkness, and then Adam, who was followed by Melchizedek, and in these days, the Son of Man. And so will my Father continue to manifest his mercy and show forth his love, even to this dark and evil world. So also will I, after my Father has invested me with all power and authority, continue to follow your fortunes and to guide in the affairs of the kingdom by the presence of my spirit, who shall shortly be poured out upon all flesh. Even though I shall thus be present with you in spirit, I also promise that I will sometime return to this world, where I have lived this life in the flesh and achieved the experience of simultaneously revealing God to man and leading man to God. Very soon must I leave you and take up the work the Father has intrusted to my hands, but be of good courage, for I will sometime return. In the meantime, my Spirit of the Truth of a universe shall comfort and guide you.

176:2.4 (1915.1) "You behold me now in weakness and in the flesh, but when I return, it shall be with power and in the spirit. The eye of flesh beholds the Son of Man in the flesh, but only the eye of the spirit will behold the Son of Man glorified by the Father and appearing on earth in his own name.

176:2.5 (1915.2) "But the times of the reappearing of the Son of Man are known only in the councils of Paradise; not even the angels of heaven know when this will occur. However, you should understand that, when this gospel of the kingdom shall have been proclaimed to all the world for the salvation of all peoples, and when the fullness of the age has come to pass, the Father will send you another dispensational bestowal, or else the Son of Man will return to adjudge the age.

176:2.6 (1915.3) "And now concerning the travail of Jerusalem, about which I have spoken to you, even this generation will not pass away until my words are fulfilled; but concerning the times of the coming again of the Son of Man, no one in heaven or on earth may presume to speak. But you should be wise regarding the ripening of an age; you should be alert to discern the signs of the times. You know when the fig tree shows its tender branches and puts forth its leaves that summer is near. Likewise, when the world has passed through the long winter of material-mindedness and you discern the coming of the spiritual springtime of a new dispensation, should you know that the summertime of a new visitation draws near.

176:2.7 (1915.4) "But what is the significance of this teaching having to do with the coming of the Sons of God? Do you not perceive that, when each of you is called to lay down his life struggle and pass through the portal of death, you stand in the immediate presence of judgment, and that you are face to face with the facts of a new dispensation of service in the eternal plan of the infinite Father? What the whole world must face as a literal fact at the end of an age, you, as individuals, must each most certainly face as a personal experience when you reach the end of your natural life and thereby pass on to be confronted with the conditions and demands inherent in the next revelation of the eternal progression of the Father's kingdom."

176:2.8 (1915.5) Of all the discourses which the Master gave his apostles, none ever became so confused in their minds as this one, given this Tuesday evening on the Mount of Olives, regarding the two-fold subject of the destruction of Jerusalem and his own second coming. There was, therefore, little agreement between the subsequent written accounts based on the memories of what the Master said on this extraordinary occasion. Consequently, when the records were left blank concerning much that was said that Tuesday evening, there grew up many traditions; and very early in the second century a Jewish apocalyptic about the Messiah written by one Selta, who was attached to the court of the Emperor Caligula, was bodily copied into the Matthew Gospel and subsequently added (in part) to the Mark and Luke records. It was in these writings of Selta that the parable of the ten virgins appeared. No part of the gospel record ever suffered such confusing misconstruction as this evening's teaching. But the Apostle John never became thus confused.

176:2.9 (1915.6) As these thirteen men resumed their journey toward the camp, they were speechless and under great emotional tension. Judas had finally confirmed his decision to abandon his associates. It was a late hour when David Zebedee, John Mark, and a number of the leading disciples welcomed Jesus and the twelve to the new camp, but the apostles did not want to sleep; they wanted to know more about the destruction of Jerusalem, the Master's departure, and the end of the world.

3   Later Discussion at the Camp

1.   176:3.1 (1916.1) As they gathered about the campfire, some twenty of them,

Thomas asked: "Since you are to return to finish the work of the kingdom, what should be our attitude while you are away on the Father's business?" As Jesus looked them over by the firelight, he answered:

176:3.2 (1916.2) "And even you, Thomas, fail to comprehend what I have been saying. Have I not all this time taught you that your connection with the kingdom is spiritual and individual, wholly a matter of personal experience in the spirit by the faith-realization that you are a son of God? What more shall I say? The downfall of nations, the crash of empires, the destruction of the unbelieving Jews, the end of an age, even the end of the world, what have these things to do with one who believes this gospel, and who has hid his life in the surety of the eternal kingdom? You who are God-knowing and gospel-believing have already received the assurances of eternal life. Since your lives have been lived in the spirit and for the Father, nothing can be of serious concern to you. Kingdom builders, the accredited citizens of the heavenly worlds, are not to be disturbed by temporal upheavals or perturbed by terrestrial cataclysms. What does it matter to you who believe this gospel of the kingdom if nations overturn, the age ends, or all things visible crash, since you know that your life is the gift of the Son, and that it is eternally secure in the Father? Having lived the temporal life by faith and having yielded the fruits of the spirit as the righteousness of loving service for your fellows, you can confidently look forward to the next step in the eternal career with the same survival faith that has carried you through your first and earthly adventure in sonship with God.

176:3.3 (1916.3) "Each generation of believers should carry on their work, in view of the possible return of the Son of Man, exactly as each individual believer carries forward his lifework in view of inevitable and ever-impending natural death. When you have by faith once established yourself as a son of God, nothing else matters as regards the surety of survival. But make no mistake! this survival faith is a living faith, and it increasingly manifests the fruits of that divine spirit which first inspired it in the human heart. That you have once accepted sonship in the heavenly kingdom will not save you in the face of the knowing and persistent rejection of those truths which have to do with the progressive spiritual fruit-bearing of the sons of God in the flesh. You who have been with me in the Father's business on earth can even now desert the kingdom if you find that you love not the way of the Father's service for mankind.

176:3.4 (1916.4) "As individuals, and as a generation of believers, hear me while I speak a parable: There was a certain great man who, before starting out on a long journey to another country, called all his trusted servants before him and delivered into their hands all his goods. To one he gave five talents, to another two, and to another one. And so on down through the entire group of honored stewards, to each he intrusted his goods according to their several abilities; and then he set out on his journey. When their lord had departed, his servants set themselves at work to gain profits from the wealth intrusted to them. Immediately he who had received five talents began to trade with them and very soon had made a profit of another five talents. In like manner he who had received two talents soon had gained two more. And so did all of these servants make gains for their master except him who received but one talent. He went away by himself and dug a hole in the earth where he hid his lord's money. Presently the lord of those servants unexpectedly returned and called upon his stewards for a reckoning. And when they had all been called before their master, he who had received the five talents came forward with the money which had been intrusted to him and brought five additional talents, saying, 'Lord, you gave me five talents to invest, and I am glad to present five other talents as my gain.' And then his lord said to him: 'Well done, good and faithful servant, you have been faithful over a few things; I will now set you as steward over many; enter forthwith into the joy of your lord.' And then he who had received the two talents came forward, saying: 'Lord, you delivered into my hands two talents; behold, I have gained these other two talents.' And his lord then said to him: 'Well done, good and faithful steward; you also have been faithful over a few things, and I will now set you over many; enter you into the joy of your lord.' And then there came to the accounting he who had received the one talent. This servant came forward, saying, 'Lord, I knew you and realized that you were a shrewd man in that you expected gains where you had not personally labored; therefore was I afraid to risk aught of that which was intrusted to me. I safely hid your talent in the earth; here it is; you now have what belongs to you.' But his lord answered: 'You are an indolent and slothful steward. By your own words you confess that you knew I would require of you an accounting with reasonable profit, such as your diligent fellow servants have this day rendered. Knowing this, you ought, therefore, to have at least put my money into the hands of the bankers that on my return I might have received my own with interest.' And then to the chief steward this lord said: 'Take away this one talent from this unprofitable servant and give it to him who has the ten talents.' *

176:3.5 (1917.1) "To every one who has, more shall be given, and he shall have abundance; but from him who has not, even that which he has shall be taken away. You cannot stand still in the affairs of the eternal kingdom. My Father requires all his children to grow in grace and in a knowledge of the truth. You who know these truths must yield the increase of the fruits of the spirit and manifest a growing devotion to the unselfish service of your fellow servants. And remember that, inasmuch as you minister to one of the least of my brethren, you have done this service to me.

176:3.6 (1917.2) "And so should you go about the work of the Father's business, now and henceforth, even forevermore. Carry on until I come. In faithfulness do that which is intrusted to you, and thereby shall you be ready for the reckoning call of death. And having thus lived for the glory of the Father and the satisfaction of the Son, you shall enter with joy and exceed-

ingly great pleasure into the eternal service of the everlasting kingdom."

176:3.7 (1917.3) Truth is living; the Spirit of Truth is ever leading the children of light into new realms of spiritual reality and divine service. You are not given truth to crystallize into settled, safe, and honored forms. Your revelation of truth must be so enhanced by passing through your personal experience that new beauty and actual spiritual gains will be disclosed to all who behold your spiritual fruits and in consequence thereof are led to glorify the Father who is in heaven. Only those faithful servants who thus grow in the knowledge of the truth, and who thereby develop the capacity for divine appreciation of spiritual realities, can ever hope to "enter fully into the joy of their Lord." What a sorry sight for successive generations of the professed followers of Jesus to say, regarding their stewardship of divine truth: "Here, Master, is the truth you committed to us a hundred or a thousand years ago. We have lost nothing; we have faithfully preserved all you gave us; we have allowed no changes to be made in that which you taught us; here is the truth you gave us." But such a plea concerning spiritual indolence will not justify the barren steward of truth in the presence of the Master. In accordance with the truth committed to your hands will the Master of truth require a reckoning.

176:3.8 (1918.1) In the next world you will be asked to give an account of the endowments and stewardships of this world. Whether inherent talents are few or many, a just and merciful reckoning must be faced. If endowments are used only in selfish pursuits and no thought is bestowed upon the higher duty of obtaining increased yield of the fruits of the spirit, as they are manifested in the ever-expanding service of men and the worship of God, such selfish stewards must accept the consequences of their deliberate choosing.

176:3.9 (1918.2) And how much like all selfish mortals was this unfaithful servant with the one talent in that he blamed his slothfulness directly upon his lord. How prone is man, when he is confronted with the failures of his own making, to put the blame upon others, oftentimes upon those who least deserve it!

176:3.10 (1918.3) Said Jesus that night as they went to their rest: "Freely have you received; therefore freely should you give of the truth of heaven, and in the giving will this truth multiply and show forth the increasing light of saving grace, even as you minister it."

4   *The Return of Michael*

176:4.1 (1918.4) Of all the Master's teachings no one phase has been so misunderstood as his promise sometime to come back in person to this world. It is not strange that Michael should be interested in sometime returning to the planet whereon he experienced his seventh and last bestowal, as a mortal of the realm. It is only natural to believe that Jesus of Nazareth, now sovereign ruler of a vast universe, would be interested in coming back, not only once but even many times, to the world whereon he lived such a unique life and finally won for himself the Father's unlimited bestowal of universe power and authority. Urantia will eternally be one of the seven nativity spheres of Michael in the winning of universe sovereignty. *

176:4.2 (1918.5) Jesus did, on numerous occasions and to many individuals, declare his intention of returning to this world. As his followers awakened to the fact that their Master was not going to function as a temporal deliverer, and as they listened to his predictions of the overthrow of Jerusalem and the downfall of the Jewish nation, they most naturally began to associate his promised return with these catastrophic events. But when the Roman armies leveled the walls of Jerusalem, destroyed the temple, and dispersed the Judean Jews, and still the Master did not reveal himself in power and glory, his followers began the formulation of that belief which eventually associated the second

coming of Christ with the end of the age, even with the end of the world.

176:4.3 (1918.6) Jesus promised to do two things after he had ascended to the Father, and after all power in heaven and on earth had been placed in his hands. He promised, first, to send into the world, and in his stead, another teacher, the Spirit of Truth; and this he did on the day of Pentecost. Second, he most certainly promised his followers that he would sometime personally return to this world. But he did not say how, where, or when he would revisit this planet of his bestowal experience in the flesh. On one occasion he intimated that, whereas the eye of flesh had beheld him when he lived here in the flesh, on his return (at least on one of his possible visits) he would be discerned only by the eye of spiritual faith.

176:4.4 (1919.1) Many of us are inclined to believe that Jesus will return to Urantia many times during the ages to come. We do not have his specific promise to make these plural visits, but it seems most probable that he who carries among his universe titles that of Planetary Prince of Urantia will many times visit the world whose conquest conferred such a unique title upon him.

176:4.5 (1919.2) We most positively believe that Michael will again come in person to Urantia, but we have not the slightest idea as to when or in what manner he may choose to come. Will his second advent on earth be timed to occur in connection with the terminal judgment of this present age, either with or without the associated appearance of a Magisterial Son? Will he come in connection with the termination of some subsequent Urantian age? Will he come unannounced and as an isolated event? We do not know. Only one thing we are certain of, that is, when he does return, all the world will likely know about it, for he must come as the supreme ruler of a universe and not as the obscure babe of Bethlehem. But if every eye is to behold him, and if only spiritual eyes are to discern his presence, then must his advent be long deferred.

176:4.6 (1919.3) You would do well, therefore, to disassociate the Master's personal return to earth from any and all set events or settled epochs. We are sure of only one thing: He has promised to come back. We have no idea as to when he will fulfill this promise or in what connection. As far as we know, he may appear on earth any day, and he may not come until age after age has passed and been duly adjudicated by his associated Sons of the Paradise corps.

176:4.7 (1919.4) The second advent of Michael on earth is an event of tremendous sentimental value to both midwayers and humans; but otherwise it is of no immediate moment to midwayers and of no more practical importance to human beings than the common event of natural death, which so suddenly precipitates mortal man into the immediate grasp of that succession of universe events which leads directly to the presence of this same Jesus, the sovereign ruler of our universe. The children of light are all destined to see him, and it is of no serious concern whether we go to him or whether he should chance first to come to us. Be you therefore ever ready to welcome him on earth as he stands ready to welcome you in heaven. We confidently look for his glorious appearing, even for repeated comings, but we are wholly ignorant as to how, when, or in what connection he is destined to appear.

Paper 177

Wednesday, the Rest Day

177:0.1 (1920.1) WHEN the work of teaching the people did not press them, it was the custom of Jesus and his apostles to rest from their labors each Wednesday. On this particular Wednesday they ate breakfast somewhat later than usual, and the camp was pervaded by an ominous silence; little was said during the first half of this morning meal. At last Jesus spoke: "I desire that you rest today. Take time to think over all that has happened since we came to Jerusalem and meditate on what is just ahead, of which I have plainly told you. Make sure that the truth abides in your lives, and that you daily grow in grace."

177:0.2 (1920.2) After breakfast the Master informed Andrew that he intended to be absent for the day and suggested that the apostles be permitted to spend the time in accordance with their own choosing, except that under no circumstances should they go within the gates of Jerusalem.

177:0.3 (1920.3) When Jesus made ready to go into the hills alone, David Zebedee accosted him, saying: "You well know, Master, that the Pharisees and rulers seek to destroy you, and yet you make ready to go alone into the hills. To do this is folly; I will therefore send three men with you well prepared to see that no harm befalls you." Jesus looked over the three well-armed and stalwart Galileans and said to David: "You mean well, but you err in that you fail to understand that the Son of Man needs no one to defend him. No man will lay hands on me until that hour when I am ready to lay down my life in conformity to my Father's will. These men may not accompany me. I desire to go alone, that I may commune with the Father."

177:0.4 (1920.4) Upon hearing these words, David and his armed guards withdrew; but as Jesus started off alone, John Mark came forward with a small basket containing food and water and suggested that, if he intended to be away all day, he might find himself hungry. The Master smiled on John and reached down to take the basket.

1. One Day Alone with God

177:1.1 (1920.5) As Jesus was about to take the lunch basket from John's hand, the young man ventured to say: "But, Master, you may set the basket down while you turn aside to pray and go on without it. Besides, if I should go along to carry the lunch, you would be more free to worship, and I will surely be silent. I will ask no questions and will stay by the basket when you go apart by yourself to pray."

177:1.2 (1920.6) While making this speech, the temerity of which astonished some of the near-by listeners, John had made bold to hold on to the basket. There they stood, both John and Jesus holding the basket. Presently the Master let go and, looking down on the lad, said: "Since with all your heart you crave to go with me, it shall not be denied you. We will go off by ourselves and have a good visit. You may ask me any question that arises in your heart, and we will comfort and console each other. You may start out carrying the lunch, and when you grow weary, I will help you. Follow on with me."

177:1.3 (1921.1) Jesus did not return to the camp that evening until after sunset. The Master spent this last day of quiet on earth visiting with this truth-hungry youth and talking with his Paradise Father. This event has become known on high as "the day which a young man spent with God in the hills." Forever this occasion exemplifies the willingness of the Creator to fellowship the creature. Even a youth, if the desire of the heart is really supreme, can command the attention and enjoy the loving companionship of the God of a universe, actually experience the unforgettable ecstasy of being alone with God in the hills, and for a whole day. And such was the unique experience of John Mark on this Wednesday in the hills of Judea.

177:1.4 (1921.2) Jesus visited much with John, talking freely about the affairs of this world and the next. John told Jesus how much he regretted that he had not been old enough to be one of the apostles and expressed his great appreciation that he had been permitted to follow on with them since their first preaching at the Jordan ford near Jericho, except for the trip to Phoenicia. Jesus warned the lad not to become discouraged by impending events and assured him he would live to become a mighty messenger of the kingdom.

177:1.5 (1921.3) John Mark was thrilled by the memory of this day with Jesus in the hills, but he never forgot the Master's final admonition, spoken just as they were about to return to the Gethsemane camp, when he said: "Well, John, we have had a good visit, a real day of rest, but see to it that you tell no man the things which I told you." And John Mark never did reveal anything that transpired on this day which he spent with Jesus in the hills.

177:1.6 (1921.4) Throughout the few remaining hours of Jesus' earth life John Mark never permitted the Master for long to get out of his sight. Always was the lad in hiding near by; he slept only when Jesus slept.

2   *Early Home Life*

177:2.1 (1921.5) In the course of this day's visiting with John Mark, Jesus spent considerable time comparing their early childhood and later boyhood experiences. Although John's parents possessed more of this world's goods than had Jesus' parents, there was much experience in their boyhood which was very similar. Jesus said many things which helped John better to understand his parents and other members of his family. When the lad asked the Master how he could know that he would turn out to be a "mighty messenger of the kingdom," Jesus said:

177:2.2 (1921.6) "I know you will prove loyal to the gospel of the kingdom because I can depend upon your present faith and love when these qualities are grounded upon such an early training as has been your portion at home. You are the product of a home where the parents bear each other a sincere affection, and therefore you have not been over-loved so as injuriously to exalt your concept of self-importance. Neither has your personality suffered distortion in consequence of your parents' loveless maneuvering for your confidence and loyalty, the one against the other. You have enjoyed that parental love which insures laudable self-confidence and which fosters normal feelings of security. But you have also been fortunate in that your parents possessed wisdom as well as love; and it was wisdom which led them to withhold most forms of indulgence and many luxuries which wealth can buy while they sent you to the synagogue school along with your neighborhood playfellows, and they also encouraged you to learn how to live in this world by permitting you to have original experience. You came over to the Jordan, where we preached and John's disciples baptized, with your young friend Amos. Both of you desired to go with us. When you returned to Jerusalem, your parents consented; Amos's parents refused; they loved their son so much that they denied him the blessed experience which you have had, even such as you this day enjoy. By running away from home, Amos could have joined us, but in so doing he would have wounded love and sacrificed loyalty. Even if such a course had been wise, it would have been a terrible price to pay for experience, independence, and liberty. Wise parents, such as yours, see to it that their children do not have to wound love or stifle loyalty in order to develop independence and enjoy invigorating liberty when they have grown up to your age.

177:2.3 (1922.1) "Love, John, is the supreme reality of the universe when bestowed by all-wise beings, but it is a dangerous and oftentimes semi-selfish trait as it is manifested in the experience of mortal parents. When you get married and have children of your own to rear, make sure that your love is admonished by wisdom and guided by intelligence.

177:2.4 (1922.2) "Your young friend Amos believes this gospel of the kingdom just as much as you, but I cannot fully depend upon him; I am not certain about what he will do in the years to come. His early home life was not such as would produce a wholly dependable person. Amos is too much like one of the apostles who failed to enjoy a normal, loving, and wise home training. Your whole afterlife will be more happy and dependable because you spent your first eight years in a normal and well-regulated home. You possess a strong and well-knit character because you grew up in a home where love prevailed and wisdom reigned. Such a childhood training produces a type of loyalty which assures me that you will go through with the course you have begun."

177:2.5 (1922.3) For more than an hour Jesus and John continued this discussion of home life. The Master went on to explain to John how a child is wholly dependent on his parents and the associated home life for all his early concepts of everything intellectual, social, moral, and even spiritual since the family represents to the young child all that he can first know of either human or divine relationships. The child must derive his first impressions of the universe from the mother's care; he is wholly dependent on the earthly father for his first ideas of the heavenly Father. The child's subsequent life is made happy or unhappy, easy or difficult, in accordance with his early mental and emotional life, conditioned by these social and spiritual relationships of the home. A human being's entire afterlife is enormously influenced by what happens during the first few years of existence.

177:2.6 (1922.4) It is our sincere belief that the gospel of Jesus' teaching, founded as it is on the father-child relationship, can hardly enjoy a world-wide acceptance until such a time as the home life of the modern civilized peoples embraces more of love and more of wisdom. Notwithstanding that parents of the twentieth century possess great knowledge and increased truth for improving the home and ennobling the home life, it remains a fact that very few modern homes are such good places in which to nurture boys and girls as Jesus' home in Galilee and John Mark's home in Judea, albeit the acceptance of Jesus' gospel will result in the immediate improvement of home life. The love life of a wise home and the loyal devotion of true religion exert a profound reciprocal influence upon each other. Such a home life enhances religion, and genuine religion always glorifies the home.

177:2.7 (1923.1) It is true that many of the objectionable stunting influences and other cramping features of these olden Jewish homes have been virtually eliminated from many of the better-regulated modern homes. There is, indeed, more spontaneous freedom and far more personal liberty, but this liberty is not restrained by love, motivated by loyalty, nor directed by the intelligent discipline of wisdom. As long as we teach the child to pray, "Our Father who is in heaven," a tremendous responsibility rests upon all earthly fathers so to live and order their homes that the word father becomes worthily enshrined in the minds and hearts of all growing children.

3   The Day at Camp

177:3.1 (1923.2) The apostles spent most of this day walking about on Mount Olivet and visiting with the disciples who were encamped with them, but early in the afternoon they became very desirous of seeing Jesus return. As the day wore on, they grew increasingly anxious about his safety; they felt inexpressibly lonely without him. There was much debating throughout the day as to whether the Master should have been allowed to go off by himself in the hills, accompanied only by an errand boy. Though no man openly so expressed his thoughts, there was not one of them, save Judas Iscariot, who did not wish himself in John Mark's place.

177:3.2 (1923.3) It was about midafternoon when Nathaniel made his speech on "Supreme Desire" to about half a dozen of the apostles and as many disciples, the ending of which was: "What is wrong with most of us is that we are only halfhearted. We fail to love the Master as he loves us. If we had all wanted to go with him as much as John Mark did, he would surely have taken us all. We stood by while the lad approached the Master and offered him the basket, but when the Master took hold

of it, the lad would not let go. And so the Master left us here while he went off to the hills with basket, boy, and all."

177:3.3 (1923.4) About four o'clock, runners came to David Zebedee bringing him word from his mother at Bethsaida and from Jesus' mother. Several days previously David had made up his mind that the chief priests and rulers were going to kill Jesus. David knew they were determined to destroy the Master, and he was about convinced that Jesus would neither exert his divine power to save himself nor permit his followers to employ force in his defense. Having reached these conclusions, he lost no time in dispatching a messenger to his mother, urging her to come at once to Jerusalem and to bring Mary the mother of Jesus and every member of his family.

177:3.4 (1923.5) David's mother did as her son requested, and now the runners came back to David bringing the word that his mother and Jesus' entire family were on the way to Jerusalem and should arrive sometime late on the following day or very early the next morning. Since David did this on his own initiative, he thought it wise to keep the matter to himself. He told no one, therefore, that Jesus' family was on the way to Jerusalem.

177:3.5 (1924.1) Shortly after noon, more than twenty of the Greeks who had met with Jesus and the twelve at the home of Joseph of Arimathea arrived at the camp, and Peter and John spent several hours in conference with them. These Greeks, at least some of them, were well advanced in the knowledge of the kingdom, having been instructed by Rodan at Alexandria.

177:3.6 (1924.2) That evening, after returning to the camp, Jesus visited with the Greeks, and had it not been that such a course would have greatly disturbed his apostles and many of his leading disciples, he would have ordained these twenty Greeks, even as he had the seventy.

177:3.7 (1924.3) While all of this was going on at the camp, in Jerusalem the chief priests and elders were amazed that

Jesus did not return to address the multitudes. True, the day before, when he left the temple, he had said, "I leave your house to you desolate." But they could not understand why he would be willing to forgo the great advantage which he had built up in the friendly attitude of the crowds. While they feared he would stir up a tumult among the people, the Master's last words to the multitude had been an exhortation to conform in every reasonable manner with the authority of those "who sit in Moses' seat." But it was a busy day in the city as they simultaneously prepared for the Passover and perfected their plans for destroying Jesus. *

177:3.8 (1924.4) Not many people came to the camp, for its establishment had been kept a well-guarded secret by all who knew that Jesus was expecting to stay there in place of going out to Bethany every night.

4 Judas and the Chief Priests

177:4.1 (1924.5) Shortly after Jesus and John Mark left the camp, Judas Iscariot disappeared from among his brethren, not returning until late in the afternoon. This confused and discontented apostle, notwithstanding his Master's specific request to refrain from entering Jerusalem, went in haste to keep his appointment with Jesus' enemies at the home of Caiaphas the high priest. This was an informal meeting of the Sanhedrin and had been appointed for shortly after ten o'clock that morning. This meeting was called to discuss the nature of the charges which should be lodged against Jesus and to decide upon the procedure to be employed in bringing him before the Roman authorities for the purpose of securing the necessary civil confirmation of the death sentence which they had already passed upon him. *

177:4.2 (1924.6) On the preceding day Judas had disclosed to some of his relatives and to certain Sadducean friends of his father's family that he had reached the

conclusion that, while Jesus was a well-meaning dreamer and idealist, he was not the expected deliverer of Israel. Judas stated that he would very much like to find some way of withdrawing gracefully from the whole movement. His friends flatteringly assured him that his withdrawal would be hailed by the Jewish rulers as a great event, and that nothing would be too good for him. They led him to believe that he would forthwith receive high honors from the Sanhedrin, and that he would at last be in a position to erase the stigma of his well-meant but "unfortunate association with untaught Galileans."

177:4.3 (1924.7) Judas could not quite believe that the mighty works of the Master had been wrought by the power of the prince of devils, but he was now fully convinced that Jesus would not exert his power in self-aggrandizement; he was at last convinced that Jesus would allow himself to be destroyed by the Jewish rulers, and he could not endure the humiliating thought of being identified with a movement of defeat. He refused to entertain the idea of apparent failure. He thoroughly understood the sturdy character of his Master and the keenness of that majestic and merciful mind, yet he derived pleasure from even the partial entertainment of the suggestion of one of his relatives that Jesus, while he was a well-meaning fanatic, was probably not really sound of mind; that he had always appeared to be a strange and misunderstood person.

177:4.4 (1925.1) And now, as never before, Judas found himself becoming strangely resentful that Jesus had never assigned him a position of greater honor. All along he had appreciated the honor of being the apostolic treasurer, but now he began to feel that he was not appreciated; that his abilities were unrecognized. He was suddenly overcome with indignation that Peter, James, and John should have been honored with close association with Jesus, and at this time, when he was on the way to the high priest's home, he was bent on getting even with Peter, James, and John more than he was concerned with any thought of betraying Jesus. But over and above all, just then, a new and dominating thought began to occupy the forefront of his conscious mind: He had set out to get honor for himself, and if this could be secured simultaneously with getting even with those who had contributed to the greatest disappointment of his life, all the better. He was seized with a terrible conspiracy of confusion, pride, desperation, and determination. And so it must be plain that it was not for money that Judas was then on his way to the home of Caiaphas to arrange for the betrayal of Jesus.

177:4.5 (1925.2) As Judas approached the home of Caiaphas, he arrived at the final decision to abandon Jesus and his fellow apostles; and having thus made up his mind to desert the cause of the kingdom of heaven, he was determined to secure for himself as much as possible of that honor and glory which he had thought would sometime be his when he first identified himself with Jesus and the new gospel of the kingdom. All the apostles once shared this ambition with Judas, but as time passed they learned to admire truth and to love Jesus, at least more than did Judas.

177:4.6 (1925.3) The traitor was presented to Caiaphas and the Jewish rulers by his cousin, who explained that Judas, having discovered his mistake in allowing himself to be misled by the subtle teaching of Jesus, had arrived at the place where he wished to make public and formal renunciation of his association with the Galilean and at the same time to ask for reinstatement in the confidence and fellowship of his Judean brethren. This spokesman for Judas went on to explain that Judas recognized it would be best for the peace of Israel if Jesus should be taken into custody, and that, as evidence of his sorrow in having participated in such a movement of error and as proof of his sincerity in now returning to the teachings of Moses, he had come to offer himself to the Sanhedrin as one who could so arrange with the captain holding the orders for Jesus' arrest that he could be taken into custody quietly, thus avoiding any danger of stirring up the multitudes or the necessity of postponing his arrest until after the Passover.

177:4.7 (1925.4) When his cousin had finished speaking, he presented Judas, who, stepping forward near the high priest, said: "All that my cousin has promised, I will do, but what are you willing to give me for this service?" Judas did not seem to discern the look of disdain and even disgust that came over the face of the hardhearted and vainglorious Caiaphas; his heart was too much set on self-glory and the craving for the satisfaction of self-exaltation.

177:4.8 (1926.1) And then Caiaphas looked down upon the betrayer while he said: "Judas, you go to the captain of the guard and arrange with that officer to bring your Master to us either tonight or tomorrow night, and when he has been delivered by you into our hands, you shall receive your reward for this service." When Judas heard this, he went forth from the presence of the chief priests and rulers and took counsel with the captain of the temple guards as to the manner in which Jesus was to be apprehended. Judas knew that Jesus was then absent from the camp and had no idea when he would return that evening, and so they agreed among themselves to arrest Jesus the next evening (Thursday) after the people of Jerusalem and all of the visiting pilgrims had retired for the night.

177:4.9 (1926.2) Judas returned to his associates at the camp intoxicated with thoughts of grandeur and glory such as he had not had for many a day. He had enlisted with Jesus hoping some day to become a great man in the new kingdom. He at last realized that there was to be no new kingdom such as he had anticipated. But he rejoiced in being so sagacious as to trade off his disappointment in failing to achieve glory in an anticipated new kingdom for the immediate realization of honor and reward in the old order, which he now believed would survive, and which he was certain would destroy Jesus and all that he stood for. In its last motive of conscious intention, Judas's betrayal of Jesus was the cowardly act of a selfish deserter whose only thought was his own safety and glorification, no matter what might be the results of his conduct upon his Master and upon his former associates.

177:4.10 (1926.3) But it was ever just that way. Judas had long been engaged in this deliberate, persistent, selfish, and vengeful consciousness of progressively building up in his mind, and entertaining in his heart, these hateful and evil desires of revenge and disloyalty. Jesus loved and trusted Judas even as he loved and trusted the other apostles, but Judas failed to develop loyal trust and to experience wholehearted love in return. And how dangerous ambition can become when it is once wholly wedded to self-seeking and supremely motivated by sullen and long-suppressed vengeance! What a crushing thing is disappointment in the lives of those foolish persons who, in fastening their gaze on the shadowy and evanescent allurements of time, become blinded to the higher and more real achievements of the everlasting attainments of the eternal worlds of divine values and true spiritual realities. Judas craved worldly honor in his mind and grew to love this desire with his whole heart; the other apostles likewise craved this same worldly honor in their minds, but with their hearts they loved Jesus and were doing their best to learn to love the truths which he taught them.

177:4.11 (1926.4) Judas did not realize it at this time, but he had been a subconscious critic of Jesus ever since John the Baptist was beheaded by Herod. Deep down in his heart Judas always resented the fact that Jesus did not save John. You should not forget that Judas had been a disciple of John before he became a follower of Jesus. And all these accumulations of human resentment and bitter disappointment which Judas had laid by in his soul in habiliments of hate were now well organized in his subconscious mind and ready to spring up to engulf him when he once dared to separate himself from the supporting influence of his brethren while at the same time exposing himself to the clever insinuations and subtle ridicule of the enemies of Jesus. Every time Judas allowed his hopes to soar high and Jesus would do or say something to dash them to pieces, there was always left in Judas's heart a scar of bitter resentment; and as these scars multiplied, presently that heart, so often wounded, lost all real affection for the one who had inflicted this distasteful experience upon a well-intentioned but cowardly and self-centered personality. Judas did not realize it, but he was a coward. Accordingly was he always inclined to assign to Jesus cowardice as the motive which led him so often to refuse to grasp for power or glory when they were apparently within his easy reach. And every mortal man knows full well how love, even when once genuine, can, through disappointment, jealousy, and long-continued resentment, be eventually turned into actual hate.

177:4.12 (1927.1) At last the chief priests and elders could breathe easily for a few hours. They would not have to arrest Jesus in public, and the securing of Judas as a traitorous ally insured that Jesus would not escape from their jurisdiction as he had so many times in the past.

5 The Last Social Hour

177:5.1 (1927.2) Since it was Wednesday, this evening at the camp was a social hour. The Master endeavored to cheer his downcast apostles, but that was well-nigh impossible. They were all beginning to realize that disconcerting and crushing events were impending. They could not be cheerful, even when the Master recounted their years of eventful and loving association. Jesus made careful inquiry about the families of all of the apostles and, looking over toward David Zebedee, asked if anyone had heard recently from his mother, his youngest sister, or other members of his family. David looked down at his feet; he was afraid to answer.

177:5.2 (1927.3) This was the occasion

of Jesus' warning his followers to beware of the support of the multitude. He recounted their experiences in Galilee when time and again great throngs of people enthusiastically followed them around and then just as ardently turned against them and returned to their former ways of believing and living. And then he said: "And so you must not allow yourselves to be deceived by the great crowds who heard us in the temple, and who seemed to believe our teachings. These multitudes listen to the truth and believe it superficially with their minds, but few of them permit the word of truth to strike down into the heart with living roots. Those who know the gospel only in the mind, and who have not experienced it in the heart, cannot be depended upon for support when real trouble comes. When the rulers of the Jews reach an agreement to destroy the Son of Man, and when they strike with one accord, you will see the multitude either flee in dismay or else stand by in silent amazement while these maddened and blinded rulers lead the teachers of the gospel truth to their death. And then, when adversity and persecution descend upon you, still others who you think love the truth will be scattered, and some will renounce the gospel and desert you. Some who have been very close to us have already made up their minds to desert. You have rested today in preparation for those times which are now upon us. Watch, therefore, and pray that on the morrow you may be strengthened for the days that are just ahead." *

177:5.3 (1927.4) The atmosphere of the camp was charged with an inexplicable tension. Silent messengers came and went, communicating with only David Zebedee. Before the evening had passed, certain ones knew that Lazarus had taken hasty flight from Bethany. John Mark was ominously silent after returning to camp, notwithstanding he had spent the whole day in the Master's company. Every effort to persuade him to talk only indicated clearly that Jesus had told him not to talk.

177:5.4 (1928.1) Even the Master's good cheer and his unusual sociability frightened them. They all felt the certain drawing upon them of the terrible isolation which they realized was about to descend with crashing suddenness and inescapable terror. They vaguely sensed what was coming, and none felt prepared to face the test. The Master had been away all day; they had missed him tremendously.

177:5.5 (1928.2) This Wednesday evening was the low-tide mark of their spiritual status up to the actual hour of the Master's death. Although the next day was one more day nearer the tragic Friday, still, he was with them, and they passed through its anxious hours more gracefully.

177:5.6 (1928.3) It was just before midnight when Jesus, knowing this would be the last night he would ever sleep through with his chosen family on earth, said, as he dispersed them for the night: "Go to your sleep, my brethren, and peace be upon you till we rise on the morrow, one more day to do the Father's will and experience the joy of knowing that we are his sons."

Paper 178

Last Day at the Camp

178:0.1 (1929.1) JESUS planned to spend this Thursday, his last free day on earth as a divine Son incarnated in the flesh, with his apostles and a few loyal and devoted disciples. Soon after the breakfast hour on this beautiful morning, the Master led them to a secluded spot a short distance above their camp and there taught them many new truths. Although Jesus delivered other discourses to the apostles during the early evening hours of the day, this talk of Thursday forenoon was his farewell address to the combined camp group of apostles and chosen disciples, both Jews and gentiles. The twelve were all present save Judas. Peter and several of the apostles remarked about his absence, and some of them thought Jesus had sent him into the city to attend to some matter, probably to arrange the details of their forthcoming celebration of the Passover. Judas did not return to the camp until midafternoon, a short time before Jesus led the twelve into Jerusalem to partake of the Last Supper.

1   Discourse on Sonship and Citizenship

178:1.1 (1929.2) Jesus talked to about fifty of his trusted followers for almost two hours and answered a score of questions regarding the relation of the kingdom of heaven to the kingdoms of this world, concerning the relation of sonship with God to citizenship in earthly governments. This discourse, together with his answers to questions, may be summarized and restated in modern language as follows:

178:1.2 (1929.3) The kingdoms of this world, being material, may often find it necessary to employ physical force in the execution of their laws and for the maintenance of order. In the kingdom of heaven true believers will not resort to the employment of physical force. The kingdom of heaven, being a spiritual brotherhood of the spirit-born sons of God, may be promulgated only by the power of the spirit. This distinction of procedure refers to the relations of the kingdom of believers to the kingdoms of secular government and does not nullify the right of social groups of believers to maintain order in their ranks and administer discipline upon unruly and unworthy members.

178:1.3 (1929.4) There is nothing incompatible between sonship in the spiritual kingdom and citizenship in the secular or civil government. It is the believer's duty to render to Caesar the things which are Caesar's and to God the things which are God's. There cannot be any disagreement between these two requirements, the one being material and the other spiritual, unless it should develop that a Caesar presumes to usurp the prerogatives of God and demand that spiritual homage and supreme worship be rendered to him. In such a case you shall worship only God while you seek

to enlighten such misguided earthly rulers and in this way lead them also to the recognition of the Father in heaven. You shall not render spiritual worship to earthly rulers; neither should you employ the physical forces of earthly governments, whose rulers may sometime become believers, in the work of furthering the mission of the spiritual kingdom.

178:1.4 (1930.1) Sonship in the kingdom, from the standpoint of advancing civilization, should assist you in becoming the ideal citizens of the kingdoms of this world since brotherhood and service are the cornerstones of the gospel of the kingdom. The love call of the spiritual kingdom should prove to be the effective destroyer of the hate urge of the unbelieving and war-minded citizens of the earthly kingdoms. But these material-minded sons in darkness will never know of your spiritual light of truth unless you draw very near them with that unselfish social service which is the natural outgrowth of the bearing of the fruits of the spirit in the life experience of each individual believer.

178:1.5 (1930.2) As mortal and material men, you are indeed citizens of the earthly kingdoms, and you should be good citizens, all the better for having become reborn spirit sons of the heavenly kingdom. As faith-enlightened and spirit-liberated sons of the kingdom of heaven, you face a double responsibility of duty to man and duty to God while you voluntarily assume a third and sacred obligation: service to the brotherhood of God-knowing believers.

178:1.6 (1930.3) You may not worship your temporal rulers, and you should not employ temporal power in the furtherance of the spiritual kingdom; but you should manifest the righteous ministry of loving service to believers and unbelievers alike. In the gospel of the kingdom there resides the mighty Spirit of Truth, and presently I will pour out this same spirit upon all flesh. The fruits of the spirit, your sincere and loving service, are the mighty social lever to uplift the races of darkness, and this Spirit of Truth will become your power-multiplying fulcrum.

178:1.7 (1930.4) Display wisdom and exhibit sagacity in your dealings with unbelieving civil rulers. By discretion show yourselves to be expert in ironing out minor disagreements and in adjusting trifling misunderstandings. In every possible way—in everything short of your spiritual allegiance to the rulers of the universe—seek to live peaceably with all men. Be you always as wise as serpents but as harmless as doves.

178:1.8 (1930.5) You should be made all the better citizens of the secular government as a result of becoming enlightened sons of the kingdom; so should the rulers of earthly governments become all the better rulers in civil affairs as a result of believing this gospel of the heavenly kingdom. The attitude of unselfish service of man and intelligent worship of God should make all kingdom believers better world citizens, while the attitude of honest citizenship and sincere devotion to one's temporal duty should help to make such a citizen the more easily reached by the spirit call to sonship in the heavenly kingdom.

178:1.9 (1930.6) So long as the rulers of earthly governments seek to exercise the authority of religious dictators, you who believe this gospel can expect only trouble, persecution, and even death. But the very light which you bear to the world, and even the very manner in which you will suffer and die for this gospel of the kingdom, will, in themselves, eventually enlighten the whole world and result in the gradual divorcement of politics and religion. The persistent preaching of this gospel of the kingdom will some day bring to all nations a new and unbelievable liberation, intellectual freedom, and religious liberty.

178:1.10 (1931.1) Under the soon-coming persecutions by those who hate this gospel of joy and liberty, you will thrive and the kingdom will prosper. But you will stand in grave danger in subsequent times when most men will speak well of kingdom believers and many in high places nominally accept the gospel of the heavenly kingdom. Learn to be faithful to the kingdom even in times of peace and prosperity. Tempt not the angels of your supervision to lead you in troublous ways as a loving discipline designed to save your ease-drifting souls.

178:1.11 (1931.2) Remember that you are commissioned to preach this gospel of the kingdom—the supreme desire to do the Father's will coupled with the supreme joy of the faith realization of sonship with God—and you must not allow anything to divert your devotion to this one duty. Let all mankind benefit from the overflow of your loving spiritual ministry, enlightening intellectual communion, and uplifting social service; but none of these humanitarian labors, nor all of them, should be permitted to take the place of proclaiming the gospel. These mighty ministrations are the social by-products of the still more mighty and sublime ministrations and transformations wrought in the heart of the kingdom believer by the living Spirit of Truth and by the personal realization that the faith of a spirit-born man confers the assurance of living fellowship with the eternal God.

178:1.12 (1931.3) You must not seek to promulgate truth nor to establish righteousness by the power of civil governments or by the enaction of secular laws. You may always labor to persuade men's minds, but you must never dare to compel them. You must not forget the great law of human fairness which I have taught you in positive form: Whatsoever you would that men should do to you, do even so to them.

178:1.13 (1931.4) When a kingdom believer is called upon to serve the civil government, let him render such service as a temporal citizen of such a government, albeit such a believer should display in his civil service all of the ordinary traits of citizenship as these have been enhanced by the spiritual enlightenment of the ennobling association of the mind of mortal man with the indwelling spirit of the eternal God. If the unbeliever can qualify as a superior civil servant, you should seriously question whether the roots of truth in your heart have not died from the lack of the living waters of combined spiritual communion and social service. The consciousness of sonship with God should quicken the entire life service of every man, woman, and child who has become the possessor of such a mighty stimulus to all the inherent powers of a human personality.

178:1.14 (1931.5) You are not to be passive mystics or colorless ascetics; you should not become dreamers and drifters, supinely trusting in a fictitious Providence to provide even the necessities of life. You are indeed to be gentle in your dealings with erring mortals, patient in your intercourse with ignorant men, and forbearing under provocation; but you are also to be valiant in defense of righteousness, mighty in the promulgation of truth, and aggressive in the preaching of this gospel of the kingdom, even to the ends of the earth.

178:1.15 (1931.6) This gospel of the kingdom is a living truth. I have told you it is like the leaven in the dough, like the grain of mustard seed; and now I declare that it is like the seed of the living being, which, from generation to generation, while it remains the same living seed, unfailingly unfolds itself in new manifestations and grows acceptably in channels of new adaptation to the peculiar needs and conditions of each successive generation. The revelation I have made to you is a living revelation, and I desire that it shall bear appropriate fruits in each individual and in each generation in accordance with the laws of spiritual growth, increase, and adaptative development. From generation to generation this gospel must show increasing vitality and exhibit greater depth of spiritual power. It must not be permitted to become merely a sacred memory, a mere tradition about me and the times in which we now live.

178:1.16 (1932.1) And forget not: We have made no direct attack upon the persons or upon the authority of those who sit in Moses' seat; we only offered them the new light, which they have so vigorously rejected. We have assailed them only by the denunciation of their spiritual disloyalty to the very truths which they profess to teach and safeguard. We clashed with these established leaders and recognized rulers only when they threw themselves directly in the way of the preaching of the gospel of the kingdom to the sons of men. And even now, it is not we who assail them, but they who seek our destruction. Do not forget that you are commissioned to go forth preaching only the good news. You are not to attack the old ways; you are skillfully to put the leaven of new truth in the midst of the old beliefs. Let the Spirit of Truth do his own work. Let controversy come only when they who despise the truth force it upon you. But when the willful unbeliever attacks you, do not hesitate to stand in vigorous defense of the truth which has saved and sanctified you.

178:1.17 (1932.2) Throughout the vicissitudes of life, remember always to love one another. Do not strive with men, even with unbelievers. Show mercy even to those who despitefully abuse you. Show yourselves to be loyal citizens, upright artisans, praiseworthy neighbors, devoted kinsmen, understanding parents, and sincere believers in the brotherhood of the Father's kingdom. And my spirit shall be upon you, now and even to the end of the world.

178:1.18 (1932.3) When Jesus had concluded his teaching, it was almost one o'clock, and they immediately went back to the camp, where David and his associates had lunch ready for them.

2   After the Noontime Meal

178:2.1 (1932.4) Not many of the Master's hearers were able to take in even a part of his forenoon address. Of all who heard him, the Greeks comprehended most. Even the eleven apostles were bewildered by his allusions to future political kingdoms and to successive generations of kingdom believers. Jesus' most devoted followers could not reconcile the impending end of his earthly ministry with these references to an extended future of gospel activities. Some of these Jewish believers were beginning to sense that earth's greatest tragedy was about to take place, but they could not reconcile such an impending disaster with either the Master's cheerfully indifferent personal attitude or his forenoon discourse, wherein he repeatedly alluded to the future transactions of the heavenly kingdom, extending over vast stretches of time and embracing relations with many and successive temporal kingdoms on earth.

178:2.2 (1932.5) By noon of this day all the apostles and disciples had learned about the hasty flight of Lazarus from Bethany. They began to sense the grim determination of the Jewish rulers to exterminate Jesus and his teachings.

178:2.3 (1932.6) David Zebedee, through the work of his secret agents in Jerusalem, was fully advised concerning the progress of the plan to arrest and kill Jesus. He knew all about the part of Judas in this plot, but he never disclosed this knowledge to the other apostles nor to any of the disciples. Shortly after lunch he did lead Jesus aside and, making bold, asked him whether he knew—but he never got further with his question. The Master, holding up his hand, stopped him, saying: "Yes, David, I know all about it, and I know that you know, but see to it that you tell no man. Only doubt not in your own heart that the will of God will prevail in the end."

178:2.4 (1933.1) This conversation with David was interrupted by the arrival of a messenger from Philadelphia bringing word that Abner had heard of the plot to kill Jesus and asking if he should depart for Jerusalem. This runner hastened off for Philadelphia with this word for Abner: "Go on with your work. If I depart from you in the flesh, it is only that I may return in the spirit. I will not forsake you. I will be with you to the end."

178:2.5 (1933.2) About this time Philip came to the Master and asked: "Master, seeing that the time of the Pass-over draws near, where would you have us prepare to eat it?" And when Jesus heard Philip's question, he answered: "Go and bring Peter and John, and I will give you directions concerning the supper we will eat together this night. As for the Passover, that you will have to consider after we have first done this."

178:2.6 (1933.3) When Judas heard the Master speaking with Philip about these matters, he drew closer that he might overhear their conversation. But David Zebedee, who was standing near, stepped up and engaged Judas in conversation while Philip, Peter, and John went to one side to talk with the Master.

178:2.7 (1933.4) Said Jesus to the three: "Go immediately into Jerusalem, and as you enter the gate, you will meet a man bearing a water pitcher. He will speak to you, and then shall you follow him. When he leads you to a certain house, go in after him and ask of the good man of that house, 'Where is the guest chamber wherein the Master is to eat supper with his apostles?' And when you have thus inquired, this householder will show you a large upper room all furnished and ready for us."

178:2.8 (1933.5) When the apostles reached the city, they met the man with the water pitcher near the gate and followed on after him to the home of John Mark, where the lad's father met them and showed them the upper room in readiness for the evening meal.

178:2.9 (1933.6) And all of this came to pass as the result of an understanding arrived at between the Master and John Mark during the afternoon of the preceding day when they were alone in the hills. Jesus wanted to be sure he would have this one last meal undisturbed with his apostles, and believing if Judas knew beforehand of their place of meeting he might arrange with his enemies to take him, he made this secret arrangement with John Mark. In this way Judas did not learn of their place of meeting until later on when he arrived there in company with Jesus and the other apostles.

178:2.10 (1933.7) David Zebedee had much business to transact with Judas so that he was easily prevented from following Peter, John, and Philip, as he so much desired to do. When Judas gave David a certain sum of money for provisions, David said to him: "Judas, might it not be well, under the circumstances, to provide me with a little money in advance of my actual needs?" And after Judas had reflected for a moment, he answered: "Yes, David, I think it would be wise. In fact, in view of the disturbed conditions in Jerusalem, I think it would be best for me to turn over all the money to you.

They plot against the Master, and in case anything should happen to me, you would not be hampered."

178:2.11 (1934.1) And so David received all the apostolic cash funds and receipts for all money on deposit. Not until the evening of the next day did the apostles learn of this transaction.

178:2.12 (1934.2) It was about half past four o'clock when the three apostles returned and informed Jesus that everything was in readiness for the supper. The Master immediately prepared to lead his twelve apostles over the trail to the Bethany road and on into Jerusalem. And this was the last journey he ever made with all twelve of them.

3 On the Way to the Supper

1. 178:3.1 (1934.3) Seeking again to avoid the crowds passing through the Kidron valley back and forth between Gethsemane Park and Jerusalem, Jesus and the twelve walked over the western brow of Mount Olivet to meet the road leading from Bethany down to the city. As they drew near the place where Jesus had tarried the previous evening to discourse on the destruction of Jerusalem, they unconsciously paused while they stood and looked down in silence upon the city. As they were a little early, and since Jesus did not wish to pass through the city until after sunset, he said to his associates:

178:3.2 (1934.4) "Sit down and rest yourselves while I talk with you about what must shortly come to pass. All these years have I lived with you as brethren, and I have taught you the truth concerning the kingdom of heaven and have revealed to you the mysteries thereof. And my Father has indeed done many wonderful works in connection with my mission on earth. You have been witnesses of all this and partakers in the experience of being laborers together with God. And you will bear me witness that I have for some time warned you that I must presently return to the work the Father has given me to do; I have plainly told you that I must leave you in the world to carry on the work of the kingdom. It was for this purpose that I set you apart, in the hills of Capernaum. The experience you have had with me, you must now make ready to share with others. As the Father sent me into this world, so am I about to send you forth to represent me and finish the work I have begun.

178:3.3 (1934.5) "You look down on yonder city in sorrow, for you have heard my words telling of the end of Jerusalem. I have forewarned you lest you should perish in her destruction and so delay the proclamation of the gospel of the kingdom. Likewise do I warn you to take heed lest you needlessly expose yourselves to peril when they come to take the Son of Man. I must go, but you are to remain to witness to this gospel when I have gone, even as I directed that Lazarus flee from the wrath of man that he might live to make known the glory of God. If it is the Father's will that I depart, nothing you may do can frustrate the divine plan. Take heed to yourselves lest they kill you also. Let your souls be valiant in defense of the gospel by spirit power but be not misled into any foolish attempt to defend the Son of Man. I need no defense by the hand of man; the armies of heaven are even now near at hand; but I am determined to do the will of my Father in heaven, and therefore must we submit to that which is so soon to come upon us.

178:3.4 (1934.6) "When you see this city destroyed, forget not that you have entered already upon the eternal life of endless service in the ever-advancing kingdom of heaven, even of the heaven of heavens. You should know that in my Father's universe and in mine are many abodes, and that there awaits the children of light the revelation of cities whose builder is God and worlds whose habit of life is righteousness and joy in the truth. I have brought the kingdom of heaven to you here on earth, but I declare that all of you who by faith enter therein and remain therein by the living service of truth, shall surely ascend to the worlds on high and sit with me in the spirit kingdom of our Father. But first must you gird yourselves and complete the work which you have begun with me. You must first pass through much tribulation and endure many sorrows—and these trials are even now upon us—and when you have finished your work on earth, you shall come to my joy, even as I have finished my Father's work on earth and am about to return to his embrace."

178:3.5 (1935.1) When the Master had spoken, he arose, and they all followed him down Olivet and into the city. None of the apostles, save three, knew where they were going as they made their way along the narrow streets in the approaching darkness. The crowds jostled them, but no one recognized them nor knew that the Son of God was passing by on his way to the last mortal rendezvous with his chosen ambassadors of the kingdom. And neither did the apostles know that one of their own number had already entered into a conspiracy to betray the Master into the hands of his enemies.

178:3.6 (1935.2) John Mark had followed them all the way into the city, and after they had entered the gate, he hurried on by another street so that he was waiting to welcome them to his father's home when they arrived.

Paper 179

The Last Supper

179:0.1 (1936.1) DURING the afternoon of this Thursday, when Philip reminded the Master about the approaching Passover and inquired concerning his plans for its celebration, he had in mind the Passover supper which was due to be eaten on the evening of the next day, Friday. It was the custom to begin the preparations for the celebration of the Passover not later than noon of the preceding day. And since the Jews reckoned the day as beginning at sunset, this meant that Saturday's Passover supper would be eaten on Friday night, sometime before the midnight hour.

179:0.2 (1936.2) The apostles were, therefore, entirely at a loss to understand the Master's announcement that they would celebrate the Passover one day early. They thought, at least some of them did, that he knew he would be placed under arrest before the time of the Passover supper on Friday night and was therefore calling them together for a special supper on this Thursday evening. Others thought that this was merely a special occasion which was to precede the regular Passover celebration.

179:0.3 (1936.3) The apostles knew that Jesus had celebrated other Passovers without the lamb; they knew that he did not personally participate in any sacrificial service of the Jewish system. He had many times partaken of the paschal lamb as a guest, but always, when he was the host, no lamb was served. It would not have been a great surprise to the apostles to have seen the lamb omitted even on Passover night, and since this supper was given one day earlier, they thought nothing of its absence.

179:0.4 (1936.4) After receiving the greetings of welcome extended by the father and mother of John Mark, the apostles went immediately to the upper chamber while Jesus lingered behind to talk with the Mark family.

179:0.5 (1936.5) It had been understood beforehand that the Master was to celebrate this occasion alone with his twelve apostles; therefore no servants were provided to wait upon them.

The Desire for Preference

179:1.1 (1936.6) When the apostles had been shown upstairs by John Mark, they beheld a large and commodious chamber, which was completely furnished for the supper, and observed that the bread, wine, water, and herbs were all in readiness on one end of the table. Except for the end on which rested the bread and wine, this long table was surrounded by thirteen reclining couches, just such as would be provided for the celebration of the Passover in a well-to-do Jewish household.

179:1.2 (1936.7) As the twelve entered this upper chamber, they noticed, just inside the door, the pitchers of water, the basins, and towels for laving their dusty feet; and since no servant had been provided to render this service, the apostles began to look at one another as soon as John Mark had left them, and each began to think within himself, Who shall wash our feet? And each likewise thought that it would not be he who would thus seem to act as the servant of the others.

179:1.3 (1937.1) As they stood there, debating in their hearts, they surveyed the seating arrangement of the table, taking note of the higher divan of the host with one couch on the right and eleven arranged around the table on up to opposite this second seat of honor on the host's right.

179:1.4 (1937.2) They expected the Master to arrive any moment, but they were in a quandary as to whether they should seat themselves or await his coming and depend on him to assign them their places. While they hesitated, Judas stepped over to the seat of honor, at the left of the host, and signified that he intended there to recline as the preferred guest. This act of Judas immediately stirred up a heated dispute among the other apostles. Judas had no sooner seized the seat of honor than John Zebedee laid claim to the next preferred seat, the one on the right of the host. Simon Peter was so enraged at this assumption of choice positions by Judas and John that, as the other angry apostles looked on, he marched clear around the table and took his place on the lowest couch, the end of the seating order and just opposite to that chosen by John Zebedee. Since others had seized the high seats, Peter thought to choose the lowest, and he did this, not merely in protest against the unseemly pride of his brethren, but with the hope that Jesus, when he should come and see him in the place of least honor, would call him up to a higher one, thus displacing one who had presumed to honor himself.

179:1.5 (1937.3) With the highest and the lowest positions thus occupied, the rest of the apostles chose places, some near Judas and some near Peter, until all were located. They were seated about the U-shaped table on these reclining divans in the following order: on the right of the Master, John; on the left, Judas, Simon Zelotes, Matthew, James Zebedee, Andrew, the Alpheus twins, Philip, Nathaniel, Thomas, and Simon Peter.

179:1.6 (1937.4) They are gathered together to celebrate, at least in spirit, an institution which antedated even Moses and referred to the times when their fathers were slaves in Egypt. This supper is their last rendezvous with Jesus, and even in such a solemn setting, under the leadership of Judas the apostles are led once more to give way to their old predilection for honor, preference, and personal exaltation.

179:1.7 (1937.5) They were still engaged in voicing angry recriminations when the Master appeared in the doorway, where he hesitated a moment as a look of disappointment slowly crept over his face. Without comment he went to his place, and he did not disturb their seating arrangement.

179:1.8 (1937.6) They were now ready to begin the supper, except that their feet were still unwashed, and they were in anything but a pleasant frame of mind. When the Master arrived, they were still engaged in making uncomplimentary remarks about one another, to say nothing of the thoughts of some who had sufficient emotional control to refrain from publicly expressing their feelings.

Beginning the Supper

179:2.1 (1937.7) For a few moments after the Master had gone to his place, not a word was spoken. Jesus looked them all over and, relieving the tension with a smile, said: "I have greatly desired to eat this Passover with you. I wanted to eat with you once more before I suffered, and realizing that my hour has come, I arranged to have this supper with you tonight, for, as concerns the morrow, we are all in the hands of the Father, whose will I have come to execute. I shall not again eat with you until you sit down with me in the kingdom which my Father will give me when I have finished that for which he sent me into this world."

179:2.2 (1938.1) After the wine and the water had been mixed, they brought the cup to Jesus, who, when he had received it from the hand of Thaddeus, held it while he offered thanks. And when he had finished offering thanks, he said: "Take this cup and divide it among yourselves and, when you partake of it, realize that I shall not again drink with you the fruit of the vine since this is our last supper. When we sit down again in this manner, it will be in the kingdom to come."

179:2.3 (1938.2) Jesus began thus to talk to his apostles because he knew that his hour had come. He understood that the time had come when he was to return to the Father, and that his work on earth was almost finished. The Master knew he had revealed the Father's love on earth and had shown forth his mercy to mankind, and that he had completed that for which he came into the world, even to the receiving of all power and authority in heaven and on earth. Likewise, he knew Judas Iscariot had fully made up his mind to deliver him that night into the hands of his enemies. He fully realized that this traitorous betrayal was the work of Judas, but that it also pleased Lucifer, Satan, and Caligastia the prince of darkness. But he feared none of those who sought his spiritual overthrow any more than he feared those who sought to accomplish his physical death. The Master had but one anxiety, and that was for the safety and salvation of his chosen followers. And so, with the full knowledge that the Father had put all things under his authority, the Master now prepared to enact the parable of brotherly love.

Washing the Apostles' Feet

179:3.1 (1938.3) After drinking the first cup of the Passover, it was the Jewish custom for the host to arise from the table and wash his hands. Later on in the meal and after the second cup, all of the guests likewise rose up and washed their hands. Since the apostles knew that their Master never observed these rites of ceremonial hand washing, they were very curious to know what he intended to do when, after they had partaken of this first cup, he arose from the table and silently made his way over to near the door, where the water pitchers, basins, and towels had been placed. And their curiosity grew into astonishment as they saw the Master remove his outer garment, gird himself with a towel, and begin to pour water into one of the foot basins. Imagine the amazement of these twelve men, who had so recently refused to wash one another's feet, and who had engaged in such unseemly disputes about positions of honor at the table, when they saw him make his way around the unoccupied end of the table to the lowest seat of the feast, where Simon Peter reclined, and, kneeling down in the attitude of a servant, make ready to wash Simon's feet. As the

Master knelt, all twelve arose as one man to their feet; even the traitorous Judas so far forgot his infamy for a moment as to arise with his fellow apostles in this expression of surprise, respect, and utter amazement.

179:3.2 (1938.4) There stood Simon Peter, looking down into the upturned face of his Master. Jesus said nothing; it was not necessary that he should speak. His attitude plainly revealed that he was minded to wash Simon Peter's feet.

Notwithstanding his frailties of the flesh, Peter loved the Master. This Galilean fisherman was the first human being wholeheartedly to believe in the divinity of Jesus and to make full and public confession of that belief. And Peter had never since really doubted the divine nature of the Master. Since Peter so revered and honored Jesus in his heart, it was not strange that his soul resented the thought of Jesus' kneeling there before him in the attitude of a menial servant and proposing to wash his feet as would a slave. When Peter presently collected his wits sufficiently to address the Master, he spoke the heart feelings of all his fellow apostles.

179:3.3 (1939.1) After a few moments of this great embarrassment, Peter said, "Master, do you really mean to wash my feet?" And then, looking up into Peter's face, Jesus said: "You may not fully understand what I am about to do, but hereafter you will know the meaning of all these things." Then Simon Peter, drawing a long breath, said, "Master, you shall never wash my feet!" And each of the apostles nodded their approval of Peter's firm declaration of refusal to allow Jesus thus to humble himself before them.

179:3.4 (1939.2) The dramatic appeal of this unusual scene at first touched the heart of even Judas Iscariot; but when his vainglorious intellect passed judgment upon the spectacle, he concluded that this gesture of humility was just one more episode which conclusively proved that Jesus would never qualify as Israel's deliverer, and that he had made no mistake in the decision to desert the Master's cause.

179:3.5 (1939.3) As they all stood there in breathless amazement, Jesus said: "Peter, I declare that, if I do not wash your feet, you will have no part with me in that which I am about to perform." When Peter heard this declaration, coupled with the fact that Jesus continued kneeling there at his feet, he made one of those decisions of blind acquiescence in compliance with the wish of one whom he respected and loved. As it began to dawn on Simon Peter that there was attached to this proposed enactment of service some signification that determined one's future connection with the Master's work, he not only became reconciled to the thought of allowing Jesus to wash his feet but, in his characteristic and impetuous manner, said: "Then, Master, wash not my feet only but also my hands and my head."

179:3.6 (1939.4) As the Master made ready to begin washing Peter's feet, he said: "He who is already clean needs only to have his feet washed. You who sit with me tonight are clean—but not all. But the dust of your feet should have been washed away before you sat down at meat with me. And besides, I would perform this service for you as a parable to illustrate the meaning of a new commandment which I will presently give you."

179:3.7 (1939.5) In like manner the Master went around the table, in silence, washing the feet of his twelve apostles, not even passing by Judas. When Jesus had finished washing the feet of the twelve, he donned his cloak, returned to his place as host, and after looking over his bewildered apostles, said:

179:3.8 (1939.6) "Do you really understand what I have done to you? You call me Master, and you say well, for so I am. If, then, the Master has washed your feet, why was it that you were unwilling to wash one another's feet? What lesson should you learn from this parable in which the Master so willingly does that service which his brethren were unwilling to do for one another? Verily, verily, I say to you:

A servant is not greater than his master; neither is one who is sent greater than he who sends him. You have seen the way of service in my life among you, and blessed are you who will have the gracious courage so to serve. But why are you so slow to learn that the secret of greatness in the spiritual kingdom is not like the methods of power in the material world?

179:3.9 (1940.1) "When I came into this chamber tonight, you were not content proudly to refuse to wash one another's feet, but you must also fall to disputing among yourselves as to who should have the places of honor at my table. Such honors the Pharisees and the children of this world seek, but it should not be so among the ambassadors of the heavenly kingdom. Do you not know that there can be no place of preferment at my table? Do you not understand that I love each of you as I do the others? Do you not know that the place nearest me, as men regard such honors, can mean nothing concerning your standing in the kingdom of heaven? You know that the kings of the gentiles have lordship over their subjects, while those who exercise this authority are sometimes called benefactors. But it shall not be so in the kingdom of heaven. He who would be great among you, let him become as the younger; while he who would be chief, let him become as one who serves. Who is the greater, he who sits at meat, or he who serves? Is it not commonly regarded that he who sits at meat is the greater? But you will observe that I am among you as one who serves. If you are willing to become fellow servants with me in doing the Father's will, in the kingdom to come you shall sit with me in power, still doing the Father's will in future glory."

179:3.10 (1940.2) When Jesus had finished speaking, the Alpheus twins brought on the bread and wine, with the bitter herbs and the paste of dried fruits, for the next course of the Last Supper.

Last Words to the Betrayer

179:4.1 (1940.3) For some minutes the apostles ate in silence, but under the influence of the Master's cheerful demeanor they were soon drawn into conversation, and ere long the meal was proceeding as if nothing out of the ordinary had occurred to interfere with the good cheer and social accord of this extraordinary occasion. After some time had elapsed, in about the middle of this second course of the meal, Jesus, looking them over, said: "I have told you how much I desired to have this supper with you, and knowing how the evil forces of darkness have conspired to bring about the death of the Son of Man, I determined to eat this supper with you in this secret chamber and a day in advance of the Passover since I will not be with you by this time tomorrow night. I have repeatedly told you that I must return to the Father. Now has my hour come, but it was not required that one of you should betray me into the hands of my enemies."

179:4.2 (1940.4) When the twelve heard this, having already been robbed of much of their self-assertiveness and self-confidence by the parable of the feet washing and the Master's subsequent discourse, they began to look at one another while in disconcerted tones they hesitatingly inquired, "Is it I?" And when they had all so inquired, Jesus said: "While it is necessary that I go to the Father, it was not required that one of you should become a traitor to fulfill the Father's will. This is the coming to fruit of the concealed evil in the heart of one who failed to love the truth with his whole soul. How deceitful is the intellectual pride that precedes the spiritual downfall! My friend of many years, who even now eats my bread, will be willing to betray me, even as he now dips his hand with me in the dish."

179:4.3 (1940.5) And when Jesus had

thus spoken, they all began again to ask, "Is it I?" And as Judas, sitting on the left of his Master, again asked, "Is it I?" Jesus, dipping the bread in the dish of herbs, handed it to Judas, saying, "You have said." But the others did not hear Jesus speak to Judas. John, who reclined on Jesus' right hand, leaned over and asked the Master: "Who is it? We should know who it is that has proved untrue to his trust." Jesus answered: "Already have I told you, even he to whom I gave the sop." But it was so natural for the host to give a sop to the one who sat next to him on the left that none of them took notice of this, even though the Master had so plainly spoken. But Judas was painfully conscious of the meaning of the Master's words associated with his act, and he became fearful lest his brethren were likewise now aware that he was the betrayer.

179:4.4 (1941.1) Peter was highly excited by what had been said, and leaning forward over the table, he addressed John, "Ask him who it is, or if he has told you, tell me who is the betrayer."

179:4.5 (1941.2) Jesus brought their whisperings to an end by saying: "I sorrow that this evil should have come to pass and hoped even up to this hour that the power of truth might triumph over the deceptions of evil, but such victories are not won without the faith of the sincere love of truth. I would not have told you these things at this, our last supper, but I desire to warn you of these sorrows and so prepare you for what is now upon us. I have told you of this because I desire that you should recall, after I have gone, that I knew about all these evil plottings, and that I forewarned you of my betrayal. And I do all this only that you may be strengthened for the temptations and trials which are just ahead."

179:4.6 (1941.3) When Jesus had thus spoken, leaning over toward Judas, he said: "What you have decided to do, do quickly." And when Judas heard these words, he arose from the table and hastily left the room, going out into the night to do what he had set his mind to accomplish. When the other apostles saw Judas hasten off after Jesus had spoken to him, they thought he

had gone to procure something additional for the supper or to do some other errand for the Master since they supposed he still carried the bag.

179:4.7 (1941.4) Jesus now knew that nothing could be done to keep Judas from turning traitor. He started with twelve—now he had eleven. He chose six of these apostles, and though Judas was among those nominated by his first-chosen apostles, still the Master accepted him and had, up to this very hour, done everything possible to sanctify and save him, even as he had wrought for the peace and salvation of the others.

179:4.8 (1941.5) This supper, with its tender episodes and softening touches, was Jesus' last appeal to the deserting Judas, but it was of no avail. Warning, even when administered in the most tactful manner and conveyed in the most kindly spirit, as a rule, only intensifies hatred and fires the evil determination to carry out to the full one's own selfish projects, when love is once really dead.

Establishing the Remembrance Supper

179:5.1 (1941.6) As they brought Jesus the third cup of wine, the "cup of blessing," he arose from the couch and, taking the cup in his hands, blessed it, saying: "Take this cup, all of you, and drink of it. This shall be the cup of my remembrance. This is the cup of the blessing of a new dispensation of grace and truth. This shall be to you the emblem of the bestowal and ministry of the divine Spirit of Truth. And I will not again drink this cup with you until I drink in new form with you in the Father's eternal kingdom."

179:5.2 (1942.1) The apostles all sensed that something out of the ordinary was transpiring as they drank of this cup of blessing in profound reverence and perfect silence. The old Passover commemorated the emergence of their fathers from a state of racial slavery into individual freedom;

now the Master was instituting a new remembrance supper as a symbol of the new dispensation wherein the enslaved individual emerges from the bondage of ceremonialism and selfishness into the spiritual joy of the brotherhood and fellowship of the liberated faith sons of the living God.

179:5.3 (1942.2) When they had finished drinking this new cup of remembrance, the Master took up the bread and, after giving thanks, broke it in pieces and, directing them to pass it around, said: "Take this bread of remembrance and eat it. I have told you that I am the bread of life. And this bread of life is the united life of the Father and the Son in one gift. The word of the Father, as revealed in the Son, is indeed the bread of life." When they had partaken of the bread of remembrance, the symbol of the living word of truth incarnated in the likeness of mortal flesh, they all sat down.

179:5.4 (1942.3) In instituting this remembrance supper, the Master, as was always his habit, resorted to parables and symbols. He employed symbols because he wanted to teach certain great spiritual truths in such a manner as to make it difficult for his successors to attach precise interpretations and definite meanings to his words. In this way he sought to prevent successive generations from crystallizing his teaching and binding down his spiritual meanings by the dead chains of tradition and dogma. In the establishment of the only ceremony or sacrament associated with his whole life mission, Jesus took great pains to suggest his meanings rather than to commit himself to precise definitions. He did not wish to destroy the individual's concept of divine communion by establishing a precise form; neither did he desire to limit the believer's spiritual imagination by formally cramping it. He rather sought to set man's reborn soul free upon the joyous wings of a new and living spiritual liberty.

179:5.5 (1942.4) Notwithstanding the Master's effort thus to establish this new sacrament of the remembrance, those who followed after him in the intervening centuries saw to it that his express desire was effectively thwarted in that his simple spiritual symbolism of that last night in the flesh has been reduced to precise interpretations and subjected to the almost mathematical precision of a set formula. Of all Jesus' teachings none have become more tradition-standardized.

179:5.6 (1942.5) This supper of remembrance, when it is partaken of by those who are Son-believing and God-knowing, does not need to have associated with its symbolism any of man's puerile misinterpretations regarding the meaning of the divine presence, for upon all such occasions the Master is really present. The remembrance supper is the believer's symbolic rendezvous with Michael. When you become thus spirit-conscious, the Son is actually present, and his spirit fraternizes with the indwelling fragment of his Father.

179:5.7 (1942.6) After they had engaged in meditation for a few moments, Jesus continued speaking: "When you do these things, recall the life I have lived on earth among you and rejoice that I am to continue to live on earth with you and to serve through you. As individuals, contend not among yourselves as to who shall be greatest. Be you all as brethren.

And when the kingdom grows to embrace large groups of believers, likewise should you refrain from contending for greatness or seeking preferment between such groups."

179:5.8 (1943.1) And this mighty occasion took place in the upper chamber of a friend. There was nothing of sacred form or of ceremonial consecration about either the supper or the building. The remembrance supper was established without ecclesiastical sanction.

179:5.9 (1943.2) When Jesus had thus established the supper of the remembrance, he said to the eleven: "And as often as you do this, do it in remembrance of me. And when you do remember me, first look back upon my life in the flesh, recall that I was once with you, and then, by faith, discern that you shall all sometime sup with me in the Father's eternal kingdom. This is the new Passover which I leave with you, even the memory of my bestowal life, the word of eternal truth; and of my love for you, the outpouring of my Spirit of Truth upon all flesh." *

179:5.10 (1943.3) And they ended this celebration of the old but bloodless Passover in connection with the inauguration of the new supper of the remembrance, by singing, all together, the one hundred and eighteenth Psalm.

Paper 180

The Farewell Discourse

180:0.1 (1944.1) AFTER singing the Psalm at the conclusion of the Last Supper, the apostles thought that Jesus intended to return immediately to the camp, but he indicated that they should sit down. Said the Master:

180:0.2 (1944.2) "You well remember when I sent you forth without purse or wallet and even advised that you take with you no extra clothes. And you will all recall that you lacked nothing. But now have you come upon troublous times. No longer can you depend upon the good will of the multitudes. Henceforth, he who has a purse, let him take it with him. When you go out into the world to proclaim this gospel, make such provision for your support as seems best. I have come to bring peace, but it will not appear for a time.

180:0.3 (1944.3) "The time has now come for the Son of Man to be glorified, and the Father shall be glorified in me. My friends, I am to be with you only a little longer. Soon you will seek for me, but you will not find me, for I am going to a place to which you cannot, at this time, come. But when you have finished your work on earth as I have now finished mine, you shall

then come to me even as I now prepare to go to my Father. In just a short time I am going to leave you, you will see me no more on earth, but you shall all see me in the age to come when you ascend to the kingdom which my Father has given to me."

The New Commandment

180:1.1 (1944.4) After a few moments of informal conversation, Jesus stood up and said: "When I enacted for you a parable indicating how you should be willing to serve one another, I said that I desired to give you a new commandment; and I would do this now as I am about to leave you. You well know the commandment which directs that you love one another; that you love your neighbor even as yourself. But I am not wholly satisfied with even that sincere devotion on the part of my children. I would have you perform still greater acts of love in the kingdom of the believing brotherhood. And so I give you this new commandment: That you love one another even as I have loved you. And by this will all men know that you are my disciples if you thus love one another.

180:1.2 (1944.5) "When I give you this new commandment, I do not place any new burden upon your souls; rather do I bring you new joy and make it possible for you to experience new pleasure in knowing the delights of the bestowal of your heart's affection upon your fellow men. I am about to experience the supreme joy, even though enduring outward sorrow, in the bestowal of my affection upon you and your fellow mortals.

180:1.3 (1944.6) "When I invite you to love one another, even as I have loved you, I hold up before you the supreme measure of true affection, for greater love can no man have than this: that he will lay down his life for his friends. And you are my friends; you will continue to be my friends if you are but willing to do what I have taught you. You have called me Master, but I do not call you servants. If you will only love one another as I am loving you, you shall be my friends, and I will ever speak to you of that which the Father reveals to me.

180:1.4 (1945.1) "You have not merely chosen me, but I have also chosen you, and I have ordained you to go forth into the world to yield the fruit of loving service to your fellows even as I have lived among you and revealed the Father to you. The Father and I will both work with you, and you shall experience the divine fullness of joy if you will only obey my command to love one another, even as I have loved you."

180:1.5 (1945.2) If you would share the Master's joy, you must share his love. And to share his love means that you have shared his service. Such an experience of love does not deliver you from the difficulties of this world; it does not create a new world, but it most certainly does make the old world new.

180:1.6 (1945.3) Keep in mind: It is loyalty, not sacrifice, that Jesus demands. The consciousness of sacrifice implies the absence of that wholehearted affection which would have made such a loving service a supreme joy. The idea of duty signifies that you are servant-minded and hence are missing the mighty thrill of doing your service as a friend and for a friend. The impulse of friendship transcends all convictions of duty, and the service of a friend for a friend can never be called a sacrifice. The Master has taught the apostles that they are the sons of God. He has called them brethren, and now, before he leaves, he calls them his friends.

The Vine and the Branches

180:2.1 (1945.4) Then Jesus stood up again and continued teaching his apostles: "I am the true vine, and my Father is the husbandman. I am the vine, and you are the branches. And the Father requires of me only that you shall bear much fruit. The vine is pruned only to increase the fruitfulness of its branches. Every branch coming out of me which bears no fruit,

the Father will take away. Every branch which bears fruit, the Father will cleanse that it may bear more fruit. Already are you clean through the word I have spoken, but you must continue to be clean. You must abide in me, and I in you; the branch will die if it is separated from the vine. As the branch cannot bear fruit except it abides in the vine, so neither can you yield the fruits of loving service except you abide in me. Remember: I am the real vine, and you are the living branches. He who lives in me, and I in him, will bear much fruit of the spirit and experience the supreme joy of yielding this spiritual harvest. If you will maintain this living spiritual connection with me, you will bear abundant fruit. If you abide in me and my words live in you, you will be able to commune freely with me, and then can my living spirit so infuse you that you may ask whatsoever my spirit wills and do all this with the assurance that the Father will grant us our petition. Herein is the Father glorified: that the vine has many living branches, and that every branch bears much fruit. And when the world sees these fruit-bearing branches—my friends who love one another, even as I have loved them—all men will know that you are truly my disciples.

180:2.2 (1945.5) "As the Father has loved me, so have I loved you. Live in my love even as I live in the Father's love. If you do as I have taught you, you shall abide in my love even as I have kept the Father's word and evermore abide in his love."

180:2.3 (1946.1) The Jews had long taught that the Messiah would be "a stem arising out of the vine" of David's ancestors, and in commemoration of this olden teaching a large emblem of the grape and its attached vine decorated the entrance to Herod's temple. The apostles all recalled these things while the Master talked to them this night in the upper chamber.

180:2.4 (1946.2) But great sorrow later attended the misinterpretation of the Master's inferences regarding prayer. There would have been little difficulty about these teachings if his exact words had been remembered and subsequently truthfully recorded. But as the record was made, believers eventually regarded prayer in Jesus' name as a sort of supreme magic, thinking that they would receive from the Father anything they asked for. For centuries honest souls have continued to wreck their faith against this stumbling block. How long will it take the world of believers to understand that prayer is not a process of getting your way but rather a program of taking God's way, an experience of learning how to recognize and execute the Father's will? It is entirely true that, when your will has been truly aligned with his, you can ask anything conceived by that will-union, and it will be granted. And such a will-union is effected by and through Jesus even as the life of the vine flows into and through the living branches.

180:2.5 (1946.3) When there exists this living connection between divinity and humanity, if humanity should thoughtlessly and ignorantly pray for selfish ease and vainglorious accomplishments, there could be only one divine answer: more and increased bearing of the fruits of the spirit on the stems of the living branches. When the branch of the vine is alive, there can be only one answer to all its petitions: increased grape bearing. In fact, the branch exists only for, and can do nothing except, fruit bearing, yielding grapes. So does the true believer exist only for the purpose of bearing the fruits of the spirit: to love man as he himself has been loved by God—that we should love one another, even as Jesus has loved us.

180:2.6 (1946.4) And when the Father's hand of discipline is laid upon the vine, it is done in love, in order that the branches may bear much fruit. And a wise husbandman cuts away only the dead and fruitless branches.

180:2.7 (1946.5) Jesus had great difficulty in leading even his apostles to recognize that prayer is a function of spirit-born believers in the spirit-dominated kingdom.

Enmity of the World

180:3.1 (1946.6) The eleven had scarcely ceased their discussions of the discourse on the vine and the branches when the Master, indicating that he was desirous of speaking to them further and knowing that his time was short, said: "When I have left you, be not discouraged by the enmity of the world. Be not downcast even when fainthearted believers turn against you and join hands with the enemies of the kingdom. If the world shall hate you, you should recall that it hated me even before it hated you. If you were of this world, then would the world love its own, but because you are not, the world refuses to love you. You are in this world, but your lives are not to be worldlike. I have chosen you out of the world to represent the spirit of another world even to this world from which you have been chosen. But always remember the words I have spoken to you: The servant is not greater than his master. If they dare to persecute me, they will also persecute you. If my words offend the unbelievers, so also will your words offend the ungodly. And all of this will they do to you because they believe not in me nor in Him who sent me; so will you suffer many things for the sake of my gospel. But when you endure these tribulations, you should recall that I also suffered before you for the sake of this gospel of the heavenly kingdom. *

180:3.2 (1947.1) "Many of those who will assail you are ignorant of the light of heaven, but this is not true of some who now persecute us. If we had not taught them the truth, they might do many strange things without falling under condemnation, but now, since they have known the light and presumed to reject it, they have no excuse for their attitude. He who hates me hates my Father. It cannot be otherwise; the light which would save you if accepted can only condemn you if it is knowingly rejected. And what have I done to these men that they should hate me with such a terrible hatred? Nothing, save to offer them fellowship on earth and salvation in heaven. But have you not read in the Scripture the saying: 'And they hated me without a cause'?

180:3.3 (1947.2) "But I will not leave you alone in the world. Very soon, after I have gone, I will send you a spirit helper. You shall have with you one who will take my place among you, one who will continue to teach you the way of truth, who will even comfort you.

180:3.4 (1947.3) "Let not your hearts be troubled. You believe in God; continue to believe also in me. Even though I must leave you, I will not be far from you. I have already told you that in my Father's universe there are many tarrying- places. If this were not true, I would not have repeatedly told you about them. I am going to return to these worlds of light, stations in the Father's heaven to which you shall sometime ascend. From these places I came into this world, and the hour is now at hand when I must return to my Father's work in the spheres on high. *

180:3.5 (1947.4) "If I thus go before you into the Father's heavenly kingdom, so will I surely send for you that you may be with me in the places that were prepared for the mortal sons of God before this world was. Even though I must leave you, I will be present with you in spirit, and eventually you shall be with me in person when you have ascended to me in my universe even as I am about to ascend to my Father in his greater universe. And what I have told you is true and everlasting, even though you may not fully comprehend it. I go to the Father, and though you cannot now follow me, you shall certainly follow me in the ages to come."

180:3.6 (1947.5) When Jesus sat down, Thomas arose and said: "Master, we do not know where you are going; so of course we do not know the way. But we will follow you this very night if you will show us the way."

180:3.7 (1947.6) When Jesus heard Thomas, he answered: "Thomas, I am the way, the truth, and the life. No man goes to the Father except through me. All who find the Father, first find me. If you know me, you know the way to the Father. And you do know me, for you have lived with me and you now see me."

180:3.8 (1947.7) But this teaching was too deep for many of the apostles, especially for Philip, who, after speaking a few words with Nathaniel, arose and said: "Master, show us the Father, and everything you have said will be made plain."

180:3.9 (1947.8) And when Philip had spoken, Jesus said: "Philip, have I been so long with you and yet you do not even now know me? Again do I declare: He who has seen me has seen the Father. How can you then say, Show us the Father? Do you not believe that I am in the Father and the Father in me? Have I not taught you that the words which I speak are not my words but the words of the Father? I speak for the Father and not of myself. I am in this world to do the Father's will, and that I have done. My Father abides in me and works through me. Believe me when I say that the Father is in me, and that I am in the Father, or else believe me for the sake of the very life I have lived—for the work's sake."

180:3.10 (1948.1) As the Master went aside to refresh himself with water, the eleven engaged in a spirited discussion of these teachings, and Peter was beginning to deliver himself of an extended speech when Jesus returned and beckoned them to be seated.

The Promised Helper

180:4.1 (1948.2) Jesus continued to teach, saying: "When I have gone to the Father, and after he has fully accepted the work I have done for you on earth, and after I have received the final sovereignty of my own domain, I shall say to my Father: Having left my children alone on earth, it is in accordance with my promise to send them another teacher. And when the Father shall approve, I will pour out the Spirit of

Truth upon all flesh. Already is my Father's spirit in your hearts, and when this day shall come, you will also have me with you even as you now have the Father. This new gift is the spirit of living truth. The unbelievers will not at first listen to the teachings of this spirit, but the sons of light will all receive him gladly and with a whole heart. And you shall know this spirit when he comes even as you have known me, and you will receive this gift in your hearts, and he will abide with you. You thus perceive that I am not going to leave you without help and guidance. I will not leave you desolate. Today I can be with you only in person. In the times to come I will be with you and all other men who desire my presence, wherever you may be, and with each of you at the same time. Do you not discern that it is better for me to go away; that I leave you in the flesh so that I may the better and the more fully be with you in the spirit?

180:4.2 (1948.3) "In just a few hours the world will see me no more; but you will continue to know me in your hearts even until I send you this new teacher, the Spirit of Truth. As I have lived with you in person, then shall I live in you; I shall be one with your personal experience in the spirit kingdom. And when this has come to pass, you shall surely know that I am in the Father, and that, while your life is hid with the Father in me, I am also in you. I have loved the Father and have kept his word; you have loved me, and you will keep my word. As my Father has given me of his spirit, so will I give you of my spirit. And this Spirit of Truth which I will bestow upon you shall guide and comfort you and shall eventually lead you into all truth.

180:4.3 (1948.4) "I am telling you these things while I am still with you that you may be the better prepared to endure those trials which are even now right upon us. And when this new day comes, you will be indwelt by the Son as well as by the Father. And these gifts of heaven will ever work the one with the other even as the Father and I have wrought on earth and before your very eyes as one person, the Son of Man. And this spirit friend will

bring to your remembrance everything I have taught you."

180:4.4 (1948.5) As the Master paused for a moment, Judas Alpheus made bold to ask one of the few questions which either he or his brother ever addressed to Jesus in public. Said Judas: "Master, you have always lived among us as a friend; how shall we know you when you no longer manifest yourself to us save by this spirit? If the world sees you not, how shall we be certain about you? How will you show yourself to us?"

180:4.5 (1949.1) Jesus looked down upon them all, smiled, and said: "My little children, I am going away, going back to my Father. In a little while you will not see me as you do here, as flesh and blood. In a very short time I am going to send you my spirit, just like me except for this material body. This new teacher is the Spirit of Truth who will live with each one of you, in your hearts, and so will all the children of light be made one and be drawn toward one another. And in this very manner will my Father and I be able to live in the souls of each one of you and also in the hearts of all other men who love us and make that love real in their experiences by loving one another, even as I am now loving you."

180:4.6 (1949.2) Judas Alpheus did not fully understand what the Master said, but he grasped the promise of the new teacher, and from the expression on Andrew's face, he perceived that his question had been satisfactorily answered.

The Spirit of Truth

180:5.1 (1949.3) The new helper which Jesus promised to send into the hearts of believers, to pour out upon all flesh, is the Spirit of Truth. This divine endowment is not the letter or law of truth, neither is it to function as the form or expression of truth. The new teacher is the conviction of truth, the consciousness and assurance of true meanings on real spirit levels. And this new teacher is the spirit of living and growing truth, expanding, unfolding, and adaptative truth.

180:5.2 (1949.4) Divine truth is a spirit-discerned and living reality. Truth exists only on high spiritual levels of the realization of divinity and the consciousness of communion with God. You can know the truth, and you can live the truth; you can experience the growth of truth in the soul and enjoy the liberty of its enlightenment in the mind, but you cannot imprison truth in formulas, codes, creeds, or intellectual patterns of human conduct. When you undertake the human formulation of divine truth, it speedily dies. The post-mortem salvage of imprisoned truth, even at best, can eventuate only in the realization of a peculiar form of intellectualized glorified wisdom. Static truth is dead truth, and only dead truth can be held as a theory. Living truth is dynamic and can enjoy only an experiential existence in the human mind.

180:5.3 (1949.5) Intelligence grows out of a material existence which is illuminated by the presence of the cosmic mind. Wisdom comprises the consciousness of knowledge elevated to new levels of meaning and activated by the presence of the universe endowment of the adjutant of wisdom. Truth is a spiritual reality value experienced only by spirit-endowed beings who function upon supermaterial levels of universe consciousness, and who, after the realization of truth, permit its spirit of activation to live and reign within their souls.

180:5.4 (1949.6) The true child of universe insight looks for the living Spirit of Truth in every wise saying. The God-knowing individual is constantly elevating wisdom to the living-truth levels of divine attainment; the spiritually unprogressive soul is all the while dragging the living truth down to the dead levels of wisdom and to the domain of mere exalted knowledge.

180:5.5 (1949.7) The golden rule, when divested of the superhuman insight of the Spirit of Truth, becomes nothing more than a rule of high ethical conduct. The golden rule, when literally interpreted, may become the instrument of great offense to one's fellows. Without a spiritual discernment of the golden rule of wisdom you might reason that, since you are desirous that all men speak the full and frank truth of their minds to you, you should therefore fully and frankly speak the full thought of your mind to your fellow beings. Such an unspiritual interpretation of the golden rule might result in untold unhappiness and no end of sorrow.

180:5.6 (1950.1) Some persons discern and interpret the golden rule as a purely intellectual affirmation of human fraternity. Others experience this expression of human relationship as an emotional gratification of the tender feelings of the human personality. Another mortal recognizes this same golden rule as the yardstick for measuring all social relations, the standard of social conduct. Still others look upon it as being the positive injunction of a great moral teacher who embodied in this statement the highest concept of moral obligation as regards all fraternal relationships. In the lives of such moral beings the golden rule becomes the wise center and circumference of all their philosophy.

180:5.7 (1950.2) In the kingdom of the believing brotherhood of God-knowing truth lovers, this golden rule takes on living qualities of spiritual realization on those higher levels of interpretation which cause the mortal sons of God to view this injunction of the Master as requiring them so to relate themselves to their fellows that they will receive the highest possible good as a result of the believer's contact with them. This is the essence of true religion: that you love your neighbor as yourself.

180:5.8 (1950.3) But the highest realization and the truest interpretation of the golden rule consists in the consciousness of the spirit of the truth of the enduring and living reality of such a divine declaration. The true cosmic meaning of this rule of universal relationship is revealed only in its spiritual realization, in the interpretation of the law of conduct by the spirit of the Son to the spirit of the Father that indwells the soul of mortal man. And when such spirit-led mortals realize the true meaning of this golden rule, they are filled to overflowing with the assurance of citizenship in a friendly universe, and their ideals of spirit reality are satisfied only when they love their fellows as Jesus loved us all, and that is the reality of the realization of the love of God.

180:5.9 (1950.4) This same philosophy of the living flexibility and cosmic adaptability of divine truth to the individual requirements and capacity of every son of God, must be perceived before you can hope adequately to understand the Master's teaching and practice of nonresistance to evil. The Master's teaching is basically a spiritual pronouncement. Even the material implications of his philosophy cannot be helpfully considered apart from their spiritual correlations. The spirit of the Master's injunction consists in the nonresistance of all selfish reaction to the universe, coupled with the aggressive and progressive attainment of righteous levels of true spirit values: divine beauty, infinite goodness, and eternal truth—to know God and to become increasingly like him.

180:5.10 (1950.5) Love, unselfishness, must undergo a constant and living readaptative interpretation of relationships in accordance with the leading of the Spirit of Truth. Love must thereby grasp the everchanging and enlarging concepts of the highest cosmic good of the individual who is loved. And then love goes on to strike this same attitude concerning all other individuals who could possibly be influenced by the growing and living relationship of one spirit-led mortal's love for other citizens of the universe. And this entire living adaptation of love must be effected in the light of both the environment of present evil and the eternal goal of the perfection of divine destiny.

180:5.11 (1950.6) And so must we clearly recognize that neither the golden rule nor the teaching of nonresistance can

ever be properly understood as dogmas or precepts. They can only be comprehended by living them, by realizing their meanings in the living interpretation of the Spirit of Truth, who directs the loving contact of one human being with another.

180:5.12 (1951.1) And all this clearly indicates the difference between the old religion and the new. The old religion taught self-sacrifice; the new religion teaches only self-forgetfulness, enhanced self-realization in conjoined social service and universe comprehension. The old religion was motivated by fear-consciousness; the new gospel of the kingdom is dominated by truth-conviction, the spirit of eternal and universal truth. And no amount of piety or creedal loyalty can compensate for the absence in the life experience of kingdom believers of that spontaneous, generous, and sincere friendliness which characterizes the spirit-born sons of the living God. Neither tradition nor a ceremonial system of formal worship can atone for the lack of genuine compassion for one's fellows.

The Necessity for Leaving

180:6.1 (1951.2) After Peter, James, John, and Matthew had asked the Master numerous questions, he continued his farewell discourse by saying: "And I am telling you about all this before I leave you in order that you may be so prepared for what is coming upon you that you will not stumble into serious error. The authorities will not be content with merely putting you out of the synagogues; I warn you the hour draws near when they who kill you will think they are doing a service to God. And all of these things they will do to you and to those whom you lead into the kingdom of heaven because they do not know the Father. They have refused to know the Father by refusing to receive me; and they refuse to receive me when they reject you, provided you have kept my new commandment that you love one another even as I have loved you. I am telling you in advance about these things so that, when your hour comes, as mine now has, you may be strengthened in the knowledge that all was known to me, and that my spirit shall be with you in all your sufferings for my sake and the gospel's. It was for this purpose that I have been talking so plainly to you from the very beginning. I have even warned you that a man's foes may be those of his own household. Although this gospel of the kingdom never fails to bring great peace to the soul of the individual believer, it will not bring peace on earth until man is willing to believe my teaching wholeheartedly and to establish the practice of doing the Father's will as the chief purpose in living the mortal life.

180:6.2 (1951.3) "Now that I am leaving you, seeing that the hour has come when I am about to go to the Father, I am surprised that none of you have asked me, Why do you leave us? Nevertheless, I know that you ask such questions in your hearts. I will speak to you plainly, as one friend to another. It is really profitable for you that I go away. If I go not away, the new teacher cannot come into your hearts. I must be divested of this mortal body and be restored to my place on high before I can send this spirit teacher to live in your souls and lead your spirits into the truth. And when my spirit comes to indwell you, he will illuminate the difference between sin and righteousness and will enable you to judge wisely in your hearts concerning them.

180:6.3 (1951.4) "I have yet much to say to you, but you cannot stand any more just now. Albeit, when he, the Spirit of Truth, comes, he shall eventually guide you into all truth as you pass through the many abodes in my Father's universe.

180:6.4 (1951.5) "This spirit will not speak of himself, but he will declare to you that which the Father has revealed to the Son, and he will even show you things to come; he will glorify me even as I have glorified my Father. This spirit comes forth from me, and he will reveal my truth to you. Everything which the Father has in this domain is now mine; wherefore did I say that this new teacher would take of that which is mine and reveal it to you.

180:6.5 (1952.1) "In just a little while I will leave you for a short time. Afterward, when you again see me, I shall already be on my way to the Father so that even then you will not see me for long."

180:6.6 (1952.2) While he paused for a moment, the apostles began to talk with each other: "What is this that he tells us? 'In just a little while I will leave you,' and 'When you see me again it will not be for long, for I will be on my way to the Father.' What can he mean by this 'little while' and 'not for long'? We cannot understand what he is telling us."

180:6.7 (1952.3) And since Jesus knew they asked these questions, he said: "Do you inquire among yourselves about what I meant when I said that in a little while I would not be with you, and that, when you would see me again, I would be on my way to the Father? I have plainly told you that the Son of Man must die, but that he will rise again. Can you not then discern the meaning of my words? You will first be made sorrowful, but later on will you rejoice with many who will understand these things after they have come to pass. A woman is indeed sorrowful in the hour of her travail, but when she is once delivered of her child, she immediately forgets her anguish in the joy of the knowledge that a man has been born into the world. And so are you about to sorrow over my departure, but I will soon see you again, and then will your sorrow be turned into rejoicing, and there shall come to you a new revelation of the salvation of God which no man can ever take away from you. And all the worlds will be blessed in this same revelation of life in effecting the overthrow of death. Hitherto have you made all your requests in my Father's name. After you see me again, you may also ask in my name, and I will hear you.

180:6.8 (1952.4) "Down here I have taught you in proverbs and spoken to you in parables. I did so because you were only children in the spirit; but the time is coming when I will talk to you plainly concerning the Father and his kingdom. And I shall do this because the Father himself loves you and desires to be more fully revealed to you. Mortal man cannot see the spirit Father; therefore have I come into the world to show the Father to your creature eyes. But when you have become perfected in spirit growth, you shall then see the Father himself."

180:6.9 (1952.5) When the eleven had heard him speak, they said to each other: "Behold, he does speak plainly to us. Surely the Master did come forth from God. But why does he say he must return to the Father?" And Jesus saw that they did not even yet comprehend him. These eleven men could not get away from their long-nourished ideas of the Jewish concept of the Messiah. The more fully they believed in Jesus as the Messiah, the more troublesome became these deep- rooted notions regarding the glorious material triumph of the kingdom on earth.

Paper 181

Final Admonitions and Warnings

181:0.1 (1953.1) AFTER the conclusion of the farewell discourse to the eleven, Jesus visited informally with them and recounted many experiences which concerned them as a group and as individuals. At last it was beginning to dawn upon these Galileans that their friend and teacher was going to leave them, and their hope grasped at the promise that, after a little while, he would again be with them, but they were prone to forget that this return visit was also for a little while.

Many of the apostles and the leading disciples really thought that this promise to return for a short season (the short interval between the resurrection and the ascension) indicated that Jesus was just going away for a brief visit with his Father,

after which he would return to establish the kingdom. And such an interpretation of his teaching conformed both with their preconceived beliefs and with their ardent hopes. Since their lifelong beliefs and hopes of wish fulfillment were thus agreed, it was not difficult for them to find an interpretation of the Master's words which would justify their intense longings.

181:0.2 (1953.2) After the farewell discourse had been discussed and had begun to settle down in their minds, Jesus again called the apostles to order and began the impartation of his final admonitions and warnings.

Last Words of Comfort

181:1.1 (1953.3) When the eleven had taken their seats, Jesus stood and addressed them: "As long as I am with you in the flesh, I can be but one individual in your midst or in the entire world. But when I have been delivered from this investment of mortal nature, I will be able to return as a spirit indweller of each of you and of all other believers in this gospel of the kingdom. In this way the Son of Man will become a spiritual incarnation in the souls of all true believers.

181:1.2 (1953.4) "When I have returned to live in you and work through you, I can the better lead you on through this life and guide you through the many abodes in the future life in the heaven of heavens. Life in the Father's eternal creation is not an endless rest of idleness and selfish ease but rather a ceaseless progression in grace, truth, and glory. Each of the many, many stations in my Father's house is a stopping place, a life designed to prepare you for the next one ahead. And so will the children of light go on from glory to glory until they attain the divine estate wherein they are spiritually perfected even as the Father is perfect in all things.

181:1.3 (1953.5) "If you would follow after me when I leave you, put forth your earnest efforts to live in accordance with the spirit of my teachings and with the ideal of my life—the doing of my Father's will. This do instead of trying to imitate my natural life in the flesh as I have, perforce, been required to live it on this world.

181:1.4 (1954.1) "The Father sent me into this world, but only a few of you have chosen fully to receive me. I will pour out my spirit upon all flesh, but all men will not choose to receive this new teacher as the guide and counselor of the soul.

But as many as do receive him shall be enlightened, cleansed, and comforted. And this Spirit of Truth will become in them a well of living water springing up into eternal life.

181:1.5 (1954.2) "And now, as I am about to leave you, I would speak words of comfort. Peace I leave with you; my peace I give to you. I make these gifts not as the world gives—by measure—I give each of you all you will receive. Let not your heart be troubled, neither let it be fearful. I have overcome the world, and in me you shall all triumph through faith. I have warned you that the Son of Man will be killed, but I assure you I will come back before I go to the Father, even though it be for only a little while. And after I have ascended to the Father, I will surely send the new teacher to be with you and to abide in your very hearts. And when you see all this come to pass, be not dismayed, but rather believe, inasmuch as you knew it all beforehand. I have loved you with a great affection, and I would not leave you, but it is the Father's will. My hour has come.

181:1.6 (1954.3) "Doubt not any of these truths even after you are scattered abroad by persecution and are downcast by many sorrows. When you feel that you are alone in the world, I will know of your isolation even as, when you are scattered every man to his own place, leaving the Son of Man in the hands of his enemies, you will know of mine. But I am never alone; always is the Father with me. Even at such a time I will pray for you. And all of these things have I told you that you might have

peace and have it more abundantly. In this world you will have tribulation, but be of good cheer; I have triumphed in the world and shown you the way to eternal joy and everlasting service."

181:1.7 (1954.4) Jesus gives peace to his fellow doers of the will of God but not on the order of the joys and satisfactions of this material world. Unbelieving materialists and fatalists can hope to enjoy only two kinds of peace and soul comfort: Either they must be stoics, with steadfast resolution determined to face the inevitable and to endure the worst; or they must be optimists, ever indulging that hope which springs eternal in the human breast, vainly longing for a peace which never really comes.

181:1.8 (1954.5) A certain amount of both stoicism and optimism are serviceable in living a life on earth, but neither has aught to do with that superb peace which the Son of God bestows upon his brethren in the flesh. The peace which Michael gives his children on earth is that very peace which filled his own soul when he himself lived the mortal life in the flesh and on this very world. The peace of Jesus is the joy and satisfaction of a God-knowing individual who has achieved the triumph of learning fully how to do the will of God while living the mortal life in the flesh. The peace of Jesus' mind was founded on an absolute human faith in the actuality of the divine Father's wise and sympathetic over-care. Jesus had trouble on earth, he has even been falsely called the "man of sorrows," but in and through all of these experiences he enjoyed the comfort of that confidence which ever empowered him to proceed with his life purpose in the full assurance that he was achieving the Father's will.

181:1.9 (1954.6) Jesus was determined, persistent, and thoroughly devoted to the accomplishment of his mission, but he was not an unfeeling and calloused stoic; he ever sought for the cheerful aspects of his life experiences, but he was not a blind and self-deceived optimist. The Master knew all that was to befall him, and he was unafraid. After he had bestowed this peace upon each of his followers, he could consistently say, "Let not your heart be troubled, neither let it be afraid."

181:1.10 (1955.1) The peace of Jesus is, then, the peace and assurance of a son who fully believes that his career for time and eternity is safely and wholly in the care and keeping of an all-wise, all-loving, and all-powerful spirit Father. And this is, indeed, a peace which passes the understanding of mortal mind, but which can be enjoyed to the full by the believing human heart.

Farewell Personal Admonitions

181:2.1 (1955.2) The Master had finished giving his farewell instructions and imparting his final admonitions to the apostles as a group. He then addressed himself to saying good-bye individually and to giving each a word of personal advice, together with his parting blessing. The apostles were still seated about the table as when they first sat down to partake of the Last Supper, and as the Master went around the table talking to them, each man rose to his feet when Jesus addressed him.

181:2.2 (1955.3) To John, Jesus said: "You, John, are the youngest of my brethren. You have been very near me, and while I love you all with the same love which a father bestows upon his sons, you were designated by Andrew as one of the three who should always be near me. Besides this, you have acted for me and must continue so to act in many matters concerning my earthly family. And I go to the Father, John, having full confidence that you will continue to watch over those who are mine in the flesh. See to it that their present confusion regarding my mission does not in any way prevent your extending to them all sympathy, counsel, and help even as you know I would if I were to remain in the flesh. And when they all come to see the light and enter fully into the kingdom, while you all will welcome them joyously, I depend upon you, John, to welcome them for me.

181:2.3 (1955.4) "And now, as I enter upon the closing hours of my earthly career, remain near at hand that I may leave any message with you regarding my family. As concerns the work put in my hands by the Father, it is now finished except for my death in the flesh, and I am ready to drink this last cup. But as for the responsibilities left to me by my earthly father, Joseph, while I have attended to these during my life, I must now depend upon you to act in my stead in all these matters. And I have chosen you to do this for me, John, because you are the youngest and will therefore very likely outlive these other apostles.

181:2.4 (1955.5) "Once we called you and your brother sons of thunder. You started out with us strong-minded and intolerant, but you have changed much since you wanted me to call fire down upon the heads of ignorant and thoughtless unbelievers. And you must change yet more. You should become the apostle of the new commandment which I have this night given you. Dedicate your life to teaching your brethren how to love one another, even as I have loved you."

181:2.5 (1955.6) As John Zebedee stood there in the upper chamber, the tears rolling down his cheeks, he looked into the Master's face and said: "And so I will, my Master, but how can I learn to love my brethren more?" And then answered Jesus: "You will learn to love your brethren more when you first learn to love their Father in heaven more, and after you have become truly more interested in their welfare in time and in eternity. And all such human interest is fostered by understanding sympathy, unselfish service, and unstinted forgiveness. No man should despise your youth, but I exhort you always to give due consideration to the fact that age oftentimes represents experience, and that nothing in human affairs can take the place of actual experience. Strive to live peaceably with all men, especially your friends in the brotherhood of the heavenly kingdom. And, John, always remember, strive not with the souls you would win for the kingdom."

181:2.6 (1956.1) And then the Master, passing around his own seat, paused a moment by the side of the place of Judas Iscariot. The apostles were rather surprised that Judas had not returned before this, and they were very curious to know the significance of Jesus' sad countenance as he stood by the betrayer's vacant seat. But none of them, except possibly Andrew, entertained even the slightest thought that their treasurer had gone out to betray his Master, as Jesus had intimated to them earlier in the evening and during the supper. So much had been going on that, for the time being, they had quite forgotten about the Master's announcement that one of them would betray him.

181:2.7 (1956.2) Jesus now went over to Simon Zelotes, who stood up and listened to this admonition: "You are a true son of Abraham, but what a time I have had trying to make you a son of this heavenly kingdom. I love you and so do all of your brethren. I know that you love me, Simon, and that you also love the kingdom, but you are still set on making this kingdom come according to your liking. I know full well that you will eventually grasp the spiritual nature and meaning of my gospel, and that you will do valiant work in its proclamation, but I am distressed about what may happen to you when I depart. I would rejoice to know that you would not falter; I would be made happy if I could know that, after I go to the Father, you would not cease to be my apostle, and that you would acceptably deport yourself as an ambassador of the heavenly kingdom."

181:2.8 (1956.3) Jesus had hardly ceased speaking to Simon Zelotes when the fiery patriot, drying his eyes, replied: "Master, have no fears for my loyalty. I have turned my back upon everything that I might dedicate my life to the establishment of your kingdom on earth, and I will not falter. I have survived every disappointment so far, and I will not forsake you."

181:2.9 (1956.4) And then, laying his hand on Simon's shoulder, Jesus said: "It is indeed refreshing to hear you talk like that, especially at such a time as this, but, my good friend, you still do not know what you are talking about. Not for one moment would I doubt your loyalty, your devotion; I know you would not hesitate to go forth in battle and die for me, as all these others would" (and they all nodded a vigorous approval), "but that will not be required of you. I have repeatedly told you that my kingdom is not of this world, and that my disciples will not fight to effect its establishment. I have told you this many times, Simon, but you refuse to face the truth. I am not concerned with your loyalty to me and to the kingdom, but what will you do when I go away and you at last wake up to the realization that you have failed to grasp the meaning of my teaching, and that you must adjust your misconceptions to the reality of another and spiritual order of affairs in the kingdom?"

181:2.10 (1956.5) Simon wanted to speak further, but Jesus raised his hand and, stopping him, went on to say: "None of my apostles are more sincere and honest at heart than you, but not one of them will be so upset and disheartened as you, after my departure. In all of your discouragement my spirit shall abide with you, and these, your brethren, will not forsake you. Do not forget what I have taught you regarding the relation of citizenship on earth to sonship in the Father's spiritual kingdom. Ponder well all that I have said to you about rendering to Caesar the things which are Caesar's and to God that which is God's. Dedicate your life, Simon, to showing how acceptably mortal man may fulfill my injunction concerning the simultaneous recognition of temporal duty to civil powers and spiritual service in the brotherhood of the kingdom. If you will be taught by the Spirit of Truth, never will there be conflict between the requirements of citizenship on earth and sonship in heaven unless the temporal rulers presume to require of you the homage and worship which belong only to God.

181:2.11 (1957.1) "And now, Simon, when you do finally see all of this, and after you have shaken off your depression and have gone forth proclaiming this gospel in great power, never forget that I was with you even through all of your season of discouragement, and that I will go on with you to the very end. You shall always be my apostle, and after you become willing to see by the eye of the spirit and more fully to yield your will to the will of the Father in heaven, then will you return to labor as my ambassador, and no one shall take away from you the authority which I have conferred upon you, because of your slowness of comprehending the truths I have taught you. And so, Simon, once more I warn you that they who fight with the sword perish with the sword, while they who labor in the spirit achieve life everlasting in the kingdom to come with joy and peace in the kingdom which now is. And when the work given into your hands is finished on earth, you, Simon, shall sit down with me in my kingdom over there. You shall really see the kingdom you have longed for, but not in this life. Continue to believe in me and in that which I have revealed to you, and you shall receive the gift of eternal life."

181:2.12 (1957.2) When Jesus had finished speaking to Simon Zelotes, he stepped over to Matthew Levi and said: "No longer will it devolve upon you to provide for the treasury of the apostolic group. Soon, very soon, you will all be scattered; you will not be permitted to enjoy the comforting and sustaining association of even one of your brethren. As you go onward preaching this gospel of the kingdom, you will have to find for yourselves new associates. I have sent you forth two and two during the times of your training, but now that I am leaving you, after you have recovered from the shock, you will go out alone, and to the ends of the earth, proclaiming this good news: That faith-quickened mortals are the sons of God."

181:2.13 (1957.3) Then spoke Matthew: "But, Master, who will send us, and how shall we know where to go? Will Andrew show us the way?" And Jesus answered: "No, Levi, Andrew will no longer direct you in the proclamation of

the gospel. He will, indeed, continue as your friend and counselor until that day whereon the new teacher comes, and then shall the Spirit of Truth lead each of you abroad to labor for the extension of the kingdom. Many changes have come over you since that day at the customhouse when you first set out to follow me; but many more must come before you will be able to see the vision of a brotherhood in which gentile sits alongside Jew in fraternal association. But go on with your urge to win your Jewish brethren until you are fully satisfied and then turn with power to the gentiles. One thing you may be certain of, Levi: You have won the confidence and affection of your brethren; they all love you." (And all ten of them signified their acquiescence in the Master's words.)

181:2.14 (1958.1) "Levi, I know much about your anxieties, sacrifices, and labors to keep the treasury replenished which your brethren do not know, and I am rejoiced that, though he who carried the bag is absent, the publican ambassador is here at my farewell gathering with the messengers of the kingdom. I pray that you may discern the meaning of my teaching with the eyes of the spirit. And when the new teacher comes into your heart, follow on as he will lead you and let your brethren see—even all the world—what the Father can do for a hated tax-gatherer who dared to follow the Son of Man and to believe the gospel of the kingdom. Even from the first, Levi, I loved you as I did these other Galileans. Knowing then so well that neither the Father nor the Son has respect of persons, see to it that you make no such distinctions among those who become believers in the gospel through your ministry. And so, Matthew, dedicate your whole future life service to showing all men that God is no respecter of persons; that, in the sight of God and in the fellowship of the kingdom, all men are equal, all believers are the sons of God."

181:2.15 (1958.2) Jesus then stepped over to James Zebedee, who stood in silence as the Master addressed him, saying: "James, when you and your younger brother once came to me seeking preferment in the honors of the kingdom, and I told you such honors were for the Father to bestow, I asked if you were able to drink my cup, and both of you answered that you were. Even if you were not then able, and if you are not now able, you will soon be prepared for such a service by the experience you are about to pass through. By such behavior you angered your brethren at that time. If they have not already fully forgiven you, they will when they see you drink my cup. Whether your ministry be long or short, possess your soul in patience. When the new teacher comes, let him teach you the poise of compassion and that sympathetic tolerance which is born of sublime confidence in me and of perfect submission to the Father's will.

Dedicate your life to the demonstration of that combined human affection and divine dignity of the God-knowing and Son-believing disciple. And all who thus live will reveal the gospel even in the manner of their death. You and your brother John will go different ways, and one of you may sit down with me in the eternal kingdom long before the other. It would help you much if you would learn that true wisdom embraces discretion as well as courage. You should learn sagacity to go along with your aggressiveness. There will come those supreme moments wherein my disciples will not hesitate to lay down their lives for this gospel, but in all ordinary circumstances it would be far better to placate the wrath of unbelievers that you might live and continue to preach the glad tidings. As far as lies in your power, live long on the earth that your life of many years may be fruitful in souls won for the heavenly kingdom."

181:2.16 (1958.3) When the Master had finished speaking to James Zebedee, he stepped around to the end of the table where Andrew sat and, looking his faithful helper in the eyes, said: "Andrew, you have faithfully represented me as acting head of the ambassadors of the heavenly kingdom. Although you have sometimes doubted and at other times manifested dangerous timidity, still, you have always been sincerely just and eminently fair in dealing with your associates. Ever since the ordination of you and your brethren as messengers of the kingdom, you have been self- governing in all group administrative affairs except that I designated you as the acting head of these chosen ones. In no other temporal matter have I acted to direct or to influence your decisions. And this I did in order to provide for leadership in the direction of all your subsequent group deliberations. In my universe and in my Father's universe of universes, our brethren-sons are dealt with as individuals in all their spiritual relations, but in all group relationships we unfailingly provide for definite leadership. Our kingdom is a realm of order, and where two or more will creatures act in co-operation, there is always provided the authority of leadership.

181:2.17 (1959.1) "And now, Andrew, since you are the chief of your brethren by authority of my appointment, and since you have thus served as my personal representative, and as I am about to leave you and go to my Father, I release you from all responsibility as regards these temporal and administrative affairs. From now on you may exercise no jurisdiction over your brethren except that which you have earned in your capacity as spiritual leader, and which your brethren therefore freely recognize. From this hour you may exercise no authority over your brethren unless they restore such jurisdiction to you by their definite legislative action after I shall have gone to the Father. But this release from responsibility as the administrative head of this group does not in any manner lessen your moral responsibility to do everything in your power to hold your brethren together with a firm and loving hand during the trying time just ahead, those days which must intervene between my departure in the flesh and the sending of the new teacher who will live in your hearts, and who ultimately will lead you into all truth. As I prepare to leave you, I would liberate you from all administrative responsibility which had its inception and authority in my presence as one among you. Henceforth I shall exercise only spiritual authority over you and among you.

181:2.18 (1959.2) "If your brethren desire to retain you as their counselor, I direct that you should, in all matters temporal and spiritual, do your utmost to promote peace and harmony among the various groups of sincere gospel believers.

Dedicate the remainder of your life to promoting the practical aspects of brotherly love among your brethren. Be kind to my brothers in the flesh when they come fully to believe this gospel; manifest loving and impartial devotion to the Greeks in the West and to Abner in the East. Although these, my apostles, are soon going to be scattered to the four corners of the earth, there to proclaim the good news of the salvation of sonship with God, you are to hold them together during the trying time just ahead, that season of intense testing during which you must learn to believe this gospel without my personal presence while you patiently await the arrival of the new teacher, the Spirit of Truth. And so, Andrew, though it may not fall to you to do the great works as seen by men, be content to be the teacher and counselor of those who do such things. Go on with your work on earth to the end, and then shall you continue this ministry in the eternal kingdom, for have I not many times told you that I have other sheep not of this flock?"

181:2.19 (1959.3) Jesus then went over to the Alpheus twins and, standing between them, said: "My little children, you are one of the three groups of brothers who chose to follow after me. All six of you have done well to work in peace with your own flesh and blood, but none have done better than you. Hard times are just ahead of us. You may not understand all that will befall you and your brethren, but never doubt that you were once called to the work of the kingdom. For some time there will be no multitudes to manage, but do not become discouraged; when your lifework is finished, I will receive you on high, where in glory you shall tell of your salvation to seraphic hosts and to multitudes of the high Sons of God. Dedicate your lives to the enhancement of commonplace toil. Show all men on earth and the angels of heaven how cheerfully and courageously mortal man can, after having been called to work for a season in the special service of God, return to the labors of former days. If, for the time being, your work in the outward affairs of the kingdom should be completed, you should go back to your former labors with the new enlightenment of the experience of sonship with God and with the exalted realization that, to him who is God-knowing, there is no such thing as common labor or secular toil. To you who have worked with me, all things have become sacred, and all earthly labor has become a service even to God the Father. And when you hear the news of the doings of your former apostolic associates, rejoice with them and continue your daily work as those who wait upon God and serve while they wait. You have been my apostles, and you always shall be, and I will remember you in the kingdom to come."

181:2.20 (1960.1) And then Jesus went over to Philip, who, standing up, heard this message from his Master: "Philip, you have asked me many foolish questions, but I have done my utmost to answer every one, and now would I answer the last of such questionings which have arisen in your most honest but unspiritual mind. All the time I have been coming around toward you, have you been saying to yourself, 'What shall I ever do if the Master goes away and leaves us alone in the world?' O, you of little faith! And yet you have almost as much as many of your brethren. You have been a good steward, Philip. You failed us only a few times, and one of those failures we utilized to manifest the Father's glory.

Your office of stewardship is about over. You must soon more fully do the work you were called to do—the preaching of this gospel of the kingdom. Philip, you have always wanted to be shown, and very soon shall you see great things. Far better that you should have seen all this by faith, but since you were sincere even in your material sightedness, you will live to see my words fulfilled. And then, when you are blessed with spiritual vision, go forth to your work, dedicating your life to the cause of leading mankind to search for

God and to seek eternal realities with the eye of spiritual faith and not with the eyes of the material mind. Remember, Philip, you have a great mission on earth, for the world is filled with those who look at life just as you have tended to. You have a great work to do, and when it is finished in faith, you shall come to me in my kingdom, and I will take great pleasure in showing you that which eye has not seen, ear heard, nor the mortal mind conceived. In the meantime, become as a little child in the kingdom of the spirit and permit me, as the spirit of the new teacher, to lead you forward in the spiritual kingdom. And in this way will I be able to do much for you which I was not able to accomplish when I sojourned with you as a mortal of the realm. And always remember, Philip, he who has seen me has seen the Father."

181:2.21 (1960.2) Then went the Master over to Nathaniel. As Nathaniel stood up, Jesus bade him be seated and, sitting down by his side, said: "Nathaniel, you have learned to live above prejudice and to practice increased tolerance since you became my apostle. But there is much more for you to learn. You have been a blessing to your fellows in that they have always been admonished by your consistent sincerity. When I have gone, it may be that your frankness will interfere with your getting along well with your brethren, both old and new. You should learn that the expression of even a good thought must be modulated in accordance with the intellectual status and spiritual development of the hearer. Sincerity is most serviceable in the work of the kingdom when it is wedded to discretion.

181:2.22 (1961.1) "If you would learn to work with your brethren, you might accomplish more permanent things, but if you find yourself going off in quest of those who think as you do, in that event dedicate your life to proving that the God-knowing disciple can become a kingdom builder even when alone in the world and wholly isolated from his fellow believers. I know you will be faithful to the end, and I will some day welcome you to the enlarged service of my kingdom on high."

181:2.23 (1961.2) Then Nathaniel spoke, asking Jesus this question: "I have listened to your teaching ever since you first called me to the service of this kingdom, but I honestly cannot understand the full meaning of all you tell us. I do not know what to expect next, and I think most of my brethren are likewise perplexed, but they hesitate to confess their confusion. Can you help me?" Jesus, putting his hand on Nathaniel's shoulder, said: "My friend, it is not strange that you should encounter perplexity in your attempt to grasp the meaning of my spiritual teachings since you are so handicapped by your preconceptions of Jewish tradition and so confused by your persistent tendency to interpret my gospel in accordance with the teachings of the scribes and Pharisees.

181:2.24 (1961.3) "I have taught you much by word of mouth, and I have lived my life among you. I have done all that can be done to enlighten your minds and liberate your souls, and what you have not been able to get from my teachings and my life, you must now prepare to acquire at the hand of that master of all teachers— actual experience. And in all of this new experience which now awaits you, I will go before you and the Spirit of Truth shall be with you. Fear not; that which you now fail to comprehend, the new teacher, when he has come, will reveal to you throughout the remainder of your life on earth and on through your training in the eternal ages."

181:2.25 (1961.4) And then the Master, turning to all of them, said: "Be not dismayed that you fail to grasp the full meaning of the gospel. You are but finite, mortal men, and that which I have taught you is infinite, divine, and eternal. Be patient and of good courage since you have the eternal ages before you in which to continue your progressive attainment of the experience of becoming perfect, even as your Father in Paradise is perfect."

181:2.26 (1961.5) And then Jesus went over to Thomas, who, standing up, heard him say: "Thomas, you have often lacked faith; however, when you have had your seasons with doubt, you have never lacked courage. I know well that the false prophets and spurious teachers will not deceive you. After I have gone, your brethren will the more appreciate your critical way of viewing new teachings. And when you all are scattered to the ends of the earth in the times to come, remember that you are still my ambassador. Dedicate your life to the great work of showing how the critical material mind of man can triumph over the inertia of intellectual doubting when faced by the demonstration of the manifestation of living truth as it operates in the experience of spirit-born men and women who yield the fruits of the spirit in their lives, and who love one another, even as I have loved you. Thomas, I am glad you joined us, and I know, after a short period of perplexity, you will go on in the service of the kingdom. Your doubts have perplexed your brethren, but they have never troubled me. I have confidence in you, and I will go before you even to the uttermost parts of the earth."

181:2.27 (1962.1) Then the Master went over to Simon Peter, who stood up as Jesus addressed him: "Peter, I know you love me, and that you will dedicate your life to the public proclamation of this gospel of the kingdom to Jew and gentile, but I am distressed that your years of such close association with me have not done more to help you think before you speak. What experience must you pass through before you will learn to set a guard upon your lips? How much trouble have you made for us by your thoughtless speaking, by your presumptuous self-confidence! And you are destined to make much more trouble for yourself if you do not master this frailty. You know that your brethren love you in spite of this weakness, and you should also understand that this shortcoming in no way impairs my affection for you, but it lessens your usefulness and never ceases to make trouble for you. But you will undoubtedly receive great help from the experience you will pass through this very night. And what I now say to you, Simon Peter, I likewise say to all your brethren here assembled: This night you will all be in great danger of stumbling over me. You know it is written, 'The shepherd will be smitten and the sheep will be scattered abroad.' When I am absent, there is great danger that some of you will succumb to doubts and stumble because of what befalls me. But I promise you now that I will come back to you for a little while, and that I will then go before you into Galilee."

181:2.28 (1962.2) Then said Peter, placing his hand on Jesus' shoulder: "No matter if all my brethren should succumb to doubts because of you, I promise that I will not stumble over anything you may do. I will go with you and, if need be, die for you."

181:2.29 (1962.3) As Peter stood there before his Master, all atremble with intense emotion and overflowing with genuine love for him, Jesus looked straight into his moistened eyes as he said: "Peter, verily, verily, I say to you, this night the cock will not crow until you have denied me three or four times. And thus what you have failed to learn from peaceful association with me, you will learn through much trouble and many sorrows. And after you have really learned this needful lesson, you should strengthen your brethren and go on living a life dedicated to preaching this gospel, though you may fall into prison and, perhaps, follow me in paying the supreme price of loving service in the building of the Father's kingdom.

181:2.30 (1962.4) "But remember my promise: When I am raised up, I will tarry with you for a season before I go to the Father. And even this night will I make supplication to the Father that he strengthen each of you for that which you must now so soon pass through. I love you all with the love wherewith the Father loves me, and therefore should you henceforth love one another, even as I have loved you."

181:2.31 (1962.5) And then, when they had sung a hymn, they departed for the camp on the Mount of Olives.

Paper 182

In Gethsemane

182:0.1 (1963.1) IT WAS about ten o'clock this Thursday night when Jesus led the eleven apostles from the home of Elijah and Mary Mark on their way back to the Gethsemane camp. Ever since that day in the hills, John Mark had made it his business to keep a watchful eye on Jesus. John, being in need of sleep, had obtained several hours of rest while the Master had been with his apostles in the upper room, but on hearing them coming downstairs, he arose and, quickly throwing a linen coat about himself, followed them through the city, over the brook Kidron, and on to their private encampment adjacent to Gethsemane Park. And John Mark remained so near the Master throughout this night and the next day that he witnessed everything and overheard much of what the Master said from this time on to the hour of the crucifixion.

182:0.2 (1963.2) As Jesus and the eleven made their way back to camp, the apostles began to wonder about the meaning of Judas's prolonged absence, and they spoke to one another concerning the Master's prediction that one of them would betray him, and for the first time they suspected that all was not well with Judas Iscariot. But they did not engage in open comment about Judas until they reached the camp and observed that he was not there, waiting to receive them.

When they all besieged Andrew to know what had become of Judas, their chief remarked only, "I do not know where Judas is, but I fear he has deserted us."

The Last Group Prayer

182:1.1 (1963.3) A few moments after arriving at camp, Jesus said to them: "My friends and brethren, my time with you is now very short, and I desire that we draw apart by ourselves while we pray to our Father in heaven for strength to sustain us in this hour and henceforth in all the work we must do in his name."

182:1.2 (1963.4) When Jesus had thus spoken, he led the way a short distance up on Olivet, and in full view of Jerusalem he bade them kneel on a large flat rock in a circle about him as they had done on the day of their ordination; and then, as he stood there in the midst of them glorified in the mellow moonlight, he lifted up his eyes toward heaven and prayed:

182:1.3 (1963.5) "Father, my hour has come; now glorify your Son that the Son may glorify you. I know that you have given me full authority over all living creatures in my realm, and I will give eternal life to all who will become faith sons of God. And this is eternal life, that my creatures should know you as the only true God and Father of all, and that they should believe in him whom you sent into the world. Father, I have exalted you on earth and have accomplished the work which you gave me to do. I have almost finished my bestowal upon the children of our own creation; there remains only for me to lay down my life in the flesh. And now, O my Father, glorify me with the glory which I had with you before this world was and receive me once more at your right hand.

182:1.4 (1964.1) "I have manifested you to the men whom you chose from the world and gave to me. They are yours—as all life is in your hands—you gave them to me, and I have lived among them, teaching them the way of life, and they have believed. These men are learning that all I have comes from you, and that the life I live in the flesh is to make known my Father to the worlds. The truth which you have given to me I have revealed to them. These, my friends and ambassadors, have sincerely willed to receive your word. I have told them that I came forth from you, that you sent me into this world, and that I am about to return to you. Father, I do pray for these chosen men. And I pray for them not as I would pray for the world, but as for those whom I have chosen out of the world to represent me to the world after I have returned to your work, even as I have represented you in this world during my sojourn in the flesh. These men are mine; you gave them to me; but all things which are mine are ever yours, and all that which was yours you have now caused to be mine. You have been exalted in me, and I now pray that I may be honored in these men. I can no longer be in this world; I am about to return to the work you have given me to do. I must leave these men behind to represent us and our kingdom among men. Father, keep these men faithful as I prepare to yield up my life in the flesh. Help these, my friends, to be one in spirit, even as we are one. As long as I could be with them, I could watch over them and guide them, but now am I about to go away. Be near them, Father, until we can send the new teacher to comfort and strengthen them.

182:1.5 (1964.2) "You gave me twelve men, and I have kept them all save one, the son of revenge, who would not have further fellowship with us. These men are weak and frail, but I know we can trust them; I have proved them; they love me, even as they reverence you. While they must suffer much for my sake, I desire that they should also be filled with the joy of the assurance of sonship in the heavenly kingdom. I have given these men your word and have taught them the truth. The world may hate them, even as it has hated me, but I do not ask that you take them out of the world, only that you keep them from the evil in the world. Sanctify them in the truth; your word is truth. And as you sent me into this world, even so am I about to send these men into the world. For their sakes I have lived among men and have consecrated my life to your service that I might inspire them to be purified through the truth I have taught them and the love I have revealed to them. I well know, my Father, that there is no need for me to ask you to watch over these brethren after I have gone; I know you love them even as I, but I do this that they may the better realize the Father loves mortal men even as does the Son.

182:1.6 (1964.3) "And now, my Father,

I would pray not only for these eleven men but also for all others who now believe, or who may hereafter believe the gospel of the kingdom through the word of their future ministry. I want them all to be one, even as you and I are one. You are in me and I am in you, and I desire that these believers likewise be in us; that both of our spirits indwell them. If my children are one as we are one, and if they love one another as I have loved them, all men will then believe that I came forth from you and be willing to receive the revelation of truth and glory which I have made. The glory which you gave me I have revealed to these believers. As you have lived with me in spirit, so have I lived with them in the flesh. As you have been one with me, so have I been one with them, and so will the new teacher ever be one with them and in them. And all this have I done that my brethren in the flesh may know that the Father loves them even as does the Son, and that you love them even as you love me. Father, work with me to save these believers that they may presently come to be with me in glory and then go on to join you in the Paradise embrace. Those who serve with me in humiliation, I would have with me in glory so that they may see all you have given into my hands as the eternal harvest of the seed sowing of time in the likeness of mortal flesh. I long to show my earthly brethren the glory I had with you before the founding of this world. This world knows very little of you, righteous Father, but I know you, and I have made you known to these believers, and they will make known your name to other generations. And now I promise them that you will be with them in the world even as you have been with me—even so."

182:1.7 (1965.1) The eleven remained kneeling in this circle about Jesus for several minutes before they arose and in silence made their way back to the nearby camp.

182:1.8 (1965.2) Jesus prayed for unity among his followers, but he did not desire uniformity. Sin creates a dead level of evil inertia, but righteousness nourishes the creative spirit of individual experience in the living realities of eternal truth and in the progressive communion of the divine spirits of the Father and the Son. In the spiritual fellowship of the believer-son with the divine Father there can never be doctrinal finality and sectarian superiority of group consciousness.

182:1.9 (1965.3) The Master, during the course of this final prayer with his apostles, alluded to the fact that he had manifested the Father's name to the world. And that is truly what he did by the revelation of God through his perfected life in the flesh. The Father in heaven had sought to reveal himself to Moses, but he could proceed no further than to cause it to be said, "I AM." And when pressed for further revelation of himself, it was only disclosed, "I AM that I AM." But when Jesus had finished his earth life, this name of the Father had been so revealed that the Master, who was the Father incarnate, could truly say:

182:1.10 (1965.4) I am the bread of life.
182:1.11 (1965.5) I am the living water.
182:1.12 (1965.6) I am the light of the world.
182:1.13 (1965.7) I am the desire of all ages.
182:1.14 (1965.8) I am the open door to eternal salvation.
182:1.15 (1965.9) I am the reality of endless life.
182:1.16 (1965.10) I am the good shepherd.
182:1.17 (1965.11) I am the pathway of infinite perfection.
182:1.18 (1965.12) I am the resurrection and the life. 182:1.19 (1965.13) I am the secret of eternal survival. 182:1.20 (1965.14) I am the way, the truth, and the life.
182:1.21 (1965.15) I am the infinite Father of my finite children.
182:1.22 (1965.16) I am the true vine; you are the branches.
182:1.23 (1965.17) I am the hope of all who know the living truth. 182:1.24 (1965.18) I am the living bridge from one world to another. 182:1.25 (1965.19) I am

the living link between time and eternity.

182:1.26 (1965.20) Thus did Jesus enlarge the living revelation of the name of God to all generations. As divine love reveals the nature of God, eternal truth discloses his name in ever-enlarging proportions.

Last Hour Before the Betrayal

182:2.1 (1966.1) The apostles were greatly shocked when they returned to their camp and found Judas absent. While the eleven were engaged in a heated discussion of their traitorous fellow apostle, David Zebedee and John Mark took Jesus to one side and revealed that they had kept Judas under observation for several days, and that they knew he intended to betray him into the hands of his enemies. Jesus listened to them but only said: "My friends, nothing can happen to the Son of Man unless the Father in heaven so wills. Let not your hearts be troubled; all things will work together for the glory of God and the salvation of men."

182:2.2 (1966.2) The cheerful attitude of Jesus was waning. As the hour passed, he grew more and more serious, even sorrowful. The apostles, being much agitated, were loath to return to their tents even when requested to do so by the Master himself. Returning from his talk with David and John, he addressed his last words to all eleven, saying: "My friends, go to your rest. Prepare yourselves for the work of tomorrow. Remember, we should all submit ourselves to the will of the Father in heaven. My peace I leave with you." And having thus spoken, he motioned them to their tents, but as they went, he called to Peter, James, and John, saying, "I desire that you remain with me for a little while."

182:2.3 (1966.3) The apostles fell asleep only because they were literally exhausted; they had been running short on sleep ever since their arrival in Jerusalem. Before they went to their separate sleeping quarters, Simon Zelotes led them all over to his tent, where were stored the swords and other arms, and supplied each of them with this fighting equipment.

All of them received these arms and girded themselves therewith except Nathaniel. Nathaniel, in refusing to arm himself, said: "My brethren, the Master has repeatedly told us that his kingdom is not of this world, and that his disciples should not fight with the sword to bring about its establishment. I believe this; I do not think the Master needs to have us employ the sword in his defense. We have all seen his mighty power and know that he could defend himself against his enemies if he so desired. If he will not resist his enemies, it must be that such a course represents his attempt to fulfill his Father's will. I will pray, but I will not wield the sword." When Andrew heard Nathaniel's speech, he handed his sword back to Simon Zelotes. And so nine of them were armed as they separated for the night.

182:2.4 (1966.4) Resentment of Judas's being a traitor for the moment eclipsed everything else in the apostles' minds. The Master's comment in reference to Judas, spoken in the course of the last prayer, opened their eyes to the fact that he had forsaken them.

182:2.5 (1966.5) After the eight apostles had finally gone to their tents, and while Peter, James, and John were standing by to receive the Master's orders, Jesus called to David Zebedee, "Send to me your most fleet and trustworthy messenger." When David brought to the Master one Jacob, once a runner on the overnight messenger service between Jerusalem and Bethsaida, Jesus, addressing him, said: "In all haste, go to Abner at Philadelphia and say: 'The Master sends greetings of peace to you and says that the hour has come when he will be delivered into the hands of his enemies, who will put him to death, but that he will rise from the dead and appear to you shortly, before he goes to the Father, and that he will then give you guidance to the time when the new teacher shall come to live in your hearts.'" And when Jacob had rehearsed this message to the

Master's satisfaction, Jesus sent him on his way, saying: "Fear not what any man may do to you, Jacob, for this night an unseen messenger will run by your side."

182:2.6 (1967.1) Then Jesus turned to the chief of the visiting Greeks who were encamped with them, and said: "My brother, be not disturbed by what is about to take place since I have already forewarned you. The Son of Man will be put to death at the instigation of his enemies, the chief priests and the rulers of the Jews, but I will rise to be with you a short time before I go to the Father. And when you have seen all this come to pass, glorify God and strengthen your brethren."

182:2.7 (1967.2) In ordinary circumstances the apostles would have bidden the Master a personal good night, but this evening they were so preoccupied with the sudden realization of Judas's desertion and so overcome by the unusual nature of the Master's farewell prayer that they listened to his good-bye salutation and went away in silence.

182:2.8 (1967.3) Jesus did say this to Andrew as he left his side that night: "Andrew, do what you can to keep your brethren together until I come again to you after I have drunk this cup. Strengthen your brethren, seeing that I have already told you all. Peace be with you."

182:2.9 (1967.4) None of the apostles expected anything out of the ordinary to happen that night since it was already so late. They sought sleep that they might rise up early in the morning and be prepared for the worst. They thought that the chief priests would seek to apprehend their Master early in the morning as no secular work was ever done after noon on the preparation day for the Passover. Only David Zebedee and John Mark understood that the enemies of Jesus were coming with Judas that very night.

182:2.10 (1967.5) David had arranged to stand guard that night on the upper trail which led to the Bethany-Jerusalem road, while John Mark was to watch along the road coming up by the Kidron to Gethsemane. Before David went to his self-imposed task of outpost duty, he bade farewell to Jesus, saying: "Master, I have had great joy in my service with you.

My brothers are your apostles, but I have delighted to do the lesser things as they should be done, and I shall miss you with all my heart when you are gone." And then said Jesus to David: "David, my son, others have done that which they were directed to do, but this service have you done of your own heart, and I have not been unmindful of your devotion. You, too, shall some day serve with me in the eternal kingdom."

182:2.11 (1967.6) And then, as he prepared to go on watch by the upper trail, David said to Jesus: "You know, Master, I sent for your family, and I have word by a messenger that they are tonight in Jericho. They will be here early tomorrow forenoon since it would be dangerous for them to come up the bloody way by night." And Jesus, looking down upon David, only said: "Let it be so, David."

182:2.12 (1967.7) When David had gone up Olivet, John Mark took up his vigil near the road which ran by the brook down to Jerusalem. And John would have remained at this post but for his great desire to be near Jesus and to know what was going on. Shortly after David left him, and when John Mark observed Jesus withdraw, with Peter, James, and John, into a near-by ravine, he was so overcome with combined devotion and curiosity that he forsook his sentinel post and followed after them, hiding himself in the bushes, from which place he saw and overheard all that transpired during those last moments in the garden and just before Judas and the armed guards appeared to arrest Jesus.

182:2.13 (1968.1) While all this was in progress at the Master's camp, Judas Iscariot was in conference with the captain of the temple guards, who had assembled his men preparatory to setting out, under the leadership of the betrayer, to arrest Jesus.

Alone in Gethsemane

182:3.1 (1968.2) After all was still and quiet about the camp, Jesus, taking Peter, James, and John, went a short way up a near-by ravine where he had often before gone to pray and commune. The three apostles could not help recognizing that he was grievously oppressed; never before had they observed their Master to be so heavy-laden and sorrowful. When they arrived at the place of his devotions, he bade the three sit down and watch with him while he went off about a stone's throw to pray. And when he had fallen down on his face, he prayed: "My Father, I came into this world to do your will, and so have I. I know that the hour has come to lay down this life in the flesh, and I do not shrink therefrom, but I would know that it is your will that I drink this cup. Send me the assurance that I will please you in my death even as I have in my life."

182:3.2 (1968.3) The Master remained in a prayerful attitude for a few moments, and then, going over to the three apostles, he found them sound asleep, for their eyes were heavy and they could not remain awake. As Jesus awoke them, he said: "What! can you not watch with me even for one hour? Cannot you see that my soul is exceedingly sorrowful, even to death, and that I crave your companionship?" After the three had aroused from their slumber, the Master again went apart by himself and, falling down on the ground, again prayed: "Father, I know it is possible to avoid this cup—all things are possible with you—but I have come to do your will, and while this is a bitter cup, I would drink it if it is your will." And when he had thus prayed, a mighty angel came down by his side and, speaking to him, touched him and strengthened him.

182:3.3 (1968.4) When Jesus returned to speak with the three apostles, he again found them fast asleep. He awakened them, saying: "In such an hour I need that you should watch and pray with me—all the more do you need to pray that you enter not into temptation—wherefore do you fall asleep when I leave you?"

182:3.4 (1968.5) And then, for a third time, the Master withdrew and prayed: "Father, you see my sleeping apostles; have mercy upon them. The spirit is indeed willing, but the flesh is weak. And now, O Father, if this cup may not pass, then would I drink it. Not my will, but yours, be done." And when he had finished praying, he lay for a moment prostrate on the ground. When he arose and went back to his apostles, once more he found them asleep. He surveyed them and, with a pitying gesture, tenderly said: "Sleep on now and take your rest; the time of decision is past. The hour is now upon us wherein the Son of Man will be betrayed into the hands of his enemies." As he reached down to shake them that he might awaken them, he said: "Arise, let us be going back to the camp, for, behold, he who betrays me is at hand, and the hour has come when my flock shall be scattered. But I have already told you about these things."

182:3.5 (1968.6) During the years that Jesus lived among his followers, they did, indeed, have much proof of his divine nature, but just now are they about to witness new evidences of his humanity. Just before the greatest of all the revelations of his divinity, his resurrection, must now come the greatest proofs of his mortal nature, his humiliation and crucifixion.

182:3.6 (1969.1) Each time he prayed in the garden, his humanity laid a firmer faith-hold upon his divinity; his human will more completely became one with the divine will of his Father. Among other words spoken to him by the mighty angel was the message that the Father desired his Son to finish his earth bestowal by passing through the creature experience of death just as all mortal creatures must experience material dissolution in passing from the existence of time into the progression of eternity.

182:3.7 (1969.2) Earlier in the evening it had not seemed so difficult to drink the cup, but as the human Jesus bade farewell to his apostles and sent them to their rest, the trial grew more appalling. Jesus experienced that natural ebb and flow of feeling which is common to all human experience, and just now he was weary from work, exhausted from the long hours of strenuous labor and painful anxiety concerning the safety of his apostles. While no mortal can presume to understand the thoughts and feelings of the incarnate Son of God at such a time as this, we know that he endured great anguish and suffered untold sorrow, for the perspiration rolled off his face in great drops. He was at last convinced that the Father intended to allow natural events to take their course; he was fully determined to employ none of his sovereign power as the supreme head of a universe to save himself.

182:3.8 (1969.3) The assembled hosts of a vast creation are now hovered over this scene under the transient joint command of Gabriel and the Personalized Adjuster of Jesus. The division commanders of these armies of heaven have repeatedly been warned not to interfere with these transactions on earth unless Jesus himself should order them to intervene.

182:3.9 (1969.4) The experience of parting with the apostles was a great strain on the human heart of Jesus; this sorrow of love bore down on him and made it more difficult to face such a death as he well knew awaited him. He realized how weak and how ignorant his apostles were, and he dreaded to leave them. He well knew that the time of his departure had come, but his human heart longed to find out whether there might not possibly be some legitimate avenue of escape from this terrible plight of suffering and sorrow. And when it had thus sought escape, and failed, it was willing to drink the cup. The divine mind of Michael knew he had done his best for the twelve apostles; but the human heart of Jesus wished that more might have been done for them before they should be left alone in the world. Jesus' heart was being crushed; he truly loved his brethren. He was isolated from his family in the flesh;

one of his chosen associates was betraying him. His father Joseph's people had rejected him and thereby sealed their doom as a people with a special mission on earth. His soul was tortured by baffled love and rejected mercy. It was just one of those awful human moments when everything seems to bear down with crushing cruelty and terrible agony.

182:3.10 (1969.5) Jesus' humanity was not insensible to this situation of private loneliness, public shame, and the appearance of the failure of his cause. All these sentiments bore down on him with indescribable heaviness. In this great sorrow his mind went back to the days of his childhood in Nazareth and to his early work in Galilee. At the time of this great trial there came up in his mind many of those pleasant scenes of his earthly ministry. And it was from these old memories of Nazareth, Capernaum, Mount Hermon, and of the sunrise and sunset on the shimmering Sea of Galilee, that he soothed himself as he made his human heart strong and ready to encounter the traitor who should so soon betray him.

182:3.11 (1970.1) Before Judas and the soldiers arrived, the Master had fully regained his customary poise; the spirit had triumphed over the flesh; faith had asserted itself over all human tendencies to fear or entertain doubt. The supreme test of the full realization of the human nature had been met and acceptably passed. Once more the Son of Man was prepared to face his enemies with equanimity and in the full assurance of his invincibility as a mortal man unreservedly dedicated to the doing of his Father's will.

Paper 183

The Betrayal and Arrest of Jesus

183:0.1 (1971.1) AFTER Jesus had finally awakened Peter, James, and John,

he suggested that they go to their tents and seek sleep in preparation for the duties of the morrow. But by this time the three apostles were wide awake; they had been refreshed by their short naps, and besides, they were stimulated and aroused by the arrival on the scene of two excited messengers who inquired for David Zebedee and quickly went in quest of him when Peter informed them where he kept watch.

183:0.2 (1971.2) Although eight of the apostles were sound asleep, the Greeks who were encamped alongside them were more fearful of trouble, so much so that they had posted a sentinel to give the alarm in case danger should arise. When these two messengers hurried into camp, the Greek sentinel proceeded to arouse all of his fellow countrymen, who streamed forth from their tents, fully dressed and fully armed. All the camp was now aroused except the eight apostles. Peter desired to call his associates, but Jesus definitely forbade him. The Master mildly admonished them all to return to their tents, but they were reluctant to comply with his suggestion.

183:0.3 (1971.3) Failing to disperse his followers, the Master left them and walked down toward the olive press near the entrance to Gethsemane Park. Although the three apostles, the Greeks, and the other members of the camp hesitated immediately to follow him, John Mark hastened around through the olive trees and secreted himself in a small shed near the olive press. Jesus withdrew from the camp and from his friends in order that his apprehenders, when they arrived, might arrest him without disturbing his apostles. The Master feared to have his apostles awake and present at the time of his arrest lest the spectacle of Judas's betraying him should so arouse their animosity that they would offer resistance to the soldiers and would be taken into custody with him. He feared that, if they should be arrested with him, they might also perish with him.

183:0.4 (1971.4) Though Jesus knew that the plan for his death had its origin in the councils of the rulers of the Jews, he was also aware that all such nefarious schemes had the full approval of Lucifer, Satan, and Caligastia. And he well knew that these rebels of the realms would also be pleased to see all of the apostles destroyed with him.

183:0.5 (1971.5) Jesus sat down, alone, on the olive press, where he awaited the coming of the betrayer, and he was seen at this time only by John Mark and an innumerable host of celestial observers.

The Father's Will

183:1.1 (1971.6) There is great danger of misunderstanding the meaning of numerous sayings and many events associated with the termination of the Master's career in the flesh. The cruel treatment of Jesus by the ignorant servants and the calloused soldiers, the unfair conduct of his trials, and the unfeeling attitude of the professed religious leaders, must not be confused with the fact that Jesus, in patiently submitting to all this suffering and humiliation, was truly doing the will of the Father in Paradise. It was, indeed and in truth, the will of the Father that his Son should drink to the full the cup of mortal experience, from birth to death, but the Father in heaven had nothing whatever to do with instigating the barbarous behavior of those supposedly civilized human beings who so brutally tortured the Master and so horribly heaped successive indignities upon his non-resisting person. These inhuman and shocking experiences which Jesus was called upon to endure in the final hours of his mortal life were not in any sense a part of the divine will of the Father, which his human nature had so triumphantly pledged to carry out at the time of the final surrender of man to God as signified in the threefold prayer which he indited in the garden while his weary apostles slept the sleep of physical exhaustion.

183:1.2 (1972.1) The Father in heaven desired the bestowal Son to finish his earth career naturally, just as all mortals must finish up their lives on earth and in the flesh. Ordinary men and women cannot expect to have their last hours on earth and the supervening episode of death made easy by a special dispensation. Accordingly, Jesus elected to lay down his life in the flesh in the manner which was in keeping with the outworking of natural events, and he steadfastly refused to extricate himself from the cruel clutches of a wicked conspiracy of inhuman events which swept on with horrible certainty toward his unbelievable humiliation and ignominious death. And every bit of all this astounding manifestation of hatred and this unprecedented demonstration of cruelty was the work of evil men and wicked mortals. God in heaven did not will it, neither did the archenemies of Jesus dictate it, though they did much to insure that unthinking and evil mortals would thus reject the bestowal Son. Even the father of sin turned his face away from the excruciating horror of the scene of the crucifixion.

Judas in the City

183:2.1 (1972.2) After Judas so abruptly left the table while eating the Last Supper, he went directly to the home of his cousin, and then did the two go straight to the captain of the temple guards. Judas requested the captain to assemble the guards and informed him that he was ready to lead them to Jesus. Judas having appeared on the scene a little before he was expected, there was some delay in getting started for the Mark home, where Judas expected to find Jesus still visiting with the apostles. The Master and the eleven left the home of Elijah Mark fully fifteen minutes before the betrayer and the guards arrived. By the time the apprehenders reached the Mark home, Jesus and the eleven were well outside the walls of the city and on their way to the Olivet camp.

183:2.2 (1972.3) Judas was much perturbed by this failure to find Jesus at the Mark residence and in the company of eleven men, only two of whom were armed for resistance. He happened to know that, in the afternoon when they had left camp, only Simon Peter and Simon Zelotes were girded with swords; Judas had hoped to take Jesus when the city was quiet, and when there was little chance of resistance. The betrayer feared that, if he waited for them to return to their camp, more than threescore of devoted disciples would be encountered, and he also knew that Simon Zelotes had an ample store of arms in his possession. Judas was becoming increasingly nervous as he meditated how the eleven loyal apostles would detest him, and he feared they would all seek to destroy him. He was not only disloyal, but he was a real coward at heart.

183:2.3 (1973.1) When they failed to find Jesus in the upper chamber, Judas asked the captain of the guard to return to the temple. By this time the rulers had begun to assemble at the high priest's home preparatory to receiving Jesus, seeing that their bargain with the traitor called for Jesus' arrest by midnight of that day. Judas explained to his associates that they had missed Jesus at the Mark home, and that it would be necessary to go to Gethsemane to arrest him. The betrayer then went on to state that more than threescore devoted followers were encamped with him, and that they were all well armed. The rulers of the Jews reminded Judas that Jesus had always preached nonresistance, but Judas replied that they could not depend upon all Jesus' followers obeying such teaching. He really feared for himself and therefore made bold to ask for a company of forty armed soldiers. Since the Jewish authorities had no such force of armed men under their jurisdiction, they went at once to the fortress of Antonia and requested the Roman commander to give them this guard; but when he learned that they intended to arrest Jesus, he promptly refused to accede to their request and referred them to his superior officer. In this way more than an hour was consumed in going from one authority to another until they finally were compelled to go to Pilate himself in order to obtain permission to employ the armed Roman guards. It was late when they arrived at Pilate's house, and he had retired to his private chambers with his wife. He hesitated to have anything to do with the

enterprise, all the more so since his wife had asked him not to grant the request. But inasmuch as the presiding officer of the Jewish Sanhedrin was present and making personal request for this assistance, the governor thought it wise to grant the petition, thinking he could later on right any wrong they might be disposed to commit.

183:2.4 (1973.2) Accordingly, when Judas Iscariot started out from the temple, about half after eleven o'clock, he was accompanied by more than sixty persons—temple guards, Roman soldiers, and curious servants of the chief priests and rulers.

The Master's Arrest

1. 183:3.1 (1973.3) As this company of armed soldiers and guards, carrying torches and lanterns, approached the garden, Judas stepped well out in front of the band that he might be ready quickly to identify Jesus so that the apprehenders could easily lay hands on him before his associates could rally to his defense. And there was yet another reason why Judas chose to be ahead of the Master's enemies: He thought it would appear that he had arrived on the scene ahead of the soldiers so that the apostles and others gathered about Jesus might not directly connect him with the armed guards following so closely upon his heels. Judas had even thought to pose as having hastened out to warn them of the coming of the apprehenders, but this plan was thwarted by Jesus' blighting greeting of the betrayer. Though the Master spoke to Judas kindly, he greeted him as a traitor.

183:3.2 (1973.4) As soon as Peter, James, and John, with some thirty of their fellow campers, saw the armed band with torches swing around the brow of the hill, they knew that these soldiers were coming to arrest Jesus, and they all rushed down to near the olive press where the Master was sitting in moonlit solitude. As the company of soldiers approached on one side, the three apostles and their associates approached on the other. As Judas strode forward to accost the Master, there the two groups stood, motionless, with the Master between them and Judas making ready to impress the traitorous kiss upon his brow.

183:3.3 (1974.1) It had been the hope of the betrayer that he could, after leading the guards to Gethsemane, simply point Jesus out to the soldiers, or at most carry out the promise to greet him with a kiss, and then quickly retire from the scene. Judas greatly feared that the apostles would all be present, and that they would concentrate their attack upon him in retribution for his daring to betray their beloved teacher. But when the Master greeted him as a betrayer, he was so confused that he made no attempt to flee.

183:3.4 (1974.2) Jesus made one last effort to save Judas from actually betraying him in that, before the traitor could reach him, he stepped to one side and, addressing the foremost soldier on the left, the captain of the Romans, said, "Whom do you seek?" The captain answered, "Jesus of Nazareth." Then Jesus stepped up immediately in front of the officer and, standing there in the calm majesty of the God of all this creation, said, "I am he." Many of this armed band had heard Jesus teach in the temple, others had learned about his mighty works, and when they heard him thus boldly announce his identity, those in the front ranks fell suddenly backward. They were overcome with surprise at his calm and majestic announcement of identity. There was, therefore, no need for Judas to go on with his plan of betrayal. The Master had boldly revealed himself to his enemies, and they could have taken him without Judas's assistance. But the traitor had to do something to account for his presence with this armed band, and besides, he wanted to make a show of carrying out his part of the betrayal bargain with the rulers of the Jews in order to be eligible for the great reward and honors which he believed would be heaped upon him in compensation for his promise to deliver Jesus into their hands.

183:3.5 (1974.3) As the guards rallied from their first faltering at the sight of Jesus and at the sound of his unusual voice, and as the apostles and disciples drew nearer, Judas stepped up to Jesus and, placing a kiss upon his brow, said, "Hail, Master and Teacher." And as Judas thus embraced his Master, Jesus said, "Friend, is it not enough to do this! Would you even betray the Son of Man with a kiss?"

183:3.6 (1974.4) The apostles and disciples were literally stunned by what they saw. For a moment no one moved. Then Jesus, disengaging himself from the traitorous embrace of Judas, stepped up to the guards and soldiers and again asked, "Whom do you seek?" And again the captain said, "Jesus of Nazareth." And again answered Jesus: "I have told you that I am he. If, therefore, you seek me, let these others go their way. I am ready to go with you."

183:3.7 (1974.5) Jesus was ready to go back to Jerusalem with the guards, and the captain of the soldiers was altogether willing to allow the three apostles and their associates to go their way in peace. But before they were able to get started, as Jesus stood there awaiting the captain's orders, one Malchus, the Syrian bodyguard of the high priest, stepped up to Jesus and made ready to bind his hands behind his back, although the Roman captain had not directed that Jesus should be thus bound. When Peter and his associates saw their Master being subjected to this indignity, they were no longer able to restrain themselves. Peter drew his sword and with the others rushed forward to smite Malchus. But before the soldiers could come to the defense of the high priest's servant, Jesus raised a forbidding hand to Peter and, speaking sternly, said: "Peter, put up your sword. They who take the sword shall perish by the sword. Do you not understand that it is the Father's will that I drink this cup? And do you not further know that I could even now command more than twelve legions of angels and their associates, who would deliver me from the hands of these few men?"

183:3.8 (1975.1) While Jesus thus effectively put a stop to this show of physical resistance by his followers, it was enough to arouse the fear of the captain of the guards, who now, with the help of his soldiers, laid heavy hands on Jesus and quickly bound him. And as they tied his hands with heavy cords, Jesus said to them: "Why do you come out against me with swords and with staves as if to seize a robber? I was daily with you in the temple, publicly teaching the people, and you made no effort to take me."

183:3.9 (1975.2) When Jesus had been bound, the captain, fearing that the followers of the Master might attempt to rescue him, gave orders that they be seized; but the soldiers were not quick enough since, having overheard the captain's orders to arrest them, Jesus' followers fled in haste back into the ravine. All this time John Mark had remained secluded in the nearby shed. When the guards started back to Jerusalem with Jesus, John Mark attempted to steal out of the shed in order to catch up with the fleeing apostles and disciples; but just as he emerged, one of the last of the returning soldiers who had pursued the fleeing disciples was passing near and, seeing this young man in his linen coat, gave chase, almost overtaking him. In fact, the soldier got near enough to John to lay hold upon his coat, but the young man freed himself from the garment, escaping naked while the soldier held the empty coat. John Mark made his way in all haste to David Zebedee on the upper trail. When he had told David what had happened, they both hastened back to the tents of the sleeping apostles and informed all eight of the Master's betrayal and arrest.

183:3.10 (1975.3) At about the time the eight apostles were being awakened, those who had fled up the ravine were returning, and they all gathered together near the olive press to debate what should be done. In the meantime, Simon Peter and John Zebedee, who had hidden among the olive trees, had already gone on after the mob of soldiers, guards, and servants, who were now leading Jesus back to Jerusalem as they would have led a desperate criminal. John followed close behind the mob, but Peter followed afar off. After John Mark's escape from the clutch of the soldier, he provided himself with a cloak which he found in the tent of Simon Peter and John Zebedee. He suspected the guards were going to take Jesus to the home of Annas, the high priest emeritus; so he skirted around through the olive orchards and was there ahead of the mob, hiding near the entrance to the gate of the high priest's palace.

Discussion at the Olive Press

183:4.1 (1975.4) James Zebedee found himself separated from Simon Peter and his brother John, and so he now joined the other apostles and their fellow campers at the olive press to deliberate on what should be done in view of the Master's arrest.

183:4.2 (1975.5) Andrew had been released from all responsibility in the group management of his fellow apostles; accordingly, in this greatest of all crises in their lives, he was silent. After a short informal discussion, Simon Zelotes stood up on the stone wall of the olive press and, making an impassioned plea for loyalty to the Master and the cause of the kingdom, exhorted his fellow apostles and the other disciples to hasten on after the mob and effect the rescue of Jesus. The majority of the company would have been disposed to follow his aggressive leadership had it not been for the advice of Nathaniel, who stood up the moment Simon had finished speaking and called their attention to Jesus' oft- repeated teachings regarding nonresistance. He further reminded them that Jesus had that very night instructed them that they should preserve their lives for the time when they should go forth into the world proclaiming the good news of the gospel of the heavenly kingdom. And Nathaniel was encouraged in this stand by James Zebedee, who now told how Peter and others drew their swords to defend the Master against arrest, and that Jesus bade Simon Peter and his fellow swordsmen sheathe their blades. Matthew and Philip also made speeches, but nothing definite came of this discussion until Thomas, calling their attention to the fact that Jesus had counseled Lazarus against exposing himself to death, pointed out that they could do nothing to save their Master inasmuch as he refused to allow his friends to defend him, and since he persisted in refraining from the use of his divine powers to frustrate his human enemies. Thomas persuaded them to scatter, every man for himself, with the understanding that David Zebedee would remain at the camp to maintain a clearinghouse and messenger headquarters for the group. By half past two o'clock that morning the camp was deserted; only David remained on hand with three or four messengers, the others having been dispatched to secure information as to where Jesus had been taken, and what was going to be done with him.

183:4.3 (1976.1) Five of the apostles, Nathaniel, Matthew, Philip, and the twins, went into hiding at Bethpage and Bethany. Thomas, Andrew, James, and Simon Zelotes were hiding in the city. Simon Peter and John Zebedee followed along to the home of Annas.

183:4.4 (1976.2) Shortly after daybreak, Simon Peter wandered back to the Gethsemane camp, a dejected picture of deep despair. David sent him in charge of a messenger to join his brother, Andrew, who was at the home of Nicodemus in Jerusalem. *

183:4.5 (1976.3) Until the very end of the crucifixion, John Zebedee remained, as Jesus had directed him, always near at hand, and it was he who supplied David's messengers with information from hour to hour which they carried to David at the garden camp, and which was then relayed to the hiding apostles and to Jesus' family.

183:4.6 (1976.4) Surely, the shepherd is smitten and the sheep are scattered! While they all vaguely realize that Jesus has forewarned them of this very situation, they are too severely shocked by the Master's sudden disappearance to be able to use their minds normally.

183:4.7 (1976.5) It was shortly after daylight and just after Peter had been sent to join his brother, that Jude, Jesus' brother in the flesh, arrived in the camp, almost breathless and in advance of the rest of Jesus' family, only to learn that the Master had already been placed under arrest; and he hastened back down the Jericho road to carry this information to his mother and to his brothers and sisters. David Zebedee sent word to Jesus' family, by Jude, to forgather at the house of Martha and Mary in Bethany and there await news which his messengers would regularly bring them.

183:4.8 (1976.6) This was the situation during the last half of Thursday night and the early morning hours of Friday as regards the apostles, the chief disciples, and the earthly family of Jesus. And all these groups and individuals were kept in touch with each other by the messenger service which David Zebedee continued to operate from his headquarters at the Gethsemane camp.

On the Way to the High Priest's Palace

183:5.1 (1977.1) Before they started away from the garden with Jesus, a dispute arose between the Jewish captain of the temple guards and the Roman captain of the company of soldiers as to where they were to take Jesus. The captain of the temple guards gave orders that he should be taken to Caiaphas, the acting high priest. The captain of the Roman soldiers directed that Jesus be taken to the palace of Annas, the former high priest and father-in-law of Caiaphas. And this he did because the Romans were in the habit of dealing directly with Annas in all matters having to do with the enforcement of the Jewish ecclesiastical laws. And the orders of the Roman captain were obeyed; they took Jesus to the home of Annas for his preliminary examination.

183:5.2 (1977.2) Judas marched along near the captains, overhearing all that was said, but took no part in the dispute, for neither the Jewish captain nor the Roman officer would so much as speak to the betrayer—they held him in such contempt.

183:5.3 (1977.3) About this time John Zebedee, remembering his Master's instructions to remain always near at hand, hurried up near Jesus as he marched along between the two captains. The commander of the temple guards, seeing John come up alongside, said to his assistant: "Take this man and bind him. He is one of this fellow's followers." But when the Roman captain heard this and, looking around, saw John, he gave orders that the apostle should come over by him, and that no man should molest him. Then the Roman captain said to the Jewish captain: "This man is neither a traitor nor a coward. I saw him in the garden, and he did not draw a sword to resist us. He has the courage to come forward to be with his Master, and no man shall lay hands on him. The Roman law allows that any prisoner may have at least one friend to stand with him before the judgment bar, and this man shall not be prevented from standing by the side of his Master, the prisoner." And when Judas heard this, he was so ashamed and humiliated that he dropped back behind the marchers, coming up to the palace of Annas alone.

183:5.4 (1977.4) And this explains why John Zebedee was permitted to remain near Jesus all the way through his trying experiences this night and the next day. The Jews feared to say aught to John or to molest him in any way because he had something of the status of a Roman counselor designated to act as observer of the transactions of the Jewish ecclesiastical court. John's position of privilege was made all the more secure when, in turning Jesus over to the captain of the temple guards at the gate of Annas's palace, the Roman, addressing his assistant, said: "Go along with this prisoner and see that these Jews do not kill him without Pilate's consent. Watch that they do not assassinate him, and see that his friend, the Galilean, is permitted to stand by and observe all that goes on." And thus was John able to be near

Jesus right on up to the time of his death on the cross, though the other ten apostles were compelled to remain in hiding. John was acting under Roman protection, and the Jews dared not molest him until after the Master's death.

183:5.5 (1977.5) And all the way to the palace of Annas, Jesus opened not his mouth. From the time of his arrest to the time of his appearance before Annas, the Son of Man spoke no word.

Paper 184

Before the Sanhedrin Court

184:0.1 (1978.1) REPRESENTATIVES of Annas had secretly instructed the captain of the Roman soldiers to bring Jesus immediately to the palace of Annas after he had been arrested. The former high priest desired to maintain his prestige as the chief ecclesiastical authority of the Jews. He also had another purpose in detaining Jesus at his house for several hours, and that was to allow time for legally calling together the court of the Sanhedrin. It was not lawful to convene the Sanhedrin court before the time of the offering of the morning sacrifice in the temple, and this sacrifice was offered about three o'clock in the morning.

184:0.2 (1978.2) Annas knew that a court of Sanhedrists was in waiting at the palace of his son-in-law, Caiaphas. Some thirty members of the Sanhedrin had gathered at the home of the high priest by midnight so that they would be ready to sit in judgment on Jesus when he might be brought before them. Only those members were assembled who were strongly and openly opposed to Jesus and his teaching since it required only twenty-three to constitute a trial court.

184:0.3 (1978.3) Jesus spent about three hours at the palace of Annas on Mount Olivet, not far from the garden of

Gethsemane, where they arrested him. John Zebedee was free and safe in the palace of Annas not only because of the word of the Roman captain, but also because he and his brother James were well known to the older servants, having many times been guests at the palace as the former high priest was a distant relative of their mother, Salome.

Examination by Annas

184:1.1 (1978.4) Annas, enriched by the temple revenues, his son-in-law the acting high priest, and with his relations to the Roman authorities, was indeed the most powerful single individual in all Jewry. He was a suave and politic planner and plotter. He desired to direct the matter of disposing of Jesus; he feared to trust such an important undertaking wholly to his brusque and aggressive son-in-law. Annas wanted to make sure that the Master's trial was kept in the hands of the Sadducees; he feared the possible sympathy of some of the Pharisees, seeing that practically all of those members of the Sanhedrin who had espoused the cause of Jesus were Pharisees.

184:1.2 (1978.5) Annas had not seen Jesus for several years, not since the time when the Master called at his house and immediately left upon observing his coldness and reserve in receiving him. Annas had thought to presume on this early acquaintance and thereby attempt to persuade Jesus to abandon his claims and leave Palestine. He was reluctant to participate in the murder of a good man and had reasoned that Jesus might choose to leave the country rather than to suffer death. But when Annas stood before the stalwart and determined Galilean, he knew at once that it would be useless to make such proposals. Jesus was even more majestic and well poised than Annas remembered him.

184:1.3 (1979.1) When Jesus was young, Annas had taken a great interest in him, but now his revenues were threatened by what Jesus had so recently done in driving the money-changers and other commercial traders out of the temple. This act had aroused the enmity of the former high priest far more than had Jesus' teachings.

184:1.4 (1979.2) Annas entered his spacious audience chamber, seated himself in a large chair, and commanded that Jesus be brought before him. After a few moments spent in silently surveying the Master, he said: "You realize that something must be done about your teaching since you are disturbing the peace and order of our country." As Annas looked inquiringly at Jesus, the Master looked full into his eyes but made no reply. Again Annas spoke, "What are the names of your disciples, besides Simon Zelotes, the agitator?" Again Jesus looked down upon him, but he did not answer.

184:1.5 (1979.3) Annas was considerably disturbed by Jesus' refusal to answer his questions, so much so that he said to him: "Do you have no care as to whether I am friendly to you or not? Do you have no regard for the power I have in determining the issues of your coming trial?" When Jesus heard this, he said: "Annas, you know that you could have no power over me unless it were permitted by my Father. Some would destroy the Son of Man because they are ignorant; they know no better, but you, friend, know what you are doing. How can you, therefore, reject the light of God?"

184:1.6 (1979.4) The kindly manner in which Jesus spoke to Annas almost bewildered him. But he had already determined in his mind that Jesus must either leave Palestine or die; so he summoned up his courage and asked: "Just what is it you are trying to teach the people? What do you claim to be?" Jesus answered: "You know full well that I have spoken openly to the world. I have taught in the synagogues and many times in the temple, where all the Jews and many of the gentiles have heard me. In secret I have spoken nothing; why, then, do you ask me about my teaching? Why do you not summon those who have heard me and inquire of them? Behold, all Jerusalem has heard that which I have spoken even if you have not yourself heard these teachings." But before Annas could make reply, the chief steward of the palace, who was standing near, struck Jesus in the face with his hand, saying, "How dare you answer the high priest with such words?" Annas spoke no words of rebuke to his steward, but Jesus addressed him, saying, "My friend, if I have spoken evil, bear witness against the evil; but if I have spoken the truth, why, then, should you smite me?"

184:1.7 (1979.5) Although Annas regretted that his steward had struck Jesus, he was too proud to take notice of the matter. In his confusion he went into another room, leaving Jesus alone with the household attendants and the temple guards for almost an hour.

184:1.8 (1979.6) When he returned, going up to the Master's side, he said, "Do you claim to be the Messiah, the deliverer of Israel?" Said Jesus: "Annas, you have known me from the times of my youth. You know that I claim to be nothing except that which my Father has appointed, and that I have been sent to all men, gentile as well as Jew." Then said Annas: "I have been told that you have claimed to be the Messiah; is that true?" Jesus looked upon Annas but only replied, "So you have said."

184:1.9 (1980.1) About this time messengers arrived from the palace of Caiaphas to inquire what time Jesus would be brought before the court of the Sanhedrin, and since it was nearing the break of day, Annas thought best to send Jesus bound and in the custody of the temple guards to Caiaphas. He himself followed after them shortly.

Peter in the Courtyard

184:2.1 (1980.2) As the band of guards and soldiers approached the entrance to the palace of Annas, John Zebedee was marching by the side of the captain of the Roman soldiers. Judas had dropped some distance behind, and Simon Peter followed afar off. After John had entered the palace court-

yard with Jesus and the guards, Judas came up to the gate but, seeing Jesus and John, went on over to the home of Caiaphas, where he knew the real trial of the Master would later take place. Soon after Judas had left, Simon Peter arrived, and as he stood before the gate, John saw him just as they were about to take Jesus into the palace. The portress who kept the gate knew John, and when he spoke to her, requesting that she let Peter in, she gladly assented.

184:2.2 (1980.3) Peter, upon entering the courtyard, went over to the charcoal fire and sought to warm himself, for the night was chilly. He felt very much out of place here among the enemies of Jesus, and indeed he was out of place. The Master had not instructed him to keep near at hand as he had admonished John. Peter belonged with the other apostles, who had been specifically warned not to endanger their lives during these times of the trial and crucifixion of their Master.

184:2.3 (1980.4) Peter threw away his sword shortly before he came up to the palace gate so that he entered the courtyard of Annas unarmed. His mind was in a whirl of confusion; he could scarcely realize that Jesus had been arrested. He could not grasp the reality of the situation—that he was here in the courtyard of Annas, warming himself beside the servants of the high priest. He wondered what the other apostles were doing and, in turning over in his mind as to how John came to be admitted to the palace, concluded that it was because he was known to the servants, since he had bidden the gate-keeper admit him.

184:2.4 (1980.5) Shortly after the portress let Peter in, and while he was warming himself by the fire, she went over to him and mischievously said, "Are you not also one of this man's disciples?" Now Peter should not have been surprised at this recognition, for it was John who had requested that the girl let him pass through the palace gates; but he was in such a tense nervous state that this identification as a disciple threw him off his balance, and with only one thought uppermost in his mind— the thought of escaping with his life—he promptly answered the maid's question by saying, "I am not."

184:2.5 (1980.6) Very soon another servant came up to Peter and asked: "Did I not see you in the garden when they arrested this fellow? Are you not also one of his followers?" Peter was now thoroughly alarmed; he saw no way of safely escaping from these accusers; so he vehemently denied all connection with Jesus, saying, "I know not this man, neither am I one of his followers."

184:2.6 (1980.7) About this time the portress of the gate drew Peter to one side and said: "I am sure you are a disciple of this Jesus, not only because one of his followers bade me let you in the courtyard, but my sister here has seen you in the temple with this man. Why do you deny this?" When Peter heard the maid accuse him, he denied all knowledge of Jesus with much cursing and swearing, again saying, "I am not this man's follower; I do not even know him; I never heard of him before."

184:2.7 (1981.1) Peter left the fireside for a time while he walked about the courtyard. He would have liked to have escaped, but he feared to attract attention to himself. Getting cold, he returned to the fireside, and one of the men standing near him said: "Surely you are one of this man's disciples. This Jesus is a Galilean, and your speech betrays you, for you also speak as a Galilean." And again Peter denied all connection with his Master.

184:2.8 (1981.2) Peter was so perturbed that he sought to escape contact with his accusers by going away from the fire and remaining by himself on the porch. After more than an hour of this isolation, the gate-keeper and her sister chanced to meet him, and both of them again teasingly charged him with being a follower of Jesus. And again he denied the accusation. Just as he had once more denied all connection with Jesus, the cock crowed, and Peter remembered the words of warning spoken to him by his Master earlier that same night. As he stood there, heavy of heart and crushed with the sense of guilt, the palace doors opened, and the guards led Jesus past on the way to Caiaphas. As the Master passed Peter, he saw, by the light of the torches, the look of despair on the face of his former self-confident and superficially brave apostle, and he turned and looked upon Peter. Peter never forgot that look as long as he lived. It was such a glance of commingled pity and love as mortal man had never beheld in the face of the Master.

184:2.9 (1981.3) After Jesus and the guards passed out of the palace gates, Peter followed them, but only for a short distance. He could not go farther. He sat down by the side of the road and wept bitterly. And when he had shed these tears of agony, he turned his steps back toward the camp, hoping to find his brother, Andrew. On arriving at the camp, he found only David Zebedee, who sent a messenger to direct him to where his brother had gone to hide in Jerusalem.

184:2.10 (1981.4) Peter's entire experience occurred in the courtyard of the palace of Annas on Mount Olivet. He did not follow Jesus to the palace of the high priest, Caiaphas. That Peter was brought to the realization that he had repeatedly denied his Master by the crowing of a cock indicates that this all occurred outside of Jerusalem since it was against the law to keep poultry within the city proper.

184:2.11 (1981.5) Until the crowing of the cock brought Peter to his better senses, he had only thought, as he walked up and down the porch to keep warm, how cleverly he had eluded the accusations of the servants, and how he had frustrated their purpose to identify him with Jesus. For the time being, he had only considered that these servants had no moral or legal right thus to question him, and he really congratulated himself over the manner in which he thought he had avoided being identified and possibly subjected to arrest and imprisonment. Not until the cock crowed did it occur to Peter that he had denied his Master. Not until Jesus looked upon him, did he realize that he had failed to live up to his privileges as an ambassador of the kingdom.

184:2.12 (1981.6) Having taken the first step along the path of compromise and least resistance, there was nothing apparent to Peter but to go on with the course of conduct decided upon. It requires a great and noble character, having started out wrong, to turn about and go right. All too often one's own mind tends to justify continuance in the path of error when once it is entered upon.

184:2.13 (1982.1) Peter never fully believed that he could be forgiven until he met his Master after the resurrection and saw that he was received just as before the experiences of this tragic night of the denials.

Before the Court of Sanhedrists

184:3.1 (1982.2) It was about half past three o'clock this Friday morning when the chief priest, Caiaphas, called the Sanhedrist court of inquiry to order and asked that Jesus be brought before them for his formal trial. On three previous occasions the Sanhedrin, by a large majority vote, had decreed the death of Jesus, had decided that he was worthy of death on informal charges of lawbreaking, blasphemy, and flouting the traditions of the fathers of Israel. *

184:3.2 (1982.3) This was not a regularly called meeting of the Sanhedrin and was not held in the usual place, the chamber of hewn stone in the temple. This was a special trial court of some thirty Sanhedrists and was convened in the palace of the high priest. John Zebedee was present with Jesus throughout this so-called trial.

184:3.3 (1982.4) How these chief priests, scribes, Sadducees, and some of the Pharisees flattered themselves that Jesus, the disturber of their position and the challenger of their authority, was now securely in their hands! And they were resolved

that he should never live to escape their vengeful clutches.

184:3.4 (1982.5) Ordinarily, the Jews, when trying a man on a capital charge, proceeded with great caution and provided every safeguard of fairness in the selection of witnesses and the entire conduct of the trial. But on this occasion, Caiaphas was more of a prosecutor than an unbiased judge.

184:3.5 (1982.6) Jesus appeared before this court clothed in his usual garments and with his hands bound together behind his back. The entire court was startled and somewhat confused by his majestic appearance. Never had they gazed upon such a prisoner nor witnessed such composure in a man on trial for his life.

184:3.6 (1982.7) The Jewish law required that at least two witnesses must agree upon any point before a charge could be laid against the prisoner. Judas could not be used as a witness against Jesus because the Jewish law specifically forbade the testimony of a traitor. More than a score of false witnesses were on hand to testify against Jesus, but their testimony was so contradictory and so evidently trumped up that the Sanhedrists themselves were very much ashamed of the performance. Jesus stood there, looking down benignly upon these perjurers, and his very countenance disconcerted the lying witnesses. Throughout all this false testimony the Master never said a word; he made no reply to their many false accusations.

184:3.7 (1982.8) The first time any two of their witnesses approached even the semblance of an agreement was when two men testified that they had heard Jesus say in the course of one of his temple discourses that he would "destroy this temple made with hands and in three days make another temple without hands." That was not exactly what Jesus said, regardless of the fact that he pointed to his own body when he made the remark referred to.

184:3.8 (1982.9) Although the high

priest shouted at Jesus, "Do you not answer any of these charges?" Jesus opened not his mouth. He stood there in silence while all of these false witnesses gave their testimony. Hatred, fanaticism, and unscrupulous exaggeration so characterized the words of these perjurers that their testimony fell in its own entanglements. The very best refutation of their false accusations was the Master's calm and majestic silence.

184:3.9 (1983.1) Shortly after the beginning of the testimony of the false witnesses, Annas arrived and took his seat beside Caiaphas. Annas now arose and argued that this threat of Jesus to destroy the temple was sufficient to warrant three charges against him:

184:3.10 (1983.2) 1. That he was a dangerous traducer of the people. That he taught them impossible things and otherwise deceived them.

184:3.11 (1983.3) 2. That he was a fanatical revolutionist in that he advocated laying violent hands on the sacred temple, else how could he destroy it?

184:3.12 (1983.4) 3. That he taught magic inasmuch as he promised to build a new temple, and that without hands.

184:3.13 (1983.5) Already had the full Sanhedrin agreed that Jesus was guilty of death-deserving transgressions of the Jewish laws, but they were now more concerned with developing charges regarding his conduct and teachings which would justify Pilate in pronouncing the death sentence upon their prisoner. They knew that they must secure the consent of the Roman governor before Jesus could legally be put to death. And Annas was minded to proceed along the line of making it appear that Jesus was a dangerous teacher to be abroad among the people.

184:3.14 (1983.6) But Caiaphas could not longer endure the sight of the Master standing there in perfect composure and unbroken silence. He thought he knew at least one way in which the prisoner

might be induced to speak. Accordingly, he rushed over to the side of Jesus and, shaking his accusing finger in the Master's face, said: "I adjure you, in the name of the living God, that you tell us whether you are the Deliverer, the Son of God." Jesus answered Caiaphas: "I am.

Soon I go to the Father, and presently shall the Son of Man be clothed with power and once more reign over the hosts of heaven."

184:3.15 (1983.7) When the high priest heard Jesus utter these words, he was exceedingly angry, and rending his outer garments, he exclaimed: "What further need have we of witnesses? Behold, now have you all heard this man's blasphemy. What do you now think should be done with this lawbreaker and blasphemer?" And they all answered in unison, "He is worthy of death; let him be crucified." *

184:3.16 (1983.8) Jesus manifested no interest in any question asked him when before Annas or the Sanhedrists except the one question relative to his bestowal mission. When asked if he were the Son of God, he instantly and unequivocally answered in the affirmative.

184:3.17 (1983.9) Annas desired that the trial proceed further, and that charges of a definite nature regarding Jesus' relation to the Roman law and Roman institutions be formulated for subsequent presentation to Pilate. The councilors were anxious to carry these matters to a speedy termination, not only because it was the preparation day for the Passover and no secular work should be done after noon, but also because they feared Pilate might any time return to the Roman capital of Judea, Caesarea, since he was in Jerusalem only for the Passover celebration.

184:3.18 (1983.10) But Annas did not succeed in keeping control of the court. After Jesus had so unexpectedly answered Caiaphas, the high priest stepped forward and smote him in the face with his hand. Annas was truly shocked as the other members of the court, in passing out of the room, spit in Jesus' face, and many of them mockingly slapped him with the palms of their hands. And thus in disorder and with such unheard-of confusion this first session of the Sanhedrist trial of Jesus ended at half past four o'clock.

184:3.19 (1984.1) Thirty prejudiced and tradition-blinded false judges, with their false witnesses, are presuming to sit in judgment on the righteous Creator of a universe. And these impassioned accusers are exasperated by the majestic silence and superb bearing of this God-man. His silence is terrible to endure; his speech is fearlessly defiant. He is unmoved by their threats and undaunted by their assaults. Man sits in judgment on God, but even then he loves them and would save them if he could.

The Hour of Humiliation

184:4.1 (1984.2) The Jewish law required that, in the matter of passing the death sentence, there should be two sessions of

the court. This second session was to be held on the day following the first, and the intervening time was to be spent in fasting and mourning by the members of the court. But these men could not await the next day for the confirmation of their decision that Jesus must die. They waited only one hour. In the meantime Jesus was left in the audience chamber in the custody of the temple guards, who, with the servants of the high priest, amused themselves by heaping every sort of indignity upon the Son of Man. They mocked him, spit upon him, and cruelly buffeted him. They would strike him in the face with a rod and then say, "Prophesy to us, you the Deliverer, who it was that struck you." And thus they went on for one full hour, reviling and mistreating this unresisting man of Galilee.

184:4.2 (1984.3) During this tragic hour of suffering and mock trials before the ignorant and unfeeling guards and servants, John Zebedee waited in lonely terror

in an adjoining room. When these abuses first started, Jesus indicated to John, by a nod of his head, that he should retire. The Master well knew that, if he permitted his apostle to remain in the room to witness these indignities, John's resentment would be so aroused as to produce such an outbreak of protesting indignation as would probably result in his death.

184:4.3 (1984.4) Throughout this awful hour Jesus uttered no word. To this gentle and sensitive soul of humankind, joined in personality relationship with the God of all this universe, there was no more bitter portion of his cup of humiliation than this terrible hour at the mercy of these ignorant and cruel guards and servants, who had been stimulated to abuse him by the example of the members of this so-called Sanhedrist court.

184:4.4 (1984.5) The human heart cannot possibly conceive of the shudder of indignation that swept out over a vast universe as the celestial intelligences witnessed this sight of their beloved Sovereign submitting himself to the will of his ignorant and misguided creatures on the sin-darkened sphere of unfortunate Urantia.

184:4.5 (1984.6) What is this trait of the animal in man which leads him to want to insult and physically assault that which he cannot spiritually attain or intellectually achieve? In the half-civilized man there still lurks an evil brutality which seeks to vent itself upon those who are superior in wisdom and spiritual attainment. Witness the evil coarseness and the brutal ferocity of these supposedly civilized men as they derived a certain form of animal pleasure from this physical attack upon the unresisting Son of Man. As these insults, taunts, and blows fell upon Jesus, he was undefending but not defenseless. Jesus was not vanquished, merely uncontending in the material sense.

184:4.6 (1985.1) These are the moments of the Master's greatest victories in all his long and eventful career as maker, upholder, and savior of a vast and far-flung universe. Having lived to the full a life of revealing God to man, Jesus is now engaged in making a new and unprecedented revelation of man to God. Jesus is now revealing to the worlds the final triumph over all fears of creature personality isolation. The Son of Man has finally achieved the realization of identity as the Son of God. Jesus does not hesitate to assert that he and the Father are one; and on the basis of the fact and truth of that supreme and supernal experience, he admonishes every kingdom believer to become one with him even as he and his Father are one. The living experience in the religion of Jesus thus becomes the sure and certain technique whereby the spiritually isolated and cosmically lonely mortals of earth are enabled to escape personality isolation, with all its consequences of fear and associated feelings of helplessness. In the fraternal realities of the kingdom of heaven the faith sons of God find final deliverance from the isolation of the self, both personal and planetary. The God-knowing believer increasingly experiences the ecstasy and grandeur of spiritual socialization on a universe scale—citizenship on high in association with the eternal realization of the divine destiny of perfection attainment.

The Second Meeting of the Court

184:5.1 (1985.2) At five-thirty o'clock the court reassembled, and Jesus was led into the adjoining room, where John was waiting. Here the Roman soldier and the temple guards watched over Jesus while the court began the formulation of the charges which were to be presented to Pilate. Annas made it clear to his associates that the charge of blasphemy would carry no weight with Pilate. Judas was present during this second meeting of the court, but he gave no testimony.

184:5.2 (1985.3) This session of the court lasted only a half hour, and when they adjourned to go before Pilate, they had drawn up the indictment of Jesus, as being worthy of death, under three heads:

184:5.3 (1985.4) 1. That he was a per-

verter of the Jewish nation; he deceived the people and incited them to rebellion.

184:5.4 (1985.5) 2. That he taught the people to refuse to pay tribute to Caesar.

184:5.5 (1985.6) 3. That, by claiming to be a king and the founder of a new sort of kingdom, he incited treason against the emperor.

184:5.6 (1985.7) This entire procedure was irregular and wholly contrary to the Jewish laws. No two witnesses had agreed on any matter except those who testified regarding Jesus' statement about destroying the temple and raising it again in three days. And even concerning that point, no witnesses spoke for the defense, and neither was Jesus asked to explain his intended meaning.

184:5.7 (1985.8) The only point the court could have consistently judged him on was that of blasphemy, and that would have rested entirely on his own testimony. Even concerning blasphemy, they failed to cast a formal ballot for the death sentence.

184:5.8 (1985.9) And now they presumed to formulate three charges, with which to go before Pilate, on which no witnesses had been heard, and which were agreed upon while the accused prisoner was absent. When this was done, three of the Pharisees took their leave; they wanted to see Jesus destroyed, but they would not formulate charges against him without witnesses and in his absence.

184:5.9 (1986.1) Jesus did not again appear before the Sanhedrist court. They did not want again to look upon his face as they sat in judgment upon his innocent life. Jesus did not know (as a man) of their formal charges until he heard them recited by Pilate.

184:5.10 (1986.2) While Jesus was in the room with John and the guards, and while the court was in its second session, some of the women about the high priest's palace, together with their friends, came to look upon the strange prisoner, and one of them asked him, "Are you the Messiah, the Son of God?" And Jesus answered: "If I tell you, you will not believe me; and if I ask you, you will not answer."

184:5.11 (1986.3) At six o'clock that morning Jesus was led forth from the home of Caiaphas to appear before Pilate for confirmation of the sentence of death which this Sanhedrist court had so unjustly and irregularly decreed.

Paper 185

The Trial Before Pilate

185:0.1 (1987.1) SHORTLY after six o'clock on this Friday morning, April 7, A.D. 30, Jesus was brought before Pilate, the Roman procurator who governed Judea, Samaria, and Idumea under the immediate supervision of the legatus of Syria. The Master was taken into the presence of the Roman governor by the temple guards, bound, and was accompanied by about fifty of his accusers, including the Sanhedrist court (principally Sadduceans), Judas Iscariot, and the high priest, Caiaphas, and by the Apostle John. Annas did not appear before Pilate.

185:0.2 (1987.2) Pilate was up and ready to receive this group of early morning callers, having been informed by those who had secured his consent, the previous evening, to employ the Roman soldiers in arresting the Son of Man, that Jesus would be early brought before him. This trial was arranged to take place in front of the praetorium, an addition to the fortress of Antonia, where Pilate and his wife made their headquarters when stopping in Jerusalem.

185:0.3 (1987.3) Though Pilate conducted much of Jesus' examination within the praetorium halls, the public trial was held outside on the steps leading up to the main entrance. This was a concession to the Jews, who refused to enter any gentile

building where leaven might be used on this day of preparation for the Passover. Such conduct would not only render them ceremonially unclean and thereby debar them from partaking of the afternoon feast of thanksgiving but would also necessitate their subjection to purification ceremonies after sundown, before they would be eligible to partake of the Passover supper.

185:0.4 (1987.4) Although these Jews were not at all bothered in conscience as they intrigued to effect the judicial murder of Jesus, they were nonetheless scrupulous regarding all these matters of ceremonial cleanness and traditional regularity. And these Jews have not been the only ones to fail in the recognition of high and holy obligations of a divine nature while giving meticulous attention to things of trifling importance to human welfare in both time and eternity.

Pontius Pilate

185:1.1 (1987.5) If Pontius Pilate had not been a reasonably good governor of the minor provinces, Tiberius would hardly have suffered him to remain as procurator of Judea for ten years. Although he was a fairly good administrator, he was a moral coward. He was not a big enough man to comprehend the nature of his task as governor of the Jews. He failed to grasp the fact that these Hebrews had a real religion, a faith for which they were willing to die, and that millions upon millions of them, scattered here and there throughout the empire, looked to Jerusalem as the shrine of their faith and held the Sanhedrin in respect as the highest tribunal on earth.

185:1.2 (1988.1) Pilate did not love the Jews, and this deep-seated hatred early began to manifest itself. Of all the Roman provinces, none was more difficult to govern than Judea. Pilate never really understood the problems involved in the management of the Jews and, therefore, very early in his experience as governor, made a series of almost fatal and well-nigh suicidal blunders. And it was these blunders that gave the Jews such power over him. When they wanted to influence his decisions, all they had to do was to threaten an uprising, and Pilate would speedily capitulate. And this apparent vacillation, or lack of moral courage, of the procurator was chiefly due to the memory of a number of controversies he had had with the Jews and because in each instance they had worsted him. The Jews knew that Pilate was afraid of them, that he feared for his position before Tiberius, and they employed this knowledge to the great disadvantage of the governor on numerous occasions.

185:1.3 (1988.2) Pilate's disfavor with the Jews came about as a result of a number of unfortunate encounters. First, he failed to take seriously their deep-seated prejudice against all images as symbols of idol worship. Therefore he permitted his soldiers to enter Jerusalem without removing the images of Caesar from their banners, as had been the practice of the Roman soldiers under his predecessor. A large deputation of Jews waited upon Pilate for five days, imploring him to have these images removed from the military standards. He flatly refused to grant their petition and threatened them with instant death. Pilate, himself being a skeptic, did not understand that men of strong religious feelings will not hesitate to die for their religious convictions; and therefore was he dismayed when these Jews drew themselves up defiantly before his palace, bowed their faces to the ground, and sent word that they were ready to die. Pilate then realized that he had made a threat which he was unwilling to carry out. He surrendered, ordered the images removed from the standards of his soldiers in Jerusalem, and found himself from that day on to a large extent subject to the whims of the Jewish leaders, who had in this way discovered his weakness in making threats which he feared to execute.

185:1.4 (1988.3) Pilate subsequently determined to regain this lost prestige and accordingly had the shields of the emperor, such as were commonly used in Caesar worship, put up on the walls of Herod's palace in Jerusalem. When the Jews pro-

tested, he was adamant. When he refused to listen to their protests, they promptly appealed to Rome, and the emperor as promptly ordered the offending shields removed. And then was Pilate held in even lower esteem than before.

185:1.5 (1988.4) Another thing which brought him into great disfavor with the Jews was that he dared to take money from the temple treasury to pay for the construction of a new aqueduct to provide increased water supply for the millions of visitors to Jerusalem at the times of the great religious feasts. The Jews held that only the Sanhedrin could disburse the temple funds, and they never ceased to inveigh against Pilate for this presumptuous ruling. No less than a score of riots and much bloodshed resulted from this decision. The last of these serious outbreaks had to do with the slaughter of a large company of Galileans even as they worshiped at the altar.

185:1.6 (1988.5) It is significant that, while this vacillating Roman ruler sacrificed Jesus to his fear of the Jews and to safeguard his personal position, he finally was deposed as a result of the needless slaughter of Samaritans in connection with the pretensions of a false Messiah who led troops to Mount Gerizim, where he claimed the temple vessels were buried; and fierce riots broke out when he failed to reveal the hiding place of the sacred vessels, as he had promised. As a result of this episode, the legatus of Syria ordered Pilate to Rome. Tiberius died while Pilate was on the way to Rome, and he was not reappointed as procurator of Judea. He never fully recovered from the regretful condemnation of having consented to the crucifixion of Jesus. Finding no favor in the eyes of the new emperor, he retired to the province of Lausanne, where he subsequently committed suicide.

185:1.7 (1989.1) Claudia Procula, Pilate's wife, had heard much of Jesus through the word of her maid-in-waiting, who was a Phoenician believer in the gospel of the kingdom. After the death of Pilate, Claudia became prominently identified with the spread of the good news.

185:1.8 (1989.2) And all this explains much that transpired on this tragic Friday forenoon. It is easy to understand why the Jews presumed to dictate to Pilate—to get him up at six o'clock to try Jesus—and also why they did not hesitate to threaten to charge him with treason before the emperor if he dared to refuse their demands for Jesus' death.

185:1.9 (1989.3) A worthy Roman governor who had not become disadvantageously involved with the rulers of the Jews would never have permitted these bloodthirsty religious fanatics to bring about the death of a man whom he himself had declared to be innocent of their false charges and without fault. Rome made a great blunder, a far-reaching error in earthly affairs, when she sent the second-rate Pilate to govern Palestine. Tiberius had better have sent to the Jews the best provincial administrator in the empire.

Jesus Appears Before Pilate

185:2.1 (1989.4) When Jesus and his accusers had gathered in front of Pilate's judgment hall, the Roman governor came out and, addressing the company assembled, asked, "What accusation do you bring against this fellow?" The Sadducees and councilors who had taken it upon themselves to put Jesus out of the way had determined to go before Pilate and ask for confirmation of the death sentence pronounced upon Jesus, without volunteering any definite charge. Therefore did the spokesman for the Sanhedrist court answer Pilate: "If this man were not an evildoer, we should not have delivered him up to you."

185:2.2 (1989.5) When Pilate observed that they were reluctant to state their charges against Jesus, although he knew they had been all night engaged in deliberations regarding his guilt, he answered them: "Since you have not agreed on any definite charges, why do you not take this man and

pass judgment on him in accordance with your own laws?"

185:2.3 (1989.6) Then spoke the clerk of the Sanhedrin court to Pilate: "It is not lawful for us to put any man to death, and this disturber of our nation is worthy to die for the things which he has said and done. Therefore have we come before you for confirmation of this decree."

185:2.4 (1989.7) To come before the Roman governor with this attempt at evasion discloses both the ill-will and the ill-humor of the Sanhedrists toward Jesus as well as their lack of respect for the fairness, honor, and dignity of Pilate. What effrontery for these subject citizens to appear before their provincial governor asking for a decree of execution against a man before affording him a fair trial and without even preferring definite criminal charges against him!

185:2.5 (1990.1) Pilate knew something of Jesus' work among the Jews, and he surmised that the charges which might be brought against him had to do with infringements of the Jewish ecclesiastical laws; therefore he sought to refer the case back to their own tribunal. Again, Pilate took delight in making them publicly confess that they were powerless to pronounce and execute the death sentence upon even one of their own race whom they had come to despise with a bitter and envious hatred.

185:2.6 (1990.2) It was a few hours previously, shortly before midnight and after he had granted permission to use Roman soldiers in effecting the secret arrest of Jesus, that Pilate had heard further concerning Jesus and his teaching from his wife, Claudia, who was a partial convert to Judaism, and who later on became a full-fledged believer in Jesus' gospel.

185:2.7 (1990.3) Pilate would have liked to postpone this hearing, but he saw the Jewish leaders were determined to proceed with the case. He knew that this was not only the forenoon of preparation for the Passover, but that this day, being Friday, was also the preparation day for the Jewish Sabbath of rest and worship.

185:2.8 (1990.4) Pilate, being keenly sensitive to the disrespectful manner of the approach of these Jews, was not willing to comply with their demands that Jesus be sentenced to death without a trial. When, therefore, he had waited a few moments for them to present their charges against the prisoner, he turned to them and said: "I will not sentence this man to death without a trial; neither will I consent to examine him until you have presented your charges against him in writing."

185:2.9 (1990.5) When the high priest and the others heard Pilate say this, they signaled to the clerk of the court, who then handed to Pilate the written charges against Jesus. And these charges were:

185:2.10 (1990.6) "We find in the Sanhedrist tribunal that this man is an evildoer and a disturber of our nation in that he is guilty of:

185:2.11 (1990.7) "1. Perverting our nation and stirring up our people to rebellion.
185:2.12 (1990.8) "2. Forbidding the people to pay tribute to Caesar.
185:2.13 (1990.9) "3. Calling himself the king of the Jews and teaching the founding of a new kingdom."
185:2.14 (1990.10) Jesus had not been regularly tried nor legally convicted on any of these charges. He did not even hear these charges when first stated, but Pilate had him brought from the praetorium, where he was in the keeping of the guards, and he insisted that these charges be repeated in Jesus' hearing.
185:2.15 (1990.11) When Jesus heard these accusations, he well knew that he had not been heard on these matters before the Jewish court, and so did John Zebedee and his accusers, but he made no reply to their false charges. Even when Pilate bade him answer his accusers, he opened not his mouth. Pilate was so astonished at the unfairness of the whole proceeding and so impressed by Jesus' silent and masterly

bearing that he decided to take the prisoner inside the hall and examine him privately.

185:2.16 (1990.12) Pilate was confused in mind, fearful of the Jews in his heart, and mightily stirred in his spirit by the spectacle of Jesus' standing there in majesty before his bloodthirsty accusers and gazing down on them, not in silent contempt, but with an expression of genuine pity and sorrowful affection.

The Private Examination by Pilate

185:3.1 (1991.1) Pilate took Jesus and John Zebedee into a private chamber, leaving the guards outside in the hall, and requesting the prisoner to sit down, he sat down by his side and asked several questions. Pilate began his talk with Jesus by assuring him that he did not believe the first count against him: that he was a perverter of the nation and an inciter to rebellion. Then he asked, "Did you ever teach that tribute should be refused Caesar?" Jesus, pointing to John, said, "Ask him or any other man who has heard my teaching." Then Pilate questioned John about this matter of tribute, and John testified concerning his Master's teaching and explained that Jesus and his apostles paid taxes both to Caesar and to the temple. When Pilate had questioned John, he said, "See that you tell no man that I talked with you." And John never did reveal this matter.

185:3.2 (1991.2) Pilate then turned around to question Jesus further, saying: "And now about the third accusation against you, are you the king of the Jews?" Since there was a tone of possibly sincere inquiry in Pilate's voice, Jesus smiled on the procurator and said: "Pilate, do you ask this for yourself, or do you take this question from these others, my accusers?" Whereupon, in a tone of partial indignation, the governor answered: "Am I a Jew? Your own people and the chief priests delivered you up and asked me to sentence you to death. I question the validity of their charges and am only trying to find out for myself what you have done. Tell me, have you said that you are the king of the Jews, and have you sought to found a new kingdom?"

185:3.3 (1991.3) Then said Jesus to Pilate: "Do you not perceive that my kingdom is not of this world? If my kingdom were of this world, surely would my disciples fight that I should not be delivered into the hands of the Jews. My presence here before you in these bonds is sufficient to show all men that my kingdom is a spiritual dominion, even the brotherhood of men who, through faith and by love, have become the sons of God. And this salvation is for the gentile as well as for the Jew."

185:3.4 (1991.4) "Then you are a king after all?" said Pilate. And Jesus answered: "Yes, I am such a king, and my kingdom is the family of the faith sons of my Father who is in heaven. For this purpose was I born into this world, even that I should show my Father to all men and bear witness to the truth of God. And even now do I declare to you that every one who loves the truth hears my voice."

185:3.5 (1991.5) Then said Pilate, half in ridicule and half in sincerity, "Truth, what is truth—who knows?"

185:3.6 (1991.6) Pilate was not able to fathom Jesus' words, nor was he able to understand the nature of his spiritual kingdom, but he was now certain that the prisoner had done nothing worthy of death. One look at Jesus, face to face, was enough to convince even Pilate that this gentle and weary, but majestic and upright, man was no wild and dangerous revolutionary who aspired to establish himself on the temporal throne of Israel. Pilate thought he understood something of what Jesus meant when he called himself a king, for he was familiar with the teachings of the Stoics, who declared that "the wise man is king." Pilate was thoroughly convinced that, instead of being a dangerous seditionmonger, Jesus was nothing more or less than a harmless visionary, an innocent fanatic.

185:3.7 (1991.7) After questioning the Master, Pilate went back to the chief priests

and the accusers of Jesus and said: "I have examined this man, and I find no fault in him. I do not think he is guilty of the charges you have made against him;

I think he ought to be set free." And when the Jews heard this, they were moved with great anger, so much so that they wildly shouted that Jesus should die; and one of the Sanhedrists boldly stepped up by the side of Pilate, saying: "This man stirs up the people, beginning in Galilee and continuing throughout all Judea. He is a mischief-maker and an evildoer. You will long regret it if you let this wicked man go free."

185:3.8 (1992.1) Pilate was hard pressed to know what to do with Jesus; therefore, when he heard them say that he began his work in Galilee, he thought to avoid the responsibility of deciding the case, at least to gain time for thought, by sending Jesus to appear before Herod, who was then in the city attending the Passover. Pilate also thought that this gesture would help to antidote some of the bitter feeling which had existed for some time between himself and Herod, due to numerous misunderstandings over matters of jurisdiction.

185:3.9 (1992.2) Pilate, calling the guards, said: "This man is a Galilean. Take him forthwith to Herod, and when he has examined him, report his findings to me." And they took Jesus to Herod.

Jesus Before Herod

185:4.1 (1992.3) When Herod Antipas stopped in Jerusalem, he dwelt in the old Maccabean palace of Herod the Great, and it was to this home of the former king that Jesus was now taken by the temple guards, and he was followed by his accusers and an increasing multitude. Herod had long heard of Jesus, and he was very curious about him. When the Son of Man stood before him, on this Friday morning, the wicked Idumean never for one moment recalled the lad of former years who had appeared before him in Sepphoris pleading for a just decision regarding the money due his father, who had been accidentally killed while at work on one of the public buildings. As far as Herod knew, he had never seen Jesus, although he had worried a great deal about him when his work had been centered in Galilee. Now that he was in custody of Pilate and the Judeans, Herod was desirous of seeing him, feeling secure against any trouble from him in the future. Herod had heard much about the miracles wrought by Jesus, and he really hoped to see him do some wonder.

185:4.2 (1992.4) When they brought Jesus before Herod, the tetrarch was startled by his stately appearance and the calm composure of his countenance. For some fifteen minutes Herod asked Jesus questions, but the Master would not answer. Herod taunted and dared him to perform a miracle, but Jesus would not reply to his many inquiries or respond to his taunts.

185:4.3 (1992.5) Then Herod turned to the chief priests and the Sadducees and, giving ear to their accusations, heard all and more than Pilate had listened to regarding the alleged evil doings of the Son of Man. Finally, being convinced that Jesus would neither talk nor perform a wonder for him, Herod, after making fun of him for a time, arrayed him in an old purple royal robe and sent him back to Pilate. Herod knew he had no jurisdiction over Jesus in Judea. Though he was glad to believe that he was finally to be rid of Jesus in Galilee, he was thankful that it was Pilate who had the responsibility of putting him to death. Herod never had fully recovered from the fear that cursed him as a result of killing John the Baptist. Herod had at certain times even feared that Jesus was John risen from the dead. Now he was relieved of that fear since he observed that Jesus was a very different sort of person from the outspoken and fiery prophet who dared to expose and denounce his private life.

Jesus Returns to Pilate

185:5.1 (1993.1) When the guards had brought Jesus back to Pilate, he went out on the front steps of the praetorium, where his judgment seat had been placed, and calling together the chief priests and Sanhedrists, said to them: "You brought this man before me with charges that he perverts the people, forbids the payment of taxes, and claims to be king of the Jews. I have examined him and fail to find him guilty of these charges. In fact, I find no fault in him. Then I sent him to Herod, and the tetrarch must have reached the same conclusion since he has sent him back to us. Certainly, nothing worthy of death has been done by this man. If you still think he needs to be disciplined, I am willing to chastise him before I release him."

185:5.2 (1993.2) Just as the Jews were about to engage in shouting their protests against the release of Jesus, a vast crowd came marching up to the praetorium for the purpose of asking Pilate for the release of a prisoner in honor of the Passover feast. For some time it had been the custom of the Roman governors to allow the populace to choose some imprisoned or condemned man for pardon at the time of the Passover. And now that this crowd had come before him to ask for the release of a prisoner, and since Jesus had so recently been in great favor with the multitudes, it occurred to Pilate that he might possibly extricate himself from his predicament by proposing to this group that, since Jesus was now a prisoner before his judgment seat, he release to them this man of Galilee as the token of Passover good will.

185:5.3 (1993.3) As the crowd surged up on the steps of the building, Pilate heard them calling out the name of one Barabbas. Barabbas was a noted political agitator and murderous robber, the son of a priest, who had recently been apprehended in the act of robbery and murder on the Jericho road. This man was under sentence to die as soon as the Passover festivities were over.

185:5.4 (1993.4) Pilate stood up and explained to the crowd that Jesus had been brought to him by the chief priests, who sought to have him put to death on certain charges, and that he did not think the man was worthy of death. Said Pilate: "Which, therefore, would you prefer that I release to you, this Barabbas, the murderer, or this Jesus of Galilee?" And when Pilate had thus spoken, the chief priests and the Sanhedrin councilors all shouted at the top of their voices, "Barabbas, Barabbas!" And when the people saw that the chief priests were minded to have Jesus put to death, they quickly joined in the clamor for his life while they loudly shouted for the release of Barabbas.

185:5.5 (1993.5) A few days before this the multitude had stood in awe of Jesus, but the mob did not look up to one who, having claimed to be the Son of God, now found himself in the custody of the chief priests and the rulers and on trial before Pilate for his life. Jesus could be a hero in the eyes of the populace when he was driving the money-changers and the traders out of the temple, but not when he was a nonresisting prisoner in the hands of his enemies and on trial for his life.

185:5.6 (1993.6) Pilate was angered at the sight of the chief priests clamoring for the pardon of a notorious murderer while they shouted for the blood of Jesus. He saw their malice and hatred and perceived their prejudice and envy. Therefore he said to them: "How could you choose the life of a murderer in preference to this man's whose worst crime is that he figuratively calls himself the king of the Jews?" But this was not a wise statement for Pilate to make. The Jews were a proud people, now subject to the Roman political yoke but hoping for the coming of a Messiah who would deliver them from gentile bondage with a great show of power and glory. They resented, more than Pilate could know, the intimation that this meek-mannered teacher of strange doctrines, now under arrest and charged with crimes worthy of death, should be referred to as "the king of the Jews." They looked upon such a remark as an insult to everything which they held sacred and honorable in their national existence, and therefore did they all let loose their mighty shouts for Barabbas's release

and Jesus' death.

185:5.7 (1994.1) Pilate knew Jesus was innocent of the charges brought against him, and had he been a just and courageous judge, he would have acquitted him and turned him loose. But he was afraid to defy these angry Jews, and while he hesitated to do his duty, a messenger came up and presented him with a sealed message from his wife, Claudia.

185:5.8 (1994.2) Pilate indicated to those assembled before him that he wished to read the communication which he had just received before he proceeded further with the matter before him. When Pilate opened this letter from his wife, he read: "I pray you have nothing to do with this innocent and just man whom they call Jesus. I have suffered many things in a dream this night because of him." This note from Claudia not only greatly upset Pilate and thereby delayed the adjudication of this matter, but it unfortunately also provided considerable time in which the Jewish rulers freely circulated among the crowd and urged the people to call for the release of Barabbas and to clamor for the crucifixion of Jesus.

185:5.9 (1994.3) Finally, Pilate addressed himself once more to the solution of the problem which confronted him, by asking the mixed assembly of Jewish rulers and the pardon-seeking crowd, "What shall I do with him who is called the king of the Jews?" And they all shouted with one accord, "Crucify him! Crucify him!" The unanimity of this demand from the mixed multitude startled and alarmed Pilate, the unjust and fear-ridden judge.

185:5.10 (1994.4) Then once more Pilate said: "Why would you crucify this man? What evil has he done? Who will come forward to testify against him?" But when they heard Pilate speak in defense of Jesus, they only cried out all the more, "Crucify him! Crucify him!"

185:5.11 (1994.5) Then again Pilate appealed to them regarding the release of the Passover prisoner, saying: "Once more

I ask you, which of these prisoners shall I release to you at this, your Passover time?" And again the crowd shouted, "Give us Barabbas!"

185:5.12 (1994.6) Then said Pilate: "If I release the murderer, Barabbas, what shall I do with Jesus?" And once more the multitude shouted in unison, "Crucify him! Crucify him!"

185:5.13 (1994.7) Pilate was terrorized by the insistent clamor of the mob, acting under the direct leadership of the chief priests and the councilors of the Sanhedrin; nevertheless, he decided upon at least one more attempt to appease the crowd and save Jesus.

Pilate's Last Appeal

185:6.1 (1994.8) In all that is transpiring early this Friday morning before Pilate, only the enemies of Jesus are participating. His many friends either do not yet know of his night arrest and early morning trial or are in hiding lest they also be apprehended and adjudged worthy of death because they believe Jesus' teachings. In the multitude which now clamors for the Master's death are to be found only his sworn enemies and the easily led and unthinking populace.

185:6.2 (1995.1) Pilate would make one last appeal to their pity. Being afraid to defy the clamor of this misled mob who cried for the blood of Jesus, he ordered the Jewish guards and the Roman soldiers to take Jesus and scourge him. This was in itself an unjust and illegal procedure since the Roman law provided that only those condemned to die by crucifixion should be thus subjected to scourging. The guards took Jesus into the open courtyard of the praetorium for this ordeal. Though his enemies did not witness this scourging, Pilate did, and before they had finished this wicked abuse, he directed the scourgers to desist and indicated that Jesus should be brought to him. Before the scourgers laid their knotted whips upon Jesus as he was bound to the whipping post, they again put upon him the purple robe, and plaiting a crown of thorns, they placed it upon his brow. And when they had put a reed in his hand as a mock scepter, they knelt before him and mocked him, saying, "Hail, king of the Jews!" And they spit upon him and struck him in the face with their hands. And one of them, before they returned him to Pilate, took the reed from his hand and struck him upon the head.

185:6.3 (1995.2) Then Pilate led forth this bleeding and lacerated prisoner and, presenting him before the mixed multitude, said: "Behold the man! Again I declare to you that I find no crime in him, and having scourged him, I would release him."

185:6.4 (1995.3) There stood Jesus of Nazareth, clothed in an old purple royal robe with a crown of thorns piercing his kindly brow. His face was bloodstained and his form bowed down with suffering and grief. But nothing can appeal to the unfeeling hearts of those who are victims of intense emotional hatred and slaves to religious prejudice. This sight sent a mighty shudder through the realms of a vast universe, but it did not touch the hearts of those who had set their minds to effect the destruction of Jesus.

185:6.5 (1995.4) When they had recovered from the first shock of seeing the Master's plight, they only shouted the louder and the longer, "Crucify him! Crucify him! Crucify him!"

185:6.6 (1995.5) And now did Pilate comprehend that it was futile to appeal to their supposed feelings of pity. He stepped forward and said: "I perceive that you are determined this man shall die, but what has he done to deserve death? Who will declare his crime?"

185:6.7 (1995.6) Then the high priest himself stepped forward and, going up to Pilate, angrily declared: "We have a sacred law, and by that law this man ought to die because he made himself out to be the Son of God." When Pilate heard this, he was all the more afraid, not only of the

Jews, but recalling his wife's note and the Greek mythology of the gods coming down on earth, he now trembled at the thought of Jesus possibly being a divine personage. He waved to the crowd to hold its peace while he took Jesus by the arm and again led him inside the building that he might further examine him. Pilate was now confused by fear, bewildered by superstition, and harassed by the stubborn attitude of the mob.

Pilate's Last Interview

185:7.1 (1995.7) As Pilate, trembling with fearful emotion, sat down by the side of Jesus, he inquired: "Where do you come from? Really, who are you? What is this they say, that you are the Son of God?"

185:7.2 (1996.1) But Jesus could hardly answer such questions when asked by a man-fearing, weak, and vacillating judge who was so unjust as to subject him to flogging even when he had declared him innocent of all crime, and before he had been duly sentenced to die. Jesus looked Pilate straight in the face, but he did not answer him. Then said Pilate: "Do you refuse to speak to me? Do you not realize that I still have power to release you or to crucify you?" Then said Jesus: "You could have no power over me except it were permitted from above. You could exercise no authority over the Son of Man unless the Father in heaven allowed it. But you are not so guilty since you are ignorant of the gospel. He who betrayed me and he who delivered me to you, they have the greater sin."

185:7.3 (1996.2) This last talk with Jesus thoroughly frightened Pilate. This moral coward and judicial weakling now labored under the double weight of the superstitious fear of Jesus and mortal dread of the Jewish leaders.

185:7.4 (1996.3) Again Pilate appeared before the crowd, saying: "I am certain this man is only a religious offender. You should take him and judge him by your law. Why

should you expect that I would consent to his death because he has clashed with your traditions?"

185:7.5 (1996.4) Pilate was just about ready to release Jesus when Caiaphas, the high priest, approached the cowardly Roman judge and, shaking an avenging finger in Pilate's face, said with angry words which the entire multitude could hear: "If you release this man, you are not Caesar's friend, and I will see that the emperor knows all." This public threat was too much for Pilate. Fear for his personal fortunes now eclipsed all other considerations, and the cowardly governor ordered Jesus brought out before the judgment seat. As the Master stood there before them, he pointed to him and tauntingly said, "Behold your king." And the Jews answered, "Away with him. Crucify him!" And then Pilate said, with much irony and sarcasm, "Shall I crucify your king?" And the Jews answered, "Yes, crucify him! We have no king but Caesar." And then did Pilate realize that there was no hope of saving Jesus since he was unwilling to defy the Jews.

Pilate's Tragic Surrender

185:8.1 (1996.5) Here stood the Son of God incarnate as the Son of Man. He was arrested without indictment; accused without evidence; adjudged without witnesses; punished without a verdict; and now was soon to be condemned to die by an unjust judge who confessed that he could find no fault in him. If Pilate had thought to appeal to their patriotism by referring to Jesus as the "king of the Jews," he utterly failed. The Jews were not expecting any such a king. The declaration of the chief priests and the Sadducees, "We have no king but Caesar," was a shock even to the unthinking populace, but it was too late now to save Jesus even had the mob dared to espouse the Master's cause.

185:8.2 (1996.6) Pilate was afraid of a tumult or a riot. He dared not risk having such a disturbance during Passover time in Jerusalem. He had recently received a reprimand from Caesar, and he would not risk another. The mob cheered when he ordered the release of Barabbas. Then he ordered a basin and some water, and there before the multitude he washed his hands, saying: "I am innocent of the blood of this man. You are determined that he shall die, but I have found no guilt in him. See you to it. The soldiers will lead him forth." And then the mob cheered and replied, "His blood be on us and on our children."

Paper 186

Just Before the Crucifixion

186:0.1 (1997.1) AS JESUS and his accusers started off to see Herod, the Master turned to the Apostle John and said: "John, you can do no more for me. Go to my mother and bring her to see me ere I die." When John heard his Master's request, although reluctant to leave him alone among his enemies, he hastened off to Bethany, where the entire family of Jesus was assembled in waiting at the home of Martha and Mary, the sisters of Lazarus whom Jesus raised from the dead.

186:0.2 (1997.2) Several times during the morning, messengers had brought news to Martha and Mary concerning the progress of Jesus' trial. But the family of Jesus did not reach Bethany until just a few minutes before John arrived bearing the request of Jesus to see his mother before he was put to death. After John Zebedee had told them all that had happened since the midnight arrest of Jesus, Mary his mother went at once in the company of John to see her eldest son. By the time Mary and John reached the city, Jesus, accompanied by the Roman soldiers who were to crucify him, had already arrived at Golgotha.

186:0.3 (1997.3) When Mary the mother of Jesus started out with John to go to her son, his sister Ruth refused to remain behind with the rest of the family. Since she was determined to accompany her mother, her brother Jude went with her. The rest of the Master's family remained in Bethany under the direction of James, and almost every hour the messengers of David Zebedee brought them reports concerning the progress of that terrible business of putting to death their eldest brother, Jesus of Nazareth.

1   The End of Judas Iscariot

186:1.1 (1997.4) It was about half past eight o'clock this Friday morning when the hearing of Jesus before Pilate was ended and the Master was placed in the custody of the Roman soldiers who were to crucify him. As soon as the Romans took possession of Jesus, the captain of the Jewish guards marched with his men back to their temple headquarters. The chief priest and his Sanhedrist associates followed close behind the guards, going directly to their usual meeting place in the hall of hewn stone in the temple. Here they found many other members of the Sanhedrin waiting to learn what had been done with Jesus. As Caiaphas was engaged in making his report to the Sanhedrin regarding the trial and condemnation of Jesus, Judas appeared before them to claim his reward for the part he had played in his Master's arrest and sentence of death.

186:1.2 (1997.5) All of these Jews loathed Judas; they looked upon the betrayer with only feelings of utter contempt. Throughout the trial of Jesus before Caiaphas and during his appearance before Pilate, Judas was pricked in his conscience about his traitorous conduct. And he was also beginning to become somewhat disillusioned regarding the reward he was to receive as payment for his services as Jesus' betrayer. He did not like the coolness and aloofness of the Jewish authorities; nevertheless, he expected to be liberally rewarded for his cowardly conduct. He anticipated being called before the full meeting of the Sanhedrin and there hearing himself eulogized while they conferred upon him suitable honors in token of the great service which he flattered himself he had rendered his nation. Imagine, therefore, the great surprise of this egotistic traitor when a servant of the high priest, tapping him on the shoulder, called him just outside the hall and said: "Judas, I have been appointed to pay you for the betrayal of Jesus. Here is your reward." And thus speaking, the servant of Caiaphas handed Judas a bag containing thirty pieces of silver—the current price of a good, healthy slave.

186:1.3 (1998.1) Judas was stunned, dumfounded. He rushed back to enter the hall but was debarred by the doorkeeper. He wanted to appeal to the Sanhedrin, but they would not admit him. Judas could not believe that these rulers of the Jews would allow him to betray his friends and his Master and then offer him as a reward thirty pieces of silver. He was humiliated, disillusioned, and utterly crushed. He walked away from the temple, as it were, in a trance. He automatically dropped the money bag in his deep pocket, that same pocket wherein he had so long carried the bag containing the apostolic funds. And he wandered out through the city after the crowds who were on their way to witness the crucifixions.

186:1.4 (1998.2) From a distance Judas saw them raise the cross piece with Jesus nailed thereon, and upon sight of this he rushed back to the temple and, forcing his way past the doorkeeper, found himself standing in the presence of the Sanhedrin, which was still in session. The betrayer was well-nigh breathless and highly distraught, but he managed to stammer out these words: "I have sinned in that I have betrayed innocent blood. You have insulted me. You have offered me as a reward for my service, money—the price of a slave. I repent that I have done this; here is your money. I want to escape the guilt of this deed."

186:1.5 (1998.3) When the rulers of the Jews heard Judas, they scoffed at him. One of them sitting near where Judas stood, motioned that he should leave the hall and said: "Your Master has already been put to death by the Romans, and as for your guilt, what is that to us? See you to that—and begone!"

186:1.6 (1998.4) As Judas left the Sanhedrin chamber, he removed the thirty pieces of silver from the bag and threw them broadcast over the temple floor. When the betrayer left the temple, he was almost beside himself. Judas was now passing through the experience of the realization of the true nature of sin. All the glamor, fascination, and intoxication of wrongdoing had vanished. Now the evil-doer stood alone and face to face with the judgment verdict of his disillusioned and disappointed soul. Sin was bewitching and adventurous in the committing, but now must the harvest of the naked and unromantic facts be faced.

186:1.7 (1998.5) This onetime ambassador of the kingdom of heaven on earth now walked through the streets of Jerusalem, forsaken and alone. His despair was desperate and well-nigh absolute. On he journeyed through the city and outside the walls, on down into the terrible solitude of the valley of Hinnom, where he climbed up the steep rocks and, taking the girdle of his cloak, fastened one end to a small tree, tied the other about his neck, and cast himself over the precipice.

Ere he was dead, the knot which his nervous hands had tied gave way, and the betrayer's body was dashed to pieces as it fell on the jagged rocks below.

2   *The Master's Attitude*

186:2.1 (1999.1) When Jesus was arrested, he knew that his work on earth, in the likeness of mortal flesh, was finished. He fully understood the sort of death he would die, and he was little concerned with the details of his so-called trials.

186:2.2 (1999.2) Before the Sanhedrist court Jesus declined to make replies to the testimony of perjured witnesses. There was but one question which would always elicit an answer, whether asked by friend or foe, and that was the one concerning the nature and divinity of his mission on earth. When asked if he were the Son of God, he unfailingly made reply. He steadfastly refused to speak when in the presence of the curious and wicked Herod. Before Pilate he spoke only when he thought that Pilate or some other sincere person might be helped to a better knowledge of the truth by what he said. Jesus had taught his apostles the uselessness of casting their pearls before swine, and he now dared to practice what he had taught. His conduct at this time exemplified the patient submission of the human nature coupled with the majestic silence and solemn dignity of the divine nature. He was altogether willing to discuss with Pilate any question related to the political charges brought against him—any question which he recognized as belonging to the governor's jurisdiction.

186:2.3 (1999.3) Jesus was convinced that it was the will of the Father that he submit himself to the natural and ordinary course of human events just as every other mortal creature must, and therefore he refused to employ even his purely human powers of persuasive eloquence to influence the outcome of the machinations of his socially nearsighted and spiritually blinded fellow mortals. Although Jesus lived and died on Urantia, his whole human career, from first to last, was a spectacle designed to influence and instruct the entire universe of his creation and unceasing upholding.

186:2.4 (1999.4) These shortsighted Jews clamored unseemlily for the Master's death while he stood there in awful silence looking upon the death scene of a nation—his earthly father's own people.

186:2.5 (1999.5) Jesus had acquired that type of human character which could preserve its composure and assert its dignity in the face of continued and gratuitous insult. He could not be intimidated. When first assaulted by the servant of Annas, he had only suggested the propriety of calling witnesses who might duly testify against him.

186:2.6 (1999.6) From first to last, in his so-called trial before Pilate, the onlooking celestial hosts could not refrain from broadcasting to the universe the depiction of the scene of "Pilate on trial before Jesus."

186:2.7 (1999.7) When before Caiaphas, and when all the perjured testimony had broken down, Jesus did not hesitate to answer the question of the chief priest, thereby providing in his own testimony that which they desired as a basis for convicting him of blasphemy.

186:2.8 (1999.8) The Master never displayed the least interest in Pilate's well-meant but halfhearted efforts to effect his release. He really pitied Pilate and sincerely endeavored to enlighten his darkened mind. He was wholly passive to all the Roman governor's appeals to the Jews to withdraw their criminal charges against him. Throughout the whole sorrowful ordeal he bore himself with simple dignity and unostentatious majesty. He would not so much as cast reflections of insincerity upon his would-be murderers when they asked if he were "king of the Jews." With but little qualifying explanation he accepted the designation, knowing that, while they had chosen to reject him, he would be the last to afford them real national leadership, even in a spiritual sense.

186:2.9 (2000.1) Jesus said little during these trials, but he said enough to show all mortals the kind of human character man can perfect in partnership with God and to reveal to all the universe the manner in which God can become manifest in the life of the creature when such a creature truly chooses to do the will of the Father, thus becoming an active son of the living God.

186:2.10 (2000.2) His love for ignorant mortals is fully disclosed by his patience and great self-possession in the face of the jeers, blows, and buffetings of the coarse soldiers and the unthinking servants. He was not even angry when they blindfolded him and, derisively striking him in the face, exclaimed: "Prophesy to us who it was that struck you."

186:2.11 (2000.3) Pilate spoke more truly than he knew when, after Jesus had been scourged, he presented him before the multitude, exclaiming, "Behold the man!" Indeed, the fear-ridden Roman governor little dreamed that at just that moment the universe stood at attention, gazing upon this unique scene of its beloved Sovereign thus subjected in humiliation to the taunts and blows of his darkened and degraded mortal subjects. And as Pilate spoke, there echoed throughout all Nebadon, "Behold God and man!" Throughout a universe, untold millions have ever since that day continued to behold that man, while the God of Havona, the supreme ruler of the universe of universes, accepts the man of Nazareth as the satisfaction of the ideal of the mortal creatures of this local universe of time and space. In his matchless life he never failed to reveal God to man. Now, in these final episodes of his mortal career and in his subsequent death, he made a new and touching revelation of man to God.

3   The Dependable David Zebedee

186:3.1 (2000.4) Shortly after Jesus was turned over to the Roman soldiers at the conclusion of the hearing before Pilate, a detachment of the temple guards hastened out to Gethsemane to disperse or arrest the followers of the Master. But long before their arrival these followers had scattered. The apostles had retired to designated hiding places; the Greeks had separated and gone to various homes in Jerusalem; the other disciples had likewise disappeared. David Zebedee believed that Jesus' enemies would return; so he early removed some five or six tents up the ravine near where the Master so often retired to pray and worship. Here he proposed to hide and at the same time maintain a center, or co- ordinating station, for his messenger service. David had hardly left the camp when the temple guards arrived. Finding no one there, they contented themselves

with burning the camp and then hastened back to the temple. On hearing their report, the Sanhedrin was satisfied that the followers of Jesus were so thoroughly frightened and subdued that there would be no danger of an uprising or any attempt to rescue Jesus from the hands of his executioners. They were at last able to breathe easily, and so they adjourned, every man going his way to prepare for the Passover.

186:3.2 (2000.5) As soon as Jesus was turned over to the Roman soldiers by Pilate for crucifixion, a messenger hastened away to Gethsemane to inform David, and within five minutes runners were on their way to Bethsaida, Pella, Philadelphia, Sidon, Shechem, Hebron, Damascus, and Alexandria. And these messengers carried the news that Jesus was about to be crucified by the Romans at the insistent behest of the rulers of the Jews. *

186:3.3 (2001.1) Throughout this tragic day, until the message finally went forth that the Master had been laid in the tomb, David sent messengers about every half hour with reports to the apostles, the Greeks, and Jesus' earthly family, assembled at the home of Lazarus in Bethany. When the messengers departed with the word that Jesus had been buried, David dismissed his corps of local runners for the Passover celebration and for the coming Sabbath of rest, instructing them to report to him quietly on Sunday morning at the home of Nicodemus, where he proposed to go in hiding for a few days with Andrew and Simon Peter.

186:3.4 (2001.2) This peculiar-minded David Zebedee was the only one of the leading disciples of Jesus who was inclined to take a literal and plain matter-of-fact view of the Master's assertion that he would die and "rise again on the third day." David had once heard him make this prediction and, being of a literal turn of mind, now proposed to assemble his messengers early Sunday morning at the home of Nicodemus so that they would be on hand to spread the news in case Jesus rose from the dead. David soon discovered that none of Jesus' followers were looking for him to return so soon from the grave; therefore did he say little about his belief and nothing about the mobilization of all his messenger force on early Sunday morning except to the runners who had been dispatched on Friday forenoon to distant cities and believer centers.

186:3.5 (2001.3) And so these followers of Jesus, scattered throughout Jerusalem and its environs, that night partook of the Passover and the following day remained in seclusion.

4 Preparation for the Crucifixion

186:4.1 (2001.4) After Pilate had washed his hands before the multitude, thus seeking to escape the guilt of delivering up an innocent man to be crucified just because he feared to resist the clamor of the rulers of the Jews, he ordered the Master turned over to the Roman soldiers and gave the word to their captain that he was to be crucified immediately. Upon taking charge of Jesus, the soldiers led him back into the courtyard of the praetorium, and after removing the robe which Herod had put on him, they dressed him in his own garments. These soldiers mocked and derided him, but they did not inflict further physical punishment. Jesus was now alone with these Roman soldiers. His friends were in hiding; his enemies had gone their way; even John Zebedee was no longer by his side.

186:4.2 (2001.5) It was a little after eight o'clock when Pilate turned Jesus over to the soldiers and a little before nine o'clock when they started for the scene of the crucifixion. During this period of more than half an hour Jesus never spoke a word. The executive business of a great universe was practically at a standstill. Gabriel and the chief rulers of Nebadon were either assembled here on Urantia, or else they were closely attending upon the space reports of the archangels in an effort to keep advised as to what was happening to the Son of Man on Urantia.

186:4.3 (2001.6) By the time the soldiers were ready to depart with Jesus for Golgotha, they had begun to be impressed by his unusual composure and extraordinary dignity, by his uncomplaining silence.

186:4.4 (2001.7) Much of the delay in starting off with Jesus for the site of the crucifixion was due to the last-minute decision of the captain to take along two thieves who had been condemned to die; since Jesus was to be crucified that morning, the Roman captain thought these two might just as well die with him as wait for the end of the Passover festivities.

186:4.5 (2002.1) As soon as the thieves could be made ready, they were led into the courtyard, where they gazed upon Jesus, one of them for the first time, but the other had often heard him speak, both in the temple and many months before at the Pella camp.

5 Jesus' Death in Relation to the Passover

186:5.1 (2002.2) There is no direct relation between the death of Jesus and the Jewish Passover. True, the Master did lay down his life in the flesh on this day, the day of the preparation for the Jewish Passover, and at about the time of the sacrificing of the Passover lambs in the temple. But this coincidental occurrence does not in any manner indicate that the death of the Son of Man on earth has any connection with the Jewish sacrificial system. Jesus was a Jew, but as the Son of Man he was a mortal of the realms. The events already narrated and leading up to this hour of the Master's impending crucifixion are sufficient to indicate that his death at about this time was a purely natural and man-managed affair.

186:5.2 (2002.3) It was man and not God who planned and executed the death of Jesus on the cross. True, the Father refused to interfere with the march of human events on Urantia, but the Father in Paradise did not decree, demand, or require the death of his Son as it was carried out on earth. It is a fact that in some manner, sooner or later, Jesus would have had to divest himself of his mortal body, his incarnation in the flesh, but he could have executed such a task in countless ways without dying on a cross between two thieves. All of this was man's doing, not God's.

186:5.3 (2002.4) At the time of the Master's baptism he had already completed the technique of the required experience on earth and in the flesh which was necessary for the completion of his seventh and last universe bestowal. At this very time Jesus' duty on earth was done. All the life he lived thereafter, and even the manner of his death, was a purely personal ministry on his part for the welfare and uplifting of his mortal creatures on this world and on other worlds.

186:5.4 (2002.5) The gospel of the good news that mortal man may, by faith, become spirit-conscious that he is a son of God, is not dependent on the death of Jesus. True, indeed, all this gospel of the kingdom has been tremendously illuminated by the Master's death, but even more so by his life.

186:5.5 (2002.6) All that the Son of Man said or did on earth greatly embellished the doctrines of sonship with God and of the brotherhood of men, but these essential relationships of God and men are inherent in the universe facts of God's love for his creatures and the innate mercy of the divine Sons. These touching and divinely beautiful relations between man and his Maker, on this world and on all others throughout the universe of universes, have existed from eternity; and they are not in any sense dependent on these periodic bestowal enactments of the Creator Sons of God, who thus assume the nature and likeness of their created intelligences as a part of the price which they must pay for the final acquirement of unlimited sovereignty over their respective local universes. *

186:5.6 (2002.7) The Father in heaven loved mortal man on earth just as much before the life and death of Jesus on Urantia as he did after this transcendent exhibition of the copartnership of man and God. This mighty transaction of the incarnation of the God of Nebadon as a man on Urantia could not augment the attributes of the eternal, infinite, and universal Father, but it did enrich and enlighten all other administrators and creatures of the universe of Nebadon. While the Father in heaven loves us no more because of this bestowal of Michael, all other celestial intelligences do. And this is because Jesus not only made a revelation of God to man, but he also likewise made a new revelation of man to the Gods and to the celestial intelligences of the universe of universes.

186:5.7 (2003.1) Jesus is not about to die as a sacrifice for sin. He is not going to atone for the inborn moral guilt of the human race. Mankind has no such racial guilt before God. Guilt is purely a matter of personal sin and knowing, deliberate rebellion against the will of the Father and the administration of his Sons.

186:5.8 (2003.2) Sin and rebellion have nothing to do with the fundamental bestowal plan of the Paradise Sons of God, albeit it does appear to us that the salvage plan is a provisional feature of the bestowal plan.

186:5.9 (2003.3) The salvation of God for the mortals of Urantia would have been just as effective and unerringly certain if Jesus had not been put to death by the cruel hands of ignorant mortals. If the Master had been favorably received by the mortals of earth and had departed from Urantia by the voluntary relinquishment of his life in the flesh, the fact of the love of God and the mercy of the Son—the fact of sonship with God—would have in no wise been affected. You mortals are the sons of God, and only one thing is required to make such a truth factual in your personal experience, and that is your spirit-born faith.

Paper 187

The Crucifixion

187:0.1 (2004.1) AFTER the two brigands had been made ready, the soldiers, under the direction of a centurion, started for the scene of the crucifixion. The centurion in charge of these twelve soldiers was the same captain who had led forth the Roman soldiers the previous night to arrest Jesus in Gethsemane. It was the Roman custom to assign four soldiers for each person to be crucified. The two brigands were properly scourged before they were taken out to be crucified, but Jesus was given no further physical punishment; the captain undoubtedly thought he had already been sufficiently scourged, even before his condemnation.

187:0.2 (2004.2) The two thieves crucified with Jesus were associates of Barabbas and would later have been put to death with their leader if he had not been released as the Passover pardon of Pilate. Jesus was thus crucified in the place of Barabbas.

187:0.3 (2004.3) What Jesus is now about to do, submit to death on the cross, he does of his own free will. In foretelling this experience, he said: "The Father loves and sustains me because I am willing to lay down my life. But I will take it up again. No one takes my life away from me—I lay it down of myself. I have authority to lay it down, and I have authority to take it up. I have received such a commandment from my Father."

187:0.4 (2004.4) It was just before nine o'clock this morning when the soldiers led Jesus from the praetorium on the way to Golgotha. They were followed by many who secretly sympathized with Jesus, but most of this group of two hundred or more were either his enemies or curious idlers who merely desired to enjoy the shock of witnessing the crucifixions.

Only a few of the Jewish leaders went out to see Jesus die on the cross. Knowing that he had been turned over to the Roman soldiers by Pilate, and that he was condemned to die, they busied themselves with their meeting in the temple, whereat they discussed what should be done with his followers.

On the Way to Golgotha

187:1.1 (2004.5) Before leaving the courtyard of the praetorium, the soldiers placed the crossbeam on Jesus' shoulders. It was the custom to compel the condemned man to carry the crossbeam to the site of the crucifixion. Such a condemned man did not carry the whole cross, only this shorter timber. The longer and upright pieces of timber for the three crosses had already been transported to Golgotha and, by the time of the arrival of the soldiers and their prisoners, had been firmly implanted in the ground.

187:1.2 (2004.6) According to custom the captain led the procession, carrying small white boards on which had been written with charcoal the names of the criminals and the nature of the crimes for which they had been condemned. For the two thieves the centurion had notices which gave their names, underneath which was written the one word, "Brigand." It was the custom, after the victim had been nailed to the cross beam and hoisted to his place on the upright timber, to nail this notice to the top of the cross, just above the head of the criminal, that all witnesses might know for what crime the condemned man was being crucified. The legend which the centurion carried to put on the cross of Jesus had been written by Pilate himself in Latin, Greek, and Aramaic, and it read: "Jesus of Nazareth—the King of the Jews."

187:1.3 (2005.1) Some of the Jewish authorities who were yet present when Pilate wrote this legend made vigorous protest against calling Jesus the "king of the Jews." But Pilate reminded them that such an accusation was part of the charge which led to his condemnation. When the Jews saw they could not prevail upon Pilate to change his mind, they pleaded that at least it be modified to read, "He said, 'I am the king of the Jews.'" But Pilate was adamant; he would not alter the writing. To all further supplication he only replied, "What I have written, I have written."

187:1.4 (2005.2) Ordinarily, it was the custom to journey to Golgotha by the longest road in order that a large number of persons might view the condemned criminal, but on this day they went by the most direct route to the Damascus gate, which led out of the city to the north, and following this road, they soon arrived at Golgotha, the official crucifixion site of Jerusalem. Beyond Golgotha were the villas of the wealthy, and on the other side of the road were the tombs of many well-to-do Jews.

187:1.5 (2005.3) Crucifixion was not a Jewish mode of punishment. Both the Greeks and the Romans learned this method of execution from the Phoenicians. Even Herod, with all his cruelty, did not resort to crucifixion. The Romans never crucified a Roman citizen; only slaves and subject peoples were subjected to this dishonorable mode of death. During the siege of Jerusalem, just forty years after the crucifixion of Jesus, all of Golgotha was covered by thousands upon thousands of crosses upon which, from day to day, there perished the flower of the Jewish race. A terrible harvest, indeed, of the seed-sowing of this day.

187:1.6 (2005.4) As the death procession passed along the narrow streets of Jerusalem, many of the tenderhearted Jewish women who had heard Jesus' words of good cheer and compassion, and who knew of his life of loving ministry, could not refrain from weeping when they saw him being led forth to such an ignoble death. As he passed by, many of these women bewailed and lamented. And when some of them even dared to follow along by his side, the Master turned his head toward them and said: "Daughters of Jerusalem, weep not for me, but rather weep for yourselves and for your children. My work is about done—soon I go to my Father—but the times of terrible trouble for Jerusalem are just beginning. Behold, the days are coming in which you shall say: Blessed are the barren and those whose breasts have never suckled their young. In those days will you pray the rocks of the hills to fall on you in order that you may be delivered from the terrors of your troubles."

187:1.7 (2005.5) These women of Jerusalem were indeed courageous to manifest sympathy for Jesus, for it was strictly against the law to show friendly feelings for one who was being led forth to crucifixion. It was permitted the rabble to jeer, mock, and ridicule the condemned, but it was not allowed that any sympathy should be expressed. Though Jesus appreciated the manifestation of sympathy in this dark hour when his friends were in hiding, he did not want these kindhearted women to incur the displeasure of the authorities by daring to show compassion in his behalf. Even at such a time as this Jesus thought little about himself, only of the terrible days of tragedy ahead for Jerusalem and the whole Jewish nation.

187:1.8 (2006.1) As the Master trudged along on the way to the crucifixion, he was very weary; he was nearly exhausted. He had had neither food nor water since the Last Supper at the home of Elijah Mark; neither had he been permitted to enjoy one moment of sleep. In addition, there had been one hearing right after another up to the hour of his condemnation, not to mention the abusive scourgings with their accompanying physical suffering and loss of blood.

Superimposed upon all this was his extreme mental anguish, his acute spiritual tension, and a terrible feeling of human loneliness.

187:1.9 (2006.2) Shortly after passing through the gate on the way out of the city, as Jesus staggered on bearing the crossbeam, his physical strength momentarily gave way, and he fell beneath the weight of his heavy burden. The soldiers shouted at him and kicked him, but he could not arise. When the captain saw this, knowing what Jesus had already endured, he commanded the soldiers to desist. Then he ordered a passerby, one Simon from Cyrene, to take the crossbeam from Jesus' shoulders and compelled him to carry it the rest of the way to Golgotha.

187:1.10 (2006.3) This man Simon had come all the way from Cyrene, in northern Africa, to attend the Passover. He was stopping with other Cyrenians just outside the city walls and was on his way to the temple services in the city when the Roman captain commanded him to carry Jesus' crossbeam. Simon lingered all through the hours of the Master's death on the cross, talking with many of his friends and with his enemies. After the resurrection and before leaving Jerusalem, he became a valiant believer in the gospel of the kingdom, and when he returned home, he led his family into the heavenly kingdom. His two sons, Alexander and Rufus, became very effective teachers of the new gospel in Africa. But Simon never knew that Jesus, whose burden he bore, and the Jewish tutor who once befriended his injured son, were the same person.

187:1.11 (2006.4) It was shortly after nine o'clock when this procession of death arrived at Golgotha, and the Roman soldiers set themselves about the task of nailing the two brigands and the Son of Man to their respective crosses.

The Crucifixion

187:2.1 (2006.5) The soldiers first bound the Master's arms with cords to the crossbeam, and then they nailed his hands to the wood. When they had hoisted this crossbeam up on the post, and after they had nailed it securely to the upright timber of the cross, they bound and nailed his feet to the wood, using one long nail to penetrate both feet. The upright timber had a large peg, inserted at the proper height, which served as a sort of saddle for supporting the body weight.

The cross was not high, the Master's feet being only about three feet from the ground. He was therefore able to hear all that was said of him in derision and could plainly see the expression on the faces of all those who so thoughtlessly mocked him. And also could those present easily hear all that Jesus said during these hours of lingering torture and slow death.

187:2.2 (2007.1) It was the custom to remove all clothes from those who were to be crucified, but since the Jews greatly objected to the public exposure of the naked human form, the Romans always provided a suitable loin cloth for all persons crucified at Jerusalem. Accordingly, after Jesus' clothes had been removed, he was thus garbed before he was put upon the cross.

187:2.3 (2007.2) Crucifixion was resorted to in order to provide a cruel and lingering punishment, the victim sometimes not dying for several days. There was considerable sentiment against crucifixion in Jerusalem, and there existed a society of Jewish women who always sent a representative to crucifixions for the purpose of offering drugged wine to the victim in order to lessen his suffering. But when Jesus tasted this narcotized wine, as thirsty as he was, he refused to drink it. The Master chose to retain his human consciousness until the very end. He desired to meet death, even in this cruel and inhuman form, and conquer it by voluntary submission to the full human experience.

187:2.4 (2007.3) Before Jesus was put on his cross, the two brigands had already been placed on their crosses, all the while cursing and spitting upon their executioners. Jesus' only words, as they nailed him to the crossbeam, were, "Father, forgive them, for they know not what they do." He could not have so mercifully and lovingly interceded for his executioners if such thoughts of affectionate devotion had not been the mainspring of all his life of unselfish service.

The ideas, motives, and longings of a lifetime are openly revealed in a crisis.

187:2.5 (2007.4) After the Master was hoisted on the cross, the captain nailed the title up above his head, and it read in three languages, "Jesus of Nazareth—the King of the Jews." The Jews were infuriated by this believed insult. But Pilate was chafed by their disrespectful manner; he felt he had been intimidated and humiliated, and he took this method of obtaining petty revenge. He could have written "Jesus, a rebel." But he well knew how these Jerusalem Jews detested the very name of Nazareth, and he was determined thus to humiliate them. He knew that they would also be cut to the very quick by seeing this executed Galilean called "The King of the Jews."

187:2.6 (2007.5) Many of the Jewish leaders, when they learned how Pilate had sought to deride them by placing this inscription on the cross of Jesus, hastened out to Golgotha, but they dared not attempt to remove it since the Roman soldiers were standing on guard. Not being able to remove the title, these leaders mingled with the crowd and did their utmost to incite derision and ridicule, lest any give serious regard to the inscription.

187:2.7 (2007.6) The Apostle John, with Mary the mother of Jesus, Ruth, and Jude, arrived on the scene just after Jesus had been hoisted to his position on the cross, and just as the captain was nailing the title above the Master's head. John was the only one of the eleven apostles to witness the crucifixion, and even he was not present all of the time since he ran into Jerusalem to bring back his mother and her friends soon after he had brought Jesus' mother to the scene.

187:2.8 (2007.7) As Jesus saw his mother, with John and his brother and sister, he smiled but said nothing. Meanwhile the four soldiers assigned to the Master's crucifixion, as was the custom, had divided his clothes among them, one taking the sandals, one the turban, one the girdle, and the fourth the cloak. This left the tunic, or seamless vestment reaching down to near the knees, to be cut up into four pieces, but when the soldiers saw what an unusual garment it was, they decided to cast lots for it. Jesus looked down on them while they divided his garments, and the thoughtless crowd jeered at him.

187:2.9 (2008.1) It was well that the Roman soldiers took possession of the Master's clothing. Otherwise, if his followers had gained possession of these garments, they would have been tempted to resort to superstitious relic worship. The Master desired that his followers should have nothing material to associate with his life on earth. He wanted to leave mankind only the memory of a human life dedicated to the high spiritual ideal of being consecrated to doing the Father's will.

Those Who Saw the Crucifixion

187:3.1 (2008.2) At about half past nine o'clock this Friday morning, Jesus was hung upon the cross. Before eleven o'clock, upward of one thousand persons had assembled to witness this spectacle of the crucifixion of the Son of Man. Throughout these dreadful hours the unseen hosts of a universe stood in silence while they gazed upon this extraordinary phenomenon of the Creator as he was dying the death of the creature, even the most ignoble death of a condemned criminal.

187:3.2 (2008.3) Standing near the cross at one time or another during the crucifixion were Mary, Ruth, Jude, John, Salome (John's mother), and a group of earnest women believers including Mary the wife of Clopas and sister of Jesus' mother, Mary Magdalene, and Rebecca, onetime of Sepphoris. These and other friends of Jesus held their peace while they witnessed his great patience and fortitude and gazed upon his intense sufferings.

187:3.3 (2008.4) Many who passed by wagged their heads and, railing at him, said: "You who would destroy the temple and build it again in three days, save yourself. If you are the Son of God, why do you not come down from your cross?" In like manner some of the rulers of the Jews mocked him, saying, "He saved others, but himself he cannot save." Others said, "If you are the king of the Jews, come down from the cross, and we will believe in you." And later on they mocked him the more, saying: "He trusted in God to deliver him. He even claimed to be the Son of God—look at him now—crucified between two thieves." Even the two thieves also railed at him and cast reproach upon him.

187:3.4 (2008.5) Inasmuch as Jesus would make no reply to their taunts, and since it was nearing noontime of this special preparation day, by half past eleven o'clock most of the jesting and jeering crowd had gone its way; less than fifty persons remained on the scene. The soldiers now prepared to eat lunch and drink their cheap, sour wine as they settled down for the long deathwatch. As they partook of their wine, they derisively offered a toast to Jesus, saying, "Hail and good fortune! to the king of the Jews." And they were astonished at the Master's tolerant regard of their ridicule and mocking.

187:3.5 (2008.6) When Jesus saw them eat and drink, he looked down upon them and said, "I thirst." When the captain of the guard heard Jesus say, "I thirst," he took some of the wine from his bottle and, putting the saturated sponge stopper upon the end of a javelin, raised it to Jesus so that he could moisten his parched lips.

187:3.6 (2008.7) Jesus had purposed to live without resort to his supernatural power, and he likewise elected to die as an ordinary mortal upon the cross. He had lived as a man, and he would die as a man—doing the Father's will.

The Thief on the Cross

187:4.1 (2008.8) One of the brigands railed at Jesus, saying, "If you are the Son of God, why do you not save yourself and us?" But when he had reproached Jesus, the other thief, who had many times heard the Master teach, said: "Do you have no fear even of God? Do you not see that we are suffering justly for our deeds, but that this man suffers unjustly? Better that we should seek forgiveness for our sins and salvation for our souls." When Jesus heard the thief say this, he turned

his face toward him and smiled approvingly. When the malefactor saw the face of Jesus turned toward him, he mustered up his courage, fanned the flickering flame of his faith, and said, "Lord, remember me when you come into your kingdom." And then Jesus said, "Verily, verily, I say to you today, you shall sometime be with me in Paradise."

187:4.2 (2009.1) The Master had time amidst the pangs of mortal death to listen to the faith confession of the believing brigand. When this thief reached out for salvation, he found deliverance. Many times before this he had been constrained to believe in Jesus, but only in these last hours of consciousness did he turn with a whole heart toward the Master's teaching. When he saw the manner in which Jesus faced death upon the cross, this thief could no longer resist the conviction that this Son of Man was indeed the Son of God.

187:4.3 (2009.2) During this episode of the conversion and reception of the thief into the kingdom by Jesus, the Apostle John was absent, having gone into the city to bring his mother and her friends to the scene of the crucifixion. Luke subsequently heard this story from the converted Roman captain of the guard.

187:4.4 (2009.3) The Apostle John told about the crucifixion as he remembered the event two thirds of a century after its occurrence. The other records were based upon the recital of the Roman centurion on duty who, because of what he saw and heard, subsequently believed in Jesus and entered into the full fellowship of the kingdom of heaven on earth.

187:4.5 (2009.4) This young man, the penitent brigand, had been led into a life of violence and wrongdoing by those who extolled such a career of robbery as an effective patriotic protest against political oppression and social injustice. And this sort of teaching, plus the urge for adventure, led many otherwise well-meaning youths to enlist in these daring expeditions of robbery. This young man had looked upon Barabbas as a hero. Now he saw that he had been mistaken. Here on the cross beside him he saw a really great man, a true hero. Here was a hero who fired his zeal and inspired his highest ideas of moral self-respect and quickened all his ideals of courage, manhood, and bravery. In beholding Jesus, there sprang up in his heart an overwhelming sense of love, loyalty, and genuine greatness.

187:4.6 (2009.5) And if any other person among the jeering crowd had experienced the birth of faith within his soul and had appealed to the mercy of Jesus, he would have been received with the same loving consideration that was displayed toward the believing brigand.

187:4.7 (2009.6) Just after the repentant thief heard the Master's promise that they should sometime meet in Paradise, John returned from the city, bringing with him his mother and a company of almost a dozen women believers. John took up his position near Mary the mother of Jesus, supporting her. Her son Jude stood on the other side. As Jesus looked down upon this scene, it was noontide, and he said to his mother, "Woman, behold your son!" And speaking to John, he said, "My son, behold your mother!" And then he addressed them both, saying, "I desire that you depart from this place." And so John and Jude led Mary away from Golgotha. John took the mother of Jesus to the place where he tarried in Jerusalem and then hastened back to the scene of the crucifixion. After the Passover Mary returned to Bethsaida, where she lived at John's home for the rest of her natural life. Mary did not live quite one year after the death of Jesus.

187:4.8 (2010.1) After Mary left, the other women withdrew for a short distance and remained in attendance upon Jesus until he expired on the cross, and they were yet standing by when the body of the Master was taken down for burial.

Last Hour on the Cross

187:5.1 (2010.2) Although it was early in the season for such a phenomenon, shortly after twelve o'clock the sky darkened by reason of the fine sand in the air. The people of Jerusalem knew that this meant the coming of one of those hot-wind sandstorms from the Arabian Desert. Before one o'clock the sky was so dark the sun was hid, and the remainder of the crowd hastened back to the city. When the Master gave up his life shortly after this hour, less than thirty people were present, only the thirteen Roman soldiers and a group of about fifteen believers. These believers were all women except two, Jude, Jesus' brother, and John Zebedee, who returned to the scene just before the Master expired.

187:5.2 (2010.3) Shortly after one o'clock, amidst the increasing darkness of the fierce sandstorm, Jesus began to fail in human consciousness. His last words of mercy, forgiveness, and admonition had been spoken. His last wish— concerning the care of his mother—had been expressed. During this hour of approaching death the human mind of Jesus resorted to the repetition of many passages in the Hebrew scriptures, particularly the Psalms. The last conscious thought of the human Jesus was concerned with the repetition in his mind of a portion of the Book of Psalms now known as the twentieth, twenty-first, and twenty-second Psalms. While his lips would often move, he was too weak to utter the words as these passages, which he so well knew by heart, would pass through his mind. Only a few times did those standing by catch some utterance, such as, "I know the Lord will save his anointed," "Your hand shall find out all my enemies," and "My God, my God, why have you forsaken me?" Jesus did not for one moment entertain the slightest doubt that he had lived in accordance with the Father's will; and he never doubted that he was now laying down his life in the flesh in accordance with his Father's will. He did not feel that the Father had forsaken him; he was merely reciting in his vanishing consciousness many Scriptures, among them this twenty-second Psalm, which begins with "My God, my God, why have you forsaken me?" And this happened to be one of the three passages which were spoken with sufficient clearness to be heard by those standing by.

187:5.3 (2010.4) The last request which the mortal Jesus made of his fellows was about half past one o'clock when, a second time, he said, "I thirst," and the same captain of the guard again moistened his lips with the same sponge wet in the sour wine, in those days commonly called vinegar.

187:5.4 (2010.5) The sandstorm grew in intensity and the heavens increasingly darkened. Still the soldiers and the small group of believers stood by. The soldiers crouched near the cross, huddled together to protect themselves from the cutting sand. The mother of John and others watched from a distance where they were somewhat sheltered by an overhanging rock. When the Master finally breathed his last, there were present at the foot of his cross John Zebedee, his brother Jude, his sister Ruth, Mary Magdalene, and Rebecca, onetime of Sepphoris.

187:5.5 (2011.1) It was just before three o'clock when Jesus, with a loud voice, cried out, "It is finished! Father, into your hands I commend my spirit." And when he had thus spoken, he bowed his head and gave up the life struggle. When the Roman centurion saw how Jesus died, he smote his breast and said: "This was indeed a righteous man; truly he must have been a Son of God." And from that hour he began to believe in Jesus.

187:5.6 (2011.2) Jesus died royally—as he had lived. He freely admitted his kingship and remained master of the situation throughout the tragic day. He went willingly to his ignominious death, after he had provided for the safety of his chosen apostles. He wisely restrained Peter's troublemaking violence and provided that John might be near him right up to the end of his mortal existence. He revealed his true nature to the murderous Sanhedrin and reminded Pilate of the source of his sovereign authority as a Son of God. He started out to Golgotha bearing his own crossbeam and finished up his loving bestowal by handing over his spirit of mortal acquirement to the Paradise Father. After such a life—and at such a death—the Master could truly say, "It is finished."

187:5.7 (2011.3) Because this was the preparation day for both the Passover and the Sabbath, the Jews did not want these bodies to be exposed on Golgotha. Therefore they went before Pilate asking that the legs of these three men be broken, that they be dispatched, so that they could be taken down from their crosses and cast into the criminal burial pits before sundown. When Pilate heard this request, he forthwith sent three soldiers to break the legs and dispatch Jesus and the two brigands.

187:5.8 (2011.4) When these soldiers arrived at Golgotha, they did accordingly to the two thieves, but they found Jesus already dead, much to their surprise. However, in order to make sure of his death, one of the soldiers pierced his left side with his spear. Though it was common for the victims of crucifixion to linger alive upon the cross for even two or three days, the overwhelming emotional agony and the acute spiritual anguish of Jesus brought an end to his mortal life in the flesh in a little less than five and one-half hours.

After the Crucifixion

187:6.1 (2011.5) In the midst of the darkness of the sandstorm, about half past three o'clock, David Zebedee sent out the last of the messengers carrying the news of the Master's death. The last of his runners he dispatched to the home of Martha and

Mary in Bethany, where he supposed the mother of Jesus stopped with the rest of her family.

187:6.2 (2011.6) After the death of the Master, John sent the women, in charge of Jude, to the home of Elijah Mark, where they tarried over the Sabbath day. John himself, being well known by this time to the Roman centurion, remained at Golgotha until Joseph and Nicodemus arrived on the scene with an order from Pilate authorizing them to take possession of the body of Jesus. *

187:6.3 (2011.7) Thus ended a day of tragedy and sorrow for a vast universe whose myriads of intelligences had shuddered at the shocking spectacle of the crucifixion of the human incarnation of their beloved Sovereign; they were stunned by this exhibition of mortal callousness and human perversity.

Paper 188

The Time of the Tomb

188:0.1 (2012.1) THE day and a half that Jesus' mortal body lay in the tomb of Joseph, the period between his death on the cross and his resurrection, is a chapter in the earth career of Michael which is little known to us. We can narrate the burial of the Son of Man and put in this record the events associated with his resurrection, but we cannot supply much information of an authentic nature about what really transpired during this epoch of about thirty-six hours, from three o'clock Friday afternoon to three o'clock Sunday morning. This period in the Master's career began shortly before he was taken down from the cross by the Roman soldiers. He hung upon the cross about one hour after his death. He would have been taken down sooner but for the delay in dispatching the two brigands.

188:0.2 (2012.2) The rulers of the Jews

had planned to have Jesus' body thrown in the open burial pits of Gehenna, south of the city; it was the custom thus to dispose of the victims of crucifixion. If this plan had been followed, the body of the Master would have been exposed to the wild beasts.

188:0.3 (2012.3) In the meantime, Joseph of Arimathea, accompanied by Nicodemus, had gone to Pilate and asked that the body of Jesus be turned over to them for proper burial. It was not uncommon for friends of crucified persons to offer bribes to the Roman authorities for the privilege of gaining possession of such bodies. Joseph went before Pilate with a large sum of money, in case it became necessary to pay for permission to remove Jesus' body to a private burial tomb. But Pilate would not take money for this. When he heard the request, he quickly signed the order which authorized Joseph to proceed to Golgotha and take immediate and full possession of the Master's body. In the meantime, the sandstorm having considerably abated, a group of Jews representing the Sanhedrin had gone out to Golgotha for the purpose of making sure that Jesus' body accompanied those of the brigands to the open public burial pits.

The Burial of Jesus

188:1.1 (2012.4) When Joseph and Nicodemus arrived at Golgotha, they found the soldiers taking Jesus down from the cross and the representatives of the Sanhedrin standing by to see that none of Jesus' followers prevented his body from going to the criminal burial pits. When Joseph presented Pilate's order for the Master's body to the centurion, the Jews raised a tumult and clamored for its possession. In their raving they sought violently to take possession of the body, and when they did this, the centurion ordered four of his soldiers to his side, and with drawn swords they stood astride the Master's body as it lay there on the ground. The centurion ordered the other soldiers to leave the two thieves while they drove back this angry mob of infuriated Jews. When order had been restored, the centurion read the permit from Pilate to the Jews and, stepping aside, said to Joseph: "This body is yours to do with as you see fit. I and my soldiers will stand by to see that no man interferes."

188:1.2 (2013.1) A crucified person could not be buried in a Jewish cemetery; there was a strict law against such a procedure. Joseph and Nicodemus knew this law, and on the way out to Golgotha they had decided to bury Jesus in Joseph's new family tomb, hewn out of solid rock, located a short distance north of Golgotha and across the road leading to Samaria. No one had ever lain in this tomb, and they thought it appropriate that the Master should rest there. Joseph really believed that Jesus would rise from the dead, but Nicodemus was very doubtful. These former members of the Sanhedrin had kept their faith in Jesus more or less of a secret, although their fellow Sanhedrists had long suspected them, even before they withdrew from the council. From now on they were the most outspoken disciples of Jesus in all Jerusalem.

188:1.3 (2013.2) At about half past four o'clock the burial procession of Jesus of Nazareth started from Golgotha for Joseph's tomb across the way. The body was wrapped in a linen sheet as the four men carried it, followed by the faithful women watchers from Galilee. The mortals who bore the material body of Jesus to the tomb were: Joseph, Nicodemus, John, and the Roman centurion.

188:1.4 (2013.3) They carried the body into the tomb, a chamber about ten feet square, where they hurriedly prepared it for burial. The Jews did not really bury their dead; they actually embalmed them. Joseph and Nicodemus had brought with them large quantities of myrrh and aloes, and they now wrapped the body with bandages saturated with these solutions. When the embalming was completed, they tied a napkin about the face, wrapped the body in a linen sheet, and reverently placed it on a shelf in the tomb.

188:1.5 (2013.4) After placing the body in the tomb, the centurion signaled for his soldiers to help roll the doorstone up before the entrance to the tomb. The soldiers then departed for Gehenna with the bodies of the thieves while the others returned to Jerusalem, in sorrow, to observe the Passover feast according to the laws of Moses.

188:1.6 (2013.5) There was considerable hurry and haste about the burial of Jesus because this was preparation day and the Sabbath was drawing on apace. The men hurried back to the city, but the women lingered near the tomb until it was very dark.

188:1.7 (2013.6) While all this was going on, the women were hiding near at hand so that they saw it all and observed where the Master had been laid. They thus secreted themselves because it was not permissible for women to associate with men at such a time. These women did not think Jesus had been properly prepared for burial, and they agreed among themselves to go back to the home of Joseph, rest over the Sabbath, make ready spices and ointments, and return on Sunday morning properly to prepare the Master's body for the death rest. The women who thus tarried by the tomb on this Friday evening were: Mary Magdalene, Mary the wife of Clopas, Martha another sister of Jesus' mother, and Rebecca of Sepphoris.

188:1.8 (2013.7) Aside from David Zebedee and Joseph of Arimathea, very few of Jesus' disciples really believed or understood that he was due to arise from the tomb on the third day.

Safeguarding the Tomb

188:2.1 (2014.1) If Jesus' followers were unmindful of his promise to rise from the grave on the third day, his enemies were not. The chief priests, Pharisees, and Sadducees recalled that they had received reports of his saying he would rise from the dead.

188:2.2 (2014.2) This Friday night, after the Passover supper, about midnight a group of the Jewish leaders gathered at the home of Caiaphas, where they discussed their fears concerning the Master's assertions that he would rise from the dead on the third day. This meeting ended with the appointment of a committee of Sanhedrists who were to visit Pilate early the next day, bearing the official request of the Sanhedrin that a Roman guard be stationed before Jesus' tomb to prevent his friends from tampering with it. Said the spokesman of this committee to Pilate: "Sir, we remember that this deceiver, Jesus of Nazareth, said, while he was yet alive, 'After three days I will rise again.' We have, therefore, come before you to request that you issue such orders as will make the sepulchre secure against his followers, at least until after the third day. We greatly fear lest his disciples come and steal him away by night and then proclaim to the people that he has risen from the dead. If we should permit this to happen, this mistake would be far worse than to have allowed him to live."

188:2.3 (2014.3) When Pilate heard this request of the Sanhedrists, he said: "I will give you a guard of ten soldiers. Go your way and make the tomb secure." They went back to the temple, secured ten of their own guards, and then marched out to Joseph's tomb with these ten Jewish guards and ten Roman soldiers, even on this Sabbath morning, to set them as watchmen before the tomb. These men rolled yet another stone before the tomb and set the seal of Pilate on and around these stones, lest they be disturbed without their knowledge. And these twenty men remained on watch up to the hour of the resurrection, the Jews carrying them their food and drink.

During the Sabbath Day

188:3.1 (2014.4) Throughout this Sabbath day the disciples and the apostles remained in hiding, while all Jerusalem discussed the death of Jesus on the cross. There were almost one and one-half million Jews present in Jerusalem at this time, hailing from all parts of the Roman Empire and from Mesopotamia. This was the beginning of the Passover week, and all these pilgrims would be in the city to learn of the resurrection of Jesus and to carry the report back to their homes.

188:3.2 (2014.5) Late Saturday night, John Mark summoned the eleven apostles secretly to come to the home of his father, where, just before midnight, they all assembled in the same upper chamber where they had partaken of the Last Supper with their Master two nights previously.

188:3.3 (2014.6) Mary the mother of Jesus, with Ruth and Jude, returned to Bethany to join their family this Saturday evening just before sunset. David Zebedee remained at the home of Nicodemus, where he had arranged for his messengers to assemble early Sunday morning. The women of Galilee, who prepared spices for the further embalming of Jesus' body, tarried at the home of Joseph of Arimathea.

188:3.4 (2014.7) We are not able fully to explain just what happened to Jesus of Nazareth during this period of a day and a half when he was supposed to be resting in Joseph's new tomb. Apparently he died the same natural death on the cross as would any other mortal in the same circumstances. We heard him say, "Father, into your hands I commend my spirit." We do not fully understand the meaning of such a statement inasmuch as his Thought Adjuster had long since been personalized and so maintained an existence apart from Jesus' mortal being. The Master's Personalized Adjuster could in no sense be affected by his physical death on the cross. That which Jesus put in the Father's hands for the time being must have been the spirit counterpart of the Adjuster's early work in spiritizing the mortal mind so as to provide for the transfer of the transcript of the human experience to the mansion worlds. There must have been some spiritual reality in the experience of Jesus which was analogous to the spirit nature, or soul, of the faith-growing mortals of the spheres. But this is merely our opinion—we do not really know what Jesus commended to his Father.

188:3.5 (2015.1) We know that the physical form of the Master rested there in Joseph's tomb until about three o'clock Sunday morning, but we are wholly uncertain regarding the status of the personality of Jesus during that period of thirty-six hours. We have sometimes dared to explain these things to ourselves somewhat as follows:

188:3.6 (2015.2) 1. The Creator consciousness of Michael must have been at large and wholly free from its associated mortal mind of the physical incarnation.

188:3.7 (2015.3) 2. The former Thought Adjuster of Jesus we know to have been present on earth during this period and in personal command of the assembled celestial hosts.

188:3.8 (2015.4) 3. The acquired spirit identity of the man of Nazareth which was built up during his lifetime in the flesh, first, by the direct efforts of his Thought Adjuster, and later, by his own perfect adjustment between the physical necessities and the spiritual requirements of the ideal mortal existence, as it was effected by his never-ceasing choice of the Father's will, must have been consigned to the custody of the Paradise Father. Whether or not this spirit reality returned to become a part of the resurrected personality, we do not know, but we believe it did. But there are those in the universe who hold that this soul-identity of Jesus now reposes in the "bosom of the Father," to be subsequently released for leadership of the Nebadon Corps of the Finality in their undisclosed destiny in connection with the uncreated universes of the unorganized realms of outer space.

188:3.9 (2015.5) 4. We think the human or mortal consciousness of Jesus slept during these thirty-six hours. We have reason to believe that the human Jesus knew nothing of what transpired in the universe during this period. To the mortal consciousness there appeared no lapse of time; the resurrection of life followed the sleep of death as of the same instant.

188:3.10 (2015.6) And this is about all we can place on record regarding the status of Jesus during this period of the tomb. There are a number of correlated facts to which we can allude, although we are hardly competent to undertake their interpretation.

188:3.11 (2015.7) In the vast court of the resurrection halls of the first mansion world of Satania, there may now be observed a magnificent material-morontia structure known as the "Michael Memorial," now bearing the seal of Gabriel. This memorial was created shortly after Michael departed from this world, and it bears this inscription: "In commemoration of the mortal transit of Jesus of Nazareth on Urantia."

188:3.12 (2016.1) There are records extant which show that during this period the supreme council of Salvington, numbering one hundred, held an executive meeting on Urantia under the presidency of Gabriel. There are also records showing that the Ancients of Days of Uversa communicated with Michael regarding the status of the universe of Nebadon during this time.

188:3.13 (2016.2) We know that at least one message passed between Michael and Immanuel on Salvington while the Master's body lay in the tomb.

188:3.14 (2016.3) There is good reason for believing that some personality sat in the seat of Caligastia in the system council of the Planetary Princes on Jerusem which convened while the body of Jesus rested in the tomb.

188:3.15 (2016.4) The records of Edentia indicate that the Constellation Father of Norlatiadek was on Urantia, and that he received instructions from Michael during this time of the tomb.

188:3.16 (2016.5) And there is much other evidence which suggests that not all of the personality of Jesus was asleep and unconscious during this time of apparent physical death.

Meaning of the Death on the Cross

188:4.1 (2016.6) Although Jesus did not die this death on the cross to atone for the racial guilt of mortal man nor to provide some sort of effective approach to an otherwise offended and unforgiving God; even though the Son of Man did not offer himself as a sacrifice to appease the wrath of God and to open the way for sinful man to obtain salvation; notwithstanding that these ideas of atonement and propitiation are erroneous, nonetheless, there are significances attached to this death of Jesus on the cross which should not be overlooked. It is a fact that Urantia has become known among other neighboring inhabited planets as the "World of the Cross."

188:4.2 (2016.7) Jesus desired to live a full mortal life in the flesh on Urantia. Death is, ordinarily, a part of life. Death is the last act in the mortal drama. In your well-meant efforts to escape the superstitious errors of the false interpretation of the meaning of the death on the cross, you should be careful not to make the great mistake of failing to perceive the true significance and the genuine import of the Master's death.

188:4.3 (2016.8) Mortal man was never the property of the archdeceivers. Jesus did not die to ransom man from the clutch of the apostate rulers and fallen princes of the spheres. The Father in heaven never conceived of such crass injustice as damning a mortal soul because of the evil-doing of his ancestors. Neither was the Master's death on the cross a sacrifice which consisted in an effort to pay God a debt which the race of mankind had come to owe him.

188:4.4 (2016.9) Before Jesus lived on earth, you might possibly have been justified in believing in such a God, but not since the Master lived and died among your fellow mortals. Moses taught the dignity and justice of a Creator God; but Jesus portrayed the love and mercy of a heavenly Father.

188:4.5 (2016.10) The animal nature—the tendency toward evil-doing—may be hereditary, but sin is not transmitted from parent to child. Sin is the act of conscious and deliberate rebellion against the Father's will and the Sons' laws by an individual will creature.

188:4.6 (2017.1) Jesus lived and died for a whole universe, not just for the races of this one world. While the mortals of the realms had salvation even before Jesus lived and died on Urantia, it is nevertheless a fact that his bestowal on this world greatly illuminated the way of salvation; his death did much to make forever plain the certainty of mortal survival after death in the flesh.

188:4.7 (2017.2) Though it is hardly proper to speak of Jesus as a sacrificer, a ransomer, or a redeemer, it is wholly correct to refer to him as a savior. He forever made the way of salvation (survival) more clear and certain; he did better and more surely show the way of salvation for all the mortals of all the worlds of the universe of Nebadon.

188:4.8 (2017.3) When once you grasp the idea of God as a true and loving Father, the only concept which Jesus ever taught, you must forthwith, in all consistency, utterly abandon all those primitive notions about God as an offended monarch, a stern and all-powerful ruler whose chief delight is to detect his subjects in wrongdoing and to see that they are adequately punished, unless some being almost equal to himself should volunteer to suffer for them, to die as a substitute and in their stead. The whole idea of ransom and atonement is incompatible with the concept of God as it was taught and exemplified by Jesus of Nazareth. The infinite love of God is not secondary to anything in the divine nature.

188:4.9 (2017.4) All this concept of atonement and sacrificial salvation is rooted and grounded in selfishness. Jesus taught that service to one's fellows is the highest concept of the brotherhood of spirit believers. Salvation should be taken for granted by those who believe in the fatherhood of God. The believer's chief concern should not be the selfish desire for personal salvation but rather the unselfish urge to love and, therefore, serve one's fellows even as Jesus loved and served mortal men.

188:4.10 (2017.5) Neither do genuine believers trouble themselves so much about the future punishment of sin. The real believer is only concerned about present separation from God. True, wise fathers may chasten their sons, but they do all this in love and for corrective purposes. They do not punish in anger, neither do they chastise in retribution.

188:4.11 (2017.6) Even if God were the stern and legal monarch of a universe in which justice ruled supreme, he certainly would not be satisfied with the childish scheme of substituting an innocent sufferer for a guilty offender.

188:4.12 (2017.7) The great thing about the death of Jesus, as it is related to the enrichment of human experience and the enlargement of the way of salvation, is not the fact of his death but rather the superb manner and the matchless spirit in which he met death.

188:4.13 (2017.8) This entire idea of the ransom of the atonement places salvation upon a plane of unreality; such a concept is purely philosophic. Human salvation is real; it is based on two realities which may be grasped by the creature's faith and thereby become incorporated into individual human experience: the fact of the fatherhood of God and its correlated truth, the brotherhood of man. It is true, after all, that you are to be "forgiven your debts, even as you forgive your debtors."

Lessons from the Cross

188:5.1 (2017.9) The cross of Jesus portrays the full measure of the supreme devotion of the true shepherd for even the unworthy members of his flock. It forever places all relations between God and man upon the family basis. God is the Father; man is his son. Love, the love of a father for his son, becomes the central truth in the universe relations of Creator and creature—not the justice of a king which seeks satisfaction in the sufferings and punishment of the evil- doing subject.

188:5.2 (2018.1) The cross forever shows that the attitude of Jesus toward sinners was neither condemnation nor condonation, but rather eternal and loving salvation. Jesus is truly a savior in the sense that his life and death do win men over to goodness and righteous survival. Jesus loves men so much that his love awakens the response of love in the human heart. Love is truly contagious and eternally creative. Jesus' death on the cross exemplifies a love which is sufficiently strong and divine to forgive sin and swallow up all evil-doing. Jesus disclosed to this world a higher quality of righteousness than justice—mere technical right and wrong. Divine love does not merely forgive wrongs; it absorbs and actually destroys them. The forgiveness of love utterly transcends the forgiveness of mercy. Mercy sets the guilt of evil-doing to one side; but love destroys forever the sin and all weakness resulting therefrom. Jesus brought a new method of living to Urantia. He taught us not to resist evil but to find through him a goodness which effectually destroys evil. The forgiveness of Jesus is not condonation; it is salvation from condemnation. Salvation does not slight wrongs; it makes them right. True love does not compromise nor condone hate; it destroys it. The love of Jesus is never satisfied with mere forgiveness. The Master's love implies rehabilitation, eternal survival. It is altogether proper to speak of salvation as redemption if you mean this eternal rehabilitation.

188:5.3 (2018.2) Jesus, by the power of his personal love for men, could break the hold of sin and evil. He thereby set men free to choose better ways of living. Jesus portrayed a deliverance from the past which in itself promised a triumph for the future. Forgiveness thus provided salvation. The beauty of divine love, once fully admitted to the human heart, forever destroys the charm of sin and the power of evil.

188:5.4 (2018.3) The sufferings of Jesus were not confined to the crucifixion. In reality, Jesus of Nazareth spent upward of twenty-five years on the cross of a real and intense mortal existence. The real value of the cross consists in the fact that it was the supreme and final expression of his love, the completed revelation of his mercy.

188:5.5 (2018.4) On millions of inhabited worlds, tens of trillions of evolving creatures who may have been tempted to give up the moral struggle and abandon the good fight of faith, have taken one more look at Jesus on the cross and then have forged on ahead, inspired by the sight of God's laying down his incarnate life in devotion to the unselfish service of man.

188:5.6 (2018.5) The triumph of the death on the cross is all summed up in the spirit of Jesus' attitude toward those who assailed him. He made the cross an eternal symbol of the triumph of love over hate and the victory of truth over evil when he prayed, "Father, forgive them, for they know not what they do." That devotion of love was contagious throughout a vast universe; the disciples caught it from their Master. The very first teacher of his gospel who was called upon to lay down his life in this service, said, as they stoned him to death, "Lay not this sin to their charge."

188:5.7 (2018.6) The cross makes a supreme appeal to the best in man because it discloses one who was willing to lay down his life in the service of his fellow men. Greater love no man can have than this: that he would be willing to lay down his life for his friends—and Jesus had such a love that he was willing to lay down his life for his enemies, a love greater than any which had hitherto been known on earth.

188:5.8 (2019.1) On other worlds, as well as on Urantia, this sublime spectacle of the death of the human Jesus on the cross of Golgotha has stirred the emotions of mortals, while it has aroused the highest devotion of the angels.

188:5.9 (2019.2) The cross is that high symbol of sacred service, the devotion of one's life to the welfare and salvation of one's fellows. The cross is not the symbol of the sacrifice of the innocent Son of God in the place of guilty sinners and in order to appease the wrath of an offended God, but it does stand forever, on earth and throughout a vast universe, as a sacred symbol of the good bestowing themselves upon the evil and thereby saving them by this very devotion of love.

The cross does stand as the token of the highest form of unselfish service, the supreme devotion of the full bestowal of a righteous life in the service of wholehearted ministry, even in death, the death of the cross. And the very sight of this great symbol of the bestowal life of Jesus truly inspires all of us to want to go and do likewise.

188:5.10 (2019.3) When thinking men and women look upon Jesus as he offers up his life on the cross, they will hardly again permit themselves to complain at even the severest hardships of life, much less at petty harassments and their many purely fictitious grievances. His life was so glorious and his death so triumphant that we are all enticed to a willingness to share both. There is true drawing power in the whole bestowal of Michael, from the days of his youth to this overwhelming spectacle of his death on the cross.

188:5.11 (2019.4) Make sure, then, that when you view the cross as a revelation of God, you do not look with the eyes of the primitive man nor with the viewpoint of the later barbarian, both of whom regarded God as a relentless Sovereign of stern justice and rigid law-enforcement. Rather, make sure that you see in the cross the final manifestation of the love and devotion of Jesus to his life mission of bestowal upon the mortal races of his vast universe. See in the death of the Son of Man the climax of the unfolding of the Father's divine love for his sons of the mortal spheres. The cross thus portrays the devotion of willing affection and the bestowal of voluntary salvation upon those who are willing to receive such gifts and devotion. There was nothing in the cross which the Father required—only that which Jesus so willingly gave, and which he refused to avoid.

188:5.12 (2019.5) If man cannot otherwise appreciate Jesus and understand the meaning of his bestowal on earth, he can at least comprehend the fellowship of his mortal sufferings. No man can ever fear that the Creator does not know the nature or extent of his temporal afflictions.

188:5.13 (2019.6) We know that the death on the cross was not to effect man's reconciliation to God but to stimulate man's realization of the Father's eternal love and his Son's unending mercy, and to broadcast these universal truths to a whole universe.

Paper 189

The Resurrection

189:0.1 (2020.1) SOON after the burial of Jesus on Friday afternoon, the chief of the archangels of Nebadon, then present on Urantia, summoned his council of the resurrection of sleeping will creatures and entered upon the consideration of a possible technique for the restoration of Jesus. These assembled sons of the local universe, the creatures of Michael, did this on their own responsibility; Gabriel had not assembled them. By midnight they had arrived at the conclusion that the creature could do nothing to facilitate

the resurrection of the Creator. They were disposed to accept the advice of Gabriel, who instructed them that, since Michael had "laid down his life of his own free will, he also had power to take it up again in accordance with his own determination." Shortly after the adjournment of this council of the archangels, the Life Carriers, and their various associates in the work of creature rehabilitation and morontia creation, the Personalized Adjuster of Jesus, being in personal command of the assembled celestial hosts then on Urantia, spoke these words to the anxious waiting watchers:

189:0.2 (2020.2) "Not one of you can do aught to assist your Creator-father in the return to life. As a mortal of the realm he has experienced mortal death; as the Sovereign of a universe he still lives. That which you observe is the mortal transit of Jesus of Nazareth from life in the flesh to life in the morontia. The spirit transit of this Jesus was completed at the time I separated myself from his personality and became your temporary director. Your Creator-father has elected to pass through the whole of the experience of his mortal creatures, from birth on the material worlds, on through natural death and the resurrection of the morontia, into the status of true spirit existence. A certain phase of this experience you are about to observe, but you may not participate in it. Those things which you ordinarily do for the creature, you may not do for the Creator. A Creator Son has within himself the power to bestow himself in the likeness of any of his created sons; he has within himself the power to lay down his observable life and to take it up again; and he has this power because of the direct command of the Paradise Father, and I know whereof I speak."

189:0.3 (2020.3) When they heard the Personalized Adjuster so speak, they all assumed the attitude of anxious expectancy, from Gabriel down to the most humble cherubim. They saw the mortal body of Jesus in the tomb; they detected evidences of the universe activity of their beloved Sovereign; and not understanding such phenomena, they waited patiently for developments.

1   *The Morontia Transit*

189:1.1 (2020.4) At two forty-five Sunday morning, the Paradise incarnation commission, consisting of seven unidentified Paradise personalities, arrived on the scene and immediately deployed themselves about the tomb. At ten minutes before three, intense vibrations of commingled material and morontia activities began to issue from Joseph's new tomb, and at two minutes past three o'clock, this Sunday morning, April 9, A.D. 30, the resurrected morontia form and personality of Jesus of Nazareth came forth from the tomb.

189:1.2 (2021.1) After the resurrected Jesus emerged from his burial tomb, the body of flesh in which he had lived and wrought on earth for almost thirty-six years was still lying there in the sepulchre niche, undisturbed and wrapped in the linen sheet, just as it had been laid to rest by Joseph and his associates on Friday afternoon. Neither was the stone before the entrance of the tomb in any way disturbed; the seal of Pilate was still unbroken; the soldiers were still on guard. The temple guards had been on continuous duty; the Roman guard had been changed at midnight. None of these watchers suspected that the object of their vigil had risen to a new and higher form of existence, and that the body which they were guarding was now a discarded outer covering which had no further connection with the delivered and resurrected morontia personality of Jesus.

189:1.3 (2021.2) Mankind is slow to perceive that, in all that is personal, matter is the skeleton of morontia, and that both are the reflected shadow of enduring spirit reality. How long before you will regard time as the moving image of eternity and space as the fleeting shadow of Paradise realities?

189:1.4 (2021.3) As far as we can judge, no creature of this universe nor any personality from another universe had anything to do with this morontia resurrection of Jesus of Nazareth. On Friday he laid down his life as a mortal of the realm; on Sunday morning he took it up again as a morontia being of the system of Satania in Norlatiadek. There is much about the resurrection of Jesus which we do not understand. But we know that it occurred as we have stated and at about the time indicated. We can also record that all known phenomena associated with this mortal transit, or morontia resurrection, occurred right there in Joseph's new tomb, where the mortal material remains of Jesus lay wrapped in burial cloths.

189:1.5 (2021.4) We know that no creature of the local universe participated in this morontia awakening. We perceived the seven personalities of Paradise surround the tomb, but we did not see them do anything in connection with the Master's awakening. Just as soon as Jesus appeared beside Gabriel, just above the tomb, the seven personalities from Paradise signalized their intention of immediate departure for Uversa.

189:1.6 (2021.5) Let us forever clarify the concept of the resurrection of Jesus by making the following statements:

189:1.7 (2021.6) 1. His material or physical body was not a part of the resurrected personality. When Jesus came forth from the tomb, his body of flesh remained undisturbed in the sepulchre. He emerged from the burial tomb without moving the stones before the entrance and without disturbing the seals of Pilate.

189:1.8 (2021.7) 2. He did not emerge from the tomb as a spirit nor as Michael of Nebadon; he did not appear in the form of the Creator Sovereign, such as he had had before his incarnation in the likeness of mortal flesh on Urantia.

189:1.9 (2021.8) 3. He did come forth from this tomb of Joseph in the very likeness of the morontia personalities of those who, as resurrected morontia ascendant beings, emerge from the resurrection halls of the first mansion world of this local system of Satania. And the presence of the Michael memorial in the center of the vast court of the resurrection halls of mansonia number one leads us to conjecture that the Master's resurrection on Urantia was in some way fostered on this, the first of the system mansion worlds.

189:1.10 (2022.1) The first act of Jesus on arising from the tomb was to greet Gabriel and instruct him to continue in executive charge of universe affairs under Immanuel, and then he directed the chief of the Melchizedeks to convey his brotherly greetings to Immanuel. He thereupon asked the Most High of Edentia for the certification of the Ancients of Days as to his mortal transit; and turning to the assembled morontia groups of the seven mansion worlds, here gathered together to greet and welcome their Creator as a creature of their order, Jesus spoke the first words of the postmortal career. Said the morontia Jesus: "Having finished my life in the flesh, I would tarry here for a short time in transition form that I may more fully know the life of my ascendant creatures and further reveal the will of my Father in Paradise."

189:1.11 (2022.2) After Jesus had spoken, he signaled to the Personalized Adjuster, and all universe intelligences who had been assembled on Urantia to witness the resurrection were immediately dispatched to their respective universe assignments.

189:1.12 (2022.3) Jesus now began the contacts of the morontia level, being introduced, as a creature, to the requirements of the life he had chosen to live for a short time on Urantia. This initiation into the morontia world required more than an hour of earth time and was twice interrupted by his desire to communicate with his former associates in the flesh as they came out from Jerusalem wonderingly to peer into the empty tomb to discover what they considered evidence of his res-

urrection.

189:1.13 (2022.4) Now is the mortal transit of Jesus—the morontia resurrection of the Son of Man—completed. The transitory experience of the Master as a personality midway between the material and the spiritual has begun. And he has done all this through power inherent within himself; no personality has rendered him any assistance. He now lives as Jesus of morontia, and as he begins this morontia life, the material body of his flesh lies there undisturbed in the tomb. The soldiers are still on guard, and the seal of the governor about the rocks has not yet been broken.

2 The Material Body of Jesus

189:2.1 (2022.5) At ten minutes past three o'clock, as the resurrected Jesus fraternized with the assembled morontia personalities from the seven mansion worlds of Satania, the chief of archangels—the angels of the resurrection— approached Gabriel and asked for the mortal body of Jesus. Said the chief of the archangels: "We may not participate in the morontia resurrection of the bestowal experience of Michael our sovereign, but we would have his mortal remains put in our custody for immediate dissolution. We do not propose to employ our technique of dematerialization; we merely wish to invoke the process of accelerated time. It is enough that we have seen the Sovereign live and die on Urantia; the hosts of heaven would be spared the memory of enduring the sight of the slow decay of the human form of the Creator and Upholder of a universe. In the name of the celestial intelligences of all Nebadon, I ask for a mandate giving me the custody of the mortal body of Jesus of Nazareth and empowering us to proceed with its immediate dissolution."

189:2.2 (2023.1) And when Gabriel had conferred with the senior Most High of Edentia, the archangel spokesman for the celestial hosts was given permission to make such disposition of the physical remains of Jesus as he might determine.

189:2.3 (2023.2) After the chief of archangels had been granted this request, he summoned to his assistance many of his fellows, together with a numerous host of the representatives of all orders of celestial personalities, and then, with the aid of the Urantia midwayers, proceeded to take possession of Jesus' physical body. This body of death was a purely material creation; it was physical and literal; it could not be removed from the tomb as the morontia form of the resurrection had been able to escape the sealed sepulchre. By the aid of certain morontia auxiliary personalities, the morontia form can be made at one time as of the spirit so that it can become indifferent to ordinary matter, while at another time it can become discernible and contactable to material beings, such as the mortals of the realm.

189:2.4 (2023.3) As they made ready to remove the body of Jesus from the tomb preparatory to according it the dignified and reverent disposal of near-instantaneous dissolution, it was assigned the secondary Urantia midwayers to roll away the stones from the entrance of the tomb. The larger of these two stones was a huge circular affair, much like a millstone, and it moved in a groove chiseled out of the rock, so that it could be rolled back and forth to open or close the tomb. When the watching Jewish guards and the Roman soldiers, in the dim light of the morning, saw this huge stone begin to roll away from the entrance of the tomb, apparently of its own accord—without any visible means to account for such motion—they were seized with fear and panic, and they fled in haste from the scene. The Jews fled to their homes, afterward going back to report these doings to their captain at the temple. The Romans fled to the fortress of Antonia and reported what they had seen to the centurion as soon as he arrived on duty.

189:2.5 (2023.4) The Jewish leaders began the sordid business of supposedly

getting rid of Jesus by offering bribes to the traitorous Judas, and now, when confronted with this embarrassing situation, instead of thinking of punishing the guards who deserted their post, they resorted to bribing these guards and the Roman soldiers. They paid each of these twenty men a sum of money and instructed them to say to all: "While we slept during the nighttime, his disciples came upon us and took away the body." And the Jewish leaders made solemn promises to the soldiers to defend them before Pilate in case it should ever come to the governor's knowledge that they had accepted a bribe.

189:2.6 (2023.5) The Christian belief in the resurrection of Jesus has been based on the fact of the "empty tomb." It was indeed a fact that the tomb was empty, but this is not the truth of the resurrection. The tomb was truly empty when the first believers arrived, and this fact, associated with that of the undoubted resurrection of the Master, led to the formulation of a belief which was not true: the teaching that the material and mortal body of Jesus was raised from the grave. Truth having to do with spiritual realities and eternal values cannot always be built up by a combination of apparent facts. Although individual facts may be materially true, it does not follow that the association of a group of facts must necessarily lead to truthful spiritual conclusions.

189:2.7 (2023.6) The tomb of Joseph was empty, not because the body of Jesus had been rehabilitated or resurrected, but because the celestial hosts had been granted their request to afford it a special and unique dissolution, a return of the "dust to dust," without the intervention of the delays of time and without the operation of the ordinary and visible processes of mortal decay and material corruption.

189:2.8 (2024.1) The mortal remains of Jesus underwent the same natural process of elemental disintegration as characterizes all human bodies on earth except that, in point of time, this natural mode of dissolution was greatly accelerated, hastened to that point where it became well-nigh instantaneous.

189:2.9 (2024.2) The true evidences of the resurrection of Michael are spiritual in nature, albeit this teaching is corroborated by the testimony of many mortals of the realm who met, recognized, and communed with the resurrected morontia Master. He became a part of the personal experience of almost one thousand human beings before he finally took leave of Urantia.

3 The Dispensational Resurrection

189:3.1 (2024.3) A little after half past four o'clock this Sunday morning, Gabriel summoned the archangels to his side and made ready to inaugurate the general resurrection of the termination of the Adamic dispensation on Urantia. When the vast host of the seraphim and the cherubim concerned in this great event had been marshaled in proper formation, the morontia Michael appeared before Gabriel, saying: "As my Father has life in himself, so has he given it to the Son to have life in himself. Although I have not yet fully resumed the exercise of universe jurisdiction, this self-imposed limitation does not in any manner restrict the bestowal of life upon my sleeping sons; let the roll call of the planetary resurrection begin."

189:3.2 (2024.4) The circuit of the archangels then operated for the first time from Urantia. Gabriel and the archangel hosts moved to the place of the spiritual polarity of the planet; and when Gabriel gave the signal, there flashed to the first of the system mansion worlds the voice of Gabriel, saying: "By the mandate of Michael, let the dead of a Urantia dispensation rise!" Then all the survivors of the human races of Urantia who had fallen asleep since the days of Adam, and who had not already gone on to judgment, appeared in the resurrection halls of mansonia in readiness for morontia investiture. And in an instant of time the seraphim and their associates made ready to depart for the mansion worlds.

Ordinarily these seraphic guardians, onetime assigned to the group custody of these surviving mortals, would have been present at the moment of their awaking in the resurrection halls of mansonia, but they were on this world itself at this time because of the necessity of Gabriel's presence here in connection with the morontia resurrection of Jesus.

189:3.3 (2024.5) Notwithstanding that countless individuals having personal seraphic guardians and those achieving the requisite attainment of spiritual personality progress had gone on to mansonia during the ages subsequent to the times of Adam and Eve, and though there had been many special and millennial resurrections of Urantia sons, this was the third of the planetary roll calls, or complete dispensational resurrections. The first occurred at the time of the arrival of the Planetary Prince, the second during the time of Adam, and this, the third, signalized the morontia resurrection, the mortal transit, of Jesus of Nazareth.

189:3.4 (2024.6) When the signal of the planetary resurrection had been received by the chief of archangels, the Personalized Adjuster of the Son of Man relinquished his authority over the celestial hosts assembled on Urantia, turning all these sons of the local universe back to the jurisdiction of their respective commanders. And when he had done this, he departed for Salvington to register with Immanuel the completion of the mortal transit of Michael. And he was immediately followed by all the celestial host not required for duty on Urantia. But Gabriel remained on Urantia with the morontia Jesus.

189:3.5 (2025.1) And this is the recital of the events of the resurrection of Jesus as viewed by those who saw them as they really occurred, free from the limitations of partial and restricted human vision.

4   *Discovery of the Empty Tomb*

1.   189:4.1 (2025.2) As we approach the time of the resurrection of Jesus on this early Sunday morning, it should be recalled that the ten apostles were sojourning at the home of Elijah and Mary Mark, where they were asleep in the upper chamber, resting on the very couches whereon they reclined during the last supper with their Master. This Sunday morning they were all there assembled except Thomas. Thomas was with them for a few minutes late Saturday night when they first got together, but the sight of the apostles, coupled with the thought of what had happened to Jesus, was too much for him. He looked his associates over and immediately left the room, going to the home of Simon in Bethpage, where he thought to grieve over his troubles in solitude. The apostles all suffered, not so much from doubt and despair as from fear, grief, and shame.

189:4.2 (2025.3) At the home of Nicodemus there were gathered together, with David Zebedee and Joseph of Arimathea, some twelve or fifteen of the more prominent of the Jerusalem disciples of Jesus. At the home of Joseph of Arimathea there were some fifteen or twenty of the leading women believers. Only these women abode in Joseph's house, and they had kept close within during the hours of the Sabbath day and the evening after the Sabbath, so that they were ignorant of the military guard on watch at the tomb; neither did they know that a second stone had been rolled in front of the tomb, and that both of these stones had been placed under the seal of Pilate.

189:4.3 (2025.4) A little before three o'clock this Sunday morning, when the first signs of day began to appear in the east, five of the women started out for the tomb of Jesus. They had prepared an abundance of special embalming lotions, and they carried many linen bandages with them. It was their purpose more thoroughly to give the body of Jesus its death anointing and more carefully to wrap it up with the new bandages.

189:4.4 (2025.5) The women who went on this mission of anointing Jesus' body were: Mary Magdalene, Mary the mother of the Alpheus twins, Salome the mother of the Zebedee brothers, Joanna the wife of Chuza, and Susanna the daughter of Ezra of Alexandria.

189:4.5 (2025.6) It was about half past three o'clock when the five women, laden with their ointments, arrived before the empty tomb. As they passed out of the Damascus gate, they encountered a number of soldiers fleeing into the city more or less panic-stricken, and this caused them to pause for a few minutes; but when nothing more developed, they resumed their journey.

189:4.6 (2025.7) They were greatly surprised to see the stone rolled away from the entrance to the tomb, inasmuch as they had said among themselves on the way out, "Who will help us roll away the stone?" They set down their burdens and began to look upon one another in fear and with great amazement. While they stood there, atremble with fear, Mary Magdalene ventured around the smaller stone and dared to enter the open sepulchre. This tomb of Joseph was in his garden on the hillside on the eastern side of the road, and it also faced toward the east. By this hour there was just enough of the dawn of a new day to enable Mary to look back to the place where the Master's body had lain and to discern that it was gone. In the recess of stone where they had laid Jesus, Mary saw only the folded napkin where his head had rested and the bandages wherewith he had been wrapped lying intact and as they had rested on the stone before the celestial hosts removed the body. The covering sheet lay at the foot of the burial niche.

189:4.7 (2026.1) After Mary had tarried in the doorway of the tomb for a few moments (she did not see distinctly when she first entered the tomb), she saw that Jesus' body was gone and in its place only these grave cloths, and she uttered a cry of alarm and anguish. All the women were exceedingly nervous; they had been on edge ever since meeting the panicky soldiers at the city gate, and when Mary uttered this scream of anguish, they were terror-stricken and fled in great haste. And they did not stop until they had run all the way to the Damascus gate. By this time Joanna was conscience-stricken that they had deserted Mary; she rallied her companions, and they started back for the tomb.

189:4.8 (2026.2) As they drew near the sepulchre, the frightened Magdalene, who was even more terrorized when she failed to find her sisters waiting when she came out of the tomb, now rushed up to them, excitedly exclaiming: "He is not there—they have taken him away!" And she led them back to the tomb, and they all entered and saw that it was empty.

189:4.9 (2026.3) All five of the women then sat down on the stone near the entrance and talked over the situation. It had not yet occurred to them that Jesus had been resurrected. They had been by themselves over the Sabbath, and they conjectured that the body had been moved to another resting place. But when they pondered such a solution of their dilemma, they were at a loss to account for the orderly arrangement of the grave cloths; how could the body have been removed since the very bandages in which it was wrapped were left in position and apparently intact on the burial shelf?

189:4.10 (2026.4) As these women sat there in the early hours of the dawn of this new day, they looked to one side and observed a silent and motionless stranger. For a moment they were again frightened, but Mary Magdalene, rushing toward him and addressing him as if she thought he might be the caretaker of the garden, said, "Where have you taken the Master? Where have they laid him? Tell us that we may go and get him." When the stranger did not answer Mary, she began to weep. Then spoke Jesus to them, saying, "Whom do you seek?" Mary said: "We seek for Jesus

who was laid to rest in Joseph's tomb, but he is gone. Do you know where they have taken him?" Then said Jesus: "Did not this Jesus tell you, even in Galilee, that he would die, but that he would rise again?" These words startled the women, but the Master was so changed that they did not yet recognize him with his back turned to the dim light. And as they pondered his words, he addressed the Magdalene with a familiar voice, saying, "Mary." And when she heard that word of well- known sympathy and affectionate greeting, she knew it was the voice of the Master, and she rushed to kneel at his feet while she exclaimed, "My Lord, and my Master!" And all of the other women recognized that it was the Master who stood before them in glorified form, and they quickly knelt before him.

189:4.11 (2027.1) These human eyes were enabled to see the morontia form of Jesus because of the special ministry of the transformers and the midwayers in association with certain of the morontia personalities then accompanying Jesus.

189:4.12 (2027.2) As Mary sought to embrace his feet, Jesus said: "Touch me not, Mary, for I am not as you knew me in the flesh. In this form will I tarry with you for a season before I ascend to the Father. But go, all of you, now and tell my apostles—and Peter—that I have risen, and that you have talked with me."

189:4.13 (2027.3) After these women had recovered from the shock of their amazement, they hastened back to the city and to the home of Elijah Mark, where they related to the ten apostles all that had happened to them; but the apostles were not inclined to believe them. They thought at first that the women had seen a vision, but when Mary Magdalene repeated the words which Jesus had spoken to them, and when Peter heard his name, he rushed out of the upper chamber, followed closely by John, in great haste to reach the tomb and see these things for himself.

189:4.14 (2027.4) The women repeated the story of talking with Jesus to the other apostles, but they would not believe; and they would not go to find out for themselves as had Peter and John.

5   *Peter and John at the Tomb*

189:5.1 (2027.5) As the two apostles raced for Golgotha and the tomb of Joseph, Peter's thoughts alternated between fear and hope; he feared to meet the Master, but his hope was aroused by the story that Jesus had sent special word to him. He was half persuaded that Jesus was really alive; he recalled the promise to rise on the third day. Strange to relate, this promise had not occurred to him since the crucifixion until this moment as he hurried north through Jerusalem. As John hastened out of the city, a strange ecstasy of joy and hope welled up in his soul. He was half convinced that the women really had seen the risen Master.

189:5.2 (2027.6) John, being younger than Peter, outran him and arrived first at the tomb. John tarried at the door, viewing the tomb, and it was just as Mary had described it. Very soon Simon Peter rushed up and, entering, saw the same empty tomb with the grave cloths so peculiarly arranged. And when Peter had come out, John also went in and saw it all for himself, and then they sat down on the stone to ponder the meaning of what they had seen and heard. And while they sat there, they turned over in their minds all that had been told them about Jesus, but they could not clearly perceive what had happened.

189:5.3 (2027.7) Peter at first suggested that the grave had been rifled, that enemies had stolen the body, perhaps bribed the guards. But John reasoned that the grave would hardly have been left so orderly if the body had been stolen, and he also raised the question as to how the bandages happened to be left behind, and so apparently intact. And again they both went back into the tomb more closely to examine the grave cloths. As they came out of the tomb the second time, they found Mary Magdalene returned and weeping before the entrance. Mary had gone to the apostles believing that Jesus had risen from the grave, but when they all refused to believe her report, she became downcast and despairing. She longed to go back near the tomb, where she thought she had heard the familiar voice of Jesus.

189:5.4 (2027.8) As Mary lingered after Peter and John had gone, the Master again appeared to her, saying: "Be not doubting; have the courage to believe what you have seen and heard. Go back to my apostles and again tell them that I have risen, that I will appear to them, and that presently I will go before them into Galilee as I promised."

189:5.5 (2028.1) Mary hurried back to the Mark home and told the apostles she had again talked with Jesus, but they would not believe her. But when Peter and John returned, they ceased to ridicule and became filled with fear and apprehension.

Paper 190

Morontia Appearances of Jesus

190:0.1 (2029.1) THE resurrected Jesus now prepares to spend a short period on Urantia for the purpose of experiencing the ascending morontia career of a mortal of the realms. Although this time of the morontia life is to be spent on the world of his mortal incarnation, it will, however, be in all respects the counterpart of the experience of Satania mortals who pass through the progressive morontia life of the seven mansion worlds of Jerusem.

190:0.2 (2029.2) All this power which is inherent in Jesus—the endowment of life—and which enabled him to rise from the dead, is the very gift of eternal life which he bestows upon kingdom believers, and which even now makes certain their resurrection from the bonds of natural death.

190:0.3 (2029.3) The mortals of the realms will arise in the morning of the resurrection with the same type of transition or morontia body that Jesus had when he arose from the tomb on this Sunday morning. These bodies do not have circulating blood, and such beings do not partake of ordinary material food; nevertheless, these morontia forms are real. When the various believers saw Jesus after his resurrection, they really saw him; they were not the self-deceived victims of visions or hallucinations.

190:0.4 (2029.4) Abiding faith in the resurrection of Jesus was the cardinal feature of the faith of all branches of the early gospel teaching. In Jerusalem, Alexandria, Antioch, and Philadelphia all the gospel teachers united in this implicit faith in the Master's resurrection.

190:0.5 (2029.5) In viewing the prominent part which Mary Magdalene took in proclaiming the Master's resurrection, it should be recorded that Mary was the chief spokesman for the women's corps, as was Peter for the apostles. Mary was not chief of the women workers, but she was their chief teacher and public spokesman. Mary had become a woman of great circumspection, so that her boldness in speaking to a man whom she considered to be the caretaker of Joseph's garden only indicates how horrified she was to find the tomb empty. It was the depth and agony of her love, the fullness of her devotion, that caused her to forget, for a moment, the conventional restraints of a Jewish woman's approach to a strange man.

Heralds of the Resurrection

190:1.1 (2029.6) The apostles did not want Jesus to leave them; therefore had they slighted all his statements about dying, along with his promises to rise again. They were not expecting the resurrection as it came, and they refused to believe until they were confronted with the compulsion of unimpeachable evidence and the absolute proof of their own experiences.

190:1.2 (2030.1) When the apostles refused to believe the report of the five women who represented that they had seen Jesus and talked with him, Mary Magdalene returned to the tomb, and the others went back to Joseph's house, where they related their experiences to his daughter and the other women. And the women believed their report. Shortly after six o'clock the daughter of Joseph of Arimathea and the four women who had seen Jesus went over to the home of Nicodemus, where they related all these happenings to Joseph, Nicodemus, David Zebedee, and the other men there assembled. Nicodemus and the others doubted their story, doubted that Jesus had risen from the dead; they conjectured that the Jews had removed the body. Joseph and David were disposed to believe the report, so much so that they hurried out to inspect the tomb, and they found everything just as the women had described. And they were the last to so view the sepulchre, for the high priest sent the captain of the temple guards to the tomb at half past seven o'clock to remove the grave cloths. The captain wrapped them all up in the linen sheet and threw them over a near-by cliff.

190:1.3 (2030.2) From the tomb David and Joseph went immediately to the home of Elijah Mark, where they held a conference with the ten apostles in the upper chamber. Only John Zebedee was disposed to believe, even faintly, that Jesus had risen from the dead. Peter had believed at first but, when he failed to find the Master, fell into grave doubting. They were all disposed to believe that the Jews had removed the body. David would not argue with them, but when he left, he said: "You are the apostles, and you ought to understand these things. I will not contend with you; nevertheless, I now go back to the home of Nicodemus, where I have appointed with the messengers to assemble this morning, and when they have gathered together, I will send them forth on their last mission, as heralds of the Master's resurrection. I heard the Master say that, after he should die, he would rise on the third day, and I believe him." And thus speaking to the dejected and forlorn ambassadors of the kingdom, this self-appointed chief of communication and intelligence took leave of the apostles. On his way from the upper chamber he dropped the bag of Judas, containing all the apostolic funds, in the lap of Matthew Levi.

190:1.4 (2030.3) It was about half past nine o'clock when the last of David's twenty-six messengers arrived at the home of Nicodemus. David promptly assembled them in the spacious courtyard and addressed them:

190:1.5 (2030.4) "Men and brethren, all this time you have served me in accordance with your oath to me and to one another, and I call you to witness that I have never yet sent out false information at your hands. I am about to send you on your last mission as volunteer messengers of the kingdom, and in so doing I release you from your oaths and thereby disband the messenger corps. Men, I declare to you that we have finished our work. No more does the Master have need of mortal messengers; he has risen from the dead. He told us before they arrested him that he would die and rise again on the third day. I have seen the tomb—it is empty. I have talked with Mary Magdalene and four other women, who have talked with Jesus. I now disband you, bid you farewell, and send you on your respective assignments, and the message which you shall bear to the believers is: 'Jesus has risen from the dead; the tomb is empty.'"

190:1.6 (2030.5) The majority of those present endeavored to persuade David not to do this. But they could not influence him. They then sought to dissuade the messengers, but they would not heed the words of doubt. And so, shortly before ten o'clock this Sunday morning, these twenty-six runners went forth as the first heralds of the mighty truth-fact of the resurrected Jesus. And they started out on this mission as

they had on so many others, in fulfillment of their oath to David Zebedee and to one another. These men had great confidence in David. They departed on this assignment without even tarrying to talk with those who had seen Jesus; they took David at his word. The majority of them believed what David had told them, and even those who somewhat doubted, carried the message just as certainly and just as swiftly.

190:1.7 (2031.1) The apostles, the spiritual corps of the kingdom, are this day assembled in the upper chamber, where they manifest fear and express doubts, while these laymen, representing the first attempt at the socialization of the Master's gospel of the brotherhood of man, under the orders of their fearless and efficient leader, go forth to proclaim the risen Savior of a world and a universe. And they engage in this eventful service ere his chosen representatives are willing to believe his word or to accept the evidence of eyewitnesses.

190:1.8 (2031.2) These twenty-six were dispatched to the home of Lazarus in Bethany and to all of the believer centers, from Beersheba in the south to Damascus and Sidon in the north; and from Philadelphia in the east to Alexandria in the west.

190:1.9 (2031.3) When David had taken leave of his brethren, he went over to the home of Joseph for his mother, and they then went out to Bethany to join the waiting family of Jesus. David abode there in Bethany with Martha and Mary until after they had disposed of their earthly possessions, and he accompanied them on their journey to join their brother, Lazarus, at Philadelphia.

190:1.10 (2031.4) In about one week from this time John Zebedee took Mary the mother of Jesus to his home in Bethsaida. James, Jesus' eldest brother, remained with his family in Jerusalem. Ruth remained at Bethany with Lazarus's sisters.

The rest of Jesus' family returned to Galilee. David Zebedee left Bethany with Martha and Mary, for Philadelphia, early in June, the day after his marriage to Ruth,

Jesus' youngest sister.

Jesus' Appearance at Bethany

190:2.1 (2031.5) From the time of the morontia resurrection until the hour of his spirit ascension on high, Jesus made nineteen separate appearances in visible form to his believers on earth. He did not appear to his enemies nor to those who could not make spiritual use of his manifestation in visible form. His first appearance was to the five women at the tomb; his second, to Mary Magdalene, also at the tomb.

190:2.2 (2031.6) The third appearance occurred about noon of this Sunday at Bethany. Shortly after noontide, Jesus' oldest brother, James, was standing in the garden of Lazarus before the empty tomb of the resurrected brother of Martha and Mary, turning over in his mind the news brought to them about one hour previously by the messenger of David. James had always inclined to believe in his eldest brother's mission on earth, but he had long since lost contact with Jesus' work and had drifted into grave doubting regarding the later claims of the apostles that Jesus was the Messiah. The whole family was startled and well-nigh confounded by the news brought by the messenger. Even as James stood before Lazarus's empty tomb, Mary Magdalene arrived on the scene and was excitedly relating to the family her experiences of the early morning hours at the tomb of Joseph. Before she had finished, David Zebedee and his mother arrived. Ruth, of course, believed the report, and so did Jude after he had talked with David and Salome.

190:2.3 (2032.1) In the meantime, as they looked for James and before they found him, while he stood there in the garden near the tomb, he became aware of a near-by presence, as if someone had touched him on the shoulder; and when he turned to look, he beheld the gradual appearance of a strange form by his side. He was too much amazed to speak and too frightened to flee. And then the strange form spoke, saying: "James, I come to call you to the service of the kingdom. Join earnest hands with your brethren and follow after me." When James heard his name spoken, he knew that it was his eldest brother, Jesus, who had addressed him. They all had more or less difficulty in recognizing the morontia form of the Master, but few of them had any trouble recognizing his voice or otherwise identifying his charming personality when he once began to communicate with them.

190:2.4 (2032.2) When James perceived that Jesus was addressing him, he started to fall to his knees, exclaiming, "My father and my brother," but Jesus bade him stand while he spoke with him. And they walked through the garden and talked for almost three minutes; talked over experiences of former days and forecast the events of the near future. As they neared the house, Jesus said, "Farewell, James, until I greet you all together."

190:2.5 (2032.3) James rushed into the house, even while they looked for him at Bethpage, exclaiming: "I have just seen Jesus and talked with him, visited with him. He is not dead; he has risen! He vanished before me, saying, 'Farewell until I greet you all together.'" He had scarcely finished speaking when Jude returned, and he retold the experience of meeting Jesus in the garden for the benefit of Jude. And they all began to believe in the resurrection of Jesus. James now announced that he would not return to Galilee, and David exclaimed: "He is seen not only by excited women; even stronghearted men have begun to see him. I expect to see him myself."

190:2.6 (2032.4) And David did not long wait, for the fourth appearance of Jesus to mortal recognition occurred shortly before two o'clock in this very home of Martha and Mary, when he appeared visibly before his earthly family and their friends, twenty in all. The Master appeared in the open back door, saying: "Peace be upon you. Greetings to those once near me in the flesh and fellowship for my brothers and sisters in the kingdom of heaven. How could you doubt? Why have you lingered so long before choosing to follow the light of truth with a whole heart? Come, therefore, all of you into the fellowship of the Spirit of Truth in the Father's kingdom." As they began to recover from the first shock of their amazement and to move toward him as if to embrace him, he vanished from their sight.

190:2.7 (2032.5) They all wanted to rush off to the city to tell the doubting apostles about what had happened, but James restrained them. Mary Magdalene, only, was permitted to return to Joseph's house. James forbade their publishing abroad the fact of this morontia visit because of certain things which Jesus had said to him as they conversed in the garden. But James never revealed more of his visit with the risen Master on this day at the Lazarus home in Bethany.

At the Home of Joseph

190:3.1 (2033.1) The fifth morontia manifestation of Jesus to the recognition of mortal eyes occurred in the presence of some twenty-five women believers assembled at the home of Joseph of Arimathea, at about fifteen minutes past four o'clock on this same Sunday afternoon. Mary Magdalene had returned to Joseph's house just a few minutes before this appearance. James, Jesus' brother, had requested that nothing be said to the apostles concerning the Master's appearance at Bethany. He had not asked Mary to refrain from reporting the occurrence to her sister believers. Accordingly, after Mary had pledged all the women to secrecy, she proceeded to relate what had so recently happened while she was with Jesus' family at Bethany. And she was in the very midst of this thrilling recital when a sudden and solemn hush fell over them; they beheld in their very midst the fully visible form of the risen Jesus. He greeted them, saying: "Peace be upon you. In the fellowship of the kingdom there shall be neither Jew nor gentile, rich nor poor, free nor bond, man nor woman. You also are called to publish the good news of

the liberty of mankind through the gospel of sonship with God in the kingdom of heaven. Go to all the world proclaiming this gospel and confirming believers in the faith thereof. And while you do this, forget not to minister to the sick and strengthen those who are fainthearted and fear-ridden. And I will be with you always, even to the ends of the earth." And when he had thus spoken, he vanished from their sight, while the women fell on their faces and worshiped in silence.

190:3.2 (2033.2) Of the five morontia appearances of Jesus occurring up to this time, Mary Magdalene had witnessed four.

190:3.3 (2033.3) As a result of sending out the messengers during the midforenoon and from the unconscious leakage of intimations concerning this appearance of Jesus at Joseph's house, word began to come to the rulers of the Jews during the early evening that it was being reported about the city that Jesus had risen, and that many persons were claiming to have seen him. The Sanhedrists were thoroughly aroused by these rumors. After a hasty consultation with Annas, Caiaphas called a meeting of the Sanhedrin to convene at eight o'clock that evening. It was at this meeting that action was taken to throw out of the synagogues any person who made mention of Jesus' resurrection. It was even suggested that anyone claiming to have seen him should be put to death; this proposal, however, did not come to a vote since the meeting broke up in confusion bordering on actual panic. They had dared to think they were through with Jesus. They were about to discover that their real trouble with the man of Nazareth had just begun. *

Appearance to the Greeks

190:4.1 (2033.4) About half past four o'clock, at the home of one Flavius, the Master made his sixth morontia appearance to some forty Greek believers there assembled. While they were engaged in discussing the reports of the Master's resurrection, he manifested himself in their midst, notwithstanding that the doors were securely fastened, and speaking to them, said: "Peace be upon you. While the Son of Man appeared on earth among the Jews, he came to minister to all men. In the kingdom of my Father there shall be neither Jew nor gentile; you will all be brethren—the sons of God. Go you, therefore, to all the world, proclaiming this gospel of salvation as you have received it from the ambassadors of the kingdom, and I will fellowship you in the brotherhood of the Father's sons of faith and truth." And when he had thus charged them, he took leave, and they saw him no more. They remained within the house all evening; they were too much overcome with awe and fear to venture forth. Neither did any of these Greeks sleep that night; they stayed awake discussing these things and hoping that the Master might again visit them. Among this group were many of the Greeks who were at Gethsemane when the soldiers arrested Jesus and Judas betrayed him with a kiss.

190:4.2 (2034.1) Rumors of Jesus' resurrection and reports concerning the many appearances to his followers are spreading rapidly, and the whole city is being wrought up to a high pitch of excitement. Already the Master has appeared to his family, to the women, and to the Greeks, and presently he manifests himself in the midst of the apostles. The Sanhedrin is soon to begin the consideration of these new problems which have been so suddenly thrust upon the Jewish rulers.

Jesus thinks much about his apostles but desires that they be left alone for a few more hours of solemn reflection and thoughtful consideration before he visits them.

The Walk with Two Brothers

190:5.1 (2034.2) At Emmaus, about seven miles west of Jerusalem, there lived two brothers, shepherds, who had spent the Passover week in Jerusalem attending upon the sacrifices, ceremonials, and feasts. Cleopas, the elder, was a partial believer in

Jesus; at least he had been cast out of the synagogue. His brother, Jacob, was not a believer, although he was much intrigued by what he had heard about the Master's teachings and works.

190:5.2 (2034.3) On this Sunday afternoon, about three miles out of Jerusalem and a few minutes before five o'clock, as these two brothers trudged along the road to Emmaus, they talked in great earnestness about Jesus, his teachings, work, and more especially concerning the rumors that his tomb was empty, and that certain of the women had talked with him. Cleopas was half a mind to believe these reports, but Jacob was insistent that the whole affair was probably a fraud.

While they thus argued and debated as they made their way toward home, the morontia manifestation of Jesus, his seventh appearance, came alongside them as they journeyed on. Cleopas had often heard Jesus teach and had eaten with him at the homes of Jerusalem believers on several occasions. But he did not recognize the Master even when he spoke freely with them.

190:5.3 (2034.4) After walking a short way with them, Jesus said: "What were the words you exchanged so earnestly as I came upon you?" And when Jesus had spoken, they stood still and viewed him with sad surprise. Said Cleopas: "Can it be that you sojourn in Jerusalem and know not the things which have recently happened?" Then asked the Master, "What things?" Cleopas replied: "If you do not know about these matters, you are the only one in Jerusalem who has not heard these rumors concerning Jesus of Nazareth, who was a prophet mighty in word and in deed before God and all the people. The chief priests and our rulers delivered him up to the Romans and demanded that they crucify him. Now many of us had hoped that it was he who would deliver Israel from the yoke of the gentiles. But that is not all. It is now the third day since he was crucified, and certain women have this day amazed us by declaring that very early this morning they went to his tomb and found it empty.

And these same women insist that they talked with this man; they maintain that he has risen from the dead. And when the women reported this to the men, two of his apostles ran to the tomb and likewise found it empty"—and here Jacob interrupted his brother to say, "but they did not see Jesus."

190:5.4 (2035.1) As they walked along, Jesus said to them: "How slow you are to comprehend the truth! When you tell me that it is about the teachings and work of this man that you have your discussions, then may I enlighten you since I am more than familiar with these teachings. Do you not remember that this Jesus always taught that his kingdom was not of this world, and that all men, being the sons of God, should find liberty and freedom in the spiritual joy of the fellowship of the brotherhood of loving service in this new kingdom of the truth of the heavenly Father's love? Do you not recall how this Son of Man proclaimed the salvation of God for all men, ministering to the sick and afflicted and setting free those who were bound by fear and enslaved by evil? Do you not know that this man of Nazareth told his disciples that he must go to Jerusalem, be delivered up to his enemies, who would put him to death, and that he would arise on the third day? Have you not been told all this? And have you never read in the Scriptures concerning this day of salvation for Jew and gentile, where it says that in him shall all the families of the earth be blessed; that he will hear the cry of the needy and save the souls of the poor who seek him; that all nations shall call him blessed? That such a Deliverer shall be as the shadow of a great rock in a weary land. That he will feed the flock like a true shepherd, gathering the lambs in his arms and tenderly carrying them in his bosom. That he will open the eyes of the spiritually blind and bring the prisoners of despair out into full liberty and light; that all who sit in darkness shall see the great light of eternal salvation. That he will bind up the brokenhearted, proclaim liberty to the captives of sin, and open up the prison to those who are enslaved by fear and bound by evil. That he will comfort those who mourn and bestow upon them the joy of salvation in the place of sorrow and heaviness. That he shall be the desire of all nations and the everlasting joy of those who seek righteousness. That this Son of truth and righteousness shall rise upon the world with healing light and saving power; even that he will save his people from their sins; that he will really seek and save those who are lost. That he will not destroy the weak but minister salvation to all who hunger and thirst for righteousness. That those who believe in him shall have eternal life. That he will pour out his spirit upon all flesh, and that this Spirit of Truth shall be in each believer a well of water, springing up into everlasting life. Did you not understand how great was the gospel of the kingdom which this man delivered to you? Do you not perceive how great a salvation has come upon you?"

190:5.5 (2035.2) By this time they had come near to the village where these brothers dwelt. Not a word had these two men spoken since Jesus began to teach them as they walked along the way. Soon they drew up in front of their humble dwelling place, and Jesus was about to take leave of them, going on down the road, but they constrained him to come in and abide with them. They insisted that it was near nightfall, and that he tarry with them. Finally Jesus consented, and very soon after they went into the house, they sat down to eat. They gave him the bread to bless, and as he began to break and hand to them, their eyes were opened, and Cleopas recognized that their guest was the Master himself. And when he said, "It is the Master —," the morontia Jesus vanished from their sight.

190:5.6 (2036.1) And then they said, the one to the other, "No wonder our hearts burned within us as he spoke to us while we walked along the road! and while he opened up to our understanding the teachings of the Scriptures!"

190:5.7 (2036.2) They would not stop to eat. They had seen the morontia Master, and they rushed from the house, hastening back to Jerusalem to spread the good news of the risen Savior.

190:5.8 (2036.3) About nine o'clock that evening and just before the Master appeared to the ten, these two excited brothers broke in upon the apostles in the upper chamber, declaring that they had seen Jesus and talked with him. And they told all that Jesus had said to them and how they had not discerned who he was until the time of the breaking of the bread.

Paper 191

Appearances to the Apostles and Other Leaders

191:0.1 (2037.1) RESURRECTION Sunday was a terrible day in the lives of the apostles; ten of them spent the larger part of the day in the upper chamber behind barred doors. They might have fled from Jerusalem, but they were afraid of being arrested by the agents of the Sanhedrin if they were found abroad. Thomas was brooding over his troubles alone at Bethpage. He would have fared better had he remained with his fellow apostles, and he would have aided them to direct their discussions along more helpful lines.

191:0.2 (2037.2) All day long John upheld the idea that Jesus had risen from the dead. He recounted no less than five different times when the Master had affirmed he would rise again and at least three times when he alluded to the third day. John's attitude had considerable influence on them, especially on his brother James and on Nathaniel. John would have influenced them more if he had not been the youngest member of the group.

191:0.3 (2037.3) Their isolation had much to do with their troubles. John Mark kept them in touch with developments about the temple and informed them as to the many rumors gaining headway in the city, but it did not occur to him to gather up news from the different groups of believers to whom Jesus had already appeared. That was the kind of service which had heretofore been rendered by the messengers of David, but they were all absent on their last assignment as heralds of the resurrection to those groups of believers who dwelt remote from Jerusalem. For the first time in all these years the apostles realized how much they had been dependent on David's messengers for their daily information regarding the affairs of the kingdom.

191:0.4 (2037.4) All this day Peter characteristically vacillated emotionally between faith and doubt concerning the Master's resurrection. Peter could not get away from the sight of the grave cloths resting there in the tomb as if the body of Jesus had just evaporated from within. "But," reasoned Peter, "if he has risen and can show himself to the women, why does he not show himself to us, his apostles?" Peter would grow sorrowful when he thought that maybe Jesus did not come to them on account of his presence among the apostles, because he had denied him that night in Annas's courtyard. And then would he cheer himself with the word brought by the women, "Go tell my apostles—and Peter." But to derive encouragement from this message implied that he must believe that the women had really seen and heard the risen Master. Thus Peter alternated between faith and doubt throughout the whole day, until a little after eight o'clock, when he ventured out into the courtyard. Peter thought to remove himself from among the apostles so that he might not prevent Jesus' coming to them because of his denial of the Master.

191:0.5 (2037.5) James Zebedee at first advocated that they all go to the tomb; he was strongly in favor of doing something to get to the bottom of the mystery. It was Nathaniel who prevented them from going out in public in response to James's urging, and he did this by reminding them of Jesus' warning against unduly jeopardizing their lives at this time. By noontime James had settled down with the others to watchful waiting. He said little; he was tremendously disappointed because Jesus did not appear to them, and he did not know of the Master's many appearances to other groups and individuals.

191:0.6 (2038.1) Andrew did much listening this day. He was exceedingly perplexed by the situation and had more than his share of doubts, but he at least enjoyed a certain sense of freedom from responsibility for the guidance of his fellow apostles. He was indeed grateful that the Master had released him from the burdens of leadership before they fell upon these distracting times.

191:0.7 (2038.2) More than once during the long and weary hours of this tragic day, the only sustaining influence of the group was the frequent contribution of Nathaniel's characteristic philosophic counsel. He was really the controlling influence among the ten throughout the entire day. Never once did he express himself concerning either belief or disbelief in the Master's resurrection. But as the day wore on, he became increasingly inclined toward believing that Jesus had fulfilled his promise to rise again.

191:0.8 (2038.3) Simon Zelotes was too much crushed to participate in the discussions. Most of the time he reclined on a couch in a corner of the room with his face to the wall; he did not speak half a dozen times throughout the whole day. His concept of the kingdom had crashed, and he could not discern that the Master's resurrection could materially change the situation. His disappointment was very personal and altogether too keen to be recovered from on short notice, even in the face of such a stupendous fact as the resurrection.

191:0.9 (2038.4) Strange to record, the usually inexpressive Philip did much talking throughout the afternoon of this day. During the forenoon he had little to say, but all afternoon he asked questions of the other apostles. Peter was often annoyed by Philip's questions, but the others took his inquiries good-naturedly. Philip was particularly desirous of knowing, provided Jesus had really risen from the grave, whether his body would bear the physical marks of the crucifixion.

191:0.10 (2038.5) Matthew was highly confused; he listened to the discussions of his fellows but spent most of the time turning over in his mind the problem of their future finances. Regardless of Jesus' supposed resurrection, Judas was gone, David had unceremoniously turned the funds over to him, and they were without an authoritative leader. Before Matthew got around to giving serious consideration to their arguments about the resurrection, he had already seen the Master face to face.

191:0.11 (2038.6) The Alpheus twins took little part in these serious discussions; they were fairly busy with their customary ministrations. One of them expressed the attitude of both when he said, in reply to a question asked by Philip: "We do not understand about the resurrection, but our mother says she talked with the Master, and we believe her."

191:0.12 (2038.7) Thomas was in the midst of one of his typical spells of despairing depression. He slept a portion of the day and walked over the hills the rest of the time. He felt the urge to rejoin his fellow apostles, but the desire to be by himself was the stronger.

191:0.13 (2038.8) The Master put off the first morontia appearance to the apostles for a number of reasons. First, he wanted them to have time, after they heard of his resurrection, to think well over what he had told them about his death and resurrection when he was still with them in the flesh. The Master wanted Peter to wrestle through with some of his peculiar difficulties before he manifested himself to them all. In the second place, he desired that Thomas should be with them at the time of his first appearance. John Mark located Thomas at the home of Simon in Bethpage early this Sunday morning, bringing word to that effect to the apostles about eleven o'clock. Any time during this day Thomas would have gone back to them if Nathaniel or any two of the other apostles had gone for him. He really wanted to return, but having left as he did the evening before, he was too proud to go back of his own accord so soon. By the next day he was so depressed that it required almost a week for him to make up his mind to return. The apostles waited for him, and he waited for his brethren to seek him out and ask him to come back to them. Thomas thus remained away from his associates until the next Saturday evening, when, after darkness had come on, Peter and John went over to Bethpage and brought him back with them. And this is also the reason why they did not go at once to Galilee after Jesus first appeared to them; they would not go without Thomas.

The Appearance to Peter

191:1.1 (2039.1) It was near half past eight o'clock this Sunday evening when Jesus appeared to Simon Peter in the garden of the Mark home. This was his eighth morontia manifestation. Peter had lived under a heavy burden of doubt and guilt ever since his denial of the Master. All day Saturday and this Sunday he had fought the fear that, perhaps, he was no longer an apostle. He had shuddered at the fate of Judas and even thought that he, too, had betrayed his Master. All this afternoon he thought that it might be his presence with the apostles that prevented Jesus' appearing to them, provided, of course, he had really risen from the dead. And it was to Peter, in such a frame of mind and in such a state of soul, that Jesus appeared as the dejected apostle strolled among the flowers and shrubs.

191:1.2 (2039.2) When Peter thought of the loving look of the Master as he passed by on Annas's porch, and as he turned over in his mind that wonderful message brought him early that morning by the women who came from the empty tomb, "Go tell my apostles—and Peter."—as he contemplated these tokens of mercy, his faith began to surmount his doubts, and he stood still, clenching his fists, while he spoke aloud: "I believe he has risen from the dead; I will go and tell my brethren." And as he said this, there suddenly appeared in front of him the form of a man, who spoke to him in familiar tones, saying: "Peter, the enemy desired to have you, but I would not give you up. I knew it was not from the heart that you disowned me; therefore I forgave you even before you asked; but now must you cease to think about yourself and the troubles of the hour while you prepare to carry the good news of the gospel to those who sit in darkness. No longer should you be concerned with what you may obtain from the kingdom but rather be exercised about what you can give to those who live in dire spiritual poverty. Gird yourself, Simon, for the battle of a new day, the struggle with spiritual darkness and the evil doubtings of the natural minds of men."

191:1.3 (2039.3) Peter and the morontia Jesus walked through the garden and talked of things past, present, and future for almost five minutes. Then the Master vanished from his gaze, saying, "Farewell, Peter, until I see you with your brethren."

191:1.4 (2039.4) For a moment, Peter was overcome by the realization that he had talked with the risen Master, and that he could be sure he was still an ambassador of the kingdom. He had just heard the glorified Master exhort him to go on preaching the gospel. And with all this welling up within his heart, he rushed to the upper chamber and into the presence of his fellow apostles, exclaiming in breathless excitement: "I have seen the Master; he was in the garden. I talked with him, and he has forgiven me."

191:1.5 (2040.1) Peter's declaration that he had seen Jesus in the garden made a profound impression upon his fellow apostles, and they were about ready to surrender their doubts when Andrew got up and warned them not to be too much influenced by his brother's report. Andrew intimated that Peter had seen things which were not real before. Although Andrew did not directly allude to the vision of the night on the Sea of Galilee wherein Peter claimed to have seen the Master coming to them walking on the water, he said enough to betray to all present that he had this incident in mind. Simon Peter was very much hurt by his brother's insinuations and immediately lapsed into crestfallen silence. The twins felt very sorry for Peter, and they both went over to express their sympathy and to say that they believed him and to reassert that their own mother had also seen the Master.

First Appearance to the Apostles

191:2.1 (2040.2) Shortly after nine o'clock that evening, after the departure of Cleopas and Jacob, while the Alpheus twins comforted Peter, and while Nathaniel remonstrated with Andrew, and as the ten apostles were there assembled in the upper chamber with all the doors bolted for fear of arrest, the Master, in morontia form, suddenly appeared in the midst of them, saying: "Peace be upon you. Why are you so frightened when I appear, as though you had seen a spirit? Did I not tell you about these things when I was present with you in the flesh? Did I not say to you that the chief priests and the rulers would deliver me up to be killed, that one of your own number would betray me, and that on the third day I would rise? Wherefore all your doubtings and all this discussion about the reports of the women, Cleopas and Jacob, and even Peter? How long will you doubt my words and refuse to believe my promises? And now that you actually see me, will you believe? Even now one of you is absent. When you are gathered together once more, and after all of you know of a certainty that the Son of Man has risen from the grave, go hence into Galilee. Have faith in God; have faith in one another; and so shall you enter into the new service of the kingdom of heaven. I will tarry in Jerusalem with you until you are ready to go into Galilee. My peace I leave with you."

191:2.2 (2040.3) When the morontia Jesus had spoken to them, he vanished in an instant from their sight. And they all fell on their faces, praising God and venerating their vanished Master. This was the Master's ninth morontia appearance.

With the Morontia Creatures

191:3.1 (2040.4) The next day, Monday, was spent wholly with the morontia creatures then present on Urantia. As participants in the Master's morontia-transition experience, there had come to Urantia more than one million morontia directors and associates, together with transition mortals of various orders from the seven mansion worlds of Satania. The morontia Jesus sojourned with these splendid intelligences for forty days. He instructed them and learned from their directors the life of morontia transition as it is traversed by the mortals of the inhabited worlds of Satania as they pass through the system morontia spheres.

191:3.2 (2041.1) About midnight of this Monday the Master's morontia form was adjusted for transition to the second stage of morontia progression. When he next appeared to his mortal children on earth, it was as a second-stage morontia being. As the Master progressed in the morontia career, it became, technically, more and more difficult for the morontia intelligences and their transforming associates to visualize the Master to mortal and material eyes.

191:3.3 (2041.2) Jesus made the transit to the third stage of morontia on Friday, April 14; to the fourth stage on Monday, the 17th; to the fifth stage on Saturday, the 22nd; to the sixth stage on Thursday, the 27th; to the seventh stage on Tuesday, May 2; to Jerusem citizenship on Sunday, the 7th; and he entered the embrace of the Most Highs of Edentia on Sunday, the 14th.

191:3.4 (2041.3) In this manner did Michael of Nebadon complete his service of universe experience since he had already, in connection with his previous bestowals, experienced to the full the life of the ascendant mortals of time and space from the sojourn on the headquarters of the constellation even on to, and through, the service of the headquarters of the superuniverse. And it was by these very morontia experiences that the Creator Son of Nebadon really finished and acceptably terminated his seventh and final universe bestowal.

The Tenth Appearance (At Philadelphia)

191:4.1 (2041.4) The tenth morontia manifestation of Jesus to mortal recognition occurred a short time after eight o'clock on Tuesday, April 11, at Philadelphia, where he showed himself to Abner and Lazarus and some one hundred and fifty of their associates, including more than fifty of the evangelistic corps of the seventy. This appearance occurred just after the opening of a special meeting in the synagogue which had been called by Abner to discuss the crucifixion of Jesus and the more recent report of the resurrection which had been brought by David's messenger. Inasmuch as the resurrected Lazarus was now a member of this group of believers, it was not difficult for them to believe the report that Jesus had risen from the dead.

191:4.2 (2041.5) The meeting in the synagogue was just being opened by Abner and Lazarus, who were standing together in the pulpit, when the entire audience of believers saw the form of the Master appear suddenly. He stepped forward from where he had appeared between Abner and Lazarus, neither of whom had observed him, and saluting the company, said:

191:4.3 (2041.6) "Peace be upon you. You all know that we have one Father in heaven, and that there is but one gospel of the kingdom—the good news of the gift of eternal life which men receive by faith. As you rejoice in your loyalty to the gospel, pray the Father of truth to shed abroad in your hearts a new and greater love for your brethren. You are to love all men as I have loved you; you are to serve all men as I have served you. With understanding sympathy and brotherly affection, fellowship all your brethren who are dedicated to the procla-

mation of the good news, whether they be Jew or gentile, Greek or Roman, Persian or Ethiopian. John proclaimed the kingdom in advance; you have preached the gospel in power; the Greeks already teach the good news; and I am soon to send forth the Spirit of Truth into the souls of all these, my brethren, who have so unselfishly dedicated their lives to the enlightenment of their fellows who sit in spiritual darkness. You are all the children of light; therefore stumble not into the misunderstanding entanglements of mortal suspicion and human intolerance. If you are ennobled, by the grace of faith, to love unbelievers, should you not also equally love those who are your fellow believers in the far-spreading household of faith? Remember, as you love one another, all men will know that you are my disciples.

191:4.4 (2042.1) "Go, then, into all the world proclaiming this gospel of the fatherhood of God and the brotherhood of men to all nations and races and ever be wise in your choice of methods for presenting the good news to the different races and tribes of mankind. Freely you have received this gospel of the kingdom, and you will freely give the good news to all nations. Fear not the resistance of evil, for I am with you always, even to the end of the ages. And my peace I leave with you."

191:4.5 (2042.2) When he had said, "My peace I leave with you," he vanished from their sight. With the exception of one of his appearances in Galilee, where upward of five hundred believers saw him at one time, this group in Philadelphia embraced the largest number of mortals who saw him on any single occasion.

191:4.6 (2042.3) Early the next morning, even while the apostles tarried in Jerusalem awaiting the emotional recovery of Thomas, these believers at Philadelphia went forth proclaiming that Jesus of Nazareth had risen from the dead.

191:4.7 (2042.4) The next day, Wednesday, Jesus spent without interruption in the society of his morontia associates, and during the midafternoon hours he received visiting morontia delegates from the mansion worlds of every local system of inhabited spheres throughout the constellation of Norlatiadek. And they all rejoiced to know their Creator as one of their own order of universe intelligence.

Second Appearance to the Apostles

191:5.1 (2042.5) Thomas spent a lonesome week alone with himself in the hills around about Olivet. During this time he saw only those at Simon's house and John Mark. It was about nine o'clock on Saturday, April 15, when the two apostles found him and took him back with them to their rendezvous at the Mark home. The next day Thomas listened to the telling of the stories of the Master's various appearances, but he steadfastly refused to believe. He maintained that Peter had enthused them into thinking they had seen the Master. Nathaniel reasoned with him, but it did no good. There was an emotional stubbornness associated with his customary doubtfulness, and this state of mind, coupled with his chagrin at having run away from them, conspired to create a situation of isolation which even Thomas himself did not fully understand. He had withdrawn from his fellows, he had gone his own way, and now, even when he was back among them, he unconsciously tended to assume an attitude of disagreement. He was slow to surrender; he disliked to give in. Without intending it, he really enjoyed the attention paid him; he derived unconscious satisfaction from the efforts of all his fellows to convince and convert him. He had missed them for a full week, and he obtained considerable pleasure from their persistent attentions.

191:5.2 (2042.6) They were having their evening meal a little after six o'clock, with Peter sitting on one side of Thomas and Nathaniel on the other, when the doubting apostle said: "I will not believe unless I see the Master with my own eyes and put my finger in the mark of the nails." As they thus sat at supper, and while the doors were securely shut and barred, the morontia Master suddenly appeared inside the curvature of the table and, standing directly in front of Thomas, said:

191:5.3 (2043.1) "Peace be upon you. For a full week have I tarried that I might appear again when you were all present to hear once more the commission to go into all the world and preach this gospel of the kingdom. Again I tell you: As the Father sent me into the world, so send I you. As I have revealed the Father, so shall you reveal the divine love, not merely with words, but in your daily living. I send you forth, not to love the souls of men, but rather to love men. You are not merely to proclaim the joys of heaven but also to exhibit in your daily experience these spirit realities of the divine life since you already have eternal life, as the gift of God, through faith. When you have faith, when power from on high, the Spirit of Truth, has come upon you, you will not hide your light here behind closed doors; you will make known the love and the mercy of God to all mankind. Through fear you now flee from the facts of a disagreeable experience, but when you shall have been baptized with the Spirit of Truth, you will bravely and joyously go forth to meet the new experiences of proclaiming the good news of eternal life in the kingdom of God. You may tarry here and in Galilee for a short season while you recover from the shock of the transition from the false security of the authority of traditionalism to the new order of the authority of facts, truth, and faith in the supreme realities of living experience.

Your mission to the world is founded on the fact that I lived a God-revealing life among you; on the truth that you and all other men are the sons of God; and it shall consist in the life which you will live among men—the actual and living experience of loving men and serving them, even as I have loved and served you. Let faith reveal your light to the world; let the revelation of truth open the eyes blinded by tradition; let your loving service effectually destroy the prejudice engendered by ignorance. By so drawing close to your fellow men in understanding sympathy and with unselfish devotion, you will lead them into a saving knowledge of the Father's love. The Jews have extolled goodness; the Greeks have exalted beauty; the Hindus preach devotion; the faraway ascetics teach reverence; the Romans demand loyalty; but I require of my disciples life, even a life of loving service for your brothers in the flesh." *

191:5.4 (2043.2) When the Master had so spoken, he looked down into the face of Thomas and said: "And you, Thomas, who said you would not believe unless you could see me and put your finger in the nail marks of my hands, have now beheld me and heard my words; and though you see no nail marks on my hands, since I am raised in the form that you also shall have when you depart from this world, what will you say to your brethren? You will acknowledge the truth, for already in your heart you had begun to believe even when you so stoutly asserted your unbelief. Your doubts, Thomas, always most stubbornly assert themselves just as they are about to crumble. Thomas, I bid you be not faithless but believing—and I know you will believe, even with a whole heart."

191:5.5 (2043.3) When Thomas heard these words, he fell on his knees before the morontia Master and exclaimed, "I believe! My Lord and my Master!" Then said Jesus to Thomas: "You have believed, Thomas, because you have really seen and heard me. Blessed are those in the ages to come who will believe even though they have not seen with the eye of flesh nor heard with the mortal ear."

191:5.6 (2043.4) And then, as the Master's form moved over near the head of the table, he addressed them all, saying: "And now go all of you to Galilee, where I will presently appear to you." After he said this, he vanished from their sight.

191:5.7 (2044.1) The eleven apostles were now fully convinced that Jesus had risen from the dead, and very early the next morning, before the break of day, they started out for Galilee.

The Alexandrian Appearance

191:6.1 (2044.2) While the eleven apostles were on the way to Galilee, drawing near their journey's end, on Tuesday evening, April 18, at about half past eight o'clock, Jesus appeared to Rodan and some eighty other believers, in Alexandria. This was the Master's twelfth appearance in morontia form. Jesus appeared before these Greeks and Jews at the conclusion of the report of David's messenger regarding the crucifixion. This messenger, being the fifth in the Jerusalem-Alexandria relay of runners, had arrived in Alexandria late that afternoon, and when he had delivered his message to Rodan, it was decided to call the believers together to receive this tragic word from the messenger himself. At about eight o'clock, the messenger, Nathan of Busiris, came before this group and told them in detail all that had been told him by the preceding runner. Nathan ended his touching recital with these words: "But David, who sends us this word, reports that the Master, in foretelling his death, declared that he would rise again." Even as Nathan spoke, the morontia Master appeared there in full view of all. And when Nathan sat down, Jesus said: *

191:6.2 (2044.3) "Peace be upon you. That which my Father sent me into the world to establish belongs not to a race, a nation, nor to a special group of teachers or preachers. This gospel of the kingdom belongs to both Jew and gentile, to rich and poor, to free and bond, to male and female, even to the little children. And you are all to proclaim this gospel of love and truth by the lives which you live in the flesh. You shall love one another with a new and startling affection, even as I have loved you. You will serve mankind with a new and amazing devotion, even as I have served you. And when men see you so love them, and when they behold how fervently you serve them, they will perceive that you have become faith-fellows of the kingdom of heaven, and they will follow after the Spirit of Truth which they see in your lives, to the finding of eternal salvation.

191:6.3 (2044.4) "As the Father sent me into this world, even so now send I you. You are all called to carry the good news to those who sit in darkness. This gospel of the kingdom belongs to all who believe it; it shall not be committed to the custody of mere priests. Soon will the Spirit of Truth come upon you, and he shall lead you into all truth. Go you, therefore, into all the world preaching this gospel, and lo, I am with you always, even to the end of the ages."

191:6.4 (2044.5) When the Master had so spoken, he vanished from their sight. All that night these believers remained there together recounting their experiences as kingdom believers and listening to the many words of Rodan and his associates. And they all believed that Jesus had risen from the dead. Imagine the surprise of David's herald of the resurrection, who arrived the second day after this, when they replied to his announcement, saying: "Yes, we know, for we have seen him. He appeared to us day before yesterday."

Paper 192

Appearances in Galilee

192:0.1 (2045.1) BY THE time the apostles left Jerusalem for Galilee, the Jewish leaders had quieted down considerably. Since Jesus appeared only to his family of kingdom believers, and since the apostles were in hiding and did no public preaching, the rulers of the Jews concluded that the gospel movement was, after all, effectually crushed. They were, of course, disconcerted by the increasing spread of rumors that Jesus had risen from the dead, but they depended upon the bribed guards effectively to counteract all such reports by their reiteration of the story that a band of his followers had removed the body.

192:0.2 (2045.2) From this time on, until the apostles were dispersed by the rising tide of persecution, Peter was the generally recognized head of the apostolic corps. Jesus never gave him any such authority, and his fellow apostles never formally elected him to such a position of responsibility; he naturally assumed it and held it by common consent and also because he was their chief preacher. From now on public preaching became the main business of the apostles. After their return from Galilee, Matthias, whom they chose to take the place of Judas, became their treasurer.

192:0.3 (2045.3) During the week they tarried in Jerusalem, Mary the mother of Jesus spent much of the time with the women believers who were stopping at the home of Joseph of Arimathea.

192:0.4 (2045.4) Early this Monday morning when the apostles departed for Galilee, John Mark went along. He followed them out of the city, and when they had passed well beyond Bethany, he boldly came up among them, feeling confident they would not send him back.

192:0.5 (2045.5) The apostles paused several times on the way to Galilee to tell the story of their risen Master and therefore did not arrive at Bethsaida until very late on Wednesday night. It was noontime on Thursday before they were all awake and ready to partake of breakfast.

Appearance by the Lake

192:1.1 (2045.6) About six o'clock Friday morning, April 21, the morontia Master made his thirteenth appearance, the first in Galilee, to the ten apostles as their boat drew near the shore close to the usual landing place at Bethsaida.

192:1.2 (2045.7) After the apostles had spent the afternoon and early evening of Thursday in waiting at the Zebedee home, Simon Peter suggested that they go fishing. When Peter proposed the fishing trip, all of the apostles decided to go along. All night they toiled with the nets but caught no fish. They did not much mind the failure to make a catch, for they had many interesting experiences to talk over, things which had so recently happened to them at Jerusalem. But when daylight came, they decided to return to Bethsaida. As they neared the shore, they saw someone on the beach, near the boat landing, standing by a fire. At first they thought it was John Mark, who had come down to welcome them back with their catch, but as they drew nearer the shore, they saw they were mistaken—the man was too tall for John. It had occurred to none of them that the person on the shore was the Master. They did not altogether understand why Jesus wanted to meet with them amidst the scenes of their earlier associations and out in the open in contact with nature, far away from the shut-in environment of Jerusalem with its tragic associations of fear, betrayal, and death. He had told them that, if they would go into Galilee, he would meet them there, and he was about to fulfill that promise.

192:1.3 (2046.1) As they dropped anchor and prepared to enter the small boat for going ashore, the man on the beach called to them, "Lads, have you caught anything?" And when they answered, "No," he spoke again. "Cast the net on the right side of the boat, and you will find fish." While they did not know it was Jesus who had directed them, with one accord they cast in the net as they had been instructed, and immediately it was filled, so much so that they were hardly able to draw it up. Now, John Zebedee was quick of perception, and when he saw the heavy-laden net, he perceived that it was the Master who had spoken to them. When this thought came into his mind, he leaned over and whispered to Peter, "It is the Master." Peter was ever a man of thoughtless action and impetuous devotion; so when John whispered this in his ear, he quickly arose and cast himself into the water that he might the sooner reach the Master's side. His brethren came up close behind him, having come ashore in the small boat, hauling the net of fishes after them.

192:1.4 (2046.2) By this time John Mark was up and, seeing the apostles coming ashore with the heavy-laden net, ran down the beach to greet them; and when he saw eleven men instead of ten, he surmised that the unrecognized one was the risen Jesus, and as the astonished ten stood by in silence, the youth rushed up to the Master and, kneeling at his feet, said, "My Lord and my Master." And then Jesus spoke, not as he had in Jerusalem, when he greeted them with "Peace be upon you," but in commonplace tones he addressed John Mark: "Well, John, I am glad to see you again and in carefree Galilee, where we can have a good visit. Stay with us, John, and have breakfast."

192:1.5 (2046.3) As Jesus talked with the young man, the ten were so astonished and surprised that they neglected to haul the net of fish in upon the beach. Now spoke Jesus: "Bring in your fish and prepare some for breakfast. Already we have the fire and much bread."

192:1.6 (2046.4) While John Mark had paid homage to the Master, Peter had for a moment been shocked at the sight of the coals of fire glowing there on the beach; the scene reminded him so vividly of the midnight fire of charcoal in the courtyard of Annas, where he had disowned the Master, but he shook himself and, kneeling at the Master's feet, exclaimed, "My Lord and my Master!"

192:1.7 (2046.5) Peter then joined his comrades as they hauled in the net. When they had landed their catch, they counted the fish, and there were 153 large ones. And again was the mistake made of calling this another miraculous catch of fish. There was no miracle connected with this episode. It was merely an exercise of the Master's preknowledge. He knew the fish were there and accordingly directed the apostles where to cast the net.

192:1.8 (2047.1) Jesus spoke to them, saying: "Come now, all of you, to breakfast. Even the twins should sit down while I visit with you; John Mark will dress the fish." John Mark brought seven good-sized fish, which the Master put on the fire, and when they were cooked, the lad served them to the ten. Then Jesus broke the bread and handed it to John, who in turn served it to the hungry apostles. When they had all been served, Jesus bade John Mark sit down while he himself served the fish and the bread to the lad. And as they ate, Jesus visited with them and recounted their many experiences in Galilee and by this very lake.

192:1.9 (2047.2) This was the third time Jesus had manifested himself to the apostles as a group. When Jesus first addressed them, asking if they had any fish, they did not suspect who he was because it was a common experience for these fishermen on the Sea of Galilee, when they came ashore, to be thus accosted by the fish merchants of Tarichea, who were usually on hand to buy the fresh catches for the drying establishments.

192:1.10 (2047.3) Jesus visited with the ten apostles and John Mark for more than an hour, and then he walked up and down the beach, talking with them two and two—but not the same couples he had at first sent out together to teach. All eleven of the apostles had come down from Jerusalem together, but Simon Zelotes grew more and more despondent as they drew near Galilee, so that, when they reached Bethsaida, he forsook his brethren and returned to his home.

192:1.11 (2047.4) Before taking leave of them this morning, Jesus directed that two of the apostles should volunteer to go to Simon Zelotes and bring him back that very day. And Peter and Andrew did so.

Visiting with the Apostles Two and Two

192:2.1 (2047.5) When they had finished breakfast, and while the others sat by the fire, Jesus beckoned to Peter and to John that they should come with him for a stroll on the beach. As they walked along, Jesus said to John, "John, do you love me?" And when John answered, "Yes, Master, with all my heart," the Master said: "Then, John, give up your intolerance and learn to love men as I have loved you. Devote your life to proving that love is the greatest thing in the world. It is the love of God that impels men to seek salvation. Love is the ancestor of all spiritual goodness, the essence of the true and the beautiful."

192:2.2 (2047.6) Jesus then turned toward Peter and asked, "Peter, do you love me?" Peter answered, "Lord, you know I love you with all my soul." Then said Jesus: "If you love me, Peter, feed my lambs. Do not neglect to minister to the weak, the poor, and the young. Preach the gospel without fear or favor; remember always that God is no respecter of persons. Serve your fellow men even as I have served you; forgive your fellow mortals even as I have forgiven you. Let experience teach you the value of meditation and the power of intelligent reflection."

192:2.3 (2047.7) After they had walked along a little farther, the Master turned to Peter and asked, "Peter, do you really love me?" And then said Simon, "Yes, Lord, you know that I love you." And again said Jesus: "Then take good care of my sheep. Be a good and a true shepherd to the flock. Betray not their confidence in you. Be not taken by surprise at the enemy's hand. Be on guard at all times—watch and pray."

192:2.4 (2047.8) When they had gone a few steps farther, Jesus turned to Peter and, for the third time, asked, "Peter, do you truly love me?" And then Peter, being slightly grieved at the Master's seeming distrust of him, said with considerable feeling, "Lord, you know all things, and therefore do you know that I really and truly love you." Then said Jesus: "Feed my sheep. Do not forsake the flock. Be an example and an inspiration to all your fellow shepherds. Love the flock as I have loved you and devote yourself to their welfare even as I have devoted my life to your welfare. And follow after me even to the end."

192:2.5 (2048.1) Peter took this last statement literally—that he should continue to follow after him—and turning to Jesus, he pointed to John, asking, "If I follow on after you, what shall this man do?" And then, perceiving that Peter had misunderstood his words, Jesus said: "Peter, be not concerned about what your brethren shall do. If I will that John should tarry after you are gone, even until I come back, what is that to you? Only make sure that you follow me."

192:2.6 (2048.2) This remark spread among the brethren and was received as a statement by Jesus to the effect that John would not die before the Master returned, as many thought and hoped, to establish the kingdom in power and glory. It was this interpretation of what Jesus said that had much to do with getting Simon Zelotes back into service, and keeping him at work.

192:2.7 (2048.3) When they returned to the others, Jesus went for a walk and talk with Andrew and James. When they had gone a short distance, Jesus said to Andrew, "Andrew, do you trust me?" And when the former chief of the apostles heard Jesus ask such a question, he stood still and answered, "Yes, Master, of a certainty I trust you, and you know that I do." Then said Jesus: "Andrew, if you trust me, trust your brethren more—even Peter. I once trusted you with the leadership of your brethren. Now must you trust others as I leave you to go to the Father. When your brethren begin to scatter abroad because of bitter persecutions, be a considerate and wise counselor to James my brother in the flesh when they put heavy burdens upon him which he is not qualified by experience to bear. And then go on trusting, for I will not fail you. When you are through on earth, you shall come to me."

192:2.8 (2048.4) Then Jesus turned to James, asking, "James, do you trust me?" And of course James replied, "Yes, Master, I trust you with all my heart." Then said Jesus: "James, if you trust me more, you will be less impatient with your brethren. If you will trust me, it will help you to be kind to the brotherhood of believers. Learn to weigh the consequences of your sayings and your doings. Remember that the reaping is in accordance with the sowing. Pray for tranquillity of spirit and cultivate patience. These graces, with living faith, shall sustain you when the hour comes to drink the cup of sacrifice. But never be dismayed; when you are through on earth, you shall also come to be with me."

192:2.9 (2048.5) Jesus next talked with Thomas and Nathaniel. Said he to Thomas, "Thomas, do you serve me?" Thomas replied, "Yes, Lord, I serve you now and always." Then said Jesus: "If you would serve me, serve my brethren in the flesh even as I have served you. And be not weary in this well-doing but persevere as one who has been ordained by God for this service of love. When you have finished your service with me on earth, you shall serve with me in glory.

Thomas, you must cease doubting; you must grow in faith and the knowledge of truth. Believe in God like a child but cease to act so childishly. Have courage; be strong in faith and mighty in the kingdom of God."

192:2.10 (2049.1) Then said the Master to Nathaniel, "Nathaniel, do you serve me?" And the apostle answered, "Yes, Master, and with an undivided affection." Then said Jesus: "If, therefore, you serve me with a whole heart, make sure that you are devoted to the welfare of my brethren on earth with tireless affection. Admix friendship with your counsel and add love to your philosophy. Serve your fellow men even as I have served you. Be faithful to men as I have watched over you. Be less critical; expect less of some men and thereby lessen the extent of your disappointment. And when the work down here is over, you shall serve with me on high."

192:2.11 (2049.2) After this the Master talked with Matthew and Philip. To Philip he said, "Philip, do you obey me?" Philip answered, "Yes, Lord, I will obey you even with my life." Then said Jesus: "If you would obey me, go then into the lands of the gentiles and proclaim this gospel. The prophets have told you that to obey is better than to sacrifice. By faith have you become a God-knowing kingdom son. There is but one law to obey—that is the command to go forth proclaiming the gospel of the kingdom. Cease to fear men; be unafraid to preach the good news of eternal life to your fellows who languish in darkness and hunger for the light of truth. No more, Philip, shall you busy yourself with money and goods. You now are free to preach the glad tidings just as are your brethren. And I will go before you and be with you even to the end."

192:2.12 (2049.3) And then, speaking to Matthew, the Master asked, "Matthew, do you have it in your heart to obey me?" Matthew answered, "Yes, Lord, I am fully dedicated to doing your will." Then said the Master: "Matthew, if you would obey me, go forth to teach all peoples this gospel of the kingdom. No longer will you serve your brethren the material things of life; henceforth you are also to proclaim the good news of spiritual salvation. From now on have an eye single only to obeying your commission to preach this gospel of the Father's kingdom. As I have done the Father's will on earth, so shall you fulfill the divine commission. Remember, both Jew and gentile are your brethren. Fear no man when you proclaim the saving truths of the gospel of the kingdom of heaven. And where I go, you shall presently come."

192:2.13 (2049.4) Then he walked and talked with the Alpheus twins, James and Judas, and speaking to both of them, he asked, "James and Judas, do you believe in me?" And when they both answered, "Yes, Master, we do believe," he said: "I will soon leave you. You see that I have already left you in the flesh. I tarry only a short time in this form before I go to my Father. You believe in me—you are my apostles, and you always will be. Go on believing and remembering your association with me, when I am gone, and after you have, perchance, returned to the work you used to do before you came to live with me. Never allow a change in your outward work to

influence your allegiance. Have faith in God to the end of your days on earth. Never forget that, when you are a faith son of God, all upright work of the realm is sacred.

Nothing which a son of God does can be common. Do your work, therefore, from this time on, as for God. And when you are through on this world, I have other and better worlds where you shall likewise work for me. And in all of this work, on this world and on other worlds, I will work with you, and my spirit shall dwell within you."

192:2.14 (2049.5) It was almost ten o'clock when Jesus returned from his visit with the Alpheus twins, and as he left the apostles, he said: "Farewell, until I meet you all on the mount of your ordination tomorrow at noontime." When he had thus spoken, he vanished from their sight.

On the Mount of Ordination

192:3.1 (2050.1) At noon on Saturday, April 22, the eleven apostles assembled by appointment on the hill near Capernaum, and Jesus appeared among them. This meeting occurred on the very mount where the Master had set them apart as his apostles and as ambassadors of the Father's kingdom on earth. And this was the Master's fourteenth morontia manifestation.

192:3.2 (2050.2) At this time the eleven apostles knelt in a circle about the Master and heard him repeat the charges and saw him re-enact the ordination scene even as when they were first set apart for the special work of the kingdom. And all of this was to them as a memory of their former consecration to the Father's service, except the Master's prayer.

When the Master—the morontia[1] Jesus—now prayed, it was in tones of maj-

1   "Morontia is a term designating a vast level intervening between the material and the spiritual. It may designate personal or impersonal realities, living or nonliving energies. The warp of morontia is spiritual; its woof is physical."

esty and with words of power such as the apostles had never before heard. Their Master now spoke with the rulers of the universes as one who, in his own universe, had had all power and authority committed to his hand. And these eleven men never forgot this experience of the morontia rededication to the former pledges of ambassadorship. The Master spent just one hour on this mount with his ambassadors, and when he had taken an affectionate farewell of them, he vanished from their sight.

192:3.3 (2050.3) And no one saw Jesus for a full week. The apostles really had no idea what to do, not knowing whether the Master had gone to the Father. In this state of uncertainty they tarried at Bethsaida. They were afraid to go fishing lest he come to visit them and they miss seeing him. During this entire week Jesus was occupied with the morontia creatures on earth and with the affairs of the morontia transition which he was experiencing on this world.

The Lakeside Gathering

192:4.1 (2050.4) Word of the appearances of Jesus was spreading throughout Galilee, and every day increasing numbers of believers arrived at the Zebedee home to inquire about the Master's resurrection and to find out the truth about these reputed appearances. Peter, early in the week, sent out word that a public meeting would be held by the seaside the next Sabbath at three o'clock in the afternoon.

192:4.2 (2050.5) Accordingly, on Saturday, April 29, at three o'clock, more than five hundred believers from the environs of Capernaum assembled at Bethsaida to hear Peter preach his first public sermon since the resurrection. The apostle was at his best, and after he had finished his appealing discourse, few of his hearers doubted that the Master had risen from the dead.

192:4.3 (2050.6) Peter ended his sermon, saying: "We affirm that Jesus of Nazareth is not dead; we declare that he has risen from the tomb; we proclaim that

we have seen him and talked with him." Just as he finished making this declaration of faith, there by his side, in full view of all these people, the Master appeared in morontia form and, speaking to them in familiar accents, said, "Peace be upon you, and my peace I leave with you." When he had thus appeared and had so spoken to them, he vanished from their sight. This was the fifteenth morontia manifestation of the risen Jesus.

192:4.4 (2051.1) Because of certain things said to the eleven while they were in conference with the Master on the mount of ordination, the apostles received the impression that their Master would presently make a public appearance before a group of the Galilean believers, and that, after he had done so, they were to return to Jerusalem. Accordingly, early the next day, Sunday, April 30, the eleven left Bethsaida for Jerusalem. They did considerable teaching and preaching on the way down the Jordan, so that they did not arrive at the home of the Marks in Jerusalem until late on Wednesday, May 3.

192:4.5 (2051.2) This was a sad homecoming for John Mark. Just a few hours before he reached home, his father, Elijah Mark, suddenly died from a hemorrhage in the brain. Although the thought of the certainty of the resurrection of the dead did much to comfort the apostles in their grief, at the same time they truly mourned the loss of their good friend, who had been their stanch supporter even in the times of great trouble and disappointment. John Mark did all he could to comfort his mother and, speaking for her, invited the apostles to continue to make their home at her house. And the eleven made this upper chamber their headquarters until after the day of Pentecost. *

192:4.6 (2051.3) The apostles had purposely entered Jerusalem after nightfall that they might not be seen by the Jewish authorities. Neither did they publicly appear in connection with the funeral of Elijah Mark. All the next day they remained in quiet seclusion in this eventful upper chamber.

192:4.7 (2051.4) On Thursday night the apostles had a wonderful meeting in this upper chamber and all pledged themselves to go forth in the public preaching of the new gospel of the risen Lord except Thomas, Simon Zelotes, and the Alpheus twins. Already had begun the first steps of changing the gospel of the kingdom—sonship with God and brotherhood with man—into the proclamation of the resurrection of Jesus. Nathaniel opposed this shift in the burden of

their public message, but he could not withstand Peter's eloquence, neither could he overcome the enthusiasm of the disciples, especially the women believers.

192:4.8 (2051.5) And so, under the vigorous leadership of Peter and ere the Master ascended to the Father, his well-meaning representatives began that subtle process of gradually and certainly changing the religion of Jesus into a new and modified form of religion about Jesus.

Paper 193

Final Appearances and Ascension

193:0.1 (2052.1) THE sixteenth morontia manifestation of Jesus occurred on Friday, May 5, in the courtyard of Nicodemus, about nine o'clock at night. On this evening the Jerusalem believers had made their first attempt to get together since the resurrection. Assembled here at this time were the eleven apostles, the women's corps and their associates, and about fifty other leading disciples of the Master, including a number of the Greeks. This company of believers had been visiting informally for more than half an hour when, suddenly, the morontia Master appeared in full view and immediately began to instruct them. Said Jesus:

193:0.2 (2052.2) "Peace be upon you.

This is the most representative group of believers—apostles and disciples, both men and women—to which I have appeared since the time of my deliverance from the flesh. I now call you to witness that I told you beforehand that my sojourn among you must come to an end; I told you that presently I must return to the Father. And then I plainly told you how the chief priests and the rulers of the Jews would deliver me up to be put to death, and that I would rise from the grave. Why, then, did you allow yourselves to become so disconcerted by all this when it came to pass? and why were you so surprised when I rose from the tomb on the third day? You failed to believe me because you heard my words without comprehending the meaning thereof.

193:0.3 (2052.3) "And now you should give ear to my words lest you again make the mistake of hearing my teaching with the mind while in your hearts you fail to comprehend the meaning. From the beginning of my sojourn as one of you, I taught you that my one purpose was to reveal my Father in heaven to his children on earth. I have lived the God-revealing bestowal that you might experience the God-knowing career. I have revealed God as your Father in heaven; I have revealed you as the sons of God on earth. It is a fact that God loves you, his sons. By faith in my word this fact becomes an eternal and living truth in your hearts. When, by living faith, you become divinely God-conscious, you are then born of the spirit as children of light and life, even the eternal life wherewith you shall ascend the universe of universes and attain the experience of finding God the Father on Paradise.

193:0.4 (2052.4) "I admonish you ever to remember that your mission among men is to proclaim the gospel of the kingdom—the reality of the fatherhood of God and the truth of the sonship of man. Proclaim the whole truth of the good news, not just a part of the saving gospel. Your message is not changed by my resurrection experience. Sonship with God, by faith, is still the saving truth of the gospel of the kingdom. You are to go forth preaching the love of

God and the service of man. That which the world needs most to know is: Men are the sons of God, and through faith they can actually realize, and daily experience, this ennobling truth. My bestowal should help all men to know that they are the children of God, but such knowledge will not suffice if they fail personally to faith-grasp the saving truth that they are the living spirit sons of the eternal Father. The gospel of the kingdom is concerned with the love of the Father and the service of his children on earth.

193:0.5 (2053.1) "Among yourselves, here, you share the knowledge that I have risen from the dead, but that is not strange. I have the power to lay down my life and to take it up again; the Father gives such power to his Paradise Sons. You should the rather be stirred in your hearts by the knowledge that the dead of an age entered upon the eternal ascent soon after I left Joseph's new tomb. I lived my life in the flesh to show how you can, through loving service, become God- revealing to your fellow men even as, by loving you and serving you, I have become God-revealing to you. I have lived among you as the Son of Man that you, and all other men, might know that you are all indeed the sons of God.

Therefore, go you now into all the world preaching this gospel of the kingdom of heaven to all men. Love all men as I have loved you; serve your fellow mortals as I have served you. Freely you have received, freely give. Only tarry here in Jerusalem while I go to the Father, and until I send you the Spirit of Truth. He shall lead you into the enlarged truth, and I will go with you into all the world. I am with you always, and my peace I leave with you."

193:0.6 (2053.2) When the Master had spoken to them, he vanished from their sight. It was near daybreak before these believers dispersed; all night they remained together, earnestly discussing the Master's admonitions and contemplating all that had befallen them. James Zebedee and others of the apostles also told them of their experiences with the morontia Master in Galilee and recited how he had three times appeared to them.

1   The Appearance at Sychar

193:1.1 (2053.3) About four o'clock on Sabbath afternoon, May 13, the Master appeared to Nalda and about seventy-five Samaritan believers near Jacob's well, at Sychar. The believers were in the habit of meeting at this place, near where Jesus had spoken to Nalda concerning the water of life. On this day, just as they had finished their discussions of the reported resurrection, Jesus suddenly appeared before them, saying:

193:1.2 (2053.4) "Peace be upon you. You rejoice to know that I am the resurrection and the life, but this will avail you nothing unless you are first born of the eternal spirit, thereby coming to possess, by faith, the gift of eternal life. If you are the faith sons of my Father, you shall never die; you shall not perish. The gospel of the kingdom has taught you that all men are the sons of God. And this good news concerning the love of the heavenly Father for his children on earth must be carried to all the world. The time has come when you worship God neither on Gerizim nor at Jerusalem, but where you are, as you are, in spirit and in truth. It is your faith that saves your souls. Salvation is the gift of God to all who believe they are his sons. But be not deceived; while salvation is the free gift of God and is bestowed upon all who accept it by faith, there follows the experience of bearing the fruits of this spirit life as it is lived in the flesh. The acceptance of the doctrine of the fatherhood of God implies that you also freely accept the associated truth of the brotherhood of man. And if man is your brother, he is even more than your neighbor, whom the Father requires you to love as yourself. Your brother, being of your own family, you will not only love with a family affection, but you will also serve as you would serve yourself. And you will thus love and serve your brother because you, being my brethren, have been thus loved and served by me. Go, then, into all the world telling this good news to all creatures of every race, tribe, and nation. My spirit shall go before you, and I will be with you always."

193:1.3 (2054.1) These Samaritans were greatly astonished at this appearance of the Master, and they hastened off to the near-by towns and villages, where they published abroad the news that they had seen Jesus, and that he had talked to them. And this was the seventeenth morontia appearance of the Master.

2   *The Phoenician Appearance*

193:2.1 (2054.2) The Master's eighteenth morontia appearance was at Tyre, on Tuesday, May 16, at a little before nine o'clock in the evening. Again he appeared at the close of a meeting of believers, as they were about to disperse, saying:

193:2.2 (2054.3) "Peace be upon you. You rejoice to know that the Son of Man has risen from the dead because you thereby know that you and your brethren shall also survive mortal death. But such survival is dependent on your having been previously born of the spirit of truth-seeking and God-finding. The bread of life and the water thereof are given only to those who hunger for truth and thirst for righteousness—for God. The fact that the dead rise is not the gospel of the kingdom. These great truths and these universe facts are all related to this gospel in that they are a part of the result of believing the good news and are embraced in the subsequent experience of those who, by faith, become, in deed and in truth, the everlasting sons of the eternal God. My Father sent me into the world to proclaim this salvation of sonship to all men. And so send I you abroad to preach this salvation of sonship. Salvation is the free gift of God, but those who are born of the spirit will immediately begin to show forth the fruits of the spirit in loving service to their fellow creatures. And the fruits of the divine spirit which are yielded in the lives of spirit-born and God-knowing mortals are: loving service, unselfish devotion, courageous loyalty, sincere fairness, enlightened honesty, undying hope, confiding trust, merciful ministry, unfailing goodness, forgiving tolerance, and enduring peace. If professed believers bear not these fruits of the divine spirit in their lives, they are dead; the Spirit of Truth is not in them; they are useless branches on the living vine, and they soon will be taken away. My Father requires of the children of faith that they bear much spirit fruit. If, therefore, you are not fruitful, he will dig about your roots and cut away your unfruitful branches.

Increasingly, must you yield the fruits of the spirit as you progress heavenward in the kingdom of God. You may enter the kingdom as a child, but the Father requires that you grow up, by grace, to the full stature of spiritual adulthood. And when you go abroad to tell all nations the good news of this gospel, I will go before you, and my Spirit of Truth shall abide in your hearts. My peace I leave with you."

193:2.3 (2054.4) And then the Master disappeared from their sight. The next day there went out from Tyre those who carried this story to Sidon and even to Antioch and Damascus. Jesus had been with these believers when he was in the flesh, and they were quick to recognize him when he began to teach them. While his friends could not readily recognize his morontia form when made visible, they were never slow to identify his personality when he spoke to them.

3   *Last Appearance in Jerusalem*

193:3.1 (2055.1) Early Thursday morning, May 18, Jesus made his last appearance on earth as a morontia personality. As the eleven apostles were about to sit down to breakfast in the upper chamber of Mary Mark's home, Jesus appeared to them and said:

193:3.2 (2055.2) "Peace be upon you. I have asked you to tarry here in Jerusalem until I ascend to the Father, even until I send you the Spirit of Truth, who shall soon be poured out upon all flesh, and who shall endow you with power from on high." Simon Zelotes interrupted Jesus, asking, "Then, Master, will you restore the kingdom, and will we see the glory of God manifested on earth?" When Jesus had listened to Simon's question, he answered: "Simon, you still cling to your old ideas about the Jewish Messiah and the material kingdom. But you will receive spiritual power after the spirit has descended upon you, and you will presently go into all the world preaching this gospel of the kingdom. As the Father sent me into the world, so do I send you. And I wish that you would love and trust one another. Judas is no more with you because his love grew cold, and because he refused to trust you, his loyal brethren. Have you not read in the Scripture where it is written: 'It is not good for man to be alone. No man lives to himself'? And also where it says: 'He who would have friends must show himself friendly'? And did I not even send you out to teach, two and two, that you might not become lonely and fall into the mischief and miseries of isolation? You also well know that, when I was in the flesh, I did not permit myself to be alone for long periods. From the very beginning of our associations I always had two or three of you constantly by my side or else very near at hand even when I communed with the Father. Trust, therefore, and confide in one another. And this is all the more needful since I am this day going to leave you alone in the world.

The hour has come; I am about to go to the Father."

193:3.3 (2055.3) When he had spoken, he beckoned for them to come with him, and he led them out on the Mount of Olives, where he bade them farewell preparatory to departing from Urantia. This was a solemn journey to Olivet. Not a word was spoken by any of them from the time they left the upper chamber until Jesus paused with them on the Mount of Olives.

4   Causes of Judas's Downfall

193:4.1 (2055.4) It was in the first part of the Master's farewell message to his apostles that he alluded to the loss of Judas and held up the tragic fate of their traitorous fellow worker as a solemn warning against the dangers of social and fraternal isolation. It may be helpful to believers, in this and in future ages, briefly to review the causes of Judas's downfall in the light of the Master's remarks and in view of the accumulated enlightenment of succeeding centuries.

193:4.2 (2055.5) As we look back upon this tragedy, we conceive that Judas went wrong, primarily, because he was very markedly an isolated personality, a personality shut in and away from ordinary social contacts. He persistently refused to confide in, or freely fraternize with, his fellow apostles. But his being an isolated type of personality would not, in and of itself, have wrought such mischief for Judas had it not been that he also failed to increase in love and grow in spiritual grace. And then, as if to make a bad matter worse, he persistently harbored grudges and fostered such psychologic enemies as revenge and the generalized craving to "get even" with somebody for all his disappointments.

193:4.3 (2056.1) This unfortunate combination of individual peculiarities and mental tendencies conspired to destroy a well-intentioned man who failed to subdue these evils by love, faith, and trust. That Judas need not have gone wrong is well proved by the cases of Thomas and Nathaniel, both of whom were cursed with this same sort of suspicion and overdevelopment of the individualistic tendency. Even Andrew and Matthew had many leanings in this direction; but all these men grew to love Jesus and their fellow apostles more, and not less, as time passed. They grew in grace and in a knowledge of the truth. They became increasingly more trustful of their brethren and slowly developed the ability to confide in their fellows. Judas persistently refused to confide in his brethren. When he was impelled, by the accumulation of his emotional conflicts, to seek relief in self-expression, he invariably sought the advice and received the unwise consolation of his unspiritual relatives or those chance acquaintances who were either indifferent, or actually hostile, to the welfare and progress of the spiritual realities of the heavenly kingdom, of which he was one of the twelve consecrated ambassadors on earth.

193:4.4 (2056.2) Judas met defeat in his battles of the earth struggle because of the following factors of personal tendencies and character weakness:

193:4.5 (2056.3) 1. He was an isolated type of human being. He was highly individualistic and chose to grow into a confirmed "shut-in" and unsociable sort of person.

193:4.6 (2056.4) 2. As a child, life had been made too easy for him. He bitterly resented thwarting. He always expected to win; he was a very poor loser.

193:4.7 (2056.5) 3. He never acquired a philosophic technique for meeting disappointment. Instead of accepting disappointments as a regular and commonplace feature of human existence, he unfailingly resorted to the practice of blaming someone in particular, or his associates as a group, for all his personal difficulties and disappointments.

193:4.8 (2056.6) 4. He was given to holding grudges; he was always entertaining the idea of revenge.
193:4.9 (2056.7) 5. He did not like to face facts frankly; he was dishonest in his attitude toward life situations.
193:4.10 (2056.8) 6. He disliked to discuss his personal problems with his immediate associates; he refused to talk over his difficulties with his real friends and those who truly loved him. In all the years of their association he never once went to the Master with a purely personal problem.

193:4.11 (2056.9) 7. He never learned that the real rewards for noble living are, after all, spiritual prizes, which are not always distributed during this one short life in the flesh.

193:4.12 (2056.10) As a result of his persistent isolation of personality, his griefs multiplied, his sorrows increased, his anxieties augmented, and his despair deepened almost beyond endurance.

193:4.13 (2057.1) While this self-centered and ultraindividualistic apostle had many psychic, emotional, and spiritual troubles, his main difficulties were: In personality, he was isolated. In mind, he was suspicious and vengeful. In temperament, he was surly and vindictive. Emotionally, he was loveless and unforgiving. Socially, he was unconfiding and almost wholly self-contained. In spirit, he became arrogant and selfishly ambitious. In life, he ignored those who loved him, and in death, he was friendless.

193:4.14 (2057.2) These, then, are the factors of mind and influences of evil which, taken altogether, explain why a well-meaning and otherwise onetime sincere believer in Jesus, even after several years of intimate association with his transforming personality, forsook his fellows, repudiated a sacred cause, renounced his holy calling, and betrayed his divine Master.

5   *The Master's Ascension*

193:5.1 (2057.3) It was almost half past seven o'clock this Thursday morning, May 18, when Jesus arrived on the western slope of Mount Olivet with his eleven silent and somewhat bewildered apostles. From this location, about two thirds the way up the mountain, they could look out over Jerusalem and down upon Gethsemane. Jesus now prepared to say his last farewell to the apostles before he took leave of Urantia. As he stood there before them, without being directed they knelt about him in a circle, and the Master said:

193:5.2 (2057.4) "I bade you tarry in Jerusalem until you were endowed with power from on high. I am now about to take leave of you; I am about to ascend to my Father, and soon, very soon, will we send into this world of my sojourn the Spirit of Truth; and when he has come, you shall begin the new proclamation of the gospel of the kingdom, first in Jerusalem and then to the uttermost parts of the world. Love men with the love wherewith I have loved you and serve your fellow mortals even as I have served you. By the spirit fruits of your lives impel souls to believe the truth that man is a son of God, and that all men are brethren. Remember all I have taught you and the life I have lived among you. My love overshadows you, my spirit will dwell with you, and my peace shall abide upon you. Farewell."

193:5.3 (2057.5) When the morontia Master had thus spoken, he vanished from their sight. This so-called ascension of Jesus was in no way different from his other disappearances from mortal vision during the forty days of his morontia career on Urantia.

193:5.4 (2057.6) The Master went to Edentia by way of Jerusem, where the Most Highs, under the observation of the Paradise Son, released Jesus of Nazareth from the morontia state and, through the spirit channels of ascension, returned him to the status of Paradise sonship and supreme sovereignty on Salvington.

193:5.5 (2057.7) It was about seven forty-five this morning when the morontia Jesus disappeared from the observation of his eleven apostles to begin the ascent to the right hand of his Father, there to receive formal confirmation of his completed sovereignty of the universe of Nebadon.

6   Peter Calls a Meeting

193:6.1 (2057.8) Acting upon the instruction of Peter, John Mark and others went forth to call the leading disciples together at the home of Mary Mark. By ten thirty, one hundred and twenty of the foremost disciples of Jesus living in Jerusalem had forgathered to hear the report of the farewell message of the Master and to learn of his ascension. Among this company was Mary the mother of Jesus. She had returned to Jerusalem with John Zebedee when the apostles came back from their recent sojourn in Galilee. Soon after Pentecost she returned to the home of Salome at Bethsaida. James the brother of Jesus was also present at this meeting, the first conference of the Master's disciples to be called after the termination of his planetary career.

193:6.2 (2058.1) Simon Peter took it upon himself to speak for his fellow apostles and made a thrilling report of the last meeting of the eleven with their Master and most touchingly portrayed the Master's final farewell and his ascension disappearance. It was a meeting the like of which had never before occurred on this world. This part of the meeting lasted not quite one hour. Peter then explained that they had decided to choose a successor to Judas Iscariot, and that a recess would be granted to enable the apostles to decide between the two men who had been suggested for this position, Matthias and Justus.

193:6.3 (2058.2) The eleven apostles then went downstairs, where they agreed to cast lots in order to determine which of these men should become an apostle to serve in Judas's place. The lot fell on Matthias, and he was declared to be the new apostle. He was duly inducted into his office and then appointed treasurer. But Matthias had little part in the subsequent activities of the apostles.

193:6.4 (2058.3) Soon after Pentecost the twins returned to their homes in Galilee. Simon Zelotes was in retirement for some time before he went forth preaching the gospel. Thomas worried for a shorter period and then resumed his teaching. Nathaniel differed increasingly with Peter regarding preaching about Jesus in the place of proclaiming the former gospel of the kingdom. This disagreement became so acute by the middle of the following month that Nathaniel withdrew, going to Philadelphia to visit Abner and Lazarus; and after tarrying there for more than a year, he went on into the lands beyond Mesopotamia preaching the gospel as he understood it.

193:6.5 (2058.4) This left but six of the original twelve apostles to become actors on the stage of the early proclamation of the gospel in Jerusalem: Peter, Andrew, James, John, Philip, and Matthew.

193:6.6 (2058.5) Just about noon the apostles returned to their brethren in the upper chamber and announced that Matthias had been chosen as the new apostle. And then Peter called all of the believers to engage in prayer, prayer that they might be prepared to receive the gift of the spirit which the Master had promised to send.

Paper 194

Bestowal of the Spirit of Truth

194:0.1 (2059.1) ABOUT one o'clock, as the one hundred and twenty believers were engaged in prayer, they all became aware of a strange presence in the room. At the same time these disciples all became conscious of a new and profound sense of spiritual joy, security, and confidence. This new consciousness of spiritual strength was immediately followed by a strong urge to go out and publicly proclaim the gospel of the kingdom and the good news that Jesus had risen from the dead.

194:0.2 (2059.2) Peter stood up and declared that this must be the coming of the Spirit of Truth which the Master had promised them and proposed that they go to the temple and begin the proclamation of the good news committed to their hands. And they did just what Peter suggested.

194:0.3 (2059.3) These men had been trained and instructed that the gospel which they should preach was the fatherhood of God and the sonship of man, but at just this moment of spiritual ecstasy and personal triumph, the best tidings, the greatest news, these men could think of was the fact of the risen Master. And so they went forth, endowed with power from on high, preaching glad tidings to the people—even salvation through Jesus—but they unintentionally stumbled into the error of substituting some of the facts associated with the gospel for the gospel message itself. Peter unwittingly led off in this mistake, and others followed after him on down to Paul, who created a new religion out of the new version of the good news.

194:0.4 (2059.4) The gospel of the kingdom is: the fact of the fatherhood of God, coupled with the resultant truth of the sonship-brotherhood of men. Christianity, as it developed from that day, is: the fact of God as the Father of the Lord Jesus Christ, in association with the experience of believer-fellowship with the risen and glorified Christ.

194:0.5 (2059.5) It is not strange that these spirit-infused men should have seized upon this opportunity to express their feelings of triumph over the forces which had sought to destroy their Master and end the influence of his teachings. At such a time as this it was easier to remember their personal association with Jesus and to be thrilled with the assurance that the Master still lived, that their friendship had not ended, and that the spirit had indeed come upon them even as he had promised.

194:0.6 (2059.6) These believers felt themselves suddenly translated into another world, a new existence of joy, power, and glory. The Master had told them the kingdom would come with power, and some of them thought they were beginning to discern what he meant.

194:0.7 (2059.7) And when all of this is taken into consideration, it is not difficult to understand how these men came to preach a new gospel about Jesus in the place of their former message of the fatherhood of God and the brotherhood of men.

1   The Pentecost Sermon

194:1.1 (2060.1) The apostles had been in hiding for forty days. This day happened to be the Jewish festival of Pentecost, and thousands of visitors from all parts of the world were in Jerusalem. Many arrived for this feast, but a majority had tarried in the city since the Passover. Now these frightened apostles emerged from their weeks of seclusion to appear boldly in the temple, where they began to preach the new message of a risen Messiah. And all the disciples were likewise conscious of having received some new spiritual endowment of insight and power.

194:1.2 (2060.2) It was about two o'clock when Peter stood up in that very place where his Master had last taught in this temple, and delivered that impassioned appeal which resulted in the winning of more than two thousand souls. The Master had gone, but they suddenly discovered that this story about him had great power with the people. No wonder they were led on into the further proclamation of that which vindicated their former devotion to Jesus and at the same time so constrained men to believe in him. Six of the apostles participated in this meeting: Peter, Andrew, James, John, Philip, and Matthew. They talked for more than an hour and a half and delivered messages in Greek, Hebrew, and Aramaic, as well as a few words in even other tongues with which they had a speaking acquaintance.

194:1.3 (2060.3) The leaders of the Jews were astounded at the boldness of the apostles, but they feared to molest them because of the large numbers who believed their story.

194:1.4 (2060.4) By half past four o'clock more than two thousand new believers followed the apostles down to the pool of Siloam, where Peter, Andrew, James, and John baptized them in the Master's name. And it was dark when they had finished with baptizing this multitude.

194:1.5 (2060.5) Pentecost was the great festival of baptism, the time for fellowshipping the proselytes of the gate, those gentiles who desired to serve Yahweh. It was, therefore, the more easy for large numbers of both the Jews and believing gentiles to submit to baptism on this day. In doing this, they were in no way disconnecting themselves from the Jewish faith. Even for some time after this the believers in Jesus were a sect within Judaism. All of them, including the apostles, were still loyal to the essential requirements of the Jewish ceremonial system.

2   The Significance of Pentecost

194:2.1 (2060.6) Jesus lived on earth and taught a gospel which redeemed man from the superstition that he was a child of the devil and elevated him to the dignity of a faith son of God. Jesus' message, as he preached it and lived it in his day, was an effective solvent for man's spiritual difficulties in that day of its statement. And now that he has personally left the world, he sends in his place his Spirit of Truth, who is designed to live in man and, for each new generation, to restate the Jesus message so that every new group of mortals to appear upon the face of the earth shall have a new and up-to-date version of the gospel, just such personal enlightenment and group guidance as will prove to be an effective solvent for man's ever-new and varied spiritual difficulties.

194:2.2 (2060.7) The first mission of this spirit is, of course, to foster and personalize truth, for it is the comprehension of truth that constitutes the highest form of human liberty. Next, it is the purpose of this spirit to destroy the believer's feeling of orphanhood. Jesus having been among men, all believers would experience a sense of loneliness had not the Spirit of Truth come to dwell in men's hearts.

194:2.3 (2061.1) This bestowal of the Son's spirit effectively prepared all normal men's minds for the subsequent universal bestowal of the Father's spirit (the Adjuster) upon all mankind. In a certain sense, this Spirit of Truth is the spirit of both the Universal Father and the Creator Son.

194:2.4 (2061.2) Do not make the mistake of expecting to become strongly intellectually conscious of the outpoured Spirit of Truth. The spirit never creates a consciousness of himself, only a consciousness of Michael, the Son. From the beginning Jesus taught that the spirit would not speak of himself. The proof, therefore, of your fellowship with the Spirit of Truth is not to be found in your consciousness of this spirit but rather in your experience of enhanced fellowship with Michael.

194:2.5 (2061.3) The spirit also came to help men recall and understand the words of the Master as well as to illuminate and reinterpret his life on earth.

194:2.6 (2061.4) Next, the Spirit of Truth came to help the believer to witness to the realities of Jesus' teachings and his life as he lived it in the flesh, and as he now again lives it anew and afresh in the individual believer of each passing generation of the spirit-filled sons of God.

194:2.7 (2061.5) Thus it appears that the Spirit of Truth comes really to lead all believers into all truth, into the expanding knowledge of the experience of the living and growing spiritual consciousness of the reality of eternal and ascending sonship with God.

194:2.8 (2061.6) Jesus lived a life which is a revelation of man submitted to the Father's will, not an example for any man literally to attempt to follow. This life in the flesh, together with his death on the cross and subsequent resurrection, presently became a new gospel of the ransom which had thus been paid in order to purchase man back from the clutch of the

evil one—from the condemnation of an offended God. Nevertheless, even though the gospel did become greatly distorted, it remains a fact that this new message about Jesus carried along with it many of the fundamental truths and teachings of his earlier gospel of the kingdom. And, sooner or later, these concealed truths of the fatherhood of God and the brotherhood of men will emerge to effectually transform the civilization of all mankind.

194:2.9 (2061.7) But these mistakes of the intellect in no way interfered with the believer's great progress in growth in spirit. In less than a month after the bestowal of the Spirit of Truth, the apostles made more individual spiritual progress than during their almost four years of personal and loving association with the Master. Neither did this substitution of the fact of the resurrection of Jesus for the saving gospel truth of sonship with God in any way interfere with the rapid spread of their teachings; on the contrary, this overshadowing of Jesus' message by the new teachings about his person and resurrection seemed greatly to facilitate the preaching of the good news.

194:2.10 (2061.8) The term "baptism of the spirit," which came into such general use about this time, merely signified the conscious reception of this gift of the Spirit of Truth and the personal acknowledgment of this new spiritual power as an augmentation of all spiritual influences previously experienced by God-knowing souls.

194:2.11 (2061.9) Since the bestowal of the Spirit of Truth, man is subject to the teaching and guidance of a threefold spirit endowment: the spirit of the Father, the Thought Adjuster; the spirit of the Son, the Spirit of Truth; the spirit of the Spirit, the Holy Spirit.

194:2.12 (2062.1) In a way, mankind is subject to the double influence of the sevenfold appeal of the universe spirit influences. The early evolutionary races of mortals are subject to the progressive contact of the seven adjutant mind- spirits of the local universe Mother Spirit. As man progresses upward in the scale of intelligence and spiritual perception, there eventually come to hover over him and dwell within him the seven higher spirit influences. And these seven spirits of the advancing worlds are:

194:2.13 (2062.2) 1. The bestowed spirit of the Universal Father—the Thought Adjusters.

194:2.14 (2062.3) 2. The spirit presence of the Eternal Son—the spirit gravity of the universe of universes and the certain channel of all spirit communion.

194:2.15 (2062.4) 3. The spirit presence of the Infinite Spirit—the universal spirit-mind of all creation, the spiritual source of the intellectual kinship of all progressive intelligences.

194:2.16 (2062.5) 4. The spirit of the Universal Father and the Creator Son—the Spirit of Truth, generally regarded as the spirit of the Universe Son.

194:2.17 (2062.6) 5. The spirit of the Infinite Spirit and the Universe Mother Spirit—the Holy Spirit, generally regarded as the spirit of the Universe Spirit.

194:2.18 (2062.7) 6. The mind-spirit of the Universe Mother Spirit—the seven adjutant mind-spirits of the local universe.

194:2.19 (2062.8) 7. The spirit of the Father, Sons, and Spirits—the new-name spirit of the ascending mortals of the realms after the fusion of the mortal spirit-born soul with the Paradise Thought Adjuster and after the subsequent attainment of the divinity and glorification of the status of the Paradise Corps of the Finality.

194:2.20 (2062.9) And so did the bestowal of the Spirit of Truth bring to the world and its peoples the last of the spirit endowment designed to aid in the ascending search for God.

3 What Happened at Pentecost

194:3.1 (2062.10) Many queer and strange teachings became associated with the early narratives of the day of Pentecost. In subsequent times the events of this day, on which the Spirit of Truth, the new teacher, came to dwell with mankind, have become confused with the foolish outbreaks of rampant emotionalism. The chief mission of this outpoured spirit of the Father and the Son is to teach men about the truths of the Father's love and the Son's mercy. These are the truths of divinity which men can comprehend more fully than all the other divine traits of character. The Spirit of Truth is concerned primarily with the revelation of the Father's spirit nature and the Son's moral character. The Creator Son, in the flesh, revealed God to men; the Spirit of Truth, in the heart, reveals the Creator Son to men. When man yields the "fruits of the spirit" in his life, he is simply showing forth the traits which the Master manifested in his own earthly life. When Jesus was on earth, he lived his life as one personality—Jesus of Nazareth. As the indwelling spirit of the "new teacher," the Master has, since Pentecost, been able to live his life anew in the experience of every truth-taught believer.

194:3.2 (2062.11) Many things which happen in the course of a human life are hard to understand, difficult to reconcile with the idea that this is a universe in which truth prevails and in which righteousness triumphs. It so often appears that slander, lies, dishonesty, and unrighteousness—sin—prevail. Does faith, after all, triumph over evil, sin, and iniquity? It does. And the life and death of Jesus are the eternal proof that the truth of goodness and the faith of the spirit-led creature will always be vindicated. They taunted Jesus on the cross, saying, "Let us see if God will come and deliver him." It looked dark on that day of the crucifixion, but it was gloriously bright on the resurrection morning; it was still brighter and more joyous on the day of Pentecost. The religions of pessimistic despair seek to obtain release from the burdens of life; they crave extinction in endless slumber and rest. These are the religions of primitive fear and dread.

The religion of Jesus is a new gospel of faith to be proclaimed to struggling humanity. This new religion is founded on faith, hope, and love.

194:3.3 (2063.1) To Jesus, mortal life had dealt its hardest, cruelest, and bitterest blows; and this man met these ministrations of despair with faith, courage, and the unswerving determination to do his Father's will. Jesus met life in all its terrible reality and mastered it—even in death. He did not use religion as a release from life. The religion of Jesus does not seek to escape this life in order to enjoy the waiting bliss of another existence. The religion of Jesus provides the joy and peace of another and spiritual existence to enhance and ennoble the life which men now live in the flesh.

194:3.4 (2063.2) If religion is an opiate to the people, it is not the religion of Jesus. On the cross he refused to drink the deadening drug, and his spirit, poured out upon all flesh, is a mighty world influence which leads man upward and urges him onward. The spiritual forward urge is the most powerful driving force present in this world; the truth-learning believer is the one progressive and aggressive soul on earth.

194:3.5 (2063.3) On the day of Pentecost the religion of Jesus broke all national restrictions and racial fetters. It is forever true, "Where the spirit of the Lord is, there is liberty." On this day the Spirit of Truth became the personal gift from the Master to every mortal. This spirit was bestowed for the purpose of qualifying believers more effectively to preach the gospel of the kingdom, but they mistook the experience of receiving the outpoured spirit for a part of the new gospel which they were unconsciously formulating.

194:3.6 (2063.4) Do not overlook the fact that the Spirit of Truth was bestowed upon all sincere believers; this gift of the spirit did not come only to the apostles. The one hundred and twenty men and women assembled in the upper chamber all received the new teacher, as did all the honest of heart throughout the whole world. This new teacher was bestowed upon mankind, and every soul received him in accordance with the love for truth and the capacity to grasp and comprehend spiritual realities. At last, true religion is delivered from the custody of priests and all sacred classes and finds its real manifestation in the individual souls of men.

194:3.7 (2063.5) The religion of Jesus fosters the highest type of human civilization in that it creates the highest type of spiritual personality and proclaims the sacredness of that person.

194:3.8 (2063.6) The coming of the Spirit of Truth on Pentecost made possible a religion which is neither radical nor conservative; it is neither the old nor the new; it is to be dominated neither by the old nor the young. The fact of Jesus' earthly life provides a fixed point for the anchor of time, while the bestowal of the Spirit of Truth provides for the everlasting expansion and endless growth of the religion which he lived and the gospel which he proclaimed. The spirit guides into all truth; he is the teacher of an expanding and always-growing religion of endless progress and divine unfolding. This new teacher will be forever unfolding to the truth-seeking believer that which was so divinely folded up in the person and nature of the Son of Man.

194:3.9 (2064.1) The manifestations associated with the bestowal of the "new teacher," and the reception of the apostles' preaching by the men of various races and nations gathered together at Jerusalem, indicate the universality of the religion of Jesus. The gospel of the kingdom was to be identified with no particular race, culture, or language. This day of Pentecost witnessed the great effort of the spirit to liberate the religion of Jesus from its inherited Jewish fetters. Even after this demonstration of pouring out the spirit upon all flesh, the apostles at first endeavored to impose the requirements of Judaism upon their converts. Even Paul had trouble with his Jerusalem brethren because he refused to subject the gentiles to these Jewish practices. No revealed religion can spread to all the world when it makes the serious mistake of becoming permeated with some national culture or associated with established racial, social, or economic practices.

194:3.10 (2064.2) The bestowal of the Spirit of Truth was independent of all forms, ceremonies, sacred places, and special behavior by those who received the fullness of its manifestation. When the spirit came upon those assembled in the upper chamber, they were simply sitting there, having just been engaged in silent prayer. The spirit was bestowed in the country as well as in the city. It was not necessary for the apostles to go apart to a lonely place for years of solitary meditation in order to receive the spirit. For all time, Pentecost disassociates the idea of spiritual experience from the notion of especially favorable environments.

194:3.11 (2064.3) Pentecost, with its spiritual endowment, was designed forever to loose the religion of the Master from all dependence upon physical force; the teachers of this new religion are now equipped with spiritual weapons. They are to go out to conquer the world with unfailing forgiveness, matchless good will, and abounding love. They are equipped to overcome evil with good, to vanquish hate by love, to destroy fear with a courageous and living faith in truth. Jesus had already taught his followers that his religion was never passive; always were his disciples to be active and positive in their ministry of mercy and in their manifestations of love. No longer did these believers look upon Yahweh as "the Lord of Hosts." They now regarded the eternal Deity as the "God and Father of the Lord Jesus Christ." They made that progress, at least, even if they did in some measure fail fully to grasp the truth that God is also the spiritual Father of every individual.

194:3.12 (2064.4) Pentecost endowed mortal man with the power to forgive personal injuries, to keep sweet in the midst of the gravest injustice, to remain unmoved in the face of appalling danger, and to challenge the evils of hate and anger by the fearless acts of love and forbearance. Urantia has passed through the ravages of great and destructive wars in its history. All participants in these terrible struggles met with defeat. There was but one victor; there was only one who came out of these embittered struggles with an enhanced reputation— that was Jesus of Nazareth and his gospel of overcoming evil with good. The secret of a better civilization is bound up in the Master's teachings of the brotherhood of man, the good will of love and mutual trust.

194:3.13 (2065.1) Up to Pentecost, religion had revealed only man seeking for God; since Pentecost, man is still searching for God, but there shines out over the world the spectacle of God also seeking for man and sending his spirit to dwell within him when he has found him.

194:3.14 (2065.2) Before the teachings of Jesus which culminated in Pentecost, women had little or no spiritual standing in the tenets of the older religions. After Pentecost, in the brotherhood of the kingdom woman stood before God on an equality with man. Among the one hundred and twenty who received this special visitation of the spirit were many of the women disciples, and they shared these blessings equally with the men believers. No longer can man presume to monopolize the ministry of religious service. The Pharisee might go on thanking God that he was "not born a woman, a leper, or a gentile," but among the followers of Jesus woman has been forever set free from all religious discriminations based on sex. Pentecost obliterated all religious discrimination founded on racial distinction, cultural differences, social caste, or sex prejudice. No wonder these believers in the new religion would cry out, "Where the spirit of the Lord is, there is liberty."

194:3.15 (2065.3) Both the mother and brother of Jesus were present among the one hundred and twenty believers, and as members of this common group of disciples, they also received the outpoured spirit. They received no more of the good gift than did their fellows. No special gift was bestowed upon the members of Jesus' earthly family. Pentecost marked the end of special priesthoods and all belief in sacred families.

194:3.16 (2065.4) Before Pentecost the apostles had given up much for Jesus. They had sacrificed their homes, families, friends, worldly goods, and positions. At Pentecost they gave themselves to God, and the Father and the Son responded by giving themselves to man—sending their spirits to live within men. This experience of losing self and finding the spirit was not one of emotion; it was an act of intelligent self-surrender and unreserved consecration.

194:3.17 (2065.5) Pentecost was the call to spiritual unity among gospel believers. When the spirit descended on the disciples at Jerusalem, the same thing happened in Philadelphia, Alexandria, and at all other places where true believers dwelt. It was literally true that "there was but one heart and soul among the multitude of the believers." The religion of Jesus is the most powerful unifying influence the world has ever known.

194:3.18 (2065.6) Pentecost was designed to lessen the self-assertiveness of individuals, groups, nations, and races. It is this spirit of self-assertiveness which so increases in tension that it periodically breaks loose in destructive wars.

Mankind can be unified only by the spiritual approach, and the Spirit of Truth is a world influence which is universal.

194:3.19 (2065.7) The coming of the Spirit of Truth purifies the human heart and leads the recipient to formulate a life purpose single to the will of God and the welfare of men. The material spirit of selfishness has been swallowed up in this new spiritual bestowal of selflessness. Pente-

cost, then and now, signifies that the Jesus of history has become the divine Son of living experience. The joy of this outpoured spirit, when it is consciously experienced in human life, is a tonic for health, a stimulus for mind, and an unfailing energy for the soul.

194:3.20 (2065.8) Prayer did not bring the spirit on the day of Pentecost, but it did have much to do with determining the capacity of receptivity which characterized the individual believers. Prayer does not move the divine heart to liberality of bestowal, but it does so often dig out larger and deeper channels wherein the divine bestowals may flow to the hearts and souls of those who thus remember to maintain unbroken communion with their Maker through sincere prayer and true worship.

4   Beginnings of the Christian Church

194:4.1 (2066.1) When Jesus was so suddenly seized by his enemies and so quickly crucified between two thieves, his apostles and disciples were completely demoralized. The thought of the Master, arrested, bound, scourged, and crucified, was too much for even the apostles. They forgot his teachings and his warnings. He might, indeed, have been "a prophet mighty in deed and word before God and all the people," but he could hardly be the Messiah they had hoped would restore the kingdom of Israel.

194:4.2 (2066.2) Then comes the resurrection, with its deliverance from despair and the return of their faith in the Master's divinity. Again and again they see him and talk with him, and he takes them out on Olivet, where he bids them farewell and tells them he is going back to the Father. He has told them to tarry in Jerusalem until they are endowed with power—until the Spirit of Truth shall come. And on the day of Pentecost this new teacher comes, and they go out at once to preach their gospel with new power. They are the bold and courageous followers of a living Lord, not a dead and defeated leader. The Master lives in the hearts of these evangelists; God is not a doctrine in their minds; he has become a living presence in their souls.

194:4.3 (2066.3) "Day by day they continued steadfastly and with one accord in the temple and breaking bread at home. They took their food with gladness and singleness of heart, praising God and having favor with all the people. They were all filled with the spirit, and they spoke the word of God with boldness. And the multitudes of those who believed were of one heart and soul; and not one of them said that aught of the things which he possessed was his own, and they had all things in common."

194:4.4 (2066.4) What has happened to these men whom Jesus had ordained to go forth preaching the gospel of the kingdom, the fatherhood of God and the brotherhood of man? They have a new gospel; they are on fire with a new experience; they are filled with a new spiritual energy. Their message has suddenly shifted to the proclamation of the risen Christ: "Jesus of Nazareth, a man God approved by mighty works and wonders; him, being delivered up by the determinate counsel and foreknowledge of God, you did crucify and slay. The things which God foreshadowed by the mouth of all the prophets, he thus fulfilled. This Jesus did God raise up. God has made him both Lord and Christ. Being, by the right hand of God, exalted and having received from the Father the promise of the spirit, he has poured forth this which you see and hear. Repent, that your sins may be blotted out; that the Father may send the Christ, who has been appointed for you, even Jesus, whom the heaven must receive until the times of the restoration of all things." *

194:4.5 (2066.5) The gospel of the kingdom, the message of Jesus, had been suddenly changed into the gospel of the Lord Jesus Christ. They now proclaimed the facts of his life, death, and resurrection and preached the hope of his speedy return to this world to finish the work he began.

Thus the message of the early believers had to do with preaching about the facts of his first coming and with teaching the hope of his second coming, an event which they deemed to be very near at hand.

194:4.6 (2067.1) Christ was about to become the creed of the rapidly forming church. Jesus lives; he died for men; he gave the spirit; he is coming again. Jesus filled all their thoughts and determined all their new concepts of God and everything else. They were too much enthused over the new doctrine that "God is the Father of the Lord Jesus" to be concerned with the old message that "God is the loving Father of all men," even of every single individual. True, a marvelous manifestation of brotherly love and unexampled good will did spring up in these early communities of believers. But it was a fellowship of believers in Jesus, not a fellowship of brothers in the family kingdom of the Father in heaven. Their good will arose from the love born of the concept of Jesus' bestowal and not from the recognition of the brotherhood of mortal man. Nevertheless, they were filled with joy, and they lived such new and unique lives that all men were attracted to their teachings about Jesus. They made the great mistake of using the living and illustrative commentary on the gospel of the kingdom for that gospel, but even that represented the greatest religion mankind had ever known. *

194:4.7 (2067.2) Unmistakably, a new fellowship was arising in the world. "The multitude who believed continued steadfastly in the apostles' teaching and fellowship, in the breaking of bread, and in prayers." They called each other brother and sister; they greeted one another with a holy kiss; they ministered to the poor. It was a fellowship of living as well as of worship. They were not communal by decree but by the desire to share their goods with their fellow believers. They confidently expected that Jesus would return to complete the establishment of the Father's kingdom during their generation. This spontaneous sharing of earthly possessions was not a direct feature of Jesus' teaching; it came about because these men and women so sincerely and so confidently believed that he was to return any day to finish his work and to consummate the kingdom. But the final results of this well-meant experiment in thoughtless brotherly love were disastrous and sorrow-breeding. Thousands of earnest believers sold their property and disposed of all their capital goods and other productive assets. With the passing of time, the dwindling resources of Christian "equal-sharing" came to an end—but the world did not. Very soon the believers at Antioch were taking up a collection to keep their fellow believers at Jerusalem from starving.

194:4.8 (2067.3) In these days they celebrated the Lord's Supper after the manner of its establishment; that is, they assembled for a social meal of good fellowship and partook of the sacrament at the end of the meal.

194:4.9 (2067.4) At first they baptized in the name of Jesus; it was almost twenty years before they began to baptize in "the name of the Father, the Son, and the Holy Spirit." Baptism was all that was required for admission into the fellowship of believers. They had no organization as yet; it was simply the Jesus brotherhood.

194:4.10 (2067.5) This Jesus sect was growing rapidly, and once more the Sadducees took notice of them. The Pharisees were little bothered about the situation, seeing that none of the teachings in any way interfered with the observance of the Jewish laws. But the Sadducees began to put the leaders of the Jesus sect in jail until they were prevailed upon to accept the counsel of one of the leading rabbis, Gamaliel, who advised them: "Refrain from these men and let them alone, for if this counsel or this work is of men, it will be overthrown; but if it is of God, you will not be able to overthrow them, lest haply you be found even to be fighting against God." They decided to follow Gamaliel's counsel, and there ensued a time of peace and quiet in Jerusalem, during which the new gospel about Jesus spread rapidly.

194:4.11 (2068.1) And so all went well in Jerusalem until the time of the coming of the Greeks in large numbers from Alexandria. Two of the pupils of Rodan arrived in Jerusalem and made many converts from among the Hellenists. Among their early converts were Stephen and Barnabas. These able Greeks did not so much have the Jewish viewpoint, and they did not so well conform to the Jewish mode of worship and other ceremonial practices. And it was the doings of these Greek believers that terminated the peaceful relations between the Jesus brotherhood and the Pharisees and Sadducees. Stephen and his Greek associate began to preach more as Jesus taught, and this brought them into immediate conflict with the Jewish rulers. In one of Stephen's public sermons, when he reached the objectionable part of the discourse, they dispensed with all formalities of trial and proceeded to stone him to death on the spot.

194:4.12 (2068.2) Stephen, the leader of the Greek colony of Jesus' believers in Jerusalem, thus became the first martyr to the new faith and the specific cause for the formal organization of the early Christian church. This new crisis was met by the recognition that believers could not longer go on as a sect within the Jewish faith. They all agreed that they must separate themselves from unbelievers; and within one month from the death of Stephen the church at Jerusalem had been organized under the leadership of Peter, and James the brother of Jesus had been installed as its titular head.

194:4.13 (2068.3) And then broke out the new and relentless persecutions by the Jews, so that the active teachers of the new religion about Jesus, which subsequently at Antioch was called Christianity, went forth to the ends of the empire proclaiming Jesus. In carrying this message, before the time of Paul the leadership was in Greek hands; and these first missionaries, as also the later ones, followed the path of Alexander's march of former days, going by way of Gaza and Tyre to Antioch and then over

Asia Minor to Macedonia, then on to Rome
and to the uttermost parts of the empire.